DATE DUE

			PRINTED IN U.S.A.

Poetry
Criticism

Guide to Gale Literary Criticism Series

For criticism on	Consult these Gale series
Authors now living or who died after December 31, 1959	*CONTEMPORARY LITERARY CRITICISM (CLC)*
Authors who died between 1900 and 1959	*TWENTIETH-CENTURY LITERARY CRITICISM (TCLC)*
Authors who died between 1800 and 1899	*NINETEENTH-CENTURY LITERATURE CRITICISM (NCLC)*
Authors who died between 1400 and 1799	*LITERATURE CRITICISM FROM 1400 TO 1800 (LC)* *SHAKESPEAREAN CRITICISM (SC)*
Authors who died before 1400	*CLASSICAL AND MEDIEVAL LITERATURE CRITICISM (CMLC)*
Black writers of the past two hundred years	*BLACK LITERATURE CRITICISM (BLC)*
Authors of books for children and young adults	*CHILDREN'S LITERATURE REVIEW (CLR)*
Dramatists	*DRAMA CRITICISM (DC)*
Hispanic writers of the late nineteenth and twentieth centuries	*HISPANIC LITERATURE CRITICISM (HLC)*
Native North American writers and orators of the eighteenth, nineteenth, and twentieth centuries	*NATIVE NORTH AMERICAN LITERATURE (NNAL)*
Poets	*POETRY CRITICISM (PC)*
Short story writers	*SHORT STORY CRITICISM (SSC)*
Major authors from the Renaissance to the present	*WORLD LITERATURE CRITICISM, 1500 TO THE PRESENT (WLC)*

ISSN 1052-4851

R

Poetry Criticism

Excerpts from Criticism of the Works of the Most Significant and Widely Studied Poets of World Literature

VOLUME 13

Jane Kelly Kosek
Christine Slovey
Editors

Gale Research

An ITP Information/Reference Group Company

I(T)P
Changing the Way the World Learns

NEW YORK • LONDON • BONN • BOSTON • DETROIT
MADRID • MELBOURNE • MEXICO CITY • PARIS
SINGAPORE • TOKYO • TORONTO • WASHINGTON
ALBANY NY • BELMONT CA • CINCINNATI OH

STAFF

Jane Kelly Kosek, Christine Slovey, *Editors*

Margaret Haerens, Jeff Hill, Drew Kalasky,
Marie Rose Napierkowski, Mary K. Ruby, Lawrence J. Trudeau,
Associate Editors

Marlene S. Hurst, *Permissions Manager*
Margaret A. Chamberlain, Maria Franklin, *Permissions Specialists*

Susan Brohman, Diane Cooper, Michele Lonoconus, Maureen Puhl,
Shalice Shah, Kimberly F. Smilay, Barbara A. Wallace,
Permissions Associates

Sarah Chesney, Edna Hedblad, Margaret McAvoy-Amato,
Tyra Y. Phillips, Lori Schoenenberger, Rita Valazquez,
Permissions Assistants

Victoria B. Cariappa, *Research Manager*

Mary Beth McElmeel, Tamara C. Nott, Michele P. Pica,
Tracie A. Richardson, Norma Sawaya, *Research Associates*

Mary Beth Trimper, *Production Director*
Deborah Milliken, *Production Assistant*

Sherrell Hobbs, *Macintosh Artist*
Randy Bassett, *Image Database Supervisor*
Robert Duncan, *Scanner Operator*
Pamela Hayes, *Photography Coordinator*

Margaret Haerens, Jeff Hill, Drew Kalasky, Michael L. LaBlanc, Marie Rose Napierkowski,
Mary K. Ruby, Christine Slovey, Lawrence J. Trudeau, *Desktop Typesetters*

Library of Congress Catalog Card Number 91-118494
ISBN 0-8103-9274-7
ISSN 1052-4851

Printed in the United States of America

10 9 8 7 6 5 4 3 2 1

I(T)P™ Gale Research Inc., an International Thomson Publishing Company.
ITP logo is a trademark under license.

Contents

Preface vii

Acknowledgments xi

Aphra Behn 1640(?)-1689 1

Li Ho 791-817 41

Amy Lowell 1874-1925 58

Eugenio Montale 1896-1981 102

Gérard de Nerval 1808-1855 171

Cesare Pavese 1908-1950 200

Wendy Rose 1948- 231

Walter Scott 1771-1832 243

Christopher Smart 1722-1771 323

Françios Villon 1431-1463(?) 372

Literary Criticism Series Cumulative Author Index 421

PC Cumulative Nationality Index 495

PC Cumulative Title Index 497

Preface

A Comprehensive Information Source on World Poetry

*P*oetry Criticism (PC) provides substantial critical excerpts and biographical information on poets throughout the world who are most frequently studied in high school and undergraduate college courses. Each *PC* entry is supplemented by biographical and bibliographical material to help guide the user to a fuller understanding of the genre and its creators. Although major poets and literary movements are covered in such Gale Literary Criticism Series as *Contemporary Literary Criticism (CLC)*, *Twentieth-Century Literary Criticism (TCLC)*, *Nineteenth-Century Literature Criticism (NCLC)*, *Literature Criticism from 1400 to 1800 (LC)*, and *Classical and Medieval Literature Criticism (CMLC)*, *PC* offers more focused attention on poetry than is possible in the broader, survey-oriented entries on writers in these Gale series. Students, teachers, librarians, and researchers will find that the generous excerpts and supplementary material provided by *PC* supply them with vital information needed to write a term paper on poetic technique, examine a poet's most prominent themes, or lead a poetry discussion group.

Coverage

In order to reflect the influence of tradition as well as innovation, poets of various nationalities, eras, and movements are represented in every volume of *PC*. Each author entry presents a historical survey of the critical response to that author's work; the length of an entry reflects the amount of critical attention that the author has received from critics writing in English and from foreign critics in translation. Since many poets have inspired a prodigious amount of critical explication, *PC* is necessarily selective, and the editors have chosen the most significant published criticism to aid readers and students in their research. In order to provide these important critical pieces, the editors will sometimes reprint essays that have appeared in previous volumes of Gale's Literary Criticism Series. Such duplication, however, never exceeds fifteen percent of a *PC* volume.

Organization

Each *PC* author entry consists of the following components:

- **Author Heading:** the name under which the author wrote appears at the beginning of the entry, followed by birth and death dates. If the author wrote consistently under a pseudonym, the pseudonym will be listed in the author heading and his or her legal name given in parentheses in the lines immediately preceding the Introduction. Uncertainty as to birth or death dates is indicated by question marks.

- **Introduction:** a biographical and critical essay introduces readers to the author and the critical discussions surrounding his or her work.

- **Author Portrait:** a photograph or illustration of the author is included when available. Most entries also feature illustrations of people and places pertinent to an author's career, as well as holographs of manuscript pages and dust jackets.

- **Principal Works:** the author's most important works are identified in a list ordered chronologically by first publication dates. The first section comprises poetry collections and book-length poems. The second section gives information on other major works by the author. For foreign authors, original foreign-language publication information is provided, as well as the best and most complete English-language editions of their works.

- **Criticism:** critical excerpts chronologically arranged in each author entry provide perspective on changes in critical evaluation over the years. All individual titles of poems and poetry collections by the author featured in the entry are printed in boldface type to enable a reader to ascertain without difficulty the works under discussion. For purposes of easy identification, the critic's name and the publication date of the essay are given at the beginning of each piece of criticism. Unsigned criticism is preceded by the title of the journal in which it originally appeared. Publication information (such as publisher names and book prices) and parenthetical numerical references (such as footnotes or page and line references to specific editions of a work) have been deleted at the editor's discretion to enable smoother reading of the text.

- **Explanatory Notes:** introductory comments preface each critical excerpt, providing several types of useful information, including: the reputation of a critic, the importance of a work of criticism, and the specific type of criticism (biographical, psychoanalytic, historical, etc.).

- **Author Commentary:** insightful comments from the authors themselves and excerpts from author interviews are included when available.

- **Bibliographical Citations:** information preceding each piece of criticism guides the interested reader to the original essay or book.

- **Further Reading:** bibliographic references accompanied by descriptive notes at the end of each entry suggest additional materials for study of the author. Boxed material following the Further Reading provides references to other biographical and critical series published by Gale.

Other Features

Cumulative Author Index: comprises all authors who have appeared in Gale's Literary Criticism Series, along with cross-references to such Gale biographical series as *Contemporary Authors* and *Dictionary of Literary Biography*. This cumulated index enables the user to locate an author within the various series.

Cumulative Nationality Index: includes all authors featured in *PC*, arranged alphabetically under their respective nationalities.

Cumulative Title Index: lists in alphabetical order all individual poems, book-length poems, and collection titles contained in the *PC* series. Titles of poetry collections and separately published poems are printed in italics, while titles of individual poems are printed in roman type with quotation marks. Each title is followed by the author's name and the volume and page number corresponding to the location of commentary on specific works. English-language translations of original foreign-language titles are cross-referenced to the foreign titles so that all references to discussion of a work are combined in one listing.

Citing *Poetry Criticism*

When writing papers, students who quote directly from any volume in the Literary Criticism Series may use the following general formats to footnote reprinted criticism. The first example pertains to material drawn from periodicals, the second to material reprinted from books:

[1]David Daiches, "W. H. Auden: The Search for a Public," *Poetry* LIV (June 1939), 148-56; excerpted and reprinted in *Poetry Criticism*, Vol. 1, ed. Robyn V. Young (Detroit: Gale Research, 1990), pp. 7-9.

[2]Pamela J. Annas, *A Disturbance in Mirrors: The Poetry of Sylvia Plath* (Greenwood Press, 1988); excerpted and reprinted in *Poetry Criticism*, Vol. 1, ed. Robyn V. Young (Detroit: Gale Research, 1990), pp. 410-14.

Comments Are Welcome

Readers who wish to suggest authors to appear in future volumes, or who have other suggestions, are cordially invited to contact the editors.

Acknowledgments

The editors wish to thank the copyright holders of the excerpted criticism included in this volume and the permissions managers of many book and magazine publishing companies for assisting us in securing reprint rights. We are also grateful to the staffs of the Detroit Public Library, the Library of Congress, the University of Detroit Mercy Library, Wayne State University Purdy/Kresge Library Complex, and the University of Michigan Libraries for making their resources available to us. Following is a list of the copyright holders who have granted us permission to reprint material in this volume of *PC*. Every effort has been made to trace copyright, but if omissions have been made, please let us know.

COPYRIGHTED EXCERPTS IN *PC*, VOLUME 13, WERE REPRINTED FROM THE FOLLOWING PERIODICALS:

American Indian Culture and Research Journal, v. 4, 1980 for "The Uses of Oral Tradition in Six Contemporary Native American Poets" by James Ruppert. Copyright © 1980 The Regents of the University of California. Reprinted by permission of the author.—*The Antioch Review,* v. 35, Spring-Summer, 1977. Copyright © 1977 by the Antioch Review, Inc. Reprinted by permission of the Editors.—*Book Forum,* v. V, 1981 for "American Indian Poets--And Publishing" by Wendy Rose. Copyright © 1981 by The Hudson River Press. Reprinted by permission of the author.—*Books Abroad,* v. 45, Autumn, 1971; v. 47, Summer, 1973. Copyright 1971, 1973 by the University of Oklahoma Press. Both reprinted by permission of the publisher.—*The Centennial Review,* v. XXIV, Winter, 1980 for "The Theme of Authority in the Works of Francois Villon" by Ann Tukey Harrison. © 1980 by *The Centennial Review.* Reprinted by permission of the publisher and the author.—*Choice,* v. 23, May, 1986. Copyright © 1986 by American Library Association. Reprinted by permission of the publisher.—*ELH,* Fall, 1974; v. 58, Spring, 1991. Copyright © 1974, 1991 by The Johns Hopkins University Press. All rights reserved. Both reprinted by permission of the publisher.—*The Emory University Quarterly,* v. XXI, Spring, 1965. Copyright © by *The Emory University Quarterly.* Reprinted by permission of the publisher.—*English Studies,* Netherlands, v. 65, February, 1984. © 1984 by Swets & Zeitlinger B.V. Reprinted by permission of the publisher.—*Etudes Anglaises,* v. XXIV, October-December, 1971. Reprinted by permission of the publisher.—*Grand Street,* v. 3, Autumn, 1983 for "An Invitation to Hope: Eugenio Montale" by Henry Gifford. Copyright © 1983 by Grand Street Publications, Inc. All rights reserved. Reprinted by permission of the publisher and the author.—*Italian Quarterly,* v. 8, Spring, 1964; v. 13, Summer, 1969. Both reprinted by permission of the publisher.—*Italica,* v. XLII, March, 1965. Reprinted by permission of the publisher.—*KUSC-FM--Los Angeles, CA,* March 11, 1981. Reprinted by permission of Jascha Kessler.—*Literature and Psychology,* v. XVII, 1967. © Editor 1967. Reprinted by permission of the publisher.—*Modern Language Quarterly,* v. XXVIII, 1967. © 1969 University of Washington. Reprinted by permission of Duke University Press.—*The Modern Language Review,* v. 66, October, 1971 for "Scott and 'Marmion': The Discovery of Identity" by John Pikoulis. © Modern Humanities Association 1971. Reprinted by permission of the publisher and the author.—*Neophilologus,* v. LXXVI, January, 1992 for "Communication and Implied Audience(s) in Villon's Testament" by Barbara N. Sargent-Baur. © 1992 by H. D. Tjeenk Willink. Reprinted by permission of the publisher and the author.—*The New York Review of Books,* v. XVIII, June 1, 1972; v. XXIV, June 9, 1977. Copyright © 1972, 1977 Nyrev, Inc. Both reprinted with permission from *The New York Review of Books.*—*PMLA,* v. LXXXII, December, 1967. Copyright © 1967 by the Modern Language Association of America. Reprinted by permission of the Modern Language Association of America.—*Proceedings of the British Academy,* v. XLVII, *1961 Lectures and Memoirs*; v. LXI, *1975 Lectures and Memoirs.* © The British Academy 1962, 1976. Both reproduced by permission of the publisher.—*The Sewanee Review,* v. LXVI, Winter, 1958 for "Eugenio Montale's Poetry: A Meeting of Dante and Brueghel" by Glauco Cambon. Copyright 1966 by Glauco Cambon. Reprinted by permission of the Literary Estate of Glauco Cambon./ v. LXXXV, Summer, 1977 for "The Poetry of Eugenio Montale" by Russell Fraser. © 1977 by The University of the South. Reprinted with the permission of the editor of *The Sewanee Review* and the author.—*The South Atlantic Quarterly,* v. 48, July, 1949. Copyright 1949 by Duke University Press, Durham, NC. Reprinted with permission of the publisher.—*Studies in English Literature, 1500-1900,* v. XII, Autumn, 1972 for "The Dilemma of History: A Reading of Scott's *Bridal of Trierman*" by Jill

COPYRIGHTED EXCERPTS IN *PC*, VOLUME 13, WERE REPRINTED FROM THE FOLLOWING BOOKS:

PHOTOGRAPHS AND ILLUSTRATIONS APPEARING IN *PC*, VOLUME 13, WERE RECEIVED FROM THE FOLLOWING SOURCES:

Aphra Behn
1640?–1689

(Pseudonym of Aphra Johnson or Aphra Amis; also Aphara, Ayfara, and Afray; also wrote under the pseudonyms Astrea and Astraea) English dramatist, novelist, poet, essayist, and translator.

INTRODUCTION

Willing to endure seventeenth-century society's disapproval of women writing for pay, Behn became the first female to earn her living solely as an author, openly competing for recognition with the male writers who comprised the English literary establishment. Her works, like the literary endeavors of her male contemporaries, catered to the libertine tastes of King Charles II and his supporters through social and political satire as well as plots involving amorous intrigues and sexual promiscuity. Behn's verse, which tends to be less coarse than her dramas, often focuses either on lovers or the historical events of the era. Her most studied poems challenge social mores by freely discussing female sexual desire and questioning gender roles.

Biographical Information

Most critical studies of Behn speculate about her early life, but Behn's birthplace and date of birth, as well as the identity of her parents, have never been conclusively established. However, it is generally agreed that she and her family sailed to Surinam in South America, most likely in 1663, and that her father, who had been appointed lieutenant-governor there, died en route. Behn lived in Surinam for several months before the Dutch takeover, and her impressions of the country were later recorded in her novel *Oroonoko; or, The Royal Slave.* It is speculated that after returning to England in 1664 she married a man of Dutch descent. At this time Behn seems to have been wealthy, popular at the court of Charles II, and well known for her charm and wit. However, her husband died shortly after their marriage and, for reasons unknown, she was left an impoverished widow. It is only after this point in her life that substantial information about Behn has been documented. In 1666, Charles II employed Behn, a staunch royalist, to spy on a disaffected English group in Antwerp. Though the mission provided the crown with valuable information, Behn was not remunerated for her espionage efforts. She returned to England in poverty and spent a brief time in debtor's prison before ultimately deciding to, as she said, "write for bread." Until this time only a few women had been writers, but they were aristocrats who merely dabbled in the arts, and their works were not taken seriously. Thus, Behn's decision to join London's Grub Street hacks was both bold and unprecedented. The popularity of her first play, *The Forced Marriage; or, The Jealous Bridegroom,* proved that a woman could successfully write the same bawdy material

that the male playwrights of the era were producing. Eventually, however, Behn's work was attacked as immoral by many of her contemporaries. Undaunted by the criticism, she continued to write and spent most of her literary career defending her works against charges of indecency; Behn claimed that critics unfairly singled her out because of her gender. Behn lived an impoverished life, and her material hardships contributed to a prolonged illness in her later years. After her death, she was honored with a burial in Westminster Abbey.

Major Works

Much of Behn's verse appears in her plays. These poems are generally valued for their musicality and their contribution to the dramas in which they are contained, but have attracted little attention as independent literary pieces. Samuel J. Rogal has stated that they "reflect [Behn's] ability to manipulate verse as a reinforcement for dramatic theme and setting," and Vita Sackville-West downplayed the consideration due these lyrics by characterizing them as songs rather than poetry. Other poems by Behn were written in honor of noted figures or for occasions such as coronations, the birth of a child in the royal family, the death of famous individuals, and other events that she deemed worth celebrating in verse. Her most discussed poems, however, depart from literary tradition by treating the subject of romantic love graphically and from a female perspective. "The Willing Mistress" serves as a counterpoint to the view of women as coquettes or passive objects of passion, depicting them instead as willful beings driven by passion in the same manner as men. "The Disappointment" presents a woman who becomes sexually aroused by her lover but is then frustrated by his impotence. "To the Fair Clarinda, Who Made Love to Me, Imagined More than Woman" has been interpreted by commentators as a celebration of lesbian love. In these poems and others, Behn challenged the orthodoxies of her day in print, just as her "writing for bread" challenged them in practice.

Critical Reception

Though Behn enjoyed some popular success during her lifetime and had early supporters, she was dogged throughout her career with charges of lewdness. Her reputation was revived in the twentieth century by Virginia Woolf, who wrote in *A Room of One's Own* (1930), "All women together ought to let flowers fall upon the tomb of Aphra Behn . . . for it was she who earned them the right to speak their minds"; since then Behn has received much attention from feminist critics, who note her subversion of the patriarchal code in her life and her writing and praise her advocation of freedom for women in matters of love, marriage, and sexual and artistic expression.

PRINCIPAL WORKS

Poetry

Poems upon Several Occasions, with a Voyage to the Island of Love 1684
The Case for the Watch (poetry and prose) 1686
La Montre: or, The Lover's Watch (poetry and prose) 1686
Lycidus; or, The Lover in Fashion (poetry and prose) 1688
The Lady's Looking-Glass, to Dress Herself By: or, The Art of Charming (poetry and prose) 1697
The Works of Aphra Behn. 6 vols. (poetry, dramas, and novels) 1915
Selected Writings of the Ingenious Mrs. Aphra Behn (poetry, novels, dramas, and essays) 1950
The Uncollected Verse of Aphra Behn 1989

Other Major Works

The Forced Marriage; or, The Jealous Bridegroom (drama) 1670
The Amorous Prince; or, The Curious Husband (drama) 1671
The Dutch Lover (drama) 1673
Abdelazar; or, The Moor's Revenge (drama) 1676
The Town Fop; or, Sir Timothy Tawdrey (drama) 1676

The Rover; or, The Burnished Cavalier, Part I (drama) 1677
Sir Patient Fancy (drama) 1678
The Feigned Courtesans; or, A Night's Intrigue (drama) 1679
The Roundheads; or, The Good Old Cause (drama) 1681
The Second Part of the Rover (drama) 1681
The City Heiress; or, Sir Timothy Treat-all (drama) 1682
The False Count; or, A New Way to Play an Old Game (drama) 1682
Love Letters between a Nobleman and His Sister (fictional letters) 1684
The Luckey Chance; or, An Alderman's Bargain (drama) 1686
The Emperor of the Moon (drama) 1687
The Fair Jilt; or, The History of Prince Tarquin and Miranda (novel) 1688
The History of the Nun; or, The Fair Vow-Breaker (novel) 1688
Oroonoko; or, The Royal Slave (novel) 1688
The Lucky Mistake (novel) 1689
The Widow Ranter; or, The History of Bacon in Virginia (drama) 1689
The Histories and Novels of the Late Ingenious Mrs. Behn (dramas and novels) 1696
Love Letters to a Gentleman (letters) 1696
The Plays, Histories, and Novels of the Ingenious Mrs. Aphra Behn. 6 vols. (dramas and novels) 1871
The Novels of Mrs. Aphra Behn (novels) 1969

CRITICISM

Kendrick (poem date 1688)

SOURCE: "To Mrs. B. on Her Poems," in *Lycidus; or, The Lover in Fashion, Together with a Miscellany of New Poems* by Aphra Behn et al., Joseph Knight and Francis Saunders, 1688, n.p.

[*In the following poem, Kendrick praises Behn in exalted terms, likening her to a goddess and declaring her verse superior to that of Orinda (Katherine Philips), Sappho, and even Ovid.*]

To Mrs. B. on Her Poems

Hail, Beauteous *Prophetess,* in whom alone,
Of all your fair Heav'ns master-piece is shewn.
For wondrous skill it argues, wondrous care,
Where two such Stars in first conjunction are.
A Brain so Glorious, and a Face so fair,
Two Goddesses in your composure joyn'd.
Nothing but Goddess cou'd, you're so refin'd,
Bright *Venus* Body gave, *Minerva* Mind.

How soft and fine your manly numbers flow,
Soft as your Lips, and smooth as is your brow.
Gentle as Air, bright as the Noon-days sky,
Clear as your skin, and charming as your Eye.

No craggy Precipice the Prospect spoyles,
The Eye no tedious barren plain beguiles.
But, like *Thessalian* Fields your Volumes are,
Rapture and charms o're all the soyl appear,
Astrea and her verse are *Tempe* everywhere.

Ah, more than Woman! more than man she is,
As *Phœbus* bright; she's too, as *Phœbus* wife.
The Muses to our sex perverse and coy
Astrea. do's familiarly enjoy.
She do's their veiled Glorys understand,
And what we court with pain, with ease command.
Their charming secrets they expanded lay,
Reserv'd to us, to her they all display.
Upon her Pen await those learned Nine.
She ne're but like the Phosph'rus draws a line,
As soon as toucht her subjects clearly shine.

The femal Laurels were obscur'd till now,
And they deserv'd the Shades in which they grew:
But *Daphne* at your call return's her flight,
Looks boldly up and dares the God of light.
If we *Orinda* to your works compare,
They uncouth, like her countrys soyle, appear,
Mean as its Pesants, as its Mountains bare,
Sappho tasts strongly of the sex, is weak and poor
At second hand the russet Laurels wore,
Yours are your own, a rich and verdant store.
If Loves the Theme, you outdo *Ovids* Art,
Loves God himself can't subtiller skill impart.
Softer than's plumes, more piercing than his Dart.

If *Pastoral* be her Song, she glads the Swains
With Livelier notes, with spritelier smiles the plains.
More gayly than the Springs she decks the Bowrs
And breaths a second *May* to Fields and Flowrs.
If e're the golden Age again return
And flash in shining Beames from's Iron Urn,
That Age not as it was before shall be,
But as th' Idea is refin'd by thee.
That seems the common; thines the Elixir, Gold,
So pure is thine, and so allay'd the old.

Happy, ye Bards, by fair *Astrea* prais'd,
If you'r alive, to brighter life you're rais'd;
For cherished by her Beames you'l loftyer grow,
You must your former learned selves outdo,
Thô you'd the parts of *Thirst* and of *Strephon* too.
Hail, mighty Prophetess! by whom we see
Omnipotence almost in Poetry:
Your flame can give to Graves *Promethean* fire,
And *Greenhills* clay with living paint inspire,
For like some Mystick wand with awful Eyes
You wave your Pen, and lo the dead Arise.

Athenian Mercury (essay date 1691)

SOURCE: An excerpt in *Athenian Mercury*, Vol. 5, No. 13, January 12, 1691, p. 2.

[*In responding to a reader's question, the editor opines that Behn's poetry is uncannily similar in spirit to that of Sappho, and wishes that Behn had produced her own translation of Sappho's verse.*]

Quest. . . . *Whether* Sappho *or Mrs.* Behn *were the better Poetess?*

Answ. We must beg the Person of Honours pardon who lent this Question, if we can't help telling a pleasant passage before we answer it, 'tis met with in the Voyages of one *Struis* a *Dutchman,* about some 10 years since translated into *English;* and 'tis this, *In the City of Ardebil in Persia are a Corporation of Whores, all Poetesses, whose chief Subject is the praise of the Emperor.* This unlucky Story was brought to mind by some woful Loyal plays, which for 2 Reigns together pester'd the Theaters and Stationers, which is all we will say of 'em, considering whose they were, but come now to the comparison: *Sappho* wrote too little, and Mrs. *Behn* too much, for us to give 'em any just or equal Character, not but that by the little, *very little* we have of *Sappho,* we believe hardly ever were 2 *Souls* more alike than Mrs. *Behns* and hers. Mrs. *Behn,* its true, has writ many things, and some of 'em excellently well, in her own *soft strain,* few coming near her; particularly in her **Lovers Watch,** which if we mistake not, we formerly mention'd. And then her **Voyage to the Island of Love,** proves her a great proficient both in the *Theory and practical part of that passion:* But yet one Fragment consisting but of a few Lines, which we have of *Sappho's,* carries something in it so soft, *lushious and charming even in the sound of the words,* that *Catallus* himself, who has endeavour'd somewhat like 'em in Latin, comes infinitely short of 'em, and so have all the rest who have writ their own thoughts on that Subject;—for which reason we cou'd wish Mrs. *Behn* her self had translated 'em before she went to *Elysium* to meet her.

V. Sackville-West (essay date 1928)

SOURCE: "Works: The Poet," in *Aphra Behn: The Incomparable Astrea,* The Viking Press, 1928, pp. 157–63.

[*Vita Sackville-West was an English poet, novelist, biographer, and essayist. In the following excerpt, she judges whether Behn should more appropriately be considered a poet or a songwriter.*]

Much has been written about Mrs. Behn as a playwright, and as a novelist she has been mentioned from time to time, but as a poet she has scarcely been mentioned at all. "Love in fantastic triumph sate,"—how many people can quote beyond that first splendid line? Yet she herself claimed that poetry was her talent, so it seems fair to examine, now that she is no longer there to speak for herself, what justification she had for that arrogance. I cannot help having some respect for the opinion that writers hold of themselves, even though their judgment almost invariably prove to be wrong. Had she said song-writer, we should be all agreement. Her songs were as good as the age allowed them to be; she was no genius to stride out beyond the conventions of her age, but as she was a perfectly competent maker of plays, so was she a perfectly competent maker of the sort of song then in fashion, and occasionally she rose above it, and produced something that was less a song than a pure lyric:

> Love in fantastic triumph sate,
>   Whilst bleeding hearts around him flowed,
> For whom fresh pains he did create
>   And strange tyrannic power he showed:
> From thy bright eyes he took his fires,
>   Which round about in sport he hurled,
> But 'twas from mine he took desires
>   Enough t'undo the amorous world.
>
> From me he took his sighs and tears,
>   From thee his pride and cruelty;
> From me his languishments and fears,
>   And every killing dart from thee.
> Thus thou and I the god have armed
>   And set him up a deity;
> But my poor heart alone is harmed,
>   Whilst thine the victor is, and free.

Yes, she could certainly write a song. She could write **"The Libertine"**:

> A thousand martyrs I have made,
>   All sacrificed to my desire,
> A thousand beauties have betrayed,
>   That languish in resistless fire.
> The untamed heart to hand I brought,
> And fixed the wild and wandering thought.
>
> I never vowed nor sighed in vain,
>   But both, though false, were well received;
> The fair are pleased to give us pain.
>   And what they wish is soon believed.
> And though I talked of wounds and smart,
> Love's pleasures only touched my heart.
>
> Alone the glory and the spoil
>   I always laughing bore away;
> The triumphs without pain or toil,
>   Without the hell the heaven of joy.
> And while I thus at random rove
> Despise the fools that whine for love.

She could write **"The Willing Mistress"** and **"When Jemmy first began to love."** But all these exercises, excellent as they are in their own way, rather recall the severe words of Hazlitt: "It should appear, in tracing the history of our literature, that poetry had . . . in general declined, by successive gradations, from the poetry of imagination in the time of Elizabeth, to the poetry of fancy in the time of Charles I, and again from the poetry of fancy to that of wit, as in the reign of Charles II." Astrea set great store by wit, and most of her poems are neat enough in consequence. Many of them are incorporated in the plays, where little more than a light and pleasant refrain was needed. It may seem surprising that she never

took to satire; but then, although often indignant, she was never spiteful. There was no real vinegar in her mockery. So her songs, let us concede, are graceful enough; pointed, gallant. But still we come back to her claim that she was a poet. The writer of **"Love in Fantastic Triumph"** was certainly a poet; what more can we bring, beyond the songs, to support her claim? what sudden accent, from the swell of her turgid Pindarics?

> So have I seen an unfit star
>   Outshine the rest of all the numerous
>   train,
> As bright as that which guides the mariner,
> Dart swiftly from its darkened sphere
> And ne'er shall sight the world again.

Is that poetry? Is this:

> By the sad purling of some rivulet
>   O'er which the bending yew and willow
>   grow,
> That scarce the glimmering of the day permit
>   To view the melancholy banks below,
> Where dwells no noise but what the mur-
>   murs make,
> When the unwilling stream the shade for-
>   sakes?

It is very seldom that her voice speaks with even this hint of the accent of poetry. The songs are, on the whole, the best that can be claimed for her, and it may be said that the claim is a modest one. Indeed, this whole estimate of Astrea's work is perhaps slightly ungracious: it is more in the nature of reproach than of praise. We concede that she did certain things well, and then immediately attack her for not having done different things better,—much as we criticise Proust to-day for not having concentrated more on the passions of the human heart, and less on certain worldly aspirations with which we are temperamentally unsuited to sympathise. We grow impatient with the gifts that she undoubtedly had, and abuse her for not having exploited other gifts which would have created for us something more to our taste. She is an example, we conclude, of those writers who preversely mistake their vocation. So be it. In the course of . . . three months spent in her company [i.e. reading her works], it is Aphra the woman of whom I have grown fond, to the extent of forgiving Aphra the writer the tedious hours she has compelled me to spend over her volumes. She has puzzled and annoyed me; but it is, in the end, with considerable affection that I record her courage and adversities. Gay, tragic, generous, smutty, rich of nature and big of heart, propping her elbows on the tavern table, cracking her jokes, penning those midnight letters to her sad lover by the light of a tallow dip,—this is the Aphra of whom one cannot take leave without respect.

Frederick M. Link (essay date 1968)

SOURCE: "The Poet," in *Aphra Behn,* Twayne Publishers, Inc., 1968, pp. 102–15.

[An American educator specializing in English literature, Link has published editions of works by Behn, John Dryden, Hannah Cowley, and Walter Scott. In the following excerpt, he provides an overview of Behn's poetry.]

Most of Mrs. Behn's poetry is occasional—the work of a professional dramatist with a considerable lyric talent and a constant need for money. For her plays she wrote prologues and epilogues, only occasionally obtaining them from a fellow writer; these works constitute a clearly defined group. A second grouping is more miscellaneous: some forty songs written to be sung within the plays, several sets of commendatory verses, a number of topical pieces, and several translations. Elegies and panegyrics, often written in the loosely organized irregular stanza popularized by Abraham Cowley a generation earlier, make up a final group. A brief study of some of these poems suggests Mrs. Behn's unusual versatility and shows the quality of her best work.

PROLOGUES AND EPILOGUES

The prologues and epilogues are typical of the period. They are always in couplets, though more triplets appear than Pope would have approved; and they are usually satiric and topical. The speaker, usually one of the important characters in the piece, addresses the audience directly; comments on the state of the theater and of the playgoers are staple fare. The audience is rarely praised for its good taste; in one prologue after another Mrs. Behn criticizes the trend toward farce and "entertainment" which she saw debasing the legitimate stage:

> Alas! a poet's good for nothing now,
> Unless he have the knack of conjuring too;
> For 'tis beyond all natural sense to guess
> How their strange miracles are brought to pass.
> Your Presto Jack be gone, and come again,
> With all the hocus art of legerdemain;
> Your dancing tester, nutmeg, and your cups,
> Outdoes your heroes and your amorous fops.

Some of the pieces document the change. The prologue to *The Emperor of the Moon,* for example, traces the progress of recent drama from heroic tragedy through "humbler comedy" to farce. The attack on the taste of the playgoer is conventional, of course, but it is made too often to have no basis in fact. The fore- and afterpieces themselves give at least two reasons for the decline in quality. One is the thinning audience, a basic economic fact which forced most playwrights to take any measures necessary to fill the house. The epilogue to *The Second Part of the Rover* speaks of the poets as kings of wit summoning their parliaments by playbill; the new play used to be "the speech that begs supply":

> But now—
> The scanted tribute is so slowly paid,
> Our poets must find out another trade;

> They've tried all ways th' insatiate clan to please;
> Have parted with their old prerogatives—
> Their birthright satiring, and their just pretense
> Of judging, even their own wit and sense—
> And write against their consciences, to show
> How dull they can be to comply with you.
> They've flattered all the mutineers i' th' nation,
> Grosser than e'er was done in dedication;
> Pleased your sick palates with fantastic wit,
> Such as was ne'er a treat before to th' pit;
> Giants, fat cardinals, Pope Joans, and friars,
> To entertain right worshipfuls and squires. . . .

The prologue to *Abdelazer* chides the gallants for having been so long absent and for coming "only on the first and second days"; the epilogue to *The Emperor of the Moon* laments that "Not one is left will write for thin third day."

The other reason suggested for the decline is the turbulent political situation. The actress Elizabeth Currer comes on stage at the start of *The Feigned Courtesans* to ask:

> Who would have thought such hellish times to've
>   seen,
> When I should be neglected at eighteen?
> That youth and beauty should be quite undone,
> A pox upon the Whore of Babylon.

Apparently, many of the audience no longer supported the Tory side, particularly in the late 1670's and early 1680's: "And yet you'll come but once, unless by stealth, / Except the author be for commonwealth."

The gallants and fops who made up a large share of the audience are often baited in a good-humored way, especially for their capriciousness and love for the cheap and spectacular: "Vain amorous coxcombs every where are found, / Fops for all uses but the stage abound." The prologue to *The Young King,* in like vein, mocks the "Sparks who are of noise and nonsense full, / At fifteen witty, and at twenty dull." But a stronger lash is reserved for country squires, city merchants, and of course Puritans. The country bumpkin "At last by happy chance is hither led, / To purchase clap with loss of maidenhead"; he comes to be "all burlesque in mode and dress," and nothing more than "mighty noise and show." The "cit" is often an upstart, and nearly always Whiggish. Satire against the Whigs is both general and specific, as in the references to the *Ignoramus* jury and to Titus Oates. Mrs. Behn follows the Tory line in identifying Shaftesbury and his group with the cant and violence of the Good Old Cause. The prologue to *The Roundheads,* a typical example, has the ghost of Hewson "Roused by strange scandal from th' eternal flame" to ask whether all the furor over Jesuit plots can "Act mischief equal to Presbytery":

> Pay those that rail, and those that can delude
> With scribbling nonsense the loose multitude.
> Pay well your witnesses, they may not run
> To the right side, and tell who set 'em on.

Pay 'em so well, that they may ne'er recant,
And so turn honest merely out of want.
Pay juries, that no formal laws may harm us;
Let treason be secured by *Ignoramus*.

The political theme appears in some form in nearly half of the twenty-two prologues and epilogues presumably written by Mrs. Behn. The epilogue to *The Rover* draws an analogy between Puritanism and those who would "with canting rule . . . the stage refine," and Mrs. Behn attacks "dull method" also in the prologue to *The Amorous Prince* and in the epilogue to *Sir Patient Fancy*. The reverse of the coin appears in the frequent panegyrics to Charles and his policies. The epilogue to *The Young King*, for example, develops a not so obscure contrast between the Arcadian shepherd in peaceful command of his flock and the chaotic state of England; the concluding reference, "And keep the golden age within our woods and plains," makes use of an image common in Tory poetry.

Many, if not all, of these themes appear frequently in prologues and epilogues by other hands; they occasionally serve to confirm and emphasize themes in the plays they accompany, but only more personal themes like the defense of women in the epilogue to *Sir Patient Fancy* and in the prologue to *The Forced Marriage* are peculiar to Mrs. Behn.

Mrs. Behn's handling of the couplet form is usually competent and often distinguished. Sustained metaphors like that in the epilogue to Part Two of *The Rover* remind one of Dryden, the greatest master of the genre. The form demands an ear for the rhythms of speech, and the technical skill to achieve variety and interest within the limitations of the two-line unit. Mrs. Behn has both. In one piece after another she manages to bring off a good-humored attack on the foibles of her audience, allude satirically to contemporary politics, and simultaneously evoke the mood most suitable for introducing her play and for bringing the evening to a close. The prologue to *Sir Patient Fancy*, spoken by the actor Thomas Betterton, adopts the bantering, familiar tone characteristic of the period:

Oh the great blessing of a little wit!
I've seen an elevated poet sit
And hear the audience laugh and clap, yet say,
Gad, after all, 'tis a damned silly play;
He, unconcerned, cries only—Is it so?
No matter, these unwitty things will do
When your fine, fustian, useless eloquence
Serves but to chime asleep a drowsy audience.
Who at the vast expense of wit would treat,
That might so cheaply please the appetite?

The positioning of *great* and *little*, the irony of *blessing*, and the pun of *elevated* are important details. The rhymes in lines 2, 3, and 4 are naturally produced without inversion of normal syntax; the use of the pyrrhic foot in line 3, forcing a slight accent on the *yet*, emphasizes the disjunction stated in the couplet and the variability of the audience. Mrs. Behn places her caesuras to achieve max-imum variety within the lines, and she guards against monotony by varying iambs with trochees (ll. 1 and 9) and by using polysyllables in almost every line. The alexandrine in line 8 is perhaps too obviously the metrical equivalent of *drowsy*, but the alliteration and accent shift in *fine fustian* produce exactly the desired effect.

Mrs. Behn rarely uses the superb organizing images which inform Dryden's best prologues. But the political situation provides her with a ready-made metaphor which she manipulates with great skill. The same prologue furnishes a good example:

But now, like happy states luxurious grown,
The monarch wit unjustly you dethrone,
And a tyrannic commonwealth prefer,
Where each small wit starts up and claims his
    share;
And all those laurels are in pieces torn,
Which did e'er while one sacred head adorn.

The *sacred head* is Dryden, but the metaphor takes the passage beyond a single literary figure. Dryden becomes Charles; his "dethronement" by a mob of hack poets and pamphleteers is made to suggest not merely the destruction of literary values but the fate of the royal martyr and its consequences in the Commonwealth period. The use of the word *sacred* establishes still another level of meaning: beyond the "death" of Dryden is the death of Charles; beyond it is that of Christ. The effect of the passage is to connect two apparently unrelated phenomena—the state of literature and the state of the nation; assert that the one is caused by the other; and use the religious image to condemn republicanism in all three areas of life.

A final example of her skill may be cited from the prologue to *The City Heiress*, which uses an extended metaphor from the business world to satirize an abortive dinner of "thanksgiving" planned by the Whigs to discomfit the Tories:

Who, but the most incorrigible fops,
For ever doomed in dismal cells, called shops,
To cheat and damn themselves to get their livings,
Would lay sweet money out in sham Thanksgivings?
Sham-plots, you may have paid for o'er and o'er;
But whoe'er paid for a sham treat before?
Had you not better sent your offerings all
Hither to us, than Sequestrators Hall?
I being your steward, justice had been done ye;
I could have entertained you worth your money.

In ten lines, Mrs. Behn identifies the leading Whigs as foppish shopkeepers, refers slyly to the collapse of the Oates plot, and wittily suggests that her Tory play would have been better entertainment for the Whigs than anything they themselves could have planned for the same money.

SONGS AND OTHER SHORT POEMS

The Restoration wits perfected a sophisticated and impersonal style which for elegance, wit, and precision of tone has seldom been surpassed in English poetry. The mode they adopted was limited and artificial, but its limits were self-imposed and its artificiality deliberate. Mrs. Behn's best songs bear comparison with those of the court poets and of Matthew Prior; few of them fail to give pleasure after nearly three hundred years.

Her lyric gift is evident from the first. The masque in Act V of *The Forced Marriage* is graceful enough, but the page's song in II.vi is at another level of achievement:

> Amintas that true-hearted swain
> Upon a river's bank was laid,
> Where to the pitying streams he did complain
> On Sylvia! that false charming maid;
> But she was still regardless of his pain.
> Oh! faithless Sylvia! would he cry,
> And what he said the echoes would reply:
>   Be kind or else I die. E[cho]. I die.
>   Be kind or else I die. E[cho]. I die.

The sophisticated pastoralism exemplified by the conscious and half-ironic use of personification (*pitying streams*) and by the light oxymoron (*false charming*) is quite typical. Mrs. Behn accepts both the language and the themes dictated by the convention; the names and the setting are as appropriate as the sentiments. The stylization is obvious, the lyric quality and the handling of rhythm exceptional.

Other fine examples are Hippolita's song in III.iii of *The Dutch Lover*, and the song for II.vi of the same play:

> His charming eyes no aid required,
> To tell their amorous tale:
> On her that was already fired
> 'Twas easy to prevail.
> He did but kiss, and clasp me round,
> Whilst they his thoughts expressed;
> And gently laid me on the ground—
> Ah! Who can guess the rest?

The later plays show no decline in Mrs. Behn's powers. The magnificent song which opens *Abdelazer*—**"Love in Fantastic Triumph Sat"**—has been often reprinted, and is probably her best known poem. The songs in *The Town Fop* are almost as good. The comic serenade in *Sir Patient Fancy* (III.ix) is deliberately bathetic and beautifully illuminates Sir Credulous' character. Both *The Second Part of the Rover* and *The City Heiress* contain fine songs: Sir Anthony's catch in Act III scene i of the latter is as appropriate for him as for the situation in which it occurs.

All of these songs come early in Mrs. Behn's career. Many of them were collected in her *Poems upon Several Occasions: With a Voyage to the Island of Love* (1684). By that time she had written a considerable number of other lyrics. Some of them, like **"Our Cabal,"** have unclear biographical significance; most are in the usual pastoral vein, as artless as art could make them, and written with that detached gaiety so typical of the Restoration period and so foreign to the twentieth century. The last stanza of **"When Jemmy First Began to Love"** is a good example:

> But now for Jemmy must I mourn,
>   Who to the wars must go;
> His sheephook to a sword must turn:
>   Alack, what shall I do?
> His bagpipe into warlike sounds,
>   Must now exchanged be:
> Instead of bracelets, fearful wounds;
>   Then what becomes of me?

Additional lyrics appeared in *Miscellany, Being A Collection of Poems by Several Hands* (1685), a volume edited by Mrs. Behn. Among them is the worst of her poems, a painful paraphrase of the Lord's Prayer, but also the excellent song, **"Cease, Cease, Aminta to Complain,"** and a graceful dialogue "made in an entertainment at court." The last substantial group of poems is found in *A Miscellany of New Poems,* appended to *Lycidus; or, The Lover in Fashion* (1688). No songs are among them, and such poems as the two to Alexis add nothing to her earlier achievements. By this time she was near death, and much involved in fiction and translation—activities that seem to have brought in more money than lyric poetry. After her death, poems by her, or attributed to her, appeared for a number of years; but none of them matches the quality of the dozen or so songs already mentioned.

Among Mrs. Behn's shorter poems are a number of narrative and satiric efforts, and a few miscellaneous pieces. The narratives are distinctly inferior to the lyrics, partly because Mrs. Behn's handling of rhythm and rhyme in them is inadequate. **"On a Juniper Tree,"** for example, is written in tetrameter couplets and seems to end every few lines. The reader comes down hard on the rhymes; only one line in six or seven has any internal pause. **"Our Cabal,"** written in the same form, is not much better. The only good narrative poem is a paraphrase of an unnamed French original, entitled **"The Disappointment."** She adopts a more flexible rhyme scheme to tell Lysander's story in stanzas, and the effect is that of a series of short lyrics held together by the sequence of action.

Satiric poems are rare outside the prologues and epilogues. **"A Letter to a Brother of the Pen in Tribulation"** is one example; the best is her verses **"On a Conventicle,"** first printed in Charles Gildon's *Miscellany Poems upon Several Occasions* (1692):

> Behold that race, whence England's woes proceed,
> The viper's nest, where all our mischiefs breed,
> There, guided by inspiration, treason speaks,
> And through the holy bagpipe Legion squeaks.
> The Nation's curse, religion's ridicule,
> The rabble's God, the politician's tool,
> Scorn of the wise, and scandal of the just,
> The villain's refuge, and the women's lust.

ELEGIES AND PANEGYRICS

The last group of Mrs. Behn's original poems—the elegies and panegyrics—bulks larger than all the rest. The poems comprising it are occasional in the strict sense of that word: they are written upon someone's birth, death, or marriage; upon a friend's departure; or perhaps upon a fellow author's new book. Most of them are addressed to members of the royal family or to the nobility and are at least semi-public in character. These circumstances dictated an elevated form. Mrs. Behn ordinarily chose the pindaric, the highest suitable form in the contemporary hierarchy of genres; less frequently, she used the couplet.

Some poems in this type appeared in the early collections. The 1684 *Poems* contains "**The Golden Age**"; "**A Farewell to Celadon, on His Going into Ireland**"; "**On the Death of Mr. Grinhil, the Famous Painter**"; "**To Mr. Creech . . . on His Excellent Translation of Lucretius**"; "**To Mrs. W. On Her Excellent Verses . . .**"; "**To My Lady Morland at Tunbridge**"; "**On Mr. J. H. in a Fit of Sickness**"; and "**To the Honorable Edward Howard. . . .**" Of these only the poem to Lady Morland is in regular couplet form; most are irregular in both rhyme scheme and meter. Most of them are conventional and overly rhetorical; they tell the reader very little about their subjects and sound, therefore, like a hundred other forgotten pieces written on similar occasions.

One, however, is of greater interest. The poem on the golden age, which opens the volume, is a free paraphrase of an English translation from the French. Its pastoral primitivism recalls Mrs. Behn's earliest plays, and adumbrates more than one passage in *Oronooko*. The versification is undistinguished; in fact, part of the first stanza is cited in *Peri Bathous* as an example of the florid style. But the poem is the author's most explicit statement of a major theme: the conflict between sex and society. In the Edenic world of the poem, in which "Right and Property were words since made," lovers are restrained only by their vows to each other, which are "inviolably true":

> Not kept in fear of gods, no fond religious cause,
>> Nor in obedience to the duller laws.
>> Those fopperies of the gown were then not known,
> Those vain, those politic curbs to keep man in,
> Who by a fond mistake created that a sin
> Which freeborn we, by right of nature, claim our own.

Honor is society's invention, designed to destroy paradise:

> Honor! that put'st our words that should be free
>> Into a set formality;
> Thou base debaucher of the generous heart,
> That teachest all our looks and actions art;
>> What love designed a sacred gift,
>> What nature made to be possessed,
>> Mistaken honor, made a theft. . . .

Honor belongs to courts and palaces, where it may disturb the politician's sleep. The natural man, aware that beyond death is an eternal night, seizes his chance for happiness: "The swift paced hours of life soon steal away: / Stint not, ye Gods, his short-lived joy."

The *Miscellany* of 1685 added four more poems to this group: "**On the Death of the Late Earl of Rochester**"; "**A Pindaric to Mr. P. Who Sings Finely**"; "**On the Author of . . . *The Way to Health* . . .**"; and "**A Pastoral to Mr. Stafford . . .**" None of these is especially good, but the poem to Rochester is remarkable for genuineness of feeling. Mrs. Behn admired him both as man and as poet: "He was but lent this duller world t' improve / In all the charms of poetry, and love." Finally, the poems at the end of *Lycidus* included "**On the Honourable Sir Francis Fane . . . ,**" "**A Pastoral Pindaric . . . ,**" and "**On Desire.**" The second of these states again the superiority of love to the restrictions of society. Dorset and his wife will be happy because their marriage was not determined by "portion and jointure" but by common interest and affection.

Many poems in the form, and particularly those written on state occasions, were published in folio or quarto shortly after the event which they celebrate. The first of these was *A Pindaric on the Death of Our Late Sovereign* (early 1685), which had a second London and a Dublin edition within the year. Mrs. Behn's Tory sentiments are nowhere more obvious than in this elegy, which compares Charles with both Christ and Moses and which draws the logical conclusion about Charles' ultimate destiny: like Christ, he fell "a bleeding victim to atone for all!" and, "transfigured all to glory, mounts to Heaven!" (st. 4). *A Poem Humbly Dedicated to the Great Pattern of Piety and Virtue Catherine Queen Dowager,* published later in 1685, indulges in hyperboles on her grief and carries on the metaphor of divine correspondence: "So the blest Virgin at the world's great loss, / Came, and beheld, then fainted at the cross."

The last, and by far the longest, of the 1685 poems is *A Pindaric Poem on the Happy Coronation of . . . James II.* Mrs. Behn's joy in the event is unfeigned; the Gods themselves are happy in her poem:

> Gay robes of light the young divinities put on,
> And spread their shining locks to outvie the sun.
> On pillows formed of yielding air they lie,
> Placed in the mid-way regions of the sky. . . .
>
>> (st. 4)

The elaborate description of the coronation is not very good. The verse is frequently stilted and artificial, the flattery gross if not fulsome, and the sentiments expressed in exaggerated diction. Occasionally the poem, like that on the death of Charles, comes alive, especially when Mrs. Behn deals with her personal feeling about the Stuarts:

> Howe'er I toil for life all day,
> With whate'er cares my soul's oppressed,
> 'Tis in that sunshine still I play,
> 'Tis there my wearied mind's at rest;
> But oh vicisitudes of night must come
> Between the rising glories of the sun!
>
>> (st. 19)

When the personal note is missing, these poems become mere hack work, praise tailored in advance of an order and perhaps never paid for. The pindaric *To . . . Christopher Duke of Albemarle* (1687) is perhaps the worst of the entire group, largely for this reason. On the other hand, the elegy *To the Memory of . . . George Duke of Buckingham,* published in May, 1687, is surprisingly good. Mrs. Behn, who obviously regarded this celebrated wit very highly, rises to her occasion. "When so much wit, wit's great reformer dies," the very muses come to his obsequies. Care may dog the steps of the ordinary statesman, but in his handling of the ship of state,

> Great Buckingham a sprightlier measure trod:
> When o're the mounting waves the vessel rod[e],
> Unshocked by toils, by tempests undismayed,
> Steered the great bark, and as that danced, he
>   played.

>   (ll. 39–42)

He was a phoenix, but with a difference:

> Thy matchless worth all successors defies,
> And scorned an heir should from thy ashes rise:
> Begins and finishes that glorious sphere
> Too mighty for a second charioteer.

>   (ll. 80–83)

During her last days, Mrs. Behn published panegyrics on every important Tory occasion, probably because her financial need was great. The Queen's pregnancy produced the appropriate congratulation, full of Tory imagery:

> Like the first sacred infant, this will come
> With promise laden from the blessed womb,
> To call the wand'ring scattered nations home.
> Adoring princes shall arrive from far,
> Informed by angels, guided by his star,
> The new-born wonder to behold, and greet;
> And kings shall offer incense at his feet.

The subsequent poem on the birth of the Prince of Wales, in its delight at the perpetuation of the Stuart line, is more than a little ironic in its references to the future of the prince who became the Pretender: "No monarch's birth was ever ushered in / With signs so fortunate as this has been" (st. 3). Sir Roger L'Estrange's *History of the Times* occasioned a poem to this loyal Tory (1688), but the events of that memorable year were fatal to Mrs. Behn's political hopes, and the two subsequent panegyrics are markedly different in tone.

A Congratulatory Poem to . . . Queen Mary upon Her Arrival in England presents its author bewailing "an unhappy dear loved monarch's fate"; her stubborn muse lay "sullen with stubborn loyalty," aroused only by the memory of Mary's blood relationship to Charles II:

> And thou, great lord of all my vows, permit
> My muse who never failed obedience yet,
> To pay her tribute at Maria's feet,
> Maria so divine a part of you,

> Let me be just—but just with honor too.

>   (ll. 54–58)

The last of these poems was written during Mrs. Behn's fatal illness. Gilbert Burnet, the great Whig divine, had considerately inquired about her health, and the pindaric to him was her response. His writings, she says, have almost persuaded her of the justice of the Glorious Revolution. But old loyalties are stronger, and in the fourth and sixth stanzas of the poem she presents her case in the most moving lines in all her poetry:

> My muse that would endeavor fain to glide
> With the fair prosperous gale, and the full driving
>   tide:
> But loyalty commands with pious force,
>   That stops me in the thriving course;
> The breeze that wafts the crowding nations o'er,
>   Leaves me unpitied far behind
>   On the forsaken, barren shore,
> To sigh with Echo, and the murmuring wind. . . .
> Thus while the chosen seed possess the promised
>   land,
>   I, like the excluded prophet, stand;
>   The fruitful happy soil can only see,
>   But am forbid by fate's decree
> To share the triumph of the joyful victory.
>   Though I the wond'rous change deplore,
>   That makes me useless and forlorn,
>   Yet I the great design adore,
>   Though ruined in the universal turn.
> Nor can my indigence and lost repose,
> Those meager furies that surround me close,
>   Convert my sense and reason more
>   To this unprecedented enterprise,
>   Than that a man so great, so learn'd, so wise,
> The brave achievement owns and nobly justifies.

>   (sts. 6, 8)

Few Whigs had so generous and sincere a compliment from an ardent Tory, and few monarchs can have had such unswerving loyalty where there was no obligation and very little reward. One must pity the blindness of Mrs. Behn's devotion, especially in the case of James II; but one cannot help admiring its integrity and strength.

The substantial poems Mrs. Behn produced for great occasions have been largely forgotten and do not merit revival. The handful of exquisite lyrics, slight as they are, have proved less ephemeral: it is owing to them and to her prologues and epilogues that she may claim a place as a minor Restoration poet.

Carol Barash (essay date 1990)

SOURCE: "The Political Possibilities of Desire: Teaching the Erotic Poems of Behn," in *Teaching Eighteenth-Century Poetry,* edited by Christopher Fox, AMS Press, 1990, pp. 159–76.

[*In the following essay, Barash argues that Behn's erotic poems contest "the heterosexual assumptions on which lovers' language is based." Barash focuses primarily on the poem "The Disappointment."*]

I have taught the erotic poems of Aphra Behn (ca. 1640–1689) in Restoration and eighteenth-century survey courses, in courses about Augustan poetry, and in surveys of literature by women. I usually assign **"The Disappointment," "To the fair Clarinda who made Love to me, imagin'd more than Woman"** and **"On Desire. A Pindarick"** as a group, with either the Earl of Rochester's erotic poems or poetry by other Restoration women for comparison. . . .

Students usually love Behn's poetry; and I begin by asking them why. Since part of my point in teaching these poems is to show the ways in which desire, particularly sexual desire—which many of them are apt to think of as something natural and unchanging—is constructed textually and historically, I begin by asking them questions about their own responses to Behn. What did they like, what did they find off-putting, for instance, in **"The Disappointment"**?

. . . . .

Students often speak first about the poem's energy, their vague sense of its sexual plot. If most of them are shocked that seventeenth-century people wrote so frankly about sex, they are even more surprised to discover that a woman could write this way. I talk briefly about the historical context of the Restoration, suggesting that the works of Behn—like those of Rochester—often depict sexual and political authority as overlapping problems. In the court masque *Sodom,* for instance, Charles II is depicted as being politically undone by his male and female lovers; and in several of Behn's political poems female monarchs pose a threat to male government. I suggest that the execution of the king in 1649 called attention to the relationship between the king's or queen's material body and their right to govern, and that the cultural preoccupation with the monarch's *body* tended, in general, to sexualize questions of authority and government.

At the same time, there was a new interest in women writers and a marked rise in the number of women writing for publication in the second half of the seventeenth century. During the civil wars and interregnum, numerous sectarian women wrote as community leaders and prophets. In addition, the literary culture in which royalists participated while in exile in France was a fundamentally gynocentric culture. The *salons* were run by women, and the writings which grew out of them make women's heroism central. Finally, when Charles II re-opened the London theatres after the Restoration, his patent to Thomas Killigrew and Charles Davenant included a provision—for the first time—that women, rather than young boys, should perform the women's parts. These various forms of attention to women's social and dramatic roles—and their potential political voices—seem to have enabled women, particularly between 1660 and 1714, not only to write, but to sign their works as women. Indeed, since the female

voice was in many ways a privileged position from which to make political and sexual claims in the Restoration and early eighteenth century, we often find men in this period writing as if they were women.

For Virginia Woolf and many later writers, it was the bold and defiant Aphra Behn who symbolized women's entrance into the public world of writing in the 1680s. Unlike Katherine Philips, who claimed that women's writing was essentially private and apolitical, and unlike Anne Killigrew, who died before her own epic and dramatic works could be completed, Behn had been a spy for Charles II in Antwerp before she returned to London and became fiercely and openly involved in the competitive marketplace of the London stage. She claimed repeatedly that she had been mistreated as a writer because she was a woman. Author of sixteen plays, many short fictional works, and numerous political poems, Behn also translated from French, edited poetical miscellanies which included works by other women, and wrote two major novels, one of which discusses the slave trade. In marked contrast to Anne Finch, Countess of Winchilsea, the most well-known of Augustan women writers and one who decorously signed the first editions of her works "by a Lady," Behn's name or initials appeared on the title page of all her major works.

Although most early eighteenth-century readers would have been familiar with Behn's poems, plays and novels, the creation of the first anthologies of "women's poetry" in the 1750s began a process which quickly excluded Behn from what we might call the "women's canon." Preoccupied with norms of female modesty and decorum, the editors of the new anthologies found Behn's work licentious, her life as a sexually independent woman a bad model for others to follow. Behn's erotic poems, which place her in the middle of Restoration debates about language and sexuality, never even made it into these eighteenth-century anthologies. To read Behn's poems now, I suggest, allows us to look at Restoration writing and Restoration culture from the position of one who is both a new, almost privileged insider, and one who often found herself—because she was a woman—excluded from the very cultural forms and cultural practices which made writing possible.

Returning to **"The Disappointment"**—and rhetorically suspending students' important questions about the poem's mythic and pastoral references—I ask them about the poem's plot: what's going on under all those slippery allusions? The more honest students will admit that they often weren't sure about what exactly *happens* in the poem, but someone is sure to have taken the "Hell of Impotence" of the final line literally and read backwards to find earlier references to sexual intercourse. After students unravel as much of the plot as they can—the poem's lack of determinacy about who does what to whom, I tell them, is part of the poem's argument—we begin working through the poem from beginning to end.

I explain that **"The Disappointment"** reworks a "libertine," or aristocratic male form: the poetic meditation on and description of premature ejaculation. The so-called "imperfect enjoyment" poem was based on French sources and translated by Rochester and other court wits of the time. In the men's poems about impotence, the male author watches the objectification of the male speaker and usually suggests that women's sexual desire and sexual forwardness—and men's fantasies about their own sexual performance—cause the man's sexual failure. Behn's **"The Disappointment"** was first published in Rochester's *Poems* (1680) and long thought to be written by him. As we work through the poem, I encourage students to pay special attention to those moments when a female speaker—or a female author—seems to intervene in this overtly male poetic form.

We look next at the poem's structure and setting. Whereas Rochester's "Imperfect Enjoyment" is written in heroic couplets, and thus marks itself as mock-heroic, Behn uses the form of the Shakespearean sonnet but fractures it in two ways. Although her rhyme scheme—*abba cddc ee*—lacks a third quatrain, I note that the underlying pattern nevertheless suggests the sonnet and its connotations as a poem of erotic address. What difference does it make, then, that Behn's lines have eight rather than ten syllables, four rather than five stresses each? And why is the final line of each stanza again pentameter? I urge students to read sections of the poem aloud, and to discuss the experience of the poem as spoken address, explaining that on the eve of the English civil wars more than fifty percent of all English men and over seventy percent of women were illiterate—that is, they could not sign their name on public records—at this time. Students describe Behn's **"Disappointment"** as simultaneously smooth and unsettling, the haltingly short lines working against the fluidity set up by the rhyme scheme, and the pentameter lines repeatedly suggesting a return to order and closure that never fully happens.

Unlike the urbane stance—and urban setting—of Rochester's "Imperfect Enjoyment," Behn's poem is pastoral, a setting which emphasizes the characters' innocence and which was used time and again by women poets of this period to challenge the cultural and linguistic codes which excluded them from writing in epic and dramatic genres. One could refer here to Anne Killigrew's "The Miseries of Man," which begins as pastoral but quickly shifts to a more sombre tone as two female figures murmur forth their "woes":

> In that so temperate Soil *Arcadia* named,
> For fertile Pasturage by Poets fam'd;
> Stands a steep Hill, whose lofty jetting Crown,
> Casts o'er the neighboring Plains, a seeming
>   Frown. . . .

> By oblique windings through this gloomy Shade,
> Has a clear purling Stream its Passage made,
> The *Nimph,* as discontented seem'd t'ave chose
> This sad Recess to murmur forth her Woes.

> To this Retreat, urg'd by tormenting Care,
> The melancholly *Cloris* did repair. . . .

> Near to the Mourning *Nimph* she chose a Seat,
> And these complaints did to the Shades repeat.

The pastoral setting seems to authorize the prophetic stance of Killigrew's speaker, which she uses to condemn state-authorized violence and warfare:

> And now, methinks, I present do behold
> The Bloudy Fields that are in Fame enroll'd,
> I see, I see thousands in Battle slain,
> The Dead and Dying cover all the Plain. . . .

The faithful wife will find her husband's "lofty Crest,"

>   And those refulgent Arms which late his Breast
> Did guard, by rough Encounters broke and tore,
> His Face and Hair, with Brains all clotted ore.
> And Warlike Weeds besmeer'd with Dust and Gore.

>   And will the Suffering World never bestow
> Upon th'Accursed Causers of such Woe,
> A vengeance that may parallel their Loss,
> Fix Publick Thieves and Robbers on the Cross?

Similarly, the speaker of Finch's "Petition for an Absolute Retreat" inhabits a landscape which figures for women's shared emotional life, a place in which the power of female friendship rescues the speaker from storms of political upheaval. Women's use of pastoral, I argue, derives from the situation of Eve in Book IX of Milton's *Paradise Lost*. Eve's pruning and tending the flowers represents ideal, unalienated labor in the world before the fall, but there is also a danger in Eve's affinity with nature, for it is her perfect labor which separates her from Adam, and it is as part of nature that Satan ultimately ensnares her.

How, specifically, does Behn rework what she takes from Milton? I might ask at this point. If Milton's sexually charged—and enticingly feminized—garden provides a point of departure for many Restoration women writers, Behn emphasizes the sexual contest at work in **"The Disappointment"** by shifting rapidly between the swain's and the nymph's points of view. The poem opens with an apparently overdetermined, unequal contest between the "Amorous" swain's "impatient Passion" and the "fair" nymph's inability to "defend her self [any] longer." Even Nature "conspire[s]" with Lysander's desire. The approach of evening and darkness compounds the apparent danger to the nymph, yet the light from her own (presumably desiring) eyes allows Behn's speaker (and her readers) quite voyeuristically to watch the scene. Up to this point, it seems that—as in other "imperfect enjoyment" poems—male sexual subjectivity and women's objectification in love will be foregrounded.

But then the reader, with Lysander, meets the willing but frightened Cloris. Working closely with stanzas III–VI, we see that Cloris's resistance is phrased in the past tense, while actions that suggest the power of her desire are expressed in the present: she "Permits his Force"; "Her Hands . . . meet" his bosom; "She wants the pow'r to say" no. The landscape—"Silent as yielding Maid's consent"—is

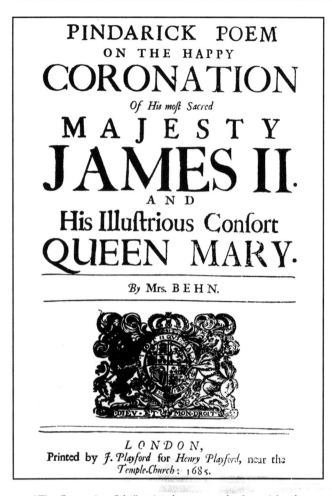

PINDARICK POEM
ON THE HAPPY
CORONATION
Of His moſt Sacred
MAJESTY
JAMES II.
AND
His Illuſtrious Conſort
QUEEN MARY.

By Mrs. B E H N.

LONDON,
Printed by *J. Playford* for *Henry Playford,* near the
Temple-Church: 168 5.

"The Coronation Ode," printed as a pamplet for quick sale.

metonym for Cloris's desire. Beautiful, alone, in a context in which silence equals consent, Cloris is caught between her sexual desire and her commitment to "Honour," which

she claims to love even more than she loves Lysander (stanza III). One might also note, at this point, that Lysander is equally confused about what is going on, alternately describing Cloris as a goddess (stanza V) and as an "Enemy" to be raped and "spoil[ed]" (stanza IV). Returning to the notion of the monarch's two bodies, one might also say here that as ruler of Lysander's heart, Cloris's body is at once a hauntingly spiritual "Altar" or "Paradice" and a material "Object" to be "seiz'd" and possessed (stanza V).

I spend some time discussing the cultural significance of women's "honor" in the seventeenth century—"honor" meaning, first and foremost, "chastity," a women's status as the sexual property of either her father or her husband—and stress Behn's distaste for this definition of "Honor." This is especially clear in the lines she added to her translation of the "Golden Age" from Tasso's *Aminta*:

> Oh cursed Honour! thou who first didst damn
>   A woman to the sin of shame;
>   Honour! that rob'st us of our gust,

> Honour! that hinder'd mankind first,
> At Love's eternal spring to quench his amorous
>   thirst.
>   Honour! who first taught lovely eyes the art,
>   To wound and not to cure the heart.
>   With love to invite, but to forbid with awe,
>   And to themselves prescribe a cruel law. . . .
> Thou miser, Honour, hord'st the sacred store,
> And starv'st thyself to keep thy votaries poor.

To lose one's Honor—one's reputation as a chaste woman—was, as Cloris says, to lose the "chiefest part" of life (stanza III). In other words, the loss of one's honor could be a form of social death for a woman in the seventeenth century. This concept of women's honor creates Cloris's predicament, requiring that "Love and Shame confus'dly strive" in the self-protective signs and whispers she extends to Lysander. Although Cloris never states her love overtly—and thus, strictly speaking, acts honorably—her desire repeatedly shifts the poem from the narrative past to the more urgent present without outwardly violating rules about women's honor. Through these shifts in tense, the poem thus dramatizes the desire which Cloris herself cannot admit.

To understand stanzas V and VI, students need some explanation of seventeenth-century theories about male and female sexuality. I explain the Galenic notion that men and women's bodies were essentially analogous—ovaries like testicles, penis like vagina, and so forth—with, it was believed, both men and women ejaculating in orgasm. Cloris and Lysander are similarly unable to experience sexual pleasure when their blood rushes from their "hinder Place"—Cloris's to her face (stanza XII), and Lysander's to his rage (stanza IX). When Cloris becomes "half dead and breathless" in the sixth stanza, there is the strong suggestion that she is experiencing sexual pleasure (though not penetration) and that her reputation has perhaps already been sacrificed.

Cloris is thus undone by the power of her own desire, not by rape; and Lysander's ejaculation—never as clearly articulated as in the men's poems, though the "Flowers bath'd in the Morning Dew" (stanza XII) suggest it has happened—is part of his own sexual timorousness, analogous in many ways to Cloris's fainting. As Cloris faints to avoid admitting (in the senses both of taking in and allowing the outcome of) her immodest desire, Lysander in stanza VIII shrinks away from her passive body rather than violate it. Here, the present tense is used to impede Lysander's sexual progress: "Too much love destroys" pleasure; "God conspires" to rescue Cloris. Lysander's flaccid penis, like Cloris's unprofessed desire, is described metonymically in references at once to human anatomy and to the landscape. Cloris's sexual desire and Lysander's unwillingness to commit rape are thus grammatically as well as figuratively parallel. Lysander is undone first by his own desire—"Excess of Love his Love betray'd"—which, when it fails to achieve its end, becomes an overwhelming anger. Neither the nymph's feigning nor her forwardness can be blamed for the swain's failure; rather, the combination of her desire and his modesty—the complete inversion of of her desire and his modesty—the complete inversion of the expected opposition between female modesty and male forwardness in love with which the poem begins—leaves the relationship unconsummated.

By this point someone is sure to have asked, well what side is Behn on anyway? It seems that for the bulk of the poem Behn describes Cloris's feigning and Lysander's sexual posturing—both of which have been learned from the conventions of love poetry—as alternately duplicitous and silly. A feminist may venture that this is in fact an anti-feminist poem, a possibility I give back to the class, reshaping the concern as a question of how one might guess **"The Disappointment"** was written by a woman if they came upon it in an anonymous edition. Returning to the mythic references with which the poems ends, how can Cloris, in running away from Lysander, be like both Daphne and Venus (stanza XIII)? Why are the male partners in these stories—Apollo and Adonis—not mentioned here by name?

Both tales come from Ovid's *Metamorphoses,* and in both cases Behn emphasizes the woman's half of the story by naming her alone. If Cloris is like the nymph Daphne, running to flee the god who wishes to rape her, she is also like the goddess Venus, who mourns the loss of her human lover. I suggest that these two myths, taken together, shift the story of premature ejaculation to the point of view of a disappointed and fearful—but still desiring—woman. Behn's emphasis can be reinforced by recalling the question, in stanza XII—"Who can the Nymph's Confusion guess?"—which is answered, in the final stanza, after the two stories from Ovid: "The *Nymph's* Resentments none but I / Can well Imagine or Condole." Behn's narrator, in these lines, authorizes herself to speak on women's behalf, giving the state of Lysander's soul back to "those who sway'd his Destiny" (stanza XIV), presumably the poets who first taught him to think of his sexual organs as godlike. A libertine ideal of sexual freedom and sexual play is still maintained in Behn's poem, but women's ambivalent relationship to sexual freedom—it is both desirable and dangerous—is also revealed in the conflicting mythic references with which **"The Disappointment"** concludes.

In the conclusion of **"The Disappointment"** Behn calls our attention to the *female sexual subject,* that is, to the desiring woman as author of a narrative of sexual desire. At this juncture I relate Behn's strategies of engendering the authorial subject in the erotic poems to the sexual attraction between woman author and woman monarch in her political poems of the 1680s. What happens, I then ask, when another woman is the object of the speaker's desire, as is the case in **"To the Fair Clarinda, who made love to me, imagin'd more than Woman"**:

> Fair lovely Maid, or if that Title be
> Too weak, too Feminine for Nobler thee,
> Permit a Name that more Approaches Truth:
> And let me call thee, Lovely Charming Youth.
> This last will justifie my soft complaint,
> While that may serve to lessen my constraint;
> And without Blushes I the Youth pursue,

> When so much beauteous Woman is in view.
> Against thy Charms we struggle but in vain
> With thy deluding Form thou giv'st us pain,
> While the bright Nymph betrays us to the Swain.
> In pity to our Sex sure thou wer't sent,
> That we might Love, and yet be Innocent:
> For sure no Crime with thee we can commit;
> Or if we should—thy Form excuses it.
> For who, that gathers fairest Flowers believes
> A snake lies hid beneath the Fragrant Leaves.

> Thou beauteous Wonder of a different kind,
> Soft *Cloris* with the dear *Alexis* join'd;
> When e'r the Manly part of thee, wou'd plead
> Thou tempts us with the Image of the Maid,
> While we the noblest Passions do extend
> The love to *Hermes, Aphrodite* the Friend.

What here characterizes the women's relationship? How is it defined in this poem? I ask. Someone usually responds by asking if Behn was *really* a lesbian. I explain that one of her male lovers was bisexual, and that she wrote many poems based on the female narrator's erotic attraction to other women (particularly to royal and aristocratic women), but the idea that lesbianism is something natural—something one "is" or "isn't"—is a notion of sexuality and sexual desire that **"To the Fair Clarinda"** vigorously rejects.

The relationship between the speaker and Clarinda is framed and defined by a world in which gender opposition is law. From the very first line gender is introduced as part of reading and relating to the other, even to another woman: "Fair lovely Maid, or if that *Title* be / Too weak . . . / Permit a *Name* that more Approaches Truth" (emphasis mine). We might say that the speaker heterosexualizes her erotic attraction to another woman by imagining first that she herself is a man and Clarinda is a woman. Then, calling Clarinda a sexually ambiguous "Charming Youth" Behn's speaker "pursue[s]" her, and thus breaks social codes about women's "modesty" or passivity in love. Clarinda's beauty is heightened by the hyperfeminine "Charms" and metamorphic "deluding Form" with which she attracts the speaker.

Behn's speaker also suggests the more problematic implications of Clarinda's "deluding Form." While it is no "Crime" for a woman to love another woman, even the speaker has not imagined that the female sexual body is snakelike, phallic, or—to be precise—clitoral:

> For sure no Crime with thee we can commit;
> Or if we should—thy Form excuses it.
> For who that gathers fairest Flowers believes
> A snake lies hid beneath the Fragrant Leaves.

While the female "Form" of Clarinda's body seems at first to mute the speaker's sexual aggression, when that "Form" is revealed to be female, it proves the relationship sexual after all. It is fairly straightforward, at this point, to show students how the poem moves from *name* to *body* as that aspect which defines the women's relationship, and it is as textual body, I argue, that the relationship is finally resolved.

When Behn invokes the mythic pair, Hermes and Aphrodite, at the end of **"To the Fair Clarinda,"** she is once again working against Ovid's *Metamorphoses.* Where Ovid's myth explains the creation of a body that is sexually both male and female, the desire of Behn's speaker for another woman playfully dismantles Ovid's Hermaphroditus into the warring intentions of his/her parents. Splitting Hermaphroditus into Hermes and Aphrodite allows the speaker to transgress the boundaries she invoked earlier between male and female. She is now able both to "[gather] . . . fairest Flowers" and to extend "noblest passions" to the "snake . . . beneath the Fragrant Leaves." Paradoxically, this love poem to another woman is more clearly encoded in terms of male and female oppositions than any of Behn's heterosexual love poems. The more rigidly gender and sexuality are mapped onto real physical bodies, the more manipulable and unstable the categories "male" and "female" become. If Clarinda *is* both maid and youth, both Hermes and Aphrodite, then men and women can no longer be understood as oppositionally "nymph" and "swain." Behn's dismantling of Ovidian myth is part of her larger contest with the heterosexual assumptions on which lovers' language is based.

Behn's erotic poems can be usefully compared here to those of Katherine Philips (1632–1664). In the 1650s and early 1660s Philips wrote numerous poems from "Orinda" to "Lucasia." The vows of devotion between Orinda and Lucasia were part of an elaborate "Society of Friendship" which mapped out an ideal, platonic friendship between women, a world free from the material constraints and obligations of heterosexual love and marriage. For instance, in "To my Excellent *Lucasia,* on our Friendship," Orinda states,

> No Bridegrooms nor Crown-conquerors mirth
>   To mine compar'd can be:
> They have but pieces of this Earth,
>   I've all the World in thee.
>
> Then let our Flame still light and shine,
>   And no false fear control,
> As innocent as our Design,
>   Immortal as our Soul.

Honor, as Philips states in "To the truly-competent Judge of Honour, *Lucasia,*" places women above the concerns of the material world:

> . . . Honour is more great and more sublime,
> Above the battery of Fate or Time. . . .
> Honour's to th' Mind as Beauty to the Sense. . . .
> But as that Beauty were as truly sweet,
> Were there no Tongue to praise, no Eye to
>   see't. . . .
> So Honour is its own Reward and End,
> And satisfied within, cannot descend
> To beg the suffrage of a vulgar tongue.

In Behn's poems, in contrast, there is no such space free from cultural and legal naming, no place in which women might define their own sexual reality and yet remain honorable.

In Behn's view women can, however, inscribe—and enact—a female sexual community which is fundamentally subversive. This is precisely what happens at the end of **"On Desire. A Pindarick."** I encourage students to discuss the various ways in which desire is addressed—disease, dream, ghost, spright—and to think about the ways in which these various figures overlap incompletely. What is the composite sense of desire one has by the end of Behn's eighth stanza? And how is that changed when the poem shifts, first to address "Philosophers" (stanza 9) and then to speak to women, "ye fair ones," in the final three stanzas? When Behn's speaker defines women's "virtue" and "modesty" as a "cheat," then urges women to continue using them as part of the "false disguise" of honor, she emphasizes the necessary doubleness at work in any public formulation of female desire.

As in **"The Disappointment"** and **"To the Fair Clarinda,"** **"On Desire"** ends with a classical allusion; and once again women's sexual desire shifts the poem—and the mythic story—from the narrative past to the more urgent present tense. Here Behn claims that Helen of Troy was not raped by Paris, but that she was secretly in love with him. This is no simple transformation: Behn is suggesting that stories about women's desire would shake not merely literary conventions about sexual love, but the foundations of epic itself. Behn's erotic poems are, finally, an excellent example of the way in which Restoration uses of classical myth were sites of cultural conflict, moments in which the stories of the past were remade in an attempt to define the cultural, political—and, indeed, sexual—reality of the present.

Bernard Duyfhuizen (essay date 1991)

SOURCE: "'That Which I Dare Not Name': Aphra Behn's 'The Willing Mistress,'" in *ELH,* Vol. 58, No. 1, Spring, 1991, pp. 63–82.

[In the following excerpt, Duyfhuizen explicates the poem "The Willing Mistress" through comparisons to other verse by Behn and to her drama The Dutch Lover, *finding that the poem is a metaphor for a woman trying to retain her identity and control in a male-dominated world.]*

In reclaiming [**"The Willing Mistress"**] for their landmark *Norton Anthology of Literature by Women,* Sandra M. Gilbert and Susan Gubar suggest the interpretive significance of **"The Willing Mistress"** when they comment that "although the Restoration circles in which she traveled permitted extraordinary licence to male artists like Behn's libertine friend and patron John Wilmont, earl of Rochester, the same circles expected women to remain decently silent about their own desires. . . . [H]owever, Behn did not maintain such silence." In an era when the major archetype for a female lover was either the "coy mistress" of poets

---

Louis Untermeyer contrasts Behn's plays and poetry:

The plays show one side of Aphra Behn, the poetry another. The plays, written cold-bloodedly for an audience whose appetites had been whetted on the gross fare supplied by Dryden, Rochester, Villiers, and Sackville, are coarse; the poetry is refined to the point of fancifulness. With the exception of a few concessions to contemporary taste, such as **"Beneath a Cool Shade,"** the lyrics are light, almost transparent. The best of them play with paradox as delicately as the well-known **"Song"** beginning:

Love in fantastic triumph sate
    Whilst bleeding hearts around him flowed,
For whom fresh pains he did create
    And strange tyrannic power showed.

Louis Untermeyer, in his Lives of the Poets, *Simon and Schuster, 1959.*

---

such as Robert Herrick and Andrew Marvell or the metonymic "cunt" of Restoration libertines such as Wilmont, Lord Buckhurst, and Sir George Etherege, control of female representation was considered a male province—as was essentially all poetry itself and all sexual feeling. Though libertines might rail against the reluctant woman, and carpe diem poets might try to persuade her to bestow her sexual favors on her eager lover, the systems of sexual exchange, in a general society that was moving its cultural norm to the more Puritan middle class, were increasingly valorizing the propriety of the non-sexual woman, the chaste wife, the ignorant virgin daughter.

In this climate, Behn's "willing mistress" (along with some of her other heroines) performs an extraordinary act in frankly proclaiming female passion. The male lover may still have to persuade and seduce his mistress through his eloquence, but the physical arguments—"kisses," the "charming" gaze, and the body "already fired"—presuppose an entailment that the mistress willingly chooses not to avoid. As Angeline Goreau observes [in *Reconstructing Aphra*, 1980], "Not only was such direct acknowledgment of her own desire considered unfeminine in a woman, but her equal activity in sexual advance—'and I returned the same'—must have been disconcerting even to the rakehell fops and seducers who pretended to disregard female honor. Aphra's poem, called 'The Willing Mistress,' was putting a period to the 'Coy Mistress.'" We will see in a moment, however, that this proclamation is far from unproblematic.

Indeed, it is necessary for us to see why conclusions about Behn's poetry such as Jeremy Treglown's patronizing, "as far as simple sexiness goes she can hold her own" ["Masculine Strokes of a Feminine Pen," *TLS* (6 February 1981)], and John J. Richetti's dismissive, "Mrs. Behn's . . . tiresome accounts of sexual disaster seem to be an artless recognition of the realities of sex for eighteenth-century women, or at least its emotional resonances" ["The Portrayal of Women in Restoration and Eighteenth-Century

English Literature," in *What Manner of Women*, edited by Marlene Springer, 1977], miss the point. To advocate the social philosophy of sexual autonomy, to speak and be heard with self-authority, women have traditionally met with male resistance that necessitated a full articulation of the difficulties social and cultural forces have inscribed in that position. To proclaim autonomy threatens the foundations of patriarchal culture built on female submission to male domination and control of all facets of life. In seventeenth-century England in particular, the cultural formation of gender dichotomies was unmistakable in the doctrine of the two spheres. As Goreau observes, the two principal inhibitions "that kept women from publishing their writing in the seventeenth century" were

the sense that wit belonged to the masculine province and the fear of violating feminine "modesty." The first is clear enough, but the second is less immediately evident. Its source lies in the complex interaction of symbolic and concrete interpretation of the concept of the feminine sphere. This division of masculine and feminine spheres of experience separated "the world" from "the domestic circle," the public from the private arena; women were denied access to the former and confined to the latter by "custom." The social hegemony of modesty and its attributes—virtue, honour, name, fame, and reputation—served to police the segregation by ascribing a sexual significance to any penetration, either from within or without, of a woman's "private circle." To publish one's work was to make oneself "public": to expose oneself to "the world." Women who did so violated their feminine modesty both by egressing from the private sphere which was their proper domain and by permitting foreign eyes access to what ought to remain hidden and anonymous. ["Aphra Behn: A Scandal to Modesty," in *Feminist Theorists*, edited by Dale Spender, 1983]

That Behn demolished this sphere for herself is clear, but the cost was enormous as she was constantly attacked by critics (mostly male) who did not hesitate to use her gender as a criterion for her worth as a poet. Exacerbating this situation were Behn's frankly sexual texts that overtly subverted both the libertine and Puritan sexual politics of her time.

Thus, if we were to look at **"The Willing Mistress"** merely in New Critical isolation, away from its historical context, and with the latest post-sexual revolution perspective, then it reads like the fulfillment of an archetypal male wish: a lover with no strings attached. But attention to women's history and the context of the cultural as well as physiological formation of female sexuality has made modern readers aware that even though the strings might be unattached to the man, they exist nonetheless, and they often form the ties that bind the woman to narrow roles in patriarchal culture. To pursue Behn's complex understanding of this dichotomy, I propose to explore the textual history of **"The Willing Mistress"** to uncover the poem's direct dialogic relationship with some of Behn's other writing, and to suggest that we can discover, in the regress of its textual production and evolution, its textual unconscious, which will take our reading well beyond merely "tiresome accounts of sexual disaster" or "simple sexiness."

Like most editors of Norton anthologies, Gilbert and Gubar provide a few glosses on phrases students might have trouble with and a snippet of textual history—"This song appears in Behn's play *The Dutch Lover,* where it is sung by a maidservant to her mistress"—which provides them with their date of publication, 1673. The text of the poem they provide, however, is not precisely as it appeared in Behn's comedy *The Dutch Lover.* Consulting Montague Summers's edition of *The Works of Aphra Behn,* we discover that the version presented is that of Behn's 1684 *Poems upon Several Occasions.* The substantive changes between these two versions are essentially lexical (1673 text/1684 text): l.11, "wanton"/"amorous"; 1.18 "amorous"/"softening"; 1.22 "they"/"those." The changes are slight, but those in lines eleven and eighteen mark a poetic "softening" from the first version's bolder "wantonness." An older Aphra Behn may have wanted to celebrate the tenderness of unconstrained sexuality and to move the poem a step away from the more subversive and paradoxical social connotations represented by the female figure of the "wanton." Additionally, as we will see, these alterations may have been necessitated by the shifting characterization of the perceived speaker.

Yet the case doesn't end in a simple textual correction; by indicating that the poem "appears in . . . *The Dutch Lover,*" Gilbert and Gubar invite us to consider Behn's third play and reinsert **"The Willing Mistress"** in one of its earlier contexts. The song is sung by Francisca to her mistress Cleonte at the opening of act 2, scene 6. Cleonte, in her chamber dressed only in her nightgown, asks for a song, lifting a prohibition on Francisca's speech, imposed because she told only stories of love and of Cleonte's (presumed) half-brother Silvio (for whom Francisca has a secret passion). Francisca picks a song (**"The Willing Mistress,"** but it does not yet have this title) that will please herself, but it also figures the plot entailment of Silvio's obsessive love for Cleonte. At the song's conclusion, Silvio enters "all undrest, gazing wildly on Cleonte; his Arm ty'd up." The dialogue that ensues makes clear to Cleonte the depth of his transgressive desire for her, yet like the mistress in the song, both Cleonte and Silvio "dare not name" the subject of their discourse:

> *Cleo*: Alas, what means my Brother?
> *Silv*: Can you not guess, fair Sister? have my Eyes
>   So ill exprest my Soul? or has your Innocence
>   Not suffer'd you to understand my Sighs?
>   Have then a thousand Tales, which I have told you,
>   Of Broken Hearts, and Lovers Languishments,
>   Not serv'd to tell you, that I did adore you?
> *Cleo*: Oh let me still remain in Innocence,
>   Rather than Sin so much to understand you. . . .
> *Silv*: Can you believe it Sin to love a Brother? it
>   is not so in Nature.
> *Cleo*: Not as a Brother, Sir; but otherwise,
>   It is, by all the Laws of Men and Heaven. . . .
>   What wou'd you have me do?
> *Silv*: Why—I would have thee do—I know not
>   what—
>   Still to be with me—yet that will not satisfy;
>   To let me—look upon thee—still that's not

> enough—
> I dare not say to kiss thee, and imbrace thee;
> That were to make we wish—I dare not tell
>   thee what—

We see in this debate a repetition of Francisca's song but the sexual politics have been reversed. One cannot say of Silvio that "His charming Eyes no aid requir'd, / To tell their amorous Tale"; nor can one say of Cleonte that she is made "willing to receive / That which I dare not name." Indeed, the libertine logic of free love, by which **"The Willing Mistress"** has been interpreted, is doubly complicated by the taboo on incest and by Cleonte's steadfast insistence on her virtuous innocence. Moreover, Silvio's injured arm serves as a metaphor for the necessary impotence of this particular desire. (Behn would subvert the masculine plot of potency more literally in such texts as **"The Disappointment"** and *Love Letters Between a Nobleman and His Sister.*) Ultimately it will be revealed that Silvio and Cleonte are not related at all, and their love becomes permissible "by all the Laws of Men and Heaven."

At this point in the play, however, Cleonte's guarding of her innocence is fully understandable because her sister, the "loose Hippolyta, was lost." We have learned in act 1, scene 2, that Hippolyta, the literal willing mistress of the play, has "fallen from Honour, and from Virtue, / And liv'st in Whoredom with an impious Villain," and that Marcel (yet another brother) vows revenge for "that Rape which [Antonio] committed on her Innocence." Significantly for our purposes of seeing the intertextuality of **"The Willing Mistress"** and *The Dutch Lover,* when Hippolyta is described by Silvio as "drest like a *Venice* Curtezan, / With all the Charmes of a loose Wanton," we see precisely the word Behn later removed in her softening of the poem.

More significant is the alignment of reiterated images among Cleonte, Hippolyta, and the song that occurs when Hippolyta, who has only appeared briefly at the opening of act 2, scene 3 (when she is weeping while fleeing with Antonio to "St. Peter's Grove"—recall the first line of the song), finally has a full scene. Act 3, scene 3, opens with Antonio sleeping and Hippolyta singing what is clearly a continuation of Francisca's song:

> Ah false Amyntas, can that Hour
>   So soon forgotten be,
> When first I yielded up my Power
>   To be betray'd by thee?
> God knows with how much Innocence
>   I did my Heart resign
> Unto thy faithless Eloquence,
>   And gave thee what was mine.
>
> I had not one Reserve in store,
>   But at thy Feet I laid
> Those Arms which conquer'd heretofore,
>   Tho now thy Trophies made.
> Thy Eyes in silence told their Tale
>   Of love in such a way,

That 'twas as easy to prevail,
   As after to betray.

After an active returning of kisses and a "willing" "yield-ing" to "that which I dare not name" and "who can guess the rest"—the unnameable delights of freely acknowledged passion—the mistress realizes her loss of the "Power" that her "Innocence" gave her. Now the betrayal latent in the fourth line of Francisca's song manifests itself in the fourth and sixteenth lines of Hippolyta's. The "false" and "faith-less" Amyntas's eyes are no longer "charming," and rath-er than an "amorous Tale," they tell "in silence" the con-ventional masculine plot of conquest and betrayal that underlies so much of Cavalier "love poetry" and that is overtly stated in the profane lyrics of the Restoration wits. At this point, Behn has undercut the image of the "willing mistress" to expose her socialized vulnerability and the logic of entailments that the "lost woman" would encoun-ter. While "willing," she could equally engage the system of sexual exchange and had "return'd the same," but now that she has given "what was mine" she has "not one Reserve in store"—in this sexual economy, the mistress has surrendered her property and now must face an empty set of prospects.

Hippolyta, in identifying with the mistress, expresses the horror of her situation:

   My Grief's too great to be diverted this way.
   Why should this Villain sleep, this treacherous Man
   Who has for ever robb'd me of my rest?
   Had I but kept my Innocence intire,
   I had out-brav'd my Fate, and broke my Chains,
   Which now I bear like a poor guilty Slave,
   Who sadly crys, If I were free from these,
   I am not from my Crimes; so still lives on,
   And drags his loathed Fetters after him.
   Why should I fear to die, or murder him?
   It is but adding one Sin more to th' number.
   This—would soon do't—but where's the Hand to
      guide it?
                                    [*Draws a Dagger, sighs*]
   For 'tis an act too horrid for a Woman.
   But yet thus sleeping I might take that Soul,
   Which waking all the Charms of Art and Nature
   Had not the Power t'effect.
   Oh were I brave, I could remember that,
   And this way be the Mistress of his Heart.
   But mine forbids it should be that way won;
   No, I must still love on, in spite of me,
   And wake him quickly, lest one Moment's thought
   Upon my Shame should urge me to undo him.

Like Hamlet who hesitates to take his revenge and is thrown back on the self to rationalize his delay in soliloquy, Hip-polyta must work through a conflicting set of emotions that chart a woman's response to her textualization by an act of love. First we feel Hippolyta's anger and rage against this "villain" who has robbed her of her rest, specifically because the sexual act that has rended her "Innocence" has also inscribed for her a "Fate" that is figured in un-mistakable images of submission: "my Chains, / Which

now I bear like a poor guilty Slave, / . . . his loathed Fetters." Momentarily she considers an escape that is no escape: suicide or murder of the sleeping Antonio. Yet her shattered sense of self requires a "Hand to guide" her, and she pauses in time to concede that "'tis an act too horrid for a Woman." At this point Hippolyta falls back on gen-der conventions; whereas it is expected that Marcel should seek revenge for the seduction of his sister (in fact Sil-vio's wounded arm resulted from a fight with Marcel over Silvio's failure to uphold the patriarchal honor and kill the transgressive lovers), for Hippolyta to avenge herself is "an act too Horrid." Instead, she considers the possibility of employing "the Charms of Art and Nature" to make her "the Mistress of his Heart," but since these "had not the Power" to channel Antonio's sexual desire into a satisfac-tory course initially, she disdains the double artifice that would now be required. Finally, since she "must still love on, in spite of" herself, she becomes the exemplary female victim of sexual domination. And with consummate irony, she decides to wake Antonio before she is further tempted "to undo him" who, in the sexual parlance of the day, has already "undone" her.

Behn now complicates the plot of this willing mistress's destiny. One senses in Hippolyta's move from justified rage to self-blame for her own victimization, her "Shame," an ironic portrait of the social constraints imposed upon woman by the patriarchal double standard that always seeks to control and to exploit female sexuality, to acknowledge it only as a projection of patriarchal desires (Antonio) or social identity (Marcel and Silvio). Upon waking, Antonio calms Hippolyta's rage and with protestations of his love "seduces" the dagger away from her. Once in possession of the dagger, the obvious symbol of the phallus, in the sexual politics their dialogue, Antonio tells her, "Stand off, false Woman, I dispise thy love." He now reveals that his carefully crafted plot to ruin Hippolyta "'twas not [because of] love to thee, / But hatred to thy Brother Don Marcel." With this complication, Behn makes clear the extent to which sexuality can become only a supplement in another system of exchange, that the sexual equality figured by the "willing mistress" is always already un-equal and subordinate to other forces driving patriarchal society. Behn makes this clear by the repeated conjoining of Hippolyta with prostitution as she and Antonio debate, with bitter irony on her part and malicious wit on his, the question of her "Price."

Through a series of plot turns, Hippolyta gets away from Antonio and then disguises herself as a man in order to challenge her "ravisher" to a duel "that will redeem / All the lost Credit of our Family." Hippolyta's soliloquy upon her changed status now that she has donned masculine attire underwrites the gendered expectations and behav-iours of the era at the same time it calls into question the dominant masculine ideology of "Love":

   Thus I dare look abroad again:
   Methinks I am not what I was,
   My Soul too is all Man;
   Where dwells no Tenderness, no womanish
      Passions.

I cannot sigh, nor weep, nor think of Love,
But as a foolish Dream that's gone and past.
Revenge has too possession of my Soul,
And drove those Shadows thence; and shows me now
Love, in so poor, so dispicable a Shape,
So quite devested of his Artful Beauty,
That I'm asham'd I ever was his Votary.
Well, here's my challenge to *Antonio*:
But how to get it to him is the Question.
Base as he is, he'll not refuse to come,
And since he never saw the wrong'd *Alonzo,*
Sure I may pass for him.

By disguising herself as Alonzo, the man to whom she was "contracted" to marry, and by relying on masculine codes of "honor" in responding to a challenge, she frames a plausible—and exemplarily patriarchal—context for the duel. Within the generic logic of the comedy, however, the shifting identities now double back as the true Alonzo (whom Hippolyta had never met before, the contract for her marriage had been negotiated by Marcel) becomes her second for the duel. Antonio, on the other hand, having been stung by "Conscience," now desires Hippolyta's "pardon" for his treachery. Significantly, their roles have reversed as she now seeks revenge whereas he seeks reconciliation. As the duel ensues, all three fight, until Marcel arrives and unwittingly joins the side of Antonio and duels his own sister. Symbolically, to fight the brother returns the plot to the basic level of its family romance and the struggle of the daughter to free herself from the destiny her family planned for her.

Since the only female responses represented for Hippolyta are submission or death, she can only act through a cross-gendered adoption of the dominant code of behavior, but without training she is finally no match for her brother, who wounds her while Alonzo disarms Antonio. In this extraordinary scene (4.3), Hippolyta, who has donned the garb of the patriarchy and sought to engage its context of "honor," is confronted with her brother, her ravisher (who is now reformed and claims her as his "Wife"), and her contracted husband—thus she forms the intersection of gendered representation as each man defines her femaleness as a projection of his own, different, desires. Against such odds, the wounded Hippolyta must submit to the negotiated reconciliation of these representations. In the end, Hippolyta is legally married to Antonio and reclaimed by her family; the plot is resolved happily under the wise eyes of Ambrosio, the father of Cleonte and Hippolyta.

With such an ending, *The Dutch Lover* veers back to the conventional, although not unproblematic, teleology of marriage as a resolution and reclamation of transgressive energies. The song which will later be titled **"The Willing Mistress"** and its continuation to a second part, marking the potential exploitation of sexual equality, now becomes a layered text that both celebrates such equality and warns the listener of its dangers. Why Behn chose to reproduce the song in her *Poems upon Several Occasions* in only the first three stanzas may reflect her relatively more established position as a writer a decade after *The Dutch*

Lover or her greater willingness to leave the question of the poem's sexual entailments indeterminate. If we see the poem in light of Behn's later novel, *Love Letters between a Nobleman and His Sister* (1684–87), we can recognize in this latter work a greater concern to explore the "willing mistress"'s destiny when marriage to the desired lover is an unavailable solution—Silvia's transgressive love with Philander, her brother-in-law, operates always outside the logic that would entail matrimony for them. But before we turn to an even earlier verston of **"The Willing Mistress"** and the question of how the poem might intersect with Behn's own sexual existence, we should briefly look at the poem that would incorporate much of the continuation: **"The Reflection: A Song."**

By all accounts, **"The Reflection: A Song"** first appeared in Behn's 1684 *Poems upon Several Occasions* although both Summers in his notes to the *The Works* and Mary Ann O'Donnell in her *Aphra Behn: An Annotated Bibliography of Primary and Secondary Sources* fail to note that lines 17–28 repeat almost verbatim lines 5–16 of the song as it appears in *The Dutch Lover.* The setting is much the same, as is the subject: the betrayed and abandoned female lover bemoaning the "Rigor of her Fate," the loss of both her virginity and her lover's love. But the implication that this "mistress" was easy in her willingness is dispelled by her assertion how "long beseig'd" her heart had been before she "was lost without Controul." Whereas the "willing mistress" boldly spoke of "return'd" kisses and of being "her that was already fir'd," the "reflecting mistress" can only reread the text of her exploited passion:

Till by such Obligations Prest,
    By such dear Perjuries won:
I heedlesly Resign'd the rest
    And quickly was undone.
For as my Kindling Flames increase,
    Yours glimeringly decay:
The Rifled Joys no more can Please,
    That once oblig'd your Stay.

The final stanza goes on to strip the Arcadian landscape of all its gayness as the "reflecting mistress" waits to die. Although such a stance seems conventional, we must remember how few were the voices speaking against the seduction poetry produced by men. If male poetry of this period is characterized by its lyric attempt to seize the moment in a pure set of images that would defy time, the female poetry of Behn and others is characterized by its inescapable narrative, by its recognition of consequences beyond the passionate moment, by the profound gender difference in the conceptualization of time.

Because Behn has other poems besides **"The Reflection: A Song"** that focus on the betrayed lover, we must recognize that the image of the "willing mistress" is informed precisely by those thematic conventions it appears so determined to break. This can be seen clearly if we examine the first version of **"The Willing Mistress,"** published in 1672 in a volume of poetry, the *Covent Garden Drolery,* which Behn appears to have edited and to which she contributed four poems. Two of the poems, **"A Song to a**

Scotish [sic] **tune"** (**"Come my Phillis let us improve"**) and **"Damon being asked a reason for Loveing,"** can be seen as conventional seduction poems within the tradition of a male speaker addressing a coy mistress with a carpe diem argument. The third, **"Song to a Scotish tune"** (**"When Jemmy, first began to Love"**), is spoken by the female lover, but her abandonment at the close of the poem is caused by a war that has forced her lover to become a soldier; nevertheless, she can only wonder what will become of her if her lover fails to return.

The fourth poem, simply titled **"Song,"** we will recognize as **"The Willing Mistress"** but with an essential change:

> I led my Silvia to a Grove,
>   Where all the Boughs did shade us,
> The Sun it self, though it had strove,
>   It could not have betray'd us.
> The place secur'd from humane eyes,
>   No other fear alows,
> But when the Winds do gently rise,
>   And kiss the yeilding [sic] Boughs.
> Down there we sate upon the Moss,
>   And did begin to play
> A thousand wanton tricks, to pass
>   The heat of all the day.
> A many kisses I did give,
>   And she return'd the same,
> Which made her willing to receive
>   That which I dare not name.
>
> My greedy eyes no ayds requir'd,
>   To tell their amorous Tale:
> On her that was already fir'd,
>   'Twas easie to prevail.
> I did but kiss and claspe her round
>   Whilst they my thoughts exprest,
> And laid her gently on the ground:
>   Oh! who can guess the rest?

A profound change occurs with the shift of speaker. In the context of the other poems by Behn in this collection, it appears that she has adopted the male voice and thus presented the masculine perspective. Indeed, the variant in line 17—"My greedy eyes"—marks a gendered internal focalization by the speaker that differs from the willing mistress's *observation*—"His charming eyes"—in the later versions. As this alteration makes clear, the difference between the versions is both in who *speaks* the discourse of desire and who *sees*: the "greedy" lover sees the Other only as a consumable object, whereas the willing mistress's observation is simultaneously a projection of her desire onto the Other—to reproduce the Other in her desired image. Yet this is not a persuasive poem, a carpe diem lyric; its sexual entailment has already occurred, and though we are still conjured to guess its nature, this song is essentially a boast. Moreover, we see in both versions the play of subjectivity and objectification. The frank avowal of returned kisses and a fully agreed to "willingness" in the later versions is here only the perception of the speaker, a perception that has no guarantee of accura-

cy beyond the speaker's specific desires. "Silvia" is an object whose sexual identity has been appropriated and transformed into a text, but as conventional as this gendered object appears, can we unqualifiedly say the same about the nature of the *gendered subject* speaking this version? Or must we read otherwise to discover an Other that the poet "dare not name"?

In reading Restoration poetry, one often confronts a system of coded naming that connects the poem directly to the poet's life. For instance, Behn referred to herself (as did her contemporaries) repeatedly as "Astrea." Within this code, scholars have identified "Amyntas" as John Hoyle, a Gray's Inn lawyer, who has been described as a "spectacular libertine" and who in "1687 was arraigned before a Grand Jury on a charge of sodomy with a poulterer, which resulted in a verdict of *Ignoramus*." Goreau, in writing her biography of Behn, relies on the version of **"The Willing Mistress"** sung in *The Dutch Lover,* and on other poems that appear to identify Hoyle, to conclude that "it seems reasonable to assume that Aphra Behn's love affair with John Hoyle began sometime in the early or middle 1670s." A piece of evidence of particular relevance to Goreau's argument and of interest to my inquiry here is the 1707 reprinting of the poem in the *Muses Mercury* under the title **"A Song for J. H.",** with an editorial gloss stating this poem is from a copy in Behn's own handwriting.

The poem printed in the *Muses Mercury* is a heavily edited version of the 1672 *Covent Garden Drolery* text, which, we can speculate, Behn may have either written for Hoyle to mark a significant moment in their relationship or copied the early version into the "Person's Book who was very much her friend [Hoyle]" before she reworked the poem for *The Dutch Lover*. In a move tellingly emblematic of Behn's evolving "displacement" to the margins of literary history, the editor of the *Muses Mercury* re-wrote Behn's poem for the following reason: "As Amorous as these Verses may be thought, they have been reduc'd to bring them within the Rules of Decency, which all Writers ought to observe, or instead of a *Diversion* they will become a *Nusance*." The changes made clearly diminish the poem's power—be it aesthetic, erotic, or subversive—and implicate the editor in an exploitation that is at the same time an erasure of Behn's **"A Song for J. H."**

I

> I led my *Sylvia* to a Grove,
>   Where ev'ry Tree might shade us;
> The Sun it self, a Foe to Love,
>   Cou'd not have there betray'd us.
> The Place secur'd from human Eyes,
>   No other Fear allows.
> But when the Zephirs gently rise
>   And kiss the yielding Boughs.

II

> Down then we sat upon the Moss,

And both began to play
A Thousand Sports we found to pass
  The sultry Heat of Day,
What Kisses did the Shepard give,
  And what the Nymph return,
They lov'd so much, they scarce cou'd live,
  So much they both did burn.

III

His greedy Eyes no Aid requir'd
  To tell their am'rous Tale,
Enough she was already fir'd,
  And he might soon prevail;
Again he kiss'd and clasp'd her round,
  And thus his thoughts exprest;
He sigh'd and laid her on the Ground,
  Let Lovers guess the rest.

It is impossible to know if any of these variants were in the manuscript of Behn's that the editor claims to be working from, but the startling shift in the middle of the poem from the first-person speaking persona (which all other versions maintain and in which Behn often worked) to the third-person speaker/narrator suggests the point at which Behn's original text violated the "Rules of Decency." Indeed, those are precisely the lines on which much of my present reading of the poem depends. The *Muses Mercury* editor has doubly displaced the textual authority by the distancing effect of the third-person perspective and by the explicit heterosexual emplotment within a teleology established by the pastoral literary tradition—indeed, "Sylvia" has been transformed into a "Nymph," a carefully distanced representation of an erotic female who will not "become a Nusance."

Despite this editorial "Diversion" and what the actual story of this textual transmission is, the addition of Hoyle to our story raises other speculations. Since Hoyle is reputed to have been a notorious libertine and, despite a reputation as an abandoning lover, of extraordinary attractiveness to women (see Behn's **"Our Cabal"**), we may speculate that when Behn writes of "that which I dare not name," she may be referring to sexual practices that extended beyond what her society would term "normal" or "natural." Indeed, the later echo of Behn's line in Lord Alfred Douglas's poem "Two Loves"—"I am the Love that dare not speak its name"—would come to haunt Oscar Wilde in his 1890s trials relating to his homosexuality. But as we move into this ambiguous territory, an even "other" reading of the *Covent Garden Drolery* version is possible. In shifting the speaker of the poem to the willing mistress in the later versions, Behn herself makes clear the heterosexual relationship of the two figures in the poem. The *Covent Garden Drolery* version is not so clear cut, and my reading so far of the speaker as male is based on the context of the poem (the other poems published with it, Hoyle's relationship with Behn, and the specific gendering of its later versions) and on a conventional reading practice that assumes a heterosexual context for love poetry. However, the "I" remains ambiguous, and

we might speculate whether the speaker could be a woman, a woman closer to Behn herself.

In 1688, late in her life, Behn published two poems, appended to her *Lycidus; or, The Lover in Fashion,* that reinscribe the doubleness of the *Covent Garden Drolery* version. The first is **"On the first discovery of falseness in Amintas. By Mrs. B."** This poem reiterates the complaints of betrayal we have already seen in the continuation verses in *The Dutch Lover* and in **"The Reflection."** Moreover, its setting is the same "solitary Grove," the same "Bed of Moss"; and as the betrayed woman speaks to her "Soul," we experience the same matrix of images as we have in **"The Willing Mistress"**:

Breath out thy Passion; tell him of his power
  And how thy flame was once by him approv'd.
How soon as wisht he was thy conqueror,
  No sooner spoke of Love, but was belov'd.
His wonderous Eyes, what weak resistance found,
  While every charming word begat a wound?

Here thou wilt grow impatient to be gone,
  And thro[ugh] my willing Eyes will silent pass,
Into the stream that gently glides along,
  But stay thy hasty flight, (my Soul,) alas,
A thought more cruel will thy flight secure,
  Thought, that can no admittance give a cure.

That last "thought more cruel" is of the faithless Amintas as "an humble suppliant at anothers feet"; and with this thought in mind the poem's speaker can take the step Hippolyta only momentarily considered: suicide. When Behn wrote this poem is probably impossible to determine, but it did appear (with variants) as **"The Disoblig'd Love"** in the March 1707 *Muses Mercury* selection from manuscript copies it is believed belonged to Hoyle. And if Hoyle's libertine reputation is accurate, and the number of poems Behn wrote addressing this Amyntas's libertine reputation tends to confirm it, then his first unfaithfulness to Behn probably occurred early in their relationship. Possibly this poem, together with **"The Reflection"** and the continuation in *The Dutch Lover,* represents Behn's working through the betrayal of her passion that fell prey to an almost archetypal Restoration Rake.

The other poem appended to *Lycidus* is **"To the Fair Clarinda, Who Made Love to Me, Imagined More than Woman,"** which Gilbert and Gubar include in the *Norton Anthology* selections. Although this poem cannot be as directly aligned with **"The Willing Mistress"** as others I've discussed, **"To the Fair Clarinda"** raises precisely the issue of a sexual politics that some "dare not name." The poem unmistakably celebrates lesbian love despite a culturally formulated discourse that cannot escape heterosexual paradigms. The poem opens with a problem of naming as the speaker underwrites the gendering of language implicit in the discursive practices of love poetry: "Fair lovely maid, or if that Title be / Too weak, too Feminine for Nobler thee, / Permit a Name that more Approaches Truth. / And let me call thee, Lovely Charming Youth." We again find ourselves in the realm of the

"Charming" in which the magic of love is conjured, but while the male lover charms by gazing eyes and words, the fair Clarinda charms through her body:

> Against thy Charms we struggle but in vain
> With thy deluding Form thou giv'st us pain,
> While the bright Nymph betrays us to the Swain.
> In pity to our Sex sure thou wer't sent,
> That we might Love, and yet be Innocent:
> For sure no Crime with thee we can commit;
> Or if we should—thy Form excuses it.

Although the speaker appears only able to express her desires via figures of a heterosexual union with Clarinda, she comes to realize that the entailment of their sexual pleasure will not result in the physical signature of heterosexual love: pregnancy. And in the operative cultural discourse of transgressive sexuality, Behn plays on whether their love would be "Innocent" or a "Crime." In this well-constructed paradox, this "Love" that Behn finally dares to name deconstructs the discursive practice of Cavaliers and Restoration wits alike—as the speaker makes clear in an image of the clitoris that is at the same time phallic, and thus powerful: "For who, that gathers fairest Flowers believes / A Snake lies hid beneath the Fragrant Leave."

"Thou beauteous Wonder of a different kind"—in the final verse, the speaker focuses on the hermaphroditic imagery that informs the poem's deconstructive paradoxes. The willing mistress Behn invokes here is an androgynous angel who can be both lover and friend, whose plot does not entail an inevitable betrayal that may or may not be put right by a rescuing patriarchy. As we saw in *The Dutch Lover,* the teleology of the marriage ending reclaimed Hippolyta from her betrayed status, and as we saw in **"The Reflection,"** the teleology of death provides the only other option Restoration culture could understand. Can we now see the betrayed willing mistress of **"On the first discovery of falseness in Amintas"** breaking the sequence of the teleologies of suicide and marriage, recognizing in the fair Clarinda a satisfying and less threatening alternative to the sexual politics of the time?

To suggest as much then as now is to undermine patriarchal structures that seek to use sexual love as a control of feminine autonomy. Behn's willing mistress strives to regain control for herself despite the cost exacted by her lover and by society. In a way, these poems can be read as metaphors for Aphra Behn the literary artist, who found both welcome and betrayal in Restoration circles, yet who also found and founded a female literary tradition that would publicly seek its subject on its own terms. The androgyny of the female writer, writing in male-dominated literary circles, is figured in the fair Clarinda, who like Behn must divide herself to give her "self" a voice that will find its own audience and that will be heard in an "other" dominated culture. As Virginia Woolf observed in *A Room of One's Own,* "All women together ought to let flowers fall upon the tomb of Aphra Behn . . . for it was she who earned them the right to speak their minds."

Ros Ballaster (essay date 1992)

SOURCE: "'A Devil on't, the Woman Damns the Poet': Aphra Behn's Fictions of Feminine Identity," in *Seductive Forms: Women's Amatory Fiction from 1684 to 1740,* Oxford at the Clarendon Press, 1992, pp. 69–113.

[*In the following excerpt, Ballaster explores the relationship between Behn's poetry and her opinions about gender roles.*]

Behn's best-known attempt at self definition is her vindication of herself as poet in the preface to a late play, *The Lucky Chance* (1687). Her writings on her writing, habitually triggered by the hostility of male 'wits', turn on the question of gender attribution. The preface to *The Lucky Chance,* a comedy of manners performed at the Theatre Royal in 1687, defines 'masculine' writing in two ways. The first definition refers solely to the question of content, and the double standard employed with regard to a woman playwright. Sexual explicitness is only permissible, she notes, for the male author. Addressing her female audience, Behn writes: 'Had I a Day or two's time, . . . I would sum up all your Beloved Plays, and all the Things in them that are past with such Silence by; because written by Men: Such Masculine Strokes in me, must not be allow'd'. Behn's second definition of 'masculine' writing raises, however, more complex issues. This time addressing her male peers in the theatre, she writes:

> All I ask is the Priviledge for my Masculine Part the Poet in me, (if any such you will allow me) to tread in those successful Paths my Predecessors have so long thrived in, to take those Measures that both the Ancient and Modern Writers have set me, and by which they have pleas'd the World so well; If I must not, because of my Sex, have this Freedom, but that you will usurp all to your selves; I lay down my Quill, and you shall hear no more of me, no not so much as to make Comparisons, because I will be kinder to my Brothers of the Pen, than they have been to a defenceless Woman; for I am not content to write for a Third Day only. I value Fame as much as I had been born a *Hero;* and if you rob me of that, I can retire from the ungrateful World and scorn its fickle favours.

Poetic genius is here firmly identified with 'masculinity', and 'heroic' male adventurism. If Behn rejects the pertinence of the double standard with regard to poetic content, these remarks suggest that she saw excellence in poetic form as an exclusively masculine quality. As a woman poet, she presents herself a divided subject, one of the female sex but with access to a 'masculine' power of poetry.

[In 'Aphra Behn: Sexuality and Self-Respect', *Women's Studies* 7 (1980)] Judith Kegan Gardiner employs this difficult passage to shed light on Behn's conception of authorial identity as a whole, arguing that 'To enable herself to write, Behn created a poetic identity for herself as Astrea, muse of a lost golden age who could combine "Female Sweetness and a Manly Grace". More fundamentally, to avoid becoming the disdainful lady or the disdained whore of male polarization, she identified with the male role while modifying its view of women.' Gardiner does not differentiate, however, between Behn's strategies of gender identification in the different genres in which she wrote. Behn only uses this language of the 'masculine part' to refer to the writing she classifies as poetry, and to discuss her interest in poetic *form*. Although her comments are made in a preface to a play the demand to 'take those Measures' literary traditions have made available to her suggests that we read them in the context of notions of creative power in metred verse. Behn, it is clear, was all too aware of the conventional polarization of the 'female' in Restoration poetry. Here, woman appears either as the ideal Petrarchan mistress, to be slavishly worshipped and anatomized from her eyebrows to her toes, or as the engulfing, destructive whore of libertine poetry. The only response to these rigid dichotomies in Restoration love poetry seems to be precisely that which Behn adopted in her poetry, that of lifting the female poet into a position which supposedly transcends the enclosures of ideologies of the 'feminine', by casting her as the possessor of a male poetic gift, or as a muse or goddess.

This is not, however, Behn's only strategy in her writing as a whole. In her preface to her first play, *The Dutch Lover,* produced at the Theatre Royal in 1673, she makes very bold claims indeed for women's literary abilities, insisting that 'Plays have no great room for that which is men's great advantage over women, that is Learning'. Noting that neither Shakespeare nor Jonson were respected for their intellectual breadth, she adds of her male contemporaries, that, with the exception of Dryden, there are 'none that write at such a formidable rate, but that a woman may well hope to reach their greatest heights'. The drama and fiction appeared far more accessible genres to Behn than poetry, since neither necessarily required a classical training. Behn consistently identifies poetry as a heroic masculine preserve. Thus, she most frequently adopts a Sapphic or oracular poetic voice in her poetry, in sharp contrast to the intimate and confiding persona of her novelistic prose, and the incisive wit of her dramatic prefaces.

Behn lifted the female poet into a position which supposedly transcends the enclosures of ideologies of the 'feminine', by casting her as the possessor of a male poetic gift, or as a muse or goddess.

—*Ros Ballaster*

This is not to say, however, that Behn's poetry is not equally inclined to exploration and subversion of gender dichotomies. Her utopian poem, **'The Golden Age',** in many ways a conventional piece of Tory pastoral nostalgia, is also a remarkable exercise in female self-creation. Behn's pastoral idyll is a world in which a female Nature cannot be constrained by the power of man:

The stubborn Plough had then,

Made no rude Rapes upon the Virgin Earth;
Who yielded of her own accord her plentious Birth,
   Without the Aids of men;
  As if within her Teeming Womb,
  All Nature, and all Sexes lay,
  Whence new Creations every day
  Into the happy World did come:
  The Roses fill'd with Morning Dew
   Bent down their loaded heads,
T'adorn the careless Shepherds Grassy Beds
While still young opening Buds each moment grew,
And as those withered, drest his shaded Couch
  anew.

In this female economy, earth/woman contains all sexual difference within herself. Both virgin and mother, Nature has the power of sexual emission and generation. She impregnates and reproduces herself, as the roses filled with morning dew dispel their liquid, die, and replenish autonomously. Once again it is the female who has access to both sides of the sexual divide. Behn's **'The Golden Age'**, in the context of her other work, can be read as a further contribution to her narcissistic exercise in female self-creation.

It is in the ambiguous poem, **'To the fair Clarinda, who made Love to me, imagin'd more than Woman'**, appended to her translation of *Lycidus,* that this narcissistic challenge to masculine exclusions reaches its height:

Fair lovely Maid, or if that Title be
Too weak, too Feminine for Nobler thee,
Permit a Name that more Approaches Truth:
And let me call thee, Lovely Charming Youth.
This last will justifie my soft complaint;
While that may serve to lessen my constraint;
And without Blushes I the Youth persue,
When so much beauteous Woman is in view.
Against thy Charms we struggle but in vain
With thy deluding Form thou giv'st us pain,
While the bright Nymph betrays us to the Swain.
In pity to our Sex sure thou wer't sent,
That we might Love, and yet be Innocent:
For sure no Crime with thee we can commit;
Or if we shou'd—thy Form excuses it.
For who, that gathers fairest Flowers believes
A Snake lies hid beneath the Fragrant Leaves.

Thou beauteous Wonder of a different kind,
Soft *Cloris* with the dear *Alexis* join'd;
When e'er the Manly part of thee, wou'd plead
Thou tempts us with the Image of the Maid,
While we the noblest Passions do extend
The Love to *Hermes, Aphrodite* the Friend.

This twenty-four line poem, like so much of Behn's work, has largely prompted biographical investigation. What, her critics ask, is the (sexual) identity of the lover?

The poem is most frequently interpreted as a panacea to lesbian desire. Thus, [in *The Incomparable Aphra*] George Woodcock sees **'Clarinda'** as proof that Behn was 'not uninterested in the predilections of the original Sappho', Angeline Goreau describes it [in *Reconstructing Aphra: A Social Biography of Aphra Behn,* 1980] as a 'playful tribute to her own sex' but devoid of the 'consuming passion' of the *Love-Letters to a Gentleman,* and Cora Kaplan sums it up as 'a witty poem about a lesbian attraction' [*Salt and Bitter and Good: Three Centuries of English and American Women Poets,* 1975]. Under the protection of the disguise of idealized female friendship, supporters of this interpretation argue, the lovers are safe from recognition of their lesbian practices ('For sure no Crime with thee we can commit; / Or if we shou'd—thy Form excuses it').

Another possible reading, however, is that the lover is a cross-dressing or transvestite man. Disguised as a woman, the male lover gains easy access to his mistress ('For who that gathers fairest Flowers believes / A Snake lies hid beneath the Fragrant Leaves'). This reading might lead us back to John Hoyle, the supposed 'Lycidus' of the *Love-Letters to a Gentleman,* for whom there is some evidence of homosexuality, although none of transvestitism.

Behn allows us no easy solution to this riddle, but rather encourages her reader to enjoy the play across both sexes and the subversive power of the image of the hermaphrodite. The rhyming couplet provides the ideal structure for the undercutting of each successive clue, and a reversal of the beloved's sexual identity ('And without Blushes I the Youth persue, / When so much beauteous Woman is in view', and 'When e'er the Manly part of thee wou'd plead / Thou tempts us with the Image of the Maid').

'To Fair Clarinda' is, I would argue, best illuminated within the context of Behn's narcissistic contemplation of her own poetic practice. The concluding line, a splitting of the term Hermaphrodite, the figure who contains both sexual morphologies, also contains an embedded pun. Aphrodite is both the goddess of love, and the lover of Aphra. Aphra is then both subject and object of her own poem. The riddling tautologies of the poet are a seductive plea to her reader to abandon the search for a unitary identity behind the writing, whether that of the lover or the beloved. The reader, like Behn's fictional lovers, is encouraged to take his or her pleasure from the pursuit of (sexual) meaning, rather than in its definitive resolution.

The complex play of gendered subjectivity to which **'Clarinda'** points us is more fully developed as the specific property of the female writer, however, in Behn's use of narrative as opposed to lyric form. Behn abandons the oracular, mythic persona of Astrea in her prose writings for a more familiar feminine subject position, that of the 'gossip' or story-teller.

Judith Kegan Gardiner (essay date 1993)

SOURCE: "Liberty, Equality, Fraternity: Utopian Longings in Behn's Lyric Poetry," in *Rereading Aphra Behn: History, Theory, and Criticism,* edited by Heidi Hutner, University Press of Virginia, 1993, pp. 273–300.

[*An American critic and educator, Gardiner has published a study on the verse of English poet and dramatist Ben Jonson and has also contributed essays to several publications devoted to feminist criticism and scholarship. In the following essay, she states that Behn expressed in her verse a desire for the liberation of women from repressive social and political norms.*]

Aphra Behn was a poet of astonishing range and accomplishment. In her own time she was praised primarily as a poet, and she hoped that posterity would place her with "Sappho and Orinda" in a female lineage of poetry and in the ageless pantheon of fame. She awed men with her talent and fluency and inspired other women to write. Her later reputation is almost entirely as a playwright and pioneer novelist, however. "With their feeble personification and insipid allegory, almost all" of her poems are "equally dull," complained critic Edward Wagenknecht [in "In Praise of Mrs. Behn," *The Colophon* 18 (1934)]. "And she—poor lady!—considered herself a poet first of all." Today's feminists prefer her vigorous polemics in behalf of herself and other women to her lyrics on more traditional topics. However, her poetry forms a distinctive part of her oeuvre that should be more highly valued.

In this poetry, traditional tropes of heterosexual love present a longing for community, for a society in which the radical values of liberty, equality, and fraternity would be possible for women and defined in women's terms. Of anomalous social position, Behn mythologized her family of origin, her personal past, and her nation's history; her poetry created a world in which a woman like herself could flourish. She contextualized her longings for a more just and fulfilling life not in Restoration England at large but only in a coterie of fellow poets and a realm of poetry, a pretty pastoral world that took shape in the printed book. In this as in many other respects, she is similar to the other best-known seventeenth-century woman poet, Katherine Philips—known as Orinda, as Behn was known as Astraea— and both women write within the traditions of seventeenth-century lyric established earlier in the century by the canonical male poets John Donne and Ben Jonson. Such similarities between the more private and more public female poets help us understand how for the seventeenth century, the public and private were overlapping rather than polarized: Behn's poetry circulated in manuscripts among friends, was sung on the stage, and reappeared in published books. Such poetry calls into question the categories of public and private often used to organize seventeenth-century literary history and also many conventional literary judgments, for example, those exalting the verisimilar over the artificial and the passionate over the playful.

Behn's best known and most widely admired poem is **"Love Arm'd,"** a song from her 1677 play *Abdelazar.*

> Love in Fantastique Triumph satt,
> Whilst Bleeding Hearts a round him flow'd,
> For whom Fresh paines he did Create,
> And strange Tyranick power he show'd;
> From thy Bright Eyes he took his fire,
> Which round about, in sport he hurl'd;

But 'twas from mine he took desire,
Enough to undo the Amorous World.

From me he took his sighs and tears,
From thee his Pride and Crueltie;
From me his Languishments and Feares,
And every Killing Dart from thee;
Thus thou and I, the God have arm'd,
And sett him up a Deity;
But my poor Heart alone is harm'd,
Whilst thine the Victor is, and free.

The poem succeeds by the standards of cavalier poetry, expressing turbulent erotic passions in elegantly concise and self-contained tetrameter quatrains. The first quatrain paints an emblem. Personified love sits in a triumphal throne or chariot as in a classical victory pageant or a Renaissance masque, both spectacles of power. Love is a conquering hero at the expense of others who have lost. His "Fantastique Triumph" is both extraordinary and imaginary: The effective trisyllabic *fantastic* implies both the exaggerated power of love and its origin in the lovers' mental constructs. Love is the creator, although he creates pain rather than the universal harmony attributed to God by Milton's *Paradise Lost,* which appeared a few years before Behn began publishing. Therefore, love's alien and uncanny "strange" power is "tyrannic"—that is, both absolute and unjust. The seventeenth-century's frequent changes of political regime would certainly have left nearly everyone in Restoration England thinking that they had recently lived under a tyranny of one sort or the other, either Puritan or Royalist. "Tyranny" would not be a dead metaphor, then, but a lively reminder of being at the mercy of people and events beyond one's individual control, of political as well as personal passions. Milton makes Satan a grand tyrant, but Behn domesticates such cosmic references; similarly, she alludes to the baroque splendors of God enthroned and Christ's bleeding heart by painting images that recall contemporary baroque churches while keeping her lyric resolutely modest and secular.

The poem's great power derives from the contrast between its painful and exaggerated sentiments and a controlled and orderly form that seems to accept this situation as proper, normal, perhaps even necessary. The beloved's eyes are the source of love's fire, and love seems to enjoy the pure exercise of his power, hurling lightning bolts "in sport," a gesture huge and reckless enough to balance the lover's eyes, which are filled with enough "desire" to "undo the amorous world." The neat balances of "from me" and "from thee" break down, however. "To undo" is the opposite of creation, perhaps a synonym for the creation of pain, though unlike the woman undone by sexual indiscretion in Restoration London, the wounded lover is not abandoned and alone but is surrounded by bleeding hearts, as though the whole universe is wounded by love.

Similar patterns remain important throughout Behn's poetry: The woman always wants reciprocity, as does the lover of either sex; the man or the beloved wants freedom. Behn frequently depicts relationships of equality that degenerate, perhaps because it is so hard for her to imagine reciprocity and equality in a society devoid of them in which only sexual passion seems to offer the possibility of ecstatic reciprocity. The carefully balanced "me" and "thee" in this poem seem to keep the relationship between the lovers as even as the meter, against the sense, so that the contrast between the poem's form and its emotional content reproduces the dilemma of the woman who is told that a relationship is equal at the same time that she feels more constrained than her lover both psychologically and socially. Equality is defined on his terms: Either lover can enter or leave the relationship at will, but the woman becomes emotionally more attached and more vulnerable because of possible pregnancy or loss of reputation—events such poems do not mention directly.

The phrase "thus thou and I" in the concluding quatrain works syllogistically in the fashion of the best seventeenth-century lyrics, although its conclusions do not spring logically from what has occurred before; instead, the logic is that implied simply by the combination "thou and I"—that is, by the desire that subordinates the lover to the beloved's power. "Thou and I" invent the god and shape its being. Without such deification, Love might be fair rather than tyrannical and sadistic. Once again the apparent union and reciprocity of the lovers breaks down into a power imbalance of female victimage. As Behn emphasizes by the pause late in the poem's last line, to be "free" from reciprocal claims is to be victorious over the committed. A poem written around the time of the English Revolution might well champion freedom although it appears equivocal about its meaning for women. Paradoxically, to be free may be possible only for the victorious, only for tyrants who keep others enslaved. Freedom may also only be possible for the dispassionate, those so cool that they do not care. Throughout her life Behn defended sexual passion as peremptory but also as central to human satisfaction. In a poem **"To Desire"** she could address it as an old but difficult friend, "thou haunts my inconvenient hours," and, in her paraphrase of the Lord's prayer, she famously expected divine indulgence for an eroticism she could not seriously believe was sinful:

> Of all my Crimes, the breach of all thy Laws
> Love, soft bewitching Love! has been the cause
> . . . That sure will soonest be forgiven of God.

In its original context, **"Love Arm'd"** opens Behn's heroic drama *Abdelazar,* where it is sung by the Queen of Spain, who is foolishly in love with a disdainful Moor who became her lover only for political reasons and who now rebuffs her. The song thus sets up Behn's goal of reciprocal emotion, indicated in meter and word patterning, against a context of power that vitiates reciprocity between men and women. Even though the woman is the active wooer and a queen, she is powerless against a foolish passion for a tyrannic man, and she thus colludes in the eroticizing of power on which this poem, and perhaps modern patriarchy, are based.

The context of that peculiar Restoration literary form, the heroic drama, mythologizes social contexts so that any heroine may be a queen; however, everyone in a play must be marked by class and gender, even if the classes and locale do not correspond to those of Restoration England. Lyric poems dissolve even this imaginary context into the freer space of the poetry anthology, in which **"Love Arm'd"** appears with no indication of who its speaker or beloved are. Even if love is tyrannical and unjust, such a world remains fair in the sense that the rules of love apparently apply to all lovers, whomever they may be. The roles are not gender-specific, and the lover clearly bears responsibility for the fix she or he is in because love's cruelty cannot exist without the cooperation of both parties. The miniature world of **"Love Arm'd"** is a cruel but meaningful one, potentially sex-egalitarian but confusing about the conventional alignments of gender.

In the double binds that Behn so frequently shows men putting women in, the man may well treat the woman as an object to be discarded when he has had his pleasure, but he blames her even more severely when he cannot have his pleasure.

—Judith Kegan Gardiner

If the central dynamic of Behn's poetry is the longing for reciprocity in a world in which men and women hold unequal power, then **"The Disappointment"** is a humorous meditation and an ironic revenge on those conditions. **"The Disappointment"** may also be seen as an opposite to **"Love Arm'd."** Where **"Love Arm'd"** may display the woman suffering from a man's power over her, **"The Disappointment"** shows a woman suffering from the one form of powerlessness that is specific to men, sexual impotence. The perfect reciprocity that Behn implies ought to exist in sexual love is denied for the woman of **"The Disappointment"** in two apparently contrasting but reinforcing ways—the man's physical power over her and his lack of power over his own body, a debility Behn heightens in comparison to her source, whose hero later becomes vigorously successful with his mistress. Thus, unlike Ovid's *Amores* book 3, poem 7, the classical precursor of such poems, or the French "L'Occasion Perdue Recouverte" that Behn's poem partly translates, or even the earl of Rochester's brutal "The Imperfect Enjoyment," Behn's poem does not contrast an incident of male impotence with his otherwise exaggerated virility.

Whereas **"Love Arm'd"** paints an emblematic fiction of a personified god, **"The Disappointment"** revels in another artificial world, one Behn creates frequently in her nondramatic verse—that of precious pastoral. Seventeenth-century pastoral is often reviled as artificial and "effeminate," because we moderns prefer forms that seem closer to a direct transcription of social life, the novel aesthetic and aesthetic of the novel form that Behn helped shape in the 1680s. In this poem, however, Behn moves away from

social realism, changing its setting from an interior "appartement" in her source to an outdoor "lone Thicket made for Love." This transformation indicates that Behn positively embraced the pastoral; it was not just something she translated for quick cash.

One twilight afternoon "Amorous *Lysander*" surprises "fair *Cloris*" in that lonely thicket, and he immediately starts making love to her. The poem's only direct discourse, which is italicized occurs when Cloris protests against her lover's advances, beginning "*Cease, Cease—your vain Desire, / Or I'll call out.*" Because we hear Cloris's words directly, we may feel that it is the woman's consciousness to which we are closest in the poem. Only she speaks directly in Behn's poem, although not in the source, where her lover is voluble; the rest of Behn's **"The Disappointment"** is reported via an apparently female narrator. Such phrasing highlights female agency in the poem, but the situation is complicated. Behn alters her source to emphasize Lysander's passivity despite the fact that he is the aggressor in the affair: He is "o'er-Ravish'd" and "too transported"; "Excess of Love his Love betray'd." Conversely, Cloris's protests against an apparent rape underline that what a woman says is not necessarily what she means, a view that may alienate Behn from today's women: The narrator insists, like the male lover in the poem, that Cloris means yes when she says no. The narrator, another woman, can correctly read a woman who is either constrained from knowing her feelings or restrained from expressing them by conventional standards of female propriety. Thus, the poem gives us two contradictory ways of reading female reliability and the correspondence of speech to feeling, of expression to passion—Cloris's and the narrator's.

What Lysander seeks is less a particular woman than a cosmic power centered in the female body:

> His daring Hand that Altar seiz'd,
> Where Gods of Love do sacrifice:
> That Awful Throne, that Paradice
> Where Rage is calm'd, and Anger pleas'd;
> That Fountain where Delight still flows,
> And gives the Universal World Repose.

Immediately thereafter, in a passage that Behn expands from her source, the lovers enjoy a union that is reciprocal, passionate, and simultaneously physical and emotional.

> Her Balmy Lips incountring his,
> Their Bodies, as their Souls, are joyn'd;
> Where both in Transports Unconfin'd
> Extend themselves upon the Moss.

The body language of the poem hints at the possibility of true reciprocity; her hand touches his breast—a touch Behn adds to the original—then his hers. In the moments building up to the humorous climax, we hear of idyllic pleasures that cannot be sustained, a wordless reciprocity where his body and hers first mirror one another and then melt and blend. The language describing their rapture echoes that of Donne's poems like "The Extasie," describing a union that transcends the mere flesh. And Cloris and

Lysander melt into just such a perfect, perhaps even idyllically infantile union, one that nostalgically recalls the poetry written before the English Civil War, the rosy Elizabethan bloom. This initial period of union in **"The Disappointment"** is mutual and consensual. The poem's references to higher loves and historical allusions help create its context, not a spiritually transcendent realm but a lost garden of earthly pleasures.

At the crucial moment, however, "The too transported hapless Swain / Found the vast Pleasure turn'd to Pain." The woman responds:

> *Cloris* returning from the Trance
> Which Love and soft Desire had bred,
> Her timerous Hand she gently laid
> (Or guided by Design or Chance)
> Upon that Fabulous *Priapus,*
> That Potent God, as Poets feign;
> But never did young Sherpherdess,
> Gath'ring of Fern upon the Plain,
> More nimbly draw her Fingers back,
> Finding beneath the verdant Leaves a Snake:
>
> Than *Cloris* her fair Hand withdrew,
> Finding that God of her Desires
> Disarm'd of all his Awful Fires,
> And Cold as Flow'rs bath'd in the Morning Dew.
> Who can the *Nymph*'s Confusion guess?
>
> Like Lightning through the Grove she hies,
> Or *Daphne* from the *Delphick* God.

The diction here is both erotic and witty. The primary joke is that the disappointed woman runs away like a frightened virgin. The encomium to Priapus, classical god of the phallus, unlike the earlier one to Cloris's "altar" of love, is both exaggerated and ironically undercut. Internal rhyme makes the "Fabulous Priapus" already comic, and the alliterations of "that potent god, as poets feign" link male poetry, faking, and the myths or fables that govern society.

If male power is the dominating fact over female life, male impotence may seem a balancing justice, a kind of cheery revenge—even though part of the joke is that male impotence becomes another kind of power, that of withholding pleasure from the woman, for whom heterosexual pleasure is only available when he wants and when he can. In the double binds that Behn so frequently shows men putting women in, the man may well treat the woman as an object to be discarded when he has had his pleasure, but he blames her even more severely when he cannot have his pleasure. This approach contrasts with Behn's source, where Cloris is angry but Lysander pledges eternal love and apologizes for his failing, explaining that her *"Beauty"* in his *"Soul . . . joynd Respect and Love in one"* to cause his embarrassment. As the woman speaker of Behn's lyric **"To *Alexis* in Answer to his Poem against Fruition"** complains, women can't win against their male lovers:

> They fly if Honour take our part,
> Our Virtue drives 'em o're the field.

> We lose 'em by too much desert,
> And Oh! they fly us if we yeild.

In Behn's version of **"The Disappointment,"** the man's anger at the woman is just as strong as if his lost satisfaction sprang from the lady's denial rather than from his own impotence. The narrator claims, "The *Nymph*'s Resentments none but I / Can well Imagine or Condole." Cloris keeps these imagined resentments to herself, in contrast to the French poem, in which she insults her lover's *"Scottish Lump"* and calls him *"weakly mann'd."* Behn's Lysander does not plead with his woman or languish in despair but "curs'd his Birth, his Fate, his Stars; / But more the *Shepherdess's* Charms." In the French source, he blames first the devil and then Cloris's heavenly beauty. In Behn, he charges that Cloris's "Charms" or spells have bewitched him to the *"Hell* of Impotence"— hardly a benign reference in an age when male impotence was a common complaint against witches and women were hanged for witchcraft. Even though the woman within the poem is disappointed and blamed, however, the female narrative voice seems just a bit gleeful at the philanderer's discomfort.

Critic Richard Quaintance assumes that when Behn varies from her source, she errs, a victim of poetic incompetence: "Checked by indifference, inability, or the economy of the stanza form she chose, she totally missed some of the sense as well as the words of her original," he lectures [in "French Sources of the Restoration 'Imperfect Enjoyment' Poem," *Philological Quarterly* 42 (April 1963)]. If we assume, however, not that she misunderstood the tradition but that she wished to redirect it, we can understand her relation to the male poetic tradition through her changes from her source. Quaintance laments that Behn "has turned a success story, prolix and jolly, into . . . an object lesson on the risk of self-absorption during love, a pragmatic warning against acting in love with love while Cloris is waiting." Behn "may be blaming" the man "out of a feminine sympathy," he says, apparently without realizing that his own disappointment with the poem may be the result of a masculine sympathy that Behn's poem deliberately invokes and then mocks. This sympathy springs from an identification with the male hero so strong that it causes the modern male critic to misread Behn's poem, in which, unlike the source, Lysander does not noticeably act self-absorbed or in love with love at all as "Mad to possess, himself he threw / On the Defenceless Lovely Maid."

Pastoral settings were associated especially with women authors and audiences in the Restoration; they were considered effete and phony by many men. It makes sense, then, to consider its advantages for a female author like Behn, who translated continental pastorals like **"The Golden Age"** and who transferred other poems into pastoral settings. One advantage of the pastoral is that it reformulates social class. Supposedly set in the lowest class of rural society and often in a purportedly primitive stage of social evolution, the pastoral masks the real class imbalances of the contemporary urban scene. The theatrical set to which Behn belonged was a privileged slice of London where the classes could mix—but only while following certain rules that traded female sexual respectability for access to men of rank and wit. Behn's pastoral games and identifications by initials play peekaboo with social class—advertising their acquaintance with titled men and women by references to "My Lady Morland" or "Sir R.O." but teasing us about unknown others so that our sexual voyeurism about who is currently sleeping with whom is conflated with our print-reading outsiders' voyeurism about the upper classes.

Modern privacy was being invented in Behn's historical period, privacy with reference to one's relations to God, to bodily functions, to reading, and to sex. One might even argue that the conventions of literary voyeurism helped create conventions of privacy and that silently watching people became assimilated with that other private and recently silent activity, reading. Pornography increased in the late seventeenth century, as did female literacy and misogyny. Earlier in the century John Donne wrote intense, passionate, and apparently private love poetry, yet in his lyrics passionate love for a woman was often predicated on the man's seduction being overheard, his erotic behavior overseen, by another man, the reader's surrogate—even in those poems that protest being looked at or talked about. "For God's sake hold your tongue and let me love," the lover tells his friend in "The Canonization." In Donne's "The Extasie," a pastoral lyric that had enormous influence on later seventeenth-century writers, the lover invokes a male spectator "by love refined" who would stand "within convenient distance" to view the lover and his beloved in an ecstatic embrace. Only in terms of this voyeurism can the world-denying perfection of Donne's sexual love be affirmed. Behn makes such hidden voyeurism explicit, often to deliberately pornographic effect; at the same time, she reveals and alters its gendered dynamics. Although the seventeenth-century woman is already accustomed to being a spectacle for male viewers, Behn's poetry subjects both men and women to the scandalizing attention accorded sexual objects. **"On a Juniper Tree, cut down to make Busks"** develops this erotic theme, covertly combining it with a convention of religious personification.

By adopting the persona of a juniper tree, Behn recalls Christian poems about the true cross while seeming to evade gender completely. The tree begins the poem by boasting that it was "The Pride and Glory of the Wood," then that its glory springs from its role in a sexual encounter between two lovers. "Beneath my shade the other day, / Young *Philocles* and *Cloris* lay." At one point the juniper sees itself as a "Rival Shade" to the lover and hence as male; it finds the woman desirable, steals kisses from her, and wants to be near her, echoing male erotic poetry from Catullus on. At another point it compares itself to women, however: "My Wealth, like bashful Virgins, I / Yielded with some Reluctancy." Insofar as Behn's voice sounds behind the personification, such allusions to virginity are ironized. The tree further claims to be the pander, duenna, and bridal chamber of the lovers all in one; the editors of *Kissing the Rod: An Anthology of Seventeenth-Century Women's Verse* (1988) note that in re-

vising the poem, Behn made the woman's role more active.

> Upon my Root she lean'd her head,
> And where I grew, he made their Bed:
> Whilst I the Canopy more largely spread.

Although by bending down its branches, the tree "had the blisse, / To rob the Shepherd of a kiss," Behn portrays the ideal sexuality between the lovers as completely mutual and reciprocal, not stealthy, a Donne-like merger of bodies and feelings:

> [The lovers] mingled melting Rays,
> Exchanging Love a thousand ways.
> Kind was the force on every side,
> . . . . .
> His panting Breast, to hers now join'd,
> They feast on Raptures unconfin'd;
> Vast and Luxuriant, such as prove
> The Immortality of Love.
> For who but a Divinitie,
> Could mingle Souls to that Degree;
> And melt 'em into Extasie?
> Now like the *Phenix,* both Expire,
> While from the Ashes of their Fire,
> Sprung up a new and soft desire.

The poem runs through a medley of motifs best-known from Donne's love poetry: melted souls, an ecstasy, a phoenix, and the play with religious language. In Behn's version, however, "immortality" alludes not to divine truth but simply to the renewed desire for sex: Her lovers "did invoke, / The God! and thrice new vigor took." After three bouts the woman humorously expresses doubts about her complaisance. Fortunately for her, her lover is still devoted to her. For him, "Loves sacred flame, / Before and after was the same"—clearly a utopian wish from Behn's viewpoint, as many of her poems register disappointment that men are so much less interested in women after than before the act.

After recording the lovers' perfect union, the tree returns to its perverse role: "The Shepherdess my Bark carest, / Whilst he my Root, Love's Pillow, kist." Andrew Marvell plays on such images of "vegetable love" more metaphysically in "The Garden," for example, in which the solitary speaker boasts that "Stumbling on melons, as I pass, / Ensnared with flowers, I fall on grass." Whereas Marvell's speaker transcends the libertine garden tradition for the purer joys of contemplation, only sexual voyeurism provides Behn's tree a semblance of pleasure. Nature in Behn's poetry has no independent joys and needs human sexual love to animate it. Behn's pastoral is antinatural and thoroughly anthropomorphic. If, in the words that Pope so memorably rewrote, Behn calls "Wit . . . no more than *Nature* well exprest," one might also say that for her, nature was little more than human wit well expressed in poetry.

After the lovers leave the woods, the juniper tree is desolate:

> And if before my Joyes were such,

Engraving from a lost portrait of Behn.

In having heard, and seen too much,
My Grief must be as great and high
When all abandon'd I shall be,
Doom'd to a silent Destinie
. . . . .
No more a joyful looker on.

Woefully isolated, the tree wants to participate not just in sex but in the human community. Bereft, the tree cries "Christal Dew" over Cloris. She responds as to a lover, with "Pity" because her "Soul is made of Love." Her loving response is ironic, however, that of a metamorphosing Ovidian god who objectifies lovers.

She cut me down, and did translate,
My being to a happier state.
No Martyr for Religion di'd
With half that Unconsidering Pride
[as the tree did].

The tree's top is burned for incense, while its

body into Busks was turn'd:
Where I still guard the Sacred Store,
And of Loves Temple keep the Door.

Thus the juniper ends up as part of a woman's corset, a homey, familiar, and humorous counterpart to other poetic metamorphoses or ways of getting near the beloved. Here

the tree continues to act as pander or duenna, the complicit third to others' erotic coupling, or as a member of the woman's family, guarding her virtue.

The entire poem is an extended personification in tetrameter couplets, a light form appropriate for a bit of pastoral pornography. As a perversely enthusiastic voyeur, Behn's juniper is not simply part of a lush, natural setting, as we would expect from a tree, but participates, like the reader, in the pleasures of vicarious sex. As frequently happens in Behn's soft porn, the tree's voyeurism is satirically presented yet not undercut, and the poem invites the reader to engage in such dubious pleasures—admittedly weaker pleasures than those the lovers experience, but stronger and more pleasant fare than readers normally receive. Such pornography celebrates the joys of peeking more than the joys of sex; it depends on and incites a sense of sexual behavior as secret, forbidden, and titillating—more so, for example, than in erotic medieval fabliaux, where sexual couples are often humourously and publicly caught in the act.

Behn writes in one tradition of Donne, the tradition of witty erotic verse. This tradition is firmly androcentric, making women its objects, and hence it is difficult for women to take it seriously. Behn does not. Instead, she uses the pastoral setting to create alternatives to the world around her. One might argue that an identification with artifice works better than an identification with nature for women because women have too often been inscribed within a restrictive definition of nature, and the social as constituted in Behn's time was no better: Appeal to an artificial nature conspicuously unlike any nature one could see in contemporary London or in the countryside around it defines her pastoral. In poems like **"The Disappointment"** and **"On a Juniper Tree,"** Behn creates a nature that responds to women's as well as men's desires; however, it never aspires, as does the nature of some male Restoration writers, to the sublime. The limits against which her poetry strives are not those of the intractable flesh, because she implies that social restrictions, not those of nature, limit women most. To concede that the limits imposed on women were natural would be to give up the possibility of being a woman poet altogether.

Behn in this respect differs dramatically from her friend and patron John Wilmot, the Earl of Rochester, a man who had everything except a conviction of the value of anything, a cynic who asked transcendental questions because social power was so clearly already his that his dissatisfaction had to reach beyond it. For Restoration women, who did not have everything and could not get it, Rochester's pose made no sense. Such women did not probe the paradoxes of embodiment in literature because they were always already assumed to be identical with their bodies; they therefore needed instead to explore the overcoming of embodiment. Moreover, women like Behn did not share male disgust with human flesh, although at the end of the century many women championed chastity over the difficulties of marriage. This disparity in the perspectives of male and female writers in the seventeenth century perhaps accounts in part for male critics' judgment that women's poetry of the period is shallow. Such critics may take the social order for granted and hence underestimate its restrictive powers on women, especially for women who do not respond to these restrictions by seeking social revolution. Restoration women did not, like some men of the time, need to seek in sexual experience a loss of identity they could find nowhere else, because they found loss of identity everywhere. Like male poets erotic and mystic, women writers did seek ideal unions. They were much more likely than the men to dwell primarily on the reciprocity within union, however, perhaps otherwise fearing that in sex and religion as well as in marriage, the one flesh and one spirit of the joined couple would always be his. For a sense of reciprocity and fluidity, some religious women turned to a flexibly gendered God. Secular women writers like both Behn and Philips instead renamed themselves and others as a way of moving out of their defined social circumstances into new and ideal imaginary communities where they could be equal participants with other artists, lovers, and friends.

Behn died as she had lived—a new woman longing for an imaginary past golden age and creating myths of a world where to be a public woman was not to be a whore but to be a hero and a poet.

—Judith Kegan Gardiner

A crucial biographical fact about Behn is her social isolation from the usual familial supports at the time she became a professional author. Whereas other women writers relied on the categories of virgin, wife, or mother to provide them acceptability, Behn had no husband and no known husband's relatives, as other widows did, no children, and no known family of origin; this apparent familial vacuum indicates deliberate effort on her part to obfuscate those facts that would fix her social identity. Instead, she springs from nowhere onto the stage, via South America, Continental spying, and jail. Gossips around her assumed that such a self-made woman must be man-made. Contemporaries alleged that her works were written by male lovers, and even some modern feminist editors cannot resist categorizing her as a prostitute: "There is no evidence that she chose the profession of writing: there is every sign that she was reduced to making a living by her wits. We may honour her for refusing the other obvious alternative, prostitution, if only we could be sure that she did" [Germaine Greer et al., eds., *Kissing the Rod*]. If we look at the literary consequences of Behn's self-creation rather than worry its sexual economics, however, we see that such self-creation in a closed and hierarchical society demands the simultaneous creation of a new social order into which the new self fits. In their oriental courts, European carnivals, and American wildernesses, Behn's plays partially reformulate their societies, but the poetry is freer still to invent idealized, imaginary worlds.

In Behn's erotic poetry, sexual knowledge creates its own community of values. In **"The Willing Mistress,"** for example, after mutual kissing, the woman is "willing to receive / That which I dare not name." Her lover's eyes alone "tell their softning Tale" to woo her; without words he "lay'd me gently on the Ground, / Ah who can guess the rest?" The poem, an entirely verbal construction, describes an experience that claims to be entirely physical, unmediated by language. But the poem works only by its appeal to a linguistic community that can freely and easily translate the physical into a shared verbal world. We all already must know what "that which I dare not name" must be, and the final rhetorical question solicits the smug answer that all of us readers can "guess the rest." The shared joke requires shared knowledge, not of the idiosyncracies of any individual lover but of physical experience common to us all, and it expects us to laugh, too, at conventional verbal and social structures that pretend that we, including the women among the poem's readers, do not all know what sex is about and enjoy it equally well.

One possible community in opposition to patriarchal Restoration society was that of closely bonded women; that is, the society that Behn's poetic predecessor Katherine Philips tried to create in her poetry and in her life. Like Philips, Behn eroticizes female friendships, most notably in **"To the Fair *Clarinda*, who made Love to me, imagin'd more than Woman."** That poem, however, equates the "weak" with the "Feminine" and assumes a heterosexual norm so strong that female bonds are necessarily "innocent" and derivative on heterosexual models:

> without Blushes I the Youth persue,
> When so much beauteous Woman is in view,
> . . . . .
> In pity to our Sex sure thou we'rt sent,
> That we might Love, and yet be Innocent.

Apparent innocence, as always in Behn, nods to the community of readers in the know: "For sure no Crime with thee we can commit; / Or if we shou'd—thy Form excuses it."

More frequently, Behn expresses ties to women not through coupled relationships but indirectly through sexual triangles in which her female speakers typically cast themselves as the other woman, a discarded mistress. Older and less attractive than her rival, such a woman ingratiates herself with the rival by praising her and complaining about the man. Because she draws herself and the fickle male lover as morally equivalent, however, such praise ejects the rival into a superior but distant position above the speaker and her former lover. This sexual triangle made up of three people of both sexes allows Behn to shift positions and identifications; she does not, like so many male poets, simply use it to elide the sexual other and return to homosocial bonding.

In **"To My Lady *Morland* at Tunbridge,"** Behn establishes a parallel between crowds who come out to admire the conquering hero who won a war and those that stare at the famous beauties of the hour: "I wish'd to see, and much a Lover grew / Of so much Beauty, though my Rivals too." Submitting to the woman rival, not the lover, the speaker judges that "Not to love you, a wonder sure would be, / Greater then all his Perjuries to me." Traditional male love poetry allows its characters only two positions, and only one of them gets to speak: Transfixed by a female beauty, the male lover gazes and spouts verse. For a woman to look at a woman's beauty in this convention turns the woman into an envious rival eager to replace the first woman. In **"To Damon,"** "Mrs. *A. B.*" rejects the position of being a sexual object lulled by "all those usual flatteries" praising her "face and Eyes." Instead, the position of rival allows her to look actively at the other woman; as in other poems, like **"To *Lysander* at the *Musick-Meeting*,"** the female speaker can gaze admiringly at a man, feeding her "greedy Eyes" with his "Heav'nly Form." In **"To My Lady *Morland*"** the speaker moves from a male erotic pose to a male heroic one, echoing Caesar's famous boast only to reverse its narcissism and grandiosity; she becomes the conquered, not the conqueror. "I came and saw, and blest my Destiny; / I found it Just you should out-Rival me." As she continues to praise the rival, however, she begins to undermine the rival's liaison with the lover to which at first she seemed to acquiesce. Claiming only the best of motives, she suggests that the rival deserves to have a better suitor than her own former lover; she deserves, in fact, a "Virgin-Heart," not that used-up old rake, who would be better off returning to the speaker, his discarded mistress. Shakespeare's sonnets accustom us to poems in which an aging lover harangues and excuses a dishonest beloved about a lovely rival, though he genders his more complicated triangles differently. Another Behn poem switches positions in the sexual triangle in comparison with **"To My Lady *Morland*."** In **"Selinda and Cloris,"** Selinda asks Cloris whether her "Friendship" or her "Jealousie" led her to confide that Selinda's lover first belonged to Cloris. Thus, Behn's poems link their female speakers with other women by means of a chain of lovers that expands into a network of complex emotional relationships.

By adopting a heroic stance, that of the brave soul who comes to see what to conquer, Behn's speakers set their loyal feudal values against greedy, selfish, and implicitly capitalistic ones. Like Donne, Behn chastises the turning of personal relationships into commodities at the same time that she uses the language of the market to denounce unfair competition: "I hate Love-Merchants that a Trade wou'd drive," the female speaker responds in **"To *Lysander*, on some Verses he writ, and asking more for his Heart than 'twas worth."** She lectures him about the true value that love should have:

> A Heart requires a Heart Unfeign'd and True,
> Though Subt'ly you advance the Price,
> And ask a Rate that Simple Love n'ere knew:
> And the free Trade Monopolize.

In this poem the speaker is explicitly a jealous woman, furious that her equally jealous male lover imposes faithful isolation on her while having affairs with other women:

> And every Hour still more unjust you grow,

> Those Freedoms you my life deny,
> You to *Adraste* are oblig'd to show,
> And give her all my Rifled Joy.

Miserable and alone, the speaker says that she feels the "Fragments" of the lover's "Softness," while the other woman, the better capitalist, "takes the welcome rich Return" on what was originally the first woman's investment. The rules are unfair, and Behn does not know how to make them fair on a woman's terms. Unable to find a vocabulary of equality that does not assume a male norm, the poem attacks the double standard:

> Be just, my lovely *Swain,* and do not take
> Freedoms you'll not to me allow;
> Or give *Amynta* so much Freedom back:
> That she may Rove as well as you.

The liberal language of freedom, justice, and equality appears to establish a fair standard, a standard to be aspired to, and Behn was clearly fascinated by the Restoration "Rover" or heroic philanderer, like the hero of her best-known play. One could not simply reverse the double standard by giving women permission to be as bad as men, however. What Behn wants instead is a community on her terms, an equality of mutual devotion that she imagines as free of capitalistic "interest": "Let us then love upon the honest Square, / Since Interest neither have designd." But the poem ends anticlimactically because the speaker can blast the hypocrisy of the double standard only by falling herself into the male role of mercenary scoundrel. "For the sly Gamester, who ne'er plays me fair / Must Trick for Trick expect to find." And, as mercenary interests are anathema to true love in Behn's scheme, so is jockeying for power: "A Pox of Foolish Politicks in Love," as **An *Ode* to Love** expostulates.

Behn's love poetry expresses a longing for community that is more overt in what we might call her fraternal poetry, and she seeks ideal reciprocity not only through sex but through the writing of poetry. She does not elaborate on the stresses the solitary poet faces while toiling to find rhymes at her lonely writing table. Instead, she describes the poetic craft as a collective one. By making explicit the favors poets do one another to give all of them more work and more pleasure, Behn produces a community of egalitarian insiders, a mutual admiration society. By publishing these poems about poetry writing, she then invites us outsiders to be provisional members of this inner community or to enviously define ourselves by our exclusion.

"A Letter to a Brother of the Pen in *Tribulation*" addresses the "Brother" from the viewpoint of one of the boys. The speaker asserts that friendship and the confraternity of writing are more important than sexual difference, although she agrees that sex can get one into trouble and, under the circumstances, the brother who caught venereal disease has a right to be angry at women: "'tis but Just thou shouldst in Rancor grow / Against that Sex that has Confin'd thee so," she comforts him, although she is a member of "that sex" herself. If liberty is a value, then, being confined is intolerable, especially being confined not to the love of one woman but to the love of none and the nasty *"Sweating-Tub"* used to cure such diseases. Although Behn commiserates with her friend, she is also razzing him about his unlucky disease, clearly the fault of his own habits as well as the woman's, and she is willing to tease him with a sibling-like rivalry that accepts the poem's readers as its confidantes. Her cozy footnotes explain the inside references to us readers: "I wanted a Prologue to a Play," she says of the occasion for the poem, and she teases the brother by revealing the secret she has just found out; "He pretended to Retire to Write" when he was really recuperating from "An Interlude of Whoring."

Another fraternal poem is more casual, less competitive. **"To *Damon*. To inquire of him if he cou'd tell me by the Style, who writ me a Copy of Verses that came to me in an unknown Hand"** links the female speaker with a male friend in a union that is more intimate than the one she may establish with her unknown suitor, the writer of an anonymous poem in her honor. The title assumes that the speaker's friend Damon knows all the likely male poets well enough to tell by the style, not just the handwriting, whose verses pique her interest, and she therefore seems to share with Damon an easy camaraderie that is itself free of sexual tensions and full of mutual confidences. The unknown lover, in turn, deserves her interest and respect because he chose to woo her entirely and unphysically through disembodied words. She says that before the poem arrived to disturb her, she was "Free as the Air, and calm as that," a perfectly inhuman kind of freedom she does not really relish, although she enjoyed a sabbatical from thinking about "the faithless sex," as she calls men, reversing their criticisms of women. That stoic composure was only a pose, she admits:

> calm and innocent I sate,
> Content with my indifferent fate
> (A Medium, I confess, I hate.)

The anonymous poem attracts her, she says, not because it was "fill'd with praises of my face and Eyes, / My verse, and all those usual flatteries" but through the quality of its verse, which she thinks reveals the "Soul" of the man. Her artistry necessarily matches his: "I drew him all the heart cou'd move." Then she falls in love with the "dear Idea" she has formed, a love that allies her with the greatest, if most foolish, of male artists, *"Pigmalion,"* who "for the charms he made, he sigh'd and burn'd." So Behn eroticizes not merely the object of poetry but also its author and poetry-making in itself. She shares a community with the recipient of her poem while asking him about the man who sent her one. Poems circulate, and Behn is both poet and subject of poetry, sender and receiver in a community of interpretation that is the basis of both love and friendship and in which Behn imagines herself in both traditionally masculine and traditionally feminine roles. Other Behn poems, too, celebrate this poetic circulation, as in **"The Sence of a Letter sent me, made into Verse; To a New Tune"** and **"On a Copy of Verses made in a Dream, and sent to me in a Morning before I was Awake."**

In comparison to these playful and erotic poems of camaraderie, **"To Mr. *Creech* (under the Name of *Daphnis*) on his Excellent Translation of *Lucretius*"** lifts the conventional pastoral disguise to praise her friend in his own name—and to comment directly on the impediments to women's equality that the other poems address imaginatively through their pastoral names and settings. Behn is unequivocal that women's faults are social rather than natural in origin, not universal but historically specific:

> Till now, I curst my Birth, my Education,
> And more the scanted Customes of the Nation:
> Permitting not the Female Sex to tread,
> The mighty Paths of Learned Heroes dead.

Taking seriously ideas about the enobling nature of literature, she once again connects the roles of poet and hero. To debar women from the one is to debase their chances of ever attaining the other. Like other feminists from the Renaissance through Virginia Woolf, she decries the meagerness of women's education, their relegation to inferior and disposable vernacular texts, and their exclusion from that classical culture that was coming to mark the English gentleman rather than the professional scholar: "The Fulsome Gingle of the times, / Is all we are allow'd to understand or hear." Then her friend Creech's translation of Lucretius

> dost advance
> Our Knowledg from the State of Ignorance,
> And equals us to Man! Ah how can we,
> Enough Adore, or Sacrifice enough to thee.

Cocky and self-confident with politicians or fellow playwrights, Behn shares some of the self-abasing admiration with which other seventeenth-century women writers treat male classicists, convinced by the culture around them that the lack of a classical education meant the lack not just of a body of knowledge but also of any possibility for full personal, intellectual, and moral development. Equality is obviously an unstable concept for Behn if women must "Adore" as a god the person who "equals us to Man" by sharing his learning.

This double assertion of equality and inferiority runs through Behn's poems to members of the nobility or clergy, like the earl of Rochester and Bishop Burnet. In thanking the poet Anne Wharton in **"To Mrs. W. On her Excellent Verses (Writ in Praise of some I had made on the Earl of *Rochester*) Written in a Fit of Sickness"** Behn again praises "The Great, the God-like *Rochester*" who spoke to her "worthless" self:

> With the same wonted Grace my Muse it prais'd,
> With the same Goodness did my Faults Correct;
> And careful of the Fame himself first rais'd,
> Obligingly it School'd my loose Neglect.

The ideological barriers to her self-esteem clearly were formidable. She responded in part by adopting both sides of many contradictions, especially those that separated feminine attitudes from "my Masculine Part the Poet in me" (preface to *The Lucky Chance*), but she had other defenses as well. One was to define herself as a woman who could simultaneously inhabit the usually masculine roles of both poet and hero, even if in subsidiary ways, a technique that resulted in Behn's seeing herself as perhaps lesser than, but not different from, the men. Thus, she commends "the Honourable Sir *Francis Fane,* on his Play call'd the *Sacrifice*" by saying that she read his poetry "with pleasure tho I read with shame" its superiority to her own. As with rival female beauties, she sustains community by praising the other and admitting her own inferiority of quantity but not of kind. When she reads his work, "the tender Laurels which my brows had drest / Flag, like young Flowers, with too much heat opprest." Bested, she is still crowned and garlanded, still one of the noble poet's guild.

In another poem celebrating a male translator of classical poetry, "**A** *Pastoral* **to Mr.** *Stafford,*" she is especially grateful for the translator's reclamation of female role models, and the classical precedent of female heroism allows her to display her own credentials as a female hero, a loyal royalist who has done her king dangerous public political service: "Once," she says

> by th' . . . Kings Commands,
> I left these Shades, to visit forein Lands;
> Imploy'd in public toils of State Affairs,
> Unusual with my Sex, or to my Years.

Her own unusual heroic experiences enable her to appreciate Stafford's translation of Virgil's Camilla, who "shews us how / To be at once *Hero* and *Woman* too." Camilla's heroism validates Behn's and makes it, though in an unbelieving and critical age, more plausible. For other models of how one can be a woman who is also a hero, Behn looks to classical history and myth, as the men did, and confirms her views by exchanging them with her brothers of the pen. Thus, she writes "**To** *Amintas.* **Upon reading the Lives of some of the** *Romans*" to laud

> That age when valor they did Beauty name,
> When Men did justly our brave sex prefer,
> Cause they durst dye, and scorn the publick shame
> Of adding Glory to the conqueror.

If the erotic triangle of the fraternal band of poets provided Behn with her best model of community and her substitute for the marital family she did not have and apparently did not want, her Tory party allegiances provided her with a voluntary substitute for a family lineage and a family name, a family of descent that bestowed at once rank and history on its members. Behn's political poetry seems silly to us in part because it was silly; praising the unpopular James II as beloved by his people or the publicly philandering Charles II as a devoted husband who died like Jesus Christ, "A Bleeding Victim to *attone* for all," seemed fatuous then, as it does now. "**A Congratulatory Poem to her most Sacred Majesty on the Universal Hopes of all Loyal Persons for a Prince of Wales**" celebrated hopes for the Roman Catholic James II's future progeny that were hardly universal in Protestant England. Modern distaste for this political poetry may also result

from the fact that the modern alignment of the political with the public was just beginning in the Restoration, yet bedroom politics still ruled the nation. Much of Behn's political verse celebrates personal female matters like pregnancy and childbirth that determined dynasties. Behn addresses royal women as wives and mothers and royal men as husbands and fathers; even her rather more successful political satire attacks political opponents through their sexual pecadilloes, as in the pleasant song "**When *Jemmy* first began to Love**" that alluded to Charles II's illegitimate son, the duke of Monmouth.

In her last sick and painful hours, political loyalty seems to have sustained Behn's sense of herself as a poet identified with a bygone age and a cause nobly lost. Behn sets this personal loyalty to the Stuart family against political expediency in her "**Pindaric Poem to the Reverend Doctor Burnet,**" written when she was dying. Although Burnet urged her to celebrate William and Mary's assumption of the crown in the Glorious Revolution of 1689, she pleaded that "Loyalty Commands with pious force" and "stops" her pen. Even with history and possibly the good of the nation arrayed against her and the Stuarts, she founds her integrity on her loyalty to them:

> Tho' I the Wond'rous Change deplore,
> That makes me Useless and Forlorn,
> Yet I the great Design Adore.

Behn died as she had lived—a new woman longing for an imaginary past golden age and creating myths of a world where to be a public woman was not to be a whore but to be a hero and a poet, someone surrounded not by creditors or catcalls on a London street but by the utopian society organized through the communal dedications in a volume of her own lyric poems.

Robert Markley and Molly Rothenberg (essay date 1993)

SOURCE: "Contestations of Nature: Aphra Behn's 'The Golden Age' and the Sexualizing of Politics," in *Rereading Aphra Behn: History, Theory, and Criticism,* edited by Heidi Hutner, University Press of Virginia, 1993, pp. 301–21.

[*In the following excerpt, the critics assess the coherence and principles of the ostensibly feminist ideology presented in Behn's poem "The Golden Age."*]

Recent feminist critiques of early modern science by Carolyn Merchant [*The Death of Nature: Women, Ecology, and the Scientific Revolution,* 1980], Brian Easlea [*Witch-Hunting, Magic, and the New Philosophy,* 1980], and Evelyn Fox Keller [*Reflections on Gender and Science,* 1985], have argued for the foundational status of the popular analogy (used by Francis Bacon, Robert Boyle, and others) that identifies "man's" exploitation of a feminized nature with the patriarchal repression of women. Although in the context of seventeenth-century natural philosophy,

Aphra Behn's 1684 poem **"The Golden Age"** similarly offers a counter to masculinist constructions of nature and of women as passive sites for the inscription of male power, her idealization of a bountiful nature that exists prior to humankind's interventions ultimately reinscribes patriarchal structures even as it seeks to validate a **"Golden Age"** of unrepressed sexuality in which distinctions of gender, class, religion, and politics are subsumed within a vision of undifferentiated pleasure, plenitude, and fulfilled desire. As her introductory essay to her translation of Fontenelle's *A Discovery of New Worlds* demonstrates, Behn was well aware of the gendering of seventeenth-century scientific discourse and its implications for the disempowerment of women and the devaluation of nature. The idea of an autonomous, self-sufficient realm of nature is crucial to feminist critiques of early modern science—in Behn's poem and in the work of twentieth-century critics and historians; if nature is independently "plentious," so the argument goes, then our self-imposed alienation from nature can and should be remedied by throwing off what Behn calls "those Politick Curbs" of both external and internalized repression. Precisely because Behn's idealization of nature reproduces, as an oppositional strategy, the binary logic of Baconian exploitation, **"The Golden Age"** reinscribes hierarchical valuations of class status and property rights—and devalues labor—even as it ostensibly exposes them as ideological constructs. If nature is instead the site of complex cultural contestations, if nature is constantly in the process of being (re)produced by human interventions, then Behn's move to return to an unrepressed sexuality and a pristine natural world does not liberate either nature or sexuality from ideology but marks their further implication in the dialogically agitated discourses of seventeenth-century literature, natural philosophy, and politics. In this regard, Behn's poem provides an opportunity to explore the complexities of seventeenth-century constructions of nature that are marginalized in both traditional and revisionist accounts of the gendering of early modern science.

"The Golden Age" ostensibly seeks to overcome the alienation of humankind from nature. In its evocation of a prefallen state, the poem describes "an Eternal Spring" where lovers "uncontroul'd did meet" with "unbounded Joyes" of sexual pleasure; a "bounteous Nature" provides a "kind increase" of "every necessary good," liberating "th'agreeing Swaines" from the need to work, to compete for food, or, significantly, to enter into a social order founded on "Right and Property." What differentiates Behn's Golden Age from the biblical Garden of Eden is precisely the absence of sin and of external forms of authority—"Monarchs" ("those Arbitrary Rulers over men"), "the Gods," and "Religion." Behn describes a post-Golden Age world in the same terms as the Christian perception of a postlapsarian world: alienation from nature, which produces the need to labor, and alienation from others, which produces the need for external forms of authority to police individual desires. Because she rejects the notion of sin, however, her analysis of the causes of the fallen states of both humanity and nature differs fundamentally from Christian narratives. In **"The Golden Age,"** alienation, labor, and repression are not the conse-

quences of an originary sin but are continually being reproduced by the repression of desire, by "Pride and Avarice," by the dissemination of "Honour" as a means to encourage individuals to police themselves in the names of religion and morality. The poem suggests that the conditions of the post-Golden Age world—individuals constrained by oppression and obedience to authority—*already* exist within the Garden of Eden in the form of divine prohibitions. In this respect, Behn's idealizing of unrepressed sexuality and pristine nature becomes a means to demystify forms of external and internalized repression that have been naturalized within religion and morality. As a counterstrategy, her poem must therefore hold open the possibility that somehow a way back to a state prior to repression can be found, that humankind is not irrevocably alienated from its desires by an originary sin. She must posit in her analysis an origin for repression that lies within the man-made realms of ideology and institutional authority.

However, Behn's idealization of sexuality and nature reveals a number of contradictions that arise from her linking of political and sexual repression. In a crucial sense, **"The Golden Age"** raises the question of whether humankind must unrepress sexuality to return to a pristine political state free from war, "Right and Property," honor, and so on, or whether a political revolution is necessary to restore humankind to a natural, unrepressed sexuality. In effect, Behn must insist on the causal link between politics and sexuality to ground her demystification of "Pride, Avarice" and "honour," but she must also separate sex and politics to avoid what, for her, would be dire social consequences: the fall from the benevolent—and ostensibly apolitical—Tory paternalism (envisioned in her comedies of the 1680s and other works) to the anarchy of a debased Hobbesian political realm, represented by her satire of the sociopolitical corruption of Whigs and Puritans in *The Roundheads, The City Heiress,* and *The Widow Ranter.* As a professional woman writer, a proponent of women's sexual freedom, and a Tory apologist, Behn must draw on a variety of incommensurate discursive strategies and political values to ground her critique of repression in representations of a sexualized self that exists in an idealized form outside of the networks of ideological constraint. Therefore, her poem does not and cannot exhibit either a formal aesthetic unity or a coherent political ideology; in fact, its theoretical and historical significance lies in its disclosure of the necessarily fragmentary ideological conditions of its production, its registering of the discursive crises within late-seventeenth-century constructions of nature, politics, and sexuality.

The opening two stanzas of **"The Golden Age"** suggest the complications that arise from the arguments and strategies Behn uses to assert the foundational status of the connections among unrepressed desire, an idealized nature, and a nonhierarchical social order. What seems to begin as a description of the Golden Age becomes a polemic against repression. Yet because Behn conflates imagistically and conceptually the eternal state of nature and the historicopolitical realm, which is irrevocably marked by hierarchies of class and gender, she can define neither a method nor an agency for re-creating the "Blest Age":

> . . . when ev'ry Purling Stream
>   Ran undisturb'd and clear,
> When no scorn'd Shepherds on your Banks were
>   seen,
> Tortur'd by Love, by Jealousie, or Fear;
> When an Eternal Spring drest Ev'ry Bough,
> And Blossoms fell, by new ones dispossest;
> These their kind Shade affording all below,
> And those a Bed where all below might rest.
> The Groves appear'd all drest with Wreaths of
>   Flowers,
> And from their Leaves dropt Aromatick Showers,
> Whose fragrant Heads in Mystick Twines above,
> Exchang'd their Sweets, and mix'd with thousand
>   Kisses,
>   As if the willing Branches strove
>   To beautifie and shade the Grove
>   Where the young wanton Gods of Love
> Offer their Noblest Sacrifice of Blisses.

As the stanza progresses, nature increasingly takes on a personified sexuality that in lines three and four had been attributed, but only by negation, to "scorn'd Shepherds . . . Tortur'd by Love, by Jealousie, or Fear"; in fact, no shepherds, whether scorned or not, actually appear until stanza six. As nature assumes the erotic energy that Behn uses to distinguish the prelapsarian from the postlapsarian world, it becomes the necessary precondition for an undifferentiated social order from which all potential for conflict has been eliminated: "All below" share equally in the boughs' shade and the bed of blossoms. The lower classes, figured as the shepherds, are written out of the poem from the outset, so that the labor required to enable the existence of a leisured class is repressed in favor of an aestheticized labor ("To beautifie . . . the Grove") in which human agency has been displaced by nature's own activity ("the willing Branches strove"). The only inhabitants of the Golden Age are idealized aristocrats, apparently unsupported by any form of labor; these "Gods of Love" ostensibly neither have nor require any economic or political function.

The nature that Behn portrays in **"The Golden Age,"** then, is not a pristine wilderness but an idealized vision of a bucolic English countryside that already has been acted upon (implicitly) by labor. Although blossoms fall in this "Eternal Spring," they are "by new ones dispossest"; this image of dispossession—of a violent renewal dependent on usurpation—marks the irruption of an economic and political lexicon ("affording," "Exchang'd," "Sacrifice") into an otherwise idyllic and ahistorical description of nature. In the next stanza, all human agency seems to disappear; even the deflected discourses of labor and politics are effaced until the closing lines of the stanza:

> While to their soft and tender Play,
>   The Gray-Plum'd natives of the Shades
> Unwearied sing till Love invades,
>   Then Bill, then sing agen, while Love and Musick
> makes the Day.

The birds' "Play" evades the negative consequences of labor (as their "Unwearied" singing suggests) until "Love invades," marking the return of the violence implied, as we discuss below, in the "Play" of unconstrained desire, in the maintenance of a hierarchical class structure and in the constant reconstruction and renaturalizing of nature.

Having described the idyllic natural conditions of the Golden Age in the first two stanzas, Behn attempts in stanza three to rewrite Genesis to promote her vision of an idealized nature prior to labor and repression:

> The stubborn Plough had then,
> Made no rude Rapes upon the Virgin Earth;
> Who yielded of her own accord her plentious Birth,
>   Without the Aids of men;
> As if within her Teeming Womb
> All Nature, and all Sexes lay,
> Whence new Creations every day
> Into the happy World did come.

The issue of labor seems to be raised precisely so that it can be dismissed; labor functions as the excluded opposite—the devalued other—of an idealized earth that is at once virginal and polymorphously sexual and fecund. Behn appropriates the simple gendered oppositions of Baconian science that privilege man's labor over nature's plenitude, but she inverts this gender hierarchy in order to redescribe technological productivity as rape and to celebrate nature's self-sustaining generative powers. Although Behn retains the Baconian trope of a masculinized enterprise and a feminized and bounteous earth, she does not follow through on the binary logic implied by this inversion: in Behn's creation myth, earth's undifferentiated sexuality subsumes the sexual, specifically reproductive, functions of both men and women without privileging either: "within her Teeming Womb . . . all Sexes lay." This vision of an undifferentiated sexuality allows Behn to attack the sexually invasive and rapacious nature of Baconian industry and to resist traditional Judeo-Christian devaluations of female sexuality authorized, in the seventeenth century, by invocations of the myth of the Garden of Eden. As part of her critique of the ideology represented by the "stubborn Plough," she explicitly revises the biblical story of Genesis in the second half of this stanza by displacing the opposition between masculine and feminine sexuality in favor of an opposition between two masculine sexualities—one aggressively phallic, the other noninvasive:

> . . . the Snakes securely dwelt,
> Not doing harm, nor harm from others felt;
> With whom the Nymphs did Innocently play,
> No spightful Venom in the wantons lay;
> But to the touch were Soft, and to the sight were Gay.

Behn insists that we recognize the traditional moral implications of these lines and then (re)read them as a demystification of the repressive, masculinist sexuality that the biblical prohibitions enforce. But her redefinition of a noninvasive male sexuality requires a logical and temporal sleight of hand: the innocence of the nymphs and snakes defines itself in opposition to a phallic sexuality that is ostensibly a consequence of the fall from the Golden Age but that in these lines *already* is inscribed in the series of negations ("Not doing harm, nor harm from others felt") used to mark their "play." Symbolically, no erection ("soft") or ejaculation ("No spightful Venom") takes place and therefore neither can sexualized procreation; the nymphs' sexuality, described by touch and sight, removes them from an economy in which "labors" mark the consequences of unconstrained desire. Women are written out of this myth of undifferentiated procreation in the Golden Age because to foreground female sexuality in the late seventeenth century—to construct a positive image of an unrepressed female desire—is to be forced to confront the consequences of their sexual activity: pregnancy, the bearing of fatherless children, and resulting challenges to the hereditary distribution of wealth, power, and prestige. Behn's fiction of a Golden Age of undifferentiated sexuality, then, derives from and reinforces an idealized image of an aristocratic and patrilineal society that must seek both to control feminine desire through marriage and the laws of primogeniture and to naturalize the coercive means by which the exploitation of labor and natural resources maintains the hierarchies of class and gender.

In the poem's opening stanzas, Behn defines politics in terms of sexuality in order to suppress as well as to defer considering the consequences of unconstrained desire. What follows, then, is a sequence of attempts to locate an origin for repression by displacing these consequences into a past—her version of the Fall—as both the causes and the effects of everything that she tries to negate in the course of the poem: labor, the mystifications of "Honour," religion, war, politics, shame, avarice, ambition, and fame. Although she describes a temporal rupture between the Golden Age and the age of repression, she can neither locate historically nor define theoretically a structure of causation. In one respect, she suggests that a hierarchical social structure comes into being as a result of repression, but in another she implies that the inequities of power serve as the origin of repression:

> Monarchs were uncreated then,
> Those Arbitrary Rulers over men:
> Kings that made Laws, first broke 'em, and the
> Gods
> By teaching us Religion first, first set the World at
> Odds:
> Till then Ambition was not known,
> That Poyson to Content, Bane to Repose;
> Each Swain was Lord o'er his own will alone,
> His Innocence Religion was, and Laws.
> Nor needed any troublesome defense
> Against his Neighbors Insolence.

Monarchs are "uncreated" and "Arbitrary"; they seem to emerge from nowhere, without explanation. There is no history, no mythology, no logic to explain or to justify the "Arbitrary" exercise of power. Ambition, similarly, seems to be a progeny without a parent. Although Behn employs a rhetoric of origins and consequences—"first . . . first,

first"—she describes no mechanism to account for the corruption of humankind and nature, that is, for the link between sexual and social repression.

Yet Behn's vision of unalienated sexuality depends on the prerequisites of social hierarchy: "Each Swain" must be "Lord" over his own "will," his own desire. The logic of this metaphor links the unconstrained exercise of pleasure to an idealized—and self-legitimating—aristocratic power, while in the next stanza Behn's attacks on "Right and Property," "Power," "Pride and Avarice" precisely recapitulate the self-aggrandizing and aristocratic values implicit in her evocation of the swain as "Lord." Her attack is based on the assumption that "Rapes, Invasions, Tyrannies" are products of the imposition of power on individuals who (then) learn to reproduce the repressions of "Tyrant Honour," internalizing them as a "Fond Idol." Her insistence on yoking power and pleasure in the figure of the swain presupposes a Hobbesian conception of atomistic individuals who are motivated by their inherent selfishness, which in Hobbes's view, leads inevitably to competition, to the conditions for "Rapes, Invasions, Tyrannies." In (re)creating the Golden Age, Behn denies both the assumptions and the consequences of the war of all against all by idealizing "bounteous Nature": in contrast to the Hobbesian state of nature, characterized by scarcity and therefore competition, Behn's prelapsarian world provides "every necessary good" as "a common Sacrifice to all th'agreeing Swaines." Behn mystifies the inequities of a hierarchical social structure predicated on coercion by idealizing the "common Sacrifice" of nature's "kind increase" in order to displace the political conflicts and sacrifices that occur when individuals act on the license of their own wills. The "common Sacrifice" of nature also mystifies its appropriation—those "rude Rapes" that are necessary to an economy of "increase." The fiction of an infinitely bounteous nature, in turn, allows Behn to write out of her history the appropriation of the labor of commoners on which the economy of a hierarchical social structure depends. She uses the construct "all th'agreeing Swaines," then, to deny the Hobbesian premises that in a state of nature competition arises as a consequence of unchecked individual desires and that community can result only from coercion or from voluntary self-restraint. However, Behn's attack on the "needless use of Arms" and her insistent denial of the need for "any troublesome defense / Against [a] Neighbors Insolence" betrays her anxiety that the only basis for a hierarchical social structure lies in the use of force.

As Behn's revision of Hobbes suggests, unrepressed sexuality and an idealized nature are constituted in the poem by the very elements that Behn ostensibly rejects—property, pride, avarice, and "Trade." Consequently, the search for the origin of repression can lead only to the reinscription of the conditions of that repression and, significantly, to the reiteration of a language that presupposes humankind's alienation from nature and from the desires that the poet continually insists are natural. In the middle of stanza five, Behn's attack shifts from external forms of repression to "Honour" as both a mystification imposed on "the slavish Crowd"—"Nonsense, invented by the Proud"—and an internalized "Poyson" that teaches individuals to police their own desires. Again, however, the origin of honor is given incommensurate explanations: It was "not known in those blest days" of the Golden Age, and yet, when "the Amorous world injoy'd its Reign," "Tyrant Honour"—already present—"strove t'usurp in Vain," although it apparently was held in check by the exercise of individual desire. "Honour" deserves its derogatory personification, according to Behn, because it creates "those Politick Curbs to keep man in." Encompassing both external and internal forms of repression, honor apparently functions in opposition to desire. But the two are related dialectically: to justify its repressions, honor must presuppose the existence of a disruptive libidinal excess, and desire must be expressed in a language that defines itself by means of its resistance to an already existing state of repression.

In this regard, desire can be described only in terms that are parasitic on—and that seek to negate—the discourse of internalized repression: "The Nymphs were free, no nice, no coy disdain; / Deny'd their Joyes, or gave the Lover pain." Throughout stanza six, Behn relies on a vocabulary of invasion and conquest, even though she claims to be depicting mutual passion and unrepressed desire:

> The yielding Maid but kind Resistance makes;
> Trembling and blushing are not marks of shame,
>   But the Effect of kindling Flame:
> Which from the sighing burning Swain she takes,
> While she with tears all soft, and down-cast-eyes,
> Permits the Charming Conqueror to win the prize.

Nothing in these lines differentiates reciprocal love from rape except the poet's insistence that the maid's resistance is "kind" and her tears are "soft." Behn's language of negation works to mystify the power she herself assumes in order to render "kind Resistance" as a display of mutual passion rather than of masculinist violence. She uses two strategies to disguise the foundational status of violence, power, and repression in the construction of sexual and political relations. First, she creates the illusion of an "objective" stance from which she apparently derives her authority to interpret the semiotics of passion, to distinguish—albeit illegitimately—between "Trembling and blushing" produced by desire and these same physiological signs produced by fear. Her ostensible detachment covers for her imposition of an authoritative interpretation of the nymph's behavior. Then she mystifies this intrusive authority as the "soft power" of the voyeuristic cupids who watch and intervene only to encourage "a Shepherd uninspir'd" to amorous action; nonetheless, the cupid's power, as represented by his shooting an arrow at the swain, is both phallic and aggressive. In both cases, Behn relies on the very strategies of assertion that she previously had characterized as evidence of the illegitimate power she ascribes to the forces of repression. In the preceding stanza, she criticizes the arbitrary signification of "words since made" that allows "Rapes, Invasions, Tyrannies" to be "miscall'd" the "gaining of a Glorious Name"; in stanza six, however, she asserts her authority to interpret similarly "miscall'd" signs without acknowledging her appro-

priation of the linguistic and political power she has attacked.

Behn's efforts to distinguish between two kinds of language—a universal semiotic that, in the act of naming, discloses the essential natures of things and the socially constructed, politicized, and therefore mystified language of "Politick Curbs"—continue in the next stanza:

> The Lovers thus, thus uncontroul'd did meet,
> Thus all their Joyes and Vows of Love repeat:
>   Joyes which were everlasting, ever new
>   And every Vow inviolably true:
> Not fear of Gods, no fond Religious cause,
> Nor in obedience to the duller Laws.
> Those Fopperies of the Gown were then not known,
> Those vain, those Politick Curbs to keep man in,
> Who by a fond mistake Created that a Sin;
> Which freeborn we, by right of Nature claim our own.
>   Who but the Learned and dull moral Fool
> Could gravely have forseen, man ought to live by Rule?

To maintain the fiction that a distinction exists between ideal and corrupt semiotics, Behn must posit the origin of repression as a "fond mistake" that gives rise to a system of morality, "obedience to the duller Laws." But the distinction itself depends on the temporal priority of this universal semiotic, a priority undermined by the contemporaneous existence of the "Learned and dull moral Fool," who "forsee[s]" the advent of the same moral codes that he himself already embodies. The truth of "every Vow"—the idealization of pristine language—depends on a strategy of negation ("Not kept in fear of Gods, no fond Religious cause") that allows Behn to idealize desire ("Joyes which were everlasting") as the basis of a community ("freeborn we") that can evade time and repression. In effect, love is described ideally and transhistorically in stanza seven precisely to mystify the Hobbesian self-interest and implicit violence of the "originary" seduction in stanza six.

The entire seventh stanza, then, ostensibly accounts for the origin of repression in terms of a historical movement from unrepressed desire to the repressions of religion and law, but this false history emerges as a displacement of the history of sexual and social violence always already present, a history Behn must deny in order to conduct her demystification of "Politick Curbs." The fallacy in her reasoning shows up in her logical and temporal markers: "The Lovers thus" seems to refer to a historical point after their initial meeting, so that "thus uncontroul'd" suggests that their sexual freedom is a result of their original encounter rather than its cause. If this is the case, then their love must exist in opposition to a state of repression that allows for the possibility of misinterpreting "kind Resistance" as a defense against rape. Or, if we accept Behn's assertion that the Golden Age did not have "Politick Curbs," then her repetition of "thus" lacks logical force. Any historical analysis of the power structure encoded in the lovers' relationship is deferred by the repetition of "thus" and the repetition of "Joyes and Vows of Love," both of which serve as a means to deny and to control the uncontrollable passion—the disruptive potential of passionate love and passionate violence—that the lovers represent. Behn's strategies of idealization and demystification are related dialectically: if the idealization of lovers and their joys and vows becomes a means to resist "duller Laws," it also describes processes of idealization that themselves repress the violence ("discord, noise, and wars") that maintains the social order. Behn's attempts to restrict the sociopolitical implications of her analysis by decoupling sexual from political repression continue to conflict with her efforts to locate a political origin for the policing of desire.

The tensions within Behn's analytic cannot be resolved because the myth of her egalitarian sexuality is founded on hierarchies of class, gender, and property. In stanza eight Behn tries to evade this contradiction by returning to an excoriation of "cursed Honour" that excludes its political dimension in order to focus on the internalizing of sexual repression. This redefinition of honor locates repression in the individual's sexual behavior rather than in cultural disseminations of power:

> Oh cursed Honour! thou who first didst damn,
>   A Woman to the Sin of shame;
>   Honour! that rob'st us of our Gust,
>   Honour! that hindred mankind first,
> At Loves Eternal Spring to Squench his amorous
>   thirst.
> Honour! who first taught lovely Eyes the art,
>   To wound, and not to cure the heart:
> With Love to invite, but to forbid with Awe,
> And to themselves prescribe a Cruel Law;
>   To Veil 'em from the Lookers on,
>   When they are sure the slave's undone,
> And all the Charmingst part of Beauty hid;
> Soft Looks, consenting Wishes, all deny'd.

As in stanza five, honor is portrayed unequivocally as the source of all constraint, the unquestioned origin of repression, sin, and violence, but in these lines Behn represses the link between the sexual and the political upon which she had insisted earlier. The "Cruel Law" is shorn of its political implications; it is no longer a literal, external form of prohibition regulating relations among people but instead operates solely within an internal realm ("and to themselves prescribe") to create self-centered, atomistic beings. In effect, Behn argues that honor objectifies the coquette, transforming her from a desiring individual into a cipher embodying a corrupt language that cannot deliver what it promises. The coquette who learns "the art to wound" becomes a product of honor's ministry of perpetually deferred desire; with her "soft Looks, consenting Wishes, all deny'd," she is "drest to Tempt, not gratify the World." But like the "yielding Maid" of stanza six and the "bounteous Nature" of stanza four, she does not exist independently of the repressive forces that constitute her as an object of desire; even in the Golden Age, she would have no purpose other than to "gratify the World."

What are presented as the aftereffects of sexual repression—"the Sin of shame," wounding, cruelty, and slavery—

in fact constitute "the Amorous world" as part of an already fallen and politicized realm. The portrait of the woman prior to her instruction in honor discloses what Behn seeks to hide—the implication of the world of politics and commerce in the construction of sexuality:

> [Honour] gathers up the flowing Hair,
>   That loosely plaid with wanton Air.
> The Envious Net, and stinted order hold,
> The lovely Curls of Jet and shining Gold;
> No more neglected on the Shoulders hurl'd:
> Now drest to Tempt, not gratify the World:
> Thou, Miser Honour, hord'st the sacred store,
> And starv'st thy self to keep thy Votaries poor.

The reification of the woman appears to be attributed to the workings of honor, that "Envious Net," but actually preexists them. Both her pre- and postlapsarian bodies are commodified: "The lovely Curls of Jet and shining Gold" define her in economic terms prior to the commercial interests of "Miser Honour" (stinting, hoarding, and storing) that postdate the Golden Age. By focusing on the woman as coquette, Behn displaces our recognition that, whether tempting or gratifying, the woman has value only within an exchange economy—the patrilineal system that objectifies her as a commodity on the marriage market. The coquette is constructed as a member of the landed classes, as her dress signifies; consequently, the temptation she offers—and the reward she withholds (until marriage, at least)—is not only sexual but also economic. Her culturally constructed motivation for frustrating the desires of men, for hoarding "the Charmingst part of Beauty," is to maintain her marketability. It is not honor that enslaves, impoverishes, and starves its victims but rather the very systems of exchange—commercial, political, and sexual—that ensure the transference of property from one generation of men to another by means of her body.

Although in the opening eleven lines of stanza nine Behn continues to revile honor (as the "base Debaucher of the generous heart" and a "Foe to Pleasure") and to define love implicitly in economic terms (as "a sacred Gift . . . made to be possest" that honor has "made a Theft"), by the middle of the stanza she has repoliticized honor ("tyrant over mighty Kings"), banishing it to "Princes Pallaces," leaving "Shepheards Cottages" free from its influence. Her insistence that honor "be gone!" marks her efforts to maintain the fiction that the Golden Age is nonpolitical and noncommercial, an idyllic space in which social status is naturalized ("the first rate of man / That nearest were to Gods Alli'd") and not a product of either the influence-peddling at the court or the vicissitudes of the market. In contrast to Behn's previous assertions that repression has a historical origin, this stanza suggests that unrepressed desire and honor exist contemporaneously but are located within different economies of political, commercial, and sexual exchange:

> What mak'st thou here in Shepheards Cottages;
> Why troublest thou the quiet Shades and Springs?
>   Be gone, and make thy Fam'd resort
>   To Princes Pallaces;

Go Deal and Chaffer in the Trading Court,
That busie Market for Phantastick Things;
Be gone and interrupt the short Retreat,
  Of the Illustrious and the Great;
  Go break the Politicians sleep,
  Disturb the Gay Ambitious Fool,
    That longs for Scepters, Crowns, and Rule,
Which not his Title, nor his Wit can keep;
But let the humble honest *Swain* go on,
In the blest Paths of the first rate of man;
    That nearest were to Gods Alli'd,
And form'd for love alone, disdain'd all other
    Pride.

Behn draws upon a traditional distinction between the values of the country and those of the court to identify the latter with trade, ambition, and the delusory satisfactions of "Phantastick Things." The country, on the other hand, is the home of the "humble honest *Swain*," who is "form'd for love alone" and rejects "Scepters, Crowns, and Rule." Historically, and implicitly within the poem, both the country and the court are the products of a patrilineal economy that must seek to repress desire to ensure the orderly transfer of land and money; the two realms, in this respect, are not sites of antithetical systems of value but projections of the same ideological imperatives of socioeconomic privilege. In the figure of the "Swain," Behn conflates two socioeconomic registers that heretofore she had kept implicitly distinct: laboring rustics and gentlemen-lovers. The ambiguity of this figure allows her to mystify both the social hierarchy that creates shepherds, who are dispossessed from the power represented by the court, and the labor that is necessary to maintain the leisure of the country aristocracy so that its members can engage in "love alone" rather than in commerce or political intrigue. Despite Behn's attempt to describe the country as free from the interventions of trade and labor, it is as dependent upon the symbolic and practical "Market" as the court. In this poem, however, labor (in the senses of both the courtiers' business and the shepherds' work) can be only a "Phantastick Thing" because Behn's moves towards a liberatory rhetoric of desire always reinscribe the conditions of a social order that seeks to negate its dependence on and exploitation of the labor of the lower classes.

At the beginning of the final stanza Behn for the third time exclaims "Be gone!" The subject of her command is not simply "Honour" but the complexities and contradictions that continually reimplicate her vision of a nonhierarchical Golden Age in economies of privilege and repression. Behn's struggle throughout the poem has been to restrict the implications of her account of the origin of sexual repression and to naturalize desire as a communitarian ideal. At the end of her poem, she retreats to a version of the carpe diem motif as though it presented an escape from the problems of order and desire that she has dealt with in the previous nine stanzas. However, her use of this conventional motif forces her to introduce into the poem a seasonal conception of nature that is at odds with the "Eternal Spring":

The Spring decays, but when the Winter's gone,
  The Trees and Flowers a new come on;
The Sun may set, but when the night is fled,
  And gloomy darkness does retire,
  He rises from his Watry Bed:
All Glorious, Gay, all drest in Amorous Fire.

Significantly, spring "decays" into the cycle of the seasons; although a renewal occurs, Behn emphasizes the inevitability of mortality in the very imagery she uses to describe Sylvia, the woman she addresses.

But *Sylvia* when your Beauties fade,
When the fresh Roses on your Cheeks shall die,
  Like Flowers that wither in the Shade,
Eternally they will forgotten lye,
And no kind Spring their sweetness will supply.

Sylvia is alienated from two natures—the "Eternal Spring" of the Golden Age and the cyclical seasons of renewal. Her sexuality and life irrevocably decay; her experience of the cyclical nature represented by the seasons is bounded by her mortality. In these lines, the implicit violence that had been figured in stanza one as the dispossession that allowed the "Eternal Spring" to renew itself is rendered imagistically as death and decay.

Behn's quest for an origin to explain humankind's fall into repression is displaced onto a nature that is continually in the process of decay and creation. From the point of view of postlapsarian humans, however, cyclical nature is experienced only as an inexorable movement towards death.

When Snow shall on those lovely Tresses lye,
And your fair Eyes no more shall give us pain,
  But shoot their pointless Darts in vain.
What will your duller honour signifie?
Go boast it then! and see what numerous Store
Of lovers will your Ruin'd Shrine Adore.
  Then let us, *Sylvia,* yet be wise,
  And the Gay hasty minutes prize:
The Sun and Spring receive but our short Light,
Once sett, a sleep brings an Eternal Night.

Significantly, the speaker's injunction, "the Gay hasty minutes prize," promises neither the satisfactions of sexual pleasure nor the rewards of idyllic existence in an eternal Golden Age; rather than emphasizing the eternity of sensual delight promised in earlier stanzas, Behn leaves Sylvia with the specter of her own mortality, whether or not she gives up the repressions of honor. Sylvia's beauties are cast in images of violence and pain that herald "an Eternal Night." In one sense, the pessimism of this stanza is a product of Behn's rejection earlier in the poem of the religion that "first set the World at Odds," leaving her in the position of a de facto mortalist. Having defined the Golden Age as a negation of the various practices and strategies of external and internal repression, Behn leaves Sylvia no way to re-create the conditions of the Golden Age; she will either follow the dictates of "duller honour" or she will experience a few "Gay hasty minutes" of pleasure bounded temporally and physically by an "Eternal Night," by the decay of her body, which has been figured metaphorically in natural terms. The "Joyes which were everlasting, ever new" of stanza seven are predicated on a rejection of individual mortality and of a history that must always be figured as postlapsarian. The joys offered Sylvia, bounded by personal and cultural history, therefore reinscribe the conditions that exist throughout the poem—the "originary" alienation of a fallen sexuality.

Sylvia, then, is alienated from nature, alienated from her "numerous Store / Of Lovers," alienated from her own sexuality, and alienated from the very processes aging her body. Her alienation is not a function of honor's repressions but of Behn's reducing individuality to less than the sum of her physical parts. Whether Sylvia is repressed or unrepressed, she exists as nothing more than the fragments of cheeks, tresses, and eyes, like the objectified women of the Petrarchan sonnet tradition. Even when Sylvia is granted the possibility of an unrepressed existence, her subjectivity is restricted to that of the atomistic, Hobbesian self whose pleasures, like her life, must be short because she has no access to an idealized, infinitely "bounteous nature." Instead, she is figured as a product of a postlapsarian and niggardly nature that "Stint[s] . . . short-liv'd joy." In previous stanzas, Behn represses the sociopolitical consequences of individualistic competition by denying the Hobbesian premise of nature's scarcity. In these lines, however, Behn acknowledges the conditions of Hobbesian conflict but depoliticizes them by displacing them onto a stinting nature. She can avoid dealing with the implications of the war of all against all, then, only by radically isolating Sylvia and by drastically limiting her agency: Sylvia's only choices are to wither and die. Behn's exhortation to Sylvia to gather her rosebuds recalls the rape of the nymph in stanza six as well as the "Sacrifice" of bounteous nature in stanza four; far from empowering them, the limited agency Behn grants to Sylvia and to prelapsarian nature at best enables their "willing" complicity in their own exploitation.

The carpe diem motif with which Behn ends the poem suggests how thoroughly she has erased the possibility of recapturing a Golden Age; sociopolitical explanations of alienation are displaced onto a stinting nature, represented as the source of all dissatisfaction. Sylvia must be introduced in stanza ten precisely to define political problems solely in terms of individual choices and to foreclose the possibility of a political rather than biological analysis of an economy of scarcity that governs the distribution of everything from food to joy. In effect, Behn places Sylvia in a position analogous to that of many of the heroines in her comedies: the woman who is seeking sexual satisfaction and the socioeconomic legitimation of her desires. In plays such as *The Rover,* part II, Behn dramatizes the issue of women's desire as necessary to a "radical" questioning of gender roles because the liberatory potential of this desire does not extend to a questioning of "Right and Property" as the bases of a patrilineal society. But at the end of **"The Golden Age,"** Behn does not have the generic trappings of comedy to distract our attention from the

ways in which a seemingly "feminist" articulation of desire reinforces the processes by which the conservative political philosophy of right and property is—as it must be, in her mind—reinscribed. In this regard, Sylvia functions almost metonymically for the processes of political analysis that occur in the poem. Behn has no trouble in identifying the sources and causes of repression and human misery—religion, kings, unequal distributions of right and property, "Rapes, Invasions, and Tyrannies"—but her Toryism precludes her adding up these local analyses into a general critique of sociopolitical alienation. The move against which she guards ferociously is the move to a world in which property and power are leveled—the brief-lived experiments in 1649 and 1650 of the Diggers, which are appropriated and satirized in her plays as the grotesque self-aggrandizing of Puritans and Whigs.

Our reading of **"The Golden Age"** suggests that Behn's work in particular and the array of texts that, in the late seventeenth and early eighteenth centuries, have been identified as "feminist" cannot be read simply as ideological counters to a dominant masculinist ideology. Her poem is significant historically precisely because it discloses the contradictions within contemporary constructions of nature, politics, gender, and identity. In its efforts to celebrate prelapsarian nature as a mode of resistance to economies of repression, Behn's poem can generate only new strategies of implication, new modes of reinscribing an ideology that takes as fundamental humankind's alienation from nature, love, and labor. In this sense, her feminism, like that of her contemporaries, cannot be separated from the ideologies of privilege and power that map its limitations.

FURTHER READING

Bibliography

O'Donnell, Mary Ann. *Aphra Behn: An Annotated Bibliography of Primary and Secondary Sources.* New York: Garland Publishing, 1986, 557 p.

   Catalogue of Behn's works and critical commentaries on her writings; includes an introduction that summarizes her career.

Biography

Cameron, W. J. *New Light on Aphra Behn.* Auckland, New Zealand: University of Auckland, 1961, 106 p.

   Cameron summarizes the study as "an investigation into the facts and fictions surrounding [Behn's] journey to Surinam in 1663 and her activities as a spy in Flanders in 1666."

Duffy, Maureen. *The Passionate Shepherdess: Aphra Behn, 1640–89.* London: Jonathan Cape, 1977, 324 p.

   Account of Behn's life based on her works and the scant extant documents relating to or by her. Duffy examines

Behn's works in so far as they offer insight into her life.

Goreau, Angeline. *Reconstructing Aphra: A Social Biography of Aphra Behn.* New York: The Dial Press, 1980, 339 p.

Portrays Behn as a woman driven by contradictory personality traits: independence and emotional neediness.

Criticism

Boehrer, Bruce Thomas. "Behn's 'Disappointment' and Nashe's 'Choise of Valentines': Pornographic Poetry and the Influence of Anxiety." *Essays in Literature* XVI, No. 2 (Fall 1989): 172–87.

Concludes that "The Disappointment" "marginalizes the male experience of anxiety and humiliation [resulting from sexual impotence], concentrating upon the ironies whereby manly poetry is made."

Greer, Germaine. "Montague Summers and *The Works of Aphra Behn.*" In *The Uncollected Verse of Aphra Behn,* edited by Germaine Greer, pp. 1–11. Stump Cross, England: Stump Cross Books, 1989.

Chastises Montague Summers for poor scholarship in his six-volume edition of *The Works of Aphra Behn,* particularly pointing out errors related to Summer's treatment of Behn's poetry. Greer states: "It is typical of Behn's chequered literary fortunes that she should have found an editor shadier than herself, who divided his intellectual attention unevenly between satanism, theatricals, and literature, in descending order of importance, and that we should be indebted to his eccentricity for the only edition of her works that we have."

Kretsch, Donna Raske. "Sisters across the Atlantic: Aphra Behn and Sor Juana Inéz de la Cruz." *Women's Studies* 21, No. 3 (1992): 361–79.

Compares Behn and Sor Juana Inéz de la Cruz, a Mexican nun and contemporary of Behn's, finding similar feminist attitudes in their works. In the course of the essay, Kretsch briefly discusses Behn's poem "To Alexis in Answer to His Poem against Fruition."

"Mrs. Behn." *Littell's Living Age,* No. 631 (28 June 1856): 800–11.

Biographical and critical overview of Behn's career reprinted from *The Dublin University Magazine.* The critic attests to the variety and profusion of poetry produced by Behn, while expressing some doubt about the quality of her verse, and proceeds to quote some notable poems by her.

Mermin, Dorothy. "Women Becoming Poets: Katherine Philips, Aphra Behn, Anne Finch." *E.L.H.* 57, No. 2 (Summer 1990): 335–55.

Attributing the scarcity of female poets in England before the nineteenth century to "cultural suppression," Mermin examines and compares the verse of Philips, Behn, and Finch in order to "clarify both the causes of the prevailing silence and the conditions under which it could be broken."

O'Donnell, Mary Ann. "A Verse Miscellany of Aphra Behn: Bodleian Library MS Firth c.16." In *English Manuscript Studies, 1100–1700, Volume 2,* edited by Peter Beal and Jeremy Griffiths, pp. 189–227. Oxford: Basil Blackwell, 1990.

Asserts that Behn authored and transcribed some of the verses in a Bodleian Library manuscript consisting of poems by various authors. According to O'Donnell, this manuscript "reminds us of how much we have yet to learn about Aphra Behn and her circle."

Robertson, Eric S. "Katherine Philips—Aphra Behn—The Duchess of Newcastle—Early Minor Writers." In his *English Poetesses: A Series of Biographies, with Illustrative Extracts,* pp. 1–36. London: Cassell & Company, Limited, 1883.

Delivers a harsh assessment of Behn's poetry and plays, dismissing all but two of her poems, "A Song" and "On the Death of Waller." Offering a partial explanation for what he perceives as the unsavory quality of her poetry, Robertson blames prevailing literary trends and Behn's position as an outsider to respected society.

Rogal, Samuel J. "Aphra Behn." In *Critical Survey of Poetry, English Language Series,* edited by Frank N. Magill, pp. 123–31. Englewood Cliffs, N.J.: Salem Press, 1982.

Overview of Behn's verse. Rogal assesses her status as a poet, stating: "Critics may defend Behn's talent for drama and prose fiction as worthy of recognition beside that of her male contemporaries. As a writer of verse, however, she cannot claim a place among the poets of the first rank."

Stiebel, Arlene. "Not since Sappho: The Erotic in Poems of Katherine Philips and Aphra Behn." In *Homosexuality in Renaissance and Enlightenment England: Literary Representations in Historical Context,* edited by Claude J. Summers, pp. 153–64. New York: The Haworth Press, Inc., 1992.

Interprets "The Disappointment" as an account of rape and argues that Behn's verse manipulated literary conventions to allow her to discuss taboo subjects such as lesbianism without alerting the audience to any breach of decorum.

Additional coverage of Behn's life and career if contained in the following sources published by Gale Research: *DISCovering Authors; Drama Criticism,* **Vol. 4;** *Literature Criticism from 1400 to 1800,* **Vol. 1; and** *World Literature Criticism.*

Li Ho
791–817

Chinese poet.

INTRODUCTION

Li Ho lived during the late T'ang period (618–907) in Chinese history and wrote poetry remarkable for blending traditional poetic forms with images of shocking violence and a general mood of pessimism. Although his verse was admired by his contemporaries despite its strangeness, it subsequently lapsed into obscurity. A revival of interest in Li Ho's poems has recently taken place, with commentators expressing admiration for the vivid imagery and evocative, haunting quality of his verse.

Biographical Information

Li Ho was born into a distant, impoverished branch of the imperial clan. According to some sources, he began writing poetry at age six. When he was still a boy his father died, leaving him solely responsible for the welfare of his large family, and at age eighteen Li Ho sought to provide for them by becoming a civil servant. He passed a provincial examination, but was blocked from taking an examination which might have secured him a more substantial position at the imperial court by a prohibition against sons using their fathers' names. (One of the characters in his name matched one of his late father's.) He eventually accepted a minor office to which he was entitled by hereditary right. While at court, Li Ho began to write about the lives of courtesans, interested in their beautiful and ceremonious lifestyles. His own circumstances proved less attractive; he suffered from chronic illness, and success continually eluded him. As a result, his poetry increasingly turned to metaphysical treatments of death in which he savagely debunked mythology and rejected religion. In 817 he returned home and died the same year.

Major Works

Only 243 of Li Ho's poems, ballads, and songs have survived. Like nearly all Chinese poets of his day, Li Ho wrote much of his verse in the traditional *shih* form, which features a controlled number of lines of a specified number of syllables. He experimented with the form, however, introducing, for instance, unusual rhyme schemes and unorthodox stanza patterns. The subjects and tone of Li Ho's poems are unconventional as well. Bitter, ironic, and frequently morbid, his works are subjective expressions, employing an idiosyncratic range of images invested with highly personal significance. Repeated references to spirits of the dead and to such elements as rain and mist, light and shadow, create a pervasive sense of melancholy throughout much of Li Ho's work and have earned him the reputation of a poet preoccupied with supernatural phenomena.

Critical Reception

To some extent Western critics have taken greater interest in Li Ho's works than have their Chinese counterparts. Scholars have accounted for this apparent anomaly by observing that Li Ho's emphasis on subjective experience places him outside the Chinese poetic tradition with its emphasis on impersonal, generalized experience, while it permits comparisons of Li Ho's poems to those of John Keats, Charles Baudelaire, and other exemplars of the Western poetic notion of the "tortured genius." J. D. Frodsham has noted several ways in which Li Ho's poems seem peculiarly modern, particularly the manner in which he "sees things in flashes, apparently disconnectedly, so that his technique is probably far more familiar to modern readers, whose eyes have been trained by years of television and cinema, than it was to his traditional audience." Several critics have pointed out that the startling juxtapositions of images in Li Ho's poems contribute to their unsettling and otherworldly qualities. Burton Watson has pointed out the poems' "deliberately disjointed, nonlogical manner of presentation," which was intended to "increase the effect of shock and surprise" felt by the reader. Commentators have also argued that, despite Li Ho's reputation for individualism and aestheticism, his poetry reflects his deep involvement in the affairs of his time. As Frodsham has emphasized, "even the most cursory reading of his verse will show that Ho was deeply concerned with the problems of his day and used his ballads, which had a wide circulation, to satirize contemporary abuses."

PRINCIPAL ENGLISH TRANSLATIONS

The White Pony 1947
Poems of the Late T'ang 1965
The Poems of Li Ho (791–817) 1970
Sunflower Splendor: Three Thousand Years of Chinese Poetry 1975

*These collections contain the work of other writers in addition to that of Li Ho.

CRITICISM

A. C. Graham (essay date 1965)

SOURCE: "Li Ho," in *Poems of the Late T'ang,* translated by A. C. Graham, Penguin Books, 1965, pp. 89–92.

[*In the following excerpt, Graham discusses the central themes in Li Ho's works.*]

Li Ho is the most remarkable case in Chinese literature of a poet recently rediscovered after long neglect. He does not appear at all in the most familiar anthologies, such as the eighteenth-century *Three Hundred T'ang Poems.* Although famous in the ninth century and never quite forgotten, he offended the conventionality of later taste by his individuality and its health and balance by his morbidity and violence. To see his peculiar qualities as virtues required the breakdown of traditional literary standards in the nineteenth and twentieth centuries. It is now widely recognized by Chinese, Japanese, and Western readers alike that he is a major poet both in his own right and as a creative influence, the link between Han Yü, who discovered his talent when he was still a boy, and the masters of the ninth century, Tu Mu, who wrote the preface to his poems, and Li Shang-yin, who wrote his biography.

Li Ho continued the cult of 'strange' imagery, but turned it into something which is strange by any standards, not merely by those of the world's most sensible and temperate poetic tradition. He also continued Han Yü's experiments in Old Style versification, showing a taste for unorthodox rhyme schemes and for sequences of three or four quatrains rather than the standard eight-line form, the transitions between lines often so abrupt that he was credited with compiling his poems out of independently written couplets. These features he combines with an extreme compression more characteristic of the New Style verse of Tu Fu.

Li Ho's central theme is the transience of life, a subject which he treats as though no one before him had ever felt the drip of the water-clock on his nerves, in a wholly personal imagery of ghosts, blood, dying animals, weeping statues, whirlwinds, the will-o'-the-wisp—the last appears in many guises, 'ghostly lamps', 'cold blue candle-flames', 'sinister fires', 'darkened torches', 'fireflies in the tomb'. He seems quite uninterested in any of the common recipes for reconciliation with death, Confucian, Taoist, or Buddhist, with the result that he is equally far from the serenity of the greatest Chinese poets and the facile melancholy of the more commonplace. Even in his recurrent visions of the Taoist paradise he imagines the immortals dying, and his fantasies of watching from heaven the land and sea changing places over thousands of years only sharpen his sense of the irrevocable passage of time on earth. In the untranslated *Second Year of Chang-ho* he wishes long life to the Emperor, yet finishes with the disturbing and characteristic qualification:

. . . Till the thread of the Seven Stars snaps and the Lady in the Moon dies.

An aphorism often repeated in various forms declares that Tu Fu's genius was that of a Confucian sage and Li Po's of a Taoist immortal, that Po Chü-i's was human and Li Ho's ghostly or daemonic. An obsession with the world of spirits and of the dead shows up in many of his poems and accounts for his interest in shamanistic seances and in the *Songs of Ch'u* of the third century B.C., almost the only earlier poetry which shows a similar concern. One has the impression that Li Ho, who died young, felt himself already half way across the boundary between the living and the dead. But being Chinese, he has no place in his imagination for our own favourite bogey, the abstraction 'Death'.

Li Ho's more characteristic poems seldom introduce him directly at all, only sights, sounds, and smells. The tears in his poems are shed by flowers, by a rainy sky, by exorcized goblins who weep blood. But in spite of this reticence one is never in doubt of the pressure of an emotion which not only selects but exaggerates, distorts, invents the impressions which the poet offers to our senses, and of a muffled violence which erupts in the paranoid fury of *Don't Go Out of the Door.* Because of this unvarying stamp of a unique personality Li Ho is detached at a much shallower level than is Tu Fu. Tu Fu, in spite of his personal references, does not at bottom ask us to be interested in anything particular to himself; he selects the universal in his experience and invites us to sympathize, not with him, but with a generalized figure of man in exile.

Li Ho reminds many readers of Baudelaire. The affinity is not altogether an illusion, but in one respect it can mislead. When we read that Li Ho was called a *kuei ts'ai,* a ghostly or daemonic genius, and notice his apparently familiar constellation of pessimism, voluptuousness, aestheticism, and an imagination haunted by dark forces, it is tempting to read him as a nineteenth-century Satanist. But the Western sense of evil of course assumes a Christian background, and the *kuei* of Li Ho's poems are generally not devils but ghosts, sad rather than malevolent beings. Nor are there any overtones of the flesh and the devil in Li Ho's sensuality, which may be disreputable for a strict Confucian, but hardly sinful. His pessimism also has none of the ambivalence which one expects in a Western artist obsessed by original sin, who is at least half on the side of the destructive element because he finds it at the bottom of his own heart.

J. D. Frodsham (essay date 1970)

SOURCE: An introduction to *The Poems of Li Ho,* translated by J. D. Frodsham, Oxford at the Clarendon Press, 1970, pp. xiii–lxiv.

[*In the excerpt below, Frodsham reviews the religious, social, and artistic influences on Li Ho's poetry.*]

Unusual as Ho's work undoubtedly is, he is nevertheless very much of his time. He does not stand apart from it in the way, say, Blake and Smart stand apart from the eighteenth century. In a sense, his verse simply carries to an extraordinary degree qualities of intensity, floridity and deep-grained pessimism already highly characteristic of T'ang verse. Only in his development of the *Ch'u Tz'u* tradition can be really be called unique. Take for example the prevailingly pessimistic tone of his verse. From the Han dynasty onwards Chinese poetry is on the whole deeply melancholy in tone. T'ang poetry was no exception to this, and even poets like Tu Fu and Li Po (699–762) write verse steeped in sadness. It was not until the Sung dynasty (960–1279) that Chinese poets rid themselves of the burden of sorrow, as the great Japanese critic, Yoshikawa Kōjirō has pointed out. In this respect Ho is typical of his age, for his verse is so imbued with melancholy that the pages seem to darken as one reads.

Any thorough study of Ho's verse would attempt to explain this fully. In doing so, it would have to account for the whole shift in outlook which took place in the poetry of the ninth century, the movement away from the outgoing, assertive verse of Tu Fu to the esoteric, withdrawn poetry of Li Shang-yin. This introduction is no place to attempt such a feat: but I should hazard the guess that the basic factors involved were the decline of the empire after the rebellion of An Lu-shan; the weakening of the central government; the increasing dominance of the enuchs and the dissociation of literary men from political power. All of these—and especially the last—resulted in what Toynbee would call 'a failure of nerve on the part of the creative minority'. This would account for the pervading sense of melancholy, nostalgia and regret that so characterizes most of the poetry of the *Yüan-ho* period (806–21). Furthermore, this was an age when none of the traditional remedies seemed to make sense any more. Taoism had degenerated into superstition; Buddhism was on the verge of collapse—the persecution of 845 finally struck it a mortal blow—and even the most ardent Confucian reformers found that the time was not yet ripe for revival of the Master's teachings.

What is peculiar, then, about Ho's verse is not his melancholy but the extent of it; not the sentiment itself but the symbols he used to express it. Wada Toshio [in *Gumma daigaku kiyō jimbun kagaku hen,* 1956] has analysed Ho's verse statistically and found that expressions directly connected with death occur 74 times; expressions hinting at death 198 times; expressions of sadness 131 times and expressions of anxiety and fear 262 times—a total of 665 in all. On an average there are three expressions concerned with death or unhappiness in every poem. Wada's analysis simply lends statistical support to what the reader had already felt in his senses; namely that Ho's verse is extraordinarily melancholy even by T'ang standards. Furthermore, the images he persistently draws on, those of ghosts, demons, spirits, bones, blood, tombs, corpses, will-o'-the-wisps and so on, are normally studiously avoided by Chinese poets, as they are avoided by ordinary Chinese, on the grounds that they are unlucky. Admittedly, during T'ang the weird tale or ghost story (*ch'uan-ch'i*)

enjoyed a great vogue; but these stories are certainly not obsessed with death and decay as is Ho's verse.

Ho's 'death-wish', as we should style it today, has been noted by the contemporary writer, Hung Wei-fa, who remarked that Ho was afraid of death, yet longed for it, for since he was sick of the world of men, he yearned for heaven. Ho's longing for death is certainly understandable. For a start, he stemmed from that most pessimistic of classes, impoverished aristocracy—people for whom the past recedes ever further in a golden haze. Secondly, he was unlucky in not being allowed to take an examination which would almost certainly have led him to fame and fortune—and for a Chinese to think himself unlucky is to have lost all hope. Finally, he was a man ravaged by disease, constantly in failing health and—to cap all this—poor, at least in comparison with his friends. Small wonder then that he found life a burden which he would gladly shake off. He would fain have fled the world—but to what?

Classical Confucianism admits of no life beyond the grave, beyond the squeaking and gibbering of ghosts. In this it is as comfortless as the religion of the ancient Greeks. Hung Wei-fa's assertion that Ho 'longed for heaven' must therefore refer to his belief in either Buddhism, or Taoism or both. Ostensibly Ho was no Taoist at least in the conventional sense, for many of his satirical poems are attacks upon Emperor Hsien-tsung, who spent a great deal of time and money which could have been better employed in the business of government in seeking for elixirs of eternal life. On the other hand, there can be no denying that Ho was fascinated with the concept of Heaven, which recurs constantly in his poems as a place of exquisite beauty, where immortals dwell.

> Là, tout n'est qu'ordre et beauté,
> Luxe, calme et volupté.

It seems to me highly probable that at one level of belief Ho was convinced of the reality of the Taoist heaven. This would help to explain the stories about his death-bed:

> When Ch'ang-chi was at death's door, suddenly, in broad day-light he saw a man in purple raiment driving a red dragon and carrying a tablet . . . who said: 'I am here to summon Ch'ang-chi' . . . Ch'ang-chi at once got down from his bed and kowtowed saying:

> 'Mama is old and ill. I don't want to leave her.'

> The man in purple raiment said with a smile: 'The Emperor [of Heaven] has just built the White Jade Tower and summons you to come at once and write a description of it. Life up in Heaven is delightful: there is no hardship there.' Ch'ang-chi only wept the more . . .

Li Shang-yin goes on [in *Li Yi-shan wen-chi, Ssu-pu ts'ung-k'an*] to state that this story was narrated to him by Mrs. Wang, Ho's sister, who was present at his death, adding that her veracity was undoubted.

Now if, in fact, Ho really believed in Heaven, then it is highly likely that during his final moments he actually saw and described the events that his sister spoke of. What we have here, indeed, is a graphic account of Ho's death-bed vision—a consoling dream as touching and as vividly colorful as many of his poems. But how can this Taoist belief be reconciled with Ho's avowed Buddhism, for he states quite plainly in his poem **Presented to Ch'en Shang** that the *Lankāvatāra-sūtra* is his constant companion, along with the *Ch'u Tz'u*?

I think the explanation lies in the fact that the *Lankāvatāra*—a work of notorious difficulty and profundity—was the principal sutra of the Ch'an (Zen) school during T'ang. Ho must therefore have been a devotee of Ch'an Buddhism, a fact which would explain the otherwise puzzling lack of overt Buddhist allusions in his verse, since this school attaches only secondary importance to the scriptures. The Heaven of Ho's visions therefore cannot have been the Western Paradise of Amitābha Buddha, for this is not a belief held by the Ch'an school. He must have envisaged Heaven in Buddhist terms as the abode of the gods, a higher race than men and seemingly immortal by comparison, who were yet doomed to perish as all things in the universe must perish since they too were bound to the Wheel of Life and Death.

When we turn from Ho's thought to a study of the actual texture of the poems themselves we find ourselves on firmer ground. Ho's poems are notoriously difficult and enigmatic. 'Li Ho's poems cannot be read without a commentary', is an old literary saw. His poems, like Li Shang-yin's, present special difficulties for a number of reasons. Firstly, the poems have a logic of their own. His imagination is neither rhetorical nor yet dramatic: it is purely visual. He sees things in flashes, apparently disconnectedly, so that his technique is probably far more familiar to modern readers, whose eyes have been trained by years of television and cinema, than it was to his traditional audience. This technique is undoubtedly connected with the method of composition described in his biographies, in which he would jot down lines and phrases as they occurred to him and then piece them together like a mosaic on his return home. As a result of this, some of his long poems, like **Ch'ang-ku** and **She Steals My Heart** tend to break down into disparate shots in which the inner unity that should bind them has been lost. In cinematic terms, Ho's camera-work—whether black-and-white or colour—is always brilliant. It is his montage that sometimes fails him.

It is this technique that leads one of his most penetrating modern commentators, Arai Ken, to complain that Ho jumps about in time and space, keeps changing his subject and in general lacks unity. Arai has failed to notice, however, that this disintegration of the continuity of exterior events is a strikingly modern characteristic, an anticipation of the Bergsonian flux of twentieth-century Western art. In Ho's verse, landmarks keep moving about in a most disconcerting fashion. As Ch'ien Chung-shu astutely observed [in *T'an-yi-lu*, 1948], his poetry is like the shifting sands of the desert—a desert, I might add, which has up

to now deterred most of those who would have liked to cross it. As may be imagined, such poetry presents formidable difficulties for the English translator, who is forced to be explicit when the original is vague because of the nature of our language.

Another source of perplexity is found in Ho's imagery. His metaphors are often difficult to follow until one has grasped their inner logic.

> He is Hsi Ho whipping up the sun
> That tinkles like glass.

This borders on the synaesthesia of the Symbolists, whom Ho so much resembles. The sun is like glass because both are white and shining (glass was an exotic substance for T'ang Chinese). Glass tinkles when shattered; the sun is being shattered by time. Therefore it tinkles as Hsi Ho—who drives the sun horse—applies the whip. Ho's verse abounds in images of this nature.

Closely connected with the problem of Ho's imagery is his fondness for kennings. Thus autumn flowers are 'cold reds'; wine is 'liquid amber'; swords are 'jade dragons', jujubes are 'hanging pearls' (or 'hanging reds'). Along with this goes a penchant for coining new words and phrases which is quite uncharacteristic of Chinese poetry. His painstaking craftsmanship, his determination to make his language fresh and novel, seems to indicate the influence of Tu Fu, who once remarked: 'Not even death would stop me from trying to startle my readers.' But Ho went a great deal further than Tu Fu ever dared. As one Chinese critic remarked: Li Ho's poetry is like the art of jade-carving. Not a single word but has been refined a hundred times. This is really the product of work that made him 'vomit out his heart' [Yeh Yeh-lan, *Li Ch'ang-chi chi-pa*]. Here again he resembles French nineteenth-century poetry, especially the Parnassians, for whom:

> L'œuvre sort plus belle
> D'une forme au travail rebelle,
> Vers, marbre, onyx, émail.

His language has a Keatsian sumptuousness, every rift loaded with ore, a 'devotion to the intensity imbedded within the concrete' giving his lines a 'heavy richness, [a] slow clogged—almost drugged—movement, [a] choked-in fullness . . . which gives him strength with all his luxury and which keeps his sensuousness firm and vital' [Walter Jackson Bate, 'Keats's Style: Evolution toward Qualities of Permanent Value', in *The Major English Poets*, ed. Clarence D. Thorpe and others, 1957].

In short then, Ho's work is closer in many respects to modern western poetry than to the classical Chinese tradition. This may explain why T'an Ssu-t'ung (1865–98), one of the martyrs of the 1898 Reform Movement and Lu Hsün (1881–1936) the greatest writer modern China has produced, both admired Ho's verse. It may also explain why so many of the traditional commentators, especially Confucian rationalists like the Ch'ing commentator Wang Ch'i, have gone so wildly astray at times in interpreting

Ho's work, since they understood neither his mystical temperament nor his patriotism.

Ironically enough, modern Chinese communist criticism, which invariably pays lip-service to Lu Hsün, has constantly ignored his praise of Li Ho. Instead the critics have accused Ho of most of the social sins—passivity, aestheticism, lack of patriotism, and a failure to get to grips with reality. Yet even the most cursory reading of his verse will show that Ho was deeply concerned with the problems of his day and used his ballads, which had a wide circulation, to satirize contemporary abuses. His attacks on the eunuch T'u-t'u Ch'eng-ts'ui in particular may have played a part in forcing the emperor to dismiss this singularly incompetent general from his command of the Armies of the Divine Plan in 809.

> A lady-general leads our Chinese soldiers.
> A dainty kerchief tucked into her quiver.
> She's not ashamed of her heavy, gold seal,
> Lurching along with bow-case at her waist.
> Simple old men, just honest villagers,
> Tested the teeth of arrow-barbs last night,
> But she sent her courier to cry victory—
> Must powder and mascara blind us all!

Even more dangerous than his attacks on the eunuchs were his scarcely veiled satires on Emperor Hsien-tsung's quest for immortality through Taoist arts—a quest which was eventually to result in his death. Taoists believed that with the aid of the proper drugs, life could be lengthened almost indefinitely. Since most of these drugs were highly toxic preparations of gold, arsenic, lead, mercury and like substances, it is hardly surprising to learn that those who sought immortality the most assiduously were frequently those who departed this life the most precipitately. As early as 810, the Emperor had evinced considerable interest in elixirs of immortality, much to the disapproval of his minister, Li Fan, who had given him a stern lecture on the folly of putting one's faith in Taoist magicians. This seems to have had little effect on Hsien-tsung's ardour, for by 819 we find him 'swallowing drugs daily and so becoming more and more bad-tempered and thirsty', a process which continued until his demise the following year.

Several writers attempted to remonstrate with the emperor on this subject, though to do so was really 'to run up against the dragon's scales', since this was a topic on which he was notoriously short-tempered. Han Yü himself, who had merely alluded indirectly to the subject in his well-known memorial on the Buddha's bone, only narrowly escaped death for his indiscretion. Po Chü-yi, Meng Chiao and other poets preferred to couch their protests in the form of verse gibing at the vain quest for immortality undertaken by previous emperors such as Ch'in Shih Huang-ti, Emperor Wu of Han and Emperor Wen of Wei. Ho himself has a large number of poems on this subject, so many in fact that one wonders how he escaped punishment, for he was undoubtedly running a risk by circulating songs dealing with such a topic. . . .

It is difficult at this remove for us to estimate just how many of the poems are to be understood as satires. Yao Wen-hsieh ascribes satirical intent to almost every verse Ho wrote, but this, of course is an exaggeration. However, it is fair to assume that a great many poems which appear innocuous enough now would have been read as satires by Ho's contemporaries. Perhaps something like 20 percent of the verse, at a conservative estimate, can even now reasonably be labelled satirical, though half the time we can never be sure just what target he is aiming at. In any case, it is certain that his involvement with the New Ballad (*hsin yüeh-fu*) Movement must not be underestimated. Po Chü-yi (772–846) and Yüan Chen had both come to the conclusion that 'the duty of literature is to be of service to the writer's generation: that of poetry to influence public affairs'. This conviction was a revival of an ancient belief, dating back to *The Classic of Poetry* and the *Ch'u Tz'u,* that the poet was the social conscience of his time. To ensure the widest possible circulation for their work, Po and Yüan cast their criticisms of existing abuses into ballad form. These ballads, which enjoyed as much vogue as the popular songs of our own time, were songs with a message. As Po puts it in the preface to his own collection of fifty ballads:

> (These songs) are concerned with ideas, not with fine phrases . . . This was the principle behind the three hundred poems (of *The Classic of Poetry*) . . . Their style is smooth and flowing, so they can easily be played and sung. In short, they have been written for the emperor, for his ministers, for the people . . . They have not been written simply for art's sake.

This manifesto of Po's may be considered as the inception of the New Ballad Movement. Po and Yüan were soon joined by a number of other writers—Li Shen, Meng Chiao, Chang Chi and Han Yü among them—who were all concerned in some degree with the use of verse as a vehicle for social criticism. Strictly speaking, the New Ballad had to conform to the criteria Po Chü-yi himself adopted. It had to be simple in expression—Po is said to have tried out all his poems on an old maidservant, deleting anything she could not understand—and conform to the ballad form, while revealing sympathy for the plight of the common people. The poetry, in fact, was in the pity. Ho has comparatively few ballads which meet all these requirements, for he was influenced more by the *Li Sao* tradition (the greatest poem of the *Ch'u Tz'u*) than by *The Classic of Poetry,* and the *Li Sao,* though critical of governmental abuses, was ornate and highly obscure. Nevertheless, Ho would have certainly subscribed to Empson's dictum:

> Politics are what verse should
> Not fly from, or it goes all wrong.

Furthermore, he did write a few ballads which fulfil all the criteria laid down by Po Chü-yi and yet carry his own inimitable stamp, as in the following song describing the miseries of the jade-gatherers, who had taken to this dangerous work to save themselves and their families from starvation:

On rainy nights, on the ridge of a hill,
He sups on hazel-nuts.
Like the blood that wells from a cuckoo's maw,
Are the old man's tears.
The waters of Indigo river are gorged
With human lives.
After a thousand years the dead
Still loathe these torrents.

A steep hillside, wind in the cypress,
Whistle of rain—
Deep in the springs he hangs from a rope,
Green curling and swirling,
Thinking of wife and children back in his poor
    village,
In a white-thatched hut.
Upon stone steps of ancient terraces
The heartbreak grows.

Though apparently simple, analysis reveals this to be a far more complex and intricately structured poem than anything Po Chü-yi ever wrote. In modern terms, we can discern within this verse something of that peculiar tension between symbolism and naturalism manifest in the work of so many writers of our own century. But I shall come back to this point later. For the moment we shall simply note that the poem makes its point dramatically and effectively and must certainly be ranked as a ballad of social protest squarely in the tradition.

These two aspects of Ho's verse, his patriotism and his protests, have not received nearly as much critical attention as has his so-called aestheticism, his preoccupation with exotic subjects and fantastic imagery. A great deal of his poetry anticipates the languid, incense-laden atmosphere of the *tz'u,* a kind of song lyric composed to fixed melodic patterns which was to come into being some fifty years or so after his death.

Clouds tumbling over her jewelled pillow,
She seeks a spring dream,
In caskets cold with inlaid sapphires
The dragon-brain grows chill?

. . . . .

She lies resentful in her net of pearls
Unable to sleep,
Beneath a robe ornate with golden phoenix
Her body is chill, . . .

. . . . .

Drowsy with wine, idle all the white day
In a moored boat,
In a plum-breeze by the ferry she waves
Her singing-fan.

. . . . .

Butterflies lighting on China pinks—
Hinges of silver,

Frozen water, duck-head green—
Coins of glass.
Its six-fold curves enclose a lamp
Burning orchid-oil.
She lets down her tresses before the mirror,
Sheds her gold cicadas,
Perfume of aloes from a warm fire,
Smoke of dogwood.

. . . . .

A single skein of perfumed silk,
Clouds cast on the floor,
Noiseless, the jade comb tumbles down
From her lustrous hair,
Delicate fingers push back the coils—
Colour of an old rook's plumes
Blue-black and sleek—the jewelled comb
And hairpin cannot hold.

. . . . .

Flowers bow down beneath light dew,
Melilote's breath,
Windlass of jade and rope of silk
Draw the dawn water,
Her powdered face, like purple carnelian,
Hot and fragrant.

Part of this verse—like the last example—is undoubtedly satiric. But in any case, even when Ho's intentions were to mock, he lingered to admire. This world of black-haired, jade-skinned beauties, blushing cheeks, perfumed silks, gauze bed-curtains, flickering tapers, carved screens, golden censers fuming with rare incense, and the mournful drip of rain on the kolanut trees, was to become the sole poetic province of *tz'u* writers like Wen T'ing-yün (812?–70?), Wei Chuang (836–910), Li Yü (937–78), and others. Such a trend was not new in Chinese verse; it had appeared for the first time some three hundred years previously, with the so-called 'palace poetry' of the last years of the Six Dynasties. Ho's natural sensuality could not resist the appeal of this glittering kingdom of pearl and aloes-wood, jasper and cassia, though he invested it with a significance lacking in later writers. Not only does Ho anticipate the great poets of the *tz'u:* he also looks forward to the two outstanding romantics of the ninth century, Tu Mu and Li Shang-yin. Like them he delights in wine and spring flowers, beautiful women and the moon on the water. Ho takes love as seriously as the Confucian poet took friendship. Li Shang-yin, one of the greatest poets of love writing in Chinese, was a devoted admirer of Ho's and must have found support for his passionate affairs of the heart in Ho's verse:

What sort of love am I seeking?
That of Hsün Feng-ch'ien.
O sun above the city wall,
Forever stay above the city wall!
Let a single day be as a thousand years,
And never sink to rest.

Some critics give the impression that Ho's love of beauty was somehow incompatible with the Confucian gravity and sense of purpose associated with the New Ballad Movement: that aestheticism and naturalism could not go together. This is a misleading dichotomy. T'ang poetry, even the best of it, is inclined to be florid: but one should never mistake this for a lack of high seriousness. One has only to look at Han Yü's own verse to see that it abounds in quaint conceits and odd expressions, breaks many of the time-hallowed rules of composition and deals with subjects which no earlier poet would have thought fit to mention in verse. I hazard the opinion that both the intricate nature of Ho's own poetry and his choice of subjects were in fact partly the result of a deliberate attempt to please his patrons. There is certainly nothing in Ho's verse which Yü or his fellows would have thought frivolous. Critics have failed to see that there is a difference between Ho's verse and the effete, palace poetry against which Yü fulminated. Palace poetry was mere empty rhetoric; once penetrate its glossy surface and there was nothing underneath. But Ho's verse, even when concerned with the very subjects that formed the sole staple of the palace poets, never wavered from the *Li Sao* tradition. Beneath the intricately patterned surface lay solid layers of meaning. Ultimately, Yü waged war on the poetry of Ch'i and Liang because not of its 'decadent' subject-matter but because it was void of social content: he praised Ho's verse because it came to grips with reality, whether it dealt with soldiers starving in a frontier-post or a princess getting drunk at a banquet. Ho was astute enough to realize, as so many later critics have not, that if verse was to mirror the complex, sophisticated and disintegrating fabric of T'ang society it could not confine itself to simple ballads. It is only because he possessed this poetic range that he could so successfully hold up the mirror to his age: and it was precisely for this quality that Yü admired him. His verse in its own way reflects the realities of T'ang life just as faithfully as the poems of Tu Fu and Po Chü-yi. The parallel with our own times when naturalism and symbolism, aesthete and realist flourish together, is quite striking. One is reminded of Mallarmé congratulating Zola on the publication of *L'Assommoir,* both having, as Durkheim pointed out, a common need to destroy the real or escape from it.

The contention that the main difference between Ho's poetry and the verse of Ch'i and Liang, which it sometimes superficially resembles, lies in their content brings us directly to the problems of meaning in Chinese verse. Ho was brought up in a poetic tradition which laid great stress on metaphor (*pi*) and allegory (*hsing*). . . .

Western sinologists have very much inclined to ignore the part played by *pi* and *hsing* in Chinese verse, largely because the tradition of a work possessing several levels of meaning died out in Europe during the seventeenth century and has only recently been revived. I. A. Richards's 'multiple definition', Kenneth Burke's 'multiple causation', William Troy's attempt to revive the medieval 'four levels of meaning' are all of them relevant to any attempt to read Chinese literature in depth. Unfortunately, very little, if anything, has as yet been done towards ap-

plying modern critical methods to the study of Chinese poetry. A. C. Graham's recent excursions into this field in his *Poems of the Late T'ang* have the distinction of being the first serious attempt of its kind. In general, due credit has not been given to traditional Chinese explanations of the meanings hidden in verse. . . .

A point closely connected with this is the question of plurisignation (a better term than 'ambiguity') in Ho's verse. Lack of literary professionalism among sinologists has all too often led to a concern with outmoded, pre-Empsonian ideas about the meaning of a poem. The notion has persisted that the denotative aspect of language is more important than the connotative: that a line—or a whole poem—must mean one thing and one thing only. In fact, Chinese poetry has consciously employed plurisignation since the Six Dynasties period; by late T'ang times, when Ho was writing, multiple meanings had become quite as involved as those of Shakespearian verse. This poses special difficulties for the translator, who is in any case forced by the very nature of the English language to be precise where Chinese is vague and suggestive. At times, he may be lucky enough to hit upon a rendering which will convey something of the ambiguity of the original; but most of the time he can only laboriously spell out the other possible meanings of the line in a footnote.

A reluctance to annotate poems copiously has been one of the main reasons, I think, why Ho has not received the attention that is his due from Western translators. From the end of the eighth century onwards, Chinese poetry becomes steadily more complex and allusive. The Chinese poet has always relied heavily for his effect on allusions. Pound's characterization of a poem as a form that should be able to do as much in a line as a whole page of prose is strikingly true of Chinese verse, which can sum up a situation, draw an analogy or reveal a contrast in the minimum of words through the use of the shorthand of allusion. As the corpus of literature increased there was a tendency on the part of poets to refer not only to the Confucian and Taoist classics but to the whole ever-growing body of earlier writings. This means that the later T'ang poets tend to be rather more difficult to read than their predecessors, if only because they have incorporated so much into their verse. This is not to say that there is a great deal of purely literary allusion in Ho's verse; on the contrary, there is far less of this than in say, the fifth-century poet Hsieh Ling-yün. But there is enough general use of allusion to ensure that there are very few poems in Ho's collected works that can be understood without at least some notes and a good many poems that require a great deal of annotation indeed.

Here the Western reader is at a considerable disadvantage compared with even the Chinese reader who has received no formal classical education; for the latter has acquired, by cultural osmosis as it were, a great deal of information which the unfortunate Westerner has painstakingly to imbibe. All this goes to swell the already excessive volume of footnotes, until the translator half begins to wonder, with Pound, whether he is not obscuring the text with philology. Nevertheless, I myself am convinced for one that this is the only way in which Chinese verse can be made intelligible to the European reader, without fobbing him off with mere *chinoiserie.*

It may be objected that a great deal of the essential poetry of the original is lost through such a method of translation. I doubt this. Such a belief can be traced back to the French Symbolist view that poetry, 'which is made with words, not ideas', as Mallarmé expressed it, must evaporate like spilt perfume when poured into the alien flask of another language. This contention has come up against some very sharp and perceptive criticism of recent years, the most telling onslaught on this cherished doctrine coming from the Chicago critics. They reject the doctrine that literature is only a question of particular arrangements of words on the page, as Leavis puts it, in favour of the view that we are moved not by words but by the things the words stand for. One can test this for oneself. Flecker's line:

> A ship, an isle, a sickle moon—
> With few, but with how splendid stars.

loses nothing when rendered into any language. The quality of the imagery here is such that it passes unscathed through the refining fires of translation. It is precisely this characteristic of Ho's verse, the giving of sharp perceptions in images of extra-ordinary colour and clarity, that makes him a peculiarly translatable poet. Whatever else may be lost, this at least is not.

But Ho has other advantages for the translator besides the vividness of his imagery. Chinese poets, on the whole, are impersonal, self-effacing and inclined to generalize in a way which sometimes muffles the impact of their verse on the Western reader, who is accustomed to as forceful a display of individualism in his poetry as in his culture. The Western poet, at least since the Romantics, has almost invariably been endowed with a personality which makes itself strongly felt through his verse. In this respect, Ho is an aberration from the Chinese standard; for though he very seldom consciously intrudes himself into his verse, the stress of his personality is there all the same. One is continually aware of a sort of controlled violence in his poems, informing even the most casual-sounding lines. He is a poet of exaggerated gestures and moods, swinging between despair and exultation in a way that leads one to guess that he must have been something of a manic-depressive. It is, I suspect, this violence of gesture that makes him so irritate his Chinese readers, who are vaguely conscious all the time that the proprieties are being offended. An image like the following illustrates what I mean:

> Like the blood that wells from a cuckoo's maw
> Are the old man's tears.

Occurring as it does in a poem of social protest, which we are accustomed to think of in terms of the gentle, conversational ironies of Po Chü-yi, this image brings one up with a start. It is altogether too vehement. What is more, it has a peculiar tellingness about it which is hard to explain. The Chinese reader would at once link this with the story of the Emperor of Shu who abdicated his throne, fled into the wilds and was changed into a cuckoo. But what has this allusion to the weeping emperor to do with an old peasant? The most likely explanation is that the blood the old man weeps (another exaggeration) makes him kin to the cuckoo and hence an animal; at the same time, the cuckoo is an emperor, so the old man's grief is imperial. Linking cuckoo, peasant and emperor in this way through the highly unpleasant image of blood flowing from the eyes and mouth works on the reader powerfully and upsettingly. For a Chinese, the implied social confusion of man with animal, peasant with Son of Heaven, would have been not the least disturbing thing about this comparison.

Another factor which is not lost in translation but can be brought over unscathed is Ho's evocative use of colour to symbolize emotion. White, gold, silver, black, red, green, yellow, blue-green, emerald, vermilion, scarlet, purple, turquoise and cinnabar run riot through his work. Furthermore, his palette is a highly idiosyncratic one in which certain colours, notably white, red and blue-green are dominant, with white standing far above the rest. . . .

Ho's liking for white, a colour associated in China not with purity and virginity but with mourning and misfortune, is highly significant. To the Chinese, white is an unlucky colour, suggesting death and old age. In the Han system of correspondences it was linked with autumn, the west (and hence the setting sun), and the element metal. . . . Moreover, since 'jade' as an adjective always means 'jade-white' in Chinese and never 'jade-green', the combination of white, metal, and jade—265 instances in all out of 613—represents a quite extraordinary preference for white. Even in the West, psychologists tend to associate a strong liking for white with psychic abnormality: in China, where white has all the emotional overtones that in Europe would be carried by black, such a predilection would be considered morbid and ill-omened.

Ho's landscapes, drenched in this white radiance, shine with an unearthly pallor.

> In the ninth month, the great wilderness is white.
>
> The entire mountain bathed in a white dawn.
>
> Horses' hooves trampling in white.
>
> Autumn whitens the infinite heavens.
>
> White grasses, dead beneath invading mist.
>
> A white sky, water like raw silk.
>
> Where endless desert merges with white sky.
>
> Vast autumn gleamed white.
>
> Jade mist over green damp
> Like pennants of white.
>
> To an islet where white duckweed grows . . .

The cloud-towers are half-revealed,
Walls slant and white.

Above cold gardens, deserted courtyards,
A limpid, white void.

The white glare returns to the Western Hills.

There seems little doubt that Ho's obsession with white
was in some way connected with the premature and sinister whitening of his own hair, a physiological quirk which
he refers to several times in his poems. He was haunted by
the mystery of whiteness as another great poet, Lorca, was
haunted by the spell of green.

Against this pallid background the other colours burn with
a brilliant flame:

Under massing clouds red nets darken,
Over broken stones slant purple coins.

Beyond the frontiers like rouge from Yen,
Night's purple congeals.

Who is this girl shedding vermilion tears?

Cold candles, kingfisher-green . . .

Smoky yellow mantles the willows.

A thousand hills of darkest emerald.

A flame-red mirror opens in the east.

His glittering sword flashes through the sky,
Turning heaven sapphire-blue.

On the scarlet walls hang girdle-gems of jade.

Under the white sun, a thousand hills
Look darkest green.

Black waters of the Pine Stream
Bear new dragon-eggs.

Emerald smoke swirling . . .

Cold reds weeping dew . . .

What hungry beetles would not eat
Piles up in broken yellows.

Twilight purple freezes in the dappled sky.

Only black waters' waves sobbing at dawn.

Pattern of golden snakes on her dancing-rug.

Along with this striking use of colour goes a wholly personal imagery which, again, is unique in Chinese if not in
world literature. The following images all occur in Ho's
verse, some of them several times: shrieking phoenixes;

lonely simurghs; ageing simurghs; shivering hares; old
fishes; gaunt dragons; crying molecrickets; weeping rac-
coons; dying foxes; white foxes barking; snarling dogs;
wailing crickets; drooling lions; slavering griffons; whin-
nying and half-starved horses; crying crows; serpents riding
a white mist; old turtles in jade wells; poisonous, horned
dragons; demon-owls and weeping bronze camels. The last
figure leads us to the next class of imagery, that of normally
inanimate objects which in Ho's verse become endowed
with a mysterious life of their own. This is the world of
T'ang ghost stories: swords that roar, swords that fly, painted dragons ridden by rain-elves, haggard straw-dogs, weeping statues and gargoyles peering out of stunted trees. It is
but a step away from the realm of gods and spirits proper,
ranging from cave-dwelling demons, mountain trolls, witches
and Weird Crones to Nü Kua, the Purple King and the
Mother who is Queen in the West. Against the flickering
background of a hallucinatory universe, where mountains
crumble away in the wind and land lurches out of the sea
only to disappear again. Ho's phantasmagoria dances wildly past. The only constant here is the inexorable passing of
time: the dripping water-clock, the booming drum mark
men's progress towards the graves where the fireflies dance
like corpse-fires and lonely candles burn. Nor are men alone
in their predicament. In the Buddhist vision of things even
the gods must perish; and Ho's heaven is a place of funerals where the blessed themselves are borne in never-ending
procession to the tomb.

Ultimately, Ho was at heart a mystic, as we might have
guessed from his preoccupation with the *Lankāvatāra,* the
central theme of which is the doctrine of self-realization
(*svasiddhānta*) and inner enlightenment (*pratyātmagati*).
Many of his poems are clearly records, not of hallucinations, but of genuine, if elementary visions, in which he
transcends the world of egoic experience, the illusions of
Maya, entering a realm in which he contemplates a higher
state of being than our own. Today, we have so completely lost touch with inner reality that very few of us can
believe in its existence, a fact that makes it difficult for us
to respond adequately to Ho's greatest poems where the
vision shines the most resplendently. Nevertheless, we must
realize that the world of his visions was not a mere fantasy
into which he retreated from the miseries of 'reality'. Rather, his Buddhist training enabled him to journey to places
far removed from 'the weariness, the fever and the fret' of
his existence without losing his orientation, while his poetic
genius enabled him to describe vividly what he had seen.

Ho's feeling for religion, whether for Zen or for Shaman-
ism, his sense of the ultimate identity (*samatā*) of the
world-of-birth-and-death (*samsāra*) and Nirvana, is central not peripheral to his poetic art. He wrote verse ultimately not for aesthetic pleasure but to express what the
Lankāvatāra calls *pratyātmāryajñānagocara*—the state of
intuitive awareness of inner truth. It is perhaps this which
makes the perceptive Western reader want to link him
with that great occult tradition which includes Baudelaire
and Blake, Rimbaud and Yeats. Though his visions are
admittedly never more than two-fold (to use Blake's term)
they are intensely felt and realized, even if they do lapse
at times when the spirit fails him into mere fantasy. His

moments of epiphany occur when he realizes—to quote his favourite sutra—that 'this world of error is eternity itself, truth itself' (*'Bhrāntih śāśvatā, bhrāntis tattvam'*); when he glimpses as Yeats puts it, 'the uncontrollable mystery on the bestial floor'.

To say this is not to overlook the fact that Ho's poetry lacks the serene assurance of the mystic who has achieved realization and enlightenment. Since for much of his life he was a sick man, a great deal of his verse betrays all the feverish and heightened sensibility of the consumptive. In this he is very much of his age. As Yoshikawa Kōjirō remarks: 'T'ang poetry burns with intensity. The moment in which the poem is born is one of the most vital instants in a man's life in his headlong plunge towards death. He must fix his eyes upon the instant and pour his feelings into it. The emotion must cohere, it must jet forth, it must explode'.

Never was this truer than of the poetry of Li Ho. In his sensuality and the despairing intensity with which he strives to hold the passing moment burning eternally in his art, like a frozen flame, he is akin to Keats: and like Keats—or Beddoes, whom he also resembles—he is half in love at times with easeful death. He wrote in the shadow of the grave: and no philosophy, no religion, no consoling belief could quite keep out its ineluctable cold. Only at the white radiance of his own poetic visions could he warm himself for a while before making his final journey to those cypress-shadowed tombs where he had wandered so often during his brief lifetime like some pallid and melancholy ghost. Yet it would have been some consolation to him, I feel, to learn that now 'after a thousand years in earth', his 'rancorous blood' shines forth in the light of day as emerald-jade.

Burton Watson (essay date 1971)

SOURCE: "Later Trends in T'ang Poetry," in *Chinese Lyricism: Shih Poetry from the Second to the Twelfth Century,* Columbia University Press, 1971, pp. 169–96.

[*In this excerpt, Watson assesses Li Ho's talent and poetic style.*]

While the Chinese poetic tradition, led by men like Han Yü and Po Chü-i, moved in the direction of a simpler, more relaxed style, greater variety of subject matter, and more discursive or philosophical treatment, bringing it momentarily, as Graham notes [in *Poems of the Late T'ang*], much closer to our own, a young writer of promise named Li Ho (791–817) was busily forging ahead on a wholly different course. He has traditionally been described as a *kuei-ts'ai* or man of "devilish talent," a term that points up both the uncanny brilliance he showed even at an early age, and the weird, otherworldly quality that informs much of his important work. We [can see] this eerie quality appearing in the late works of Tu Fu; Li Ho explored it to the full, filling his more daring poems with images drawn from mythology and folk religion or the

shaman songs of the *Ch'u Tz'u*. From the late poetry of Tu Fu he took also a fondness for extreme compression of language, which in his own work assumes the form of a deliberately disjoined, nonlogical manner of presentation. To increase the effect of shock and surprise which such a style was clearly designed to arouse in the reader, he employed odd diction, new and peculiar expressions that he invented to replace conventional ones. Finally, from the late Tu Fu he took a highly personal tone and a mood of unrelieved pessimism that in time was to become characteristic of nearly all poetry of the closing years of the T'ang.

Had Li Ho lived beyond his twenty-sixth year, he might have matured into a figure of major importance and influenced the entire course of later Chinese poetry. As it is, his work stands as something of an isolated oddity in the literary tradition. Though praised by T'ang writers, its mood of eeriness and violence seemed to repel later readers, who allowed it to sink into relative neglect. Recently there has been a considerable revival of interest, the oddness and obscurity that were once regarded as the defects of Li Ho's poetry being now very much in fashion. Its greatest asset remains its vivid, haunting imagery, which can be appreciated without undue concern for what it all may mean. . . .

Though Li Ho, because of his untimely death, technically belongs to the Middle T'ang period, his work in many ways foreshadows the poetry of the period to follow. His pessimism, as we have seen, became in time the prevailing mood, his fondness for compressed, highly polished language, the ideal in diction. But what in Li Ho had been a search for new and striking effects devolved into mere fussiness and preoccupation with surface ornament. Whereas he had, like Han Yü, experimented in the irregular forms of the *ku-shih,* delighting in the deliberate repetition of words which they allow, the Late T'ang poets turned once more to the *lü-shih* and other modern style forms. They no doubt hoped in this way to recapture something of the brilliance that Tu Fu and others had earlier achieved in these forms. Unfortunately, they succeeded for the most part in reproducing only the ornateness and technical dexterity of the earlier age. In theme and feeling their works seemed unable to rise above a shallow and world-weary mannerism.

Edward H. Schafer (essay date 1973)

SOURCE: "The Goddess Epiphanies of Li Ho," in *The Divine Woman: Dragon Ladies and Rain Maidens in T'ang Literature,* University of California Press, 1973, pp. 104–14.

[*In the following excerpt, Schafer examines Li Ho's treatment of the mythological figures of water goddesses and dragon women.*]

It was Li Ho who took it upon himself to oppose the tendency to secularize the water goddesses and to humanize the dragon women of antiquity.

Because Li Ho is now at last in vogue, it would be pointless here to recapitulate the meager details of his biography, to refine appreciations of his writings, or even to attempt a superficial survey of his poetic work. Efforts at achieving all of these aims have already appeared in many languages. Rather I shall concentrate on only one aspect of his genius, which has so recently come to be appreciated after the neglect, misunderstanding, or obloquy of centuries of critics who were blind equally to his love of ancient goddesses and to his gift for exploiting the rich resources of his language. The dour and puritanical judges of the post-Sung era interpreted and dismissed both subject and treatment as mere frivolity.

Li Ho's interest in this subject was not unrelated to his linguistic preferences. If he rejoiced in dark thoughts about divine apparitions, it was partly because these personae gave him rich opportunities to indulge his preferences for particular color words. He liked those related to the blue-green part of the spectrum, and also white, the color of metal, of death, of specters, of stark dreamworlds. It is curious that the climax of his preoccupation with the divine world came during the last year of his life, during and after his return to his home from the capital—a time when, renewing the *Ch'u tz'u* tradition, he wrote his poems **"Hsiang Consort," "Shaman Mountain is High,"** and **"Lady of Cowrie Palace."** This set forms a subdivision of the class of bizarre and supernatural themes that make up a large part of his surviving verse—poems full of bogles, shamankas, haunted animals, enchantments, nightmares, and frightful atmospheres. Long after his death it was usual for critics to write of his "talent for specters." Accordingly, he loved the ancient poems of Ch'u and the divine water women that inhabited them.

The shamanistic tone of much of his work, evident both in his goddess poems and in those plainly labeled as shaman songs (for instance, the pair of "Divine Strings" poems) is due not only to Li Ho's love of the *Ch'u tz'u,* but to the influence on him of the old *yüeh fu* songs, particularly those made in the Wu area during the early part of the Six Dynasties period. But it seems almost ludicrous to speak of "influence" on Li Ho. These same ancient songs "influenced" other T'ang poets. But there is a wide difference between, on the one hand, borrowing classical themes as good, reliable stereotypes or capturing brilliant images to convert to one's secondary purposes, and, on the other hand, taking a personally treasured image and renovating it completely—making it blossom, as it were, for the first time. What Shakespeare did to Italian stories is what Li Ho did to the shaman songs. Although his poems drew on the past, he was the opposite of an imitator—he was a highly original creator. If he resorted to the linguistic imagery of those old poems, he did not fail to reorchestrate them and so to transform them into something entirely his own. Compare Brahms, "Variations on a Theme by Haydn." There is nothing pedantic, familiar, or "archaistic" about his re-creations.

Indeed, some of Li Ho's water women have no obvious classical antecedents; they are as fresh as if born yesterday. They are Li Ho's own artifacts, suggested perhaps by

a phrase in one of the old rhapsodies. These new evocations carry an almost overwhelming conviction of the reality of the divine beings they describe. These are no conventional deities, nor are they usually flattering masks for popular courtesans, as in the manner of so many of his contemporaries. They are truly strange, inhuman, and—except for Li Ho's talent—ineffable. The poet somehow manages to express their remoteness from all normal experience. In a sense, he is himself a possessed shaman, describing his vision of a unique supernatural protectress. His language is not the hysterical chant of a shaman, however, but elegantly phrased in the most difficult and fantastic imagery. At the same time, he reveals himself as the mortal lover of an immortal being, who is ultimately unattainable. He was trying passionately to revivify and actualize a dream of beauty and to demonstrate his devotion to a quasi-religious ideal—an ambition quite out of step with the literary life of his times, when the ancient goddesses could only be fossilized relics or trite topics for the amorously inclined. Li Ho at least could breathe life into their faded figures—an unparalleled achievement for a Chinese mythographer. Li Ho was, on a particularly magnificient scale, in the class of the "enamored" bards of Turkey, who put their mystical visions of beloved women, whom they sought delightly in the real world, to words and music. These poets followed an ancient shamanistic tradition in using a syllabic kind of verse, ignoring the quantitative rules followed by the Ottoman court poets. But they were closer to folk poetry than Li Ho was to the popular poets who stood behind the *yüeh fu.*

I am compelled to disagree in part with Professor Hawkes who, while acknowledging the brilliance of Li Ho's semi-erotic fantasies, takes pains to state that the poet did not "believe" in the divine figures he evoked [David Hawkes, "The Supernatural in Chinese Poetry," *The Far East: China and Japan,* 1961]. He must, in my view, have believed in them in some sense in order to infuse such vivid life in them. While adhering to the opinion that a good poet is primarily a linguistic craftsman—a creator of word artifacts—I cannot help finding something of the magician and the priest in Li Ho. I am convinced that he believed in the ultimate reality of his own re-creations: for him, in *some* magic world, the goddesses existed.

Li Ho seems to have been entranced with the sounds of words more than most of his better-known contemporaries. It is not my intention here to analyze this aspect of his poetry in any detail, but simply to take note of a fact that needs much more study. Because Professor Pulleyblanks has elucidated them for us, we can now hear the rhymes of Li Ho's verses much as men of the ninth century heard them, without having them filtered through the early seventh-century phonology reconstructed by Professor Karlgren. However, I suspect that Li Ho may sometimes have adhered to rhyme tables that represented speech already out of use in his own times. For instance, although the rhymes of **"The Departure Song of the Divine Strings"** are clear only in terms of Pulleyblank's ninth-century reconstructions, the rhymes of **"The Song of God's Child"** follow *Ch'ieh yün* categories exactly [E. G. Pulleyblank, "The Rhyming Categories of Li Ho (791–817)," *The Tsing*

Hua Journal of Chinese Studies, August 1968]. Pulley-blank's labors also help to vivify imitative effects, such as the ringing metallic sonorities of **"Lady of Cowrie Palace"** in the second and fourth positions (immediately before the caesura) and in **"The Departure Song of the Divine Strings"** before the caesura.

Possibly the best resumé—admittedly an impressionistic one—of the power of Li Ho's words is an encomium attributed to his older friend, Han Yü:

> The unbroken filiations of clouds and smoke are not up to their manner;
> The profound remoteness of the waters is not up to their passion;
> The brim-fullness of spring is not up to their harmonies;
> The clear purity of autumn is not up to their style;
> A mast in the wind or a horse in battle line is not up to their boldness;
> Tile and coffin, seal and cauldron are not up to their antiquity;
> Flowers in season and beautiful women are not up to their color;
> Wasted nations, ruined basilicas, thorns and brush, hillocks and dunes are not up to their indignation, their animosity, their sorrow, and their misery;
> The sucking of the whale, the leaping of the giant turtle, the ox demon, the snake god are not up to their desolation, their wildness, their distortions and their illusions. . . .

But it is time to turn directly to some of these poems.

Li Ho could hardly have neglected the most powerful and persistent of the ancient river goddesses, the goddess of the Hsiang, whose sway also extended up and down the Yangtze for an indeterminate distance. She was also sometimes identified, as in a prose story . . . , with the venerable goddess of the Lo, and with the goddess of Wu shan. So much has already become clear: she had become the mistress of all of the waters of Central China. Like many of his poems, Li Ho's **"Hsiang Consort"** is knotty, intricate, and almost untranslatable because of its complex allusions and uncompromising reliance on metaphor. A commentary is essential. But first the basic poem:

> Spotted bamboo of a thousand years—aging but undying.
> Long companying the houri of Ch'in—a canopy on Hsiang Water.
> The incantations and provocations of the maids of the Man fill the chilly void.
> The Nine Mountains—unmoving green; the tear flowers—red.
>
> A parted simurgh, a separated phoenix, she—deep in misty Ts'ang-wu.
> Like cloud of Wu and rain of Shu—communion achieved from afar.
> While dark and dismal the autumn breath ascends the blue-green sweetgums

> In cool night—among the waves—she enchants that ancient dragon.

And now a short explication:

> Since the death of Shun, the tear-spotted bamboos have survived the centuries.
> The bamboos, like the spirit of the goddess ("houri of Ch'in"), have long hovered over the river.
> The aboriginal ("Man") shamankas still mourn for Shun; they try to lure him back with their spells.
> "The Nine Mountains" are the supposed burial place of Shun, carpeted with evergreen vegetation, spotted by the goddess's tears.
>
> The goddess is a divine bird, parted from her mate in the humid forests of subtropical Ts'ang-wu.
> "Cloud of Wu" is the mist goddess of Wu shan; "Rain of Shu" is the impregnating spirit of her lover, the king of Ch'u, come from afar to join her. They are here identified with the Hsiang goddess and her lover Shun.
> Even the breath of autumn—cold, sad, and deadly—forces the sap up into the liquidambar trees which symbolize the divine king.
> In the river the bull alligator—king, rain summoner, ancient dragon—is invigorated by the chant of the shamanka who impersonates the goddess mistress. Compare with *ku lung* "ancient dragon" as a phonetic transcription of Cambodian *kurung* "king."

In another poem, **"Song of God's Child,"** Li Ho has celebrated the goddess of the Hsiang under the alternate title given her in the "Nine Songs." The reader will also recognize allusions to Wang Po's famous ode on the gallery of the Prince of T'eng, both in the use of the term *ti tzu* "god's child" and in the reference in both to the old *yüeh fu* "Young Gentleman of the White Rock":

> The Gentleman of White Rock dwells by the Kiang,
> Guided before by the Sire of the Kiang, followed behind by fishes.

"Dwells by the Kiang" (which could just as well be "dwells overlooking the Kiang") becomes "looked out on a holm in the Kiang" in Wang Po's masterpiece; in Li Ho's transmutation, the phrase is merely suggested by the reference to the mysterious esquire. But beyond the classical allusions, the poem teems with ghostly lights, alarming cries, and supernatural vapors. It goes like this:

> God's Child from Tung-t'ing—a thousand miles.
> Cool winds, a wild-goose cry—sky lies on water.
> Nine-jointed sweet flags die on the stones.
> The Hsiang Deity strums a zither—invites God's Child.
>
> In aged cinnamons on the hill's crest old aromatics alter.
> A woman dragon chants plaintively—cold water lights up.

The fish run by sandy reach: it is the Gentleman of
  White Rock!
Lazily he takes a true pearl—hurls it into the
  dragon hall.

In this complicated poem the goddless calls to her counterpart, a river god (under the old name of Young Gentleman of White Rock), possibly represented by a shaman.
Here is a line-by-line commentary:

The Hsiang goddess can fly out a thousand miles
  from her headquarters in Lake Tung-t'ing.
The call of a goose in the cool autumn air passes
  over the sky-reflecting lake: she is in flight!
Wild plants shrivel on lakeside stones at the touch
  of the cold divine presence.
Her sister calls to her with the sound of music. Or
  is it a male deity?

Cinnamon wood matures—the sacred odor of the
  southland.
The dragon lady is the goddess in her serpentine
  form—she calls for her mate.
He appears as a mysterious figure from a folk
  poem,
But he is contemptuous: a dragon pearl is his for
  the asking, but he tosses it back.

This fantasy is a translation into medieval terms of the
mood of the old shaman poems of the "Nine Songs," in
which the pleading shaman is left hopeless. But here Li
Ho reverses the roles of lover and beloved. The white
rock man is the alter ego of Shun: unexpectedly he disdains
the divine pearl—his ages-old dragon wife.

It is necessary to mention in passing a poem in which Li Ho
alludes not to one, but to many supernatural figures, among
whom are the Hsiang Consort, in her inflated guise as "houri
of the Kiang," and Nü Kua. Both, cloaked in appropriate
imagery, appear in his paean to the famous harper Li P'ing,
whose music had power over the worlds of men and gods
alike. Although the poem celebrates primarily the magical
talent of a virtuoso musician—and Li Ho was fascinated by
music—it is laden with images characteristic of his goddess
poems—cold, white, metallic, draconic, and watery. In
these verses there is the full diapason: autumn, towering
clouds, the White-silk Woman (another goddess), jade,
lotus, dew, "cool light," stars, Nü Kua's stones, rain, krak-
ens, moon, dampness. A typical line describes the cumu-
lus clouds frozen in place by the divine energy of the harp
strings:

The void is white with clotted clouds, sprawled and
  driftless.

But here now is an attempt to put a poem devoted to a
single goddess, the **"Lady of Cowrie Palace,"** into English. Ultimately it is a hopeless task, because the T'ang
original rings with metallic sounds that cannot be transferred to English from Chinese. The multiple allusions and
double images, too, can only be hinted at. Some European

cognates may serve as a fanfare or eye-opening prelude to Li
Ho's presentation of the aqueous domain and palatial residence of an immortal queen, both more icy and free of passion than the Snow Queen of Hans Christian Andersen and
her frosty palace. Li Ho conjures up a vivid picture of a
frozen, immobile, ageless, silvery, petrified, static, metallic,
crystalline being. The goddess is deathless; she fears no change
nor corruption—and can share nothing with a mortal creature. There are intimations of the mineral immortality of such
a creature in our own literary heritage. Erasmus Darwin, for
instance, the bard of triumphant science, wrote of her:

Call from her crystal cave the Naiad Nymph,
Who hides her fine form in the passing lymph.

But this nymph is an artificial nymph—a nymph of the
head, not of the heart. Then there is the nymph of the soul
and religious fantasy, not unknown to William Blake:

But silken nets and traps of adamant with Oothoon
  spread,
And catch for thee girls of mild silver, or of furious
  gold. ["Visions of the Daughters of Albion"]

Others of the breed would not have astonished Li Ho,
however. One such is the unlucky heroine of the fairy
story "Undine," written by Friedrich Baron de la Motte-
Fouqué. . . . Just so was the shelly palace of the god of
the Yellow River, the crystalline habitat of the Chinese
ondines—cold, beautiful, ophidian nixies.

These frigid creatures have a long and lively history in
Chinese literature. Sometimes they resemble the adaman-
tine fairies and silvery sylphs of Taoist mythology, "whose
flesh and skin resemble ice and snow"; sometimes they are
like the "jade women" of Li Po's vision of T'ai shan, the
sacred mountain. Above all, the elegant Ch'an monk, Kuan-
hsiu, who illuminated the court of Shu in the tenth century,
was conscious of the mineral nature of transcendent beings
such as these: "The entities which populate this dreamland
are realized stalactites, coagulated salts, or gems crystallized out of the primordial magma." (The words are my
own, commenting on Kuan-hsiu's remarkable paradise poems.) But despite these very respectable antecedents and
analogues, no goddess of jade was ever realized so brilliantly as Li Ho's **"Lady of Cowrie Palace."** It is a poem
of a kind rare not only in Chinese literature, but in world
literature:

Clink! clink! the Lake Woman toys with metal
  bangles.
A birdlike headpiece—cocked tail, folded wings.
In her six palaces there is no speech—all life is
  leisure.
High hangs a silver plate, reflecting blue hills.

Long eyebrows of frozen green—how many thousand
  years?
Pure and cool, indifferent to age—though a simurgh
  in her mirror.
Her autumn skin hardly feels the cold of a jade
  dress.

The light of the void is fast and firm—water like
   sky.

This deserves some interpretation:

> The goddess has nothing to do but to finger her
> jewelry, unchangeable metal like herself.
> Her headdress is a bird of metal, like the crown of a
> medieval princess. (This line echoes the description
> of the headdress of Yang Kuei-fei as described in
> Po Chü-i's *Ch'ang hen ko*: "halcyon-blue tail
> cocked—a golden bird.")
> Even palace gossip does not exist—everything was
> said eons ago.
> A fairy reflector of metal shows the blue hills of
> mutable earth, here transformed into a static,
> impalpable scene.

> The goddess herself is immortal—her green eye
> makeup needs no changing.
> Unlike the vain simurgh who, watching its aging
> figure in a mirror (metal!) trembles with fear, the
> goddess, contemplating herself, is unmoved.
> (Simurgh is a Persian word naturalized in English.
> I use it as an equivalent of the fantastic Chinese
> *luan*—"phoenix" having been preempted for *feng*. I
> am pleased that Frodsham has adopted it in his
> translation of this poem [*The Poems of Li Ho
> (791–817)*].)

> "Autumn" regularly connotes "white" and "cool"—
> and even "death," the changeless state. Her
> costume is not only jadelike in color and beauty,
> but is as rigid and cold as jade—and like ice and
> glass.
> Her sky yields a fixed and unchanging light—it is
> the deep blue of the watery abyss.

There appears to be at least one important exception to Li
Ho's seeming aversion to the common ninth-century practice of disguising courtesans, singing girls, mistresses, and
court beauties as once popular goddesses who had fallen
into neglect in upper-class religion. This is the poem titled
"True Pearl—Belle of the Lo." Inspecting the poem itself, it seems hard to avoid agreeing with the conclusion
of Arai Ken, the Japanese Li Ho specialist, that this lovely
pearl, like the moon maidens of Li Shang-yin, was an
actual beauty of Lo-yang. This decision is arrived at with
some reluctance, in view of the fact that the great *T'u shu
chi ch'eng* anthology lists the poem under the rubric of
water goddesses. It begins with a pearl maiden flying down
to Lo-yang out of the blue sky. She wears a bird-shaped
crown, like the Lady of Cowrie Palace, and she dreams of
her mountain in Szechwan, like the Wu shan goddess. She
is a simurgh and a phoenix—indeed she has all of the
attributes of a river fairy. But in the last four quatrains she
is compared with the light ladies of Lo-yang—to their
disadvantage. Is, then, a particular woman concealed here,
or is Li Ho telling us that no mortal woman can compare
with the divine creature of his linguistic epiphanies? In
any case, his courtesan, if such she is, appears in supernatural guise. She is adorable—but strange and aloof, like
a creature out of an ancient myth.

Kuo-Ch'ing Tu (essay date 1979)

SOURCE: "Li Ho's *Kuei-ts'ai*: An Evaluation of His
Poetic Genius," in *Li Ho*, Twayne Publishers, 1979, pp.
121–31.

[*In the excerpt below, Kuo-Ch'ing Tu surveys the characteristic features of Li Ho's poetry.*]

[Li Ho's] poetic characteristics can be generalized as
follows:

1) Li Ho's poetic worlds have three dimensions: the celestial world of immortals or divine spirits, the shadowy world
of the dead, and the human world of reality. As a matter
of fact, Li Ho lived an unhappy life of thwarted ambitions
and constant frustration, and many of his works are strongly
tinged with his sufferings at the hard hands of fate or his
resentment against social injustice, although many of his
poems express purely aesthetic experience. As the modern
critic Hung Wei-fa, author of Li Ho's chronological biography, has aptly remarked, "Li Ho was much afraid of
death, yet frequently referred to death because he could
not resign himself to it." On the other hand, "He was tired
of and averse to the bitterness of this world; therefore he
often fancied Heaven as well." However, it seems to me
that even his poems about Heaven and graves have at
heart a this-wordly attitude. In his poems about immortals,
even as his mind soars into Heaven, he often looks down
upon this world; therefore, his celestial poems are different from ordinary roaming-with-immortals poems (*Yu-hsien
shih*), which describe the wandering of a poet's mind in
supernatural realms where, frolicking with immortals, it
forgets all wordly affairs. The surrealistic worlds of Li
Ho's poetry often betray the poet's anguish of despair and
his dissatisfaction with this world. When despair and dissatisfaction have reached the extreme, they tend to bring
about a mental explosion which threatens to involve the
entire universe in the poet's ruin. In this sense, some of Li
Ho's poetry can certainly be seen to produce a pathos of
cosmic proportions.

2) With regard to the art of expression, Li Ho completely rejects the seven-syllable regulated verse, a poetic form
flourishing at that time. Most of his poems are written in
the style of *yüeh-fu* and Ancient Verse: lines are irregular, rhymes are changed frequently, and rhyme words in
oblique tones are preferred. As a result, variety in the
musical flow is increased and the surprising effect of the
images is enhanced. It is this kind of free verse that
serves most properly to express the poet's profound feelings and sensitive impressions. Li Ho's poetry abounds
in sensuous experiences and visual images, and at the
same time possesses very strong musical qualities. The
fact that many of Li Ho's *yüeh-fu* poems were sung to
the accompaniment of wind and string instruments by
musicians should not be disregarded. In addition, Li Ho's
poetic styles have both simple and obscure aspects, just
as his poetic worlds have bright and dark dimensions.
The obscurity of his poetry does not so much derive
from elaboration in diction or syntax as from his extraordinary associations and from the inner logic of his origi-

nal ideas. If the reader has an insight into this inner logic, he will appreciate that Li Ho's poetry, in most cases, is consistent in development and well organized in terms of putting the best words in the best order.

3) From an aesthetic point of view, the intrinsic nature of Li Ho's poetry can be summed up in four words: *yu* (dark), *ming* (bright), *ch'i* (startling or extraordinary), and *li* (colorful or splendid). *Yu* and *ming* refer to Li Ho's poetic worlds, which are symbolized by his own line:

> The sputtering taper laughs in the night,
>   congealing the dark and the light.

The poet's life resembles a lingering taper burning out its orchid oil and flickering with a dark and bright flame. Like the poet struggling with adversity, the taper sputters in the night, now and then bursting into tears and laughter, sometimes remaining still as if trying to congeal the dark and the light. In Chinese, *yu-ming* as a compound also means the human world and the nether world. Just as the taper flickering in the night simultaneously casts light and shadow, so the poet's mind projects contrasting feelings—feelings of day and night, joy and anger, life and death.

On the other hand, *ch'i* and *li* refer to Li Ho's use of language, which can be typically interpreted by such a line as: "The pen complements creation: Heaven has no merit." Li Ho's images often take people by surprise; his rhymes are abrupt and full of changes, his diction is colorful and strongly emotive, his language is sometimes very elaborate. All of these features are the marvelous work of his creative pen, which strives to perfect nature's creation, to startle Heaven and the gods by depriving them of credit, or even to make jealous demons cry over its exquisite workmanship. . . .

These four characteristic features of Li Ho's poetry seem to me to be essentially derived from the intrinsic nature of his genius: *kuei*. After the Sung dynasty, Li Ho was dubbed a *kuei-ts'ai,* a genius of *kuei*. The word *"kuei"* in Chinese has two basic meanings: 1) as a noun referring to a ghost, a departed spirit, as in *kuei-hun* (disembodied spirits); 2) as an adjective meaning "clever," "crafty," or "artful" as in *kuei-fu shen-kung* (extremely skillful workmanship). Accordingly, *kuei-ts'ai* as a description of Li Ho's poetic genius has two major implications: Li Ho was a poet who was fond of describing "ghostly" scenes or the world of the dead, and many of his poems do evoke "ghostly" feelings in the reader's mind; and he possessed an almost demonic genius, which enabled him to write wonderful poems so skillful in the use of language and so surprising in the poetic worlds explored that he might have been a devil himself or at least as clever as a devil.

Wada Toshio in his article about Li Ho's kuei poetry and its formation is in basic agreement with these ideas, although he summarizes Li Ho's usage of the word *kuei* in four ways: 1) referring to the dead or a departed spirit, as in "In an autumn graveyard, ghosts chant Pao Chao's poems" (*Ch'iu fen kuei ch'ang Pao chia shih*); 2) refer-

---

Kuo-Ch'ing Tu on Li Ho's imagery:

In the poetic sky of the T'ang dynasty, Li Ho's poetry sometimes glitters with a carefree combination of synaesthetic images that have puzzled many critics; sometimes it glimmers ghostlike in the wind and rain, making the blood run cold; sometimes it sparkles distantly like an eternal jewel against the darkness of the past; sometimes it glistens like morning dewdrops on the leaves, delicate and dazzling, pleasing to the aesthetic eye; and sometimes it reflects the realities of this earth, exposing life's seamy underside and casting a clear light on human ugliness and greed.

Kuo-Ch'ing Tu, from "Light and Shadows: His Worlds, in Li Ho, *Twayne Publishers, 1979, p. 83.*

---

ring to a phenomenon which occurs in connection with the dead, as in "Ghostly rain sprinkles the empty grass" (*Kuei yü sa k'ung ts'ao*); 3) referring to the gods of common belief, as in "Sea gods and mountain spirits come to sit in seats" (*Hai shen shan kuei lai tso chung*); 4) As an adjective describing exquisite, almost inhumanly perfect workmanship, e.g., "On the thousand-year-old stone bench, devil weavers cry" (*Ch'ien sui shih ch'uang t'i kuei kung*). Wada considers the second usage (descriptive of ghostly phenomena) to be a subordination of the first (references to the dead or departed spirits), and the fourth usage (inhuman perfection) to be irrelevant to *kuei* poetry as practised by Li Ho. Therefore, he concludes that "in the final analysis what is expressed by the word '*kuei*' in Li Ho's usage is of two kinds only: the first and the third," It seems to me, however, that such a conclusion is not justified. Rather, it is the third category (references to gods) that is an elaboration of the first (references to the dead). The divine and evil spirits of common religious belief are, in many cases, transformed from disembodied spirits of human beings or animals, gods and ghosts inhabiting a common world of fantasy and imagination.

The second category (descriptive of ghostly phenomena), on the other hand, is quite different from the first and perhaps better than the other classifications exemplifies the mysterious *kuei* quality of Li Ho's poetry. In Wada's second usage, *kuei* often serves to establish a mood of gloom or eeriness that has captivated readers for centuries. In the first usage (references to the dead), there is no common effect on the reader from the specific terms. Just as in the West various ghosts have an individual character, some being mischievous, some sorrowful, some glorious (poltergeists, the ghost of Hamlet's father, and the headless horseman), a specific *kuei* may or may not conjure up an effect of "ghostliness." So, it is the ghostly mood or sense of eeriness (Wada's second category) that a poem suggests rather than the specific subject matter it describes that impresses the mind of Li Ho's reader. Far from being a mere elaboration, the second usage of the term indicates the essential quality of his poetic world, just as the fourth usage (inhuman perfection) rather than being irrelevants is characteristic of his poetic language.

Such being the case, I believe that Li Ho has been branded a *kuei-ts'ai* for two reasons: because of the consciously ghostly and eerie atmosphere of his poems and because of their suprisingly ingenious qualities. Generally speaking, *kuei-shih* strongly appeals to the senses rather than the intellect; it is more emotive than rational. Therefore, sensuous experiences and elaborate expressions result in a passionate and resplendent style—dazzlingly beautiful words strongly appealing to the senses. For, if words are not beauteous and colorful, they cannot express the poet's feelings strongly enough to satisfy his own aesthetic instinct; if words do not strongly appeal to the senses, they probably cannot conceal the poet's inner uneasiness or cover up the bleakness of his mind. Li Ho often uses sensuous or emotive adjectives to modify colors, such as "aged red" (*lao-hung*) or "crumbling green" (*t'ui-lü*), and thus suggests a gloomy, grievous feeling against ostensibly colorful diction, achieving a ghostly or doleful atmosphere in his poetic lines. Li Ho's *kuei-shih* are, substantially as P'an Te-yü (1785–1839) has stated, "all written with extremely colorful words, about extremely gloomy scenes; as when in a short story, a woman ghost in red makeup and dress appears among ancient palaces and desolate gardens and sends a chill through the reader's frame; if he reads under a single lamp at night, his hair will stand on end."

As a kuei-ts'ai, Li Ho has been often mentioned together with Li Po, the poet-immortal (*shih-hsien*), and Tu Fu, the poet-sage (*shih-sheng*). I think these three T'ang poets represent three different poetic worlds: the nether, the celestial, and the terrestrial, respectively. . . .

Li Ho's world is pleasure-seeking, hedonistic, but ends on a somewhat gloomy note. It strongly appeals to sensuousness; all the senses, visual, auditory, olfactory, tactile, and gustatory, play in concert in this poem. It seems that only through his senses is the poet able to grasp the world, that only through sensuous stimulations is he able to enjoy life to his heart's content, to forget human sufferings even if only temporarily, and to escape from the relentless plunder of time. His eyes look downward to the grave. Even at the height of enjoyment, he never fails to remind himself of the end of all pleasures, because he knows well that time is constantly extorting life from humankind and the world; both are destined to come to an end. This poem shows that the poet, however hard he tries to enjoy life, is always oppressed by the passage of time and haunted by the shadow of death.

In terms of the breadth and variety of poetic worlds explored, Li Ho's poetry cannot compare with Li Po's or Tu Fu's, for he has left behind only two hundred and forty-two poems, while to Li Po and Tu Fu 1,004 and 1,455 poems are attributed respectively. As Suzuki Torao maintains, Li Ho is only an illustrious poet (*ming-chia*) rather than a great master (*ta-chia*). A *ta-chia* demonstrates versatility in varied accomplishments: many-sided subject matter, wide-ranging poetic worlds, and diverse forms; an adept not only in quantity but also in the quality of poetry, not only in the worlds originally explored but also in the use of language successfully explored. A *ming-chia* excels other poets in his speciality. Li Ho is best known for his *kuei* poetry which is full of ghostly atmosphere and startling images. Although he can hardly be recognized as a great master, Li Ho's position in the history of Chinese literature is unique and beyond question.

In the past several decades Li Ho has been compared to or mentioned together with many Western poets and considered, as the modern poet-critic Yü Kuang-chung puts it [in "To the White Jade Palace: A Critical Study of Li Ho," in *Tamkang Journal,* No. 7, 1968], an "unintended precursor" of many Western literary "isms." Professor David Ch'en [in "Li Ho and Keats; Poverty, Illness, Frustration, and a Poetic Career," in *Tsing Hua Journal of Chinese Studies* ns V, No. 1, 1965] has also likened his life to John Keats's (1795–1821) in its "poverty, illness, frustration," causing these two poets to be "congenial in spirit and similar in style," because "the essential and common experience of life of the two poets is suffering, and suffering in a devoted and persistent poetic career has refined their works into a poetry of intensity." According to A. C. Graham [in *Poems of the Late T'ang,* 1968] Li Ho reminds many Western readers of Baudelaire or a nineteenth-century Satanist, because of "his apparently familiar constellation of pessimism, voluptuousness, aestheticism, and an imagination haunted by dark force." It has also been pointed out [by William C. Golightly] that Li Ho's imagery is Surrealistic, because it is congruent with the "classifications of Surrealistic, images" developed by André Breton (1896–1966), especially the image which "possesses the character of a hallucination." and "implies the negation of some elementary physical property." Thus he is further seen to be a Surrealist because he was "able to organize heterogeneous images into a homogeneous mood with a way of imagination which Shakespeare calls 'fine frenzy'" [Yü Kuang-chung]. By the same token, he is taken to be an Imagist because "of the six credos of Imagism, Li Ho anticipated all except the one that insists on the use of daily speech." Moreover, many Chinese scholars consider him an aesthete because his poetry aims only at "beauty" and is richly stored with "sheer silk and perfume," "romantic moods and sensuous feelings" as well as "beauteous words and sonorous rhymes"; in short, because he "tried to build a palace of art in this human world." In addition, Li Ho is seen to "have a prophetic place in the niche of Symbolism. For we find in Li Ho two remarkable traits of the school: suggestiveness and fusion of sense experiences" [Yü Kuang-chung].

Thus, Li Ho proves to be a most interesting subject for the comparative study of Chinese and Western literatures. The fact that Li Ho's poetry can give rise to such different interpretations reflects the multifaceted nature of his poetry. Although there is some truth in each comparison mentioned above, these are no more than impressionistic comments, none being based on a comprehensive and thorough study of the poets compared or the theories adduced. Strictly speaking, an extensive and detailed study of Li Ho in comparison with various Western poets or in terms of modern Western literary theory still remains to be done.

FURTHER READING

Biography

South, Margaret Tudor. *Li Ho: a Scholar-official of the Yüan-ho Period (806–821)* Adelaide: Libraries Board of South Australia, 1967, 495 p.

    An examination of Li Ho's life and works.

Criticism

Chow, Clayton. Review of *The Poems of Li Ho 791–817,* translated by J. D. Frodsham. *The Journal of Asian Studies* XXX, No. 1 (November 1970): 431–32.

    Favorable assessment of Frodsham's translation, observing that Li Ho "proves himself to be one of the rare poets who can pass relatively unscathed through the fires of translation."

Fish, Michael B. "Yang Kuei-Fei as the Hsi Wang Mu: Secondary Narrative in Two T'ang Poems." *Monumenta Serica* XXXII (1976): 337–54.

    Reads Li Ho's "Jasper Flower Music" as a retelling of the legendary romance between the Queen Mother of the West (Hsi Wang Mu) and Emperor Mu (Mu T'ien-tzu).

Amy Lowell
1874–1925

American poet, critic, biographer, and essayist.

INTRODUCTION

The leading proponent of Imagism in American poetry, Lowell is remembered for her forceful theorizing on poetics, her eccentric, outspoken personality, and her iconoclastic approach to poetic form. Her experimentation led her to create what she called polyphonic prose, a form similar to free verse that employs intermittent rhyme, changing points of view, and the repetition of images or ideas. Although she was Ezra Pound's successor as chief advocate of Imagism—a movement that stressed clarity and succinctness in presenting the poetic image—Lowell is herself generally categorized as a minor, though versatile, poet, whose work displays occasional bursts of brilliance. Influenced in both style and theme by her studies of Far Eastern verse, she also sought to liberate poetry from the strictures of meter, using as her vehicles free verse, polyphonic prose, and haiku in such volumes as *Sword Blades and Poppy Seed, Pictures of the Floating World*, and *What's O'Clock*. This last volume, containing the best of Lowell's late work, was posthumously published and awarded the Pulitzer Prize in poetry in 1926.

Biographical Information

Lowell was born of a distinguished New England family whose wealth and position provided her with opportunities for a good education and travel in Europe. In later years, the proper, conservative values Lowell acquired in her youth clashed with her naturally independent and domineering personality, creating an unresolved conflict that is reflected in her life and work. In her late twenties Lowell decided to become a poet, and during the next few years she used her wealth, industry, and intimidating personality to accomplish that end. Her first volume (except for an early vanity press publication) appeared in 1912. *A Dome of Many-Coloured Glass* is conventional and undistinguished, exhibiting nothing of the experimental form that characterizes Lowell's later volumes. In 1913 she met Pound and immediately embraced Imagism, a style applied successfully in her next collection, *Sword Blades and Poppy Seed*. With this widely acclaimed work, Lowell moved to the forefront of American poetry, a position from which she lent support to other writers, among them D. H. Lawrence. During the next decade, she wrote several books of criticism and over six hundred poems, edited three Imagist anthologies, and became a popular speaker at American universities. Accompanying Lowell during her last years was Ada Russell, a former actress who became Lowell's secretary, close friend and inspiration for several love poems. Lowell died in 1925, shortly after completing her *John Keats*, a biography of the poet whom she saw as her greatest influence.

Major Works

While *A Dome of Many-Coloured Glass* was the first published of her serious poetry, Lowell's adoption of the Imagist precepts in 1913 marks a dramatic change from the conventional poetry of this early volume. *Sword Blades and Poppy Seed* is characteristic of this new poetry, which abounds in sensuous imagery, a precise economy of words, and a delight in texture and color. The collection also represents Lowell's first experiments with polyphonic prose, a form that she used to its greatest effect in the dramatic monologues in rustic New England vernacular of *Men, Women and Ghosts* and the historical narratives of *Can Grande's Castle*. The former work contains "Patterns"—a dramatic monologue that examines the clash between duty and desire—which is considered one of Lowell's most important poem. In the latter, the theme of civilization at war, exemplified in the acclaimed "Bronze Horses," predominates. Lowell's interest in Asian literature is evident throughout her canon, reaching its height in the "Lacquer Prints" of *Pictures of the Floating World* and in the interpolated Chinese poetry of *Fir-Flower Tablets,* written with the aid of translator Florence Ayscough. In *Legends,* she returns to the mythical-historical vein of

Can Grande's Castle by exploring the poetic possibilities of folklore, while *A Critical Fable,* which was published anonymously in 1922, is Lowell's satirical look at twenty-one poets: herself and twenty of her contemporaries. The poetry of *What's O'Clock, East Wind,* and *Ballads for Sale,* although uneven in places, contains some of her most accomplished lyrics. Among Lowell's critical works, poetry is the dominant concern. *Six French Poets* introduced American audiences to the chief post-symbolist artists. *Tendencies in Modern American Poetry* is, likewise, less a critical study than an introduction to a larger public of several American poets, including the Imagists H. D. and John Gould Fletcher. Her biography *John Keats* is valued as a landmark work for its wealth of previously unpublished material gathered from Lowell's private collection on the Romantic poet.

Critical Reception

Overall, the reaction to Lowell's poetry has been decidedly mixed. Many of her works, including *Sword Blades and Poppy Seed, Can Grande's Castle,* and *What's O'Clock,* met with great success upon publication, but this acclaim soon faded. In addition, Lowell's works have consistently elicited negative responses from several critics, who have seen her poetry as lacking in depth, originality, and genuineness. Others have admired her range and technical skill, but have continued to see her work as superficial. In 1975 Glenn Richard Ruihley pushed for a reconsideration of her work that emphasizes the significance of her poetic voice; still, while contemporary commentators have acknowledged her importance as the innovator of polyphonic prose and as a spokesperson for the Imagist movement, most limit her lasting contribution to a handful of poems.

PRINCIPAL WORKS

Poetry

Dream Drops: or, Stories from Fairy Land, by a Dreamer
  1887
A Dome of Many-Coloured Glass 1912
Sword Blades and Poppy Seed 1914
Men, Women and Ghosts 1916
Can Grande's Castle 1918
Pictures of the Floating World 1919
Fir-Flower Tablets 1921
Legends 1921
A Critical Fable 1922
What's O'Clock 1925
East Wind 1926
Ballads for Sale 1927
Fool o' the Moon 1927

Other Major Works

Six French Poets (criticism) 1915
Tendencies in Modern American Poetry (criticism) 1917
John Keats (biography) 1925

Poetry and Poets (essays) 1930

CRITICISM

The Literary Spotlight (essay date 1924)

SOURCE: "Amy Lowell," in *The Literary Spotlight,* edited by John Farrar, George H. Doran Company, 1924, pp. 51–64.

[*In the following essay, the anonymous critic studies Lowell's works, focusing on the themes characteristic of her poetry.*]

Amy Lowell towers above most contemporary versifiers like a sort of nineteenth century Savonarola, exhorting them to beware the pitfalls of sin and the ways of the devil. She is the sternest of Puritans; but over her gray sense of duty she wears a multitude of jewels. She wreathes herself in flowers, exotic colors flame from her hair, and while she consigns lust to the bonfire she makes sure that both lust and the bonfire are attractively tricked out with pretty words. Probably no great woman ever so successfully concealed herself by elaborate trappings. The poetical Miss Lowell reminds me occasionally of a wholehearted and beautiful dowager who, afraid that her own person will fail to charm, hedges herself about with silks and satins, perfumes, flowers, jewels, and clanking metals, until she seems a veritable museum of *objets d'art,* and the real woman beneath, fine and true as she is, becomes discernible only to those who are patient enough to look and to wait. The genius of Miss Lowell is based on a conflict—it is the quarrel of New England conservatism with an almost pagan love of the beautiful—and the result is, naturally enough, a firm code of denial, of duty in the strictest sense.

I do not purpose to ridicule Amy Lowell in these paragraphs, nor to belittle her literary powers. Any one so vital as she is, so tremendously active, gives broad chance for the cheap journalist and punster to indulge himself in comic regard. All her life she has been subject for such attacks; but those who have attacked her have not retired unscathed. In 1914 she was limned by *Town Topics* which said, among other vicious things: "It is reported that the Macmillans will publish a book of Miss Lowell's verses. Poor Old Boston." F.P.A., from his scornful heights of columny, parodied her again and again and even resorted to personal jibes. It was not the real poets, however, nor the real critics who bombarded her with criticism. It was the little versifiers and wits, who found the marching cadences of Miss Lowell's verses and the virile rush of her imagination easy to parody and to criticize. The firm quality of her work can be judged easily from the list of her critics. Radicals like Max Eastman attacked her, yet in 1915 W. D. Howells gave her high praise. Professor John Erskine and J. C. Squire still look askance at her, yet in

1921 even H. L. Mencken admitted grudgingly that she had "undoubted talents." Clement Shorter compared her to Dr. Johnson as the "unacknowledged head of Literary America." In 1913 Louis Untermeyer referred to her slightingly, but he has since paid her many glowing tributes. Her championship of the imagists brought down showers of controversy about her, which she weathered with little apparent effort. That she actually likes a good argument there is no doubt; but her hates are more intellectual than personal, and her raillery is most often leveled at dunderheads and dodos. She is forever sweeping out dusty minds, and her broom is more vigorous than cruel.

Miss Lowell has published six volumes of her own poetry. Two critical books, adaptations of Chinese translations and of two French operettas, critical pieces, and essays form the enormous body of her work. Before me now, in uniform size and with bright gemlike bindings, lies the complete set of her poems. After rereading them all I confess myself thoroughly humbled. There has never lived a woman poet of such range, versatility, and power. She reminds one of Byron or Browning. I am convinced that future time will find in her one of the literary giants of our time, and that, in spite of her overpowering personality, she will be known for her *poetry*. I know of only one way of phrasing my belief. She is a great poet.

Consider the poems. They range from the delicate, sometimes trite lyrics of *A Dome of Many-Coloured Glass* to the passionate virtuosity of *Can Grande's Castle* and the more closely knit dramas of *Legends*. There are pieces as fragile and as finely wrought as Italian glass. Pieces like the serene and musical **"Patience"** or **"Madonna of the Evening Flowers"** or **"White and Green"**:

> Hey! My daffodil-crowned;
> Slim and without sandals!
> As the sudden spurt of flame upon darkness
> So my eyeballs are startled with you,
> Supple-limbed youth among the fruit-trees,
> Light runner through tasselled orchards.
> You are an almond flower unsheathed,
> Leaping and flickering between the budding
>   branches.

There are pieces of atmospheric description that startle by their trueness and glow with imagery. Turn to **"Motor Lights on a Hill Road,"** or **"Before the Storm."** There is humor, even in such grim New England tragedies as those Yankee dialect poems in **"The Overgrown Pasture."** There is the perhaps more characteristic drama of **"Patterns,"** of **"The Cremona Violin,"** or **"The Cross-Roads"**; and, most important of all, Miss Lowell's imaginative grasp of historical events, her linking of them to human passion as in the epical **"Bronze Horses"** or that great portrait of Lady Hamilton, **"Sea-Blue and Blood-Red."** She sees often not one country but several, and their contrasted events of the same epoch.

Are these six books, these hundreds of poems, and the many others known to be in existence but still unpub-

lished, the unrelated effusions of a vigorous mind and a prolific pen, or are they related by some deep philosophy of life? To me Miss Lowell, in even firmer accents than Robert Frost or than Stuart Pratt Sherman, is preaching the philosophy of Puritanism and is at the same time, especially in her earlier volumes, longing to escape from it. This regard for morality, this stern preaching of duty, this conviction that moral laws infringed lead only to punishment by nature or by God, is evident in every one of her books. I do not think that she has been unaware of her doctrines; but I fancy she has not realized how much of a propagandist for them she is. In her early work she was quite unashamed. She spoke occasionally almost with the accents of Gipsy Smith or Billy Sunday. In **"Azure and Gold"** we find a trite stanza that might come almost from a Y. M. C. A. hymn book:

> Centre Stone of the Crown of the World,
>   "Sincerity" graved on your youth!
> And your eyes hold the blue-bird flash,
>   The sapphire shaft, which is truth.

Here is philosophy concealed by no Maeterlinckian gauzes. Again we have it in **"Fatigue"**:

> Dower me with strength and curb all foolish
>   eagerness—
> The law exacts obedience. Instruct, I will conform.

She doesn't particularly wish to conform, mind you; but *she will!*

Over and over in the dramatic poems the story reiterates this idea of retribution for sin or dalliance. **"The Great Adventure of Max Breuck"** has it—Max loses all that is best to him in life because he tarries a moment by the way. Paul Jannes in **"The Shadow"** is turned from the pathway of sanity by his absorption in a shadow on his wall, the image of his own desire, the image from which he cannot escape. Lady Hamilton and Nelson are victims of their passion. Their tragedy is the most moving in **"Can Grande's Castle."** In **"Guns as Keys: and the Great Gate Swings"** Admiral Perry seizes on and opens to the world the mysteries of Japan—but what will be the consequences, Miss Lowell asks:

> Occident—Orient—after fifty years.

In **"A Tale of Starvation"** the old man gives up life in his quest for the beautiful and, as he finds, the foolish. Napoleon is a figure which appeals to Miss Lowell as a symbol of lofty ambition brought low. In **"Hammers"** she paints him magnificently.

Unfaithfulness, adultery, she again and again uses as the theme for grim tragedy: in **"Pickthorn Manor,"** in **"The Cremona Violin,"** in **"Reaping,"** in **"The Ring and the Castle,"** and others. Along with this is the other motif, the longing for escape, the desire to flee from the standards that life imposes. In the early books she feels this more keenly. Twice, she compares this mood to a pathway, leading somewhere. Where? In **"The Way"** she sees

. . . spanning the river a bridge, frail promise to
    longing desire

and in **"A Coloured Print by Shokei"**—

For it must lead to a happy land,
This little path by a waterfall spanned.

Even more definitely personal she repeats this longing for
change in **"The Starling."**

I weary for desires never guessed,
For alien passions, strange imaginings,
To be some other person for a day.

In her latest volumes her philosophy of retributive justice
is thoroughly crystallized. With the exception of two pieces of purely descriptive writing, all of the verses in *Legends* are on the one theme. **"Memorandum Confided by
a Yucca to a Passion-Vine"** is the story of the fox who
was desirous of the moon, and the consequences of his
fearful quest. Says the fox:

"And I have come here to drink this poison and
   die."

"A Legend of Porcelain" is the story of expiation for
sin—

Snared by beauty, she permitted her august father's
   house to go unguarded.

"Many Swans," an Indian variant of the Prometheus story, tells how "Many Swans" desired the possession of a
gift of Heaven against which fate had warned him and
which, then, accomplished the destruction of himself and
his people.

"The thing I wanted is bad," but he had the thing
   and
   he could not part from it.

"Witch-Woman" is the bizarre story of evil love—

These kisses shot with poison,
These thoughts cutting me like red knives.

"The Ring and the Castle" is a terrifying study of insanity and murder resulting from adulterous love:

"Benjamin Bailey, Benjamin Bailey, sinners repent
   when they come to die."

"The Statue in the Garden" is not unlike **"The Shadow"** in its symbolism—a man is again absorbed in a concrete image of ideal beauty or love, and is pursued by this
image.

In the vivid and almost brutal **"Dried Marjoram,"** a mother tries to expiate her son's sin. **"Before the Storm"** is
the legend of old Peter Rugg who is trying to find his
destination through the ages—it is perhaps humorous that

the object of the search is in this case not love nor beauty—but Boston! **"Four Sides to a House"** is a story of
revenge, and of the ultimate disaster which a murdered
man brings upon his murderers. There it is! Take it for
what you will—obsession or philosophy—it is the secret
of Miss Lowell's work; and yet, though she shrinks from
seizing the object of desire, though she shows the retribution that inevitably follows, she admires those who seize
it.

There is not so much of the prude in Miss Lowell as I may
appear to think. She does not say, "Don't! Don't! Don't!"
She simply sees with terrible clarity what is likely to happen to you if you do. She cannot bring herself to believe
that happiness ever follows fulfilled desire. It is destruction to "follow your instincts." Napoleon fires her imagination. "Impudent! Audacious! But, by Jove, he blinds
the eyes!" And for John Keats, who is almost her greatest
hero, she has a wistful regard—he found beauty and seized
it, in spite of all.

Now comes a sprig little gentleman,
And turns over your manuscript with his mincing
   fingers,
And tabulates places and dates.
He says your moon was a copy-book maxim,
And talks about the spirit of solitude,
And the salvation of genius through the social
   order.
I wish you were here to damn him
With a good, round, agreeable oath, John Keats,
But just snap your fingers,
You and the moon will still love,
When he and his papers have slithered away
In the bodies of innumerable worms.

Miss Lowell's own life has been fulfilled by the most
rigorous discipline. Ever since she undertook to write
poetry, she has made its creation, its entertainment, and its
criticism her entire existence. She spends at least half her
days in one of the most beautiful private libraries in the
world—her own. Her life is organized for literature and is
arranged to meet the demands made of it by the instinct to
create! She understands *life* thoroughly; but she is afraid
of it. She has spent her whole poetical career in disciplin-
ing her emotions. It is her mind only that wanders far
afield. She has more intellectual curiosity than any other
woman I have ever known. If she were a man, she would
probably employ the best athletic trainer in the country to
keep her in shape for her greatly varied tasks, tasks which
she imposes on herself, like *The Life of John Keats*. These
tasks are exacting and worth while, and in accomplishing
them she never pauses midway. She has been known to
read hundreds of reference books to obtain the atmosphere
for one poem. If you should tell her that she could have
achieved the same effect with less use of accurate detail,
she would give you the retort courteous that a poem, to be
a poem to her, must be intellectually satisfying; that half-
truths do not satisfy her.

Although she is constantly picturing the downfall of arro-
gant power, she is herself an aristocrat of no mean posi-

tivity. While she recognizes the worth of democracy, beauty, to her, is possible only through the refinements of life. She is intolerant; but, in the main, of one thing only—stupidity. Her mind works with almost miraculous rapidity. Those who arrive at conclusions more slowly, often find themselves lost in the maze of her questioning. She occasionally forgets that conclusions reached more slowly may be quite as sound.

Her thirst for constructive thinking has made necessary her critical writings and her interest in the spread of enthusiasm for poetics. It is the same interest that prompts her to devour practically all of the new detective novels. It is the same instinct which led her to undertake the writing of a biography—which is, after all, the detection and reconstruction of a series of facts grouped around a working theory, then a proof of that theory by a proper presentation of the facts.

Her enemies—and she has many—are mostly those who resent her intolerance of intellectual sloppiness and her strong sense of moral values. She attends many banquets and her presence is often the cause of a torrent of disagreement.

What are her critical opinions of her contemporaries? You may find them in *Tendencies in Modern American Poetry* or, better still, in the anonymous *A Critical Fable,* a pamphlet written in the tradition of Miss Lowell's greatuncle's *A Fable for Critics.* In this are recorded her latest critical ideas. She denies that she wrote the screed, and for present purposes I accept the denial. Nevertheless, its dicta are from the oracle of Brookline—her sibylline accents breathe through its pages. It is thoroughly in the Amy Lowell tradition. Its author has sat before the Lowell hearth and has heard the flow of brittle wisdom that greets the crackling flames and assaults the orchids from the Lowell greenhouses. Yes—it is as much in the Lowell tradition as are the family heirlooms and the orchids.

Her imagery, careful, direct, vivid, according to the imagist creed, occasionally takes the breath away by its strangeness. She tends to choose a hard image for representing soft things. She is forever comparing people to flowers, natural objects to jewels—

> . . . and one Rubens dame,
> A peony just burst out,
> With flaunting crimson flesh.

Or

> The notes rose into the wild sun-mote
> Which slanted through the window.
> They lay like coloured beads a-row,
> They knocked together and parted,
> And started to dance . . .

Her style is varied and practically always musical. For one who has been noted for her championship of free rhythms, she is remarkably devoted to form. Even her poems which at first reading seem chaotic gain in structur-

al roundness as they are studied. She has molded her mind carefully to the pattern she desires, and it is according to this pattern that her poetry is made. Her rhythms vary from the boom and surge of polyphonic prose such as we find in the memorable close of **"The Bronze Horses"**—

> The boat draws away from the Riva. The great bronze horses mingle their outlines with the distant mountains. Dim gold, subdued green-gold, flashing faintly to the faint, bright peaks above them. Granite and metal, earth over water. Down the canal, old, beautiful horses, pride of Venice, of Constantinople, of Rome. Wars bite you with their little flames and pass away, but roses and oleanders strew their petals before your going, and you move like a constellation in a space of crimson stars.
>
> So the horses float along the canal, between barred and shuttered palaces, splendid against marble walls in the fire of the sun.

—to lilting delicacies such as the following:

> It is Chou-Kiou who paints the fighting crickets
> On the egg-shell cups;
> Who covers the Wa-Wa cups
> With little bully boys;
> Who sketches Manchu ladies, Tartar ladies,
> Chasing crimson butterflies with faint silk fans,
> On the slim teapots of young bamboo.
> Chou-Kiou,
> Bustling all day between the kilns and the
>   warehouses.
> A breath of peach-bloom silk
> Turning a pathway—
> Puff! She is gone,
> As a peach-blossom painted on paper
> Caught in a corner of the wind.

This suiting of mood and story to rhythm is characteristic of Miss Lowell and is one of her greatest gifts as a poet.

Her best work is her latest. In a certain sense she will probably never surpass the vision and the execution of **Can Grande's Castle,** but in **Legends** and in new poems not yet gathered in book form, she exhibits a smoothness and a dramatic fervor greater than in any previous work. She gives way with infrequency to the sharp, muted, and sometimes inept phrases which marred many early poems. She has not written so thoroughly prosaic a piece as **"The Forsaken"** in many years—nor do we now find such unfortunate couplets as

> And fragrant as fir-trees are
> When breezes in their needles jar.

Her later style is fluid and gracile, the thought deeper, the dream clearer. She deals with life more directly, as if she had suddenly come to understand both herself and the world better and was no longer afraid to speak boldly and truly. She puts down the veil. She comes out from her harem of fretwork and jewels, from her passionate absorption in gardens, from her wayward habit of being distracted from the point by the sudden sight and smell of flowers. She speaks with accents which are at the same time firm and beautiful. So great is the vitality possessed by her, that this progress has been possible. Heaven grant that she will use all her energy from now on in creating poetry and criticisms and in delivering her fervid lectures, that she may not again feel that literature and life require her to propagate a "school" of poetry or nourish another flock of poets. No matter how great her influence may have been in producing the new poetry in America, she has never furthered a poet greater than herself; and to herself, rather than to Johnny Jones or even John Keats, she should turn the efforts of what should prove her most productive years—the next ten!

John Livingston Lowes (essay date 1925)

SOURCE: "The Poetry of Amy Lowell," in *Essays in Appreciation,* Houghton Mifflin Company, 1936, pp. 157–74.

[*In the following essay, originally published in 1925, Lowes describes Lowell's enduring contribution to English poetry.*]

We are still far too close to the brilliant and arresting personality which was Amy Lowell for a dispassionate appraisal of the one thing for which above all else she cared—her poetry. She was herself, through her vividness and force, the most disturbing factor in our judgment, and no one who knew her can write with entire detachment about her work. One can only speak with sincerity, and trust that one's opinions are not too far from the truth. What, then, accepting once for all these limitations, has she left which has enduring value? All else is after all of secondary moment, and for our purpose we may disregard it here.

When an eager intellectual curiosity is coupled with a spirit of adventure and an indomitable will, things will happen. And when with these qualities there is conjoined a no less eager sense of beauty as revealed in line and light and colour and the potentialities of words and rhythms, the thing that happens will be poetry. And the poetry so engendered will be apt to add to the sum of beauty and to enrich our sense of it in unexpected and sometimes disconcerting ways. And it will also inevitably, in common with all adventuring (and with most things else), fail twice to once that it triumphantly succeeds. Those are the glories—attainment and attempts alike—of the spirit of adventure, and in that inextinguishable spirit the poetry of Amy Lowell is steeped.

I am not sure that this is not indeed its most distinctive characteristic. It flashes like a banner through the pages of **Can Grande's Castle,** and **Legends,** and **Men, Women and Ghosts**. But I suspect that its even more significant expression is found in poems which to all seeming are utterly bare of it. Let me quote one of them which happens to be explicit in its title:

Dawn Adventure

I stood in my window looking at the double cherry:
A great height of white stillness,
Underneath a sky the colour of milky grey jade.
Suddenly a crow flew between me and the tree—
Swooping, falling, in a shadow-black curve—
And blotted himself out in the blurred branches of a
    leafless ash.
There he stayed for some time, and I could only
    distinguish
        him by his slight moving.
Then a wind caught the upper branches of the
    cherry,
And the long, white stems nodded up and down,
    casually,
        to me in the window.
Nodded—but overhead the grey jade clouds passed
    slowly,
        indifferently, toward the sea.

—High, white stillness, cut suddenly by a falling curve of black; then a wind in the whiteness, and the friendly signal of the earthborn height, set over against the slow, indifferent movement of the higher height out toward a kindred deep: first a picture, succinct and sparing as a Chinese print; then all at once a touch which opens vistas—in that moment at the window is the sudden thrill of unforeseen experience which is at the heart of all adventure. And the poem is typical of a hundred others. At any moment the familiar may assume one of a thousand fleeting aspects of freshness or surprise. To catch this evanescence, above all to fix it, is perennial adventure and an endless quest. Often enough the swift irradiation is uncaptured, or it dims beneath the intractable medium of words, or in the effort to escape that dulling its intensity is overwrought. But all that is part of the adventure. And more than any recent poet Amy Lowell sought and missed and won triumphantly experience and expression of those flashes of sudden beauty which pass before most of us can say: 'Lo! there!'—which pass before many of us even know they *are.*

For she has been for years enlarging our boundaries through her own keen, clear perceptions of beauty that most of us have missed, and through her fearlessness in saying precisely what she saw. It was very often not what we saw, and we were apt to question its existence, or at best to dub the thing extreme. It often was; all ardent spirits overshoot the mark. But when the mark was hit (and that is the sole matter of importance), some familiar, even hackneyed object or experience stood sharply out in fresh and often startling beauty. No poet writing today, I think, save Thomas Hardy, saw and heard with more acute perception, or saw and heard and felt so many shades and tones and shapes of things—brilliant and subtle and fugitive and firm. And joined with this quick sensitiveness to physical impressions was an intellectual honesty as sensitive—a passion for truth which never knowingly falsified the report of what was seen. And that alert and vivid sense of beauty, restless with a poet's craving for expression, yet in expression lucidly exact, has schooled us, skeptical and reluctant scholars, to a quickened vision of strange loveliness in familiar things.

I know that to some this emphasis on the familiar will seem capriciously misplaced. But Amy Lowell lived with equal intensity in two worlds. One was the world of the crowded pages of **'The Bronze Horses,'** and **'Sea-Blue and Blood-Red,'** and **'Guns as Keys; and the Great Gate Swings,'** and **'Witch-Woman,'** and [**'Memorandum Confided by a Yucca to a Passion-Vine,'**] and **'Many Swans'**: the world of the Orient, and of strange legends and superstitions, and of a Past which lay as in a mirror before her, dazzling in its brilliancy and tumultuous with movement—a world as remote as the planet Mars from Brookline Village, Massachusetts. The other was rooted deep in those things which were to her the centre—the things which were *her own*. And the poems which are touched with perhaps the most enduring beauty are those at the heart of which are the objects of her passionate attachment: her garden, the great room in which from sunset till sunrise she lived and talked and wrote, the shifting play of light and colour on trees and birds and sky outside her window, and (merged with all and crowning all) she to whom was dedicated, in *John Keats,* 'This, and all my books.' **'Madonna of the Evening Flowers,' 'Vernal Equinox,' 'Bright Sunlight,' 'July Midnight,' 'The Garden by Moonlight,' 'A Sprig of Rosemary,' 'Penumbra,' 'Prime,' 'Vespers,' 'Summer Night Piece'; 'The Corner of Night and Morning,' 'Beech, Pine, and Sunlight,' 'Planning the Garden,' 'Dog-Days,' 'To Winkey,' 'Lilacs,' 'Purple Grackles'**—behind these lies a depth and inwardness unborrowed of the eye:

> A black cat among roses,
> Phlox, lilac-misted under a first-quarter moon,
> The sweet smells of heliotrope and night-scented
>   stock.
> The garden is very still,
> It is dazed with moonlight,
> Contented with perfume,
> Dreaming the opium dreams of its folded poppies.
> Firefly lights open and vanish
> High as the tip buds of the golden glow,
> Low as the sweet alyssum flowers at my feet . . .
> Only the cat, padding between the roses,
> Shakes a branch and breaks the chequered pattern
> As water is broken by the falling of a leaf.
> Then you come,
> And you are quiet like the garden,
> And white like the alyssum flowers,
> And beautiful as the silent sparks of the fireflies.
> Ah, Beloved, do you see those orange lilies?
> They knew my mother,
> But who belonging to me will they know
> When I am gone?

No one can read that and fail to understand that it was through no happy accident but by virtue of a subtle kinship that the poems of *Fir-Flower Tablets* are, in their exquisite art, among the masterpieces of their kind. They are unique, I suppose, in that their translator knew no Chinese. There is no need to rehearse the story which the

book tells for itself of the intimate collaboration with Mrs. Ayscough, who, through her insight into the genius of the language, was to her friend 'the pathway to a new world,' so that the long and arduous task became 'an exciting and inspiring thing.' It was one of the great adventures. And in nothing that Miss Lowell did are the finest qualities of her art more unerringly displayed. Its clarity is no less luminous, but its incised sharpness of line is softened, and its vividness acquires a purer tone. It is as if the mellow serenity of the age-old Orient had descended upon the more restless, keen-edged beauty of a newer world:

> The village is hazy, hazy,
> And mist sucks over the open moor. . . .
> My private rooms are quiet,
> *And calm with the leisure of moonlight through an*
>   *open door.*

Something of the magic of that tranquil line pervades the volume. And paradoxical as it may seem, more than anywhere else except in her own garden or her own high-walled room, one feels that here Amy Lowell was at home. And one feels, too, that had she lived in the eighth century, by the Peach-Flower Pool and the Swallow Mountains and the Yellow Crane Tower, she would have seen essentially what Li T'ai-po and Tu Fu saw, and would have expressed its breath and finer spirit in a fashion fundamentally the same.

> The house of the lonely scholar is in the winding
>   lane.
> The great scholar's gate is very high.
> The garden pool lies and shines like the magic gall
>   mirror;
> Groves of trees throw up flowers with wide, open
>   faces;
> The leaf-coloured water draws the Spring sun.
> Sitting in the green, covered passage-way, watching
>   the strange,
>   red clouds of evening,
> Listening to the lovely music of flageolets and
>   strings,
> The Golden Valley is not much to boast of.
>
> The clear spring reflects the thin, wide-spreading
>   pine-tree—
> And for how many thousand, thousand years?
> No one knows.
> The late Autumn moon shivers along the little water
>   ripples,
> The brilliance of it flows in through the window.
> Before it I sit for a long time absent-mindedly
>   chanting,
> Thinking of my friend—
> What deep thoughts!
> There is no way to see him. . . .
>   . . . But already the bright hills hold half of the
>   sun between
>   their lips. . . .
> And, rising, one can see the Autumn moon sliding
>   beneath the
>   ripples of the river,

While slowly the sun mounts in the East—
What hope for the revels now?

Precisely what is Amy Lowell and what Li T'ai-po, I neither know nor greatly care. But I do know that she has taken things of beauty which to their readers for centuries were (as they felt them) 'like Spring flowers,' 'like the branches of trees reflected in water—the branches of still trees,' and through her unison with their spirit has recreated their delicate, lingering charm.

I have dwelt on the later lyrics because I believe that among them are the poems which are most surely marked for immortality. But these moments when swift, penetrating vision is subdued to keeping with the mood which it has stirred are but one element in an astonishing profusion. Those of us who have followed the rapid sequence of Miss Lowell's books—or rather, the succession of absorbing interests out of which they sprang—have marvelled at the unabated zest with which fresh fields were entered, searchingly explored, and then annexed. For Amy Lowell had to a high degree the instincts of the scholar bound up, in a nature of singular complexity, with the spirit of adventure and the artist's compelling bent. Sometimes one quality was uppermost, sometimes another; custom never staled her infinite variety. But in the longer, more ambitious poems the student in her, for both good and ill, walked *pari passu* with the adventurer and the poet. In the difficult art of research she was self-taught, but no trained investigator ever brought to his task more tireless energy or a more obstinate determination to find out everything which for the purpose of the moment could be learned. That I know, for I have seen it. What it gave to her poems was a veracity in fundamentals as remarkable as it is by most of her readers unsuspected. For necessarily the artist has transmuted what the investigator brought. Between what I have been saying and this declaration of her own in *Legends* there is not the slightest inconsistency:

> I have changed, added, subtracted, jumbled several together at will, left out portions; in short, made them over to suit my particular vision. . . . The truth of poetry is imaginative, not literal, and it is as a poet that I have conceived and written my book.

So did Chaucer, so did Coleridge, so did Keats. Read side by side with **'Many Swans'** the stark, primitive Kathlemet legend which so kindled Amy Lowell's imagination; compare with the **'Legend of Porcelain'** the books on Chinese pottery which gave to it its lavishness of exquisite detail—do this (to take no more examples), and there will come fresh understanding of the ways of the imagination with its delved and garnered stuff. 'Not that exact knowledge could help the act of creation,' wrote Miss Lowell of Keats, 'but that, with knowledge as a springboard, imagination could leap with more certainty of aim.' One could reconstruct Amy Lowell's ripest *Ars Poetica* from passages scattered through the pages of *John Keats,* and that last sentence reflects her own experience.

Heaven forbid, however, that I should convey to anyone (if such there be!) who does not know *Can Grande's Castle*

or *Legends* the notion that they are academic. They exhaust, on the contrary, one's adjectives (Miss Lowell's were inexhaustible) even to suggest their flashing, impetuous movement, the gaiety and gusto with which their bright, pure, sharply cut images pour along, their combined sweep and concentration, the dramatic contrasts and the stir and tumult of their incidents. I know no writer of English whose command of the rich vocabulary of sensuous impressions approaches Amy Lowell's; the almost physical impact of it startles one each time one turns her pages. But just these qualities which I have mentioned constitute, and always have, a peril to the artist.

There is in Miss Lowell's *Critical Fable* a *tour de force* of self-portraiture—or rather, a gay, sparkling, whimsical portrait of herself as she knew that others saw her. It was not meant to be taken too seriously. But behind its 'gorgeous nonsense' (to use a phrase of Coleridge's) is the humorous detachment of a keen intellect turned with disarming candour upon itself. And one stroke of characterization is particularly apposite here:

> Armed to the teeth like an old Samurai,
> Juggling with jewels like the ancient genii,
> Hung all over with mouse-traps of metres, and
>   cages
> Of bright-plumaged rhythms, with pages and pages
> Of colours slit up into streaming confetti
> Which give the appearance of something sunsetty,
> And gorgeous, and flowing—a curious sight
> She makes in her progress, a modern White Knight,
> Forever explaining her latest inventions. . . .

Nobody who knows the most engaging figure in 'Alice Through the Looking Glass' will miss the half-rueful, half amusedly tolerant point of that. It reminds one irresistibly of an equally candid remark of Coleridge's about his talk:

> The second sort [of talkers] is of those who use five hundred more ideas, images, reasons, etc., than there is any need of to arrive at their object, till the only object arrived at is that the mind's eye of the bystander is dazzled with colours succeeding so rapidly as to leave one vague impression that there has been a great blaze of colours all about something. Now this is my case, and a grievous fault it is. My illustrations swallow up my thesis.

It was Coleridge, as it happens, who, in 'The Rime of the Ancient Mariner' and 'Christabel' and 'Kubla Khan,' was to Amy Lowell the supreme artist of them all; and both he and she were clear-sighted enough to recognize, the one in his conversation and the other in her verse, the common defect of their quality, which was a too free spending of their affluence—an excess sometimes magnificent, but still excess. And one feels this in Miss Lowell's poetry, I think, precisely where the check of the familiar is withdrawn, and her intensely pictorial imagination revels at will in the exercise of its visualizing energy upon objects and events which (as she says in the Preface to *Can Grande's Castle*) she 'cannot have experienced,' yet which 'seem as actual as [her] own existence.' Of their vivid actuality there can be no question, but we are often dazzled by the unrelieved profusion of brilliant imagery, and instead of the sense of a large simplicity which the Chinese poems leave, we carry away that other impression of the 'great blaze of colours all about something,' which succeeded the most amazing talk of modern times. But that after all is not quite the whole story. I must once more fall back upon Coleridge—who in some mysterious fashion has taken possession of this paragraph! He is speaking of the hero of Miss Lowell's own **'Sea-Blue and Blood-Red'**: 'To the same enthusiastic sensibilities,' he observes, 'which made a fool of him with regard to his Emma, his country owed the victories of the Nile, Copenhagen, and Trafalgar.' Very well! To the same enthusiastic sensibilities which sometimes overloaded every rift with ore, we owe the thronging impressions which are elsewhere wrought with sovereign restraint into close-girt, straight-sandalled verse.

No poet writing today . . . saw and heard with more acute perception, or saw and heard and felt so many shades and tones and shapes of things—brilliant and subtle and fugitive and firm.

—John Livingston Lowes

I am keeping clear of all the theories, whether of Imagism, or cadenced verse, or polyphonic prose. Provocative ideas shot like sparks from an anvil when Amy Lowell talked or wrote, and, being half superb free-lance and half crusader, she delighted in the clash of controversy which she stirred. But I think she had herself ceased to care greatly for what, in effect, were battles long ago. Her past work spoke for itself; there were endless fresh experiences to capture and interpret; and her invincible alacrity of spirit turned to those. The period of dashing swordplay had served its turn. The thing that matters now is the beauty which has emerged serenely from the practice of the theories which once evoked the flashing of so many harmless blades. And this peculiar beauty at its rarest (for perfection is an angel visitant) suggests the clarity of radiant air, and the pure lines of a pattern cut in polished stone—'clear, reticent, superbly final.'

> For me,
> You stand poised
> In the blue and buoyant air,
> Cinctured by bright winds,
> Treading the sunlight.
> And the waves which precede you
> Ripple and stir
> The sands at my feet.

If those eight lines of **'Venus Transiens'** were the only fragment left of an unknown poet, we should recognize that the craftsmanship which wrought their cool, controlled, and shining beauty was unique. And one of the paradoxes of genius is the fact that the most prodigal of poets in her

diction could vie, when her art was surest, with the most restrained. Set over against the gorgeous panorama of any section of **Can Grande's Castle** this:

> I might be sighting a tea-clipper,
> Tacking into the blue bay,
> Just back from Canton
> With her hold full of green and blue porcelain,
> And a Chinese coolie leaning over the rail
> Gazing at the white spire
> With dull, sea-spent eyes.

One would not give up either; together they sum up in little the two ruling impulses, peripheral and central (to use a critic's phraseology) of a poet who (to use her own!) 'when not hurricaning's astoundingly terse.' She is, at will, precisely that. Every volume is packed with undetachable examples, succinct, crisp, often trenchant; bright and brief (in the words of a poet whom Miss Lowell did not love!)— bright as 'the flashing of a shield.' But for renewed assurance one need only turn, in **What's O'Clock**, to **'The Anniversary,'** and **'Twenty-Four Hokku on a Modern Theme,'** and (for that matter) **'Evelyn Ray.'** Moreover, the exactness which Miss Lowell loved is nowhere more remarkable than in her sense of the savour and 'feel' of words:

> I want to be a carpenter,
> To work all day long in clean wood,
> Shaving it into little thin slivers
> Which screw up into curls behind my plane;
> Pounding square, black nails into white boards,
> With the claws of my hammer glistening
> Like the tongue of a snake.
> I want to shingle a house,
> Sitting on the ridge-pole in a bright breeze. . . .
> I want to draw a line on a board with a flat pencil,
> And then saw along that line,
> With the sweet-smelling sawdust piling up in a
>   yellow heap
>   at my feet.

Or (as Keats would say), 'Look at flowers—you know what she says about flowers': blue bells that are 'Deep tunnels of blue and white dimness, Cool wine-tunnels for bees'; 'a tide of poppies, Crinkled and frail and flowing in the breeze'; 'The scent of hyacinths, like a pale mist'——

Yes, I know that it will be said again and yet again that all this is but the beauty of the senses, 'untouched by solemn thought.' I shall not argue that. Perhaps '[Its] nature is not therefore less divine.' At all events Miss Lowell found sufficient answer in a Chinese print:

> Red foxgloves against a yellow wall streaked with
>   plum-
>   coloured shadows;
> A lady with a blue and red sunshade;
> The slow dash of waves upon a parapet.
> That is all.
> Non-existent—immortal—
> As solid as the centre of a ring of fine gold.

But in this last book one feels, I think, a deepening of experience, and a beauty less dependent on the eye. The poignant susceptibility to sense impressions is still there:

> Yet there are sights I see and sounds I hear
> Which ripple me like water as they pass.

There is still the delight in words that are carven and vivid and luminous as gems; the delight in rhythms as free yet as poised as the flight of a gull. And at times there is prodigality in each. But there has been nothing before in Miss Lowell's poetry quite like the 'half quizzical, half wistful,' altogether winning self-revelation in **'The Sisters'**; or the mocking lightness of touch and ironic suggestion of **'The Slippers of the Goddess of Beauty'**; or the breadth and warmth and (in its true sense) homeliness of **'Lilacs,'** or the sheer lyric intensity of **'Fool o' the Moon.'** I am not forgetting **'Meeting-House Hill'**; **'Purple Grackles'**; that buoyant skit on John Keats which bears the title **'View of Teignmouth in Devonshire'**; the **'Summer Night Piece'** which, like **'Madonna of the Evening Flowers,'** is a dedication; **'Prime'** and **'Vespers'**; the lines **'To Carl Sandburg'**; the sonnets to Eleanora Duse. But these bear, some in rare degree, the stamp of a familiar loveliness. It is the new paths broken that are significant—now sadly so. For the ripest years, with disciplined powers and deepening experience behind them and fresh fields before, were yet to come. *Dis aliter visum.* She has added new beauty to English poetry. How great that contribution is will first be clearly seen when time has winnowed, and her enduring work is brought together in one rare and shining book. It would have been still richer had she lived. For to the very end her gallant banner flew. And two lines in this last volume sum up alike what was and might have been:

> I ride, ride,
> Seeking those adventures to which I am dedicate.

Amy Lowell (essay date 1930)

SOURCE: "Why We Should Read Poetry," in *Poetry and Poets,* Houghton Mifflin Company, 1930, pp. 1–9.

[In the following essay, Lowell delivers her thoughts on the value of poetry.]

Why should one read Poetry? That seems to me a good deal like asking: Why should one eat? One eats because one has to, to support life, but every time one sits down to dinner one does not say, 'I must eat this meal so that I may not die.' On the contrary, we eat because we are hungry, and so eating appears to us as a pleasant and desirable thing to do.

The necessity for poetry is one of the most fundamental traits of the human race. But naturally we do not take that into account, any more than we take into account that dinner, and the next day again, dinner, is the condition of our remaining alive. Without poetry the soul and heart of man starves and dies. The only difference between them is that all men know, if they turn their minds to it, that without food they would die, and comparatively few people know that without poetry they would die.

When trying to explain anything, I usually find that the Bible, that great collection of magnificent and varied poetry, has said it before in the best possible way. Now the Bible says that 'man shall not live by bread alone.' Which, in modern words, means—cannot live on the purely material things. It is true, he cannot, and he never does. If he did, every bookshop would shut, every theatre would close its doors, every florist and picture dealer would go out of business, even the baseball grounds would close. For what is baseball but a superb epic of man's swiftness and sureness, and his putting forth the utmost of the sobriety and vigour that is in him in an ecstasy of vitality and movement? And the men who watch are carried away by this ecstasy, out of themselves and the routine of their daily lives, into a world romantic with physical force. But you object that they don't think of it in this way. Of course they don't; if they did they would be poets, and most men are not poets. But this is really what stirs them, for without it, throwing a little ball about a field, and trying to hit it with a stick, isn't really very interesting. A baseball game is a sort of moving picture of what Homer wrote in his *Iliad.* I do not believe there is a boy in America who would not like Butcher and Lang's translation of the *Odyssey,* if no one had ever told him it was a schoolbook.

That is what poetry really is. It is the height and quintessence of emotion, of every sort of emotion. But it is always somebody feeling something at white heat, and it is as vital as the description of a battle would be, told by a soldier who had been in it.

I do not wish to be misunderstood. I do not mean that every book, or every play, contains this true poetry. Many, most, alas! are poor imitations; some are merely sordid and vulgar. But books and plays exist because man is groping for a life beyond himself, for a beauty he needs, and is seeking to find. And the books and plays which live are those which satisfy this need.

Somebody once said to me that to make goodness dull was a great crime. In poetry, those men who have written without original and vital feeling, without a flaming imagination, have much to answer for. It is owing to them that poetry has come to mean a stupid and insipid sort of stuff, quite remote from people's lives, fit only for sentimental youth and nodding old age. That sort of poetry is what is technically called 'derivative,' which means that the author copies some one else's emotion, often some one else's words, and commonplace verses are written about flowers, and moonlight, and love, and death, by people who would never be moved by any of these things if sincere poets had not been writing about them from the beginning of the world. People who like to hear the things they are used to repeated say, 'That is beautiful poetry'; simple, straightforward people say, 'Perhaps it is. But I don't care for poetry.' But once in a while there comes along a man with knowledge and courage enough to say, 'That is not poetry at all, but insincere bosh!'

Again I do not mean that all poetry can be enjoyed by everybody. People have different tastes and different training. A man at forty seldom cares for the books which delighted him as a boy. People stop developing at all ages. Some men never mature beyond their teens; others go on growing and changing until old age. Because B likes a book is no reason why A should. And we are the inheritors of so splendid a literature that there are plenty of books for everybody. Many people enjoy Kipling's poems who would be confused by Keats; others delight in Burns who would be utterly without sympathy for Blake. The people who like Tennyson do not, as a rule, care much about Walt Whitman, and the admirers of Poe and Coleridge may find Wordsworth unattractive, and again his disciples might feel antagonized by Rossetti and Swinburne. It does not matter, so long as one finds one's own sustenance. Only, the happy men who can enjoy them all are the richest. The true test of poetry is sincerity and vitality. It is not rhyme, or metre, or subject. It is nothing in the world but the soul of man as it really is. Carlyle's *French Revolution* is a great epic poem; so are Trevelyan's three volumes on *Garibaldi and the Italian War of Independence*. That they are written in prose has nothing to do with the matter. That most poems are written rhythmically, and that rhythm has come to be the great technical fact of poetry, was, primarily, because men under stress of emotion tend to talk in a rhythmed speech. Read Lincoln's 'Address at Gettysburg' and 'Second Inaugural,' and you will see.

Nothing is more foolish than to say that only such and such forms are proper to poetry. Every form is proper to poetry, so long as it is the sincere expression of a man's thought. That insincere men try bizarre forms of verse to gain a personal notoriety is true, but it seems not very difficult to distinguish them from the real artists. And so long as men feel, and think, and have the need of expressing themselves, so long will their modes of expression change. For expression tends to become hackneyed and devitalized, and new methods must be found for keeping the sense of palpitant vigour.

There are signs that we are living at the beginning of a great poetic renaissance. Only three weeks ago the *New York Times* printed some remarks of Mr. Brett, the head of The Macmillan Company, in which he said that poetry was pushing itself into the best-seller class. And the other day a London publisher, Mr. Heinemann, announced that he should not publish so many novels, as they were a drug on the market. England has several magazines devoted exclusively to poetry and poetic drama. Masefield is paid enormous sums for his work, and a little book entitled *The Georgian Book of Poetry*, containing the work of some of the younger men, which has been out barely two years, is already in its ninth edition. Here, in America, we have *The Poetry Journal*, published in Boston, and *Poetry*, published in Chicago. England counts among her poets W. B. Yeats, Robert Bridges, John Masefield, Wilfred Wilson Gibson, D. H. Lawrence, F. L. Flint, James Stevens,

Rudyard Kipling, and, although on a somewhat more popular level, Alfred Noyes. England also boasts, as partly her own, the Bengal poet, Rabindranath Tagore, who has just been awarded the Nobel Prize, and Ezra Pound, who, although an American by birth and happily therefore ours to claim, lives in London. In America we have Josephine Preston Peabody, Bliss Carman, Edwin Arlington Robinson, Anna Hempstead Branch, Hermann Hagedorn, Grace Fallow Norton, Fanny Stearns Davis, and Nicholas Vachel Lindsay. These lists represent poets with many differing thoughts and modes of thought, but they point to the great vitality of poetry at the moment.

Have I answered the question? I think I have. We should read poetry because only in that way can we know man in all his moods—in the most beautiful thoughts of his heart, in his farthest reaches of imagination, in the tenderness of his love, in the nakedness and awe of his soul confronted with the terror and wonder of the Universe.

Poetry and history are the textbooks to the heart of man, and poetry is at once the most intimate and the most enduring.

Lowell's penchant for self-promotion:

Lowell's reputation, although colored by her flamboyance, was based on real literary criteria, her own prolific output as well as a certain literary tycoonism made possible by her fabulous wealth. She apparently had a knack for placing herself at the heart of controversy, and a hunger for performance and self-display, as well as the economic means to accomplish both. . . . She handled poetry—writing, publication, promotion—with the talent of a business entrepreneur. "I made myself a poet," she reportedly said to her rival Harriet Monroe, editor of *Poetry,* "but the Lord made me a business man."

Celeste M. Schenk, "Amy Lowell," in Modern American Women Writers, *edited by Elaine Showalter and others, Charles Scribner's Sons, 1991.*

Glenn Hughes (essay date 1931)

SOURCE: "Amy Lowell: The Success," in *Imagism & the Imagists: A Study in Modern Poetry*, 1931. Reprint by The Humanities Press, 1960, pp. 197–223.

[*In the following essay, Hughes surveys Lowell's literary career, evaluating each of her poetry collections and critical works.*]

Amy Lowell was born at Brookline, Massachusetts, February 9, 1874, the descendant of a long line of well-bred New Englanders, several of whom were men of letters. Her mother's father was Minister to England, and her paternal grandfather's cousin was the distinguished poet, James Russell Lowell. Her mother was a highly cultivated woman, a musician and a linguist, and it was from her that Miss Lowell derived much of her interest in the arts and her early knowledge of the French language and literature. She was educated privately, and spent a great deal of time, even as a child, traveling abroad. As a young woman she continued her travels, spending one winter on the Nile, another in California, and still another in Greece and Turkey, not to mention several summer trips to the principal European countries.

It is not at all strange that in this environment, and with such rich experiences, Miss Lowell should have tried her hand at literary expression. Yet the fact is that the creative impulse developed in her slowly. She is said to have begun writing poems at the age of thirteen (like most other girls), but it was not until she was twenty-eight that she decided to become a poet, and she was thirty-four when her first poems appeared in print. Two years later she gathered into a volume all her early poetic efforts which she considered worthy of preservation, and these were published as *A Dome of Many-Coloured Glass*. This book did not startle anyone. It contained only conventional poems: uninspired lyrics on the usual themes, a group of sonnets, and some children's verses. It was exactly the sort of first book of poems to be expected from a young woman of Miss Lowell's social and intellectual class. Louis Untermeyer, in his *American Poetry Since 1900,* says it is so trite that one can hardly believe Amy Lowell the author of it. He thinks it showed no promise of the originality which distinguished much of her later work. Most critics, I believe, held the same view, though it has been suggested by one that in the poem which opens the volume, **"Before the Altar,"** we have a definite indication of the author's tendency toward free verse and an individual technique.

What we can say certainly is that in these trial verses Miss Lowell showed an authentic, if not extraordinary, poetic sensibility; that she proved herself a conscientious craftsman; and that she revealed several of her major passions: Keats being one, Japanese art another, and colorful gardens a third. These passions were lifelong with Miss Lowell, and recur regularly in her writing.

In *A Dome of Many-Coloured Glass* Amy Lowell paid her tribute to poetic convention. Never again was she to accept so complacently the patterns and the diction of popular English verse. Henceforth she was to play the part of chief experimenter in the laboratory of Anglo-American poetry—experimenter and interpreter both. She was always willing to employ fixed forms, and to write in perfect meter with perfect rime, but after 1912 she strove for newer imagery and diction, and her best energy went toward the making of vers libre and the still more radical polyphonic prose.

Two things conspired to drive Miss Lowell from the sanctuary presided over by Keats and his fellow romanticists. One was her study of modern French poetry; the other was her association in London with Ezra Pound and those who were to become the imagists. She visited London during

the summer of 1913. She came in contact with poetic minds more original than her own. She saw the stirrings of a new force. What she had learned from reading the French poets (the Parnassians and the symbolists) helped her to grasp the theories advanced by the London group, and presently she found herself an absolute convert to the principles of the "new" poetry. Before leaving America she had written one poem in free form, unrimed. This she gave to Pound for use in *Des Imagistes,* and at once set about writing others of the same sort.

A year later she was in London again. This time she was surer of herself and of her mission. She had been asked to deliver in Boston a series of lectures on modern French poetry, and the summer trip to Europe was to provide her with additional knowledge of the subject. Also she had been thinking about the poets whom Pound had gathered around him. Her typically American flair for organization and promotion had set her imagination working, and she now had plans for advancing the cause of imagism. . . .

In October 1914, shortly after Miss Lowell returned to America with the manuscript of *Some Imagist Poets* in her bag, a new volume of her own verse was published. This was **Sword Blades and Poppy Seed,** an assortment of work which demonstrated clearly all the new interests and influences to which her poetic consciousness had been subjected during the preceding two years. In her preface to the book, she states her "immense debt" to the French—particularly in the matter of technique; and declares herself to be strongly under the spell of the Parnassians. She does not mention imagism, but she discusses briefly the principles of vers libre, and suggests that Flint's phrase, "unrimed cadence," is an appropriate English equivalent for the French term. She mentions also that three of the poems in the book are written in a form which, so far as she knows, "has never before been attempted in English." She means, of course, what later came to be known as "polyphonic prose." The invention of the form she ascribes to Paul Fort. But nowhere in the preface does she mention any of the London poets—perhaps because no one of them was well known, perhaps because she was not quite conscious of her indebtedness to them. Yet anyone who reads through the book can see that she owed something to several of her fellow imagists. Take an obvious example:

White and Green

Hey! My daffodil-crowned,
Slim and without sandals!
As the sudden spurt of flame upon darkness
So my eyeballs are startled with you,
Supple-limbed youth among the fruit trees,
Light runner through tasseled orchards.
You are an almond flower unsheathed
Leaping and flickering between the budded
   branches.

This is not derived from the French. Nor is it original Amy Lowell. It is simply a poem in the manner of H. D., bungled slightly by the imitator's hand. **"The Pike"** is in Flint's style:

In the brown water,
Thick and silver-sheened in the sunshine,
Liquid and cool in the shade of the reeds,
A pike dozed.
Lost among the shadows of stems
He lay unnoticed.
Suddenly he flicked his tail,
And a green-and-copper brightness
Ran under the water.

In other poems one may easily find traces of Pound and Aldington and Fletcher. It was natural for Amy Lowell to imitate—her curiosity was extraordinary, and her love of experiment amounted to a passion. What she admired she emulated, and she was not always scrupulous in the matter of acknowledgments. Catch any one of the other imagists off guard and he will confess that some time or other he has been startled to find Miss Lowell proudly exhibiting jewels filched from his own store. I do not mean to imply that the other imagists never borrowed methods—some of them even borrowed in return from Miss Lowell, but they were at great pains to say so; and besides, her indebtedness was always greater than theirs. Her most distinctive contribution to the imagist movement (in the opinion of her colleagues) was her business sense and her indefatigable enthusiasm for propaganda. She was their Barnum. They were amused by her flamboyant methods; they were content to profit from her success.

What impressed them most in her poetry was her polyphonic prose. Not that they all liked it, but they felt that in spite of what it owed to Saint-Pol-Roux and Paul Fort, it was an actual contribution to modern poetic technique. John Gould Fletcher was so struck by the effectiveness of this method that he adopted it in several of his own compositions (see *Breakers and Granite*), and Richard Aldington, writing in the *Egoist* for November 16, 1914, not only praises the polyphonic prose pieces included in *Sword Blades and Poppy Seed,* but advises "all young poets to study these poems attentively," and adds "I am not a bit ashamed to confess that I have myself imitated Miss Lowell in this, and produced a couple of works in the same style."

It is easy to understand how any writer interested in new effects would be tempted to essay the polyphonic form, if for nothing more than his own amusement. No medium offers better opportunity for a display of virtuosity. Particularly arresting, and probably most successful of Miss Lowell's early examples of the method, is the melodramatic narrative, **"In a Castle,"** wherein cadence and rime are cunningly interwoven. This is the opening movement:

Over the yawning chimney hangs the fog. Drip—hiss—
drip—hiss—fall the raindrops on the oaken log which
burns, and steams, and smokes the ceiling beams.
Drip—hiss—the rain never stops.

The wide, state bed shivers beneath its velvet coverlet.
Above, dim, in the smoke, a tarnished coronet gleams
dully. Overhead hammers and chinks the rain. Fearfully
wails the wind down distant corridors, and there comes

the swish and sigh of rushes lifted off the floors. The arras blows sidewise out from the wall, and then falls back again.

It is my lady's key, confided with much nice cunning, whisperingly. He enters on a sob of wind, which gutters the candles almost to swaling. The fire flutters and drops. Drip—hiss—the rain never stops. He shuts the door. The rushes fall again to stillness along the floor. Outside, the wind goes wailing.

Even so brief an extract is enough to demonstrate the extraordinary scope of this "many-voiced" form, this omnibus capable of carrying at one time all the devices of poetic expression: meter, cadence, prose rhythms, assonance, alliteration, rime, and return. Amy Lowell was peculiarly fitted to do the pioneer work in English polyphonic prose, for she was nothing if not a virtuoso. Her pleasure was to make words dance surprisingly; to startle her readers with pyrotechnic displays of color and curious medleys of sound. Depth she sometimes attempted, but seldom attained. Brilliance was her forte. And so it was that although **Sword Blades and Poppy Seed** contained many varieties of verse, conventional and otherwise, its significance centered in these introductory specimens of a novel and exotic technique.

A year after the appearance of these poems, Miss Lowell brought out her valuable essays, *Six French Poets,* which grew from the series of lectures she delivered in Boston during the winter of 1914–1915. In the brief preface she deplores the ignorance of Englishmen and Americans in the matter of contemporary French poetry and dedicates her own abilities to its correction. How enthusiastically she approached her subject may be judged from her statement that "France has just been passing through one of the great poetical epochs of her career—one of the great poetical epochs of the world." The six essays of the book deal in turn with Emile Verhaeren, Albert Samain, Remy de Gourmont, Henri de Régnier, Francis Jammes, and Paul Fort. Miss Lowell does not give her reasons for choosing these particular poets; she leaves us to assume that they are the best representatives of their period. With this choice F. S. Flint, for one, takes issue. In the *Egoist* for January 1, 1916, he writes reminiscently of a discussion he and Miss Lowell had on the subject, and restates his position.

When, in the summer of 1914, she told me of her intention to write this book and of the names of the poets she had chosen, I objected to Samain. Samain, I said, was exquisite, but not important; and he could only be read a few pages at a time without weariness. Stuart Merrill and Francis Vielé-Griffin, I went on, are both more considerable poets; both are Americans, and the public to which you make your first appeal is American; if you will not have them, Rimbaud and Laforgue are immensely more important than Samain; and since you insist on including Remy de Gourmont as one of your poets, you might increase your number to seven, in many ways an appropriate number where poets are concerned; and so on. But she would hear nothing of it.

Yet he thinks that the book is in the main excellent, and he bestows particular praise on the prose translations which Miss Lowell made from the work of the six poets and which she included as an appendix. "The best translations," he says, and in this field Flint's word must be considered authoritative, "the best translations into English that so far exist of the six poets in question, or, it might truly be said, of the French poets of the symbolist generation."

Elsewhere in the same article he speaks of Miss Lowell's devotion to the French poets, and takes the opportunity to describe the strong effect created upon him and other members of the London group by her informal readings of French poetry. He recalls the scenes at the Berkeley Hotel:

> No one, I suppose, will have listened to Miss Lowell's causerie in so happy a setting as the sitting-room of her hotel, where she talked to us in the August of 1914. Through the long French window open in the corner could be seen the length of Piccadilly, its great electric globes, its shiny roadway, and, on the left, the tops of the trees of Green Park, dark grey in the moonlight; the noise of the motor-buses and of the taxis reached us in a muted murmur, and at the corner of the park opposite, beneath a street lamp, stood a newsboy, whose headlines we strained our eyes from time to time to catch. It was in this tenseness created by the expectation of news that Miss Lowell read Paul Fort or Henri de Régnier to us (she reads French beautifully); and it is the emotions of those evenings, more than anything else, that her book brings back to me.

The War shortened Miss Lowell's stay in London, but it did not interfere with her work. If anything it increased her productivity, for her next book of original verse, *Men, Women, and Ghosts,* exhibited a tremendous amount of writing done in a relatively short space of time. Too much writing, probably, for the actual amount of legitimate emotion behind it. But Miss Lowell was always brimming over with energy, and at that stage of her career when she had just caught the public attention she was totally unrestrained. *Men, Women, and Ghosts* includes three hundred and sixty pages of verse, yet we are told in the preface that the author has excluded "all purely lyrical poems," leaving only "stories." But the "stories" are more varied than one would suppose. There are narratives in conventional form, others in free verse, and still others in polyphonic prose. There are short pieces, primarily descriptive, in which there is certainly no story, except by vague implication. There are historical romances (swiftly impressionistic), New England dialect tales (not-too-successful tours de force) and modern war episodes. In fact there is a vast array of miscellaneous subjects, strung on a thread of theory. Miss Lowell had dedicated herself to the task of exploring the possibilities of rhythm—particularly the rhythms of free verse—and she was therefore ranging far in search of material. One day she would attempt to reproduce "the circular movement of a hoop bowling along the ground," again "the suave, continuous tone of a violin." From an effort to capture the grace of eighteenth-century Venice

she would turn to the angularity of rustic New England, and thence to the Aquarium or a Boston drawing-room. It was certainly cold-blooded, this combination of note-taking and laboratory transcription. The surprising thing is that its results were so animated. Amy Lowell herself was so vital that she imparted warmth to the most mechanical exercise. When emotion was lacking she created the illusion of emotion—which is almost the same thing in a work of art.

"Patterns" . . . is an outstanding example of Miss Lowell's skill in the manipulation of free-verse rhythms and of her effective use of color and form to convey emotion.

—Glenn Hughes

There are, I think, many poems in *Men, Women, and Ghosts* which are mediocre or worse. They represent the inevitable failures of the prolific and experimental poet. But there there are a few which "come off" excellently, and which represent minor triumphs in the field of modern poetry. **"Patterns"** is one of these, and **"Malmaison"** is another. Both are stories in the true sense, the former an outstanding example of Miss Lowell's skill in the manipulation of free-verse rhythms and of her effective use of color and form to convey emotion, the latter a proof of the adaptability of polyphonic prose to the requirements of dramatic narrative. Both are interesting, also, as specimens of sustained imagistic writing.

Never was Miss Lowell more deft than in **"Patterns,"** where cadence follows the shifting mood as easily, as infallibly, as its shadow follows a bird; and the curves of the song are tipped with felicitous rime. The setting is a garden, the time is summer, and the speaker a maiden of an earlier century, whose lover is fighting in Flanders:

> I walk down the garden paths,
> And all the daffodils
> Are blowing, and the bright blue squills.
> I walk down the patterned garden paths
> In my stiff, brocaded gown.
> With my powdered hair and jeweled fan,
> I too am a rare
> Pattern. As I wander down
> The garden paths.

The fullness of summer, the beauty and softness of the flowers, waken her passion, which "wars against the stiff brocade," and listening to the "splashing of waterdrops in the marble fountain," she dreams of herself as a bather, spied upon by her lover:

> What is Summer in a fine brocaded gown!
> I should like to see it lying in a heap upon the
> ground.
> All the pink and silver crumpled up on the ground.

I would be the pink and silver as I ran along the
    paths,
And he would stumble after,
Bewildered by my laughter.
I should see the sun flashing from his sword-hilt
    and the
        buckles on his shoes.
I would choose
To lead him in a maze along the patterned paths,
A bright and laughing maze for my heavy-booted
    lover.
Till he caught me in the shade,
And the buttons of his waistcoat bruised my body
    as he
        clasped me,
Aching, melting, unafraid.
With the shadows of the leaves and the sundrops,
And the plopping of the waterdrops,
All about us in the open afternoon—
I am very like to swoon
With the weight of this brocade,
For the sun sifts through the shade.

But the dream is a pathetic one, for her lover has been
killed in action, and now her proud fidelity gives rise to
a cruel vision of the future:

In Summer and in Winter I shall walk
Up and down
The patterned garden paths
In my stiff, brocaded gown.
The squills and daffodils
Will give place to pillared roses, and to asters, and
    to
        snow.
I shall go
Up and down,
In my gown.
Gorgeously arrayed,
Boned and stayed.
And the softness of my body will be guarded from
    embrace
By each button, hook, and lace.
For the man who should loose me is dead,
Fighting with the Duke in Flanders,
In a pattern called a war.
Christ! What are patterns for?

Apart from the technical expertness of this poem, and its
resultant emotional force, there are other reasons for considering it representative of Miss Lowell's best poetic vein.
First, it has a garden setting; second, it deals with persons
of refinement; third, its action is laid in the romantic past.
With such elements she was always happy, and always
reasonably competent. Instinctively and by familiarity with
them, she understood them. With coarser and more typically modern elements she was not at ease—in spite of
much determination and good will.

After this third book of verse, which on the whole tended
to strengthen her literary position in America, Miss Lowell published another volume of prose criticism, in *Ten-*

dencies in Modern American Poetry, by means of which
she hoped to clarify the confusion which existed in the
public mind regarding the poets of the American renaissance. As in the case of her treatment of French poetry,
she here limits herself to six representative figures, and
devotes to each a combined biographical and critical analysis. Imagism she treats as the third stage in the development of the new poetry, and after giving considerable space
to the imagist principles and something of the history of
the movement, she examines in detail the lives and poetic
works of H. D. and John Gould Fletcher.

The book was found useful, and still is—although its real
mission was an ephemeral one. Its chief value today is
historical, for as a document it is important; as criticism
it has been superseded by more discriminating works. At
the time of writing this book, Miss Lowell was too much
a part of the general movement, and of the imagist movement in particular, to be a thoroughly just interpreter of
the new American poetry. She strove for impartiality, but
in vain. Consequently, those critics who desired to do so,
found it comparatively easy to demonstrate her critical
faults and to show her in the rôle of propagandist.

Perhaps the most annoyed of the critics was Conrad Aik-
en, who [in his *Scepticisms,* 1919] found the book intolerably egotistical, colloquial to the point of vulgarity, malicious in its partisanship, and fundamentally false in its
logic. After perusing it carefully he concluded that "a certain intellectual unripeness and sketchiness, a proneness
to hasty and self-satisfying conclusions without careful or
accurate survey of the facts, make of Miss Lowell an amateur rather than a serious critic. She is engaging, clever,
an industrious assimilator of current ideas, and to some
degree she sifts among them the bad from the good; but
the instant she enters the psychological or philosophical
or reflective spheres she proves herself a child, swayed
very largely by her emotions and desires."

And T. S. Eliot, reviewing the book in the *Egoist* for April
1918, greatly deplored its bad taste and its nationalism. It
strikes him as "a most unfortunate thing that this all-Amer-
ican propaganda should continue," and he believes that
"Literature must be judged by language, not by place. . . .
Provinciality of material may be a virtue. . . . ; provinciality of point of view is a vice."

Having done what she deemed her duty by the principal
American poets of the time, Miss Lowell lost not a moment in pursuing her own creative career. *Can Grande's
Castle* revealed her at the height of her enthusiasm for
polyphonic prose. Four long poems made up the book—
poems which gave the author full scope for her ambitions
as a narrator and as a technical experimentalist. **"Sea-
Blue and Blood-Red"** retells, with the dexterous speed of
a motion picture, the story of Lady Hamilton and Lord
Nelson. **"Guns as Keys: and the Great Gate Swings"**
gives a kaleidoscopic picture of the emergence of Japan
from her state of isolation, and indicates by cleverly arranged incidents and symbols, the spiritual conflicts and
tragedies resulting from the commercial invasion of the
Orient by the nations of the West. **"Hedge Island"** at-

Sevenels, Lowell's estate in Boston.

tempts to portray the passing of Old England, and to bring into the net of rhapsody all the bits of landscape, the snatches of song, the city scenes and sounds, which can serve to awaken memories of an England that is now little more than a dream, and which can form a poetic contrast with the modern order. **"The Bronze Horses"** is the most ambitious of the four narratives, and occupies nearly half the book. Its conception is unusually good, I believe, and its execution, though uneven, is at times brilliant. Miss Lowell takes as her theme the four horses of Saint Mark's Church, Venice, and from their history weaves a rich tapestry of color and movement. From the days of ancient Rome and Constantinople, we follow the destiny of these horses, finding in them the never-changing symbol of glory and victory, watching with them the rise and fall of empires. We leave them in 1915, when Venice is endangered by German bombs and it is decreed that the beautiful bronze horses must be sent to Rome for safety:

> The boat draws away from the Riva. The great bronze horses mingle their outlines with the distant mountains. Dim gold, subdued green-gold, flashing faintly to the faint, bright peaks above them. Granite and metal,

earth over water. Down the canal, old, beautiful horses, pride of Venice, of Constantinople, of Rome. Wars bite you with their little flames and pass away, but roses and oleanders strew their petals before your going, and you move like a constellation in a space of crimson stars.

> So the horses float along the canal, between barred and shuttered palaces, splendid against marble walls in the fire of the sun.

It was a good choice of theme for a pretentious piece of polyphonic writing. It lent itself perfectly to the orchestral effects which Miss Lowell set out to achieve, and it brought into happy union her technical virtuosity and her considerable knowledge of the European scene.

Inasmuch as both *Men, Women, and Ghosts* and *Can Grande's Castle* were limited almost entirely to narrative poems, Miss Lowell now found herself burdened with a tremendous accumulation of lyrics. For at no time had she ceased writing in lyric vein. In the spring of 1919, therefore, she issued as *Pictures of the Floating World,* a collection of short poems written during the preceding five years. As the title indicates (it is a rendering of the Japanese *Ukiyo-e,* a name commonly applied to the realistic color-prints of which Miss Lowell was so fond), many of the poems in this book are on Oriental themes, and some of them are written in imitation of Oriental style. Since the beginning of her career as a poet, Miss Lowell had manifested an unusual interest in the poetry and painting of China and Japan, but not until the publication of *Pictures of the Floating World* did she reveal the full extent of that interest. The short poems which begin the volume are called "Lacquer Prints," and are in the spirit of Japanese *hokku* and *tanka,* though no effort is made to reproduce the actual syllabic pattern of these exotic forms. In most instances Miss Lowell succeeds admirably in attaining the compression as well as the psychological values of her models, and although experts have detected non-Japanese characteristics in some of them, they agree that on the whole the poems are valuable examples of the influence of Japanese art on a Western mind. In such fancies as the following we have the authentic spirit of the *hokku*:

To A Husband:

Brighter than fireflies upon the Uji River
Are your words in the dark, Beloved.

Ephemera

Silver-green lanterns tossing among windy branches:
So an old man thinks
Of the loves of his youth.

The pieces written under Chinese influence—"Chinoiseries"—are fewer in number, and perhaps less convincing in effect. Still, they have considerable charm, and their composition was useful to Miss Lowell as a preparation for her more extended effort in the same field which resulted in *Fir-Flower Tablets,* a collection of translations from the Chinese, made in collaboration with Mrs. Florence Ayscough.

Whatever else may be said of Amy Lowell as a poetic interpreter of the Orient, it is undeniable that she went to great pains to fit herself for such an office. She steeped herself in the pictorial art of both countries, and read innumerable books relating to their history, life, and culture. She was in close association with several Orientalists of Boston (including her brother Percival, who had lived for several years in Korea and Japan and was the author of four books dealing with the Far East); she learned what she could from Ezra Pound, John Gould Fletcher, and other contemporary poets interested in Oriental poetry; and she derived a considerable amount of help from the French writers of the nineteenth century who had participated in the movement called "Japonisme." This last-named source has been skilfully traced in a recent study by Professor William Leonard Schwartz, and now appears more important than one might have suspected. [In *Modern Language Notes,* March, 1928] Professor Schwartz proves, among other things, that in at least three of Miss Lowell's poems she paraphrased prose passages from the work of Edmond de Goncourt, and although she did not attempt to conceal the fact (so literal are the renderings from the French), she made no mention of her indebtedness.

Only a small proportion of *Pictures of the Floating World* is written in actual imitation of foreign models, yet the Oriental influence is dominant throughout the book. Fantastic imagery conveying evanescent moods is the artistic aim involved; an aim which sometimes carried the poet too far, and seduced her into conceits which even to a tolerant reader appear absurd. Such incongruous similes as:

My thoughts
Chink against my ribs
And roll about like silver hailstones.

and

Little hot apples of fire,
Burst out of the flaming stem
Of my heart,

give no pleasure to the discriminating mind, nor do they plead well the cause of imagism. Fortunately, they are not really typical of the book, though they do illustrate its chief weakness, which is the tendency toward far-fetched and rather puerile imagery.

Miss Lowell's next venture was a return to narrative. Having treated in *Can Grande's Castle* the historical themes which appealed most to her, she now determined to exploit the field of folklore, and the result was a collection of eleven rather long poems published as *Legends.* Some were based on familiar tales, others were inventions. Their settings include China, Peru, Yucatan, England, New England, and the Indian country of North America. How many and what varied sources contributed to their making is indicated in the author's preface, where she specifies a number of reference books, and emphasizes the fact that those unspecified are much more numerous. In other words we have in *Legends* one more example of Miss Lowell's indefatigable curiosity and energy. She was an inveterate explorer of literature, and a tireless creator, or perhaps we should say, re-creator. So fanatical was she on the subject of writing, so ardent in her search for material, that she could not bear to let even the slightest fluttering idea escape her net. The poems in *Legends* are not by any means her worst work, nor are they her best. They stand upon a level of mediocre competency. They represent maturity of technique (in all Miss Lowell's favorite modes), and their subject-matter is legitimate. Yet somehow, it seems to me, they do not get beyond the category of tours de force. Artful but uninspring, they neither add to nor detract from her reputation as a poet.

Her next appearance before the public was in a mask, and Harlequin as Critic was her rôle. Taking her cue from her illustrious relative, James Russell Lowell, whose *Fable for Critics* had appeared more than sixty years before, she composed *A Critical Fable,* in which she exhibited twenty-one modern American poets (including herself) impaled on the needles of a flashing wit. The book was published anonymously, and so ingeniously had Miss Lowell concealed her personal characteristics of thought and style that few readers guessed the truth of its authorship. Two years later the truth came from the author herself.

A Critical Fable presents Miss Lowell in her most joyous mood, a mood of utter abandon. Taking the rollicking measure of "'T was the night before Christmas," and riming in couplets and triplets, with plenty of ear-tickling feminine rimes to break the monotony, she races and cuts capers until one is dizzy with following her. How easily she could do this sort of stunt, and what pleasure it afforded her, can be sensed by any reader. But as an amusing comment on her technical facility, I reproduce here a letter (now published for the first time) which Miss Lowell wrote to John Gould Fletcher from her home at Brookline, Massachusetts, on December 6, 1915:

DEAR J. G. F.: Tonight you said a thing
Which left me much upset and wondering.

You seemed to feel that riming was so hard,
To have the knack made any man a bard.

To turn out couplets fast as you could think
Was quite a worthy use of printer's ink.

But pointing to your friend whom I'll not name
I said his verse would put a child to shame.

To reach the end within a given time
And wind up sharply on a tidy rime

Seemed to call forth a terrible commotion
And make his brain whirl like a stormy ocean.

Such tricks he used to cause his words to fall
Each on its accent! And that isn't all.

Some verbs expanded with that fearful "did,"
Others condensed; and nothing neatly hid.

Was that a style of which one could be proud?
I asked you, and my horror cried out loud.

You shook your head. "He rimes so easily,"
You sadly murmured, "it amazes me."

I vowed to you that I could do it too.
"But he does not repeat his rimes," said you.

I told you I could rime for half a day,
You doubted me. And now, behold my way!

Not wishing to admit that I'm defeated
I've done the thing, and not a rime repeated.

I could go on like this till you were dead,
But it is late and I must go to bed.

I've proved my point and if these lines don't go
well
They took me just ten minutes.

                                        AMY LOWELL.

P.S. The postscript holds the letter's kernel,
So tell me, did you take the Poetry Journal?

It must be admitted that in *A Critical Fable* she did not allow her pleasure in riming to run away with her intellect. The fact that the rimes came so easily made it possible for her to concentrate on what she had to say. And she had plenty to say. She packed more solid stuff into this crazy jingle than she ever had into her serious prose works. And she was wittier than she had ever been. The frenzied pace of the poem, together with the wild music of its unrestrained rimes, seems to have intoxicated her mind to a degree of extraordinary brilliance.

Particularly interesting to us at this time, of course, is the passage relating to herself. In order to safeguard her anonymity she had, naturally, to adopt the attitude most likely to throw readers off the track leading to her own door. She therefore composed a spirited eulogy of her work, and pooh-poohed those critics who denied her a place among the immortals. The ruse (not unlike those to be found in detective stories) worked admirably. She describes herself as a powerful, bewildering poet, whom few can appreciate:

Conceive, if you can, an electrical storm
Of a swiftness and fury surpassing the norm;
Conceive that this cyclone has caught up the
    rainbow
And dashed dizzily on with it streaming in tow.
Imagine a sky all split open and scissored
By lightnings, and then you can picture this
    blizzard.
That is, if you'll also imagine the clashes
Of tropical thunder, the incessant crashes
Which shiver the hearing and leave it in ashes.
Remember, meanwhile, that the sky is prismatic
And outrageous with color. The effect is erratic
And jarring to some, but to others ecstatic,
Depending, of course, on the idiosyncratic
Response of beholders. When you come to think of
    it,
A good deal is demanded by those on the brink of
    it.

Yet she is careful to note that technical brilliance does not substitute for, but merely conceals, emotional integrity.

Despite her traducers, there's always a heart
Hid away in her poems for the seeking;
    impassioned,
Beneath silver surfaces cunningly fashioned
To baffle coarse pryings, it waits for the touch
Of a man who takes surfaces only as such.

She is very insistent on the subtlety of her poetry, and expresses much pity for him who cannot divine it. She also spends some time defending her erudition and bestowing praise on her versatility. As for the final judgment on the value of her contribution to American literature:

> The future's her goose and I dare say she'll wing it.
> Though the triumph will need her own power to
>   sing it.
> Although I'm no prophet, I'll hazard a guess
> She'll be rated by time as more rather than less.

Just how much of this egotism was assumed for the occasion and how much was honestly felt is a question which I cannot answer. It must be admitted, however, that Miss Lowell was never lacking in self-confidence.

A Critical Fable was the last book of verse published by Amy Lowell before her death from a paralytic stroke on May 12, 1925. But the last few years of her life were crowded with work. She completed in time for publication shortly before her death a monumental biography and critical analysis of John Keats, and she composed enough poems to form the three volumes which were published posthumously. One of these, *What's O'Clock?,* she herself prepared for the press; the other two, *East Wind,* and *Ballads for Sale,* were edited by her literary executors. On the whole these later poems are less daring than their predecessors. Their tone is quieter, their moods more tender. They reveal less of the note-taking method of composition, and more meditation. The peace of garden-flowers has closed in on the poet's mind and softened the edges of her fancy. She still turns to the far corners of the earth for symbols of beauty:

> So I start, but never rest
> North or South or East or West.
> Each horizon has its claim
> Solace to a different aim.
> Four-soul'd like the wind am I,
> Voyaging an endless sky,
> Undergoing destiny.

But she brings them all back to the New England garden. She will gather pearls from the Orient, and coral from distant seas, but their exotic beauty cannot match the beauty of lilacs:

> Heart-leaves of lilac all over New England,
> Roots of lilac under all the soil of New England,
> Lilac in me because I am New England,
> Because my roots are in it,
> Because my leaves are of it,
> Because my flowers are for it,
> Because it is my country
> And I speak to it of itself
> And sing of it with my own voice
> Since certainly it is mine.

It *was* her country. And when she sang of it she was at her best. It was then that she sang most with her own voice. In the eleven volumes of her poetry there are many voices, and sometimes hers is not the strongest. It is hard to estimate even now the value of her contribution, for al-

though the total of her work is before us, its diversity is baffling, and the personality behind it is still too strongly felt. So dominant a woman was she, so persuasive a propagandist, so clever a poetic craftsman, that one prefers to evade the critical issue, and leave it all to time. Louis Untermeyer once said, "No poet living in America has been more fought for, fought against, and generally fought about than Amy Lowell." That is true, and we are still somewhat blinded by the smoke of battle.

To Miss Lowell's strongest admirers she was a great poet, the greatest woman poet of her time; to her detractors she was only a side show, a specimen of blatant Americanism—dynamic, superficial, and, in its worst sense, successful. At any rate she was, by popular standards, a success. Everything she touched prospered. She was a born promoter, and she was in the right country for the exercise of her talent. But it is not necessary either to elevate to elevate her to the plane of the immortals or to set her down a wearer of false fame. One may take a middle course, and agree with D. H. Lawrence that "In everything she did she was a good amateur." That is the course I am inclined to take.

S. Foster Damon (essay date 1935)

SOURCE: *"Men, Women and Ghosts,"* and *"Can Grande's Castle,"* in *Amy Lowell: A Chronicle, with Extracts from Her Correspondence,* 1935. Reprinted by Archon Books, 1966, pp. 375–83, 467–80.

[*In the following excerpt, originally published in 1935, Damon examines Lowell's narrative poetry of the years 1914–1918, collected in* Men, Women and Ghosts *and* Can Grande's Castle.]

[*Men, Women and Ghosts*] is a collection of the narrative poems which Amy Lowell had written since she sent off the manuscript of *Sword Blades and Poppy Seed.* The earliest was probably '**The Allies,**' which is dated August 14, 1914; the last were written while she was assembling the book. All lyrics were purposely excluded, as being out of key. Already there were enough of them for a volume by themselves, but Miss Lowell was more interested in acquainting the public with the larger forms she was developing. A half of her new book was in free verse; a third was in rhymed meter; and the rest was polyphonic prose.

Of the thirty titles, twelve deal with war, including the four '**Bronze Tablets**' about Napoleon and the five contemporary '**War Pictures.**' Three of these, and five others, are studies of love and passion. Except for the ghost-story, '**Cross-Roads,**' love is treated exclusively from the woman's point of view.

'**Patterns,**' the first poem in the book, and the first of her poems to become very popular, remains as great as it seemed on first reading. A dramatic monologue expressing the tragedy of woman in wartime, it transcends both war and love, and is ultimately an expression of the repressed rebellion against the conventions and laws of life that bind the heart of every living soul. As though aware of this universal application, Miss Lowell translated it from the present time back into the Queen Anne period, the 'stiff brocaded gown' of those years being a symbol at once handsomer and more expressive. The dextrous use of the paeonic meter (which usually is light and tripping) to convey the despair of a ruined life, and the balancing of irregular lines to produce a sense of regularity, could have been done only by an expert craftsman. The emotional structure of the poem, including the drop of the voice almost a minor third at the beginning of the third strophe, and the brief interruption of the prose (the letter), culminating in the strangled explosion, half oath, half prayer, 'Christ! What are patterns for?' at the end, is sheer genius. This dramatic appeal of a universal subject, with the honesty of the treatment and the glamour of the setting, triumphed completely over what in 1916 seemed like daring frankness. It has always been a favorite with readers, and once, in a western convent, it was even acted, a little girl being cast as 'Pink and Silver.'

'Pickthorn Manor' also deals with woman's love in a period also vaguely Queen Anne. The heroine of **'Patterns'** loses her betrothed in Flanders; the Lady Eunice is a bride who falls helplessly in love while her husband is fighting in the same fatal place. He returns, and in a scuffle drowns with his bride. The central meaning of the poem, however, 'pertains entirely to the realm of psychology'; it is that of—

> a person allowing his mind to dwell for so long upon a thing that he becomes as it were hypnotized into believing his dream actual. This is the meaning of Eunice taking Gervais for her husband. It is as it were an *idée fixe* which blinds her to reality, and around that obsession, grown horrible by its result, the poem is woven. [according to Lowell in a letter to Winifred Bryher, June 29, 1918.]

'The Cremona Violin,' the third poem in the book, is another study of the neglected woman who falls into adultery. Her husband, however, is not a soldier: he is a concert-master, wholly devoted to his music.

> In **'The Cremona Violin,'** my idea was not so much that Herr Altgelt's music absorbed him away from his wife, as it was that she was held in subjection to him by this same music. I think my sympathies were not entirely with Charlotta, for, if a person marries an artist, it is quite clear that they must admit the position of art in the other's life to be paramount; and this does not at all mean that the artist does not give all of himself to the person he loves, but simply that he is dedicated to an ideal which includes the person he loves, and carries him, and the object of his love, beyond. I think Herr Altgelt was extremely fond of his wife; I think, in fact, that he adored her; but it was also a condition of his being that he was forced to give himself to his music. This she failed to understand, and put down as neglect. It was merely a necessity of the situation, and which in marrying him she should have firmly recognized and agreed to. In other words, she was too

selfish to be the wife of an artist, although she had enough artistic feeling to be attracted and held by this very art, which, in the final count, she was so terribly jealous of. She broke the violin, not in a rage at him, but in a rage at its being the reason that kept her from following her own purely selfish inclinations.

The concert-master's profession allowed Amy Lowell to experiment in extending the effects of free verse. As she explained in her Preface, Debussy's piano-pieces had suggested using the movement of poetry much as the composer uses the movement of music. This was not the Imagist method of approximating the sister art: it was more directly imitative; but it brought into her work the ever-changing motility which the Imagists had overlooked. The Imagist lyrics are static in mood from the first line to the last; Amy Lowell's experiments were deliberately dynamic. In **'The Cremona Violin,'** the story proper is told in rime royal, while the passages describing the concert run through all meters and rhythms into free verse. In the poem on Stravinsky's **'Grotesques,'** she set herself to translating a real piece of music into free verse, with such remarkable success that those who have read the poem have no difficulty with the quartet. In **'A Roxbury Garden,'** Amy Lowell tried a cognate experiment: that of reproducing the rhythm of hoops and of battledore and shuttlecock in free verse.

'The Cross-Roads' is a tale of a suicide's ghost which waits with its rotting body in its cross-roads grave until the funeral of the woman passes; the poem ends as his avenging ghost pursues her out of sight. Miss Lowell was all but a complete sceptic about the supernatural. She had a famous story about her reading with Evangeline Adams, the astrologer, who told her that she was very soothing to insane persons, and that all the other members of her family were mad. Another time, the daughter of her scrub-woman developed such mediumistic powers that the police were called in; but Miss Lowell walked with the girl in the garden until she confessed the fraud and never attempted it again. Yet the subject fascinated Miss Lowell, none the less: she knew and could discuss all the theories. While she ridiculed the ordinary evidence which such authorities as Sir Oliver Lodge and Sir Arthur Conan Doyle offered as proof of an after-life, she insisted that there were some things which had not yet been explained. She believed in the secret room at Glamis Castle: her parents had been visiting there at a time when the age-old mystery was told the heir, and they had watched his light-heartedness vanish and his disposition sadden. Within a few months she was to visit Patience Worth. *An Adventure,* by C. A. E. Moberly and E. F. Jourdain, which had been published anonymously in 1911, interested her strongly, though she declared that if psychic auras could really saturate physical surroundings, she would have seen her father, whose coffin once stood in the very room where she worked night after night. Her own nerves were capable of affecting her imagination (she knew that Blake was speaking truth when he said he could stare at a knot-hole until he became terrified); but she was too interested in such tendencies not to enjoy them. In **'The Cross-Roads,'** for the first time in her poetry, she expressed this side of her nature; while in **'Nightmare,'** inspired by the letter N of George Cruikshank's *Comic Alphabet,* she expressed her delight in a playful supernaturalism which always pleased and never disturbed her.

The poems about the World War speak for themselves. **'The Allies'** represents a serpent of men marching to destroy the red eagle of militarism. In the long column are a teacher, poet, mill-owner, and others, all determined to make the world safe again. **'The Bombardment'** depicts the destructiveness of war: the inspiration of the poet, the life-work of the scientist, the arts (represented by the cathedral), and the crafts (the bohemian glass) are all destroyed, while the lives of women and children are threatened, in a conflagration under a heavy rain shot through with shells. The childishness of the whole thing is symbolized in **'Lead Soldiers,'** where the problem is reduced to the microcosm of a nursery. Tommy playing with his soldiers is the spirit of militarism; the nursery fire is patriotism; the china mandarin on the bookcase is the inherited wisdom of mankind; the rose he holds represents the arts. In the manoeuvres against an imaginary enemy, Tommy slips and upsets the pitcher on the wash-stand; but it is blood, not water, that flows. Meanwhile the mandarin bleeds helplessly to death, his rose broken.

'Bronze Tablets' is a series of poems written around one of Miss Lowell's great heroes, Napoleon, whom she admired, not so much as general or emperor as liberator and personality. He appears in only one of the poems—**'Malmaison';** and in that he hardly speaks, for the real subject is the tragedy of the Empress Josephine. (When Miss Lowell saw **'Malmaison'** featured in the *Little Review,* she thought it the best poem she had ever written; and indeed it drew quite a little sheaf of congratulatory letters from strangers.) In **'The Fruit Shop,'** an impoverished aristocrat, spending her last coins for fruit, just catches a glimpse of Napoleon's chaise as he departs for the war. **'The Hammers'** is a sequence of sound-pictures of events connected with his fall: the building of the British ships; the destruction of his emblems on the Paris shop-signs; the eradication of the names of his victories from the arch in the Place du Carrousel; the flight after Waterloo; the making of his coffin. But in the last of the **'Bronze Tablets,'** his statue on the Place Vendôme column dizzies the travellers. **'Malmaison'** and **'The Hammers'** are in polyphonic prose, from the changing rhythms of which Amy Lowell developed a new way of telling her story; she evoked it through a series of dissolving views, which imply the history without stating it.

'1777,' another historial poem, contrasts revolutionary Boston with decadent Venice—a contrast of two republics, two kinds of women, two seasons, two sets of color. The garden in **'1777'** was her own garden at Sevenels, which also inspired **'A Roxbury Garden'** with its little girls at play. Besides this poem, and **'Lead Soldiers,'** there are two other poems about children. **'The Paper Wind Mill'** recounts a child's tragedy that actually happened to August Belmont at the Hague, while his father was Minister there; in Miss Lowell's poem, it becomes the tragedy of grasping the ideal and finding it dead. **'The**

Red Lacquer Music Stand' is the episode which terminates the first book of Goethe's autobiography, retold in an American setting. It becomes a symbol of the destructive effect of even the most spontaneous religion upon the joys of childhood.

'The Overgrown Pasture' is a group of four dramatic monologues in Yankee settings. Miss Lowell believed that the New England countryside had been drained twice of its best blood (by the westward emigration and the Civil War), and that this draining accounted for its decadence. Frost once asked her what was wrong with the place; she replied, 'Read your own poems and find out.' When Ellery Sedgwick, of the *Atlantic Monthly,* was dubious about the dialect of **'Off the Turnpike,'** she wrote him (October 26, 1915):

> But I must defend myself against your strictures about New England dialect. As a matter of fact, there is not a single expression in that poem that I did not find precedent for in Alice Brown's 'Meadow Grass.' After I had written it, I carefully took out her books and went through them with a view to correcting my own expressions, and I was astonished to find how very accurate I had been. I think it must be atavism, for although you yourself may have been brought up nearer the pumpkin fields than I, do not forget that my grandfather Lawrence was a farmer boy; and also I have been living cheek by jowl with the natives every summer for fifteen years.

Mary Aldis planned to present the first three of these pieces in her experimental theater with Mrs. Russell acting at least one of them; unfortunately, the scheme was never carried through, because of Miss Lowell's inability to arrange a date. On August 22, 1916, Miss Lowell wrote Mrs. Aldis:

> In regard to the place in **'Off the Turnpike'** where the woman sits down hard on pulling the hand, which you

and Mr. Brown are afraid may bring a laugh, I can only say that it depends entirely upon the actress. A good actress ought to be able to command laughs or prevent them, as she chooses. I have never had anybody laugh in that place when I have read the poem, and it seems to me that if you take the part of the woman, there will be no difficulty there; and if anyone else takes the part, perhaps I could coach her so as to prevent the thing from appearing humorous. The peculiar quality of the Yankee mind is this constant darting from humor to tragedy, what one might almost call humor in tragedy; and without it, one does not have quite the proper psychology. But if we find in rehearsal that the thing does not get over in the right way, it will be quite easy to delete that line or substitute another. I am not at all pigheaded about such things. . . .

You do not say anything about **'Number 3 on the Docket'** in this letter. But I trust you are going to give that too, as it is far and away the most popular of that Yankee series. I have received quite a number of letters from people, speaking of its absolute truth.

Only one poem in the book can really be called personal; that is **'The Dinner-Party,'** where Miss Lowell expresses the helpless rage of all original thinkers amongst the polite sceptics 'mildly protesting against my coarseness in being alive.' It was inspired by a dinner she had attended that spring in New York. **'Spring Day'** (which begins with the famous bathtub) really belongs to the group **'Towns in Colour,'** a series which is primarily visual, and thus allied to and yet contrasted with her experiments in music. The Preface acknowledges the influence of Fletcher's unrelated method, especially in his 'London Excursion.'

'Red Slippers,' the first of this group, contrasts the conventional ideal of beauty with its reality. One sleety December dusk, waiting in her automobile on Washington Street for Mrs. Russell, who was Christmas-shopping, Miss Lowell saw a window display of red slippers. The handsome colors and forms stirred her well-stored memory to its depths, raising momentarily to the threshold glints and gleams of many beautiful 'unrelated' things—stalactites of blood, crimson Japanese bridges, scarlet tanagers, firecrackers. It was the first stage of the creative process, which she caught as part of the poem itself. But past her vision the crowd hurried, to stare in an adjoining window, where an artificial lotus opened to reveal a doll, then shut again. This contraption was awkward, sentimental, tawdry, and meaningless; but it fitted the crowd's idea of what beauty ought to be, so they accepted it as such, never perceiving its real ugliness. 'One has often seen shoes, but whoever saw a cardboard lotus bud before?' Amy Lowell asked ironically.

'Afternoon Rain in State Street' is another color-study of Boston; so is **'The Aquarium,'** which was written 'after many visits to City Point.' **'An Opera House'** and **'Thompson's Lunch Room'** are similar studies of New York subjects.

Sometimes travellers from a rise look back to their starting point, and are surprised to see how far they have gone

already; and if Miss Lowell looked back from **'Towns in Colour,'** to **'New York at Night'** in her first book (a conventional protest against a city more like nineteenth-century London than twentieth-century New York), she was entitled to congratulate herself on her amazing progress; for then she was behind the times, now she was ahead of it. But more likely, she was merely distressed that she had ever let herself print that insincere thing.

So rapidly did *Men, Women and Ghosts* sell that on October 26, the eighth day after publication, a second edition of six hundred copies was ordered.

. . . . .

Can Grande's Castle

Every poet who is seriously interested in literature as an art, sooner or later gets tired of the constant implication that he must have experienced personally everything of which he writes; therefore, to offset this vulgar error (that his works are fragments of a veiled autobiography) he attempts something that he could not possibly have experienced. Amy Lowell had been particularly plagued by this attitude. Friends and foes, too often overlooking the essentially dramatic (or objective) nature of her work, identified poet and poem so much, that the person of the one obscured the sincerity of the other. The columnists, for example, were still filling their daily inches with mechanical guffaws over the thought of Amy Lowell shingling a roof, Amy Lowell taking a bath, and so on. Perhaps this was one reason why she chose subjects so remote from Brookline. The castle of Can Grande was the refuge of Dante; in her title it represents the poet's refuge from the world, and the high point from which he can view it. (But it is a tower of stone, not of ivory.) The motto of her book she took from Aldington's 'At the British Museum.' 'That simply means, as you will observe,' she wrote Untermeyer on May 14, 1918, 'that I could not possibly have experienced these things: I must have read about them; but that the reading becomes real.'

And any poet who is not content to remain definitely minor must progress beyond the brief poems which are all he can manage at first. The lyric points toward the character sketch, the character sketch toward the drama. And in those tragic years 1914–18, every headline in every newspaper pointed daily toward the Titanic drama of the nations. Dante began with Hell and attained Heaven; Amy Lowell began with War and attained Art. As she explained in her Preface, the four poems—

all owe their existence to the war, for I suppose that, had there been no war, I should never have thought of them. They are scarcely war poems, in the strict sense of that word, nor are they allegories in which the present is made to masquerade as the past. Rather, they are the result of a vision thrown suddenly back upon remote events to explain a strange and terrible reality. 'Explain' is hardly the word, for to explain the subtle causes which force men, once in so often, to attempt to break the civilization they have been at pains to rear, and so oblige other, saner, men to oppose them, is scarcely the province of poetry. Poetry works more deviously, but perhaps not less conclusively.

. . . For an artist to shut himself up in the proverbial 'ivory tower' and never look out of the window is merely a tacit admission that it is his ancestors, not he, who possess the faculty of creation. This is the real decadence: to see through the eyes of dead men. Yet today can never be adequately expressed, largely because we are a part of it and only a part. For that reason one is flung backwards to a time which is not thrown out of proportion by any personal experience, and which on that very account lies extended in something like its proper perspective.

Circumstances beget an interest in like circumstances, and a poet, suddenly finding himself in the midst of war, turns naturally to the experiences of other men in other wars. He discovers something which has always hitherto struck him as preposterous, that life goes on in spite of war. That war itself is an expression of life, a barbaric expression on one side calling for an heroic expression on the other. It is as if a door in his brain crashed open and he looked into a distance of which he had heard but never before seen. History has become life, and he stands aghast and exhilarated before it.

The subject of her book, then, is war—not the World War, nor war in the abstract, but a study of various wars in the past. Inevitably, Amy Lowell's conceptions were affected by the Boston historians. Parkman, Prescott, and Motley had viewed history as a series of picturesque scenes, which they re-created in a highly literary form. John Fiske was transitional to the Adams brothers, Henry and Brooks, who philosophized on the hidden laws of history. The earlier group treated it artistically, the latter reduced it to a science; and Amy Lowell combined the brilliant presentation of the one with the analytic intelligence of the other. In *Can Grande's Castle*—particularly in **'The Bronze Horses'**—she accepts Brooks Adams's theory that civilizations arise cyclically upon economic success, then decay as the racial energy runs out; she also accepts Henry Adams's theory that international crises recur more and more frequently as the speed of history accelerates. But Amy Lowell, in organizing and completing her theory, won a place of her own amongst the historical philosophers. To her, art was not only the expression of a civilization: it was life's highest achievement and its only permanence—it was almost civilization itself. The economic system is the root, the popular pleasures are the transient flower, and the arts are the seed-bearing fruit. In giving art this importance, she was unknowingly reviving, secularizing, and extending the old Puritan theory that man was created for the purpose of being happy, and that individual happiness was proof of a life in accord with the will of God.

Her method of presenting her material was predetermined by this philosophy of history. The surface of these poems is a brilliant series of magic-lantern dissolving views of the past. They depict various civilizations at those critical points when one is hurled against another, to the subjugation and even the destruction of the physically weaker. But the real subject is not historical: it is rather the sur-

vival of civilization in the eternal struggle against war. The superficial pictures are splendid with the colors of life; they represent the arts and amusements which constitute a civilization; but behind these pictures are at work the acquisitive and destructive forces which give meaning to the poems—a meaning anything but splendid. The surface is life, the depths are death; combined, the result is history.

In reading *Can Grande's Castle,* then, one must watch the flow of seemingly unrelated pictures of carnivals and triumphs and love-affairs and horse-races with an eye to what they signify in human society, for they were selected to illustrate and explain the civilization under discussion. The flow is life itself; war is the death-force that destroys them. The splendor of the surface sheds no glamour upon the meaning; Amy Lowell was not glorifying war.

Carlyle's *French Revolution* (which she had called 'a great epic poem'), Hardy's *Dynasts* (which so curiously anticipated the moving eye of the cinema), and Griffith's mammoth films (*Intolerance* had been released in 1916) may be considered as precursors of her method of presentation. Nevertheless, springing as it did from her own conception of history, it was entirely original, and so completely expressive of her meaning and appropriate to her poems as to be inevitable. Its validity is amply proved by the many later writers, in both prose and verse, who have used it for their own historical writings.

Her metrical form was equally her own: it was her 'polyphonic prose,' now developed so far beyond Paul Fort's alternation of alexandrines and prose, that the fundamental conception was entirely different. In a later lecture she described her search for a measure that would be epical:

For years, I had been pondering this difficulty. How to get the breadth, the serious scope and grandeur, into the new work that the old had. We could do much with our medium that the older poets could not do; but they could do things with theirs which we could not touch . . .

It was this very pattern-weaving I was seeking when I hit upon what has most misleadingly come to be called 'polyphonic prose.' . . .

. . . The work of the French poet, Paul Fort, gave me my first inkling of a new form. Working from his advance, I gradually evolved a system of verse which should make use of the old as well as the new, and so, employing all the voices proper to poetry, should at once fuse them to its purpose and create a new medium out of the result. I wanted an orchestral effect, and the delicate flute-notes of *vers libre* must be augmented by other instruments, no matter where I got them.

. . . The object was to find a new form for epic poetry . . . The modern epic, as I conceived it, should be based rather upon drama than upon narrative. This came partly from the greater speed and vividness demanded today of all the arts; and partly from the realization that, without the formality of metre, a sustained narrative of considerable length tends to become prose . . . Epic poems on the old pattern did not seem to fit in with the workings of the modern poet's mind. At least it would appear so, since he was not moved to write them. But I was moved; I had conceived some subjects which could come under no other head. I believed that the musicians had got hold of the right idea, and in 'polyphonic prose' it seemed to me that I had stumbled upon a form which could sustain the grandeur of a large conception, and treat it at once musically, dramatically, lyrically, and pictorially. . . .

Amy Lowell's narrative structures also were original; but as each poem has an architecture of its own, and as that architecture is the final expression of her meaning, each must be discussed separately.

'Sea-Blue and Blood-Red,' the first of these poems, is a tale of the love of Lord Nelson and Lady Hamilton, admiral and actress, from the Battle of the Nile and their first meeting, to his death at Trafalgar and her miserable grave in the lumber-yard at Calais, with its wooden marker slowly being chipped away by souvenir-hunters. It is a poem color-saturated and choral, a series of glowing historical frescoes. Nelson's triumphs are those of reactionary England crushing French liberalism: he is the 'Savior of banks'; his victories 'stamp out liberty'; or, as he sees it, 'It is Duty and Kings. Caste versus riff-raff.' Amy Lowell's enthusiasm for Napoleon (who does not appear in this poem) was that of Beethoven's when he dedicated the Heroic Symphony to the Liberator—a dedication he blotted out when Napoleon was crowned.

The lovers are the other side of the two makers of history; and their tale is a queer mixture of coarseness and idealism. Amy Lowell's attitude towards 'quivering, blood-swept, vivid Lady Hamilton' is best summed up in 'The woman is undoubtedly mad, but it is a madness which kindles.' The whole poem is kindled by her; yet Miss Lowell also felt her to be somewhat of a fool. 'A fig for good taste!'—and the exuberance of her frocks and deeds cancels their vulgarity; but there is sure misery at the end. 'Wife in the sight of Heaven'—but the rest of Nelson's letter (which Miss Lowell owned) has never been printed, is perhaps unprintable; and Parliament was not to see with Heaven's eyes.

'I have been very accurate in these historical poems,' Miss Lowell wrote Barrett Wendell, 'perhaps more accurate than a poet has any business to be. In fact, fearing in some way to travesty my originals, every remark that Lord Nelson and Lady Hamilton make in the first poem has been copied from their letters. My facts are correct throughout; my fancies—do they equal them?'

Only a scholar could have been so accurate and so thorough; yet the scholarship is always subordinate to the poetry, and never intrudes; wherefore Miss Lowell was hardly of the 'Erudite School of Poetry.'

The structure of the poem is comparatively simple, being the tale of this single love affair at the focus of imperial conflicts. But the ordinary way of telling a story would not do; instead, we are given a series of pictures, through which one guesses at the amour, much as persons in Neapolitan society doubtless did. The admiral's ships anchor under the flaming mountain ('the red thread to the blue thread cleaves'); he presents the Ambassadress with a satinwood table; they are seen much together; they are missed from a reception, and glimpsed disappearing through a postern; there is gossip. . . . So the tale continues. Realism merges into symbolism, then re-emerges; for Nelson himself is the blue of the sea, Emma the blood-red Vesuvian flame. They are two threads, red and blue, whose interweaving and unravelling is the *leitmotif* marking the beginning and end of episodes, and binding the whole poem together. In fact, the significance of each event becomes so intense as to make that event a symbol, which is in turn a stage in the story. Thus the admiral's ship coming to anchor beneath the volcano is no mere preparation for the meeting of the lovers: it is Nelson himself as lover—the warrior, after his great achievements, returning to haven for rest, restoration, happiness, which he finds through a woman. Only by following the series of symbols can the plot be followed; but such was Amy Lowell's skill, that no audience ever was baffled by the meaning of the poems in *Can Grande's Castle*.

'Guns as Keys: and the Great Gate Swings' takes us from Europe to the other side of the world, in 1853–54, when Occident and Orient—America and Japan—meet. It is the first momentous confronting of the white and yellow races in modern times. The United States sees the chance to acquire another market, and sends Perry to obtain a treaty by means of a show of warships, which he does, thus ending the seclusion behind which Japan has lived its idyllic life.

The theme is Commercialism versus Art. 'I wanted to place in juxtaposition the delicacy and artistic clarity of Japan and the artistic ignorance and gallant self-confidence of America. . . . Which of them has gained most by this meeting, it would be difficult to say.' The poem leaves no doubt. America gained its market, but at what cost!

> Commerce-raiding a nation; pulling apart the curtains
> of a temple and calling it trade. Magnificent mission!
> . . . Romance and heroism; and all to make one dollar
> two. For centuries men have pursued the will-o'-the-
> wisp—trade. And what have they got?

What indeed but an exchange? While Japanese art inspired a Whistler in America, American guns inspired a Japanese army and navy.

> The sands of centuries run fast, one slides, and another,
> each falling into a smother of dust.

> A locomotive in pay for a Whistler; telegraph wires
> buying a revolution; weights and measures and Audubon's
> birds in exchange for fear. Yellow monkey-men leaping
> out of Pandora's box, shaking the rocks of the Western
> coastline. Golden California bartering panic for prints.
> The dressing-gowns of a continent won at the cost of

security. Artists and philosophers lost in the hour-glass sand pouring through and open Gate.

'You have blown off the locks of the East, and what is coming will come.' The war which inspired this poem is still in the future.

It is divided into two parts. Part I alternates polyphonic prose (the voyage of the dynamic, aggressive, commercial Americans) with free verse lyrics (the life of the static, pacific, aesthetic Japanese). As there was no communication between the two countries, there was the more reason for not relating the stages of the sea-voyage to events in Japan. The print-like lyrics, therefore, summarize Japanese civilization in its respective attitudes towards nature, sex, popular and aristocratic entertainments, the state, the church, the stage, politics, and death. Part II is a pictorial narrative of the negotiations. The Postlude, dated 1903, partially answers the questions: 'Then wait—wait for fifty years—and see who has conquered.' In Japan, a disillusioned student commits suicide; in America, crowds throng the memorial exhibition of Whistler's paintings. These two episodes 'are facts, but they hardly epitomize the whole truth. Still they are striking, occurring as they did in the same year.'

> What I meant to give in both those postludes was the effect that each country had upon the other. In the Japanese section, how difficult it was for the Oriental to assimilate the Occidental habits of thought, how he broke in the effort; in the American part, how, in conquering Japan for our commerce, as we thought, we had ourselves been conquered on the aesthetic plane, and our habits of thought insensibly modified by contact with the Japanese.

'Hedge Island, a Retrospect and a Prophecy,' the third and shortest of the four poems, is a paean over the vitality of England in the Napoleonic days—the England of hedges (which always impress the New Englander used to rambling stone walls) and of coaches, which had been her love ever since as a young girl she had persuaded her mother to give her W. Outram Tristram's anecdotal *Coaching Days and Coaching Ways.*

The hedgerows, starring out from London, are the setting; between them roll the coaches to the compass-points. We ride in the Glasgow mail through its first night as far as Derby. Then follows a series of pictures, hearty as Rowlandson, lively as Cruikshank, quaint as Hugh Thomson, summarizing English civilization: romance, in an elopement to Gretna Green; literature, agriculture, religion, and fashion, as travellers; eating, in a dinner at the *George;* drinking; Christmas, a fog, a gibbet, snow, as they affect the coaches; royalism, in a procession of the mails to celebrate the King's birthday; and physical courage, in all England driving to a prize-fight.

But everything changes; a warning tone is heard, repeated:

> Ah, hedges of England, have you led to this? Do you always conduct to galleried inns, snug bars, beds hung with flowered chintz, sheets smelling of lavender?

What of the target practice off Spithead? . . .

It is the navy. Some pages on, the army appears:

> 'Damn the soldiers! Drive through them, Watson.' A fine, manly business; are we slaves? 'Britons never— never—' Waves lap the shore of England, waves like watchdogs growling; and long hedges bind her like a bundle. Sit safe, England, trussed and knotted; while your strings hold, all will be well.

A puff of steam—Industrialism—and the coaches disappear. Soldiers marching—to the World War. But the Prophecy is a cheer, a triumphant 'England forever!' gathering volume as the poem ends.

'The Bronze Horses' is the last poem of the book, and the longest.

Can Grande's Castle **was Amy Lowell's first completely original book. . . . Never did she produce anything more purely splendid.**

—S. Foster Damon

In 'Guns as Keys' Amy Lowell had stated her belief: 'Your gains are not in silver, mariners, but in the songs of violins, and the thin voices whispering through printed books.' In 'The Bronze Horses' we behold Art, the climax of civilization, triumphing across centuries, surviving the wreck of empires; the one thing permanent in the course of war and greed.

The conception is enormous. Four civilizations are represented, four different ideals of happiness; they are contrasted with opposing civilizations; the more vigorous triumphs; and the conquered collapses under stress of war, evades it, or endures it. The four wars are respectively wars of conquest, of religion, of liberation, of mere madness; but all are destructive and glut the greed of the conquerors. Yet the bronze horses, always the spoil, survive unharmed.

The poem begins at the center of civilization, Rome under Vespasian, in 71 A.D. Patrician (the languid lady in her bath) and plebeian (the bored workman) are alike spoiled, stale, enervate, for the armies ravage the rest of the world to provide them with luxuries. These wars are the Roman economic system. Now the city is regaled with a triumph: Titus has conquered Judea, whose most sacred treasures are paraded through the streets. Jehovah has fallen before Jupiter; but that overthrow reminds us that Jupiter also will fall to another god, under the onslaught of other armies. And the bronze horses, who placidly watch the procession, have also been spoils of war—a glance backward, showing that the beginning of the poem is hardly the be-ginning of the subject.

In the second section, the poem leaps forward to the East-ern Empire, Constantinople of A.D. 1204. It is a city made enormously rich by commerce; its chief amusement is bet-ting on the races. But the Fourth Crusade is launched; the Roman Church conquers the Greek Church, and the city of gold is destroyed for its gold by the pious crusaders.

The third section describes Venice of A.D. 1797, with its carnivals and frivolous love-making, under the tyranny of a corrupt oligarchy, aided by the Inquisition. General Bonaparte's armies try to liberate the Venetians, but they bewail the loss of their beautiful horses more than they rejoice over freedom; and 'tomorrow come the Austrians.'

The last section leaps forward only a comparatively few years (so fast has history speeded up) to Venice again in 1915, at the time of Italy's break with Austria and her entry into the World War. Venice is bombed. Her church-es are banked with sandbags, and the bronze horses are sent to Rome for safe-keeping. The poem ends as they glide down the canals, completing a cycle, as it seems, by returning to the city where they stood nearly two thousand years before.

But the ending is no ending, as the beginning was no beginning. The horses are not to remain there; and the poem stops with a glance forward. 'For how long? Ask the guns . . . '

Framing the poem, so to speak, are four preludes on elemental themes: fire, the life-giver and transmuter, in which the metals, rising from the other three elements, take forms which endure until the fire comes again. It would seem as if each section were dominated by an element; for clearly Rome is of the earth, Constantinople perishes in a conflagration, Venice is built upon the waters, and her last trial comes from the air. But Miss Lowell, while she admitted the fact, denied that it was intentional. Yet how far unconscious intent builds a struc-ture is yet to be determined.

Can Grande's Castle was Amy Lowell's first completely original book—original in meter, method, structure, and meaning. It has a glory and exultation to it that reminds one of Blake's *America:* turning the pages is like an in-crease of light on the retina. Never did she produce any-thing more purely splendid, though some of her later work was richer.

Eric W. Carlson (essay date 1949)

SOURCE: "The Range of Symbolism in Poetry," in *The South Atlantic Quarterly,* Vol. 48, No. 3, July, 1949, pp. 442–51.

[*In the following excerpt, Carlson discusses Lowell's var-ied use of symbolism in her poetry.*]

Taken as a whole, Amy Lowell's verse represents the rich and significant variety of symbolism in modern poetry. In some, especially the early derivative pieces like **"Before the Altar"** and **"Fool o' the Moon,"** the symbols are conventional and allegorical; the same is true of the short symbolical tales like **"The Fool Errant," "On the Man-telpiece," "The Shadow,"** and **"The Way."** More fre-quently, however, conventional and creative symbols are interwoven, as in **"In a Time of Dearth,"** where sand, caravan, Arab horses, and mirage suggest lack of inspira-tion, romantic splendor, free abandon, and illusion respec-tively; and the matches and newspapers signify artifical stimulation and the attempt to shut out the fact that the creative springs have dried up. **"The Poem"** illustrates the same dramatic interplay of conventional and realistic symbols: the twig, a literary symbol of the poem properly nourished, and the nail, an original symbol of poetic stim-ulus neglected and withered. **"Pyrotechnics"** contrasts natural, ideal beauty—stars, rockets—and the display of the tawdry and the artificial—the set pieces, King, Queen, Generals. **"The Precinct. Rochester"** also, for purposes of contrast and irony, combines traditional, creative, and realistic elements: the Roman wall symbolizes the protec-tive barriers around institutional religion, whereas the shel-tered, wasted life within is suggested by the overripe, unplucked fruit; the living needs of humanity are repre-sented by the discontented people, clamoring for the ne-cessities of life; and the patchwork of religious solutions, by the restored cathedral.

A conscious symbolist, Amy Lowell devoted one of her books, *Legends,* almost solely to symbolical tales and leg-ends. In its Preface she stated that "stories, as such, they emphatically are not," but rather "speculative or appre-hended truth" with a "curious substratum of reality," which when remolded gives insight into life for the contempo-rary reader. "I have changed, added, subtracted, jumbled several together at will, left out portions; in short, made them over to suit my particular vision." Since most of these legends are retold so as to suggest the author's meaning, the symbols may be called augmented myth symbols. In **"Many Swans"** an Indian sun-myth is used to interpret a theme similar to that of Steinbeck's *The Pearl:* the achievement of an ideal that conflicts with an estab-lished way of life results in a loss of both the culture and the ideal. Amy Lowell described **"Many Swans"** as "a double allegory, the sun-myth being one, and the other being the destruction of the Indian races through the all-imposing power and intelligence of the white man." One lyric, she explained, "was meant to show the fatal and cruel blunder of trying to do away with the religion and ritualistic dances of the Indians" by means of "a debauched and poisoned form" of Christianity.

In his comments on **"Sea-Blue and Blood-Red"** S. Foster Damon points out (*Amy Lowell,* 1935) yet another kind of symbolism. Two threads, red and blue, are interwoven in this poem as leitmotifs at the beginning and end of each episode and as symbols integrating the series of historical scenes into one whole. Blue is associated with Lord Nel-son, the sea, masculine power, and virility; red, with Lady Hamilton, Vesuvius smoldering, femininity, passion. "The significance of each event becomes so intense as to make that event a symbol, which is in turn a stage in the story. . . . Only by following the series of symbols can the plot be followed. . . ." For example, in Naples, Nelson and Lady Hamilton ride by as the living exemplars of courage, daring to be themselves in the here and now, amid a setting of effete and impotent Catholicism.

A predilection for the dramatic symbol is also apparent in **"A Tale of Starvation," "Astigmatism," "After Hearing a Waltz by Bartok," "Dreams in War Time,"** and **"Patterns."** In **"The Coal Picker"** the story is a symbol of the transcendental idea that beauty may be found in everything, however commonplace. In **"1777"** an effective dramatic contrast of American and Mediterranean civilizations is unified by the dominant symbolic motif of the trumpet-vine, sounding forth the promise of a vigorous, revolutionary, self-reliant nation, and by the falling leaves, brown and yellow, suggesting a decadent and dying culture. A variant of this inductive dramatization of a realized value is Miss Lowell's use of a sequence of apparently unrelated scenes to suggest an underlying truth. **"Malmaison,"** for example, traces the decline and loss of the love between Napoleon and Empress Josephine in a series of dramatic pictures or conversations that convey the emotive and psychological meaning of the experience as well as the known facts.

The highest creative symbolism is to be found in two of Amy Lowell's most powerful poems, **"Patterns"** and **"Lilacs."** In the former the garden paths, the stiff brocaded gown, and the war represent the larger social pattern symbolized by the drama itself: the social convention that makes woman a victim of man's tragic folly in a man's world. Out of historically accurate materials, the author has woven a pattern of symbols into a symbol of patterning pressures, making the title word and idea a new symbol in literature. Similarly in **"Lilacs,"** a Persian flower imported by the Puritans becomes the symbol of New England culture and its quiet sense of beauty. In these two poems the symbol functions on the highest creative level.

Of psychological and Freudian symbolism there is a good deal in Amy Lowell's poetry. **"The Doll"** and **"Pity 'Tis, 'Tis True"** deal with the mother complex or obsession to have a child. **"The House in Main St."** has to do with "a sort of Freudian complex." Frustration is the subject of **"The Red Knight," "Appuldurcombe Park,"** and **"The Basket,"** as well as **"Number 3 on the Docket,"** which involves a persecution complex. Tragedies of abnormal fixation form the central themes in **"After Hearing a Waltz by Bartok," "The Real Estate Agent's Tale,"** and **"Pickthorn Manor."** For a phobia that leads to suicide, there is **"The Notebook in the Gate-legged Table."**

In **"The Book of Hours of Sister Clothilde"** the basic idea seems to be that the worship of the Virgin is a sublimated adoration of sex fulfilment. The unconscious, Freudian symbolism is subtly handled. Although Miss Lowell refused to explain this poem, she admitted that the key to its meaning was the use of a poisonous snake for the Virgin's robe. Clothilde's subconscious sexual excite-

ment is suggested by such details as the "simple green" changing to hot flames; Clothilde's queer and trembling excitement of waiting, her indifference to the bite of the snake; "the red spots, in a flushed excess, pulse and start"; and her treasuring of the snake skin later, its dazzling sensuous appeal worshiped by Clothilde. Clothilde symbolizes the young natural self that cannot be entirely sublimated, and of course the snake is a traditional symbol of sex. Old François, the gardener, also seems to be a symbol; perhaps he represents the censorship of conventional morality: he kills desire (the snake), protects the innocent against further ill effects (sucks the wound), and makes an object lesson of the incident (warns the other sisters).

The most ambitious and the most obscure of the symbolical poems, however, is without doubt **"The Basket."** Here the poet deals in the cryptic, striking image-symbols of the surrealist. A young man, a poet, is passionately in love with Annette; but Annette is unresponsive to his ardor, "And he, the undesired, burns and is consumed." The silver thread separating their shadows on the wall suggests their spiritual separation; the nuts in the basket, the dried fruits of his desire; their shells, the husks of his passion; the eyes that she quietly consumes, the excessive admiration that she thrives on. Her embroidery, upon which she lavishes her energy and interest, has a religious motif: here again probably the author wished to put in opposition the sentimentality of formal religion and the reality of art and love. After the fire destroys Annette and the house, leaving a ruin of ice, he sees eyes of geranium red (the symbols of his unquenched desire, of his futile, unrequited love).

Although this poem has been called "a symbolic puzzle," to the reader familiar with the range and variety of symbolism in modern art **"The Basket"** probably offers little difficulty. Certainly the symbols used do not depend upon any private experience of the poet's or upon acquaintance with a special background of literature. For that reason they are not really cryptic, however obscure they may seem to the reader not accustomed to this mode of symbolic expression. The symbols in this poem may be called contextual, because within the context of the emotional experience described they are consistent and meaningful without benefit of footnotes or exegesis by the author.

Glenn Richard Ruihley (essay date 1975)

SOURCE: "John Keats and High Noon—Last Poems: 1922–1925," in *The Thorn of a Rose: Amy Lowell Reconsidered,* Archon Books, 1975, pp. 139–75

[*In the following excerpt, Ruihley analyzes Lowell's later poetry, describing developments of form, style, and theme.*]

In the years which immediately followed [Amy Lowell's] death, three new volumes were issued, *What's O'Clock,* 1925, *East Wind,* 1926, and *Ballads For Sale,* 1927, all taken from her bulging folders of unpublished material. Though they varied a great deal in quality, each gave evidence of the new powers of expression which the poet had acquired in the last few years of her life.

The poems of *East Wind* were the first in order of time, the poet having worked on this manuscript as early as 1921. A collection of tales of rural New England life, the thirteen poems continue the vein of gloom begun in **"The Overgrown Pasture"** sequence of *Men, Women, and Ghosts*. The peculiarity of these compositions is the lack of poetic quality in their form. In her zeal for innovation, Amy Lowell had devised a flat, free verse monologue whose jaggedness and use of dialect she hoped to turn to expressive account. The form justifies itself to a certain extent in **"Off The Turnpike"** and **"Number Three On The Docket"** from the earlier book. Both of these poems are studies of mental derangement produced by loneliness and emotional repression. As characters, Hiram's widow in the first and the husband-slayer in the second poem are well realized and the emotional force the poems generate is due in part to the blighted quality of their speech. This was the poet's expressive intention, but her successes in the form are few in number, while the extreme irregularity of the lines cancels all poetic effect.

In the poems collected in *East Wind* the direction of advance was in the tightening of form. Nearly half of the thirteen poems are now written in meter. Moreover, **"The Doll"** is a further departure in that the woman who speaks the lines is a sophisticated artist instead of an unlettered country person. This *persona*, never used before, allowed the poet a new refinement and range of observation. The story she recounts is that of two old maids with a pathological attachment to a large French doll, and the tale of the two starved lives is controlled and filtered by the speaker's urbane wit.

"[That] Day That Was That Day," the second notable poem in *East Wind,* is an advance for another reason. Written in the shapeless verse of the earlier work, it is the story of a woman driven to suicide by the emotional poverty of her life. Like Hiram's widow and the husband-killer mentioned above, Minnie Green is one of Miss Lowell's few successes in realizing human character. The same pinched quality of speech used in the other poems contributes to our sense of her plight, but this is relieved here by three interludes of a highly poetic quality. At first glance it would seem that the poet is merely sketching in some decorative background for her tale, but this does not account for the deep resonance of the lines,

> *The wind rose, and the wind fell,*
> *And the day that was that day*
> *Floated under a high Heaven.*
> *"Home! Home! Home!"*
> *Sang a robin in a spice-bush.*
> *"Sun on a roof-tree! Sun on a roof-tree!"*
> *Rang thin clouds*
> *In a chord of silver across a placid sky. . . .*

In their proper setting in the poem the three interludes are very striking. Their effect is to place these meager lives in a cosmic setting. In contrast to Minnie's choked life, Miss Lowell gives us the largeness and mystery of man's natural setting.

Ballads For Sale was the last of Miss Lowell's books to be published. This thick miscellany was well edited by Mrs. Russell, but the task she undertook was not solvable in any way that would do justice to Miss Lowell's gifts and the artistic stage she had reached at the end of her life. The poems consisted of the overflow from the poet's files, including many rejects from books she had published early in her career. Had Miss Lowell lived to fulfill her promise, it is likely that most of these poems would have been destroyed, but Mrs. Russell did not have that option.

> **Nothing else Lowell wrote equals "Paradox" in its ability to fuse a jewel-like hardness and brilliance with a compelling statement of her feelings about the would-be Beloved.**
>
> **—*Glenn Richard Ruihley***

Among these slight and brittle pieces there were a few poems of real substance, including some representing her most accomplished technique. One such poem is **"Paradox,"** a lyric of extraordinary evocative power. Nothing else she wrote equals this poem in its ability to fuse a jewel-like hardness and brilliance with a compelling statement of her feelings about the would-be Beloved. Part of the beauty of expression consists in the gradual building of linked images of the Beloved and a fantastic jeweled garden so that a very complex structure of poetic associations emerges.

> You are an amethyst to me,
> Beating dark slabs of purple
> Against quiet smoothnesses of heliotrope,
> Sending the wine-color of torches
> Rattling up against an avalanche of pale windy
>   leaves. . . .
> An amethyst garden you are to me,
> And in your sands I write my poems,
> And plant my heart for you in deathless yew-trees
> That their leaves may shield you from the falling
>   snow. . . .

Other poems of interest in the book include a full and literal account of Amy's relationship with Mrs. Russell written for her **"On Christmas Eve"** as a gift, an elaborate love lyric, **"Thorn Piece,"** the terse eroticism of **"Carrefour,"** and a caustic self-portrait in **"New Heavens For Old."** In addition to these there is also the fine lyric, **"On Looking at a Copy of Alice Meynell's Poems"** which seems to belong among the poems of this kind collected in *What's O'Clock*. This last named volume, which won the Pulitzer Prize in 1926 and has been the most popular of her books as well, is the vindication of Miss Lowell's belief in the value of unhurried development and accumulation of powers. Its quality consists of a heightening of all that had gone before. It is not the journey completed but the sun at high noon after which there was to be the softened forms and golden light of afternoon.

Polyphonics

One of the reasons for her success was that Miss Lowell had found a means to do justice to her impressions and, at the same time, to integrate these with reflective, ratiocinative, and more purely emotive elements. That this was possible was due to her ten years of continual experimentation with novel forms of verse, which gained her a reputation as literary radical and filled her volumes with hundreds of pages of verbal exercises, all of which were needed to bring her designs to completion. But this does not mean that Miss Lowell ever devised one all-purpose formula for her work. It was not a question of a single method she consciously developed but rather of the possibility of composing in polyphonic sequence.

Already in her pre-Imagist period she was writing in the rhymed *vers libre* of the French, a mixed form seen at its best in **"Patterns."** Somewhat later, in 1913 and 1914, she wrote extensively both in strict meters and in free verse of a high technical quality. Next came the quasi-epics in polyphonic prose, 1917–1918, with their requirement that she deal with a great variety of complex material within a single poem. As she was successful in doing this, she gained skill in the control of unwieldy subject matter, and her composition gained a fluidity corresponding to these demands. All that remained was to use this suppleness to combine the various "voices"—her term for the different modes and devices of poetry—and one could have a poem which expanded and contracted, alternating between meter and free verse, as well as the many variations of these Miss Lowell herself had devised.

Quite often rhymed metrical verse was used as a point of departure for a delicate music which hovers above the banality of strict design as the rhythms stretch to fit each expressive purpose and rhyme-words fall expectedly like bell-notes. Examples of this technique can be found in **"Texas," "Fool O' The Moon," "The Swans,"** and **"Merely Statement."** But this is one limited use of the form and its essential characteristic is its variability. One of the fullest uses of her technique can be found in the elegiac poem, **"The Vow,"** inspired by a visit the poet made to Charleston, South Carolina in 1922.

As Foster Damon has pointed out [in *Amy Lowell: A Chronicle,* 1935] Miss Lowell had lively feelings about the Civil War as the result of the animated family discussions of it she recalled from her childhood. In **"The Vow"** these memories combined with her taste for tropical richness and the sentiment which is best expressed in her line, "O loveliness of old, decaying haunted things" from another poem on Charleston's past. Moreover, Amy Lowell could identify with her subjects: the two proud ladies who sacrificed themselves by vowing never to leave their own garden until the South was free of Northern rule. The fact that both their ideals and their conduct were unrealistic merely added to the poignancy of the situation.

On the basis of these fused meanings and the impressions she gathered during her visit, Miss Lowell sets out to organize her far-ranging poem. The subject is the Pringle sisters and their useless defiance, but the note struck is that of human incompletion, a theme enlarged and dignified by association with the events of the Civil War:

> Tread softly, softly,
> Scuffle no dust.
> No common thoughts shall thrust
> Upon this peaceful decay,
> This mold and rust of yesterday.
> This is an altar with its incense blown away
> By the indifferent wind of a long, sad night;
> These are the precincts of the dead who die
> Unconquered. Haply
> You who haunt this place
> May deign some gesture of forgiveness
> To those of our sundered race
> Who come in all humility
> Asking an alms of pardon.
> Suffer us to feel an ease,
> A benefice of love poured down on us from these
>   magnolia-trees.
> That, when we leave you, we shall know the bitter
>   wound
> Of our long mutual scourging healed at last and
>   sound. . . .

The elegaic tone is sustained here in lines whose very appearance suggests the reticence of the emotions involved. As she tells us, her words are directed by the need she feels for reconciliation of the "sundered race," and this has its verbal counterpart in the widely separated end-rhymes: softly, haply, humility, magnolia-trees—which drop down through the passage drawing it together with the most tenuous of bonds. In the last three lines quoted above there is a reference to love pouring down from the magnolias, and here the lines expand in summary of what has been said and in anticipation of the descriptive and narrative section that follows:

> Through an iron gate, fantastically scrolled and
>   garlanded,
> Along a path, green with moss, between two rows
>   of high magnolia-trees—
>   *How lightly the wind drips through the*
>   *magnolias.*
>   *How slightly the magnolias bend to the wind.*
> It stands, pushed back into a corner of the piazza,
> A jouncing-board, with its paint scaled off,
> A jouncing-board which creaks when you sit upon
>   it.
>   *The wind rattles the stiff leaves of the*
>   *magnolias:*
>   *So may tinkling banjos drown the weeping of*
>   *women.*

The poem continues in this vein, giving us the story of the Pringle sisters detail by detail, and with the curious, abrupt interruptions of thought seen above: *"How lightly the wind . . ."* which hold the poem to a high level of lyrical intensity. The vow having been made for so high a cause, the sisters play their chosen role to the end and leave their home and garden only in death. The beautiful conclusion of the poem is a variant of the opening, but its tone is more gathered, more firm, and more hurried. The poet reflects now that it is her obligation to find a moral in this gloomy story and press on with her other concerns.

I have given this account of the poem in order to show the diverse parts of which it is composed. In the opening passage Miss Lowell uses the rhymes and strongly marked stresses found in meter to concentrate and heighten her emotional statement. But she has also used her freedom as a *vers-libriste* to bend and reorder the lines to match the shifting content of her thought. We find her doing this in the three long lines in the middle of this section. As her subject changes in the stanza that follows, so does her style, the lines exploding into energetic free verse as she turns to the tropical setting and the heroic acts and attitudes of the sisters. In this section the poet makes use of lyrical interjections in the style of her coruscating polyphonic prose developed some years earlier. Reduced in this way to short, disconnected passages and exploited for its brilliance, the high intensity form adds measurably to the poem's expressive effect. At the end of the long poem the verses are rounded by a return to the pattern of the opening, as noted above, but with the shift to a changed point of view as the result of the completed experience.

Part of the appeal of **"The Vow"** consists in a rhetorical excellence I have not described, but the purpose here is to illustrate the polyphonic sequence. Miss Lowell's most mature technical achievement, it is a real innovation which appears to be unique in English verse. By this means, the many "voices" of poetry—rhyme, meter, stanza, refrain, free verse, the intricate sound patterns of her polyphonic prose, and, finally, the use of key images or ideas which she called "return"—became fully available to catch the fleeting shapes of her thought. If this suggests clutter, it should be remembered that the technique consisted in the selection of those voices appropriate to the subject and that these are used in the polyphonic sequence required. There is also the element of spontaneity mentioned above. Had this technique been the result of a calculated plan, the freshness and charm inherent in it would have vanished.

One is led to this conclusion by a careful reading of polyphonic pieces such as **"Purple Grackles."** Here the artistry consists in the alternation of descriptive passages of colloquial tone, like stanza one, with statements of a higher order of intensity and poetic form, as in stanza two. These components are drawn together by an effective use of refrain, "The grackles have come," and in the conclusion there is a marked alteration in mood as the poet ponders the meaning of seasonal change. What had been a festive and humorous mixing between the poet-hostess and a horde of kingly guests changes to a lesson in the nature of things when they suddenly disappear. At this point in the poem, the witty and loosely structured lines contract and harden—become, in a word, the perfect expression of the sharpened awareness she now turns on the scene about her. The section is introduced by a last use of

her refrain and a subtle intrusion of rhyme in "purple head" and "flower beds," very widely separated, which adds to the sense of finality in the passage:

> Come! Yes, they surely came.
> But they have gone.
> A moment ago the oak was full of them,
> They are not there now.
> Not a speck of a black wing,
> Not an eye-peep of a purple head.
> The grackles have gone,
> And I watch an Autumn storm
> Stripping the garden,
> Shouting black rain challenges
> To an old, limp summer
> Laid down to die in the flower-beds.

"Lilacs," also written at this time, is another New England poem of complex intentions. As we see in the opening lines, it is more austere than **"Purple Grackles,"** the poet achieving the ultimate simplication by reducing her statement to the naming of a series of distinct but somehow evocative colors. This passage is followed by other sharply focused images which are rendered with an uncanny purity and freshness of line. So true are all these pictures that the objects appear in a new light—and what is usually taken as a miscellaneous catalogue turns out to be the features of a "face." It is the face of New England, and through the key symbolism of the lilac blooms Miss Lowell has elicited the spirit of a land and a people—

> You are brighter than apples,
> Sweeter than tulips,
> You are the great flood of our souls
> Bursting above the leaf-shapes of our hearts.

Somehow, the many bright images forming the body of this poem coalesce into a coherent design, and the division of the lines into three distinct movements makes possible the gradual rise to the assertion of a mystical identity between poet and country.

The merit of **"Lilacs"** consists in the discovery of oneness under the veil of diverse appearances, and it does this partly by the use of a unifying design. In **"East, West, North, and South of a Man"** the poet begins with a closely delimited theme, the four aspects of *a man,* and moves outward to diversity in a poem consisting of four loosely related movements. In fact, one may wonder if this is a single poem at all, or at least if this could be one man as the poet tells us in her title. But the purpose here is to dramatize her subject by the use of extreme instances presented in brilliant and contrasting images. Three of her portraits are in free verse but in the portrait of the itinerant peddler, the poet has used a jingling, broken-ended meter to suggest the inconsequence of the merchant's concerns. For the others, the warrior, the lover, and the scholar, she has used an expansive form of free verse and sumptuous settings to turn our thought in a transcendental direction. We can see this in the similes she uses in the opening lines of the poem, with their echo of the rhythm and refrain of the medieval ballad:

He rides a white horse,
  Mary Madonna,
Dappled as clouds are dappled,
  O Mary, Mary,
And the leather of his harness is the colour of the
  sky.

Beginning with a knight seated on a horse, a practical man of action, we have next a reference to clouds and already in the fifth line of this poem, rhythm and image are intended to suggest infinite dimensions. Dimensions of this kind are also attributed to the handsome, gorgeously arrayed lover—"His voice is the sun in mid-heaven/Pouring on whirled ochre dahlias"—and in the climactic portrait of the scholar, said to be Miss Lowell herself, the poet sets before us the infinitude of the mind as the final measure of man:

  The walls of forbidden cities fall before him;
  He has but to tap a sheepskin to experience kingdoms,
  And circumstance drips from his fingers like dust. . . .
  He eats the centuries
  And lives a new life every twenty-four hours,
  So lengthening his own to an incalculable figure. . . .

The sense of magnitude we have in this poem is expressed in **"The Green Parakeet"** as well, but in the latter poem it is an ironic commentary on a story of tragic deprivation. On the one hand we see the world of nature with its startling beauty and freshness, symbolized by the parakeet as well as by talking and whimsical vines, trees, and barberry bushes. On the other, there is the mixed nature of man. As the poem begins, the protagonist ravishes a young, innocent girl. Although she does not resist and she conceives a love for him at once, the hero has deprived the girl of her purity, represented here by the death of the pet parakeet. Stricken by guilt, the lover first runs away to watch her from a distance.

  I stared at her from the farther side
  Of Hell, no space is great beside
  This space. I could not see her face
  Across such vastitude of space,
  And over it drowsed a darkened thing:
  A monster parakeet's green wing,
  The air was starred with parakeets.
  I turned and rushed into the streets. . . .

After a few days of covert observation of the deserted girl, some "odd obedience" in his feet compels him to rush out into the country. He then wears out his life moving restlessly from one place to another, "Bent double underneath the load / Of memory and second sight," while the specter of the bird haunts him. The story of guilty love is told in tight tetrameter couplets. Opening out from this are a number of polyphonic interludes developed along highly fanciful lines, whose effect is to interweave this tragedy with the life of natural things. At the conclusion of the poem the poet gives us a final image of the innocent creatures of nature set in contrast with the fevered state of man.

  The man scuffed across a bridge and up a steep hill.
  "Quietly, quietly," whispered the barberrybushes, and

hid their scarlet tongues under their leaves. "Weep, Tree-Brothers," said the grapevines. But the long lines of trees only rustled and played hide and seek with the peeping moon. They were too tall to pay much heed to anything so small as an old man limping up a hill.

Asepsis

Besides the impressions and combined forms we find in these polyphonic sequences, Amy Lowell was also writing many lyrics during the last years of her life. Some of these are among her best work of this type. The emotions are very fully developed and the content is matched by a corresponding richness of poetic invention. Perhaps the best single example would be **"Song for a Viola D'Amore."** Like many other lyrics she wrote at this time, the **"Song"** was inspired by Miss Lowell's feelings for her companion [Ada Russell], but there is another and contrasting group even more expressive of the poet's inner history. These are the poems of asepsis: the bleeding of life by the denial of vital experience.

The sense of tragic incompleteness, Miss Lowell's foremost theme, is presented with great emphasis in her poem, **"New Heavens For Old."**

  I am useless.
  What I do is nothing,
  What I think has no savor.
  There is an almanac between the windows:
  It is of the year when I was born.

  My fellows call me to join them. . . .
  They are indecent and strut with the thought of it. . . .
  Young men with naked hearts jeering between iron
    house-fronts,
  Young men with naked bodies beneath their clothes
  Passionately conscious of them,
  Ready to strip off their clothes,
  Ready to strip off their customs, their usual routine,
  Clamoring for the rawness of life,
  In love with appetite. . . .
  They call for women and the women come,
  They bare the whiteness of their lusts to the dead
    gaze
    of the old house-fronts,
  They roar down the street like flame,
  They explode upon the dead houses like new, sharp
    fire.
  But I—
  I arrange three roses in a Chinese vase. . . .
  I fuss over their arrangement.
  Then I sit in a South window. . . .
  And think of Winter nights,
  And field-mice crossing and re-crossing
  The spot which will be my grave.

The poem is somewhat theatrical and over-drawn but it is interesting as a revelation of Miss Lowell's attitudes. Her description of the youth, "her fellows" who shout for her in this poem bearing "vermilion banners," defying the propriety represented by "the iron fronts of the houses"— this description is interesting in that it does not apply at all to her own time, but it is an accurate account of developments forty-five years after her death. There is an element of clairvoyance and even of prophecy here; but she does not tell us to what extent she sympathizes with the rebelliousness of her fellows. What is clear is that she places herself on the side of adventure and self-expression and equates excessive constraints with death.

The stiffling of the inner self is also her theme in the deeply meditated lyric, **"On Looking at a Copy of Alice Meynell's Poems, Given Me Years Ago By A Friend."** This poem, treating Miss Lowell's loveless state, was inspired by news of the death of Alice Meynell and is addressed to Frances Dabney, a close friend who had died many years before. The history to which it refers concerns Miss Lowell's visit to Devonshire in 1899, in the company of Miss Dabney, when the future poet was suffering from a nervous breakdown. As stated above, the illness persisted through the remainder of Miss Lowell's youth, and in this poem she tells of the cause of the malady. It was not the English sea air which she required but a chance at life. For this reason Miss Dabney's gift of the book of poems was ironic. The theme of Miss Meynell's verse was the very experience through which Miss Lowell was passing, and reading the poems only sharpened her sense of loss:

> Silent the sea, the earth, the sky,
> And in my heart a silent weeping,
> Who has not sown can know no reaping
> Bitter conclusion and no lie. . . .
> No future where there is no past!
> O cherishing grief which laid me bare,
> I wrapped you like a wintry air
> About me. Poor enthusiast!

These are the unpromising ingredients the poet transmutes into a preternatural radance. But it would be wrong to assume that this is so because the feelings involved are in some way pleasing to her or that her exaltation is due to the stoic fortitude she expresses at the end of the poem. Instead, we must look for the answer in another order of experience she also traces in the poem. This reveals itself in the hypnotic or hallucinatory quality of the images with which she evokes the Devonshire sea-coast, the poetry of Miss Meynell:

> . . . like bronze cathedral bells
> Down ancient lawns, or citadels
> Thundering with gongs where choirs sang. . . .

and the act of remembrance itself that she compares to a winking, spectral light. This experience of a deeper order of existence cannot be described, except as she suggests it in her images, but its importance lies in the fact that it has invested and transformed the pain and deformity of life with which this poem began.

The same process is at work in **"Nuit Blanche,"** one of the most accomplished of Amy Lowell's lyrics. The French

title means "white night" or sleeplessness, but the meaning is modified if we reflect that Miss Lowell slept during the day and worked in quiet and seclusion at night. Taking these circumstances into account, the poem would seem to express a total vacancy of life, the exhaustion of normal interests and energies. However, the withdrawal of feeling does not include indifference to sexual passion. And we learn as well that it is not satiety that has inspired her fatigue but a long-continued incompletion. Out of this basic discord, the poet has fashioned a superb glissando, sound and image being molded into a single seamless whole.

> I want no horns to rouse me up tonight,
> And trumpets make too clamorous a ring
> To fit my mood, it is so weary white
> I have no wish for doing any thing.
>
> A music coaxed from humming strings would
>   please;
> Not plucked, but drawn in creeping cadences
> Across a sunset wall where some Marquise
> Picks a pale rose amid strange silences.

The predominance of single syllable words here is important to her esthetic design. Along with the drawn-out pentameters, this slows the movement of her lines, the pronounced end-rhymes in alternate succession having the same retarding effect. The purpose is to suggest a slow awakening, and the mood set for this is symbolized by a continual stress on whiteness beginning with the title of the poem and ending with its last syllable. Nevertheless, her subject is not whiteness or nullity of life. Though this is the poet's mood, the scene to which she awakes is a romantic one, and we are aware from the first syllables that it is not an earthly ground.

This is expressed, first of all, by the sounds of music which recall the concerts Miss Lowell gave in her white and crystal library. In the poem, as it did in real life, the music stretches to enclose a garden, and here we have the heroine of **"Patterns"** again, now very subdued, but engaged in the same task of defining herself and the terms of her existence. It is sunset here, not the brilliant daylight of **"Patterns,"** and there is no defiance at all. The brisk-paced sweep through a spring-time garden is replaced by lanquid movements whose meaning is focused in the pale rose the heroine picks "amid strange silences." If the rose symbolizes the bloodlessness of her life, the "strange silences" suggest her suffocated state, and in the third stanza this tragic figure dissolves completely into the twilight landscape:

> Ghostly and vaporous her gown sweeps by
> The twilight dusking wall. I hear her feet
> Delaying on the gravel, and a sigh,
> Briefly permitted, touches the air like sleet.

After this there is a transition to night and the poet herself reappears.

> And it is dark. I hear her feet no more.
> A red moon leers beyond the lily-tank,

Amy Lowell as a debutante.

A drunken moon, ogling a sycamore,
Running long fingers down its shining flank.

A lurching moon, as nimble as a clown,
Cuddling the flowers and trees which burn like
    glass.
Red, kissing lips I feel you on my gown—
Kiss me, red lips, and then pass—pass.

Music, you are pitiless tonight,
And I so old, so cold, so languorously white.

At first sight it seems that there has been a falling away
from the elevation of the first three stanzas. Here we have
the moon as clown in lustful relation with the objects of
the garden. But then we notice the artistry that moves the
poem first from humming strings to the faded marquise
and finally embraces a sharply contrasting scene. The subject now is the pain of bondage to the flesh. This is vividly expressed in the most poignant passage in the poem:
"Red, kissing lips I feel you on my gown— / Kiss me, red
lips, and then pass—pass." At this point there is a sudden
break in the form and tone of the poem, which is the
verbal equivalent of the snapping of her mood. No longer
equal to the spirituality of the music and the harmonies of
the moonlit scene, there is a collapse to awareness of the
discords of her life.

"Nuit Blanche" and "Alice Meynell" can be seen in
this way as admixtures of tragic incompletion and the
glimpsing of transcendent design. In "Folie de Minuit,"
on the other hand, we have a direct challenge to the
flawed state in which man finds himself. In the poem she
wrote to a pious friend many years earlier ("To Elizabeth Ward Perkins"), Miss Lowell had stood uneasily
outside a church door incapable of the surrender of her
viewpoint for the sake of the comfort inside. In "Folie
de Minuit," she enters a cathedral as an invader with the
purpose of summoning God with an offering of music
which she is still playing, now hopelessly, at the end of
the poem.

As the poem implies, man not only suffers personal unful-
filment, but as sentient and rational being, he suffers also
because of the withdrawal of the fatherhood of his Creator. Unique and isolated in the natural scheme of things,
man can only complete his own selfhood in converse with
the *corresponding* Power he expresses. To speak in monologue is unsatisfying. Only the responses of an equal can
tell us of ourselves. "Folie de Minuit" was a reaction, in
part, to an earnest rereading of the Bible Miss Lowell
undertook at this time. In her conception, the god-man
Christ bears unmistakable signs of divinity. But Jesus lived
long ago and since the passing of that era God has been
noticeably quiescent. At least, this was Miss Lowell's view
and the cathedral we enter in her poem is a cold and
untenanted religious museum.

The quality of her emotion is given at once in a fervid
opening passage where trochaic accents, emphatic rhymes
(word-lord, city-pity, cold-boldest), and the insistence on
o and or combinations, as in snow and lord, all contribute
to the intensity of effect:

> No word, no word, O Lord God!
> Hanging above the shivering pillars
> Like thunder over a brazen city.
> Pity, is there pity?
> Does pity pour from the multiform points
> Of snow crystals?
> If the throats of the organ pipes
> Are numb with cold,
> Can the boldest bellows' blast
> Melt their now dumb hosannas?

We notice first the explosive energy which seems to top-
ple or transform the holy precincts around the poet. Part
of this establishment or religious machinery is the idea of
the loving God, but the Deity which is conceived here is
a remote and terrifying power like "thunder over a brazen
city." In contrast, man has a need for pity—not because
he is weak but because he is in darkness. This darkness
hangs over the whole poem, filling the cathedral and acting as the backdrop to the theatrical "midnight burials" of
stanza four. In this context, the poet asks how man can
expect pity in a universe symbolized by the icy perfection
of the snowflake. Such hopes are illusory, it seems, but
these same "multiform points," obviously the product of
intelligence, show that the universe is "haunted."

Since this is her conviction, a possibility that remains is to dwell on those precincts and those passages of history where the Divine was manifest in another form. This would seem to be true of ancient Palestine and the European "age of faith" which furnish the content for the section which follows, including its effulgent image of Christ:

> No word, august and brooding God!
> No shriveled spectre of an aching tone
> Can pierce those banners
> Which hide your face, your hands,
> Your feet at whose slight tread
> Frore water curds to freckled sands
> Seaweed encrusted. . . .

In this passage the use of s sounds which unify the section as a whole, the use of the dental sounds d and t in the last three lines, and the unexpected rhyme in sands-hands add to the tightness of design. Following on this, the poet says that she had hoped to break the silence of the church with golden anthems of the kind sung by the victorious Hebrews.

Though this was her purpose, everything she sees in the cathedral is choked with silence and dust, and this has affected her as well. In an extraordinary image, "My fingertips are cast in a shard of silence," she gives us her sense of the spiritual impotence of man. Without an answer from the God of the shadows, there is no possibility of communion or means by which man may truly define himself. This is the cause for the despair of the poem:

> Pity me, then,
> Who cry with wingless psalms,
> Spellbound in midnight and chill organ pipes. . . .

But it is also important to note that none of these considerations deters the poet, who is still playing religious anthems at the end of the poem.

Transcendence

The failure of the spiritual quest that Miss Lowell describes in **"Folie de Minuit"** must be qualified by reference to the mystical order of experience we have traced in her poetry. Mystic awareness is the implied subject of many poems in **What's O'Clock** and it is the predominate note of the volume. First of all, it is at the center of her long, blank-verse narrative, **"Which Being Interpreted Is As May Be or Otherwise,"** whose setting is the belfry of a cathedral and whose story is a symbolic contest between earth forces, represented by the statute of a satanic king, and the forces of spiritual aspiration, represented by the frail and other-worldly scholar, Neron. In the vividly imagined **"In Excelsis,"** remarkable for its ability to sustain the note of rapture or ecstasy, adoration of the beloved one becomes fused with religious emotion. And **"Evelyn Ray,"** a narrative lyric, interweaves a stark human tragedy with one of the poet's most evocative numinous landscapes.

This same dual theme is found in the six sonnets written for **"Eleonora Duse,"** that may be considered a conscious summation of the thought and experience of the poet. The occasion that inspired them favored this purpose. The poems were composed in December, 1923, at the height of her powers and in her last recorded "burst" of poetic creativity. Because of her circumstances at this moment and the circumstances of Duse, it was natural that the poet would be led to a special view of life and the place of the artist. However, the reader of these sonnets should not be misled into seeing them as a romanticizing of the lives and attitudes described. The strangeness of the poem is not due to sentimental distortion but rather to its fidelity to the nature of the two women involved. For this reason, we are obliged to accept these revelations in the character and form which Miss Lowell gave them.

The history began in the Boston theater in 1902 when a performance by Duse stirred new life in the neurasthenic, twenty-eight year old Miss Lowell. In terms of tragic deprivations there were similarities in the lives of the two women. We know from Miss Lowell's earliest poem that she saw in Duse the mastery and transcendence of this experience. That it could produce an awareness that would serve the purposes of art was a second discovery for her. For this reason it was Duse—with her uncanny power to detect and transmit the spiritual vibration—and not a poet of impressive formal achievement who always remained Miss Lowell's artistic ideal.

Nevertheless, Miss Lowell was unable to see Duse from 1902 to 1923 and when she encountered her again both of them were drawing to the close of their lives. Though these facts do not appear in her poem, Duse at this time was broken by age and ill health and accepted the hardships of an American tour only to gain funds for an art theater she hoped to establish in Italy. In view of these handicaps, the emaciated and white-haired actress must have made a remarkable effort. The tour calling for her appearance even as a young woman, became a succession of triumphs. Near the close of her New York engagement, Amy saw her in two performances, and then again on December 4 and 6 in Boston. The two had exchanged letters and after the second of the Boston appearances Duse came to spend a day at Sevenels. The day-long visit was a success, and that encounter, plus other performances Miss Lowell was able to see before the sudden death of the actress a few months later, furnished the inspiration for her poem:

> Seeing's believing, so the ancient word
> Chills buds to shrivelled powder flecks, turns flax
> To smoky heaps of straw whose small flames wax
> Only to gasp and die. The thing's absurd!
> Have blind men ever seen or deaf men heard?
> What one beholds but measures what one lacks.
> Where is the prism to draw gold from blacks,
> Or flash the iris colors of a bird?
> Not in the eye, be sure, nor in the ear,
> Nor in an instrument of twisted glass,
> Yet there are sights I see and sounds I hear
> Which ripple me like water as they pass.
> This that I give you for a dear love's sake
> Is curling noise of waves marching along a lake.

The dematerialization of vision, an important element in this poem, is supported by a sound-patterning which stresses high, light sounds (chills, shrivelled, iris, eye, twisted, blind, etc.) as well as a pattern of images which suggest an airy dryness: "Chills buds to shrivelled powder flecks." Emerging from this is the affirmation of the mystical insight on which Duse's power is based. Through this gift we become aware of the incompleteness of the phenomenal world which is shown to depend on essences of which we have no direct sensory awareness. In spite of its limitations, the world of sense participates in the transcendent design and is capable of stirring profound emotions: "Yet there are sights I see. . . ." After this amendment of her thesis, the poet concludes the sonnet by saying that she is writing these poems to express her love for Duse.

In sonnet two we are told of the poem's character as a letter to her friend; and there is a second challenge to the empiricist who would confine the world to what we can see:

> Seeing's believing? What then would you see?
> A chamfered dragon? Three spear-heads of steel?
> A motto done in flowered charactry?
> The thin outline of Mercury's winged heel?
> Look closer, do you see a name, a face,
> Or just a cloud dropped down before a holy place?

The images have the crisp, linear quality we found in sonnet one and we find again in lines six and seven with their account of the decisive effect of Duse on her life: "Like melted ice/I took the form and froze so" . . . Given the facts of their encounter, we are able to accept the note of worship in the last line as well as the reverence she expresses in sonnet three:

> Lady, to whose enchantment I took shape
> So long ago, though carven to your grace,
> Bearing, like quickened wood, your sweet sad face
> Cut in my flesh, yet may I not escape
> My limitations: words that jibe and gape
> After your loveliness and make grimace
> And travesty where they should interlace
> The weave of sun-spun ocean round a cape. . . .

Eloquent as these lines are, they are a *diminuendo* from the fever of the two preceding sonnets in which the poet affirms her transcendental vision. The headlong rush there is replaced by a slow, curved movement as the poet goes on to describe the meaning of Duse for her life and what Duse is in herself. For this purpose abstract or conceptual language is inadequate, so she turns to nature to suggest the qualities of the artist, concluding with a statement of Duse's affect on her world: "All that you are mingles as one sole cry/To point a world aright which is so much awry."

These lines anticipate the theme Miss Lowell develops in the two sonnets that follow. The first of these, number four, emphasizes the special character of Duse's art. So great is the understanding of this artist that it seems to embrace the whole experience of mankind. Because of her

awareness of human nature and its needs, Duse acts as a moral force which calls men to their higher selves, being picked, the poet says:

> . . . to pierce, reveal, and soothe again.
> Shattering by means of you the tinsel creeds
> Offered as meat to the pinched hearts of man.
> So, sacrificing you, she fed those others
> Who bless you in their prayers even before their
>   mothers.

The somewhat flattened tone of the last line calls attention to a peculiarity of her form. In all six sonnets the last line is drawn out by an extra two or four syllables like a whip snapped at the end, breaking the symmetry for a moment and propelling the reader to the next sonnet. It is likely that the device originated by accident when the poet found she had twelve syllables, an alexandrine, at the end of sonnet one. But from that point forward its use is deliberate, and it achieves her purpose in giving added weight to the final statement.

Sonnet five extends and varies the treatment of the theme introduced in three, but there is a new inrush of feeling as the poet turns to consider Duse in the character now of prophetess.

> Life seized you with her iron hands and shook
> The fire of your boundless burning out
> To fall on us, poor little ragged rout
> Of common men, till like a flaming book
> We, letters of a message, flashed and took
> The fiery flare of prophecy, devout
> Tourches to bear your oil, a dazzling shout,
> The liquid golden running of a brook.
> Who, being upborne on racing streams of light,
> Seeing new heavens sprung from dusty hells,
> Considered you, and what might be your plight,
> Robbed, plundered—since Life's cruel plan compels
> The perfect sacrifice of one great soul
> To make a myriad others even a whit more whole.

This is the most declamatory of the six sonnets, if that word can be taken in a favorable sense, the purpose of the poet being to proclaim the transcendent stature of Duse. The sense of urgency which fills her mind is expressed in the strongly marked accents and rhymes ("Robbed, plundered"—"Life seized you"; shook - book - brook etc.), but it comes as well from the meaning of her statements. There is an urgent need to affirm, for the experience involved turns on a tragic opposition. As men are drawn up by the fire of the prophetess and her revelation of a divine message, so they become her "torches" and finally are "upborne on racing streams of light"—this same process of spiritualization exacts unfulfillment and exhaustion for Duse, a tragedy which the poet generalizes as a law of the race in the concluding three lines of the poem.

This being true, Duse is both victor and vanquished as we reach the last section of the poem. But sonnet six, very likely the peak of Miss Lowell's art, is informed by a profundity of vision which transforms once more our view of Duse and permits the poet to conclude her poem on a note of somber exaltation:

> Seeing you stand once more before my eyes
> In your pale dignity and tenderness,
> Wearing your frailty like a mistry dress
> Draped over the great glamor which denies
> To years their domination, all disguise
> Time can achieve is but to add a stress,
> A finer finess, as though some caress
> Touched you a moment to a strange surprise.
> Seeing you after these long lengths of years
> I only know the glory come again,
> A majesty bewildered by my tears,
> A golden sun spangling slant shafts of rain,
> Moonlight delaying by a sick man's bed,
> A rush of daffodils where wastes of dried leaves
>   spread.

Taking account of this sonnet as a whole, we notice first the perfect correspondence between idea and form. Since her purpose is to express a rarefied state of mind, she has given her lines the same delicate tonality that we found in sonnet one. This is emphasized by the lightness and the chiming of the sounds—dignity, frailty, and misty all falling together in a sequence of two lines—as well as the graceful pauses in rhythm which follow the final word of nearly every line. The image which this sonnet evokes is that of the beauty of Duse as she appeared before her audiences in 1923, audiences which were often discomfited by her thinness and pallor but stayed on to be caught in the web woven by her hands and the rapt perfection of her movements. As always, she had refused to wear makeup on this last tour. "I make myself up morally," she said, and did nothing to disguise her white hair.

It is essential to know these facts in order to do justice to the poet's conception. Duse, never posessed of physical allure, was now the shell of her former self. But it does not follow from this that the poet was deceived or deceiving. Rather, this *was* her meaning in a deeper sense. The beauty that she saw in Duse was not in the flesh at all, and the passage of years had only accentuated it. *This* is the "great glamour" which enchanted her, which can annul time, and which she hastens to conjoin with those superb images of renewal and healing in the concluding lines of the poem. In doing this she crystalizes the main theme of her poetry: divinity is one whether glimpsed in a sunset, a landscape, or a human face. But this perception is not new to poetry. What is unique here is the evidence of her experience. If we look back now to the glowing images of this poem and ponder what she tells us there about her response to Duse, we can only conclude that she was participating in an exalted spiritual reality and this ecstasy is the record she left of it in her poetry.

Richard Benvenuto (essay date 1985)

SOURCE: "Imagist and Impassionist: The Major Lyrics," in *Amy Lowell*, Twayne Publishers, 1985, pp. 120–39.

[*In the following essay, Benvenuto examines the stylistic and thematic aspects of Lowell's lyrical poetry in the collections,* Pictures of the Floating World *and* What's O'Clock.]

While [Amy] Lowell was writing the dramatic and narrative poems of ***Men, Women and Ghosts, Can Grande's Castle,*** and ***Legends,*** she was developing steadily as a lyric poet as well. . . . [Her] discovery of imagism resulted in such finely wrought lyrics as **"Taxi"** and **"Aubade"** in ***Sword Blades and Poppy Seed.*** And although she often wrote with other ends in mind than those of imagism, the imagist principles taught her to focus on relevant detail and on sensory, nondiscursive language, and to value such qualities as concision and vividness as the identifying traits of modern poetry. ***Pictures of the Floating World,*** published in 1919, and ***What's O'Clock,*** published posthumously in 1925, show her often achieving these effects in her major lyrics—both in the shorter, suggestive picture poems most often associated with imagism, and in her longer lyrical meditations. By 1919, moreover, Lowell had begun to study seriously Japanese and Chinese poetry, a lifelong interest that would culminate in the collaborative translation with Florence Ayscough of Chinese lyrics in ***Fir-Flower Tablets*** (1921). The reticence, economy, and suggestiveness that Lowell found in such Oriental forms as the Japanese haiku reinforced the lessons of the imagists. Also, the emphasis, in imagist and much Oriental poetry, on objectivity, nuance, and exact language, taught Lowell to write of her own inmost feelings with greater detachment and to evoke, even from some of her most personal poems, strong transpersonal emotions.

IMAGIST ICONS: "WRITTEN PICTURES"

Although the imagists had denied that they were a school of painters, one of their aims was surely to make the reader "see"—to render particular moments and scenes out of colors and objects. And Lowell, who explored the analogies between poetry and music, was equally interested in what poetry could learn from painting—as her title, ***Pictures of the Floating World,*** suggests. While writing ***Fir-Flower Tablets,*** moreover, she had to work with a form of verse that Florence Ayscough translates as "Hanging-on-the-Wall Poems," or "Written Pictures," a form that specifically identifies poetry as a pictorial or visual art: "A beautiful thought perpetrated in beautiful handwriting and hung upon the wall to suggest a mental picture." Lowell was not concerned with only the surface of things, but she was drawn to sensory and especially visual experience, and she wrote a number of descriptive poems that read essentially like word-paintings, such as **"A Bather,"** from ***Pictures of the Floating World:***

> Thick dappled by circles of sunshine and fluttering
>   shade,
> Your bright, naked body advances, blown over by
>   leaves,
> Half-quenched in their various green, just a point of
>   you showing,
> A knee or a thigh, sudden glimpsed, then at once
>   blotted into

The filmy and flickering forest, to start out again
Triumphant in smooth, supple roundness, edged
  sharp as white ivory,
Cool, perfect, with rose rarely tinting your lips and
  your breasts,
Swelling out from the green in the opulent curves
  of ripe fruit,
And hidden, like fruit, by the swift intermittence of
  leaves.

Subtitled "After a Picture by Andreas Zorn," and delicately colored with green, ivory, and rose, **"A Bather"** is clearly more impressionistic than imagistic. It is also a composition, in the pictorial sense, using light and shade to reveal and obscure the body of the woman, which we see only in fragments or as ivorylike points in the flickering green. In the poem, of course, as opposed to the painting, the woman can move; and as she approaches the stream in which she will bathe, she weaves in and out of the forest, showing a sudden glimpse of knee or thigh, then blending black into the vegetation, only to start out again.

This image of the weaving human figure is carried beyond the purposes and the possibilities of mere surface description, however; it reveals the poem's theme, a vision of the woman's body as interwoven with nature—distinct like a bright thread in a dark cloth, but inseparable from the cloth. The woman's breasts are not merely like ripe fruit, but swell out of the leaves in the place where fruit would naturally be, suggesting that the woman is herself a tree of life. Her approach to the stream is accompanied by an urgency in the landscape for her to merge totally with it. The water is "impatient" to take her; the sky floats "solemnly" over her beauty; the river attempts to keep her "submerged and quiescent," while over her "glories / The Summer." Fusing with nature to become its spirit or life-force, she does not lose her identity as a woman but expands the significance of womanhood, becoming a symbol that Lowell discovers and examines:

Oread, Dryad, or Naiad, or just
Woman, clad only in youth and in gallant
  perfection,
Standing up in a great burst of sunshine, you dazzle
  my eyes
Like a snow-star, a moon, your effulgence burns up
  in a halo,
For you are the chalice which holds all the races of
  men.

The verbal picture has gone beyond sense experience to a mental image, to a sacramental attitude.

The difference between **"A Bather"** and an early poem like **"Teatro Bambino"** is not difficult to see. Besides a more natural language in **"A Bather,"** its mythological allusion grows organically out of the poem instead of being forced on it. Similarly, the bather who is the chalice of the human race is a more substantial and a more symbolic figure than an earlier and similar portrait of a woman—the fountain siren of **"Clear, with Light Variable Winds."**

"A Bather" is typical of Lowell's growing power, but it represents only one of several kinds of lyrics that she wrote extensively. The imagist influence, which is not strong in **"A Bather,"** is much more pronounced in the shorter haikulike poems that appear in *Pictures of the Floating World* and *What's O'Clock*. Many of these, although they have the gemlike hardness and exact language favored by the imagists, admittedly give little more than surface description—miniature pictures of trees, leaves, rivers, the sky:

Circumstance

Upon the maple leaves
The dew shines red,
But on the lotus blossom
It has the pale transparence of tears.

Others end with an idea or a symbol that their material does not justify, as in **"Ombre Chinoise,"** which is nonetheless a beautiful poem:

Red foxgloves against a yellow wall streaked with
  plum-coloured shadows;
A lady with a blue and red sunshade;
The slow dash of waves upon a parapet.
That is all.
Non-existent—immortal—
As solid as the centre of a ring of fine gold.

But we must approach even these miniature picture poems with some care, as Foster Damon illustrates in his reading of **"Outside a Gate"**: "On the floor of the empty palanquin / The plum-petals constantly increase." It is, as Damon points out [in *Amy Lowell: A Chronicle,* 1935], an imagist love poem: "The plum-petals indicate that it is spring; the palanquin is the equipage of a noble; its place at the gate shows that he is visiting; the accumulation of petals shows that his visit is a long one—and to whom does one pay long visits in spring but to one's beloved?" The so-called thinness, that is, of a number of Lowell's lyrics can be more apparent than real, and surface details can signal the presence of underlying emotions or events.

For precise description, with details that are hard and clear and yet suggestive, **"Wind and Silver,"** from *What's O'Clock,* is one of Lowell's best short lyrics and one of the most purely imagistic:

Greatly shining,
The Autumn moon floats in the thin sky;
And the fish-ponds shake their backs and flash their
  dragon scales
As she passes over them.

The poem suggests a unity in nature, a oneness between sky and earth, moon and pond. The moon "floats," as if it were in water, or as if the ponds were reflected and repeated in the sky. The fish-ponds become fish and assume the denser materiality of animal bodies. But as they "shake their backs and flash their dragon scales," the ponds also take on the property of the moon, reflecting and repeating its light on earth. . . . [The] moon is an important symbol in Lowell's poetry, and it is often described in goddess-like terms or as an unattainable enchantress. The metaphorical dragon, on the other hand, evokes the familiar beast from folklore and legend that holds the princess captive or guards the entrance to a magic castle or cave. Frazer says that dragons are often identified in folktales as water spirits inhabiting and controlling fountains or lakes, and that young women were sometimes sacrificed to them as brides. **"Wind and Silver"** at least hints at such associations. The moon, a feminine symbol and identified as "she," transforms the ponds into something bestial and alive, a dragon that flashes at her as if to allure or pursue.

And yet the floating moon and the lit ponds have exchanged identities. A similar idea informs **"The Sand Altar,"** which is on the same page as **"Wind and Silver"** in *The Complete Poetical Works,* and which can be taken as a companion piece to it.

> With a red grain and a blue grain, placed in
>   precisely the proper positions, I made a beautiful
>   god, with plumes of yard-long feathers and a
>   swivel eye.
>
> And with a red grain and a blue grain, placed in
>   precisely the proper positions, I made a dragon,
>   with scaly wings and a curling, iniquitous tail.
>
> Then I reflected:
> If, with the same materials, I can make both god
>   and dragon, of what use is the higher
>   mathematics?
>
> Having said this, I went outdoors and stood under a
>   tree and listened to the frogs singing their
>   evening songs in the green darkness.

"The Sand Altar" focuses on the very activity that creates a unity of opposites, thus bringing to consciousness the submerged imaginative operations that resulted in the unifying images and metaphors of **"Wind and Silver."** In both poems, however, the interconnection or common origin of bestial and ideal images questions the dualistic view of the universe as divided between divine and demonic forces. **"The Sand Altar,"** with its moral (as well as mathematical) perplexity, is a more explicit challenge than **"Wind and Silver,"** but neither poem attempts to state a particular philosophy. Rather, Lowell retreats from her discovery that the same materials produce "both god and dragon," back to external nature, to the neighborhood of ponds, as suggested by the frogs. They sing undisturbed, not to a contrasting image of light, but within a green, encompassing darkness.

We do not always find such suggestiveness and depth in Lowell's pictorial lyrics, but for that matter we do not always find them in any poet. The longer written pictures range from the self-conscious word-painting of the poem immediately preceding **"A Bather"** and aptly named **"Impressionist Picture of a Garden"**:

> Give me sunlight, cupped in a paint brush,
> And smear the red of peonies
> Over my garden.
> Splash blue upon it,
> The hard blue of Canterbury bells . . .

—where there is little more than an itemization of colors and flowers—to the sexually suggestive, eerie garden in **"Sultry"**:

> To those who can see them, there are eyes,
> Leopard eyes of marigolds crouching above red
>   earth,
> Bulging eyes of fruits and rubies in the heavily-
>   hanging trees,
> Broken eyes of queasy cupids staring from the
>   gloom of myrtles.
> I came here for solitude
> And I am plucked at by a host of eyes.

The imagery recalls Lowell's earlier poem, **"The Basket,"** in which a woman eats human eyes as calmly as if they were shelled nuts. Here, a garden of eyes threatens to devour a woman. Seeking solitude, she finds herself the focus of a cunning, waiting nature which, with its eyes of leopards and cupids and bulging red fruit, surrounds her with images of fecundity and an intimidating, almost certainly sexual, power.

At the center of the picture, pointing at her, is a statue of Hermes, a god notorious for his amorous interests and called the "ever-smitten Hermes" by Keats in "Lamia." Lowell would surely be aware of the parallel between her poem and the opening scene of Keats's, in which an invisible, shy nymph is revealed to Hermes by a lamia whose body is marked with leopardlike spots and peacock eyes—after which Hermes sexually possesses the nymph. Lowell's Hermes, in a garden where eyes pluck at her and all of nature seems lewdly voyeuristic, is satyrlike and "more savage than the goat-legged Pan." He catches "men's eyes" with his youth, his manhood, and the reticence of [his] everlasting revelation. Capturing her attention, Hermes forces Lowell to see, to become "a cunning eye" and thus partake in the sexual character of the garden; and he awakens her imagination, causing her to seek in the distant past for the original Hermes, in an attempt to enter the world or reality of his revelation.

She finds the hidden, original force that this "time-gnawed" statue reveals, but it does not renew her:

> Yours are the eyes of a bull and a panther,
> For all that they are chiselled out and the sockets
>   empty.
> You—perfectly imperfect,
> Clothed in a garden,
> In innumerable gardens,
> Borrowing the eyes of fruits and flowers—
> And mine also, cold, impossible god,
> So that I stare back at myself
> And see myself with loathing.

Having originally gone to the garden to be alone, she now sees herself as others, or as nature and Hermes, see her. The intense self-consciousness of staring at herself results in a self-rejection that recalls her fearful prophesy in **"A Fairy Tale,"** that she would "never . . . be fulfilled by love." But of course **"Sultry"** is considerably more complex than the early autobiographical poem; Hermes, the object and the cause of sexual awareness, is at once predatory, fruitful, and an empty ruin. And it is not clear whether Lowell's self-hatred results from her admission of her sexual unattractiveness to a Hermes or to any man, or from her rejection of his intimidating and sexually restrictive point of view—a refusal to see herself as a sexual object. Whether the mode of seeing is loathsome, or the woman seen, or both, the experience is destructive, reducing Lowell to a "shadow, tortured out of semblance," who can "see nothing." The vivid picture of a garden of eyes ends in sightlessness.

LOVE POEMS: THE LADY OF HER CHOICE

The single most important figure in Lowell's lyrics is Ada Dwyer Russell, her housemate and companion for the last decade of her life. Dwyer unquestionably gave Lowell emotional ballast and crucial support in the years of controversy and illness that followed 1914. Lowell nicknamed her friend "Peter"—the rock; and she resented and feared the separations caused by Dwyer's occasional visits to her family. Whether the two women were physical lovers has not, to my knowledge, been confirmed. Jean Gould [in *Amy: The World of Amy Lowell and the Imagist Movement,* 1975] refers to, but does not elaborate upon, Lowell's "bisexual tendencies" and "psychosexual conflict." Many of Lowell's narratives and monologues . . . deal with male-female relations, but the tendency of these is to end in frustration (**"The Cremona Violin," "The Rosebud Wall-Paper"**); bitterness (**"Patterns"**); or psychic or physical destruction (**"The Basket," "The Great Adventure of Max Breuck"**). Of course, conflict, tension, and even violence are common elements of narrative, and Lowell's men are as likely to become victims as are her women. Still, just as there is a great difference between the female-centered, nurturing nature of **"A Bather"** and Hermes' leering, aggressive garden in **"Sultry,"** so the contrast between the narratives about heterosexual love and the love lyrics to Ada Dwyer is striking. The Ada Dwyer poems are marked by tenderness and fulfillment, and often rise to a tone of rapturous adoration.

As the loved one, Dwyer takes on several roles or identities, which Lowell develops in some detail in the section of *Pictures of the Floating World* called **"Two Speak Together,"** a collection of poems dealing with her and her companion. Dwyer is nature's symbol, a presence that combines and evokes the beautiful flowers and trees in Lowell's garden:

> When I think of you, Beloved,
> I see a smooth and stately garden
> With parterres of gold and crimson tulips
> And bursting lilac leaves.
>
>   (**"Mise en Scene"**)

In **"Wheat-in-the-Ear,"** where she is a radiant gem, a spear that burns, Dwyer combines matter and light, form and energy.

> You flash in front of the cedars and the tall
>   spruces,
> And I see that you are fire—
> Sacrificial fire on a jade altar,
> Spear-tongue of white, ceremonial fire.

She is, in the metaphoric **"The Weather-Cock Points South,"** like an unblemished white flower from which Lowell carefully peels the petals.

> One by one
> I parted you from your leaves,
> Until you stood up like a white flower
> Swaying slightly in the evening wind.

Again, but even more explicitly than in **"A Bather,"** a woman's body becomes and takes the place of a plant.

The nakedness in **"Wheat-in-the-Ear"** and the sensuous, figurative disrobing here recall Lowell's fascination with the nude female body. At the same time, Ada Dwyer was past fifty when the **"Two Speak Together"** poems appeared, and it is unlikely that Lowell meant the nakedness to be taken literally. Rather, her love for the other woman has stripped their relationship of the patterns that restrain and war against passion; or, to take another idea from **"Patterns,"** Dwyer acts out the desire to become one with nature and to reveal her hidden self. She thus shows Lowell a fresh, ageless beauty. Moreover, an image of a jade cup in **"Wheat-in-the-Ear"** connects her to the more universal symbol of womanhood in **"A Bather"**—the "chalice" that "holds" the human race.

Ultimately, Dwyer's nakedness is that of an ideal made flesh, a sacramental revelation of holiness or even divinity in human form, and with very different associations from those of Hermes. In **"Mise en Scene,"** Dwyer's shawl flares behind her like the "draperies of a painted Madonna." Two poems later in the sequence, Dwyer is the **"Madonna of the Evening Flowers,"** at whose feet Lowell longs "to kneel." She is also a modern Venus in **"Venus Transiens"**:

> Tell me,
> Was Venus more beautiful
> Than you are,
> When she topped
> The crinkled waves,
> Drifting shoreward
> On her plaited shell?

By finding in Dwyer the beauty of the Madonna and of a goddess of love, Lowell combines two usually opposed images of woman.

The religious associations suggested by the Madonna and Venus are carried even further and made more explicit. Dwyer—whose beauty inspired Lowell the poet and whose love sustained Lowell the person—becomes a source of sacramental nourishment, the bread and wine of Lowell's life:

> When you came, you were like red wine and honey,
> And the taste of you burnt my mouth with its
>   sweetness.
> Now you are like morning bread,
> Smooth and pleasant.
> I hardly taste you at all for I know your savour,
> But I am completely nourished.
>
> ("**A Decade**")

Only a letter distinguishes between "savour" and "Saviour," thus strengthening the associations with Christ of the bread and wine. In **"Orange of Midsummer,"** Lowell goes beyond the symbolic bread and wine to blood itself, which Dwyer, like Christ, gives her to drink in a cup—in effect, the chalice, which Lowell identifies with womanhood.

> "Are you thirsty?" said you,
> And held out a cup.
> But the water in the cup was scarlet and crimson
> Like the poppies in your hands.
> "It looks like blood," I said.
> "Like blood," you said,
> "Does it?
> But drink it, my Beloved."

Not surprisingly, when Ada Dwyer is separated from her, Lowell feels empty and desolate; the nights frighten her, and nature seems meaningless or incomplete, as in **"Left Behind"**:

> I cannot look at the flowers,
> Nor the lifting leaves of the trees.
> Without you, there is no garden,
> No bright colours,
> No shining leaves.
> There is only space,
> Stretching endlessly forward. . . .

Without Dwyer, a city she is visiting seems "incoherent" and "trivial," and Lowell's "brain aches with emptiness" (**"The Sixteenth Floor."**) In **"Autumn,"** someone brings Lowell a bright yellow dahlia, an image of "Fecundity." But Dwyer's absence makes Lowell barren, and she offers to send the flower to her friend, who has taken with her "All I once possessed." With Ada Dwyer gone, the center of the garden, of life, falls apart; without its symbolic flower, its nourishing cup, imagination remains passive before the fecund dahlia. In **"Frimaire,"** the last of the **"Two Speak Together"** poems, Lowell imagines herself and Dwyer as the last two flowers in a late autumn garden, and wonders anxiously about their final separation: which one of them will die first, leaving the other alone? But a haiku, from **"The Anniversary"** in *What's O'Clock,* states an even closer relationship to her friend, and keeps the flower (and the nourishment) metaphor:

> You wrong me, saying:
> One death will not kill us both.
> Your veins hold my sap.

What's O'Clock also contains the beautiful **"Song for a Viola D'Amore,"** which begins, "The lady of my choice is bright / As a clematis at the touch of night," and which is almost certainly an Ada Dwyer poem; and **"Vespers,"** in which Dwyer is again necessary for nature to have meaning. The foxgloves in the poem would burn to her, as to a Venus or Madonna:

> Last night, at sunset,
> The foxgloves were like tall altar candles.
> Could I have lifted you to the roof of the
>   greenhouse, my Dear,
> I should have understood their burning.

"Vespers" is followed by **"In Excelsis,"** the most comprehensive of the Ada Dwyer love poems, the one in which Lowell brings together the various images, symbols, and intimations of the others:

> You—you—
> Your shadow is sunlight on a plate of silver;
> Your footsteps, the seeding-place of lilies;
> Your hands moving, a chime of bells across a
>   windless air.

A profusion of images and details portrays the "you," the loved one, as an encompassing, pervasive force, so that Dwyer's presence—which is like sunlight and water, the sound of bees and wasps, "the perfume of jonquils"—is as close and as vast as that of nature's. As the central figure in the garden, she makes it fruitful—her footsteps are "the seeding place of lilies"; and she feeds, with a sacramental meal, Lowell the gardener: "I drink your lips, / I eat the whiteness of your hands and feet." Though inaccessible as the clouds, the loved one touches the heart mysteriously, like a rainbow. Gould calls **"In Excelsis"** an "adoration." And in fact, more than anything else, it resembles a modern psalm, a devotional hymn not just to Ada Dwyer, who is not named in any of these poems, but to the redeeming power of love—a human force that virtually takes the place of God and gives meaning and beauty to life, prompting Lowell to respond with "those things" that make her a poet.

But though the lover feels the wonder and power of love, the experience is not the transcendental visitation that came upon the early romantics; nor does Lowell, who once thought of writing a book on Matthew Arnold, seek relief from a Victorian crisis of faith. The experience remains finite, within the familiar world of earth and sky, and the lovers do not have to remain true to each other for protection against a world that is not as true or beautiful as it seemed. Rather, Lowell sings "Glory! Glory!" because Dwyer's presence and love have lit the darkling plain.

SPRING AND FALL:
INTIMATIONS OF MORTALITY

In **"Frimaire,"** as already mentioned, Lowell wonders whether she or Ada Dwyer will be the first to die. In **"Penumbra,"** the poem immediately preceding **"Frimaire,"** Lowell thinks of her own death, and wonders what it will be like for Dwyer then. Lowell claims that she will not really be absent, because her house and garden, her pictures and books, which she has known so long and loved so well, will speak to Dwyer for her. But in **"The Garden by Moonlight,"** Lowell directs her companion to a row of orange lilies. "They knew my mother," she says, "But who belonging to me will they know / When I am gone." Despite the high spirits that she showed almost to the end, Lowell thought about mortality more as she grew older and more infirm, and in some of the finest of her later lyrics she took up such issues as the possibilities of permanence in a world governed by change, and explored the connections between time present and time lost.

Lowell thought about mortality more as she grew older . . . , and explored the connections between time present and time lost.

—Richard Benvenuto

Two companion poems in *What's O'Clock,* **"Lilacs"** and **"Purple Grackles,"** juxtapose the two seasons spring and fall, with **"Lilacs"** celebrating the spring that the flower stands for—"May is lilac here in New England"—and **"Purple Grackles"** memorializing the death of summer as signaled by the birds clustering in the fall. From May in the one poem to September in the other, a season of fulfillment changes into a time portending decay.

"Lilacs" represents the best of the familiar Lowell, the Lowell commonly identified as a word-painter, or imagist turned into an elaborate chronicler of bright surfaces:

> Lilacs,
> False blue,
> White,
> Purple,
> Colour of lilac,
> Your great puffs of flowers
> Are everywhere in this my New England.

But the lilacs provide more than a colorful picture. As the lilacs "are everywhere" now, so they "were everywhere" in the past, thus connecting the present with an earlier New England. Now they watch a deserted house. Earlier, they "tapped the window when the preacher preached his sermon," and "flaunted the fragrance" of their blossoms "Through the wide doors of Custom Houses . . . When a ship was in from China." Like sirens of nature, the lilacs tempt the "quill-driving" Custom House clerks until they writhe on their high stools and write poetry "on their letter-sheets behind the propped-up ledgers." The scene is like a page out of Wordsworth. Quit your books, the lilacs seem to be saying, "May is a month for flitting." But unlike Wordsworth, Lowell makes no claim for a greater

moral wisdom in nature. The lilacs simply oppose their beauty to the pursuit of profit, as they stir the restless imaginations of a people devoted to commerce.

Immigrants themselves, moreover, like the New Englanders, the lilacs have spread "From Canada to Narragansett Bay" to become the symbol or emblem of the region's inner self: "You are the great flood of our souls / Bursting above the leaf-shapes of our hearts." Lowell's language makes one body, one being, out of the flowers and the people—the "heart-shaped leaves" of the one matching and mirroring the leaf-shaped "hearts" of the other. The common identity is pressed even closer in the "heart-leaves" of the poem's beautiful final lines:

> Heart-leaves of lilac all over New England,
> Roots of lilac under all the soil of New England,
> Lilacs in me because I am New England,
> Because my roots are in it,
> Because my leaves are of it,
> Because my flowers are for it,
> Because it is my country
> And I speak to it of itself
> And sing of it with my own voice
> Since certainly it is mine.

As the speaker turns herself into a lilac, thus both personifying the flower and using it as a metaphor for herself, self-discovery and the recognition of a collective, lasting regional identity take place together.

In *What's O'Clock,* **"Lilacs"** is immediately followed by **"Purple Grackles,"** and as the season changes from May to September, so does the color of the landscape to the darker purple and black of the grackles. Unlike the deep-rooted, permanent lilacs, moreover, the grackles are only temporary visitors, stopping each year for a short stay in Lowell's garden on their migration south. Their sudden appearance startles and delights her, and though its meaning is essentially somber, the poem opens with an amused, celebratory welcoming of the birds:

> The grackles have come.
> The smoothness of the morning is puckered with
> 　　their incessant chatter.
> A sociable lot, these purple grackles,
> Thousands of them strung across a long run of
> 　　wind,
> Thousands of them beating the air-ways with quick
> 　　wing-jerks,
> Spinning down the currents of the South.

Her attitude even becomes whimsical as Lowell wonders if the grackles are perhaps really blackberries, they cluster in the trees so thickly, or like highwaymen and thieves, except that they are so loud and unstealthy. Only when she realizes that they are stealing her summer does a different note enter, for the dark birds force her to see that her "hydrangea blooms are rusty," that the golden hearts of the flowers are changing to "lusterless seeds," and that the sun is as pale as a shrinking lemon. She "did not see this yesterday, / But to-day the grackles have come."

Though the seasonal changes are taking place as close to Lowell as her own garden, and though the grackles envelop her, she does not become one with them or their world as she did with the lilacs. Even when the antics of the birds delight her, as when they use her rainfilled gutter for bathing because she has not provided them with a suitable bath, her language suggests that she remains indoors, watching them from behind the safety of her window. She speaks of herself as their host, but knows that they do not take her into account or consider her important:

> Tyrian-feathered freebooter,
> Appropriating my delightful gutter with so
>   extravagant an ease,
> You are as cool a pirate as ever scuttled a ship,
> And are you not scuttling my Summer with every
>   peck of your sharp bill?

It is an amusing, even a touching scene, and the one in which Lowell comes closest to the foreign, animal independence of the grackles—to the otherness of nature. She addresses the bird, as she repeatedly did the lilacs, with the conversational "you." Elsewhere in the poem she uses the more distant and impersonal "they." But Lowell can come this close to the grackles because her window separates her from them; and the scene as a whole, an incident in the "scuttling" of her summer, underscores her helplessness as a human to do anything about the changes that nature brings.

While she can "only stare stupidly out of the window," the grackles depart as suddenly and mysteriously as they arrived, "and it is a year gone by":

> And I watch an Autumn storm
> Stripping the garden,
> Shouting black rain challenges
> To an old, limp Summer
> Laid down to die in the flower-beds.

Tragedy has evolved out of whimsical, comic beginnings, as a world full of movement and sound becomes old and limp, and as a deadly black rain replaces the lively black birds. The world of **"Lilacs"** seems far removed, yet its companion poem mourns for the world that poem celebrated.

Taken together, **"Lilacs"** and **"Purple Grackles"** encompass the spring and fall of external nature. **"On Looking at a Copy of Alice Meynell's Poems"** moves the cycle inward to the soul's experiences of youth and age, past and present. Lowell's friend Frances Dabney had given her the volume of Meynell's poems in the late 1890s, while the two of them were in Devonshire, England, where Lowell hoped to shake off a severe nervous depression. Reading the book again, after Meynell's death in 1922, Lowell recalls that earlier painful time when she and Dabney read it first:

> You gave this book to me to ease
> The smart in me you could not heal.
> Your gift a mirror—woe or weal.
> We sat beneath the apple-trees.

> And I remember how they rang,
> These words, like bronze cathedral bells
> Down ancient lawns, or citadels
> Thundering with gongs where choirs sang.

> Silent the sea, the earth, the sky,
> And in my heart a silent weeping.
> Who has not sown can know no reaping!
> Bitter conclusion and no lie.

> O heart that sorrows, heart that bleeds,
> Heart that was never mine, your words
> Were like the pecking Autumn birds
> Stealing away my garnered seeds.

> No future where there is no past!
> O cherishing grief which laid me bare,
> I wrapped you like a wintry air
> About me. Poor enthusiast!

Lowell remembers her early womanhood, not as the traditional springtime of youth, but as a barren, bitter season. The Meynell poems, in which she sees herself as in a "mirror," are like a "wintry air," or "Autumn birds" stealing the last of her pent-up, unfruitful feelings. The silent, almost colorless landscape of the beginning of the poem also mirrors, and is made the projection of, her silent suffering, while a ship that "sleeps" motionlessly for three hours symbolizes the inertia of her feelings, the state she is stuck in. Yet while the landscape portrays her, her condition remains invisible to her friend. Instead of intimacy and sharing between the two women, there is separation and blindness. Lowell remembers Dabney with kindness, but a harsh accusation—were you made of "wood or stone?"—reveals her essential loneliness, her sense of being in the company of a stranger instead of a friend. Even Meynell's poems, in which Lowell finds a fellow sufferer in a stranger, seem distant and of another time, like cathedral bells over "ancient lawns" or thunderings in empty choir lofts—with Lowell's image echoing Shakespeare's powerful metaphor for the autum of life: "those boughs which shake against the cold / Bare ruin'd choirs, where late the sweet birds sang." Lowell's fear, moreover, in what should be the springtime of her life, is that she will have no harvest, will "know no reaping." In 1899 she had not yet discovered the outlet of poetry, but rather finds her feelings appropriated and expressed in the verses of another. In more than one sense of the term, then, she has come to a "Bitter conclusion."

The last stanzas of the poem return to the present. The episode seems "strange" in 1922, when Lowell can remember but is no longer possessed by the griefs of 1899. Meynell's poems do not move her as they did, or ring like bells, but are simply well-crafted lines fading into the past they belong to: "The ink is pale, the letters fade. / The verses seem to be well made." Reminding her that the time that they mirrored is dead, they lead her to think of death—first Dabney's, then Meynell's:

> And you are dead these drifted years,
> How many I forget. And she

Who wrote the book, her tragedy
Long since dried up its scalding tears.

I read of her death yesterday,
Frail lady whom I never knew
And knew so well. Would I could strew
Her grave with pansies, blue and grey.

Would I could stand a little space
Under a blowing, brightening sky,
And watch the sad leaves fall and lie
Gently upon that lonely place.

So cried her heart, a feverish thing.
But clay is still, and clay is cold,
And I was young, and I am old,
And in December what birds sing!

In effect, the poem portrays a spiritual wasteland, the soul's encounter with desolate or destructive truths. Though the present has moved beyond the past, there is little indication of a change for the better in the quarter century since Lowell first read Meynell. If anything, as the last surviver of the trio in the poem, her loneliness is even more complete. Time brings death, not renewal, and the autumn landscape remains or edges closer to winter, when the autumn of harvesting birds changes into birdless December. Like the motionless ship, like Lowell's old nervous prostration, the seasonal cycle gets stuck and breaks down.

Thus, the *In Memoriam* stanza that Lowell had used in one of her earliest poems is particularly appropriate for this, one of her last. For **"On Looking at a Copy of Alice Meynell's Poems"** is a memorial to all three of the women in it: to the well-meaning but imperceptive friend who became a stranger, to the poet whose tragedy has long since cooled, and to the earlier self from whom Lowell is as separated now as she is from the other two. Not only have past emotions and relationships died, they have left little trace in the present; their having been brings little comfort. Hence, Lowell does not recall the past to keep it in memory, but to have done with it:

Go, wistful book, go back again
Upon your shelf and gather dust.
I've seen the glitter through the rust
Of old, long years, I've known the pain.

I've recollected both of you,
But I shall recollect no more.
Between us I must shut the door.
The living have so much to do.

Perhaps not all is dark in this essentially dark and troubled poem, which is itself a hard-won harvest of the past, despite Lowell's fear that she would know no reaping of her old suffering. The distant emotions still glitter through the rust of time, even if they can no longer be felt. And she looks ahead to the business of living. But even here, Lowell speaks with more resignation than eagerness or sense of triumph over mortality, in a tone not unlike that

of Hopkins when, in another poem about isolation and hoarded pain, he called himself "a lonely began."

The **"Alice Meynell"** poem is powerful in its very negations—its sense of helplessness, loss, and the corroding, killing years. A sonnet to Eleanora Duse, one of six written at about the same time as **"Alice Meynell,"** deals just as honestly with similar ideas, but celebrates the power of a soul to survive the years and even grow more luminous as mortality approaches:

Seeing you stand once more before my eyes
In your pale dignity and tenderness,
Wearing your frailty like a misty dress
Draped over the great glamour which denies
To years their domination, all disguise
Time can achieve is but to add a stress,
A finer fineness, as though some caress
Touched you a moment to a strange surprise.

Lowell had not seen Duse since 1902, when she was inspired by the actress to write her first poem. Now, in 1923, Duse was sixty-five years old, gaunt, white haired, and, like Lowell, near death. But in the sonnet, the frail body is only an outward, almost transparent dress, through which Lowell can see and affirm something that is permanent or eternal, so that "after these long lengths of years . . . the glory come[s] again"—thus uniting past and present as one time. Duse, though not idealized as a Madonna or a Venus, but merely human, becomes Lowell's symbol of man's victory over time. Though the body ages, it is not vanquished by time, but becomes more spiritual. And all time can do to the soul is give a finer edge to its power to transcend time.

In what G. R. Ruihley aptly calls "those superb images of renewal and healing in the concluding lines of the poem," [in *The Thorn of a Rose: Amy Lowell Reconsidered,* 1975] Lowell extends the power to defeat time into nature, making it a natural principle or force—in the sun that shines through shafts of rain; in the moon, Lowell's familiar symbol of transcendent beauty, lighting up a sick man's bed; in the daffodils, flowers of spring, growing in a waste of leaves. Images of spring and fall, the promising and the perishing, appear together in a beautifully written traditional sonnet in which Lowell uses the precision and natural speech of the New Poetry. And like most of Lowell's best work, it is faithful to the appearance and inquiring into the mysteries of life.

FURTHER READING

Biography

Gould, Jean. *Amy: The World of Amy Lowell and the Imagist Movement.* New York: Dodd, Mead & Company, 1975, 372 p.
    Biography of Lowell that emphasizes her role as a leading figure among the Imagist poets.

Sprague, Rosemary. "Amy Lowell." In *Imaginary Gardens: A Study of Five American Poets*, pp. 49–96. Philadelphia: Chilton Book Company, 1969.

Largely biographical exploration of Lowell's career that highlights her efforts as a poetic innovator and experimenter.

Criticism

Aiken, Conrad. "The Technique of Polyphonic Prose: Amy Lowell." In *Scepticisms: Notes on Contemporary Poetry*, pp. 115–25. New York: Alfred A. Knopf, 1919.

Outlines the artistic limitations of Lowell's *Can Grande's Castle*.

Ambrose, Jane P. "Amy Lowell and the Music of Her Poetry." *The New England Quarterly* LXII, No. 1 (March 1989): 45–62.

Analysis of musical elements in Lowell's poetry.

Ayscough, Florence. "Amy Lowell and the Far East." *The Bookman* LXIII, No. 1 (March 1926): 11–18.

Overview of Lowell's Oriental poems in which Ayscough recounts the experiments in technique Lowell conducted during their collaboration.

Flint, F. Cudworth. *Amy Lowell*. Minneapolis: University of Minnesota Press, 1969, 48 p.

Biographical and critical assessment of Lowell's literary career.

Katz, Michael. "Amy Lowell and the Orient." *Comparative Literature Studies* XVIII, No. 2 (June 1981): 124–40.

Discusses Far Eastern influences in Lowell's poetry as far back as *Sword Blades and Poppy Seed* (1914).

Macleish, Archibald. "Amy Lowell and the Art of Poetry." *North American Review* CCXXI (March 1925): 508–21.

Praises Lowell's talents and asserts her poetic significance.

Schwartz, William Leonard. "A Study of Amy Lowell's Far Eastern Verse." *Modern Language Notes* XLIII, No. 3 (March 1928): 145–52.

Concludes that Lowell was more a propagandist than an interpreter of Far Eastern poetry.

Untermeyer, Louis. "Amy Lowell." In *American Poetry Since 1900*, pp. 135–56. New York: Henry Holt and Company, 1923.

Lauds Lowell's poetic versatility and technical virtuosity.

Walker, Cheryl. "Amy Lowell and the Androgynous Persona." In *Masks: Outrageous and Austere: Culture, Psyche, and Persona in Modern Women Poets*, pp. 16–43. Bloomington: Indiana University Press, 1991.

Interprets Lowell's poetry from a feminist perspective, analyzing the politics of gender in her writings.

Wood, Clement. *Amy Lowell*. New York: Harold Vinal, 1926, 185 p.

Critical study of Lowell that reveals a consistent contempt for her work.

Interviews

Kilmer, Joyce. "The New Spirit in Poetry: Amy Lowell." In *Literature in the Making by Some of Its Makers*, pp. 253–62. New York: Harper & Brothers, 1917.

Interview in which Kilmer elicits Lowell's theories of poetry.

Additional coverage of Lowell's life and career is contained in the following sources published by Gale Research: *Contemporary Authors*, Vol. 104; *Dictionary of Literary Biography*, Vols. 54, 140; and *Twentieth-Century Literary Criticism*, Vols. 1, 8.

Eugenio Montale
1896–1981

Italian poet, critic, journalist, essayist, translator, and short story writer.

INTRODUCTION

Recipient of the 1975 Nobel Prize for literature, Montale affirmed through poetry a belief in human dignity and the ultimate value of existence, but also expressed pessimism at the disparity between human spiritual aspirations and the reality of our condition. His existentially profound poetry is conveyed in deeply personal and impressionistic terms, which contrasted with the embellished, formal style that predominated in Italy in the early decades of the twentieth century. According to Montale, "I wanted to free the music in words, apply them to reality, and in transcending mere depiction, capture what is essential." Because of its subjectivity, Montale's verse often verges on impenetrable, leading some critics to label him a hermetic poet.

Biographical Information

Montale was born in Genoa in 1896 into a wealthy family. He attended school until the age of fourteen, when poor health prevented further formal education. Montale entered the army in 1917 and published his first poems that same year. Upon leaving the military after World War I, he returned to Genoa, where he co-founded a short-lived literary journal and began contributing poems, articles, and reviews to newspapers and magazines. After relocating to Florence, where he worked for the publisher Bemporad from 1927 to 1928, Montale assumed the directorship of the Gabinetto Vieusseux Library, a position he held for a decade before being forced to resign due to his anti-Fascist sympathies. In spite of this occurrence, biographers note that he avoided direct political involvement throughout his life. Montale worked primarily as a translator and as the poetry critic of *La fiera letteraria* during World War II. He joined the staff of a Milan daily paper, *Corriere della sera* in 1948. During his career with *Corriere della sera,* Montale functioned as a literary editor and music critic and served in the latter capacity until his death.

Major Works

Montale published five major verse collections: *Ossia di seppia* (*Cuttlefish Bones*), *Le occasioni* (*The Occasions*), *La bufera e altro* (*The Storm, and Other Poems*), *Satura* (*Miscellany*), and *Diario del '71 e del '72*. In the first, *Cuttlefish Bones*, the sea and rugged shore of the Ligurian coast near Genoa serve as symbols of the poet's emotional and mental states. The bleak and harsh landscape not only conveys the ethical and metaphysical anguish that was palpable in the aftermath of World War I but also represents

what Montale perceived as ungovernable forces that shape human experience. The poems register loneliness, exhaustion, and despair, and ultimately offer no resolutions to the poet's anxiety. Later volumes incorporate some of these motifs and introduce new emphases as well. *The Occasions* examines love and the relationship of the individual to the whole of humanity and history; *The Storm, and Other Poems* explores the significance of personal values and integrity, especially in the tumult of modern times. In several poetry collections Montale speaks to a symbolic female figure, sometimes identified as Clizia or Volpe, who is an idealized lover or the embodiment of goodness and strength. The poet addresses his deepest concerns for himself and humanity to these angelic beings and draws hope and inspiration from them.

Critical Reception

Cuttlefish Bones established Montale's reputation as a fresh new voice in Italian poetry, but it was after *The Storm, and Other Poems* that he received considerable public recognition. His disinterest in realism and his use of external phenomena—landscape, historical events, and physical objects—as a means of revealing thoughts and states of mind has led commentators to observe the influence of the Symbolist poets in his work. Montale's focus on psychological and emotional states renders his verse subjective and sometimes inscrutable, leading to occasional accusations of intentional obscurity. Readers generally agree that the work composed later in his career is more accessible, particularly the ruminations about his deceased wife in *Xenia*. When comparing Montale to other poets, critics usually mention T. S. Eliot and Dante Alighieri. They observe in *Cuttlefish Bones* the stark, apocalyptic imagery, the bleak view of modern life, and the persistent hope that characterize Eliot's *The Wasteland*. Commentators perceive that Beatrice, about whom Dante wrote love poetry, served as a model for the female figures in Montale's verse; furthermore, both poets are recognized for their command of the Italian language, treatment of horror, solitude, and misery, and images of purgatory and hell.

PRINCIPAL WORKS

Poetry

Ossi di Seppia [*Cuttlefish Bones*] 1925
*La casa dei doganieri e altri poesie [*The Customs House, and Other Poems*] 1932
Le occasioni [*The Occasions*] 1939
*Finisterre [*Land's End*] 1943
Poesie 1948
Poesie 1949
La bufera e altro [*The Storm, and Other Poems*] 1956
Poesie 1957
Poems from Eugenio Montale 1959
Accordi e pastelli [*Harmony and Pastels*] 1962
Satura [*Miscellany*] 1962
Poesie: Poems 1965
Selected Poems 1965
Il coplevole [*The Offender*] 1966
*Xenia 1966
Eugenio Montale: Selected Poems 1970
Provisional Conclusions: A Selection of the Poetry of Eugenio Montale, 1920–1970 1970
Satura: 1962–1970 1971
Diario del '71 e del '72 1973
Motetti: The Motets of Eugenio Montale 1973
Trentadue variazioni 1973
†New Poems 1976
Quaderno di quattro anni [*It Depends: A Poet's Notebook*] 1977
Tutte le poesie [*All the Poems*] 1977
L'Opera in versi [*Poetical Works*] 1980
Altre versi e poesie disperse [*Otherwise: Last and First Poems of Eugenio Montale*] 1981
Poesie inedite. 6 vols. 1986–

*These three collections of poems also appeared in other volumes as follows: *La casa dei doganieri e altri versi* in *Le occasioni*; *Finisterre* in *La bufera e altro*; and *Xenia* in *Satura*.

†Selections from *Satura: 1962–1970* and *Diario del '71 e del '72*.

Other Major Works

Omaggio a Italo Svevo (criticism) 1925
La storia di Billy Budd [translator; from the novella *Billy Budd* by Herman Melville] 1942
Strano interludio [translator; from the drama *Strange Interlude* by Eugene O'Neill] 1943
Quaderno di traduzioni [translator; from works by various authors] 1948
Amleto, principe di Danimarca [translator; from the drama *Hamlet* by William Shakespeare] 1949
Al dio sconsciuto [translator; from the novel *To a God Unknown* by John Steinbeck] 1954
La farfalla di Dinard [*The Butterfly of Dinard*] (short stories, prose poems, and sketches) 1956
Auto de fé: Cronache in due tempi [*Act of Faith: Chronicles from Two Periods*] (essays) 1966
Eugenio Montale/Italo Svevo: Lettere, con gli scritti de Montale su Svevo [*Eugenio Montale/Italo Svevo: Letters, with Montale's Writings on Svevo*] (letters and essays) 1966
Fuori di case [*Away from Home*] (travel essays) 1969
La poesia non esiste [*Poetry Does Not Exist*] (short fiction) 1971
Nel Nostro Tempo [*Poet in Our Time*] (prose) 1972
E ancora possible la poesie? [*Is Poetry Still Possible?*] (Nobel Prize speech) 1975
Sulla poesia [*On Poetry*] (essays) 1976
Selected Essays (essays) 1978
Montale comenta Montale [*Montale Speaks on Montale*] (interview) 1980
Prime alla Scala [*Opening Nights at La Scala*] (prose) 1981
Lettere a Salvatore Quasimodo [*Letters to Salvatore Quasimodo*] (correspondence) 1981
The Second Life of Art: Selected Essays of Eugenio Montale (essays) 1982
Quaderno genovese [*Genoan Diary*] (diary) 1983

CRITICISM

Glauco Cambon (essay date 1958)

SOURCE: "Eugenio Montale's Poetry: A Meeting of Dante and Brueghel," in *The Sewanee Review*, Vol. LXVI, No. 1, 1958, pp. 1–32.

[*An Italian-born educator and critic, Cambon has written extensively on Montale and edited his* Selected Poems *(1966). Joseph Brodsky called him Montale's "most perceptive critic." In the following essay, Cambon comments on the style and worldview of Montale's early poetry.*]

If there ever was a writer who found himself entirely in his first essays and never betrayed himself afterwards, it is the author of ***Ossi di Seppia*** (***Cuttlefish Bones***, 1925), ***Le Occasioni*** (***The Occasions***, 1939) and ***Finisterre*** (1942). And this Conradian attitude is fully recognizable in the stoical Montale of ***La Bufera e Altro*** (***The Storm and Other***

Things), published in Venice by Neri Pozza in 1956. Montale never wavered in his style, and thanks to this firmness of expression has been able to face his psychological, moral and metaphysical worries without disintegrating either as an artist or as a man. From this angle *La Bufera* can be said to continue *Le Occasioni*; whoever might expect a "new" Montale from the new booklet would be disappointed. His novelties are no news to us: the storm does not prevail on him, the game between him and time goes ceaselessly on, and the "bottle from the sea" hasn't come to shore yet. Montale isn't the man to bring his poetry "up to date." No need for that, since the two essential terms of his discourse are the world and the self, in the dimension of time. Between these two poles there flares up now and then a metaphysical lightning, to punctuate a colloquy lasting a whole life; it will be the revelation of nothingness, or the antithetical one of a transcendent mystery, but certainly human history (in the sense of public events) has little to do with it, being at most a secondary component, an occasional background. Montale lives time with great intensity, but his is fundamentally a time alien to historiography, it is the individual's memory and the crumbling up of the world. If facts and figures of contemporary history appear in his poetry, it is only as a function of his personal drama; such is the case of **"Primavera hitleriana"** ("Hitlerian Spring"), **"Piccolo Testamento"** ("A Small Will"), and **"Il Sogno del Prigioniero"** ("The Prisoner's Dream"). Here, in the second half of the present collection, the poet, confronted by the public world, withdraws from it in horror or mistrust; whether Hitler or "red or black clerics" are involved, his conclusion is always the same: to defend the inner stronghold of the self from public encroachments, for the public world is always cruel, or false:

> Ognuno riconosce is suoi: l'orgoglio
> non era fuga, l'umiltà non era
> vile, il tenue bagliore strofinato
> laggiù non era quello di un fiammifero.

> Everyone recognizes his kindred: pride
> was no flight, humility
> was not cowardly, the thin gleam scratched up
> down there was not of a burning match.

Montale's historical pessimism is absolute: in **"Piccolo Testamento"** he evokes a hellish Apocalypse shadowing our history with the wings of Dante's Lucifer, and the defense of values is entrusted to the individual, private and precarious, with a matchless effect of sorrowful contrast:

> Solo quest'iride posso
> lasciarti a testimonianza
> d'una fede che fu combattuta,
> d'una speranza che bruciò più lenta
> di un duro ceppo nel focolare.
> Conservane la cipria nello specchietto
> quando spenta ogni lampada
> la sardana si farà infernale
> e un ombroso Lucifero scenderà su una prora
> del Tamigi, del Hudson, della Senna

> scuotendo l'ali di bitume semi-
> mozze dalla fatica, a dirti: è l'ora.

> Only this iris can I bequeath to you
> to witness a faith that was fought,
> a hope that burned slower
> than a hard log on the hearth.
> Keep its powder in your handbag mirror
> when, in the general blackout,
> the dance will get infernal
> and a shadowy Lucifer will descend on a prow
> the Thames, Hudson or Seine,
> shaking his tar wings half maimed by
> fatigue, to tell you the time is up.

The myth of this black Apocalypse becomes Kafkian in **"Sogno del Prigioniero"** where the victory of public evil is complete, the "purge has been going on forever" and the protagonist does not know whether "at the banquet" he is going to devour others, stuffed gooselike, or be devoured in his turn. His judgment on our age is clear: in Montale's view, our civilization is going to founder in an anonymous collectivism where there will be no place for the real carrier of values—the individual. These are the ideas Montale personally confirms in his fireside talk.

But, however we may evaluate these particular texts, the protest against the world of organized politics is no accidental motif in him, for it issues directly from his *Weltanschauung*. At the roots of Montale's stoicism there lies the sense of time as a steady consumption, of existence as entropy, as a process of decay not to be reversed. In such Lucretian and Leopardian perspective, the soul has no way out, and it can find itself only in the utter intensity with which it experiences the events of climactic instants and of memory. Refusing the dispersal entailed by an official calendar, it will secede further and further into that authentic history which is the labyrinth of inwardness, ceaselessly questioned in suffering and dream. Montale's hermeticism has nothing whatever to do with a literary fashion; it is an existential attitude, a defense of the self, a veiling and unveiling of his spiritual integrity. That is why his voice remains actual today when the hermetic fashion is over. In Montale, faithfulness to the self and faithfulness to language are one and the same; if his message is one of despair, his honesty is rocklike, and one cannot say too often that after the corruption of Dannunzian influence, which had boned the Italian literary language, he has signally contributed to endow it with a new spinal cord. As Luciano Anceschi remarks in his preface to the anthology of modern Italian poetry, *Lirica del Novecento* the "Crepuscolari" and Giovanni Pascoli are two recognizable strains in his discourse, which owed something to them in its moulding phase, but—and this is what matters—he overstepped any provincial boundary to obey his European and cosmic feeling; and he could accomplish that because, beyond the worn, uncertain or convulsive vocabulary of the moment, he found an access to Dante's rugged language. If Mario Praz (in "T. S. Eliot and Eugenio Montale," published in *Symposium*, London 1948) and more recently a young critic, Sergio Pannella (in the December 1954 issue of the magazine *Galleria*), have been able to draw a persuasive parallel between the poet of **"Il Male di vivere"** (**"The Harm of Living"**) and the creator of "Prufrock" and *The Waste Land,* such undeniable parallelism must also be recognized as something more than a mere fact of "waste land," for it is rooted in their *Wahlverwandschaft* for Dante—an affinity openly proclaimed by the Anglo-American poet and implied by the Italian one in his word-choices, sound-orientations, and love for clearcut vision, or even in some functional quotation, as happens for instance in **"Mottetto" No. 8** (from *Le Occasioni*), starting with an obvious echo of the Dantesque lizard which "sotto la gran fersa / dei dì canicular, cangiando siepe, / folgore par se la via attraversa" (under the great flail / of dog-days heat, moving from hedge to hedge, / flits lightning-like across the path) and ending on a note from Shakespeare's *The Tempest.*

Normally Montale's language has a vertebrate compactness going back to Dante's; fighting shy of the all-too-obvious music into which the Italian lyrical tradition had come to melt, it lowers its tone to become an intimate conversation averse to epic peals, high-strung melody or set cadences. Montale came thus to disjoint verse and freely treat the eleven-syllable line; shrinking discourse into a sequence of intense hard passages (see **"Mottetti"** for that); and he transposed sound onto an inner level, varying rhyme with dissonance, shifting it into the body of the line, where it will exercise a more secret charm, and often seeking in alliteration a sound-unity for the context—a unity to be reconstructed from within, by valuing syllables and consonants to the extent of making them the vertebrae of a poetical organism. In **"Scirocco"** (**"Sirocco"**), for instance (from *Ossi di Seppia*):

l'agave che s'abbarbica al crepaccio
dello scoglio
e sfugge al mare da le braccia d'alghe
che spalanca ampie gole e abbranca rocce.

the vertebrae are contained in these words: *abbarbica* (strikes root, clings), *braccia* (the arms), *spalanca* (throws open) and *abbranca* (clutches). But the secret thread of this discreet music is also intertwined with the recurrence of the vowel *a* (to be pronounced, of course, like the English broad *a*), so full of breath, whether by itself or linked with an *l* consonant:

oh alide ali dell'aria
ora son io
l'agave che s'abbarbica al crepaccio
'dello scoglio
etc., etc.

Oh, dry wings of the air
now am I
the agave that clings to a crevice
of the sea-cliff
and escapes the seaweed-armed sea
opening wide gorges and clutching rocks

We thus have an internal play on *alide* (dry), *ali* (wings),

aria (air), *agave* (agave), *alghe* (seaweed), *spalanca* (throws open); the skeleton of verse is clad with sound-flesh. Likewise, see the play of *l* sounds (*mollemente* = softly, *flabello* = fan, *redola* = grassy path, *libellule* = dragonflies, *fardel-lo* = burden) in "Mottetto" No. 17; or in the ending of "Buffalo," the echoes of dry, plosive sounds (*specchi* = mirrors, *schiante secchi* = dry crashes, *schiene* = backs); or again, in the ending of **"Corno Inglese"** (**"English Horn"**), the counterpoint of sibilant and plosive consonants:

nell'ora che lenta s'annera
suonasse te pure stasera
scordato strumento,
cuore.

in the slowly darkening hour
would it were playing you too tonight
instrument out of tune,
heart.

Or again, in **"Meriggiare pallido e assorto"** (**"Pale, Intent Noontide"**), aridity changed to syllable (*sterpi* = briar, *schiocchi* = clacks, *serpi* = snakes, *crepe* = cracks, *scaglie* = flakes, *scricchi* = creakings, *Cicale* = cicadas, *calvi* = bald, *picchi* = peaks, *cocci* = shards, *aguzzi* = sharp); and in the first stanza of the next poem in the same collection, the telling insistence on *f* sounds:

Non rifugiarti nell'ombra
di quel folto di verzura
come il falchetto che strapiomba
fulmineo nella caldura.

Do not seek shelter in the shade
of that thick greenery
like the headlong hawk that plunges
lightning-like through the heat.

We are not here in the domain of an obvious, all-too-external onomatopoeia, as so often happens in Pascoli, but in the field of a sound-magic which stakes all on the "atomic" element of the word to make speech "scabro ed essenziale" (rugged and essential), as the poet himself has it. That rugged essentialness, to be sure, which strengthens Dante's verse—as Ugolino's and Pier delle Vigne's cantos will abundantly show. Many are the clues to Dante's blood-inheritance in Montale; for instance, the sad solemnity of **"I Morti"** (**"The Dead"**) in *Ossi di Seppia,* and even more **"Tramontana"** (**"North Wind"**), from the same collection:

Ed ora sono spariti i circoli d'ansia
che discorrevano il lago del cuore
e quel friggere vasto della materia
che discolora e muore.
Oggi una volontà di ferro spazza l'aria,
divelle gli arbusti, strapazza i palmizi

. . . . .

Ogni forma si squassa mel subbuglio

degli elementi; è un urlo solo, un muglio
di scerpate esistenze: tutto schianta
l'ora che passa . . .

And now have vanished the rings of anxiety
that rippled the lake of my heart
and the vast seething of matter
that fades out to die.
Today an iron will sweeps the air,
uproots bushes, fatigues palmtrees,

. . . . .

Every shape is shaken in the turmoil
of elements; it is one shriek, one bellow
of uprooted existences: everything is torn
by the passing hour . . .

Canto I of *Inferno* is here intentionally brought up by that "lake of the heart" which is a metaphor Montale seems to cherish, and then the ghost of Pier delle Vigne speaks up in two verbs (*scerpare* = to uproot, and *schiantare* = to tear up) to invest all of existence with a tragic meaning. For the poem deals with the horror of uprooting, and its concluding note signs love for the roots a wild wind threatens to break; therefore the Dante reference, whether conscious or casual, focusses our modern situation in a total vision. Attention should not be denied, in this poem, to the initial alliterations (*spazza* = sweeps, *strapazza* = fatigues, *palm-izi* = palmtree clumps), which illustrate the above remarks on the sound-harshness used to give new bones to verse; but what is still more important, Pier delle Vigne shows up again in a poem from *Finisterre* (included, of course, in the present volume): **"Personae Separatae."** We are in a hellish wood of "skeleton locusts" where hell is made by the estrangement of two human beings who formerly communicated and loved each other. But all at once their private sorrow widens to enclose the universal tragedy of mankind at war (*Finisterre* came into being during World War II), and the momentous passage is accomplished by a clipped hint, almost casually:

. . . Troppo
straziato è il umano, troppo sorda
quella voce perenne . . .
The human wood is too much torn,
too hollow that perennial voice . . .

The skeleton trees become Pier delle Vigne's wood, i.e., the whole human race—suicidal like Pier, and just as hardly punished and broken up. A remembrance of Paradise emphasizes horror:

La tua forma
passò di qui, si riposò sul riano
tra le nasse atterrate, poi si sciolse
come un sospiro, intorno—e ivi non era
l'orror che fiotta, in te la luce ancora
trovava luce, oggi non più che al giorno
primo già annotta.

Your shape
was seen here to rest in the small gorge

among the stranded nets, then it dissolved
like a sigh all around—and there was not
the welling horror, in you light still found light,
today no longer, when at the blush of dawn
night already looms.

This poem is among the most sustained in the whole book, and all of *Finisterre,* as a matter of fact belongs to the best Montale. The poet of **"Casa dei Doganieri"** (**"House of the Customs Men"**), **"Dora Markus," "Eastbourne," "Notizie dall'Amiata"** (**"News from Mount Amiata"**) and **"Nuove Stanze"** (**"New Stanzas"**) has lived up to his own accomplishment, just because he has not violated his nature or tried to be different from what he is. He has added valid items to his former poetical inventory, without straying from the variously deep, delicate or fitful vein which as yet shows no signs of exhaustion. The "occasions" of poetry are numberless, as many as the moments of life. Joyce's epiphany is always possible to the Genoese metaphysical realist, who has no need to re-invent himself at each season because he is what he is, as irreducibly as his native sea-cliffs. Never mind if, in the present collection, certain diary pages from **"Intermezzo," "Flashes e dediche"** (**"Flashes and Dedications"**) and **"Madrigali privati"** (**"Private Madrigals"**) remain too private to deserve comparison with the strong pieces. In Montale the man, side-by-side with the stern metaphysical mind that has seen through anguish, there is an elf often unexpectedly gleaming in his blue eyes and inducing him to cherish light or even frivolous things; there is the humorist who never takes himself seriously and who loves animals, and the whimsical boy who may like operettas, street songs and Gozzano's baubles, and the ephemeral occasion. And there is, finally, a coyness compelling him to veil his own intense feelings, afterwards to liberate them in some cryptic line which is meant both as confession and concealment. These components of his personality are all to be found, in quaint or subtly creative synthesis, in the body of his poetry.

A poetry where obscurity is never a trick, and where occasional signs of involution never betray complacent mannerism, but are part of the poet's inner drama: "Do not ask us for the word hewing from all sides / our formless soul . . . Do not ask us for the formula apt to open up worlds to you, / but only for some crooked syllable, dry like a withered branch," he has said in *Cuttlefish Bones.* An existence as poverty, which when confronted by nothingness, indefiniteness, shapelessness, can only rely on the props of *hic* and *nunc,* on the objects whose individuality is felt as utter suffering; but this sense of the individual as ineffable, though minimal, reality, carried away by time, this Heideggerian *Dasein als Nichtigkeit* must try conclusions with the ghost of Otherness threatening it from the outside as well as from within. Memory is the shelter of existence, private history in the chaos of public history, that *sensus sui* which alone can save us; yet memory itself ends up undermining the individual's identity, changing him into something else than himself:

Trema un ricordo nel ricolmo sechio;
nel puro cerchio un'immagine ride.

Accosto il volto a evanescenti labbri:
si deforma il passato, si fa vecchio,
appartiene ad un altro . . .

A memory quivers in the full pail,
in the pure ring an image laughs.
I accost my face to evanescent lips:
the past is distorted, it ages,
it belongs to another . . .

This was *Ossi di Seppia* (*Cuttlefish Bones*); and **"Due nel Crepuscolo"** (**"Two in the Twilight"**), from *La Bufera,* deepens the same experience in a turn of classic accomplishment:

        . . . Ed io riverso
nel potere che grava attorno, cedo
al sortilegio di non riconoscere
di me più nulla fuor di me: s'io levo
appena il braccio, mi si fa diverso
l'atto, si spezza su un cristallo, ignota
e impallidita sua memoria, e il gesto
già più non m'appartiene;
se parlo, ascolto quella voce attonito.

       . . . And I, lying back
in the impending power, yield
to the spell of not recognizing
aught of myself out of myself: if only
I raise my arm, the act turns different,
it breaks on a crystal, its memory
paling unknown, and my very gesture
belongs to me no more;
if I talk, I listen to that voice astonished.

Estranging himself from himself in time, the individual cannot help estranging himself from his beloved, who suddenly becomes a cryptic Unknown, a disquieting Other, or an empty remainder:

       . . . Ti guardo
in un molle riverbero. Non so
se ti conosco; so che mai diviso
fui da te come accade in questo tardo
ritorno. Pochi istanti hanno bruciato
tutto di noi: fuorché due volti, due
maschere che s'incidono, sforzate,
di un sorriso.

       . . I look at you
in a soft glimmer. I don't know
if I know you; I know I never was
so divided from you as happens in this belated
return. Few instants have burned up
all of us: save two faces, two
masks on which, with effort,
a smile is engraved.

The sense of spiritual event, even though as destruction, is here expressed with utter force, subtly grasping the unseizable metamorphoses of consciousness. We are on the line of **"Arsenio"** and of the other poem as above

quoted; for **"Due nel crepuscolo"** dates back from 1926. Struggle against the formless, identity that alienates itself, metamorphosis of memory, threat or splendor of otherness: these are the main themes of Montale's last phase, and they account for his apocalyptic thrusts. His speech is interspersed with negative epiphanies:

Il soffio cresce, il buio è rotto a squarci,
e l'ombra che tu mandi sulla fragile
palizzata s'arriccia. Troppo tardi
se vuoi esser te stessa!

The wind gets stronger, darkness is ripped by gusts,
and the shadow you cast on the shaky fence
curls up. Too late now
if you want to be yourself!

Since our fellow-being's estrangement from ourselves into a complete otherness makes the distance between him and us yawn infinite, the message never arrives, the letter remains "unwritten," and life becomes an inability to disappear:

Sparir non so né riaffacciarmi; tarda
la fucina vermiglia
della notte, la sera si fa lunga,
la preghiera è supplizio e non ancora
tra le rocce che sorgono t'è giunta
la bottiglia dal mare. L'onda, vuota,
si rompe sulla punta, a Finisterre.

I cannot vanish or lean out again; belated
is the ruddy workshop of night,
evening draws intolerably on,
prayer is torture and not yet
among the rising cliffs has come to you
the bottle from the sea. The empty wave
breaks on the headland at Finisterre.

The image of that bottle entrusted to the surf explains the nature of Montale's poetical utterance; it is in a way the poet's self-consciousness, but not only on the purely aesthetic level, since it is broadly human, existential; it expresses the desperate desire and inability to communicate. In Italian poetry, this is one of the most intense passages the writer knows. Aesthetically less achieved, but motivated by the same dramatic experience of otherness, is the surrealist poem **"Nel Sonno"** (**"In Sleep"**), where we feel as strangely persuasive, like a De Chirico without trickery, the focal image of that "adversary" that "snaps his helmet shut / on his face." It is another mask of otherness, the impenetrable face reality opposes to an individual estraged from everything; it is the price of self-isolation. But the mask of an inimical otherness covers other moments of experience as well; in **"Serenata indiana"** (**"Indian Serenade"**), for instance, it is the unforgettable horror of a hidden identity of the beloved woman with the octopus, the greedy and shapeless monster of the abyss:

Fosse tua vita quella che mi tiene
sulle soglie—e potrei prestarti un volto,
vaneggiarti figura. Ma non è,

non è così. Il polipo che insinua
tentacoli d'inchiostro fra gli scogli
può servirsi di te. Tu gli appartieni

e non lo sai. Sei lui, ti credi te.

If it was yours, this life that holds me
on the thresholds—then I could lend you a visage,
fancy you as a figure. But it is not so,

it is not so. The octopus that pushes
inky tentacles into the reef
can use you. Unawares you belong

to him. You are he, you think you are yourself.

The horror of this black witchcraft is utterly convincing; the self is undermined, and the poet struggles in the impossible endeavor to define the formless. We are in a decidedly Melvillian and Dickinsonian atmosphere, though Montale is not indebted to those masters. The theme of threatening otherness arising as a ghost before or within ourselves is basic in the two American poets, who on the other hand, as to style, temper, and background, would seem absolutely unlinked with each other; but such a link, and the independent affinity of the Italian contemporary poet, are fully clarified by Eliot's words when, in *The Three Voices of Poetry,* he says poetry is a fight of Jacob against the angel, that is, a struggle against formlessness.

Ghosts of sea-animals (medusae) appear in the magic mirror of **"Gli orecchini" ("The Earrings"),** where their presence is conjured, in the ambiguous twilight atmosphere, by the corals of the earrings which defenseless feminine hands (sharply defined as "bleak" and "overwhelmed") are buckling on. A double threat is presented by formlessness (the sea of twilight) and war (". . . the crazy funeral booms / and knows that two lives don't matter"); how could we help remembering the demoniac moth of **"Vecchi Versi" ("Old Lines")**, in *Le Occasioni*?—though war was only a dark foreboding there.

Otherness as the black witchcraft of memory inspired **"Il ventaglio" ("The Fan"),** also concerned with war. It is perhaps a rather unachieved poem, for the author left too much out of the page (a fault imputed to him also by Mr. Williamson in the documented articles on Italian contemporary poetry that he published in *Poetry,* Winter 1951–2 issues); but the central image, of memory visualized as a fan that opens and closes up, and frightens us with a spell, is very original. The concluding question (Muore chi ti riconosce?=Does whoever recognizes you have to die?) brings us back to the fundamental theme of sphinx-like otherness. In the fond **"Ballata scritta in una clinica" ("Ballad Written in a Clinic"),** the experience of Otherness is given by the threat of death:

Attendo un cenno, se è prossima
l'ora del ratto finale;
son pronto e la penitenza
s'inizia fin d'ora nel cupo

singulto di valli e dirupi
dell'*altra* Emergenza.

I await a sign, if the hour
of final abduction is near;
I am ready and penance
begins right now in the hollow
sobbing of valleys and cliffs
of the *other* Emergence.

Here the small things of his sick wife (her tortoise-rimmed eye-glasses, her wooden bulldog, her alarm-clock with phosphorescent dial-hands), making the protagonist a recognizable portrait, emphasize the sad contrast with looming death, which Montale, obeying his unpredictable inspiration, embodies in the mythical figure of Jupiter changed into a bull to abduct Europa. In view of Montale's refined cultural background, would it be allowed to read in this mythical "final abduction" a quick oblique hint at the tragedy of Europe, momentarily identified with the lady who shares the poet's life? But the "bull-like god" isn't only death; it is also a heathen totem of vital urge; and the ambiguity is one of Montale's most intriguing, for it springs from an invocation to the god both as death-giver and savior of life. In **"Gallo cedrone" ("Black Cock"),** another fine poem of this volume, Jupiter is a black cock killed and buried in the womb of earth like a seed.

The final stanzas of **"Ballad"** show Montale at his very best:

Hai messo sul comodino
il bulldog di legno, la sveglia
col fosforo sulle lancette
che spande un tenue lucore
sul tuo dormiveglia,

il nulla che basta a chi vuole
forzare la porta stretta;
e fuori, rossa, s'inasta,
si spiega sul bianco una croce.

Con te anch'io m'affaccio alla voce
che irrompe nell'alba, all'enorme
presenza dei morti; e poi l'ululo
del cane di legno è il mio, muto.

You have put on your night-table
the wooden bulldog, the alarm-clock
with phosphorescent hands
that cast a faint glimmer
on your halfwaking,
the nothing that suffices to any who want
to break through the narrow gate;
and outside there goes up on the flagstaff
a fluttering cross, red on white.

With you I too lean out to meet the voice
that breaks out in sunrise, the enormous
presence of the dead; and then the howl

of the wooden bulldog is mine, mute.

These lines need no comment; they take the soul by surprise. That movement from the small real and emblematic objects (the wooden bulldog is still to be found at the Montales') to the enormity of death, and then the return from that glimpse of immensity to the helpless bauble—the wooden bulldog—which is charged with the poet's whole sorrow to the extent of becoming himself, his own fidelity! The two things—toy dog and alarm-clock—are photographed, but not casually; they are emblems of faithfulness and of patient time about to end. That is clarified by the unexpected finale, which owes most of its poetical efficiency to the complex play of sounds and pauses. It is all a counterpoint of *u*'s, *l*'s; and *m*'s; there is an utterly poignant caesura between "mio" (mine) and "muto" (mute), like a sob and a prolongation of the line beyond itself, in a heavy suspense. The vowel-echo arising from the strees on "ululo" (howl) and "muto" (mute) could not be more powerful, and at the same time it is of a rare subtlety. For it evokes a hallucination only to negate it right away, but the negation retains an echo of the notion denied. The word "muto," though it means "silent," ends up howling too; silence becomes an internalized shriek.

> **Normally Montale's language has a vertebrate compactness going back to Dante's; fighting shy of the all-too-obvious music into which the Italian lyrical tradition had come to melt, it lowers its tone to become an intimate conversation averse to epic peals, high-strung melody or set cadences.**
>
> —*Glauco Cambon*

Though it does not make easy reading, **"Ezekiel Saw the Wheel,"** inspired by a spiritual and through it by the Bible, is choice Montale, and it deals with his Leitmotives: the spell of memory, the effort to dig up the image of a beloved dead from the "mound of sand" time's hourglass had heaped up in his heart, the assault of otherness as a ghost of the past in the present, the vision of the "threatening Wheel" which is not only Ezekiel's wheel, but also **"Eastbourne"**'s desperate symbol ("Evil wins . . . the wheel won't stop") in *Le Occasioni,* Leopardi's closed circle "of all heavenly and terrestrial things" which "ceaselessly turn around always to revert to their starting point," as drawn in **"Canto Notturno di un Pastore Errante nell'Asia" ("Night Song of an Asiatic Wandering Shepherd").** The initial "foreign hand" is menacingly transmogrified, it becomes a "claw" in the end, and the peachtree's petals are "turned to blood." Doubtlessly hermetic as it is, this poem cannot be denied a sufficient internal motivation, being full of human suffering. Montale is all genuine, even when he does not yield himself; and he is not the man ever to yield his own secret easily.

It is interesting to notice that the image of the wheel as Karma, ineluctable fatality, appears also at the end of **"L'orto" ("The Garden"),** one of the best poems in this collection:

> . . . Se la forza
> che guida il disco *di già inciso* fosse
> un'altra, certo il tuo destino al mio
> congiunto mostrerebbe un solco solo.

> . . . If the force
> that guides the record *already incised*
> were another, certainly your lot and mine
> would be joined in one groove.

When the late critic Pancrazi stated his acceptance of Montale's "physical" poetry as given in *Ossi di Seppia* and his refusal of the "metaphysical" *Occasioni,* he failed to see how our poet's existential symbolism spontaneosly issued from his cosmic, physical sensibility and was at bottom the same thing.

"La primavera hitleriana" ("Hitlerian Spring") pushes to another limit the experience of otherness, as mystical nihilism in which to find a shelter from the horror of a perverted present:

> Oh la piagata
> primavera è pur festa se raggela
> in morte questa morte! Guarda ancora
> in alto, Clizia, è la tua sorte, tu
> che il non mutato amor mutata serbi,
> fino a che il cieco sole che in te porti
> si abbàcini nell'Altro e si distrugga
> in Lui, per tutti . . .

> Oh, the wounded spring
> is still a feast if it freezes
> this death to death! Look on high,
> Clizia, it is your destiny, you
> who, yourself changed, keep unchanged love in you,
> until the blind sun you carry in yourself
> may be dazzled in the Other and destroy
> itself in Him, for all . . .

In **"Ezekiel Saw the Wheel"** otherness was death, memory, woman, sphinx and destiny; here it is the experience of Being itself; and here the affinity with Heidegger's development is conspicuous, though Montale owes nothing to the German thinker. The author of *Sein und Zeit (Being and Time)* started with a philosophy of existence as finitude grounded upon nothingness, but in his last works, especially from the Hoelderlin essay on, he has evidenced different motifs, turning upon the experience of Being as participation in a horizon of possibility through language. From nihilism to mysticism is not an inconceivable step; and Montale, even though he does not rely on an organized system of orthodoxy like Eliot, proves occasionally open to luminous apocalypses. The visage of Christ dawns in his verse: in **"Iride" ("Iris")** as Holy Shroud, in **"Sulla colonna più alta" ("On the Highest Pillar"),** in **"L'ombra della magnolia" ("The Magnolia Shadow")** as "the Bridegroom's stigmata." God is now mentioned as possibility: see **"Verso Siena" ("Toward Siena"):**

La scatola a sorpresa ha fatto scatto
sul punto in cui il mio Dio gittò la maschera
e fulminò il ribelle.

The jack-in-the-box has clicked open
at the point when my God threw down His mask
to blast the rebel.

And see further **"Vento sulla mezzaluna"** (**"Wind on the Crescent"**), **"Nella serra"** (**"In the Greenhouse"**), **"Incantesimo"** (**"Spell"**), **"Verso Finistère"** (**"Toward Finistère"**) and the surprising **"Anniversario"** (**"Anniversary"**), where the poet kneels to adore a young life that blossoms to give him joy and salvation, but finally despairs of any possibility to share his own revelation with his fellowmen, and for an instant sees himself as

>   . . . Dio diviso
> dagli uomini, dal sangue raggrumato
> sui rami alti, sui frutti.

>   . . . God secluded
> from men, from the blood curdled
> on the high branches, on the fruits.

Is this a momentary sin of Lucifer? The poet would personally confirm such interpretation (for that "secluded God" might also be read as a vocative, thereby eliminating the narcissistic attitude); but even here, after all, he only lives with extreme sincerity his own inner experience; and his identification with the suffering god is characterized by the grief of being separated from mankind, not by any complacent pride.

Therefore, if Otherness can manifest itself as demoniac outbreak, alienation, threatening madness, it also has a divine and angelic visage. Like a "Dolce Stil Nuovo" poet—say, Guinizelli or the early Dante—our poet repeatedly perceives the winged figure of an angelic woman. Thus **"L'orto"** (**"The Garden"**) starts with a "messaggera" (harbinger) which closely recalls the etymology of "angel":

> Io non so, messaggera
> che scendi, prediletta
> del mio Dio (del tuo forse) se nel chiuso
> etc . . .

> I don't know, harbinger
> who descendest, beloved
> of my God (of thine perhaps) if in the enclosure
> etc . . . .

and in its last stanza speaks of "incarnate demons" and "foreheads of fallen angels." The garden is the spellbound precinct of memory; the unknown visitor, probably the Clizia of other poems, is both a Mnemosyne and a soothsayer who had foretold the disaster of war:

> L'ora della tortura e dei lamenti
> che s'abbatté sul mondo,
> l'ora che tu leggevi chiara come in un libro
> figgendo il duro sguardo di cristallo

bene in fondo, là dove acri tendine
di fuliggine alzandosi su lampi
di officine celavano alla vista
l'opera di Vulcano,
il dì dell'Ira che più volte il gallo
annunciò agli spergiuri . . .

> The hour of torture and lament
> that fell on the world,
> the hour you clearly read as in a book
> prying with your hard crystal look
> down where sour curtains
> of soot rising on lightnings
> of workshops hid from sight
> the work of Vulcan,
> the Day of Wrath that the cock often
> announced to perjurers . . .

The conclusion is a desperate affection changed into Weltschmerz:

> O labbri muti, aridi dal lungo
> viaggio per il sentiero fatto d'aria
> che vi sostenne, o membra che distinguo
> a stento dalle mie, o diti che smorzano
> la sete dei morenti e i vivi infocano,
> o intento che hai creato fuor della tua misura
> le sfere del quadrante e che ti espandi
> in tempo d'uomo, in spazio d'uomo, in furie
> di démoni incarnati . . .

> O silent lips, dry from the long
> journey through the path of air
> that sustained you, o limbs I hardly
> can tell from mine, o fingers that allay
> the thirst of dying people and inflame the living,
> o intention that created out of your measure
> the dial hands and now expand yourself
> into human time, human space, furies
> of demons incarnate . . .

Another angelic epiphany flashes in **"L'ombra della magnolia"** (**"The Magnolia Shadow"**) as "cesena," a migratory bird unconquered by the "shudder of frost"; and the flight of the mysterious creature invites the poet to leap into transcendence:

> . . . Gli altri arretrano
> e piegano. La lima che sottile
> incide tacerà, la vuota scorza
> di chi cantava sarà presto polvere
> di vetro sotto i piedi, l'ombra è livida,—
> è l'autunno, è l'inverno, è l'oltrecielo
> che ti conduce e in cui mi getto, cèfalo
> saltato in secco al novilunio.
>   Addio.

> . . . The others fall back
> and surrender. The file that thinly engraves
> will hush, the empty husk
> of the singer will be soon glassy dust
> under our feet, the shadow is livid,—

it is autumn, it's winter, the Further sky
that leads you, and into it I throw myself,
a mullet leaping onto dry land at the new moon.

                                                                      Good-bye.

That may mean he tries to conquer otherness by facing migration into death. And he gives us a magnificent ending, due to the inner understanding the poet has of animal life. This "mullet" leaps with no less force than the Eel ("**L'Anguilla**") which is among Montale's perfect things. The eel is understood in its mystery of living creature, ocean-traveller, and its irresistible penetration into the hardest upland recesses represents an inverted transcendence, a victory of life over death:

l'anima verde che cerca
vita là dove solo
morde l'arsura e la desolazione,
la scintilla che dice
tutto comincia quando tutto pare
incarbonirsi, bronco seppellito;

the green soul that seeks
life where only parched desolation bites,
the spark that says
everything begins when everything seems
to burn to charcoal, a buried stick;

It would be useless pedantry to read Montale—or any other artist of the word—in the light of systematic Freudianism; but can we exclude that under the triumphant vitality of these lines there may seethe a phallic image, motivated by the explicit ritual of regenerating fecundation?

L'anguilla, torcia, frusta,
freccia d'Amore in terra
che solo i nostri botri o i disseccati
ruscelli pirenaici riconducono
a paradisi di fecondazione . . .

The eel, a torch, a whip,
a dart of Love on earth
which only our ravines or the dried-up
Pyrenea brooks lead back
to paradises of fecundation . . .

Such hypothesis is not based on intellectualistic assumptions, but on a concrete reading of details and whole. But let us revert to angels. "**La frangia dei capelli**" ("**The Bangs**") pivots on an angelic feminine apparition:

. . . l'ala onde tu vai,
trasmigratrice Artemide ed illesa,
tra le guerre dei nati-morti; e s'ora
d'aeree lanugini s'infiora
quel fondo, a marezzarlo sei tu, scesa
d'un balzo, e irrequieta la tua fronte
si confonde con l'alba, la nasconde.

. . . the wing that carries you,
migrating Artemis and unhurt
among the wars of stillborn people; and if

that lake-bottom blossoms with airy down
it's you who marble it, coming down
at a jump, and your restless forehead
merges with dawn, and hides it in itself.

And here the expression "the wars of stillborn people" contains a dreadful judgment on our age, similar to the one Eliot issued with his "hollow men" fantasy. "**Giorno e Notte**" ("**Day and Night**") states a vague identity between woman and skylark:

Anche una piuma che vola può disegnare
la tua figura, o il raggio che gioca a rimpiattino
tra i mobili, il rimando dello specchio
di un bambino, dai tetti . . .

Even a flying feather can draw your figure,
or the ray playing at hide-and-seek
in the furniture, the light rebounding
from a child's mirror on the roofs . . .

Then the sunrise-announcing bird, that is the angelic harbinger of light and vanquisher of darkness (as the title itself points out), is shot down to death:

. . . —e ancora le stessa grida e i lunghi
pianti sulla veranda
se rimbomba improvviso il colpo che t'arrossa.
la gola e schianta l'ali, o perigliosa
annunciatrice dell'alba, . . .

. . . —and the same screams again and the long
crying on the verandah
if there suddenly bursts the shot that reddens
your throat and breaks your wings, O daring
herald of dawn . . .

and then daybreak is no longer a triumph of light, but a Doomsday blared by barracks bugles on the silent waiting of cloisters and hospitals:

e si destano i chiostri e gli ospedali
a un lacerìo di trombe . . .

and cloisters and hospitals are awakened
by a rending blare of bugles . . .

The emblematic background of the poem, a pretty obvious one, is another implicit judgment passed on the evil of this age, on the violence of soul-killing war; in "**Black Cock**" the poet recognizes himself in the sumptuous wild bird mangled by a gunshot, and in "**Omaggio a Rimbaud**" ("**Homage to Rimbaud**") he describes the adventure of the author of *Illuminations* as a "grey-partridge flight." The image of angelic woman mysteriously dominates "**Il tuo volo**" ("**Your Flight**"), in a hermetic fire of disdain; but here perhaps "trobar clus" has been pushed too far, as well as in "**Iride**" ("**Iris**"), a poem avowedly transcribed from a dream, which gives us the real Montale only by fits and starts, without bringing to the surface its inner motivation. But "**Sulla colonna più alta**" ("**On the Highest Pillar**"), which portrays a victory of Christ in half-apocalyptic, half-Franciscan terms, has a beautiful angelic swallow that makes Christmas, transforming "the black diadems of briars into mistletoe":

> Ma in quel crepuscolo eri tu sul vertice:
> scura, l'ali ingrommate, stronche dai
> geli dell'Antilibano . . .

> But in that twilight you were on the top:
> dark, wings encrusted, exhausted by
> Antilebanon frost . . .

In this "illumination" one should notice the nice color-play on black: first we have a "self-humiliation of ravens and black-caps" (sedentary and scavenger birds), then the black wings of the obliquely mentioned swallow, and finally the "black diadems of briars." In **"Proda di Versilia"** (**"Versilian Shore"**), one of the best pieces in the whole collection, the spell of memory which brings back the dead is wrought by a white sail, visually changed into a Dantesque angel from *Purgatorio*:

> I miei morti che prego perché preghino
> per me, per i miei vivi com'io invece
> per essi non resurrezione ma
> il compiersi di quella vita ch'ebbero
> inesplicata e inesplicabile, oggi
> più di rado discendono dagli orizzonti aperti
> quando una mischia d'acque e cielo schiude
> finestre ai raggi della sera,—sempre
> più raro, astore celestiale, un cutter
> bianco-alato li posa sulla rena.

> My dead, whom I pray that they may pray
> for me, for my dear living ones as I in my turn
> for them invoke not resurrection but
> only completion of the life they had
> unexplained and inexplicable, today
> more seldom descend from the open horizons
> when an affray of waters and sky discloses
> windows to evening beams,—ever more seldom,
> celestial hawk, a white-winged cutter
> lays them down on the sand.

(Canto VIII of *Purgatorio,* at line 104, tells of two angels who, like "astor celestiali" or celestial hawks, rout the tempting snake; while Canto II sings of the pilot-angel who ferries the souls to shore.) The three stanzas following this superb introductory one (which is directly linked to **"I Morti," "The Dead,"** from *Ossi di Seppia*) minutely evoke a particular landscape together with the poet's childhood. There are three fundamental effects, or rather three tones which by their succession create the magic of this poem: the lofty Purgatorial one of the beginning; the realistic one of the middle (where Montale paints in Brueghelian vein, and Brueghel happens to be a favorite painter with him), and finally the fable of the last stanza, with its allusion to Alice in Wonderland and the gloomy ending:

> . . . tempo che fu misurabile
> fino a che non s'aperse questo mare
> infinito, di creta e di mondiglia.

> . . . a time that was measurable
> until there yawned this boundless sea
> of clay and slush.

It is again the threat of formlessness; "evil wins." And Brueghel, incidentally, seems to me a good clue to Montale's minute realism, ever ready to surrealist outlets: those objects lovingly painted, those cold or intimate and brown tones, those warm homely interiors, so busy, those birds etched in flight . . . The reader is referred to the central part of this poem for telling details, keeping in mind that the comparison aims at far more than a precious critical delight, for it means to throw light on an inner quality of Montalian art: the accurate realism behind its metaphysical soarings. It isn't for nothing that our poet cultivates painting too.

Conversation with the dead has inspired two more classical jewels: **"To my mother"** (in Foscolo's cadence) and **"Voce giunta con le folaghe"** (**"Voice Coming with the Moorhens"**). To speak with his father, for Montale, is to speak with Dante, as the style of the following lines will show:

> L'ombra che mi accompagna
> alla tua tomba, vigile,

>   . . . . .

> l'ombra non ha più peso della tua
> da tanto seppellita, i primi raggi
> del giorno la trafiggono, farfalle
> vivaci l'attraversano, la sfiora
> la sensitiva e non si rattrappisce.

> L'ombra fidata e il muto che risorge,
> quella che scorporò l'interno fuoco
> e colui che lunghi anni d'oltretempo
> (anni per me pesante) disincarnano,
> si scambiano parole che interito
> sul margine io non odo; l'una forse
> ritroverà la forma in cui bruciava
> amor di Chi la mosse e non di sè,
> ma l'altro sbigottisce e teme che
> la larva di memoria in cui si scalda
> ai suoi figli si spenga al nuovo balzo.

> The shadow that accompanies me,
> watchful, to your grave,

>   . . . . .

> the shadow has no more weight than yours
> now buried for so long, the first beams
> of day transfix it, lively butterflies
> cross it, the sensitive plant
> skims it without crumpling.

> The trusty shadow and the dumb man resurrected,
> the one consumed by its internal fire
> and he whom long years of trans-time
> (years for me who weigh) are disembodying,

exchange words I cannot hear
stiffening on the bank; perhaps the former
will find again the form in which burned
love of Its Mover and not of itself,
but the other is dismayed and fears
lest the ghost of memory in which he is warmed
for his children be extinguished at the new jump.

The *Purgatorio* reference is motivated by the very nature of memory: a fire assiduously purifying the image of our beloved ones when their presence is denied to us forever. And in memory it is possible, at long last, to find a heaven, i.e. to find ourselves again:

Così si svela prima di legarsi
a immagini, a parole, oscuro senso
reminescente, il vuoto inabitato
che occupammo e che attende fin ch'è tempo
di colmarsi di noi, di ritrovarci . . .

Thus is revealed before being tied up
to images and words, dark reminiscent sense,
the uninhabited void that we occupied
and that waits until it is time
to be filled with us, to find us again . . .

This rendezvous with the dead and the past is catalyzed by a storm in **"L'arca"** (**"The Ark"**), a thing painted with firm brush and ending on the note of the dog as a voice of fidelity:

. . . La tempesta
primaverile scuote d'un latrato
di fedeltà la mia arca, o perduti.

. . . The Spring storm shakes
with a bark of fidelity
my ark, O lost ones.

Here too, that copper kettle steaming in the kitchen is poignantly Brueghelian, and it acts as a foil, with its warm intimacy to the sorrow of final bereavement. **"La Bufera"** (**"The Storm"**), which gives the book its title, is a developed metaphor which might comment a famous Montalian line from **"Dora Markus"** in *Le Occasioni*:

è una tempesta anche la tua dolcezza

your very sweetness is a storm

because it concentrates on a woman the gleam of lightning (her white forehead) and the black gloom of stormclouds (the "cloud" of her hair). Like a flash of lightning, that woman vanished "into darkness," and we don't know whether such darkness is death or home; perhaps the ambiguity is intentional. Storm, apocalypse, black (or white) witchcraft of memory; transfiguration (see **"Il Giglio Rosso," "The Red Lily"**) and passage, grief of the instant, ecstasy and pain of remembrance: **"Da una torre"** (**"From a Tower"**), with that Brueghelian blackbird soaring from the lightning rod, and that unforgettable dog Piquillo leaping up from his tomb "joyous and long-eared,"

moves from an initial upward flight to a resurrection in memory and to be finally ship-wrecked in a vision of death ("a country of skeletons," "a lip . . . getting muter"), and could be antiphonal to **"Mottetto" No. 8,** from *Le Occasioni,* which plays on the instant and on the vanity of its metamorphoses in memory.

From a thorough reading, we may conclude, there emerges perhaps the best lyrical poet of the Italian twentieth century (with the possible exception of Ungaretti), one belonging to the great Western tradition which, with Proust, Joyce, Eliot and Faulkner, has explored the paradoxes of time, existence, finitude and memory, expressing outspokenly the impending disintegration of our civilization. History is thus experienced in a deeper way.

. . . ma una storia non dura che nella cenere
e persistenza è solo l'estinzione.

. . . but a history can only endure in ash
and the only persistence is extinction.

That is what Montale says in **"Piccolo Testamento,"** in keeping with his vision of historical and cosmic entropy. And certainly we will not ask him for the consolation of new gospels; it is enough that, in times of rhetoric and confusion, he taught us to see clearly the most frightening realities and to love things for what they are, in their poverty so much richer than the winged horses, eagles and lions with which the Italy of King Umberto the First, during the Nineties, and Fascist Italy after World War I, stifled Risorgimento Italy. Montale will never give us programs, only "occasions." Occasions of wonder, sorrow and dream; unexpected colloquies with reality, lightnings of revelation not to be reduced to dogma; his limit is also his worth. What else should we ask of a poet? Faith in our world, or rather in the possibility of living in and improving it, is something we shall have to find in ourselves.

Maria Sampoli Simonelli (essay date 1959)

SOURCE: "The Particular Poetic World of Eugenio Montale," in *Italian Quarterly,* Vol. 3, No. 10, Summer, 1959, pp. 42–55.

[*In the following essay, Simonelli holds that the foundation of Montale's poetics was established in* Cuttlefish Bones *and developed in later works.*]

To talk about Montale's poetics is above all to talk about his *Ossi di seppia* (1925). His later collections of poems—*Occasioni* (1939), *Bufera* (1956)—do not modify the position assumed and lived by Montale from his very early poetic experiences: "Meriggiare pallido . . ." (*Ossi di seppia*), dated 1916. In the collections following the *Ossi* the poet merely continues to investigate his problem more profoundly and to develop his particular poetic language further. It is in his particular poetic language rather than in his subjects that Montale attempts modification. He adopts a more extensive and more narrative style, which remains open to exterior happenings. But in speaking of such a modification, one must proceed with caution, for even in the *Ossi,* created during a moment in which Italian poetry in its search for the purely essential shunned any type of narrative expedient, Montale's narrative taste is already evident; not so much in the poems themselves as in the concious construction of the collection. It is not unusual for the "opera prima" of a poet to represent a fixed point in the spiritual life of the poet. Moreover, in most cases the "opera prima" is something more than an attempt: it is the presentation and clarification of the particular poetic world of the writer. Once formulated and expressed through various sounds and images, this poetic world unconsciously restricts the poet and often prevents an interior development by fixing him once and for all in the position which he himself has created.

This, in a way, has happened to Montale. After the *Ossi* Montale's poetry always found itself faced with a hopeless ontological limit established by the poems themselves. He had two choices: either to negate his earlier works, or in some way to repeat in continuous prismatizations the same inevitable ideas. He has chosen the latter path. And perhaps it is for this reason that the name Montale immediately brings to mind the *Ossi di seppia,* just as the name Leopardi immediately brings to mind the *Idilli.* Only on second thought does one recall the *Occasioni* (and certain poems of this collection such as **"Dora Markus"** or **"La casa dei doganieri"**) and the recent *Bufera*. Montale's "stuttering language" ("balbo parlare"), so rich and carefully thought out, is already to be found in *Ossi* as is his equilibrium, "uneven and essential" at the same time; his poetic world as well is expressed (and always in such a way as to remain in accord with his basic premises). In the *Ossi,* too, Montale's particular "philosophy" first presented itself, already inevitably closed to any development whatsoever.

That Montale's poetry originates from a negative position, from a belief in non-existence or from a non-gnosis, has been known for some time now. But to write poetry is always a gnosis or way of becoming conscious; a way of learning about oneself and the world which surrounds one, one's own drama in relation to the self as well as in relation to external realities. To arrive at such a consciousness Montale looks inside himself with a searching and pitiless glance until he feels or even sees a terrible anguish from which there is no hope of escape: he sees the evil of life itself. For him, all of nature suffers. And each thing suffers in accordance with its capacity to suffer, in its own particular way:

> it was the strangled stream that gurgles,
> it was the crumbling of the leaf
> dried-out, it was the horse fallen battered.
>
> *(Ossi di seppia)*

In man this suffering becomes intellectual, metaphysical. His doom consists of aspiring for a happiness which is pure illusion; in aspiring for it and at the same time being fully aware that it is an illusion; in searching for a truth which continually escapes him, a truth which is always beyond his grasp. The human condition is symbolized as the useless strain of searching for a "broken thread in the net which encloses us" (**"In limine"**); "the link which does not hold, / the thread to disentangle, which finally places us / in the middle of a truth" (**"I limoni"**); "the apparition that saves you." During certain vague moments of lucidity ("and in the breast a sweetness rains") it seems that man almost understands this elusive mystery: but it is an illusion which immediately dissolves and the "blue" once again "shows itself only in pieces," "the light becomes meager—mean the soul" (**"I limoni"**). It is the illusion of a moment which betrays and disheartens but nevertheless encourages man to take up the search once again, because it leaves behind the desire for a lost promise, for the solarity of the golden horns.

This is subject matter quite close to that of Leopardi. It lacks, however, the vague, "il pellegrino," the melancholy of Leopardi; it has become pure dialectic which lives and thrives on the intelligence, almost eliminating all sentiment "a priori." The affective life is as if darkened; the very words have become meager, pale, fit for the posing of the same agitating, unsolved and unsolvable problem: the cognitive or ontological problem. If Leopardi sought for the "why" of the universe and the life of man, to conclude that "perhaps in whatever form, in whatever / condition he may exist, in cot or cradle / it is a gloomy birthday for the one just born" ("Canto notturno di un pastore errante dell'Asia"); Montale does not even bother to search, because he assumes the answer to be true from the start. What Montale asks is rather, Of what does this "suffering" consist? that is, he asks the "why" of this suffering, only to conclude that it is a suffering without reason and without purpose; it is an unquenchable thirst for knowledge, a painful desire or longing for something that can never be attained and which resolves itself only in nothing:

> And walking in the dazzling sun
> to feel with sad bewilderment
> what all of life is and its struggle
> in this following along a wall
> which has on top sharp broken bits of bottle.
>
> *(Ossi di seppia)*

It is superfluous to point out how much that is "romantic" is to be found in the content of Montale's poetry. But expressions, the poetic images dissolve into a suffocating weariness of despairing monotony. Things seem always alike but unrelated: they are pure apparitions lacking any deep meaning. Montale's universe is a chaos of monotony which offers no relief. The poetry of the *Ossi* is fixed in the blinding atmosphere of a sultry midday: an atmosphere which renders barren every source of sentiment. It is a midday "tense and burned" of which the early Leopardi already had captured the surprising static quality and in which things appear isolated, detached, desiccated. Their moment is mere apparition, their variation is pure contingency, which returns to present the same vexing problem of staticity.

It is at this point that Montale introduces the most concrete and fascinating of his symbols: the sea. In its continuous flowing movement the sea combines the absolute staticity or motionlessness of man and his appearance of being in continuous movement. The clarification of this symbol comes in that group of nine poems which in the *Ossi* give life to an extensive colloquy with the sea. **"Mediterraneo"** is almost a "poemetto" in which the sea has a concealed symbolic value. But it is not an abstract or intellectually forced symbol, rather it is a symbol which is born spontaneously from the very nature of the sea and from Montale's special reaction to it. The sea is life; it is the essence of humanity, dynamic and static at the same time; and the voice of the sea is the very voice of humanity "vast and manifold and at the same time confined" (**"Antico, sono ubriacato della tua voce"**). In continuous movement, in letting oneself be seized by life, like a pebble or sunflower there is the hope of finding the essential, freedom, "the dreamed-of homeland," "the uncorrupted country." Montale fully understands the problem, but he refuses to accept it. It is his intelligence that does not permit him to abandon himself to life. To the poet the right "to observe" alone is conceded, to view powerlessly the miracle of life without being part of it: he is the "desolate plant," "the dried-out earth," which opens up to allow the blossoming of a pale flower: his poetry, which is powerless to capture the truth and which functions only as a means for relieving his "rancor."

His doom consists of aspiring for a happiness which is pure illusion; in aspiring for it and at the same time being fully aware that it is an illusion; in searching for a truth which continually escapes him, a truth which is always beyond his grasp.

—*Maria Sampoli Simonelli*

An emotion from which there is no escape, which every Montale poem reveals and almost puts on a level with pleasure, is the joy of self-destruction: "because in confidence, my dear friend, I believe that you are happy and that everyone else is happy; but as far as I am concerned, with your permission and that of the century, I am very unhappy; and I believe myself to be so; and all the newspapers of two worlds will not convince me to the contrary." (G. Leopardi, *Operette morali*, "Dialogo di Tristano e di un amico"). The Leopardian position is adapted to the new drama. Life is for the others; it is for those like Esterina, who find in the sea "the force which tempers" her, and says "in the water you discover yourself and you renew yourself," but it is not for one who "of a race of those who remain earth-bound" is capable only of "watching." Montale knows that he is incapable of solving the cognitive problem, yet he never gives up trying. It is a titanic battle between his desire to know, which is his intellectual pride, and the limit of knowledge imposed upon every man. Yet **"Falsetto"** is the most and at the same time the least Leopardian of Montale's po-

ems. That is to say, it is the poem which best reflects Leopardi's imagery and at the same time best reveals Montale's difference from it. Esterina is, in some ways, daughter to Silvia: both are fixed in eternal youth. Esterina, whose twenty years of age threaten her in the form of a rosy-grey cloud which little by little encloses her; Silvia, who is fixed in the memory "when beauty splendored in your laughing, agile eyes" and "happy and thoughtful you ascended the threshold of youth." But Silvia already lives in a myth, in the absolute immobility of bland thought, of dreams, of vague expectations. Silvia is an integral part of the poet who created her. Esterina, even though idolized, remains outside the poet: she is of that part of the world which is in opposition to the Montalian "I." Montale can pray for her as he can for the others, but he cannot reassure her in her ignorance of life:

> Tomorrow's doubt does not frighten you.
> Happily you stretch out
> on a reef glistening of salt
> and in the sun you burn your body.
> You bring to mind the lizard
> paused on the barren rock;
> for you youth lies in wait
> for him the little boy's lasso of grass.
>   (**"Falsetto,"** *Ossi*)

The instinctive knowledge that things possess is the very essence of Esterina: it is a particular way of knowing or understanding that really belongs exclusively to childhood, when

> Every moment burned
> in the succeeding moments without trace
> to live was a venture too new
> hour by hour, and it made the heart pound.
>   (**"La fine dell'infanzia,"** *Ossi*)

Death is not a threat to Silvia but rather a redemption or solution. But Esterina does not die, rather she lives in an inconceivable nightmare, not forthcoming but present. And Montale captures all of the suffering in this. "Go, for you I have prayed"; those most appropriate words from **"In limine,"** are recapitulated at the end of the first stanza of **"Falsetto"**: "I pray it be / for you an ineffable concert / of tiny bells." The intense cleavage between the poet and his image is still more evident in the closing:

> We watch you, we of a race
> of those who remain earth-bound.

Esterina does not represent a happiness completely lost, a dream which could have been realized but was not, like Leopardi's Silvia. Rather, she represents a happiness which is denied to whoever desires to know it. To want to know or understand life, the essence of things, is already in itself a denial of our ability to know. To abandon oneself to life and with a "shrug of the shoulders" destroy the fortresses of an obscure tomorrow signifies a capturing of the essence of life without knowing or understanding it; and this is the only way to be able to live beyond the negation.

More than once Montale has attempted the theme of childhood, the age of illusion. Above all, he has attempted to capture the moment of fracture, the breaking point, the painful passage from the naiveté or unawareness of childhood to the unarmed, defeated consciousness of adulthood. from **"Falsetto"** to **"La farandola dei fanciulli,"** from **"Arremba sulla strinata proda"** to **"La fine dell'-infanzia,"** the same theme is dealt with: perhaps salvation consists in the ability to fix one's very self in eternal childhood, in a long sleep in which "the evil spirits that sail in fleets" can never catch up with one. An impossible means of salvation!

> The moment which destroys the slow work of
>   months arrives: now secretly it cracks, now rends
>   it in a tempest.

Life presses down on us: the break from the fallible "certitudes" of childhood "arrives," sometimes slowly and mysteriously, other times suddenly and violently, but to escape the break is an impossibility.

> The fracture comes: perhaps without a fracas.
> Who has constructed feels his condemnation.
>   **("Arremba sulla strinata proda,"** *Ossi*)

In **"La fine dell'infanzia"** the break is lived as personal memory, and is no longer feared or suffered through another. This poem is among the best constructed and most rich in thought of Montale's first collection. In it the themes which Montale has been unravelling throughout the *Ossi* are recapitulated and clarified in the loose and sad narrative tone of the central part of the poem. The image of the sea in a tempest, which opens and closes the poem, gives it a circular construction. But this image has an analogical value which surpasses its constructive value. The tempest signifies the breaking point in which "the deception was evident," and it is the indication of a painful existence which lasts beyond the breaking point in a world which no longer has "a center." Uncertainty, uneasiness, cognitive impotency accompany "the hour of searching." Everything becomes extraneous, unconceivable, mysterious, closed in upon itself like a raincloud.

> Heavy clouds upon a troubled sea
> which boiled in our face, soon appeared.

And childhood died in a ring-around-the rosy:

> Remote also the place
> of childhood which explores
> a blocked-in yard as a world.

The Leopardian theme of the illusion, the delightful deception, which accompanies childhood, becomes in Montale the theme of the imaginative consciousness of astonished childhood, when

> Things dressed themselves with names,
> our world had a center.

Life, after the passage from childhood to adulthood, is nothing more than a fatiguing and useless searching for this "center;" a spasmodic waiting for the miracle of insight, the sudden ripping away of the veil behind which the truth of all things is hidden. This is a return, therefore, to the central point of Montale's poetry.

A particular moment is expressed in the poems entitled **"Sarcofaghi."** Here Montale groups together four poems of a particular tone which deal with one poetic motif: the eternal, happy, stable life of art as opposed to the ever-changing, unhappy, uncertain life of man. The relationship with Pirandello is more than evident. Human existence in its continuous and fatal flowing, in its participation in form without ever *becoming* form is a slow and daily death. Montale lingers:

> man who passes by . .
> Then goes on: in this valley
> there is no exchange of dark and light.
> Along this way your life has led you,
> there is no refuge for you, you are too dead.
>   **("Sarcofaghi,"** *Ossi*)

The creatures of art glory in an immutable existence. Perceived during a sudden illumination, "in a bland minute"—when nature functions mysteriously through the fantasy of the poet—these creatures remain fixed eternally in their happiness. They are the work of nature and therefore they are life, but a life which *is* form and for this reason stable and eternal.

> . . . in a bland
> minute illuminating nature
> molds her happy
> creatures, mother not step-mother,
> in levity of form.
> World that sleeps or world that glories
> in immutable existence: who can say?

The same conception of art guides both Montale and Pirandello. "Nature serves as the instrument of the human fantasy in order to continue or carry higher her work of creation," explains Pirandello through the Father in *Six Characters in Search of an Author*. But that which in Pirandello is reasoning and dialectics in Montale dissolves into lyrical afterthoughts and images. The very question: "who can say?" shadows the concept with a halo of doubt. Pirandello affirms; Montale doubts. And from this doubt is born that sad and lyrical tone which Pirandello rejects.

But this is not the only point of contact between the two authors. By contact I do not mean a direct Pirandellian influence on the formation of Montale's thought, but rather an independent working-out of the same problem, the conception of which depends on the particular historical-philosophical atmosphere of each author while the affinity of the solutions depends on a certain spiritual affinity between the two. Pirandello and Montale are certainly the Italian writers most representative of an epoch and of a crisis of moral values. But knowledge or cognizance is at the base of ethics: a gnostic solution is also always a solution which implies a human norm of existence, and therefore the solution is a moral one.

The problem or theme of the "truth" is at the center of both Pirandello's art and Montale's poetry. It arises from the search for a plausible reason for the "fear of living." Pirandello, in his last essay on Verga written five years before his death, makes a nearly open confession of the problem: "Almost all the Sicilians," he writes, "have an instinctive fear of life which causes them to close themselves within themselves, lonely, contented by little, so long as it gives them a sense of security" (*Saggi,* Mondadori). This fear of life is the hidden poetical core of Pirandello's work, and he feels and suffers this fear in all of its destructive force while he insistently searches for the "why." In Montale the "fear of living" becomes the "evil of living" ("male di vivere"): but his reason for searching for the "why" is analogous to Pirandello's. Pirandello in his inquiry gathers the roots of the drama through the conflict between "life which continuing moves onward and changes, and form which fixes life making it immutable." But the drama remains beyond the philosophical solution, and it is the drama of man who aspires to life and at the same time fears it. These premises lead to Pirandello's relativism concerning truth. If man could only arrive at *a* truth, stable, certain, unchangeable, a true, undoubtable truth, he could conquer his "fear of living." The norm of his actions would be based on this unchangeable truth finally realized. But the only truth which man is capable of arriving at is a subjective, individual, changeable truth. "The reality of today will be the illusion of tomorrow; and the reality of tomorrow will become even a more fleeting illusion at some future time," Pirandello had written in *Il fu Mattia Pascal,* anticipating the words of the Father in *Six Characters.* Every man, therefore, has his own truth, but it is a truth which naturally and instinctively cannot satisfy him: man desires not *a* truth but rather *the* truth. Human existence is nothing more than a fatiguing and useless search for an unattainable mystery which perhaps exists within but which presents itself to man behind a thick, impenetrable black veil just as Signora Ponza is presented to the public in the last act of *Così è (se vi pare).* In Montale relativism disappears, and in its place appears the "contingent" as a moment which passes and is to be grasped; not truth certainly, but rather the complete renunciation of possibility of possessing truth. In Montale, Pirandello's gnosic pessimism is sharpened beyond the point of relativism. There remains only a lyrical opening of disillusioned hope for a miracle. Everyone who lives—by the very fact that he is alive—tends toward movement: towards a movement which gives the sense of life although it is mere appearance or a "glimmer of life." The *Occasioni,* Montale's second collection of poems, are born from this state of mind. In this collection Montale attempts to capture in pure poetry this fleeting moment, the "occasion," the contingent. And his style becomes always more narrative; he makes the momentary impression the only thing that counts and that has an absolute value. Like Arsenio, the most dramatic and autobiographical character in the *Ossi,* Montale now attempts to let himself be taken by the sea, by life; he attempts to leave the "race of those who remain earthbound." But "all becomes strange and difficult"; "everything is impossible" (**"Carnevale di Gerti"**). For a man who thinks or even for a man who has once attempted this road to the mystery, the contingent life is an empty passing of images that have neither sense nor reason. And perhaps this is really the profound reason: one lives thanks to a "tailsman," like Dora Markus, like every man. In accepting the cognitive limit a sporadic and absurd hope gave temporary light. Now this too gives way, and "hell is certain."

One cannot talk about Montale without at least mentioning the value of recollection or memory in the poems of this poet. Memory is the very life of Montale's present poetics: a life which is a "screen of images," which has in itself "the signs of death and of the past." The Montalian memory gathers both past and future, resolving both in pure detached images. If in the *Ossi* Montale had captured the universal chaos of things: each thing independently static, without order and without a goal; in the *Occasioni* he captures the interior chaos of human existence: a collection of separate, unattached images, lacking in both order and aim. Man in his deepest soul mirrors the useless universal life. This is the new and more disconcerting position of Montale, who is so capable of translating into poetry a crisis of faith in oneself and a "transcendency" which may be cause, order, and harmony of things.

One can scarcely find, among the prominent poets of this century, one who has used metaphysics as intensively as Montale. His poetry is essentially a metaphysical search for a way of life.

—Arshi Pipa, in Italica, March, 1962.

In the *Bufera,* Montale's most recent collection, the two motifs are interwoven, and they mirror each other without finding a solution of "glimmer of light." Montale, like his poetry, develops in an apparition of continual movement, which, in reality, remains in the fixed staticity of everything. Perhaps because of this, the poetical discovery of the sea, which appears in the *Ossi* as pure symbol and pure transfiguration of reality, is so right for Montale. It is a sea outside of us; it is a sea deep within us: all sound and all movement, all changing colors and tones, yet it is always the same. And nothing makes sense; neither the staticity nor the movement. One cancels the other without ever satisfying or being satisfied.

Glauco Cambon   (essay date 1967)

SOURCE: "Eugenio Montale's 'Motets': The Occasions of Epiphany," in *PMLA,* Vol. LXXXII, No. 7, December, 1967, pp. 471–84.

[*In the following excerpt, Cambon arques that thematic and formal unity links the "Motets" in* The Occasions.]

The Centrality of the twenty "Mottetti" to Montale's decisive second book, *Le Occasioni* (1939), has been noted by such critics as Ettore Bonora and Silvio Ramat [in *La poesia di Montale* (1965) and *Montale* (1965), respectively]. Despite their probings, however, much remains to be done towards an organic understanding of this remarkable series of poems. Since this part of Montale's work relates to much else he has written before and after, I shall not attempt to isolate it from the rest of the *Occasioni* book, but merely to keep my focus on what is after all a kind of book within the book. A tighter unity prevails among the "Motets" than among the other poems in the volume, both because the former all turn on the constant of love for Clizia in the variations of worldly vicissitudes, and because they match this thematic constancy by a relative constancy of form.

The author himself, in his awareness of their interdependence, rearranged their sequential order to fit a dialectic of the heart rather than a strict chronological succession. The first three "Motets" (I take these details from the latest Mondadori edition, the fifth, of 1962) are dated 1934, and the last one 1937, with a prevalence of intermingled 1937 and 1938 datings in between. **"Motet" No. 5** is of 1939, and therefore should come at the very end, if compositional chronology were the dominant consideration; it is arguable that the author shifted this utterly despondent piece backwards to fifth position to avoid concluding the whole sequence on the hell-haunted keynote on which it had started, especially since he then chose for an epilogue the ironically resigned ". . . ma così sia" of 1937, which changes the entire perspective. Instead of a development coming around full circle to seal a history of despair, we now have a precariously open line of spiritual dynamics.

Inner time thus supersedes factual time in the final arrangement of artistic experience, as specifically shown by the reshuffling of past and present which, within the magic circle of **"Motet" No. 3,** results in a suspension of time. Timelessness, however, is never durably grasped, just fleetingly glimpsed; it is as if the experiencing persona swam underwater in the stream of time only to surface momentarily into the timeless sphere where he cannot finally breathe—and this metaphor actually materializes in a later, thematically related poem from *La Bufera e altro* (**"L'ombra della magnolia"**), with the poet seeing himself as a fish jumping on dry land at the call of his beloved from "l'oltrecielo," the sky beyond the sky. Here is one source of epiphany, "the point of intersection of the timeless / with time," to say it with Eliot, and it helps us to understand why in the end time will be accepted.

The experience of time is primary, intense to the point of making a reference to Bergson's concept of felt duration almost inevitable. Temporality as a form of consciousness involves a keen sense of the uniqueness of each fully lived moment, and thereby places a special emphasis on contingency, as in the philosophy of Emile Boutroux, another thinker who is relevant to Montale's poetical world; the poet himself publicly acknowledged his strong interest in Boutroux's *philosophie de la contingence* during his formative years. Each contingent moment (in Montale's language, "occasion") being unrepeatable, the intimate story outlined by these poems unfolds as a progression from a state of haunted deprivation to a substantially different one, though within this open pattern there occur, analogically speaking, seasonal cycles of the soul, winter to spring and summer, bereavement to budding hope, and plenitude and bereavement once again. Even if the analogy is imperfect, as Walter Ong would warn us, it nevertheless operates; analogies are not identities, and this means that the spiritual movement embodied in the overall design of the "Motets" is neither linear nor circular, but spiral.

Montale concentrates on private history, since public history in his opinion has become the domain of falsity and injustice. The several poems count as heartbeats of the mind engaged in the quest for personal truth and happiness: a fulfilling illumination to exorcize the *idola fori* of the age. Hence the markedly "occasional" nature of the "Mottetti," in accordance with the programmatic title of the whole book, *Occasioni*: in a historically deranged world (it's the middle-to-late thirties and the sky is darkening over Europe), in a naturally unyielding cosmos, a possible order of higher truth may reveal itself only by fleeting chance, and obliquely. The "occasional" mode of epiphany determines the rhapsodically loose structure within whose range each "Motet" can best function as an individual climax of perception that mirrors the previous ones and leads up to the next.

The poet's openness to experience will not guarantee an abundance of reliable occasions, yet he will keep trying, for he knows that his only chance (both as man and as poet) is to hope against hope: "Sobre el bolcán la flor," his epigraph from Bécquer has it, and it reads like a summary of Leopardi's "La Ginestra," that sober celebration, as a foil to man's disastrous history, of the unconquerable flower which no eruption will finally evict from Vesuvius' inhospitable slopes. The first poem of the sequence voices the despair of an excruciating loss which leaves only "the certainty of hell":

Lo sai: debbo riperderti e non posso.
Come un tiro aggiustato mi sommuove
ogni opera, ogni grido e anche lo spiro
salino che straripa
dai moli e fa l'oscura primavera
di Sottoripa.

Paese di ferrame e alberature
a selva nella polvere del vespro.
Un ronzio lungo viene dall'aperto,
strazia com'unghia ai vetri. Cerco il segno
smarrito, il pegno solo ch'ebbi in grazia
da te.
    E l'inferno è certo.

You know it: I must lose you again and I cannot.
Like an accurate shot every action
startles me, every shout, and even the salty
breeze which brims over
the docks and makes the murky Spring
of Sottoripa.

Landscape of iron structures and of ship-masts
thick like a forest in the evening's dust.
A long whir comes from the open,
grates like a nail on windowpanes. I seek the lost
sign, the only pledge I received as a grace
from you.
     And hell is certain.

Everything conspires to make this "Motet" one of the strongest poetical statements of the century, whether we take it by itself, or as a prologue to the whole allusive story, or as the epilogue of an antecedent development: its dramatic abruptness, its clipped syntax like a gasping breath, its sharp imagery and crackling syllables interwoven with hidden rhymes (*tiro-spiro, lungo-unghia, strazia-grazia, segno-pegno*). Word economy reaches a maximum without impinging on the naturalness of utterance; Genoa's harbor is rapidly etched, a merciless landscape (for this contingency) even in the midst of spring, since it can be the scene of unbearable farewells. Spiritual derangement wreaked on the persona by such a departure culminates in the forecast of "hell" at the end, but it has already come through in those poignant similes of the "accurate shot" and of the "prolonged whir like a nail grating on the panes." Nothing in Auden or Eliot, nothing in Benn surpasses this nervous incisiveness, this assurance of diction which stands out as one exemplary embodiment of modern sensibility at its harrowing best. One thinks of the "Preludes," of "Rhapsody on a Windy Night"; and yet somehow Montale's piece throbs with greater urgency.

Nothing is explained and everything counts; as so often with Leopardi (an undoubted ancestor), the energy of utterance arches into an I-Thou address which must bridge a gap of absence (whether temporary or final), and leaves room only for the essentials of inner existence. We do not *see* the addressed person, we are not *told* who she is, only her importance to the speaker. The following "Motets" will make clearer why she is so important, without really violating the initial reticence. One thing we know: she is very human and real, yet somehow superhuman, if she can give "pledges of grace." These are of course the hyperboles of love, but in the course of the sequence they will develop into metaphysical attributes. She is not a stable presence; she has come and gone and is going once again, forever—a detail concisely expressed by that verb (*riperderti*) which makes the whole difference between rhetoric and passion. She is the exceptional visitor from another world (and in more than one sense, as the sequel will show), and she changes everything for our poet, who is left seeking for the "sign" of redemptive power.

Cavalcanti's, Dante's, Petrarch's ladies likewise brought peace and torment to their worshipers; the link is not casual, for it does not take long to see how Montale's language is steeped in *Dolce Stil Nuovo* and (even more) mature Dantesque style. The counterpoint of salvation and damnation appears in the very rhymes of this poem: *tiro* (shot) evokes *spiro* (breath, breeze), *strazia* (tortures) elicits *grazia* (grace), *aperto* (open) is echoed by *certo* (the certitude of hell), while *segno* (sign) instead tends tonally and semantically to coalesce with *pegno* (pledge), thus

giving a musical resolution to the dissonant chords. In other poems of the series, or of the book, the dissonance coagulates into an oxymoron, such as "la tua cara minaccia" (your cherished menace) in **"Motet" No. 7,** the war described in terms of "night games of Roman candles" and "a feast" in **"Motet" No. 3,** or (elsewhere in *Le Occasioni*) "è una tempesta anche la tua dolcezza" (your very sweetness is a storm) in **"Dora Markus."** . . .

Coming to our first "Motet" with Dante in mind will result in an enriching recognition of the poem's qualities *per se* as well as of its structural function in the series. The cutting sounds, the concrete, localized words, the cruel metaphors call to mind the percussive alliterations of *Inferno* with its concomitantly astringent similes: "come coltel di scardova le scaglie"; "si dileguò come da corda cocca"; "come d'un stizzo verde ch'arso sia"; "tal che se Tambernicchi / vi fosse su caduto, o Pietrapana, / non avrìa pur da l'orlo fatto cricchi." The harbor's "wood of masts and iron" might almost arouse overtones of the Dark Wood; indeed a subjective "hell" is "certain," while the persona appropriately keeps looking for the "lost sign," for "the pledge of grace" his troubling Beatrice had given him. Like the *Inferno*'s prologue, this "Motet" consummates a catastrophe and ushers in the possibility of a renewal by way of a perilous quest which should lead the bewildered poet back to his Lady. By the same token, it is the questing attitude that makes poetry possible, it describes the nature of Montale's poetry, as **"Motet" No. 9** (coincidentally starting on an intentional reference to Dante) may exemplify, on the most intellectual level, a relentless search for meaning in the wilderness of phenomena. Ever since **"I Limoni"** (the opening piece of *Ossi di seppia,* 1925) he had hoped to disentangle "the thread . . . / that may instal us in the quick of a truth." . . .

It is the personal intimacy of a specific love rapport that dominates the "Motets" sequence and is itself heaven and hell to the poet's persona. The "prologue," we saw, has set the scene for the development of love's vicissitudes, and the next poem, composed in the same year, begins to explore them backwards by venturing into the region of memory and thereby supplying some antecedents to the predicament previously expressed. We hear of a crucial year of suffering (disease, as the following poem will show) at a "foreign" (Swiss?) lake, whence his elusive lady came down to her poet with a heraldic token (the "sign" and "pledge" mentioned in Poem No. 1?):

> Molti anni, e uno più duro sopra il lago
> straniero su cui ardono i tramonti.
> Poi scendesti dai monti a riportarmi
> San Giorgio e il Drago . . .

> Many years, and one, harder, on the foreign
> lake where sunsets blaze.
> Then you descended from the mountains to bring
>   back
> Saint George and the Dragon to me . . .

If it is true, as Bonora says [in *La poesia di Montale*], that the heraldry refers to Genoa's patron saint, to signify a love tryst which took place there, we can hardly miss the larger significance of the symbol. As the rest of the poems variously hint, and the whole of *Le Occasioni* makes unequivocally clear (especially in elegies like **"Eastbourne"** or **"Nuove Stanze,"** thematically related to "Motets"), the world is out of joint around the two lovers, and the condition of hell is no idiosyncrasy of the poet's mind; his lady often appears as defiant prophetess or fighting angel against the forces of evil, and thus St. George killing the dragon (of political obscurantism) makes the perfect icon for her to "bring back" to her devotee. It does not matter that the icon is no material object but (given Montale's psychological use of verbs like *riportare* and *ritornare*) simply the enshrined memory of a private occurrence. On the trans-narrative level, the force of style itself makes it announce emblematically the desperate fight for reason and justice, which concerns both parties here along with the largely unaware world around them. The persona, then, has more than one good reason to wish he "could imprint" the significant image on the "banner" he feels flapping at the seawind "in the heart":

> Imprimerli potessi sul palvese
> che s'agita alla frusta del grecale
> in cuore . . . E per te scendere in un gorgo
> di fedeltà, immortale.
> Would I were able to imprint them on the flag
> which flutters at the whip of the seawind
> in my heart . . . And to descend for your sake into
>   a whirlpool
> of faithfulness, immortal.

Not victory, but fidelity to the point of sacrifice is the thing for our poet who would joust for his lady's emblem. While still keeping his guard up against any encroachment of pompousness, he has come a long way from **"Arsenio"**'s paralyzing dubitation; for her he would readily go down in a whirlpool of self-purified passion. The extreme concision makes for mythical focus, climaxing in the very Dantesque metonymy (cf. "San Giorgio e il Drago" with "Caino e le spine" in *Inf.* XX. 126, or "il gallo di Gallura" in *Purg.* VIII. 81) which gives this personal story a decisive turn for the legendary. There is enough precision to individualize the persons involved, and enough narrative vagueness to evoke the mysterious aura of a fairytale; a marked success, to be sure, of the tendency to retreat from the explicit into the resourceful realm of the implicit. The rhymes, as usual, reinforce a semantic point, and this is particularly true of "tramonti" (sunsets) and "monti" (mountains), where a sunlike halo accrues to the Transalpine visitor. "Drago" (dragon) shocks us into sharper awareness when we realize its consonance with "lago" (lake). We could even speak of semantic rhyme in the case of the twice used verb "scendere" (to descend), which in Stanza 2 echoes, on the part of the speaker, the ritual action performed by his lady in Stanza 1.

This leads us to see the responsorial symmetry of the two stanzas, the first of which centers on the lady's person and actions, the second on her poet's response; and the response endures, as the verb tenses show—indefinite present

offsetting the definite past of Stanza 1: "scendesti" (you descended) . . ."potessi" (could I) . . . "scendere" (descend). Thus memory prolongs and develops the erstwhile occasion into epiphany. The "lake" of Stanza 1 makes room for a "whirlpool" (*gorgo*) in Stanza 2; our lady really came as an angel to stir the waters, since everything (St. 2) is now in commotion in the poet's own self; he views his commitment to her as a tempestuous, dangerous, if enlivening state: "gorgo di fedeltà" (whirlpool of fidelity), a unique, and uniquely motivated, paradox. If any "Motets" justify their musical title by verbal counterpoint and polyphonic structure, this one does.

"Motet" No. 1 generated **"Motet" No. 2** by way of associative reminiscence, and the latter in turn provides a further invitation to memory, thereby giving rise to **"Motet" No. 3**. Genoa was the clue **No. 1** afforded to the subsequent piece, and hospital and war develop as a contrapuntal poetical situation in **No. 3** from the apposite intimations of **"Motet" No. 2**. The mind keeps going back into a further past on the thread of restless memory. Brief mention of the lady's sick confinement now summons the vision of her monotonous life in the uncommunicative plight of an Alpine sanitarium. The vision arises as an indefinite present, for the noun-ridden style of Stanza 1 admits of no verbs. At the end (St. 4) this syntax will focus on a historical present expressing the continuity of memory once struck by the significant moment:

> E' scorsa un'ala rude, t'ha sfiorato le mani,
> ma invano: la tua carta non è questa.
>
> A rough wind has brushed past, skimming your
>   hands,
> but in vain: this was not your card.

And remembrance once again transforms the occasion (solitary card games in the hospital) into epiphany (Death's wing brushing past, but to indicate the wrong card; our lady's allegiance is not to death, and her hour has not struck; hope nestles in the nest of pain). Meanwhile, this "exile" of hers in the foreign hospital has reminded the poet of his own exile: the predicament of war by now long weathered. Two manners of solitude, two ways of confronting death; the separately endured ordeals were eventually to bring the two lovers together.

So he endured, but to what purpose, asks the poet in the next "Motet" (**No. 4**). His purpose was and is to know her, to be with her; the time spent in ignorance of her now appears wasted, and war ("il logorio / di prima," the distress of *the time before*) "spared" him only to let him see what an irremediable loss this was. Nevertheless, as memory pushes into door after door of the *temps perdu*, he is able to say that physical absence did not prevent his being spiritually with her when another ordeal, her father's death, tried her. Everything comes back to him from long ago, and war especially, as he knew it in a given region of the Alps ("Cumerlotti o Anghébeni"). The particulars of chance, expressed by these odd names of Alpine villages, add a weird note of individually felt reality to the scene. War in a way has not ended for him since "the distress of the time *before*" knowing his woman has been followed by a presumable "distress of the time *after*" losing her—who could alone be his peace, who alone could make sense of his life. "Ridiculous the waste sad time / Stretching before and after," as the conclusion of "Burnt Norton" has it. Also, war and love have been intertwining fugally through three of these four "Motets" like complementary themes which contrast each other but may tend to a resolving fusion; the fusion, indeed, that will take place in the final stanza of **"Notizie dall' Amiata"** at the end of *Le Occasioni,* where the key expression is "rissa cristiana," Christian strife, anticipating the even bolder synthesis of "L'ombra della magnolia" in La Bufera e altro: "perché la guerra fosse in te e in chi adora / su te le stimme del tuo Sposo" (that war might be in you and in whosoever worships / in you the stigmata of your Bridegroom). Love may bring peace, but in a psychological and even more in a mystical sense it is also "war." The two descanting themes transform each other in the course of Montale's poetical career.

Here it was the verb of active memory ("mi riporta Cumerlotti," etc.) that released a kind of purgatorial revelation by matching different levels of past experience; but we are back in hell with **"Motet" No. 5,** which rephrases in an even starker way the situation of **"Motet" No. 1**: an ineluctable parting, this time by train, and a hopelessness investing the whole world. Metallic onomatopoeia (of the kind Carducci had already essayed in his "Alla stazione in una mattina d'autunno" ["At the Station in an Autumn Morning"]) concurs with coughing asyndeton to structure the infernal vision:

> Addi, fischi nel buio, cenni, tosse
> e sportelli abbassati. E' l'ora . . .

> Goodbyes, whistles in the dark, nods, coughing,
> and windows lowered in the train. It is time . . .

It is, indeed, the time of parting, of loss, of infernal epiphany:

> . . . Forse
> gli automi hanno ragione. Come appaiono
> dai corridoi, murati!

> . . . Perhaps
> the automatons are right. How they appear
> walled in, from the aisles!

"Walled-in automatons": a dehumanized mankind appears, dominated by mechanical power.

In the second stanza, this sinister music becomes a dance of death:

> Presti anche tu alla fioca
> litania del tuo rapido quest'orrida
> e fedele cadenza di carioca?

> Are you too lending to the dim
> litany of your express train this horrid
> and faithful cadence of a carioca dance? . . .

The first four "Motets" make a cycle which is sealed by the fifth. Then from the zero point another season of the soul begins; and we go through the odyssey of waiting and hope and loss, all the stations of the search. But since the departure has been physically final, our poet looks for his lady's symbolic presence; everything may become a token, an embodying sign of her. And in this way the process of erotic apotheosis starts, with the absent lady taking on more and more metaphysical attributes. First (as in "Motet" No. 6) she is what gives a meaning to our poet's life, then she becomes the source of all meaning and life, to culminate in the frankly deifying myths of **"Eastbourne," "Nuove Stanze," "L'orto,"** and **"Iride."** The ecclesiastical connotation of the title "Motets" makes itself felt, the more so as we connect the "Mottetti" with those other (thematically related) lyrics.

"Motet" No. 6 still delves in memory, since only from the past can the poet's light come now that his woman is removed from contact:

> La speranza di pure rivederti
> m'abbandonava;

> e mi chiesi se questo che mi chiude
> ogni senso di te, schermo d'immagini,
> ha i segni della morte o dal passato
> è in esso, ma distorto e fatto labile,
> un *tuo* barbaglio . . .

> The very hope to see you again
> was abandoning me;

> and I wondered if this thing which blocks
> any sense of you, this screen of images,
> bears the signs of death or, from the past,
> it has retained, though distorted and fleeting,
> a glimmer of *you* . . .

In the barrier of blind phenomena ("schermo d'immagini," screen of images) which threaten death because they seem to shut him off from any "sense of" (his lady), the poet wonders whether "a gleam" (*barbaglio*) of her can still be found, however "faint and distorted." He is once again in the purgatorial plight of looking for his salvation, as it were, against odds; and it is against odds that the invoked sign comes, in the unlikeliest form of epiphany. "Cerco il segno / smarrito . . . ," he said in **"Motet" No. 1**; and at times the symbol is not certain, as in the present case, where Clizia is epiphanized by a liveried lackey pulling two jackals on a leash:

> (a Modena, tra i portici,
> un servo gallonato trascinava
> due sciacalli al guinzaglio).

> (at Modena, in the porticoes,
> a liveried servant was dragging
> two jackals on a leash).

Even the fact that this particular remembrance is set in parentheses makes it a problematical epiphany. The revelatory sign generally comes at the unexpected moment, in the chance place, in the unforeseen way; here (*if* it is the sign), the exotic animals from Africa and the Orient, connected with the sun, remind the poet of sunflower-like Clizia. They are as incongruous to the scene as was Clizia herself, the visitor from another world. Incongruity may signalize transcendence, as **"Motet" No. 9** will show.

Animals abound and tend to be magic vehicles in Montale's world, and if right now this function has accrued to the exotic jackals, in the next "Motet" (**No. 7**) it will be the familiar swallows that evoke his faraway lady. They are familiar, but winged and migratory; remember the heroic stork of **"Sotto la Pioggia,"** and the many birdlike incarnations of the transcendental lady in *La Bufera e altro*. The swallows' joyful shuttling between telegraph poles and the sea, however, is not enough to bring her bodily back. She does not cease to be a real woman, and here the persona cannot do with anything less than her physical presence. Such oscillations of the heart contribute to the drama of occasion and epiphany. After a rainstorm, the "truce" of the elements is "menaced" by the pervasive thought of her:

> Già profuma il sambuco fitto su
> lo sterrato; il piovasco si dilegua.
> Se il chiarore è una tregua,
> la tua cara minaccia la consuma.

> Already the thick elderberry exhales its scent
> on the dug up earth; the shower fades away.
> If the light is a truce,
> your cherished menace now consumes it.

In **"Motet" No. 2** she had come to stir the waters; to have known her is to have lost one's peace, and no peace would be welcome or indeed possible without her.

With **"Motet" No. 8** she appears symbolically, but (this time) unmistakably, in the tracing of a palm tree's shadow cast on a wall by the sunrise:

> Ecco il segno: s'innerva
> sul muro che s'indora:
> un frastaglio di palma
> bruciato dai barbagli dell'aurora.

> Here is the sign: it innervates
> the wall being gilded by the sun:
> an arabesque of palm leaves
> burned by the dazzle of the dawn.

The Orient sun and the palm tree have to do with Clizia's sunny nature and with her Palestinian ancestry (as indicated by other poems like **"L'orto"** and **"Iride"**). For once the epiphany coincides immediately with its occasion, and the poet knows a fulfillment; one might say that he has momentarily left hell and purgatory itself behind, though heaven here and now can only be a matter of privileged instants, a dimension tangential to the historically fallen human condition.

The sunny sighting conjures auditory and tactile phenomena to make the absent one a total inner presence:

> Il passo che proviene
> dalla serra sì lieve,
> non è felpato dalla neve, è ancora
> tua vita, sangue tuo nelle mie vene.

> The footstep approaching
> from the hothouse so lightly
> is not muffled by the snow, it is still
> your life, your blood within my veins.

The hypostasis of love is here strongly physical, immanent, personal, climaxing in the erotic fusion. Snow and sun, Orient and North make a polarity of milieux to reinforce the rapture, as in Heine's love poem of the pine tree consumed by love for the remote palm tree in the East; but what sets off the modern poem from its Romantic counterpart is a sensual chord produced by the counterpoint of physiological density and airy fantasy. The body, the here and now, the realm of occasion are never abandoned forever, and such swayings confer on Montale's sequence its unique dynamics, to preserve it from anaemic rarefaction.

If this fine "Motet" is the first fulfilling response to the search announced by **"Motet" No. 1** ("cerco il segno / smarrito"), in the next poem the situation is reversed. While **"Motet" No. 9** is undoubtedly the most abstract and intellectual of the "Mottetti," passion is not excluded; the search for meaning has come to involve the speculative mind along with the heart. In a way, **"Motet" No. 9** marks the beginning of still another cycle within the sequence, by picking up the doctrinal cue of **"Motet" No. 6,** for here we find the questing poet engaged in sifting the phenomena for an evidence of the highest value that only Clizia can impart. The first cycle had culminated in the hellish nightmare of **"Motet" No. 5,** the second has consummated itself in the momentarily attained heaven of **"Motet" No. 8,** and after the respective zero point and high point of moral experience we find the persona resuming his relentless search, swaying between utter alienation and fulfillment, the two experiential thresholds of the mind. "Lo sguardo fruga d'intorno, / la mente indaga accorda disunisce . . . / . . . Sono i silenzi in cui si vede / in ogni ombra umana che si allontana / qualche disturbata Divinità" (The eyes keep scanning all around, / the mind investigates, harmonizes, disjoins . . . / . . . These are the silences in which one sees / in each self-distancing human shadow / some disturbed Godhead). These lines from Montale's **"I limoni,"** the opening lyric of *Ossi di seppia* (1925), could provide an epigraph for whole present sequence and for the specific "Motet" under consideration.

The heavenly epiphany of the previous poem bore the earmarks of immediacy, now the mind recoils into the mediating act of thought which negates the *occasions* supplied by sensory reality to rise to a glimpse of the ineffable. The "screen of images" that makes the world of phenomena might be pierced to attain the noumenal. The poet probes a set of privileged phenomena from various areas of sensory experience within the range of a Ligurian seascape for traces of the transcendent entity his lady seems to have become. But even though their shared quality of instantaneousness made them all candidates to revelatory power, they fail in the end when tested against the utterly "other" nature of the noumenal Thou she is. Whether visual or auditory, the phenomenon consummating itself in the moment is both in and out of time, it verges on the timeless, therefore could somehow manifest transcendency; but not so here, where each event remains closed in itself, an opaque monad (as Franco Fortini wrote [in *Comunità,* August 1954] when analyzing "Estate"):

Il ramarro, se scocca
sotto la grande fersa
delle stoppie—

la vela, quando fiotta
e s'inabissa al salto
della rocca—

il cannone di mezzodì
più fioco del tuo cuore
e il cronometro se
scatta senza rumore—

. . . . .

e poi? Luce di lampo
invano può mutarvi in alcunché
di ricco e strano. Altro era il tuo stampo.

The green lizard, should it dart
under the great whiplash
of sunburnt stubblefields—

the sail, when it flutters
and falls at the steep
cliff headland—

the noontide cannon shot
feebler than your heart
and the chronometer if
it noiselessly clicks—

. . . . .

and then? A lightning glory
in vain could change you all into something
rich and strange. Thy kind was other.

The suddenly darting lizard (a Dantesque reference), the sail vanishing behind a rock, the noontime cannon shot, and finally the ticking of the chronometer: these events can only add up to a series, horizontally as it were, but since they are still circumscribed by time (and the series happens to end with the action of a mechanical timepiece), the question remains open: "what then?" The poet has weighted them one by one to find them wanting *even if they are susceptible of esthetic transfiguration* ("in vain a lightning glory could change you into something rich and strange"). At this point we realize that the quotation from

Shakespeare's *Tempest* is made to carry a definition of the poetic process, and in a poem which questions the ultimate value of esthetic experience, one can go no further than to begin with Dante and conclude with Shakespeare, the highest authorities of poetry.

The religious hypostasis of love has gone to a dizzy height; if the Absent Lady is not even accessible to poetical revelation, because her essence "was wholly other," she is godlike, or partakes of godhead. The poem's procedure in reaching that level presents some (probably not fortuitous) similarity to the Negative Way of the mystics who strove to express the ineffability of God by successively discarding every created aspect of beauty or power that could seem to approach Him: God is not this, nor that, nor even that . . . Like Dante in *Purgalorio* here Montale is a poet exploring the limits of his own art and humbly declaring it (along with Nature) unable to capture the transcendent. For the transcendent would be a steady plenitude of light, and poetic epiphanies are intermittent gleams only. The act of sifting and discarding what nature and art have to offer is underscored by the gesture of pronouns: in the two concluding lines the persona first addresses all the pondered phenomena collectively ("mutarvi," change you all), then turns away from them to speak to his lady ("Altro era il tuo stampo," quite other was thy cast). Notice should also be taken of how the enumerative, suspended rhythm of this poem conveys a tone of progressive meditation, unlike the fast and melodious rhythm of the previous one which suited the immediacy of enjoyed epiphany.

The metaphysical failure of Nature and Art does not stop our poet from pursuing his quest of revelatory analogies in the surrounding cosmos; for, should he cling forever to any kind of Negative Way, he would have to renounce poetry altogether. In **"Motet" No. 10** (which is also chronologically later then **No. 9**) we see him again waiting for the appearance of his lady. "Why are you delaying?" ("Perché tardi?") he asks her; the scene is set, a squirrel is knocking on the tree, the half-moon is vanishing in the triumphant sun, day has started. But she, now appropriately disembodied into pure light, is hidden in a cloud:

A un soffio il pigro fumo trasalisce,
si difende nel punto che ti chiude.
Nulla finisce, o tutto, se tu fòlgore
lasci la nube.

At a gust the sluggish smoke startles,
to defend itself at the point which encloses you.
Nothing will end, or everything, if you, lightning-
    like, leave the storm cloud.

Her appearance in the world of time-bound phenomena can only be lightning-like; essence manifests itself tangentially in our opaque reality. We do not know if the apocalyptic rendezvous will be kept, we are left to share the waiting. The lightning image harks back to the foregoing "Motet," though with reverse import; the "nothing will end, or everything" implies that the longed-for revelation will either save or consume the world. . . .

Musical epiphany is indeed what we have in **"Motet" No. 11,** where the absent lady makes her presence felt as a disembodied voice which is the soul of the world:

La tua voce è quest'anima diffusa.
Su fili, su ali, al vento, a caso, col
favore della musa o d'un ordegno,
ritorna lieta o triste . . .

Your voice is this diffusive soul.
On wires, on wings, at the wind, at random, with
the help of the Muse or of an engine,
it returns, joyous or sad . . .

The poet's communion with her through the medium of music (no matter how produced) is rigorously private, and he defends it against intruding interlocutors:

Parlo d'altro,
ad altri che t'ignora e il suo disegno
è là che insiste *do re la sol sol* . . .

I speak of other things,
to another man, who has no idea of you, and its
    design
is there, insistent: *do re la sol sol* . . .

And so the passion of faith has overcome the ascetic denials of the intellectual **"Motet" No. 9.** Reality does hold cues to the intangible, but, of course, both in this **"Motet" No. 11** and in the next one, the intangible is subjective, a revelation the persona refuses to share. **No. 12** sings the angelic transfiguration of his woman:

Ti libero la fronte dai ghiaccioli
che raccogliesti traversando l'alte
nebulose; hai le penne lacerate
dai cicloni, ti desti a soprassalti.

I rid your forehead of the icicles
you gathered winging through the lofty
nebulae; your feathers are torn
by cyclones, you awaken by fits and starts.

That incongruity which manifests transcendence is here stressed by opposing the richness of imaginative subjectivity to the imperiousness of external, social reality:

Mezzodì: allunga nel riquadro il nespolo
l'ombra nera, s'ostina in cielo un sole
freddoloso; e l'altre ombre che scantonano
nel vicolo non sanno che sei qui.

Noontime: in the window frame the medlar tree
lengthens its black shadow, a shivering sun
persists up there; and the other shadows turning
into the alley do not know you are here.

Epiphany here (as given in the previous stanza of **"Motet" No. 12**) precedes outer reality instead of springing from its cues, and the two moments neatly offset each other. In the process, though, and just because inner reality has

been affirmed without qualification, external reality loses its firmness to dissolve (not only optically) into shadows ("l'ombra nera . . . ; l'altre ombre"). It is noon (*mezzodì*), the hour of plenitude, but plenitude comes to the poet only subjectively, from another sphere than that of physical presences; which is perhaps another way of restating the inadequacy of nature to his glimpsed revelation. "Things as they are," Stevens would say, "are changed upon the blue guitar." Or can they be? Here, at least, things as they are prove irreducible to the substance of a poet's dream.

Thus the troubadour must repeatedly exile himself from the certitude of unshared vision, to be lost among men and things: **"Motet" No. 13** features him in an ambiguous Venice à la Offenbach, where a vision of his lady once taken away from him by demoniacally laughing carnival masks confounds him. What is left but some intermittent spurts of life? In watching on the now deserted scene a fisherman with his writhing eel catch, he emotionally identifies with the man and ultimately with the doomed fish:

una sera tra mille e la mia notte
è più profonda! S'agita laggiù
uno smorto groviglio che m'avviva
a stratti e mi fa eguale a quell'assorto
pescatore d'anguille dalla riva.

an evening like countless others and my night
is deeper! There stirs yonder
a bleak tangle which rouses me
by fits and starts and makes me identical
to that intent fisher of eel on the bank.

Visionary Venice of remembered love with incidents worthy of *Tales of Hoffmann* abruptly dissolves into a quotidian, dull, realistic Venice, and the two contradictory moments of experience, appropriately assigned each to one stanza of the poem (in keeping with the dominant pattern of "Motets"), bring forth two opposite epiphanies: the nightmare of loss at the peak of merriment, and the desolation of fading vitality, as if the persona were reentering the world of **"Arsenio."**

Yet Queen Mab is at work and will not let him rest. **"Motet" No. 14** breaks the spell to grasp the analogic presence of the remote lady in the music of hailstorm, whose destructiveness competes with, and finally melts into, her sprightly song of days gone by. The polyphonic resolution of that contrast through ambivalence aptly crowns this poem marked by musical references to a solemn Debussy (*The Submerged Cathedral*) and the lighter "Aria of the Campanulas." As usual, private reference serves to pinpoint the individual nature of the emotional situation; for all the mythical developments or mystical hypostases that situation fosters, it is not just any two lovers who are involved, but *these* two. The lady used to impersonate, in her private singing, the light opera character of Lakmé.

The whimsical operation of memory here—from the hailstorm-battered campanulas of a garden to the "Campanulas Aria," from hailstorm patter to mechanical keyboard ("la pianola degli inferi") to the trilling of the now remote singer—fits the fanciful manifestation of womanhood, which oddly conquers (by transforming them) the forces of destruction. But **"Motet" No. 11** had said how any given occasion could evoke her voice: "on wires, on wings, in the wind at random, with the help of the Muse or of an engine."

No. 15 returns to a grave note. The beginning of day and the beginning of night, the turning points of man's daily activity, can only receive a human meaning (in the mechanical dispersal of work) from the poet's lady, who keeps threading together the contrary moments of time:

> al chiaro e al buio, soste ancora umane
> se tu a intrecciarle col tuo refe insisti.

> in daylight or in darkness, pauses still human
> if you keep interlacing them with your thread.

This is not the most perspicuous or convincing of the "Motets," but for all that it lends itself to interpretation. We notice that (in Stanza 1) daybreak carries with it a noise of trains in a tunnel, while in Stanza 2 nightfall brings the woodworm's creaking in the writer's desk and an ominous "watchman's step"; in both cases, an oppressive image of somber closure ("chiusi uomini in corsa," cf. the "automatons" of **No. 5**). Since Stanza 2 gives us the poet's own study (rather menaced than protected by the approaching "watchman" in whose custody this prison like world apparently is), and Stanza 1 a slice of the humdrum outside world, an opposition arises between public and private reality, outside hustle-and-bustle and interior meditation. The writer is alienated from the surrounding world, and the only way to heal this wound in experience is for him to heed the constant inspirations of his Muse (who handles a thread in a very womanly yet very Fatelike fashion). The transcendental seamstress (unlike her other avatars) appears as a steady presence.

Since in this poetry trains seem generally to function as instruments of alienation or separation, it is not surprising to find a funicular railway, in the next poem, once more parting the two lovers. A forget-me-not brings up this further painful memory in what could have become an all-too-obvious sentimental piece in hands less expert than Montale's; actually, the poem has a captivating simplicity and a freshness all its own. The following poem instead (**"Motet" No. 17**) requires some comment, though it is every bit as vivid and far more painterly. Taken by itself, it belongs to Montale's most characteristic achievement; a chastened, yet prehensile sensuousness enables the language to grasp the essentials of a rural scene: late summer fields in the imminence of a storm. Few, sober yet dense brushstrokes as if from the palette of Fattori or Tosi, and tingling pizzicato sounds in a sustained metrical-syntactic flow outline a world peopled only by minimal creatures, with an effect of increased atmospheric vastness. There is no stanza break (unlike the pattern of the other "Motets"), and one effect is to stress the suspense of weather; but the coming storm already makes itself felt in a gradual hush, and in no time at all it will burst upon the deceptive peace:

> dove spenge le sue fiaccole
> un sole senza caldo, tardo ai fiori
> ronzìo di coleotteri che suggono
> ancora linfe, ultimi suoni, avara
> vita della campagna. Con un soffio
> l'ora s'estingue: un cielo di lavagna
> si prepara a un irrompere di scarni
> cavalli, alle scintille degli zoccoli.

> where a sun without warmth
> snuffs out its torches, there lingers in the flowers
> a hum of insects that still suck
> nectar: last sounds, niggardly life
> of the countryside. With a gust
> the hour dies out: a slate-gray sky
> gets ready for the irruption of lean
> horses, for the spark-striking hoofs.

The "lean horses" about to break into the sky, scattering "sparks from their hoofs," are a demonic, and rurally fitting, metaphorization of the galloping thunderclouds.

Nothing more need be said if we take the poem by itself, as the self-contained piece it can certainly be. But, as part of the "Motet" series, it must possess a resonance far beyond the limited scope of an Impressionist vignette. Those threatening "lean horses" have to do with the Horsemen of the Apocalypse. The storm (it is 1938) is overshadowing human history and is not just a part of local Nature. The piece is apocalyptic, not impressionist, its contextual position coming to strengthen the intrinsic clue. We may also call to mind the symbolic value of storms in Montale's poetry, all the way down to *La Bufera e altro*. A striking trait in this **"Motet" No. 17** (and one that tends to set it rather apart from the rest) is the absence of any allusion to Clizia; it is an "It," not a "Thou" poem as all the others are. Even at the risk of overly rationalizing what brooks little or no rationalization, I would connect that unique trait with the drama of light and darkness, good and evil, whose positive protagonist Clizia has come to be. Where she is absent, no angel will be left to fight the forces of destruction; and the world is here abandoned to the coming ravage (which may also have a purifying effect, since open war seems better than oppressive stagnation).

Although composed in 1937, a year before its predecessor in the series as we now have it, **"Motet" No. 18** seems to form a corollary to the one we have just discussed. It is fall now, and the summer storms are past; another kind of desolation looms on the November landscape where the woodcutter's axe hits the acacia tree:

> Non recidere, forbice, quel volto,
> solo nella memoria che si sfolla,
> non far del grande suo viso in ascolto
> la mia nebbia di sempre.

> Un freddo cala . . . Duro il colpo svetta.
> E l'acacia ferita da sé scrolla
> il guscio di cicala
> nella prima belletta di Novembre.

Do not cut off, scissors, that visage
now left alone in my unpeopled memory,
do not make of her great, listening face
my perennial fog.

Cold weather settles down . . . Hard
    swings the blow.
And the wounded acacia shakes off
the cicada shell
in the first mire of November.

By one of the unpredictable analogies on which poetry thrives, the axe's blade arouses in the poet's mind the echo of an inner blow; and we know what blow, for in the "Motet" sequence "quel volto" can be only one visage, Clizia's. He fears for her life (hence the prayer to an Atropos figure to stop its murderous scissors, or, more simply, to Time itself, which Dante personified as a ruthless gardener "going around with his shears," "lo tempo va dintorno con le force," *Par.* XVI.). But to pray for her life is to pray for his own, especially in the spiritual sense; no wonder, then, that he should implicitly recognize himself in the "wounded acacia" of Stanza 2. Poems emblematizing himself or the other humans as plants abound in all of his three books of verse, witness **"Tramontana," "Scirocco," "Arsenio"** in *Ossi de Seppia*, **"Tempidi Bellosguardo"** in *Le Occasioni*, **"Personae Separatae"** in *La Butera e altro*. The cicada shell, likewise emblematic (in Anceschi's sense of the term), adds its funereal note to the realistic aspect of the scene. As a more explicit motif, symbolizing the doomed singer, it will recur in **"L'ombra della magnolia,"** a passionate lyric of La Bufera e altro:

    Vibra intermittente
in vetta una cicata . . .
    . . . La lima che sottile
incide tacerà, la vuota scorza
di chi cantava sarà presto polvere,
è l'autunno, è l'inverno. . . .

    On the treetop intermittently
a cicada shrills . . .
    . . . The thin cutting file
will soon be hushed, the empty husk
of the erstwhile singer will soon be dust,
it is autumn, it is winter. . . .

We have come again to a threshold of negative experience, signalized by the fact that the speaker no longer addresses Clizia directly, but only speaks *of* her as an imperiled memory (as he does in the following "Motet"); in the last one, it is an open question whether the only possible mention of her there ("[il] tuo fazzoletto," your handkerchief) really refers to Clizia or to the persona talking to himself. Be that as it may, the two remaining poems of the sequence mark an emotional epilogue of renumciation. In **No. 19,** a remarkable accomplishment to be compared with the pictorial apocalypse of **No. 17,** we see a spring which is no spring because the inspiring lady has receded into unattainable distance to leave the poet dejectedly scanning the sky for a sign of her in the midst of a gloomy landscape. Time goes on, inexorably, to corrode

existence; Clizia was the counteracting force capable of (momentarily at least) reversing that entropy:

    La canna che dispiuma
    mollemente il suo rosso
    flabello a primavera;
    la rédola sul fosso, su la nera
    correntìa sorvolata di libellule;
    e il cane trafelato che rincasa
    col suo fardello in bocca,
    oggi qui non mi tocca riconoscere;
    ma là dove il riverbero più cuoce
    e il nuvolo s'abbassa, oltre le sue
    pupille ormai remote, solo due
    fasci di luce in croce.

                    E il tempo passa.

    The reed that deplumes
    languidly its red
    flabellum in spring;
    the grass tufts on the ditch banks, over the black
    stream overflown by dragonflies;
    and the panting dog that comes home
    with the day's catch in his mouth,

    not these here, now, do I have to recognize;
    but there where the heat reverberates most sharply
    and the clouds come closer down, beyond
    her pupils already vanished, only two
    crossed beams of light.

                    And time wears on.

In Stanza 1 the recent manifestations of inviting Nature reborn are considered only to be rejected afterwards ("oggi qui non mi tocca riconoscere," "today here I don't have to recognize"): the strong prolepsis helps the dialectical inversion of theme, with the key verb "to recognize" acting as the syntactical and semantic hinge of the whole sweeping sentence). What the persona has to "recognize" here and now, in a sultry, cloudy landscape, is the negative sign coming from a chance event in the real scene: "due / fasci di luce in croce," "two crossed beams of light." These beams literally "cross her out," they appear "beyond her now remote pupils." As a cross, they also portend suffering, the suffering that goes with this irretrievable loss, and more.

In the twentieth **"Motet,"** the concluding piece of the series, an ironic resignation prevails:

    . . . ma così sia. Un suono di cornetta
    dialoga con gli sciami del quercheto.
    Nella valva che il vespero riflette
    un vulcano dipinto fuma lieto.

    La moneta incassata nella lava
    brilla anch'essa sul tavolo e trattiene
    pochi fogli. La vita che sembrava
    vasta è più breve del tuo fazzoletto.

    . . . but so be it. A sound of cornet
    converses with the swarms of the oakwood.

In the seashell that mirrors the twilight
a painted volcano gaily smokes.

The coin encased in lava
likewise shines on the desk and holds down
few sheets of paper. Life which seemed
vast is smaller than your handkerchief.

"Così sia," "so be it"; life blossoms around the poet, and even his paperweights on the desk—a seashell and an ancient coin encased in a lava chunk—shine serenely. The prayerlike words of the opening (they are the Italian *Amen*) reveal their irony when we come to the sharp end: "Life, which seemed so vast, is smaller than your handkerchief." Even if by that "you" the poet means distant Clizia, it is as if he were talking to himself; he accepts his deprivation and is aware (with a certain detachment) of the joyously reawakened life around him. A painted volcano on the seashell, a piece of hardened lava on the desk remind him that his own life no longer seethes with the ardors of youth (just as the fiery youth of the world seemed inexorably past in "Sul muro grafito," an early *Ossi di seppia* piece which appears to foreshadow the present "Motet" in more than one respect). The painted volcano (no less than the coin) may also point to the resolution of art which immobilizes riotous life and makes it viable as pure image. Another probable implication of the two focal objects is the chance cooperation of human art and elemental nature: the destructive lava has preserved the precious coin, the shell so beautifully designed by other than human forces has become the receptacle of a diminutive painting. But the main point is the retreat from the infinity youth had promised under Clizia's inspiration into the frame of the finite; one thinks of the second stanza of **"Notizie dall'Amiata,"** with its invocation to the north wind that "endears to us our chains." The epiphany afforded by this last "Motet" is of the phenomenal, of the limited reality—not of the noumenal, as was formerly the case.

Through the ups and downs of inner experience, the persona has known heaven and hell and purgatory; the threshold of hell was touched with **"Motet" No. 5,** heaven was felt in **"Motet" No. 8,** and the threshold of spiritual death was sighted in **"Motet" No. 18;** now only the stoic acceptance of slowly dwindling life is left, with whatever minor consolations it may offer: neither heaven nor hell, a purgatory perhaps, but with no goal to the purging except death. It would seem that the poet's persona has grown from passionate youth to the sad wisdom of age, through the cycles of experienced time. Goethe's concept of *Entsagung* comes to mind, a renunciation made harder by that poet's cult of *das ewig Weibliche*. Montale too, in his less ambitious compass, has shown a deep fascination with the myth of the Eternal Feminine, and a comparable ability to accept limits and renunciation. It might be added here that Montale pointedly refers to Goethe in one of the *Occasioni* poems, **"Nel parco di Caserta,"** and that his choice of such a title for the whole book probably stems from Goethe's dictum that his own poetry in a way is all *Gelegenheitsdichtung*, poetry of occasion. That the German humanist poet would not have concurred with Montale's elliptical style, or sympathized with his frequent

distrust of Nature's regenerative powers, is beside the point. Montale voices the modern temper, with all the hardships it is heir to.

In spite of the unspectacular nature of his life, however, Montale has been a powerful catalyst in the process of revivification of the Italian idiom as an instrument of significant literary production, a process especially visible in this century, and especially in the Italian lyric.

—*Rebecca West*, in Chicago Review, Winter 1975–76.

Joseph Cary (essay date 1969)

SOURCE: "Eugenio Montale," in *Three Modern Italian Poets: Saba, Ungaretti, Montale,* New York University Press, 1969, 235–329.

[*In the following excerpt, Cary explicates poems from Montale's "war-book," Land's End (Finisterre).*]

Dismissed from the directorship of the Gabinetto Vieusseux in 1938—the year of "Notizie dall'Amiata"—and forced to take on a heavy load of translation (chiefly from the English language, mostly Shakespeare plays) in order to survive, Montale stayed in Florence and wrote the poems to be gathered in the small war-book called *Finisterre*.

With its pointed epigraph taken from Agrippa D'Aubigné's "À Dieu"

> Les princes n'ont point d'yeux pour voir ces grands merveilles,
> Leurs mains ne servent plus qu'à nous persécuter. . . .

Finisterre was unpublishable in the Italy of this tormented period. The manuscript was smuggled out to Switzerland where an edition of 150 copies was published in Lugano in 1943 just before the *coup d'état* of July 25th which marked the beginning of the end of Mussolini.

In his essay on "Eliot and Ourselves," Montale has remarked on the *stilnovismo* of Eliot and Pound, their common cult of Dante and their *docte* allusiveness that "works itself out in inlay work and the glittering game of quotations and recollections." The same might be said of *Finisterre*; it is entirely appropriate that the second edition of this book (Florence, 1945) included a facsimile of Montale's never-finished translation of the first two stanzas of *Ash-Wednesday*, Eliot's stilnovistic season in purgatory. The poems are similar in their tendency towards recondite allusion, occult citation, a certain exclusive and "aristocratic" approach to the traditions involved. The themes of course are entirely different, and Montale's style has grown increasingly compressed and elliptical. *Finisterre,* he writes in "Intenzioni."

> is a matter of a few poems, born under the incubus of the years '40–42, perhaps the freest I have ever written, [in which] the research effected in *Le occasioni* is carried to its extreme consequences, the interlacings of rhymes and assonances become even more dense, and I am surprised that nobody has brought up the name of Gerard Manley Hopkins. In a certain fashion I too was searching for my own "sprung rhythm."

Montale conceives of sprung rhythm as involving not only the *crammed* quality of much of Hopkins' (and his own) verse but as a dramatic instrument: "the musical investiture of the act of inspiration that doesn't degrade music to a simplistic 'auroral' ineffability."

Another facet of this heightened "interlacing" is Montale's use of the sonnet for the first and only time in his published career—seven out of the fifteen short lyrics in *Finisterre* move in some sort of relation to the form. In several the sonnet is only there as a covert allusion or witty possibility, identifiable only in the context of other definitely "committed" sonnets on either side. Thus **"Serenata Indiana"** (Indian Serenade: given what happens here the allusion to Shelley's breathless lyric can only be sardonic) is made of fourteen hendecasyllables exactly halved (that is, between lines seven and eight) by a large space. The lyric, then, is broken into two sub-lyrics of seven lines apiece, and these in turn—perfectly symmetrically—into two triads and a concluding single line. The rhyming is largely slanted (*sera-mare-potere, aloè-follia*), irregularly placed but as noticeable as is generally the case with sonnets. Each of the two halves is devoted to a contrasting perception of Clizia's power. [Clizia is a mythical hero-female ideal-feminine principle in Montale's poetry]. The first celebrates her domination of reality, the second unhappily evokes her as a victim of brutal natural forces ("the inky tentacles of the polyp") in a reversal kin to that of "unarmed goodness" by Evil in **"Eastbourne."** Thus this sonnet bisects into sections of ecstasy and anguish, unified by adoration, with the halfway break working something like the hinge of alteration between octave and sestet in the orthodox model. Pursuing Montale's citation of Hopkins, one could call **"Serenata indiana"** a sprung- or curtal-sonnet, where the various pleasures of symmetry, sound-chiming and thematic modulation are cultivated in a drastically restricted area.

More characteristic of *Finisterre* sonnetry, however, are poems like **"Nel sonno"** (**"In Sleep"**), **"Gli orecchini"** (**"The Earrings"**), **"La frangia dei capelli"** (**"The Bangs"**), and **"Il ventaglio"** (**"The Fan"**), where Montale's familiarity with the so-called Shakespearian sonnet is apparent. . . . (He has published translations of sonnets 22, 33, and 48 in the *Quaderno di traduzioni*).

"Gli orecchini" is one of Montale's . . . sonnets written on the Shakespeare model. It focuses on one of the talis-

manic appurtenances—signs, icons—belonging to Clizia: her earrings.

> Non serba ombra di voli il nerofumo
> della spera. (E del tuo non è piú traccia.)
> È passata la spugna che i barlumi
> indifesi dal cerchio d'ora scaccia.
> Le tue pietre, i coralli, il forte imperio
> che ti rapisce vi cercavo; fuggo
> l'iddia che non s'incarna, i desiderî
> porto fin che al tuo lampo non si struggono.
> Ronzano èlitre fuori, ronza il folle
> mortorio e sa che due vite non contano.
> Nella cornice tornano le molli
> meduse della sera. La tua impronta
> verrà di giú: dove ai tuoi lobi squallide
> mani, travolte, fermano i coralli.

> The tarnished mirror does not conserve the shadow / of flights. (And of yours there is no longer a trace). / The sponge has passed over that / hunts out defenseless glimmerings from the circle of gold. / Your stones, the corals, the strong imperium / that snatched you—I search for them there: I flee / that goddess who is disincarnate, I bear my desires / until they are consumed in your lightning. / Outside the coleoptera are buzzing, the mad cortège is buzzing /—it knows two lives don't count. / Within the mirror-frame the jellied / medusae return. Your seal / will come from below: where, at your earlobes, emaciated / anguished hands affix the corals.

Beyond the prosodic features of Shakespearean sonnet **"Gli orecchini"** has other high-Renaissance qualities. *Concettismo,* the athletically deployed conceit, is very evident in the modulations of imagery through which a gold-framed looking-glass becomes a well of prophetic memory yielding first blackness (absence) then a murky subhumanity (the low-level organic activity of beetles and jellyfish whose technical name, *medusae,* adds a classic danger to the forces beleaguering the poet and his *donna*), and finally, in the strange triumphant couplet, the regal insignia of Clizia attended by her people, the poor and wretched, the sacrificed ones of this world. Language too is remote from "spoken" Italian—either aureate (such as *spera* which is a literary Tuscan archaicism for "mirror," *cerchio d'oro* and *cornice* for the "frame," *forte imperio, iddia*) or unusual technical terms like *èlitre,* "elytra," the hard outer wing-casings of beetle-like insects which cover and protect the hindlegs, and vibrate and "buzz"—here intended to suggest the subhuman sound of war-mechanisms like tanks and planes.

The coral earclips of **"Gli orecchini"** are a good example of "private" objects treated by Montale in such a way that they preserve their occult meanings for "two lives" while simultaneously working as public emblems for a great humane ideal. Indeed, there is an heroic equivalence between the images of the pale martyred hands attending the toilette of Clizia and the arming of Achilles. Another *Finisterre* sonnet, **"Il ventaglio,"** demonstrates the virtù of her fan, amounting to a holy relic in time of war. It is also a perfect example of the allusive density, transitional-abruptness and nervous intensity of tempo of the Montale of this phase.

The poem must begin with its title, since the fan, never mentioned in the sonnet *per se,* is surely not only the source of the mother-of-pearl in line nine, contributing several associative functions (wings, wind), but is the *là* of line three whereon the poet vainly tries to "paint" or fix his memories of happier, prewar days of love.

> *Ut pictura . . .* Le labbra che confondono,
> gli sguardi, i segni, i giorni ormai caduti
> provo a figgerli là come in un tondo
> di cannocchiale arrovesciato, muti
> e immoti, ma piú vivi. Era una giostra
> d'uomini e ordegni in fuga tra quel fumo
> ch'Euro batteva, e già l'alba l'inostra
> con un sussulto e rompe quelle brume.
> Luce la madreperla, la calanca
> vertiginosa inghiotte ancora vittime,
> ma le tue piume sulle guance sbiancano
> e il giorno è forse salvo. O colpi fitti,
> quando ti schiudi, o crudi lampi, o scrosci
> sull'orde! (Muore chi ti riconosce?)

Ut pictura . . . Lips that mingle, / gazes, signs, days now fallen away / —I try to fix them there as in an eyepiece / of a reversed telescope, mute / and immobile, but more living. There was a whirling clashing [*giostra* combines "joust" and "carousel": we should probably think of the wheeling motion of Evil in poems like **"Eastbourne"** or, in the *Silvae,* **"Ezekial Saw the Wheel"**] / of men and machines fleeing in that smoke / that Eurus [god of the cold southeast wind; probably also meant to suggest sonically a wind-beaten "Europe"] flailed, and already the dawn empurples it [*inostrare* can also mean: "grant the hat of the cardinalate to" as well as, in pun, "in-Auster," i.e. "dawn sponsors a warmth-bearing counterwind to chilling Eurus"] / with a bound and breaks up those wintrinesses. / The mother-of-pearl grows resplendent, the dizzy / vortex [*calanca* is literally a little bay or cove; I associate it here with the *giostra* of line five] still swallows victims, / but your feathers whiten on their cheeks [*le guance* leaves *whose* cheeks an open question; I would say both Clizia's and the victims'] / and perhaps the day is saved. Oh the steady strokes, / when you reveal yourself, oh the raw flashes, oh the roars / above the horde! (Does he who recognizes you die?)

Even providing a fairly literal translation, one can see, involves real difficulties, so dense with associative energy are the words. And there are some authentic obscurities in this dense sonnet which so admirably illustrate Dr. Johnson's witty definition of the metaphysical poem [That is, ". . . a kind of *discordia concors*; a combination of dissimilar images, or discovery of occult resemblances in things apparently unlike . . . ; nature and art are ransacked for illustrations, comparisons, and allusions; their learning instructs, and their subtlety surprises; but. . . ."]. Yet the main action seems clear enough. The poem is about the power residing in Clizia's fan which, since it is present (*là*), she has presumably left behind her—as it turns out, as a sign of her mission. **"Il ventaglio"** is also a triumphant

affirmation of her genuine and abiding presence—as contrasted with the sad images of her, lips, gazes, reduced and crystallized by memory.

Ut pictura . . . : the sonnet starts with Horace's famous phrase from the epistle *Ad Pisones* ("Art of Poetry," line 361: *Ut pictura poesis*—"As with painting, so with poetry") which serves as a stage-direction for what follows: the poem-image of the loveable past that the poet is occupied in trying to "fix" on his absent lady's fan. The desperation informing this effort to take refuge in the past is indicated in the first clause of the second sentence with its references to military debacle and the heavy clouds of war and winter storm, while the second clause, with its startled *già* and shift into the present tense shows the miracle of the relic as it starts—not a return via memory but a resurrected presence in a replenished present. Thus "already" through the mere contemplation of her fan the light begins to dawn, the storm begins to abate, while simultaneously the fan assumes—kin in this to the various *éventails* of Mallarmé—its coordinate roles as purveyor of winds (here a beneficent southern variety) and wing carrying back the angel of the storm. But no longer is she a mere "refuge," a fixed image or snapshot which the poet projects for the sake of his sanity. Here toward the poem's climax she is present, is directly addressed, and the miraculous possibility dawns that she is able to alter the balance of things (". . . il giorno è forse salvo"). The wing feathers that were her fan now bear light to the drowning visages of "the victims" and also retributive justice to the fleeing hordes of Ahriman. The extraordinary *mana* of her coming prompts the final question. What is the fate of those, like the Nestorian or the guilty ones, who must sustain her radiance face to face? The query, and its strenuous abruptness after the string of exclamations preceding it, sounds out the panting ecstasy with which, fanlike, the poem snaps shut.

One more remark should be made on the point and pertinence of the Horatian citation at the beginning. Besides setting the scene for subsequent action, *Ut pictura* also suggests that this poem should be seen as a picture—which it is; indeed, it is a succession of them. The full passage in the epistle deals with the matter of perspective, how poems, like pictures, vary with distance, with conditions of light and shadow, with familiarity. But **"Il ventaglio"** itself incorporates several perspectives and viewpoints—contrasting chiefly the tiny "plane" of fixed memory with the immense living present that succeeds it. That is to say, the citation functions not only to place the action of the poem but to capsulize a major thematic concern of the poem itself. One has to know Horace to get the full point, but this is part of the instructive surprise and "scholastic" pleasure offered by the Montale of *Finisterre.* For some—for Montale in fact—such poems are "of a texture possibly too rigorous," as he puts it in "Intenzioni." Surely **"Il ventaglio"** qualifies as one of the microfilmed "euphuistic sonnets" over which Clizia dozes in one of the poet's last testaments, **"Botta e risposta."**

Such is *Finisterre.* The title itself is self-explanatory and familiar: land's end, the Breton cape looking westward from Europe "roughly three thousand miles" across the sea to Clizia—an emblem of terminus, an end of one world and expectation of another. From here as before, he searches for signs: her earrings or her fan:

> Anche una piuma che vola può disegnare
> la tua figura, o il raggio che gioca a rimpiattino
> tra i mobili, il rimando dello specchio
> di un bambino, dai tetti. . . .

> Even a feather floating in the air can trace / your shape,
> or the ray that plays at hide-and-seek / among the
> furniture, reflection from a child's / mirror on the roofs.

Later her features will be found in an eel, a fox, a torpedofish; this weird totemism founds its surreal climax in the search-poem **"Per album"** (**"Lines for an Album"**) written in the early 1950's:

> . . . Ho continuato il mio giorno
> sempre spiando te, larva girino
> frangia di rampicante francolino
> gazzella zebú ocàpi
> nuvola nera grandine. . . .

> . . . I resumed my day / forever spying on you, larva
> tadpole / fringe of ivy ptarmigan / gazelle zebu okapi
> / black cloud hailstone. . . .

But Montale's *Revelation,* his personal apocalypse of signs, will be found in the oneiric **"Iride"** (**"Iris"**).

The second edition of **Finisterre** was augmented by several autograph reproductions (one of them the *Ash-Wednesday* fragment), two prose-pieces and four poems of varying length. *In chiave, terribilmente in chiave* (key to it all, terribly so) as Montale writes in "Intenzioni" was **"Iride,"** "a poem I dreamed [twice] and then translated from a nonexistent tongue; I am perhaps more the medium than the author." **"Iride"** does not constitute a "key" that opens, or unlocks or in any way defines the poet's relation to his *donna*; even Montale, usually scornful of his readers' perplexities, grants that it might legitimately be considered obscure—"but even so I see no reason to throw it away."

Nor do I. How after all does one correct a dream? Certainly **"Iride"** is a poem that is extremely dependent upon the reader's knowledge of Montale's prior work—it does not stand by itself. But fragmentary and genuinely obscure as it frequently is, it is also a poem in which many of the strands of *l'affaire Clizia* come to their exacerbated and "heretical" conclusion, and in this sense is indeed *terribilmente in chiave.*

"Iride" is a diptych representing two aspects of the cult of Clizia. The first is composed about her annunciatory signs, this time drastically occult and as "closed" to her priest, apparently, as to ourselves. Here, for example, is **"Iride I"**'s extremely convoluted opening clause, deployed over three verse paragraphs in a labyrinthine series of imagistic amplifications and qualifications:

> Quando di colpo San Martino smotta
> le sue braci e le attizza in fondo al cupo
> fornello dell'Ontario,
> schiocchi di pigne verdi fra la cenere
> o il fumo d'un infuso di papaveri
> e il Volto insanguinato sul sudario
> che mi divide da te;

> questo e poco altro (se poco
> è un tuo segno, un ammicco, nella lotta
> che me sospinge in un ossario, spalle
> al muro, dove zàffiri celesti
> e palmizi e cicogne su una zampa non chiudono
> l'atroce vista al povero
> Nestoriano smarrito);

> è quanto di te giunge dal naufragio
> delle mie genti, delle tue. . . .

> When all of a sudden Saint Martin shifts / his embers
> and kindles them deep in the dark / furnace of Ontario,
> / snapping of green pinecones in the ashes / or the
> steam from a poppy infusion / and the bloody Face on
> the napkin / that —divides me from you / —this and
> little else (if little / is a sign of yours, a wink, in the
> struggle / that condemns me to an ossuary, back / to
> the wall, where celestial sapphires / and palm trees
> and storks on one foot don't shut out / the atrocious
> sight from the poor / strayed Nestorian)—this is how
> much of you gets here from the wreck / of my people,
> of yours. . . .

A heretic's dream of salvation, expressed in the images of the orthodoxy from which he is excommunicate—that would be one way of describing what is going on here. **"Iris,"** the title of the poem and the *donna*'s newest *senhal,* is not only a flower and thus part of the company of floral presences with which the poem is tissued, not only synecdoche for the eye of *coscienza* which is one of her main signs, not only the name of the rainbow goddess and messenger for the Olympians, but also and above all—as the poem will say—*Iri del Canaan,* the rainbow of the Promised Land, the Lord's own sign of covenant with the lost and wandering.

The first three lines of the passage cited lend the dream a cryptic time and place; St. Martin's summer (our "Indian" summer) is the brief period of mild weather that can occur in late autumn, so that St. Martin's intervention in chilly Ontario implies a kind of trans-Atlantic thaw which joins the western world in a brief season of saving warmth. But grammatically it is not the season but the saint who performs this miracle, and we are reminded of his cloak and mission of holy and heroic charity. In this context even *braci* may have dream-connections with the Ember Days of fasting and prayer that frame autumn in the church calendar.

Or, to take the signs themselves, the first—the crackling pinecones in the ashes—is introduced by St. Martin's fires and its connotation of renewal (green against grey, sudden explosive energy out of depletion) is familiar enough to the attentive reader of Montale. But those that immediately follow are more strange, though they clearly function to remind us of the visionary sphere in which the poem operates. The poppy infusion (whose fumes are produced by the same heat that cracks the pinecones) is at once an extract that is part of the poem's "botanical" collection, an opiate and pain-killer possibly suggested, if we go outside the poem, by the medications required by Montale's very sick wife in the same year, 1943 (see **"Ballata scritta in una clinica" ["Ballad Written in a Clinic"]**) and a producer of other, exalted states of consciousness. This last can guide us to the third sign, and second saint; the sudarium or sweatcloth with the face of suffering Christ upon it, Clizia's napkin which—like Saint Martin's cloak and Saint Veronica's handkerchief—testifies to her mission of pity and ministration to the sick and suffering, as well as to the perfect faith that divides her from the "poor strayed Nestorian" dreaming her.

The remaining images are less recondite. That of the prisoner (whose prison is, appropriately enough for an Italian and European in 1943, a morgue or charnel house) is an old one. What I take to be the sardonically listed images of traditional otherworldly consolation (the celestial sapphires will be found in Dante—*Para.* XXIII, 101–2—though the reference is not needed to comprehend this Blue Heaven; the storks and palms seem out of some child's guide to the Holy Land) are too out of phase and insubstantial to blinker the wretched Nestorian to atrocity—the mangled bones and torn flesh of Europe, the suffering God consubstantial with a wrecked humanity. The long parenthesis of stanza two not only identifies the dreamer but underlines his desperate need for signs of his angel's immanence, the "rosary" of sacred images that he may hold and count over to stave off his rational despair.

At the same time the prisoner's cult is no longer private. Its erotic origins have been sublimated into a complicity with her mission whose blazon is—as **"Iride II"** dealing with the prisoner's recognition and renunciation informs us—the Face, "that effigy in purple on the white cloth."

> . . . Perché l'opera tua (che della Sue
> è una forma) florisse in altri luci
> Iri del Canaan ti dileguasti. . . .

> . . . So that your work (which is a form / of His)
> might flower in other lights, / Iris of Canaan you
> disappeared. . . .

The old images, so much a part of the erotic texture of the *Ossi* poems of the late 1920's and the earlier *Occasioni,* are now swiftly recapitulated: the garden where they were together, "our river," the lonely shore, the disappearing boat—and are found to be irrelevant to the new dispensation. "If you return you are not you, your terrestrial story is changed . . ."; or, as the poem concludes (italics are the dreamer's):

> . . . non hai sguardi né ieri né domani;

> *perché l'opera Sua* (che nella tua
> si trasforma) *dev'esser continuata.*

. . . you have no eyes [that is, for me], no yesterdays, no tomorrows; / *because His work* (which transforms itself / into yours) *must be continued.*

Glauco Cambon (essay date 1971)

SOURCE: "The New Montale," in *Books Abroad,* Vol. 45, No. 4, Autumn, 1971, pp. 639–45.

[*In the following excerpt, Cambon states that* Miscellany (Satura)*departs from the style of Montale's earlier poetry.*]

The poet himself once intimated that his three major books of verse, *Ossi di seppia* (1925), *Le occasioni* (1939), and *La bufera e altro* (1956), had vaguely rehearsed a Dantesque pilgrimage finally rewarded by glimmers of paradise. If so, what place can this fourth book, *Satura,* take in the overall sequence? In what sense, if at all, can it go further than its predecessors and thus refocus the whole itinerary? These are no idle questions, especially with a writer like Eugenio Montale, who is chary of his word. We might have been forgiven if we had taken at face value the finality of **"Provisional Conclusions"** with which he chose to end his third volume in 1956; they did sound like poetical epitaphs. Then came the improbable *Satura* of 1962, a thin sheaf of lyrics, part new and part exhumed from remote decades, to weaken any such surmise. The scant poems were so inconspicuously printed that they looked like a mimeograph for private circulation. In fact the were not for sale; and the self-deflating tone of the leading piece, **"Botta e risposta"** (**"Thrust and Riposte"**), combined with the elusive format to suggest the idea of a literary postscript to **"The Storm and Other Things"**; a trifle, of the kind Montale likes to disseminate in his verse ("nugae" is his word) as a insurance against pomposity. *Satura* did not align with the previous trinity, and as a consequence Montalians began to look to his prose for telling expression. For the first time Montale the prose writer outweighed Montale the poet, a natural outcome of old age and artistic maturity. What else should one expect of a poet who had attained his fulfilment? The sixties saw the publication of a substantially enriched second edition of the short stories, *Farfalla di Dinard* (*Butterfly of Dinard*); of the correspondence with, and essays on, Italo Svevo; of the volume of general essays, *Auto da fè*; and finally, of the lively travelogue, *Fuori di Casa,* the harvest of Montale's journalism. More collections of literary essays were (and are) known to be in the works. Prose it was to be from now on, wasn't it?

But the sixties also saw something happen to Montale the man which shook him out of his growing indifference: the death (1963) of his wife Drusilla, better known as "la Mosca," the Fly. He had shared so much with her; thus the blow was hard even if not unexpected. I have a personal letter from him which tells of his distress and more recently (winter 1970–71) he writes me: "My loneliness is really dreadful." La Mosca's death drove Montale into poetry again—a feat quite consistent with the mercurial personality of a lady who, when she chose to, could punctuate with fitfulness her remarkable charm. From 1964 to 1967 the shy flowers of *Xenia* cropped up, short poems all addressed to the dead woman who gently haunted the survivor. They appeared in two literary magazines and eventually were collected in an out-of-the-way edition similar to *Satura*'s. By now the prospect of a new book loomed large, though I heard of it from Montale only in April 1970 during a conversation we had in Rome. And so it is that *Satura* has appeared in January 1971, collecting the post-*Bufera* pieces with considerable new additions.

Its very publication has been the author's way of sidetracking ("depistare") his critics, as the introductory piece states in a different sense. The sidetracking in **"Il Tu" "The Thou"** concerns the dogmatizing attitude of a few readers apropos of one central feature of Montale's style, the use of a sometimes unspecifiable Thou to elicit self-revelation on the part of the lyrical persona. The critics, he says, repeat that this Thou is "an institution"; and while he takes the blame for sidetracking them, he rebukes them for missing the basic point that in him "the many are one even if they appear / multiplied by mirrors." What he resents is the tendency on the part of some of us to harden his existential utterances into rhetorical formulas and thereby superimpose a preconceived mold on the rediscovery each poem is intended to be. For he is a man of few, if any, certainties; and those few he can never take for granted; they seem to require endless verification in the face of a mystifying reality behind which perhaps a terrifying (or consoling) Reality yawns. The poem concludes as follows:

> . . . The trouble
> is that the bird lured by mirrors in the snare
> does not know if he is he or one of his too many
> duplicates.

If this refers only to the critics sidetracked by the poet, it amounts to a complacent game of revenge. Is that all, and would it justify the keynote placement of the poem? I suspect there is more to it. I am tempted to play into the hands of the sidetracking poet (and may His Naughtiness forgive my naïveté) by reading the effective image on a broader scale, to include all the people who claim to decipher reality on the strength of some final formula while they are decoyed by the protean nature of appearances to the point of not even knowing who they are any more. Against this mundane pretentiousness the poet sets up his own Augustinian doubt and, as a perfect complement to it, the infallible insight of his late wife, who turned the tables against the "blahblah of high society" by seeing through the blind smugness of so many cheap detractors; she helped him to unmask the mystifications erected by people believing "that reality is what one sees" because hers, though dimmed, were "the only true eyes"; she also had the gift of "incredible recognitions" and could burst out into the kind of laughter that anticipates a "private Doomsday."

She had a secret affinity for the tameless hawks seen in France and Greece, for she liked "la vita fatta a pezzi, quella che rompe dal suo insopportabile / ordito" (in Singh's version, "life torn to shreds, / life breaking out from its unbearable weft"). Like the Clizia of "Motets" (to which *Xenia* antiphonally corresponds), la Mosca seems

endowed with clairvoyance. She archly dismissed life's "vanity fairs" and funerals, thereby making it a "tabula rasa," yet one point mattered to her, a point "not intelligible" to him. She gave him the courage to defy an oppressive, counterfeit reality, of which the Florence flood of November 1966, so destructive of many cherished keepsakes in the Montales' house, was only a climactic manifestation. She alone knew "that motion / is not different from stillness, / that void is plenitude and a serene sky / is the diffusest cloud." Such mystic wisdom made her the principle of poetry itself, of at least the catalyst of Montale's own poetry, for regardless of critical allegations to the contrary, this poetry was not branded by "inappartenenza": it did *belong* to her. More than the defensive rejoinder (and this is the first book where Montale talks back to his critics), what arrests my attention is the assertion that la Mosca, having died, is "no longer form, but essence," a line the author revised from an earlier printed version, still appearing in Singh's bilingual edition, to avert any equivocations about who the subject of those predicates is supposed to be. The lyrical intensity matches the metaphysical deftness of the phrase, which could satisfy both an ontological believer and a skeptic of Santayana's stripe. "Essence" may be read subjectively or otherwise. The enhancing negation contained in that concept fits one remembered trait of la Mosca's which won such respect from Montale that he even suspected his own art of vulgarity: her refusal to write for a literary public. Now it is only her word, "so stinted and imprudent," that satisfies him.

Obviously la Mosca fulfills in *Xenia* a function analogous to that of Clizia in "Motets" and in various other poems from *Le Occasioni* and *La Bufera*: to provide a focal Thou that draws the persona out, to conquer his reticence about what really matters, to embody the unseizable reality of what is personal. Distance, absence, memory are a prerequisite of such polar tension, as they were for Dante and Petrarch. In Clizia's case distance is geographic, while in la Mosca's case it is metaphysical, being provided by death. With both ladies memory engenders transfiguration. Prophecy becomes, retrospectively, one of their common attributes. Like Clizia, indeed, la Mosca now appears to be that *unicum,* the fully developed consciousness that challenges the world; she alone can attain the noumenal sphere and make it accessible to her lover. But because the "Thou" is no "institution," as the poet warned us, there is no confusing the two women. They are not identical; they participate in the same fund of ultimate knowledge and being. They remain sharply individualized, and this is particularly true of la Mosca. No other condition would hold in Montale's cosmos.

For one thing, la Mosca is physically impaired, a constant victim of sickness and pain, half blind, or sheathed in a cast, while Clizia is angelically invulnerable. Both women are creatures of flesh and blood to begin with, but Clizia soars into bolder metamorphoses to the point of divine hypostasis; la Mosca instead remains somehow terrestrial, or should I say chthonic, and is far less protean, even in her apparitions as a ghost. The diminutive transformation into the insect which fits her nickname with its correlates of humor, affection and eeriness, marks her distinctive nature vis-à-vis imperious Clizia, who alone can become a skylark, a bolt of lightning, or a sun goddess. One couldn't possibly imagine her endowed with a "bat-like radar" as la Mosca is in *Xenia*; but then la Mosca is mostly associated with night, blindness, fluttering smallness, as against the solar halo of her angelic counterpart who ranges cosmic spaces; and if la Mosca can understand the liberty of hawks, it is only at a distance, without direct identification. They are what she cannot, physically, ever hope to be, though they figure forth the hidden freedom of her unimpaired mind. Clizia appears as a visitor from another continent or even from outer space, and her contacts with the worshiping persona of "Motets" are always momentary; they take place as epiphanies of transfiguring memory, but their occasion in "real life" has always been tangential to the time of quotidian duration. La Mosca instead, no matter how instantaneous her postmortem avatars, has always inhabited a continuous, domestic time. She, in fact, stands to her poetical rival as the quotidian (the authentically lived quotidian) stands to the exotic. In death, she has accordingly become one and the same thing with the *Lares* and *Penates* of the Montale household—a function hardly conceivable for Clizia.

A formal consequence of these thematic differences might be seen in the quite dissimilar treatment of rhythm and tone. Both cycles, "Motets" and *Xenia,* are analogous in the sense that each constitutes a self-contained series of lyrics from which no single piece should be excerpted, for even those individual poems that show a high degree of autonomy stand to lose something when removed from their context. An extreme example of what happens to a pithy epigram if uprooted from context is to be seen in *Xenia* I, 9:

> Ascoltare era il solo tuo modo di vedere.
> Il conto del telefono s'è ridotto a ben poco.

In Singh's translation:

> Listening was your only way of seeing.
> The telephone bill now amounts to very little.

The structural analogy between the two cycles emphasizes by contrast their divergence of texture and meter; the musical implications of the term "Motet" are borne out by Montale's rhythmic execution in "Motets," while the gnomic import of the term "Xenia" is as clearly realized in Montale's *Xenia* as it was in Goethe's poems by the same title. The low-keyed tone of the "Xenion" I quoted above is typical of the whole cycle, and to quite a large extent, of all of *Satura*, where the high register of "Motets" and the occasional hymnic élan of *La Bufera* are not at home. For *Satura* as a whole is played out on a deliberately prosier key than any of Montale's previous verse books. In his old age he has carried out more radically than even before the policy of a *talking* style (the policy that quickened *Ossi di seppia* forty-six years ago). It was perhaps the only new departure open to him after the singing performance of *La Bufera*—which brings us closer to answering the question initially raised in this paper: how is *Satura* integrated into the overall sequence of

Montalian poetry and how can it go beyond its immediate predecessor in the series? To go any further was out of the question. Clizia was not to be out-Cliziaed; so the only way was to retrace one's steps and speak with the voice of one who had returned from her lofty regions a wiser and a sadder man. There is in fact a posthumous tone to *Satura,* a tone appropriate to the man who had had Clizia and la Mosca as guides to the other world hidden behind the facade of this world; and that other world is hell or paradise, as the pointed references in "Motets" (and in *Xenia,* with an ample dose of sidetracking humor) show. The surviving persona actually says he hopes "that we are all dead without knowing it." Dead, namely, to the mundane world, to the world of mystification he and la Mosca jointly inhabited in a protective armor of mocking defiance.

Elsewhere ("**Gli uomini che si voltano**") he calls another personal Muse, maybe Clizia herself, "the only living one" in contrast to the many who are spiritually dead, "cadaveri in maschera" (masked corpses). Being dead to the world means being alive spiritually; but Montale's unworldliness lacks the mediaeval monk's comforts—the assurance of a revealed faith culminating in the approaching millennium—for his way is entirely tentative, and if God dawns in his universe through the good offices of Clizia or (in the present book) la Mosca, He is in the lower case, and is envisaged as a merciless Argus rather than as the conventional merciful Daddy. On page 56 we find the Nietzschean title "**La morte di Dio**" ("**The Death of God**"), where the irreverently bureaucratic language in which this stale piece of news is conveyed to (of all people) the Pope makes a mockery of institutionalized religion. Here it is la Mosca's demonic laughter that precipitates the Götterdämmerung of ossified monotheism, but in the "**Xenion**" mentioned above, her refusal to name God smacked of some secret reverence toward the irreducible mystery which our poet prefers to leave inviolate for the same reason that he resents, as we saw, any reduction of his (or any) poetry to institutionalized rhetoric or to a pretext for glosses. To define, then, is to violate, yet Montale's attitude in these matters escapes any type of easy agnosticism. In "**Divinità in incognito**" he pleads for a Hölderlinian kind of polytheism: he has actually sensed tangible divinity in some human beings he has met. Here one is well advised to remember his prefatory hint that in him "the many are one," otherwise one risks being sidetracked into institutionalizing his latter-day polytheism. He is probably saying that personal meetings can bring forth epiphany, the revelation of higher values, and the epiphany can attain such an intensity as to deserve the name of theophany. With all due apologies for thus intruding with my "explanation" on the immediacy of Montale's poetry, I think such a reading may give a good retrospective clue to that enigmatic poem in *La Bufera,* "**L'orto**" ("**The Garden**"), where Clizia becomes, after being angel and prophet, an actual godhead with creative attributes.

But what of the recipient and celebrant of such fitful revelation? The Montalian persona can indeed take on priestly connotations, as "**Intercettazione telefonica**" ("**Wiretapping**") says in the tongue-in-cheek style to be expected from much of *Satura*. He thought he was "a bishop *in partibus* [*infidelium*]," but he finds he was "probably a cardinal *in pectore*"; only the Pope, dying, forgot to tell him, and he can thus live "with or without faith," but "outside history" and "in mufti." The humor hides an earnestness of sorts. He is in the world, but not of it. Montale's unworldliness, as I noted earlier, is of a special kind, the kind that prefers secrecy to open profession, because it must live in and with the world. Thus, signally in the present book, he will have to use the language of the world as a mask. Dare we call him a newfangled Jesuit? Both the hairsplitting casuistry and the pragmatic aims of Jesuits are alien to him; in fact he even takes to task one famous contemporary Jesuit, Teilhard de Chardin, for having given (in Montale's opinion) a gross vulgate of spiritual philosophy. At any rate, Montale's appropriation of current ideological clichés or of small talk trivialities is an exposure, a satire ("Satura," of course). Masks can expose, as Hamlet knew. Hence that outburst of mundane slogans, **"Fanfara,"** which takes issue with the triumphant certainties of dialectical materialism. Its companion piece is **"La storia,"** articulated in two complementary parts. Here Montale speaks in his own gnomic voice instead of mimicking the public voice of one touted ideology for parodistic purposes. We notice the series of iterative negations in Part I and the qualified affirmations of Part II. The old devotee of Boutroux's contingentist philosophy with a tinge of Crocean idealism pops up again to blast away at any form of hard-and-fast historicisms that amounts to an idolatry of History. He defends the unpredictable against any form of wholesale dialectic that insists on preempting the future. I daresay this poem counts doctrinally more than aesthetically, and I would even incline to tilt the scales in a comparable direction with the three **"Botta e risposta"** (**"Thrust and Riposte"**) pieces, which are heavily weighted on the confessionally autobiographical side; I am uneasy about their mixture of self-irony and defensiveness.

Less explicit, less diffuse statements like **"Fine del '68"** (**"End of 1968"**) achieve much greater poignancy. This is where I recognize Montale's major voice—beyond all masks; this is where his seemingly casual dryness cuts deeper; a recognition I find inevitable with epigrams like the **"Xenion"** of the hawks, or the **"Xenion" No. 7** of the first part, not to mention others, and with the Clizia-oriented sequence **"Dopo una fuga"** (**"After a Flight"**). I don't mean that Clizia is necessarily the subject, biographically speaking; that will be left for biographers to delve. In any case "Ex-voto" certainly has to do with Clizia, with the essence of her meaning for the poet; and it ranks with Montale's strongest pieces:

> Insisto
> nel ricercarti nel fuscello e mai
> nell'albero spiegato, mai nel pieno, sempre
> nel vuoto: in quello che anche al trapano
> resiste . . .

> I insist
> on seeking you in the shoot, never
> in the full grown tree, never in fullness, always

in the void: in what resists
even in the drill . . .

Whether Clizia herself, or the creative principle one could call divine, is meant, matters little since here the two are one. The flashbacks to *Ossi di seppia*, pieces like **"Fuscello teso"** and **"Delta,"** do not amount to passive echoes of erstwhile creativity. They recapitulate a primal motif and in doing so tap the undrying source.

While the gnomic bent was implicit in much of Montale's early work, one salient trait of *Satura* seems by and large new: the frequency of syntactical parallelism, often reinforced by anaphora, as a structuring metric pattern. We find it, to an extent nobody could have anticipated from certain embryonic foreshadowings, in **"La storia,"** in **"Prima del viaggio"** (**"Before the trip"**), in **"L'angelo nero"** (**"The Black Angel"**), in **"Le parole"** (**"The Words"**), in **"Un mese fra i bambini"** (**"A Month Among Children"**), in **"Piove"** (**"It is raining"**), a witty parody of d'Annunzio's lovely "Alcyone" lyric (but d'Annunzio is not the real target), to name the most conspicuous examples. This is what prompted my friend Franco Fido of Brown University, in a private conversation, to mention Prévert as a possible influence—not a far-fetched idea, especially if we take into account the impish naughtiness that goes with much of this style in *Satura*. The elfish wit reaches a surreal peak in **"The Black Angel,"** a welcome surprise from the aging Montale, something to offset the thoroughly self-deflating stance of **"Botta e risposta."** Not only Prévert, but also Rafael Alberti comes to mind when we read this rejuvenated Montale. It is the reward of his dogged fight for the unpredictable. What a relief to find him still capable of vital contradictions! After the somber skepticism he voiced about language in **"Incespicare"** (**"Stumbling"**), where according to him we must be resigned to a "half-way speaking" since the one man who did speak out in full, once, turned out to be "incomprehensible," our poet can forget himself anew in the exhilaration of the singing word. Perhaps words can still recapture a fleeting resonance of the unique Word. And so even *Satura* is far from limited to the prose-like low pitch I have described as its basic strategy.

Stephen Spender (essay date 1972)

SOURCE: "The Poetry of Montale," in *The New York Review of Books*, Vol. XVIII, No. 10, June 1, 1972, pp. 29–32.

[*Spender was an English man of letters who rose to prominence during the 1930s as a Marxist lyric poet and as an associate of W. H. Auden, Christopher Isherwood, C. Day Lewis, and Louis MacNeice. His poetic reputation has declined in the postwar years, while his stature as a prolific and perceptive literary critic has grown. In the following excerpt, Spender celebrates Montale's ability as a poet, finding that he unsentimentally captured the essence of life.*]

Mosca (meaning "fly")—as everyone called her—was the wife of Eugenio Montale, the most famous living Italian poet and the incomparable ironic literary commentator of *Corriere della Sera*. She was a small, auburn-haired, rather heavily made-up lady who wore spectacles with thick lenses that magnified the gaze with which she looked out at the world. She took people in amusedly—not unkindly—but with no illusions about them. Her laugh was of the sort that used to be described as "tinkling." There was certainly something old-fashioned about her, like a watchful guest at a corner table of a boardinghouse on the sea coast. Perhaps she was called Mosca (Montale seems in his poetry to wonder why) because she seemed glinting and flickering: a firefly rather than just a fly, I would have thought.

It was she who told me one May morning in 1947 in Florence how Montale, having invited Dylan Thomas to dinner, had called on the great young English poet then visiting the city—and had entered his hotel room just in time to observe him scrambling into a clothes cupboard to escape dining with Italy's foremost poet. Dylan did various things of the same kind in Florence that week. The critic Luigi Berti (whom Dylan insistently called "Berty") objected to such behavior, on the rather surprising grounds that it was snobbish. I asked him why. Berti said he thought that the moment had arrived in history when English poets traveling in Italy should no longer give themselves the airs of "milords"—behave like Lord Byron, that is to say.

Mosca recounted Dylan's adventures joyously. *"Il était très étrange,"* she said. Now, a quarter of a century later, after Mosca's death in 1963, Montale has written a volume of poems about her which are both gravely sad and evocatively humorous. Having the appearance almost of a pendant or postscript to the main body of his work, nevertheless in some ways they serve almost as introduction to it. They have all its qualities with none, or few, of the difficulties; and thus they clarify problems for the reader of the previous work. One of these is the question of whom the poet is addressing in certain of his poems when he uses the pronoun *tu*. As Edith Farnsworth points out in the Introduction to ***Provisional Conclusions*** (the selection of Montale's poems which she has translated), "'You' is one or it may be all; it is the companion, even though, as in the case of Dora Markus, it may be personally unknown. It is the creature, or the essence, to be adored . . . and yet . . . it is hard to think of any love poem in any previously accepted sense."

In some of these poems there is such a feeling of the isolation of the poet that, whether the "you" is intended as Dora Markus, as the unknown, unproved, and withdrawn God, or as a friend, it seems ultimately the poet himself, because there is no communication for him with "another."

In the first "Sequenza" in *Xenia,* Montale disposes of this suspicion when he writes:

> Dicono che la mia
> sia una poesia d'inappartenenza.
> Ma s'era tua era di qualcuno.

(In G. Singh's translation: They say that mine / is poetry that belongs to no one. / But if it was yours, it was someone's.)

In *Xenia* the "thou" has clarified and hardened, like an outline emerging from mist into clear light, into the character of Mosca. This character has certain properties, such as spectacles, halting speech, a brother who died young; also a history of hotel rooms and conversations on telephones. However, the lines quoted above continue: "era di te non più forma ma essenza" ("not your form but your essence"). Although we see Mosca everywhere in this poetry—flitting through it in her bright insect way—the quintessential is what survives: It is here that her being shares unique consciousness with the poet:

> Tu sola sapevi che il moto
> non è diverso dalla stasi,
> che il vuoto è il pieno e il sereno
> è la più diffusa delle nubi.

(You alone knew / that motion is not different from stillness, / that the void is the same as fullness, / that the clearest sky is but / the most diffused in clouds.)

This revealing poem also throws light on Montale's method of working and approach to poetry when, continuing his dialogue with the quintessential Mosca, he contrasts her understanding of him with the attitudes of those who say that "poetry at its highest / glories the Whole in its flight, and deny / that the tortoise is swifter than the lightning" ("negano che la testuggine / sia più veloce del fulmine"). One looks at the photograph of the poet on the cover of the New Directions edition of ***Selected Poems*** and sees that—suede-skinned, wrinkled, with bright eyes of vision contrasted with a mouth that is ironic—it is indeed the face of an angelic tortoise.

The most difficult task for the writer of an elegy is, it seems, to evoke the figure of the one mourned. In most elegies we are made perhaps to share the grief of the poet, which is generalized, but the character of the person mourned seems abstract or a stereotype, like a marble urn. Milton follows classical models in giving us in *Lycidas* nothing of the character of Edward King. Wordsworth's "Lucy" poems evoke poignantly the dissolution of Lucy into impersonal nature, without giving us any idea what she was like. Tennyson communicates an almost intolerable grief but makes little more of Hallam than a discreet mixture of King Arthur and Albert, Prince Consort. Only Thomas Hardy effectively puts touches into his poems about his dead first wife which make us see a real woman. We learn that she had whims such as that of packing her luggage and leaving the house, in order to go on a suddenly wished for journey, without informing anyone. Although only lightly sketched, she is a ghost whose warm breath one feels on one's cheek. Hardy can give the reader strange Douanier Rousseau-like shocks of a naïve reality, as when he addresses her:

> —yes, as I knew you then,
> Even to the original air-blue gown.

In *Xenia,* Mosca flits and glints from poem to poem.

I began this article with the anecdote about Dylan Thomas and Montale because reading *Xenia* acted on my mind like a thread pulled which led to the long-forgotten anecdote. At this distance of time, I may indeed have recalled it incorrectly. It may have been Montale or Luigi Berti and not Mosca who told it to me. The point is though that these short poems restore to Mosca the voice and look with which she might have told it. The opening of the first poem brings her back speaking:

> Caro piccolo insetto
> che chiamavano mosca non so
>   perchè,
> stasera quasi al buio
> mentre leggevo il Deuteroisaia
> sei ricomparsa accanto a me,
> ma non avevi occhiali,
> non potevi vedermi,
> nè potevo io senza quel luccichio
> riconoscere te nella foschia.

(Dear little Mosca, / So they called you, I don't know why, / this evening almost, in the dark, / while I was reading Deutero-Isaiah / you reappeared beside me, / but without your glasses, / so that you could not see me, / nor could I recognize you in the haze / without that glitter.)

These poems are in no way excessive or rhetorical. Montale records the bare truth: the reflexes of the senses—the nerves—from which the wife who is one flesh with him has been removed; after that the continued communication between them which is of the essence of their relationship. Beyond her presence he knows though that Mosca is changing, altering, altered:

> La tua parola così stenta e impru-
>   dente
> resta la sola di cui mi appago.
> Ma è mutato l'accento, altro il
>   colore.

(Your speech so halting yet unguarded / is the only thing left / with which to content myself. / But the accent is changed and the color is different.)

There are doubts and wonderings about the plane of existence on which lovers meet in a marriage which is that of essential being:

> Pietà di sè, infinita pena e angoscia
> di chi adora il *quaggiù* e spera e
>   dispera
> di un altro. . . . (Chi osa dire un
>   altro mondo?)

(Self-pity, infinite pain and anguish / his who worships what's *here below* / and hopes and despairs of something else. . . . [And who dare say another world?])

Another book that throws light on Montale's poetry is the

collection of stories and sketches written for the *Corriere della Sera,* entitled *The Butterfly of Dinard.* . . . In a Preface specially written for this English edition, Montale states that his aim was to write "about those silly and trivial things that are at the same time important: to project the image of a prisoner who is at the same time a free man."

One of the most revealing of these "trivia" is a story entitled "Sul Limite." It opens with the description of a taxi accident in which the passenger, who is the narrator, leaves the scene of the disaster, gets onto a train, and arrives at a place where he is greeted by a comrade who was killed in the war. Nicola, as this wartime comrade is called, has collected together pets that the narrator had when he was a child, with which to greet him. His pet guinea pig Mini, Nicola tells him, is being looked after by Giovanna. The narrator's heart sinks. "'Is she dead?' I asked. ' . . . She's alive,' he retorted sharply; 'though you can call her dead if you like, the same as you and me. . . .'"

Montale's prose style is distinct from his poetry and well within the conventions of the French or Italian *feuilleton.* Nevertheless this sketch takes us to the center of his poetic world which is the twilight one—between day and night, between death's and life's kingdom—of Dante's *Purgatorio.* It is the dusk through which men peer and see each other's features sharply: a world of looming, effulgent minutiae, stony and human things, surrounded by a vastness in which the visible changes into the invisible, the invisible into the visible, I into thou, thou into I.

In the New Directions selection Maurice English translates **"Motet XX"** (from *Le Occasioni*) which gives very well this sense of the relation between the definite detail and the undefined vastness. I give it only in translation because the New Directions paperback, which is bilingual, is readily obtainable:

> . . . Well, be it so. The sounding of
>   the horn
> answers the bee-swarm in the
>   grove of oaks.
> On the sea-shell which takes the
>   evening's gleam
> a painted volcano gaily smokes.
> In the lava paperweight, a coin,
>   stuck fast,
> gleams also on the table, and holds
>   down a sheaf
> of papers. Life, which had seemed
>   so vast,
> is a tinier thing than your hand-
>   kerchief.

Montale has been compared to Eliot and it is true that like Eliot he seems a spiritual inhabitant of *The Divine Comedy.* However, there is this great difference: the voice of Montale speaks like that of a man finding himself situated in a circle which is that of the modern world, and from which he does not seek to escape. He defines this condition and although he would like to get beyond it (believe, for example, in an existence where he will be reunited with Mosca) truth for him consists of not believing what he does not know or experience. He exists within time, which is now.

He does not use Virgil as Dante does, or use Dante as Eliot does, to get outside the circle of the contemporary condition into eternity, even though he measures the living instant against the whole tradition. He is closer to Samuel Beckett than to Eliot or Yeats because although he is conscious of vastness outside his time and space, he uses that knowledge to define his own limited time and space. Like Beckett, he finds freedom in measuring his prison cell and his consciousness as its prisoner. He writes in "Casa sul Mare":

Tu chiedi se così tutto vanisce
in questa poca nebbia di memorie;
se nell'ora che torpe o nel sospiro
del frangente si compie ogni destino.
Vorrei dirti che no, che ti s'appressa
L'ora che passerai di là dal tempo;
forse solo chi vuole s'infinita,
e questo tu potrai, chissà, non io.
Penso che per i più non sia
      salvezza,
ma taluno sovverta ogni disegno,
passi il varco, qual volle si ritrovi.

. . . . .

You ask if all must disappear
in this residual mist of recollection;
if in this torpid hour or in the
      breath
of every breaker, all destinies must
      be fulfilled.
I long to tell you not, that close
      to you
is the hour which you will pass
      within a sphere
outside of time; it may be that
      only the one
who wants to, lives forever; you
      may be he;
I do not know. I think that for
      the most of us
there is no salvation, but who
      subverts each
plot, eludes each ambush
is he who finds himself.

Vorrei dirti che no: I would like to be able to reassure you and to dispel your doubts. This is the language of a man who, although he lives on a plane of intense spirituality, nevertheless cannot cheat himself by denying the evidence of argument that seems to him rational and of his senses. He cannot concentrate immortality into a moment of vision or of prayer, or thrust himself upon dogmas that give life the significance of myth come true. Montale belongs, I suppose, to the tradition of anticlerical and agnostic Italians who do not believe in God but nevertheless see heaven and hell as a metaphor for life:

Il vinattiere ti versava un poco
d'Inferno. E tu, atterrita: Devo
      berlo? Non basta
esserci stati dentro a lento fuoco?

(The wine-waiter poured into your glass / some Inferno. And you, all fright: Must I drink it? Isn't it enough to have been in it—burning slowly?)

The general tenor of Montale's poetry is of a man talking quietly aloud (his voice sometimes taking off from talk to sing the fragment of an aria), resonant to himself and to his readers who overhear him.

—Stephen Spender

Like Rilke, he describes faithfully the landscape of suffering, but cannot accept the official theological explanations, or go on a Dante-conducted tour through the universe. He sees the truth but not the Truth, though he, rather sadly, denies denying it. There are glimmerings, rumors, rumblings, and illuminations off-stage in his poetry. But the idea of a world of spiritual certainties is only a memory among others.

The general tenor of this poetry is of a man talking quietly aloud (his voice sometimes taking off from talk to sing the fragment of an aria), resonant to himself and to his readers who overhear him. He has the kind of sensuous intelligence that observes everything and instinctively places it within an order of the mind which does not have to be stated. He is the poet of the sea, and of rocks and plants along the shore, and of desolate places at the mouths of rivers (like that salsified landscape at the mouth of the Po which I once visited).

Sere di gridi, quando l'altalena
oscilla nella pergola d'allora
e un oscuro vapore vela appena
la fissità del mare.

(Evenings of cries, when the swing / rocks in the pergola of long ago, / and a dark vapour slightly / veils the quiet sea.)

One would be inclined to call him a great nature poet, were not the nature he describes so often denatured. In the English language the closest poetry to this is the desolate landscape of Browning's "Childe Roland to the Dark Tower Came."

He is not, though, without humor and an affectionate playfulness, like that of one going over the old tunes of the operas which he learned when he was training to be a singer, or of the narrator surrounded by the toys of his childhood in "Sul Limite."

Montale is, it seems, an amateur painter; and his poetic landscapes remind me of the monochromatic, highly simplified, yet marvelously "placed" landscapes of Giorgio Morandi, a painter whom, I believe, he admires. He has a melancholy which is shared by many Italian writers and which is in some ways the consequence of having his whole sensibility forced into a minor key to avoid the great major key effects of the Italian language. All the same, in his secrecy, his closeness to the minute particulars, he can, like Blake, make passionate statements. They are likely to blast through even his quieter poems. Here are the impassioned concluding lines of **"The Sunflower"** . . . :

> Bring me within your hands that
>   flower which yearns
> up to the ultimate transparent
>   white
> where all of life into its essence
>   burns:
> Bring me that flower impassioned
>   of the light.

(Portami tu la pianta che conduce dove sorgono bionde transparenze e vapore la vita quale essenza; portami il girasole impazzito di luce.)

G. Singh (essay date 1973)

SOURCE: "Wit, Understatement, and Irony: Montale's Sixth Book of Poems," in *Books Abroad,* Vol. 47, No. 3, Summer, 1973, pp. 507–10.

[*An Indian-born educator, critic, and poet, Singh has translated several selections of poems by Montale and is the author of* Eugenio Montale: A Critical Study of His Poetry, Prose, and Criticism *(1973). Other book-length studies by Singh focus on A. C. Swinburne, Giacomo Leopardi, Ezra Pound, and T. S. Eliot. In the following excerpt, he assesses the style and tone of the poems in* Diario del '71 e del '72.]

The first part of Montale's fifth book of poems, **Diario del '71,** appeared in a private, limited edition of 100 copies, published by Vanni Scheiwiller, Milan, 1971. To this has now been added **Diario del '72** to form a new book [**Diario del '71 e del '72**] (The fourth book **Satura** came out in 1971; see Glauco Cambon, "The New Montale," in *Books Abroad,* 45:4). There are about 90 poems, most of them short, some of them even epigrammatic.

There are two distinct strains running through this book: the lyric strain and the ironic-satirical strain. The two sometimes merge with each other; at other times they don't so much exclude as dominate one another. One can divide the book into two groups of poems—one where the lyric strain prevails and the other where the ironic strain does. As to the poems written in the predominantly lyrical key, they, for the most part, belong to the **Xenia** group, both by virtue of the inspiration behind them and their technique, diction and the realistic-evocative manner of narration or discourse. Such poems are **"L'arte povera," "a C.," "I**

nascondigli," "Il Pirla" and "Il lago di Annecy" (*Diario del '71*); and "Ancora ad Annecy," "Annetta," "Diamantina," "Sorapis, 40 anni fa" and "Al mio grillo" (*Diario del '72*).

In "L'arte povera" ("Poor Art"), while recounting the various materials he used in painting—blue sugar bags or wrapping paper, and "wine and coffee for the colors / and smears of toothpaste if the background was / a tassled sea"—the poet suddenly turns to the woman loved who is no more, with an emotionally subdued yet morally pregnant constatation:

> È la parte di me che riesce a sopravvivere
> del nulla ch'era in me, del tutto ch'eri
> tu, inconsapevole.

> (This is all that has managed to survive
> of the nothing that was in me and
> of everything that you were without knowing it.)

In "I nascondigli" ("Hiding Places"), some of the objects that belong to the world of *Xenia* and even earlier poems, and that, for all their triviality, have an emotionally charged association in the poet's mind, return: "my wife's little wooden dog, her brother's / obituary, three or four / pairs of her glasses, the cork / of a bottle that long ago / struck her on the forehead at the New Year's / *cotillon* at Sils Maria" and have "formed a conspiracy to sustain" the poet after his wife's death. In "Ancora ad Annecy" ("Still at Annecy"), revisiting this lake in France after his wife's death, the poet does not—deliberately, as it were—recall "the stately abode that sheltered you / before the coastguards' house was built, / almost like a cliff, in memory." But the very fact of recalling the coastguards' house (in the poem "La casa dei doganieri") in preference to the stately abode of an earlier period is itself a poetically effective way of linking two important episodes from the past which have become one, each adding to the evocative poignancy and richness of the other. And if in his recollection today, especially now that the object of love is dead, the poet considers youth to be "the most ridiculous season in life" ("Annetta"), it is not only his way of vindicating what is no more or of resuscitating someone who was "a genius of pure inexistence" but also of re-living in the only way possible what was once something ineffably sweet and poignant: "something so poignant that / it almost made me bleed."

It is, however, in "Sorapis, 40 anni fa" ("Sorapis, 40 Years Ago") that the distinction between age and youth is completely annulled, annulled by the absorbing recollection of fully realized love. But such a feeling is by its very nature inextricably linked with the nature of what is being experienced on a given occasion, *while* it is being experienced:

> Poi ti guidai tenendoti per mano
> fino alla cima, una capanna vuota.
> Fu quello il nostro lago, poche spanne d'acqua,
> due vite troppo giovani per essere vecchie,
> e troppo vecchie per sentirsi giovani.

Scoprimmo allora che cos'è l'età,
Non ha nulla a che fare col tempo, è un miracolo
che ci fa dire siamo qui, è un miracolo
che non si può ripetere. Al confronto
la gioventù è il più vile degl'inganni.

(And then I led you by the hand
to the summit, to an empty hut.
That was our lake, a few spans
of water, two lives too young
to be old, and too old to feel
themselves young. It was then that we
discovered what age means; it
has nothing to do with time,
it is something which makes us say
we are here, a miracle that
cannot be repeated. By contrast
youth is the vilest of all illusions.)

The other and more numerous poems in *Diario del '71 e '72,* on the other hand, are inspired by the poet's moral, philosophical and metaphysical reflections as well as by his pregnantly witty and sarcastic comments on the various aspects of the *Zeitgeist.* Montale's verbal and conceptual inventiveness is to be seen at its best in these cerebral or neo-metaphysical poems, parodies and epigrams. At times wit and irony are directed by the poet at himself, but most of the time at others and at the ethos, values or nonvalues, myths and illusions of contemporary civilization. In such poems, therefore, the poet, the moralist and the journalist join hands and what comes out is something impressively new, at least in Italian poetry. In **"A Leone Traverso,"** Montale's literary friend and a distinguished translator, the poet says how, like Traverso, he too dreamt of being one day "mestre de gay saber," but it was a vain hope: "A dried up laurel / doesn't put forth leaves even for the roast." In **"La mia musa"** (**"My Muse"**) Montale compares his muse to "a scarecrow standing precariously / on a checker-board of vines":

Un giorno fu riempita
di me e ne andò fiera. Ora ha ancora una manica
e con quella dirige un suo quaretto
di cannucce. È la sola musica che sopporto.

(One day it was filled with me and went away
proudly. Now it still has a sleeve
with which it directs its quartet of straws.
It's the only music I can bear.)

In **"Il terrore di esistere"** (**"The Terror of Existing"**) the poet's summing up of his life's possessions—he who in **"Mia vita a te non chiedo lineamenti"** (*Ossi di seppia*) had said he didn't need "lineamenti / fissi, volti plausibili o possessi"—is both witty and characteristic of the tone, inflexion and ethos of a great many poems in this book.

Nell'anno settantacinquesimo e più della mia vita
sono disceso nei miei ipogei e il deposito
era là intatto. Vorrei spargerlo a piene mani
in questi sanguinosi giorni di carnevale.

(In the seventy-fifth year or so of my life
I've gone down to look into the safe
and find that the deposit is intact.
I would like to scatter it freely
in these bloody days of the carnival.)

The note of self-irony turns, at times into self-denigration as in the poem **"King-fisher,"** with its subtle, moral and symbolic undertones.

Praticammo con curo il carpe diem,
tentammo di acciuffare chi avesse pelo o
    escrescenze,
gettammo l'amo senza che vi abboccasse
tinca o barbo (e di trote non si parli).
Ora siamo al rovescio e qui restiamo attenti
se sia mai una lenza che ci agganci.
Ma il Pescatore nicchia perchè la nostra polpa
anche al cartoccio o in carpione non trova più
    clienti.

(We practiced carefully *carpe diem*;
tried to catch whoever had skin
or excrescences, cast the hook
without tench or barbel, (not to mention
trout) biting at the hook.
Now the situation is reversed and we
are anxiously waiting for a line to catch us.
But the Fisherman shilly-shallies because
even in a paper-bag or as a picked carp
our pulp no longer attracts clients.)

Thus, although in an altogether different mode and key, the poet's quest for self-identity, self-exploration and self-differentiation—differentiation, for instance, from what he calls "the swarm of automatons called life" (**"Sono pronto ripeto, ma pronto a che?"**)—which started with *Ossi di seppia,* continues. But both the language, the imagery and the rhythmic suppleness have acquired a new verve and a new impetus, partly due to Montale's having achieved to the full the kind of maturity, stoicism or divine indifference which he had outlined in *Ossi di seppia* and which makes him feel, more than ever before, that in "the restless round of life / honey and absinth have the same taste." And now, having lived most of his life, the poet finds that he is still "uncertain as to the rules of combat":

Non era tanto facile abitare
nel cavallo di Troia.
Vi si era così stretti da sembrare
acciughe in salamoia.
Poi gli altri sono usciti, io restai dentro,
incerto sulle regole del combattimento,

(It wasn't so easy to live
in the horse of Troy.
They were so congested inside
as to seem like sardines. Then
the others stepped out but I
stayed in, uncertain as to the rules of combat.)

And the book closes with a characteristic poem **"Finis"**

which is still another example of Montalian wit, understatement and irony all rolled into one:

Raccomando ai miei posteri
(se ne saranno) in sede letteraria,
il che resta improbabile di fare
un bel falò di tutto che riguardi
la mia vita, i miei fatti, i miei nonfatti.
Non sono un Leopardi, lascio poco da ardere
ed è già troppo vivere in percentuale.
Vissi al cinque per cento, non aumentate
la dose. Troppo spesso invece piove
sul bagnato.

(I charge posterity [if I have
any, which is rather improbable],
on the literary plane, to make
a big bonfire of all that concerns me—
my life, my experiences, my non-experiences—
I'm no Leopardi,
I leave little behind me to be burnt
and it's already too much to live
in percentages. I for my part
lived five per cent; don't augment
the dose. It often rains
on what's already wet.)

Wallace Craft (essay date 1976)

SOURCE: "Openness to Life: The Poetry of Eugenio Montale, 1975 Nobel Laureate for Literature," in *Books Abroad,* Vol. 50, No. 1, Winter, 1976, pp. 7–15.

[*In the following excerpt, Craft highlights dominant subjects in Montale's poetry: contemporary values, the human condition, and the search for meaning in life.*]

In October the Swedish Academy announced that the 1975 Nobel Prize for Literature would be bestowed upon the poet Eugenio Montale, the fifth Italian writer to receive the honor. In 1906, the sixth anniversary of the award, Giosué Carducci (1835–1907), neoclassical poet of Italy's post-unification era, was the first Italian Nobel winner. Twenty years later the laureate was Grazia Deledda (1871–1936), author of more than twenty-five novels, most of which are set in Sardinia. Many will doubtless recognize the name of the poet and playwright who received the prize in 1934: Luigi Pirandello (1867–1936), a writer known throughout the world for his philosophical plays *Henry IV* and *Six Characters in Search of an Author.* It is interesting to observe that these earlier awards did not raise the bitter feelings and controversy that attended the presentation in 1959. In that year the prize went to the poet Salvatore Quasimodo (1901–68), who, like Pirandello, was born in Sicily. In 1959 many felt that Eugenio Montale, this year's recipient, was somehow slighted by the Nobel committee's decision. Others were of the opinion that the older Giuseppe Ungaretti (1888–1970) was more deserving than either Quasimodo or Montale. While this matter will always remain open to debate, it is perhaps well to recognize the fact that five of Italy's most

distinguished writers—three of them poets—have been honored, if not at the proper time, then at least in the proper manner. . . .

Within the limits of Italian literature Montale is generally thought to belong to a triumvirate of poets which includes Giuseppe Ungaretti and Salvatore Quasimodo. These writers, plus a few others, are often referred to as the "hermetic" poets. The term "hermetic" was first applied to the deceptively simple, condensed poetry of Ungaretti, although since the 1930s it has been applied to any verse which literary critics find obscure or "difficult." In a broader sense, however, when critics refer to Montale as a hermetic poet they are suggesting a literary debt or relationship to the development of so-called "pure poetry" (*poésie pure*) in Europe. "Pure poetry" is, of course, that type of highly musical, radically imaginative poetry which evolves from Mallarmé to and beyond such poets as Valéry, Eliot and Lorca. In a strict sense Montale did not write *poésie pure,* although a few characteristics of such poetry may also be observed in his verse: e.g., rich musicality, private symbolism and reduced emphasis on sentimentality.

> Montale may be the most humane poet of the century so far, his humility before the perfect devolving into a brilliant energy of imperfection. But he was also a deeply non-contacting, unconsoling artist, nearly as much so as Proust.
>
> —*Ross Feld, in* Parnassus, *Spring–Summer 1983.*

Montale's oeuvre invites comparison with various American and European writers such as Paul Valéry and Jorge Guillén, although recent critical attention has often focused on the likeness of T. S. Eliot to the Italian poet. The comparability of these poets is mainly based upon their respective modes of description. In the verse of each author nature is consistently presented kaleidoscopically as a mosaic of fragments or broken images. Both Eliot and Montale explore this fragmented world in order to fathom the mystery of human life. It must be pointed out, however, that Eliot emerges from his existential wilderness or wasteland to find resolution in the framework of Christianity. Montale's quest, on the other hand, never leads to final answers. The fundamental questions regarding life, death and human fate posed in the early poetry are deepened, repeated but not resolved in later verse.

With regard to the relationship between poetry and life, Montale is conspicuously comparable with Saint-John Perse, the French Nobel winner of 1960. Like Montale and Eliot, Perse views poetry as quest, a mode of investigating the natural world. The eclectic presentation of images gleaned from various fields of study is a striking stylistic feature in the work of both the Italian and the Frenchman. Though the spirit of Perse's work may be considered a bit more optimistic than that of Montale, in the final analysis, I believe the similarities outweigh the differences. To date, Montale's writings have been likened to those of several poets in the Italian tradition (Dante, Gozzano, D'Annunzio), but few studies have been conducted to determine the poet's significance in the total context of Western literature. Hopefully this year's Nobel award will serve to stimulate comparative studies of such international scope.

In considering the art of any poet the reader's first instinct is to look for those themes or leitmotifs which may lend unity and coherence to the opera omnia. In the case of Montale, however, the reader cannot expect too much consistency or evidence of systematic belief. Furthermore, the poet has commented that a precise ideological stance never ensures the value or survival of any art. Where, then, is the reader to begin? What is the primary focus of Montale's five slim collections of verse? Fortunately Montale has been fairly responsive to these questions. The human condition, or, more precisely, the maladjustment (*disamonia*) associated with the human condition is the subject of this poetry. The term "maladjustment" is used in reference to man's inability to find meaning in a physical world of which he may be considered the solitary prisoner. As one critic puts it, the problem at the heart of Montale's poetry is that man feels out of harmony with the natural elements which swirl about him in an endless process of transformation. At times the phenomenal world seems to be only an infernal machine which happens to include man in its meaningless and relentless patterns of movement.

Montale has responded to the existential quandary in two ways: first, he has attempted to achieve a sense of harmony or identity with the natural world; and second, he has sought to discover a higher order of existence (metaphysical level of being) which might illuminate man's life in the immediate physical ambience. In certain of Montale's early poems one observes a longing to be at one with the elements and thus to escape the sense of malaise and contingency. The sea, that eternal limit of the poet's childhood region, the Ligurian coast, becomes a symbol of primeval nature within which the poet experiences alienation. Verses contained in the poem **"Naked and Essential"** from the collection *Cuttlefish Bones* (1925) give poignant expression to this desire for harmonius marriage with the sensuous environment:

> My desire was to be naked and essential
> like bits of shell
> tormented by your motion,
> and melted into your salty depths;
> a splinter beyond the cage of time,
> witness of iron law that will not yield.

Again in **"Antico"** (**"Ancient One,"** an epithet for the sea) the poet yearns for release into cosmic freedom:

> It was you who first told me
> that the tiny ferment
> of my heart was but a moment
> of yours; that your uncertain law

> sleeps deep within me:
> to know at once variation and unity:
> and thus to rid myself of all waste,
> as you do, casting upon the shore
> among bits of cork, seaweed, starfish,
> the spent tokens of your abyss.

Montale's desire to escape a sense of homelessness and alienation within the physical world will, in truth, never be satisfied, for man is permitted neither to recover his past nor to understand fully the roots of his existence.

In other moments of his quest Montale attempts to transcend human disharmony vis-à-vis reality through perception of a metaphysical order of truth. Whether we, his readers, consider this source of truth God, First Cause or some other Absolute is really not so important. The point is that the poet is seeking breakthrough or revelation as an avenue to greater understanding of life—an understanding which cannot be achieved by means of reason alone. Images of light or movement toward light often reflect the Montalean search for transcendence. One of the most strikingly beautiful compositions dramatizing the poet's ontological inquiry is **"The Sunflower."** The humble plant turns upward, toward the source of its life, until it seems maddened in the intensity of sun-worship:

> Bring me the plant that leads
> to where transparency is born
> and life appears as essence;
> bring me the flower maddened by the light.

Just as the sunflower turns worshipfully upward to regard the sustaining force of its life, so, too, earthbound Montale turns outward to scan nature in the effort to glimpse a truth perhaps hidden behind or beyond the veil of the physical order.

Regardless of the Montalean themes mentioned here, it would be incorrect to imply that the poet's work is limited to consideration of the existential dilemma. Especially in poems from the collections *The Occasions* (1939) and *The Storm and Other Things* (1956) Montale speaks passionately and convincingly of perplexing ethical and social problems in the contemporary world. Underlying the ethical dimension of Montale's poetry is the belief that various evils witnessed in the twentieth century, especially the regimentation and annihilation of men, can be overcome or at least challenged if each individual will but offer resistance and say "no" to the masters of totalitarian systems. In the first collection, *Cuttlefish Bones,* this lesson in ethics is given as a lyrical formula: "Today we can only tell you this, / what we are *not,* what we do *not* accept." In the thirties Montale obeyed his own moral imperative and refused to join the Fascist Party.

In the articles of prose collected in *Auto da fé* and *In Our Time* Montale has much to say regarding moral issues relevant to the contemporary world. The poet has always believed that the individual has a responsibility to recognize and to resist certain forces or trends which erode human freedom and challenge the idea that man is an end, valid per se. The chief danger today, as Montale sees things, is that we may be moving gradually into an era of civilization in which the machine will replace man as the point of reference for all values. At that point in the future tyranny will not exist as a man-controlled, man-centered structure similar to the forms of fascism and communism of past years, but rather will arise as a result of what man himself (homo faber, technological man) has made. In Montale's opinion the main problem stemming from technology is that the "free time" which machines make possible does not necessarily lead to genuine freedom. On the contrary, such unlimited leisure may lead to a disintegration of society or at least to a replacement of those values held sacred in the West since the Renaissance:

> One day, it is said, man will be able to work three or four hours a day, thus increasing his free time for almost unlimited leisure and amusement. But already there arises the possibility that many people, sensing an obligation to consume free time, may become frustrated or even delinquent citizens.
>
> (*In Our Time*)

It may be, as Montale repeatedly suggests, that *otium* or leisure, technological man's gift to himself, is actually a Pandora's box capable of releasing more curses than blessings. For example, if homo ludens cannot find sufficient means to "kill" his free time, then he may become *homo destruens* and turn, out of ennui and frustration, to the destruction of himself and his own world. Furthermore, there is danger that art itself may fall victim to an age of leisure. Montale reasons that when man becomes afraid of time—that is, when time is thought of negatively or as a void to be filled at any cost—then art will be viewed only as a "standard commodity" designed to fill instances of released time. Of course if civilization reaches that point, homo sapiens will no longer exist as we know him today. Sadly, man will have lost the ability to learn from his past and to contemplate his future.

It must be emphasized that Montale's purpose in examining the quality and direction of modern civilization is not, certainly, to pose as a kind of *vates,* the poet-prophet who predicts doom and holds no hope for the future. The essays do not, in fact, reveal an outlook that is fundamentally pessimistic as regards the future of civilization. Rather, his words are a plea for resistance to the concept of a technocentric in place of an anthropocentric society. Montale addresses problems of culture and civilization as a humanist, for he believes that only as long as man is considered the end of progress and not the means thereto can civilization as we now envision it survive. In short, only man himself can ensure that he, not the machine, will remain the measure of all things.

In announcing the Nobel Prize in Literature for 1975 the Swedish Academy appraised Eugenio Montale's work as "an interpretation of values in our time." The values of which Montale's writings are the interpretation and endorsement may be reduced to a simple phrase: fidelity to life. In an interview held in 1966 the poet declared that he

has been able to survive through the tumultuous years of the twentieth century primarily because he has always sustained a faith in life. The poet lives, to use his own words, in "the hope that life has meaning." Though the ultimate significance of life may remain forever beyond the reach of human reason, the challenge that life presents to each individual has always been considered worthwhile. It would be wrong, then, to concur with those critics who can view Montale's work only as a literature of crisis or pessimism. On the contrary, the poet's words imply and inspire a degree of optimism, for they suggest that in spite of human tragedy life must hold meaning.

Openness to life is perhaps the poet's most significant achievement, for adherence to this principle has enabled him to avoid two temptations to which many, if not the majority of modern artists, have fallen prey. The first temptation, common especially in the first half of this century, is that tendency to withdraw from life into an ivory tower of theory or subjectivity (Valéry and also the Italian disciples of Mallarmé are included here). Second, there is the opposite trend to "engage" or enslave art in conformity to a particular ideology. Remaining beyond these limiting spheres of the subjective and ideological, Montale demonstrates great concern for the freedom and survival of art. For many years now the poet has realized that the genuine knowledge sought by poets—that is, knowledge of universal scope and implication—can only be found at the heart of life itself, within the act of living, a gesture which Eugenio Montale has always considered the supreme act of faith:

> And well I know: to burn,
> this, and nothing else, is my significance.

Joseph Brodsky (essay date 1977)

SOURCE: "The Art of Montale," in *The New York Review of Books,* Vol. XXIV, No. 10, June 9, 1977, pp. 35–9.

[*Brodsky is a Russian poet and critic who emigrated from the Soviet Union in 1972 and became an American citizen in 1977. His view of poetry as a relief from the horrors and absurdities of life and the meaningless vacuum of death has led critics to link him with the modern school of existentialism. In the following excerpt from a review of* New Poems, *Brodsky notes distinguishing characteristics of Montale's poetry and praises the verse written about his deceased wife.*]

Ever since the Romantics, we have been accustomed to the biographies of poets whose startling careers were sometimes as short as their contributions; in this context, Montale is a kind of anachronism, and the extent of his contribution to poetry has been anachronistically great. A contemporary of Apollinaire, T. S. Eliot, Mandelstam, and Hart Crane, he belongs more than chronologically to that generation. Each of these writers wrought a qualitative change in his respective literature, as did Montale, whose task was much the hardest.

While it is usually chance that brings the English-speaking poet to read a French poet (Laforgue, say), an Italian does so out of a geographical imperative. The Alps, which are now a two-way route for all sorts of "isms," used to be a one-way route going north. For any Italian poet to take a new step, he must lift up the load amassed by the traffic of the past and the present. The load of the present was, perhaps, the lighter for Montale to handle.

During the first two decades of this century the situation in Italian poetry was not much different from that of other European literature. By that I mean that there was an aesthetic inflation caused by the absolute domination of the poetics of Romanticism (whether in its naturalistic or symbolist version). The two principal figures on the Italian poetic scene at that time—the *"prepotenti"* Gabriele D'Annunzio and Marinetti—did little more than manifest that inflation, each in his own way. While D'Annunzio carried inflated harmony to its extreme (and supreme) conclusion, Marinetti and the other Futurists were striving for the opposite, to disintegrate that harmony. In both cases it was a war of means against means; i.e., a conditioned reaction which marked a captive sensibility. It now seems clear that it required three poets from the next generation, Giuseppe Ungaretti, Umberto Saba, and Eugenio Montale, to make the Italian language yield a modern lyric.

In a spiritual odyssey there is no Ithaca, and even speech is but a means of transportation. A stern metaphysical realist with an evident taste for extremely condensed imagery, Montale managed to create his own poetic idiom through the juxtaposition of what he called "the aulic"—the courtly—and the "prosaic"; an idiom which as well could be defined as *"amaro stile nuovo"* (the bitter new style), in contrast to Dante's formula which reigned in Italian poetry for more than six centuries. The most remarkable aspect of Montale's achievement is that he managed to push forward despite the grip of the *dolce stile nuovo*. In fact, far from trying to loosen this grip, Montale constantly refers to or paraphrases the great Florentine both in imagery and vocabulary. His allusiveness is partially responsible for the charges of obscurity that critics occasionally level against him. But references and paraphrases are the natural elements of any civilized discourse (free—or "freed"—of them, discourse is but gesticulation), especially within the Italian cultural tradition: Michelangelo and Raphael, to cite only two instances, were both avid interpreters of *La Divina Commedia*; one of the purposes of a work of art is to create dependents; the paradox is the more enslaved the artist, the freer he is.

The maturity that Montale displayed in his very first book—*Ossi di Seppia,* published in 1925—makes it more difficult to account for his development. Already here he has subverted the ubiquitous music of the Italian hendecasyllabics, assuming a deliberately monotonous intonation that is occasionally made shrill by the addition of feet or is muted by their omission—one of the many techniques he employs in order to avoid prosodic inertia. If one recalls Montale's immediate predecessors (and the flashiest figure among them is certainly D'Annunzio), it becomes clear that stylistically Montale is indebted to nobody—or to everybody he bounces up against in his verse, for polemic is one form of inheritance.

This continuity through rejection is evident in Montale's use of rhyme. Apart from its function as a kind of linguistic echo, a sort of homage to the language, a rhyme lends a sense of inevitability to the poet's statement. Advantageous as it is, the repetitive nature of a rhyme scheme (or for that matter, of any scheme) creates the danger of overstatement. To prevent this, Montale often shifts from rhymed to unrhymed verse within the same poem. His objection to overstatement is clearly an ethical as well as an aesthetic one—proving that a poem is a form of the closest possible interplay between ethics and aesthetics.

This interplay, lamentably, is precisely what tends to vanish in translation. Still, despite the loss of his "vertebrate compactness" (in the words of his most perceptive critic, Glauco Cambon), Montale survives translation well. By lapsing inevitably into a different tonality, translation—because of its explanatory nature—somehow catches up with the original by clarifying those things which could be regarded by the author as self-evident and thus elude the native reader. Though much of the subtle, discrete music is lost, the American reader has an advantage in understanding the meaning, and would be less likely to repeat in English an Italian's charges of obscurity. . . .

Perhaps the term "development" is not applicable to a poet of Montale's sensitivity, if only because it implies a linear process; poetic thinking always has a synthetic quality and employs—as Montale himself expresses it in one of his poems—a kind of "bat-radar" technique, i.e., thought operates in a 360 degree range. Also, at any given time a poet is in possession of an entire language and his preference for an archaic word is dictated by his subject matter or his nerves rather than by a preconceived stylistic program. The same is true of syntax, stanzaic design, and the like. For sixty years Montale has managed to sustain his poetry on a stylistic plateau, the altitude of which one senses even in translation.

> **If one recalls Montale's immediate predecessors (and the flashiest figure among them is certainly D'Annunzio), it becomes clear that stylistically Montale is indebted to nobody—or to everybody he bounces up against in his verse, for polemic is one form of inheritance.**
>
> **—*Joseph Brodsky***

New Poems is, I believe, Montale's sixth book to appear in English. But unlike previous editions which aspired to give a comprehensive idea of the poet's entire career, this volume contains only poems written during the last decade, coinciding thus with Montale's most recent (1971) collection—*Satura*. And though it would be senseless to view them as the ultimate word of the poet, still—because of their author's age and their unifying theme, the death of his wife—each conveys to some extent an air of finality. For death as a theme always produces a self-portrait.

In poetry, as in any other form of discourse, the addressee matters no less than the speaker. The protagonist of the *New Poems* is preoccupied with the attempt to estimate the distance between himself and his interlocutor and then to figure out the response "she" would have made had she been present. The silence into which his speech necessarily has been directed harbors, by implication, more in the way of answers than human imagination can afford, a fact which endows Montale's "her" with undoubted superiority. In this respect Montale resembles neither T. S. Eliot nor Thomas Hardy, with whom he has been frequently compared, but rather Robert Frost of the "New Hampshire period," with his idea that woman was created out of man's rib (a nickname for heart) neither to be loved nor to be loving, nor to be judged, but to be "a judge of thee." Unlike Frost, however, Montale is dealing with a form of superiority that is a *fait accompli*—superiority *in absentia*—and this stirs in him not so much a sense of guilt as a feeling of disjunction: his persona in these poems has been exiled into "outer time."

This is, therefore, love poetry in which death plays approximately the same role as it does in *La Divina Commedia* or in Petrarch's sonnets to Madonna Laura: the role of a guide. But here quite a different person is moving along familiar lines; his speech has nothing to do with sacred anticipation. What Montale displays in *New Poems* is that tenaciousness of imagination, that urge to outflank death, which might enable a person, upon arriving and finding "Kilroy was here," to recognize his own handwriting.

But there is no morbid fascination with death, no falsetto in these poems; what the poet is talking about here is the absence which lets itself be felt in exactly the same nuances of language and feeling as those which "she" once used to manifest "her" presence—the language of intimacy. Hence the extremely private tone of the poems in their technique and in their close detail. This voice of a man speaking—often muttering—to himself is generally the most conspicuous characteristic of Montale's poetry, but this time the personal note is enforced by the fact that the poet's persona is talking about things only he and she had knowledge of—shoehorns, suitcases, the names of hotels where they used to stay, mutual acquaintances, books they had both read. Out of this sort of *realia,* and out of the inertia of intimate speech, emerges a private mythology which gradually acquires all the traits appropriate to any mythology, including surrealistic visions, metamorphoses, and the like. In this mythology, instead of some female-breasted sphinx, there is the image of "her," minus her glasses: this is the surrealism of subtraction, and this subtraction, affecting either subject matter or tonality, is what gives unity to this collection. (See the accompanying selection.)

Death is always a song of "innocence," never of experience. And from the beginning of his career Montale shows

his preference for song over confession. Although less explicit than confession, a song is less repeatable; as is loss. Over the course of a lifetime psychological acquisitions become more real than real estate. There is nothing more moving than an alienated man resorting to elegy:

> With my arm in yours I have de-
>   scended at least a million stairs,
> and now that you aren't here, a
>   void opens at each step.
> Even so our long journey has been
>   brief.
> Mine continues still, though I've no
>   more use
> for connections, bookings, traps,
> and the disenchantment of him who
>   believes
> that the real is what one sees.
>
> I have descended millions of stairs
>   with my arm in yours,
> not, of course, that with four eyes
>   one might see better.
> I descended them because I knew
> that even though so bedimmed
> yours were the only true eyes

Other considerations aside, this reference to a continuing solitary descent of stairs echoes something in *La Divina Commedia,* **"Xenia I"** and **"Xenia II,"** as well as **"Diary of 71"** and **"Diary of 72,"** the poems that make up the present volume, are full of references to Dante. Sometimes a reference consists of a single word, sometimes an entire poem is an echo—like No. 13 of **"Xenia I"** which echoes the conclusion of the twenty-first Song in the *Purgatorio,* the most stunning scene in the whole *Cantica.* But what marks Montale's poetic and human wisdom is his rather bleak, almost exhausted, falling intonation. After all, he is speaking to a woman with whom he has spent many years: he knows her well enough to realize that she would not appreciate a tragic tremolo. He knows, certainly, that he is speaking into silence; the pauses that punctuate his lines suggest the closeness of that void which is made somewhat familiar—if not inhabited—because of his belief that "she" might be there. And it is the sense of her presence that keeps him from resorting to expressionistic devices, elaborate imagery, catch-phrases, and the like. She who died would resent verbal flamboyance as well. Montale is old enough to know that the classically "great" line, however immaculate its conception, flatters the audience and is a kind of shortcut to self-deception. He is perfectly aware of where his speech is directed. . . .

New Poems provides an idiom which is clearly new. It is largely Montale's own idiom, but some of it derives from the act of translation, whose limited means only increase the original austerity. The cumulative effect of this book is startling, not so much because the psyche portrayed in *New Poems* has no previous record in world literature, as because it makes it clear that such a mentality could not be expressed in English as its original language. The question "why" may only obscure the reason; because even in

Montale's native Italian such a mentality is strange enough to earn him the reputation of an exceptional poet.

Poetry in itself is a translation; or, to put it another way, poetry is one of the faculties of the psyche translated into language. It is not so much that poetry is a form of Art as that Art is a form to which poetry often resorts. Essentially, poetry is a verbalization of perception, the translation of that perception into a full harmony (or disharmony) of language—language is, after all, the best available tool. But for all the value of this tool in ramifying and deepening perceptions—revealing sometimes more than was originally intended, which, in the happiest cases, merges with the perceptions—every more or less experienced poet knows how much is left out or has suffered because of it.

This suggests that poetry is somehow also alien or resistant to language, be it Italian, English, or Swahili, and that the human psyche because of its synthesizing nature is infinitely superior to any language we are bound to use (having somewhat better chances with inflected languages). To say the least, if the psyche had its own tongue, the distance between it and the language of poetry would be approximately the same as the distance between the latter and conversational Italian. Montale's idiom shortens both trips.

New Poems ought to be read and reread a number of times, if not for the sake of analysis, the function of which is to return a poem to its stereoscopic state—the way it existed in the poet's mind—then for the fugitive beauty of this subtle, muttering, and yet firm stoic voice, which tells us that the world ends with neither a bang nor a whimper but with a man talking, pausing, and then talking again. When you have had such a long life, anticlimax ceases to be just another device.

The book is certainly a monologue; it couldn't be otherwise when the interlocutor is absent, as is nearly always the case in poetry. Partly, however, the idea of monologue as a principal device springs from the "poetry of absence," another name for the greatest literary movement since Symbolism—a movement which came into existence in Europe, and especially in Italy, in the Twenties and Thirties—"Hermeticism." The following poem, which opens the present collection, is testimony to the main postulates of the movement and is itself its triumph. (*Tu* in Italian is the familiar form of "you.")

The Use of "Tu"

Misled by me
the critics assert that my "tu"
is an institution, that were it not
for this fault of mine, they'd have
    known
that the many in me are one,
even though multiplied by the
    mirrors.
The trouble is that once caught in

the net
the bird doesn't know if he is
    himself
or one of his too many duplicates.

Montale joined the Hermetic movement in the late Thirties while living in Florence, where he moved in 1927 from his native Genoa. The principal figure in "Hermeticism" at that time was Giuseppe Ungaretti, who took the aesthetics of Mallarmé's *"Un Coup de Dés"* perhaps too much to heart. However, in order to comprehend the nature of Hermeticism fully it is worthwhile to take into account not only those who ran this movement, but also who ran the whole Italian show—and that was Il Duce. To a large degree, Hermeticism was a reaction of the Italian intelligentsia to the political situation in Italy in the second and third decades of this century and could be viewed as an act of cultural self-defense—linguistic self-defense, in the case of poetry—against Fascism. At least, to overlook this aspect of Hermeticism would be as much a simplification as stressing it would be.

Although the Italian regime was far less carnivorous toward Art than were its Russian and German counterparts, the sense of its inconsistency with the traditions of Italian culture was much more apparent and intolerable than in those countries. It is almost a rule that in order to survive under totalitarian pressure Art should possess density in direct proportion to the magnitude of that pressure. The whole history of Italian culture supplied part of the necessary density; the rest of the job fell to the Hermeticists, little though their name implied it. What could be more odious for those who stressed literary asceticism, compactness of language, emphasis on the word and its alliterative powers, sound versus—or rather, over—meaning, and the like, than the propaganda verbosities and state-sponsored versions of futurism?

Montale has the reputation of being the most difficult poet of this school and he is certainly more difficult—in the sense of being more complex—than Ungaretti or Salvatore Quasimodo. But for all the overtones, reticence, merging of associations or hints of associations in his work, its hidden references, substitutions of general statements for microscopic detail, elliptical speech, etc., it was he who wrote **"La primavera Hitleriana"** (**"The Hitler Spring"**), which begins:

The dense white cloud of the
    mayflies crazily
whirls around the pallid street
    lamps and over the parapets
spread on the ground a blanket on
    which the foot
grates as on sprinkled sugar; . . .

This image of the foot grating on the dead mayflies as on sprinkled sugar conveys such a toneless, deadpan unease and horror that when some fourteen lines below he says:

. . . and the water continues to eat at
    the

shoreline, and no one is any more
  blameless
                              (translated by Maurice English)

it sounds like lyricism. Little in these lines recalls Hermeticism, that ascetic variant of Symbolism. Reality was calling for a more substantial response, and World War II brought with it a "dehermetization." Still, the "hermeticist" label became glued to Montale's back, and he has, ever since, been considered an "obscure" poet. But whenever one hears of obscurity, it is time to stop and ponder one's notion of clarity, for it usually rests on what is already known or preferred, or, in the worst cases, remembered. In this sense, the more obscure, the better. In this sense, too, the obscure poetry of Montale still carries on a defense of culture, this time against a much more ubiquitous enemy:

> The man of today has inherited a nervous system which cannot withstand the present conditions of life. While waiting for the man of tomorrow to be born, the man of today reacts to the altered conditions not by standing up to them or by endeavoring to resist their blows, but by turning into a mass.

There is something remarkable about the almost simultaneous appearance of these two books; they seem to merge. In the end, *Poet in Our Time* makes the most appropriate illustration of the "outer time" inhabited by the persona of the *New Poems*. Again, this is a reversal of *La Divina Commedia* where this world was understood as "that realm." "Her" absence for Montale's persona is as palpable as "her" presence was for Dante's. The repetitive nature of existence in this after-life-now is, in its turn, kindred to Dante's circling among those "who died as men before their bodies died." *Poet in Our Time* supplies us with a sketch—and sketches are always somewhat more convincing than oils—of that rather overpopulated spiral landscape of such dying yet living beings.

This book doesn't sound very "Italian," although the old civilization contributes a great deal to the accomplishment of this old man of letters. The words "European" and "International" when applied to Montale also look like tired euphemisms for "universal." Montale is one writer whose mastery of language stems from his spiritual autonomy; thus, both *New Poems* and *Poet in Our Time* are what books used to be before they became mere books: chronicles of souls. Not that they need any. The last of the *New Poems* goes as follows:

To Conclude

I charge my descendants (if I have
any) on the literary plane
which is rather improbable, to make
a big bonfire of all that concerns
my life, my actions, my non-
      actions.
I'm no Leopardi, I leave
little behind me to be burnt,
and it's already too much to live

by percentages. I lived at the rate
of five per cent; don't increase
the dose. And yet
it never rains but it pours.

Russell Fraser (essay date 1977)

SOURCE: "The Poetry of Eugenio Montale," in *The Sewanee Review,* Vol. LXXXV, No. 3, Summer, 1977, pp. 411–29.

[*Fraser is an American educator and critic specializing in the works of William Shakespeare. In the following essay, he argues that Montale takes an agnostic stance in his poetry by raising issues without drawing conclusions: "Montale, venturing the question, doesn't venture an answer. No answer is likely, unless an irreducible surd."*]

My subject is Montale's poetry and the peculiar configuration that it makes.

Poems like Wallace Stevens's "The Ordinary Women" baffle exegesis, but when you say them over and over, they describe a configuration or form: "The lacquered loges hunddled there / Mumbled zay-zay and a-zay, a-zay." Other poems such as "Hugh Selwyn Mauberley" present difficulty which is all at the exegetical level. Only read what Pound has read or let the commentators do that for you; this superficial labor accomplished, the rest is easy going. Montale's poetry lives in its own place—call it a midden—between these different kinds. It smells of ebbtide and detritus like the early poetry of T. S. Eliot, which means it is bookish poetry and smells of the lamp:

> The happiness of cork abandoned to the current
> that melts around tumbledown bridges.
>   ("**Boats on the Marne**")

Or it smells of the ditch whence private memory springs, the foul rag-and-bone shop of the heart:

> *nella fossa*
> *che circonda lo scatto del ricordo.*
>   ("**Voice Arriving with the Coots**")

Montale is not a discursive poet, so the clarity you expect in the poetry of linear progression is wanting, the Comedian as the Letter C making his soul, where C is the peregrine hero and the cursus that he negotiates. In this poetry of innuendo motion belies itself or goes downward to darkness. Falling leaves describe a helix, spiraling like arrows in their descent. Revolving doors appear to communicate as they pass on their metaled ways. The look of communication is an optical illusion. The swallow, faithful to instinct, builds its nest, wanting life to endure. The squirrel, presenting life, still flames in the pine tree.

> But over the dikes, at night, the dead water
> wears down the stones.
>   ("**Lindau**")

"Botta e Riposta": the title to which Montale twice returns in his poetry of the 1960s elucidates the strategy—it is perhaps a psychological imperative—of these earlier pieces. **"Blow and Counterblow"**:

> Now the minutes are equal and fixed
> like the turns of a pump wheel.
>
> ("House by the Sea")

Thesis and antithesis confront one another. From the confrontation no synthesis ever emerges.

> Desolate the leaves
> of the living who lose themselves
> in the prism of the minute,
> the fevered limbs devoted
> to the motion that repeats itself
> in a brief circle.
>
> ("Times at Bellosguardo")

We need the Italian for the beating of the metronome, then the subsidence:

> *atti minuti spechiati,*
> *sempre gli stessi—*

"acts minutes mirrored, always the same." Nothing happens. This poetry cries for apocalypse.

Time, passing, is static, and it moulders (*"funghisce su sè"*) as it dotes on the past. But Montale in the same context suggests that "memory is not a sin so long as it avails." To turn from the past—old fathers, grandfathers—is to abjure reality, always understood as refreshment, hence to insure the sterility of the present. Montale disinters the past, not as he is morbid or molelike (*"di talpe, abiezione"*), but as he is heuristic. Like the eel in the great poem of that title he learns by fronting death and still-luminous decay to thread the slime and granite of life.

The learning in which he instructs us—*"la mia lezione"*—is not intellectual but is felt in the blood. This is certainly a kind of heuristics but is expressible only as it makes a figure. You cannot express the yield, as in a cento of available truths. Memory, dazzling in sleep, irradiates the waking day. The pulsing of the sea, remembered, evokes consternation. These are powerful words—*"abbagliante,"* *"sbigottimento"*—but peculiar to the event which is their occasion. The sun is an event, also an adventure (*"evvenimento"*), and it riddles us with light. This riddling sums but does not explicate our being: *"bruciare, / questo, non altro, è il mio significato."* The voice that pours from the green bells of the sea, whelming the heart, throbs with ardor, then is stilled: *"il bollore / della vita fugace."* The eel against the river, narrowing down and down, presents a torch, a lash, Love's arrow on earth, a rainbow that vanishes in the moment of its apparition. Always the apparition is violent and necessarily itself, *"su sè."* Montale is a parochial poet, and he is loath to debase the linguistic currency in which he trades.

Having said this much, let me go against the drift of the argument. Montale's poems make a composition analogous to music. His motets of the 1930s, antiphonal in structure, this voice against that one and both voices recurring, suggest a generic title for the whole. In the poetry conceived as "mottetti," recurring figures do duty for plot. As they recur they constitute this writer's poetics; so they give us liberty to say what he attempts. The substantive *"solco,"* a thing plowed and prospectively bearing, signals to the reader who has met it before the accession at least the potentiality of knowledge. *"Nel solco dell'emergenza"*: in the furrow of emergency we encounter, unexpectedly, our own tormented being, coming out of darkness into light.

Poetics is not the same as philosophy. Montale, working his furrow or little patch of ground and so getting to know it, does not pretend to generalize from what he knows. I suppose that we who read him are more ambitious. If our ambition is not wholly out of the way, that is because what is most parochial is most likely to ramify or breed.

In this obdurately analytic or personal poetry, the buried life is everywhere, rooted way down in quick recollection, so that often you want a gloss, though knowing you are not going to get one. **"Arsenio"** enacts the plight of the dislocated man (*"sperso"*), whose alienation is qualified as he drags his roots with him. Viscid and tentacular, they eddy beneath turbid water—like the seaweed that Montale remembers persistently from his boyhood on the Ligurian coast—menaced by the water but still trembling with life as they cling to the source which guarantees their being:

> giunco te che le radici
> con sè trascina, viscide, non mai
> svelte, tremi di vita.

I take it that Arsenio, an obscure monastic of the early Christian centuries, is lifted from the hagiography and meant to emblematize, in humility and mock humility, this poet of holes and corners. It is more pertinent to say, as particulars ramify, that he is emblematic of ourselves.

I cannot name the woman tenacious memory exhumes, save as Montale names her. She is Clizia the heliotrope, transformed by Apollo, or Diana Artemis, the embodiment of purity to which the fierceness of the hunter is allied, or she is Diotima who discourses to the wise man on the nature of love, or the devotee Veronica who tenders Christ her veil. Maybe, like Petrarch's Laura, this woman is begotten by the poet on his muse. The commentators think otherwise and are willing to come to specific matters. What they have to tell us in this particular doesn't signify. Montale, reflecting on Cavafy's poetry, suggests why this is so. "Cavafy's erudition was that of an artist who takes what he needs wherever he finds it and who could not really care less for historical exactitude." Better to go or stay with the reticent poet and see him as manipulating personae. I think of Shakespeare at sonnets and what we don't know about the life that goes into the poetry or from which the poetry appeals. Montale is less favored than Shakespeare; he is, however, more favored than most modern makers—Yeats, for example—in that the essential biography is dim. He thinks—meeting Brancusi, whose vociferous ego is everywhere in the room: "This is precisely the problem of our time: art 'with anecdote' (that is, with something that recalls the life of the man)." Joyce says that Shakespeare's poetry is written by another man who bears the same name. It is a just rejoinder to the biographical critics—and as valid for Montale as for Shakespeare. The effect in either case is ardent and impersonal, the artist like the Creator, impassioned but discreet, hiding himself in his elliptical handiwork. The impersonality authorizes the passion.

The function of the poet as he descends on the world is, by convention, pentecostal. Like the messengers of Tobias in **"The Hitler Spring"** he touches with fire and so resuscitates the living dead. Or he is the diviner who with rod or wand locates the life-giving spring beneath our stony soil: *"per i sempreverdi / bruciati e le cavane avide d'aqua."* In Montale's poetry the divining is potential, rarely accomplished. The gullies still clamor for rain, the evergreens wither. The dominant landscape (*"greti arsi del sud"*) is Eliotic:

> A heap of broken images, where the sun beats,
> And the dead tree gives no shelter, the cricket no
>   relief,
> And the dry stone no sound of water. Only
> There is shadow under this red rock.

Further back is Dante, the common property of both poets (they use him with a difference), discerning no shade, no sign, only the bank and the bare road and the livid color of the stone (*Purgatorio* 13). Dante's progress is, however, ineluctably upward. Purgatory wants its transcendent conclusion. Montale cannot see so far. He prays for the dead that they may pray for him—he is pious and self-regarding—and for the living

>   not because
> I hope for their resurrection, rather
> for the fulfilling of that life they have had,
> unexplained and inexplicable.
>
>   (**"Beach at Versilia"**)

The living are only hypothetically alive. The past absolute (*"ebbero"*) renders their present existence. It says that the present is moribund already. No celestial kingdom is in prospect.

Mostly the life of which the poetry is made declares its humdrum condition. It is not a clamant storm, Dante's *"bufera infernal, che mai non resta,"* but is offhandedly *La Bufera e Altro* ("and other things"). The last sounds (*"ultimi suoni"*) that assault us might portend Armageddon; they are only a buzzing, as of bluebottle flies. "We are all already dead without knowing it" (quoting from *Satura*), and this buzzing is our requiem. Life is only scribbling on a blackboard. Or it is a letter not written or a bottle in the sea that never finds its destination. Like Matthew Arnold's protagonists we are sundered from each other, "in the sea of life enisled." Arnold, however, is proffering answers. Never mind that the answers are bleak.

Montale is prodigal of questions, he is a niggard of answers, but I think that the answers are implicit in his country of the mind. The characteristic mise-en-scène is a garden burned with salt, or a funicular in which the travelers sit passive and alone, or a forest of iron masts in the dusty evening. The reminiscence is of Dante's *"selva oscura,"* and it emphasizes the distance between these two poets. In the hell through which Montale ventures to lead us—he assumes the role of Virgil to our modern Dante-pilgrim, but unlike Virgil he does not bring us out on the heights of theology—there is no *contrapasso* or apportioning of just desserts. His protagonists are aloof from good and evil, like the cripples and old folks and little children of **"Eastbourne,"** who inhabit a gaudy pavilion erected on piles above the eroding and victorious sea. Or they are denatured, no longer human beings but red ants

> In the cracks of the soil, amidst the tares . . .
> That now break ranks and now reform themselves
>   On the summit of a miniscule hill.
>
>   (**"The Wall"**)

The psychological tenor is superficially the same as Valéry's in his fragments from "The Youngest of the Fates" (*La Jeune Parque*). Valéry, like Montale, tastes ashes in his mouth, so enjoins on himself his own annihilation: *"Forme-toi cette absence . . . Abandonne-toi vive aux serpents."* But in the end denaturing, *"malgré moi-même,"* is impossible to this poet of affirmations: "It is necessary, O Sun, / That I adore my heart wherein you are confirmed." Valéry is countervailing—or in any case he is counterpointing—the injunction to descend and to sleep. Montale in comparison seems perversely uninventive, harping continually on the one string.

Rising and falling, the sound of a cruel gigue stings us to the quick. The analogy is to "the long wave of my life," the up and down of it, a pattern and divested of meaning. So the crashing noises come to crescendo, then close without interval in muteness. *"I fragori si distendono, / si chiudono in sordina"* (**"Eastbourne"**). Syntax is mimetic; it authenticates the dreary round. Conjunctions are omitted, as betokening sequence. There is no sequence, no heightening or depressing, so resort is to the paratactic style. The vocabulary works to present deliquescence. *"Chiudere"* (to close) is the apposite verb; elsewhere—since the emotional weather seems not to change—are similar words and phrases on its semantic or connotative periphery.

> Veiled trembling of lights beyond the closed
>   windows,
> silhouetting the profiles of women at dusk.
>
>   (**"Café at Rapallo"**)

The windows are always closed. Passion is a shut-in (*"chiusa passione"*), rarely loosed or unfolded. The redressing of the negative words—*"sciolta"* or *"schiude"*—is not often conceded. Its occasion is not often perceived. Silence, like a cloud, immures us, or lazy smoke, or we are carried on a train (*"chiusi uomini"*) through a dark tunnel, anticipating the ultimate immuring or interring: *"chiusa di cimento."*

Barricades seal off our salvation. What the deity has in store for us, nobody can say. His fuliginous operations—*"di fuliggine,"* suggesting a divinity of hell—are hidden from view; and when we put the portentous question he shuts up his face like an ambush.

The hardness of Montale—*"come un ramo,"* like the limbs of a tree whose fibers are inextricably twisted—verges on opacity, not simply on the surface but all the way through, so mingling gnomic Stevens and recondite Pound. Only rarely is the sense or saying in the music, in "the beauty of inflections." Form and content bristle with mutual antipathy. Or say that the form, which asserts meaning exactly as it is formal, and the content, in which meaning is often to seek, are immiscibles that fuse to create a third thing which has not existed yet in the standard taxonomies.

In poetry where the corrosive idea does not translate, as when the word becomes flesh, this forcible joining of opposites-by-convention is surprising, but like an affront. The poet is jejune: Hart Crane comparing love to a burnt match skating in a urinal, Pound in his hysterical fourteenth canto scoring off the Georgians who thought poetry was beautiful:

> Above the hell-rot
> the great arse-hole,
> 　broken with piles,
> hanging stalactites,
> 　greasy as sky over Westminster.

Oxymoron when it works effects a chemical change, the poet exploiting latent energies, as of fire and powder, but to an end which is not combustion but annealing. Surprise attends the recognition of what you had not noticed before, the integrity of the compound that the poet makes or discovers. To read Montale successfully you need a new set of terms. That is one measure of his greatness.

All poetry is bringing order to experience, but this is more or less true, and it depends on whose poems are to hand. Montale is not so much rationalizing his uncomely material as enunciating and honoring the figure that it makes. In his best poems—**"The Lemons," "The Sunflower," "To My Mother," "The Hawks"** (to name only a few of them)—he so countenances actuality—this time, these trivia—as to confer reality upon it. The conferring is like a sacrament, but it works from within. The phenomenal world is made abruptly incarnate, not declared to be noumenal or real. That is why paraphrase fails. "The perception of the intellect is given in the words" (Pound is introducing the poems of Cavalcanti), "that of the emotions in the cadence." Something like that.

In Montale's poetry there is a felt oxymoron between the congealing form and the content that threatens to unfix it. Often the poetry wears the favor of consecutive argument. The pattern "since . . . then" is syllogistic. Since the road taken, should I turn back, is longer than the road ahead; since the palliatives that present themselves along the way do not palliate: then let us push on to the bound of the

waste. This is the expectation the syntax engenders, as the poet apostrophizes his dead father (**"Voice Arriving with the Coots"**). But logical structure functions as a blind, and the corollary tells us, in the teeth of expectation, that there is no golden underground where spirits gat them home. *"Eccoti"*: Here you are, father, not there. The end of the journey that we think we are pursuing is independent of the end. But go to the poem and see how the conclusion is augured and mandated by the indulgent particulars of which the dependent clauses are made. Since they are indulgent, they are logically off the point. At the same time they are indispensable to the life of the whole, where life is not a paradigm but the pressing on form of the indigenous thing.

Philosophy and politics are prone to general statement, science also, and poetry of the second rank. Montale's poetry, like that of his master Dante, is innervated (to translate his verb *"sinnerva"*), gives nerves to ideas, so making them things. Revivification is an idea, but it is presented metaphorically. The returning year fords the heavens, pillaging the heart (**"Autumn Cellars"**). That is tenable of springtime in the year 19__, and in the little town of _____, and only as the poet perceives it. You cannot elevate metaphor to preceptorial status.

If we agree that disembodied ideas do not signify, let us also agree that the imitation of life is a gudgeon not worth taking. Montale in his craft is not looking to render our ephemeral business; in any case the rendering is not where we come out. Naturalism is all-in-all sufficient only for the art of trompe l'oeil. It is a minor art. The stuff in which Montale deals is ugly only in the first place, as nature yields it up to his inspection. His flaccid or seamy data, since they are naturalistic, are nothing. "Dark things strain towards brightness"—to quote from **"The Sunflower"**—and in their straining are perdurably changed. The poet is the instrument of this unlikely metamorphosis. He is Proteus the shifty god, neither fish nor flesh; but what he is changing, or melding rather, as one thing merges with another thing, is not himself but his materials: bodies in their drossy solidity diffused, exhausting themselves in a flowing of colors, thence in a flowing of music: *"si esauriscono i corpi in un fluire / di tinte: queste in musiche."* This is not Ovid, the conjuring poet, turning Daphne as by magic to the laurel tree. I see Montale, more augustly, as presenting Apollo, but not now ambitious or balked of his own ends. The loving magic that he works on the heliotrope is disinterested, thus magnanimous. He is not displacing what he touches but making it greater. He burns with auroral light the nondescript particular (*"bruciato dai barbagli dell'aurora"*) and creates in the process not another thing but the thing itself, as it might be. *"Ecco il segno."* In the bread and wine, the body and blood are already there. Only you have to enlarge them. This is the poetry of transubstantiation, where the mystery, in the accepted sense, is still dark to the priestcraft that performs it.

In the title poem of *La Bufera,* the running together of *"marmo* [marble] *manna e distruzione"* articulates a unity of disparate things. The poetry is saying that the bane and the yield (or manna) are the same. Against the harmony of the amaranth moon, redolent of romance, recalling the flower that never fades, is set the tumult in the blood, which discomposes all that famous harmony (**"In Sleep"**). Prosody emphasizes the connection or disjunction. Prosodically the poem is like a Shakespearian sonnet and is written in verse that is basically hendecasyllabic, the standard linear form of Italian poetry to the present. It begets expectations, even as the sonnet form begets and belies them. (See **"Leda and the Swan."**) There is no prosodic reticule more aggressively formal, and here we feel it brimming with inchoate substance, the shrieking of nightbirds, error that strangles, hideous apparitions thrusting upward from dream. Assonance, alliteration, medical and interior rhyme—the staple techniques of conventionally mellifluous poetry—as they are levied on in this poetry, work against the conventional grain. They are the music or the threads on which the tassel of the verse is caught, or they are the tassel of experience itself, strung or reveled out into hours and years.

Convention yokes together similar sounds to make the lines cohere: pity thrilling in the air, for the greedy roots, for the tumid bark: *"per l'avide / radici, per le tumide cortecce."* Montale prefers the refracting of convention. Like and like come together but to mock the resemblance—or like and unlike to find out their identity. You can make a facile rhyme of *"frastaglio"* and *"abbaglio,"* the slashed or broken thing and the quality of wonder (**"Autumn Cellars"**). But the yoking together is more than homophonic, or rather in this case the sonantal correspondence argues that splendor is discovered in prosaic materials and corruption is its warrant and even its condition. "For nothing can be sole or whole / That has not been rent." The flock or palpable aggregate is also the mist in which it dissolves: *"greggia"* and *"nebbia"* are heard and felt to associate, as clouds associate with carob trees, solidity with its obverse (*"e nubi . . . dei carrubi"*), and the serene and transpicuous ether with the entombing darkness below: *"nell'aria ancora serena . . . / nel ventre della balena."*

In **"The Shorewatchers' House"** the pleonastic particle (*"Ne,"* meaning, gratuitously, "of it") is twice repeated, and it signals affirmation. Then follows a perfect homonym, complementary in sound, antithetic in sense, and turning the prior sequence out of doors.

Ne tengo ancora un capo. . . .
Ne tengo un capo; ma tu resti sola
nè qui respiri nell' oscurità.

Memory is a thread:

I still hold an end of it. . . .
I hold an end of it; but you remain alone
nor do you breathe here in the dark.

Substantially the poem is saying: after all you are not here, and memory fails. Under the skin the sequence of meaning goes: Yes . . . yes; but: no. So meaning is discountenanced as the form asserts it.

Meaning in this poetry is occulted on the premise that not much is open to rationalization. Perception is a screen of images—*"schermo d'immagini"*—where the screen is like that in the movies; it is also a moat defending against the sensory world. The adverbial phrase which locates us is *"nel crepuscolo."* We move in a twilight or crepuscular kingdom. Thought or memory assails us, but like a "swarm" or "fog." Reality is "muffled"; it only grazes or touches us lightly, like a puff of air or diaphanous cloud. More figures recur here: *"sfiora," "un soffio."* The words bespeak ephemerality and compose a gravid presence, tolling us back to our soul's self, the clog to which we are fettered. So perception, communion also, is partial.

The mirror breaks that signalizes apprehension. Blind shears, like Milton's shears but with no Christian succor behind, reduce our experience to fragments. Between you and me a subaqueous brightness, occluding and deforming, insinuates itself. "I do not know if I know you." Its uncanny power—*"sortilegio"*—consigns us to solipsism— this, on the one hand, on the other to a horrid autonomy which entails not freedom but a shivering of the whole into parts. The man alone surrenders; dwelling in this country he has no option:

To the sorcery of not recognizing
Anything of myself outside of myself.
                    (**"Two in the Twilight"**)

What we recognize is like the lightning in the collied night, a gesture without provenance against a background that is always running away. The indicated words are *"sfuggevole," "reciso."*

Dubiety is where we live, so wan hope is native to us.

The hope of ever seeing you again
was fleeing from me.
                    (**"Motet VI"**)

Here seeing means partly metaphysical seeing, grasping the quiddity or quick. Memory tuning out, the sovereign presence of distortion, is the business of the poem. But who is the protagonist, an equivocal creature and possibly inimical, and how is it that memory grows tenuous? Here are two answers. The first is from Yeats, who saw a monkey on a chain but never said a thing.

So I have picked a better trade
And night and morning sing:
Tall dames go walking in grass-green Avalon.

And here is Montale, turning it around in the concluding stanza of his motet:

At Modena, among the porticoes,
a servant in livery was dragging
two jackals on a leash.

The connection between the stanzas is suppressed, so the mind labors to enforce it. Perhaps the connection is inconsequent, syntactical merely? I suppose that we divine it as we take the force of the antecedent details. From one point of view, divining is not so good as declarative statement.

"I don't know." The declarative phrase rejects the possibility of declaring or affirming, and in the poem called **"The Garden"** it recurs like witless music when the needle is stuck in the groove. The repetitions simultaneously assert and gainsay. Structure and substance are at a mortal war. The anaphoric mode, repeating the same grammatical sequence, makes an order. The direction is centripetal. Concurrently it says the poem, whose purport is subversive of order. The metaphysical direction is centrifugal. The object of the verb, which is the subject or point, is withheld, but not costively. Maybe there is no point. Deific design, the fingering that we hear or think we hear on the heavenly keyboard, is perhaps an imposition, man creating God after his own proclivities. At any rate, "*Io non so.*" The path that bears us is fashioned of air, or too narrow to prosecute, perhaps no path at all. Or if it exists it carries us to hell where we shall melt like wax against the fire.

Evidently Montale is not an optimistic poet. He does not beat the big drum like D'Annunzio, who wants us to march with him into the future. But neither does he indulge the pessimism-by-rote of his predecessor Carducci to whom, in an amusing poem, he hears himself compared. In his poetry revealed truth is unavailing. But skepticism avails. For once that dismal Pyrrho is approved. "Every doubt takes you by the hand like a friendly little girl" (**"Portovenere"**). Customary formulations and responses—"*per assumere un volto*": preparing a face to meet the faces that you meet—are put away. This poet must purge himself, like the cleansing sea, of "*lordura,*" "*macerie*"—intellectual shibboleths. He is the maimed man who is aggrandized as he witnesses to his affliction. The poetry presents him or his different guises, the wounded acacia that shakes loose its outworn husks in the time of storms, the eel that inhabits fruitfully where everything is burned. The blow he takes is hard, but what it lops away ("*svetta*") is excrescent. The path he pursues is harder—"*la via più dura*"—but as he transacts it he withers into the truth, "leaping into dryness under the new moon." He creates, lock, stock, and barrel from his incessant probing and his resinous heart, a personal order, however tentative, and free from religious or political persuasion, "*chierico rosso, o nero,*" the red shirt or the clerical habit.

As a gloss on Montale, the metonymic poet who puts the parts for the whole, see Montale the translator, who discerns a kindred spirit in Emily Dickinson or Gerard Manley Hopkins. Here, from one of Dickinson's poems, is an apparent connection: "The missing All prevented me / From missing minor things." If you fail to apprehend or believe in the total congeries—what Montale caricatures as the intolerable sleight of hand of the stars, and Dickinson sees as manifest only "inscrutably"—you are driven back on the minute particular. Hopkins at a guess commends himself to Montale as the questions he raises are answerable only in terms of the phenomenal world. Hopkins the eschatological poet is the invention of Professor X, altogether a less mettlesome person. Rightly read, his appeal,

Montale's also, is to the discordant-seeming matrix from which we take our being.

> All things counter, original, spare, strange;
> whatever is fickle, freckled (who knows how?)

> *e tutto ch'è*
> *fuor di squadra, difforme, impari e strambo.*
> *Tutto che muta, punto da lentiggini (chissà come?)*

Life comes, unbidden, to the dark corner where the eremite—it is Arsenio—cultivates his garden (**"Chrysalis"**). His only light ("*la sola luce*") is personal and veiled but indemnifies his isolation and declares it gracious. He is a man of silences but not deprived as he is silent. Quench the clamant birdsongs and you begin to hear. The yield of this hearing and seeing, as passion's war is intermitted, is the replenishing of our poverty with riches, "*l'odore dei limoni.*" What the tacit observer discovers—more precisely and soberly: what, one day, he might discover—is the dead point of the world ("*il punto morto del mondo*"). It is the chink in the armor or the half-closed gate which allows us to glimpse and savor, for an ecstatic instant, the divinity that inheres in common things.

> He gripped more closely the essential prose
> As being, in a world so falsified,
> The one integrity for him, the one
> Discovery still possible to make.

So after all he is like Crispin, the Comedian as the Letter C, and his poetry also is a vale of soul-making. That is not as he aspires to the role of the magus, looking into the heart of the mystery, rather as he trusts (gingerly, for want of a better) to his senses:

> Gladly I will read the black
> signs of the branches on the white snow
> like an essential alphabet.
>
> (**"Almost a Fantasy"**)

The essential alphabet or the essential prose is cryptic and not readily construed—this, as we are human, so purblind. We see piecemeal, "*illuminato a tagli,*" where the pieces make a unity that is only supposititious. On this sour cross the poetry leaves us.

But not quite. To the quiescent man, a cantle of the truth is conceded, or the cantle which is the truth, as he declines to put himself forward. He stretches out, so makes a lengthened shadow, as he disburdens himself of himself: "*mi allungo disfatto di me*" (**"In the Park"**). Like the Snow Man in Stevens's poem, he is

> The listener, who listens . . .
> And, nothing himself, beholds
> Nothing that is not there and the nothing that is.

To listen, to watch, to lie in shadow ("*Meriggiare pallido e assorto*"): the infinitives on which this early poem is strung are like a rosary that the poet tells, keeping time to his salvation. He attains to salvation, the "delirium of immobility" by which Arsenio is recognized, as he contemplates the rock that covers the world, or the swallow's black flight,

> un solco
> a imbuto, il volo nero d'una rondine.
>   ("Sulla Greve")

This is the furrow that bears.

> And I have no other rosary
> to finger, nor pillar of fire
> if not this, of resin and berries.
>   ("Iris")

Common things, acknowledged—a rosary of cautious drops sparkling on the hayfork—confer the gift of grace. The obscure idea of God descends on the saving remnant ("*sui pochi viventi*"), who are alive as they want prepossession.

Where are the bread and wine of this poetry, "*la nostra parte di richezza*"? Bread is the velvet bud, and wine the profound breathing of the sea. The redemptive rite in which they participate is the achieving of peculiarity in this temporal place, the tenacious gangue or veinstone that associates the living and the dead (**"Eastbourne"**).

Peculiarity, the irrefrangible thing, must suffice us. That is the burden of Montale's music and denotes its acrid color, the inflection of it, the figure it makes. To encapsulate this figure I am drawing on intimations from *Satura* and *Diario,* the last of Montale's five volumes. They reveal a poet who is fiercely self-occupied yet insistently remote, hiding himself in underground places. He refuses with horror the glosses of the scholiast. By and large he is resolutely antipoetic, not gay or wise or celestial. He entertains ugliness with something more than equability: poetry and the sewer are two problems that he is unwilling to disjoin. Sweet and sour, beauty and terror constitute for him an inextricable harmony ("*una sola musica*"). He is wanting in "philosophy." Brothers, he says, don't look to me for tears or succor. So far as he knows, man is the unlikely product of a game of chance ("*lotteria*"), so there isn't much profit in agitating metaphysical questions. Children don't inquire if another life exists, and as they are incurious, they are right. This reticent poet is, however, not phlegmatic or impervious to divinity; only he finds it in a droplet or crumb. He is the man whose eyes have opened for a moment, "*e tanto basta.*" It is enough.

The triumphant conclusion of Montale's poem **"To My Mother"** gives the sense and the strength-in-weakness of this provisional poet. The "disencumbered highway," the path the eschatologist is pursuing,

> is not a path, only two hands, a face,
> *those* hands, *that* face, the gesture of one life
> that is not any other but itself,
> only this puts you into elysium,
> thick with the souls and voices in which you live.

The gesture the spirit makes as the poem sinks to silence is ambiguous. But it remains. "*E il gesto rimane*":

> it measures
> the void, sounds the boundaries of it:
> the unknown gesture that expresses
> itself and nothing else.
>   ("Times at Bellosguardo")

Perhaps, like a picklock, it forces open the closed place or secret point of the world. Montale, venturing the question doesn't venture an answer. No answer is likely, unless an irreducible surd.

Jascha Kessler (broadcast date 1981)

SOURCE: A review of *It Depends: A Poet's Notebook,* in a radio broadcast on KUSC-FM,—Los Angeles, CA, March 11, 1981.

[*Kessler is an American educator, poet, short story writer, translator, and screenwriter. In the following excerpt from the transcript of a radio broadcast, he states that Montale is more "outspoken and direct" in* It Depends: A Poet's Notebook *than in his previous works.*]

We have still among us today the great Italian poet, Engenio Montale, who won the Nobel Prize for Literature in 1975. And, perhaps it's not surprising that he continues to produce poetry that is full of interest and power, although he keeps changing its qualities and its direction. Not surprising, because of the nature of this great poet. Ever since his first book came out in 1925, Montale's most recurrent theme has been the mediation of our present lives, that is, our personal identities, by our links to the past. Of course, one has to have *had* a past, and Italy is the European country *par excellence* with a past. I suppose that there is another, and somewhat ironical, aspect to this situation of Italy in our Western Civilization's heritage: for Italy is also one of the last Western nations to have entered the Modern Age, for it was only unified as a nation during the past century, lagging long behind even Germany. As anyone who has travelled and lived in Italy knows, it is a very varied and very complex society, and Italians are Milanese, Venetians, Tuscans, Abruzzese and Sicilians, for example, before they are Italians. And in fact, Italy has a long way to go, perhaps luckily so, before the people of its many regions become, if they ever do, more or less one people.

At any rate, there are extremes of contrast always present to the minds of Italian artists, ranging from the most primitive and poverty-stricken backwardness to the most contemporary and sophisticated mentalities. And even in the hills of Sicily, or the mountains of the Marche, the poorest peasants live among the ruins and relics of what was Classical Roman Civilization, bad before Roman, Etruscan and Greek. Not only is the past so rich and complex, but the swiftly-changing 20th Century can be seen as its mirror opposite, or even contrary: unstable and beset by extraordinary pressures. For a meditative poet like Montale, whose lifelong effort has been to express the vision of the constancies of Italian life, and to stabilize himself in order to offer a spiritual structure to the mind of our time, or, rather, to the diverse minds of our time, the challenge has been enormous, and it is what has made his poetry what it is. And Montale, being a great poet, has been seeking constancies to live by. Therefore, during the long aberration of Italian Facism, from 1922 to 1945, the period of his principal works, he stood firmly opposed to the regime, its theatrical impostures and vanities, its parody of Socialist ideals, and its essentially vulgar shoddiness and had to live outside of its force unlike our American Ezra Pound, who, living in Italy, believed that Mussolini's regime was really the modern way to go, and that its delirious propaganda of energy, athleticism and Futurist worship of power, speed, and technological brutality was the promise of the new day for Europe. As Montale remarks in his new book, we find that "precariousness (is) the muse of our time."

Montale's new book is called *It Depends: A Poet's Notebook*. It was published in 1977 in Italy, with the title *Quaderno di quattro anni,* or, *The Four Years' Notebook,* to translate it roughly, when Montale was in his 82nd year.

Montale can speak through wit, pun and parody and sardonicism, he can speak, not oracularly and desperately as Yeats did, and as Roethke did, or even tragically and despondently as Thomas Hardy did, but directly out of the fullness of his life.

—Jascha Kessler

I can summarize the thrust of these 75 pages of poems by saying that whereas Montale was always a subtle, dense, rich and rare poet of deep meditative vision, he has, in his old age, become most casual, most outspoken and direct in his manners. Although a collection of what is called poems out of his writing notebooks over four years would seem to be private jottings, what we do in fact have here is a very various collection of humorous, critical, sardonic and often wittily editorial comments on contemporary life by a mind that has grown ever more clear, ever more direct and forceful. It is the poetry of old age; but every bit of it is the consequence of a poetic life lived in the moral and intellectual realm. When Yeats, for example, entered old age, he was quite different. Yeats spoke up at one point, and declared that it was time to be "making the soul," and his poetry became increasingly passionate, sensuous, and was built up on and out of the extreme tension of trying to resolve the realms of the flesh and the spirit into a unity. Montale, coming from a land of crystalline light, and not from the dark and moist foggy ambiguities of Northern Europe, is quite another sort of poet in old age, as though his Classical temperament and inheritance

had accepted the identity of flesh and spirit from the outset. So that, in old age, all that passionate confusion and struggle had long ago been outgrown; he had long ago found his satisfactions and fulfillment in love and marriage, in life and the political struggle: that is, he had grown up and through his life. When one regards Yeats, however, one sees a poet who remained in many ways adolescent and terribly incomplete, unfulfilled, until he entered old age, whereupon there was the desperation of having to begin to live as a man, a whole man, when there was hardly any time left at all. Montale's character, in contrast, has always been marked by a certain Italian kind of integrity and sobriety; and his efforts have been to find a way to live and be a man in a world that denies both being and humanity.

Now, in these notebook poems of his late 70's and early 80's, Montale discourses quite informally and freely: we see here the results of his quest for modernity, and for *being here now,* which is fundamentally a Classical kind of way of looking at our moments of life, Classical and perhaps even pagan. He can speak through wit, pun and parody and sardonicism, he can speak, not oracularly and desperately as Yeats did, and as Roethke did, or even tragically and despondently as Thomas Hardy did, but directly out of the fullness of his life. He can look at the present, and, being old, call up odd vagrant memories from the remote past. His voice is even, his eye cold and clear. He remembers, for instance, Aspasia:

> Late in the night
> men used to enter her room
> by the window. She lived on the ground floor.
> I had named her Aspasia and she was pleased.
> Then she left us. She worked as a barmaid,
> a hairdresser and other things. It rarely happened
> that I met her. But when I did,
> I called out Aspasia! and she
> would smile without stopping. We were
> the same age, she must be long since dead.
> When I enter Hell,
> almost from force of habit I shall shout
> Aspasia at the first shade that smiles.
> Naturally she will keep on walking.
> We shall never know who was and who wasn't
> that butterfly who had just a name
> chosen by me.

And in another poem, the poet prays, with devastating irony:

> Protect me
> my silent custodians
> because the sun is turning cold
> and the last leaf of the laurel
> was dusty
> and couldn't be used
> even for the roast *en casserole*—
> protect me from this
> halfpenny film
> which is being projected
> before me

and presumes to involve me
as an actor or extra
not provided for by the script—
protect me even
from your own presence
almost always useless
and inopportune
protect me
from your terrifying absences—
from the void which you create
around me
protect me from the Muses
whom I saw roosting
or reduced to their half busts
in order to hide better
from my ghost's step—
protect me or better still
ignore me
when I enter the urn
I have been praying for for years—
protect from the face/farce
which gained me entry into the illustrated Larousse
only to be omitted from
the new edition—
protect me
from those who beseech your presence
around my catafalque—
protect me with your forgetfulness
if it can help me keep on my feet
poor household gods always locked
in your dubious identity—
protect me without
anyone knowing about it
because the sun is turning cold
and he who knows it is
maliciously pleased
o my little gods
third-rate divinities
driven out of the ether.

And finally, though there are dozens of short poems that are deceptively simple, with the deadly simplicity of old age's devastating and ruthless probity, here is an example of what I mean . . . :

The dead poets sleep peacefully
under their epitaphs
and they only start with indignation
when a worthless writer
recalls their names.
And so do the flowers thrown into the rubbish heap
if someone should pick them up by chance.
They were on their way
to their mother but now
they are on their way to no one
or to a bunch held together by a string
or by silver paper and to the nearby garbage can
to the joy not even of a child or a madman.

To recur once again to the old Yeats, in one of his most famous poems, "Lapis Lazuli," the poet speaks of ancient sages who are full of laughter. Yeats was not really, at the

end, full of laughter, I think. But the gaiety of which Yeats dreamed, that gaiety is actually here in Montale, and even these private, these notebook poems, so called, are full of that strange, and really almost ineffable gaiety of the very old poet.

Rebecca J. West (essay date 1981)

SOURCE: "Prose Glosses: Is Poetry Still Possible?" in *Eugenio Montale: Poet on the Edge,* Cambridge, Mass.: Harvard University Press, 1981, pp. 136–54.

[*An English journalist, novelist, and critic, West championed equality for women and other liberal political views. In the following excerpt, she studies Montale's prose writings for insights into his thoughts about the function of poetry.*]

In his career as a journalist Montale wrote innumerable prose pieces, some of which have already been anthologized in *Auto da fé* and *Sulla poesia,* others of which have still to be gathered. He has published two collections of short prose: *Farfalla di Dinard,* which is made up of stories and prose pieces, and *Fuori di casa,* which consists of his travel pieces. . . .

I should like to concentrate attention on a few texts that are particularly revealing of Montale's poetics and of his beliefs concerning the function and meaning of poetry. These prose pieces are not necessarily explicit or direct commentaries on individual poems or collections of poetry, although as Cesare Segre and others have shown, this is a legitimate and profitable way of using the prose [Segre, "Invito alla 'Farfalla di Dinard," in *I segni e la critica,* 1970]. However, these pieces do provide us with further insight into Montale's attitudes toward life and art and can be considered, therefore, as *ancilla poesis,* leading to a deeper understanding of his poetry's origins and goals.

The short essay-story "La poesia non esiste" ("Poetry Does Not Exist") was originally published in *Corriere della Sera* on October 5, 1946. It is directly tied to the war, which was an immediate reality in the Italy of 1944, the year in which the story takes place. The setting of the story, Montale's apartment in Florence, draws into its walls the dangers assailing the world outside while containing the more truly interior preoccupations of the poet concerning poetry and its function within the collectivity of people to whom its existence matters. The setting serves as a frame that comments ironically on the dialogue, the former being realistic, very much down-to-earth, and fraught with a sense of the immediate contigencies of personal threat—of the war, in short—while the latter is of the much less tangible realm of intellectual, philosophical discourse, abstract and remote from the battles raging outside. The two are played off one another in a vivacious, even humorous manner, but the essential seriousness of both cannot be ignored.

The season is "the dark winter" of 1944. The narrator has opened his home to those Italians who are being sought by the German army for their partisan activities. These guests include Brunetto, a friend, and several others whom Montale calls, in English, "flying ghosts," men who come and go each evening and whose identities remain unknown to their host. The evening in question is being passed by the radio and the electric heater when suddenly the concierge calls up to warn the men of the arrival of a German soldier. The moment is tense, and the tension is heightened by such phrases as "there was no time to waste"; "what would the friends do?"; "perhaps the German wasn't alone." The frightened guests hasten to hide in a darkened room as their host moves slowly toward the door. He opens it to find a young German officer, "a youth of little more than twenty years of age, almost two meters tall, with a hooked nose like a bird of prey, and two eyes, both timid and wild, under a disordered, brushlike lock of hair." He is holding a roll of paper, which he points toward the narrator as if it were a "colubrina" (a sort of musket). Up to this point in the story we are in the world of action, threat, and uncertainty. The scene might be likened in impact to the opening shorts of Rossellini's *Città aperta* (*Open City*), a film concerning the partisan fight, which depicts men in a situation analogous to that of the three men in Montale's narrative. These first few paragraphs are in fact cinematographic in style. There is sparse descriptive detail, only enough information about the men and the room as is minimally necessary to establish a picture of them. Then come several swift movements or pans: the answering of the telephone, the men's disappearance, the host's quick switching of radio stations, the sound of the doorbell, the unbolting of the door. There is no dialogue. The reader's attention is completely fixed on the opening door and the figure standing at the threshold.

The description of the German, whose appearance reminds the narrator of a "bird of prey" and who points a threatening-looking object at the host, is a masterful cliché in either film or fiction: the climax of suspense, the moment in a movie when the music would swell dramatically and the camera fix on the frightened face of the Italian. The suspense is broken in a most unorthodox fashion by the German's first words: "I am a literary, and I bring you the poems you asked me for." In its tense context this declaration takes on a humorous aspect, so completely inappropriate and unexpected is it. Not only has the German brought poems rather than guns, but he has introduced himself incorrectly as a *letterario,* a "literary." The narrator immediately comments: "Certainly he meant a man of letters." The absurdity of the moment is intensified by this correction, for even in a state of fear the narrator hastens to correct in a mental note the German's bad Italian. This is our first glimpse of the host's dry wit, which becomes more obvious as the story advances. We must now begin to reorient ourselves, just as the narrator must do, for the classic wartime drama has taken a decidedly original turn.

All of this is accomplished in a page and a half; Montale's prose, like his poetry, tends to the understated, using the swift stroke, the minimal. The dialogue, introduced by the German's words, continues in the host's response. "Very flattered," he remarks that the young man's name is not unknown to him: "This is a great honor for me. How

might I be of service?" At this point begins a long paragraph, the essential one, constructed entirely of description and "indirect free discourse." We learn that the German, Ulrich, had written to the narrator several years before concerning his translations of some Italian poetry, and the narrator had in turn asked that the young man send him a collection of Hölderlin's lyrics that were not available in Italy at that time. Ulrich never answered his request but, ironically, has turned up two years later and under the most inappropriate of circumstances with a typed copy of some three hundred pages of the poetry. He apologizes for having based his transcription on the Zinkernagel edition rather than on that of Hellingrath but is confident that "sein gnädiger Kollege" (his esteemed colleague) will be able to order the poems correctly with a few months' work. Ulrich asks for nothing in return, except perhaps for copies of some Italian poems. The irony of the situation is by now rampant; the two scholars are politely exchanging notes while Montale remarks in parentheses that he is in a cold sweat, "and not only in view of the hard work" of selecting appropriate "illustrious moderns" for the eager young German.

The visitor settles in to tell his life story. He says that he arranges concerts on the piazza of the Italian city where he is now stationed; he himself is a musician who plays, the narrator vaguely recalls, "the bugle or the fife." Before the war he was a student of philosophy, dedicated to finding and explaining "the essence of Life" and to disproving the assertion that philosophic speculation is a vicious circle that "bites its own tail, a whirling of thought around itself." He had been disillusioned in his search, however, for the professor under whose tutelage he explored the possibility of the *Dasein*, the "existential I in flesh and blood," took a dislike to him and kindly showed him the door. What was left to him was poetry, which however proved equally disenchanting. A brief if devastating survey follows: Homer was not a man, "and everything that departs from the human results as extraneous to man." The Greek lyrics are hopelessly fragmentary; Pindar's mythical, musical world is no longer ours; Latin oratory is equally out of our reach. Dante, whose name is brought up by the narrator in what one must imagine as a hesitant question, is "grandissimo," but one reads him as a *pensum*; Shakespeare is too natural, Goethe not natural enough. So much for the entire Western poetic tradition. "And the moderns?" the narrator asks, as he pours out the last of the Chianti that has accompanied their conversation. The young man dismisses them with equal dispatch: "They never give the impression of stability; we are too much a party to them to be able to evaluate them." He concludes: "Believe me, poetry doesn't exist . . . and then, then . . . a perfect poem would be like a philosophic system that completely satisfies, it would be the end of life, an explosion, a collapse, and an imperfect poem is not a poem. Better to struggle . . . with the girls."

With these words Ulrich stands, wishes his host a good digestion of Hölderlin, while Montale tells us that he hadn't the courage to reveal that he had stopped studying German two years before, and takes his leave. The narrator then goes into the darkened room where the men have been hiding, and Brunetto asks: "Has your German gone away then? And what did he have to say to you?" The answer is succinct: "He says that poetry doesn't exist." Brunetto's response to this is a simple "ah," accompanied by Giovanni's snores; the two men are sleeping, we are told, "in a very narrow bed."

This story is surely one of the most original and striking illustrations of the dichotomy between art and life as well as a subtly humorous depiction of the ironic relationship of the active to the contemplative life. The evaluation of poetry is presented through several filters: the wartime setting, the tense realities of the apartment hideout, the German's youth and naïveté, the narrator's essential silence, and the partisans' reactions to the German's conclusion that poetry does not exist. Had Montale presented these thoughts on the existence or nonexistence of poetry in a straightforward essay, as in fact he has done elsewhere to some degree, our reception of them would have been entirely different. Here we see the vacuity of the discussion, given the very real issues and threats assailing the men and given Ulrich's extreme youth and idealism. Yet we also understand the human import of the meeting; the enemy is a twenty-year-old boy who has made the trip to the narrator's apartment not to conquer him and his concealed guests but rather to bring him Hölderlin's poetry and perhaps simply to find a kindred soul with whom to discuss those things most real and most essential to him. In spite of Ulrich's negative conclusions concerning the life of poetry, the story shows just how persistently poetry does in fact exist, not certainly as a perfected abstraction, "un'esplosione," but as an eccentric, unexpected, even inappropriate gift emerging out of the darkness of the Florentine evening and disappearing back into it. Nor does poetry in any way alter the reality surrounding it, a reality that turns its back and begins to snore. There is good reason for this indifference: Brunetto and Giovanni have no reason to care about the existence of poetry when their lives are at stake. There are no grand gestures here, no clearly defined heroes or villians. The narrator is a gracious host to the Italian partisans and to the German alike. He is neither a hero nor a coward but quite simply a man capable of seeing the inadequacies of both life and art. The story is a perfect example of Montale's very basic belief in daily decency and a masterful dramatization of his self-portrait as expressed in "Intervista immaginaria": "I have lived my time with the minimum of cowardice that had been allowed to my weak powers, but there are those who did more, even if they did not publish books."

Montale rarely wrote poems as explicitly tied to the war as this prose piece, although **"Finisterre"** and *La bufera* are deeply imbued with the horror and tragedy of the war years. There is, however, a poem in *Quaderno,* written in 1975, which harks back to the First World War, in which Montale saw action. In **"L'eroismo"** (**"Heroism"**) the poet reveals his dreams of glory, encouraged by his beloved Clizia: "Clizia mi suggeriva di ingaggiarmi / tra i guerriglieri di Spagna . . ." (Clizia suggested that I might enlist / with the guerrilla fighters of Spain). But no such glory was his, and he remembers little of his actual military experience except for "futile exertions," "the irksome /

clicking of the gunners." He also recalls "Un prigioniero *mio* / che aveva in tasca un Rilke e fummo amici / per pochi istanti" (*My very own* prisoner / who had Rilke in his pocket and we were friends / for a few instants). Ulrich and the prisoner are spiritually one and the same. Both men emerge from the generalizations of war as sparsely sketched and yet unforgettable human beings, one lugging around his three-hundred-page typescript of Hölderlin and the other his small Rilke. This is where poetry exists not only for Montale but for anyone who recognizes that, as Montale writes in **"The Truth"** in *Quaderno* existence is often nothing more than "una tela di ragno" (a spider's web), infinitely tenuous, subjective, and minimal.

The essay "Tornare nella strada" (To Go Back to the Street) was first published in 1949. It is not, like "Style and Tradition" or "The Solitude of the Artist," usually singled out as an important statement by Montale worthy of translation and redistribution; yet I believe that it is highly revealing of Montale's attitude toward art and art's continuing life. The piece is in part a polemic against what Montale calls "current art," which is characterized by its rejection of form and its attachment to the concepts of immediacy, the ephermal, and the solipsistic. In contrast Montale offers a conservative view of art, which is fully incarnated in form and which truly exists only when it attains "its second and greater life: that of memory and of individual, small circulation."

The essay consists primarily of a definition of this second life as proposed by Montale. He begins by emphasizing the necessity of created art: "The uncreated work of art, the unwritten book, the masterpiece that could have been born and was not born are mere abstractions and illusions." But art does not end with the creation of works, for a work does not fully live until it is "received, understood, or misunderstood by someone: by the public." This public can consist of only one person, "as long as it is not the author himself." Furthermore, the success of art does not depend on the immediate consumption or enjoyment of the work of art "with an instant relationship of cause and effect," but rather "its obscure pilgrimage across the consciousness and the memory of people, its complete reflux back into life whence art itself drew its first nourishment." Montale states, "It is this second moment, of minute consumption and even of misunderstanding, that makes up what interests me the most in art."

The poet then goes on to give several examples of this phenomenon in his own experience: Svevo's *Zeno* always comes to mind when he sees a group of indifferent people following a funeral procession or when the north wind blows; he always sees a face of Piero or Mantegna or thinks of Manzoni's line "era folgore l'aspetto" (her face was a lightning flash) when he meets Clizia or other beloved ladies; Paul Klee's *Zoo* comes to mind when he thinks of strange animals, "zebra or zebu." The issue is not that of easy memorability, for if this were the case "Chiabrera would beat Petrarch, Metastasio would outsell Shakespeare," but of art, which can give to someone a sense of "liberation and of comprehension of the world." What Montale believes in is the essential importance of the "incalculable and absurd existence" of art, which is not necessarily equal to "an objective vitality and importance of art itself." Another series of examples follows: someone can face death for a noble cause while whistling "Funiculì funicolà"; Catullus can come to mind in an austere cathedral, and conversely a religious aria of Handel can accompany a "profane desire"; we can remember a poem by Poliziano "even in days of madness and slaughter." Montale concludes that "everything is uncertain, nothing is necessary in the world of artistic refractions; the only necessity is that such refraction sooner or later be rendered possible."

The essay was written for a newspaper and not as a fully developed excursus on art; I do not therefore want to inflate its content or the depth of its argumentation. It is written well, alternating between discursive prose and striking concrete examples of what Montale himself has experienced as the second life of art. It reveals Montale's readiness to engage in polemics, his ability to take a stand and unequivocally argue its virtues. But what he is arguing here is also very much tied to the values at work in his equivocal, understated poetry: the importance of the marginal, the individual, the incalculable in art as well as in life. These eccentric and minimal qualities must, however, be fully expressed in artistic forms and cannot have meaning if they remain in the realm of the abstract or the mystical. Emotions and virtues or vices are highly abstract things, as are general concepts such as Life and Art, but they can be concretized not in order that their true essence be fixed once and for all but rather to enable them to be shared by others living through them. Given Montale's views on the unreliability of language and his uncertainty concerning history, either individual or collective, it is not surprising that he clings to this essentially minimal life of art, which can be as fraught with "misunderstandings" and contingencies as any communicative act. The central concern is that one be committed to the possibility of some sort of exchange in spite of the necessarily partial and imperfect nature of it.

Montale's own poetry has itself taken on this second life. His flora and fauna (the sunflower, the eel, the mouse, the butterfly); his locales (the customs house, the garden, the seashore); his talismanic objects (the ivory mouse, the shoehorn, the earrings); his beloved women (Clizia, Dora Markus, Gerti, Mosca, Annetta): all these and many more have entered into the psyches and hearts of his readers. I for one experience them as as much a part of my life as actual people, places, and things I know firsthand. They all serve as points of contact; they have taken hold and have thus reentered the cycle of life from which they emerged. They have the power to inform life because they themselves live in poems that make them matter. An indifferent or mediocre rendering of any individual experience or insight will condemn it to death no matter how intensely meaningful it might have been for the author. All people take with them to the isolation and silence of the grave the vital diversity and uniqueness of their own lives unless they are communicated and passed on through words and acts that transcend the death of the body. Like all great artists Montale leaves behind an indelible mark: his art,

which is thoroughly imbued with "that ultimate hypothesis of sociality that an art born from life always has: to return to life, to serve man, to count as something for man."

"Farfalla di Dinard" ("Butterfly of Dinard") is a very brief story that provides the title of the collection of stories first published in 1956. It is the final story of the collection, and its last sentence is beautifully closural: "I bent my head and when I lifted it again I saw that on the vase of dahlias the butterfly was no more." Given the symbolic value of the butterfly in Montale's poetry—in **"Vecchi versi"** and **"Omaggio a Rimbaud"** especially but implicitly in the figure of Clizia, who is herself a creature of flight—the disappearance of this butterfly signifies much more than is expressed on the simple denotative level. The story is both allusive and concrete, as Cesare Segre has pointed out in his article "Invito alla 'Farfalla di Dinard'" [in *Per conoscere Montale*]. It seems almost a poem in prose in its movement from the initial "horizontality" of the opening lines to the "rare and expressive adjectives" and "unexpected metaphors" of its development. But it is also rooted in the terra firma of prosaic irony and the common sense of the waitress who sees no butterfly at all. The story relates the following: A "little saffron-colored butterfly" has visited the narrator each day at his table in a café in Brittany. On the eve of his departure he is seized with the desire to know if it is a sign from his beloved, a "secret message." He decides to ask the waitress if she will check to see if the butterfly continues to appear after his departure, writing him a simple yes or no. "Stuttering," he explains that he is "an amateur entomologist" and asks the favor. The waitress responds in French: "A butterfly? A yellow butterfly?" and adding in Italian, "But I see nothing. Look closer." The butterfly is nowhere to be seen.

The butterfly can be interpreted on many levels: it is a secret message, a mysterious connective link between distant persons, hope, nostalgia, love, poetry. It is also simply a butterfly, a purely coincidental presence that is as meaningless, and eventually as nonexistent, as the waitress's casual comments indicate. This mixture of the real and the imaginary, of tenuous and unironic hope and ironic deflation, is the essential tenor of Montale's poetry from the very first. "Farfalla di Dinard" can therefore be read as a sort of summation in miniature of a poetics centering around a search for some tangible, sure reality to which emotions and images can be attached.

The reality in question is that of the butterfly itself, which might be "*la* farfalla," or "*the* butterfly" (Montale's italics); the search is posited in clearly defined terms of yes and no. The narrator calls the problem "il punto da risolvere" (the point to be resolved). This point concerning the butterfly's existence is related to other points in Montale's poetry: "Ricerco invano il punto onde si mosse / il sangue che ti nutre" (I search in vain for the point whence was moved / the blood that nourishes you); "Una tabula rasa; se non fosse / che un punto c'era, per me incomprensibile, / e questo punto *ti riguardava*" (A tabula rasa; if it weren't / for the fact that there was a point, incomprehensible for me, / and this point *had to do with you*); "A un

157

soffio il pigro fumo trasalisce, / si difende nel punto che ti chiude" (At a puff the lazy smoke quivers, / but persists at the point that hides you), of which Montale wrote in a letter to Bobi Bazlen, "It is clear that *at the point* can have two meanings: *at the moment in which* and *at the place in which,* both legitimate. For Landolfi, this doubt is horrible; for me it is a richness." In the recent poem **"A questo punto"** (**"At This Point"**) in *Diario del'71* the phrase "a questo punto smetti" (at this point stop) is repeated three times and then resolved in the final lines, "A questo punto / guarda can i tuoi occhi e anche senz'occhi" (At this point / look with your own eyes and even without eyes). Certainly not all of these usages of the word are identical, but they are all joined by their essentiality, their use as a term of either temporal or spatial quidity or as the desired resolution of some tension or doubt. But the point cannot be resolved in the story; an unequivocal answer is not possible, perhaps because the butterfly exists only for Montale, perhaps because it flew away before the waitress could note its presence. Its very existence is put in doubt, and the essential question of the meaning of its presence is thus vitiated and rendered unanswerable.

As Segre points out in his article, *Farfalla di Dinard* as a collection provides us with "a precious hermeneutical instrument" in our comprehension of Montale's poetry, in part because the "motive-occasion" for what will eventually be elaborated into poetry is almost always explicitly given in the stories. In the title story we are told about the butterfly and its importance to the poet in an open manner that helps us determine its symbolic significance in the less accessible poems. This is the only kind of biography that can provide meaningful illumination of the poetry. In his explanation of the "Motet" that begins "La speranza di pure rivederti" (The hope of even seeing you again), Montale also provides some information as to the autobiographical origins of the highly elusive series. He was forced to do so given the erroneous critical attempts to explain so many elements in the poems, especially the "two jackals on a leash" of the above mentioned "Motet." The jackals that Montale actually saw in Modena he experienced as "an emblem, an occult citation, a *senhal*," just as the butterfly of the story is felt to be an omen, the immediate reason for such a reaction being the fact that "Clizia loved odd animals." Montale bewails the "mental torpidity" of critics not because they did not come up with the correct explanation of the "Motet" but because they asked the wrong questions. He admits that there may have been too much "concentration" in his poetic rendering of the experience but counters:

> In the face of this poem criticism acts like that visitor at an art show who, looking at two paintings, for example a still life of mushrooms or a landscape with a man who is walking along holding an open umbrella, might ask himself: How much do those mushrooms cost per kilo? Were they gathered by the painter or bought at the market? Where is that man going? What's his name? Is the umbrella made of real silk or a synthetic?

Montale concludes the article arguing for a *juste milieu* between understanding nothing and understanding too much, for "on either side of this mean there is no salvation for poetry or for criticism."

Taking off from this defense of the so-called obscure "Motet" Claire Huffman asked Montale if the reader must "limit his response to the poems to the connotative and Montalian levels of poetic meaning, or is there a middle ground? Can one assign a referential value to the 'ideological phantasmata,' and perhaps even to the 'facts, situations and things' of the poetry?" Montale answers that "an explanation is always possible as long as one does not go as far as chronicle. (Who was Clizia? Who was the Fox? Who was the girl of **"After a Flight"**?) I myself could not say, since they were transformed unbeknownst to them" ["Eugenio Montale: Questions, Answers, and Contexts," in *Yearbook of Italian Studies* (1973–1975)]. The point is to ask questions pertinent to the poetry and not to the satisfaction of extraliterary curiosity concerning the life of the poet. In this sense "Butterfly of Dinard" provides us with essential directives in our approach to the poetry, for the disappearance of the butterfly—of the real, seen butterfly, that is—is inevitable and even necessary to its elaboration into poetic symbol. The butterfly, Clizia, the Fox, even Mosca are all part of a stylistic adventure; and although they, like unnumerable other figures, places, and occurrences in the poems, were no doubt real and directly experienced, they all took flight away from chronicle and toward the realm of a lyrical existence. This is an opposite, although not opposing movement from the one described in "Tornare alla strada": there art was seen as feeding back into life; here, life feeds into art. The space of conjunction must be understood as betwixt and between the two, in that zone in which both the radical disjunctions and the vital links between life and art can be sought out, expressed, and nourished.

> **One important point is that Montale must be seen as a European writer, both as poet and critic, rather than as a regional or even an Italian one**.
>
> —*Rebecca West*

Montale's Nobel Prize speech "É ancora possible la poesia?" ("Is Poetry Still Possible?") was made on December 12, 1975. It is a curious piece, lacking the organized and cohesive quality of so much of Montale's critical writing. This can be explained, at least in part, by the fact that it was written in some haste and in the emotion of the moment. The poet writes in it that he had thought of entitling the talk "Will Poetry Be Able to Survive in the Universe of Mass Media?" and this interest in the world of today with its plethora of mass media is evident throughout the speech. But it also looks back to the poetry of the past and to Montale's conception of the origins of poetry.

Montale begins with the assertion that the world may soon experience "a historic shift of colossal proportions." This change, he insists, will signal not the end of man but rather the end of communal and social systems as we know them. What the result of such a change will be for mankind is not clear, although Montale suggests that the "age-old diatribe as to the meaning of life" may well cease, at least for a few centuries. He does not develop these thoughts any further, being "neither a philosopher, sociologist, nor moralist." He turns rather to his own area of competence: poetry, "an absolutely useless product, but scarcely ever harmful and this is one of its claims to nobility." In response to the judgment of his own production as being meager, he counters that "fortunately poetry is not merchandise." But what is it then? Originally it was the result of the desire to join a vocal sound to the beat of primitive music; "only much later could words and music be written down in some way and distinguished one from the other." So poetry is first sound; then it becomes visual, with "its formal schemes" having much to do with its "visibility." After the invention of printed books poetry can be defined as that which is "vertical" and does not fill up all the "blank space" (as Montale insists, "even certain empty spaces have a value"), unlike prose, which fills up all the space of a page and gives no indications as to its "pronounceability." Around the end of the nineteenth century the established forms of poetry no longer satisfied either the eye or the ear, and the crisis of form began, extending into all of the arts. Montale wonders what "rebirth or resurrection" might arise out of the so-called death of art, art that has become "consumer items, to be used and then thrown away."

The next section of the talk begins with a critique of the negative effect the contemporary attitudes of despair, confusion, and immediate gratification have had on art, which today, Montale asserts, has become "a show . . . that performs a kind of psychic massages on the spectator or listener or reader." This art is "sterile" ' and shows "a tremendous lack of trust in life." What can be the place of poetry, "the most discreet of the arts . . . the fruit of solitude and of accumulation?" Poetry has kept up with the times, insisting on its purely visual or purely auditory nature; it has also broken down the old barriers between itself and prose. Montale insists that there are innumerable roads open to this "mainstream" poetry but that it will no doubt be ephemeral, producing few works that will survive the test of time. There will also be created an art, however, that is "control and reflection," a marginal art that "refuses with horror the term *production*; that art that rises up almost by a miracle and seems to fix an entire epoch and an entire linguistic and cultural situation." This poetry will be capable of surviving its own time and even of returning many years after its birth to influence the art of the future.

Montale next cites a poem by Du Bellay that found in Walter Pater its interpreter, and thus in a certain sense its life, centuries after its composition, proving that "great poetry can die, be reborn, die again, but it will always remain one of the highest accomplishments of the human spirit." The poet concludes that many contemporary books of poetry "might endure through time," yet there is still the question of what that endurance will mean. Will these

books be able to bring anything meaningful to the future? The answer not only for poetry but for all art is directly tied to "the human condition." For Montale the destiny of art must be seen as analogous to the destiny of mankind, the ultimate question remaining whether "the people of tomorrow . . . will be able to resolve the tragic contradictions with which we have struggled from the very first day of Creation."

This speech is disturbing and unsatisfactory in many ways: first because it shows Montale at his most querulously conservative; second because it raises questions and issues that are not answered in any truly illuminating manner. It is clear that Montale does not like contemporary experiments in art, which he considers for the most part to be empty and self-indulgent. This is certainly his prerogative. I take issue not with his view but rather with the way in which he presents it. Either a satiric or parodic portrait of the contemporary artist or a full-fledged, developed critique would have been much more effective. What we have instead are potshots—brief sallies and equally swift retreats from the subject at hand. For example, Montale speaks of the "portrait of a mongoloid" on display in an art show, "a subject *très dégoutant*," and even more so when it was discovered to be not "a portrait at all, but the unfortunate one in the flesh." The poet ironically comments, "But why not? Art can justify anything." The poet also criticizes contemporary music that is "solely noisy and repetitive" and appeals to young people who "come together in order to exorcise the horror of their solitude." These examples of the degradation of art are the kind that bring knowing and even complacent nods of recognition and agreement from certain members of the audience but that do not push the implications of their assertion far enough. Why should we refuse to accept such portraits and such music as art? The ironic "art can justify everything" means its opposite of course; but if art does not justify anything and everything, who determines its limits, who polices its borders? If experimentation is disallowed, might not the very vitality of art be destroyed? In playing devil's advocate I am myself committing the very sin of which I accuse Montale in not offering answers to these and other fundamental questions raised in his speech. Yet I believe that the criticism stands: having decided to confront such vast issues as the present and future status of art and the survival of poetry in today's and tomorrow's world of mass communication, Montale ought to have equivocated less and provided more than the very general, although not untrue, conclusion that great art is always privileged and "rises up almost miraculously."

These last comments point to the essential defect of the speech. It is an example of what is atypical of Montale, both in his prose writings and his poetry: that is, an inclusive, panoramic theme and the epigrammatic, generalizing style that results. Thus the Nobel speech is a sort of negative reinforcement of that which is strong in and vital to Montale's work: the specific, the minimal, the concrete, the eccentric. The first three prose pieces I have discussed are all excellent examples of these virtues on both a thematic and a stylistic level. They all treat circumscribed topics using either fictional or discursive particulars that illustrate convincingly the issues in question. They are all brief, concise, and minimal, not in the subjects or experiences they deal with but in the presentation of them. Perhaps sensing the momentous quality attached to the Nobel speech, Montale sought to universalize his usually very particularized tone, with less than convincing results.

This criticism pertains to the last collections of poetry also; the poems in *Diario* and *Quaderno* that are least successful are those in which Montale gives in to a sententious, moralizing tone and encapsulates his thoughts in aphoristic verses. Irony and flashes of lyricism save the collections from this tendency, but in this essay such elements are missing. It is understandable that the poet should feel the push to summarize; the weight of more than sixty years as a poet and his tremendous reputation conspire toward that end. In the recent interview with Claire Huffman, Montale was asked: "What things (or questions) interest you the most? What things don't interest you at all?" He laconically answered: "Practical issues, concerning survival (material survival). The fortunes of humanity are outside my area of competence." In the speech just discussed he says he is no philosopher, no moralist. Both of these assertions are somewhat contradicted by Montale's recent poetry, his comments on his work, and the Nobel speech. I have chosen to criticize the speech in particular not because it has some sort of eminent position in Montale's prose, although I fear that many people will read it in isolation and thus assign special weight to it, but because it represents those philosophizing, moralizing stands in the late Montale that do not lead to felicitous artistic or critical products.

There are many provisional conclusions concerning Montale's prose that can be offered even after limiting the discussion to only a few examples of his fiction and critical writings. One important point is that Montale must be seen as a European writer, both as poet and critic, rather than as a regional or even an Italian one. When *Ossi di seppia* first appeared there was a tendency to see it as a volume that fit into a Ligurian tradition, but it was soon recognized that such an approach was much too limiting, if not erroneous. Already in the first collection Montale's ties to a much wider poetic and philosophical tradition were evident, in spite of his undeniable interest in writing of his place of birth, the sea, and the particular local landscape of which he later wrote in **"Dov'era il tennis"** (**"Where the Tennis Court Was"**) in *La bufera e altro*: "It is strange to think that each of us has a landscape like this, event if very different, that will have to remain *his* own immutable landscape."

Le occasioni and *La bufera* made it even more evident that Montale was a cosmopolitan poet participating in a much broader tradition than simply the Italian one, a fact explicitly pointed out by the poet himself in his choice of epigraphs for these collections from Spanish, English, and French literature as well as in his mention of the French symbolists, Gerard Manley Hopkins, Keats, and others in his explications of certain of the poems contained therein. His *Quaderno di traduzioni* (*Translation Notebook*) also reveals his very active interest in the poetry of other

Western traditions, as do his many pieces on poets from Valéry and Prévert to Ezra Pound, Auden, Roethke, and T. S. Eliot. The prose pieces discussed here are typical in the range of interests they reveal: German poetry in "La poesia non esiste"; travel in France in "Farfalla di Dinard"; modern painting and music in "Tornare nella strada"; contemporary art in "É ancora possibile la poesia?" Even more so than in the poetry it is in the prose that we see the eclectic and wide-ranging culture of Montale, which inevitably feeds his verses and gives his work a frame of reference far beyond the confines of Italy. The Italian lyric tradition is of course an extremely rich and varied one, ranging from Dante to Petrarch to the Baroque poets to Leopardi and the great triumvirate of Carducci, Pascoli, and D'Annunzio, not to mention the moderns—futurists, crepuscularists, hermeticists, and so on. I am not suggesting that Montale has divorced himself from this tradition or that he did not make use of it in elaborating his own poetry. But what is so clearly evident, especially in his autobiographical, fictional, and critical writings, is his assimilation of other linguistic, literary, and cultural materials and his constant view of artistic activity as transcending national boundaries.

This cosmopolitan orientation is no doubt motivated in part by temperament and purely personal tastes. In a general sense Montale's recourse to other traditions and cultures is also tied to what he has called "an unfittedness . . . a maladjustment both psychological and moral" that from the first made him feel in disharmony with his immediate environment. In a more specific sense we can see in his view of the Italian language another source of discontent, for he says of it, "I wanted to wring the neck of the eloquence of our old aulic language," using interestingly enough a Verlainian turn of phrase. He further comments on his attitude toward Italian that "in the new book [*Occasions*] I continued my battle to dig out another dimension from our heavy polysyllabic language, a language that seemed to me to refuse an experience such as mine . . . I have often cursed our language, but in it and through it I came to recognize myself as incurably Italian: and without regrets." Here is evident a combative resistance to Italian, Montale's native language, as well as a final capitulation without regrets to its inevitable hegemony.

A humorous piece included in the collection *Farfalla di Dinard* reveals Montale's rather shamefaced admiration of the English style. I say "shamefaced" because the self-parody is rampant, and yet the very real attachment to such a style is equally evident. The story is entitled "Signore inglese" ("English Gentleman"), and this gentleman practices a new sport: that of being a "fake Englishman." He does this in Switzerland because an Englishman in England is nothing special and because he needs a neutral space in which to carry out his fiction. Montale writes that he has been trying for years to emulate the man but without success. What follows is a merciless depiction of English habits: the renunciation of any athletic activities, the daily consumption of tea and cakes, the maintenance of a stoic silence broken only by some *chiú* (a clipped "thank you") if anyone should speak to him or do him some small service. Montale concludes that "in an imaginary club of fake Englishmen the presidency would be his and the vice-presidency would be mine." The story is entirely humourous but it has its origins in the poet's real fascination with and admiration for the laconic, absolutely un-Mediterranean English style.

If Montale can be associated with a European perspective, it is very much an old-world one—that is, of a culture and style particular to the nineteenth- and early-twentieth-century intellectual. The new world, America, held great interest for many Italian writers of the thirties and forties, especially Cesare Pavese, and that interest resulted in the translation of American classics, in travel books, and in the general elaboration of a myth of America. Although Montale translated some American literature, both prose and poetry, and spent a few days in New York, he never shared this American fever, a fact entirely consonant with his conservative and deeply old-world character. The world and culture in which he feels most at home are those of the people evoked in the poem **"Lettera" ("Letter")** in *Satura*: "i veri e i degni avant le déluge" (the true and the deserving *avant le déluge*). This may seem at odds with his modernity as a poet, but I do not believe that we must see a contradiction here, for his conservation has always been tempered with a most acute awareness of the present moment. Montale does not express a belief in the superiority of the good old days but rather points to and seconds certain fundamental values and styles as timeless and therefore universally valid. His distrust of and even disdain for contemporary manifestations of power, immediacy, speed, and self-gratification show by contrast his sustained belief in the minor virtues of patience, painstaking care in and dedication to one's craft, awareness of one's limits, and daily decency. There is undeniably a bit of the snob in Montale, but he has never sought to hide this facet of his personality. His prose works display his European, cosmopolitan, conservative, and even slightly aristocratic tastes and interests. In them we see a mind that has certain affinites with the poetic genius behind the collections of verse; we also learn much from them of the man behind the hermetic, ironic poetic *I*.

In his fictional-autobiographical prose in the collections *Farfalla di Dinard* and *Fuori di casa* Montale reveals his penchant for sature, irony, and humor, a voice that is fully developed poetically in the latest poems. In his journalistic and critical writings he shows his constant involvement in the past, present, and future of art in the Western world. It is clear that his greatness lies in his poetry, for although he is an accomplished raconteur and a perceptive critic, he is not exceptionally gifted as either. This is understandable, for sustained and rich prose demands a synthetic vision of a believed and believable reality—not realism necessarily but the ability to build a complete world. Montale's description of the stories of *Farfalla* as "culs-de-lampe" (vignettes) is apt. They are *occasioni,* more discursively presented than in the poems of course but nonetheless brief and sketchy pieces that find their total meaning in their collectivity and in their interrelationship with the poetry they directly or indirectly gloss. The poet's critical writings also tend toward the sketch, the single insight, the unsystematic presentation of the opinions

and insights of a cultivated but not especially privileged reader of both texts and events. This emphasis on the seemingly minimal in both his poetry and prose is perhaps the most essential aspect of the Montalian voice. Thematically, stylistically, and philosophically his writing is the expression of a long dedication to the value, and indeed necessity, of what is individual and unique in both art and life. For Montale, if poetry is still possible it is because it is born, lives, dies, and is born again through wars, great social, cultural, and even spiritual upheavals, not as an essential issue or as a force for change and final revelation but as "an entity of which we know very little." This phrase could well be applied to the human race itself, so convinced are we of our central and superior position, "our certainty or illusion of believing ourselves to be privileged," when in fact our salvation, and poetry's, lies instead in the courageous recognition of how minimal is our self-knowledge, how deeply marginal and inevitably ambiguous is that which we seek to make essential and unequivocal: our own existence.

Henry Gifford (lecture date 1983)

SOURCE: "An Invitation to Hope: Eugenio Montale," in *Grand Street,* Vol. 3, No. 1, Autumn, 1983, pp. 91–111.

[*An English educator and critic, Gifford has written extensively about Russian literature. In the following essay, he provides an overview of Montale's verse, noting a message of hope implicit in his works.*]

The critic Sergio Solmi, long acquainted with Eugenio Montale and much appreciated by him, opens an account of his poetry with these words:

> There were few things we believed in when young; but among those few we certainly did believe in poetry.
> ["La poesia di Montale" (1957), in *Scrittori negli anni,* 1963]

He spoke for a generation that had seen two different kinds of disaster befall Italy: the defeat and demoralization of Caporetto; the triumph, and the moral degradation following upon it, of Fascism. His statement recalls the question once put to Nadezhda Mandelstam by a woman teacher in the provinces: how was it that "all those students who thirst after truth and righteousness are always so keen on poetry?" Living through the black comedy of Italian Fascism is not to be compared with what Russian intellectuals had to endure in the same years. Until the Republic of Salò, set up in 1943, the oppression in Italy had more in common with the rule of the Romanovs than with that of Stalin. This can be illustrated from an incident in Montale's own life. In 1929 (the very year when Soviet writers first came to feel the intimations of terror) he was appointed director of a famous library in Florence, where Leopardi had once held a post. Three names were submitted for a final choice to the *podestà,* Count Giuseppe della Gherardesca, who asked if it could be assumed that all belonged to the party. After some hesitation the scholar reporting to him had to confess that the third candidate, Montale, did not. Whereupon Della Gherardesca said, with a smile: "*E allora nominiamo il terzo.*" It was not until the end of 1938 that "*il terzo*" was dismissed as unfit to carry out the duties incumbent upon him, "for political reasons."

Still, even if Montale was in acute danger from the regime only during the last months of Fascist rule, his poetry meant so much to those of the same generation and others that followed, because it expressed with a "relentless lucidity" the moral predicament of all Italians who "thirsted after truth and righteousness." From the moment when his first book, *Ossi di seppia,* appeared in 1925, Montale became the poet with most to say to contemporaries who would heed him. A man who accepted—and valued—isolation, he yet found himself at the center of imaginative life in his country. This was a paradox Montale understood very well.

A "relentless lucidity"—that phrase is from an article he wrote soon after the death of Italo Svevo, whose characteristic he held it to be. Mainly owing to a couple of appreciative notices by Montale, late in 1925 and early in 1926, Svevo at last achieved recognition throughout Italy—although as a native of Trieste this could never have come to him easily, living partly as he did in a Germanic culture to which writers like Kafka and Musil also belonged. What Montale admired above all in Svevo was the willingness to abide his time. The two novels he wrote in the 1890s had sunk without trace, except in his native city. Then, after twenty-five years, he published *La coscienza di Zeno* in 1923, and the two earlier novels did what Henry James had hoped for one day in the case of his own unappreciated novels in the 1880s: they "kicked off their tombstones." Svevo thus demonstrated, according to Montale, his "timeliness," and that is "always, in art, the sign of an authentic figure." Those who take immense pains to "fabricate" their literary selves "always arrive a minute late. Laboriously they seize fortune by the forelock. To others Poetry (even without fortune) simply offers herself." Svevo did not care for verse—he hoped Montale would soon "pass on to a more rational form of expression." But Montale recognized in him "the poet that he was even though thinking he abhorred poetry." Svevo impressed Montale as a man "always basically sure of having trodden the right road, the road of truth." He had been ruled by the necessities of his art, as every poet must be.

A writer from Trieste, Montale maintains, is "closely tied to the life, the usage and the difficult destiny of his city." Montale himself had an intimate but not constricting bond with a particular region, the Ligurian coast, where for a few miles north of Spezia are to be found the Cinque Terre, rocky, still fairly inaccessible in the days of his youth, the haunt of fishermen and peasants who had to work a soil as sparse as any in the peninsula. It might have been in Calabria; it might even, he adds, have served as a substitute for Castile: "here Pabst's Don Quixote could have found his most suitable setting." The hint of Castile is enough to recall another poet who encountered his personal landscape in such a primitive scene—Antonio

Machado. As a boy Montale left Genoa every year to spend his summers there, and the austerity of the Ligurian littoral, with its "nests of falcons and gulls," seems to have determined, or perhaps confirmed, a tone in Montale, a regard for harsh fact, a distrust of unthinking fluency. This earned him the reputation of a "negative" poet, deliberately prosaic, whose work imparted, in Gianfranco Contini's words, "the sense of a life and nature" that were "*petrose*" ["Introduzione a *Ossi di seppia*," *Esercizi di lettura,* 1974], of a stony intransigence, like the terrain that had fostered him. Who could have guessed that Montale's first ambition had been to appear on the opera stage, with a strong temptation, as he confesses, to the histrionic?

Svevo, Montale notes, had to endure the dominance in fiction, after the first two novels had failed, of Gabriele D'Annunzio with his cult of the superman. All the more remarkable was the "nervous modernity" of those neglected novels. Montale himself in the early 1920s found it necessary to free his imagination from the oppressive eloquence of D'Annunzio, as theatrical a figure as any exponent of *bel canto* in the opera house. It is, of course, to Giuseppe Ungaretti that the credit belongs for having brought back to Italian poetry emphasis on the individual words in sparse clauses, so that maximum meaning could be restored to them. Ungaretti published his collected verse for the years 1914 to 1919, mostly on wartime experience as an infantryman, under the title *L'Allegria.* It has been said by Arshi Pipa, in his book *Montale and Dante* that, whereas Ungaretti performed "a kind of laboratory work" with poetic language, "dissolving the lyric phrase into its elements," Montale "dug beneath, and discovered its roots." Both men were concerned to make, as Montale says in an essay of 1925, "Style and Tradition," "an effort towards simplicity and clarity, at the cost of seeming poverty-stricken." Twenty years later, in another article, "Intentions"—an interview of the most satisfactory kind, being written by himself with every question reduced to a row of dots—Montale said: "I wanted to wring the neck of the eloquence in our old courtly language, even at the risk of a counter-eloquence."

Ossi di seppia means "cuttlefish bones." In a somewhat early poem **"Riviere"** (**"Shores"**) which Montale placed at the end of the volume perhaps because of its optimism, which he later dismissed as "premature," the image makes an appearance:

> Oh allora sballottati
> come l'osso di seppia dalle ondate
> svanire a poco a poco . . .
>
> [Oh then thrown about
> like the cuttlefish bone by the waves
> to fade away little by little . . .]

G. S. Singh in *Eugenio Montale,* his detailed survey of Montale's poetry, prose, and critical writings up to 1973, indicates that the phrase "*gli ossi delle seppie*" may have drifted to him out of a poem by D'Annunzio. It is a deliberately prosaic title for the collection, yet in this concluding poem, which looks back to his boyhood, when he was "a bewildered adolescent," the image has been transformed by a romantic dream, of merging ("fading away," and elsewhere "slowly dying with a smile") into the coastal scene. The poem, with its hope of healing and restoration—"my spirit no longer divided"—cannot bear up against the force of denial in the rest of the volume, which it tries to reverse. Montale had found the essential note of *Ossi di seppia* in a very well-known lyric, the only one surviving from the period before he entered the army in 1917. This had been written in the previous year, when he was twenty, and Singh justly notes the "maturity and self-control" of the poem. It describes a desolate and sultry scene on the Ligurian coast, at noon, when all the poet can do is *"Meriggiare pallido e assorto,"* "pale and preoccupied" seek the shade from a garden wall, listening, not unlike Leopardi in *L'infinito,* to the small sounds of life in a solitary place. But whereas Leopardi was content to drown his thought in the contemplation of infinity, Montale is left with a *"triste meraviglia,"* a sad wonderment that human existence should mean no more than *"questo seguitare una muraglia / che ha in cima cocci aguzzi di bottiglia":* "following a wall / topped with jagged pieces of bottle-glass."

There is good reason to bring in Leopardi when considering Montale's first book. What he may have owed to certain immediate predecessors or to older contemporaries like the other Ligurian poets should not be overlooked; but the challenging presence over against, rather than in, *Ossi di seppia* is Leopardi. Ugo Foscolo, twenty years senior to Leopardi, was also much admired by Montale as a writer who never repeated himself, thus giving "a prodigious lesson." But Leopardi's unflinching endurance, the classical serenity of his despair, appealed to Montale's own instincts. Matthew Arnold greatly respected Leopardi for "a grave fulness of knowledge, an insight into the real bearings of the questions which as a sceptical poet he raises, a power of seizing the real point, a lucidity . . ." All this issued in "the sense for form and style." Only one of those phrases should, I think, be modified for Montale—"a *grave* fulness of knowledge." The adjective betrays that inveterate wish for the ennoblement of poetry by a critic who thought "seriousness" must always be "high." Otherwise, even the incomplete Montale of *Ossi di seppia* is well described. His skepticism was shared, as Solmi has testified, by a whole generation, and it became more than ever needful under the mendacious rule of Fascism. Montale's declaration in the poem that opens the section of *Ossi di seppia* from which the book takes its title defines a poetic method and accordingly a moral stance:

Non domandarci la formula che mondi possa aprirti,
sì qualche storta sillaba e secca come un ramo.
Codesto solo oggi possiamo dirti,
cio che *non* siamo, cio che *non* vogliamo.

[Don't ask from us the formula that can reveal
     worlds to you,
rather a few deformed syllables dry as a branch.
This is all that today we can tell you,
What we are *not,* and do *not* desire.]

The first stanza of this poem dismisses a kind of verse that Montale feels can no longer be written, whereby the formless modern spirit (*"l'amino nostro informe"*) would, through ministration of the word, stand foursquare and self-assured. Even so, in the glory of self-affirmation, it would resemble "a crocus / lost in the middle of a dusty meadow." Sappho once compared a bride to the hyacinth in the hills which the shepherds tread down. Montale's crocus is not necessarily pathetic in that way, but its appearance in such arid surroundings may be called ironic. Yet to "declare and shine forth" might seem the natural ambition of a poet, especially when he uses the language that had been Dante's. The path of negation, though the one honorable path for that time, must lead eventually to some kind of transcendent vision, if the poetic impulse is not to be deeply frustrated.

[In *Esercizi di lettura*] Gianfranco Contini has discussed this problem in relation to Ungaretti. He quotes various comments from Leopardi about the necessity, even when a work describes "the nullity of things," for some "passion or illusion" that may console. Leopardi saw clearly that the imagination cannot achieve anything without "an air of prosperity," "a vigor of spirit"—more than that, a "gleam" of "gaiety" (*allegrezza*). It is precisely such animation and buoyancy that enabled Samuel Johnson to tread briskly the dark corridors of *The Vanity of Human Wishes.* Montale's attitude in *Ossi di seppia* is rather one of *atonia,* "want of tone," or depression. He has "often met with the evil of life" (*"Spesso il male di vivere ho incontrato"*); he can foresee, in these years, only one "miracle," which would be the revelation of "the nothingness" at his back (*"il nulla alle mie spalle"*) and how, after this, accept the "customary deception" of trees, houses, and hills?

The image that best conveys his sense of being condemned to impotence without hope is that of the wheel, stamped indelibly in the line from a later poem, on Bank Holiday 1933 at Eastbourne:

Vince il male . . . La ruota non s' arresta.

[Evil prevails . . . The wheel is not stayed.]

Ossi di seppia, anticipating this in one of its most memorable lyrics, *"Cigola la carrucola del pozzo"* ("Creaks the pulley of the well"), describes a fleeting vision that memory brings up with the full bucket. When he leans forward to the girl's image there, the wheel scrapes once more, distance intervenes, and she is lost in the black depths:

Ah che già stride
la ruota, ti ridona all' atro fondo,
visione, una distanza ci divide.

It was, of course, far from true that the language of this first volume would be only "a few deformed syllables dry as a branch." Montale, we know, had suspected that the strangling of eloquence could make room for "a countereloquence." His diction was "dry" in the sense of being restrained and very accurate; "deformed" only in the eyes of contemporary readers who were shocked by his literalness—how could he end the poem **"Delta,"** so full of passionate longing, with "the whistle of a tug," or write of little boys looking out for a stray eel in half-dried-up puddles? When **Ossi di seppia** came out, Croce's famous distinction between "poetry" and "non-poetry" made the understanding of Montale's purpose difficult. Yeats complained of T. S. Eliot that "in describing this life that has lost heart his own art seems grey, cold, dry." It seems more than the coincidence it must be that Eliot in his "Rhapsody on a Windy Night" should have given prominence to an image recalling Montale's definition of his own style:

> The memory throws up high and dry
> A crowd of twisted things;
> A twisted branch upon the beach . . .

Neither Eliot nor Montale was satisfied to wander perpetually in the desert. Their "stony" despair was impatient for affirmation; and when such moments became possible—"the infirm glory of the positive hour"—the poetic cripple (as Montale pretends to define himself) would throw away his crutches and stride into a new and legitimate eloquence.

At this stage he still has to proceed by hints and gestures:

> Bene non seppi, fuori del prodigio
> che schiude la divina Indifferenza:
> era la statua nella sonnolenza
> del meriggio, e la nuvola, e il falco alto levato.
>
> [Good I have not known, apart from the marvel
> that reveals the divine Indifference:
> it was the statue in the drowsiness
> of noonday, and the cloud, and the hawk lifted high.]

There is a complete mastery in those lines. Montale, as Singh observes, must be counted among the poets who are "born mature." This very modest epiphany follows upon three images of the evil in life he has met with ("*il male di vivere . . . incontrato*"): a stream choked in spate, a leaf scorched and rolled up like paper, a felled horse. The "divine Indifference" may sound like one of Hardy's abstractions, yet Montale's doubt is more delicately held in play—there has been a "marvel" however ambiguous; the capital letter of Indifference seems not the product of an ironic scheme like Hardy's but a concession to the possibly divine. Both **"Cigola la carrucola del pozzo"** and **"Vento e bandiere"** (**"Wind and Flags"**) tell of a moment that is then swept away—as the latter poem protests, "Alas, never twice in the same way / does time order the grains." Here the "marvel" is suggested by the gathering confidence of that last line:

> del meriggio, e la nuvola, e il falco alto levato,

as it rises to soar with the bird.

The amplest gesture in the volume takes the form of a lyrical sequence—nine poems which resemble nine stanzas of a formal ode—addressed to the Mediterranean. The sea is nearly always within sight in **Ossi di seppia**: "The house of my faraway summers," he tells it, "was beside you, as you know, / in the land where the sun burns / and midges cloud the air." For Montale it is an "ancient" sea, and the language it has given him, "words . . . nourished by fatigues and silences," can be recognized by "a fraternal heart" as "tasting of Greek salt." He would like to feel "rough and essential" like the pebbles rolled by the sea, instead of "a man who intently studies / in himself, in others, the tumult / of fleeting life"—this "petty ferment of my heart" which is but a moment of the sea's greater turmoil. From the sea he has learned to find also in himself its "perilous law: to be vast and manifold / and at the same time stable." It had given him once visions of "*la patria sognata*," "the homeland of which you dream." Out of its upheaval has risen the "evidence," and the exile has gone back once more to an innocent world, "*nel paese incorrotto*." The sea may scatter, if it so cares, "*questa debole vita che si lagna*," "this puny life that complains," as a sponge cancels the scrawl on a blackboard. But in the last lines of the sequence Montale has discovered his purpose:

> Bene lo so: bruciare,
> questo, non altro, è il mio significato.
>
> [I understand it well: to burn,
> this, nothing else, is what I am here for.]

The Mediterranean is undoubtedly a tour de force, and its flowing energy and articulated grace deny everything he says in the sequence about his "stunted rhythm" and "stammering utterance" (*"balbo parlare"*), the "wornout dictionary letters," the only words available to him which like a prostitute are there for the first bidder to take. However, the sequence, in spite of its powerful affirmation at the end, has not overcome the doubts that recur with the latest poem in the volume, **"Arsenio,"** whose protagonist, "a reed that drags along its own roots," (*"giunco . . . che le radici / con se trascina"*), is one too familiar with "the fever of immobility" (*"delirio . . . d'immobilità"*). In **"The House by the Sea,"** (**"Casa sul mare"**), written one year after *The Mediterranean,* he is once more resigned to the rigor of senseless time, like the waterwheel that turns and turns. His companion asks him whether all things vanish in the mist of memory. He would like to reply that they do not, but all he can do is give her the "avid hope" which he has exhausted for himself:

> Il cammino finisce a queste prode
> che rode la marea col moto alterno.
> Il tuo cuore vicino che non m'ode
> salpa già forse per l'eterno.
>
> [The journey ends on these shores
> which the tide erodes with alternate motion.
> Your heart at my side that does not hear me
> already perhaps weighs anchor for the eternal.]

Not the journey itself, but one important stage of it, had ended with **Ossi di seppia**. It was a remarkable first book, so fully realized that its effect was irresistible. *Ossi di seppia,* like Pasternak's *My Sister Life* in those years, or Eliot's *Poems 1909–1925,* announced a new presence in poetry, a voice whose authority was not to be disputed, because it spoke not only for itself but intuitively for the time. Like the other two, Montale had created a personal style which others found themselves fascinated by: it became the poetic primer, as Osip Mandelstam said of Pasternak's volume, for a generation. Montale had greatly enlarged the scope of verse, by his readiness to combine the prosaic with the learned. Like the other two poets, he knew instinctively how to innovate with an underlying sense of tradition. But *Ossi di seppia,* out of which grows the achievement of his next two volumes, *Le occasioni* (1928–1939) and *La bufera e altro* (1940–1954), still had not discovered what he spoke of in the poem **"On the Threshold"** (**"In limine"**) that opens this first book—"the saving phantom," (*"il fantasma che ti salva"*).

From the moment when his first book, *Ossi di seppia,* appeared in 1925, Montale became the poet with most to say to contemporaries who would heed him. A man who accepted—and valued— isolation, he yet found himself at the center of imaginative life in his country.

—Henry Gifford

Now he must recognize and seize the "occasions" on which this phantom reveals itself. The poetry that results is more difficult than *Ossi di seppia*: Montale's quest is almost bafflingly personal, it no longer permits him the logical ordering and firm declarations of his first volume. Always in himself withdrawn and rather inscrutable, he had felt like one living in a glass bell, and during his twenty years in Florence he tried, as he says, "to live with the detachment of a foreigner, a Browning." At the same time he wanted to write a "purer" poetry, one that would "contain its motifs without revealing them, or rather blurting them out."

[In "Le occasioni di Montale," in *Scrittori negli anni*] Sergio Solmi remarked that in *Le occasioni* "the dimensions of a personal destiny" begin to show themselves. He quoted an observation of Rilke's, about the "unique reality," not fully comprehensible and rightly so in Rilke's opinion, which is expressed by art the deeper it goes. Montale says in his "imaginary interview" that for modern man there is no distinction between the outside world and his inner self; and "the poet's task is to find an exact truth (*una verità puntuale*), not a general truth." The notation of Montale's exact personal truth becomes very fine—the more elusive their import, the more salient and clear his images. This is particularly the case in the second part of *Le occasioni,* entitled **"Mottetti."** The term denotes not so much "a vocal composition in harmony," since there is

only one voice, that of Montale meditating, even though a plurality of images is harmonized in them. Rather it means a brief epigrammatic statement, on the scale of Goethe's and Schiller's *Xenien* (though without their satirical thrust) or the *Xenia* Montale himself wrote after his wife's death. In these little poems the "screen of images" (*"schermo d' immagini"*) is sometimes impassable, even when Montale has given their origin elsewhere. Thus in the Motet from which that phrase comes, the last three lines remain an enigma, even though as Montale has recorded they describe a real incident:

(a Modena, tra i portici,
un servo gallonato trascinava
due sciacalli al guinzaglio).

[(At Modena through the colonnades
a servant in braided livery dragged along
two jackals on a leash.)]

In these years during which he wrote what is probably his finest verse, constituting the second and third volumes of the original "trilogy," Montale comes much nearer to Dante than to Leopardi. This is the burden of the elaborate study by Arshi Pipa which relates his poetry at many points to the *Divine Comedy* and also to the *Vita Nuova*. It has to be made clear, however, that the parallel, like all such parallels when major poets are in question, should not be seen as complete. Pipa is scrupulous in noting the differences. But for every Italian poet the encounter with Dante must befall him at some point in his career, and to consider it briefly may bring a useful perspective.

There are two aspects that press for attention. The first is the condition of exile—not that Montale was ever subjected to it in the fullest sense, but he could admit no reconciliation with Fascist Italy. As he had said in one of the later poems of *Ossi di seppia,* **"Incontro"** (**"Meeting"**), now he was going down into the Dantesque gloom (*"aria persa"*) of his future, this must be his prayer: *"ch'io / scenda senza viltà"*—that he did this without concession to cowardice. By the time he is engaged on his third volume, Montale has become inevitably a political poet, and some of his most telling indictments, like **"La primavera hitleriana,"** on Hitler's visit to Florence (a final step toward the ruin of Italy), could not be published until after the war. Montale was to write in a poem of 1961, **"Botta e risposta"** (**"Blow and Counterblow"**), that half his life had been spent in the Augean stables. Nor, unfortunately, were his hopes of the postwar republic to be realized. So personal integrity—the avoidance at any cost of *viltà*— compelled him to political utterance. His intimate love poems in the first part of *La bufera,* which is entitled **"Finisterre"** (and the ambiguity seems ominous), have as their inevitable background "a cosmic and terrestrial war without object or reason." Montale, as he asserts in **"Piccolo testamento,"** written in 1953 by way of an "interim conclusion," was opposed to "red cleric or black." For him political utterance is really moral condemnation, a warning against the persistence of evil, "the menacing Wheel" in the poem with its title **"Ezekiel Saw the Wheel"** from a Negro spiritual, the "foul jig" (*"sozzo trescone"*) of **"The Hitlerian Spring."** In all this frenzy of approaching destruction, Montale had the benefit of Dante's example, a lesson in fortitude and in preservation of the true self as a form of national conscience.

This may seem an extravagant claim for Montale, and one that builds too much on his allusions, often no more than glancingly made, to Dante. But the "pattern of persistence" in his poetry, to quote a phrase of Glauco Cambon's [in "Eugenio Montale: An Introduction," in *Selected Poems* by Eugenio Montale, 1965], was of inestimable value at that time, and it is impossible not to recognize in Montale's concern for "exact truth" a sense of responsibility that aligns him with Dante.

The second aspect to reveal their affinity was not, like the first, largely incidental to the period. Montale, as Pipa emphasizes, is a metaphysical poet, and ultimately engaged with religious issues. His skepticism, apparently so debilitating in **Ossi di seppia,** proceeds like Eliot's from a profound desire for the certainties that once were possible. His negation was that of a spirit reluctant to deny. In the Dante centenary lecture of 1965, Montale concluded that "Dante remains extraneous to our times, to our subjective and fundamentally irrational civilization, because he puts his faith in facts and not in ideas. And it is precisely the logic behind these facts that escapes us today." Montale is not happy with the "vast heap of notions provisional in nature" replacing the ordered system of the past in "a world which is moving progressively away from the center." He looks urgently for some form of salvation; and it is Dante and Petrarch who encourage him to put his trust in the celebration of transcendental love.

Several women are addressed in **Le occasioni.** Three of them can be identified. Gerti in the poem about her "carnival" was an Austrian from Graz whom he had known in Florence. She was blended to make "a single phantom" with Dora Markus, the subject of a much anthologized poem in two parts, the first dating from 1926, the second from 1939. Dora, like "Liuba who is leaving" in a neighboring poem of that name, was Jewish. Montale has recorded this fact of both women, and their significance—neither comes back elsewhere in his poetry—rests above all on that. Their problem, like his own, is one of survival in an increasingly hostile world. Dora impresses him by the power she showed to resist, however stormy her life—*"Non so come stremata tu resisti . . ."*; and in the second poem, with its twice-repeated warning that it is "late, always more late," he honors her example: *"Non si cede / voce, leggenda o destino."* Voice, legend, destiny: what we affirm, what has made us, and what we must endure—these things are not to be sacrificed.

The figure corresponding to Beatrice in Montale's devotion is named Clizia, and she is to be found in many poems of **Le occasioni,** particularly the Motets; in the Finisterre sequence; in **"The Hitlerian Spring"** and **"The Little Testament"**; and elsewhere too. She also was Jewish, on Montale's avowal to Silvio Guarnieri; but this cannot be inferred from the poetry. More important is her role as Christophora, "a bearer of Christ." The name Clizia is apparently derived from the mythological Clytie [Klutie], a daughter of Oceanus who was changed by Apollo into a sunflower. Montale records a different change for Clizia: she has become a Christian, and in **"The Hitlerian Spring"** he speaks of her unaltered love, and of the "blind" solar radiance within her which is consumed in God. Another poem **"Iris"** (**"Iride"**)—which for once he had "dreamed and transcribed," being more a medium than its author—presents her as carrying on the work of Christ; while the poet himself, "a poor bewildered Nestorian," is separated from her because he cannot contemplate "the bloody Face on the sudarium," the veil of Veronica.

The poems addressed to Clizia are poignant and often difficult. The revelations granted to him arise from his own memory: the "phantom that saves" has to be recovered from the past. Montale's imagination feeds upon retrospect, and in this he resembles Thomas Hardy. But he differs from Hardy in not forever regretting a significance lost at the time, in not haunting with wistful obstinacy a vanished scene. As Solmi has expressed it [in "La poesia di Montale"], Montale's "flashes" of vision (one series of poems in **La bufera** is entitled **"'Flashes' and Dedications"**) must be understood as "countersigns of an individual story which at the same time aspires to reveal its structure as a story over and above this [*una soprastoria*] of everyone."

In the later poems of **Le occasioni** and more insistently in **La bufera** the hints of that common story are manifest. It was not possible for him to use the direct language of Agrippa d'Aubigné, the protestant satirist and historian three hundred years earlier, in the quotation placed as epigraph to the Finisterre poems which had to be published in Switzerland:

> The princes have no eyes to see these great marvels,
> Their hands now serve only to persecute us . . .

By the time of **"Finisterre"** the war—Montale's "storm" in the initial poem—had already come, and his own despair in separation from Clizia may be understood also as depicting the plight of a captive Europe, indeed of humanity itself, "in the nightmare years '40 to '42":

> . . . tarda
> la fucina vermiglia
> della notte, la sera si fa lunga,
> la preghiera è supplizio e non ancora
> tra le rocce che sorgono t' è giunta
> la bottiglia dal mare. L'onda, vuota,
> si rompe sulla punta, a Finisterre.

> [. . . lingers on
> the vermilion forge
> of night, the evening lengthens,
> prayer is torment, and not yet
> among the rocks that rise up has reached you
> the bottle from the sea. The wave, empty,
> breaks on the headland, at Finisterre.]

Clizia, whose significance is ultimately perhaps that of Montale's Muse, alternates with another enigmatic figure, "*la volpe,*" the vixen of "**'Flashes' and Dedications**" and of the "**Madrigali privati**" forming the penultimate section of *La bufera*. But apart from these two personages is another, to whom he dedicated his "**Ballad Written in a Clinic,**" which is dated January 1945. It looks back to an experience of the previous year, soon after the liberation of Florence, but when Italy continued to be "*nel solco dell' emergenza,*" in the furrow of the emergency. Montale speaks here of their shared misery to his wife, Drusilla Tanzi, who was undergoing treatment for what had been at first wrongly diagnosed as a brain tumor. The tone of this poem is quite unlike that of any other in the volume:

Hai messo sul comodino
il bulldog di legno, la sveglia
col fosforo sulle lancette
che spande un tenue lucore
sul tuo dormiveglia,

il nulla che basta a chi vuole
forzare la porta stretta . . .

[You have set on the bedside cupboard
the wooden bulldog, the alarm-clock
with phosphorus on its hands
which spreads a faint light
over your drowsiness,

the nothing that suffices one who wants
to force the strait gate . . .]

Other poems by Montale had mentioned a little talisman like the bulldog: Dora Markus kept a white ivory mouse in her bag. Elsewhere he recalls characteristic details (like his father's "shawl and beret") evoking a particular and often repeated scene. But in the lines quoted from the "**Ballad**" something else is at work—the abandonment of that reserve which had never before allowed him to bring his wife directly into a poem, or to reveal a private act of consolation, like placing the bulldog beside her bed. The poem ends with an admission of uncontrollable grief: "*e poi l'ululo / del cane di legno è il mio, muto.*" The howling of the wooden dog has become his own, voiceless.

It was in 1963 that his wife died. The poems he wrote under the shock of this inaugurated a fourth volume and with it an entirely new phase in his poetry.

Both Singh and F. R. Leavis have compared Montale's two sets of fourteen poems each—he called them *Xenia,* "gifts" or "offerings"—with Hardy's *Poems of 1912–13,* written after a similar bereavement at the same age [F. R. Leavis, *The Listener,* December 16, 1972]. Those by Hardy are recognized as the most impressive single body of work from a poet who had produced much verse, never trivial and often arresting. They record a personal crisis in which a very private man—like Montale—has been brought face to face with his own sufferings, the pangs of a conscience awakened too late. Montale, of course, did not share Hardy's predicament: he was free from remorse. And it cannot be claimed for *Xenia,* as it reasonably may for *Poems of 1912–13,* that in their sudden visitation they

revealed to the poet a more profound knowledge of himself and gave to his poetry a new timbre, a more urgent resonance.

Carlo Bo, in reviewing in 1971 the volume that contains *Xenia,* called by Montale *Satura,* in the sense of "a medley," spoke of Yeats and Machado as other poets who had surprised their readers by a fresh development of style and outlook late in life. He detected in Montale a freedom that must be "the fruit of an assuredness which until now had remained under constraint of a certain embarrassment" ["Montale poeta-critico," *Nuova Antologia,* July 1971]. The change of tone (though it had been anticipated in the "**Ballad Written in a Clinic**") is startling for this poet:

Caro piccolo insetto
che chiamavano mosca non so perché,
stasera quasi al buio
mentre leggevo il Deuteroisaia
sei ricomparsa accanto a me,
ma non avevi occhiali,
non potevi vidermi
né potevo io senza quel luccichìo
riconoscere te nella foschia.

[Dear little insect
whom they called "Mosca," why I don't know,
this evening almost in the dark
while I was reading Deutero-Isaiah
you reappeared beside me,
but you had no glasses,
you couldn't see me
nor could I without that glistening
recognize you in the dimness.]

The many recollections on which these poems are founded could hardly be more prosaic, more banal to the outside world: the steep reduction of his telephone bill, now Mosca has gone; the cheap little shoehorn they left behind in a Venetian hotel; the need now to book single rooms when he visits Paris. Montale confides things he would never have mentioned in his poetry before—the whistle that was to be their sign of recognition in the other world, her habit of praying to Saint Anthony for lost umbrellas and other items from her wardrobe, or the list of their belongings ruined by the flood of November 1966 in Florence. He had sometimes written of his personal life, directly or under light fictional disguise, in prose sketches. *La farfalla di Dinard (The Butterfly of Dinard)* contains some of these. But in *Xenia,* and in other poems scattered through the volume, he accepts the compulsion to speak openly, under the immediate onset of feeling, about their life together and his unbearable loss. Anything can stir Montale to this. He remembers that the gulls will be waiting for him to throw them crumbs so that she may hear their screaming:

Oggi manchiamo all' appuntamento tutte e due
e il nostro breakfast gela tra cataste
per me di libri inutili e per te di reliquie
che non so: calendari, astucci, fiale e creme.

[Today we miss the appointment both of us
and our breakfast grows cold among piles
for me of useless books and for you of relics
I don't know: calendars, cases, phials and face-
creams.]

He was to publish two further books—*Diary of '71 and '72* and, in 1977, *Notebook of Four Years*. The description of these poems as forming a diary is accurate. Many of them are jottings, reflections on his own work, the nature of his life, the events of the day, the course that it seems to him the world is taking. The tone is relaxed but never nerveless—he remains astringent to the last. An old man's view of our present situation is not likely to be cheerful, yet the "vigor of spirit" that Leopardi said is requisite in the poetry of disillusionment still runs through his verse. It flickers into warmth with mention of Mosca; it is at its coldest and most detached when he considers the age itself, or his own achievement. In one poem he describes his Muse as a scarecrow; in another, by way of farewell, "*Per finire,*" he advises his successors (if any there are) to "make a good bonfire of everything that concerns / my life, my actions and my non-actions." He had been no Leopardi but had "lived at five per cent."

Montale spoke more justly of himself some twenty years earlier, in the **"Little Testament,"** which was to be "evidence / of a faith that was fought for, / of a hope that burned more slowly / than a hard log on the hearth." Poetry, as he says in **"A questo punto,"** from the *Diary of '71 and '72,* had been "the shadow that accompanied [him] in war and peace, and also / in the time between." Now this shadow was to drop its mask, and to declare itself as "your thought, / . . . your non-necessity, your useless rind."

> T'ho ingannato
> ma ora ti dico a questo punto smetti.
> Il tuo peggio e il tuo meglio non t'appartengono
> e per quello che avrai puoi fare a meno
> di un' ombra.

> [I have deceived you
> but now I tell you at this point give up.
> Your worst and your best do not belong to you
> and for what you shall have you can do without
> a shadow.]

Montale, it need hardly be said, ignored this advice. The shadow was repeating what he had maintained in the "imaginary interview," that "art is the form of life for one who truly does not live: a compensation or a surrogate." He also said this provides no excuse for an ivory tower: the poet "must not renounce life," even if life evades him.

But indeed life did not evade Montale. His isolation was that of a mind actively engaged in watching, and making its judgment of, the world. The great poets, necessarily few, are alive, fully alive as men of action seldom are, through their integrity. Solmi in 1957 quotes [in "La poesia di Montale"] the observation of Vittorio Sereni that "the name of a poet seems ever more difficult to carry and sustain even inside the normal limits of literature." Mon-

tale gave a supreme example of how to carry that name with honor, and to resist those "voices of temptation" in the desert which Eliot warned against.

FURTHER READING

Bibliography

Ricciardelli, Michael. "Montale in the U.S.A. (1936–1971)." *Books Abroad* 45, No. 4, Autumn, 1971, pp. 645–48.
Index of criticism by American commentators.

Craft, Wallace. "Eugenio Montale in *Books Abroad* (1947–1975)." *Books Abroad* 50, No. 1 (Winter 1976): 15.
Lists articles and reviews on Montale that have appeared in the periodical.

Criticism

Almansi, Guido. "Earth and Water in Montale's Poetry." *Forum for Modern Language Studies* 2, No. 4 (October 1966): 377–85.
Discusses the interrelation of water and earth symbolism in Montale's verse.

Almansi, Guido, and Merry, Bruce. *Eugenio Montale: The Private Language of Poetry.* Edinburgh: Edinburgh University Press, 1977, 167 p.
Study divided into sections focusing on each of Montale's five major verse collections. According to the authors, "More than any other poet in the twentieth century, . . . Montale has become the messenger of our existential and sentimental uncertainty. Here we recognized a voice which spoke our own moral cowardice, our own aesthetic perplexity."

Baranski, Zygmunt. "Dante and Montale: The Threads of Influence." In *Dante Comparisons: Comparative Studies of Dante and: Montale, Foscolo, Tasso, Chaucer, Petrarch, Propertius and Catullus,* edited by Eric Haywood and Barry Jones, pp. 11–48. Dublin: Irish Academic Press, 1985.
Examines the impact of Dante's verse on the work of Montale.

Becker, Jared M. "What We Are Not: Montale's Anti-Fascism Revisited." *Italica* 60, No. 4 (Winter 1983): 331–39.
Contends that Montale was not a political poet, despite his anti-Fascist sympathies.

————. "Decadence Defended: Montale's 'Botta e risposta I'." *Italian Quarterly* 27, No. 106 (Fall 1986): 25–32.
Interprets the first poem in Montale's "Thrust and Parry" series as a defense against Benedetto Croce's post-war attacks on writers deemed "decadent," a term used to describe "one who absents himself from the real and present world."

————. *Eugenio Montale.* Twayne's World Authors Series:

Italian Literature, edited by Anthony Oldcorn. Boston: Twayne Publishers, 1986, 154 p.

  Biographical and critical study of Montale's career.

Brose, Margaret. "The Spirit of the Sign: Oppositional Structures in Montale's *Ossi di Seppia.*" *Stanford Italian Review* 4, No. 2 (Fall 1984): 147–75.

  Studies *Cuttlefish Bones* in order to highlight traits common to Montale's poetry from the beginning of his career through *The Storm, and Other Poems* in 1956.

Burnshaw, Stanley, and others, eds. "Eugenio Montale." In *The Poem Itself*, pp. 316–325. Reprint. New York: Schocken Books, 1967.

  Poem-by-poem explication of "Meriggiare pallido e assorto," "Arsenio," "La casa dei doganieri," and "L'anguilla."

Cambon, Glauco. *Eugenio Montale's Poetry: A Dream in Reason's Presence.* Princeton, N.J.: Princeton University Press, 1982, 274 p.

  Comprehensive analysis of Montale's verse. A friend of Cambon, Montale reviewed the manuscript of this study prior to publication.

Caprioglio, Giuliana. "Intellectual and Sentimental Modes of Rapport with Reality in Montale's *Ossi* and *Occasioni.*" *Italian Quarterly* 13, No. 50 (Fall 1969): 51–66.

  Maintains that *Cuttlefish Bones* and *The Occasions* are contrasting statements arising from Montale's "meditation on the life of man, on the precariousness of the peace which is allowed him, on his fate of death, on the discordance between an active and contemplative life."

Feld, Ross. "Montale." *Parnassus* 11, No. 1 (Spring–Summer 1983): 33–57.

  Traces the evolution of Montale's poetry.

Flint, R. W. "Montale's *New Poems* and *Pequod.*" *The American Poetry Review* 7, No. 6 (November–December 1978): 20–2.

  Presents an overview of Montale's poetry.

Fraser, Russell. "Montale's Night Music." *The Southern Review* 14, No. 3 (Summer 1978): 449–59.

  Endeavors to demonstrate that Montale is a very hard poet to define because he is, according to Fraser, paradoxically "anti-romantic" and "the legatee and perpetuator of the romantic tradition."

Huffman, Claire de C. L. "The Poetic Language of Eugenio Montale." *Italian Quarterly,* Nos. 47–8 (Winter–Spring 1969): 105–28.

  Asserts that Montale "seeks to reject language which is weighed down by cultural incrustations." Huffman explains that he avoids rhetoric and ornamentation while conveying the universal significance of his subjects.

————. "Structuralist Criticism and the Interpretation of Eugenio Montale." *The Modern Language Review* 72, No. 2 (April 1977): 322–334.

  Presents structuralism as a preferred framework for analyzing the stylistic aspects of Montale's verse but also acknowledges weaknesses in this critical approach.

————. *Montale and the Occasions of Poetry.* Princeton, N. J.: Princeton University Press, 1983, 293 p.

  Though a broad study of Montale's poetry, this study employs *The Occasions* as "a lens through which to discern the undoubted distinction of individual poems and the larger poetic tendencies as they have manifested themselves over the years."

————. "Montale for the English-Speaking: The Case of 'In Limine.'" *Forum Italicum* 23, Nos. 1–2 (Spring–Fall 1989): 121–46.

  Illustrates the difficulties of translating Montale's poetry through the example of "In Limine."

McCormick, C. A. "Sound and Silence in Montale's *Ossi di seppia.*" *The Modern Language Review* 62, No. 4 (October 1967): 633–41.

  Examines the interplay between silence and sound in Montale's first verse collection as it is expressed in imagery and diction.

Pacifici, Sergio. "Poetry: Eugenio Montale, The Quest for Meaning." In his *A Guide to Contemporary Italian Literature: From Futurism to Neorealism*, pp. 177-87. Cleveland: Meridian Books, 1963.

  Introduction to Montale in which Pacifici states: "Man, for the poet, is a being aspiring naturally to a condition of unachievable harmony within and without. He longs to 'know,' yet he is fully aware that *the* reasons of existence will always escape him."

Perella, Nicolas J. "Eugenio Montale." In his *Midday in Italian Literature: Variations on an Archetypal Theme*, pp. 240–328. Princeton, N.J.: Princeton University Press, 1979.

  Explores the philosophical and religious implications of the theme of noontime in *Cuttlefish Bones,* finding that it connotes ambivalence about existence.

Pipa, Arshi. "The Message of Montale." *Italica* 34, No. 1 (March 1962): 239–55.

  Noting Montale was a poet preoccupied with the metaphysical dimension of life, Pipa suggests that *Cuttlefish Bones, The Occasions,* and *The Storm, and Other Poems* record an ongoing quest for spiritual fulfilment.

————. "Memory and Fidelity in Montale." *Italian Quarterly* 10, Nos. 39–40 (Winter–Spring 1967): 62–79.

  Acknowledging the disparate critical perceptions of the role of memory in Montale's verse, Pipa attempts "to explore and map out the domain of memory in the work of Montale, in the hope of arriving at a conclusion that brings together and explains these and other conceptions of the Montalean memory."

Singh, G. "Eugenio Montale." *Italian Studies* 28 (1963): 101–37.

  Attempts to define Montale's poetics and philosophy as expressed through his verse.

————. *Eugenio Montale: A Critical Study of His Poetry, Prose, and Criticism.* New Haven, Conn.: Yale University Press, 1973, 297 p.

> Commenting on the intent of his study of Montale's work, Singh states: "It doesn't purport to offer any specialized thesis or exegesis concerning any one particular aspect. Its aim is to provide a general critical account of Montale's *oeuvre* in its totality."

Solmi, Sergio. "The Poetry of Montale." *Quarterly Review of Literature* XI, No. 4 (1962): 221–38.

> Claiming that Montale best expressed the spiritual condition of his generation, Solmi traces the poet's accomplishment through the collections *Cuttlefish Bones, The Occasions,* and *The Storm, and Other Poems.*

West, Rebecca. "On Montale." *Chicago Review* 27, No. 3 (Winter 1975–76): 14–24.

> An introduction to Montale's poetry. According to West, "Montale has been a powerful catalyst in the process of revivification of the Italian idiom as an instrument of significant literary production."

————. "Montale's 'Care Ombre': Identity and Its Dissolution." *Forum Italicum* 23, Nos. 1–2 (Spring–Fall 1989): 212–28.

> Contends that Montale's poetry addressed to deceased loved ones "recognizes the inevitable dissolution of 'mortalia' ['mortality'] and embodies, in its abiding beauty, a form of continuing life that prolongs 'beyond the threshold of death' conversation, communion, and love."

Williamson, Alan. "Montale and the Screen of Images." *Parnassus* 13, No. 2 (Spring–Summer 1986): 179–92.

> Assesses the significance that images hold for Montale. According to Williamson, Montale "shows that even a poem as small as the Sixth Motet can give an account—however compressed—of the ontological status it assigns to images in general, as well as of the emotional complex that makes a particular image inevitable."

Additional coverage of Montale's life and career is contained in the following sources published by Gale Research: *Contemporary Authors,* Vols. 17–20 (rev. ed.); *Contemporary Authors New Revision Series,* Vol. 30; *Contemporary Literary Criticism,* Vols. 7, 9, 18; *Dictionary of Literary Biography,* Vol. 114; and *Major 20th-Century Writers.*

Gérard de Nerval
1808–1855

(Born Gérard Labrunie) French poet, short story writer, playwright, translator, novelist, essayist, and critic.

INTRODUCTION

Nerval is recognized as one of the most influential French poets of the nineteenth century. One of the first writers to explore the realm of the subconscious, he is noted for the innovative use of illusory states such as dreams and hallucinations in his work. The themes and imagery in Nerval's poetry were directed by several persistent personal obsessions, and originated in such diverse sources as art, mythology, religion, fantasy, and the occult.

Biographical Information

Nerval was a small child when his mother died while assisting her husband, a surgeon in the Napoleonic army, on his tours of Germany. He was raised by a great-uncle in the Valois, the rural region of France that was to remain in his memory—and appear in his poetic works—as an idyllic landscape of childhood perfection. During his schooling in Paris, he displayed precocious literary talent, publishing at age twenty a translation of Johann Wolfgang von Goethe's *Faust*, which the great poet himself acclaimed. Nerval became a member of the *Jeune-France*, a group of Romantic artists and writers who challenged the established classical school not only with radical artistic theories but with flamboyant dress and eccentric behavior. But Nerval's carefree Bohemian life became troubled as increasingly severe money problems and mental difficulties befell him. Biographers allege that the fact that Nerval had never known his mother led to intense infatuations with women later in life; in his writing, women are depicted in various guises as unattainable embodiments of ideal femininity. The most enduring of his unrequited passions was for an actress, Jenny Colon, whose aloofness and early death hastened the deterioration of Nerval's mental health. Ironically, the madness which plagued Nerval heightened his artistic sensibility, and it was in his final years that he produced his greatest poetry. At the age of forty-six, Nerval committed suicide by hanging himself from a railing in a Paris alley.

Major Works

Published in 1854, *Les Chiméres* is considered by most critics to be Nerval's greatest poetic accomplishment. The sequence is composed of twelve sonnets, each imbued with mythological and religious imagery, as well as themes

derived from Nerval's own life. The poems are interwoven, with recurring characters and allusions that parallel religious history and the alchemist's process of turning base metals into gold. The first sonnet, "El Desdichado," introduces a character called the black prince; the second, his feminine counterpart "Myrtho." The result of their union is described in the third sonnet of the sequence, "Horus"; this offspring is viewed not only as a symbol of the birth of Christ, but also the product of combining two metals in alchemy. In addition, "Horus" is seen by commentators to represent the revival of Nerval's interest in new poetic forms and techniques. In the remaining sonnets comprising *Les Chiméres*, Nerval continues to develop several spiritual, mythological, and autobiographical themes, creating what critics consider a dense, highly evocative work.

Critical Reception

Nerval is praised for the far-reaching influence of his artistic vision which is manifest in the work of many notable French writers of the Symbolist and Surrealist literary periods, including Guillaime Appollinaire, Charles Baudelaire, Arthur Rimbaud, Marcel Proust, and Théophile

Gautier. When discussing Nerval's body of work, critics have focused on his innovative use of dreams and visions, the semiotic qualities of his language, his copious references to mythology and religon, and the extensive incorporation of events and characters from his own life.

PRINCIPAL WORKS

Poetry

Les Chiméres [*The Chimeras*] 1854; published in *Les Filles du feu*
Les Filles du feu [*Daughters of Fire*] (poetry and novellas) 1854
Le Rêve et la Vie [*Dreams and Life*] (poetry and short stories) 1855
Selected Writings (poetry and short stories) 1957

Other Major Works

Faust de Göthe [translator] (poetry) 1828
Léo Burckart (drama) 1839
Voyage en Orient [*Journey to the Orient*] (short stories) 1851
Les Illuminés (sketches) 1852
Lorely: souvenirs d'Allemagne (travel essays) 1852
Sylvie: Recollections of Valois (short stories) 1887
Œuvres Complètes. 10 vols. (short stories) 1926–32
Aurélia [*Aurelia*] (short stories and sketches) 1932
Œuvres 2 vols. (short stories) 1960–61

CRITICISM

Wallace Fowlie (essay date 1948)

SOURCE: "Nerval: The Poet's Uncrowning," in *Love in Literature: Studies in Symbolic Expression,* Indiana University Press, 1965, pp. 58–63.

[*Fowlie is one of the most respected and versatile critics of French literature. His works include translations of major dramatists and poets of France as well as critical studies of the major figures and movements of French letters. In the following excerpt, Fowlie speaks of the life and works of Nerval as those of a man inhabiting a dream world.*]

For most of the romantics, the dream world was a second domain of consciousness to which they escaped with pleasure, where they fought reason and reasoning, and where they bedecked, according to their desires, the real world. The dream for Chateaubriand, Lamartine, and de Musset was a band they put over their eyes to blot out the vulgar world of the bourgeois. For only one of the romantics was the dream what it should have been: the world of the

subconscious controlled by its own laws, where the inhabitants are indigenous and bear the recognizable traits of fantastic and fairy-like creatures. The name of this romantic, Gérard de Nerval, is as unreal as the visions which compose his dreams, and after one hundred years, we say today 'Gérard de Nerval' and read the sonnets of his *Chimères* and his short novels, as if his true name and real life outside his writings had never existed. The dream of Nerval has triumphed. His work, rather than being an obviously symbolic transcription of his life, is his life. Everything has been reversed in Nerval, because his life is a faint transcription of his dream.

As the popular ballad reveals the heart of a people more accurately than any historical narration of events, as mythology alone really penetrates the meaning of history, Nerval's work, and especially the sonnets called *Les Chimères,* form a more authentic record of his life than any biography could. The sonnets are much more than a distillation of experiences. They create the new compact life where the settings are more real than the landscapes of the Valois and the Orient, where the characters are more living than Adrienne in the children's dance in the park of the château, and more real than Jenny Colon on the stage of the Paris theatres. The voyages in *Les Chimères* are the only ones we need to follow. The madness of this poet undertook voyages less exaggerated than the real voyages in which Nerval, incited by his studies of the cabala, of magic, and mystical initiations, destroyed the real worlds. His wisdom was obscure because it was composed of magnetism, esoterism, and occultism, but his madness was lucid because it constructed the limitless and perfect world of dreams. As a traveller, Nerval pursued the symbolism of numbers and the memories of magic and of cabala, but as a poet, he constructed the existence of a man who loves and suffers. Any historical or psychological method used to explain Nerval will fail, because reality for him existed as the substance of a dream, as a substance to be modified and remodelled. His writings are therefore as invulnerable as a dream. Any explication is less than approximate. In order to read Nerval, it is a question of living a dream and feeling its beauty. It is not a question of dissecting it.

The figures of the women who inhabit his work resemble those phantoms who are always the same phantom of a dream. Adrienne, Jenny Colon, the Neapolitan girl, the English girl, are all synthesized in Aurélia, the only woman Gérard could love since, never having seen her in life, he was able to make her divine. The conscious life of the poet was composed of departures, of voyages, of peregrinations, and only in his dreams did he remain immobilized before the ideal form of the woman he was seeking. A poet of love, Nerval always remained a poet of metempsychosis: he was never sure of loving, he was never sure of having loved, and only in his dreams was his former existence of Eden purity, of innocency, and of happiness reproduced. Nerval encouraged his madness because it abolished time and plunged him into a distant past where all was illuminated with joy. The children's dance during which he received a kiss from yellow haired Adrienne marked the beginning of an experience in metempsychosis in which he believed he was all the youthful dancers of former times and in which so ancient a ceremonial kiss symbolized perfect happiness. The moment of ecstasy in our childhood, which was perhaps in Gérard de Nerval's case, Adrienne's kiss, is the supreme moment in our amorous experience which we try during the rest of our life to recognize, to recapture, to re-live in other forms and with other beings. The spiritual experience alone of love is tenacious. It inevitably triumphs over physical experience in binding us to time which has gone by, to a past which becomes present and future. Love is metempsychosis. It is the same experience we re-live ceaselessly.

La treizieme revient . . . C'est encor la première.

The sumptuous resonances of this sonnet of **"Artémis,"** while knowingly falsifying the truth, reduce the fragments of real experiences into a single experience as simple as it is profound, as permanent as it is inaccessible.

As the popular ballad reveals the heart of a people more accurately than any historical narration of events, as mythology alone really penetrates the meaning of history, Nerval's work, and especially the sonnets called *Les Chimères*, form a more authentic record of his life than any biography could.

—Wallace Fowlie

"Artémis" is a luminous example of lyric creation in which the entire life of the poet is recast: all the idealisms and all the failures. The sonnet not only contains direct reminiscences of nocturnal life, of death, of youth, and of maturity—it reproduces at the same time, and through that miracle of coincidence and evocation which art alone can construct, the universal experience of all men. **"Artémis"** diminishes life, in re-creating it, by use of the simplest words in all languages: 1. treize et premier; 2. reine et roi; 3. berceau et bière; 4. aimer et mourir; 5. rose et sainte. Paradoxically speaking, Nerval succeeds in doing in his sonnet what James Joyce does in *Finnegans Wake,* in the numerous closely covered pages of a long work: the re-creation of a life and of life. In each group of these primitive words of the sonnet there exist worlds of involuntary memory. The subject matter of *Finnegans Wake* is these worlds, silenced in Nerval's sonnet but obscurely living in the imagination of each reader. A work of art, truly, is not constructed on a subject matter; it is infallibly constructed on an absence. The void left by a completed experience is the authentic subject matter of art, and in a literary work, words come to fill this void without however building a real substance. An experience becomes spiritual especially from the moment it is translated into a language. Art

consecrates the spirituality of life by giving it a form, as the body consecrates the spirituality of the soul.

The principle of metempsychosis (revealed in the first line of **"Artémis,"** in the meaning of the words 'treizième' and 'première') abolishes, by surpassing it, the tragic notion of love.

Et c'est toujours la seule—ou c'est le seul moment.

'The one moment' referred to was that love always sought by Nerval because it had once existed and because it continued to exist in his dreams. This dream is as imperishable as life itself, bequeathed to all men according to the mysterious principle of the survival of souls and things. Tragedy is therefore only the arresting of life and the death of dreams. Nerval never entered tragedy because his dream was an uninterrupted communication with the past, the survival of experience, the reality he asked of every day and every night. Nerval's poetry first abolished tragedy because of the fact that experience is never terminated, and then abolished time, effaced by the very character itself of dreams.

I am ready to believe that Nerval was one of those very exceptional men whose thoughts are always pure. The purity of his imagination is almost unique in literature. It prevented him from becoming tragic. The tragic hero is the victim who has encountered his executioner. But Nerval was the victim without an executioner, eternally extended on the altar, living, behind his closed eyes, the drama of life and death. Both his dream and his sorrow were virginally modest. Lying on his altar where all possible voyages haunted him, he could see in his mind's eye the subtle skies of the Valois, the foggy forests of Ermenonville, the campestral landscapes of Mortefontaine and Loisy. Incapable of living or dying, Gérard tried to identify himself with all the characters in life and in death, and to feel the destiny of each one in order to fill the abyss extending around him in all directions.

Si je meurs, c'est que tout va mourir

he said in one of his sonnets on **"Le Christ aux Oliviers,"** and therein stated one of his most purely nihilistic philosophical thoughts. In this line, he expresses his identity with the cosmos. In him cohabit the natural and the supernatural, and after him all will cease existing. The dreamer is a victim, and the worlds of his dream gravitate around the void. Nerval's work was an appeal, not for the purpose of justifying before his friends and physicians the attacks of madness which constantly threatened him, but for justifying his thought on the abyss and on renascent love. As the perpetual vagrancy of his life led to suicide, his limitless dreams coincided with the death of the worlds, with the extinction of the dark suns of melancholy. Metempsychosis ceased to be for Nerval a religious principle and became a principle of delirium and poetry. I believe that Nerval didn't like living. He had no real desire to live, as most men have. His mind, ornamented solely with his dreams, lived by not living. As Jews are specialists in catastrophes, as Americans are specialists in optimisms,

Gérard de Nerval was a specialist in dreams. He knew neither sun-fed passions, nor obscure loves. He only dreamed passionately, obscurely, wilfully exhausting the vision of a children's dance which appears both so darkened and illuminated that it is accepted as an incomprehensible rite of some lost truth. Nerval played the rôle of lover as a guardian or a priest who had never seen his goddess or his god. Nothing existed for him in time: neither heaven nor earth; neither love nor faith.

The tragic hero of antiquity, of the 'chansons de geste', and of the classical theatre, is abstemious of words, but Nerval, in pursuing the reality of language, pursued at the same time the reality of dreams and avoided the tragic or glorious conclusions with which life is composed. Thereby Nerval is the ancestor of *Le Grand Meaulnes,* of Proust, of Bloom. No modern poetry is more 'narrative' than *Les Chimères*. The principle of illuminism penetrates the entire work of Nerval and is opposed to any ultimate light, either tragic or sanctified. Nothing ends, neither life nor death, because men and gods equally never cease being absorbed in the universe. The final substance of the sonnets—all the very simple words and the pauses between the words and the lines—is the only immobile element in Nerval's work. This substance chained to the white pages sings of perpetual becoming and recommencing where tragedy is an episode, where glory is a disappearance, where death is life.

Romanticism, of all the centuries and not solely of the nineteenth, is the dream of life, the harsh and provocative disproportion which exists between imagined life and daily life. Rousseau, in certain pages of his *Rêveries,* bequeathed to the hypersensitive hearts of the nineteenth and twentieth centuries, ways and exercises by which to attain the ecstasy of dreams, but the Rousseauistic romantics in their dream of life are today replaced by Gérard de Nerval in his life of dreams. The climate desired by Jean-Jacques was the dream of nature, but the climate desired by Nerval was the nature of dreams. The human solitude of Rousseau gave way to the mortal solitude of Nerval who felt, more profoundly than the Swiss writer, the desert truth of the cosmos.

The love expressed by Nerval at the inception of the modern era is love of eternity, love of that force which bends trees and men, but which also straightens them up thanks to the indestructible truth of dreams. The poet Nerval knew himself as a living man and as a future dead man: he did not distinguish in himself the two rôles which are measured by the two rites of life and death. Uncrowned by life, this prince of Aquitania was crowned by death. It was fitting that at the birth of the theatrical romantic pessimism in the century which has given the greatest number of dreamers to the world, a single writer should cease contemplating from his real site the clouds of his dreams in order to live in his dreams the transfigured image of his life. Like Plotinus who, immobile, contemplated the drama of his being, Nerval contemplated love, without loving, without living in love. Like the heroes of Corneille who, forging the destiny of their duty, dream of the love which will one day be accessible to

them, Nerval dreamed of what a calm and reasonable life might resemble, while forging the limitless kingdom of his dreams.

John W. Kneller   (essay date 1960)

SOURCE: "The Poet and His Moira: 'El Desdichado'," in *PMLA,* Vol. LXXV, No. 4, September, 1960, pp. 402–09.

[*An English-born critic and educator specializing in French literature, Kneller is the coauthor of* Introduction à la poésie francaise *(1962) and a former editor of* French Review. *In the following essay, he provides an exegesis of "El Desdichado," finding the sonnet to be an expression of Nerval's belief about his lot in life.*]

Concerning Gérard de Nerval it has been said, of late, that the hour of synthesis is at hand. This is particularly true of **"El Desdichado,"** for most authors of the increasingly voluminous literature devoted to this sonnet have taken an extrinsic approach; that is, they have applied techniques of other fields, such as psychiatry, biography, astrology, and alchemy. At best they have helped to elucidate hitherto obscure symbols; at worst they have made of their thesis a kind of Procrustean bed on which the poem has been either stretched to death or decapitated.

In this richly connotative piece, almost every word is a symbol evoking a cluster of ideas and feelings, and, because of this, the reader has frequently selected, according to his lights, the meaning which is appropriate for him. Enlightened by Dante's *Convivio,* Nerval did indeed want his later poems to have not one meaning, but several, and this fact lends credence to a multi-level exegesis, such as Jean Richer's ["Le luth constellè de Nerval," *Cahiers du Sud,* No. 331 (1955)]. The problem here, however, is to determine whether each of several interpretations of a given symbol is equally important to an appreciation of the work as a whole, or whether there is a basic meaning for each word-symbol to which all others are subsidiary. An oversimplified example from music theory may help to explain why the second of these alternatives is preferable. As everyone knows, a musical theme consists of a series of notes, one following the other. This theme, or melody, may have contrapuntal melodies, and each of its notes will have almost an infinity of harmonics which give it its timbre and characteristic quality. To play the theme correctly, one must, of course, play the right notes, not the harmony, and above all, one must not reach for the harmonics. Since poets are dealing with words, and since each of these contributes to the total significance of the poem, it is incumbent upon the critic to find the basic meaning, the fundamental tone, of each word-symbol, and to relegate other meanings to their proper secondary role.

If we risk restating the obvious in this connection, it is because a substantial amount of Nerval criticism, ignoring the fact that this poem like all the other *Chimères,* is a coherent, unified statement of an experience, has tended to reduce explication to the finding of a precise biographical event or specific written source for a given word or image.

But Gérard cannot be charged with a disdain for syntax, nor with a desire to squander the true poetic meaning of words on a multiplicity of autobiographical or literary associations. He has compressed years of experience into a few words, but these words are the quintessence of that experience, not a series of clues to events in his own life.

It seems appropriate, therefore, that a fresh interpretation of this sonnet be made in the light of these observations and taking into account the illuminating and suggestive, though often fragmentary, discoveries of the past decade. We shall not attempt to demonstrate the beauty of this work. For this reason our comments on form will be restricted to those which have a direct bearing on our subject, the meaning of **"El Desdichado."** But it is our belief that a full appreciation of that beauty can come only after a proper interpretation of its symbols, towards which this study is intended to contribute.

Ample justification for interpreting **"El Desdichado"** as the statement of a poetic experience can be found in the nineteenth letter to Jenny Colon: "Il y a des années d'angoisses, de rêves, de projects qui voudraient se presser dans une phrase, dans un mot. . . ." But this poem is more than a distillation of "years of anguish, dreams, and plans." For the Greeks, every human being had his *moira*—his share of life, happiness, sorrow, glory, despair—neatly carved out for him by the gods, and he was instinctively aware of it, even though he could not always discern its shape. The subject of **"El Desdichado"** is this *moira,* or, more precisely, Gérard de Nerval's *moira,* the line drawn around his fate, the closed book of his spiritual autobiography. Just as a constellation in Greek mythology is the eternal symbol of a hero's life, so this poem is the essence of Nerval's. That he could have left it as a calling card in the offices of the *Mousquetaire,* a newspaper directed by his friend Alexandre Dumas, is only an admirable example of his disarming modesty.

It has been many times repeated that the title was taken from chapter eight of *Ivanhoe,* where Scott describes a mysterious young knight ready to do battle. Since this attribution of influence has some bearing upon the meaning of the title, it will be appropriate to review certain important but as yet unobserved details, gleaned from this well-known novel about England in the twelfth century. In the first place, the knight in question turns out later to be Wilfred of Ivanhoe. In the second place the cause of Ivanhoe's sorrow is not simply, as Mme. Moulin assumes, that he has been dispossessed of his manor by King John. It is true that the manor in question had been possessed "in free and independent right" by his ancestors, had been taken away by Richard the Lion-Hearted, then restored to Ivanhoe in return for the latter's services to his king. It is also true that during Richard's absence King John gave the fief of Ivanhoe to Reginald Front-de-Bœuf. But to be stripped of his estate by John would cause no more than a passing concern to a confident supporter of Richard. The real cause of Wilfred's dismay is a conflict with his father, Cedric, on two basic issues: first, that he had "stooped to hold, as a feudal vassal the very domains which his fathers possessed in free and independent right"

(chapter 14); second, and more important, that he had fallen in love with Lady Rowena, Cedric's ward, whom his father had destined for Althelstane of Coningsburgh (chapter 18). The unfortunate young hero, banished from his ancestral home and forbidden to love his fair mistress by an intransigent, disapproving father is a striking variation of a basic Oedipal pattern observed by Charles Mauron in Nerval's writings ["Nerval et la psycho-critique," *Cahiers du Sud,* No. 293 (1949)]. With these facts in mind we can see more clearly why Nerval, an avid reader of Scott, could have identified himself with the dark warrior of chapter eight. Finally, a word must be said about the appearance of the title in the novel itself. In the chapter in question, Scott describes the mysterious knight as follows: "His suit of armor was formed of steel, richly inlaid with gold, and the device on his shield was a young oaktree pulled up by the roots, with the Spanish word *Desdichado,* signifying 'Disinherited'." Must we assume, as Mme. Moulin [*Les Chimères: Exégèses de Jeanine Moulin,* 1949] and others do, that Nerval was as ignorant of the Spanish language as the Scottish bard seems to have been in this instance? *Desdichado* means "unfortunate," "unhappy," "unlucky," "distressed," "miserable"—not "disinherited" (*desheredado*). By adding the article, Nerval has personified all the meanings of this word, and let it stand for himself, the hero of this poem.

> Je suis le Ténébreux,—le Veuf,—l'Inconsolé,

The ease of transforming an adjective into a noun in French and other Romance languages by simply prefixing the definite article provides Nerval with a device rarely available to the English poet and translator (cf. the good, the true, the beautiful). The full significance of this device can be appreciated if we compare a similar verse from Victor Hugo's *Booz Endormi*: "Je suis seul, je suis veuf et sur moi le soir tombe." Where Hugo is content with a banal, prosaic statement, Nerval is seeking a much greater intensity of expression. There are numerous examples in Greek mythology of an idea's becoming incarnate. Gérard seems to be striving for such an ideal, for by adding the article and capitalizing the adjectival nouns, he is saying that he is the incarnation of everything dark and gloomy ("ténébreux"), widowed and alone ("veuf"), unconsoled and disconsolate ("inconsolé"). One could, of course, multiply the secondary meanings in each case, but basically (in a remarkable ambiguity which William Empson would surely admire) they all mean the same thing: "bereft" (of light, of love, of solace).

> Le Prince d'Aquitaine à la Tour abolie:

The first hemistich does not refer to Waifre d'Aquitaine, nor to Gaston III, Count of Foix, nor to any other prince or hero with whom Nerval may have at one time or another associated himself. The fact that Gérard claimed to have descended from Périgordian ancestry may have led him to choose the ancient kingdom to which Périgord was enfeoffed; but one could make an equally strong case for the evocative power and sonorous quality of the word, "Aquitaine." It is, by the same token, interesting but not indispensable to note that the sixteenth card in the game of tarots is called "la maison-Dieu ou la foudre," or, according to Le Breton, "la maison-Dieu ou la Tour foudroyée" ["La Clef des *Chimères,* l'Alchimie," *Fontaine,* No. 44, 1945]. Analyzing the component parts of the verse, we find, simply, that the poet is *the* Prince of Aquitaine bereft of his tower. The word, "tower," stands for castle, and the synecdoche is especially appropriate since the keep (*donjon*) was the tallest, most solid part of the building, the place where the medieval lord kept his family, his treasures, and his archives. As E. Noulet has already observed, the word, "aboli"—which previously applied only to abstractions, as, for example, in "to abolish a law, a right, a privilege"—took on a broader meaning with the publication of this poem, entered the poetic language of the nineteenth century, and was used by Mallarmé no less than six times [*Etudes littéraires,* 1944]. In this context it could mean "the tower which had been brought down," but symbolically it surely signifies "the Prince of Aquitaine whose rights, privileges, and property have been abolished." What is more unfortunate than to be *the* Prince of Aquitaine with no land, no home, no defenses—to be deprived of light, of love, of consolation? The importance of the definite article in these first two verses cannot be exaggerated, for, as Henri Meschonnic has remarked in connection with other sonnets of **Les Chimères,** it is employed by Nerval to "establish the serenity of an eternal order" ["Essai sur la poétique de Nerval," *Europe,* No. 353 (1948)]. The entire verse, seen as a single concept, thus becomes a kind of adjectival noun in apposition with and completing the three elements of the preceding one. The poet has said what he is. In the next two verses he will say why.

> Ma seule *Etoile* est morte,—et mon luth constellé
> Porte le *Soleil* noir de la *Melancolie.*

Here we must again distinguish between the genesis of an image and its meaning. In 1837, it may be recalled, Gérard fell in love with the actress, Jenny Colon. In February or March 1838, Jenny broke off the affair, and two months later married a flutist in the orchestra that accompanied the theatrical group in which she was employed. She died in 1842. An idea of the emotional impact that this liaison had on Nerval may be formed by reading the *Lettres à Jenny Colon,* which, as Jean Richer has shown, were written during the winter of 1837-38. It has been said that she was the only woman he deeply loved in real life. It would be more accurate to observe that she was the only one who seemed to respond fully to a feminine ideal which he nourished all his life. An apt disciple of Goethe, he loved only one woman in many forms. In the *Promenades et souvenirs* her names were Héloïse, Fanchette, and Célénie; in the **Filles du feu** her names were Angélique, Sylvie, and Adrienne; later on she was identified with Balkis, the Queen of Sheba, and with the goddess, Artemis; finally she became the ever vanishing and reappearing Aurélia, who in the mysteriously poetic narrative of that name, guides him through a series of trials to salvation.

There is no doubt that the death of Jenny Colon in 1842 contributed to the poet's increasingly morbid state of melancholy, and that this mental state, in one of its recur-

ring forms, could many years later have contributed to the mood of this poem. But the image, "Ma seule *Etoile* est morte," does not *mean* that Jenny Colon is dead; it is the distillation of that and other experiences. Likewise the seventeenth tarot card does not explain this image, though it may have helped to inspire it. On this card, Nerval could have been struck by the large star surrounded by seven smaller ones, could have considered the large one as the "only" star (because of its size which differentiated it from the others), and could have imagined a situation wherein such a body could have been the source of light for the smaller ones, which would then by definition be planets. But again we are dealing with sources rather than meanings. Upon close reading, it appears that, in the kind of ambiguity Nerval employed in the first two verses, he is saying the same thing twice in these two. In other words, "Ma seule *Etoile* est morte et mon luth constellé / Porte le *Soleil* noir de la *Mélancolie*" are two different ways of saying the same thing. Nerval shares the ancients' belief that the end of the world will come when the sun's fire dies out. The dead star and the black sun are thus, on the metaphysical level, symbols of the poet's deep despair. On the affective level, *"Etoile"* symbolizes the poet's one love in all its forms. A germ of this idea is found in the following passage from *Sylvie*: "Ermenonville . . . tu as perdu ta *seule étoile,* qui chatoyait pour moi d'un double éclat. Tour à tour bleue et rose comme l'astre trompeur d'Aldébaran, c'était Adrienne ou Sylvie—c'était les deux moitiés *d'un seul amour.*" It is by reference to an eternal feminine principle, not to a particular woman, that the word *"Etoile"* in this verse takes on its full affective meaning. Finally, if we think of part one, chapters 2 and 3 of *Aurélia,* where the star, the poet thinks, is guiding him towards his destiny, we see a third level of meaning for this symbol. Whatever guidance he may have hoped for has disappeared; he can no longer see his star in the heavens.

Nerval has compressed years of experience into a few words, but these words are the quintessence of that experience, not a series of clues to events in his own life.

—John W. Kneller

In the only enjambment of the entire poem, the second hemistich of this line is syntactically connected to the final verse of the quatrain, and although its meaning is the same as that of the hemistich just discussed, it contains images which shade that meaning and require explanation. For Jean Richer, *"le luth* means not only the musical instrument traditionally attributed to the poet, but 'the wood' (*al-ūd,* in Arabic) which is living matter and specifically an engraved wood ('constellé'), that is to say on which are probably carved the stars naming the man Gérard Labrunie, therefore his horoscope" [*Cahiers du Sud,* No. 331 (1955)]. This explanation is not only in genious but plausible, if we remember that the subject of the poem is the poet's destiny. Since the visual aspect of this astral imagery is secondary to the symbolic, the adjective *constellé* means "fated."

That the fourth verse could have been inspired by Dürer's *Melancholia* cannot be denied. But if we refer to the enigmatic engraving, we see that what Nerval calls a "*Soleil noir*" is probably a comet, and the comet is spreading light. Without going beyond the circle of Nerval's close friends, one can find the reason for his interpretation. For, as Jean Richer has noted, Théophile Gautier, in a poem called "Mélancholia," described the painting as follows: " 'Dans le fond du tableau, sur l'horizon sans borne, / Le vieux père Océan lève sa face morne, / Et dans le bleu cristal de son profond miroir / Réfléchit les rayons d'un grand soleil tout noir.' " Suggestive of the image are these two verses by Nerval in **"Le Christ aux Oliviers"**: "En cherchant l'œil de Dieu, je n'ai vu qu'une orbite / Vaste, noire, et sans fond, d'où la nuit qui l'habite." In the *Voyage en Orient,* he makes a precise reference to the engraving: "Le soleil noir de la mélancolie, qui verse des rayons obscurs sur le front de l'ange rêveur d'Albert Dürer, se lève aussi parfois aux plaines lumineuses du Nil, comme sur les bords du Rhin, dans un froid paysage d'Allemagne." In *Aurélia,* the black sun symbolizes the end of the world. Thus the poet's anguish, reaching a climax, becomes identical with the tragic fate of the universe.

> Dans la nuit du Tombeau, Toi qui m'as consolé,
> Rends-moi le Pausilippe et la mer d'Italie,

In a letter to Jenny Colon (1837), in the "Roman à faire," published in the periodical, *La Sylphide* (1842), and in **"Octavie,"** one of the *Filles du Feu* (1854), Nerval tells of an incident which happened to him during a stay in Italy in 1834. Having encountered a young Englishwoman, Octavie, he arranged to meet her again the next day at Portici. As a diversion he then went to spend the night with a gypsy. Overcome by a mood of depression, however, he left the house where he was being entertained, wandered about the city of Naples, then began to walk up Mount Posilippo. Reaching the top, he looked down over a steep cliff toward the sea, and was tempted to take his life. He resisted the temptation, however, and, suddenly remembering his engagement with Octavie, he was rescued from the despondency in which he had almost committed suicide. On the basis of such facts as these, Mme. Moulin interprets the "Toi" in the first verse of the stanza to mean Octavie. But bearing in mind Nerval's respect for syntax, we see that there are two possible readings for these verses: (1) "you who are now in the tomb, and who once consoled me when I was in despair . . ."; (2) "now that I am in the darkness of the tomb, you, who once consoled me, give me back. . . ." M. Cellier is right in opting for the second reading, since it is in keeping with the point of view of the poem, a kind of epitaph sonnet in which the poet speaks from beyond the ivory gate ["Sur un vers des *Chimères:* Nerval et Shakespeare," *Cahiers du Sud,* No. 311 (1952)]. The puzzling inconsistency of "consolé" after the "inconsolé" of the first verse can be explained by assuming an ellipsis and adding "autrefois"

before the last word. The "Toi" here does not, therefore, refer to Octavie. Such an interpretation unnecessarily restricts the meaning. The fact that it is capitalized confirms the interpretation that it is the "seule *Etoile*" of line three, the "Reine" of verse ten, the only woman the poet ever loved, the principle which Goethe, in *Faust,* calls *das Ewig-Weibliche.* He is beseeching guidance toward the light, the love, and the consolation, the absence of which he poignantly regrets in the first quatrain. In the Nervalian personal mythology, Italy (particularly the area around the bay of Naples) represents light, life, happiness, whereas Germany represents the opposite. The fact that Posilippo was supposed to mean, etymologically, "surcease of cares" was undoubtedly taken into account by the poet, and provides a valid secondary meaning to the verse.

> La *fleur* qui plaisait tant à mon cœur désolé,

The Eluard manuscript bears the word "ancolie" over the word "*fleur.*" Even though this flower is the symbol of melancholy according to some, and the emblem of madness according to others, it is clear why it never reached the final version. At the end of the verse it would have been a facile rhyme for "*Mélancolie*"; within, it would have been an interior cacophony unacceptable to Nerval's pure classical ear. Nor is it the anxoka which appears in *Aurélia,* as Jean Richer avers. The best explanation of "la fleur," and one which is in keeping with the rest of the poem is found in Mallarmé's *Crise de vers*: "Je dis: une fleur! et, hors de l'oubli où ma voix relègue aucun contour, en tant que quelque chose d'autre que les calices sus, musicalement se lève, idée même et suave, l'absente de tous bouquets." "La *fleur*" is indeed the one that is absent from any bouquet: it is *the* flower, the quintessence of "flowerness," all flowers purified into a symbol.

> Et la treille où le Pampre à la Rose s'allie

Underneath the visual image, which needs no explication, is the Dionysiac fertility symbol—the union of the rose and the vine. The rose, attribute of Venus, and the vine, attribute of Dionysos, render the symbolism of this verse unmistakable. A secondary resonance of meaning may be discerned if we recall that Nerval always had a predilection for creeping or climbing plants. In chapter three of *Sylvie* he writes: "Je revois sa fenêtre où *le pampre s'enlace au rosier.*" In *Aurélia* I, V, he speaks of "perspectives reliées par de longues traînées de verdure grimpante." Later in the same work when recalling his childhood he describes the "festons de l'aristoloche et du lierre." Since these creepers are all associated with the calm pleasures of childhood, it is not inappropriate to find in this verse a secondary nostalgic significance.

In the first quatrain the poet has consistently used symbols of darkness; in the second, it is the light imagery which dominates. In the first he has stated all that he is bereft of, in the second he asks that they be given back. The second stanza thus develops exactly opposing, but at the same time complementary, themes to those of the first. The poet who has known love, happiness, and light in the past feels all the more poignantly their absence in the present.

> Suis-je Amour ou Phébus? . . . Lusignan ou Biron?

Breaking the regular rhythm of the first two strophes, the poet now asks, "Am I Eros or Phoebus? . . . Lusignan or Biron?" Exegetes have had great difficulty with this verse. It is the only one that Le Breton does not attempt to coerce into his alchemistic hypothesis. The interpretations have varied widely; indeed the only item on which there seems to be substantial agreement is "Lusignan." All Nervalians agree that this refers to the mortal with whom the legendary mermaid, Mélusine, fell in love. The family name derives from the fairy palace which she created, and in which they lived after their marriage. Wishing to conceal from her husband the fact that she was a mermaid and at times had the tail of a fish, she exacted from him the promise that he would not intrude upon her on Saturdays. When he broke the promise and discovered her secret, she left him forever. According to legend, she returned whenever the lord of the castle or the king of France was dying, at which time she was supposed to appear, shrieking, on the castle wall. There is no doubt that the Lusignan intended here is the legendary one, and not one of the members of the historical family, particularly since, in the Eluard manuscript of this poem, Nerval wrote the name of Mélusine in the margin next to the word "Fée" in line fourteen.

The identification of Lusignan gives a clue to an interpretation of "Amour." Amour is not simply a "dieu grec," as Mme. Moulin is satisfied to assume, nor the character of that name in the *Roman de la Rose,* as André Lebois avers [in "Vers une élucidation des Chimerès de Nerval," *Archives des Lettres modernes,* March, 1957], nor the beautiful, winged boy, blindfolded and shooting his arrows to left and right, nor yet love in general. What undoubtedly attracted Nerval in this god was that he was the lover of Psyche. In later Greek literature, it will be recalled, Cupid (or Eros) secreted Psyche in a beautiful palace. Since he was a god, he forbade her to look at him when he visited her at night. She disobeyed, and he left her. Eros, the lover of Psyche, and Lusignan, the lover of Mélusine, have this in common: a restrictive condition is placed on their love. Eros must not be seen by Psyche; Lusignan must not attempt to see Mélusine on Saturdays. In each case the restriction is broken, and the lovers are bereft of their loved ones.

"Phébus" cannot refer here to Gaston III (1331-91), Count of Foix, given the sobriquet because of his handsome appearance. It is true that Nerval claimed descendancy from the counts of Foix in the sonnet **"A Madame Sand"** and signed a letter dated 22 November 1853 to the same person, "Gaston Phébus d'Aquitaine." But internal evidence argues cogently for another interpretation. Just as the somber night imagery of the first strophe stands out in contrast with the brilliant light imagery of the second, so Eros, the nocturnal lover, must here be contrasted with Phoebus Apollo, god of light and poetry.

Concerning Biron, there are, again, many suggested interpretations. According to Pierre Audiat [in his *L'Aurélia de Gérard de Nerval,* 1926], Nerval is referring here to Charles, duke of Biron, born in 1562, marshal of France, who served Henry the Fourth faithfully for a while, then conspired with the Duke of Savoy and Spain against France, was condemned to death and decapitated 31 July 1602. Mme. Moulin believes, on the other hand, that "Biron refers to the father of the above, Armand de Gontaut, Baron de Biron, who was born in Périgord, served valiantly as a marshal under Henry the Fourth, and was killed in the siege of Epernay" [*Les Chimères: Exégèses de Jeanine Moutin,* 1949]. This is the Biron immortalized in the song, "Quand Biron voulut danser," which Gérard included in his article, "Chansons et légendes du Valois," published with the **Filles du feu**. Léon Cellier is convinced that "Biron" refers to the character of this name in Shakespeare's *Love's Labour's Lost,* and supports his thesis by showing that Nerval was under the influence of the Bard of Avon at the time he wrote the scenario for *La Polygamie est un cas pendable.*

There is no evidence in this poem or elsewhere in Nerval's works that he ever considered himself treacherous; the Audiat thesis is therefore without foundation. There is no doubt, on the other hand, that Shakespeare's madcap young lord, in attendance on Ferdinand, king of Navarre, would greatly appeal to Gérard, especially in the scene where he is being put to the test by his beloved. The image of Gérard as a *fol délicieux* is not entirely without foundation. But does it fit in with the context of the poem? Since Eros and Phoebus, as Greek gods, can be logically compared, it is unlikely that Nerval, in the same verse, would compare the legendary founder of a historical family with a character in a Shakespearian play. Lusignan must therefore be compared with another historical and legendary figure, the Périgordian hero, celebrated in the Valois folk song. Taken as a symbol this "Biron" would possess, in addition to his own, some of the characteristics of the Shakespearian hero. In this way the second two interpretations are reconciled, and our understanding of the word itself is enriched.

If our identification of these four figures is correct, what then does the verse signify? An extremely wooden translation of the first hemistich, but perhaps a fairly accurate one, would be: "Am I basically a poet or a lover?" Or: "Am I poetry and light, or love and darkness?" At certain periods of his life, Gérard was very modest about his poetic gifts. In the preface to **Les Filles du feu** he says in connection with his later sonnets, including this one, " . . . la dernière folie qui me restera probablement ce sera de me croire poète." But since the first stanza of the poem itself argues even more cogently against any identification with Phoebus, and since there is no idle punctuation in **"El Desdichado,"** we may assume that the suspension points between the two hemistichs indicate a true ellipsis, and that Gérard, in at least a temporary answer to the question he has just asked, assumes that his is not the *moira* of a poet, but that of a lover. That being the case, the next question comes into better focus. "If I am under the ascendancy of Eros, is it then my destiny to have strange, enchanted loves (Lusignan) or successful, happy, courtly ones (Biron)? Shall I, like Lusignan, offend my beloved and be sad? Or shall I, like Biron, dance and be happy?" Such is the sense of this verse, with all the secondary clusters of meaning. As we shall see, the remaining verses indirectly answer the questions raised here.

Mon front est rouge encor du baiser de la Reine;

It is nearly impossible to read this greatly esteemed and frequently quoted line, whose density of expression is so Mallarmean, without thinking of the faun's reflection: "Mon sein, vierge de preuve, atteste une morsure / Mystérieuse, due à quelque auguste dent." For we have here no simple allusion to a courtly experience such as that of Alain Chartier, who was kissed on the brow by Margaret of Scotland for having written "La Belle Dame sans merci." We have, rather, a distillation of the experience previously related in *Sylvie,* where the young hero, after having kissed Adrienne, confesses, "De ce moment, un trouble inconnu s'empara de moi." "La *Reine*" is not Balkis, Candace, or any other specific queen; analogous to "la *fleur*" of verse nine, she is all of these and none at the same time; she is the first, the preëminent one of her sex, the "seule Etoile" of verse three, the heroine of this poem. The ascendancy of Eros seems at this point complete.

J'ai rêvé dans la Grotte où nage la Sirène . . .

As with other verses one must not debate whether "Grotte" here refers to the *grotta azzurra* on Capri or to the cave of the Villa Gregoriana at Tivoli, near Rome. The fact that both "Grotte" and "Sirène" are capitalized indicates that Gérard is interested in the symbol rather than any reference—the generic rather than the specific. If the preceding verse is, in a sense, an answer to the question, "Amour ou Phébus?" then this one responds to the query, "Lusignan ou Biron?" We know of Nerval's fascination for legends about mermaids from his commentary on "La Reine des poissons," a variation on the romance of Mélusine. We know that in his affective life, he was always seeking an unattainable ideal. The sense of this verse is then a confession that he is a nympholept, not in the pejorative, but rather in the literal or etymological sense of the word. Besides being kissed by the queen, he has been caught by the nymphs (*nymphólēptos*).

Et j'ai deux fois vainqueur traversé l'Achéron:

The suspension points of the preceding verse indicate not only the trailing off of a reverie, but a break in thought. The theme of love makes way for that of poetry. It has been said that he is referring here to two attacks of madness. We now know that he had many more such attacks. We also know from his correspondence, and particularly from *Aurélia,* that he considered them as quasi-mystical experiences during which he seemed to know and understand everything in the universe. Contrary, therefore, to the ancient belief so aptly expressed by Phèdre, "On ne voit point deux fois le rivage des morts . . . Et l'avare Achéron ne lâche point sa proie," Gérard, assuming now a much more heroic tone, declares that he has survived death. He

affirms that his experiences have qualified him as a seer (this is the correct inference of the word "vainqueur"), and thus reinforces the point of view of this epitaph sonnet.

Modulant tour à tour sur ma lyre d'Orphée
Les so upirs de la Sainte et les cris de la Fée.

The preceding verses take on their full significance in the light of the final two. Consistent with our previous observations, we may conclude that "la Sainte" is not the Adrienne of *Sylvie,* who became a nun and supposedly died at Saint Sulpice in 1832. She is, instead, the "sainte de l'abime" of the sonnet, **"Artémis"**; she is all that is personified by the myth of Eurydice. "La Fée" is not merely Mélusine or the "Reine des poisons" of the Valois legend; she is *the* fairy, the nymph, the sister to all mermaids. The final tercet stands in contrast with the first. In the first he says that he is under the ascendancy of Eros and Lusignan; but in the second he seems to be asserting that Biron (the hero) and Phoebus (the god of poetry) have predominance over his *moira.* He is then the hero-poet, who, like Orpheus, has through a transgression brought about the death of his loved one, and who, again like the Thracian bard, has transformed his experience into poetry. He has sung of a dual aspect of one great love ("Sainte-Fée").

The sonnet is, clearly, not an enigma in which hieroglyphic figures are used to conceal its true meaning from all but the initiate. Nor is it an example of "pure poetry," a kind of exorcism which is read solely for its incantatory power. It does have many hidden meanings, and its verses do have a magical charm for a large number of people. But it is fundamentally a poem of expression, albeit indirect, a kind of meditation in which we can participate by reading its lines. The use of italics and capitals, the presence of the words "seule" (whose importance is attested to by the fact that it appears no less than eleven times in the *Chimères*), and the frequent repetition of the definite article all indicate a striving for the essential, the general, the eternal, the absolute. The verses are spoken almost as oracular pronouncements, and these pronouncements make sense. It is possible to shed some light on the poem by reference to alchemy, to astrology, to psychology, and especially to the poet's biography and writings. But **"El Desdichado"** is complete in itself; it contains its own meaning. It is Gérard de Nerval's *moira.*

Gwendolyn Bays (essay date 1964)

SOURCE: A preface and "The Seer in French Romanticism," in *The Orphic Vision: Seer Poets from Novalis to Rimbaud,* University of Nebraska Press, 1964, pp. vii–ix, 68–128.

[*Bays is an American educator and critic specializing in French literature. In the following excerpt, she asserts that Nerval attempted to unify myth, the occult, and religion in* Les Chimères.]

In the literature of Romanticism the theme of the poet as seer is not the large and all-embracing subject it might appear to be at first glance. It is, in fact, a small branch of a much larger current of thought known as Illuminism, which was extremely rich and complex and which affected, to a greater or lesser degree, the majority of writers from the middle of the eighteenth century to the end of the nineteenth. . . .

The intellectual curiosity of the Romantics toward the phenomenon of voyance, it may be noted, has an exact parallel in present-day interest in such subjects as hypnosis, telepathy, and extrasensory perception. . . .

As an esthetic theory, the idea of the poet as seer is not one which passed away quickly in the nineteenth century. It has survived and has many modern adherents, who, although they state the theory in different terms, still hold to its essential tenet that art is not an end in itself but a valid means of arriving at new knowledge. As such, the doctrine lies midway between two extreme esthetic viewpoints of today. On the one hand are the purists who hold tenaciously to the doctrine of art for art's sake and do not want their literature contaminated with ideas; at the other extreme are the advocates of "committed art" who contend that serious art should ally itself with the political and social causes of the times. The first view tends to relegate the artist to the ivory tower where he can remain less affected by the events which take place around him and therefore more capable of producing "pure art"; the second view subjects the artist too much to the hue and cry of the masses. In its more extreme form, the latter view destroys both the artist and his art, when both must become the mouthpiece of a particular government. The conception of the poet as seer, which lies between these two extremes, neither separates the artist from the human lot nor subjects him to mob thinking for, like the priest, he has been in touch with something larger than individual existence, but is not for this reason exempt from the human condition. Translated into the modern philosophical terminology of F. S. C. Northrop, this larger existence would be best called "the esthetic continuum," with the meaning which he ascribes to it. Rimbaud and the German Romantics called it the "World Soul" but, in any case, the creative process is conceived as a dynamic one, in that the role of the poet is passive as well as active and proceeds by an incoming as well as by an outgoing method. In his outgoing active capacity the poet is a "stealer of fire" in the Rimbaldian sense, whereas in his passive role he is an instrument for the reception of ideas from the Beyond. But it is the passive role of the artist which is usually overlooked, and this is the very one which must precede, for the poet cannot seize Eternity until Eternity has first seized him.

The true seer must be able to decipher myth and legend, especially those of the ancient world, since early peoples concealed their most profound truths under the guise of a simple story. An understanding of the essence of myths was therefore desirable, if not indispensable, in providing the adept with a key to ancient wisdom. Through his assiduous pursuit of occult stud-

ies, Nerval possessed and assimilated the symbols of magic more thoroughly than any other seer poet. . . .

Nerval's belief in the dream as a means of knowing, of exploring the unconscious and of entering into communication with a spirit world, as related in *Aurélia,* was based upon his personal experiences. Here we shall be concerned with Nerval the syncretist and interpreter of myths who, inspired by his occult research, undertook in 1842 an eleven-month trip to the Middle East. This is the Nerval of *Le Voyage en orient* (1851) and of the twelve cryptic sonnets, *Les Chimères* (1854).

Behind all the picturesque detail of the landscape and the people of the Middle East, as Nerval saw it, lies the mystery of the Orient with its strange and secret doctrines, its initiation into the mysteries which professed to link modern man to the beginnings of his race. In this world charged with mystery the most common events of everyday life are not isolated and without meaning, but possess a secondary or transcendental significance. Second sight in the Nervalian sense means the ability to see and to decipher the spiritual significance of events. Extending further than the Swedenborg-Baudelaire correspondence, in which only objects signify, Nerval's second sight is much more uncanny, but it never produces a shock because the supernatural is treated as if nothing in the world could be more natural. . . .

It is probable that the twelve sonnets composing *Les Chimères* received this title because each possesses a multiple meaning, as the body of the mythical Chimera was said to have triple form. Not only do the events of Nerval's personal life signify, but they also form a pattern parallel to the various steps of the alchemical process and also to the religious past of man. The sonnets are twelve in number, suggesting the twelve steps considered essential in the alchemical process of changing the baser metals into gold. Although the cryptic allusions of a personal and alchemical nature have been worked out with much care and precision by Jeanine Moulin and Le Breton, the relationship of the poems to each other and the overall pattern of their progression has not yet been shown by other critics. It is this which will be pointed out here.

> In *Les Chimères,* Nerval has interwoven the events of his life and the transcendental fabric of his mystical research so skilfully that philosophy, art, and the personal events of his life form a closely knit whole.
>
> —*Gwendolyn Bays*

The first three poems, **"El Desdichado," "Myrtho,"** and **"Horus,"** correspond to the Kabbalistic tradition, to the alchemical process, and to the poet's own life. El Desdichado, the black and melancholy prince, is the primordial chaos, the masculine principle with relation to Myrtho, "the divine enchantress," the feminine principle of the second poem. Their union produces "Horus," the divine child, or the third emanation, which in Kabbalistic symbolism is called the "Word." In alchemical symbols, the black prince is the disintegrated matter as it descends into the crucible; in terms of the poet's own life, it is Nerval bereft of his two loves, Adrienne and Jenny Colon, who died prior to the composition of these poems. It is for this reason that Nerval says, comparing himself with Orpheus, that he has twice crossed the Acheron. But as the black metal of the alchemical process begins to whiten in the heat, the poet begins to find consolation in "the pale hortensia" of the second poem, who is Octavie in his personal life. As the white metal begins to turn red in the crucible, so the pale hortensia becomes entwined with the myrtle, the red flower sacred to Venus. In the poet's own life his love for the pale and pure Octavie becomes mingled with the more carnal love for the Neapolitan girl whom he encountered on his travels.

Horus, the divine son of Isis and Osiris, was considered by syncretists to have been a prefiguration of Christ and one of the incarnations of God. His birth in the primitive world, marking the end of that epoch, was said to be comparable to the coming of Christ in the Greco-Roman world. As his birth marked the beginning of a new religion so, in alchemical terms, the "philosophic child" or "the treasure of the philosophers" meant the first suggestion of the appearance of gold, which was preceded by a rainbow of colors. This is suggested by Nerval in the last line of the poem with his allusion to the "scarf of Iris." In terms of the poet's personal life, the philosophic child was born when, after a series of disappointments in love, he dedicated himself seriously to the discovery of a synthesis of occult symbols to serve as a basis for solving the mystery of existence. From this point on the sonnets indicate the religious evolution of man:

"Horus"—*The Egyptian Religion.* It marks the end of the more primitive gods.

"Anteros"—*Greek Polytheism.* Anteros was the son of Aphrodite and Ares, born of the union of opposites which was said to have created the harmony of Grecian culture. Anteros is the champion of ancient polytheism in its struggle against monotheism. Compared in the poem with Cain, Anteros is considered by Nerval to be another revolter who has "sown the dragon's teeth" which will produce a race of intellectual giants. The last tercet of this poem contains a reference to the alchemical process of the triple absolution of the philosophic mercury, necessary for its purification. This would seem to correspond with the three stages of religious development—Egyptian, Grecian, and Roman—through which religious thought had to pass in the process of its purification.

"Delfica"—*The Roman Religion.* As the name Delphica implies, this religion developed from the Greek. As Daphne was changed into a laurel, so the Grecian religion changed into the Roman which finally "sleeps

under the arch of Constantine." The poet prophesies that the ancient gods will return, just as he and Octavie have found again, in Pompeii, the temple of the Egyptian goddess, Isis. In his references to the laurel (Apollo), the myrtle (Venus), the olive (Minerva), and the sycamore (Christianity), Nerval suggests that it will be through the syncretism of ancient thought with Christianity that this return will occur.

"Artemis"—*The Virgin.* Between the ancient world and the Christian world about to be born comes another manifestation of Isis, the queen of heaven, who is also the queen of the night and its mysteries. In the person of the Virgin, past and future are contained, since the pagan goddess prefigures the mother of Christ. Thus Nerval asks: "The first or the last?" The number thirteen is associated with Artemis because there are thirteen lunations annually. Thirteen is considered an unlucky number because, in the tarot cards, it is the symbol of death. For the poet, it means the death of Aurélia. We know he associated Aurélia with Artemis because he first gave the title *Artemis ou le rêve et la vie* to his work *Aurélia.* Aurélia-Artemis is the actress Jenny Colon who, the poet says, belonged to him more in her death than in her life (Cf. *"C'est la mort—ou la morte"*). In her hand, Artemis carries the *rose trémière* (hollyhock), the rose of the Orient, which suggests again the poet's idea of syncretism. In the last stanza, the poet orders the white roses to fall—that is, the two early Christian women saints mentioned in the preceding stanza—since he considers the pagan Artemis, "saint of the abyss" and goddess of the night, to be preferable to them. In alchemical terms, the white roses refer to the matter which has become volatilized. As the alchemist urges the volatilized matter to fall back to the bottom of the crucible lest it escape upon the world, so the poet is somewhat reluctant to see the birth of Christianity.

Le Christ Aux Oliviers (5 sonnets)—*Christianity.* Nerval's Christ in Gethsemane is unmistakably the Christ of the syncretists—the eternal victim who has had other incarnations (Cf. Sonnet 5). The real agony of Nerval's Christ is that he is torn between two worlds, one dying and the other in the process of being born. In the third sonnet, his is the only breath of life in this intermediary stage of civilization. All in the universe is dead except Christ. Only he is aware that if he dies everything is dead. Like Vigny's Christ, Nerval's is also an anguished being who doubts the existence of God, but who, unlike the former, does not become an embittered revolter before the abyss surrounding him. Particularly dramatic are the last two stanzas of the fifth sonnet, in which the oracle invoked by Caesar is forever silenced. Now only Christ can explain the mysteries.

"Vers dorés"—*Syncretism.* One would have expected the sonnets to end with the five mentioned above. What, then, is the significance of this one added on at the end? Since a progression has been noted in the other sonnets, it would seem logical for this one not to lack connection with the others, but to represent what Nerval believes will follow Christianity—a rediscovery of the spiritual essence of the ancient mysteries. The true gold of the alchemist or "the mystery of the metal" mentioned in this sonnet, is spiritual in nature. It consists in man's realization that everything in the universe is alive—mineral and metal, plant and animal—that in the most obscure human being "a hidden God dwells," and finally in man's perception of his identity with this totality of life through love (Adonis).

As Nerval sought a common denominator to reconcile all religions, he also attempted to fit the events of his personal life into this meaningful whole. *Les Chimères* are the bright and many-faceted jewels formed from the slowly deposited sum of his research and experience—the jewels of the alchemist in search of perfection. In these sonnets, he has interwoven the events of his life and the transcendental fabric of his mystical research so skilfully that philosophy, art, and the personal events of his life form a closely knit whole. For this reason, a slight flaw anywhere in the warp or woof of his existence could result the more easily in a break of this unity. No conflict existed for him between his vocation as artist and as seer.

Walter A. Strauss (essay date 1965)

SOURCE: "Gérard de Nerval," in *The Emory University Quarterly,* Vol. XXI, No. 1, Spring, 1965, pp. 15–31.

[*Strauss is a German-born American critic and educator. In the following excerpt, he summarizes Nerval's philosophical orientation and discusses* Les Chimères, *focusing on the poems "El Desdichado" and "Artemis."*]

Between the years 1798 and 1800 a group of German poets and critics launched a journal known as the *Athenäum,* which became the first platform of the continental Romantic movement. The leading critic of the group, Friedrich Schlegel, declared, "Only he who has a religion of his own, an original view of the Infinite, can be an artist"; and the leading poet of the group, Novalis, proclaimed, "Poetry is that which is genuinely and absolutely real. This is the core of my philosophy: the more poetic, the truer."

These new assertions about the nature of art and poetry are indices of a profound change taking place in the notion of poetry in Europe, and their effect was to be far-reaching. This phenomenon, generally referred to as Romanticism, marks the moment at which the poet ceases to regard himself as an interpreter or servant of the society and its world-outlook, and invests himself with the new role of transformer, legislator, visionary—either as Orphic metamorphoser or as Promethean rebel, reconciler or destroyer. . . .

[In] Germany the Romantic movement tended toward abstraction because men like Schlegel, Novalis, and Schelling attempted to transform the new aesthetic into a revolutionary *Weltanschauung:* or better, they saw the world with different eyes and called for a new expressive style

and aesthetic to register this change. Whereas in England Romanticism makes no real attempt to transform theology (or science, for that matter), the German Romantics envisioned a new romantic science, a poetic physics, a fusion between the modes of poetic and scientific knowledge, a "universal encyclopedia of knowledge," as Novalis put it, in which the severed or severing realms of science, philosophy, politics, theology, and poetry would once more be reconciled, harmonized, and unified. . . .

The poet who will occupy us tonight, Gérard de Nerval, belongs to the category of the harmonizers. I have chosen him for two reasons: he was the only French Romantic poet who profoundly understood, and suffered from, the Romantic separation of man from world, and of rational self from mystical self; and going as far as he did in an attempt to bridge these gaps, he illustrates better than perhaps anyone else the hazards of the Romantic-Orphic alchemical quest for reintegration.

Biographical data can be reduced to a minimum. Nerval's dates are 1808-1855. His temperament was a deceptively quiet and gentle one. His first decade as a man of letters, which coincided with the heyday of French Romanticism, was relatively undistinguished. But behind the modest and amiable exterior, three great passions—all of which are really aspects of the same all-encompassing passion—remained concealed, at least in part: the restless hunger for travel, the quest for a unification of knowledge, the anticipation of a great love. When Nerval found this love in the person of an actress named Jenny Colon, and when he was forced to suffer the death of his beloved, the other passions were fertilized: Nerval traveled to the Orient to unlock its mysteries, and he attempted to use the keys provided by travel, experience, and extensive readings to create for himself and within himself a comprehensive world view. The quest necessitated not only a voyage outward but also a voyage inward, a descent into himself, in analogy with Orpheus' descent into Hades. This search took the form of an exploration *to the limits* of the borderland between reality and dream, and had for its concomitant a series of lapses into madness, the final result being suicide at the age of 46. In the last few years, however, between attacks of insanity, Nerval found the courage and energy to compose a number of works, of which the two most important, an autobiographical fantasy-novel entitled *Aurélia* and a group of twelve sonnets entitled *Les Chimères* will be of particular interest to us tonight.

Fundamental to an understanding of Nerval's intellectual dilemma is his own critique of the religious situation; and reflections of this nature are scattered throughout his later work. Meditating near the Temple of Isis at Pompeii, he writes:

> As a child of a skeptical rather than unbelieving century, floating between two contrary educations, that of the revolution which denied everything, and that of the social reaction, which claims to be restoring the entirety of Christian beliefs, shall I see myself brought to the point of believing everything, as our forefathers the 18th century philosophers had denied everything?

The problem is, however, only partially stated, because Nerval, in reaction to these eighteenth century *philosophies,* aligned himself with the so-called "illuminists" of that period; and this orientation throws light on his early Utopian Socialism, particularly the religious or pseudo-religious elements inherent in the Fourierist movement. But Nerval's early interest in Utopian Socialism was more a characteristic of the atmosphere of French Romanticism, and of the imprint that Victor Hugo had left upon the movement during its years of growth; in his later years the illuministic and religious interests took the upper hand.

> There is certainly—he wrote—something more frightening in history than the fall of empires, and that is the death of religions. . . . The true believer may be spared that impression, but, with the skepticism of our epoch, you sometimes shudder to find so many gloomy doors opening upon nothingness. . . .
>
> The art of the Renaissance had finished off the old dogma and the holy austerity of the Church before the French Revolution swept away its débris. Allegory, following in the footsteps of primitive myth, had done the same thing with the old religions. . . . In the end there is always a Lucian who writes the *Dialogues of the Gods*—and later on, a Voltaire who pokes fun at the gods and at God Himself.

The essential question, then, for Gérard de Nerval becomes the task of rebuilding upon the ruins of skepticism, a task which necessitates the closing of the "doors of nothingness." For Nerval the answer is his protracted espousal of the illuministic tradition, from Pythagoras and the Neoplatonists, by way of the Kabbala and the alchemists, to the Swedenborgians and Martinists of the eighteenth century. In this quest he was both aided and hindered by the rapidly developing interest in archaeology and comparative religion during the late eighteenth and early nineteenth century. For, whereas on the one hand the materials of ancient civilizations and cults became more readily available to him, the tendency of such accumulations of facts is to lead the reader into a more devastating skepticism. But the problem does not end there. Nerval maintained throughout his life an attachment to the Christian faith and consequently felt more than once that his skepticism as well as his experiments with magic were rebellious or sinful. In other words, he had moments of remorse for his Faustian-Promethean curiosity: the magic synthesis of religions toward which his thinking gravitated appeared to him like a violent transgression into a forbidden world.

Since Nerval saw in his religious syncretism not so much an intellectual edifice as an attempt to reconstruct his personal life in harmonious relation to an ordered cosmos—that is to say, a renewal of self through a renewal of vision—the figure of Orpheus becomes increasingly the model to which Nerval relates his experience:

> It seems to me that I have died and that I am accomplishing this second life of God.

> The Scriptures say that one act of repentance suffices to be saved, but that it has to be sincere. What if the event which strikes you keeps you from repenting? What if you are put in a state of fever or of folly? What if the gates of redemption are closed off to you?

These two reflections show Nerval's willingness to assume the burden of the descent into darkness, and the inner obstacle that would have to be surmounted. In order to understand the situation better, we must first say a few words about Nerval's syncretism.

Despite Nerval's encyclopedic hunger for the writings of the mystics and the illuminists, the interpreter of his work must not be led astray into excessive source-hunting. Nerval, as did Yeats some seventy years later, found in occult writings a partial confirmation and explanation for his own experiences and aspirations. Beginning with the declaration, quoted above, that the nineteenth century found itself face to face with the death of religion, Nerval sees himself, as a man and as a poet, confronted with a fragmented cosmos, whose pieces he tries to reassemble. The quest for unity of cosmos—of microcosm and macrocosm—begins first of all with an awareness of the dichotomies *here and now*. The most pervasive of all these is that of the divided self, long an appanage of the Romantics, consecrated particularly by *Faust I,* by Heine's *Doppelgänger,* and by E. T. A. Hoffman, and echoed and ratified by virtually all writers of the first half of the nineteenth century. A step beyond the personal "double" is Nerval's generic division of the human race into two types, "les enfants du limon" (the children of the slime)—the damned, those who cannot liberate themselves from the earth; and "les enfants du feu" (the children of fire)—those who are open to redemption, through art, through magic, through the "dream." The activity of the "children of fire" has its origins in the center of the earth, underground, in the preserve of the forgers and alchemists, and this activity often encroaches on forbidden terrain because it tends to interfere with the normal processes of nature. Moreover, redemption cannot take place without the Woman. Here Nerval, following once more the theosophists, elevates the figure of the goddess—mother—beloved into the figure of redemptress, identifying her variously as the idealized form of all the beloved women (Jenny Colon, Aurélia, etc.), plus the divine figures of the Virgin, Aphrodite, Demeter and finally Isis. (To quote Nerval: "Is it not true that we must combine all these different modes of the same idea, and that it has always been an admirable theogonic idea to give men a celestial Mother to worship, whose child is the hope of the world?") It is the belief in the reality of the unified redemptive figure of the Eternal Feminine who is simultaneously wife, mother and goddess, that guarantees the integration of the "double" inner man: if the Eternal Feminine is allowed to lead, she will redeem her lover-worshipper. But since the image of Isis must be recovered through a lost beloved, such as the actress Jenny Colon, the lover must become Orpheus: he must make the descent into the darkness of deprivation and dereliction, to reclaim his Eurydice, who, though she cannot accompany him back to earth, at least can give meaning and direction to his terrestrial life, precisely because she has opened the vistas of celestial life to Orpheus. Such is the general pattern of Nerval's Orphic experience, and, because of the crucial emphasis placed on Eurydice, it is worth noting that the experience also has a number of close parallels with Dante's *Vita nuova*, which, too, is an account of a life almost wasted yet miraculously redeemed by Beatrice.

The first part of the autobiographical dream-fantasy *Aurélia* describes a dream-curve that extends the horizon of the dream into the very substance of waking life and engulfs it. This extension of dream into waking life intensifies the visionary, the *shamanic* faculties of the dreamer, but because of its all-pervasiveness alienates the self from the processes of the world, even to the point of folly. The self becomes further and further divided and Part I of the work ends on the note of damnation and loss. The second part begins in anguish, describes the same curve as Part I but with a greater awareness of the error committed, then rises to a new and more complete vision whose final outcome, however, is not the integration of the self, but madness, not the achievement of redemption, but merely a vision of it glimpsed from a distance.

In the sense that *Aurélia,* like the *Vita nuova,* is a spiritual diary, a book of memory read retrospectively for signs, a discipline and initiation into the true way of salvation, the analogy of the two books is sufficiently apparent. So are the role played by Beatrice in Dante's work and the role played by the beloved, who becomes indirectly identified with Eurydice, in Nerval. But Beatrice leads Dante upward from the Garden of Eden through the circles of Paradise in the *Divine Comedy*; whereas Eurydice becomes identified in Nerval with all the mother-goddesses, most specifically with Isis, and leads Nerval upward as well as downward, into an ambiguous Gnostic purgatory whose dimensions are those of a no-man's land. The essential difference, then, between the two works is that Dante moves from a zone of illumination through darkness into greater and greater luminosity, while Nerval moves through a darkness occasionally touched by a radiance that never succeeds in abolishing the blackness. And whereas in Dante the function of dreamer is distinctly placed in a context of experience that assigns to reality and to the dream their proper respective places, in Nerval the dream tends at every point to obliterate reality and make it oneiric. These differences between Dante and Nerval may be used to illustrate rather succinctly the vast differences in perspective between a coherent world-order and a fragmented and labyrinthine universe.

The sonnet sequence **Les Chimères,** to which we must now turn, is a group of lyrical and mythical poems that grow out of Nerval's preoccupation with religious, personal and poetic synthesis during the last 12 years of his life. This sequence has always been regarded as extremely hermetic and therefore impenetrable to the uninitiated intelligence. Nerval was somewhat more modest about the poems than his critics. He speaks of the sonnets as having been "composed in a state of *super-naturalistic* revery"; insisting that they are hardly more obscure than Swedenborg or Hegel, he says they "would lose their charm by

being explicated, if such a thing were possible." The key word in this sentence seems to me to be "charm" (in the sense in which Baudelaire and the Symbolists and particularly Valéry liked to use the word in its root meaning of "incantation"). Whatever one makes of this somewhat cryptic remark, one must in any case note how far this is from the critical and intellectual clearsightedness of Dante. Dante's work is built around a center; Nerval's is an attempt to look for a new center. It is not accidental that the sonnet **"Delfica"**:

> Ils reviendront, ces Dieux que tu pleures toujours!
> Le temps va ramener l'ordre des anciens jours;
> La terre a tressailli d'un souffle prophétique. . . .

> (They will return, these gods for whom you still
>   weep!
> Time will restore the order of former days;
> The earth has trembled with a prophetic
>   breath. . . .)

anticipates Yeats' famous poem, "The Second Coming": both are poems about a missing center.

The culmination of the Chimères series is to be found in the two sonnets entitled **"El Desdichado"** and **"Artemis,"** in which the quest for the missing center is precariously achieved—and lost again. The former exalts the reborn Orpheus and the regained Eurydice; the latter places Eurydice into the total constellation of the Feminine Archetype. Here is **"El Desdichado"**:

> Je suis le Ténébreux,—le Veuf,—l'Inconsolé,
> Le prince d'Aquitaine à la Tour abolie:
> Ma seule *Etoile* est morte,—et mon luth constellé
> Porte le *Soleil* noir de la *Mélancolie.*

> Dans la nuit du Tombeau, toi qui m'as consolé,
> Rends-moi le Pausilippe et la mer d'Italie,
> La *fleur* qui plaisait tant à mon coeur desolé,
> Et la treille où le pampre à la rose s'allie.

> Suis-je Amour ou Phébus? . . . Lusignan ou Biron?
> Mon front est rouge encor du baiser de la Reine;
> J'ai rêvé dans la Grotte où nage la Sirene . . .

> Et j'ai deux fois vainqueur traversé l'Achéron:
> Modulant tour à tour sur la lyre d'Orphée
> Les soupirs de la Sainte et les cris de la Fée.

> (I am the Shadowy One—the Widowed—the
>   Unconsoled,
> The Prince of Aquitania of the ruined Tower:
> My only *Star* is dead—and my starred lute
> Bears the black *Sun* of *Melancholy.*

> In the night of the Tomb, You who consoled me,
> Give me back Posilippe and the Italian Sea,
> The *flower* that pleased my desolate heart so much,
> And the arbor where the Vine and the Rose are
>   entwined.
> Am I Eros or Phoebus? . . . Lusignon or Biron?

My brow is still red with the kiss of the Queen;
I have dreamed in the Cave where the Mermaid
    swims . . .

And twice victoriously have I crossed the Acheron:
Modulating in turn on the Orphic lyre
The sighs of the Saint and the cries of the Fairy.)

An alternate title of the poem (in a manuscript version) is "Le Destin"—Destiny. The sonnet stands under the shadow of a black destiny, the destiny of misfortune and disinheritance (those are the meanings of the Spanish word *desdichado*: note the words "ténébreux," "morte," "Soleil noir," "Mélancolie," "tombeau," plus the extraordinary dark resonances that abound in the first part of the poem), until they are gradually dissipated in lines 6–8, giving way to the brighter colors (especially lines 7, 8, and 10) and ending in a note of triumph (lines 12–14).

Without attempting to use extraneous aids, such as alchemical lore or the Tarot pack of cards (which may find their reflection in the poem, but which illuminate only facets of secondary importance), we note that in this sonnet the poet defines his present state—widowerhood, disconsolateness—in relation to his past: the death of his beloved and of his religious belief (the "seule Etoile" refers to both the guide-star and the Woman-guide), the memory of a comforter in a previous descent into the realm of death. Confrontation of present with past gives rise to the crucial question that opens the first tercet: What sort of lover am I? What sort of poet am I? The first question is in terms of Amor-Eros-Bacchus against Phoebus-Apollo; *i.e.*, it poses the question of relationship between the experience of love and the transmutation of the experience into beauty. The Lusignan-Biron contrast connects with the prince of Aquitania, the mythical ancestor of Nerval himself, who claimed to be descended from the Lusignan family of Poitou, and with the actual roots in Valois, Nerval's home region, Biron being a hero of Valois folk legends. (Lusignan is also the King of Cyprus, husband of the enigmatic mermaid Melusina in line 11.) But the point is not so much geographical: the question is rather whether the poet is to find his identification in legendary persons of the past or in the gods. The answer is, I think, that neither set of contrasts, nor the two sets of dilemma, predominate, and that the final identification, as a kind of coincidence of opposites, is to be found in Orpheus, who is at the same time divine (the subject of the ancient Orphic cult) and human, as well as the subject of legends, and who in his descent (as a "widower" and "shadowy") recovers not so much Eurydice herself but Orpheus's lyre, the power of song that Eurydice vouchsafes. The three lines that follow the double inquiry are significant in the assertions that they make: First of all, there are still imprinted on his forehead the memory and proof of the experience of love, the Eros-mark. Secondly, the dream (the Apollonian element) is, or has been, equally present all along, the poetic disposition has always been there; the experience prolongs itself into the present to activate the poetic urge. And finally, the role of Orpheus has been assumed before on two occasions (these two occasions are usually equated with Nerval's two major lapses into in-

sanity prior to 1853) with victorious results: the metamorphosis into song of the quintessence of the Feminine, in its sacred ("les soupirs de la Sainte") and in its secular and magic ("les cris de la Fée") components. In brief: Orpheus transmutes Eurydice into song. It is, I think, important to insist on the essential unity of the Orpheus figure as presented in the sonnet: the mediator between Dionysus and Apollo, the divine and human, the contemporary and the legendary, the defeated and the victorious, the widower and the husband.

Against **"El Desdichado"** we must set **"Artémis"**, which has certain resemblances to *Aurélia*, previously summarized. **"El Desdichado"** inquired into the destiny of the poet by examining the past with relation to the present. **"Artémis,"** (whose alternate title, in another manuscript version, is "Ballet des Heures," "Ballet of the Hours") is the existential collapse of Orpheus, in a confrontation of the actual present with the eternal present. Whereas the movement of **"El Desdichado"** was down and then up, from "ténébreux" to "vainqueur" (*i.e.*, the Orphic victory), the movement of **"Artémis"** is simply downward, the words "tombez" and "abîme" absorbing the precipitous impact of the poem.

La Treizième revient . . . C'est encor la première;
Et c'est toujours la seule,—ou c'est le seul moment;
Car es-tu reine, ô toi! la première ou dernière?
Es-tu roi, toi le seul ou le dernier amant? . . .

Aimez qui vous aima du berceau dans la bière;
Celle que j'aimai seul m'aime encor tendrement:
C'est la mort—ou la morte . . . O délice! ô
    tourment!
La rose qu'elle tient, c'est la *Rose trémière*.

Sainte Napolitaine aux mains pleines de feux,
Rose au coeur violet, fleur de sainte Gudule:
As-tu trouvé ta croix dans le désert des cieux?

Roses blanches, tombez! vous insultez nos dieux,
Tombez, fantômes blancs, de votre ciel qui brûle:
—La sainte del'abime est plus sainte à mes yeux!

(The Thirteenth returns . . . It is still the first;
And it is still the Only one—or it is the only
    moment:
For are you Queen, O You! the first or the last?
Are you King, you [who are] the sole or the last
    lover?

Love the one who loved you from the cradle in the
    grave;
Her whom I alone loved still loves me tenderly:
She is Death—or the Dead One . . . O delight! O
    torment!
The rose that she holds is the hollyhock Rose.

Neapolitan saint with hands full of fires [lights],
Rose of the violet heart, Saint Gudula's flower:
Did you find your Cross in the desert of the

heavens?
White roses, fall! You insult our Gods,
Fall, white phantoms, from your burning sky:
—The saint of the abyss is holier in my eyes.)

The inquiry here comes at the very beginning; and here again, as in line 9 of **"El Desdichado,"** the convergence of opposites (première ou dernière, etc.) provides the answer, in this case clearly affirmed by the words "seul" and "seule." But the poem is more complex, just as *Aurélia* is more complex than the preceding prose works. Lines 1 and 2 are concerned with the circularity of time; a note in the Eluard manuscript version of the poem makes this clear: "la XIIIe Heure (pivotale)"; the thirteenth is the hour which designates the repetition of the cycle, the pivot, from the standpoint of which time is arrested, suspended. The key word "moment" is also axial: it pivots from the experience *of* time to the experience of love *in* time, and by an analogous movement sets up a suspension of the lovers into one archetypal unit—queen and king.

The second quatrain pursues the feminine Archetype across this suspension of time-space, by expanding the image of the queen into that of mother-spouse, that is to say: going beyond the confines of the poem for a moment, into Aurélia-Isis. This excursus is all the more justifiable since the hollyhock rose is specifically associated with Aurélia, but also, as Nerval indicates in a note to the Eluard manuscript, with Saint Philomène (meaning "Beloved"), a Neapolitan saint who is represented as holding a rose, probably a hollyhock rose.

This saintly essence of the Archetypal Beloved accounts for the other saints, one southern (Saint Rosalie, a saint associated with Palermo) and one northern (Saint Gudule, associated with Brussels). These three incarnations of the saintly woman bring the poet to the all-important question: "As-tu trouvé ta croix dans le désert [a variant has 'l'abîme'] des cieux?" (Did you find your Cross in the desert of the heavens?) The question is a challenge, the negative answer being foreshadowed by the word "désert." The final tercet marks the lapse and the collapse of the poet's vision: the conflict between the deities on high, in the upper abysses of the saints, and "nos dieux," the deities down below, this conflict between the Christian version and the pantheistic-magic version of the world, culminates in the final desperate challenging assertion that the Eurydice of the downward way of the nocturnal realm is holier to him than the transfigured Aurélia-Isis, that the transfiguration of Aurélia-Isis takes place in Hades.

There is, as it were, a gap between **"El Desdichado"** and **"Artémis"**: it is as though Nerval had written **"El Desdichado"** in preparation for another Orphic descent, trying to assure himself of the victorious outcome by recalling the two earlier plunges. With **"Artémis"** the poet remains fixed in the underworld: just as time is suspended in the poem, so the "Orphic" is suspended at the edge of Hades. Whereas in **"El Desdichado"** the poet underwent the spell of Aphrodite-Eros, the later sonnet is under the ban of Artémis the virgin goddess (and also the moon-goddess, one of whose avatars is Hecate, goddess of un-derworld spirits). Thus Nerval has moved from an impending eclipse (the "Soleil noir" of Desdichado) to beyond the eclipse (the realm of night). Whether the final commitment to a dark Eurydice constitutes in itself an admission of failure, or a realization that only the way down is the way out, that in a state of darkness the poet can only sing the darkness, is difficult to say. If we go by Nerval's biography, then we must conclude that Artémis ends in a recognition of failure. In a letter written at that moment of personal crisis, Nerval states: "All is fulfilled. I have only myself to blame any my impatience for being expelled from Paradise. From now on I toil and give birth in pain." However, biographical criteria are never altogether reliable, since biography treats a man's life from the outside and merely conjectures about the inner life. We have seen that the conclusion of *Aurélia* leaves Gérard in a state of suspension also, but in a suspension between the light and the dark, between paradise and hell.

The causes for this unresolved dilemma lie in the very substance of Nerval's thought and experience, in what Georges Poulet calls the disaster that threatened Nerval's imagination. The constant tendency of Nerval to absorb greater and greater areas in his imagination by a process of concentric expansion, Poulet notes, results in a vanishing: "The aggrandizement is a fading-out. . . . Nothing is more poignant than this relation between magnitude and loss." Thus he delineates the two facets of Nerval's thought:

> Its glorious facet: the truly divine movement whereby his creative thought develops farther and farther and more and more triumphantly in the nature that it absorbs. Yet this is also a tragic movement at the same time, since by dint of absorbing everything the thought becomes no longer thinkable. It vanishes in its own greatness, leaving the inner universe in death and in night.

This, I propose, is essentially the dynamic of **"Artémis,"** reversing the upward dynamics of **"El Desdichado"**: As the outer vision fades, the inner unity fades: the double is in control once more. On the cosmic level, this means that the syncretistic vision of the cosmos gives way once more to the very force that brought the vision into being: the gnostic conviction of the split between spirit and matter that needed to be repaired by magic and esoteric techniques. The Orphic vision of harmonizing the world, restoring its pristine unity, was one of the major ingredients of the syncretistic urge. But when the vision fades, all that remains is the derelict figure of Orpheus, left with a derelict Eurydice at the upper edge of the abyss. It now no longer really matters whether Orpheus turns back to look at Eurydice at the risk of losing her.

In a sense this also marks the failure of realization of an Orphic synthesis in the first part of the nineteenth century. Poulet notes that "the spiritual history of Nerval is the history of a being that wanted to get along without the world in order to bring *his own* world into existence." The final result, as we know, in Nerval's case was exhaustion and folly. "I feed on my own substance and cannot renew myself," he wrote in December, 1853. Thirteen months later he committed suicide.

Here, then, ends a journey that I regard as exemplary in illustrating the hazardous enterprise that the act of laying the foundations for poetry and belief on private soil constitutes. It is exemplary because Nerval was willing to plunge into the unconscious reservoir of the psyche to try to discover the innermost reality that would validate existence and the Orphic celebration of Being. Madness and suicide were the biographical results. Yet they do not negate the quest, for there was also the vision and the precarious certitude. The night before his suicide he wrote to his aunt, "When I have triumphed over everything . . . Do not expect me tonight, for the night will be black and white." It is this chiaroscuro quality that defines the vulnerable and ambiguous situation of poetry, of all the arts, of man himself, in the contemporary world.

William C. Strange (essay date 1967)

SOURCE: "The Proper Marriage of Allegory and Myth in Nerval's 'Horus'," in *Modern Language Quarterly,* Vol. XXVIII, 1967, pp. 317–28.

[*In the following essay, Strange contends that the allegorical dimension of "Horus" is augmented by the mythology employed in the poem.*]

Although overshadowed by **"El Desdichado"** and **"Artémis,"** the great pieces in Gérard de Nerval's *Les Chimères,* the sonnet **"Horus"** does have a certain charm of its own and a particular usefulness, for few poems demonstrate so clearly just what allegory is and what it is not.

Horus

Le dieu Kneph en tremblant ébranlait l'univers:
Isis, la mère, alors se leva sur sa couche,
Fit un geste de haine à son époux farouche,
Et l'ardeur d'autrefois brilla dans ses yeux verts.

"Le voyez-vous, dit-elle, il meurt, ce vieux pervers,
Tous les frimas du monde ont passé par sa bouche,
Attachez son pied tors, éteignez son œil louche,
C'est le dieu des volcans et le roi des hivers!

L'aigle a déjà passé, l'esprit nouveau m'appelle,
J'ai revêtu pour lui la robe de Cybèle . . .
C'est l'enfant bien-aimé d'Hermès et d'Osiris!"

La déesse avait fui sur sa conque dorée,
La mer nous renvoyait son image adorée,
Et les cieux rayonnaient sous l'écharpe d'Iris.

Even without the incentives of theoretical demonstration and argument, **"Horus"** is a perfectly mannered invitation to a long reading that few could refuse. The poem is so attractive and it bristles with so many questions, partly because it is dense with allusion, but more because it alludes to such strange and difficult gods. For all his good will, Boccaccio once looked at the figure of Io-Isis and

threw up his hands with "The inquiry for the truth in this matter may be left to experts," [*Boccaccio on Poetry,* trans. Charles C. Osgood, 1956]. And that from a mythographer at the beginnings of modern scholarship.

Today, intricacies have multiplied, and truth seems farther away. Students of Nerval's poem tend to recognize that the Isis myth, as we receive it, is highly eclectic and to treat it eclectically, usually taking something from Rome and more from alchemy, but seldom dealing within the Egyptian basis of the myth. The decision to slight the myth in its original forms in favor of materials that were nearer to Nerval and more directly available to him is quite understandable. Given the state of Egyptology during his lifetime, Nerval had to know Isis primarily as a European phenomenon, an immigrant who had not quite lost her accent, but very nearly. And besides, the Egyptians who lived this myth for thousands of years never bothered to tell it; at least, no coherent Egyptian version of it has survived. Our earliest complete account of the Isis myth is to be found in Plutarch.

Yet there is a sense in which **"Horus"** chafes under this load of gnostic fossil and Enlightenment allegoric, for Nerval does better by the myth than that. His handling of its materials is remarkably sympathetic, and it results in an imaginative embodiment of the Isis story that is original and much more historical than any mid-nineteenth century student of the myth could have guessed. For example, Nerval's sonnet seems to focus on the woman, Isis, yet for some reason he calls it after the son, Horus. Rudolf Anthes maintains that Horus is in fact the central, even the germinal, character of the myth and that its other persons come into being as elaborations backward into time from him ["Mythology in Ancient Egypt," in *Mythologies of the Ancient World,* edited by Samuel Noah Kramer, 1961].

The same sympathy and near prescience characterize Nerval's feeling for the free and lively sense of the ancient story. Coleridge mused over Io-Isis as if she were a personification couched in some unknown tongue: if only we could read her name, we would have her secret. And Richard Payne Knight, in many respects a most atypical man, became in these matters a typical mythographer of the late Enlightenment. He wanted desperately to understand this myth, and for him—as, apparently, for Coleridge—that meant to find out what each figure in it stood for. Hence, in his *Discourse on the Worship of Priapus and its Connection with the Mystic Theology of the Ancients* (1786), [reprinted in *Sexual Symbolism: A History of Phallic Worship,* 1957], Knight claims that Osiris represents a "generative and prolific power," Set (Typhon in the Greek) represents a counter or destructive power or principle, and Isis is "the prolific material upon which both the creative and the destructive attributes operated."

Even Plutarch—especially Plutarch, rather—does better than this with the Isis story, for he insists that the myth is richly significant and that its figures are knots of meaning, as it were. Untie them if you must, but do not expect to be left with a single strand. In his presentation of the myth, Plutarch attempts to label these gods, but he does not simplify them. Osiris is the moisture that brings generation, and Set is the drought ["Isis and Osiris," *Moralia*, V, 1936]. Osiris is the moon, and Set is the sun; Osiris is reason and intelligence, and Set is the violence of passion. We could go on listing Plutarch's approximations or we could turn to other sources for other equivalences and labels, but we have enough to make the point that, for centuries before Nerval, there was a constant desire to "translate" this myth, to find somewhere a key to its mysteries. Why bother with such reductions? Precisely because Nerval will have none of them! Refusing all labels, he lets the myth mean in its own terms by making of it a perfectly formed sonnet of ever-shifting figures—figures that cast a shadow in the poem and then become the shadow they have cast.

Attempting to characterize that intelligence which formed these myths, once, and was formed by them, John A. Wilson singles out two characteristics of these ancient minds: the Egyptian's "love of symmetrical balance" and his belief that "there was . . . a continuing substance across the phenomena of the universe, whether organic, inorganic, or abstract" [*Intellectual Adventure of Ancient Man*, 1957]. A mind fascinated by symmetry and consubstantiality—could there be a more apt description of the imagination that gave us **"Horus"** or more striking evidence of Nerval's remarkable antique sense? From a world his own time scarcely knew, he has borrowed a myth and the temper that made it live. Knight is too sure that there are secrets here ever to find them; Plutarch, tolerant and tactful, comes much closer to the heart of the mystery; but Nerval touches the thing itself.

If **"Horus"** is a direct and vital encounter with the Isis myth, we are probably mistaken if we hope to find a key to its mysteries in some arcane manual. All that we need is the bare letter of the myth, and Plutarch gives us that. Jealous of the good king, his brother, and angry because he fears that Osiris may have cuckolded him, Set tricks Osiris into a large chest which he then seals and throws into the Nile. After a long search, which Plutarch lingers over in fond detail, the faithful Isis recovers her husband's body and returns with it. But Set attacks the dead Osiris more savagely than he had the living king, dismembers the corpse, and scatters it. Once more, Isis must go in search of her husband's remains to honor them and to conceal them from Set's anger. So ends the part of the myth that most interests Plutarch. He remarks that there is more to tell, that the ghost of Osiris will appear to his son Horus and ask for vengeance, and that Horus will defeat and humiliate Set in a series of varied encounters, but this last portion of the myth is too obscene for Plutarch's liking. One can understand Plutarch's reluctance to add such details to the substance of a myth whose seriousness and holiness he was about to maintain. Even my skimpy outline of Plutarch's selective presentation gives us all the help we need to start with Nerval's poem, not by offering a set of mechanical equivalences, a list of what sense is revealed by which god, but by forcing upon us a whole series of questions.

Coming to **"Horus"** from Plutarch, we note immediately that there was no Kneph in the story of Isis and Osiris. Plutarch does mention this puzzling figure once, but only in calling attention to the fact that not all Egyptians worshiped the dying Osiris. Specifically, "the inhabitants of the Theban territory . . . believe in no mortal god, but only in the god whom they call Kneph, whose existence had no beginning and shall have no end." Does Nerval mean for us to recognize "le dieu Kneph" as this undying Theban god, who is in every way the opposite of Osiris and remarkably out of place in this context, or has he intentionally left the figure of Kneph suggestive but vague so that he can use this vagueness, dispelling it when and how he will? And what of Kneph's cosmic palsy? His trembling shakes the universe, apparently because in some way he supports all being; but why does he tremble? Is he the frightened spectator of some birth or death, or is he being born or dying—or both? All of these questions would settle themselves if only we could establish Kneph's relationship to the usual characters and events of the Isis story.

The simple coherence of the narrative line, here at the beginning of the poem, suggests one answer. Kneph's trembling awakens Isis, who turns angrily toward that which has roused her from her sleep. Hence, Kneph is, in Nerval's poem at least, "son époux farouche." Nerval seems to have substituted Kneph for Osiris, the brother-husband of Isis and father of Horus. But things are not that simple, for "farouche" is a remarkably inappropriate epithet for Isis' husband, regardless of his name. According to Plutarch, Osiris is always the civilizer, the good king who lifts his people up from savagery, and the entire myth depends upon his beneficence to motivate Set's jealousy, Isis' grief, and Horus' extreme anger:

> One of the first acts related of Osiris in his reign was to deliver the Egyptians from their destitute and brutish manner of living. This he did by showing them the fruits of cultivation, by giving them laws, and by teaching them to honour the gods. Later he travelled over the whole earth civilizing it. . . .

The brother Set is the savage who murders this good man, but he is never Isis' husband.

"Horus" is so attractive and it bristles with so many questions, partly because it is dense with allusion, but more because it alludes to such strange and difficult gods.

—William C. Strange

Only Isis is identified with any certainty in this first quatrain, and she is far from simple. Why are her eyes green: is their color meant to qualify her supine motherness, is she the earth? And what is the old passion that burns so new in them? It could be hatred for Set, who, having killed her husband, somehow fuses with the brother whom he has murdered and she mourns. Or it could be her love for the dead Osiris about to flare into love for the new son, Horus. Her emotion rises from gesture to passionate speech without ever resolving these ambiguities. "Le voyez-vous, dit-elle, il meurt, ce vieux pervers. . . ." Is she speaking with a frosty formality, or does "vous," here, share the same antecedent with "nous" in the final lines? If it is the former, then Kneph apparently is being asked to cast out that which is dying, an appropriate task for an immortal god; but if it is the latter, then readers of the poem are charged with this task. And who is dying? Can it be the trembling Kneph? In Plutarch his one characteristic is that he cannot die. Can it be Set? The myth characterizes him just as Isis does here: his combat with Horus reveals him to be, literally, the old pervert, and he is often thought of as the god of winters and volcanoes. But he is also the deadly god, the murderer, not the victim, while Osiris is the god who dies. Only once is Set threatened with death. Horus overpowers him and delivers him in chains to Isis, but rather than gloat over his impending death, she frees him!

In short, to bring a temporary end to all this questioning, the octave of "Horus" seems quite carefully ambiguous, and the more familiar one is with the materials it draws upon, the more ambiguous it becomes. Apparently, Nerval has fused the dying husband Osiris and the savage murderer Set into the single figure of Kneph, who contains them both within his own immortality. As the octave closes, this crossing or merging of roles is pointed by one reference to the more familiar materials of Greek myth. Like Hephaestus, Set is a god with a twisted foot; but, like Osiris, Hephaestus is the damaged husband, not the deadly rival.

The sestet, too, begins by taking us outside of Egyptian myth proper with "L'aigle a déjà passé. . . ." Generally, the eagle is a symbol of kingship; it is the bird of Zeus, Jove, and Odin. More particularly, it is a Roman symbol on standard, coin, and scepter—as in Romulus' envisioning Rome's twelve centuries of power and greatness in the figure of twelve eagles. And Cybele, whose robes Isis now assumes, was the first of the great mother goddesses to be brought to pagan Rome. But does this eagle's passing signify the death of an old king, the birth of a new one, or both? Osiris has died, Horus reigns, and both are Kneph. That could be it. Nerval expands that multiple masculine identity met in the preceding stanzas, only now it is the son Horus, not the murderer Set, who is brought forward. So the eagle who passes and the new spirit that calls to Isis could be either Osiris, cut down in his prime, or Horus, casting off his childhood and emerging as king and powerful god. Or perhaps the eagle is Osiris and the spirit Horus, who succeeds him. In point of fact, the poem will not let us choose between these senses. The line implies them all, and Isis, in putting on the robes of Cybele, responds to them all—mourning as Cybele mourned the death of her love in the very fullness of his life and strength, but also protecting and serving as the great mother served the young, reborn god.

Surely, this last sense becomes strongest in the final line of Isis' speech. No longer bitterly cursing, she announces with evident pride, "C'est l'enfant bien-aimé d'Hermès et d'Osiris!" And then she flees. But why? What is she fleeing from? The savage husband is gone; there are no gods left here. Perhaps that is why she flees; she is running away from mortality and death, from us, in other words. The gods leave us when they die; the gods leave us when they are reborn as gods. The final tercet describes her flight in terms that remind us of Botticelli's "Birth of Venus": the goddess on a golden shell, the scarf full of light, the sky, and the reflecting sea. But in Nerval's poem the central figure of the painting has been erased, leaving only a suggestion of her image in the sea when *la mère* becomes *la mer* in what has to be the most astonishing fusion in this remarkably synthetic poem. Isis has become Venus-Aphrodite, the foam-born, though in Nerval's imagination she comes alive only to vanish back into the sea. But then Plutarch told us that Osiris vanished into the sea, and he even suggested that Set, in dismembering Osiris, became the sea swallowing the genial Nile.

Clearly, any attempt to force upon "Horus" a single set of exact labels or equivalences is quite impossible. The poem blocks such mechanical readings at every turn, offering familiar names in contexts that are never quite what we expect them to be or evoking distinct cultural contexts only to disengage itself from them. Evoke, then disengage: this is Nerval's poetic strategy, and it results in "Horus," a poem as evocative as a song of Schumann but as precise as a mathematical formula. Earlier, I suggested that Nerval's imagination was characterized by his feeling for the consubstantial and the symmetrical. We have been struggling with the consubstantiality of this poem, and it dazzles us; but there is symmetry in it, too. Look at the perfect manners of this sonnet or at the clear lines of the structure that emerges even from the opaque mass of questions "Horus" has made us ask. The poem combines the cyclical movement inherent in the traditional story of Osiris, who dies and is reborn in his son, with the linear movement of religious history, suggested by the pattern of references unfolded in its several stanzas. Though the primary allusion is to the Isis story, this basic myth is elaborated by references: first, to timeless Kneph of Thebes; then, to Hephaestus, Ares, and Aphrodite of Greece; then, to Cybele and Rome; and, finally, to a Venus born in the Renaissance and vanishing into our own time. The series is too long and its progress too regular for us to ignore this parade of castoff gods.

So "Horus" really has two stories to tell: one of a god who dies and is reborn in a myth, and the other of gods whose demise is a matter of historical fact. The product of this double plot is an insistently dialectical movement, complex but easily seen in the narrative sway of the poem. Disregard, for the moment, all questions of reference and identification, and this is what you will find: He trembles and wakes her. She lashes out at him. She rejoices that he is dying. She assumes motherhood because he has been born. She assumes divinity to answer his call, to follow him as mistress or as mother or as Iris, the hope and promise of both. In this scheme he is eternal Kneph, Osiris the dead husband, Set the deadly rival, and Horus the new king and son. She is always Isis, but an Isis who grows in response to this evolving masculine principle: the mother who sleeps, the wife roused to hatred, the mother who loves, the goddess adorable and vanishing. What could be more simple—or more symmetrical?

Complexity stems from the way that Nerval forces us to apply this symmetry. A pattern of action and reaction emerges sharply within his poem, but the precise agencies that act do not. Within certain limits, they are left for us to specify. It is as if Nerval had ground a lens with carefully designed properties and then had said, "Look through this until you see something." But look where and at what? **"Horus"** does tell a tale of vanishing gods. Perhaps we are meant to turn it on the present religious situation and see compressed within it, as through the wrong end of a telescope, centuries of the death of gods. Perhaps **"Horus"** is meant to make visible that which Matthew Arnold could but hear in the sea's melancholy roar. Even Kneph must die when he is only art, and this is precisely the transformation that we see in this poem: eternal Kneph elaborated into the figures of the Isis myth that pass, allusively, through Athens and Alexandria into a Rome boiling with religious change and then are stilled and vanish in lovely Botticellian froth.

But this recognizable and dour prospect is not all that we see through Nerval's poem. Consider these complicating factors. First, the straight line of history is met by the circling plot of myth with its dying and reborn gods. Then, simple history is complicated further by the omission of any reference to the Judaeo-Christian tradition with its masculine Godhead. Nerval seems to want only those ancient goddesses that the Old Testament condemns in others and represses in itself. Father Kneph is dead, and Nerval wants the beginning and that realm of the mothers where old gods rest and the new are born. Finally, as religious history moves to its mordant close, Isis' imperatives, explicit and implied, simply contradict it: "Cast him out: adore me."

Let all of these complicating factors come together, as the poem would have them, and we have something much more profound, I think, than a simple story of the secularization of nature or of the death of gods:

> The immediate reaction of human nature to the religious vision is worship. Religion has emerged into human experience mixed with the crudest fancies of barbaric imagination. Gradually, slowly, steadily the vision recurs in history under nobler form and with clearer expression. It is the one element in human experience which persistently shows an upward trend. It fades and then recurs. But when it renews its force, it recurs with an added richness and purity of content. The fact of the religious vision, and its history of persistent expansion, is our one ground for optimism. Apart from it, human life is a flash of occasional enjoyments lighting up a mass of pain and misery, a bagatelle of transient experience. [Alfred North Whitehead, *Science and the Modern World,* 1953]

Whitehead's noble generalities march toward the same ends as Nerval's images, but with one large difference. The poet's images are really much more general than the philosopher's statements. Whitehead describes the pulsing life of religious vision in a manner that clearly should have consequences for psychology, ethics, and theology, though they are not worked out. On the other hand, Nerval presents a model of vision itself, and because vision is not only a religious matter, **"Horus"** takes up directly all that wide relevancy that Whitehead's propositions can only imply. Put it this way: Wherever there is visionary experience, Nerval's poem has meaning, clarifying that one moment of vision and relating it to all the other like moments where **"Horus"** may be applied.

For a quick example, take the psychological sense this poem can make. **"Horus"** fairly begs to be read in Jungian terms. The conscious Ego and the Shadow, our personal darkness, appear quite typically as two mythical brothers, the civilizing Osiris and the barbarous Set. Together, they define a single masculine identity at war with itself, the old pervert Kneph, who is dying as the poem begins. But **"Horus"** records a cure, not a shattering descent into madness. And it comes about, as Jung says it must, when this faulty, masculine consciousness encounters the feminine unconscious it needs to complement it, to give it back the range and balance that constitute health. In this context Isis is clearly what Jung has called the Anima, manifest most often in the rich intricacies of a woman's being. Isis appears first as the angry widow/wife who hates the old pervert, but she joins with him to bear a new spirit she can love and serve as mother, mistress, and priestess. When the distress that brings about her intervention disappears, she, too, vanishes back into the sea which bore her, still to be known but not so directly, still to support our lives.

Such a brief gloss inevitably appears too slick, too easy, but it should be enough to demonstrate that **"Horus"** can make psychological as well as historical sense and to suggest that it may make sense in other ways if we let it. Simply generalize these specific patterns of religious history and psychological growth into statements of the principles they so obviously enjoin, into rules of conduct in other words, and **"Horus"** will make sharp ethical sense, punctuated by those imperatives we have already recognized in the poem. Or turn away from both principle and event within the natural world and apply **"Horus"** instead to the supernatural. Then it permits us to see, however dimly, a profoundly moving conception of a God who dies into our life and being and is born anew out of it. This is not quite the familiar mystery of incarnate and triumphant Christ, but something more like that strange and tragic God that Jakob Böhme knew. But we need not go on elaborating these senses or applications of **"Horus,"** for our analysis of the poem already has brought us back full circle. We began with a discussion of allegorical approaches to **"Horus"**; once more, we are considering **"Horus"** as allegory, though in a fashion that does greater justice both to the idea of allegory and to Nerval's poem.

Of course, with the modern distaste for things allegoric, there are those who would object to the justness or the usefulness of calling **"Horus"** an allegorical poem. But

John Cassian would have understood, and so would Aquinas, and Dante, and Boccaccio, and any others who were trained during the more than one thousand years when the classrooms of Europe echoed with "Littera gesta docet, quid credas allegoria. / Moralis quid agas, quo tendas anagogia." Because it asks for applications rather than explications, **"Horus"** is allegorical. To use it properly, one describes its literal substance—its diction, imagery, structure, etc.—which one then applies in as many ways as one can. Such successive applications yield a rich but single sense. As this sense accumulates, it will order itself more and more in a kind of ever-increasing generality until it becomes useful to pretend that this outward thrust of sense is really static and that it consists of several distinguishable levels of meaning. In effect, we bring clarity to our thought about such a poem by working with a series of cross sections of its meaning. What are the often maligned levels of allegory but those somewhat arbitrary points at which one interrupts and examines a single expanding significance, fixed in one common form in the schoolboy's jingle, and emerging, without strain or forcing, from our analysis of **"Horus"**? In discussing its problems of allusion and structure, the historical and psychological events it suggests, the principles it advocates, and the dim outline of God that it reveals, we have been moving simply and directly through the old scheme of the four levels in its most common form.

John W. Kneller (essay date 1984)

SOURCE: "Anteros, Son of Cain?" in *Writing in Modern Temper: Essays on French Literature and Thought in Honor of Henri Peyre,* edited by Mary Ann Caws, Anma Libri, 1984, pp. 91–101.

[In the following essay, Kneller explicates the poem "Anteros" as the protagonist's announcement of his revolt against God.]

The Chimeras of Gérard de Nerval continue to fascinate us because they are both hermetic and startlingly clear. These sonnets invite us to wonder about their sources, their genesis, and their hidden meanings. They move us by the cogency of their own poetic statement.

Unlike Wordsworth, Coleridge, Shelley, Hugo, and Baudelaire, Nerval did not write about theories of poetry. Even if he had, he probably would have departed from the generalizations and principles he had developed as he went about the practice of poetry. Here and there throughout his prodigious and varied literary output he scattered traces which have been pursued with sometimes successful and sometimes uncertain results. If it is true that no gap separates Nerval's sources from his writings—or his writings from one another—it is also true that none of the mythological, historical, or biblical figures that stand out in his poems conforms to the accepted characterization of that figure. Their names may well be Artemis, Amor, Phoebus, Orpheus, Isis, or Daphne, or even Caesar, Pilate, or Christ—

in which instances we had better know our Sir James George Frazer or our Bible. And if their names are Myrtho, Kneph, Lusignan, Biron, or Delfica, we ought to scurry to more recondite source books. To attempt, however, to resolve these figures into their antecedents is to be guilty of the genetic fallacy.

No belief or attitude of Nerval exists prior to or after any of his works. His figures are new. At the moment of creation, they assume an existence quite apart from their historical, literary, or mythological models and quite apart from the poet himself.

Although Nerval developed no theory of poetry, he did leave us two important passages which can serve as lanterns to guide us through the labyrinth of images in *The Chimeras*.

At the end of *Aurelia,* in the "Memorabilia," he writes:

> I resolved to fix my dream-state and learn its secret. I wondered "Why should I not break open those mystic gates, armed with all my will, and master my sensations instead of being subject to them? Is it not possible to overcome this enticing, formidable chimera, to lay down a rule for the spirits of the night which make game of our reason?"

This passage states the author's purpose in writing *Aurelia.* The presence in it of the word "chimera" provides a clue not only to the title of the group of sonnets in which **"Anteros"** appears, but also to the experimental, exploratory nature which the sonnets share with the prose narrative.

Another passage, earlier in *Aurelia,* is even more explicit: "Then I saw plastic images of antiquity vaguely taking shape before me, at first in outline, and then more solidly: they seemed to represent symbols, whose meanings I grasped only with difficulty." This sentence tells us much about the process that crystallized out into *The Chimeras.* The process seems to evolve through the following steps: (1) the fixing of an image associated with a vague spiritual state; (2) the molding of the image and the state into sonnet form; (3) the independent existence of the poem. Such a succession of steps relies heavily on the recapturing of dream-states and the discovery of their meaning.

But Nerval's sonnets are not simply the artistic ordering of recaptured dream-states. Each one of them is a coherent—albeit obscure—statement. Not the expression of an emotion, but, as T.S. Eliot would later say, "the creation of a new emotion."

By creating a new emotion, rather than reflecting a prior emotion, Nerval parts company with prevailing expressive theories of poetry during the Romantic period. He probably never read Wordsworth's Preface to the *Lyrical Ballads,* and, in any case, would surely have rejected the formulation that poetry "is the spontaneous overflow of powerful feelings." His great appeal for us today is—to modify the last two lines of the "Ars Poetica" of Archibald MacLeish—is that for him "a poem must not only mean but be." His sonnets are the forms he gave to his discoveries—the transformed plastic images of antiquity. Our approach to them must respect the unity of each of these forms, the oneness of each experience.

The experience, or new emotion, which concerns us here is metaphysical revolt, about which herewith some background.

Metaphysical revolt was given great currency and put in historical perspective by Albert Camus in *The Rebel.* Camus would have it go back to the Old Testament account of the Lord's refusal of Cain's offering and Cain's subsequent murder of Abel. It is inseparable from the belief in a personal God, who is not only the creator of all beings but also responsible for all evil. Its development in the history of ideas parallels that of Christianity in the western world. The New Testament, according to Camus, can be considered "as an attempt to reply in advance to all the Cains of the world by mitigating God's countenance, and by creating an intercessor between God and man" [*Essais,* 1965]. In Camus's logic, Jesus Christ came to solve the two principal concerns of the world's rebels— evil and death: "Only the sacrifice of an innocent God could justify the long, universal torture of innocence."

Metaphysical revolt during the Romantic period merges into satanism and owes much to the writings of John Milton, particularly as emphasized by William Blake. Blake's interpretation of *Paradise Lost* may very well be challenged today; he nevertheless set the keynote of the Romantic attitude when he declared in *The Marriage of Heaven and Hell* that Milton was "of the Devil's party without knowing it." This interpretation was probably never questioned by the Romantics themselves, who noted that Satan, not Adam, was the central figure of *Paradise Lost,* and that after the fall he was—in Milton's own terms— "majestic though in ruins." By espousing the right of human beings to redeem themselves, by making an apology for the right to revolt, and by placing humanity at the center of the universe, Milton, with Blake's assistance, opened the way to Romantic satanism.

> **The Chimeras of Gérard de Nerval continue to fascinate us because they are both hermetic and startlingly clear. These sonnets invite us to wonder about their sources, their genesis, and their hidden meanings. They move us by the cogency of their own poetic statement.**
>
> *—John W. Kneller*

The affinity for Satanism and metaphysical revolt, as Mario Praz and Max Milner have shown [in *The Romantic Agony* (1956) and *Le diable dans la littérature française* (1960), respectively], appears almost everywhere from the end of the eighteenth century on: in Schiller's *Die Räuber*

(1781); in Ann Radcliffe's *The Italian, or the Confessional of the Black Penitents* (1787); in Matthew Gregory Lewis' *The Monk* (1796); in Shelley's *Defense of Poesy* (1821); and especially in Lord Byron's *Lara* (1814), *The Corsair* (1814), *Manfred* (1817), *The Giaour* (1813), and *Cain* (1821). Jean Richer and Max Milner have discussed these works and their influence on Nerval [Richer, *Nerval: Expérience et création,* 1963].

There can be little doubt that Gérard, more often than not, adhered to Romantic satanism—that, like so many of his contemporaries and immediate literary forbears, he denied that the devil was wicked, that he considered evil as an active force produced by energy, and traditional good as a passive element whose principal characteristic was to follow reason. The sonnet, **"Anteros,"** first published in **Daughters of Fire** (1853), is—and expresses—Nervalian satanism in its purest form.

Because **"Anteros,"** like all other poems of **The Chimeras,** is complete in itself and in its order, we shall present it in the original French, which the reader will, we trust, read along with our English approximation and our comments.

Antéros

Tu demandes pourquoi j'ai tant de rage au coeur
Et sur un col flexible une tête indomptée;
C'est que je suis issu de la race d'Antée,
Je retourne les dards contre le dieu vainqueur.

Oui, je suis de ceux-là qu'inspire le Vengeur,
Il m'a marqué le front de sa lèvre irritée,
Sous la pâleur d'Abel, hélas! ensanglantée,
J'ai parfois de Caïn l'implacable rougeur!
Jéhovah! le dernier, vaincu par ton génie,
Qui, du fond des enfers, criait: "O tyrannie!"
C'est mon aïeul Bélus ou mon père Dagon . . .

Ils m'ont plongé trois fois dans les eaux du Cocyte,
Et protégeant tout seul ma mère Amalécyte,
Je ressème à ses pieds les dents du vieux dragon.

The Anteros of the title has, of course, a mythological ancestor. The Greek Anteros does not appear in early myths. He seems to have been shaped late in the cult of the Gymnasia when the ancients, wishing to depict the struggle of passionate instincts which attract or repel, divided Eros into two gods: Eros as consummated love and Anteros as unfilfilled love. The name, which means literally "against love"—ant(i)-Eros—lends itself admirably to ambiguity, since it connotes the negation of love as well as the reciprocity of love. Anteros was the quintessential *deus ultor* ("avenging god")—the avenger of those whose love has been spurned. As such, he had an altar dedicated to him by the metics, or alien residents, in Athens. On this altar, according to Pausanias, artistic figures told a legend. The Athenian, Meles, was loved by Timagoras, a metic, but returned the love only with scorn and according to his whims. One day he dared Timagoras to plunge from the rocks of the Acropolis. Timagoras was accustomed to gratifying the young man's every whim; feeling in this instance that he should prove his love at the expense of his life, he threw himself headlong to his death. Meles was so shocked and ashamed that he too climbed the rocks to die in the same manner.

Nerval read the consulted Pausanias. He could therefore have known this legend. He might also have seen the passage in which Pausanias describes a bas-relief in a palestra of Elis showing Eros and Anteros wrestling, the former holding a palm branch and the latter trying to get it away from him. He could have seen a marble relief in Naples and especially a bas-relief in the Palazzo Colonna depicting Eros and Anteros wrestling during a torch race. But even granting some prior knowledge on his part of myths or legends concerning Anteros—especially those depicting wrestling matches with Eros—and acknowledging that some familiarity with the stories can enrich our understanding as readers, it is fruitless to see the meaning of Anteros and other figures of this poem beyond the poem itself.

(1) You ask me why my heart rages so (2) And why my head remains unconquered on my flexible neck; (3) It's because I am sprung from Antaeus' race, (4) I hurl back the darts against the conquering god. Who is the *tu* of the first line? An anonymous interlocutor? The *Jehovah* of verse nine? If *tu* is an indefinite person who has asked Anteros the question which has inspired the poem, then the point of view must necessarily shift from the two quatrains, in which Anteros would be speaking of this *tu,* and the tercets, in which he unambiguously addresses Jehovah. But if we let the *tu* of the first line be the Jehovah of line nine, the poem acquires not only unity of point of view, but richer connotation.

The mingling of Greek mythology with Old Testament religion becomes more acceptable if we remember that Anteros—and, later, Antaeus—are avatars of their Classical prototypes, playing fresh roles in the world of this poem. The muffled fury of the first two lines goes far beyond Genesis 4:5-7: "but for Cain and his offering he had no regard. So Cain was very angry and his countenance fell. The Lord said to Cain, 'Why are you so angry and why has your countenance fallen?'"; and even beyond Isaiah 48:4, when the prophet berates the people of Israel: "Because I know that you are obstinate, and your neck is an iron sinew and your forehead brass . . ." The neck and the head become symbols of his revolt. The neck may have been all too ready to yield, may not have been invincibly rigid; but the head, unabashed, unsubdued, bespeaks eternal resistance to the power of Jehovah.

Throughout the rest of the poem, Anteros gives his reasons. His heart seethes with rage, first, because he is descended from Antaeus. Son of Poseidon and Gaea—God of the Sea and Mother Earth—Antaeus, let us remember, was the giant Libyan king and wrestler whose strength revived every time he touched the earth. Heracles took him on and soon realized that the only way to beat the giant was to lift him high into the air and thus prevent him

from renewing contact with Mother Earth, the source of his strength. Holding him aloft, Heracles succeeded in strangling him. Heracles, son of Zeus, kills Antaeus, son of Mother Earth—by trickery. But Antaeus lives on as do all creatures whose destiny was to be slain by the God of Heaven or his delegates, Anteros, descendant of Antaeus, does not shoot arrows at potential or actual lovers; he hurls them back at the "conquering God," who is not Eros but the archetypal embodiment of the victorious sons of heaven.

(5) Yes, I am one of those whom the Avenger inspires, (6) He has put a mark on my brow with his angry lip, (7) Beneath Abel's—alas!—blood-stained paleness, (8) I sometimes show (literally: have) the implacable redness of Cain!

To say that the Avenger of verse five is the conquering god of the previous line is to accuse the poet of redundancy. The Avenger is on the other side. He drives Anteros to revolt against Jehovah, to fling back the arrows and javelins against the conquering god. He has branded Anteros with his angry lip.

Nor can he be the Cain of verse eight. "The Avenger" is indeed an epithet frequently applied to Cain during the Romantic period. Byron so regarded him in *Cain: A Mystery,* which was lavishly praised by Goethe, Shelley, and Scott, as well as by Nerval. But, again, if Nerval had wanted the Avenger to be Cain, he would have found a better way to do it. The Avenger is the personification of all the meanings of that word—a new figure created by the poet. He is the progenitor of the race of Antaeus, the one from whom Anteros is sprung.

"Cain-colored" is red, since the color of Cain's hair is reputedly red—just as Judas' beard is supposedly red. The Cainites are a heretical sect of the second century, so-named because they held that Cain was created by a powerful force (fire) and Abel by a weak one (heaven). The Cain-Abel opposition parallels the Avenger-Jehovah struggle. Abel's paleness, or whiteness (the color of heaven) has been bloodied over and over again by the wrathful Jehovah of this poem who has unleashed great evil upon innocent people. Perceiving humanity as being divided into two groups, the chosen and the damned, the sons of Abel and the sons of Cain, Anteros declares his filiation from Cain/Antaeus and his opposition to Abel/Heracles. That his brow should be marked by the Avenger's angry lip is a nice twist. If the Almighty could set a mark on Cain to provide divine protection from physical harm to the first son of Adam, then why couldn't his rival, the Avenger, do the same for Anteros? The Almighty's power to bestow immunity is stolen from him, just as the sacred fire was stolen from Zeus by Prometheus. The mark of Anteros guarantees protection from the despotic abuse of celestial authority. It assures that his head will be unbowed.

Although the entire poem is addressed to him, Jehovah does not appear until verse nine. In this run-on position at the beginning of the first tercet, he serves as a semantic and syntactical linchpin holding the parts of the sonnet together. (9) Jehovah! the last one conquered by your spirit (literally: genius), (10) Who, from the depths of hell, cried out: "O tyranny!" (11) Is my grandfather Belus or my father Dagon . . .

The last one to be conquered by Jehovah—*le dernier*—has been identified variously as Dante's, Milton's, or Blake's Satan, and as Julian the Apostate. But a careful reading of the tercet provides a more accurate identification. He is, as Anteros clearly states, Belus—a Babylonian cognate of Baal—or Dagon. Baal is the name used throughout the Old Testament for the deity or deities of Canaan. Among the many biblical stories on this subject, the one depicting the contest between Elijah, representing the God of Israel, and Ahab, fighting for the Canaanite Baal is especially pertinent. Ahab's prayers were ignored, while Elijah's supplication was answered by the "fire of the Lord." Thereupon Elijah ordered the prophets of Baal to be killed and ran seventeen miles before the chariot of Ahab to announce to the people of Jezreel the victory over the forces of Baal (I Kings 18:20-46).

One of the nicknames of Baal was Baalzebub (or Beelzebub), which came to mean "lord of the flies" (a mocking distortion of Baal-zebul—"lord of the divine abode") and was used in the New Testament as a synonym for Satan. This association and the various biblical stories depicting the struggles between the God of Israel and Baal provide a rich historical background for Belus, whose identity is shaped by the context of his poem.

Dagon was an ancient Semitic deity whose cult was adopted by the Philistines. Although he was originally thought to be a fish-god, it is more probable that he was an agricultural deity—the root meaning of the word being "grain." According to many authorities, Dagon is supposed to have taught the use of the plough to humanity; he was considered germane to agricultural fertility. His connection with Cain and Antaeus is thus apparent. Like Gaea, he causes the earth to yield its strength to them. According to most accounts, Dagon was the father of Baal, not vice versa, as in some other versions, and in this poem. But *aïeul* and *père* can each mean "one who is the head of a long line of descendants" (*Littré*) and this meaning makes the most sense here. Jehovah may have vanquished them, but their seed survives in Anteros.

(12) They have plunged me three times into Cocytus' waters, (13) And, quite alone, protecting my Amalekite mother, (14) I sow anew at her feet the teeth of the ancient dragon. By some miracle, Belus and Dagon have immersed Anteros in the wailing waters of the Cocytus, the river tributary to the Styx, in order to protect him from the wrath of Jehovah and to safeguard the smoldering fires of his revenge. This act of triple immersion has, of course, nothing to do with the Christian ceremony of baptism, which is for the remission of sins. It is more akin to the dipping of Achilles in the Styx by his mother, Thetis, in order that Achilles be rendered invulnerable—except at the heel, by which he was held. But instead of being protected by his mother, as Achilles was by Thetis, Anteros defends *her* against extinction. As with other figures of

this poem, we must not try to place an identification tag on this mother. For Anteros, she is the one who takes from the earth, not from heaven, the fiery principle of the Avenger and passes it on from generation to generation. She is an Amalekite, a member of an aboriginal people descended from Esau. Since Esau sold his birthright to his brother Jacob for pottage, he is a proper ancestor for the world's disinherited. The Amalekites waged constant war against the Hebrews until they were wiped out by the Hebrews during the reign of Hezekiah.

On the order of Athene, the goddess of wisdom, Cadmus sowed the dragon's teeth in the soil, whereupon Sparti (or "Sown Men") sprang up and looked menacingly at the hero. Cadmus tossed a stone among them, and each of the Sparti accused the other of having thrown it. The javelins began to fly and in the battle that ensued only five survived. These five offered their services to Cadmus.

In another sonnet of *The Chimeras,* **"Delifca,"** "the conquered dragon's ancient seed" sleeps in the cave, which is "fatal to rash visitors," and "the Sibyl . . . lies asleep under the arch of Constantine." These images signify the eternal return of religious ideas and they are implied but not clearly stated in **"Anteros."**

Anteros is silent about slaying dragons and about the role of Athene. But he knows that if he plants the dragon's teeth in the earth mother—or, more precisely, at her feet, as she lies asleep (like the Sibyl)—she will give birth to warriors who will fight on his side against Jehovah, the oppressor.

The sonnet **"Anteros"** is, thus, a second sowing of the dragon's teeth. No commentaries or prose equivalents can ever explain the enchantment of these fourteen lines. The enchantment can, however, be transformed into deeper pleasure and appreciation by a proper interpretation of the poem's discursive meaning. Such an interpretation must be enriched by an understanding of the mythological, historical, or biblical forbears of the images, symbols, metaphors, and myths which figure in this the best balanced and the most tightly constructed of all the sonnets of Nerval.

Anteros is indeed a son of Cain. He prefigures Camus's rebel. He is the man who says no. He says no to the conquering god, to Abel, and to Jehovah. No to the chosen, but yes to the damned. Yes to Antaeus, to Cain, to Belus, to Dagon, to his Amalekite mother, and, above all, to the Avenger.

The sonnet **"Anteros"** may not negate, but certainly does contradict, important passages of *Aurelia,* where the narrator appears to have opted for Christianity. It is the stone and marble of Gérard de Nerval's metaphysical revolt.

John W. Kneller (essay date 1986)

SOURCE: "Nerval's 'Artémis'," in *Textual Analysis: Some Readers Reading,* edited by Mary Ann Caws, The Modern Language Association of America, 1986, pp. 26–32.

[*In the following essay, Kneller studies the language, imagery, and literary devices used in "Artémis" and asserts that Nerval's poem is "the most ambitious, the most carefully elaborated, and the most beautiful of this great poet's writings."*]

The approaches to *Les chimères* of Gérard de Nerval have followed rather than anticipated the successive stages of literary criticism in France, Great Britian, and the United States. In brief, they have been extrinsic, intrinsic, and structural. For current purposes, extrinsic method will be synonymous with projection; intrinsic procedure will also go by the name of explication or commentary; and structural system will include not only structuralism but also semiotics and theories of reading.

After the thunderous silence of late nineteenth- and early twentieth-century Lansonian literary historians, who hardly mentioned Nerval in their manuals, practitioners of extrinsic methods prevailed after World War II and took two different courses. Some applied techniques of other fields, such as psychiatry, biography, astrology, and alchemy. Others attempted to use texts or parts of texts as a means of obtaining access to obscure parts of the poet's life. The first group, in their procrustean determination to make the evidence fit the theory, often stretched the text to death or cut off its head and feet. The second, by resolving a word, phrase, or sentence into an antecedent person, object, or event, fell into the genetic fallacy.

In the fifties, following the centennial of Nerval's death, intrinsic approaches took over and summoned their practitioners to eschew genetic, affective, intentional, and historical fallacies, to affirm the interiority of the text, and to illuminate its meaning and form. Projection was clearly put to rout by explication and structuralism. In 1960, I characterized **"El Desdichado"** as "a coherent, unified statement of an experience. . . . {It} is complete in itself; it contains its own meaning" ["The Poet and His Moira: 'El Desdichado,'" *PMLA* 75]. Three years later, studying the same sonnet, Albert S. Gérard wrote: "le poème, pour être valable, doit contenir une signification perceptible sans références excessives à autre chose qu'à lui-même" ["Images, structure et thèmes dans 'El Desdichado,'" *Modern Language Review* 58 (1963)]. Eight years after the 1963 study by Jakobson and Lévi-Strauss of Baudelaire's "Les chats," Jacques Geninasca, inspired by Jakobson, published his *Analyse structurale des "Chimères" de Nerval.* For Geninasca, analyzing a text meant dismantling its system to expose its literary devices, while respecting the specific character of its poetic language and symbolic thought. His ultimate goal was to arrive at the author's total system through the properties of literary discourse uncovered in the process. Thanks to him and to other structuralists and semioticians, it was no longer necessary to plead for the validity and value of detailed poetic analysis.

Today everyone treats projection with the neglect it deserves. Two generations of Americans schooled in the methodology of the New Criticism and many more generations of French reared on explications de texte have seen to that. Some Nervalists now prefer structural approaches; others continue to practice explication. When most successful, the former have shown that it is possible to be systematic without being totally scientific, and the latter have demonstrated their ability to be interpretive without being utterly intuitive. All, let us presume, would agree that no one can really appreciate a work of art without understanding its form and its matter. For my part, I am willing to be called eclectic. Like explicators and semioticians, I am swayed most of all by the imperatives of the text itself, but I would insist that these imperatives include not only careful analysis of each word or symbol but a respect for the order in which they were written.

Since **"Artémis,"** like the other sonnets of *Les chimères,* is a coherent, ordered statement, I shall try to elucidate its words, images, and devices in the order set forth by the poet. Beginning with the circumstances surrounding its publication, I propose to discuss the title and then take the poem from top to bottom, the way it was written.

Artémis

La Treizième revient . . . C'est encore la première;
Et c'est toujours la seule,—ou c'est le seul moment:
Car es-tu reine, o toi! la première ou dernière?
Es-tu roi, toi le seul ou le dernier amant? . . .

Aimez qui vous aima du berceau dans la bière;
Celle que j'aimai seul m'aime encore tendrement:
C'est la mort—ou la morte . . . O délice! o tourment!
La rose qu'elle tient, c'est la *Rose trémière.*

Sainte napolitaine aux mains pleines de feux,
Rose au coeur violet, fleur de sainte Gudule:
As-tu trouvé ta croix dans le désert des cieux?

Roses blanches, tombez! vous insultez nos dieux:
Tombez fantômes blanches de votre ciel qui brûle:
—La sainte de l'abîme est plus sainte à mes yeux.

"Artémis" was first published, with other sonnets, in *Les filles du feu,* in 1854, while the poet was still alive. Although the manuscript of this version has not come to light, the text, as it appeared, was undoubtedly reviewed by Nerval and is therefore definitive.

The original title of *Aurélia* was *Artémis ou le rêve et la vie.* This datum not only invites us to link the sonnet with the récit but also eliminates any remote possibility that "Artémis" could be an invented masculine form of "Artémise." True, the speaker of **"El Desdichado"** thinks of himself as a widower ("Je suis le ténébreux, le veuf . . ."). True, the gloss "olim mausole" appears in the margin of the Eluard manuscript next to the word "veuf" of that sonnet. But even if El Desdichado's widowerhood could be compared, mutatis mutandis, to that of Artemisia—the widow of Mausoleus, in whose memory she erected the mausoleum of Halicarnassus, one of the seven wonders of the ancient world—there can be no question about the sex of Artemis or Aurelia. This Artemis is an avatar of the moon deity, a new being whose identity and essential qualities are determined not by classical antiquity but by the sonnet that bears her name. She is "La Treizième" and "la première" of the first line; "la seule" of the second; "la première ou dernière" of the third. She is the one that the speaker loves and "la morte" of the second quatrain. She is, above all, "la sainte de l'abîme" of the last line.

> The Thirteenth One returns . . . once more she is
>   the first;
> And she is still the only one—or this is the only
>   moment:
> For are you queen, oh you! the first or last?
> Are you king, the sole or last lover? . . .

The Eluard manuscript bears a reference near "Treizième" to a note in Nerval's own handwriting: "La XIIIe heure (pivotale)." It is tempting to let this note be an exclusive identification of the "Thirteenth One." Doing so, however, would rob the poem of its inherent richness and complexity. **"La Treizième"** unfolds the major themes of the sonnet—love, time, number, death, and religion—all at once. The ordinary language of analysis will force us to take them up seriatim, but this simultaneity is fundamental, not only here but elsewhere in the text.

"La Treizième" calls forth a woman. Obviously not anybody's thirteenth mistress, she is the heroine of this poem, already named in the title. She is thirteenth because she is "unique" and "fated." She is endowed, further on, with the common love superlatives "first," "last," "always," and "only": Nerval used these superlatives in the ninth letter to Jenny Colon and in the third chapter of *Sylvie*, and he repeats them here as a kind of exorcism to bring back together the myriad aspects of love that have disintegrated in the inexorable course of time.

Since adjectival nouns in French are more effective in presenting poetic ambiguity than is any possible English equivalent, "La Treizième" not only evokes the goddess and queen but also introduces the "thirteenth hour," because time and love are considered indissoluble. Science easily relates time to space; poetry can, as it does here, relate time to love. Instructive in this matter are two passages in Nerval's *Sylvie*. In this récit, the speaker pauses in the third chapter to describe a tortoiseshell Renaissance clock, whose gilded dome is topped by the figure of Time. On the face of this clock, in bas-relief, Diana, leaning on her stag, is surrounded by the enameled figures of the hours. The clock has not been rewound for two centuries and was not acquired to tell the time. In the first chapter of *Sylvie*, the speaker, describing the actress with whom he is infatuated, extols her perfections and compares her to the "divine Hours, which stand out so clearly, with stars on their foreheads, against the brown backgrounds of the Herculaneum frescoes." If we bear in mind that **"Artémis"** was published in the same volume as *Sylvie*, we cannot doubt that Nerval was preoccupied with the reck-

oning of time and that he associated it with the goddess Artemis when he wrote this poem.

The Lombard manuscript of **"Artémis"** bears the title "Ballet des heures." This fact makes some examination of the word *heures* essential. The Greek and Latin *Horae* were divinities of the seasons; only by an improper translation from Latin to French have they come to be confused with the hours of the day. The Hours, as they appear in art and the dance, may depict the seasons, the day, or parts of the day: they do not depict any particular hour. In Ponchielli's *La gioconda*, for example, the Hours portray the first faint glimmerings of dawn, then high noon, twilight, and finally night; victory goes to the Hours representing light over the Hours representing darkness. Nerval could well have been unaware of the etymology of this word; he was no scholar. He certainly did not know Ponchielli's opera, which was first performed at La Scala in Milan in 1876, long after his death. But as an enthusiastic and informed devotee of music, dance, and theater, he could not have ignored the meaning of the Hours for the arts. Nor should we.

"Artémis" is a profound meditation on time, love, faith, life, and death. Not a word in it is haphazard or empty of meaning. In my view, it is the most ambitious, the most carefully elaborated, and the most beautiful of this great poet's writings.

—*John W. Kneller*

If the Thirteenth One is nobody's mistress, it is certainly not one o'clock in the afternoon. Rather, it is the pivotal hour, season, or year. Like the small hand on the old Renaissance clock or the shadow on a sundial, time completes one span at a certain instant, then passes on to the next. Depending on whether it is seen ending a cycle or beginning a new one, it is the thirteenth hour or the first—or both.

In the history of humanity, time has been reckoned on the basis of either the solar or the lunar cycle. As early as the fifth millenium BC, in matriarchal Sumer, time was based on lunations, or lunar months—the time from one full moon to another. This period was approximately twenty-eight days. Analogies with the menstrual cycle are inescapable. There were thirteen lunations, or thirteen times twenty-eight days, in a year. To that total was added the extra day between the thirteenth and first month—a unique day that was both the end and the beginning. In the ancient lunar calendar, thirteen was the number of the sun's death month, when the days are the shortest of the year. As a result, it has always had ominous overtones for the superstitious. In fortune-telling tarots, thirteen is the death card. This pivotal, fated, and mysterious number is central in importance and function in **"Artémis"**; the symbols and themes revolve around it, as the planets revolve around the sun.

The exact meaning of "ou," which appears three times in the first stanza and once in the second, invites scrutiny. It does not indicate an alternative between different or unlike things (the only moment, but not the only woman). It indicates, rather, the synonymous, equivalent, and substitutive character of two ideas (the only woman *is* the only moment). "Ou" enriches the polysemous nature of the entire sonnet. For the thirteenth woman is also the first, as the thirteenth hour is the first. First and thirteenth merge with last and, with the help of "encore" and "toujours," introduce the themes of cyclic movement, recurrence, and permanence.

The suspension points after "revient" and "amant" ask the reader to pause and wonder what is left out, signaling a change of thought. They emphasize the importance of the Thirteenth One, relate her or it to the title, and invite us to ponder all the resonances of meaning that this woman, this period in time, and this number beget. Time fades in the third and fourth lines, as love takes over again. Opposite this "queen"—the multiple Artemis of the poem—the speaker looks at a projection of himself and asks whether he is "king," the first, the last, the unique love, the hero of this drama.

Paradoxically, these complex ideas are expressed in simple language. The stanza contains only two verbs: "revenir," which, followed by the suspension points, evokes cyclic movement, and "être," which appears five times, expressing permanence and essential being. The rhyme scheme (abab) departs from the traditional sonnet form (abba) and emphasizes the oscillation of themes in this quatrain.

> Love the one who loved you from the cradle to the
>   grave;
> The one I alone loved still loves me tenderly;
> She is death—or the dead one. . . . Oh delight! Oh
>   torment!
> The rose that she holds is the *Rose mallow.*

In the first line of the second stanza, taking an aphoristic tone, the speaker tells all living beings to love the unique woman of many names and attributes who figures in this sonnet. To the boldness of simplicity and repetition in the first stanza is added the temerity of the cliché in the first line of the second. The time-worn locution "from the cradle to the grave" relates the apparent polarities of "first" and "last" to human existence, as the speaker strives to resolve them into eternal principles.

This unique woman resides in the realm of the dead. She is the personification of death ("la mort") or the incarnation of death ("la morte"). This juxtaposition is matched by another ("délice" and "tourment"), and the pairs can be shuffled: "La mort-tourment" may be death without expectation of survival of soul; "la morte-délice" may portray the deceased beloved who, as in *Aurélia,* will guide

the speaker through a series of trials to salvation. The pair "mort-délice" bespeaks physical death, a joy, with certainty of afterlife; "mort-tourment," physical death, an intense suffering, if not perceived as a transition to another life. Pervading all the couplings is the painful uncertainty concerning death.

This woman, whether death itself, or the deceased beloved, appears in line 8 holding a flower in her hand. The flower she holds is the very one held by Aurélia in the garden scene of the récit that bears her name. Coming at the end in italics, *"Rose trémière"* recalls "bière," with which it forms a rich rhyme—as well as with "première" and "dernière" in the first stanza. Unlike many saints in Christian iconography and many heroines in German romanticism, the bearer of this flower must be associated with the multiple Artemis of this poem, who opposes them. That is the significance of *"Rose trémière."* Standing midway in the sonnet, the one who holds it embodies the themes presented in the first part and those that will appear in the second.

A frequent attribute of saints in Christian iconography, "rose" appears four times in the sonnet: twice here; once in line 10; once, in the plural, in line 12. By metonymy, it is manipulated to stand for Artemis, for saints who oppose her, and ultimately for the opposing religions that those saints embrace.

> Neapolitan saint with hands full of fires,
> Violet-hearted rose, flower of Saint Gudula:
> Have you found your cross in the wilderness of
>   heaven?

In Nerval's sonnets, the first two lines of the sestet often contain the key to the entire poem. These two are perhaps the most famous that he ever wrote. Maurice Barrès supposedly took delight in repeating them; Tristan Derème honored them with a poetic "garland"; François Constans considered them to be at the heart of Nerval's thought. The repetition of vowel sounds ("s*ainte*-m*ains*," "napolit*aine*-pl*eines*") explains some of that charm, but to appreciate the verses fully, one must read them in context.

The "Neapolitan saint" cannot possibly be the one who holds the rose mallow in line 8, nor can she be the saint of the abyss in the last line. On the Eluard manuscript—which, let us recall, is not the basis for the final version of this poem—the name "Rosalie" appears next to "la sainte de l'abîme" of line 14, leading some commentators to assume that the Neapolitan saint, the saint of the abyss, and Saint Rosalie were all one and the same. Such an interpretation pushes poetic ambiguity to the brink of chaos. The memories that might have gone into the making of these tercets are legion. Rosalie (in reality a Sicilian saint) appears in works that Nerval read, as well as in works that he wrote. But even if my approach did not exclude extrinsic matters of this sort, except where they are essential to an understanding of the text itself, I could not avoid the observation that if Nerval had wanted Rosalie in this poem, he would not have taken such pains to keep her out.

The Neapolitan saint is, on the contrary, a person consecrated in this poem to arouse devotional memories or feelings of holiness. Instead of bearing a flower, as one might expect, she holds a lantern, or lights. This is a nice twist, because Gudula, patron saint of Brussels, is usually represented with a lantern. According to tradition, this lantern, symbolizing the faith, went out and was then miraculously relit by Gudula's prayer. On the Lombard manuscript, Nerval originally wrote "soeur de Sainte Gudule." By replacing "soeur" with "fleur," he not only avoided sibilant cacophony but also achieved a synthesis of the two saints, the Latin and the Nordic. This new saint stands in opposition to the Artémis of this poem.

The eleventh line completes the apostrophe. The speaker asks the combined saint of the previous two lines whether she has found her cross (her salvation), in the wilderness of heaven. Has she been as fortunate, for example, as Saint Helena, mother of Constantine I, who, according to tradition, found a relic of the true cross near Calvary in 326 (an event usually called the invention of the cross)? Obviously not, since the heavens are empty. The ironic tone here recalls the defiance of Nerval's **"Antéros,"** the despair of his **"Le Christ aux oliviers,"** and Musset's 1842 satire, "Sur la paresse": "Et, pour qui joint les mains, pour qui lève les yeux, / Une croix en poussière et le désert aux cieux. . . ."

Nerval originally wrote, "l'abîme des cieux." Let's be grateful for the change, for the ambiguity of associating "abîme" with a saint of heaven as well as with the saint of the last line would have been sloppy rather than poetic.

> White roses fall! You insult our gods:
> Fall, white phantoms, from your burning heaven:
> The saint of the abyss is saintlier in my eyes!

Falling roses constitute a familiar symbol of the victory of Christian faith over death. When Saint Rosalie died, cherubs are said to have rained roses upon her body. In the denouement of Goethe's *Faust,* part 2, after the death of the hero, Mephistopheles speaks ironically of his disciple's fate. The angels answer with hymns, and a shower of roses falls on the ground, signifying that Faust, who has repented at the last moment of his life, will be saved. Even Mephistopheles is moved by the scene and, for a moment, begins to doubt his own denial of faith. The sense of this sonnet is, however, quite different. The speaker doubts the efficacy of forgiveness symbolized by falling roses. For him they are "white ghosts" ("fantômes blancs"), and they insult his gods—that is, the gods who preceded monotheism. It is Artemis, the saint of the abyss, who is holier in his eyes, for she has twofold saintliness: she is the symbol of pre-Christian, polytheistic faith and the embodiment of an eternal beloved woman.

Some of Nerval's works lie close to the events that he witnessed, encountered, underwent, or lived through as he wrote them, but this poem does not. **"Artémis"** is not the transcript of a particular poetic experience, nor is it a "song without words" or "pure poetry," as some readers have suggested. It is a profound meditation on time, love, faith, life, and death. Not a word in it is haphazard or empty of meaning. In my view, it is the most ambitious, the most carefully elaborated, and the most beautiful of this great poet's writings.

FURTHER READING

Bibliography

Villas, James. *Gérard de Nerval: A Critical Bibliography, 1900 to 1967.* Columbia: University of Missouri Press, 1968, 118 p.
> Annotated bibliography of criticism on Nerval published from 1900 to 1967.

Biography

Rhodes, S. A. *Gérard de Nerval, 1808-1855: Poet, Traveler, Dreamer.* New York: Philosophical Library, 1951, 416 p.
> The only full-length English biography of Nerval. The author presents critical commentary incidental to biographical information.

Symons, Arthur. "Gérard de Nerval." In his *The Symbolist Movement in Literature*, pp. 10-36. New York: E. P. Dutton, 1908.
> Surveys Nerval's life and writings and describes the author's role in the Symbolist movement.

Whitridge, Arnold. "Gérard de Nerval." In his *Critical Ventures in Modern French Literature,* pp. 45-64. New York: Charles Scribner's Sons, 1924.
> Largely biographical essay offering brief critical commentary.

Wood, Michael. "Gérard de Nerval: (1808-1855)." In *European Writers: The Romantic Century,* edited by Jacques Barzun, pp. 943-69. New York: Charles Scribner's Sons, 1985.
> Capsule of Nerval's life and career.

Criticism

Engstrom, Alfred G. "The 'Horus' of Gerard de Nerval." *Philological Quarterly* XXXIII, No. 1 (January 1954): 78-80.
> Addresses religious myths and syncretism as well as Nerval's concepts of the mystic and the seer in "Horus."

Gilbert, Claire. *Nerval's Double: A Structural Study.* University, Miss.: Romance Monographs, Inc., 1979, 199 p.
> Contemplates the theme of the double, or doppelganger, in Nerval's poetry and fiction.

Knapp, Bettina L. *Gérard de Nerval: The Mystic's Dilemma.* University: The University of Alabama Press, 1980, 372 p.
   Critical study of Nerval's works.

Kneller, John W. "Gerard de Nerval: 'Delfica.'" In *The Poem Itself*, edited by Stanley Burnshaw, pp. 2-5. 1960. Reprint. New York: Schocken Books, 1967.
   Examines the Nerval's use of symbolism and syncretism in "El Desdichado" and "Delfica."

Lokke, Kari. "History: Myth as Prophecy." In *Gerard de Nerval: The Poet as Social Visionary*, pp. 104-44. Lexington, Ky.: French Forum Publishers, 1987.
   Explores the symbols and myths in Nerval's poetry and other works to demonstrate his "egalitarian, pantheistic and feminist vision."

Martin, David. "Melancholy of Being, or 'I have sought the "I" of God': Genre, Gender, and Genesis in Nerval's 'El Desdichado.'" *French Forum* 15, No. 1 (July 1990): 25-36.
   Discusses Nerval's conception of the metaphysical, gender roles, and religion as evinced in his sonnet "El Desdichado".

Quennell, Peter. "Books in General." *The New Statesman and Nation* XLI, No. 1055 (26 May 1951): 596, 598.

Reviews S. A. Rhodes's biography on Nerval and provides a capsule of Nerval's life and literary achievements.

Rhodes, S. A. "Poetical Affiliations of Gerard de Nerval." *PMLA: Publications of the Modern Language Associations of America* LIII, No. 4 (December 1938): 1157-171.
   Traces the influence of Nerval's poetry on Théophile Gautier, Charles Baudelaire, Arthur Rimbaud, Andre Breton, and other French writers.

Ridge, George Ross. *The Hero in French Romantic Literature.* Athens: University of Georgia Press, 1959, 144 p.
   Explores Nerval's portrayal of hero and discusses his reputation as visionary.

Warren, Rosanna. "The 'Last Madness' of Gérard de Nerval." *The Georgia Review* XXXVII, No. 1 (Spring 1983): 131-38.
   Attempts to provide a better understanding of Nerval's works. Warren contends that "all too often [Nerval's] devotees only manage to present him as a crazed packrat of esoteric lore."

Winston, Phyllis Jane. *Nerval's Magic Alphabet.* New York: Peter Lang, 1989, 135 p.
   Considers the role of language in depicting madness in Nerval's works.

Additional coverage of Nerval's life and career is contained in the following sources published by Gale Research: *Nineteenth-Century Literature Criticism,* Vol. 1; and *Short Story Criticism*, **Vol. 18.**

Cesare Pavese
1908–1950

Italian novelist, poet, short story writer, essayist, translator, and critic.

INTRODUCTION

A transitional figure in twentieth-century Italian poetry, Pavese departed from the ornate style and linguistic complexity used by his contemporaries to veil hermetic ideas and subjects, forging instead a more straightforward, unadorned style distinguished by use of vernacular. Considered Pavese's greatest accomplishment as a poet, the collection *Lavorare stanca* (*Hard Labor*) best evinces his descriptive, naturalistic approach and his themes of solitude and alienation—which recur throughout his works—while his later verse is more conventional, lyrical, and figurative.

Biographical Information

Pavese was born in Santo Stefano Belbo, a rural town in the Piedmont region of northern Italy. The lifestyle and people of this fertile and hilly agricultural area later became strong influences on his poetry and fiction. His father died when Pavese was young; by most accounts his mother, a quiet and severe woman, provided little affection for her son. He attended high school in the cosmopolitan northern city Turin and, in 1927, enrolled at the University of Turin, where he devoted himself to the study of literature. After graduating, he published translations of works by such authors as Sinclair Lewis, Herman Melville, Sherwood Anderson, and John Dos Passos, introducing the Italian public to major contemporary western writers. In 1935, after marginal involvement in political causes, he was convicted of anti-Fascist sympathies and confined to house arrest for eight months in the remote town Brancaleone Calabro, on the southeastern peninsula of Italy. His imprisonment provided the basis for the novel *Il carcere* (*The Political Prisoner*) and for themes and images in some of his subsequent writings. Upon his release, Pavese was devastated to learn that he had been rejected by a woman with whom he had fallen in love prior to his incarceration. He continued his work translating and helped found the publishing house Einaudi, where he promoted and oversaw the publication of important European works in the social sciences. Pavese met and fell in love with an American actress in 1949 but the relationship failed. In 1950 he received the Strega Prize, Italy's most prestigious literary award, for *La bella estate: Tre romanzi* (*The Beautiful Summer: Three novels*). That same year, at the height of his literary reputation, he committed suicide.

Major Works

In *Hard Labor* Pavese offers reflections on post-World War II Italian society by means of narrative poems set in

the Piedmont, specifically the city of Turin and the surrounding countryside bordering on the mountains and the sea. In telling of the country people and urban working class of the Piedmont region, Pavese used the speech patterns and idiom of his subjects. He contrasts the solace of country life with the alienation of existence in the city, and also comments on rural culture, human relationships, the physical demands of rural life, the beauty of the land and nature, and perennial themes such as sex, death, and the human condition. The verse of *Hard Labor* employs vernacular language and long verse lines, but Pavese's later poems are more lyrical and generally composed of short verse lines. Characterized by a highly personal and subjective tone, these poems are allusive and demonstrate little concern for relating a story. The love poems of *Verrà la morte e avrà i tuoi occhi* treat his feelings for the American actress and his disillusionment at the end of their relationship. Commentators have repeatedly attributed much of the loneliness and misogynistic undertones expressed in Pavese's works to his unhappy relationships with his mother and other women.

Critical Reception

Hard Labor was poorly received when initially published in Italy. In contrast, Pavese's subsequent verse collections—published more than a decade later—received immediate praise, especially *Verrà la morte e avrà i tuoi occhi*. However, *Hard Labor* is now generally accepted as his most important collection, and English-language commentators on his poetry have concentrated almost exclusively on his first volume.

PRINCIPAL WORKS

Poetry

Lavorare stanca [*Hard Labor: Poems*] 1936
Feria d'agosto (short stories and poems) 1946
La terra e la morte [*Earth and Death*] 1947
Verrà la morte e avrà i tuoi occhi 1951
Poesie edite e inedite [*Published and Unpublished Poems*] 1962
Ciau Masino (short stories and poems) 1968
A Mania for Solitude: Selected Poems, 1930–1950 1969
**Poesie del disamore e altre poesie disperse* [*Poems of Estranged Love, and Other Scattered Poetry*] 1973

*Includes the previously published collections *La terra e la morte* and *Verrà la morte e avrà i tuoi occhi*.

Other Major Works

Paesi tuoi [*The Harvesters*] (novel) 1941
La spiaggia [*The Beach*] (novel) 1942; published in journal *Lettre D'oggi*
Il compagno [*The Comrade*] (novel) 1947
Dialoghi con Leucò [*Dialogues with Leucò*] (fictional dialogues) 1947
Opere. 16 vols. [partially translated as *Selected Works*] (novels, poems, short stories, essays, diaries, and criticism) 1947–68
†*La bella estate: Tre romanzi* [*The Beautiful Summer: Three Novels*] (novels) 1949
Il carcere [*The Political Prisoner*] (novel) 1949
La casa in collina [*The House on the Hill*] (novel) 1949
La luna e i falò [*The Moon and the Bonfires*] (novel) 1950
La letteratura americana e altri saggi [*American Literature: Essays and Opinions*] (essays) 1951
Il mestiere di vivere: Diario 1935–1950 [*The Burning Brand: Diaries of 1935–1950*] (journal) 1952
Notte di festa [*Festival Night, and Other Stories*] (short stories) 1953
Racconti [*Told in Confidence, and Other Stories*] (short stories) 1960
The Leather Jacket: Stories (short stories) 1980
‡*Stories* (short stories) 1987

†Comprises the novels *La bella estate* (*The Beautiful Summer*), *Il diavolo sulle colline* (*The Devil in the Hills*), and *Tra donne solo* (*Among Women Only*).

‡Comprises the translations *Festival Nights, and Other Stories* (1964) and *Summer Storm, and Other Stories* (1966).

CRITICISM

Davide Lajolo (essay date 1960)

SOURCE: "The Woman with the Hoarse Voice," in *An Absurd Vice: A Biography of Cesare Pavese*, edited and translated by Mario Pietralunga and Mark Pietralunga, New Directions, 1983, pp. 62–77.

[*In the excerpt below, originally published in Italian in 1960, Lajolo discusses Pavese's portrayal of women in his writings.*]

During his final university years, Pavese had an encounter that would affect his entire existence. He met the only woman he would ever really love. Until then his relations with women, although followed by acts of desperation and fainting fits, were manifestations of his exaggerated emotion, not of love. It was with this woman that Pavese experienced the fullness of his feelings. He was captivated by her from the day they met.

We shall give no other name to this woman than the one used by Pavese in the poems of **Work Wearies**: "the woman with the hoarse voice." The harmony of Pavese's life was broken by his involvement with her; it was a crucial turning point. In losing her, he would lose his hope, his tenderness toward women, his sense of masculinity, his hope for fatherhood and family. He would even see his childhood in a different light, and all his works would reflect this love, betrayal, and disenchantment.

The woman with the hoarse voice was not very beautiful, but she had a firm, cool, and strong-willed personality. She was as good as a man in sports, and her chosen field at the university, mathematics, was the opposite of Pavese's choice in the humanities.

It was not difficult to recognize when Pavese was in love. But this time he kept the name of his loved one secret and remained impenetrably silent at his friends' curiosity. He confided in Sturani only when he thought that she returned his love, but as soon as his friend advised him to be cautious, he brusquely refused to listen to him anymore.

For Pavese, this woman was different from the others. Her fascination came from her strength, masculine attitudes, hard features, and decisive, self-assured character. The timid Pavese felt he had a companion and a protector who encouraged and defended him. His weak character and the constant doubts that tormented him found a solution and strength in her. With her he felt that he could hope, that he could live and think without fears for the future.

Here we must refer back to the letter written to Professor Monti after the lyceum final exam in which Pavese tried to show, through the episode of the Horatian student, that he was a man as able and virile as others. Evidently the love he felt for the woman with the hoarse voice gave him the assurance that he could behave like the man described in that letter. Perhaps only at this time did he believe

---

himself able to learn the "business of living" not only in books, work, and self-doubt.

Throughout the time he felt that he had this woman beside him, Pavese appeared more human, natural, and happy than in any other moment of his life. His timidity became tenderness; his discomfort in front of women turned into confidence. His tragedy would begin as soon as he realized that this woman would reject and leave him without pity.

After that betrayal, Pavese would present every woman in his short stories and novels as only a creature of flesh, or as the embodiment of indifference and infidelity. The shadow that would weigh heavily upon women would always be that of pain and desperate contempt. Some of the most intense themes of *Work Wearies* derive from Pavese's relationship with the hoarse-voiced woman. Here is a poem that was part of the first edition of *Work Wearies,* but excluded from the second Einaudi edition. Under its dramatic title, it evokes images of Pavese in a boat on the Sangone River, with his woman.

Betrayal

This morning I am no longer alone. A new woman
lies here and burdens the prow
of my boat which moves slowly in the water now
    tranquil
after an icy and turbulent night.
I came from the Po that roared in the sun
with echoes of rapid waves and workers,
I made, teetering, the difficult turn
into the Sangone. "What a dream!" she observed
without moving her supine body, her eyes at the sky.
There is not a soul around and the banks are high
and narrower upstream, crowded by poplars.

How awkward the boat is in this tranquil water!
Standing at the stern to keep it in balance,
I see that the boat advances slowly: the prow is
    sinking
under the weight of a woman's body, wrapped in
    white.
She told me that she is lazy, and she has not yet
    stirred.
She remains reclining and gazes, alone, at the tops
    of the trees
as if she were in bed, and she burdens my boat.
Now that she has put a hand in the water and lets it
    skim,
she is also crowding my river. I cannot look at her—
on the prow where she stretches her body—as she
    turns her head
and curiously stares at me from below, moving her
    shoulders.
When I asked her to come in the center, leaving the
    prow,
she answered me with an impish smile: "You want
    me near you?"

Other times, drenched from a violent plunge among
    the trunks and the stones,

I continued to push toward the sun, until I was
    drunk,
and landing here in this spot, I hurled myself to the
    ground
blinded by the water and the rays, the pole thrown
    away,
to calm my fatigue at the breath
of the plants and in the embrace of the grass.

Now the shade is oppressive
on the sweat which burdens the blood, and on the
    tired limbs;
and the vault of the trees filters the light
of an alcove. I sit on the grass, not knowing what
    to say,
and I hug my knees. She has disappeared
into the forest of poplars, she is laughing and I
    must pursue her.
My skin is darkened by the sun and uncovered.
My companion, who is blonde, in placing her hands
into mine to land on the bank, has made me
    perceive,
with her delicate fingers, the perfume
of her hidden body. Other times the perfume
was the water dried on wood and the sweat in the
    sun.
My companion calls me with impatience. Dressed in
    white
she wanders among the tree trunks and I must
    pursue her.

The obsession with an adverse destiny, the fear of tiring her, the terror of losing her, heightened the poem and gave it more warmth. That woman brought back to him the enchantment of his childhood in the hills of the Langhe. Let us read **"Encounter,"** a poem from *Work Wearies,* dated 1932:

These hard hills that have made my body
and stir it with so many memories, opened to me
    the wonder
of this woman, who does not know I live her and
    cannot understand her.
I met her one evening: a lighter speck
under the ambiguous stars, in the haze of summer.
Around there was the smell of these hills,
deeper than shadow, and suddenly rang out,
as if it had come out of these hills, a voice both clear
and harsh, a voice of lost times.

Sometimes I see her, and she comes before me
defined, immutable like a memory.
I have never been able to grasp her: her reality
eludes me every time and takes me far away.
I don't know if she is beautiful. Among women she
    is very young:
so young that I am caught, thinking of her, by a
    distant memory
of childhood spent in these hills.
She is like the morning. Her eyes suggest
all the distant skies of those faraway mornings.

And she has in her eyes a firm purpose: a light
  clearer
than the dawn has ever had on these hills.

I created her from the depths of all things
that are most dear to me, and I cannot understand
  her.

Pavese thus gathered his entire world in the hands of his woman: the hills, his childhood, the sky, and the mornings, limpid and remote, because "she is like the morning." Her harsh voice was the voice of the hills, of nature. With her, even the landscape acquired a human aspect.

Pavese remained attached to the woman with the hoarse voice even when he became afraid of losing her. She returned in his dreams, memories, and hallucinations. We see her again in **"A Memory"**:

There is no man who can leave a trace
on her. What has been dissolves like a dream
in the morning, and only she lasts.
If, for a moment, a light shadow did not touch her
  brow,
she would always seem startled. Each time there is
  a smile
on her face.

Not even the days amass on her face
to alter the light smile
that radiates around her. She is firm
in all that she does, and each time seems the first;
yet she lives every moment.
Her hard body and her reticent eyes
unfold in a voice that is low and a little hoarse: the
  voice
of a tired man. And no tiredness can touch her.

If one stares at her lips, she cautiously offers
a waiting glance: no one dares a bold act.
Many men know her ambiguous smile,
the sudden shadow on her brow. If there is a man
who knew her moaning, humbled by passion,
now he suffers for it day after day, not knowing for
  whom
she is living today.

She smiles to herself
the most ambiguous smile, as she walks.

Suffering, disappointments, and betrayals would injure both the man and the poet. But if there were something for which he could hope, only that woman could awaken it. If he was still living, it was because she was still the life: "she lives every moment." And she alone was the family, when he burned with loneliness, longing for a child. Here are some verses from **"Fatherhood"**:

A man alone facing the useless sea,
  waiting for the evening, waiting for the morning.

There are children playing, but this man would like
to have a child of his own, to watch him play.

. . . . .

. . . From the dark window
comes a hoarse gasping, and no one hears it
but the man, who knows all the tedium of the sea.

Again the hoarse voice. And it was again to this woman that Pavese returned in the poem **"Work Wearies"**:

. . . . .

Is it worth being alone to be always more lonely?
When you just wander through the squares and
  streets,
they're empty. You must stop a woman,
talk to her and persuade her to live with you.

. . . . .

. . . If they were two,
even when he walked down the street, his home
  would be
where the woman was and it would be worth it.

Perhaps no other writing by Pavese expresses his awareness of hopeless loneliness as much as this writing. It was still the hoarse-voiced woman who provided him with that awareness.

After the woman with the hoarse voice, at the center of Pavese's life would be only Pavese himself: his torment, and his poetry.

—Davide Lajolo

Other women had relationships with Pavese, and some appeared able to make him believe he was once again in love. However, these women, and those from his books, would be linked to that first unforgettable love. Often they served as outlets for his rancor. They became a pretext for his contempt and represented the weak beings on which he released his wrath, his disappointments, and his defeats. After the woman with the hoarse voice, at the center of Pavese's life would be only Pavese himself: his torment, and his poetry.

One cannot understand Pavese's expressions of anger without trying to penetrate his most secret side and grasp the consequences of his failure with the hoarse-voiced woman. Pavese wanted to succeed both in literature and with women. There is no short story, novel, or page in which the memory, the face, or the desire for a woman does not arise. His continuous anxiety was undoubtedly also due to his obstinate will to scourge himself and to curse his solitude, but its primary cause was always the woman.

Each new encounter was a painful effort to rediscover love and to reconcile sex and emotion, life and abandonment. It was a cruel drama that slowly affected his body, until he became convinced that he was sexually impotent. I remember the occasions when he would confide in me with shame on this subject. It was always at night, while we strolled in the darkness of the Turin boulevards. It was hard for me to free him from that concern, to find words of reassurance, or to recommend that he see a doctor. In his diary he wrote similar confessions with obstinate cruelty and perhaps he did so just because his fear of being impotent was unfounded. In fact, Pavese had the habit of assuming a role with others and with himself. He enjoyed performing this role in order to more painfully degrade himself.

Of the women who entered Pavese's life, at least five, after the woman with the hoarse voice, were able to give him some strength. The beautiful woman he encountered shortly before his death came from America and brought with her all the fascination Pavese felt for that country. During this period he wrote me that he received "an unexpected lark from America." Immediately he added, almost as if to diminish the happiness of his announcement: "She stopped near my sheaf of grain, only because she feels lost and wants me to help her fly in the skies of our country. But she will soon leave, I feel it. I will hear her wings flapping, and I will lack the strength to attempt a cry to call her back."

Pavese seemed transformed once again by that last love. He was able to abandon his increasingly modest and severe habits. Leaving his work behind, he ran to Rome with the American woman. He once again wandered through the streets, proud to know he still could walk hand in hand with a woman. From the city he went to the sea and to the mountains, always with her. In her, even if only briefly, he found trust and, perhaps, the illusion he could finally overcome the memory of the other woman.

I remember that in a photograph Pavese showed me in July 1950, during his last trip to Milan, his eyes were blissful as he stood next to her in front of the mountains. However, it was a brief time, just the space of a season. Like the woman with the hoarse voice, the lark from America had grown tired of the little warmth he could offer her, and she flew away.

I have never forgotten what he told me late one night in Milan: "She fled at night from my bed at the hotel in Rome and she went to bed with another, with that actor you know. Like the other woman, even worse. Do you remember the one from Turin? She is the one who ended it between me and women."

If a woman was not the sole cause of Pavese's suicide, she was the most immediate and constant inspirer of his suicidal thoughts. This was apparent from his youth on, from his letters to Sturani, through the last part of his life, when he wrote in his diary: "One does not kill oneself for the love of *a* woman. One kills oneself because a love, any love, reveals us in our nakedness, our misery, our impotence, our nothingness."

His persistent search for a woman, even after all the torments of betrayal and the desertion, must also be considered in measuring his struggle to learn "the business of living" and to resist his fascination with suicide. Undoubtedly, he realized more each day, while he felt more involved in the business of writing, that literature would not be sufficient to save him. Nor could he be rescued by political involvement or by those people to whom he attempted to attach himself at times, through sacrifices and difficult compromises.

He might possibly have been saved by the tenderness of a woman he could call his own, and by the warmth of a home life. Pavese, who regarded himself and wanted to be regarded only as a suffering man, rather than a complex man, probably needed the simplicity of a vital experience so common to others. His inability to realize this experience turned his feelings toward women from yearning to anger. This attitude is already apparent in some poems of *Work Wearies*. In **"Ancestors"** the women of the family are defined in the following way:

> And women do not count in our family,
> I mean, our women stay home
> and bring us into this world and say nothing,
> they just do not count and we forget them.
> Each woman puts in our blood something new,
> but they efface themselves in the process. . . .

In **"Landscape I,"** the peasants of the village,

> sneer at the groups of women
> and ask when, dressed in goatskin,
> they will loaf in those hills and get black in the sun.

In the poem **"He-goat God,"** women are represented as animals, and Pavese, between myth and reality, sees himself as the he-goat god "who sought the she-goat and butted his head against the tree trunks."

Pavese's schoolmates at the lyceum remembered that he behaved in a similar manner when, closed in his house, "tormented" by love, he beat his head against the walls.

The woman is identified with his solitude: bitter, both present and distant, untouchable and necessary. In **"Landscape VII,"** he wrote:

> Everything in the sun ripples at the thought
> that the street is empty except for her.

And when the woman, here the hoarse-voiced woman, seems to withdraw from him, he identifies her with the disappearing moon, as in **"Passionate Women"**:

> That unknown woman, who swam at night
> alone and naked, in the darkness when the moon
>   changes,

disappeared one night and has never returned.
She was tall and she must have been dazzling white
for those eyes to reach her from the bottom of the
    sea.

In **"Burnt Lands"** we encounter those women of the city
who "know how to enjoy love":

One arrives in Turin at night
and sees at once along the streets
the flirtatious women, dressed for the eyes, walking
    alone.

. . . . .

. . . These women, who wait
and feel they're alone, know life in depth.

And again, in **"Tolerance"**:

. . . The shutters
on the house are closed, but inside there is a bed
and on the bed a blonde earns her living.
The whole town rests at night,
everyone but the blonde
who washes in the morning.

In **"Deola Thinking"**:

At the house she had to sleep at this hour
to regain her strength: the mat by her bed
was always soiled by the dirty shoes of workers and
    soldiers,
the clients who wore out her back.

It was the time when Pavese desired and needed even
casual encounters to somehow reassure his manhood. In
"Adventures" he described a boy spying on the furtive
love of cats:

. . . At the first light of dawn
also closed are the eyes of those cats in love
whom the boy used to spy on. The female cat wails
for she is without her mate.
Nothing is worthwhile—
neither the treetops nor the red clouds—
she wails at the bright sky, as if it were still night.

But the love bought on the street, although better for Pavese
than the total absence of love, begins to draw his contempt, as in these verses from **"Portrait of the Author"**:

I don't smell because I'm not hairy. The stone
    freezes
my bare back that women like
because it's smooth: is there anything women don't
    like?

And again in **"Ballet"**:

. . . The woman does not count,
each night she is different, but she is always the

small girl
who laughs, and her little bottom dances when she
    walks.

It is the same motif in **"Instinct"**:

. . . She too,
like all bitches, did not want to hear of it,
but she had the instinct. The old man—
not yet toothless—sniffed it and when night came
they went to bed. It was beautiful, the instinct.

It is always the woman: bitch, she-goat, cat, lust, but always present and indispensable in his mind. She is present
even in the noise of a cart rumbling along the road, in
"The Wagoner":

With the wagon moves a warmth
that smells of taverns,
of pressed breasts and clear nights

When the woman leaves, all becomes useless: nature, the
trees, the sea, and the lights. From **"Sad Supper"**:

. . . It's cold at dawn,
and the embrace of a body would be life.

In spite of the contempt, as soon as the face of a woman
appears, a faint hope returns and with it a sense of attachment to life. The following are verses taken from **"Nocturnal Pleasures"**:

We all have a home that awaits in the dark
and we return there: a woman waits for us in the
    dark
lying alseep: the room is warm with smells.

. . . . .

We will return tonight to the woman who sleeps,
to search her body with ice-cold fingers
and a warmth will stir our blood, a warmth
of dark wet earth: a breath of life.

There is no poem in **Work Wearies** that does not carry the
mark of a woman—and it is almost always that of the
woman with the hoarse voice.

Giose Rimanelli (essay date 1964)

SOURCE: "Conception of Time and Language in the
Poetry of Cesare Pavese," in *Italian Quarterly*, Vol. 8,
No. 29, Spring, 1964, pp. 14–34.

On October 28, 1935 Pavese made the following entry in
his diary: "Poetry begins when a simpleton says of the
sea: 'It looks like oil!'" [*The Burning Brand*, translated
by A. E. Murch, 1961]. Immediately, however, he added
that this discovery actually is not the most precise description of a flat calm. It is merely the pleasure of having

perceived the similarity, the titilation provided by the establishment of a mysterious relation between the thing perceived and the idea of the thing, between the man who sees the object and his unconscious need to express it with a parallel, an image, a symbol. Pavese points out that this is how a typical poem begins, it is based on an idea. But then it is necessary to finish it. How? He says:

> Having started the poem, one must finish it, work up the idea with a wealth of associations and skillfully arrive at an assessment of its value. . . . But usually the writing stems from sentiment—the exact description of a flat calm—that occasionally foams with the discovery of relationships. The typical poem may possibly be remote from reality, consisting up to now (just as we can even live on microbes) of mere odds and ends of similarities (sentiment); constructive thought (logic); and associations caught at random (poetry).

Nonetheless this wealth of associations or relations must be "allusive and all-pervading," wholly fused in the image. Otherwise the poem does not become flesh, it does not take on the blood of life and become history.

In another entry, October 10, 1935, Pavese writes: "Why cannot I write about these red, moonlit cliffs? Because they reflect nothing of myself. The place gives me a vague uneasiness, nothing more, and that should never be sufficient justification for a poem. If these rocks were in Piedmont, though, I could very well absorb them into a flight of fancy and give them meaning. Which comes to the same thing as saying that the fundamental basis of poetry may be a subconscious awareness of the importance of those bonds of sympathy, those biological vagaries, that are already alive, in embryo, in the poet's imagination before the poem is begun."

These two observations shed light not only on the orientation of the Pavesian poetics and the critical effort that has shaped it, but also on an aspect of the creative act. It is a weary pleonasm to assert that art is born of the relation between man and reality. But the dimensions, the intensity that this relation can assume reside exclusively in the personal sensibility (intelligence) of the artist. He is aware of this bond in his subconscious. Now the language of the unconscious is the image, the symbol. The unruffled sea that "looks like oil." The word is the language of the poet. Thus the awareness of the thing becomes poetry when the intuition of the thing becomes expression, when content, in short, becomes style. Which is to say when the poet succeeds in merging *mythos* and *logos,* image and word. It is well, therefore, to repeat that *mythos, epos* and *logos* represent the three stages of linguistic evolution: 1) language understood as a spontaneous representation of reality (intuition); 2) as a representation of events in time (narration); 3) as a form of rational inquiry (idea). These three phases constitute the creative process. The transformation now proceeds from an attitude towards reality which could be called the poet's "mythic vision." What is immediately striking in Pavese's poetry is precisely this mythic vision in communion between *man* and the *natural-ferine* world, a time "that gives us a glimpse of the community of interests between man and wild beasts."

It is from this intuition that Pavese develops his theory of the equation between savagery and superstition. The *selvaggio* celebrates his most terrifying rites before an impassive nature which, in turn, is a collection of myths. What else is ritual if not the mythic repetition of an event that has occurred and that continues to preserve its uniqueness in the very act of repeating itself? The example of the myth which occurs and reoccurs in a ritual form is offered to us every day by the Mexican *fiesta.* One must be there, as spectator or actor, to bear witness to its sacral, hence tragic uniqueness because "the savage is not picturesque but tragic," foretold, that is, as in Greek tragedy. The *fiesta* is the advent of the unusual. Time is annihilated, it no longer exists. Or it is transformed into a mythic past or total present. It makes use of sensations and of atmospheres. Space is the setting of the *fiesta,* which becomes a colorful and fantastic world, existing by itself. The persons who take part in it lose their own human and social characteristics and are transformed into living fancies. Everything happens as in a dream, and death has never brushed so close. Everything attracts its opposite. The *fiesta,* inasmuch as it is a cosmic experience, is an experience of disorder which unites contradictory elements in itself, the selfsame ones that will engender a rebirth of life. It is "a return to a remote and undifferentiated state, prenatal or presocial. It is a return that is also a beginning, in accordance with the dialectic that is inherent in social processes" [Octavio Paz, *The Labyrinth of Solitude; Life and Thought in Mexico,* 1961]. Hence myth is symbolic language, like the dream which is the same for myth (at least in reference to Freud in respect to this last observation). Both function as channels of communication from ourselves to ourselves, and express deep-seated experiences, sentiments and ideas in the form which they at first had in the external world. Dream and myth are united, they have a visionary character. Obviously, however, the dream concerns the problems of the individual, whereas the myth—which implies religion and society—reveals the characteristics of the community and endows them with importance.

The journeys of Odysseus, of Jason and of Jonah, which are considered as myths, can differ from Ahab's journey which is also mythic. But the truth is that there is always a particular adventure for every man, a particular setting which is delineated as the fancy of his secret life. This particular adventure, this particular setting will become myth (it already was), and therefore language. This language can be handed down, and it becomes poetry because myth explains it.

Pavese focuses his poetic attention on the myth-superstition ritual which always sits on the shoulders of the "*selvaggio.*" And he explains [in *The Burning Brand*] that all such things (the most terrifying rites) "are superstitious only if they strike us as unjust, forbidden by conscience, savage. Then savagery is overruled by conscience. As long as we believe in superstition, we are not superstitious. To be superstitious is essentially retrospective, in the realm of memory, an apt subject for poetry; like evil, which is always in the realm of past remorse." There is, however, a transition of common interest between primitiveness (superstition) and savagery (overruled by conscience). There is the primitive expression of the myth which, in turn, is the expression of the pre-rational ages of man.

As far as is known man had not yet developed any rational faculties in the pre-historical period. No distinction was made between feeling and volition. Man lived without self-questionings. He found himself in a world which he did not understand, but which for him was the only existent reality. It was an ordered reality. Thus the life of primitive man was lived in conformity with those early laws of survival which he accepted unconsciously. Sometimes, however, something occurred in nature which did not repeat the order, and which man could not manage to assimilate. Earthquakes and thunderbolts were events of an ultra-real character beyond his comprehension. They were the expressions and emanations of some supernatural being or power. Gods or demons. Myth was born when man consecrated as sacred a locus in which he found refuge against the unknown evil. Thus he could hope. Man gave a name to these events. Hence the appearance of language coincides with the birth of myth. In fact *mythos* means word. Myths were not mythology or legend. They were reality. What had no name had no existence. Primitive man gave life to objects. By so doing he fulfilled a creative function. Persons with more experiences gave names to things unknown by others, and as a result they were considered magical. They were respected by the community for the very reason that they extended the frontiers of reality.

Primitive man did not possess analytical faculties. For him causality and other logical categories did not exist. It was only through myth that he learned to acquire a knowledge and an awareness of reality. Symbology was the method with which he reorganized the world in his image. This is tantamount to saying that nature no longer existed in itself but in man and for man, by way of fantastic configurations. In other words nature forced man to create symbols which were naught else but the metaphorical representation of his experience of reality. The myth of Leda, violated by Zeus in the form of a swan, is the representation, not the logical description, of the conception that reality is conditioned, fertilized by spiritual, ultra-terrestrial forces.

It has already been said that primitive man lived unconsciously, and that there was a mystic reciprocal penetration between subject and object. Now it is necessary to add that he not only lived in a pre-rational, pre-logical and pre-adult age, but also in a pre-individual age. The process of individuation had not yet begun. Probably the person as such did not even have (not yet) a logical name, but existed as a function of the community. Whatever had a tribal value also had individual value. For the individual's attitude towards life, his knowledge was the very same as that held by the tribe. The symbol represented individual and collective experiences. By way of the symbol the individual identified himself with a place, with a time and a society. The individual's life had a communal character. By way of the individual the objective unconscious, that is the psychic patrimony of the tribe, was handed down

from generation to generation. Every man, in the depths of his being, is a primitive. Vestiges of communal experiences exist in the sub-stratum of the psyche, which Jung calls the collective unconscious. Later, this was to find expression in dreams, in legends, in religion and in art in the form of archetypes, i.e. images that repeat primordial situations. The poet is a primitive who expresses his experiences by using the language of a civilization. Everybody has experiences. Everybody, therefore, has a relation with reality. One among all these is a poet because he feels the reciprocal reactions between man and object more intensely, more primitively.

Mythos also means mystery: the two words have the same etymological root. For the poet the world is a mystery, something sketched out only very vaguely which he discovers every time he writes a poem. Objects have an animistic and spiritual value above all. And this awareness, this "sub-conscious awareness" of which Pavese speaks in the aforementioned passage on the red, moonlit cliffs the poet must translate into intelligible phrases.

Pavese says of his poems [in *Poesie,* 1962] that they were "an attempt to express a cluster of fantastic associations, of which one's own perception of reality consists, with a sufficient wholeness." They are also an effort (and later an actualization) of man's pre-natal and pre-social transition, as exemplified in Vico's cyclical theory, of the primitive as opposed to the savage; the *rus* as opposed to the *ars,* of the "hick, the rustic, the boor, as opposed to the citizen" [*The Burning Brand*]. The mythic unity of these stages of transition is indissoluble. And this is also the mythic unity on which Pavese's poetry is engendered and developed, assuming a substantiality of an unprecedented character.

A first exploration of Pavese's poems leads to an observation that is also a revelation, namely that they are "felt," *i.e.* they have rhythm. Let us dwell for a moment on this two-fold insight, leaving a particular and detailed analysis for later. They are suffused with an ineffable feeling that transcends reason. Rhetoric is the most certain (and obvious) repetition of a solid, critical contact that has been established with expressed ideas. Here no rhetoric is perceptible. The rhythm is constant and reflects the development of a situation that is always concrete, as are its particular elements themselves. But the relation between object and subject, between character and landscape is ungraspable because it is seamlessly fused together. As has been said Pavese's concern was to suggest at first sight only an indistinct rhythm, an atmosphere which after all is naught else but a symbolic and primitive reality. These poems are primarily a series of landscapes at once governed and united by a primordial rhythmic background which creates and recreates the myth of existence. The character of the "poesia-racconto" strips himself of his rational individuality and becomes a very part (he is part) of reality. In **"Il Dio-Caprone"** (**"The God-goat"**), for example, the boy protagonist barely exists as a ratiocinating person. All we have are his impressions of the countryside. For him existence is nature. From this perspective the boy perceives with his instinct, like a primitive. Immediately the image is born. The countryside, for him, is "a country of green mysteries," a sensual landscape possessed by a spirit that also possesses the rustics (" . . . their faces are burnt, the color of earth"). The girls who make love are "in heat," they too act by instinct. Like the animals they too seem to be in the grip of the moon's influence. The God-goat is merely an evocation of the primitive. For his part, the boy sees the countryside shimmering in the summer-light. Summer means heat and harvest-time. This event is celebrated like the vintage and corn-cobbing, it is a ceremony of consecration or *fiesta*. In primitive societies it actually was a rite which was concluded with an unconscious release of every inhibition. Rite and magic persist in the countrysides now in the form of customs and beliefs. Customs and beliefs which Pavese, in an entry dated July 1, 1942 (referring to customs and beliefs of his native village of Santo Stefano Belbo) transcribes as follows:

When the moon is old:	When the moon is new:
	Sowing flowers They come
Beautiful and With thick stems	Sickly and slim and elegant
	Cutting down trees, they will be
Healthy	Worm-eaten
	Except the pine tree which will be
Worm-eaten	Healthy
	Washing the sheets with ashes will make them
Clean and good	dirty—the ashes will filter through
	Pruning the vine and the buds will be
Harmful	Fruitful

The moon is the static symbol of rites and of magic. Thus also the excitement of animals coincides with the moon's rising (which like a rite precisely accentuates the supernatural and the powerlessness of the will). The atmosphere, already frenetic becomes increasingly tense, oppressive.

> And the bitches howl under the moon,
> because they've heard the large goat who leaps
> over the top of the hills, and sniffed the smell of
>   blood.
> Beasts stir in the stables.
> Only the big and stronger dogs bite at the rope.
> Some free themselves and run to follow the large
>   goat
> who sprays them with blood redder than fire,
> intoxicating them.
> Then, standing upright, they all dance,
> baying at the moon.

The large goat (who suggests the sorcerer of the tribe) performs the ceremony of anointment, he allows the other animals to participate in the rite. He is like a god. The

rustics, for their part, work with their hoes under the moon. At the end of the harvest they dance and drink wine. The boy feels the sexuality of the countryside. Instead of expressing it with descriptions or concepts (qualities that come with adulthood), he defines it by the fantastical vision of the large goat (which for him has the feeling of absolute uniqueness) and by drawing the parallel with the rustics.

The mythic vision is established here by the connection of the events and by the objective movement of the sober style. But Pavese manages to establish the same dimension by virtue of a "tangle of fantastical associations" [*Poesie edite e inedite,* 1962], recounting situations that are often trite, as in **"La cena triste" ("The Sad Supper")**. This poem could be defined as a painting, a still-life. The male protagonist "has thoughts" and feels the surrounding countryside. He is sitting down to a meal in the countryside under a bower, with a woman. She embodies a season, a whole experience now past which remains alive in her: "The solid shoulders and the tanned cheeks again lock up the whole summer." At the end of the supper, only the tang of grape and of woman, of vintage and of life, remains in the air.

> We are still, listening to and watching the sound
> made by the water while passing in the track of the
>   moon.
> This tarrying is the sweetest.
>   The countryside that tarries,
> still seems to be biting that cluster of grapes,
> so alive is its mouth. The tang lingers
>   like the yellowish moonlight . . .

The two persons are "watching" the sound of the water as if it were another person. The objects and abstract things around them become animated. "The chairs look at each other, deserted." "Neither the grapes nor the bread have moved." There is the implication that even the two persons are animated objects, mere presences in the vast rhythm of the countryside. They merge with that atmosphere of solitude and silence, losing themselves therein. It is night, perhaps autumn and there is no stir of life. "It's cold in the dawn, and the tight embrace of a body would be life." Even things "feel" it. "Tangs torment the famished shade." The being of the two persons mutually penetrates things. The woman and the water "tarry," the shade "does not even succeed in licking the dew already condensing on the cluster of grapes." There is a desire for contact that remains ungratified. The moon-beams seek the water and, perhaps, the man seeks the woman. Objects are persons and persons are objects. As in a painting by Giorgio Morandi objects and light are fused. In this poem persons, things and landscapes have a life, utterly unique in point of time and place.

Even in the progression in the poems from the countryside to the city, from life as instinct to life as order, the poet's transcendent vision creates and recreates the associations and cadences of time as a dimension of absolute uniqueness. In the characters who have moved to the city there is always a sovereign need for release which remains ungratified. The boy, in **"Atavismo,"** sees a horse on a deserted street. The horse is bare, and absorbs all the warmth of the sun, as though the animal were in the countryside "bare and unrestrained," where the motionless plants "look." The boy too has a body but he must cover it, hide it under clothes. "If one has a body, it must be seen," and one must go out naked to "drown in the sun." The characters, in short, would like to act in the city, where "it isn't done" as they do in the countryside where "it is done," because in the countryside life is in direct communication with objects. There one is a primitive, one has a body and one therefore is a boy. The city, instead, is a concept, practicality; it is another superstition but not memory. The countryside, however, persists in those who have moved to the city. Sometimes an object, a light suffices to bring everything to life again. In **"Il Tempo Passa"** (**"Times Passes"**) the little old man must beg for alms whereas before he would go into the fields and gorge himself with fruits. Fruits in the fields belong to him who needs them, so true is it that they don't grow behind closed doors. . . . Serenely, the little old man used to look for the blackest vine and there he would "sit in the shade," without stirring, until he was full—as if the vine were the mother, the wet-nurse, which repeats the sacral function of existence. The gift is now substituted by the wine from the tavern which reminds him of the time of his freedom in the fields. He gets drunk here and then the tavern-keeper kicks out the drunken oldster

> who sings and shouts,
> who wants a pumpkin
> and to stretch himself out under a vine.

These are events that have been transferred to the memory and that, through some mysterious mechanism (the wine, the drunkenness which is the same as the orgy and the release of inhibitions, though more artificial) return to be lived all over again. As in a dream, the little old man who sings and shouts, "re-feels," as it were, a point in time when, stretched out at his ease in a field, he was talking with a boy who was carrying a pumpkin.

The dramatization of the myth, the establishment of relations between myth and temporal things and especially between myth and people are the constituitive elements of *Lavorare stanca*.

—Giose Rimanelli

The past is contemporaneous with the present in these confrontations that spring up spontaneously. A story unfolds as if the characters were confessing and laying bare their lives. Pavese's mythic time is not nostalgia, neither is it the Proustian "time of the mind," *i.e.* involuntary memory. These characters never experience the scene of the "madeleine dipped in tea." Nonetheless, for them, there is always an inner flux which brings those particular strat-

ifications of the inner life to the surface in a vibrant and fresh form. But they are linked to the thrill of the unique feeling rather than to the remembrance of things past. For them, however, memory is a psychic kaleidoscope which is continually being reshaped within grooves that were staked-out in the consciousness in a pre-rational age. Thus for Pavese the return of a "unique event" to the memory does not mean to isolate it in time and to contemplate it. Rather, it means to live it now, as if it were happening now for the first time. Only memory-images are tied to that "subjective life" of which William James speaks [in *The Principles of Psychology*, Vol. 1, 1907]. The very rhythm of Pavese's poems, seemingly tranquil but unbroken, which immediately remind us of prose narratives, conceals a rhythm which confirms the artist's objectification with the material being dealt with. If story-telling means progression in time, Pavese understands this as a psychic progression, that is to say as a relation between consciousness and reality, an "inner relation between things." The singular quality of these poems lies precisely in their thought, a series of fantastical relations that constitute a total reality, namely duration in the Bergsonian sense. This technique on occasion is reminiscent of a similarity with the "stream of consciousness." If, however, as Bergson admits [in *Matter and Memory*, 1913], the Lockean theory of the "association of ideas" lies at the base of the stream of consciousness, here there is the dynamic factor of the "all-pervading" which is neither a fantastication of, nor a re-connection or a remembrance, of events and things, but a form of *cognition*. Now Proust, who also has something in common with Pavese, reconstructs experience on the basis of "momentary feelings." Despite the fact that he constructs his book not on mnemonic recalls from one experience or feeling to the other, "but on planes of conceptualism and mystical knowledge that reduce them to material for research" [*The Burning Brand*], Proust does not succeed in giving (or does not so wish) an absolute content to situations and people (themselves consequences of practical causes, as has been noted by Pavese himself). Instead, Pavese's conception of time is the identification of the absolute between the "sacral" character of the first infantile identification of the unknown (that which occurred in an absolute sense in the boy's preconsciousness), and living or re-lived reality (which is the knowledge of experience).

Thus for Pavese story-telling is tantamount to the invention of a landscape, which is the story itself. A hill, a landscape, a myth are fixed symbols. They exist indefinitely, in an absolute state. Myth is also the desire to endow the particular with an absolute value. This signifies making the profane sacred. Thus a hill becomes "all" hills, a sea "all" seas, etc. This is precisely what took place in the mind of primitive man (or of the boy). Myth, says Pavese, "is a norm, the schema of an event that has occurred once for all time, and which derives its value from this absolute uniqueness which lifts it out of time and consecrates it as revelation" [*La letteratura americana e altri saggi*, 1960]. With myth time comes to a stop and space is abolished. A whole existence is immobilized. Time is reduced to an image and to a "tang." What is felt once is felt again throughout the whole of life. Here is an example taken from the *Racconti*: "It is as though I were talking with her, even though the conversation had taken place many years ago and even the words have been lost. For me that furtive look, which I have mentioned, suffices and suddenly the empty sky is peopled with hills and presences."

The dramatization of the myth, the establishment of relations between myth and temporal things and especially between myth and people are the constituitive elements of the epic. In the poems of *Lavorare stanca* the epic consists in reviving images of the past as over against the present. But this is not remembrance. Rather, it is a psychic process by means of which what occurred in the past invests the reality of the present. It is an evocation, not a re-evocation. It is enough for an old woman to lie down in the sun and to stretch her arms in order to effect the return of the "vibrant day in which the body also was young, more torrid than the sun" [*Poesie*]. "The flesh becomes remembrance," and the old woman gets drunk, inebriated, as though she felt her body rejuvenating. Her father and her husband, who also died old and worn out, live again. Past and present merge, becoming one. Thus also in **"La puttana contadina"** (**"The Peasant Whore"**) the woman wakes up in a room in the city. The smell of the bed, the dawn's hay-like color, make her re-live her adolescence and other awakenings in a stable in the countryside. A whole life elapses in the image, in this specific image.

Lavorare stanca is an epic, as has been said. Pavese defines the book as the "adventure of the adolescent who, proud of his countryside, imagines the city to be similar. Instead in the city he finds solitude and seeks a remedy for it in sex and passion which serve only to de-racinate him and hurl him far from both the countryside and the city into an even more tragic solitude which is the end of adolescence."

This is evident from the titles of the different sections of the book (Forefathers, After, City in the Countryside, Maternity, Green Wood, Paternity) in which the chronological progression remains implicit. There is no temporal development from poem to poem because Pavese is not "telling a story" about the physical evolution of a person in time. There are so many characters. What he registers is an attitude of the characters towards fixed symbols: hill, sea, city, countryside, etc. The interchangeable value which these symbols have for the boy, the adult and the old man constitute the unity of the book. Pavese learned this lesson from Homer.

On February 17, 1936 Pavese wrote the following in his diary:

> It is good to go back to Homer. What is the unity of his poems? Each book has its own; unity of sentiment, of attitude, whereby it is read harmoniously, as well as physically, as a whole. *Odyssey,* Book VIII: the pleasure of poetry, dancing, rivalry; song, the lighthearted golden myth; a vindication of the nobility of life, in an oasis of pleasure and idyllic tears. *Odyssey,* Book X: adventure, the succession of obstacles, human weeping, the

growing callousness. *Iliad,* Book III: the beautiful woman, the war over her, and ennervating love. And so on. Did Homer, or the man we call Homer, think of these definitions? I believe not, but it is a revealing thing that the book wherein all Greece comes to life is composed in this way, or which comes to the same thing, that it can be so interpreted.

> But let us be careful. The great fascination of the two poems lies in the material unity of their characters, which time after time flares up in a blaze of poetic fire. Which means that even from the first example of great poetry, written intentionally as such, we have this double play: a natural unfolding of events (which could be doubled or halved without adversely affecting the issue), and successive, fundamental poetic beams of light. The story and the poetry. The union of the two elements is merely a matter of aptitude, of skill.

> This opens up the problem of whether it may not be possible to recreate the miracle in separate poems, for the very reason that the mind, in all its manifestations, strives towards unity. To compose with inspiration, but with an underlying skill that merges the various fragments together to form a poem.

In the poem-narrative of *Lavorare stanca* the miracle has happened in terms of *unity,* by means of epic, ideal links which tie one poem to another poem, bringing up and developing different themes through time.

The book's orientation appears from the time of the publication of **"Mari del sud"** (**"South Seas"**). In the boy's eyes his cousin is "a giant dressed in white," a modern Ulysses returning to his native Ithaca (he recalls Anguilla, the "American" in *La luna e i falò* [*The Moon and the Bonfires*]). For the boy the cousin represents a whole exotic world, of pearl-fishers and of extraordinary adventures in distant seas. He has been away from the village yet he has remained a simple man, rooted forever in the hills, the *langhe.* He is a legendary character, a whole childhood for the youth who now needs merely to go to the city to feel himself to be without roots. For now he has grown up and begins to feel the imperatives of life. He finds himself before "thoughts and dreams." Thus for the boy the cousin exists only as an invented reality.

If there is a "meaning" in *Lavorare stanca,* it is that contained in the last lines of **"Mari del sud"** and in the poem **"Mito"**.

> But when I tell him
> that he is among the happy few who have seen the dawn
> on the most beautiful islands of the earth,
> he smiles at the memory and replies that the sun
> was rising but the day was old for them.

Life appears like an adventure to the boy. For the cousin life is experience, hard work. But in the poem **"Mito"** the "meaning" appears even more explicit. The protagonist notices that everything has changed since youth is over like summer. He no longer "feels" things as before. Before he seemed to be a young god, a being in contact with the spirit of things:

> Weariness now
> weighs on all the man's members,
> painlessly; the calm weariness of the dawn
> which ushers in a day of rain. The dark beaches
> know not the youth, for whom once it sufficed
>   merely
> to look at them. Nor does the sea re-live in the air
> upon breathing. Resigned, the man's lips
> fall back to smile before the earth.

The youth is now alone. Even things are alien to him. He has lost his innocence. He is cut off from his Eden. Life is no longer an emotive, sensual-spiritual apprehension of things. Experience is concept and category. And it is also time. He feels the weariness which is the day-to-day weariness of life. To work with weariness (*lavorare stanca*) means to live. It is only when the awareness that man is mortal sets in that there comes the realization that life is not a dream, when existence is accepted with all its burdens and sufferings, that maturity succeeds adolescence, and the young god becomes a man. By the gesture of his suicide it appears that Pavese, in one stroke, might have wanted to wipe out the existential view glimpsed in this poem and restore himself to the origins of innocence, and thus become once more the boy, the young god, and no longer be a grown man. But myth is also destiny.

For the reason that the mythic vision is an intuition, a mystical participation in reality, these poems cannot be reduced to an idea and to a formulation. If this happens it is only because the poet has explained to himself the "meaning" of his intuition. He has tried, that is, to transform a sentiment, something unconscious, into something completely conscious. For primitive man to transform a feeling into a word, to give a name to an object, was tantamount to living them. Language was the myth itself because nothing existed if he—primitive man—did not give it a reality, a representation. Language was experience. The word co-existed with the image of god or demon. By way of language primitive man transformed a subjective emotion into something of an objective character. Thus reality was at once personal and impersonal, an inner world and an outer world. It is different for modern man. Language is something completely objective. By way of language modern-day man does not feel but contemplates reality. Which is to say he is separated, alienated from it. The concept precedes the image. Man thinks in words which represent images. By way of the concept man can think of things which he has not even seen. Instead, primitive man did not think. He expressed himself instinctively in words which at the same time were feeling and experience. He spoke only of things that he could perceive. Concepts lend themselves to relations and implications. They are an inducement to expansion. They are system. Myth is coalition. It is something that happens in a time, in a place and in a peculiar way. What the poet feels is similarly unique, and essential. This is the lesson of *Lavorare stanca.*

The words with which the poet expresses himself are connotative. They represent something indistinct, but it exists for a person, in a situation. And reality, the "meaning" of the poem, it is what is felt while reading it. The greater part of Pavese's poetry makes no sense if it is read literally. Pavese expresses himself by way of an invented jargon which is metaphor. It is only with metaphor, however, that the immediacy of perception can be retained, and form (style) becomes the medium between *mythos* and *logos*. Metaphor is endowing material things with immaterial relations. The originality of the poet consists in discovering new relations among things (*mythos*), and in giving a new meaning to language (*logos*), and in the invention of new metaphors. Now in Pavese's poems the language is pruned of all those rhetorical and quotidian growths. It retains its pristine meaning, which is precisely slang. But in this slang the metaphors are wholly new and imbued with feeling. Two examples follow:

> A tender moon and hoar-frost on the fields in the
>   dawn,
> murder the wheat.
> You are but a cloud of the most gentleness, white,
> entangled one night among the ancient branches.

At a certain point some of these comparisons no longer seem even to be metaphors, and they acquire a direct value by virtue of their simplicity:

> Dawn squats on the black hill
> and cats doze on the rooftops.

Thus the epic unity of *Lavorare stanca* is also given by the linguistic unity which consists of the repetition of adjectives, nouns, expressions, and of correspondences in punctuation and of images converging on a common and single progressive unfolding of all the poems. Even the characters are compared with situations that are nearly similar. In a page of his diary (October 14, 1936) Pavese writes:

> . . . it remains true that only what we think actually exists (our style, our time = the object of our knowledge) is worth writing about. If we are aiming at pointing out a new way of seeing things, and, therefore, a new reality, it is evident that our style must be accepted as part of the *truth,* making its influence felt beyond the printed page.

Which implies the Pavesian principle of *cognition.* At this point it is obvious to assert that in *Lavorare stanca* (the singular, *i.e.* the most unique book of the whole of modern literature) there exists a unified, firm construction, not only of an intuitive but also of a logical character.

David William Foster   (essay date 1965)

SOURCE: "The Poetic Vision of 'Le colline': An Introduction to Pavese's *Lavorare stanca,*" in *Italica,* Vol. XLII, No. 1, March, 1965, pp. 380–90.

[*In the following excerpt, Foster examines Pavese's use of "the hills" as both a poetic setting and as a basis for reality in* Lavorare stanca.]

> Non resta,
> di quel tempo di là dai ricordi, che un vago
> ricordare.

Cesare Pavese in ***Lavorare stanca*** (1936; 1931–35) chooses to limit his poetic perspective in an attempt to capture the many facets of a restricted reality. His native countryside, the hills around Turin, serve as the thematic orientation for his poems. In this his first book of poetry as in his work as a whole, Pavese turns a coldly critical eye upon his material, ruthlessly scrutinizing it and unmercifully portraying the bitterest of realities. Although the poet is cynical and sophisticated, his material is not, and it is from the interplay of these two oppositions that the poetry's interest arises. While we may say that the poet is sophisticated, we do not mean to imply that he imposes an array of dazzling worldly trappings or elegant poetic devices upon his material. As the poet who may or may not choose to deny it, he is conscious of the significance of what he is describing, and that he has selected with deliberation his narrative and is in command of its presentation. At the same time the poet is both a participant and a spectator in his poetry as well as being its creative mainspring. In so doing, Pavese most often represents himself as a little boy:

> Per la vuota finestra
> il bambino guardava la notte sui colli
> freschi e neri, e stupiva di trovarli ammassati:
> vaga e limpida immobilità. Fra le foglie
> che stormivano al buio, apparivano i colli
> dove tutte le cose del giorno, le coste
> e le piante e le vigne, eran nitide e morte
> e la vita era un'altra, di vento, di cielo,
> e di foglie e di nulla.

The hills are the entire poetic canvas of the poet. They encircle the little boy, and make up an entire world beyond which his imagination cannot pass. The limited perspective of the poet as a child is seen in the first poem of the collection, **"I mari del Sud,"** which relates the adventures of a cousin returned home from the war and the impressions he makes upon the child. The setting is the invariable setting of the poems: "Camminiamo una sera sul fianco di un colle, / in silenzio." The places which the cousin has visited, his adventures and the extent of his travels are foreign to the little boy, foreign as they would be to any child:

> [. . .] "Tu che abiti a Torino . . . "
> mi ha detto " . . . ma hai ragione. La vita va
>   vissuta
> lontano dal paese: si profitta e si gode
> e poi, quando si torna, come me a quarant'anni,
> si trova tutto nuovo. Le Langhe non si perdono."
>
> [. . .] Ma quando gli dico
> ch'egli è tra i fortunati che han visto l'aurora

> sulle isole più belle della terra,
> al ricordo sorride e risponde che il sole
> si levava che il giorno era vecchio per loro.

However, the hills do not serve only as a background for other poetic material. There is a series of eight "Paesaggi" in which the poetic setting is of primary importance, with Pavese evoking various aspects and moods of his native countryside. He is at once pastoral, as in **"Paesaggio I,"** as well as nocturnal and pathetic, as in **"Paesaggio II."** In **"Paesaggio III"** the poet is again nocturnal; but here the hillsides are seen enveloped in a kind of night mystery. The poet speaks of the worn and wasted man upon the countryside, a recurring theme in his poetry:

> L'uomo lacero pare un villano, nell'ombra,
> ma rapisce ogni cosa e i cagnacci non sentono.
> Nella notte la terra non ha piú padroni,
> se non voci inumane [. . .]

In **"Paesaggio VII, V, VIII"** (they do not appear in numerical order), the poet defines further aspects of the hills. The last poem of the series expresses what is almost a poetic genesis for the work:

> I ricordi cominciano nella sera
> sotto il fiato del vento a levare il volto
> e ascoltare la voce del fiume. L'acqua
> è la stessa, nel buio, degli anni morti.

For Pavese, his poetry is not one of organized, logical progressions of emotional visions. Rather it is suggestive images born at twilight when they are most ephemeral and subjective.

In addition to being the background for the bulk of the poetry or poetic landscapes of intrinsic beauty which merit descriptions of their own, "le colline" serve to preserve an adolescent reality which is of constant interest throughout the poetry. These landscapes are far from being Arcadian poetic settings. They are a palpable reality which, in lieu of the wider range of experiences of the outerworld unknown to the poet-child, furnish him with imaginative variations:

> La campagna è un paese di veri misteri
> al ragazzo, che viene d'estate.

Pavese's style is often lightly tinged with melancholy. His chief poetic staple is the cadenced series of images, vague and enigmatic, pregnant with a meaning which derives from the setting rather than from any innate mystery. We are constantly reminded that these are remembrances, and as such are vague and ill-defined as we would expect from the mind of an adult who is striving to re-evoke his childhood—striving to accomplish the seemingly impossible task of conveying the naiveté which was his as he lived the life he is describing. The blended and irregular perception proceeds not from an imperfect *present* perception, but from an imperfect perception at that time. It is for this reason that the hills are so many sided: not because they are now (although they may be), but rather because they were so then. Therefore, his function is that of a mere chronicler:

> [una macchia] L'ho creata dal fondo di tutte le cose
> che mi sono piú care, e non riesco a comprenderla.

In the title poem **"Lavorare stanca,"** the author sees himself as he sees the little boy. Both are fugitives upon the scene. However, as an adult, and as one who has gone beyond merely escaping from the domestic confines of the house, and as a man who has seen the world, his sentiment is neither melancholic nor nostalgic. It is a simple statement vibrant with a sense of futile despair:

> Traversare una strada per scappare di casa
> lo fa solo un ragazzo, ma quest'uomo che gira
> tutto il giorno le strade, non è più un ragazzo
> e non scappa di casa. [. . .]
>
> Non è certo attendendo nella piazza deserta
> che s'incontra qualcuno, ma chi gira le strade
> si sofferma ogni tanto. [. . .]

Pavese does not project his personality upon his subject matter. We are pointedly aware of the fact that his personality instead derives from his poetic material. In the instances in which he plays his emotions as a poet against the native landscapes, the sentiment is one of futility arising from the peasant reality—a reality which is left to the reader to surmise from the contemplative experiences and revelations seen through the eyes of a child.

The instances are few in which the poet fuses different temporal levels as he does above. Pavese relies on the imagination of his reader to grasp the significance of the bifurcated point of view in which his perceptions belong to past experiences while his interpretation and organization belong to the moment of the poem. Significantly, in **"Una generazione,"** the two points of view are played against each other in an attempt not only to continue the impressions and images of the "hillside" landscapes which are his poetic commonplace, but also to convey this feeling of a lack of progress, of a sort of spiritual ennui which produces a vague despair and creates a reflective mood near nostalgia.

One of the themes in *Lavorare stanca* which apparently runs through all of Pavese's work is the theme of natural instinct, represented by fresh carnality and sun-worshipping nudity. In his earthy thematic orientation, the poet finds the opportunity to contrast the vitality of the earth with the vitality of its inhabitants:

> Nel ricordo compaiono le grandi colline
> vive e giovani come quel corpo, e lo sguardo
>   dell'uomo
> e l'asprezza del vino ritornano ansioso
> disiderio: una vampa guizzava nel sangue
> come il verde nell'erba. Per vigne e sentieri
> si fa carne il ricordo. La vecchia, occhi chiusi
> gode immobile il cielo col suo corpo d'allora.

The sensuality of the people who appear upon the poetic canvas is intensified by Pavese's constant reference to silence and the instances in which the noun "silenzio" or its adjective "silenzioso" are used are too numerous to cite. Moreover, the lack of violence and nervous action serve to create a mood of silence where such a mood is not established in so many words.

One manifestation of the emphasis on the "natural instinct" is an insistence upon the active role of the woman. Note the description in the following stanza, created with the aid of particular natural and at the same time sensuous images:

> Le ragazze han paura delle alghe sepolte
> sotto le onde, che afferrano le gambe e le spalle:
> quant'è nudo, del corpo. Rimontano rapide a riva
> e si chiamano a nome, guardandosi intorno.
> Anche le ombre sul fondo del mare, nel buio,
> sono enormi e si vedono muovere incerte,
> come attratte dai corpi che passano. Il bosco
> è un rifugio tranquillo, nel sole calante,
> piú che il greto, ma piace alle scure ragazze
> star sedute all'aperto, nel lenzuolo raccolto.

Attention is also directed to **"Ritratto d'autore"** in which the poet's discussions are of a franker nature. One of the most interesting poems of the collection is **"L'istinto,"** in which the reader is presented with the memories of an old man, interesting because this is one of the few instances in which the poet concerns himself with the aged or the infirm. Here the disillusions of an old man contrast with the vitality and biological intensity prominent in the other poems. Yet this old man represents one of the personalities which Pavese chooses to populate his "hills," and it is from an interest in the poetic setting to an examination of a few of the human types which are outlined against this setting that we now turn.

Pavese is particularly preoccupied with procreation. A look at some of the titles and divisions of his poetry indicates this interest. There are two poems entitled **"Paternità,"** one entitled **"Maternità."** One of the six divisions of the collection carries the heading "Maternità" (10 poems) and another "Paternità" (8 poems). In the poem **"Maternità"** the poet describes a man who may well be taken as his prototype of the country peasant:

> Questo è un uomo che ha fatto tre figli: un gran
>   corpo
> poderoso, che basta a sé stesso; a vederlo passare
> uno pensa che i figli han la stessa statura.
> Dalle membra del padre (la donna non conta)
> debbon esser usciti, già fatti, tre giovani
> come lui. Ma comunque sia il corpo dei tre,
> alle membra del padre non manca una briciola
> né uno scatto: si sono staccati da lui
> camminandogli accanto.
>
>   La donna c'è stata,
> una donna di solido corpo, che ha sparso
> su ogni figlio del sangue e sul terzo c'è morta.

Pare strano ai tre giovani vivere senza la donna
che nessuno conosce e li ha fatti, ciascuno a fatica
annientandosi in loro. La donna era giovane
e rideva e parlava, ma è un gioco rischioso
prender parte alla vita. È cosí che la donna
c'è restata in silenzio, fissando stravolta il suo
     uomo.

I tre figli hanno un modo di alzare le spalle
che quell'uomo conosce. Nessuno di loro
sa di avere negli occhi e nel corpo una vita
che a suo tempo era piena e saziava quell'uomo.
Ma, a vedere piegarsi un suo giovane all'orlo del
     fiume
e tuffarsi, quell'uomo non ritrova piú il guizzo
delle membra di lei dentro l'acqua, e la gioia
dei due corpi sommersi. Non ritrova piú i figli
se li guarda per strada e confronta con sé.
Quanto tempo è che ha fatto dei figli? I tre giovani
vanno invece spavaldi e qualcuno per sbaglio
s'è già fatto un figliolo, senza farsi la donna.

Despite the title the focus of interest is the man "(la donna non conta)", and it is he who is credited with the creation of his sons, as though the man and not his wife had brought forth the three. The poem is organized so that in the first stanza we have a "vignette" of the man, and in the second of his wife. It is interesting to note that the peasant man is described in terms of an intense vitality while the woman appears as tired and worn-out. Again Pavese makes use of the quality of silence in accentuating the woman's present moral and physical exhaustion. In the third stanza not only does the poet give a picture of the three sons, but presents us with a cruel reality of the hills: the disintegration of this family unit from a lack of communication between them. Or put more simply, they ignore each other because they have no reason to do otherwise. Silence again predominates not only as a descriptive quality but as well as the motivation of the stanza.

Pavese's women are usually described in the same terms as the mother above. Women are not usually given prominence, but when they are the poet endows them with both an earthy sensuousness and an instinctive maternal feeling. The peasant men figure as prototypic images, and little boys predominate, representing Pavese as a child and therefore one facet of his critical vision of his subjects. In one instance one type of woman, the prostitute, is dwelt upon in a poem which is one of the best in the collection in terms of representation and interpretational organization. In **"Pensieri di Deola,"** Pavese has introduced, by means of the "pensieri" all of the "stanchezza" and disillusionment which constitute his vision of life in this region. The theme of the prostitute whose entire existence and occupation are a mockery of the normal biology of life is always effective when it is not romanticized, and here in the context of this collection it is a point well taken. The particular intensity of this presentation arises from the fact that the normal biological fulfillment of the peasants is presented as futile and unproductive. To juxtapose to this fact a description of the town prostitute whose function in any environment is productively useless ex-

presses all of Pavese's frustrations and cynicism in the presence of sex.

One of the most prevalent human types in *Lavorare stanca* is the drunken man who appears enough times in the role of father to make us suspect that he was a childhood reality for Pavese:

> Papà beve al tavolo avvolto da pergole verdi
> e il ragazzo s'annoia seduto. Il cavallo s'annoia
> posseduto da mosche: il ragazzo vorrebbe
>   acchiapparne,
> ma Papà l'ha sott'occhio. [. . .]
>
>   Il ragazzo s'annoia,
> il suo sorso Papà gliel'ha già fatto bere.
> Non c'è piú che guardare quel bianco maligno,
> sotto il nero dell'afa, e sperare nell'acqua.

Aside from any biological significance, the poet employs these people to carry his theme of degenerate humanity even farther (see also **"Indisciplina," "La vecchia ubriaca,"** among others). A depressing and unpleasant picture given by the ignorant and almost vegetable-like beings who form the majority of the population of the hills is compounded by descriptions of individuals who increase their impotency by perpetual drunkeness: **"Papà beve sempre."**

Pavese's descriptions and evocations have as a primary objective the portrayal of the two related moods of aboulia and atavism. Aboulia is a psychic-spiritual condition which the poet presents as emotionally inherent in his landscapes and its people. Aboulia may have two manifestations: either as the result of existentialistic failure where the aboulic possesses an ennui resulting from total resignation, or as an intrinsic characteristic, a particular personality trait, in which case it represents a negative value antithetical to human action and effectiveness. It is the latter aboulia which is here depicted, and, as such, seems almost psychosomatically linked with the second trait, atavism, or biological regression. In **"Atavismo"** the poet, while he does not present a particularly remarkable development of this theme, by his choice of title indicates his express interest in the subject. If we were to take the liberty of seeing atavism as the underlying motif for any poem with similar content, we would be aware of an outlook dwelling upon degeneracy and impotency as the poet sees his personages as human beings regressed, or regressing, to animal states:

> Ho trovato una terra trovando i compagni,
> una terra cattiva, dov'è un privilegio
> non far nulla, pensando al futuro.
> Perché il solo lavoro non basta a me e a miei;
> noi sappiamo schiantarci, ma il sogno piú grande
> dei miei padri fu sempre un far nulla da bravi.
> Siamo nati per girovagare su quelle colline,
> senza donne, e le mani tenercele dietro la schiena.

With aboulia and atavism Pavese achieves an uncomplimentary portrait of the country peasant through a stark style which swiftly blocks out his subject matter and then leaves it riven upon the page for us to contemplate, but never to partake of. Occasionally, one notes a light touch of melancholy or nostalgia on the part of the poet towards his own personification as a boy who silently awakens to behold the life around him.

Because of the poet's objective treatment of his subject matter, his poetic style is not luxuriantly "poetic." One notes the absence of poetic recourses which would animate the verses. While it is not the immediate attempt of this paper to examine the diction of the poet, a few comments in relation to the thematic orientations which have been mentioned are appropriate. In order to produce his poetic presentations Pavese has relied upon a stark narration in which sensory perceptions are almost entirely absent. Silence pervades and predominates while the poet describes and occasionally narrates in irregular verses which are verses only by virtue of an internal rhythm which rises and falls with their graphic arrangement upon the page. A principal poetic device is the rhetorical question which the poet would have contributed to the obscured and vague awareness which he feels is his. Because of the absence of "artistic" poetry, the emphasis falls hard upon the thematic content of the seventy poems in the collection, a content which is limited in scope but which serves to articulate the harshest of human experiences: a man's bitter disenchantment and quiet despair in his land and his people.

One must not make the mistake of accusing Pavese of being merely a local poet who is bound to a limited panorama of scenes, themes and emotions. The poet approaches a particular reality which is entirely familiar to him with the intention of depicting a gallery of often-conventional human types. Yet, what is important is not who is presented, but the purpose for which he is presented: to create a picture of human stagnation which is not only at home on Pavese's hills.

In one of the last poems of the collection Pavese speaks of the young god become man in order to walk the shores of the world which he will no longer be sure is his own. Pavese, the poet, the mythic "young god," returns to the land and, understanding, charged with the sadness and the weariness of man, smiles—smiles a smile for the irony of mankind:

> Verrà il giorno che il giovane dio sarà un uomo,
> senza pena, col morto sorriso dell'uomo
> che ha compreso. Anche il sole trascorre remoto
> arrossando le spiagge. Verrà il giorno che il dio
> non saprà piú dov'erano le spiagge d'un tempo.
>
> Ci si sveglia un mattino che è morta l'estate
> e negli occhi tumultuano ancora splendori
> come ieri, e all'orecchio i fragori del solo
> fatto sangue. È mutato il colore del mondo.
> La montagna non tocca piú il cielo; le nubi
> non s'ammassano piú come frutti; nell'acque
> non traspare piú un ciottolo. Il corpo di un uomo
> pensieroso si piega, dove un dio respirava.

> Il gran sole è finito, e l'odore di terra,
> e la libera strada, colorata di gente
> che ignorava la morte. Non si muore d'estate.
> Se qualcuno spariva, c'era il giovane dio
> che viveva per tutti e ignorava la morte.
> Su di lui la tristezza era un'ombra di nube.
> Il suo passo stupiva la terra.
>
>   Ora pesa
> la stanchezza su tutte le membra dell'uomo,
> senza pena: la calma stanchezza, dell'alba
> che apre un giorno di pioggia. Le spiagge oscurate
> non conoscono il giovane, che un tempo bastava
> la guardasse. Né il mare dell'aria rivive
> al respiro. Si piegano le labbra dell'uomo
> rassegnate, a sorridere davanti alla terra.

Pavese's particular anguish is that of the poet who is both a part of and external to his poetic world. In describing the reality of the "piccolo mondo" of his childhood, the poet realizes that he is no longer an integral part that he once was, but is an outsider who sees the nature of his people too clearly at times for comfort. Trapped in the limiting confines of their valley, symbolized by "le colline," the peasants are unaware of the extent of their lot. The pity and despair which they inspire in the more "civilized" beholder springs from the latter's contemplation of the base instincts of man which his civilization attempts to cover with an insufficient garment. In Pavese's case, his poetic contemplation is tinged with the melancholy of his exclusion and the defensive irony which he assumes. However, in the last analysis, Pavese's irony of superiority is a weak defense against the more basic irony of life underlying his melancholy: that his civilization, while it may not have given him a better life, has incapacitated him forever from returning to the primitive world of "le colline."

Giose Rimanelli (essay date 1969)

SOURCE: "Myth and De-Mythification of Pavese's Art," in *Italian Quarterly*, Vol. 13, No. 49, Summer, 1969, pp. 3–39.

[*In the following excerpt, Rimanelli compares Pavese to his Italian contemporaries and discusses the use of myth in* Lavorare stanca.]

In *A proposito di certe poesie non ancora scritte* Pavese says that "only critical awareness brings a poetic cycle to an end" [*Poesie*, 1962]. In this sense that which had been the poetry of modernism, that is to say the poetry of the '20's, already in 1936 represented a period that had come to a close. A closed period which—at best—allowed only variations on its main themes.

The greatest living poets of the time—[Ezra] Pound, [T. S.] Eliot, [Paul] Valery—had already formulated their experiences and now they merely amplified them. For their part the young poets were taking other directions. In England the Oxford group was decisively in favor of a poetry of social significance. In Italy, the advent of [Salvatore] Quasimodo registered the first indications of a poetry that was galvanized and reinforced by the war and not, as was held by many critics, transformed by it. Although W. H. Auden and his friends, Quasimodo included, tried to give new contents to poetry, they nevertheless wrote in the modernistic hermetic idiom. In every case, the critics were conscious of the new orientation, albeit not exactly convinced.

Modern poetry achieved recognition when the critics perceived that it not only responded to the questions and urgencies of the time, but that it also represented the end phase of an evolution that had begun with romanticism. In this sense *Lavorare stanca* was and remains a novelty. It cannot be set within the frame of the cultural background. The hesitations of the critics in judging the book are to be attributed precisely to this fact. To cite an example, let us recall that in 1936 nobody, or almost nobody, took note of *Lavorare stanca,* while the general attention was drawn to a study by Francesco Flora in which he deluded himself that he was announcing a new phase, the "hermetic" phase of Italian poetry. And when Pavese was discovered in the confusion of the immediate post-war period, another perspective loomed on the horizon and it brought other exigencies in its train. The poetry of *Lavorare stanca* was grouped together with the poetry of social significance and of commitment, with which it did share actual similarities. But it did not have a common pre-history, nor even a common orientation.

Definitively the difficulties that the critic has in approaching Pavesian poetry are above all to be attributed to the fact that Pavese did not participate in the experiments of his contemporaries, nor did he seem coinvolved in their vicissitudes. The poetics of Italian hermeticism evolved within the terms established by [Giuseppe] Ungaretti and by [Eugenio] Montale. Composition is Ungaretti's main preoccupation, and as such his poetry is autonomous, it obeys a rhythm, a syntax, a sound peculiar to it. Content and form draw increasingly closer to each other to the point of interpenetration. The words are counted, they do not crowd the page, but are wrested from silence almost painfully, and with all their meaning. Avoiding adjectives, arbitrariness, Ungaretti retains the virginal and conceptual value of the word which, isolated in the space of the page, becomes a hieroglyphic, an ideogram. In this poetry, harsh, bitter real sounds are rarely found; just as rare are onomatopoeic metaphors which spray color and emotion, and forcibly intrude on the reader. The word has a sound because it has weight and a violence at the moment it reaches the reader. Ungaretti's poems lack sonorousness. They suggest contemplation rather than sensation, a lament rather than a strident shout. The dimension of this poetry is the order of silence, a reality that presents itself as eternal, immutable and irreversible like a melody, a dimension that surpasses life and which at the same time contains its reflections. Ungaretti's encounters—his reality—are evening and morning, empty spaces, islands outside time. This contemplation by Ungaretti is virility in contrast to the symbolists who represents a contemplated reality.

Montale constitutes the other pole of Italian modernistic poetry, and it has nothing in common with Ungaretti. If behind the latter there are French cultural experiences, both the *Calligrammes* of [Guillaume] Apollinaire and the echo of [Stephane] Mallarme, Montale has a plasticity of verse and visual qualities which bring him close to the Imagists. If Eliot can describe with a new taste the dawns of an English slum in contrast to the idyllic images of the Victorians, Montale's poetry becomes thuds, whirlpool, noise, matter that beats against matter, rolling rafters, flotsam and jetsam among the algae. The word resumes its imitative and onomatopoeic function, while the detail becomes minute and the desolation is graphic. The glance, as though it were the eye of a camera, falls here and there, restless, and then comes to a halt on the Ego. The object is Montale's obsession and in contact with it the poet receives a profound impact, a metaphysical anxiety. But Montale's object does not rest upon a benevolent nature, nor does it reflect a cosmic order. He is very far from the *pathetic fallacy* of the romantics. Montale's nature is sterile and decomposed, it is made of "slime" and of "moulds," and discloses the horror of an immobility without end. Montale lives in a de-humanized present, where only the Ego and reality exist. Hence his frantic rummaging in space, in the cavities of his memory in order to bring a relic of the past to the surface, becomes an anxiety-ridden search for time, for roots. Montale's anguish is the anguish of the poet who feels himself to be incarnate, to be a body. It is the anguish of man who is prey to a historical recurrence that does not justify being. It is that *osso di seppia* without a causality, buffeted and worn out to the point of agony by the eternal waves.

Pavese's orientation, instead, rejects modernism and also rejects the poetic experiences of the past. His purpose is "to begin again at the beginning." Dissatisfied with his youthful attempts, he tried to turn to the origins of poetry. On the other hand his translations of American novels, putting him in touch with a young literature, confirmed his convictions. When Massimo Mila, in his preface to *Lavorare stanca* notes that a genre of folklorist story-telling in dialect still exists in Piedmont, which is a Celtic substratum, an epic vein which is not found in the southern regions, he simply indicates that Pavese already had a regionalistic tradition in his bones.

The first poems, which are the fruit of this search, are descriptive and naturalistic. Pavese does not waste words, but the construction remains linear, simple. The hermetic poet, on the contrary, tries to present an emotion directly, to objectify. Hence the importance of structure, of language which intensifies expression.

In the poem-narratives emotion is presented indirectly by the events that have been dramatized. Therefore the emphasis is not on the plastic-evocative value of the individual word but on the development of the narration. In other words, while the hermetics reconstruct an emotion, Pavese also invents a reality. Both the "I" who speaks, for example, and the cousin of **"Mari del Sud"** are presented by Pavese objectively, as characters. If the cousin is indirectly the subject of the second or third stanza, in the fourth

Pavese at Langhe in the Italian Piedmont, shortly after World War II.

whole cosmos: essences and archetypes. The object, therefore, does not become an end in itself but is in relation with the man who gives it life. If Pavese never goes in for minute description, and instead makes use of substantives, it is because the object represents an essence.

As everybody knows, the section *Antenati* is the prologue of *Lavorare stanca*. The myth is presented and the protagonist defined. In the poem **"Forebears"** he says: "I found companions finding myself."

What he means to say is that he found himself in the myths but that he also found the others: the myth has universal value. The protagonist lives the fundamental traumas, the core experiences. His fate has already been marked in childhood because all the contingencies of future life have filtered into the myth. The myth transforms the quotidian, *history,* into legend, and gives a form to the future.

The section *Dopo* contains, *in nuce,* all the rest of *Lavorare stanca*. It begins with the poem **"Incontro"** and it is singular because the adventures of the adolescent and of the adult will always be fugitive encounters in the street, in the journey that leads far away from the country. Nevertheless the problem of the protagonist is not the country because he is never entirely cut off from it. Rather it is the city because here he does not feel in harmony with himself. He does not succeed in possessing it and therefore *belonging* because he will never be able to raise the city to the level of myth. Now he is a grown man conscious of his actions, who investigates and analyzes. The city has no mysteries, and mystery is the pre-condition of myth. It has no mysteries because man builds it and understands it. For the boy who runs away from home the street is a mystery because he does not know where it leads. In the city, however, everything is explained because life is an eternal present, a prison. The countryman who comes to the city suffers the anguish of being identified, recognized. It is an anguish that is different from that of [Jean-Paul] Sarte's characters, or from the "I" of Montale who are citizens, people without a fate. They are in the grip of the real, of the object because they live in a de-mythified reality.

the boy, the "I," speaks of himself. In the poems the words are precise and concrete but not denotative. In practice the phrases "on the side of a hill," "late twilight" do not specify or photograph. Instead the ambiences and atmospheres are perceived. The "I," the protagonist, does not disjoin the attribute of the thing from the thing itself because he assimilates the things in their substance. When Montale says "era il rivo strozzato che gorgoglia" [*Ossi di seppia,* 1963] he attributes to the brook functions that do not belong to it, but by so doing he tries to reproduce something of an objective character glimpsed in an emotion: the dried-out brook. Pavese, on the other hand, does not have recourse to emotion and presents things objectively as though it were not he who is describing them, as though things presented themselves naturally, by themselves.

Pavese had assimilated the culture of his time but he rejected hermetic poetry because, based as it was on the concept image—language, it remained a subjective, lyrical form and therefore too often a gratuitous expression. Now Pavese's preoccupation is not a question of genre, but one having much deeper roots. We must bear in mind that the hermetic poet reduces himself to a relativistic, nauseous and contingent reality with its search for objective reality. For both Ungaretti and Montale the anguish of living derives from a lack of form. Their a-historicism is caused by an attitude towards reality that does not change, that cannot change, whereas Pavese's reality is a

Lavorare stanca speaks of a journey, as do all the epics. The hero at times descends into the Avernus, into the kingdom of the dead, before concluding his adventures. It is a journey into the unconscious, for this after all is what the caverns, the sea, etc., represent. The adventure comes to an end only when the hero returns to the world. He returns, that is to say, when the spiritual is in harmony with the real, when the unconscious and the conscious manage to maintain proper proportions, when the personality achieves full integration. Now in the descriptions of the protagonist of *Lavorare stanca* the hills are almost always enveloped in darkness, or submerged in the moonlight. They could represent his unconscious. The impossibility of renewing the myth of the country in the city represents the impossibility of establishing a normal relation between the conscious and the unconscious. The result is not a complete personality, but a sundered one. This is why the hero in the epic of *Lavorare stanca* never obtains the state of grace as instead happens in the ancient epic when the hero, after overcoming all obstacles, happily concludes the cycle of his experiences: Ulysees by finding Ithaca, Aeneas his fatherland, Dante by arriving in the sight of God. The cousin did not find the exotic world of the southern seas, peopled with islands and whales, and he returns home with the meditative air of tired peasants. The adolescent leaves the hills in search of something new and violent, as though he wanted to overcome his personal fate, and instead loses himself in the very search to find himself. At bottom he is part of the modern epic. His transcendence is in recurrence, because for Pavese life signifies precisely recurrence, ritual; the fundamental encounters repeat themselves.

The difference between Pavese and his contemporaries is that the latter used the mythic past (consider Eliot) as a simile in that, for them, to believe in history transformed into legend would have been equivalent to a rejection of their poetics. Instead Pavese, with the help of myth, dramatizes the experiences of his contemporaries, and encompasses them within himself.

Ira Sadoff (essay date 1977)

SOURCE: A review of *Hard Labor,* in *The Antioch Review,* Vol. 35, Nos. 2–3, Spring–Summer, 1977, pp. 239–41.

[*In the following excerpt, Sadoff lauds William Arrowsmith's English translation of* Hard Labor *and explores various aspects of Pavese's poetry.*]

The great Italian poet, Cesare Pavese, has finally found an able translator in poet William Arrowsmith. The translations in **Hard Labor** are direct and emulate Pavese's flatness of style and diction. Arrowsmith's critical introduction is simultaneously scholarly and informal, providing as substantial a critical overview of Pavese the man and poet as we are likely to get for some time to come. Based on the provided selection of poems, however, Arrowsmith has a tendency to overpoliticize Pavese's work; no doubt Pavese's opposition to fascism and his exile played a central part in his life and concerns, and there are a few poems from the collection **"Green Wood"** which are explicitly political, but for the most part Pavese's work centers rather on the austere Italian landscape and its effect on the people:

All I see is hills, their long, clean, flanking lines
everywhere, far and near, filling my earth and sky.
  But my hills
are harsh, with terraces and vineyards men have
  sweated to build
on that scorched ground.

—**"Displaced People"**

and, from **"People Who've Been There"**: "Sun and rain are only kind to weeds, nothing else. And now, of course, / now that the wheat's dead, the frost is over."

Pavese's real strengths lie in his supreme powers of description, his attention to narrative, and his praise of the senses.

There comes a moment when everything stands still
and ripens. The trees in the distance are quiet,
their darkness ripens, concealing a fruit so ripe
it would drop at a touch. The occasional clouds
are swollen and ripe.

—**"Grappa in September"**

The creaking wagon shakes the street. Dawn.
Somebody's lying there in the sacks of grain,
    sleeping,
dreaming of night. No lonelier bed than this.
Under the wagon a lantern dangles, night and day.
The light's out, you can tell from the sky.

—**"The Teamster"**

The characters who appear in Pavese's poems could almost have come from the paintings of Millet or early Manet: farmers, peasants, prostitutes, drunkards, workers, people who have either experienced the necessity and futility of work or who have been outcasts from the social world. In illuminating their lives, Pavese makes his real political contribution. Given the history of Italian poetry, its dedication to elegance of form and subject matter, Pavese's poems are daring indeed, as daring as Delacroix's paintings must have seemed to the classicists. "The peasants fed / their fields manure, and now their crops are nothing / but manure. No use looking. Everything will be black / with rot. . . . "

Most essential to Pavese's vision, however, is his dialogue with solitude: on the one hand he loves the purity, the meditative expansiveness of solitude; on the other, he is totally overwhelmed by feelings of endless wandering, of loneliness and disconnection. "Here, in the dark alone, / my body rests and feels the master of itself," he says, and in a persona poem titled **"People Who Don't Understand,"** he writes:

That's what Gella wants. She wants to be alone
in the fields, in the loneliest, wildest places, even
  the woods.
She'd wait until night, then wallow around in the
  grass,
even the mud. She'll never go back to the city.
  What she'd like
is doing nothing. What's the use of doing anything,
  for anyone?

And, on the other hand, he writes, "I'll wander around the streets till I'm dead tired," and "We were born to wander and ramble around these hills, / with no women, our hands folded behind our backs."

No discussion of Pavese's work would be complete without mentioning his concern with, and his ambivalence toward, women. A bachelor, Pavese in his work often reflects a strong feeling for male community and views women as "the other," always out of reach, incomprehensible, having no part in the communion of labor: "The outsider was stuffy, / tightfisted, cruel: a woman." When women are not criticized, they are often idealized, either mythically (compared to the sea or land) or archetypically (the angel or whore). But Pavese also devotes considerable attention, usually in persona poems, to women's plight, their suffering and victimization. Speaking of **"The Country Whore,"** he says, "No man can see, beyond the body lying there, / the need, the anguish, of those fumbling adolescent years." And later, more ambivalently:

> In our family women don't count . . .
> they just don't matter, and we don't remember
>   them.
> but there's one disgrace we've never known:
> we've never been women, we've never been
>   nobodies.

If *Hard Labor* suffers a weakness, it is that Pavese's sameness of flat style and diction tends to make many of the poems indistinguishable from one another, to diffuse the individual power of the poems. But in this remarkable volume there are probably a dozen inexhaustibly powerful poems which create unforgettable emotional experiences, and no one can ask for more than that from any poet.

Doug Thompson (essay date 1982)

SOURCE: "*Lavorare stanca* and the Evolution of Pavese's Verse in the Nineteen-Thirties," in *Cesare Pavese: A Study of the Major Novels and Poems,* Cambridge University Press, 1982, pp. 13–39.

[*In the following excerpt, Thompson surveys Pavese's early poetry, finding the works a means by which Pavese examined difficult periods in his life.*]

Only in 1962, with the publication by Einaudi of *Poesie edite e inedite (Published and Unpublished Poems*), did it become possible to trace the development of Pavese's poetry during the nineteen-thirties. Up to then there had been two editions of the verse he had written in the thirties—the Solaria edition of *Lavorare stanca (Working Is Tiresome*) of 1936 and the Einaudi edition of 1943. Even these had revealed substantial differences in tone, point of view and technique, although about half the poems in the second edition had made up the bulk of those in the first. Of the one hundred and four poems in *Poesie edite e inedite* written before 1940, twenty-seven of them were published for the first time. In addition, there were six poems which had appeared in the Solaria *Lavorare stanca* (a limited edition, soon exhausted) but which had been excluded from the Einaudi edition. Thus about a third of the poems belonging to that all-important decade were to all intents and purposes unknown until well after Pavese's death. Had *Poesie edite e inedite* gone no further than bringing these poems to light its contribution to Pavese scholarship would have been considerable. However, it also provided first drafts of individual poems, often reconstructed, with some difficulty, from Pavese's own papers. Thus

in a good number of cases it is possible to see how the poem gradually took shape in the poet's mind. The edition drew attention to the connection between certain poems, or groups of poems, and the events of Pavese's life, by establishing in many cases their date and place of composition. This was particularly important with regard to the troubled period in Pavese's life between August 1935 and the end of 1937. Of the twenty-eight poems belonging to that period eleven, including almost all of the group which Pavese called the *Poesie del disamore (Poems of Disaffection*), were published for the first time in 1962.

How then did Pavese's verse develop and what did he hope to achieve in it? One of the most valuable sources when seeking to answer these questions is *Il mestiere di poeta (The Poet's Craft*). This short commentary on his own work was written by Pavese at the end of November 1934, when all but eight of the forty-five poems which were to make up the Solaria edition of *Lavorare stanca* had already been composed. In those poems, we are told, the guiding principle had been 'every poem a story' (*poesia-racconto*), whilst technically Pavese had sought to make his verse 'clear and distinct, muscular, objective, essential'. He explains that what he had tried to achieve, almost instinctively, had been 'an essential expression of essential facts' without falling into what he called 'the usual introspective abstraction, expressed in a language which, because it is bookish is allusive, and masquerades all too easily as essential'. The word 'usual' needs explanation, for what Pavese is referring to is the type of poetry which was being written contemporaneously in Italian, that which Francesco Flora dubbed 'poesia ermetica' ('hermetic poetry').

As Fascism gradually tightened its grip on every aspect of Italian life, writers whose views conflicted with the 'official' views of the Regime found it increasingly difficult to write with reference to their own society lest they become victims of persecution. Some went into exile, either for the duration of the Regime, like Silone, or temporarily, like Moravia. However, others, although unwilling to compromise themselves with the Regime, did continue to write. Their poetry tended to be introspective, often abstruse, as they sought refuge from the forbidden territory of contemporary society as they saw it in delicate creations of musical words, rhythms and personal symbols. Since the fall of Fascism, debate has continued about the ethical and the poetical significance of Hermetic poetry. Whether or not it represented moral and political cowardice is irrelevant to the present discussion, but there can be no doubt at all that it played a part in refining the language, technique and sensibility of many poets, amongst them Ungaretti, Sereni, Montale and Quasimodo, so that when at last comparative freedom had been restored they were fully equipped to produce their most mature work.

Pavese, to judge from what he says about his poems in *Il mestiere di poeta* and, more importantly, from the poems themselves, refused to be restricted by current circumstances. For him the 'basic condition of every attempt at poetry, however sophisticated, is always a close reference to the ethical, and of course, practical demands of the environment in which one is living'. Thus when Italian poetry was undergoing a period of withdrawal, Pavese was taking a 'committed' stand which, although not overtly political, nonetheless raised embarrassing questions so far as the Regime was concerned. In accordance with this commitment he endeavoured to avoid certain traditional features of Italian poetry in his own verse, notably with regard to the use of imagery and metre. His poems he saw, with some justification, as 'a linguistic creation which is fundamentally dialectal or at least based on the language of speech'. With its insistence upon objects, rather than images, upon the language of speech rather than that of any literary tradition, the verse Pavese wrote between 1930 and the time of his arrest in May 1935 was fundamentally Naturalistic. In this, the two most recognisable influences upon his work are those of Walt Whitman, whose poetry he had carefully studied to write his degree thesis, and, to a somewhat lesser degree, his own earlier fellow-Piedmontese, Guido Gozzano. His debt to Whitman is manifold, even though the influence is wholly absorbed and transformed into a style which is uniquely Pavese's own. The opening sequence of Whitman's 'There was a child went forth' highlights this influence, and not only with regard to the long line which both poets favoured; indeed, in his degree thesis, Pavese had referred to 'the gaze which was serene yet full of surprise of "There was a child went forth"', and this seemingly paradoxical combination was to become an ideal at the centre of Pavese's own verse:

> There was a child went forth every day,
> And the first object he look'd upon, that object he became,
> And that object became part of him for the day or a certain part of the day,
> Or for many years or stretching cycles of years.
> The early lilacs became part of this child,
> And grass and white and red morning-glories, and white and red clover, and the song of the phoebe-bird,
> And the Third-month lambs and the sow's pink-faint litter, and the mare's foal and the cow's calf,
> And the noisy brood of the barnyard or by the mire of the pond-side,
> And the fish suspending themselves so curiously below there, and the beautiful curious liquid,
> And the water-plants with their graceful flat heads, all became part of him.

Structural features such as the copious use of parataxis, the repetition of words, phrases and specific rhythms are obvious enough, but Whitman's influence in general, though particularly on this poem, extends well beyond these. Though temperamentally very different—Pavese certainly did not share the American's cosmic optimism in his own 'myth of discovery'—themes and motifs found here are often echoed or developed in Pavese's verse which, like Whitman's, is consciously 'primitive', attempting to see with the 'occhio vergine' ('virgin eye') of the child. Pavese transforms the central image of the child, who goes out each day and discovers the world and in discovering it both creates and discovers himself, into 'lo scappato di casa' ('the runaway child'), the *fons et origo* of

the theory of myth which he developed later. Other motifs were perhaps first suggested by Whitman's 'the father, strong, self-sufficient, manly', 'men and women crowding fast in the streets', 'the light falling on roofs', 'the village on the highland seen from afar at sunset', 'all the changes of city and country', 'the old drunkard staggering home' and 'the horizon's edge'—all from this one poem. In his thesis on Whitman, Pavese continually draws attention to 'the discovery of mysterious influences in ordinary things—even the sea and the daily monotony experienced by the sailors—and the consequent serenity and joy of life and song' ('Thesis' fols 63–4) and 'the tone of amazed simplicity with which objects, the appearances of the world, are noted and made to follow endlessly, one after the other' ('Thesis' fol. 66), so that it becomes impossible not to connect this tendency with Pavese's *stupore*. There is too a strong sense of continuity and tradition, such as is found in **'I mari del Sud'** (**'The South Seas,'** *Poesie*) and **'Antenati'** (**'Forbears,'** *Poesie*).

In 'Song of Myself' and many other of Whitman's poems, there is a conscious didacticism which Lorenzo Mondo rightly connected with **'Antenati'** and with **'Paesaggio I'** (**'Landscape I'**) [*Cesare Pavese,* 1961], and which is often expressed aphoristically:

> Apart from the pulling and the hauling stands what I am

or authoritatively:

> Do you guess I have some intricate purpose?
> Well I have, for the Fourth-month showers have, and the mica on the side of a rock has

where, incidentally, the first suggests that separation of *essere* and *fare* which Pavese was to insist on later ('A person counts for what he *is,* not for what he *does*'—*Il mestiere di vivere,* 22 October 1940) and which is reflected even in his earliest poems in the contemplative observer, Pavese's narrator, a not too distant cousin of Whitman's 'loafer' or 'magnificent idler'. It would have been strange indeed had Pavese not absorbed some of the lessons he observed and analysed in Whitman's poetry and prose. The tone of his thesis is one of admiration, and the degree of identification with the American's purposes is striking.

A tendency 'to name objects and events stripped to the banality of the everyday and commonplace', common in Whitman's verse, suggested to Lorenzo Mondo a certain influence of Gozzano on Pavese, and this possibility is further strengthened when we recall the habit of the earlier poet of incorporating place names and direct speech into his poems, both devices which Pavese used in his own, earlier verse, notably in **'I mari del Sud',** though even before that. However, in spite of other obvious similarities such as the simplicity of Gozzano's language and style in his homely, discursive poetry, which frequently focuses on aspects of the provincial life of Piedmont, it is all too easy to overstate his impact on Pavese's work.

Technically, his poetry is for the most part very different, adhering as it does to more traditional verse forms and length of line than does Pavese's, and relying much on rhyme for its effects. In tone, it is usually far removed from Pavese, whose verse does not have that lugubrious sentimentalism, that penchant for melodrama, which, Gozzano indulges in poems such as 'Invernale' (Wintertime), 'La signorina Felicità ovvero la Felicità!' (Miss Felicity, or Happiness), 'Il gioco del silenzio' (The Play of Silence) and many others. Montale has rightly characterised Gozzano's verse as 'that poetry of the *faux exprès,* of semitones and harmonies in grey, that poetry which is clearly not heroic but rather *en pantoufles*', and in so doing has incidentally emphasised its difference from Pavese's. The motif which is perhaps most typical of Gozzano is the relationship between a man and a woman, either realised or potential, remembered now, years after, as though it had been the unrecognised threshold of paradise. The poems are full of naturalistic detail, and Pavese's earliest attempts at poetry are frequently reminiscent of them in this respect. However, he had already managed to control any inclination towards sentimentalism by the time he came to write **'I mari del Sud'**, where a much greater sense of emotional detachment is in evidence than in most of Gozzano's verse. It is only in fleeting moments that we glimpse any point of contact between them, and even then, despite the major differences already observed in that field, it is in the realm of *tecnica* rather than *Weltanschauung.* Mondo's suggestion that Gozzano provides 'the missing link which joins [Pavese's] youthful, emotional outpourings to **"I mari del Sud"**' seems greatly exaggerated. Indeed, Gioanola's claim that Gozzano's influence furnished 'a negative model revealing to Pavese how he couldn't write, rather than a positive model to imitate' [*Cesare Pavese: la poetica dell'essere,* 1977] seems nearer the mark. Pavese's most typical poetry between 1930 and 1935 is very different from what is most typical of Gozzano. Admittedly, the two poets move in the same provincial world, but Gozzano's attention is continually riveted on its middle-class inhabitants and their day-to-day concerns, whereas Pavese focuses on the outdoor world of the peasant or of those who live on the margins of urban society. With Pavese the whole poem grows out of memory, usually without any special emphasis on the 'act' of remembering, whereas with Gozzano the subject of the poem is a *specific* memory, and even though a lost innocence or new innocence are sometimes implicit in Pavese's material, it is never weighed down with remorse, regret or irony which colour Gozzano's harking back. There is considerable difference in tone and purpose in their approach to past experience, as a direct comparison between an early poem of Pavese's, **'Le maestrine'** (**'The School-mistresses'**)—chosen because its subject could well have appealed to Gozzano—and the closing section of **'Paolo e Virginia'** will illustrate.

'Le maestrine' (*Poesie*), like many of Pavese's earlier poems, reconstructs the process whereby a personal myth is created—that of the relatively well-to-do young women schoolteachers so much a part of, and yet so out of place in, the rural setting of the narrator's childhood:

> Le mie terre di vigne, di prugnoli e di castagneti
> dove sono cresciute le frutta che ho sempre
>   mangiato,
> le mie belle colline—hanno un frutto migliore
> che fantastico sempre e non ho morso mai.

> (these lands of vines, sloes and chestnut trees, where grow the fruits that I have always eaten, these beautiful hills of mine—they have a better fruit which I dream about continually and have never tasted.)

Here, 'frutto' is synonymous with 'myth', that which recurs 'seasonally', continually renewing that sense of joy in vitality, associated with the 'maestrine', the subject of the poem. The contradiction is highlighted between these young schoolteachers and their environment, whether human or natural; they are fixed forever in their youthfulness—indeed the narrator refuses to think of them as ever growing old—and they are left in our mind's eye 'with their fine parasols and dressed in bright colours', and we are fully aware of that sense of delight in them, which is eternally renewable for the narrator, 'my own fruit, the best, which every year returns'. Wretchedness and beauty coexist in the poem but, significantly, it is the latter which is exalted.

Such optimism—or indeed, such an organic style—are not found in the closing lines of **'Paolo e Virginia'**; life goes on, certainly, but diminished, for the richness of the love experience is not carried forward into the future, only the oppressive awareness that 'there hath passed away a glory from the earth':

> Il mio sogno è distrutto
> per sempre e il cuore non fiorisce più.

> (My dream is destroyed for ever and my heart no longer blooms.)

It is in this final stanza, with its insistent, dead ring—'morii', 'distrutto', 'per sempre', 'non . . . più', 'invano', 'lutto', etc.—that the preceding narrative finds its *raison d'être,* being entirely at the service of Paolo's personal 'unburdening'—not for the *loss* of Virginia, but for the *effect* her death has had upon him—'il cuore non fiorisce più'—the real subject and purpose of the poem. With few exceptions, Pavese did not publish this kind of 'poetry of unburdening' during his *poesia-racconto* period (roughly speaking, that of the pre-Brancaleone poems) and when he did write *and* publish poems which expressed a personal sense of desolation (1935–8) they were rarely in the narrative vein. On the contrary, they achieved a much greater compression through the *immagine-racconto,* in which objects and the relationships between them became symbols of the instinctive, essential self; landscapes of the soul. For Pavese, poetry was ever an instrument of self-discovery; for Gozzano, a catharsis and a consolation.

Although Pavese was to modify his views in the intervening years, particularly with regard to the image, he eventually came to realise that the poems of the Solaria edition of *Lavorare stanca* had represented an extraordinary moment in the history of modern Italian poetry:

At a time when Italian prose was a 'weary discussion with itself' and poetry was 'a painful silence', I was talking in prose and in verse with peasants, labourers, sand-diggers, prostitutes, prisoners, factory girls and young people. I wouldn't dream of boasting about it. I liked them and still like them. They were my sort of people ['L'influsso degli eventi' (The Influence of Events) in *La letteratura americana e altri saggi,* 1962].

Lavorare stanca was an attempt, whatever its shortcomings, at a direct confrontation with reality; more specifically, with the life and problems of the people of Piedmont and Turin. Indeed, its significance would seem to lie more in its moral and historical perspective than in any intrinsically poetic merit it might have, for technically it raised as many problems for Pavese as it solved and eventually he abandoned it in favour of prose. It was more the idea than the practice of great poetry. Nonetheless it clearly defined, once and for all, the content of Pavese's poetical world. He himself recognised its relevance in his work when he referred to it as the 'grosso monolito' (great monolith) from which all his most important works had been 'chipped'. The Soliara *Lavorare stanca* has therefore a twofold importance in contemporary Italian literature, the one historical, as the first sustained attempt at *neo-realismo* in verse, the other personal.

Lavorare stanca was an attempt, at a direct confrontation with reality; more specifically, with the life and problems of the people of Piedmont and Turin. Indeed, its significance would seem to lie more in its moral and historical perspective than in any intrinsically poetic merit it might have, for technically it raised as many problems for Pavese as it solved and eventually he abandoned it in favour of prose.

—Doug Thompson

If the whole work is indeed the 'great monolith', then—to continue the metaphor—the poem which opens the collection, **'I mari del Sud'**, is the 'plinth' on which it stands. It contains almost everything which was to be typical of Pavese's writing, and yet, in itself, it is not a consistently good poem:

Camminiamo una sera sul fianco di un colle,
in silenzio. Nell'ombra del tardo crepuscolo
mio cugino è un gigante vestito di bianco,
che si muove pacato, abbronzato nel volto,
taciturno.

(We walk one evening up the side of a hill, in silence.
In the late twilight shadows my cousin is a giant dressed

in white, who moves silently; his face is sunburnt and he does not speak.)

Two features of the poem become apparent in its opening section: the conversational tone and the unusually long line which is employed. In his attempt to sever all links with traditional verse forms, Pavese sought space in which to develop the *racconto* (*story*) aspect of each poem, and quite by chance (so he would have us believe) he stumbled across the thirteen-syllable line. Occasionally, as in the sixth line, it becomes stretched to as many as sixteen syllables, and proves extremely unwieldy, loosening the bonds of poetic form until the verse becomes indistinguishable from prose. The majority of the poems in the Solaria edition of *Lavorare stanca* are based on the thirteen-syllable line, and there are very few where the poet is entirely in control. The main problem is the caesura, which often reveals that the line is in reality two lines of shorter duration, both of which are common traditional types; for example,

Camminiamo una sera   sul fianco di un colle

Here, the first part of the 'line' is a perfectly regular seven-syllable line (*settenario*), stressed on the third and sixth syllables, whilst the second part is of six syllables (*senario*), having its stress on the second and the fifth.

Mio cugino ha parlato stasera. Mi ha chiesto
se salivo con lui: dalla vetta si scorge
nelle notti serene il riflesso del faro
lontano, di Torino. 'Tu che abiti a Torino . . . '
Mi ha detta ' . . . ma hai ragione. La vita va vissuta
lontano dal paese: si profitta e si gode
e poi, quando si torna, come me a quarant'anni,
si trova tutto nuovo. Le Langhe non si perdono.'
Tutto questo mi ha detto e non parla italiano,
ma adopera lento il dialetto, che, come le pietre
de questo stesso colle, è scabro tanto
che vent'anni di idiomi e di oceani diversi
non gliel'hanno scalfito. E cammina per l'erta
con lo sguardo raccolto che ho visto, bambino,
usare ai contadini un poco stanchi.

(My cousin has spoken this evening. He asked me if I would go up the hill with him. From the top, on clear nights, you can see the reflection of the far-off beacon of Turin. 'You who live in Turin . . . ,' he said to me, ' . . . but you're right. Life goes on far away from home, you profit from it and enjoy it and then, when you come back, like I did at the age of forty, you find everything is new. You don't lose the Langhe.' He said all this to me, but he doesn't speak Italian; speaking slowly, he uses the dialect which, like the stones of this very hill, is so rugged that twenty years of different languages and different parts of the world have left no mark on it. And he walks up the slope with that look of concentration on his face that I saw him turn on the peasants who were a bit tired, when I was a child.)

The verbal theme of the first section, that of silence ('silenzio', 'taciturno', 'tacere'), is taken up again here only to be broken. But the fact that the cousin 'has spoken' is, to the mind of the narrator, worthy of comment. There is about it that mild sense of *stupore* (amazement) which often accompanies the observation (often by children in Pavese's poems) of an event or state of affairs which would normally pass without comment. One of the most notable features of this poem is the sense of awe in which the narrator holds his cousin, and what the poem relates, almost as an undercurrent, is the myth-making process which had been going on for him for as long as he could remember. The cousin is, for the narrator, a living myth.

In this part of the poem, the two poles of Pavese's world, the Piedmontese countryside (*campagna*) and the city of Turin (*città*), are present, but at a great distance from each other. Later, they develop as two totally different worlds in Pavese's writing, and it is interesting that even here the city, which came to represent history, progress and civilisation in his mind (as opposed to the prehistory represented by *campagna*), should be described in terms of light—the 'far-off beacon' whose reflection may be seen only 'on clear nights'.

For the cousin, what is important is the sense of belonging which has accompanied him wherever he has travelled in the world and which has ultimately determined his return to the Langhe. His return involves both memory and discovery, and an awareness of something immutable. In the Langhe, the alienation of man from the world of nature has never taken place.

In the third section ('Vent'anni è stato in giro per il mondo'), the narrative swings away from the present to the past and memory, from the cousin to his continuous absence and its myth-making significance in the childhood of the narrator.

The personal memories of the narrator in the third section become a definite introspection in the fourth ('Oh da quando ho giocato ai pirati malesi'), and the objective-present with which the poem began has by this time developed into the subjective-past, a movement which, after 1935, had taken place in the whole of Pavese's poetry. The desired objectivity and immediacy of the Solaria poems were achieved only through a tremendous effort of self-discipline, and proved impossible to maintain in his isolation at Brancaleone. The lament in this part of **'I mari del Sud'** is for the lost world of childish illusion and innocence, a world which has been supplanted by the intangible, almost inexpressible horrors of modern city life:

> La città mi ha insegnato infinite paure:
> una folla, una strada mi han fatto tremare,
> un pensiero talvolta, spiato su un viso.
> Sento ancora negli occhi la luce beffarda
> dei lampioni a migliaia sul gran scalpiccio.

> (The city has taught me countless fears: a crowd or a street have made me tremble; sometimes even a thought glimpsed on someone's face. In my eyes I still feel the mocking light of thousands of street-lamps way above the great shuffling of people in the streets.)

This stanza proves to be parenthetic, though developing naturally enough out of the circumstances dealt with in the first three. Pavese himself rightly spoke of **'I mari del Sud'** as being 'a poem which is somewhere between the psychological and reportage'. In the fifth section ('Mio cugino è tornato, finita la guerra'), the events of the cousin's life return, whilst the pessimism of his relatives continues, providing a thematic link with the third section.

> Mio cugino ha una faccia recisa. Comprò un
>   pianterreno
> nel paese e ci fece riuscire un garage di cemento
> con dinanzi fiammante la pila per dar la benzina
> e sul ponte ben grossa alla curva una targa reclame.
> Poi ci mise un meccanico dentro a ricevere i soldi
> e lui girò tutte le Langhe fumando.

> (My cousin has a determined face. He bought a piece of land in the village and had a garage built there out of concrete, and he put a shiny petrol pump in front of it, and on the bend at the bridge a great big placard. Then he put a mechanic in the garage to collect the money whilst he wandered all over the Langhe smoking.)

The garage, which was to return in the poem **'Atlantic Oil'** (*Poesie*), becomes a symbol of modern, urban society and of change being imposed upon the almost timeless atmosphere which characterises the Langhe in Pavese's poetry. But in **'I mari del Sud'** the resistance to change is evidently too great, and the failure of the project emphasises the cousin's ever-increasing awareness of himself and the tradition to which he belongs:

> al mattino batteva le fiere e con aria sorniona
> contrattava i cavalli. Spiegò poi a me,
> quando fallì il disegno, che il suo piano
> era stato di togliere tutte le bestie alla valle
> e obbligare la gente a comprargli i motori.
> 'Ma la bestia' diceva 'più grossa di tutte,
> sono stato io a pensarlo. Dovevo sapere
> che qui buoi e persone son tutta una razza.'

> (he would scour the markets in the mornings, and, with an air of cunning about him, would bargain for horses. He explained to me later, after the plan had failed, that his intention had been to buy up all the animals in the valley, and in that way force people to buy cars from him. 'But the biggest animal of the lot', he said, 'was me, for having thought of it. I should have known that here people and animals are all the same race.')

From his experience he has also learnt that there are more important values in life than financial gain. He has to accept the region as it is, for he cannot change it, and this realisation makes him more human. Here, as earlier in the poem, there are hints that the cousin is still regarded as a rolling stone. The details which the narrator tells about him are suggestive of the air of myth and mystery which surrounds him in the narrator's own consciousness. There is almost a reluctance to admit that the cousin has returned for good, that he is human after all, and therefore the narrator, though perhaps not consciously, tries to persuade us and himself that his cousin is continuing his exotic life, albeit on a smaller scale. He wanders all over the Langhe, he marries a woman who is not typical of the region, he tries to introduce modern 'city' ideas and, perhaps most important of all, he maintains that solitude and taciturnity which have been the fertile ground upon which the myth has flourished. But the sense of the exotic, if ever it existed at all for the cousin, no longer plays any significant part in his life. It is only for those who, like the narrator, have not travelled and have not seen for themselves, and who have lived the far away places only in their imagination, that a sense of the exotic exists.

The next stanza ('Camminiamo da più di mezz'ora') moves, once again, to the present, for the cousin's life, a denial of the narrator's myth of it, is always lived for the present, without nostalgia or regret. For Pavese, the cousin of '**I mari del Sud**' (an actual relation of Pavese's) remained always the model of strength and self-sufficiency to which he aspired. Almost at the end of his life, in a letter to his cousin's daughter, he still referred to him as 'the only one of the Paveses who has counted for something up to now and who was a real man'.

> Mio cugino si ferma d'un tratto e si volge:
>   'Quest'anno
> scrivo sul manifesto: *Santo Stefano*
> *è sempre stato il primo nelle feste*
> *della valle del Belbo*—e che la dicano
> quei di Canelli.'
>
>   e io penso alla forza
> che mi ha reso quest'uomo, strappandolo al mare,
> alle terre lontane, al silenzio che dura.
> Mio cugino non parla dei viaggi compiuti.
> Dice asciutto che è stato in quel luogo e in
>   quell'altro e pensa ai suoi motori.

(Suddenly my cousin stops and turns to me: 'This year I'll write on the placard: *The Festival of Santo Stefano has always been the best in the Belbo valley*—and that they admit it even in Canelli' . . . and I think about the strength that this man has given me, tearing himself away from the sea, from distant lands, from the endless silence. My cousin doesn't talk about the voyages he has made. He says drily that he's been in this place or that, and he thinks about his motors.)

From the proud words to be inscribed on the placard, we realise that the cousin has in truth arrived home. The narrator derives an inner strength from the knowledge that his cousin, who has been everywhere and seen everything, has finally rejected a life of adventure in returning to what was always his deepest reality—the only reality the narrator has ever known. Yet the cousin, though a realist, is by no means insensitive for he does have one special memory, though like everything else in his life it too is controlled. It is a memory devoid of nostalgia, and it lives on in him because of its suggestiveness—of beauty, of struggle and of strength:

> e ha veduto volare i ramponi pesanti nel sole,
> ha veduto fuggire balene tra schiume di sangue
> e inseguirle e innalzarsi le code e lottare alla lancia.
> Me ne accenna talvolta.

(he saw heavy harpoons flying in the sun, he saw whales fleeing in the foam lathered with blood and saw the chase and the lifted tails and the struggle with the lance. He mentions it to me sometimes.)

One is reminded of Hemingway in the motif of the bloody struggle to the death, but the original here, as indeed with Hemingway, is Herman Melville, whose *Moby-Dick* Pavese was soon after to translate into Italian. The fascination which America and its writers had for Pavese in the years when he was composing the first *Lavorare stanca* is often present in one way or another in those poems. . . .

Certain features of '**I mari del Sud**' make it quite unlike any other Italian poetry being written at the time. Firstly, its language. There is nothing abstruse, nor even allusive. What few images there are do not serve as nuclei around which the poem is constructed. Pavese later explained in *Il mestiere di poeta* that he did not want them in his poetry because they would jeopardise his 'adored immediacy' and because he wanted to avoid the 'facile, gushing lyricism of the imagists'. Indeed, the sparseness of formal imagery suggests the language of prose rather than that of poetry; little meaning is evoked, rather is it described and explained. Nevertheless, this is poetry because, quite apart from the intricate rhythms, other formalising elements are at work, and it is in these that we best see Pavese's 'essential expression of essential facts'. An organic unity is created by the repetition of key words or phrases (*riprese*). Reference has already been made to the verbal theme of 'silence' in the first stanza and this appears yet again in the 'endless silence' of the seventh. There is a whole network of such themes, amongst them the 'dressed in white' and 'sunburnt face' of the first and sixth stanzas, the 'hilltop' of the second and seventh, 'the slope' which appears again in the second and seventh, and so on. Quite apart from these *riprese* there are others which are, like the 'silence' of the first, characteristic of one stanza; amongst these are 'far-off' and 'Turin' in the second; 'women', 'stamp', 'they forgot' and the derivatives of 'morte' (death) in the third; the 'quanto(a) tempo (vita) è trascorso(a)' (what a long time / how much life has passed) and the rhetorical use of 'altri' (others) in the fourth. This was to prove a constant and unifying feature in Pavese's poetry, the *riprese* being carried over from one work to another.

Another interesting aspect of this poem is its use of near-authentic speech within the metric scheme—a moderately successful experiment which is repeated occasionally in later poems, notably '**Estate di San Martino**' ('**Indian Summer,**' *Poesie*) and '**Il vino triste**' ('**Sad Wine,**' *Poesie*), while the use of place names has already been noted in the context of Pavese's debt to Gozzano.

The Naturalistic character of the poetry of the first *Lavorare stanca* lies not only in the use of regional Italian (occasionally dialectal) and regional topics but in the great attention paid to descriptive detail. The cousin

> è un gigante vestito di bianco,
> che si muove pacato, abbronzato nel volto,
> taciturno

whilst the arrival of the postcard triggers off the boyish flight of fancy, in which place names and their associations are sufficient to set his heart beating faster:

> veniva da un'isola detta Tasmania
> circondata da un mare più azzurro, feroce di squali,
> nel Pacifico, a sud dell'Australia.

> (It had come from an island called Tasmania, which was surrounded by the bluest of seas, teeming with sharks, in the Pacific, to the south of Australia.)

One significant feature of **'I mari del Sud'** is sharply at variance with the theories of Naturalism—the involvement of the story-teller in the events he is narrating. Pavese's narrator is not the protagonist, yet the poem is as much about the protagonist's effect on the narrator as it is about the cousin himself. There is some detachment, but nothing like that found in the chief exponents of Naturalism. Shortly after the end of this decade, Pavese realised the value of incorporating his narrator, as a character in his own right, into his novels, and after *La spiaggia* (*The Beach*), written in 1940–1, this became his common practice.

Pavese, as is clear from his diary and the poems of his youth, was extremely introverted, and it is not surprising that in several poems, even in his emotionally most controlled period 1930–5, the narrator and the protagonist are one and the same. However, the resultant poetry is rarely, if at all, morbidly subjective. Poems such as **'Antenati'** (**'Forbears'**) and **'Mania di solitudine'** (**'Mania for Solitude'**, *Poesie*) define the links between the narrator-protagonist and his environment; they are not concerned with his alienation—which, generally speaking, becomes the chief preoccupation of Pavese's poetry for a long time after the events of 1935.

The more or less Naturalistic standpoint taken in **'I mari del Sud'** was precariously maintained in **'Donne perdute'** (**'Fallen Women'**, *Poesie*), **'Fumatori di carta'** (**'Smokers of Cheap Cigarettes'**, *Poesie*) and other compositions of the years 1930–31, but even in many of those poems there is an undercurrent of *inquietudine* (anxiety) which stems primarily from the sexual preoccupations of their narrators.

It was in a poem written in 1933, **'Paesaggio I'** (**'Landscape I'**, *Poesie*), that Pavese first noted any substantial development in his verse. It was here, he tells us in *Il mestiere di poeta,* that he first 'discovered' the image. Nevertheless, he refused to admit to himself that he was using the image in a conventional manner. He claimed, instead, to have created a 'fanciful relationship' between the hermit, the subject of the poem, and the landscape in

which he had placed him. This relationship consisted simply in the direct application to the hermit of words used first of all to describe the landscape ('le felci'; 'bruciate':)

> Quando fuma la pipa in disparte nel sole,
> se lo perdo non so rintracciarlo, perchè è del colore
> delle felci bruciate.

> (When he's smoking his pipe away from his cave, in the sun, if I lose sight of him he's difficult to find again, because he is the same colour as the *scorched bracken.*)

As a result of this discovery, though he misunderstood it, Pavese came to see poetry as 'a complex of fanciful relationships which constitute one's own perception of a reality', and he began consciously to move away from an objective towards a subjective viewpoint. It was in **'Paesaggio I'** that the first world of Pavese's poetry, the countryside of the Langhe, became established in the 'punti di riferimento' ('objective correlatives') already referred to as *riprese,* though without example. It is an elemental-natural world consisting of 'la collina' ('the hill'), 'la roccia' ('rock'), 'terra' ('earth'), 'cespugli' ('shrubs and bushes'), 'sole' ('sun'), 'vigne' ('vines'), 'il cielo' ('the sky'), 'le valli' ('valleys'), 'la pianura' ('the plain'), 'foglie' ('leaves'), 'acqua' ('water'), 'pioggia' ('rain') and 'pozzi' ('pools'), a world inhabited by 'la capra' ('the goat'), 'la biscia' ('the snake'), 'villani' ('peasants') and 'vagabondi' ('tramps').

In this early period, Pavese frequently achieves a suggestiveness which is a kind of optimism at the root of the poem: for example, the opening lines of **'Due sigarette'** (**'Two Cigarettes'**, *Poesie*), composed in 1933:

> Ogni notte è la liberazione. Si guarda i riflessi
> dell'asfalto sui corsi che si aprono lucidi al vento.
> Ogni rado passante ha una faccia e una storia.
> Ma a quest'ora non c'è più stanchezza: i lampioni a migliaia
> sono tutti per chi si sofferma a sfregare un cerino.

> (Freedom comes every night. You look at the reflections on the asphalt along the streets which open out, glistening in the wind. Each rare passer-by has a face and a story. But by this time you are no longer tired. The street-lamps in their thousands are for anyone who stops to strike a match.)

In the poem that optimism is justified, for the story-teller meets a woman with whom he smokes a cigarette and talks a while, and in the last line goes off to spend the night with her. The street or the piazza, in the Solaria *Lavorare stanca,* is the place where 'ogni cosa può accadere' (anything might happen), and this is in sharp contrast with the constricted world of the post-1935 poems, for there, only the child can still feel that unlimited possibility is offered by each street. For the grown man the street becomes a place in which his solitude is emphasised, and even in the poem **'Lavorare stanca'** (*Poesie*), which dates from 1934, there is an evident retreat from the mood of **'Due sigarette'**, and the poem ends on a note of desperate optimism:

> Non è giusto restare sulla piazza deserta.
> Ci sarà certamente quella donna per strada
> che, pregata, vorrebbe dar mano alla casa.

(It isn't right to stay in the empty piazza. Surely, somewhere in these streets there is a woman who, if she were asked, would like to lend a hand in the house.)

The opening line of **'Due sigarette'** touches on one of the most prominent themes of the first *Lavorare stanca,* that of freedom. The majority of characters encountered live outside, or on the very edge of, moral or social normality. They are, for the most part, solitary figures whose outstanding characteristic is generally their self-sufficency. Many reveal a definite antipathy towards organised work, which is regarded as a limitation, whilst others, like the sanddiggers of **'Crepuscolo di sabbiatori'** (**'The Sand-Diggers' Twilight'**, *Poesie*) or the cousin of **'I mari del Sud'**, tend to be isolated by the work they do. There are also those who are morally unacceptable, the prostitutes Dina and Deola, the drunkards of **'Disciplina antica'** (**'Ancient Discipline'**, *Poesie*), and **'Indisciplina'** (**'Lack of Discipline'**, *Poesie*), the tramps of **'Casa in costruzione'** (**'House Under Construction'**, *Poesie*) and **'Il tempo passa'** (**'Time Goes By'**, *Poesie*), and even the hermit of **'Paesaggio I'**. The frequency with which they occur, in one form or another, makes it difficult not to see Pavese himself behind these various *personae*. This feeling is reinforced when we realise that another great limiting factor in *Lavorare stanca* is the question of sexual relationships, for there is enough documentary evidence, letters and diary entries, to show that Pavese always found this an insurmountable problem in his life. It is so for the narrators of **'Tradimento'** (**'Betrayal'**, *Poesie*) and **'Lavorare stanca'** (*Poesie*), and if these poems are an expression of Pavese's own difficulties, then we can also perhaps understand the compensatory significance of the virile, self-sufficient 'giants' such as the one described in **'Balletto'** (**'Dance'**, *Poesie*):

> Il gigante s'avvia e la donna è una parte di tutto il
>   suo corpo,
> solamente più viva. La donna non conta,
> ogni sera è diversa . . .

(The giant moves and the woman is a part of his whole body, only more alive. The woman doesn't matter, every evening she is a different one . . .)

This virility is often manifested as a scorn for women, which at its most extreme represents a petulant misogyny. A key poem in this context, in that it links the themes of the sexual giant, the insignificance of woman and the opposition to work, is **'Antenati'**:

> E le donne non contano nella famiglia.
> Voglio dire, le donne da noi stanno in casa

> E ci mettono al mondo e non dicono nulla
> e non contano nulla e non le ricordiamo.
>
>   . . .
>
> il solo lavoro non basta a me e ai miei;
> noi sappiamo schiantarci, ma il sogno più grande
> dei miei padri fu sempre un far nulla da bravi.

(And women don't matter in the family. What I mean is that with us women stay inside and bring us into the world and have no say in anything and no meaning and we don't remember them . . . work by itself isn't enough for me and my family. We know how to work till we drop, but the grandest dream that my forbears had was to do nothing at all just like the well-to-do.)

The 'sogno' (dream) voiced here is one of many which underlie the attempted objective presentation of real situations in *Lavorare stanca*. The compensatory principle, present in the virile 'giant', can also be extended to the kind of situation outlined in **'Due sigarette'** or **'Piaceri notturni'** (**'Night Pleasures'**, *Poesie*) which, whatever else, certainly have the appearance of dream fulfilments. This attitude towards women may be interpreted in the same way. Women, the object of desire and the denial of its fulfilment for Pavese, are frequently humbled and made the tool or scapegoat of his men. It seems that only in this way can woman be possessed and her mystery be destroyed. However, it is not my intention to imply that Pavese's poems are interesting only as case histories; but it is an aspect which cannot be ignored.

The notion of freedom depending on a rejection of the fundamental condition of the individual's participation in society—that of work—coupled with the strength associated with solitude, leads one to suspect that Pavese himself aspired, as a writer, to just such a position. Assuming its feasibility, does this represent an espousal of something akin to d'Annunzio's poet—superman, or a less than conscious reaction to the pressures on the writer under Fascist rule? In other words, was it a choice Pavese would have made whatever the historical circumstances or *force majeure*—that is, no choice at all? Pavese eventually rejected the negative attitude to work which is characteristic of *Lavorare stanca,* yet he continued to see himself as an outsider. His youthful letters to Sturani suggest that he inherited and unquestioningly accepted the *fin de siècle* notion of the artist, refusing to be possessed by a vulgar, materialistic society, seeing his artistic freedom in his rejection of its values. Between 1930 and 1935, Pavese found himself in a historical situation in which those circumstances actually prevailed. Whether consciously or not, he had schooled himself for a role he was called upon to play. His poetry began to look more and more like that of the *ermetici,* but once the historical pressures were removed then *as a writer* he took up a more or less 'committed' stand, though *as a human being* he continued to see himself as an outsider.

His sense of alienation was real enough, and more and more he came to see his writing as a means of breaking through the barriers which stood between himself and his fellow men. It is obvious from those poems in which sex is seen as the basis of a relationship that doubt and anxiety increase in Pavese's mind, so that within the space of one year he moves from the apparently sure standpoint of **'Due sigarette'** (1933) to that of **'Lavorare stanca'** (1934). The events of 1935 hit Pavese at a time when he had already begun to sense the inevitability of his own inadequacy as a man, and undermined the confidence and harmony which his earlier poems had sought to create. To make distinctions between man and writer may seem heretical; but Pavese himself does just this in the penultimate entry in his diary, for there he says:

> In my work, then, I am king. I've done it all in ten years. Just think of the hesitations I experienced then.

> In my life I am more desperate and lost than ever I was then. What have I constructed? Nothing. For several years I have ignored my defects and have lived as though they didn't exist. I have been stoical. Was it heroism? No, it cost me nothing. Then at the first assault of the 'restless anxiety' I have fallen back into quicksand. Since March I've been floundering in it. Names don't matter. Are they anything other than names turned up by chance, accidental names—if not those, wouldn't there have been others? It happens that now I know which is my greatest triumph—and this triumph lacks flesh, lacks blood, is lifeless.

> There is nothing more I want on this earth, except that which fifteen years of failure have put beyond my reach.
>
> (*Il mestiere di vivere*, 17 August 1950)

A comparison of the poems written before and after Pavese's arrest in 1935 reveals that in the earlier poems solitude is a source of strength and is therefore desired, whilst in the later ones it is seen as an inescapable weakness which is interpreted as personal failure. Having once experienced an imposed solitude, it seems he was unable to see it in the same light as before. Ironically, Pavese's success as a writer is achieved as an observer who stands on the edge of a world and reveals it, and his failure at the personal level comes from the self-same standpoint, for he is unable to enter that world and participate in it.

Freedom, with which this discussion began, became noticeably associated with children, and also with old men, in a small group of poems composed in 1934 and early 1935. Because they do not work, children and old men have time to observe and savour the world about them. However, real freedom exists only for the child, because life, for him, is still anticipation, whilst for the old it is memory and the realisation that active participation is forever past. Both enjoy a measure of peace, the child in that he does not yet know the frustrations and anxieties which stem from work and sexuality, and the old man in that those torments, once experienced, now lie behind him. These poems suggest Pavese had begun to believe that adult life was all restriction and suffering because it was then that one lost the self-sufficiency of the child and depended, for the fulfilment of one's greatest needs, particularly sexual, upon the will of others. Brancaleone and

its tragic personal sequel for Pavese confirmed him in this view, and set him searching for 'l'isolamento che basta a se stesso' (solitude which is self-sufficiency) which became his definition of 'maturity'.

The inevitable suffering associated with work and with sex is also present in those poems which bring together *compagna* and *città* in individual lives. In **'Gente che non capisce'** (**'People Who Don't Understand,'** *Poesie*) the girl Gella works in the city but travels back and forth each day, for her home is in the country. She experiences a different way of life but at the same time a growing sense of alienation, in that she can no longer identify with the countryside to which her family belongs. Her reaction—'she sits in silence' whilst they discuss their work in the country—is symptomatic of her withdrawal, illustrated by the fantasies she creates to solve her problem. Environment and tradition represent security for the characters in Pavese's poems, so that change is followed by bewilderment and suffering. It is the same in **'Città in campagna'** (**'City in the Country'**, *Poesie*), where the child, returning home to the country after a visit with his father to the city, experiences a sense of dissatisfaction; as a result of this visit his life will never again resume the tranquillity and balance it has had before. An apparently absolute reality has been shown to be merely relative.

Change, of whatever sort, assumes the character and mask of injustice in Pavese's poetry. Human life has thus a built-in element of injustice and suffering, quite apart from those injustices like work, which man imposes on himself, or sex, which is imposed on him by nature. Here Pavese draws close to Leopardi, for both poets recognise a tragic human condition which can never be substantially altered but whose suffering could perhaps be alleviated if men were to make a real effort to minimise their injustices to each other. In **'Fumatori di carta'**, Pavese makes as impassioned a plea as does the Leopardi of 'La ginestra' ('The Broom-Flower') for an improvement of man's lot through human solidarity. Pavese's poem speaks of the poverty and wretchedness of life in the city of Turin:

> Imparò a lavorare
> nelle fabbriche senza un sorriso. Imparò a misurare
> sulla propria fatica la fame degli altri,
> e trovò dappertutto ingiustizie.

> (He learned how to work in the factory without a smile. He learned how to measure the hunger of others by his own labour, and everywhere he found injustices.)

Then a statement which is untypically—if ingenuously—bold for the Pavese of 1932:

> Accettava il lavoro
> come un duro destino dell'uomo. Ma tutti gli uomini
> lo accettassero e al mondo ci fosse giustizia.

> (He accepted work as the harsh destiny of mankind. But if only all men would accept it there might be justice in the world.)

The worker curses his destiny which compels him and his brother to toil day in and day out to feed their ageing parents. The fatalism seems to have emerged as a sense of powerlessness in the face of Destiny, but this is not final, for at the end of the poem there is a statement which signals nothing less than the awakening of a political consciousness:

> D'un tratto gridò
> che non era il destino se il mondo soffriva,
> se la luce del sole strappava bestemmie:
> era l'uomo colpevole. *Almeno potercene andare,*
> *far la libera fame, rispondere no*
> *a una vita che adopera amore e pietà,*
> *la famiglia, il pezzetto di terra, a legarci le mani.*

(All of a sudden he cried out that it wasn't Destiny that made the world suffer, that caused the sunlight to bring forth nothing but curses, it was man who was to blame. 'If only we could go away, be hungry in freedom, say no to a life which uses love and pity, the family or a bit of land to tie our hands.')

It is not surprising that this poem was omitted from the Solaria *Lavorare stanca,* for whether Pavese's intention had been overtly anti-Fascist (which seems unlikely) or a general statement about the human lot, the case dealt with in the poem was typical of too many in Fascist Italy for it not to have landed Pavese and the Solaria Press in trouble.

The sixteen poems which Pavese wrote whilst he was detained at Brancaleone reveal a more obvious subjectivity than those composed before. There is an insistence on nostalgia and memory, solitude and disillusionment and an all-pervading sense of futility and stagnation. The world of these poems is one of 'pioggia' (rain), 'mare' (sea), 'fumo' (smoke), 'nebbia' (mist), 'freddo' (cold) and 'ombra' (shadow), and a sad reflective music runs through them.

Turin becomes the focus of nostalgia and loses the 'infinite paure' (numberless fears) which had been identified with it in 'I mari del Sud'. In 'Paesaggio VI' ('Landscape VI', *Poesie*) it becomes 'la bella città, in mezzo a prati e colline' (the beautiful city, set among meadows and hills) and 'le donne dai vivi colori / vi camminano' (women in bright colours walk there). That sense of possibility which had been a significant element in 'Due sigarette' returns here, but no longer with reference to the here and now. This Turin is the city of earlier memories, considered from the other end of Italy, and is mythologised into something resembling the earthly paradise. It becomes the place of memory, of reality, of security; the future to which he will one day return:

> Ogni via, ogni spigolo schietto di casa
> nella nebbia, conserva un antico tremore:
> chi lo sente non può abbandonarsi.

(Every street, every angle of a house showing through the mist retains a ripple of memory from days gone by: no-one who feels it can let himself go.)

The theme of childhood and freedom (and its obverse—adulthood and limitation) continues in 'Poetica' ('Poetics,' *Poesie*) and 'Mito' ('Myth,' *Poesie*); and is most fully developed in the latter, where the connection between childhood and the immortality of the gods, to emerge later in *Dialoghi con Leucò,* is made. The poem turns on the contrast between a child and the man he will become, and the note of disillusionment and resignation predominates.

Reference has already been made to the 'sad, reflective music' of the Bracaleone poems, and this raises the question of Pavese's versification once again. The poem 'Mito' illustrates the many weaknesses in Pavese's poetic technique. He had begun by aiming at a verse which was 'naked and almost prose-like' to avoid the niceties of traditional metres, verse forms and imagery as they were being used by the *ermetici*. However, he had found the balance difficult to achieve because of the many restraints he imposed upon himself. The long line easily became disjointed, not only because of the sense stops (including punctuation), but because of the inevitable caesuras and awkward enjambements. What becomes evident in 'Mito' is that Pavese had opened the door to all kinds of effects that at one time he would never have admitted into his verse. We find him using rhyme, as in the second stanza ('splendori' / 'Fragori' / 'colore'), or introducing alliteration, as in

> il cor*p*o di un uomo
> *p*ensieroso *si* *p*iega, dove un dio re*s*pirava

where there is interplay between the 's' and 'p' sounds, or in

> t*r*ascor*r*e *r*emoto/a*rr*o*s*sando la *s*piaggia

where the relevant sounds are the 'r' and the 's', whilst in the third stanza generally there is a preponderance of 'r' and 'v' sounds. A word repeated more than once in close proximity, noted in connection with the fourth stanza of 'I mari del Sud', makes a double appearance here—once at the beginning of the third stanza ('è . . . e . . . e') and, perhaps more noticeably, in the second with the word 'più'. This second example has added interest in that on all three occasions it is followed by a caesura, two words of three or four syllables and a substantial marked stop. The effect is to break up the rhythm and to give an emphatic sense of finality which is in keeping with the sense of collapse conveyed semantically.

Attention has already been drawn to the strong tendency of the thirteen-syllable line to divide into what are, in effect, two lines of shorter duration. The third stanza of 'Mito' is a good example, being made up almost entirely of *settenari* (seven-syllable lines). The fourth stanza, like the second, is disjointed. Only two lines (including the last one) are end-stopped, and yet the stanza contains three other full stops and a colon. Pavese's intention, it would seem, was to isolate each unit of meaning in areas of silence so as literally to give pause for thought, but once again the rhythm disintegrates and form almost collapses, so that it is debatable whether this stanza is verse at all.

On the positive side, there is an undeniable organic unity which springs, as ever, from reliance upon the *riprese*. In this poem they are mainly single words which appear both within the individual stanza and outside it; occasionally they recur in the same position in the line, like 'uomo', which is found five times in the end position. Besides the many single words (amongst which 'spiagge', 'estate', 'sole', 'dio', 'terra') there are also phrases or clauses which have a similar function, notably 'senza pena' found in an identical position in the first and fourth stanzas; 'il giovane dio' with its additional divisions into its single components; 'ignorava la morte' which occurs at the end of contiguous sentences; and, with perhaps more significance than Pavese (who in his early verse is rarely allusive) intended to give it, the opening 'Verrà il giorno', which seems to echo all the foreboding and prophecy with which Fra Cristoforo's 'Verrà un giorno' is charged in Manzoni's *I promessi sposi* (*The Betrothed*).

The disillusionment which colours **'Mito'** is there too in **'Semplicità'** (**'Simplicity,'** *Poesie*). In this poem, the sense of futility and the motif of the 'uomo solo' ('man who is alone') suggest the idea that it is far better to remain in prison and dream of life outside than to experience release and the inevitable collapse of the dream. This latter theme was to become central to the short stories which Pavese wrote between 1936 and 1938, and to his first novel, *Il carcere* (*The Political Prisoner*).

The theme of futility is best seen in **'Paternità'** (**'Paternity,'** *Poesie*) and **'Lo steddazzu'** (**'The Morning Star,'** *Poesie*), where 'l'uomo solo' reflects and waits and feels no hope. In the former he is

> dinanzi all'inutile mare,
> attendendo la sera, attendendo il mattino

(before the useless sea, waiting for evening, waiting for morning).

The poem has an ominous, dead ring in its adjectives— 'inutile' ('useless'), 'torbido' ('gloomy'), 'madide' ('soaked'), 'sola' ('alone'), 'stanco' ('tired'), 'nera' ('black')—and is reminiscent of Leopardi in its insistence on 'il gran vuoto ch'è sotto le stelle' ('the great emptiness beneath the stars') and 'le stelle, che non odono nulla' ('the stars, which hear nothing').

'Lo steddazzu' reaches the most extreme point of despair expressed in these poems. There is the futility associated with the sea, and the desperate sense of solitude, but also the destruction of the traditional symbols of hope, 'le stelle' ('the stars') and 'l'alba' ('the dawn'):

> Domani tornerà l'alba tiepida con la diafana luce
> e sarà come ieri e mai nulla accadrà.
> L'uomo solo vorrebbe soltanto dormire.
> Quando l'ultima stella si spegne nel cielo,
> l'uomo adagio prepara la pipa e l'accende.

(Tomorrow the tepid dawn will return with its diaphanous light and will be just like yesterday and nothing will ever happen. The man who is alone would like only to sleep. When the last star goes out in the sky, the man slowly fills his pipe and lights it.)

Many of the poems have a delicate beauty which derives from the pathos and suggestiveness of the images which they create. In **'Lo steddazzu'** the 'pipa' (pipe) which 'tra i denti / pende spenta' (hangs unlit between his teeth) becomes a symbol of the stagnation which the sense of futility imposes, and this is echoed and extended a little later in

> Pende stanca nel cielo
> una stella verdognola, sorpresa dall'alba.

(a greenish star hangs tired in the sky, surprised by the dawn.)

Of the poems written after Brancaleone little need be said. The *Poesie del disamore* Pavese regarded as a means of coming to terms with a personal tragedy, and never intended them for publication. In them, the motif of the return, the search for a new beginning, is prominent—in one poem, **'Ritorno di Deola'** (**'Deola's Return'**, *Poesie*), it is, perhaps significantly, the return of another 'outsider', a prostitute—but it is shot through with the realisation that something vital has disappeared forever. No attempt is made to escape from the memories of the past, nor to disguise the longing for its return, but at the same time the futility of this obsessive preoccupation is fully acknowledged. There is the realisation that actions and people and places can no longer have the same significance in his future life as they had in his past. The sense of stagnation persists:

> La notte avrà il volto
> dell'antico dolore che riemerge ogni sera
> impassibile e vivo. Il remoto silenzio
> soffrirà come un'anima, muto, nel buio.
> Parleremo alla notte che fiata sommessa.

(The night will have the face of a former grief which re-emerges every evening, impassive though living. The remote silence will suffer like a soul, unspeaking in the darkness. We shall speak to the night which breathes softly.) (**'L'amico che dorme'**—**'The Friend Who Is Sleeping'**—*Poesie*)

The tone, lexis and imagery of this poem resemble those of the much later *Verrà la morte e avrà i tuoi occhi* (*Death Will Come and Its Eyes Will Be Yours*), though technically the latter are far superior. The last of these poems, **'Risveglio'** (**'Reawakening'**, *Poesie*), announces;

> E' finita la notte
> dei rimpianti e dei sogni. Ma quel giorno non torna.

(The night of dreams and remorse is over. But that day will not come back.)

This recalls the end of summer as the end of childhood, found in **'Mito'**,

La breve finestra
beve il freddo sapore che ha dissolta l'estate.
Un vigore ci attende, sotto il cielo deserto.

(The window, barely glimpsed, absorbs the cold taste
that has dissolved the summer. Strength awaits us
beneath the empty sky.)

The poems written between the end of 1937 and 1940 slip gradually away from the old ideals of 'immediatezza' and 'oggetto' into *poesia ermetica*. Poems such as **'La notte'** (**'Night'**, *Poesie*), **'Mattino'** (**'Morning'**, *Poesie*) and **'Notturno'** (**'Nocturne'**, *Poesie*) are full of music and suggestion, but there is little in them that is tangible; they speak of 'voci e risa remote' (far-off laughter and voices—**'Paesaggio VIII,'** *Poesie*), of 'le voci morte' which 'asso-migliano al frangersi di quel mare' (the dead voices . . . resemble the breaking of the sea), of 'un'ombra fuggevole, come di nube' (a fleeting shadow, like that of a cloud—**'Mattino'**). We learn that by this time,

Non resta,
di quel tempo di là dai ricordi, che un vago
ricordare.

(Nothing remains of that time beyond memory, but a vague remembering)
                                                                —**'La notte'**

The woman whom these poems speak of is

Come una nube
intravista fra i rami

(like a cloud glimpsed through the branches)
                                                                —**'Notturno'**

and in the same poem 'una nube dolcissima' (a very gentle cloud). The accent is always on her insub-stantiality. She is seen as an illusion, always far away beyond his reach. She is associated with silence and a 'vano dolore' (useless grief): the time of unconscious happiness, the 'vivere assorto' (living absorbedly) that is connected with childhood in the poems of 1934–5, is merged in Pavese's fantasy 'nel ricordo d'allora' (in the memory of that time) when she was still his and the events of 1935–6 had yet to happen.

Although there is a tenuous beauty in these poems, they seemed to Pavese to lead nowhere. For five years almost, poetry was called upon to clarify or at least to examine the poet's personal difficulties—a far narrower task than he had originally envisaged for it. In the three years between 1938 and 1940 he composed very little in verse: in

Poesie edite e inedite there are only fourteen poems dating from those years. By that time too he had turned to writing in prose, particularly the short story form, between 1936 and 1938, and had gone on to experiment with the novel. At the time when **'Notturno'**, chronologically the last poem in this decade of verse, was being written, Pavese had already completed three novels and was probably engaged upon the fourth, *La spiaggia*. When he turned again to writing in verse, in 1945, it was technically far superior to any of that written earlier—for one thing, he had learned how to create real, unself-conscious images—but one thing that verse did have in common with the majority of poems dating from 1937 to 1940 was that it was written about a woman and his inability to comprehend her. Never again was he to attempt to tell a story in verse, for that became, with ever-increasing success, the business of Pavese's novels.

FURTHER READING

Biography

Lajolo, Davide. *An Absurd Vice: A Biography of Cesare Pavese*. Edited and translated by Mario Pietralunga and Mark Pietralunga. New York: New Directions, 1983, 255 p.

> Portrays "not only Pavese the writer but also the man who lived with extraordinary intensity many of the existential problems and vicissitudes his generation of intellectuals encountered." In the chapter entitled "The Lyceum Poems and the 'Absurd Vice'," Lajolo cites writings and correspondences by Pavese indicating his thoughts during his earliest efforts at composing poetry.

Criticism

Cipolla, Gaetao. Review of *Hard Labor*. *Canadian Journal of Italian Studies* 7, Nos. 26–7 (1984): 65–73.

> Focuses on William Arrowsmith's translation of *Lavorare stanca*. Cipolla finds that Arrowsmith gives Pavese "an English voice that rings true."

Galassi, Jonathan. Review of *Hard Labor*. *New York Times Book Review* (26 September 1976): 26.

> Comments on the themes and interrelationship of the poems in *Hard Labor*.

O'Healy, Áine. *Cesare Pavese*. Boston: Twayne Publishers, 178 p.

> Critical overview of Pavese's life and writings. O'Healy includes a selected bibliography of works by and about the author.

Additional coverage of Pavese's life and career is contained in the following sources published by Gale Research: *Contemporary Authors*, Vol. 104; *Dictionary of Literary Biography*, Vol. 128; *Short Story Criticism*, Vol. 19; and *Twentieth-Century Literary Criticism*, Vol. 3.

Wendy Rose
1948–

(Born Bronwen Elizabeth Edwards; also wrote under the pseudonym Chiron Khanshendel) American poet, nonfiction writer, artist, educator, and anthropologist.

INTRODUCTION

Born and raised in an urban setting far removed from reservation life and the influence of her Native American relations, Rose is noted for poetry that examines the experiences of mixed-blood Native Americans estranged from both Native and white societies. A well-regarded anthropologist and an accomplished visual artist, Rose is additionally known for her ardent support of efforts to establish a place for Native literature within the American literary canon.

Biographical Information

Born in Oakland, California, Rose is of Miwok and Hopi ancestry. Raised in a predominantly white community near San Francisco, she was alienated from her Native roots throughout her youth. Her mother, who was of Miwok heritage, refused to acknowledge her Amerindian ancestry, and although Rose's father was a full-blooded Hopi, she was denied membership in her father's tribe because acceptance is matrilineally determined. Furthermore, Rose's childhood peers, mimicking the prejudices of their parents, often teased her about her heritage; the resulting sense of loneliness prompted Rose to express herself through writing, painting, drawing, and singing. After dropping out of high school, she joined the American Indian Movement—an activist, sometimes radical, political organization—and later took part in their protest occupation of Alcatraz. Her professional writing career began with the publication of poetry in journals and anthologies under the pseudonym Chiron Khanshendel. In 1976 she graduated with a B.A. in anthropology from the University of California, Berkeley, where she also earned an M.A. in 1978, and later became a lecturer in Native American studies. Rose occasionally exhibits her artwork around the United States and provides designs for various Native American organizations.

Major Works

In addition to treating ecological and feminist issues, Rose's poetry incorporates her own experiences and those of other mixed-blood Native Americans who, separated from their tribal culture and alienated from the white society in which they live, are searching for a sense of identity and community. For example, in such poems as "The well-intentioned question," from the Pulitzer Prize-nominated *Lost Copper* (1980), Rose documents her feelings of marginal-

ization and her desire to be part of the Native community: "My Indian name listens / / for footsteps / stopping short of my door / then leaving forever." Her experiences in academia—where, she argues, Native writings are viewed as a fad and not serious literature—are captured in *Academic Squaw* (1977), and her background in anthropology and involvement with various Native American organizations inspires much of the imagery and history employed in her poetry. In *The Halfbreed Chronicles, and Other Poems* (1985), written while she was studying anthropology as an undergraduate at Berkeley, Rose's focus on the marginalized mixed-blood Amerindian is expanded to include other minorities, such as Japanese Americans and Native Americans from Mexico. She has stated: "You don't think of these people in the same sense as you usually think of half-breeds. But my point is that, in an important way, the way I grew up is symptomatic of something much larger than Indian-white relations. History and circumstance have made half-breeds of all of us."

Critical Reception

Rose's poetry has been praised for capturing the pain and

confusion of the Native American experience and for making it accessible to a non-Native audience. Critics note that much of Rose's work employs elements of Native American songs and chants and is preoccupied with spirituality, communion with the natural world, and the encroachment of white culture on Native society. Although some commentators assert that Rose's use of language masks her feelings, others note a sense of urgency and bitterness in her work and maintain that it is fueled by raw, unbridled emotion. Jamake Highwater has commented: "[Rose's] lines are haunted by an unresolved search for a personal as well as a tribal sense of identity. That search gives her words strength and spirit. It dissolves the barrier of race with which she cautiously surrounds [herself], and it gives us access to her pain. In that pain we are all related."

PRINCIPAL WORKS

Poetry

Hopi Roadrunner Dancing 1973
Long Division: A Tribal History 1976
Academic Squaw: Report to the World from the Ivory Tower 1977
Builder Kachina: A Home-Going Cycle 1979
Lost Copper 1980
What Happened When the Hopi Hit New York 1982
The Halfbreed Chronicles, and Other Poems 1985
Going to War with All My Relations: New and Selected Poems 1993
Bone Dance: New and Selected Poems, 1965–1993 1994

Other Major Works

Aboriginal Tattooing in California (nonfiction) 1979

CRITICISM

James Ruppert (essay date 1980)

SOURCE: "The Uses of Oral Tradition in Six Contemporary Native American Poets," in *American Indian Culture and Research Journal,* Vol. 4, No. 4, 1980, pp. 87–110.

[*In the following excerpt, Ruppert assesses Rose's efforts to write poetry that serves as a "modern correlative to the traditional functions of song" in Native American culture.*]

Wendy Rose's poetry outlines a growth process through which song becomes an important and determining aspect of modern Native American experience. The task posited is to find for the urban Indian a modern correlative to the traditional functions of song. In this she tries to merge the directions of the personal lyric with the communal song. Implicit in this endeavor, as with most

of the poets here, is the assumption that the processes of modern poetry and the traditions of song are similar. The initial position of the growth process is one in which Indians of today—especially urban Indians—find themselves without the knowledge and cut off from song and the oral tradition; [as Rose notes in **"Vanishing Point: Urban Indian"** from *Long Division: A Tribal History*] they are metaphorically dispossessed of the elements of the tradition which would connect them firmly to an intact culture and place them inside social structures: "it is I / without learning, I without song, who / dies and cries the death time." Imagistically the traditional songs seem thrust into non-receptive space, powerless. The sense of the lost force of the songs looms large [in *Long Division*] because of the remnants of culture and song that now lie in ruin. "We die in granite scaffolding / on the shape of the Sierras and lay down / with lips open thrusting songs on the / world. Who are we / and do we still live? The shaman sleeps / and says no."

Here in the present the poet discovers she has been left out: she has not only missed the impelling continuity of an intact oral tradition, but personally she is too late, too old to be "kiva-whipped" and thus incorporated into the communal life, taught the songs and welcomed into the tradition. The poet dwells with a dual depletion, both of the individual and of the oral tradition as expressed by the present condition of the tribes. The poet sees the world animated by frozen words that confine growth and retard understanding. These words are politically powerful, but the result is devastating for the tribal cultures. Songs can only crawl out of the confines like worms out of the stomach of a decaying body. [She writes in **"Trickster 1977"** in Geary Hobson's *The Remembered Earth* that] "The whole world is made-up / of words, mountain-thick, that wait / to cave in with edges that squeeze / hurt and reason into separate sounds / The songs become tons / of bilingual stuff to reckon with." To the poet the songs are almost like painful understandings and knowledge that she shies away from because of the extreme effort needed to build on them. The effort would make her vulnerable while she tried to master the words and subsequently herself. The poet retreats internally. However, an important insight has been wrought away from the conflict—words are life, or bits of life, of food that sustains life, growth and insight. The function of the frozen words must be turned around. Indian poets must become what Vizenor calls "word warriors" fighting the "word wars" with "word arrows" to bring language back into the service of tribal cultures and the oral tradition.

As the poet moves inside herself, she sees that songs and words are integral to changes and growth and that the relationship between the two is dynamic. In **"How I Came to be a Graduate Student,"** the songs lie just under the surface of her life, ready to burst forth as growth and understanding blossom. Here the poet realizes a modern equivalent to the older use of song as a codifier and guide for growth and change in a social setting. Personal changes such as birth, puberty, marriage, initiation and death are encouraged and structured by song, and the poet begins to identify her insights and changes with words and song. One might say that the poet is making herself out of words.

As this goes on internally, the image of the oral tradition changes. The songs trail after the people like whispers wherever they may go. Those who hear are tied back to the old understandings. As in **"For a few Hopi ancestors"** the songs are not lost, but ready to affect those who listen because they are an undercurrent of power and strength. It is left for the poet to discover the true power of the word and of song through the influence of other singer/poets. In two poems in ***Long Division,*** the poet is instructed by other singers outside the dominant word structure who effect miracles: one brings a dead child to life, another drags the stars around. Their language is powerful and effective. It expresses their cultural values and harkens back to the power of song in oral tradition.

The poet has now been instructed by her own growth process, by other word warriors and by those whispers of traditional song. Her own song is now brought back to the crucible of the people, for here it must be tested. It must stand with the people, help them understand the world, give them words to use, give them power, and bring them together. In **"Hopi Overlay"** [from ***Academic Squaw: Report to the World from the Ivory Tower***] her unfinished songs are given to those who are most purely oral—the children, and it is they who weave them into a final shape.

> My songs seem undone
> when they stomp-dance naked
> in the moonlight but
> children peeping from under
> dark porches laugh all
> the ups and downs in together.
> I'll take my old age early
> and watch them
> play my poems into
> cat's cradles.

The interaction with the people tests and solidifies the words. They are true and strong. The poet's growth is confirmed in song, and as the individual grows the tradition becomes stronger. The miracle has been accomplished, for the understanding of one is the understanding of the many. The words and songs guide and confirm. The songs let all participate in the process. We humans have achieved harmony with each other in song and with the world around us [as she notes in **"Walking on the Prayerstick"** from *Academic Squaw*].

> This is where we must learn
> to sing as we walk
> because our skin is
> red sand, because our pain
> is made up of burdens
> bound in corn husks,
> because our joy
> flows over the land,

because
touching ourselves
we touch everything

Wendy Rose (essay date 1981)

SOURCE: "American Indian Poets—And Publishing," in *Book Forum,* Vol. V, No. 3, 1981, pp. 400–02.

[*In the following excerpt, Rose comments on the experience of Native American writers in the literary world.*]

I have a vivid memory of walking into a bookstore in San Francisco that is well known for small press books, especially poetry, in order to buy a copy of the then-new book *The Names,* a literary autobiography, by Kiowa author, N. Scott Momaday. Having no luck in locating it on the shelves, I asked the clerk. He suggested that I look in the anthropology section or perhaps in the section especially set aside for works by and about American Indians. Sure enough, a variety of novels and poetry collections could be found under "anthropology" in that store; a quick check in the "poetry" section revealed that they could be found *only* under "anthropology." When I returned to the clerk, I pointed out (with a smile) that the books were incorrectly shelved. No, I was told, they were placed where they were because the authors were Indian. Therefore, it must be anthropology. When I replied that these authors were *not* anthropologists and the works not anthropology, he simply said that it didn't matter because, after all, there was not enough literature by Indian writers to worry about where to shelve it and would I please leave the premises. I left. In answer to the man's statement on Indian literature, I began compiling a bibliography of book-length works by American Indian and Eskimo authors; today, less than three years later, I have over 3000 entries, some of them going back into the eighteenth century.

Another event, much more recent, is similar. I was asked, several months ago, to do a poetry reading at a Bay Area bookstore that also specialized in small press publications. I accepted and was then asked who I would like to read with. I gave the name of a young (non-Indian) woman whose work I admire and who needs the exposure and experience of reading in public. She was rejected as my co-reader because she is not Indian. A quick look over my reading schedule over the years confirmed that almost always I have read with other Indian poets or, sometimes, with other writers of another ethnic minority. Almost never with whites. When I told the organizers of this particular reading that I would prefer to choose my own co-reader and that I did not care if this person was Indian or not, they canceled my reading and replaced me with a white man. The message is clear: be the ethnic curio that we want you to be or else we will not let you in at all.

What does this mean? It means that the literary world is, like the "real" world, full of backlash (against apparent progress by minority writers), of colonial thinking, and of an imperialist mentality characterized by Cherokee writer,

Geary Hobson, as "white-shamanism." The two examples cited above are simply from my personal "repertoire" and readers might be asking at this point why I objected to these situations. The segregation of Indian-authored literature in the bookstore is not only philosophical, but economic. If you are looking for poetry, you are not likely to look in the "anthropology" section. In the case of reading, it is perhaps more subtle. Most writers, I believe, would rather be judged on the quality of their work than on the set of attributes with which they were born. When I read a review of one of my books and find that the reviewer never gets past my ethnicity, I am offended even if what is said is "positive." I did not write that book in order to announce that I am Indian; I wrote it because I am a poet. Poetry is what I do. Indian is how I was born and how I see my world. I believe that my work is no more nor less "ethnic" than anyone else's. *Everyone's* work is saturated with ethnicity because our backgrounds are context for our works. *All* of us; not just the dark ones or the ones with funny names.

Let me use a few more examples from my personal experience. There was the large university press that turned down my manuscript (after saying that they were interested in it) because they had already contracted with an Indian writer that year (on another subject). And the journal that requested "Indian poems" but rejected all the work they received from Indian writers because it did not fit their idea of what "Indian poetry" should be; they ended up publishing work by non-Indians who thought they were using "Indian" styles. And the non-Indian poet who asked me to read with him because he was going to wear his paper-mache coyote mask and read his "Indian" poems and he appreciated the atmosphere of authenticity provided by having a living, breathing Indian on the same platform. And the editors who neglected to gain permission to use some of my work in a massive textbook. I found out about their copyright infringement when the book was in its third printing. When I asked for compensation, they wrote to an Indian newspaper attempting to "expose" me as one who was hurting the Indian movement by insisting on being treated as a professional. After all, how *else* would my work get published? The paper published my views alongside those of these editors and sided with me. If you are beginning to perceive a pattern, then you are quite right.

Between 1969 and 1976, Indian-authored work was (briefly) in fashion. Virtually every publisher in the country produced at least one anthology of Indian work. Many of us saw our first major exposure in such anthologies which was double-edged, both good and bad. It was good in that we were being published. Most of us were young and new at writing; we did not expect any publisher to roll out a red carpet. We knew that we would have to pay our dues like other writers. Yet the publishers were writing to us and asking for our work. What writer would not jump at the chance to be anthologized at the age of 18 or 20? It was bad in that many of us, myself included, were simply not ready for any kind of national exposure. The resulting anthologies were uneven in quality because so many of us were so young; some of us submitted

poems written in high school which would then be used by critics around the country to evaluate us as writers. No one would take our age and lack of experience into consideration—after all, our work amounted to nothing more than curios. Few critics bothered to look at it at all. Further, once a publisher produced an "Indian" book, they would never again feel the "urge" to produce another one. Having once gotten into print, the circumstances made it much more difficult for us to publish again. Our general tendency at the time toward immature work (with some notable exceptions who, also, were older) coupled with the "timeliness" of the anthologies (it was, after all, a brief fad) ensured that critics would dismiss them. Now that we have grown up we are still dismissed—to an extent far exceeding other young writers. No manuscript by an Indian author was considered on strictly literary grounds. In the reviews of our work (both anthologies and books by single authors), if the review was negative it was because we were part of that inconsequential, low-quality flood of Indian writing that the readers were so tired of; if the review was positive, it was because we were spokespeople for an entire aboriginal population. Our work appeared analyzed in sociological and anthropological journals and was compared with other writers on the basis of tribe, or against oral literature from one's own tribe. We were categorized as thoroughly, measured as carefully, and put away as finally as any skeleton from an archaeological dig.

So who are we—really? What are we doing? What are we trying to achieve? Why do we write? We are all different. Being Hopi does not automatically give me anything in common with a Seminole. There is not and never has been an "Indian" culture; there have always been hundreds of them. What we are doing is we are writing because that is what we choose to do. We write for highly individualistic reasons. We are trying to achieve many kinds of things; again this is an individual matter. Some of us have altruistic kinds of goals about helping to continue a particular literary tradition in a tribal context. Others have selfish kinds of goals about being rich and famous. Most of us write because we *have* to—that is what we do. If you have an idea in mind of what "Indian literature" is, I suggest that you reconsider. If your idea is based on the Indian-authored works you have read, consider the fact that it is often chosen according to editors' stereotypes. If your idea is based on a solid academic background about tribal literatures, consider that many of us do not speak our native language, were not raised on our ancestral land, and have no literary tradition other than what we received in some classroom. If your idea is based on the observation of certain themes or images, consider that there is no *genre* of "Indian literature" because we *are* all different. There is only literature that is written by people who are Indian and who, therefore, infuse their work with their own lives the same way that you do.

B. Almon (essay date 1986)

SOURCE: A review of *The Halfbreed Chronicles and*

Other Poems, in *Choice,* Vol. 23, No. 9, May, 1986, p. 1392.

[*In the following review, Almon praises* The Halfbreed Chronicles *and the "elegance and precision" of Rose's poetry.*]

[**The Halfbreed Chronicles and Other Poems** is a] strong and well-crafted collection of poems on Native American subjects. Rose writes with elegance and precision: her images are brilliant and her lines move with sureness. Rose's use of parallelism links her work to Native American models, while her diction manages to be fresh (because it is vivid) and traditional (because it evokes fundamentals of life and earth in the Indian tradition). She writes protest poems that avoid attitudinizing and easy rhetoric. Most of Rose's work has an objective flavor, but when it takes on a personal tinge, it comes across as genuine and lacking in self-pity even when the material is distressing ("**The Building of the Trophy**"). The last section of the book, "**The Halfbreed Chronicles**," moves from Native themes to a worldwide perspective: there are compassionate and angry poems about such figures as Truganinny, the last Tasmanian, Yuriko, a Hiroshima victim, Kitty Hart (who survived Auschwitz), and Isamu, a Japanese American sculptor rejected by his Japanese father. These poems are imagined from within: the subjects are not reduced to texts for sermons.

Joseph Bruchac (interview date 1987)

SOURCE: "The Bones Are Alive," in *Survival This Way: Interviews with American Indian Poets,* Sun Tracks and The University of Arizona Press, 1987, pp. 249–69.

[*In the following interview, Rose discusses her poetry, the influences of her mixed origins and the frustrations of being a Native American writer.*]

[Bruchac]: *In his preface to your collected poems—***Lost Copper***—N. Scott Momaday said that it was a book, "not made up of poems, I think, but of songs." Would you agree with that distinction of Momaday's?*

[Rose]: In a subjective sense, yes. I don't think that the poems are literally songs the way that we usually understand the term. But I use them the way that many Indian people traditionally use songs. They, in a sense, mark the boundaries of my life.

So that would be one of the differences between your poetry and traditional English verse.

Yeah, I think so. My perception of them. The way that they function in my life.

Is there any other way in which they're song?

I think oftentimes that audiences feel them that way. People sometimes call them songs when they talk about them but, I don't know, I couldn't speak for what it is they are

perceiving. I couldn't really put words in their mouths to try to clarify what they mean, but people call them songs and maybe they're feeling the internal parts of it the way that they have meaning for me.

In that same introduction Momaday also spoke of your language, saying "it has made a clear reflection of American Indian oral tradition." Do you perceive a relationship between your writing and that oral tradition?

I would like to but I would have to say probably not too much. I think that there are some important differences, and I think that my particular work probably leans more toward European-derived ideas of what poetry is and of who poets are than Native American in spite of the subjective feeling that I have of the way that the poems are used in my life. There are some important differences, one of which is the sense of self-expression. The need to express the self, the need to make one's own emotions special and to explain it to other people, I don't think really exists in most Native American cultures. And I think that is an important component in my work.

Are there any other distinctions that you'd see or any other things that you would use as definitions of the American Indian interpretation as opposed to the Western interpretation of the use of song or poetry?

One way that I think perhaps they do function, and I hope it doesn't sound like I'm contradicting myself too much, is that gradually the various Native American communities are re-establishing links with people using oral tradition. And sometimes this extends even to those of us who use the printed word and who publish. So in recent years I'm finding that the poet is right there with the orators and is speaking in council. I'm finding more and more that, when there are gatherings of Indian people, there will be poets who will contribute to what's happening. This was lost for a while because of the effect of the white man's education in that for a while Indian people were discounting the contribution that poets were making in the same way that the white man discounts the contributions of his own poets. But increasingly I think that contemporary poets in Native American communities are coming to be valued in a traditional sense even though the work itself might be different.

What are the roots of your poetry? How did you personally become a writer—and then a writer who identifies so strongly with your Native American roots?

That's a complex question. Influences as far as poetry are concerned—they're just so multiple. Perhaps the earliest one that I remember is Robinson Jeffers, who of course was not an Indian poet. But some of the first published poetry I was ever exposed to was his and that was important to me, and I think it was my first sense of being able to think in terms of putting a poet in a landscape that's familiar, because the area that he was writing about was where I grew up—the northern California and central California coast. That was an early influence. Other influences that were fairly early—I figured out that it was okay to be an Indian and a writer at the same time probably, as many of us did, through the influence of Scott Momaday. His getting a Pulitzer prize in fiction made a real difference to us because I think so many of us had assumed that no matter what our individual goals might be, we had to somehow choose between fulfilling the goal and having any degree of integrity as Indian people. Whatever influences there are from Native American culture—I'm being fairly careful not to cite tribe here because I was born and grew up at a distance from my tribe, so I'm trying to deliberately separate myself from saying Hopi literature or Miwok literature—my community is urban Indian and is *pan* tribal. But whatever Native American traditional influences that might be in my work, I don't know if I can pick them out individually. I missed out on a great deal by not being exposed to tribal traditions as a child. In the city I was exposed on the one hand to a great many traditions and on the other hand to nothing that was really complete. I don't know. Perhaps that's an unanswerable question. I know that there was also this: in terms of identifying as an Indian writer, that was partly and perhaps mostly a function of how literature is published and distributed in this country—which is that in this particular instance if you are of a minority group and you are a writer, you are simply not allowed to do anything other than be a minority writer.

I think this would be a good place to ask you this question. In your poem **"Builder Kachina,"** *you have these lines—"a half breed goes from one-half home to the other." And of course* **The Halfbreed Chronicles** *is the name of the collection you just read that first poem from. That word "halfbreed" seems to be very important to you. What is it? What does that mean?*

Well, again, I have to answer on at least two different levels. One is the obvious thing of being biologically halfbreed, being of mixed race. I was in a situation where I was physically separated from one-half of my family and rejected by the half that brought me up. And in this case it was because of what there is in me that belonged to the other half. The way that a lot of us put it is you're too dark to be white and you're too white to be Indian. James Welch expressed it well in *The Death of Jim Loney* where Jim Loney answers someone who says to him (to paraphrase), "oh, you're so lucky that you can have the best of both worlds and choose whether or not at a given moment you will be Indian or you will be white." And he says, "It's not that we have the best of both worlds, it's that we don't really have anything of either one." I think that's really a very true statement. You don't get to pick and choose but rather you're in a position where you have no choice whatsoever. I was in that situation where the white part of my family had absolutely no use for any other races that came into the family. The white part of the family had no use for it. The Indian half is in a situation where, among the Hopi, the clan and your identity comes through the mother, and without the Hopi mother it doesn't matter if your father was fullblooded or not, you can't be Hopi. So that left me in that situation. The first years of writing, perhaps, the motivation from the very beginning was to try to come to terms with being in that impossible situation. But then maturing as a person, halfbreed takes

on a different connotation and that's where **The Halfbreed Chronicles** are coming from. Now **The Halfbreed Chronicles** depict a number of people, and genetics doesn't have a great deal to do with it. For instance, the poem **"Georgeline"** is relating to people who are a fullblood Lakota family. There are other people who are depicted in **Halfbreed Chronicles** who would not be identified as halfbreed. People who are Japanese-American. People who are Mexican-Indian but spent their lives as sideshow freaks. People like Robert Oppenheimer. You don't think of these people in the same sense as you usually think of halfbreeds. But my point is that, in an important way, the way that I grew up is symptomatic of something much larger than Indian-white relations. History and circumstances have made halfbreeds of all of us.

Then maybe you wouldn't be offended by my bringing in something I just thought of . . . a quotation from Matthew Arnold. He described himself back in the Victorian era— "one half dead, the other powerless to be born." There seems to be, as you see it, a world dilemma not just of people of mixed Indian and white ancestry but of the modern culture that we find ourselves faced with.

Yeah, and I think that the point does come out in **The Halfbreed Chronicles** because one of the responses that I get is from people who are genetically all Caucasian, or all black, or all Indian; people who are genetically not of mixed race come up to me afterwards and say I know just what you mean by those poems. I feel like a halfbreed, too. So I know the message is getting through. We are now halfbreeds. We're Reagan's halfbreeds and Dukmejian's halfbreeds.

I find it interesting, too, that that poem, which I cited a quotation from, is called **"Builder Kachina"** *and there is no Builder Kachina as I understand it.*

No there isn't.

But you have imagined a Builder Kachina?

In a sense, yes, but based on things that my father really said to me. The poem is based on an actual conversation that I had with my biological father, which is the Hopi side of the family. And the conversation was basically my going down to the reservation and sitting down and talking to him and presenting the situation to him at a point where I was in crisis over it and saying what can I do because I can't be a member of a clan, because I can't have your clan? You're my father, not my mother, I'm not entitled to any land or any rights or any privileges on the reservation. Yet, at the same time, my mother's family doesn't accept me, never has, probably never will, because of the fact that you are my father. So what do I do? His answer to me was, "Well, sometimes it's difficult, sometimes people don't point out to you what your roots are but your roots are on this land, and you just have to stand here yourself on this Hopi land and build them," and from that came the imagined person of Builder Kachina. I've invented lots of Kachinas. I hope that it's not thought of as being too sacrilegious. But I've invented Kachinas that go into outer space. I've invented Kachinas that are in the ocean and a lot that have appeared in the visual arts. This particular one appeared in poetry.

Yes, the Kachinas are something I find occurring again and again in your writing. What are the Kachinas to you? How would you define them. I know there's a definition on strictly a tribal level . . .

Well, there's no real agreement even on that definition because they aren't any one thing. They're not strictly nature spirits and they're not strictly gods. They're not strictly ancestral spirits and yet they're all of that. They are spirit beings who grow and evolve and have families and live and possibly die. Humans have to communicate with them and have to relate to them. One way that they can be thought of is if you think of the entire earth as being one being and we as small beings living on that large being like fleas on a cat. The Kachinas in a sense are aspects of that cat that are communicating with us. This is one way to look at it.

I see then in your "Builder Kachina" a sort of balance emerging out of that duality and chaos caused by the conflict between two forces which seem to be mutually exclusive. The two worlds of the European Indian. The two worlds of the two parents that you describe in your own life.

Well, of course, one thing also is that the Hopis say that the Europeans being on this continent is something that isn't all that important in the long run, that eventually the continent will be purified. The evil parts of that influence will be gone, and things will eventually return as they were and the cycle will continue. This is really only a small thing that we inflate with our own self-importance into meaning more than it does. For those of us who are in my position, I don't know whether I'm supposed to be saved with the Hopi or wiped away with the whites.

Thinking of evils, I've seen several particular evils singled out numerous times in your writings. Let me give you some examples—the California missions, the attitude of anthropology toward Indian people in general, cities and the concept of modern cities. Why do you choose those particular targets?

I don't see cities as evil first off. I don't think there should ever be more than, at most, a couple of thousand people living in one unit. I think beyond that it's impossible to be governed with any sense of integrity when you don't recognize each other and have no obligation to each other. But in any case I don't see cities as evil per se. They're evil for me. I'm not able to adapt to living in cities even though I've tried. I become intensely uncomfortable in cities and I see cities destroy people that I love. As for the other things, the California missions, of course, were not a spiritual endeavor; they were an economic endeavor. They had more to do with the conquest of a new bunch of natural resources by the Spanish crown than they did with the saving of souls. The point behind incarcerating Indian people there was to have a cheap labor force, a slave force if you will, to make blankets and to make pots and

pans and various kinds of things for the Spanish settlers, for the colonist. Also to have everybody in one place so there wouldn't be any Indian people to stop settlement and there wouldn't be any Indian people out there able to act on their own. So they were incarcerated. Reduced is the actual Spanish term, the *reducciones*. It killed off some incredible number, something like during just ten years alone, in the early nineteenth century, the California Indian population was reduced by some incredibly high number like 80 percent. It was because of a combination of disease, of unnatural living conditions, and the punishment for running away. What a lot of people don't realize is there were a number of revolts against the Spanish mission by the Indians. But they don't tell you this in the museums. In fact, the museum right here in Oakland paints a ridiculous picture of the missions with the happy little natives making baskets in the shade of the adobe with the benevolent padres walking around rattling their rosaries. That just is not the way that the missions were.

And then there is the attitude of anthropology toward the Indian people. It seems linked to what we were just talking about with the missions.

In fact there's a saying that—I've heard versions of this saying from people from Africa, from Australia, from New Zealand, various American Indian people—first comes the explorer, then comes the military, then comes the missionary, then comes the anthropologist, then comes the tourist. Actually, though, as you know, in one sense it's ironic that I should be so highly critical of the field since at the moment I am teaching lower division anthropology at a junior college. However, I'm teaching it in an unorthodox way, and I hope I don't get in too much trouble for it. But, yeah, anthropologists have certainly been one of the main targets of some of my anger, probably stemming from my intimate association with them as a Ph.D. student in anthropology at Berkeley which contains both the best and the worst. I've run into some incredible racism in that department and, as faculty now, I see my Indian students running into situations that are even more bizarre than things I had experienced because it's becoming increasingly okay among the general population to become racist again or to express the racism that was always there. It's no longer cool to try to be tolerant or understanding or liberal or even to recognize that America is a plural country. There are a number of anthropologists, however, who are very, very good people and are sensitive to these issues. Unfortunately, I think they are still in a minority probably because anthropology is part of a European-derived institution run by the white male power structure. So Indian people along with many other kinds of people—women, gay people, people from fourth world nations and from third world nations—all of these people are coming into anthropology now and changing the face of it. But it's very slow because that old guard of course is still there. A lot of Indian people are going into anthropology just to become super informants and don't realize it.

In part two of **Lost Copper** *there are some poems that were originally published as a chapbook under the title*

Academic Squaw: Reports to the World From the Ivory Tower. *I'm always interested in titles. What did you intend by it?*

Well, obviously, it was intended as ironic. The publisher inadvertently left off a postscript that was supposed to be on the title page. I think in **Lost Copper** they did put the postscript in. In the chapbook it originally appeared in, it was inadvertently left off. It explained how the term "squaw" is used in a purely ironic sense. That was really an important thing for two reasons. One is because "squaw" is an offensive term, regardless of its origin. It is now and has been for many, many years an offensive term much like "nigger" or "spic" and has been degrading not only in a racist way but in sexual ways as well. Because the image of the so-called "squaw" is a racist and a sexist image. So, on the one hand, people who are aware of that might otherwise think that I was using it without any kind of clarification, that it was just as if it were part of my vocabulary. As if I really saw myself that way. And people who don't know any better might assume the same thing not realizing there's anything special about the word. I have run into people who simply think that that is a word for Indian women. Just like they think that "papoose" is a word for Indian children and so forth.

Or "pickaninny" is a word for a black child.

Yeah. I know a man who thought that Jewish men really were called Jewboys and would call people that to their faces in total innocence because that's the only way he had ever heard Jewish men referred to. Things like this. So there is an innocence there in one sense but there's also a maliciousness.

I meant the title, of course, in a completely ironic sense and the poems were written in that context because I had just spent two years as an undergraduate at the University of California at Berkeley in anthropology and had just, in fact, by the time the book came out entered graduate school as a Ph.D. student. So the book encompasses experiences at both the graduate and undergraduate level as an anthropology major. And, as I was saying, there were some racist things that happened. There were a lot of things that happened that I had to come to terms with. There were many times when I almost dropped out. I spent the entire first year at Berkeley, in my junior year as a transfer student from a junior college, huddling in a corner in Native American Studies drinking tea and trembling. This is all coming from somebody who was raised in a relatively urban area right next to the university all her life, so I can't imagine what it must be like coming from a reservation, from someplace that's very different from Berkeley. The poems were written as a survival kit, really. And in fact one of the most pleasant things I have ever done was the day that the book came out from Brother Benet's press, I went and stuck copies of it in all my professors' mailboxes.

Why have you chosen to enter that Ivory Tower world? That world of the academic?

I'm not in the Ivory Tower. I'm a spy.

Okay, good. You say also in the poem "Handprints," "in this university I am a red ghost."

I'm a spy.

A spy. Great.

Don't blow my cover.

Oh, no. No, we'll never tell. (laughter) Let me move on to another area, Wendy. How has your art affected your writing? You now have a reputation both as an illustrator and as a writer. In fact, in some of your poems you speak directly of that world of art in rather magical terms. Sometimes you even speak as a mother speaks of her children. I'm thinking of the poem "Chasing the Paper Shaman," or the poem "Watercolors." How has your art affected your writing and how do they work together?

I can't imagine them really working apart. Nobody bothered to tell me until I was an adult that there was anything wrong with being both a visual and a verbal artist. I think that's the only reason why that isn't the case with more people, and I think that's the reason why it is the case for so many Native American people. Look at the number of Native American authors who illustrate their own work and who illustrate other people's work. There is a tremendous number. There is nothing unusual about it among Native American people at all. There's a tremendous percentage of writers who do so in contrast to the non-Indian writers, where it's very seldom the same person who does both. But the way I think of it—now I don't really know where the poems or where the art comes from, I don't know where the images come from—but however they come or wherever they come from is like communicating with a person. It's a whole person. That person shows you things and has a certain appearance but also tells you things. So as you receive images, they are either received through the ear or through the eye or through the tongue and that's just the way it feels.

Another thing that I find different about your work and also that of a number of American Indian writers (as compared to the typical writer of the traditional English mold) is your attitude toward death. Death seems to be very important in your work. Why is that so?

I don't know. I never really thought of it as being important to the work. I guess if I really think about it, yeah, I've got a lot of bones rattling around in there. I guess there's a sense of feeling—sometimes I feel like I'm dead. Like I'm a ghost. Similarly, sometimes I feel that I'm alive but there are ghosts all around me, so that's part of it. But as far as the symbols go, of things like the bones for instance, I think maybe it's argument against death. Maybe what I'm saying is that the bones are alive. They're not dead remnants but rather they're alive.

You have these images of returning to the earth and images of bones. These don't strike me as morbid images, as they would be in, say, a poem written in the eighteenth century in England.

Well, you know, the rocks are alive and all the components of a tree, for instance, live. A pine cone falls down from the tree and it's alive. It carries the life of the tree in the seeds that are in the pine cone. And I think the parts of the body must be the same way. The brain isn't all there is to human life. The consciousness that's inside the skull is not all there is.

There is a poem of yours in **What Happened When the Hopi Hit New York**—*"Cemetery, Stratford, Connecticut"*—*with these lines: "I know that what ages earth has little to do with things we build to wrinkle her skin and fade her eyes." You also say, "I have balanced my bones between the petroglyph and the mobile home." These different things, balanced in some way, seem bound to lead in a different direction than just finality.*

Well, that's really what we are, isn't it? We're bones that are just covered with flesh and muscle. The part of us that is spirit is just a component that is part of that entirety. We are parts of the earth that walk around and have individual consciousness for awhile and then go back.

I could see someone looking at your poems and saying these are evidences of bitterness, of hopelessness, of a very dark perception of life.

That's what a lot of white people see in them. Indian people almost never do.

As a matter of fact, I'm playing the devil's advocate because I think there is a question we may have to address. What do you think American Indian poems have to offer to non-Indians? Are there problems of perception like this which may make them inaccessible to the non-Indian reader?

I don't know. I want to say no, they're not inaccessible because it's a great frustration when people won't review our work, for example, in the usual professional way, saying that they don't have "the ethnographic knowledge" to do it or something. That's a frustration to me because some of us—people like Joy Harjo or any number of other people that actually have M.F.A.s from prestigious writing schools—come out and then find that they're being told that they're culturally too obscure to be reviewed as a real writer. That isn't true. I think that a person does need to stretch the imagination a little bit, perhaps, or to learn something about Native American cultures or Native American thought systems or religion, or philosophy. Just a little bit. But I don't think any more so than you need to become a Kabbalistic scholar in order to understand Jerry Rothenberg. This is a plural society and all of us have to work at it a little bit to get the full flavor of the society. I have to. Boy, do I have to work at trying to understand the Shakespearean stuff! I have students in my creative writing classes who are into Shakespeare and write tight verse and rhyme and do it very, very well. They're not doing it unsuccessfully, but I have to really work to understand where they're coming from. Just simply that what they're expressing is a dominant cultural mode in this particular country is not sufficient reason to say that that

is the only way it should be. If I have to work at understanding that stuff, then I don't see why they shouldn't work a little bit to understand mine.

Hasn't it often been the other way? Literary critics have celebrated the greatness of someone like James Joyce because Finnegan's Wake *and his other books are so complicated.*

If they think the complication is individual rather than cultural, then they really love it, sure.

Good point.

But if they think it's cultural then they think that we're insulting them somehow by expecting them to understand it. That we're asking them to go out of their way. And of course, really, we're not asking any more of them than they ask of us when we pick up books in this society and read them.

What images, aside from those I've already mentioned, seem to be recurrent in your poetry?

I think I have a lot of female images. A lot of times I think that just talking about rocks or trees or spirits, where there's no real reason to put a gender on them, I automatically tend to make them female. I think that's something I've noticed more recently. Themes? I've been writing a little bit of science fiction poetry lately about colonizing other planets. But of course it's not from the colonizing viewpoint, it's from the viewpoint of the people on the planet. But that's sort of off the wall. I don't know, it's pretty hard to see the themes in your own work. I'm always amazed at what other people see in them. At first I don't believe them, and then I go back and I read it again and I realize they were right. Sometimes.

Which of your already published poems express most clearly for you what you want to say as a writer?

As a writer? Oh, boy! Of the published poems? I don't know. I guess the things that are most current in my mind or the things that I most want to say are what I've said most recently, which usually isn't published at that time. I guess what I want to say is bound up in ***The Halfbreed Chronicles,*** and as of now few of them have been published. One of the major focal points in ***The Halfbreed Chronicles*** section was published in *Ms. Magazine* in the June 1984 issue. That's kind of exciting to me to finally get a "pop" readership.

Is this the one about the woman who was . . .

The woman in the circus, about Julia Pastrana, yeah. They're publishing that one.

That's a particularly powerful poem, to me, for any number of reasons. I heard you read it about a year ago and was very moved by it.

Well, it's about a Mexican Indian woman who was born

physically deformed. Her face was physically deformed to where her bone structure resembled the caricature of Neanderthal man that you sometimes see in museums. She had hair growing from all over her body including her face. So she was Neanderthal looking and hairy in visual appearance, but she was also a graceful dancer and a singer in the mid-nineteenth century. She was a very young woman. She was billed as the World's Ugliest Woman and put on exhibit, where she would sing for the sideshow. The poem is not just about the exploitation of her being in the circus but is like a step beyond that. It's an ultimate exploitation. Her manager married her and it was, presumably, in order to control her life in the circus. She believed that he loved her, though, and really, what choice did she have emotionally? When she finally had a baby, the baby looked just like her. The baby had all the same deformities, but also had a lethal deformity of some kind and died just shortly after birth. Then she died a day or two after that. And her husband—and here's where the real *Halfbreed Chronicles* come in—her husband had her and the baby stuffed and mounted in a wood and glass case and continued to exhibit them in the circus even though she couldn't sing anymore. There was just something about the horror of that which in *The Halfbreed Chronicles* is coupled with the poem called **"Truganinny"** about an Aborigine woman who happened to be the last living Tasmanian native.

Truganinny went through a similar situation. She had seen her husband stuffed and mounted by the British museum people as the last Tasmanian man. She asked her aboriginal friends to please make sure that when she died that didn't happen to her. She wanted to be buried way out someplace where they couldn't find her body or just be thrown into the sea or something. And they tried but they were caught, and so she was actually stuffed and put in a museum too. Just like her husband, as the last specimen of a Tasmanian human being. The two of them together, Julia and Truganinny, represent the ultimate colonization. They're not side by side in *The Halfbreed Chronicles*. They're separated slightly by a couple of other poems. But they're intended as a pair in a sense because of the similar fate and because the circus treatment of the so-called freaks is another kind of colonization. Then too, what is it that happens to the colonized if not being made into a sideshow? So that's basically the point behind the Julia Pastrana poem and also the Truganinny poem. We are all in that situation. We are all on display that way.

There seems to be a growing consciousness on the part of American Indian women, both as writers and as people speaking up. In the postscript poem in **Lost Copper** *you say "Silko and Allen and Harjo and me—our teeth are hard from the rocks we eat." What do you have in common and why choose those particular women?*

This will sound sort of funny, I guess, but I could have gone on and named many, many more Indian women writers. I chose those particular ones because I felt that they were fairly well known, that a reader who has been reading very much contemporary Indian literature will immediately recognize the names. I feel that they have all

made strong statements about being Indian writers, both in their creative work and peripheral statements in interviews or in articles that they have written. The actual fact of the matter is that I stopped after naming just those ones because that was the meter of the poem. (laughter) What I intend there is to go on with the list—and Hogan and northSun and Burns and Tapahonso and so on and so on. They're in there.

What is exciting about their work for you?

I know that when I read their work it makes chills go up and down my spine in a way that really most other people's work doesn't. It's not just Indian women's work, but work by minority American writers, by writers of color in general. It very often has that effect on me. When I read work that does have that effect on me, it is usually by such a writer. I tend to be terribly bored by the writing of white academic poets. Hopelessly bored. I really don't care how many sex fantasies they had watching a bird on a fence. If you'll pardon the phrase, I think in academia, in English departments, that the writers are just masturbating.

Of course there are also the writers who are putting on headdresses.

Yes. Yeah. There are those, but even they are not generally in the academic situation. Even they are a little too peripheral for academe.

Um. Those white poets who would be Indian as you title that one poem of yours.

Yeah. And of course that needs some clarification too because it's widely misunderstood—the whole thing about the "white shaman" controversy that Geary Hobson and Leslie Silko have addressed themselves to, that I have addressed myself to. It's widely misunderstood. It's assumed that what we're saying is that we don't want non-Indian people to write about Indians. That's not it. Many non-Indian people have written beautifully and sensitively about Indian people. Even in persona. The difference is that there are those who come out and say that they are Indian when they are not, in the case of some. There are those who come out and do not claim to be genetically Indian, but who do claim that what they write is somehow more Indian, or more legitimately Indian, than what real Indian people are writing. There are these people who claim to be what they're not. They claim to be shamans and it's impossible to be a self-declared shaman. Your community has to recognize you. And we know that the word is Siberian but we also know what is meant by it in popular usage. Yeah, it's directed toward these people and it's a matter not of subject matter but of integrity in the way in which the subject matter is approached.

You've been editor of The American Indian Quarterly, *taught Native American Literature, worked on a major bibliography of Native American writing. What do you see happening with American Indian writing today?*

Well, I think that there is a small nucleus of people who are primarily associated with the Modern Language Association who are acknowledging that it is a legitimate field of study. People like Karl Kroeber and LaVonne Ruoff and Andrew Wiget, Larry Evers. There's a whole crew there. These are people who have been interested in it all along. But through their influence and the influence of Indian writers who have become involved in that end of the writing business, the scholarship end of it, it's becoming better accepted in academe. But it's very slow as in the fact, for example, in the University where I taught (Berkeley), we were just recently told by the English Department that they would not hire people to teach anything about American Indian literature "because it's not part of American Literature." So, it's very slow. But it's gradually happening because of people like the scholars that I named . . . although it took a long time even to get to where Indian people could go speak for themselves, where Indian writers could go deal with their own work even in the Modern Language Association because the tradition for so many years was that the white scholars would sit around and talk about the work without having the writers there to deal with it themselves. That's changing.

You feel then that the current small popularity of American Indian contemporary writing is more than just a fad? That its message is large enough to go beyond this moment?

The message is large enough to go beyond the moment—whether anyone is listening or not, I'm not sure. I think that the way that a lot of us started, particularly those that are around my age in their thirties and forties, was on the basis of a fad. We were brought into it, many of us, before we were mature enough as writers, really, to do it. We were brought into anthologies and so forth, and our work was exposed to critical masses, so to speak. But I think that maybe if we work hard enough at it that we will somehow be able to make sure that it is incorporated into general American literature. And here I'm not just talking about Native American, I'm talking about Afro-American, I'm talking about Asian-American, I'm talking about Chicano and Puerto Rican, Indochinese. All of the various cultural elements have their literature that becomes modified and yet retains its cultural integrity as they come into America. Or as they leave the reservations and go into the cities that are in America. I think this is going to happen, whether anyone is out there listening or not, it's going to happen. And I know that the Indian communities respect their writers more now and that's the part that's really important to me. I would much rather be respected by the Indian community through my writing than to have my books reviewed in the *New York Times*. I really would.

Last question. What would you say to young American Indian writers now in the way of advice?

Like that old civil rights song says, don't let nobody turn you 'round. Although they probably never heard the song. (laughter)

Robert L. Berner (essay date 1994)

SOURCE: A review of *Going to War with All My Relations,*

in *World Literature Today,* Vol. 68, No. 2, Spring, 1994, pp. 408–09.

[*In the following review, Lerner presents a favorable assessment of* Going to War with All My Relations.]

Because Wendy Rose is both a poet and a professional anthropologist and is acutely conscious of both her Indian and her European ancestry, she is uniquely situated to perceive both analytically and imaginatively the complexities of Indian experience in America. Her eighth book [*Going to War with All My Relations*], balancing characteristic earlier poems and recent uncollected work, is a valuable survey of her poetic career and an indication of her present concerns.

Rose has always revealed a true lyric gift, but it has been accompanied by a considerable moral energy, as in **"Notes on a Conspiracy,"** written in 1977 and reprinted here. This poem originated in her indignation at archeological and commercial exploitation of Indian burial remains. What makes it an important text in the canon of American Indian literature is its balance—its dismay not only at the callousness of the commerce but also at the past failure of Indian resistance—and its haunting perception that perhaps the saddest figure is the archeologist who, digging in sacred ground, cannot understand his own fate: "He does not feel the point of his own probing trowel."

Much of Rose's energy originates in painful memory of her mixed origins (Indian, German, English, Scottish). Her father gave her a Hopi identity which was only racial, and her fate—to discover Hopi culture only by an act of will and professional study—is reflected in the last line of an early poem about her father: "I grow but do not live." In spite of this, her mixed ancestry has always been a source of her strength and wisdom. A recent poem, significantly titled **"If I Am Too Brown or Too White for You,"** makes clear her recognition that her impulse to poetry derives from that complex ancestry, and her beautiful tribute to a German pioneer great-great-grandmother ends with her recognition that German and American Indian historical experience, though not simultaneous, are parallel: "Do you remember the tribes / that so loved their land / before the roll / of Roman wheels?"

These poems seem more effective, both as art and as moral statement, than those which are more consciously and explicitly "social." **"Yellow Ribbons, Baghdad 1991,"** for example, is an attempt—unsuccessful in my view—to equate Iraqi civilians killed in the Gulf War with the victims of the Sand Creek massacre. Much more successful and certainly more moving are those poems which derive from the concerns expressed in her explanation in her preface of the terms of the book's title. The "war" is our common struggle to maintain our "relations" to one another, to all living things, and to the maternal earth. The maternal principle appears again and again in the poems and is implicit in **"To the Vision Seekers, Remember This,"** in which scientists are asked to remember that all science derives from the earth itself: "it is women, / all women, where you come from, / Earth the one to remember."

Going to War with All My Relations, a significant achievement by an important poet, suggests that the revelation of the ambiguities inherent in the historical interrelationship of Indian and European elements in our culture continues to be the great task for American poets.

FURTHER READING

Criticism

Jacob, John. Review of *Long Division: A Tribal History. Booklist,* September 15, 1977, p. 133.
    Jacob offers a short synopsis of *Long Division: A Tribal History.*

Lincoln, Kenneth. "Finding the Loss." *Parnassus,* Vol. 10, No. 1, Spring/Summer 1982.
    Lincoln discusses the diversity of present-day Native Americans and how this heritage affects Rose's writing and self-concept.

Ratner, Rochelle. Review of *The Halfbreed Chronicles and Other Poems,* by Wendy Rose. *Library Journal,* Vol. 111, No. 1, January 1986, p. 89.
    Positive assessment of *The Halfbreed Chronicles.*

Interviews

Coltelli, Laura. "Wendy Rose." In her *Winged Words: American Indian Writers Speak.* Lincoln: University of Nebraska Press, 1990, pp. 121–33.
    Rose discusses themes and images in her work and her background in anthropology.

Hunter, Carol. "A MELUS Interview: Wendy Rose." *MELUS* 10, No. 3, Fall 1983, p. 67–87.
    Rose reflects upon her life, works, and political beliefs.

Additional coverage of Rose's life and career is contained in the following sources published by Gale Research: *Contemporary Authors,* Vols. 53-56; *Contemporary Authors New Revision Series,* Vol. 5; *Native North American Literature;* and *Something about the Author,* Vol. 12.

Sir Walter Scott
1771–1832

Scottish poet, novelist, short story writer, biographer, historian, critic, and editor.

INTRODUCTION

Scott is an early representative of the Romantic Movement in English literature. His poems relate tales of heroic adventure set in the idealized past and emphasize detailed descriptions of the poet's Scottish homeland. This combination proved exceedingly popular in the early 1800s; the sales of his verse narratives established a new standard for British poetry and set the stage for the subsequent popularity of other Romantic poets such as Lord Byron. Scott's appeal as a poet was followed by his overwhelming success as a fiction writer. During his lifetime, he was the most popular author the world had ever known, and modern scholars consider him both the inventor of the historical novel and the first best-selling novelist. Despite the unprecedented success of his writings in the 1800s, Scott's reputation has diminished with the passage of time. Once a staple of English literary studies, his works—especially his poems—are now largely left to scholars and historians of literature.

Biographical Information

Scott was born in Edinburgh, Scotland, to middle-class parents, the fourth surviving child of Walter Scott and Anne Rutherford. At the age of two, he suffered an attack of polio that rendered him lame for the rest of his life. Biographers point out, however, that in spite of this handicap, Scott led an active outdoor life during his childhood and developed an appreciation for picturesque scenery that later figured prominently in his writings. As a child, Scott also displayed a deep fascination with Scottish history and literature, along with an ability to retain everything he learned about his country's past, whether it was the details of an important battle or the lines of a lengthy ballad. According to critic Ian Jack, "It was Scott's good fortune as a boy to be surrounded by a sort of Greek chorus of Scots antiquaries [individuals who study the past]." These people gave Scott knowledge of and an enthusiasm for history that would directly translate to his writings. He enrolled in Edinburgh High School in 1778 and five years later entered the University of Edinburgh, studying history and law. In 1786 he was apprenticed to his father's legal firm and was called to the bar in 1792.

While serving his apprenticeship, Scott traveled extensively in the Scottish Border Country and Highlands, where he delighted in the regions' natural settings and rural inhab-

itants. In 1800 he began collecting and editing the traditional ballads of the areas he visited, combining his love for Scottish lore and literature with his ongoing excursions in the countryside. His work in this area resulted in his first major publication, *Minstrelsy of the Scottish Border,* a collection of Scottish ballads that was accompanied by imitation ballads written by Scott and others. Although it produced only modest sales, the collection enjoyed critical favor. More importantly, with the *Minstrelsy,* as John Lauber has pointed out, Scott "discovered his proper subject, Scottish history and tradition." The positive reception of the *Minstrelsy* and the encouragement of his friends prompted Scott to attempt an original work based on Scottish themes. His efforts resulted in *The Lay of the Last Minstrel,* a narrative poem set in medieval times that, in Scott's words, was "intended to illustrate the customs and manners which anciently prevailed on the Borders of England and Scotland." The success of the *Lay* when it appeared in 1805 was immediate and substantial. Determined to earn a living through his writings, Scott gave up law as a full-time profession and concentrated on the series of narrative poems that soon brought him great fame and wealth.

In the early 1810s, Scott revised and completed a fragment of a novel that he had begun many years earlier, the story of an Englishman who travels to the Scottish Highlands and becomes involved in the Jacobite Rebellion of 1745. *Waverly; or, 'Tis Sixty Years Since* proved a popular sensation when it was issued in 1814. It quickly became the most successful work of its kind and brought huge profits to Scott and his publishers. Buoyed by his prosperous first venture as a novelist, Scott began writing at a rapid pace; over the next seventeen years, he produced more than two dozen novels and tales in a series that has since become known as the *Waverly Novels.* When the first *Waverly* book was published, writing novels was considered less respectable than writing poetry, and Scott chose to issue the book anonymously. Though the popularity of the series changed the stature of novelists, Scott chose to retain his anonymity for many years. Biographers have traced this decision both to Scott's love of secrecy and to his perception that the mystery surrounding the creator of the novels contributed to their sales. Many of the books in the series were attributed to "the author of *Waverly,*" and he was often referred to simply as the "Great Unknown." Despite this approach, numerous readers and critics knew of his authorship; he became the most popular writer in England and a highly respected and admired figure throughout Europe. In 1818 he accepted a baronetcy, becoming Sir Walter Scott.

Scott was able to keep up his prolific output of books because he never plotted out his works before writing, seldom revised, and because he maintained a strenuous work schedule even when gravely ill. Many biographers and critics have tied these work habits to his desire for material gain. Scott had purchased a farm in 1811 and, after renaming the property Abbotsford, began devoting huge sums of money to building and planting on his property, and collecting relics from Scotland's past. Thus, though his income was large, his financial situation was often precarious. Disaster struck in 1826; a publishing house that Scott was financially involved with went bankrupt. Though he was a silent partner in the enterprise, Scott's debt amounted to over one hundred thousand pounds. Instead of declaring bankruptcy, Scott arranged to work off the debt through his writings. The last years of his life were devoted to the increasingly difficult task of producing salable works in a variety of genres. Beginning in 1830, he suffered a series of strokes as he labored to pay his creditors. A trip to the Mediterranean in 1831 to regain his health proved unsuccessful, and after further strokes which led to paralysis, he died at Abbotsford in 1832.

Major Works

The Lay of the Last Minstrel first established the innovative formula that Scott would employ in all of his major poetic works. The book utilizes a loose metrical construction to relate a tale of adventure and romance involving two families in sixteenth-century Scotland. Scott drew on several sources in constructing his poem. The meter was modeled on William Coleridge's then-unpublished poem

Christabel, which Scott had heard recited the year before he began the *Lay.* The subject and narrative structure of Scott's poem had much to do with the traditional Scottish ballads he had been collecting. The story is recited by the aging "Last Minstrel," who sings for an audience of Scott's contemporaries, and the poem moves back and forth in time, relating details of the Minstrel and his performance and the past events of the bard's tale. By inventing a character who is a ballad singer, Scott was able to present much of the poem in the form of an extended song that the Minstrel sings. This open structure also allowed Scott to indulge in extended description and the discussion of antiquarian details, elements that would figure prominently in his subsequent poetic works.

Marmion: A Tale of Flodden Field, his next major work, centers on the hostilities between the Scottish and English in the early 1500s and culminates in an extended description of the Battle of Flodden, where English forces defeated the Scots under King James IV. Scott drew on the conventions of the Gothic novel in writing *Marmion,* emphasizing macabre settings and the sinister actions of the title character. He also includes autobiographic reflections in the epistles that precede each canto of the poem. Though these sections have been criticized as being an unnecessary distraction from the central narrative, other critics have found them an interesting departure for Scott, arguing that the poet used these epistles to articulate his personal relationship with his historical material.

The Lady of the Lake, published in 1810, is frequently cited as Scott's most accomplished poem in terms of plot. The narrative takes place in the Scottish Highlands and concerns the adventures of a number of characters, including the chivalric hero James Fitz-James, the hero-villain Roderick Dhu, and the heroine/love interest Ellen Douglas. As Fitz-James and his forces attempt to establish a centralized Scottish kingdom, they come into conflict with Dhu's Highland clan. The story features elements of Arthurian romance, as well as extensive descriptions the mountainous countryside.

Over the next seven years, other verse narratives followed, namely *The Vision of Don Roderick, Rokeby, The Bridal of Triermain, The Field of Waterloo, The Lord of the Isles,* and *Harold the Dauntless.* Sales began to falter for the later volumes, and Scott became prone to repeating the situations and ideas of his previous poems. For instance, *Rokeby* includes an epic battle description much like the one in *Marmion.* Furthermore, two of his verse publications, *The Bridal of Triermain* and *Harold the Dauntless,* were written as imitations of his own work and published anonymously, though Scott meant these books to be taken, at least partly, in jest. After 1813, he became more involved with writing novels than poetry. His move to fiction was brought about in part by the success of Lord Byron's *Childe Harold* and Scott's belief that he could not compete with the younger poet. Though he eventually gave up the epic verse narratives of his early career, Scott composed many short poems for his novels. These include "Proud Maisie," published in *The Heart of Mid-Lothian,* often considered one of Scott's finest verse compositions.

Critical Reception

The decline of Scott's reputation among critics, especially in the twentieth century, has been widely discussed. It should also be noted that his poems were not especially popular with the reviewers of his own day. Francis Jeffrey was among the first to point out Scott's careless composition that resulted in glaring flaws in the meter and grammar of the poems. Scott was also taken to task for creating implausible plots and for interrupting the narrative story line with extended considerations of antiquarian details, folk ballads, and—in the case of the *Marmion* epistles—Scott's addresses to his friends. Critics of the time did applaud the poet's originality, however, and found his descriptive passages highly evocative. In the mid-1800s John Ruskin voiced a thorough appreciation of Scott's imagery and his relationship to nature, but such praise was rare by the turn of the century. The unadorned natural description that Ruskin had admired emphasized surface details rather than emotional depth, and most critics of the modern era were unimpressed with this approach; in 1904 Arthur Symons questioned whether the narrative verse that Scott produced even qualified as poetry. The increased attention critics have paid to language in the latter half of the twentieth century has led to several considerations of Scott's grammatical constructions. These studies have sounded a tentative vindication of Scott's methods, but the relative scarcity of critical debate has tended to keep his verse from being widely studied by contemporary readers.

PRINCIPAL WORKS

Poetry

The Eve of St. John: A Border Ballad 1800
Minstrelsy of the Scottish Border. 3 vols. [editor and contributor] (ballads and poetry) 1802–03
The Lay of the Last Minstrel 1805
Ballads and Lyrical Pieces 1806
Marmion: A Tale of Flodden Field 1808
The Lady of the Lake 1810
The Vision of Don Roderick 1811
Rokeby: A Poem 1813
*The Bridal of Triermain; or, The Vale of St. John 1813
The Field of Waterloo 1815
The Lord of the Isles 1815
*Harold the Dauntless 1817
The Poetical Works of Walter Scott. 12 vols. 1820
The Complete Poetical Works of Sir Walter Scott. 5 vols. 1894

Novels

*Waverly; or, 'Tis Sixty Years Since 1814
*Guy Mannering; or, The Astrologer 1815
*The Antiquary 1816
†*The Black Dwarf* 1816; published in *Tales of My Landlord, first series*

†*Old Mortality* 1816; published in *Tales of My Landlord, first series*
†*Tales of My Landlord, first series* 1816
†*The Heart of Mid-Lothian* 1818; published in *Tales of My Landlord, second series*
*Rob Roy 1818
†*Tales of My Landlord, second series* 1818
†*The Bride of Lammermoor* 1819; published in *Tales of My Landlord, third series*
*Ivanhoe 1819
†*A Legend of Montrose* 1819; published in *Tales of My Landlord, third series*
†*Tales of My Landlord, third series* 1819
*The Abbot 1820
*The Monastery 1820
*Kenilworth 1821
*The Pirate 1821
*The Fortunes of Nigel 1822
*Peveril of the Peak 1822
*Quentin Durward 1823
*St. Ronan's Well 1823
*Redgauntlet: A Tale of the Eighteenth Century 1824
*‡Tales of the Crusaders 1825
*Woodstock; or, The Cavalier: A Tale of the Year Sixteen Hundred and Fifty One 1826
*St. Valentine's Day; or, The Fair Maiden of Perth 1828; published in *Chronicles of the Canongate, second series*
*Chronicles of the Canongate, second series 1828
*Anne Geierstein; or, The Maiden of the Mist 1829
Waverly Novels. 48 vols. 1829–33
†*Castle Dangerous* 1832; published in *Tales of My Landlord, fourth and last series*
†*Count Robert of Paris* 1832; published in *Tales of My Landlord, fourth and last series*
†*Tales of My Landlord, fourth and last series* 1832

Other Major Works

Halidon Hill (sketch) 1822
The Life of Napoleon Bonaparte (biography) 1827
*Chronicles of the Canongate, first series (short stories) 1828
Letters on Demonology and Witchcraft (letters) 1830
The Miscellaneous Prose Works of Sir Walter Scott. 30 vols. (biographies, essays, sketches, histories, and criticism) 1834–46
The Journal of Sir Walter Scott (journal) 1890
The Letters of Sir Walter Scott. 12 vols. (letters) 1932–37
Scott on Himself: A Collection of Autobiographical Writings of Sir Walter Scott (autobiography) 1981

*These works were published anonymously.

†These works were attributed to the pseudonym Jedediah Cleishbotham.

‡This work contains the novels *The Betrothed* and *The Talisman.*

CRITICISM

Francis Jeffrey   (essay date 1805)

SOURCE: A review of *The Lay of the Last Minstrel,* in *Contributions to the Edinburgh Review,* D. Appleton and Company, 1860, pp. 359–67.

[*Jeffrey was a founder and editor of the* Edinburgh Review, *one of the most influential magazines in early nineteenth-century England and a periodical that Scott was also involved with for a time. Jeffrey was a liberal Whig who often allowed his political beliefs to color his critical opinions. He is nevertheless considered an insightful contemporary critic of Scott's work, though Scott's political views were more conservative than Jeffrey's. In the following review, which was originally published in the* Edinburgh Review *in April, 1805, the critic finds the plot of* The Lay of the Last Minstrel *to be poorly constructed and its diction to be inconsistent. The originality of Scott's conception is praised, however, along with the "spirit and force" of the poem.*]

We consider [*The Lay of the Last Minstrel*] as an attempt to transfer the refinements of modern poetry to the matter and the manner of the ancient metrical romance. The author, enamoured of the lofty visions of chivalry, and partial to the strains in which they were formerly embodied, seems to have employed all the resources of his genius in endeavouring to recall them to the favour and admiration of the public; and in adapting to the taste of modern readers a species of poetry which was once the delight of the courtly, but has long ceased to gladden any other eyes than those of the scholar and the antiquary. This is a romance, therefore, composed by a minstrel of the present day; or such a romance as we may suppose would have been written in modern times, if that style of composition had continued to be cultivated, and partaken consequently of the improvements which every branch of literature has received since the time of its desertion.

Upon this supposition, it was evidently Mr. Scott's business to retain all that was good, and to reject all that was bad in the models upon which he was to form himself; adding, at the same time, all the interest and beauty which could possibly be assimilated to the manner and spirit of his originals. It was his duty, therefore, to reform the rambling, obscure, and interminable narratives of the ancient romancers—to moderate their digressions—to abridge or retrench their unmerciful or needless descriptions—and to expunge altogether those feeble and prosaic passages, the rude stupidity of which is so apt to excite the derision of a modern reader. At the same time, he was to rival, if he could, the force and vivacity of their minute and varied representations—the characteristic simplicity of their pictures of manners—the energy and conciseness with which they frequently describe great events—and the lively colouring and accurate drawing by which they give the effect of reality to every scene they undertake to delineate. In executing this arduous task, he was permitted to avail himself of all that

variety of style and manner which had been sanctioned by the ancient practice; and bound to embellish his performance with all the graces of diction and versification which could be reconciled to the simplicity and familiarity of the minstrel's song. . . .

[Mr. Scott] has produced a very beautiful and entertaining poem, in a style which may fairly be considered as original; and which will be allowed to afford satisfactory evidence of the genius of the author, even though he should not succeed in converting the public to his own opinion as to the interest or dignity of the subject. We are ourselves inclined indeed to suspect that his partiality for the strains of antiquity has imposed a little upon the severity of his judgment, and impaired the beauty of the present imitation, by directing his attention rather to what was characteristic, than to what was unexceptionable in his originals. Though he has spared too many of their faults, however, he has certainly improved upon their beauties: and while we can scarcely help regretting, that the feuds of Border chieftains should have monopolised as much poetry as might have served to immortalise the whole baronage of the empire, we are the more inclined to admire the interest and magnificence which he has contrived to communicate to a subject so unpromising.

Whatever may be thought of the conduct of the main story, the manner of introducing it must be allowed to be extremely poetical. An aged minstrel who had "harped to King Charles the Good," and learned to love his art at a time when it was honoured by all that was distinguished in rank or in genius, having fallen into neglect and misery in the evil days of the usurpation, and the more frivolous gaieties or bitter contentions of the succeeding reigns, is represented as wandering about the Border in poverty and solitude, a few years after the Revolution. In this situation he is driven, by want and weariness, to seek shelter in the Border castle of the Duchess of Buccleuch and Monmouth; and being cheered by the hospitality of his reception, offers to sing "an ancient strain," relating to the old warriors of her family; and after some fruitless attempts to recall the long-forgotten melody, pours forth *The Lay of the Last Minstrel,* in six cantos, very skilfully divided by some recurrence to his own situation, and some complimentary interruptions from his noble auditors.

The construction of a fable seems by no means the *forte* of our modern poetical writers; and no great artifice, in that respect, was to be expected, perhaps, from an imitator of the ancient romancers. Mr. Scott, indeed, has himself insinuated, that he considered the story as an object of very subordinate importance; and that he was less solicitous to deliver a regular narrative, than to connect such a series of incidents as might enable him to introduce the manners he had undertaken to delineate, and the imagery with which they were associated. . . .

[However well calculated the story] may be for the introduction of picturesque imagery, or the display of extraordinary incident, it has but little pretension to the praise of a regular or coherent narrative. The magic of the lady, the midnight visit to Melrose, and the mighty book of the enchanter, which occupy nearly one-third of the whole poem, and engross the attention of the reader for a long time after the commencement of the narrative, are of no use whatsoever in the subsequent development of the fable, and do not contribute, in any degree, either to the production or explanation of the incidents that follow. The whole character and proceedings of the goblin page, in like manner, may be considered as merely episodical; for though he is employed in some of the subordinate incidents, it is remarkable that no material part of the fable requires the intervention of supernatural agency. The young Buccleuch might have wandered into the wood, although he had not been decoyed by a goblin; and the dame might have given her daughter to the deliverer of her son, although she had never listened to the prattlement of the river and mountain spirits. There is, besides all this, a great deal of gratuitous and digressive description, and the whole sixth canto may be said to be redundant. The story should naturally end with the union of the lovers; and the account of the feast, and the minstrelsy that solemnised their betrothment is a sort of epilogue, superadded after the catastrophe is complete.

But though we feel it to be our duty to point out these obvious defects in the structure of the fable, we have no hesitation in conceding to the author, that the fable is but a secondary consideration in performances of this nature. A poem is intended to please by the images it suggests, and the feelings it inspires; and if it contain delightful images and affecting sentiments, our pleasure will not be materially impaired by some slight want of probability or coherence in the narrative by which they are connected. The *callida junctura* of its members is a grace, no doubt, which ought always to be aimed at; but the quality of the members themselves is a consideration of far higher importance; and that by which alone the success and character of the work must be ultimately decided. The adjustment of a fable may indicate the industry or the judgment of the writer; but the Genius of the poet can only be shown in his management of its successive incidents. In these more essential particulars, Mr. Scott's merits, we think, are unequivocal. He writes throughout with the spirit and the force of a poet; and though he occasionally discovers a little too much, perhaps, of the "brave neglect," and is frequently inattentive to the delicate propriety and scrupulous correctness of his diction, he compensates for those defects by the fire and animation of his whole composition, and the brilliant colouring and prominent features of the figures with which he has enlivened it. . . .

In the very first rank of poetical excellence, we are inclined to place the introductory and concluding lines of every canto; in which the ancient strain is suspended, and the feelings and situation of the Minstrel himself described in the words of the author. The elegance and the beauty of this *setting,* if we may so call it, though entirely of modern workmanship, appears to us to be fully more worthy of admiration than the bolder relief of the antiques which it encloses; and leads us to regret that the author should have wasted, in imitation and antiquarian researches, so much of those powers which seem fully equal to the task of raising him an independent reputation. . . .

The ancient romance owes much of its interest to the lively picture which it affords of the times of chivalry, and of those usages, manners, and institutions which we have been accustomed to associate in our minds, with a certain combination of magnificence with simplicity, and ferocity with romantic honour. The representations contained in those performances, however, are for the most part too rude and naked to give complete satisfaction. The execution is always extremely unequal; and though the writer sometimes touches upon the appropriate feeling with great effect and felicity, still this appears to be done more by accident than design; and he wanders away immediately into all sorts of ludicrous or uninteresting details, without any apparent consciousness of incongruity. These defects Mr. Scott has corrected with admirable address and judgment in the greater part of the work now before us; and while he has exhibited a very striking and impressive picture of the old feudal usages and institutions, he has shown still greater talent in engrafting upon those descriptions all the tender or magnanimous emotions to which the circumstances of the story naturally give rise. Without impairing the antique air of the whole piece, or violating the simplicity of the ballad style, he has contrived in this way, to impart a much greater dignity, and more powerful interest to his production, than could ever be attained by the unskilful and unsteady delineations of the old romancers. Nothing, we think, can afford a finer illustration of this remark, than the opening stanzas of the whole poem; they transport us at once into the days of knightly daring and feudal hostility; at the same time that they suggest, and in a very interesting way, all those softer sentiments which arise out of some parts of the description. . . .

In [numerous] passages, the poetry of Mr. Scott is entitled to a decided preference over that of the earlier minstrels; not only from the greater consistency and condensation of his imagery, but from an intrinsic superiority in the nature of his materials. From the improvement of taste, and the cultivation of the finer feelings of the heart, poetry acquires, in a refined age, many new and invaluable elements, which are necessarily unknown in a period of greater simplicity. The description of external objects, however, is at all times equally inviting, and equally easy; and many of the pictures which have been left by the ancient romancers must be admitted to possess, along with great diffuseness and homeliness of diction, an exactness and vivacity which cannot be easily exceeded. In this part of his undertaking, Mr. Scott therefore had fewer advantages; but we do not think that his success has been less remarkable. . . .

The whole night-journey of Deloraine—the opening of the wizard's tomb—the march of the English battle—and the parley before the walls of the castle, are all executed with . . . spirit and poetical energy, . . . and a great variety of short passages occur in every part of the poem, which are still more striking and meritorious, though it is impossible to detach them, without injury, in the form of a quotation. It is but fair to apprise the reader, on the other hand, that he will meet with very heavy passages, and with a variety of details which are not likely to interest any one but a Borderer or an antiquary. We like very well to hear "of the Gallant Chief of Otterburne," or "the Dark Knight of Liddisdale," and feel the elevating power of great names, when we read of the tribes that mustered to the war, "beneath the crest of old Dunbar, and Hepburn's mingled banners." But we really cannot so far sympathise with the local partialities of the author, as to feel any glow of patriotism or ancient virtue in hearing of the *Todrig* or *Johnston* clans, or of *Elliots, Armstrongs,* and *Tinlinns*; still less can we relish the introduction of *Black John of Athelstane, Whitslade the Hawk, Arthur-fire-the-braes, Red Roland Forster,* or any other of those worthies who

Sought the beeves that made their broth,
In Scotland and in England both,

into a poem which has any pretensions to seriousness or dignity. The ancient metrical romance might have admitted those homely personalities; but the present age will not endure them: And Mr. Scott must either sacrifice his Border prejudices, or offend all his readers in the other parts of the empire.

There are many passages, as we have already insinuated, which have the general character of heaviness, such is the minstrel's account of his preceptor, and Deloraine's lamentation over the dead body of Musgrave: But the goblin page is, in our opinion, the capital deformity of the poem. We have already said that the whole machinery is useless: but the magic studies of the lady, and the rifled tomb of Michael Scott, give occasion to so much admirable poetry, that we can on no account consent to part with them. The page, on the other hand, is a perpetual burden to the poet, and to the reader: it is an undignified and improbable fiction, which excites neither terror, admiration, nor astonishment; but needlessly debases the strain of the whole work, and excites at once our incredulity and contempt. He is not a "tricksy spirit," like Ariel, with whom the imagination is irresistibly enamoured; nor a tiny monarch, like Oberon, disposing of the destinies of mortals: He rather appears to us to be an awkward sort of a mongrel between Puck and Caliban; of a servile and brutal nature; and limited in his powers to the indulgence of petty malignity, and the infliction of despicable injuries. Besides this objection to his character, his existence has no support from any general or established superstition. Fairies and devils, ghosts, angels, and witches, are creatures with whom we are all familiar, and who excite in all classes of mankind emotions with which we can easily be made to sympathise. But the story of Gilpin Horner can never have been believed out of the village where he is said to have made his appearance; and has no claims upon the credulity of those who were not originally of his acquaintance. There is nothing at all interesting or elegant in the scenes of which he is the hero; and in reading those passages, we really could not help suspecting that they did not stand in the romance when the aged minstrel recited it to the royal Charles and his mighty earls, but were inserted afterwards to suit the taste of the cottagers among whom he begged his bread on the Border. We entreat Mr. Scott to inquire into the grounds of this suspicion; and to take advantage of any decent pretext he can lay hold of for purging *The*

Scott on *The Lay of the Last Minstrel*:

The poem now offered to the public is intended to illustrate the customs and manners which anciently prevailed on the borders of England and Scotland. The inhabitants, living in a state partly pastoral and partly warlike, and combining habits of constant depredation with the influence of a rude spirit of chivalry, were often engaged in scenes highly susceptible of poetical ornament. As the description of scenery and manners was more the object of the author, than a combined and regular narrative, the plan of the ancient metrical romance was adopted, which allows greater latitude in this respect than would be consistent with the dignity of a regular poem. The same model offered other facilities, as it permits an occasional alteration of measure, which, in some degree, authorises the changes of rhythm in the text. The machinery, also, adopted from popular belief, would have seemed puerile in a poem which did not partake of the rudeness of the old ballad, or metrical romance.

For these reasons, the poem was put into the mouth of an ancient Minstrel, the last of the race, who, as he is supposed to have survived the Revolution, might have caught somewhat of the refinement of modern poetry, without losing the simplicity of his original model. The date of the tale itself is about the middle of the 16th century, when most of the personages actually flourished. The time occupied by the action is three nights and three days.

Sir Walter Scott, in the preface to The Lay of the Last Minstrel; *printed in* The Monthly Review; *Vol. 49, March, 1806, p. 295.*

Lay of this ungraceful intruder. We would also move for a *Quo Warranto* against the spirits of the river and the mountain; for though they are come of a very high lineage, we do not know what lawful business they could have at Branksome castle in the year 1550.

Of the diction of this poem we have but little to say. . . . [The] versification is in the highest degree irregular and capricious. The nature of the work entitled Mr. Scott to some licence in this respect, and he often employs it with a very pleasing effect; but he has frequently exceeded its just limits, and presented us with such combinations of metre, as must put the teeth of his readers, we think, into some jeopardy. He has, when he pleases, a very melodious and sonorous style of versification, but often composes with inexcusable negligence and rudeness. There is a great number of lines in which the verse can only be made out by running the words together in a very unusual manner; and some appear to us to have no pretension to the name of verses at all. What apology, for instance, will Mr. Scott make for the last of these two lines?—

For when in studious mood he pac'd
St. Kentigern's hall.

or for these?—

How the brave boy in future war,
Should tame the unicorn's pride.

We have called the negligence which could leave such lines as these in a poem of this nature inexcusable; because it is perfectly evident, from the general strain of his composition, that Mr. Scott has a very accurate ear for the harmony of versification, and that he composes with a facility which must lighten the labour of correction. There are some smaller faults in the diction which might have been as well corrected also: there is too much alliteration; and he reduplicates his words too often. We have "never, never," several times; besides "'tis o'er, 'tis o'er"—"in vain, in vain"—"'tis done, 'tis done"; and several other echoes as ungraceful.

We will not be tempted to say any thing more of this poem. Although it does not contain any great display of what is properly called invention, it indicates perhaps as much vigour and originality of poetical genius as any performance which has been lately offered to the public. The locality of the subject is likely to obstruct its popularity; and the author, by confining himself in a great measure to the description of manners and personal adventures, has forfeited the attraction which might have been derived from the delineation of rural scenery. But he has manifested a degree of genius which cannot be overlooked, and given indication of talents that seem well worthy of being enlisted in the service of the epic muse.

The Eclectic Review   (essay date 1808)

SOURCE: A review of *Marmion: A Tale of Flodden Field,* in *The Eclectic Review,* Vol. IV, May, 1808, pp. 407–22.

[*Here, the reviewer complains about the "impertinent intervention" of the various epistles included in* Marmion, *but finds other passages in the poem exciting and entertaining, despite several flaws that are detected in Scott's writing.*]

Public expectation is seldom so highly excited by the promise of a new poem, as it has been, for some time past, by the repeated annunciation of *Marmion, a Tale of Flodden Field,* by the author of *The Lay of the last Minstrel.* Mr. Scott is probably the most popular poet living in this country, even in an age distinguished for poets of various and eminent talents. Without presuming to depreciate him in comparison with any of his less fortunate contemporaries, we may attribute a portion of his fame to the felicitous circumstance of his style and subjects being peculiarly calculated to fascinate two classes of readers, the one very select and the other very numerous, who are not generally attached to the Muses; we mean, the *Black-letter-men* and the *Novel-readers* of the age: the admirers of border antiquities, and the lovers of romantic adventures. Thus trebly armed with true powers of poetry to delight the refined and susceptible heart, with skill in obsolete literature to attract the antiquary, and with a form of language

so plain, yet so fluent, as to make the novel-reader forget that his tales are in verse, Mr. Walter Scott stands unrivalled among his brethren. How far the present work may gratify that curiosity, which the somewhat officious predictions of its approach awakened, we shall not pretend to anticipate. Had *Marmion* appeared before the author, by his *Minstrelsy of the Scottish Border,* had prepared the public mind for the Gothic inroad which he meditated against the feeble provinces of modern poetry, and which he successfully accomplished in *The Lay of the last Minstrel;*—such a phenomenon of grotesque verse as is here exhibited would have staggered the critics, who would scarcely have ventured to declare a free opinion of its merits (though they might have found less difficulty in carping at its faults) till the public, the slow but finally infallible judge of literary excellence, had sentenced it to oblivion or immortality. As the case stands, both the critics and the public will judge *Marmion* in comparison with the author's former and favourite production; and it is not improbable that some disappointment may be felt, for eager and long-waiting expectation is always unreasonable. In the *Lay of the last Minstrel,* the poet rode triumphantly through a field in which there was no competitor; on the present occasion, it is true, he has only *one* rival, but that rival is the most formidable with whom *he* could be compelled to enter the lists, for that rival is himself; and unless he has greatly surpassed his own former achievements, he must be contented till the next generation at least, with the credit of having adventured bravely, but failed.

Perhaps the most captivating charm of the *Lay of the last Minstrel* may be found in the pleasing introduction of "the last Minstrel" himself, in the scene and the company where he carolled his "Lay," and in the compassionate interest awakened in the reader's breast for the old man, when, at the opening and conclusion of every canto, he recalls his own joys and sorrows, and unbosoms his individual feelings, in spontaneous and irresistibly-affecting rhapsodies. By the admirable art of the poet, the *Tale* or "Lay" itself is delivered in the presence of a party, of which every reader imagines himself one; even in perusal, therefore, the story seems rather to be *listened to* than *read.* It was not to be expected that Mr. Scott should be so fortunate as to invent a vehicle equally advantageous for another poem of similar character: but no one could doubt that he was capable of selecting and adorning a theme of higher dignity, and more exquisite intrinsic interest, than the *Lay.* Such a theme, and so executed, is *Marmion;* and bad the author trusted it with its own insulated merits to the public, it would have been welcomed and honoured with unhesitating applause. But being determined to encumber it with the most unnecessary support that could well be imagined, he has thrust between the six Cantos six long Epistles to friends, modern in style, subject, and embellishment; which might as well have been interpolated with the old chronicle of the *"Battle of Flodden"* as with this new *Tale of Flodden Field.* The author needs not be proud of the plaudits, nor sore at the sarcasms, of any one who can patiently read this book according to the order in which it is printed; for *Marmion* will have little power to dazzle or delight him, who can endure the impertinent intervention of the epistles in the most sublime and interesting pauses of the narrative. Convinced of the extraordinary worth of the latter, and the comparative insignificance of the greater part of the former, we have little doubt that the fortune of this volume will be the reverse of its predecessor:—*there* the interludes afforded the highest gratification; *here* they will not only miss due praise, but escape just censure; for as it will require very little additional trouble to turn over twenty pages instead of one, from Canto to Canto, few readers will grudge their pains to do this; but it will be much indeed if one reader in twenty will remember or care to turn back, at the conclusion, to peruse the omitted interlopers, as all interest in the book itself will expire with the hero from whom it is denominated. We are sorry to notice so palpable a piece of book-making, (and so miserably managed too, that the very artifice by which it is attempted to be concealed only exposes it the more to observation) in the work of an author who has no occasion to resort to any tricks of trade to acquire sufficient fame and profit by his labours.

We do not complain of the publication of the *"Epistles"* in the same volume with **Marmion** but of the pitiful device *to make them go down with it,* under the pretence that they are essentially connected with the story: when it is nearly self-evident that they were written without any specific reference to the piece, on which they are now most awkwardly botched by a few lines at the end of each, in some instances absolutely deteriorating their *own,* and we presume their *original,* effect; while whatever forced alliance is made between them and the grand poem, the poem has not in a single case the slightest dependence on them. If the writer was really bound to furnish a certain quantity of verse for a certain sum of money, why could he not have printed the epistles distinctly, either at the beginning or at the end of the volume?—Or why did he not chuse subjects for his preambles from the Cantos of the poem to which they are given as preludes? For with suitable themes arising out of the story itself (particularly from the *scenes* of action and the *manners* of the time) he might have been abundantly supplied, as every one may perceive on reading over the following heads, annexed to each Canto: *"The Castle;—the Convent;—the Hostel or Inn;—the Camp;—the Court;—the Battle."* As they now stand confounded together, what congeniality of feeling, or coincidence of circumstance, can possibly be imagined, between the interment of Pitt and Fox in Westminster Abbey, and the magnificent feasting of Lord Marmion at Norham Castle? or between a facetious description of Christmas gambols, and a terrific display of Flodden Field covered with contending armies? We should have preferred it, however, had the author lengthened his tale, or rather had he unfolded it more amply through *ten* or *twelve* Cantos, instead of *six.* This he might easily and advantageously have done; for his fable is so rich in materials, powerful in interest, various and intricate in incident, and animated with characters so strongly contrasted, that instead of having exhausted his subject on his present plan, we are inclined to complain that he has not sufficiently brought forward and relieved the scenes and the figures which he has here sketched with the hand of a master.

There are many things of which we wish to know more, and few on which we can justly say that the author, who has the rare talent of never being dull, has dwelt too long. Perhaps no modern poem could be so much improved by expansion, (not in *description, but in narrative,*) as the piece before us. We, will not acknowledge that we have, in any instance, been wearied with antiquarian minuteness and border garrulity; but we could very well have spared many exquisite details of the pageantry of dress, the fashion of flags, and the devices of arms, to have been compensated with further information concerning Constance, Clara, and De Wilton; and we should have been better pleased, if, with less of the pantomimical magnificence of heraldry, we had found more of human actions and passions exhibited in very strange and heroic situations.— Were the subject worth a conjecture, we should suspect that the Epistles were written with immediate reference— to certain political events—to the author's private habits of study and amusement—to the peculiar style and subjects of his poetry—and in memory of former feelings and friendships. The union of these with **Marmion** was an after-thought, and was unworthy of a skilful writer, for each might have stood alone to greater advantage. Interwoven as they are, they will be read in comparison with each other, by the few who peruse both; and we are confident in predicting that the majority of these will pronounce the epistles to be much inferior, both in energy and elegance, to the main poem. They will form this decision for a very plain, if not a very just reason; because Mr. Scott in his own style appears inimitable, but when he writes in the language of his contemporaries he immediately becomes one of them, and must then be placed in the rank which belongs to him,—a high rank we acknowledge, but certainly not the highest. In **Marmion** the expression and cadence of verse are varied and irregular to suit the thoughts and the subjects; the occasional meanness of phraseology, ruggedness of metre, vulgarity of allusion, frivolity, feebleness, or superfluity of sentiment and description, are scarcely felt as faults, because the reader is carried back to an antiquated age, and imagines himself not only hearing the story of obsolete personages, but hearing it from the lips of a minstrel who records what occurred within his own memory. Now as in Mr. Scott's *romantic poems* the beauties outweigh the blemishes, as much as, in the lays of the bards whom he assumes to imitate, the blemishes outweigh the beauties, his good natured readers, (for the readers of other poets are seldom *so* good natured,) feel continually more disposed to relish the excellencies of these compositions, than to nauseate their defects. But when, as in the epistles, he relinquishes his factitious style, and casts away his antique attire, he is listened to only as a *minstrel of the present day;* then are his uncouth and languid lines, his barbarous and tramontane rhymes, insufferable on this side of the Tweed, as readily detected and condemned as severely, as if they were found in the pages of any other living bard. We do not mean to charge Mr. Scott with negligence in these epistles; on the contrary, we are persuaded that some of the weakest passages in them have cost him more hard labour than the noblest flights that occur in the **Lay of the last Minstrel,** and the metrical romance of **Marmion.** Hence indeed we conclude, that with more credit and facility to himself, and with more delight to the public, he might have extended his great work to twelve cantos, than he has compounded the heterogeneous volume now before us.

We should not have expatiated so much on this monstrous connection between **Marmion,** and the *"Six Epistles from Ettrick Forest,"* (which were announced in the literary journals for speedy publication, long before there was any rumour of such a poem as the former being in embryo,) had it not afforded us an opportunity of distinguishing and contrasting their respective characters and pretensions to public favour. We shall have no further occasion to consider them in contact, or rather in opposition, with each other; but shall briefly point out a few of the prominent features of each, dispatching the epistles first.

The first epistle is addressed to W. S. Rose, Esq. the ingenious versifier of *Amadis de Gaul.* It appears to have been written in November, 1806; and after a good winter-piece of description, the poet, by an easy transition, recurs to his country's wintry state, and takes occasion to eulogize the memory of Lord Nelson, Mr. Pitt, and Mr. Fox, all recently lost to the nation. Though patriotism is inspiration to every true poet, yet personal and party politics in general furnish meagre and miserable subjects for the lyre; none but the muse of satire being ever genially kindled by those flames that consume the domestic tranquillity of governments. Mr. Scott, it is true, praises and mourns the dead with all his might; but we have been more affected by ten lines on the *Love of Country* in the **Lay of the last Minstrel,** than with all the "fine frenzy" of panegyric on departed statesmen, that rages through as many pages of this epistle. Ought not the awful reflection, that Mr. Pitt and Mr. Fox are reposing till the day of judgement under the same roof, almost in the same grave, to have awakened some sentiment more sublimely affecting than can be found either in the prettiness of the first four, or the common-place of the six last lines in the following extract?

> Drop upon Fox's grave the tear,
> 'Twill trickle to his rival's bier;
> O'er PITT's the mournful requiem sound,
> And Fox's shall the notes rebound.
> The solemn echo seems to cry,—
> "Here let their discord with them die;
> "Speak not for those a separate doom,
> "Whom Fate made brothers in the tomb.
> "But search the land, of living men,
> "Where wilt thou find their like agen?"

But if the poet transgressed his own boundaries in his first epistle, in the second he is entirely and most happily at home. The prospect of Ettrick Forest, now shorn of its trees and dispeopled of its savage inhabitants, as compared with its ancient glories, is admirably delineated; the ramble and the *brown-study* on the border of St. Mary's Lake are finer than any thing of the kind that we have hitherto met with in Mr. Scott himself. Even the additional scene of contrasted horror, introduced purely for the sake of connecting this epistle with the second canto of

Marmion, gives no offence, though it does not heighten the effect of the preceding descriptions. The simile, toward the conclusion, of a rivulet-cataract to a *"grey mare's tail"* though sanctioned it seems by vulgar usage, and dignified with uncommon pomp of versification, is too low and ludicrous to please in the passage where it occurs. We give the following beautiful specimen from this epistle.

> Nought living meets the eye or ear,
> But well I ween the dead are near;
> For though, in feudal strife, a foe
> Hath laid Our Lady's chapel low,
> Yet still, beneath the hallowed soil,
> The peasant rests him from his toil,
> And, dying, bids his bones be laid,
> Where erst his simple fathers prayed.
>   If age had tamed the passion's strife,
> And Fate had cut my ties to life,
> Here, have I thought, 'twere sweet to dwell,
> And rear again the chaplain's cell,
> Like that same peaceful hermitage,
> Where Milton longed to spend his age.
> 'Twere sweet to mark the setting day,
> On Bourhope's lonely top decay;
> And, as it faint and feeble died,
> On the broad lake, and mountain's side,
> To say, "Thus pleasures fade away;
> Youth, talents, beauty, thus decay,
> And leave us dark, forlorn, and grey;"—
> Then gaze on Dryhope's ruined tower,
> And think on Yarrow's faded flower;
> And when that mountain-sound I heard,
> Which bids us be for storm prepared,
> The distant rustling of his wings,
> As up his force the Tempest brings,
> 'Twere sweet, ere yet his terrors rave,
> To sit upon the Wizard's grave;
> That Wizard Priest's, whose bones are thrust
> From company of holy dust;
> On which no sun-beam ever shines—
> (So superstition's creed divines,)
> Thence view the lake, with sullen roar,
> Heave her broad billows to the shore,
> And mark the wild swans mount the ga'e,
> Spread wide through mist their snowy sail,
> And ever stoop again, to lave
> Their bosoms on the surging wave:
> Then, when, against the driving hail,
> No longer might my plaid avail,
> Back to my lonely home retire,
> And light my lamp, and trim my fire:
> There ponder o'er some mystic lay,
> Till the wild tale had all its sway,
> And, in the bittern's distant shriek,
> I heard unearthly voices speak,
> And thought the Wizard Priest was come,
> To claim again his ancient home!
> And bade my busy fancy range,
> To frame him fitting shape and strange,
> Till from the task my brow I cleared,
> And smiled to think that I had feared.

The third epistle contains a sprightly and ingenious vindication of the writer's peculiar poetical pursuits. There are in it some picturesque allusions to romantic scenery, which in early youth warmed his imagination with the enthusiastic love of Border themes. An author is seldom so eloquent as when he talks of himself, and perhaps never more pleasing than when he recals his infantine feelings and amusements.

In the fourth epistle we find many charming recollections, awakened by the occurrence to his mind of the simple expression of an "ancient minstrel,"

> Where's now the life which late we led?

The reader will sympathize delightfully with the author, if he should find some dear remembrances of his own past days renewed in the perusal of this retrospective poem.

The fifth epistle celebrates the praises of Edinburgh, in which the introduction of Britomarte, the heroine of Spenser, is very lively and appropriate. The sixth and last epistle describes Christmas gambols: the tale of the demon who keeps the chest of treasure at Franchemont is neither well told nor well applied. On the whole, the *second* and *third* of these epistles are, in our estimation, the best.

We now proceed to make a few comments on the chief poem of this volume. Marmion is a fictitious personage; the imaginary descendant of a family of that name, which became extinct in the reign of Edward IV. His adventures in this poem are grafted on a pretended mission, which he undertakes by order of Henry VIII, to James IV king of Scotland, to demand the cause of the immense preparations for war, which he was making, apparently with the view of invading England. The poem opens with the arrival of Lord Marmion and his train at Norham Castle, on the borders; in the course of the following cantos he proceeds to the Scotish camp and capital, where he has an interview with James at a ball, receives an answer of defiance, returns toward England, and joins the army under the Earl of Surrey just marching to battle against the Scots at Flodden Field. They fight—he falls. This journey affords the author a series of scenes, in which he displays, with his wonted skill and vivacity, the manners and characters of the rival nations, particularly of the Scotch, in that ferocious age of declining chivalry. But had this been all, the "progress of Lord Marmion" would have been more worthy to be celebrated by *John Nicholls* than *Walter Scott*. Out of the private history of the hero arises a deep, mysterious, and impassioned interest, which gives warmth, colouring, and animation, to what would otherwise have been a frigid and frivolous chronicle. Marmion is a hero of the highest order in war; a villain of the darkest turpitude in private life. He seduces and debauches a nun named Constance; afterwards he falls in love with the rich inheritance of Clara, a lady of splendid connexions, who is previously betrothed to De Wilton, a young and noble knight. Marmion by forged letters attaints the character of De Wilton, as a traitor; fights with him and overcomes him in single combat. Though supposed to be slain, De Wilton, on being carried from the field of tournament to

the cottage of his old beadsman, recovers and is healed of his wounds. Then assuming the garb of a Palmer, he travels from shrine to shrine on the continent, for several years, and returns to England at the commencement of Lord Marmion's mission. Meeting with the latter accidentally at Norham Castle, and being perfectly secure in his disguise, De Wilton consents to be his conductor to Edinburgh. Meanwhile Clara, supposing De Wilton dead, has taken refuge from Lord Marmion's persecuting addresses in the convent of St. Hilda at Whitby, from whence Constance had been seduced by him. Constance knowing her asylum, conspires with a monk to poison her rival. The plot is discovered, and Constance, is surrendered by her seducer, for whose sake she had attempted the atrocious deed, into the hands of the spiritual powers. While Marmion is on his journey to Scotland, Constance and the monk are prisoners at Holy Island, whither they are followed by the Abbess of Whitby, Clara, and some of the sisters of St. Hilda. Constance and the monk are tried, condemned, and immured alive within the wall of St. Cuthbert's abbey in Holy Island. The Abbess, Clara, and their companions, on their return to Whitby, are captured at sea by a Scotish vessel, and carried to Edinburgh, while Lord Marmion is there. The Abbess obtains an interview with De Wilton, disguised as a Palmer, and places in his hands certain papers, delivered to her by the condemned Constance, in which his own innocence and Marmion's treachery are fully exposed. On the marching of the Scotish army, the Abbess and her companions are sent back under safeguard to England, but Clara is committed, or rather betrayed, to the protection of Lord Marmion, to be by him delivered to her kindred, instead of being restored to the convent, in which she was only a novice. Meanwhile De Wilton casts away his Palmer's weeds, is knighted anew by Douglas, earl of Angus, and suddenly quits Tantallon castle, after being recognized by Clara. Having joined the English army, and performed miracles at the battle of Flodden, he finds Clara, after the death of Marmion; they are, of course, married, and the poem ends.

After this sketch of the fable, we shall not pretend to follow the poet through his details. The first canto presents little beside descriptions of barbarian pageantry and magnificence, in ceremony, feasting, and arms; but the imagination of the reader is filled, and his mind is prepared to expect high entertainment from a story that opens under such splendid auspices. The person and appearance of Lord Marmion are spiritedly pourtrayed in the following passage.

> Along the bridge Lord Marmion rode,
> Proudly his red-roan charger trod,
> His helm hung at the saddle bow;
> Well, by his visage, you might know
> He was a stalworth knight, and keen,
> And had in many a battle been;
> The scar on his brown cheek revealed
> A token true of Bosworth field;
> His eye-brow dark, and eye of fire,
> Shewed spirit proud, and prompt to ire;
> Yet lines of thought upon his cheek,
> Did deep design and counsel speak.

His forehead, by his casque worn bare,
His thick moustache, and curly hair,
Coal-black, and grizzled here and there,
    But more through toil than age;
His square-turned joints, and strength of limb,
Shewed him no carpet knight so trim,
But, in close fight, a champion grim,
    In camps, a leader sage.
Well was he armed from head to heel,
In mail, and plate, of Milan steel;
But his strong helm, of mighty cost,
Was all with burnish'd gold emboss'd;
Amid the plumage of the crest,
A falcon hovered on her nest,
With wings outspread, and forward breast;
E'en such a falcon, on his shield,
Soared sable in an azure field:
The golden legend bore aright,
"WHO CHECKS AT ME, TO DEATH IS DIGHT."
Blue was the charger's broidered rein,
Blue ribbons decked his arching mane;
The knightly housing's ample fold
Was velvet blue, and trapp'd with gold.

In the second canto, the ghostly tribunal, before which
Constance and the monk are tried, and sentenced to be
buried alive in the Abbey walls, though it reminds us of
Mrs. Radcliffe's Inquisition, has features of strange horror, and a gloomy sublimity peculiarly its own. The scene
is wrought up to the highest pitch of agony that can be
borne by a reader of romance: and though it is marked
with all the minuteness that characterizes the author, we
confess that in none of his former poems have we met
with any passage that struck us with a more powerful
conviction of his talents: the distress is so awful, and the
interest so excruciating, that we forgot both the *Minstrel*
and the *Mannerist,* which rarely happens in reading Mr.
Scott's artificial verse, and were entranced for a while in
the realised presence of the merciless judges, and the
despairing criminals. When we recovered our recollection, we felt as the latter might be supposed to feel, had
they escaped by miracle from the dungeon, and found
themselves breathing at liberty beyond the walls that were
to have been their grave. We can present our readers with
no abstract of this terrific scene. The following picture of
Constance will however be a proof of the extraordinary
merit of this part of the poem.

When thus her face was given to view,
(Although so pallid was her hue,
It did a ghastly contrast bear,
To those bright ringlets glistering fair,)
Her look composed, and steady eye,
Bespoke a matchless constancy;
And there she stood so calm and pale,
That, but her breathing did not fail,
And motion slight of eye and head,
And of her bosom, warranted,
That neither sense nor pulse she lacks,
You might have thought a form of wax,
Wrought to the very life, was there;
So still she was, so pale, so fair.

And now that blind old Abbot rose,
    To speak the Chapter's doom,
On those the wall was to inclose,
    Alive, within the tomb;
But stopped, because that woeful maid,
Gathering her powers, to speak essayed;
Twice she essayed, and twice, in vain,
Her accents might no utterance gain!
Nought but imperfect murmurs slip
From her convulsed and quivering lip:
    'Twixt each attempt all was so still,
    You seemed to hear a distant rill—
        'Twas ocean's swells and falls;
    For though this vault of sin and fear
    Was to the sounding surge so near,
    A tempest there you scarce could hear,
        So massive were the walls.
At length, an effort sent apart
The blood that curdled to her heart,
    And light came to her eye,
And colour dawned upon her cheek,
A hectic and a fluttered streak,
Like that left on the Cheviot peak,
    By Autumn's stormy sky;
And when her silence broke at length,
Still as she spoke, she gathered strength,
    And arm'd herself to bear.
It was a fearful sight to see
Such high resolve and constancy,
    In form so soft and fair.

The third canto *"the Hostel or Inn"* is very entertaining
and miscellaneous. Lord Marmion's midnight adventure is
fearfully imagined; but in this, as in all those apparently
supernatural events, which abound in modern romance,
when the secret is explained, the interest ceases, and can
never be renewed: a riddle can only please so long as it
puzzles. The song of Constance, in the same canto, has a
much more natural and enduring charm; it is as sweetly
wild, as if it had been sung by the unfortunate victim of
seduction to the spontaneous music of the Æolian harp, on
an autumnal evening.

SONG.

Where shall the lover rest,
    Whom the fates sever
From his true maiden's breast,
    Parted for ever?
Where, through groves deep and high,
    Sounds the far billow,
Where early violets die,
    Under the willow.
CHORUS. *Eleu loro,* &c. Soft shall be his pillow.

There, through the summer day,
    Cool streams are laving;
There, while the tempests sway,
    Scarce are boughs waving;
There, thy rest shalt thou take,
    Parted for ever,
Never again to wake,

Where hedge-rows spread a verdant screen
And spires and forests intervene
And the neat cottage peeps between?
No, no! for these will he exchange
His dark Lochaber's boundless range
Nor for gay Devon's meads forsake
Benneuis grey and Garry's lake.

Thus, while I ape the measure wild
Of tales that charmed me yet a child
Rude though they be still with the *chime*
Returns the thoughts of early time
And feelings wakened in lifes first day
Glow in the line and prompt the lay
Then rise that hill, that mountain tower
That fixed Attentions dawning hour
Where no broad river swept along
To wake perchance heroic song
Where sighed no groves in summer gale
To prompt of love a softer tale
Where scarce a puny streamlets speed
Claimed homage from a shepherds reed
It was a *lonely* scene and wild
Where naked rocks were rudely piled
But ever and anon between
Lay velvet tufts of loveliest green
And well the lonely infant knew
Recesses where the woodbine grew

Page from the manuscript of Marmion.

Never, O never.
CHORUS. *Eleu loro,* &c. Never, O never.

    Where shall the traitor rest,
       He, the deceiver,
    Who could win maiden's breast,
       Ruin, and leave her?
    In the lost battle,
       Borne down by the flying,
    Where mingles war's rattle,
       With groans of the dying.
CHORUS. *Eleu loro,* &c. There shall he be lying.

    Her wing shall the eagle flap,
       O'er the false-hearted;
    His warm blood the wolf shall lap,
       Ere life be parted.
    Shame and dishonour sit
       By his grave ever;
    Blessings shall hallow it,—
       Never, O never.
CHORUS. *Eleu loro,* &c. Never, O never.

The fourth and fifth cantos consist chiefly of curious de-lineations of the camp, the army and the clans that com-posed it, the city, the court, and in a word the whole *costume* of the age: the eye of the imagination is glorious-ly entertained, but the heart and the affections meanwhile are utterly unengaged. The ball-scene, in the fifth canto, is very lively and amusing. The gallant deportment and fiery volatile disposition of James IV are characterized with great spirit. The midnight conversation piece between the abbess of St. Hilda and the Palmer (De Wilton) is *toler-ably* dull and prosaic, but it is indispensable toward the development of the plot. The mysterious rewarning of the fatal issue of the expedition against England, though strik-ingly introduced, ought perhaps to be censured, as a vio-lation of propriety, in a poem into which no other super-natural event is admitted, although this grand circumstance is founded on popular tradition.

In the sixth canto the poet has put forth all his strength, and in one instance only has it failed him. In the sublimely imagined and skilfully executed interview between De Wilton and Clara, by moon-light, on the rocks of Tantal-lon, when they encounter and recognize each other, the minstrel, who could paint Constance equally affecting in her silence and in her speech before her remorseless judg-es, ignobly shrinks from the delicate and exquisitely dif-ficult duty of describing the emotions and language of these lovers thus romantically restored to each other. Can the following flat lines be allowed by any reader, as an apology for his indolent evasion of the finest opportunity that occurs in the whole poem of touching the tenderest strings of the heart?

    She raised her eyes in mournful mood,—
    WILTON himself before her stood!
    It might have seemed his passing ghost;
    For every youthful grace was lost,
    And joy unwonted, and surprise,
    Gave their strange wildness to his eyes.—

    Expect not, noble dames and lords,
    That I can tell such scene in words:
    What skilful limner e'er would chuse
    To paint the rainbow's varying hues,
    Unless to mortal it were given
    To dip his brush in dyes of heaven?

The appearance of the battle of Flodden, overlooked from an eminence by Clara, under the guard of Eustace and Blount, Lord Marmion's squires, is depicted with vigour and animation. But the death of Lord Marmion, as it ought to be, is the climax of the poem and of the author's art. We shall quote two passages from this mournful and ter-rible scene;—the death of an-unrepenting sinner is almost too dreadful to be contemplated even in romance! But we must mention with unqualified disapprobation the wretch-ed conceit of giving the inscription on the well in *black letter.* The inscription itself is impertinently introduced; did Clara stop to read it? How *could* the author, in the fervour of composition, in the very soul of the most pa-thetic scene of his poem, *think* of such a puerility? and *having thought* of it, why did he not spurn it as a golden apple thrown in his way, to make him stumble in the last moment, at the last step, of a victorious race? But the trick itself is absurd, and unworthy even of antiquarian frivol-ity; the minstrel is continually reminding us that we are in his presence, *hearing his lay*:—how does he contrive to sing these lines in *Old English*?

Lord Marmion, mortally wounded in the battle, is brought by his squires (who had precipitated themselves into the midst of it, when they saw his standard in danger) and laid down on the hill where Clara stood: in his fiery zeal for the honour of his country, he compels them by his irresist-ible command to return to the fight, and leave him to perish alone.

    They parted, and alone he lay;
    Clara drew her from the sight away,
    Till pain wrung forth a lowly moan,
    And half he murmured,—"Is there none,
       Of all my halls have nurst,
    Page, squire, or groom, one cup to bring
    Of blessed water, from the spring,
       To slake my dying thirst!"—
    O, woman! in our hours of ease,
    Uncertain, coy, and hard to please,
    And variable as the shade
    By the light quivering aspen made;
    When pain and anguish wring the brow,
    A ministering angel thou!—
    Scarce were the piteous accents said,
    When, with the Baron's casque, the maid
       To the nigh streamlet ran:
    Forgot were hatred, wrongs, and fears,
    The plaintive voice alone she hears,
       Sees but the dying man.
    She stooped her by the runnel's side,
       But in abhorrence backward drew,
    For, oozing from the mountain's side,
       Where raged the war, a dark red tide
       Was curdling in the streamlet blue.

Where shall she turn!—behold her mark
  A little fountain-cell,
Where water, clear as diamond-spark,
  In a stone bason fell.
Above, some half-worn letters say,
Drink weary pilgrim, drink and pray
For the kind soul of Sybil Grey,
Who built this cross and well.
She filled the helm, and back she hied,
And with surprise and joy espied
  A Monk supporting Marmion's head:
A pious man, whom duty brought
To dubious verge of battle fought,
  To shrieve the dying, bless the dead.

We are sorry to omit a fine passage which intervenes betwixt these and the following lines.

With fruitless labour, Clara bound,
And strove to staunch, the gushing wound:
The Monk, with unavailing cares,
Exhausted all the Church's prayers;
Ever, he said, that, close and near,
A lady's voice was in his ear,
And that the priest he could not hear,
  For that she ever sung,
"In the last battle, borne down by the flying,
Where mingles war's rattle with groans of the
  dying!"
  So the notes rung;
"Avoid thee, Fiend!—with cruel hand,
Shake not the dying sinner's sand!—
O look, my son, upon yon sign
Of the Redeemer's grace divine;
  O think on faith and bliss!—
By many a death-bed I have been,
And many a sinner's parting seen,
  But never aught like this."—
The war, that for a space did fail,
Now trebly thundering swelled the gale,
  And—STANLEY! was the cry;—
A light on Marmion's visage spread,
  And fired his glazing eye:
With dying hand, above his head
He shook the fragment of his blade,
  And shouted "Victory!—
"Charge, Chester, charge! On, Stanley, on!"—
Were the last words of Marmion.

We have not room for another quotation, and scarcely for another remark. In the plan and the characters, as well as in the fashion of the verse, *Marmion* departs from the most approved precedents: there is nothing resembling *poetical justice* in the story. The hero, a monster of wickedness, not only escapes the punishment due to his crimes from the hands of those whom he had injured, but dies gloriously in the field of battle, in defence of his invaded country! De Wilton (except in the disguise of the Palmer, wherein he provokes an interest which is afterwards disappointed) is a tame common place gentleman, who does nothing worthy of the high rank that he holds in the poem, or of the lovely lot assigned to him at last. He takes no step to rescue Clara from the power of Marmion, nor to avenge his own wrongs publicly on the head of the wretch, who had openly vanquished him in single combat and secretly branded him as a traitor. Their midnight recountre, in the third canto, is too ambiguous and too extravagant to satisfy the reader. Constance we apprehend will be the favourite heroine;—perhaps it is only her cruel fate that makes her such, for Clara her rival is charmingly pourtrayed, and engages our sympathy whenever she appears. But to tell the plain truth, though the author himself might perhaps be very much surprised to hear us say so,—old Angus *"Bell-the-Cat,"* is prominently the noblest character in the poem. His conduct at the ball, his appearance in the chapel when he knights De Wilton, and his parting quarrel with Marmion, all display him to the highest advantage, and reflect lustre on the talents of the poet. . . .

In this work the versification is in general more stately, and less rambling and rugged, than in the *Lay of the last Minstrel,* but we have observed that the stanzas often close with very feeble couplets. The rhymes must not be too rigidly scrutinized; the epithet *"fair"* seems to be a favourite with the author in all his poems; and in this volume, we should not be far from the truth if we were to affirm, at a round guess, that it occurs a hundred times as a rhyme.

Of the notes, we can only add that they will be found as numerous in proportion, and as entertaining in matter, as those in Mr. Scott's former publications.

Francis Jeffrey (essay date 1810)

SOURCE: A review of *The Lady of the Lake,* in *The Edinburgh Review,* Vol. XVI, No. 32, August, 1810, pp. 263–93.

[*In this review, Jeffrey comments on the Scott's ability to create verse that appeals to a wide audience. Though the reviewer detects a number of imperfections in* The Lady of the Lake, *including its similarity to Scott's other poetic works, he finds the book superior to* The Lay of the Last Minstrel *and* Marmion.]

[Mr] Scott, though living in an age unusually prolific of original poetry, has manifestly outstripped all his competitors in the race of popularity; and stands already upon a height to which no other writer has attained in the memory of any one now alive. We doubt, indeed, whether any English poet *ever* had so many of his books sold, or so many of his verses read and admired by such a multitude of persons, in so short a time. We are credibly informed, that nearly thirty thousand copies of [*The Lay of the Last Minstrel*] have been already disposed of in this country; and that the demand for *Marmion,* and the poem now before us, has been still more considerable,—a circulation, we believe, altogether without example, in the case of a bulky work, not addressed to the bigotry of the mere mob, either religious or political.

A popularity so universal is a pretty sure proof of extraordinary merit,—a far surer one, we readily admit, than would be afforded by any praises of ours: and, therefore, though we pretend to be privileged, in ordinary cases, to foretel the ultimate reception of all claims on public admiration, our function may be thought to cease, where the event is already so certain and conspicuous. As it is a sore thing, however, to be deprived of our privileges on so important an occasion, we hope to be pardoned for insinuating, that, even in such a case, the office of the critic may not be altogether superfluous. Though the success of the author be decisive, and likely to be permanent, it still may not be without its use to point out, in consequence of what, and in spite of what, he has succeeded; nor altogether uninstructive to trace the precise limits of the connexion which, even in this dull world, indisputably subsists between success and desert, and to ascertain how far unexampled popularity implies unrivaled talent. . . .

[We think] that few things are more curious than the singular skill, or good fortune, with which [Mr Scott] has reconciled his claims on the favour of the multitude, with his pretensions to more select admiration. Confident in the force and originality of his own genius, he has not been afraid to avail himself of common-places both of diction and of sentiment, whenever they appeared to be beautiful or impressive,—using them however, at all times, with the skill and spirit of an inventor: and quite certain that he could not be mistaken for a plagiarist or imitator, he has made free use of that great treasury of characters, images and expressions, which had been accumulated by the most celebrated of his predecessors;—at the same time that the rapidity of his transitions, the novelty of his combinations, and the spirit and variety of his own thoughts and inventions, show plainly that he was a borrower from any thing but poverty, and took only what he could have given if he had been born in an earlier generation. The great secret of his popularity, however, and the leading characteristic of his poetry, appear to us to consist evidently in this, that he has made more use of common topics, images and expressions, than any original poet of later times; and, at the same time, displayed more genius and originality than any recent author who has worked in the same materials. By the latter peculiarity, he has entitled himself to the admiration of every description of readers;—by the former, he is recommended in an especial manner to the inexperienced, at the hazard of some little offence to the more cultivated and fastidious.

In the choice of his subjects, for example, he does not attempt to interest merely by fine observation of pathetic sentiment, but takes the assistance of a story, and enlists the reader's curiosity among his motives for attention. Then his characters are all selected from the most common *dramatis personae* of poetry;—Kings, warriors, knights, outlaws, nuns, minstrels, secluded damsels, wizards, and true lovers. He never ventures to carry us into the cottage of the peasant, like Crabbe or Cowper; nor into the bosom of domestic privacy, like Campbell; nor among creatures of the imagination, like Southey or Darwin. Such personages, we readily admit, are not in themselves so interesting or striking as those to whom Mr Scott has devoted himself; but they are far less familiar in poetry—and are therefore more likely, perhaps, to engage the attention of those to whom poetry is familiar. In the management of the passions, again, Mr Scott appears to us to have pursued the same popular, and comparatively easy course. He has raised all the most familiar and poetical emotions, by the most obvious aggravations, and in the most compendious and judicious way. He has dazzled the reader with the splendour, and even warmed him with the transient beat of various affections; but he has nowhere fairly kindled him with enthusiasm, or melted him into tenderness. Writing for the world at large, he has wisely abstained from attempting to raise any passion to a height to which worldly people could not be transported; and contended himself with giving his reader the chance of feeling, as a brave, kind and affectionate gentleman should often feel in the ordinary course of his existence, without trying to breathe into him either that lofty enthusiasm which disdains the ordinary business and amusements of life, or that quiet and deep sensibility which unfits for all its pursuits. With regard to diction and imagery, too, it is quite obvious that Mr Scott has nor aimed at writing either in a pure or a very consistent style. He seems to have been anxious only to strike, and to be easily and universally understood; and, for this purpose, to have culled the most glittering and conspicuous expressions of the most popular authors, and to have interwoven them in splendid confusion with his own nervous diction and irregular versification. Indifferent whether he coins or borrows, and drawing with equal freedom on his memory and his imagination, he goes boldly forward, in full reliance on a neverfailing abundance; and dazzles, with his richness and variety, even those who are most apt to be offended with his glare and irregularity. There is nothing, in Mr Scott, of the severe and majestic style of Milton—or of the terse and fine composition of Pope—or of the elaborate elegance and melody of Campbell—or even of the flowing and redundant diction of Southey.—But there is a medley of bright images and glowing words, set carelessly and loosely together—a diction, tinged successively with the careless richness of Shakespeare, the harshness and antique simplicity of the old romances, the homeliness of vulgar ballads and anecdotes, and the sentimental glitter of the most modern poetry,—passing from the borders of the ludicrous to those of the sublime—alternately minute and energetic—sometimes artificial, and frequently negligent—but always full of spirit and vivacity,—abounding in images, that are striking, at first sight, to minds of every contexture—and never expressing a sentiment which it can cost the most ordinary reader any exertion to comprehend. . . .

Mr Scott has many other characteristic excellences; but we have already detained our readers too long with this imperfect sketch of his poetical character, and must proceed, without further delay, to give them some account of the work which is now before us. Of [*The Lady of the Lake*], upon the whole, we are inclined to think more highly than of either of his former publications. We are more sure, however, that it has fewer faults, than that it has greater beauties; and as its beauties bear a strong resemblance to those with which the public has already been made familiar in these celebrated works, we should not be surprised if its popularity were less splendid and remarkable. For our own parts, however, we are of opinion, that it will be oftener read hereafter than [*The Lay of the Last Minstrel* and *Marmion*]; and that, if it had appeared first in the series, their reception would have been less favourable than that which it has experienced. [*The Lady of the Lake*] is more polished in its diction, and more regular in its versification; the story is constructed with infinitely more skill and address; there is a greater proportion of pleasing and tender passages, with much less antiquarian detail; and, upon the whole, a larger variety of characters, more artfully and judiciously contrasted. There is nothing so fine, perhaps, as the battle in *Marmion*—or so picturesque as some of the scattered sketches in the *Lay*; but there is a richness and a spirit in the whole piece, which does not pervade either of these poems,—a profusion of incident, and a shifting brilliancy of colouring, that reminds us of the witchery of Ariosto,—and a constant elasticity, and occasional energy, which seem to belong more peculiarly to the author now before us. . . .

That the story [in *The Lady of the Lake*], upon the whole, is well digested and happily carried on, is evident from the hold it keeps the reader's attention through every part of its progress. It has the fault, indeed, of all stories that turn upon an *anagnorisis* or recognition, that the curiosity which is excited during the first reading, is extinguished for ever when we arrive at the discovery. This, however, is an objection which may be made, in some degree, to almost every story of interest; and we must say for Mr Scott, that his secret is very discreetly kept, and very felicitously revealed. If we were to scrutinize the fable with malicious severity, we might also remark, that Malcolm Græme has too insignificant a part assigned him, considering the favour in which he is held both by Ellen and the author; and that, in bringing out the shaded and imperfect character of Roderick Dhu, as a contrast to the purer virtue of his rival, Mr Scott seems to have fallen into the common error, of making him more interesting than him whose virtues he was intended to set off, and converted the villain of the piece in some measure into its hero. A modern poet, however, may perhaps be pardoned for an error, of which Milton himself is thought not to have kept clear, and for which there seems so natural a cause, in the difference between poetical and amiable characters. There are several improbabilities, too, in the story, which might disturb a scrupulous reader. Allowing that the king of Scotland might have twice disappeared for several days, without exciting any disturbance or alarm in his courtiers, it is certainly rather extraordinary, that neither the Lady Margaret, nor old Allan-bane, nor any of the attendants at the isle, should have recognized his person; and almost as wonderful, that he should have found any difficulty in discovering the family of his entertainer. There is something rather awkward, too, in the sort of blunder or misunderstanding (for it is no more) which gives occasion to Sir Roderick's Gathering and all its consequences; nor can any machinery be conceived more clumsy for effecting the deliverance of a distressed hero, than the introduction of a mad woman, who, without knowing or caring about the wanderer, warns him, *by a song,* to take care of the ambush that was set for him. The Maniacs of poetry have

indeed had a prescriptive right to be musical, since the days of Ophelia downwards; but it is rather a rash extension of this privilege to make them sing good sense, and to make sensible people be guided by them.

Before taking leave of the fable, we must be permitted to express our disappointment and regret at finding the general cast of the characters and incidents so much akin to those of Mr Scott's former publications. When we heard that the author of the [*The Lay of the Last Minstrel*] and of *Marmion* was employed upon a *Highland* story, we certainly expected to be introduced to a new creation, and to bid farewell, for a while, to knights, squires, courtiers, and chivalry;—but here they are all upon us again, in their old characters, and nearly in their old costume. The same age—the same sovereign—the same manners—the same ranks of society—the same tone, both for courtesy and for defiance. Loch-Katrine, indeed, is more picturesque than St Mary's Loch; and Roderick Dhu and his clan have some features of novelty;—but the Douglas and the King are the leading personages; and the whole interest of the story turns upon persons and events having precisely the same character and general aspect with those which gave their peculiar colour to the former poems. It is honourable to Mr Scott's genius, no doubt, that he has been able to interest the public so deeply with this third presentment of the same chivalrous scenes; but we cannot help thinking, that both his glory and our gratification would have been greater, if he had changed his hand more completely, and actually given us a true Celtic story, with all its drapery and accompaniments in a corresponding style of decoration.

Such a subject, we are persuaded, has very great capabilities, and only wants to be introduced to public notice by such a hand as Mr Scott's, to make a still more powerful impression than he has already effected by the resurrection of the tales of romance. There are few persons, we believe, of any degree of poetical susceptibility, who have wandered among the secluded vallies of the Highlands, and contemplated the singular people by whom they are still tenanted—with their love of music and of song—their hardy and irregular life, so unlike the unvarying toils of the Saxon mechanic—their devotion to their chiefs—their wild and lofty traditions—their national enthusiasm—the melancholy grandeur of the scenes they inhabit—and the multiplied superstitions which still linger among them,—without feeling, that there is no existing people so well adapted for the purposes of poetry, or so capable of furnishing the occasions of new and striking inventions. The great and continued popularity of Macpherson's Ossian, (though discredited as a memorial of antiquity, at least as much as is warranted by any evidence now before the public), proves how very fascinating a fabric might be raised upon that foundation by a more powerful or judicious hand. That celebrated translation, though defaced with the most childish and disgusting affectations, still charms with occasional gleams of a tenderness beyond all other tenderness, and a sublimity of a new character of dreariness and elevation; and, though patched with pieces of the most offensive plagiarism, still maintains a tone of originality which has recommended it in every nation of the civilized world. The cultivated literati of England, indeed, are struck with the affectation and the plagiarism, and renounce the whole work as tawdry and factitious; but the vulgar at home, and almost all classes of readers abroad, to whom those defects are less perceptible, still continue to admire; and few of our classical poets have so sure and regular a sale, both in our own and in other languages, as the singular collection to which we have just alluded. A great part of its charm, we think, consists in the novelty of its Celtic characters and scenery, and their singular aptitude for poetic combinations; and therefore it is that we are persuaded, that if Mr Scott's powerful and creative genius were to be turned in good earnest to such a subject, something might be produced still more impressive and original than even this age has yet witnessed.

It is now time, however, that we should lay before our readers some of the passages in the present poem which appear to us most characteristic of the peculiar genius of the author;—and the first that strikes us, in turning over the leaves, is the following fine description of Sir Roderick's approach to the isle, as described by the aged minstrel, at the close of his conversation with Ellen. The moving picture—the effect of the sounds—and the wild character and strong peculiar nationality of the whole procession, are given with inimitable spirit and power of expression.

> —"But hark, what sounds are these?
> My dull ears catch no faltering breeze,
> No weeping birch, nor aspens wake,
> Nor breath is dimpling in the lake;
> Still is the canna's hoary beard,
> Yet, by my minstrel faith, I heard—
> And hark again! some pipe of war
> Sends the bold pibroch from afar."—
>
> Far up the lengthened lake were spied
> Four darkening specks upon the tide,
> That, slow enlarging on the view,
> Four manned and masted barges grew,
> And bearing downwards from Glengyle;
> Steered full upon the lonely isle;
> The point of Brianchoil they passed,
> And, to the windward as they cast,
> Against the sun they gave to shine
> The bold Sir Roderick's bannered Pine.
> Nearer and nearer as they bear,
> Spears, pikes, and axes flash in air.
> Now might you see the tartans brave,
> And plaids and plumage dance and wave;
> Now see the bonnets sink and rise,
> As his tough oar the rower plies;
> See, flashing at each sturdy stroke,
> The wave ascending into smoke;
> See the proud pipers on the bow,
> And mark the gaudy streamers flow
> From their loud chanters down, and sweep
> The furrowed bosom of the deep,
> As, rushing through the lake amain,
> They plied the ancient Highland strain.
>
> Ever, as on they bore, more loud
> And louder rung the pibroch proud.

> At first the sounds, by distance tame,
> Mellowed along the waters came,
> And, lingering long by cape and bay,
> Wailed every harsher note away;
> Then, bursting bolder on the ear,
> The clan's shrill Gathering they could hear;
> Those thrilling sounds, that call the might
> Of old Clan-Alpine to the fight.
> Thick beat the rapid notes, as when
> The mustering hundreds shake the glen,
> And, hurrying at the signal dread,
> The battered earth returns their tread.
> Then prelude light, of livelier tone,
> Expressed their merry marching on,
> Ere peal of closing battle rose,
> With mingled outcry, shrieks, and blows;
> And mimic din of stroke and ward,
> As broad-sword upon target jarred;
> And groaning pause, ere yet again,
> Condensed, the battle yelled amain;
> The rapid charge, the rallying shout,
> Retreat borne headlong into rout,
> And bursts of triumph, to declare
> Clan-Alpine's conquest—all were there.
> Nor ended thus the strain; but slow,
> Sunk in a moan prolonged and low,
> And changed the conquering clarion swell,
> For wild lament o'er those that fell. . . .

One of the most striking passages in the poem, certainly, is that in which Sir Roderick is represented as calling up his men suddenly from their ambush, when Fitz-James expressed his impatience to meet, face to face, that murderous chieftain and his clan.

> "Have, then, thy wish!"—He whistled shrill,
>   And he was answered from the hill;
>   Wild as the scream of the curlieu,
>   From crag to crag the signal flew.
>   Instant, through copse and heath, arose
>   Bonnets and spears and bended bows;
>   On right, on left, above, below,
>   Sprung up at once the lurking foe;
>   From shingles grey their lances start,
>   The bracken-bush sends forth the dart,
>   The rushes and the willow-wand
>   Are bristling into axe and brand,
>   And every tuft of broom gives life
>   To plaided warrior armed for strife.
>   That whistle garrison'd the glen
>   At once with full five hundred men,
>   As if the yawning hill to heaven
>   A subterranean host had given.
>   Watching their leader's beck and will,
>   All silent there they stood and still.
>   Like the loose crags whose threatening mass
>   Lay tottering o'er the hollow pass,
>   As if an infant's touch could urge
>   Their headlong passage down the verge,
>   With step and weapon forward flung,
>   Upon the mountain-side they hung.
>   The mountaineer cast glance of pride

Along Benledi's living side,
Then fixed his eye and sable brow
Full on Fitz-James—"How say'st thou now?
These are Clan-Alpine's warriors true;
And, Saxon,—*I* am Roderick Dhu!"—
Fitz-James was brave:—Though to his heart
The life-blood thrilled with sudden start,
He mann'd himself with dauntless air,
Returned the Chief his haughty stare,
His back against a rock he bore,
And firmly placed his foot before:—
"Come one, come all! this rock shall fly
From its firm base as soon as I."—
Sir Roderick marked—and in his eyes
Respect was mingled with surprise,
And the stern joy which warriors feel
In foeman worthy of their steel.
Short space he stood—then waved his hand:
Down sunk the disappearing band;
Each warrior vanished where he stood,
In broom or bracken, heath or wood;
Sunk brand and spear and bended bow,
In osiers pale and copses low;
It seemed as' if their mother Earth
Had swallowed up her warlike birth.
The wind's last breath had tossed in air,
Pennon, and plaid, and plumage fair,—
The next but swept a lone hill side,
Where heath and fern were waving wide;
The sun's last glance was glinted back,
From spear and glaive, from targe and jack,—
The next, all unreflected, shone
On bracken green, and cold grey stone.

The following picture is of a very different character, and touched with the hand of a true poet.

Yet ere his onward way he took,
The Stranger cast a lingering look,
Where easily his eye might reach
The Harper on the islet beach,
Reclined against a blighted tree,
As wasted, grey, and worn as he.
To minstrel meditation given,
His reverend brow was raised to heaven,
As from the rising sun to claim
A sparkle of inspiring flame.
His hand, reclined upon the wire,
Seemed watching the awakening fire;
So still he sate, as those who wait
Till judgment speak the doom of fate;
So still, as if no breeze might dare
To lift one lock of hoary hair;
So still, as life itself were fled,
In the last sound his harp had sped.
Upon a rock with lichens wild,
Beside him Ellen sate and smiled, . . .

These passages, though taken with very little selection, are favourable specimens, we think, on the whole, of the execution of the work before us. We had marked several of an opposite character; but, fortunately for Mr Scott, we have already extracted so much, that we shall scarcely have room to take any notice of them; and must condense all our vituperation into a very insignificant compass. One or two things, however, we think it our duty to point out. Though great pains have evidently been taken with Brian the Hermit, we think his whole character a failure, and mere deformity,—hurting the interest of the story by its improbability, and rather heavy and disagreeable, than sublime or terrible in its details. The quarrel between Malcolm and Roderick, in the second canto, is also ungraceful and offensive. There is something foppish and out of character in Malcolm's rising to lead out Ellen from her own parlour; and the sort of wrestling match that takes place between the rival chieftains on the occasion, is humiliating, and indecorous. The greatest blemish in the poem, however, is the ribaldry and dull vulgarity which is put into the mouths of the soldiery in the guard-room. Mr Scott has condescended to write a song for them, which will be read with pain, we are persuaded, even by his warmest admirers: and his whole genius, and even his power of versification, seems to desert him when he attempts to repeat their conversation. Here is some of the stuff which has dropped, in this inauspicious attempt, from the pen of one of the [finest] poets of his age or country.

"Old dost thou wax, and wars grow sharp;
Thou now hast glee-maiden and harp,
Get thee an ape, and trudge the land,
The leader of a juggler band."—

"No, comrade;—no such fortune mine.
After the fight, these sought our line,
That aged harper and the girl;
And, having audience of the Earl,
Mar bade I should purvey them steed,
And bring them hitherward with speed.
Forbear your mirth and rude alarm,
For none shall do them shame or harm."—
"Hear ye his boast!" cried John of Brent,
Ever to strife and jangling bent,—
"Shall he strike doe beside our lodge,
And yet the jealous niggard grudge
To pay the forester his fee?
I'll have my share howe'er it be."

His Highland freebooters, indeed, do not use a much nobler style. For example—

"It is, because last evening-tide
Brian an augury hath tried,
Of that dread kind which must not be
Unless in dread extremity,
The Taghairm called; by which, afar,
Our sires foresaw the events of war.
Duncraggan's milk white bull they slew,"—
"Ah! well the gallant brute I knew;
The choicest of the prey we had,
When swept our merry men Gallangad.
Sore did he cumber our retreat;
And kept our stoutest kernes in awe,
Even at the pass of Beal'maha."

Scarcely more tolerable are such expressions as—

> For life is Hugh of Larbert lame;—

or that unhappy couplet, where the king himself is in such distress for a rhyme, as to be obliged to apply to one of the most obscure Saints on the kalendar.

> 'Tis James of Douglas, *by Saint Serle*;
> The uncle of the banish'd Earl.

We would object, too, to such an accumulation of strange words as occurs in these three lines.

> Fleet foot on the *correi;*
> Sage counsel *in Cumber;*
> Red hand in the foray,

Nor can we relish such babyish verses as

> He will return:—dear lady, trust:—
> With joy, return. He will,—he must.

> . . . . .

> Nay, lovely Ellen! Dearest! nay.

These, however, and several others that might be mentioned, are blemishes which may well be excused in a poem of more than five thousand lines, produced so soon after another still longer: and though they are blemishes which it is proper to notice, because they are evidently of a kind that may be corrected, it would be absurd, as well as unfair, to give them any considerable weight in our general estimate of the work, or of the powers of the author. Of these, we have already spoken at sufficient length; and must now take an abrupt leave of Mr Scott, by expressing our hope, and tolerably confident expectation, of soon meeting with him again. That he may injure his popularity by the mere profusion of his publications, is no doubt possible; though many of the most celebrated poets have been among the most voluminous: but, that the public must gain by this liberality, does not seem to admit of any question. If our poetical treasures were increased by the publication of **Marmion** and the **Lady of the Lake,** notwithstanding the existence of great faults in both these works, it is evident that we should be still richer if we possessed fifty poems of the same merit; and, therefore, it is for our interest, whatever it may be as to his, that their author's muse should continue as prolific as she has hitherto been. If Mr Scott will only vary his subjects a little more, indeed, we think we might engage to insure his own reputation against any material injury from their rapid parturition; and, as we entertain very great doubts whether much greater pains would enable him to write much better poetry, we would rather have two beautiful poems, with the present *quantum* of faults—than one, with only one tenth part less alloy. He will always be a poet, we fear, to whom the fastidious will make great objections; but he may easily find, in his popularity, a compensation for their scruples. He has *the jury* hollow in his favour; and though *the court* may think that its directions have not been sufficiently attended to, it will not quarrel with the verdict.

Samuel Taylor Coleridge on Scott's Poetry:

I am reading Scott's **Lady of the Lake,** having had it on my table week after week till it cried shame to me for not opening it. But truly as far as I can judge from the first 98 pages, my reluctance was not unprophetic. Merciful Apollo!—what an easy pace dost thou jog on with thy unspurred yet unpinioned Pegasus!—The movement of the Poem (which is written with exception of a multitude of Songs in regular 8 syllable Iambics) is between a sleeping Canter and a Marketwoman's trot—but it is endless—I seem never to have made any way—I never remember a narrative poem in which I felt the sense of Progress so languid—. There are (speaking of the first 90 pages) two or three pleasing Images—that of the Swan, p. 25.—is the best—the following seems to me to demand something more for it's introduction than a mere description for description's sake supplies—

> With boughs that quaked* at every breath   *!
> Gray Birch and Aspen wept beneath;
> Aloft, the ash and warrior Oak
> Cast anchor in the rifted Rock—

I wish, there were more faults of this kind—if it be a fault—yet I think, if it had been a beauty, it would not have instantly struck a perplexed feeling in my mind—as it did, & continues to do—a *doubt*—I seem to feel, that I could have used the metaphor; but not in that way, or without other images or feelings in tune with it. . . .

In short, what I felt in **Marmion,** I feel still more in the **Lady of the Lake**—viz. that a man accustomed to cast words in metre and familiar with descriptive Poets & Tourists, himself a Picturesque Tourist, must be troubled with a mental Strangury, if he could not lift up his leg six times at six different Corners, and each time p— a canto.

> *Samuel Taylor Coleridge, in a letter to William*
> *Wordsworth written early October 1810,*
> *published in* Collected Letters of Samuel
> Taylor Coleridge Volume III: 1807-1814,
> *edited by Earl Leslie Griggs, Oxford at*
> *the Clarendon Press, 1959, pp. 290-92.*

John Ruskin (essay date 1856)

SOURCE: "Of Modern Landscape," in *The Works of John Ruskin* Vol. 5, edited by E. T. Cook and Alexander Wedderburn, George Allen, 1904, pp. 317–53.

[*Ruskin was an English critic, essayist, historian, poet, novella writer, autobiographer, and diarist. Endowed with a passion for reforming what he considered his "blind and wandering fellow-men" and convinced that he had "perfect judgment" in aesthetic matters, Ruskin was the author of over forty books and several hundred essays and lectures that expounded his theories of aesthetics, morality, history, economics, and social reform. Although his views were often controversial and critical reception of his works was frequently hostile, Ruskin became one of the Victorian era's most prominent and influential critics of art and society. Perhaps as well known today for the eloquence of his prose as for the content of his works, Ruskin is considered one of the greatest prose stylists in the English language. In this excerpt, first published in Volume III of Ruskin's* Modern Painters *(1856), the critic discusses Scott as a figure who embodied the most important social and artistic elements of his era. Ruskin notes Scott's "pure passion for nature" and praises his use of color imagery to depict the natural world.*]

I think it probable that many readers may be surprised at my calling Scott the great representative of the mind of the age in literature. Those who can perceive the intense penetrative depth of Wordsworth, and the exquisite finish and melodious power of Tennyson, may be offended at my placing in higher rank that poetry of careless glance, and reckless rhyme, in which Scott poured out the fancies of his youth; and those who are familiar with the subtle analysis of the French novelists, or who have in anywise submitted themselves to the influence of German philosophy, may be equally indignant at my ascribing a principality to Scott among the literary men of Europe, in an age which has produced De Balzac and Goethe.

So also in painting, those who are acquainted with the sentimental efforts made at present by the German religious and historical schools, and with the disciplined power and learning of the French, will think it beyond all explanation absurd to call a painter of light water-colour landscapes, eighteen inches by twelve, the first representative of the arts of the age. I can only crave the reader's patience, and his due consideration of the following reasons for my doing so, together with those advanced in the farther course of the work.

I believe the first test of a truly great man is his humility. I do not mean, by humility, doubt of his own power, or hesitation in speaking his opinions; but a right understanding of the relation between what *he* can do and say, and the rest of the world's sayings and doings. All great men not only know their business, but usually know that they know it; and are not only right in their main opinions, but they usually know that they are right in them; only, they do not think much of themselves on that account. Arnolfo knows he can build a good dome at Florence; Albert Dürer writes calmly to one who had found fault with his work, "It cannot be better done;" Sir Isaac Newton knows that he has worked out a problem or two that would have puzzled anybody else,—only they do not expect their fellow-men therefore to fall down and worship them; they have a curious under-sense of powerlessness, feeling that the greatness is not *in* them, but *through* them; that they could not do or be anything else than God made them. And they see something Divine and God-made in every other man they meet, and are endlessly, foolishly, incredibly merciful.

Now, I find among the men of the present age, as far as I know them, this character in Scott and [English painter J. M. W.] Turner pre-eminently; I am not sure if it is not in them alone. I do not find Scott talking about the dignity of literature, nor Turner about the dignity of painting. They do their work, feeling that they cannot well help it; the story must be told, and the effect put down; and if people like it, well and good; and if not, the world will not be much the worse.

I believe a very different impression of their estimate of themselves and their doings will be received by any one who reads the conversations of Wordsworth or Goethe. The *slightest* manifestation of jealousy or self-complacency is enough to mark a second-rate character of the intellect; and I fear that, especially in Goethe, such manifestations are neither few nor slight.

Connected with this general humility, is the total absence of affectation in these men,—that is to say, of any assumption of manner or behaviour in their work, in order to attract attention. Not but that they are mannerists both. Scott's verse is strongly mannered, and Turner's oil painting; but the manner of it necessitated by the feelings of the men, entirely natural to both, never exaggerated for the sake of show. I hardly know any other literary or pictorial work of the day which is not in some degree affected. I am afraid Wordsworth was often affected in his simplicity, and De Balzac in his finish. Many fine French writers are affected in their reserve, and full of stage tricks in placing of sentences. It is lucky if in German writers we ever find so much as a sentence without affectation. I know no painters without it, except one or two Pre-Raphaelites (chiefly Holman Hunt), and some simple water-colour painters, as William Hunt, William Turner of Oxford, and the late George Robson; but these last have no invention and therefore . . . are excluded from the first rank of artists; and of the Pre-Raphaelites there is here no question, as they in no wise represent the modern school.

Again: another very important, though not infallible, test of greatness is, as we have often said, the appearance of Ease with which the thing is done. It may be that, as with Dante and Leonardo, the finish given to the work effaces the evidence of ease; but where the ease is manifest, as in Scott, Turner, and Tintoret, and the thing done is very noble, it is a strong reason for placing the men above those who confessedly work with great pains. Scott writing his chapter or two before breakfast—not retouching; Turner finishing a whole drawing in a forenoon before he goes out to shoot (providing always the chapter and drawing be good), are instantly to be set above men who confessedly have spent a day over the work, and think the hours well spent if it has been a little mended between sunrise and sunset. Indeed, it is no use for men to think to appear great by working fast, dashing, and scrawling; the thing they do must be good and great, cost what time it may; but if it *be* so, and they have honestly and unaffectedly done it with *no effort,* it is probably a greater and better thing than the result of the hardest efforts of others.

Then, as touching the kind of work done by these two men, the more I think of it I find this conclusion more impressed upon me,—that the greatest thing a human soul ever does in this world is to *see* something, and tell what it *saw* in a plain way. Hundreds of people can talk for one who can think, but thousands can think for one who can see. To see clearly is poetry, prophecy, and religion,—all in one.

Therefore, finding the world of Literature more or less divided into Thinkers and Seers, I believe we shall find also that the Seers are wholly the greater race of the two. A true Thinker who has practical purpose in his thinking, and is sincere, as Plato, or Carlyle, or Helps, becomes in some sort a seer, and must be always of infinite use in his generation; but an affected Thinker, who supposes his thinking of any other importance than as it tends to work, is about the vainest kind of person that can be found in the occupied classes. Nay, I believe that metaphysicians and philosophers are, on the whole, the greatest troubles the world has got to deal with; and that while a tyrant or bad man is of some use in teaching people submission or in-dignation, and a thoroughly idle man is only harmful in setting an idle example, and communicating to other lazy people his own lazy misunderstandings, busy metaphysi-cians are always entangling *good* and *active* people, and weaving cobwebs among the finest wheels of the world's business; and are as much as possible, by all prudent persons, to be brushed out of their way, like spiders, and the meshed weed that has got into the Cambridgeshire canals, and other such impediments to barges and busi-ness. And if we thus clear the metaphysical element out of modern literature, we shall find its bulk amazingly dimin-ished, and the claims of the remaining writers, or of those whom we have thinned by this abstraction of their straw stuffing, much more easily adjusted.

Again: the mass of sentimental literature, concerned with the analysis and description of emotion, headed by the poetry of Byron, is altogether of lower rank than the lit-erature which merely describes what it saw. The true Seer always feels as intensely as any one else; but he does not much describe his feelings. He tells you whom he met, and what they said; leaves you to make out, from that, what they feel, and what he feels, but goes into little de-tail. And, generally speaking, pathetic writing and careful explanation of passion are quite easy, compared with this plain recording of what people said and did, or with the right invention of what they are likely to say and do; for this reason, that to invent a story, or admirably and thor-oughly tell any part of a story, it is necessary to grasp the entire mind of every personage concerned in it, and know precisely how they would be affected by what happens; which to do requires a colossal intellect: but to describe a separate emotion delicately, it is only needed that one should feel it oneself; and thousands of people are capa-ble of feeling this or that noble emotion, for one who is able to enter into all the feelings of somebody sitting on the other side of the table. Even, therefore, where this sentimental literature is first-rate, as in passages of Byron, Tennyson, and Keats, it ought not to be ranked so high as the Creative. . . .

Having, therefore, cast metaphysical writers out of our way, and sentimental writers into the second rank, I do not think Scott's supremacy among those who remain will any more be doubtful; nor would it, perhaps, have been doubt-ful before, had it not been encumbered by innumerable faults and weaknesses. But it is pre-eminently in these faults and weaknesses that Scott is the representative of the mind of his age; and because he is the greatest man born amongst us, and intended for the enduring type of us, all our principal faults must be laid on his shoulders, and he must bear down the dark marks to the latest ages; while the smaller men, who have some special work to do, per-haps not so much belonging to this age as leading out of it to the next, are often kept providentially quit of the encumbrances which they had not strength to sustain, and are much smoother and pleasanter to look at, in their way: only that is a smaller way.

Thus, the most startling fault of the age being its faithless-ness, it is necessary that its greatest man should be faith-less. Nothing is more notable or sorrowful in Scott's mind than its incapacity of steady belief in anything. He cannot even resolve hardily to believe in a ghost, or a water-spirit; always explains them away in an apologetic man-ner, not believing, all the while, even in his own explana-tion. He never can clearly ascertain whether there is any-thing behind the arras but rats; never draws sword, and thrusts at it for life or death; but goes on looking at it timidly, and saying, "It must be the wind." He is educated a Presbyterian, and remains one, because it is the most sensible thing he can do if he is to live in Edinburgh; but he thinks Romanism more picturesque, and profaneness more gentlemanly; does not see that anything affects hu-man life but love, courage, and destiny; which are, indeed, not matters of faith at all, but of sight. Any gods but those are very misty in outline to him; and when the love is laid ghastly in poor Charlotte's coffin; and the courage is no more of use,—the pen having fallen from between the fingers; and destiny is sealing the scroll,—the God-light is dim in the tears that fall on it.

He is in all this the epitome of his epoch.

Again: as another notable weakness of the age is its habit of looking back, in a romantic and passionate idleness, to the past ages, not understanding them all the while, nor really desiring to understand them, so Scott gives up near-ly the half of his intellectual power to a fond, yet purpose-less, dreaming over the past, and spends half his literary labours in endeavours to revive it, not in reality, but on the stage of fiction; endeavours which were the best of the kind that modernism made, but still successful only so far as Scott put, under the old armour, the everlasting human nature which he knew; and totally unsuccessful, so far as concerned the painting of the armour itself, which he knew *not*. The excellence of Scott's work is precisely in propor-tion to the degree in which it is sketched from present nature. His familiar life is inimitable. . . . But his romance and antiquarianism, his knighthood and monkery; are all false, and he knows them to be false; does not care to make them earnest; enjoys them for their strangeness. . . .

Again: more than any age that had preceded it, ours had been ignorant of the meaning of the word "Art." It had not a single fixed principle, and what unfixed principles it worked upon were all wrong. It was necessary that Scott should know nothing of art. He neither cared for painting nor sculpture, and was totally incapable of forming a judgment about them. He had some confused love of Gothic architecture, because it was dark, picturesque, old, and like nature; but could not tell the worst from the best, and built for himself perhaps the most incongruous and ugly pile that gentlemanly modernism ever designed; marking, in the most curious and subtle way, that mingling of reverence with irreverence which is so striking in the age; he reverences Melrose, yet casts one of its piscinas, puts a modern steel grate into it, and makes it his fireplace. Like all pure moderns, he supposes the Gothic barbarous, notwithstanding his love of it; admires, in an equally ignorant way, totally opposite styles; is delighted with the new town of Edinburgh; mistakes its dulness for purity of taste, and actually compares it, [in **Marmion**], in its deathful formality of street, as contrasted with the rudeness of the old town, to Britomart taking off her armour.

Again: as in reverence and irreverence, so in levity and melancholy, we saw that the spirit of the age was strangely interwoven. Therefore, also, it is necessary that Scott should be light, careless, unearnest, and yet eminently sorrowful. Throughout all his work there is no evidence of any purpose but to while away the hour. His life had no other object than the pleasure of the instant, and the establishing of a family name. All his thoughts were, in their outcome and end, less than nothing, and vanity. And yet, of all poetry that I know, none is so sorrowful as Scott's. Other great masters are pathetic in a resolute and predetermined way, when they choose; but, in their own minds, are evidently stern or hopeful, or serene; never really melancholy. Even Byron is rather sulky and desperate than melancholy; Keats is sad because he is sickly; Shelley because he is impious; but Scott is inherently and consistently sad. Around all his power, and brightness, and enjoyment of eye and heart, the faraway Æolian knell is for ever sounding; there is not one of those loving or laughing glances of his but it is brighter for the film of tears; his mind is like one of his own hill rivers,—it is white, and flashes in the sun fairly, careless, as it seems, and hasty in its going, but

> Far beneath, where slow they creep
> From pool to eddy, dark and deep,
> Where alders moist, and willows weep,
>   You hear her streams repine.
>   [*Marmion*]

Life begins to pass from him very early; and while Homer sings cheerfully in his blindness, and Dante retains his courage, and rejoices in hope of Paradise, through all his exile, Scott, yet hardly past his youth, lies pensive in the sweet sunshine and among the harvests of his native hills.

> Blackford, on whose uncultured breast,
>   Among the broom, and thorn, and whin,
> A truant boy, I sought the nest,
> Or listed as I lay at rest,
>   While rose on breezes thin
> The murmur of the city crowd,

> And, from his steeple jangling loud,
>   St. Giles's mingling din!
> Now, from the summit to the plain,
> Waves all the hill with yellow grain;
>   And on the landscape as I look,
> Naught do I see unchanged remain,
>   Save the rude cliffs and chiming brook;
> To me they make a heavy moan
> Of early friendships past and gone.
>   [*Marmion*]

Such, then, being the weaknesses which it was necessary that Scott should share with his age, in order that he might sufficiently represent it, and such the grounds for supposing him, in spite of all these weaknesses, the greatest literary man whom that age produced, let us glance at the principal points in which his view of landscape differs from that of the mediævals.

I shall not endeavour now . . . to give a complete analysis of all the feelings which appear to be traceable in Scott's allusions to landscape scenery,—for this would require a volume,—but only to indicate the main points of differing character between his temper and Dante's. Then we will examine in detail, not the landscape of literature, but that of painting, which must, of course, be equally, or even in a higher degree, characteristic of the age.

And, first, observe Scott's habit of looking at nature neither as dead, or merely material, in the way that Homer regards it, nor as altered by his own feelings, in the way that Keats and Tennyson regard it, but as having an animation and pathos of *its own*, wholly irrespective of human presence or passion,—an animation which Scott loves and sympathises with, as he would with a fellow-creature, forgetting himself altogether, and subduing his own humanity before what seems to him the power of the landscape.

> You lonely Thorn,—would he could tell
> The changes of his parent dell,
> Since he, so grey and stubborn now,
> Waved in each breeze a sapling bough:
> Would he could tell, how deep the shade
> A thousand mingled branches made,
> How broad the shadows of the oak,
> How clung the rowan to the rock,
> And through the foliage show'd his head,
> With narrow leaves and berries red!
>   [*Marmion*]

Scott does not dwell on the grey stubbornness of the thorn, because he himself is at that moment disposed to be dull or stubborn; neither on the cheerful peeping forth of the rowan, because he himself is at that moment cheerful or curious: but he perceives them both with the kind of interest that he would take in an old man or a climbing boy; forgetting himself, in sympathy with either age or youth.

> And from the grassy slope he sees
> The Greta flow to meet the Tees;
> Where issuing from her darksome bed,

She caught the morning's eastern red,
And through the softening vale below
Roll'd her bright waves in rosy glow,
All blushing to her bridal bed,
Like some shy maid, in convent bred;
While linnet, lark, and blackbird gay
Sing forth her nuptial roundelay.

[*Rokeby*]

Is Scott, or are the persons of his story, gay at this moment? Far from it. Neither Scott nor Risingham is happy, but the Greta is; and all Scott's sympathy is ready for the Greta, on the instant.

Observe, therefore, this is not *pathetic* fallacy; for there is no passion in *Scott* which alters nature. It is not the lover's passion, making him think the larkspurs are listening for his lady's foot; it is not the miser's passion, making him think that dead leaves are falling coins; but it is an inherent and continual habit of thought, which Scott shares with the moderns in general, being, in fact, nothing else than the instinctive sense which men must have of the Divine presence, not formed into distinct belief. In the Greek it created . . . the faithfully believed gods of the elements; in Dante and the mediævals, it formed the faithfully believed angelic presence: in the modern, it creates no perfect form, does not apprehend distinctly any Divine being or operation; but only a dim, slightly credited animation in the natural object, accompanied with great interest and affection for it. This feeling is quite universal with us, only varying in depth according to the greatness of the heart that holds it; and in Scott, being more than usually intense, and accompanied with infinite affection and quickness of sympathy, it enables him to conquer all tendencies to the pathetic fallacy, and, instead of making Nature anywise subordinate to himself, he makes himself subordinate to *her*—follows her lead simply—does not venture to bring his own cares and thoughts into her pure and quiet presence—paints her in her simple and universal truth, adding no result of momentary passion or fancy, and appears, therefore, at first shallower than other poets, being in reality wider and healthier. "What am I?" he says continually, "that I should trouble this sincere nature with my thoughts. I happen to be feverish and depressed, and I could see a great many sad and strange things in those waves and flowers; but I have no business to see such things. Gay Greta! sweet harebells! *you* are not sad nor strange to most people; you are but bright water and blue blossoms; you shall not be anything else to me, except that I cannot help thinking you are a little alive,—no one can help thinking that." And thus, as Nature is bright, serene, or gloomy, Scott takes her temper, and paints her as she is; nothing of himself being ever intruded, except that far-away Æolian tone, of which he is unconscious; and sometimes a stray syllable or two, like that about Blackford Hill, distinctly stating personal feeling, but all the more modestly for that distinctness, and for the clear consciousness that it is not the chiming brook, nor the cornfields, that are sad, but only the boy that rests by them; so returning on the instant to reflect, in all honesty, the image of Nature, as she is meant by all men to be received; nor that in fine words, but in the first that come;

nor with comment of far-fetched thoughts, but with easy thoughts, such as all sensible men ought to have in such places, only spoken sweetly; and evidently also with an undercurrent of more profound reflection, which here and there murmurs for a moment, and which, I think, if we choose, we may continually pierce down to, and drink deeply from, but which Scott leaves us to seek, or shun, at our pleasure.

And in consequence of this unselfishness and humility, Scott's enjoyment of Nature is incomparably greater than that of any other poet I know. All the rest carry their cares to her, and begin maundering in her ears about their own affairs. Tennyson goes out on a furzy common, and sees it is calm autumn sunshine, but it gives him no pleasure. He only remembers that it is

Dead calm in that noble breast
Which heaves but with the heaving deep.

[*In Memoriam*]

He sees a thundercloud in the evening, and *would* have "doted and pored" on it, but cannot, for fear it should bring the ship bad weather. Keats drinks the beauty of nature violently; but has no more real sympathy with her than he has with a bottle of claret. His palate is fine; but he "bursts joy's grape against it" ["Ode to Melancholy"], gets nothing but misery, and a bitter taste of dregs, out of his desperate draught.

> **Instead of making Nature anywise subordinate to himself, Scott makes himself subordinate to her—follows her lead simply—does not venture to bring his own cares and thoughts into her pure and quiet presence—paints her in her simple and universal truth, adding no result of momentary passion or fancy.**
>
> **—John Ruskin**

Byron and Shelley are nearly the same, only with less truth of perception, and even more troublesome selfishness. Wordsworth is more like Scott, and understands how to be happy, but yet cannot altogether rid himself of the sense that he is a philosopher, and ought always to be saying something wise. He has also a vague notion that nature would not be able to get on well without Wordsworth; and finds a considerable part of his pleasure in looking at himself as well as at her. But with Scott the love is entirely humble and unselfish. "I, Scott, am nothing, and less than nothing; but these crags, and heaths, and clouds, how great they are, how lovely, how for ever to be beloved, only for their own silent, thoughtless sake!"

This pure passion for nature in its abstract being, is still increased in its intensity by the two elements above taken notice of,—the love of antiquity, and the love of colour and beautiful form, mortified in our streets, and seeking for food in the wilderness and the ruin: both feelings, observe, instinctive in Scott from his childhood, as everything that makes a man great is always.

> And well the lonely infant knew
> Recesses where the wallflower grew,
> And honeysuckle loved to crawl
> Up the low crag and ruin'd wall.
> I deem'd such nooks the sweetest shade
> The sun in all its round survey'd.
>
> [*Marmion*]

Not that these could have been instinctive in a child in the Middle Ages. The sentiments of a people increase or diminish in intensity from generation to generation,—every disposition of the parents affecting the frame of the mind in their offspring; the soldier's child is born to be yet more a soldier, and the politician's to be still more a politician; even the slightest colours of sentiment and affection are transmitted to the heirs of life; and the crowning expression of the mind of a people is given when some infant of highest capacity, and sealed with the impress of this national character, is born where providential circumstances permit the full development of the powers it has received straight from Heaven, and the passions which it has inherited from its fathers.

This love of ancientness, and that of natural beauty, associate themselves also in Scott with the love of liberty, which was indeed at the root even of all his Jacobite tendencies in politics. For, putting aside certain predilections about landed property, and family name, and "gentleman-liness" in the club sense of the word,—respecting which I do not now inquire whether they were weak or wise,—the main element which makes Scott like Cavaliers better than Puritans is, that he thinks the former *free* and *master-ful* as well as loyal: and the latter *formal* and *slavish*. He is loyal, not so much in respect for law, as in unselfish love for the king; and his sympathy is quite as ready for any active borderer who breaks the law, or fights the king, in what Scott thinks a generous way, as for the king himself. Rebellion of a rough, free, and bold kind he is always delighted by; he only objects to rebellion on principle and in form: bareheaded and open-throated treason he will abet to any extent, but shrinks from it in a peaked hat and starched collar: nay, politically, he only delights in kingship itself, because he looks upon it as the head and centre of liberty; and thinks that, keeping hold of a king's hand, one may get rid of the cramps and fences of law; and that the people may be governed by the whistle, as a Highland clan on the open hill-side, instead of being shut up into hurdled folds or hedged fields, as sheep or cattle left masterless.

And thus Nature becomes dear to Scott in a threefold way; dear to him, first, as containing those remains or memories of the past, which he cannot find in cities, and giving hope of Prætorian mound or knight's grave, in every green slope and shade of its desolate places;—dear, secondly, in its moorland liberty, which has for him just as high a charm as the fenced garden had for the mediæval;

> For I was wayward, bold, and wild,
> A self-will'd imp—a grandame's child:
> But, half a plague, and half a jest,
> Was still endured, beloved, caressed.
> For me, thus nurtured, dost thou ask
> The classic poet's well-conn'd task?
> Nay, Erskine, nay. On the wild hill
> Let the wild heathbell flourish still;
> Cherish the tulip, prune the vine;
> But freely let the woodbine twine,
> And leave untrimm'd the eglantine:
>
> [*Marmion*]

—and dear to him, finally, in that perfect beauty, denied alike in cities and in men, for which every modern heart had begun at last to thirst, and Scott's, in its freshness and power, of all men's, most earnestly.

And in this love of beauty, observe, that . . . the love of *colour* is a leading element, his healthy mind being incapable of losing, under any modern false teaching, its joy in brilliancy of hue. Though not so subtle a colourist as Dante, which, under the circumstances of the age, he could not be, he depends quite as much upon colour for his power or pleasure. And, in general, if he does not mean to say much about things, the *one* character which he will give is colour, using it with the most perfect mastery and faithfulness, up to the point of possible modern perception. For instance, if he has a sea-storm to paint in a single line, he does not, as a feebler poet would probably have done, use any expression about the temper or form of the waves; does not call them angry or mountainous. He is content to strike them out with two dashes of Tintoret's favourite colours:

> *The blackening wave is edged with white,*
> To inch and rock the seamews fly.
>
> [*The Lay of the Last Minstrel*]

There is no form in this. Nay, the main virtue of it is, that it gets rid of all form. The dark raging of the sea—what form has that? But out of the cloud of its darkness those lightning flashes of the foam, coming at their terrible intervals—you need no more.

Again: where he has to describe tents mingled among oaks, he says nothing about the form of either tent or tree, but only gives the two strokes of colour:

> Thousand pavilions, *white as snow,*
> *Chequered* the borough moor below,
> Oft giving way, where still there stood
> Some relies of the old oak wood,
> That darkly huge did intervene,
> *And tamed the glaring white with green.*
>
> [*Marmion*]

Again: of tents at Flodden:

> Next morn the Baron climbed the tower,
> To view, afar, the Scottish power,
>   Encamped on Flodden edge.

The white pavilions made a show,
Like remnants of the winter snow,
    Along the dusky ridge.

Again: of trees mingled with dark rocks:

Until where Teith's young waters roll
Betwixt him and a wooded knoll,
That graced the *sable* strath with *green,*
The chapel of St. Bride was seen.
                    [*The Lady of the Lake*]

Again: there is hardly any form, only smoke and colour,
in his celebrated description of Edinburgh:

The wandering eye could o'er it go,
And mark the distant city glow
    With gloomy splendour red;
For on the smoke-wreaths, huge and slow,
That round her sable turrets flow,
    The morning beams were shed,
And tinged them with a lustre proud,
Like that which streaks a thunder-cloud.
Such dusky grandeur clothed the height,
Where the huge Castle holds its state,
    And all the steep slope down,
Whose ridgy back heaves to the sky,
Piled deep and massy, close and high,
    Mine own romantic town!
But northward far, with purer blaze,
On Ochil mountains fell the rays,
And as each heathy top they kissed,
It gleamed a purple amethyst.
Yonder the shores of Fife you saw;
Here Preston Bay and Berwick Law:
    And, broad between them, rolled
The gallant Frith the eye might note,
Whose islands on its bosom float,
    Like emeralds chased in gold.
                            [*Marmion*]

I do not like to spoil a fine passage by italicizing it; but
observe, the only hints at form, given throughout, are in
the somewhat vague words, "ridgy," "massy," "close," and
"high"; the whole being still more obscured by modern
mystery, in its most tangible form of smoke. But the *colours* are all definite; note the rainbow band of them—
gloomy or dusky red, sable (pure black), amethyst (pure
purple), green, and gold—a noble chord throughout; and
then, moved doubtless less by the smoky than the ame-
thystine part of the group,

Fitz Eustace' heart felt closely pent,
The spur he to his charger lent,
    And raised his bridle hand,
And making demivolte in air,
Cried, 'Where's the coward that would not dare
    To fight for such a land?'
                            [*Marmion*]

I need not multiply examples: the reader can easily trace
for himself, through verse familiar to us all, the force of
these colour instincts. I will therefore add only two passages, not so completely known by heart as most of the
poems in which they occur.

Twas silence all. He laid him down
Where purple heath profusely strown,
And throatwort with its azure bell,
And moss and thyme his cushion swell.
There, spent with toil, he listless eyed
The course of Greta's playful tide;
Beneath her banks, now eddying dun,
Now brightly gleaming to the sun,
As, dancing over rock and stone,
In yellow light her currents shone,
Matching in hue the favourite gem
Of Albin's mountain diadem.
Then tired to watch the currents play,
He turned his weary eyes away
To where the bank opposing show'd
Its huge, square cliffs through shaggy wood.
One, prominent above the rest,
Rear'd to the sun its pale grey breast;
Around its broken summit grew
The hazel rude and sable yew;
A thousand varied lichens dyed
Its waste and weather-beaten side;
And round its rugged basis lay,
By time or thunder rent away,
Fragments, that, from its frontlet torn,
Were mantled now by verdant thorn.
                            [*Rokeby*]

Note, first, what an exquisite chord of colour is given in
the succession of this passage. It begins with purple and
blue: then passes to gold, or cairngorm colour (topaz
colour); then to *pale grey,* through which the yellow passes into black; and the black, through broken dyes of li-
chen, into green. Note, secondly,—what is indeed so manifest throughout Scott's landscape as hardly to need pointing out,—the love of rocks, and true understanding of
their colours and characters, opposed as it is in every
conceivable way to Dante's hatred and misunderstanding
of them.

I have already traced, in various places, most of the causes of this great difference; namely, first, the ruggedness of
northern temper (compare [paragraph] 8 of the chapter on
the Nature of Gothic in the *Stones of Venice*); then the
really greater beauty of the northern rocks, as noted when
we were speaking of the Apennine limestone; then the
need of finding beauty among them, if it were to be found
anywhere,—no well-arranged colours being any more to
be seen in dress, but only in rock lichens; and, finally, the
love of irregularity, liberty, and power springing up in
glorious opposition to laws of prosody, fashion, and the
five orders.

The other passage I have to quote is still more interesting;
because it has *no form* in it *at all* except in one word
(chalice), but wholly composes its imagery either of colour, or of that delicate half-believed life which we have
seen to be so important an element in modern landscape.

The summer dawn's reflected hue
To purple changed Loch Katrine blue;
Mildly and soft the western breeze
Just kissed the lake, just stirred the trees;
And the pleased lake, like maiden coy,
Trembled but dimpled not for joy;
The mountain-shadows on her breast
Were neither broken nor at rest;
In bright uncertainty they lie,
Like future joys to Fancy's eye.
The water-lily to the light
Her chalice rear'd of silver bright;
The doe awoke, and to the lawn,
Begemm'd with dew-drops, led her fawn;
The grey mist left the mountain side;
The torrent show'd its glistening pride;
Invisible in fleckèd sky,
The lark sent down her revelry;
The blackbird and the speckled thrush
Good-morrow gave from brake and bush;
In answer coo'd the cushat dove
Her notes of peace, and rest, and love.

[**The Lady of the Lake**]

Two more considerations are, however, suggested by the above passage. The first, that the love of natural history, excited by the continual attention now given to all wild landscape, heightens reciprocally the interest of that landscape, and becomes an important element in Scott's description, leading him to finish, down to the minutest speckling of breast, and slightest shade of attributed emotion, the portraiture of birds and animals; in strange opposition to Homer's slightly named "sea-crows, who have care of the works of the sea," and Dante's singing-birds of undefined species. Compare carefully a passage too long to be quoted,—the 2nd and 3rd stanzas of Canto VI. of **Rokeby**.

The second and the last point I have to note, is Scott's habit of drawing a slight *moral* from every scene, just enough to excuse to his conscience his want of definite religious feeling; and that this slight moral is almost always melancholy. Here he has stopped short without entirely expressing it—

The mountain shadows
. . . lie
Like future joys to Fancy's eye.

[*Rokeby*]

His completed thought would be, that those future joys, like the mountain shadows, were never to be attained. It occurs fully uttered in many other places. He seems to have been constantly rebuking his own worldly pride and vanity, but never purposefully:

The foam-globes on her eddies ride,
Thick as the schemes of human pride
That down life's current drive amain,
As frail, as frothy, and as vain.

Foxglove, and nightshade, side by side,
Emblems of punishment and pride.

Her dark eye flashed; she paused, and sighed;—
'Ah what have I to do with pride!'

[**The Lady of the Lake**]

And hear the thought he gathers from the sunset (noting first the Turnerian colour,—as usual, its principal element):

The sultry summer day is done.
The western hills have hid the sun,
But mountain peak and village spire
Retain reflection of his fire.
Old Barnard's towers are purple still,
To those that gaze from Toller Hill;
Distant and high, the tower of Bowes
Like steel upon the anvil glows;
And Stanmore's ridge, behind that lay,
Rich with the spoils of parting day,
In crimson and in gold array'd,
Streaks yet awhile the closing shade:
Then slow resigns to darkening heaven
The tints which brighter hours had given.
Thus, aged men, full loath and slow,
The vanities of life forego,
And count their youthful follies o'er
Till Memory lends her light no more.

[*Rokeby*]

That is, as far as I remember, one of the most finished pieces of sunset he has given; and it has a woful moral; yet one which, with Scott, is inseparable from the scene.

Hark again:

'Twere sweet to mark the setting day
On Bourhope's lonely top decay;
And, as it faint and feeble died
On the broad lake and mountain's side,
To say, 'Thus pleasures fade away;
Youth, talents, beauty, thus decay,
And leave us dark, forlorn, and grey.'

[*Marmion*]

And again, hear Bertram:

Mine be the eve of tropic sun!
With disk like battle-target red,
He rushes to his burning bed,
Dyes the wild wave with bloody light,
Then sinks at once—and all is night.

[*Rokeby*]

In all places of this kind, where a passing thought is suggested by some external scene, that thought is at once a slight and sad one. Scott's deeper moral sense is marked in the *conduct* of his stories, and in casual reflections or exclamations arising out of their plot, and therefore sincerely uttered; as that of Marmion:

Oh, what a tangled web we weave,
When first we practise to deceive!

But the reflections which are founded, not on events, but on scenes, are, for the most part, shallow, partly insincere, and, as far as sincere, sorrowful. This habit of ineffective dreaming and moralizing over passing scenes, of which the earliest type I know is given in Jaques, is . . . usually the satisfaction made to our modern consciences for the want of a sincere acknowledgment of God in nature: and Shakspere has marked it as the characteristic of a mind "compact of jars" (Act II. Sc. VII., *As You Like It*). That description attaches but too accurately to all the moods which we have traced in the moderns generally, and in Scott as the first representative of them.

Arthur Symons (essay date 1904)

SOURCE: "Was Sir Walter Scott a Poet?" in *The Atlantic Monthly,* Vol. XCIV, No. 5, November, 1904, pp. 664-69.

[*Symons was a critic, poet, dramatist, short story writer, and editor who first gained notoriety in the 1890s as an English decadent. Eventually, he established himself as one of the most important critics of the modern era. Symons provided his English contemporaries with an appropriate vocabulary with which to define the aesthetic of symbolism in his book* The Symbolist Movement in Literature *(1899); furthermore, he laid the foundation for much of modern poetic theory by discerning the importance of the symbol as a vehicle by which a "hitherto unknown reality was suddenly revealed." Here, he argues that the qualities often praised in Scott's verse—narrative and description—have little to do with quality poetry. Symons also compares Scott's work to that of other poets, including Homer and Geoffrey Chaucer, and finds Scott's poetry much inferior.*]

Scott was twenty-six, the age of Keats at his death, before he wrote any original verse. He then wrote two poems to two ladies: one out of a bitter personal feeling, the other as a passing courtesy; neither out of any instinct for poetry. At twenty-four he had translated the fashionable *Lenore* of Bürger; afterwards he translated Goethe's youthful play, *Goetz von Berlichingen*. In 1802 he brought out the first two volumes of the *Minstrelsy of the Scottish Border,* in which the resurrection of the old ballad literature, begun in 1765 by Percy's *Reliques,* was carried on, and brought nearer to the interest of ordinary readers, who, in Scott's admirable introductions and notes, could find almost a suggestion of what was to come in the *Waverley Novels.* The *Lay of the Last Minstrel* was begun in 1802, and published, when Scott was thirty-four, in 1805. It was begun at the suggestion of the Duchess of Buccleugh, and continued to please her. Lockhart tells us: "Sir John Stoddart's casual recitation of Coleridge's unfinished *Christabel* had fixed the music of that noble fragment in his memory; and it occurred to him that, by throwing the story of Gilpin Horner into somewhat similar cadence, he might produce such an echo of the later metrical romances as would seem to connect his conclusion of the primitive *Sir Tristrem* with the imitation of the popular ballad in the *Grey Brother* and the *The Eve of St. John*." Its success

was immediate, and for seven years Scott was the most popular poet in England. When the first two cantos of *Childe Harold's Pilgrimage* appeared in 1812, there was a more popular poet in England, and Scott gave up writing verse, and, in the summer of 1814, took up and finished a story which he had begun in 1805, simultaneously with the publication of the *Lay of the Last Minstrel,*—the story of *Waverley*. The novelist died eleven years later, in 1825; but the poet committed suicide, with *Harold the Dauntless,* in 1817.

Until he was thirty-one Scott was unconscious that he had any vocation except to be a "half-lawyer, half-sportsman." At forty-three he discovered, sooner than all the world, that he had mistaken his vocation; and with that discovery came the other one, that he had a vocation, which he promptly adopted, and in which, with his genius for success, he succeeded, as instantaneously, and more permanently. He was always able to carry the world with him, as he carried with him his little world of friends, servants, dogs, and horses. And how deeply rooted in the work itself was this persuasive and overcoming power is proved by the fact that *Waverley* was published anonymously, and that the other novels were only known, for many years, as by the author of *Waverley*. None of the prestige of the poet was handed over to the novelist. Scott attacked the public twice over, quite independently, and conquered it both times easily.

Success with the public of one's own day is, of course, no fixed test of a man's work; and, while it is indeed surprising that the same man could be, first the most popular poet and then the most popular novelist of his generation, almost of his century, there is no cause for surprise that the public should have judged, in the one case, justly, and in the other unjustly. The voice of the people, the voice of the gods of the gallery, howls for or against qualities which are never qualities of literature; and the admirers of Scott have invariably spoken of his verse in praise that would be justified if the qualities for which they praise it were qualities supplementary to the essentially poetic qualities: they form no substitute. First Scott, and then Byron, partly in imitation of Scott, appealed to the public of their day with poems which sold as only novels have sold before or since, and partly because they were so like novels. They were, what every publisher still wants, "stories with plenty of action;" and the public either forgave their being in verse, or for some reason was readier than usual, just then, to welcome verse. It was Scott himself who was to give the novel a popularity which it had never had, even with Fielding and Richardson; and thus the novel had not yet flooded all other forms of literature for the average reader. Young ladies still cultivated ideals between their embroidery frames and their gilt harps. An intellectual democracy had not yet set up its own standards, and affected to submit art to its own tastes. This poetry, so like the most interesting, the most exciting prose, came at once on the wave of a fashion: the fashion of German ballads and "tales of wonder" and of the more genuine early ballads of England and Scotland; and also with a new, spontaneous energy all its own. And it was largely Scott himself who had helped to make the fashion by which he profited.

The metrical romance, as it was written by Scott, was avowedly derived from the metrical romances of the Middle Ages, one of which Scott had edited and even concluded in the original metre: the *Sir Tristrem* which he attributed to Thomas of Ercildoune. This *Sir Tristrem* is but one among many fragmentary versions of a lost original, giving the greatest of all legends of chivalry, the legend of Tristan and Iseult. The most complete and the finest version which we have is the poem in octosyllabic couplets written in German by Gottfried of Strassburg at the beginning of 1200. In this poem we see what a metrical romance can be, and it is no injustice to Scott if we put it for a moment beside his attempts to continue that heroic lineage.

A friend of mine, an Irish poet, was telling me the other day that he had found himself, not long ago, in a small town in the West of Ireland, Athenry, a little lonely place, with its ruined castle; and having to wait there, because he had taken the wrong train, he took out of his pocket a prose version of Gottfried's poem, and sat reading it for some hours. And suddenly a pang went through him, with an acute sense of personal loss, as he said to himself: "I shall never know the man who wrote that; I have never known any man who was such a gentleman." The poem, with all its lengthy adventures, its lengthy comments, is full of the passion of beauty; the love of Tristan and Iseult is a grave thing, coming to them in one cup with death. "Love," says the poet, "she who turneth the honey to gall, sweet to sour, and dew to flame, had laid her burden on Tristan and Iseult, and as they looked on each other their colour changed from white to red and from red to white, even as it pleased Love to paint them. Each knew the mind of the other, yet was their speech of other things." And, at their last parting, Iseult can say: "We two have loved and sorrowed in such true-fellowship unto this time, we should not find it over-hard to keep the same faith even to death. . . . Whatever land thou seekest, have a care for thyself—*my* life; for if I be robbed of that, then am I, *thy* life, undone. And myself, *thy* life, will I for thy sake, not for mine, guard with all care. For thy body and thy life, that know I well, they rest on me. Now bethink thee well of me, thy body, Iseult." This, remember, is in a metrical romance, written in the metre of the *Lady of the Lake*. Now turn to that poem, and read there:—

> Nor while on Ellen's faltering tongue
> Her filial welcomes crowded hung,
> Marked she, that fear (affection's proof)
> Still held a graceful youth aloof;
> No! not till Douglas named his name,
> Although that youth was Malcolm Graeme.

Much has been claimed for Scott's poetry because of its appeal to unpoetical persons, who, in the nature of things, would be likely to take an interest in its subject matter; and it has been thought remarkable that poetry composed, like much of *Marmion,* in the saddle, by one "through whose head a regiment of horse has been exercising since he was five years old," should have seemed genuine to sportsmen and to soldiers. A striking anecdote told by Lockhart allows us to consider the matter very clearly. "In the course of the day, when the *Lady of the Lake* first reached Sir Adam Ferguson, he was posted with his company on a point of ground exposed to the enemy's artillery, somewhere no doubt on the lines of Torres Vedras. The men were ordered to lie prostrate on the ground; while they kept that attitude, the captain, kneeling at the head, read aloud the description of the battle in Canto VI, and the listening soldiers only interrupted him by a joyous huzza when the French shot struck the bank close above them." "It is not often," says Mr. Hutton in his *Life of Scott,* "that martial poetry has been put to such a test." A test of what? Certainly not a test of poetry. An audience less likely to be critical, a situation less likely to induce criticism, can hardly be imagined. The soldiers would look for martial sentiments expressed with clear and matter-of-fact fervor. They would want no more and they would find no more; certainly no such intrusion of poetry as would have rendered the speech of Henry V before the battle of Agincourt but partially intelligible to them, though there Shakespeare is writing for once almost down to his audience. Scott's appeal is the appeal of prose, the thing and the feeling each for its own sake, with only that "pleasurable excitement," which Coleridge saw in the mere fact of metre, to give the illusion that one is listening to poetry.

Let me give an instance from another art. If, on his return to England, you had taken one of Sir Adam Ferguson's soldiers into a picture gallery, and there had been a Botticelli in one corner, and a Titian in another, and between two Bellini altar-pieces there had been a modern daub representing a battle, in which fire and smoke were clearly discernible, and charging horses rolled over on their riders, and sabres were being flourished in a way very like the trooper's way, is there much doubt which picture would go straight home to the soldier? There, it might be said, is a battle-piece, and the soldier goes up to it, examines it, admires it, swears that nothing more natural was ever painted. Is that a "test" of the picture? Are we to say: this picture has been proved to be sincere, natural, approvable by one who has been through the incident which it records, and therefore (in spite of its total lack of every fine quality in painting) a good picture? No one, I think, would take the soldier's word for that: why should we take his word on a battle-piece which is not painted, but written?

A great many of the merits which people have accustomed themselves to see in Scott come from this kind of miscalculation. Thus, for instance, we may admit, with Mr. Palgrave, that Scott "attained eminent success" in "sustained vigour, clearness, and interest in narration." "If we reckon up the poets of the world," continues Mr. Palgrave, "we may be surprised to find how very few (dramatists not included) have accomplished this, and may be hence led to estimate Scott's rank in his art more justly." But is not this rather a begging of the question? Scott wrote in metre, and in some of his metrical narratives attained "sustained vigour, clearness, and interest in narration." But is there anything except the metre to distinguish these stories in verse from what, as Scott himself afterwards showed, might have been much better if they had been told in prose? Until this has been granted, no merit in narration will mean anything at all, in a consideration of poetry as poetry; any more than the noughts which you may add to the left of your figure 1, in the belief that you are adding million to million.

The fact is, that skill in story-telling never made any man a poet, any more than skill in constructing a drama. Shakespeare is not, in the primary sense, a poet because he is a great dramatist; he is a poet as much in the sonnets as in the plays, but he is a poet who chose to be also a playwright, and in measuring his greatness we measure all that he did as a playwright along with all that he did as a poet; his especial greatness being seen by his complete fusion of the two in one. And it is the same thing in regard to story-telling. Look for a moment at our greatest narrative poet, Chaucer. Chaucer tells his stories much better, much more pointedly, concisely, with much more of the qualities of the best prose narrative, than Scott; who seems to tell his stories rather for boys than for men, with what he very justly called "a hurried frankness of composition, which pleases soldiers, sailors, and young people of bold and active dispositions." Chaucer is one of the most masculine of story-tellers, and if you read, not even one of the *Canterbury Tales,* but a book of *Troilus and Cressida,* you will find in it something of the quality which we applaud in Balzac; an enormous interest in life, and an absorption in all its details, because those details go to make up the most absorbing thing in the world. But in Chaucer all this is so much prose quality added to a consummate gift for poetry. Chaucer is first of all a poet; it is almost an accident, the accident of his period, that he wrote tales in verse. In the Elizabethan age he would have been a great dramatist, and he has all the qualities that go to the making of a great lyrical poet. His whole vision of life is the vision of the poet; his language and versification have the magic of poetry; he has wisdom, tenderness, a high gravity, tinged with illuminating humor; no one in our language has said more touching and beautiful things, straight out of his heart, about birds and flowers and grass; he has ecstasy. In addition to all this he can tell stories: that was the new life that he brought into the poetry of his time, rescuing us from "the moral Gower" and much tediousness.

Now look at Scott: I do not say, ask Scott to be another Chaucer; but consider for a moment how much his admirers have to add to that all-important merit of "sustained vigour, clearness, and interest in narration." Well, it has been claimed, first and most emphatically, I think, by Sir Francis Doyle, that his poetry is "Homeric." Sir Francis Doyle says, in one of his lectures on Scott, given when Professor of Poetry at Oxford: "Now, after the immortal ballads of Homer, there are no ballad poems so full of the spirit of Homer as those of Scott." Homer, indeed, wrote of war and warriors, and so did Scott; Homer gives you vivid action, in swiftly moving verse, and so does Scott. But I can see little further resemblance, and I can see an infinite number of differences. No one, I suppose, would compare the pit-a-pat of Scott's octosyllabics with "the deep-mouthed music" of the Homeric hexameter. But Sir Francis Doyle sees in the opening of the *Lay of the Last Minstrel,* and not in this alone, "the simple and energetic style of Homer." Let me, then, take one single sentence

from that battle in Canto VI of the *Lady of the Lake,* and set against it a single sentence from one of the battle-pieces in the Iliad, in the prose translation of Mr. Lang. Here is Scott's verse:—

> Forth from the pass, in tumult driven,
> Like chaff before the wind of heaven,
>   The archery appear;
> For life! for life! their flight they ply,
> And shriek, and shout, and battle-cry,
> And plaids and bonnets waving high,
> And broadswords flashing to the sky,
>   Are maddening in the rear.

And here is Homer in English prose: "And as the gusts speed on, when shrill winds blow, on a day when dust lies thickest on the roads, even so their battle clashed together, and all were fain of heart to slay each other in the press with the keen bronze." Need I say more than these extracts say for themselves? What commonness and what distinction, what puerility of effort and what repose in energy!

Then there is Scott's feeling for nature. The feeling was deep and genuine, and in a conversation with Washington Irving Scott expressed it more poignantly than he has ever done in his verse. "When," he said, "I have been for some time in the rich scenery about Edinburgh, which is like ornamented garden land, I begin to wish myself back again among my own honest grey hills; and if I did not see the heather at least once a year, *I think I should die!"* There is a great deal of landscape painting in Scott's verse, and it has many good prose qualities: it is very definite, it is written "with the eye on the object," it is always sincere, in a certain sense; it is always felt sincerely. But it is not felt deeply, and it becomes either trite or generalized in its rendering into words. Take the description of Loch Katrine in the third canto of the *Lady of the Lake,* the final passage which Ruskin quotes for special praise in that chapter of *Modern Painters* which is devoted to a eulogy of Scott as the master of "the modern landscape" in verse. It gives a pretty and, no doubt, accurate picture, but with what vagueness, triteness, or conventionality of epithet! We get one line in which there is no more than a statement, but a statement which may have its place in poetry:—

> The grey mist left the mountain side.

In the next line we get a purely conventional rendering of what has evidently been both seen clearly and felt sympathetically:—

> The torrent showed its glistening pride.

How false and insincere that becomes in the mere putting into words! And what a *cliché* is the simile for the first faint shadows on the lake at dawn:—

> In bright uncertainty they lie,
> Like future joys to Fancy's eye.

Even in better landscape work, like the opening of the first introduction to *Marmion,* how entirely without magic is the observation, how superficial a notation of just what every one would notice in the scenery before him! To Ruskin, I know, all this is a part of what he calls Scott's unselfishness and humility, "in consequence of which Scott's enjoyment of Nature is incomparably greater than that of any other poet I know." Enjoyment, perhaps; but we are concerned, in poetry, with what a poet has made out of his enjoyment. Scott puts down in words exactly what the average person feels. Now it is the poet's business to interpret, illuminate, or at the least to evoke in a more exquisite form, all that the ordinary person is capable of feeling vaguely, by way of enjoyment. Until the poet has transformed enjoyment into ecstasy there can be no poetry. Scott's genuine love of nature, so profound in feeling, as his words to Washington Irving testify, was never able to translate itself into poetry; it seemed to become tongue-tied in metre.

And, also, there was in Scott a love of locality, which was perhaps more deeply rooted in him than his love of nature, just as his love of castles and armor and the bricabrac of mediævalism which filled his brain and his house was more deeply rooted than his love of the Middle Ages. "If," said Coleridge to Payne Collier, "I were called upon to form an opinion of Mr. Scott's poetry, the first thing I would do would be to take away all his names of old castles, which rhyme very prettily, and read very picturesquely; next, I would exclude the mention of all nunneries, abbeys, and priories, and I should then see what would be the residuum—how much poetry would remain." In all these things there was personal sincerity; Scott was following his feeling, his bias; but it has to be determined how far, and in how many instances, when he said nature he meant locality, and when he said chivalry or romance, he meant that "procession of my furniture, in which old swords, bows, targets, and lances made a very conspicuous show," on the way to Abbotsford.

Ruskin's special praise of Scott, in his attitude toward nature, is that Scott did not indulge in "the pathetic fallacy" of reading one's own feelings into the aspect of natural things. This, in the main, is true, in spite of those little morals which Scott attaches to what he sees. But it is hardly more than a negative merit, at the best; and it is accompanied by no intimacy of insight, no revealing passion; aspects are described truthfully, and with sympathy, and that is all.

Throughout the whole of his long poems, and throughout almost the whole of his work in verse, Scott remains an improviser in rhyme, not a poet. But in a few of the songs contained in the novels, songs written after he had practically given up writing verse, flickering touches of something very like poetry are from time to time seen. In one song of four stanzas, **"Proud Maisie,"** published in 1818 in the *Heart of Midlothian,* Scott seems to me to have become a poet. In this poem, which is like nothing else he ever wrote, some divine accident has brought all the diffused poetical feeling of his nature to a successful birth. Landor, who seems to have overlooked this perfect lyric, thought there was one line of genuine poetry in Scott's verse, which he quotes from an early poem on Helvellyn.

But I cannot feel that this line is more than a pathetic form of rhetoric. In **"Proud Maisie"** we get, for once, poetry.

For the rest, all Scott's verse is written for boys, and boys, generation after generation, will love it with the same freshness of response. It has adventure, manliness, bright landscape, fighting, the obvious emotions; it is like a gallop across the moors in a blithe wind; it has plenty of story, and is almost as easily read as if it were prose. The taste for it may well be outgrown with the first realization of why Shakespeare is looked upon as the supreme poet. Byron usually follows Scott in the boy's head, and drives out Scott, as that infinitely greater, though imperfect, force may well do. Shelley often completes the disillusion. But it is well, perhaps, that there should be a poet for boys, and for those grown-up people who are most like boys; for those, that is, to whom poetry appeals by something in it which is not the poetry.

The deeds, not the thoughts of men, are Scott's matter; passions expressed in action, not passions analysed in the poetic laboratory. So potent was his genius, so inspiring the martial tramp and clang of his measures, that he made the new world listen to the accents of the old.

—*Andrew Lang, in his introduction to* **The Lyrics and Ballads of Sir Walter Scott,** *edited by Lang, J. M. Dent and Co., 1894.*

W. J. Courthope (essay date 1910)

SOURCE: "The Romance of History," in *A History of English Poetry* Vol. VI, Macmillan and Co., Limited, 1910, pp. 381–417.

[*Courthope was an English educator, poet, literary critic, and biographer whose most notable work is his six-volume* History of English Poetry (1895–1910). *Described by Stuart P. Sherman as a confirmed classicist in poetical theory, Courthope reacted against Romantic theory and practice and advocated a return to the heroic couplet and the satiric poetry characteristic of the age of Alexander Pope, whose collected works he edited. Courthope's criticism tends to center on the extent to which authors reflect the English character and traditions that had enabled the British empire to arise from the institutions of the Middle Ages. Below, he discusses the historic and social factors that played a role in Scott's immense popularity and comments on the poetic style that Scott developed and refined in response to these factors.*]

In considering the character of the metrical romantic movement, initiated by Scott, it would be idle to judge it by a purely external standard. On the first appearance of *The Lay of the Last Minstrel,* [Francis] Jeffrey, puzzled by the novel features of the poem, nevertheless attempted to subject them to the canons he had recently been endeavouring to formulate in *The Edinburgh Review.*

> "Our readers," says the New-Whig critic, "will easily perceive, that, however well calculated it may be for the introduction of picturesque imagery, or the display of extraordinary incidents, it has but little pretension to the praise of a regular or coherent narrative. The magic of the lady, the midnight visit to Melrose, and the mighty book of the enchanter, which occupy nearly one-third of the whole poem, and engross the attention of the reader for a long time after the commencement of the narrative, are of no use whatever in the subsequent development of the fable, and do not contribute either to the production or explanation of the incidents that follow" [*Edinburgh Review,* April 1805].

Marmion, which was guilty of the unpardonable sin of continuing to defy the new "Rules," fared even worse:

> "Though," says Jeffrey, "we think this last romance of Mr. Scott's about as good as the former, and allow that it affords great indications of poetical talent, we must remind our readers that we never entertained much partiality for this sort of composition, and ventured on a former occasion to express our regret that an author endowed with such talents should consume them in imitations of obsolete extravagances, and the representation of manners and sentiments, in which none of his readers can be supposed to take much interest except the few who can judge of their accuracy." [*Edinburgh Review,* April 1808]

The shrewdness, and, as far as they went, the justice of Jeffrey's strictures on *The Lay of the Last Minstrel,* were undeniable. But the delight with which the public received this poem and *Marmion* must have caused him, in spite of his self-sufficiency, to suspect that his purely negative method of criticism had scarcely enabled him to give an adequate appreciation of the new departure in taste, and when *The Lady of the Lake* presented itself for judgment, he showed himself rather more sympathetic.

> "There is nothing," he says, "cold, creeping, or feeble in all Mr. Scott's poetry; no laborious littleness or puling classical affectation. He has his failings, indeed, like other people, but he always attempts vigorously, and never fails in his immediate object, without accomplishing far beyond the reach of an ordinary writer. Even when he wanders from the paths of pure taste, he leaves behind him the footsteps of a powerful genius, and moulds the most humble of his materials into a form worthy of a nobler substance. Allied to this inherent vigour and animation, and in a great degree derived from it, is that air of facility and freedom which adds so peculiar a grace to most of Mr. Scott's compositions. He seems, indeed, never to think either of himself or his reader, but to be completely identified and lost in the personages with whom he is occupied; and the attention of the reader is consequently either transferred, unbroken, to their adventures, or if it glance back for a moment to the author, it is only to think how much more might be done by putting forth that

strength at full which has, without effort, accomplished so many wonders." [*Edinburgh Review,* August 1810]

Had Jeffrey been less absorbed in his Whig exclusiveness, he must have seen, first, that the characteristics of Scott's genius, which he noted with such admirable precision, could not be brought within the scope of his stereotyped system of criticism, and, next, that the unexampled popularity of the new style of poetry was in itself a phenomenon requiring separate attention. The tendencies of popular enthusiasm might no doubt misdirect the genius of the poet; but it was no less certain that so vast a volume of instinctive feeling could never have proceeded from a mere caprice of fashion, but must have somewhere a source deep in nature; and that, before an accurate judgment could be passed on the form of the poet's art, it was necessary to account for the great movement of the public taste.

The success of Scott's metrical romances was in fact due to this, that he was the first to discover a natural poetic form for the expression of mediæval tendencies which, though they had been submerged since the Revolution of 1688 by the inflowing tides of the Renaissance, formed an integral part of the historic life and imagination of the English people. . . . [The Romantic revival in English poetry] had its fountain-head in a certain reaction of the imagination against the regularity of civil order, and in a desire to restore the liberty and simplicity of an earlier stage of social life. This feeling welled upwards into light through a number of poetical and literary springs. It showed itself first in the revival of lyrical composition by Joseph Warton, Gray, and Collins. The stream thus formed was enlarged by various affluents. Thomas Warton contributed to the change of taste by his commentaries on *The Faery Queene* and Milton's early poems, as well as by his *History of English Poetry.* Bishop Percy popularised the idea of the Ballad by his *Reliques of Early English Poetry.* Macpherson and Chatterton strove to imitate the character of Ossianic sentiment or the idiom of monkish manuscripts. A host of explorers burst into "the silent sea" of Scandinavian mythology. The aim of all these writers was simply to satisfy the craving of the public imagination for novelty; none of them showed any desire to undermine the foundations of social order.

But the progress of events in the last quarter of the eighteenth century inflamed the passions of men; and just as the outbreak of the French Revolution produced a rupture of the Whig party in politics, so did it operate to break up the course of the Romantic movement in the region of imagination. One section of writers . . . allied themselves with the Revolution on its intellectual side, and adopted its ideas of sentiment and morality. Their chief aim was the emancipation of thought and taste from all traditional restrictions. In a crude and vulgar form the romantic tendency had already been foreshadowed by the revived Petrarchism of the Della Cruscan school of poetry, but it found a larger channel of expression in the fictions of the numerous men of letters who fell under the influence of Rousseau, and followed the lead of William Godwin in his speculations on Political Justice.

In the imagination of society at large, however, the influence of the French Revolution was chiefly manifested by the impulse it gave to ideas of action and adventure. If the source of inspiration for the philosophers of the Romantic school was French, Germany provided new materials for the dramatist and the lyrical poet. A certain amount of popularity was obtained on the stage by plays constructed after the fashion of Schiller's *Robbers* and Kotzebue's *Stranger*; but the poems which fell in most congenially with the new conditions of English taste were the wild ballads of Bürger. Matthew Lewis was the first to introduce his countrymen to the new legendary school of German lyrical composition, which seems itself to have been set in motion by the fame of Bishop Percy's *Reliques*; and imagination having been once infected with a taste for spectres, demons, and other mediæval superstitions, the German epidemic soon became universal. As Scott's example shows, the new impulse was felt by men whose conservative instincts in all matters of Church and State were deeply rooted, and whose taste was grounded on long study of the English classical style inaugurated by the Revolution of 1688: the author of *The Lay of the Last Minstrel* made his first modest appearance before the public as a translator of German ballads and a contributor to Lewis' *Tales of Wonder*.

But the invention of Scott was far too large and representative to restrict itself for long to so limited a sphere. In his temperament were happily blended all the conflicting energies by which the action of his age and nation was inspired. Whig by paternal connection and training, he was Tory by ancestral tradition and personal inclination, Jacobite by imagination and sentiment. While his education had made him historian, antiquary, and lawyer, his genius transmuted all the knowledge gained in these various departments into poetry. As a poet, he united Wordsworth's love of wild nature with Byron's passion for energetic action, and to Campbell's martial patriotism he added an intense enthusiasm for the soil of his country, which recalls Virgil's praises of Italy in the Second Georgic.

> O Caledonia! stern and wild,
> Meet nurse for a poetic child!
> Land of brown heath and shaggy wood,
> Land of the mountain and the flood,
> Land of my sires! what mortal hand
> Can e'er untie the filial band
> That knits me to thy rugged strand!
> Still, as I view each well-known scene,
> Think what is now, and what hath been,
> Seems as, to me, of all bereft,
> Sole friends thy woods and streams were left;
> And thus I love them better still,
> Even in extremity of ill.
> By Yarrow's streams still let me stray,
> Though none should guide my feeble way;
> Still feel the breeze down Ettrick break,
> Although it chill my withered cheek,
> Still lay my head by Teviot Stone,
> Though there, forgotten and alone,
> The Bard may draw his parting groan.
> [*The Lay of the Last Minstrel,* Canto VI.]

The personal passion which animates all Scott's best poetry has this peculiarity, that it is not conceived like the lyrics of most of his contemporaries in an egotistic but in a social and patriotic spirit. It is easy to see that it would have been impossible to express such an overmastering feeling in a shape which—to quote Jeffrey's phrase—would entitle it "to the praise of a regular or coherent narrative." The form that Scott found for his inspirations was in fact the result of a slow, almost an accidental, development, adapting itself instinctively to the windings of the public taste. Even in his early stage of ballad-imitation we find a mood quite different from that of the first pioneers of romantic revival like Hamilton of Bangour: his imitations show no trace of any effort to sustain the archaic effect of the old ballad style: he is interested in the action and incident of the story, and seeks to tell it in the way which he feels will appeal most strongly to a modern audience. Let the reader compare, for example, the first (or ancient) and the third (or modern) parts of *Thomas the Rhymer,* and he will note the germs and trace the genesis of the style which at a later date culminated in *The Lay of the Last Minstrel*. The ancient part of the poem is characterised by the genuine *naïveté* of a rude minstrel singing to an assembly of peasants; the modern, professing to be a reproduction of the tale of Tristrem and Iseult, as told by Thomas the Rhymer himself to knights and ladies, really reflects the feelings of a latter-day audience, sophisticated and sentimental, whose imaginations are tinctured indeed by a literary acquaintance with Percy's *Reliques,* but require a mediæval love-story to be presented to them in the full dress of the eighteenth-century assembly and ball-room. Scott's supplement contains a sprinkling of old words; the names of places, familiar and dear to the poet, are woven into the narrative, in a manner anticipating *The Lay of the Last Minstrel*; a *précis* is given of the story of Tristrem and Iseult; but how little he cared to preserve a superficial appearance of antiquity in his imitation may be judged by the stanzas in which True Thomas's style of narrative is described:

> Through many a maze the winning song
>   In changeful passion led,
> Till bent at length the listening throng
>   O'er Tristrem's dying bed.
> His ancient wounds their scars expand,
>   With agony his heart is wrung:
> O where is Isolde's lilye hand,
>   And where her soothing tongue?
> She comes! she comes! like flash of flame
>   Can lover's footsteps fly:
> She comes! she comes!—she only came
>   To see her Tristrem die.
>
> She saw him die; her latest sigh
>   Joined in a kiss his parting breath;
> The gentlest pair that Britain bare,
>   United are in death.

On the other hand, Thomas the Rhymer's fate, which is supposed to be recorded by a modern minstrel, is thus narrated:

Then forth they rushed: by Leader's tide
  A selcouth sight they see—
A hart and hind pace side by side
  As white as snow on Fairnalie.

. . . . .

To Learmont's tower a message sped,
  As fast as page might run;
And Thomas started from his bed,
  And soon his clothes did on.

First he woxe pale, and then woxe red;
  Never a word he spake but three:—
"My sand is run; my thread is spun;
  This sign regardeth me."

Finding that this mixture of the ancient style with the modern was highly acceptable to the public taste, Scott gradually extended his practice in the manner described by Lockhart and illustrated in the structure of *The Lay of the Last Minstrel*. Into the person of the Minstrel he projected his own feelings; and the conscious outbursts of sentiment with which the Minstrel opens each canto of his narrative have nothing in common with the rude simplicity of the old Ballad style. What ancient bard would have written?

Breathes there a man, with soul so dead,
Who never to himself hath said,
  "This is my own, my native land!"
Whose heart hath ne'er within him burned,
As home his footsteps he hath turned
  From wandering on a foreign strand!
If such there breathe, go, mark him well;
For him no Minstrel raptures swell;
High though his titles, proud his name,
Boundless his wealth as wish can claim;
Despite those titles, power, and pelf,
The wretch, concentred all in self,
Living, shall forfeit fair renown,
And, doubly dying, shall go down
To the vile dust, from whence he sprung,
Unwept, unhonoured, and unsung.

The harp may be that of the aged Minstrel who is supposed to have played before

King Charles the Good
When he kept court in Holyrood;

but the voice is the voice of the quarter-master of the Edinburgh Light Horse, raised in 1797 to defend the country against the invasion of the French; the style is that of the author of the vigorous war-song, "To horse! to horse! the standard flies," etc.

The poetic merit of *The Lay of the Last Minstrel* lies in its descriptions—descriptions either of scenery, such as William of Deloraine saw in his ride through Teviotdale, the neighbourhood of Melrose Abbey, and the various landscapes of the river Ettrick on which the poet's imag-

ination had dwelt from his boyhood; or of the times of chivalry, which his reading in ancient deeds and chronicles had made as familiar to him as contemporary manners. It was inevitable that a story composed in the piecemeal method of *The Lay* should want unity and consistency of action. As Jeffrey says, the different romantic episodes on which the poet expatiates "are of no use whatever in the subsequent development of the fable"; and the Whig reviewer showed much sagacity in detecting the want of connection in the original design between the story of Gilpin Horner and the other portions of the poem.

"The story of Gilpin Horner," he objects, "was never believed out of the village where he is said to have made his appearance, and has no claim upon the credulity of those who were not originally of his acquaintance. There is nothing at all interesting or elegant in the scenes of which he is the hero; and in reading those passages we really could not help suspecting that they did not stand in the romance which the aged Minstrel recalled to the royal Charles and his mighty earls, but were inserted afterwards to suit the taste of the cottagers, among whom he begged his bread on the Border." [*Edinburgh Review,* April 1805]

Scott felt the justice of Jeffrey's criticism, and having now formed a new style of epic narrative, sufficiently grounded in nature to hold the interest of the public, he resolved in his next romantic experiment to bring its original features into closer conformity with the requirements of art. The structure of *Marmion* is quite different from that of *The Lay of the Last Minstrel*. The essential materials of both poems are indeed the same. *Marmion,* like *The Lay,* depends for much of its effect upon descriptions of scenery and chivalrous manners; we at once detect in the narrative the author's recollections of his own excursions in Northumberland and in the country districts between Berwick and Edinburgh; the multiformity of his antiquarian knowledge is displayed in the Notes to the Cantos describing the Castle of Norham and the Court of King James. But these picturesque details are now organised round a plot resembling in all its characteristic features the plan of romance adopted in Mrs. Radcliffe's novels. The crimes of Marmion and the adventures of Ralph de Wilton recall the artifices employed by the authoress of *The Mysteries of Udolpho* and other contemporary romance-writers to engross the attention of their readers. By these means *Marmion* attains more unity of action than *The Lay of the Last Minstrel*. But the increased interest of the narrative entails a certain sacrifice of verisimilitude in the poem as a whole. It is felt that the poet has not been entirely successful in blending the probabilities of fiction with the truth of history. William of Deloraine is an ideal representative of Border warfare, no less probable than picturesque; but Marmion, the forger of deeds, the traitor to love, "not quite a felon, yet but half a knight," as Byron justly calls him, is neither a worthy specimen of the feudal age nor a hero suitable to the atmosphere of poetry. The merits of the poem still lie in its detached episodes—in the portraits of the devil-may-care Captain of Norham Castle and Archibald Bell-the-Cat, or in the splendid description of the Battle of Flodden. Scott's poetical style reaches its highest point in his description of the flank march by which Surrey turned the position of the Scots before the commencement of the battle.

> Even so it was. From Flodden ridge
>   The Scots beheld the English host
>   Leave Barmore-wood, their evening post,
>   And heedful watched them as they crossed
> The Till by Twisel Bridge.
>   High sight it is, and haughty, while
>   They dive into the deep defile;
>   Beneath the caverned cliff they fall,
>   Beneath the castle's airy wall.
> By rock, by oak, by hawthorn-tree,
>   Troop after troop are disappearing;
>   Troop after troop their banners rearing,
> Upon the eastern bank you see.
> Still pouring down the rocky den,
>   Where flows the sullen Till,
> And rising from the dim-wood glen,
> Standards on standards, men on men,
>   In slow succession still,
> And, sweeping o'er the Gothic arch,
> And pressing on, in ceaseless march,
>   To gain the opposing hill.
> That morn to many a trumpet clang,
> Twisel! thy rock's deep echo rang;
> And many a chief of birth and rank,
> Saint Helen! at thy fountain drank.
> Thy hawthorn glade, which now we see
> In spring-tide bloom so lavishly,
> Had then from many an axe its doom,
> To give the marching columns room.
>
> And why stands Scotland idly now,
> Dark Flodden! on thy airy brow,
> Since England gains the pass the while,
> And struggles through the deep defile?
> What checks the fiery soul of James?
> Why sits that champion of the dames
>   Inactive on his steed,
> And sees, between him and his land,
> Between him and Tweed's southern strand,
>   His host Lord Surrey lead?
> What 'vails the vain knight-errant's brand?—
> O Douglas for thy leading wand!
>   Fierce Randolph for thy speed!
> O for one hour of Wallace wight,
> Or well-skilled Bruce, to rule the fight,
> And cry "Saint Andrew and our right!"
> Another sight had seen that morn,
> From Fate's dark book a leaf been torn,
> And Flodden had been Bannockbourne!—
> The precious hour has passed in vain,
> And England's host has gained the plain;
> Wheeling their march, and circling still,
> Around the base of Flodden hill.

A third experiment enabled Scott to overcome the defects in the structure of his narrative style due to its fortuitous development. *The Lady of the Lake* has its groundwork in the same motives that inspired *The Lay of the Last Minstrel* and *Marmion*—a passionate love of romantic

scenery and an imaginative sympathy with ancient and primitive manners; but it is not disfigured either by the incoherence of form which is felt to be a drawback in the first of Scott's romances, or by the inconsistency between the fiction and the history which is a blot on the second. Action and character in *The Lady of the Lake* are beautifully blended with the description of the district in which the incidents of the story are supposed to take place.

> "This poem," says Scott [in the preface to *The Lady of the Lake,* edition of *Poetical Works,* 1830], "the action of which lay among scenes so beautiful, and so deeply imprinted on my recollection, was a labour of love, and it was no less so to recall the manners and incidents introduced. The frequent custom of James IV., and particularly of James V., to walk through their kingdom in disguise, afforded me the hint of an incident which never fails to be interesting, if managed with the slightest address or dexterity."

"Address and dexterity" are exhibited throughout this poem in their finest form. The complication and explication of the plot, disguise and recognition, . . . all the features, in fact, characteristic of romance from its first beginnings in the Greek novel, are managed with perfect propriety; without exception, the personages of the tale are interesting and play their parts in the way that probability requires; and an air of charming grace and vivacity animates each description, up to the admirable *dénouement*:

> Within 'twas brilliant all and light,
> A thronging scene of figures bright;
> It glowed on Ellen's dazzled sight,
> As when the setting sun has given
> Ten thousand hues to summer even,
> And from their tissue fancy frames
> Aerial knights and fairy dames.
> Still by Fitz-James her footing staid;
> A few faint steps she forward made,
> Then slow her drooping head she raised,
> And fearful round the presence gazed
> For him she sought, who owned this state,
> The dreaded prince whose will was fate.
> She gazed on many a princely port,
> Might well have ruled a royal court;
> On many a splendid garb she gazed,
> Then turned bewildered and amazed,
> For all stood bare; and, in the room,
> Fitz-James alone wore cap and plume.
> To him each lady's look was lent;
> On him each courtier's eye was bent;
> Midst furs and silks, and jewels sheen,
> He stood, in simple Lincoln green,
> The centre of the glittering ring,—
> And Snowdoun's Knight is Scotland's King.

A triumph to which the happiness of the subject, the genius of the poet, and the taste of the public all contributed, could hardly be repeated. The number of themes suitable for treatment in the new romantic manner was limited. Even in *The Lady of the Lake* the poetry is seen to spring rather out of the skill with which the writer handles his materials than from the matter itself. Scott had assumed the spontaneous air of the ancient bard; but in reality he showed himself the brilliant successor of polished *trouvères,* Chaucer, Boccaccio, Ariosto; and however he might enliven his narrative manner with simplicities of diction borrowed from the ballad, he knew well that the artificial revival of the long-decayed oral minstrelsy would fail in its effect so soon as it ceased to be a novelty. In *Rokeby* he applied his sophisticated style to an uncongenial subject, and the public, without understanding the cause, instinctively felt that the poetical propriety of the new minstrelsy had vanished. The poet, himself with a judicious respect for the unconscious judgments of his readers, began to examine critically the foundations of his own metrical manner. He asked himself whether there was any fundamental reason why he should not apply to romantic composition in prose the principles which had proved so popular in verse; perceiving that if this way were open to him, he would be in possession of an almost unlimited supply of subjects in place of the mine which he felt to be nearly exhausted. His meditations encouraged him to resume the narrative of *Waverley,* which he had laid aside during the inspired period of his "Minstrelsy"; and the delight with which that romance was hailed by the public, compared with the comparatively cold reception of *The Lord of the Isles,* confirmed him in his determination henceforth to exchange the methods of the poet for those of the novelist.

Donald Davie   (lecture date 1961)

SOURCE: "Chatterton Lecture on an English Poet: The Poetry of Sir Walter Scott," in *Proceedings of the British Academy,* Vol. XLVII, 1962, pp. 61–75.

[*An English poet, critic, educator, and translator, Davie is well-respected for both his creative and critical contributions to literature. In his first critical work,* The Purity of Diction in English Verse *(1952), he argued for a return to the prose-like syntax, formal structures, and conservative metaphors of the eighteenth-century Augustan poets. During the 1950s Davie was associated with the Movement, a group of poets whose number included Philip Larkin, Kingsley Amis, and Thom Gunn, who believed in the importance of these qualities. In contrast to English poets of the 1940s, who were influenced by imagism and symbolism, the Movement poets emphasized restrained language, traditional syntax, and the moral and social implications of poetic content. In the following lecture, delivered in 1961, Davie analyzes several technical aspects of Scott's poetry, including grammatical arrangement and color imagery. Though Davie concedes that Scott's verse often lacks structure, the critic also stresses the creative energy expressed in many of the poems and Scott's direct, nonmetaphoric depiction of nature and society.*]

Lockhart tells a story of how Scott, in the midst of writing *The Lady of the Lake,* decided to measure his own fiction by the facts. He threw himself on horseback and, in Lockhart's words, 'put to the test the practicability of riding from the banks of Loch Vennachar to the Castle of Stirling within the brief space which he had assigned to Fitz-James's Grey Bayard, after the battle with Roderick Dhu'.

It is the sort of anecdote which delighted those many admirers of Scott throughout the nineteenth century who applauded in such episodes of Scott's life, as in the poems themselves, Scott's robust and virile, extroverted attitude to the business of writing. The most authoritative expression of this was Byron's, in *Beppo:*

> One hates an author that *all author,* fellows
>   In foolscap uniforms turn'd up with ink,
> So very anxious, clever, fine and jealous,
>   One don't know what to say to them, or think,
> Unless to puff them with a pair of bellows;
>   Of coxcombry's worst coxcombs e'en the pink
> Are preferable to these shreds of paper,
> These unquench'd snuffings of the midnight taper.

> Of these same we see several, and of others,
>   Men of the world, who know the world like men,
> Scott, Rogers, Moore, and all the better brothers,
>   Who think of something else besides the pen;

This account of Scott, which ranges him, if with Byron himself, also with Samuel Rogers and Tom Moore as against Coleridge and Wordsworth, is in line, so far as I can see, with our current estimate of Scott as poet. In the present century the case often goes by default; Scott's poetry is quite simply overlooked. But I dare say, if challenged, the instructed reader today would agree with Byron, though not in Byron's spirit nor on his grounds, that Scott as poet stands nearer to Rogers than to Wordsworth. However, anyone who thinks it worth while talking about Scott's poetry at all cannot be satisfied with this estimate of Scott as just a representative Regency versifier, and of his poetry as having therefore, by and large, only historical importance.

The reader who on the other hand endorses this estimate will think he finds confirmation if he turns to the passage in question, the account of Fitz-James's ride:

> Along thy banks, swift Teith! they ride,
> And in the race they mock'd their tide;
> Torry and Lendrick now are past,
> And Deanstown lies behind them cast:
> They rise, the banner'd towers of Doune,
> They sink in distant woodland soon;
> Blair-Drummond sees the hoof strike fire,
> They sweep like breeze through Ochtertyre;
> They mark just glance and disappear
> The lofty brow of ancient Keir;
> They bathe their coursers' sweltering sides,
> Dark Forth! amid thy sluggish tides.
> And on the opposing shore take ground,
> With plash, with scramble, and with bound.
> Right-hand they leave thy cliffs, Craig-Forth!
> And soon the bulwark of the North,
> Grey Stirling, with her towers and town,
> Upon their fleet career look'd down.

We may relish the exultation of this, the swing and fire of the rhythm, and still find ourselves thinking that it is essentially, necessarily trivial. One way to disturb this impression is to read on in Lockhart, who remarks, 'the principal landmarks in the description of that fiery progress are so many hospitable mansions all familiar to him at the same period—Blair-drummond, the residence of Lord Kaimes; Ochtertyre, that of John Ramsay, the scholar and antiquary . . . and "the lofty brow of ancient Keir", the splendid seat of the chief family of the name of Stirling . . . . The names then were not chosen at random, nor just for euphony and rhyme. And if we read the passage again with this information to assist us, we can indeed envisage the possibility—that the litany of place-names has such pace and stir, not only because they mark the stages in a furious ride against time, but also because of the fellow-feeling and the patriotic excitement which their associations awake in the poet. However, this remains only a possibility. The example is not at all conclusive. And no doubt the passage cannot count for much one way or the other.

But perhaps the unsympathetic reader will object to more in this passage than what he sees as its triviality. One can imagine the objection, 'But how wasteful this is! so many ways of saying simply that they galloped past or galloped through!' This seems to me a more profound misunderstanding. At their least considered such objections reveal a misunderstanding not just of Scott's poetry but of all poetry; they strike at and strike down not just the habit of Scott's imagination, but the act of the poetic imagination as such. I should like to dwell on this.

The ride to Stirling comes in Canto V of *The Lady of the Lake*; what follows is from Canto III, which as a whole is a good deal finer. It is a description of an ancient battlefield; or rather, more precisely, a meditation upon it—

> The Knot-grass fettered there the hand,
> Which once could burst an iron band;
> Beneath the broad and ample bone,
> That buckler'd heart to fear unknown,
> A feeble and a timorous guest,
> The field-fare framed her lowly nest;
> There the slow blind-worm left his slime
> On the fleet limbs that mock'd at time;
> And there, too, lay the leader's skull,
> Still wreath'd with chaplet flush'd and full,
> For heath-bell with her purple bloom
> Supplied the bonnet and the plume.

Clearly the reader who complained, 'So many ways of saying only that they galloped!' could complain of this, 'So many ways of saying only that they are dead and gone!' And yet I think he would be more reluctant in this case, would feel uneasily that to complain on these grounds might be to miss the point of poetic perception altogether.

For the way in which syntax and word-order in this passage are continually varied so as to mask, and yet to assert, the identity of the relationships—as knot-grass is to the hand, so field-fare to the heart, blind-worm to the limbs, and heath-bell to the head—this is an example of what may be called 'elegant variation', simply the saying of one thing many ways. And such variation is a constant and governing feature of Scott's style. Another name for it, perhaps a better one, was found by Roman Jakobson when he spoke of the 'poetry of grammar' [in a paper delivered to the International Conference of Linguistics and Poetics, 1960]. Following Sapir, Jakobson would say that grammatically each of the clauses in this passage is identical with all the others. They differ not grammatically but lexically; an identical grammatical structure is differently 'filled out', but the difference is only in the trappings as it were, and in the disposition. In much ancient poetry such grammatical parallelism, often in a more elementary form, serves as a self-sufficient principle of poetic ordering—as it does once again in some modern *vers-libre*. By Scott, of course, it is used only in conjunction with other ordering principles, the traditional ones of rhyme and imagery and metre. But Scott seldom uses these traditional devices with real power; by the time he wrote *The Lady of the Lake* Scott was, for instance, a dexterous but also a very unsubtle metrist. In any case it is when the traditional principles of order are reinforced by grammatical patterning and parallels that we recognize a poetry thoroughly achieved, structured through and through; and elegant variation, the saying of one thing many ways, brings with it for Scott this additional source of order.

When we speak of such variation as 'elegant', we should not seem to imply that it is peculiarly characteristic of late sophisticated styles. On the contrary, repetition with variation, riddles, and grammatical parallels are staple features of primitive forms like the ballad and the lay and the song; indeed the device of the refrain has meaning and power only in relationship to this principle. And so the distinction of this passage about the battlefield is the same in principle as that of the incomparable **'Proud Maisie'**, or of a much more relaxed but still wonderfully achieved song, the exquisite **'Brignall Banks are wild and fair'** in Canto Third of the otherwise tedious *Rokeby*. The augmented and diverted significance with which on each repetition the refrain is endowed—this is, in poems of this kind, a stroke of the highest art.

Poetry of grammar enters also into rhyme, for the rhyming of a verb with a noun has a more striking and normally a more artistic effect than the rhyming of verb with verb or (but this is different again) of noun with noun. And thus elegant variation or the poetry of grammar is present in the sophisticated rhyming poetry of Pope as in the riddle and the kenning or those other ancient poetic forms which Scott encountered in the ballad-collections of Ritson and Bishop Percy, which he encountered at first hand for himself when he compiled *Minstrelsy of the Scottish Border*. On the other hand, rhyme is rather a special case, since it involves direct repetition only of sound, not of sense. And the good poets of the eighteenth century, Scott's predecessors, tended to look askance at manœuvres which involved repetitions of sense, for the sufficient and admirable reason that they valued very highly the qualities of terseness, rapidity, and compactness. Modern poetic the-

An engraving of Scott's study at his estate, Abbotsford.

ory, because it similarly places a high premium on these qualities, is ill placed to acknowledge as legitimate, still less to enjoy and admire, the sort of talent in Scott which produces his meditation on the ancient battlefield. And Scott himself appears to have held that the terseness and compactness of *The Vanity of Human Wishes* made it poetry of a higher order than any he wrote himself. What needs to be insisted on, however, when we notice the lack of these qualities in Scott's poetry, is that Scott's leisurely and expansive narration can achieve effects which are as foreign to Johnson's style as Johnson's pithiness is foreign to the style of Scott. These are the effects of that gift which seems to figure in our older criticism as 'copiousness of invention'. Not only has this expression disappeared from our criticism, but I do not see what other expression has taken its place. And it puzzles me how we manage without it, or something like it, except by growing blind to that range of poetic effects which it used to denote, ancient and universal as those are. Certainly this, the copiousness of his invention, is the greatest thing in Scott, in poetry and prose alike; and so when we find him saying 'they rode on' in seven different ways, one after the other, we should not suppose that this is wasteful superfluity, but direct creative energy revelling in its own fecundity. If any one protests that this is Art for Art's sake, I would retort that it is rather Nature for Nature's sake; Pasternak has a profound passage in his autobiography, *Safe Conduct,* where he says that just as a physicist plots upon squared paper the track followed by a unit of physical energy such as an electrical charge, so the poet plots in a poem the track followed among images by that psychic energy which we call 'feeling'.

This answer is effective, if only because it is the same copiousness of invention in Scott which elaborates sentiments through variation and contrives one grammatical pattern after another, which elaborates his plots and contrives episode after episode. But the argument is not quite fair, still less conclusive. For the fact is, of course, that very little of *The Lady of the Lake* is so well written as the passages I have so far considered. George Ellis, in his *Quarterly* review of *The Lady of the Lake,* noted, as new developments since *Marmion* and *The Lay of the Last Minstrel,* 'a profusion of incident, and a shifting brilliancy of colouring that reminds us of the witchery of Ariosto'. That 'shifting brilliancy' can be illustrated, more literally perhaps than Ellis intended, by a passage such as this, from the first Canto:

The western waves of ebbing day
Roll'd o'er the glen their level way;
Each purple peak, each flinty spire,
Was bathed in floods of living fire,
But not a setting beam could glow
Within the dark ravines below,
Where twined the path in shadow hid
Round many a rocky pyramid,
Shooting abruptly from the dell
Its thunder-splinter'd pinnacle;
Round many an insulated mass,
The native bulwards of the pass,
Huge as the tower which builders vain
Presumptuous piled on Shinar's plain.
The rocky summits, split and rent,
Form'd turret, dome, or battlement,
Or seemed fantastically set
With cupola or minaret,
Wild crests as pagod ever deck'd,
Or mosque of Eastern architect.
Nor were these earth-born castles bare,
Nor lacked they many a banner fair;
For, from their shiver'd brows display'd
Far o'er the unfathomable glade,
All twinkling with the dew-drops sheen,
The brier-rose fell in streamers green,
And creeping shrubs, of thousand dyes,
Waved in the west-wind's summer sighs.

This is wretched work. It is no good asking the affronted reader not to look in a long poem for a compactness of sentiment, for a weight and also a polish in the expression, which only the short poem can give him. He may be thus outflanked, he is not convinced. And he is right. Such verse as this is not to be excused by any talk of energetic invention, or of bluff appetite and gusto too caught up in its own narrative to pause for effeminate niceties. On the contrary, what is disastrously lacking to this writing is precisely masculinity, masculinity as Pater defined it when he spoke of 'manliness' in art as 'a full consciousness of what one does, of art itself in the work of art, tenacity of intuition and of consequent purpose'. It lacks that 'masterly execution' which, to Hopkins too, as Pater's pupil, 'is a kind of male gift'. It lacks precisely that structuring through and through which appears in the passage about the battlefield. It is this, an energy of apprehension which, so far from running wild, seeks out of itself the structures to control it, which makes a piece of writing masculine or manly, as Pater and Hopkins understood those terms. And I hope it is plain that their understanding of masculinity is more serious, more ancient (for it goes back, I think, to 'Longinus'), and also far more relevant to poetry as poetry, than Byron's liking for 'men of the world, who know the world like men' or, to take another example, the 'virility' which W. M. Rossetti in 1870 allowed to Scott, as something implied by calling him 'spirited'. And if Scott always has Byron's and Rossetti's kind of masculinity, only seldom does he rise to the manliness demanded by Hopkins and Pater.

The effeminacy of this last passage, the absence from it of the truly masculine, the *truly* robust, appears in nothing so

clearly as in the handling of the metre. It was Ellis again, reviewing the poem on its first appearance, who was sorry to see it cast into octosyllabic couplets. If one speaks, in a time-honoured phrase, of the 'fatal fluency' of this metre, one ought to mean, I think, that the metrical norm asserts itself so insistently as to iron out any play of spoken stress against that norm. Thus in the case of 'The brier-rose fell in streamers green', the interesting rhythm of that line in isolation, with its hesitation on the very weak second syllable of 'brier', and the breath-pause that must intervene between the stressed syllables 'rose' and 'fell', is subjugated entirely when the line is read in the context, so that we read Thē Bríēr rōse féll; the stressed syllable 'rose' being crammed into the weak supposedly unstressed place in an iambic foot, while the frailty of the second syllable of 'brier' is drowned out completely. (This is a good example, incidentally, of how delicacy with metre assists diction also, for if Scott had respected the innate rhythm of his words he would have noticed how 'rose' and 'fell' lived awkwardly together because of the other 'rose' that comes from 'to rise'.) 'Earth-born castles' and 'the west-wind's summer sighs' are two other phrases whose rhythms are stunned by the metre. And in fact, scansion reveals that, throughout, the disposition of stress against the syllables is insensitive, arbitrary, slipshod, and improvised.

And yet this is the poet who wrote **'Proud Maisie'**; who wrote also this—

From the sound of Teviot's tide,
Chafing with the mountain's side,
From the groan of the wind-swung oak,
From the sullen echo of the rock,
From the voice of the coming storm,
  The Ladye knew it well!
It was the Spirit of the Flood that spoke,
  And he called on the Spirit of the Fell
    . . . 'Sleep'st thou, Brother?' . . .

The shock which this gives us (it is from *The Lay of the Last Minstrel*) is almost entirely a matter of rippling, resilient movement; it has to do with the accentual, rather than accentual-syllabic, metre. Not only is it more resilient and sprightly; the rhythms are given more margin to gather power before being reined back. Then too, the wandering of the stress keeps us alert so as to find it, never in each new line quite where it was in the line before. Scott, we are told, took the hint for this from Coleridge; but he deserves credit for having of himself a sufficiently inward aliveness to verse-movement to be able to profit from Coleridge's rediscovery of this ancient music. And in any case, to some extent this new alertness and unpredictability of rhythm were characteristic of all the good verse from the first phase of the English Romantic Movement, when it was still close to Percy's *Reliques*. Professor Josephine Miles in her very instructive and learned *Eras and Modes of English Poetry*, sets these lines from the *Lay* along with stanzas from Blake, from Burns, and from Tom Moore, to recreate very challengingly our sense of what a new departure was inaugurated when these poets and others began writing in this way at various dates in the 1790's. We are so aware of the confusingly many things that Romanticism later became, that we are in every danger of forgetting what a simple and salient thing it must have appeared to start with; and most of our difficulties with, for instance, the masterpiece of this first phase, *The Rime of the Ancient Mariner,* come when we try to read that poem as if it belonged to a later Romanticism which trafficked in allegory. But this is to stray from considerations simply of metre. And as to this, I am glad to borrow Professor Miles's authoritative account, when she speaks of 'a varied and broken line pattern, the constant remission of four stresses to three, with consequent effects of easy repetition or wordlessness, the lightness of assonance as the shading of rhyme, feminine as the shading of masculine endings, shadings of echo and progression from stanza to stanza, and indeed in every new form of modification in sound, the quality of shadow, echo, or answer, rather than the massed and cumulative forces of the old pentameters'. This is a description of the musical dimensions of *The Lay* and, not so exactly but still substantially, of *Marmion* also. Such fineness in the texture of sound is absent from *The Lady of the Lake*; and in fact it may well be maintained that by the time Scott wrote *The Lady,* the third of his narrative poems, his most original work was already behind him. Certainly, although there are interesting things in later narratives such as *The Lord of the Isles* and *Harold the Dauntless,* there are the clearest indications in his long poems after *The Lady of the Lake* that the resources of the author's most vivid imaginative life were already being husbanded against the time when he would draw upon them for his novels. And equally certainly some of the most impressive characteristics of *Minstrelsy of the Scottish Border,* of *The Lay of the Last Minstrel* and *Marmion,* have already disappeared from *The Lady of the Lake*.

We see this in another way, at the level of diction rather than metre, if we go back for a moment to what Ellis said of 'the shifting brilliancy of colouring' in *The Lady of the Lake*. In the passage I quoted from this poem it is indeed the 'purple peak', the brier-rose which is *'twinkling* with the dew-drops' sheen', and the 'creeping shrubs, *of thousand dyes',* which are the clearest symptoms of the loss by Scott of his initial vision and impetus. It is not that these notations are inaccurate or imprecise. For neither an Imagist exactitude nor a Keatsian full vividness of sensuous register was at any time part of Scott's purpose. In his earlier poems, as in the ballads which inspired them and (what should give us pause) in the heroic poetry of the ancient world, colours for instance have a function as much emblematic or heraldic as descriptive. Quite simply, in *The Lay* and in *Marmion* as opposed to *The Lady of the Lake* or *Rokeby,* Scott used a far more restricted palette of bold primary colours, and so achieved a more severe effect:

When red hath set the beamless sun,
Through heavy vapours dark and dun:

or:

Till, dark above, and white below
Decided drives the flaky snow, . . .

(where 'Decided', I think, is very fine); or else (Flodden field seen from afar):

And, first, the ridge of mingled spears
Above the brightening cloud appears;
And in the smoke the pennons flew,
As in the storm the white sea-mew . . . ,

where the diverse colours of the pennons are strangely and emblematically bleached to a uniform white.

Ruskin in volume III of *Modern Painters* takes another example from the description of Flodden:

The white pavilions made a show
Like remnants of the winter snow
  Along the dusky ridge.

And Ruskin makes a great deal of Scott's use of colour:

in general, if he does not mean to say much about things, the *one* character which he will give is colour, using it with the most perfect mastery and faithfulness, up to the point of possible modern perception. For instance, if he has a sea-storm to paint in a single line, he does not, as a feebler poet would probably have done, use any expression about the temper or form of the waves; does not call them angry or mountainous. He is content to strike them out with two dashes of Tintoret's favourite colours:

'The blackening wave is edged with white,
To inch and rock the sea-mews fly.'

And—

Again: where he has to describe tents mingled among oaks, he says nothing about the form of either tent or tree, but only gives the two strokes of colour:

'Thousand pavilions, *white as snow,*
Chequered the borough moor below,
Oft giving way, where still there stood
Some relics of the old oak wood,
That darkly huge did intervene,
And tamed the glaring white with green.'

But this last example is something different, as Ruskin should have acknowledged. 'And tamed the glaring white with green'—this is too painterly, too precious I had almost said, for comfort.

There are other places where Scott shows this sort of preciousness in stylized patterning of colour. A place where it causes no discomfort is the first stanza of Canto Second of *The Lay*:

If thou would'st view fair Melrose aright,
Go visit it by the pale moonlight;
For the gay beams of lightsome day
Gild, but to flout, the ruins grey.
When the broken arches are black in night,

And each shafted oriel glimmers white;
When the cold light's uncertain shower
Streams on the ruin'd central tower;
When buttress and buttress, alternately,
Seem fram'd of ebon and ivory; . . .

This domino pattern of black and white, with the painterly perception of 'cold light' in the fine line, 'When the cold light's uncertain shower', has not at all the severe effect of the whites and blacks at Flodden. On the contrary this is plainly a perception of the Regency man of letters, not of any belated harpist of the Scottish border. It is none the worse for that; indeed it comes conveniently to remind us that *The Lay* for all its loving re-creation of the conventions of late medieval romance, is by no means a simple pastiche, however expert, like some of Scott's art-ballads. The distinction of the poem is precisely that its author, while not pretending to be other than he is, a man of the Regency, can nevertheless assimilate into that modern posture habits of thought and feeling from an older and very different age.

The quite different colour-effect which Scott brings over from the ballads appears at its most impressive, as I think, in the introduction to the third Canto of *Marmion*. Here, in an epistle to William Erskine, Scott excuses himself for having deserted classical precedents of form, of genre, and of subject ('Brunswick's venerable hearse'). The emphasis falls on structure, as Scott vindicates the rambling development of 'the romance' against the classical requirement of a single unified great action. But the verse comes to life when the alternative unclassical inspiration is seen in terms not of structure but of *hue:*

Yet was poetic impulse given
By the green hill and clear blue heaven.

And the other example which Scott gives, besides the green and blue of his native Scotland, of how early environment moulds the poet beyond what precept can later correct, is similarly seen in terms of primary colour:

Look east, and ask the Belgian why,
Beneath Batavia's sultry sky,
He seeks not eager to inhale
The freshness of the mountain gale,
Content to rear his whiten'd wall
Beside the dank and dull canal?
He'll say, from youth he loved to see
The white sail gliding by the tree.

The surely unpremediatated repetition here—'whiten'd' and 'white'—has a mysterious purity and force which imprint it on the mind as the metrical resilience and eagerness imprint 'By the green hill and clear blue heaven'. What both passages have is a simplicity which is not Wordsworth's simplicity, though related to his. For it is a definitive characteristic of English Romanticism as the literary historian knows it in its earliest phase, when it is the deliberate revival, not just in subject and mood, vocabulary and metre, but also in *morality,* of the poetic style of the ballad.

When I speak of morality, I have not in mind codes or habits of morality between man and man, such as the code of chivalry to which Scott pays tribute when William of Deloraine stands over the body of his enemy Richard Musgrave. Rather I mean the sort of morality which particularly concerned Ruskin, the morality of man's relation to the non-human Creation. Accordingly I return to Ruskin for a statement of the morality implicit in Scott's way of seeing and Scott's way of writing:

> Scott is able to conquer all tendencies to the pathetic fallacy, and instead of making Nature anywise subordinate to himself, he makes himself subordinate to *her*—follows her lead simply—does not venture to bring his own cares and thoughts into her pure and quiet presence—paints her in her simple and universal truth, adding no result of momentary passion or fancy, and appears, therefore, at first shallower than other poets, being in reality wider and healthier.

It is generally held, I suppose, that 'the pathetic fallacy' is a bee which never buzzed in any bonnet but Ruskin's. And for my part I have no wish to bring back the days when the first thing to do with any poet was to inquire after his 'feeling for nature'. Yet ours is an age when we are invited to see the non-human world for purposes of poetry as merely a repertoire of 'objective correlatives', of potential symbols ready to 'stand in' for the human reality which, on this showing, alone deserves the poet's attention. In such a period we may indeed dismiss as shallow what is simply sane and truly robust.

For here I believe 'manliness' appears again, with yet another meaning. When Byron said of Keats, 'Such writing is a sort of mental masturbation . . . I don't mean he is indecent, but viciously soliciting his own ideas', he was surely defending his own practice as the author of such lines as these:

It was the cooling hour, just when the rounded
  Red sun sinks down behind the azure hill,
Which then seems as if the whole earth it bounded,
  Circling all nature, hush'd, and dim, and still,
With the far mountain-crescent half surrounded
  On one side, and the deep sea calm and chill,
Upon the other, and the rosy sky,
With one star sparkling through it like an eye.

This stanza from *Don Juan* is, as usual with Byron, extremely careless. But 'the deep sea calm and chill' represents a strength which Byron shares with Scott and with no one else among his contemporaries. The bold and simple epithets—'deep', 'calm', 'chill'—are like Scott's greens and blues, whites and reds and blacks, his bright and dark and cold. They represent a morality in respect of the natural world which is incompatible with the Keatsian morality, but not necessarily inferior. Such a brave risking of the obvious which issues for both Scott and Byron (notably in *Don Juan*) in simple naming of objects and their appearances, seems to testify to a straightforward gratitude for the pleasures of sense, and a fear that to probe them too nearly, on the one hand so far from heightening will tarnish them, on the other hand will seem ungrateful. There are several reasons for calling this refusal to fuss and probe a masculine attitude. For one thing such a casual registering of only the broad appearance is appropriate to the horseman or the traveller, the man in active life; whereas the more sedulous analysis and enumeration of Keats, of Coleridge, Tennyson, Hopkins (different as these are) is plainly, by contrast, sedentary. The modern writer who at his best shares this attitude is a self-consciously masculine author, Ernest Hemingway.

It may have appeared perverse in me to dwell so long on what must be called, however loosely, the descriptive element, in what are after all narrative poems. But Scott himself, in a headnote to *The Lay of the Last Minstrel,* declared that 'the description of scenery and manners was more the object of the author than a combined and regular narrative'. For narrative in the narrow sense of an unpredictable but probable story suspensefully told, *The Lady of the Lake* is the best of the poems; but then it is also the poem of which one feels that the story would do better as a Waverley novel, in prose. On the other hand, the clumsy and improbable plot of *Marmion,* though it is irritating, is less so in verse than it would have been in prose. In *The Lay of the Last Minstrel* the story is so slight and simple, so patently only the vehicle for other matters, that it does not get in the way. This is as much as we ask, and it is what we get; though particular episodes, such as Deloraine's visit, in Canto II, to the tomb of Michael Scott in Melrose Abbey, are well and suspensefully handled. In none of the poems is the plot itself the symbol of the issues being debated, as it is, for instance, in *Waverley.* But this would be to ask of Scott what neither he nor any other poet in English has provided, the novel in verse such as Pushkin provided with *Eugene Onegin,* and Mickiewicz in Poland with *Pan Tadeusz.* If we did have such works in English poetry, we should be hard pressed to know what to do with them, so readily do we assume that plot is trivial, so eagerly do we probe behind the literal meaning, and the subject overtly offered, to the 'theme' which we suppose lies behind it. It is this which makes us treat *The Ancient Mariner* as if it were a poem *about* the alienation of the artist from society, or *about* Christian redemption, or *about* neurosis and its cure; so far are we from seeing it as about a mariner and the strange voyage he took. Only if we recover the conviction that the meaning at the literal level is at any rate part, and a principal part, of the total meaning of a poem, only then shall we be in a position to appreciate a poem like *The Lay of the Last Minstrel,* the literal meaning of which is all the meaning there is (and quite sufficient too), a poem which is 'about' no more than what it is overtly about, that is, a foray into the Scottish lowlands in the sixteenth century. It is true, moreover, that in *The Lay of the Last Minstrel* Scott did aim at what has come to be accepted as a principal function of the European novel—the substantiation of a whole provincial society. And I think he succeeded, for we do indeed realize an image, convincing to the imagination, of the society of the Border in the sixteenth century, at every social level from the brutalized smallholder Watt Tinlinn, through the man at arms William of Deloraine, and the monk of Melrose, to the nobility. If I have

said little of this, where Scott (it is clear) laid great store by it, it is partly because it is difficult to illustrate in any way that illuminates equally matters of diction, syntax, and metre. Moreover, this delineation of manners is something which the Waverley novels do sometimes better and nearly always equally well; whereas my object has been to show that Scott is a poet, not merely a novelist who also wrote verse.

John Pikoulis (essay date 1971)

SOURCE: "Scott and *Marmion*: The Discovery of Identity," in *The Modern Language Review,* Vol. 66, No. 1, October, 1971, pp. 738–50.

[*Pikoulis is a Zimbabawean critic and educator. In the following essay, Pikoulis maintains that* Marmion *serves as a "poetic autobiography" for Scott. The critic analyzes the introductory epistles in the poem as well as the central tale of* Marmion, *concluding that the two parts work together to present the primary elements of the poet's identity.*]

It is part of the difficulty of the romance that its characteristic mode of operation strikes the modern reader as altogether foreign, the product and expression of an alien sensibility. It is not as if the ideas or the play of ideas fail to interest the writer of romances but that they need an embracing context of a lively and suspenseful plot and an amplitude of exposition which allows the writer's creative energy sufficient scope within a framework firm enough to hold the piece together but at the same time flexible enough to allow for digression and variation. Such, at any rate, is true of *Marmion* which is content to give the appearance of unconcern for 'hidden' meanings beyond the surface detail it relates and its placing of the intense, private emotion firmly within the context of overmastering public events. Its length, its seemingly rambling structure, its unimpressive technical resources and verbal texture would be sufficient to dismay the reader, let alone its subject matter.

But even if this were not the case, its being a romance would provide the most difficult challenge since, by its very nature, the romance represents that preemptive raid on the emotions which Henry James noted in his preface to *The Americans,* 'experience liberated . . . disengaged, disembroiled, disencumbered, exempt from the conditions that we usually know to attach to it'. For James, the romance deals with things 'we never *can* directly know; the things that can reach us only through the beautiful circuit and subterfuge of our thought and our desire'. Wordsworth, paying a last visit to his friend Scott in 1831, with whom he spent a morning seeing Newark, recorded the event in 'Yarrow Revisited', a verse of which is specially relevant:

> Nor deem that localized Romance
>   Plays false with our affections;
> Unsanctifies our tears—made sport
>   For fanciful dejections:

> Ah, no! the visions of the past
>   Sustain the heart in feeling
> Life as she is—our changeful Life,
>   With friends and kindred dealing.

It is not that the romancer is uninterested in things intelligent; it is, rather, that such ideas as interest him do so obsessively, are driven so deep and wide, and are full of such loaded, suggestive meaning that he cannot directly broach them without betraying their essence; what the romancer requires above all is the liberating *context,* for it is context alone that, of all things literary, most nearly approximates to the pulse and temper of his poetic vision and may accommodate and reflect most effectively the stress and tug of his feelings. Neither the packed lyric nor the elevated and expansive epic will quite do; the wrought intensity of the former is too detached from the romancer's ever-pressing sense of a community's whole life from which grow his profoundest insights, and the assurance and sweep of the latter quite confound his sense of things lost, or nearly grasped, receding into the past to leave a world strained by their promise and their memory.

Apparently, this temper of mind, this complex of emotion, can no longer provoke that imaginative leap on the part of a reader which is necessary for their appreciation, for far from impressing him by the maturity and poise of its bearing, the romance, because it is concerned with the problem of both private and public identity and self-hood, has an especial affinity with what may be termed an adolescent frame of mind, as the ballad is the product of the young community coming to a consciousness of itself. (Pushed a little, the romance becomes the romantic, with its affinity with states of childlike perception.) It is conscious at the source of its being of the impossibility of achieving a state of civilized grace and assurance, very often associated with the myth of a golden age or a nation at crucial points in its history. It is related to the time of shifting states of being, of the momentous choice which involves nothing less than the identity of self and society. That assumption of common interest, of a common fate, is crucial.

For Scott, it was made possible partly by his prodigiously retentive memory—so retentive as to be almost another sense, a creative faculty with which he could absorb, record, and explore reality. There was also his even more remarkable attachment to the fabular past of his country which began, according to a recent biographer, Arther Melville Clark [in *Sir Walter Scott: The Formative Year,* 1969], when he was as young as three or four with the ballads he listened to and retained, reinforced by tales of the past he picked up from the older people who dominated his childhood and by his turning to a mass of literature with the undiscriminating, passionate zeal of the solitary. This, in turn, was accentuated by his dislike for legal studies and his failure to enter into any very serious engagement with the classics or, indeed, with any of the regular subjects taught in his school, university, or the various classes he attended, save as they heightened his involvement with the past. What effect his lameness and the absence from his family had in all this is a matter for conjecture. What

is certain is that the influence of the past—not so much the facts but the romance of it—ran wide and deep in the young boy, so much so that he was mastered by its imaginative appeal: the fable of his country became a part of his sensibility, a possession of his personality. There may well have been some compensatory drive which urged him to take on something so massively complex as a country's past life, but that scarcely affects the significance of the alliance which was forged so early in his life. From this grew the power of Scott's best poetry, an amalgam of fact and myth in which simplicity and plainness of address produced a complexity and grandness of effect. Nor is it surprising that Scott the adult should prove to be so implacably opposed to Whiggery; he more than most could be described as conservative in life, radical in his art, for, like a good Tory, he revered the traditional in the world about him, which left the good poet in him to wander freely and brilliantly in that tradition. The society which knew Scott as the genial, outgoing man in love with legend and ballad could hardly know what he declares in a crucial passage in *Marmion*:

> That secret power by all obey'd,
> Which warps not less the passive mind,
> Its source conceal'd or undefin'd;
> Whether an impulse, that has birth
> Soon as the infant wakes on earth,
> One with our feelings and our powers,
> And rather part of us than ours;
> Or whether fitlier term'd the sway
> Of habit, form'd in early day?
> Howe'er deriv'd, its force confest
> Rules with despotic sway the breast,
> And drags us on by viewless chain,
> While taste and reason plead in vain . . .
>
>   Thus while I ape the measure wild
> Of tales that charm'd me yet a child,
> Rude though they be, still with the chime
> Return the thoughts of early time;
> And feelings, rous'd in life's first day,
> Glow in the line, and prompt the lay . . .
> Yet was poetic impulse given,
> By the green hill and clear blue heaven.
>   (Canto III, Introduction)

Friends and acquaintances may have read that as an agreeable exaggeration, so courteous is the manner and so conventionally worded is the declaration. We need to take it as literally true, indicating the poetic sensibility which was formed in infancy and childhood and the trigger ('poetic impulse') which later called forth its expression. The whole passage, which goes on to amplify the source of the impulse by recalling the tales which 'bewitch'd my mind', is a remarkable one, not least for its intimation of the essential solitariness of the young Scott until he was almost out of his teens, divided between adults, especially those in the family circle, who were of necessity at some distance from him, and the mere acquaintances (other than John Irving, who shared his enthusiasm for romances) of his school, his first university days and his apprenticeship. So keen was the solitude and so pervasive the inward imagination that Scott could write in a journal entry of 1825 that his life 'though not without its fits of waking and strong exertion, has been a sort of dream spent in "Chewing the cud of sweet and bitter fancy"'. He goes on to declare: 'Since I was five years old I cannot remember the time when I had not some ideal part to play for my own solitary amusement' [*The Journal of Sir Walter Scott, 1825–26,* edited by J. G. Tait, 1939]. Marmion, as we shall see, was just such a part, transfigured from fancy into art.

Scott's intimate sense of community was complicated by the ambiguous relationship between past and present, between the Scotland of before and after Union. He accepted change by placing it in the context of the development of a nation's manners, customs, institutions, and morality which satisfied his sense of an accumulated tradition. But there was at the same time a difficult awareness of the presence of loss. In **Marmion,** Scotland is infirm of purpose and weakened by dissension, yet the defeat of the Scottish army is recorded with a reticent, noble sorrow. Marmion's death, the defeat of valour, elicits from him an unexpected warmth of feeling. Both have the status of a common identity, varying expressions of the fitness of such events, of the eminently comparable spirit of the adversaries. The rottenness within each is expunged and the great march of conventional life resumes, with who knows how many unresolved emotions germinating beneath the surface. It is as if future events are being anticipated and rationalized: the sin of the English warrior is expiated, the essential character of Scottish life preserved. Compassion and grief modulate into a relieved happiness that the future of both countries is assured, an attitude which amounts to something like the impossible feat of *ante hoc ergo propter hoc,* in which different concepts of defeat and of endurance try to account for all that happened and was to happen. The assurance seems all the more necessary because of the undercurrents of feeling which are anything but consoling. It is all rather like the guilty hero of **Rokeby** (how many of Scott's warriors are guilty!) whose sleep came

> but with a train
> Of feelings true and fancies vain,
> Mingling, in wild disorder cast,
> The expected future with the past.
> Conscience, anticipating time,
> Already rues the enacted crime,
> And calls her furies forth . . .
>   (Canto I, ii)

As V. S. Pritchett has shrewdly remarked [in *The Living Novel,* 1961], 'history meant simply [Scott's] preoccupation with what is settled . . . A period has ended . . . Now he can survey . . . Scott does not revive the past or escape into it; he assimilates it for his own time and for his own prejudices. He writes like a citizen. He asserts the normal man, the man who has learnt to live with his evil. That is of the later novels; part of the interest of the poetry is precisely its delineation of Scott's struggle 'to live with his evil', to identify himself and his country, by expressing his profoundest and most ambiguous emotions. Like

many a modern romancer, he appeared to be a man of unshakeable conservatism and equanimity, whose character masked visions of the most profoundly radical kind, and whose colourful romancer's world could most nearly accommodate them to public utterance. This was so because Scott could subvert a conventional mode of expression to his own purposes, working by clairvoyancy and rhetoric, the clairvoyancy of sudden, inspired collocations of men, events, emotion, and thought which directly stand out from their surroundings and illuminate a whole way of life with an unexpected flood of light. A good deal of poetry works in something like this way, the direct shaft of a revealed insight lighting the poem, but none with this particular sense of release, of an uncontrollable rush of feeling. Of necessity, such perception cannot be altogether consciously worked for; the romancer bides his time, plods on until he can seize the moment of release. Thus, the often long-winded poem which fills in a context in great detail (important to the communal aspect of his art) is simultaneously a validation of and preparation for his insights—if, that is, they come. We may struggle through **The Lay of the Last Minstrel,** but it is not transformed as **Marmion** is transformed or as at least the first half of **The Lady of the Lake** is transformed, especially in the brilliant first canto which, with its crowded pattern of contrasts and revelatory juxtapositions, is one of Scott's finest achievements.

If the genuinely poetic insight works in this distinctive way, then its framing in poetic language is also distinctive in that it is 'rhetorical', a private deployment of words. It is not merely what Ruskin meant [in *Modern Painters*] by drawing attention to Scott's use of colour, the bold, simple adjectives of a man 'subordinate to' nature, the transparency of naming things, nor only what Donald Davie [in *Proceedings of the British Academy,* 1962] referred to as the 'poetry of grammar', of repetition with variation where each clause is grammatically identical with another though differing lexically: a form of elegant variation. Of course, many poets use a language which embodies private emotion and is edged with suggestive nuance or implication. Usually, the reader trains himself to read this language. With Scott, the language shifts from stock response to private vision unexpectedly, depending on the pressure of the poetic experience at a given time. The formal compliment or the straightfaced epithet may, in stretch after stretch, remain just that; at particularly slack moments, when the path seems more winding than usual, they may have the hollow ring of language responding to no very great stimulus in a tired, limp manner. Where the stimulus is real, however, something very like a sea-change comes over the language which it is impossible to capture exactly, a falling away of habituated response, a shifting clarity which carries us to the imaginative core of the work, each familiar word now direct and importunate.

The peculiar structure of **Marmion** and the slow, devious manner of its development prepare the ground. The long introductions to each canto, far from being conventional pieties, underpin the poem firmly and persuasively, while the introduction of the poet *in propria persona* at his task of writing the poem has the effect of making Scott at least as important a figure in the poem as anyone else. Indeed, the result is a twin focus—Marmion as a figure central to the events surrounding the battle at Flodden and Scott as his imaginative creator and interpreter and diminished heir. The last note is struck at once—cold November, twilight, a bare and bleak landscape steeling itself 'As deeper moans the gathering blast'. The comfort of the eventual return of spring lends no joy since there is no such assurance to relieve 'my country's wintry state'; the tributes to Pitt and Fox, unremarkable in themselves, offer an entry by their insistency of feeling into the legendary past and the poem itself:

> Warm'd by such names, well may we then,
> Though dwindled sons of little men,
> Essay to break a feeble lance
> In the fair fields of old romance.
> (Canto I, Introduction)

It is through such a mood of enervation that the antitheses of time, change, decay, and rebirth are intimated and the fact that they are related to a particular person in a specific situation establishes the fact that the tale must be seen frankly as an artefact through which his inmost feelings will be mediated, much as an image or symbol might mediate another poet's feelings. Having thus declared himself, Scott sets the perspective in a fine passage on the transience of the romantic, legendary vision, a cyclical pattern in the poet's imagination which draws from the parallel with the cycle of nature touched on earlier to which it is united in a moment of sombre recognition:

> For all the tears e'er sorrow drew
> And all the raptures fancy knew,
> And all the keener rush of blood,
> That throbs through bard in bard-like mood,
> Were here a tribute mean and low,
> Though all their mingled streams could flow—
> Woe, wonder, and sensation high,
> In one spring-tide of ecstasy!
> It will not be, it may not last,
> The vision of enchantment's past:
> Like frostwork in the morning ray,
> The fancied fabric melts away;
> Each Gothic arch, memorial-stone,
> And long, dim, lofty aisle, are gone;
> And, lingering last, deception dear,
> The choir's high sounds die on my ear.
> Now slow return the lonely down,
> The silent pastures bleak and brown,
> The farm begirt with copsewood wild,
> The gambols of each frolic child,
> Mixing their shrill cries with the tone
> Of Tweed's dark waters rushing on.
> (Canto I, Introduction)

Each emotion, each scene, has drawn from it by the steadily mounting variations a substantial imaginative life while the suppleness of the four-stress line, with its splendid modulations into five-stress, together with the shifting emphasis of the stress and the distinctive variations in cadence this allows, gives it a remarkable quality of feel-

ing and achieved expression. The personal accent clings tenaciously to the stresses, so that the directly uttered emotion and its formal embodiment in verse set up a dual harmony. This does not always sound, for Marmion's adventures are for the most part in uninspired octosyllabics which flatten the speaking voice; it is in the introductions that it appears most consistently and, as the poem progresses, the music is firmly fixed and relates the quintessence of Scott's involvement with time. It is as if the legendary past has to be expressed as a stiff, chivalric quantity before it can be taken up, before its strangely obsessive inward emotions can be absorbed. The scale in the cantos is much larger; the sedentary, isolated figure of the poet gives way to a broader canvas. One is pitched into an enfolding tale whose effects are cumulative, whose personal emotions are projections of those Scott declares in the introductions and which, in turn, point to the more embracing issue of national destiny of which they are a part. The resolution of the private affairs of the protagonists is swallowed up in the gathering climax of the battle since it is not the finding or winning of love but the world of preternatural emotion, of great heavings of compulsive feeling which accompany a nation's travail, the dreadful signs of a larger-than-human conflict dwarfing the players, which engages Scott's attention. It is, indeed, the very mark of the sympathetic anxiety which involves him in his country's past. The events rather than the verse retain a singular, luminous force and it is their eruption, once they have been gathered up into a liberating contextual pattern, that matters.

What may seem merely the colourful pageant of the past—stately, heraldic events and personages together with the trappings of the occult—begins to resolve itself into an intimation of the major theme, the state of Scotland at a time of crisis and the nature of its inheritance. It is the same principle which A. O. J. Cockshut [in *The Achievement of Sir Walter Scott*, 1969] has noticed in *The Bride of Lammermoor*:

> Read in one way, it is a perfectly clear account of a chapter of social history . . . But in actually reading the story one is constantly distracted from this sombre and simple line of intelligible events by sibyls muttering dark prophecies, by wells to which strange legends attach, and by scraps of verse that prefigure the story . . . Scott was not really writing about prophecies and the preternatural at all. Still less was he writing allegory. He was writing with great intelligence and control about the relation between fact and legend. But instead of analysing the difference . . . he places the fact and the legend side by side at every point of the story . . . By this method superstition is humanized, legend is shown to be relevant to the deepest concerns of the society that produces it.

We may at first be unattracted by the slow unfolding of Marmion's tale, but we are soon enough discomforted by the emergence of an undercurrent of strong feeling apparently in excess of what the situation demands; the hero's guilty conscience spreads like a hidden stain, rising to the surface whenever some suprarational event or story occurs (unsurprisingly, since these are in fact its counters).

Scott's brooding introductions, full of a passionate melancholy, counterpoint the tale from without while the suffering of judgement in the convent introduces a divine dispensatory justice which it is impossible not to feel dominating affairs as fate might superintend human activity. It is as if a natural scene—the landscape of a country and its popular figures—were gradually dimmed, the darkening movement punctuated by tremors of a supernatural kind, unexpected lunges of feeling. These disruptions are concentrated mainly in yet another division of the poem, the tales interposed within all but two of the cantos. (Even then, these cantos have flashbacks which add to much the same kind of inset: in Canto I, the Palmer's religious wanderings, and in Canto II the history of St Hilda's.) In Canto III, the host's tale relates the appearance of a demon warrior, in Canto IV Sir David Lindesay's tale concerns a ghostly creature warning the King to avoid war, in Canto V 'Lochinvar' tells of a romantic elopement and in the last Canto, De Wilton's History reveals the living presence of the man. At first, these insets may seem unrelated, but not for long. The demon warrior whom Marmion is impelled to challenge materializes as the man he once wronged, the herald suing for peace prefigures the more forbidding messenger whose dire warning interrupts De Wilton's conversation with the Abbess as it does the battle, while De Wilton's History lays bare the personal situation which is to reach its conclusion shortly after. Each emanation of the ghostly compels the tale into a tighter and more urgent unity. This is especially true of 'Lochinvar', whose dramatic placing of tale and teller comments effectively enough on the state of affairs at court, a certain sapping of integrity and resolution, while at the same time forecasting De Wilton's rescue of Clare. The anapaestic run of the metre perfectly traces the romance of the poem whose straightforward feeling and quick, lively action has an extraordinary liberating effect in the context of Marmion's struggles. Like the other insets, it crystallizes the chief issues and impels the poem to its resolution.

Marmion **is a poem exploring the identity of self, a poetic autobiography which serves to locate the creative principle in oneself, to determine one's subject matter for a life's work.**

—John Pikoulis

The triple focus of the poem presents an ever-deepening theme being richly worked. We might, with some justification, add a fourth, the voluminous notes Scott attached at the end. These are not superfluous even if only because they give the reader a glimpse of the variety of information Scott lived with and hence an insight into the temperament of the man. They also show how prodigious was the imagination which transformed this vast seam of history and legend into poetry and how intricately a part of his achievement they were. From this multiple focus, then, grows our understanding of the pattern formed by the

epistolary introductions, each dedicated to a different friend. It is his recording of the landscape which allows Scott entry first into his childhood and adolescence and then into the romances he encountered. It was in recording the scenery at Ashestiel and elsewhere while writing the poem that he could recall Sandy-Knowe ('It was a barren scene and wild, / Where naked cliffs were rudely pil'd' [Canto III, Introduction]) where he lived after his first serious illness; this then modulates with a revealing logic into his adolescence and the time of his second illness, when he turned to reading of military exploits. Hence,

> While stretch'd at length upon the floor,
> Again I fought each combat o'er,
> Pebbles and shells, in order laid,
> The mimic ranks of war display'd.

The quick, strong verse—what R. H. Hutton in his remarkable book [*Sir Walter Scott,* 1888] called a 'hurrying strength'—leads us to the personal emotion, the balance, stress and slowing music of

> For I was wayward, bold, and wild,
> A self-will'd imp, a grandame's child;
> But half a plague, and half a jest,
> Was still endur'd, belov'd, caress'd.

Scott's memoir tells of the severe difficulty he had in adjusting to the change 'from being a single indulged brat, to becoming a member of a large family' on his return to his mother's charge and how his enthusiasm 'was chiefly awakened by the wonderful and the terrible—the common taste of children, but in which I have remained a child even unto this day' [published in *The Life of Sir Walter Scott* by J. G. Lockhart, 1871]. He also tells us of the life of a boy of much animation who was essentially a solitary (at no time, we may infer, close to either his mother or his father and left to make the most of his own resources). Such relationships as he entered into seem always to have been directed at objectives other than those primarily related to the ordinary exchanges of life. It may well be that Scott was so absorbed in the fruits of his imagination that he hardly knew himself to be alone, a fact which later success obscured further. Even the six dedicatees of the introductory epistles appear so that they may sharpen the point of Scott's writing the poem. It was, for example, through Richard Heber that Scott met John Leyden, another collector of ballads; George Ellis published anthologies of old romances; and William Erskine both shared and stimulated Scott's enthusiasm for lore and legend, especially in the German drama, in which particular James Skene also figured. He does not mention other friends, William Clerk, James Ballantyne, Laidlaw, or James Hogg, say, who seemed less intimately involved in his poetic tastes and researches; and if the classicist Richard Heber seemed not so much taken by border ballads as by Homer and Virgil, that, too, could be turned to good account as defining Scott's interests more sharply (as in the beautiful passage concerning the treasure of Franchémont).

The introduction to the second canto, set against the now-vanished Ettrick Forest, is full of loss, not only of the pleasures the forest afforded and of the 'fiercer game' which once could be found there, but also of the poet's own past:

> Just at the age 'twixt boy and youth
> When thought is speech, and speech is truth.

As he traces the 'mingled sentiment, / 'Twixt resignation and content' and the loneliness he feels at St Mary's Lake, whose scene he describes with the great effect of the singleness of a refined emotion directly engaged, thoughts of transience and decay well up, in marked contrast to the 'ruder and more savage scene' of the following canto for which it prepares with gripping force:

> Thence view the lake with sullen roar
> Heave her board billows to the shore;
> And mark the wild-swans mount the gale,
> Spread wide through mist their snowy sail,
> And ever stoop again to lave
> Their bosoms on the surging wave.

This particularity of response (especially as the metre modulates into a more responsive rhythm) and concentration of energy is striking, but the description as a whole is remarkable more for its overall grasp than for such particularity and concentration, for the atmosphere it infuses, for the integrity of the personal statement it suggests.

The third introductory epistle returns to the justification for his writing a tale like **Marmion** and locates it in the helpless impulse which he harbours for legend, an impulse associated once more with childhood and its primary response to the Scottish landscape ('Yet was poetic impulse given / By the green hill and clear blue heaven') which Donald Davie rightly links with the simplicity of the earliest romantics, who returned to the '*morality* . . . of the poetic style of the ballad' and which he locates in the above-quoted lines as indicating the strength of one who records without insistence or pushing beyond surface meanings. It is the strength of this straightforwardness which is one aspect of his literary sensibility which Scott declares in the introductions; the other is his love for 'old tales' which he goes on to relate. All this constitutes the very pitch and reel of an imagination anything but literal; it gives his straightforwardness the validity it has.

The next epistle (introducing Canto IV) deepens this duality of directness and imaginative fervour in the contrasts it draws, most memorably in the contrast between the actuality of a shepherd frozen to death ('If fails his heart, if his limbs fail, Benumbing death is in the gale') and the contradictory reality of the blithesome shepherd who figures in 'all Arcadia's golden creed', between 'youthful summer' and 'the winter of our age'—as the tale of Marmion shows, between the past and the present. It is precisely this correspondence of complementary realities, equivalent states of being, that gives the poem its central tension and its structural principle. Marmion's progress is animated by its triple theme of human guilt, the omnipresence of the occult and of war, and the bargaining of national iden-

tity that it entails. The introductions point those themes, ground them in the living presence of their creator with the despondent lament for 'the ravages of time' with which the succeeding introduction is weighed. As with Newark and Ettrick, so Dun-Edin has fallen:

> How gladly I avert mine eyes,
> Bodings, or true or false, to change,
> For Fiction's fair romantic range,
> Or for tradition's dubious light,
> That hovers 'twixt the day and night:
> Dazzling alternately and dim,
> Her wavering lamp I'd rather trim,
> Knights, squares, and lovely dames to see,
> Creation of my fantasy,
> Than gaze abroad on reeky fen,
> And make of mists invading men.
>   (Canto V, Introduction)

Again, so tactful and solid is the courtesy of the expression that its acknowledgements almost slip by; we need not believe the disingenuous distinctions as anything other than different parts of the same feeling, his imaginative involvement in time and the obscuring light both of the past and of the present he plunges into. It is the same with the memorable Christmas scene he draws in the final introduction and the contrast there between the communal, levelling cheer of remembered holidays, their pagan origin ('grim delight', 'barbarous mirth') and such a bond of kinship inspired by them, whose spirit continues in Scotland alone. From that, it is an easy move to justifying the 'omens drear / . . . legends wild of woe and fear' and the ghostly visitations, especially as they interrupt the habituated pomp and chivalry of the public scene with pregnant force. It is this close correlation between the parts of the poem and the interpenetrating realities which vivify it, which leads us to understand how it is that the tale is that creation with whose help Scott can uncover and discover the feelings which obsess him and which, by their very nature, cannot be directly seized. This turning of himself into Marmion's story and vice versa, this activation of the fabular as reality, is the mainspring of the poem.

The mainspring is released in the Battle of Flodden by the clairvoyant act wherein Marmion is presented as the awakened hero. It is an altogether surprising reversal. The battle itself clearly engages Scott's deepest sympathies. Their pressure informs the whole description, whose clarity and concerted brevity lift it quite above the more detailed and active account of Bannockburn which closes **The Lord of the Isles**. We are divided between the wrenching pathos of the Scots' defeated valour and the admiration we are led to feel for the dying Marmion, torn by his guilt for Constance and the necessity he feels to continue directing operations. He has an electric energy which is quite other than the moody vacillation of the King, whose failure to seize the moment foredooms the issue. Scott establishes the reality of the defeat with as much pity as if it were a personal loss, but the admiration for the elemental Marmion is something more curious. De Wilton's return from the dead to rescue Clare and challenge him again, which we had been led to expect as the major resolution of the personal conflicts, passes for next to nothing in the light of the recrudescent Marmion. So, too, does the idea of religious retribution, of which the Palmer's disguise is an important part. The scene in which a monk appears to minister to Marmion and Clare to pity him in his death-throes is an extraordinary instance of transparent emotion:

> Forgot were hatred, wrongs and fears;
> The plaintive voice alone she hears,
>   Sees but the dying man.
> She stoop'd her by the runnel's side . . .
> Where raged the war, a dark-red tide
>   Was curdling in the streamlet blue.
>   (Canto VI, XXX)

That brilliantly limned moment is the vital turning point; by an act of associative magic (emphasized by the location of Sybil Grey's fountain), the broad stain of the battle encompasses Marmion in the painful destruction of 'Our Caledonian pride' as it does the comparably blemished King, whose bravery 'beseem'd the monarch slain'.

Yet Marmion is ennobled beyond even this, for, after his death, his body is mistaken for that of his faithful follower (another surprising character who appears from nowhere and contributes to the stirring collocation at the end); it is the latter's body which is buried beneath the sculptured tomb, while Marmion rests anonymously in the earth. It is a defeat—De Wilton regains his heritage and Clare—as Flodden is an abject defeat for Scotland. Yet Marmion rises above the lovers' happy return and focuses, more than anyone else, the impact of the defeat of the Scots. How an Englishman fighting against the King's army comes to share its fate in this way and how a man who had clearly wronged others comes closer to Scott's (and our) compassion rests on those competing dualities the poem had earlier explored. We may see in this confounding resolution the appearance of the Romantic hero, one who is to be measured by the dynamism with which he expresses himself and cuts through opposition, the man of action whose life is an intensely imaginative one, muscling through between the real and legendary worlds in his great solitude so as to make them seem coterminous and realize himself as a higher essence of life to be judged less by the conventional standards of morality than by what he is at heart, an imposed, personal standard which wakes in us an instinctive sympathy. Where Marmion first appeared a mysterious and blemished man, distinctly unheroic, now he is transformed into someone if not fully heroic at least of heroic proportions. It is this shifting nature of Marmion's depiction which Byron perceived in his *English Bards and Scotch Reviewers* when he writes of 'The golden-crested haughty Marmion':

> Not quite a felon, yet but half a knight,
> The gibbet or the field prepared to grace;
> A mighty mixture of the great and base.

As such, Marmion is the hero of that unreconciled contradiction which marks Scott's own personality as it does his involvement in the relationship of past and present, Scotland and England, fact and fable. The English warrior who is to some extent the centre of his own displaced emotional reaction to the defeat of his countrymen partakes of that paradoxical attitude to his country's absorption into a United Kingdom which David Daiches long ago described ['Scott's Achievement as a Novelist', *Literary Essays,* 1956], especially in his location of the figure of the Englishman in the novels, going to Scotland and, as detached observer, witnessing a nation's struggles before retiring once more to England. The fact that a man like Waverley has not a little of Scott in him and that Scott enters the past as one entering territory he has perforce made his own tightens the analogy. In the poem, projected through a keener vision, Marmion becomes the burden of sorrow. (The same may be felt about Roderick Dhu in **The Lady of the Lake,** whose fierce, compulsive belligerence dominates the poem.) **Marmion,** however, ends with the lovers living happily ever after. This is no mere flourish since, as R. H. Hutton pointed out, Scott's interest in the supernatural or that in the outsider, the down-and-out, was 'the very sign of his conventionalism . . . He widened rather than narrowed the chasm between the outlaw and the respectable citizen, even while he did not disguise his own romantic interest in the former' (*Sir Walter Scott,* p. 122). Whatever Marmion's end, the outcome of the struggles is a fit one, justly advancing the prospects of all concerned. It is as if history were being validated, Marmion taking upon himself all the contrary, almost uncontrollable feelings of a man like Scott who *feels* history should be so trusted, of one whose emotions are stirred by other, more private affections. He may well have been predisposed to the continuance of established society guided by the trusted traditions of its faith—life goes on—but society's eruptions moved him none the less. The verse by John Leyden which prefaces the poem may thus be seen to take on, intentionally or not, ironic overtones of the most animating kind:

> Alas! that Scottish maid should sing
>   The combat where her lover fell!
> That Scottish Bard should wake the string
>   The triumph of our foes to tell!

Perhaps the internal contradiction in the Scottish camp which opened it to defeat and Scott's complicated reaction to it, as to the guilty deeds of Marmion, demanded the kind of structure the poem possesses. Why else weave the tale of Englishmen searching for their true rewards and happiness round the defeat of Flodden Field and yet make so compelling a poetic argument from the resulting contradiction? Its resolution could follow, granted that Scott understood all too well how an individual's fate could be enmeshed in that of his society and granted the situation of an older man's consideration of his country's history in terms of promise and loss and his more inward sense of a childhood in which a fantasy figure like Marmion—tormented, solitary, brave, guilty, and finally ascendent in the anguish of defeat—could complement the vision of a society which is high, proud, and unstable and driven to irrevocable defeat in which its highest qualities yet survived.

It is difficult to do more than state it thus since the clairvoyancy, like the poetry, is primarily contextual, to be taken at a stretch and so discoverable only in terms of the pattern formed by the conflicts and catalyzing tensions and by their steadily cumulating impact. It is not that Scott's eye was only for the general scene or broad effect; on the contrary, the interest is often directed at the particular but in such a way as to demand a mastering perspective, as with these lines in which he defends his pursuing his natural genius against the imagined complaints of Erskine:

> Look east, and ask the Belgian why,
> Beneath Batavia's sultry sky,
> He seeks not eager to inhale
> The freshness of the mountain gale,
> Content to rear his whiten'd wall
> Beside the dank and dull canal?
>   (Canto III, Introduction)

The romancer is ever an irregular experimenter, and one needs a supporting sense when regarding these lines of Scott's apologies for an unclassical raggedness of form, his unpainterly proportions and wilfulness of procedure which he declares, with not a little self-satisfaction, in the introductions as he does in his autobiographical memoir [published in Lockhart's *The Life of Sir Walter Scott*]: 'If I have since been able in poetry to trace with some success the principles of [a sense of the picturesque in scenery], it has always been with reference to its general and leading features, or under some alliance with moral feeling.' It is the structure rather than the music or the detail which predominates, the structure not only of the poem but ultimately of a way of life, and it is that which demands from the reader his imaginative response. The words Scott used to describe his memory of the past might serve as a description of how his best work was achieved: 'like one of the large, old-fashioned stone-cannons of the Turks, very difficult to load well and discharge, but making a powerful effect when by good chance an object did come within range of its shot' (Lockhart, p. 50). The 'object' in *Marmion* was Scott himself. The identity of interest uniting the poet and his created figure was made possible by that extra dimension of Scott's sensibility whereby past and present were truly coterminous and their inhabitants part of a continuum as real to him as any of the evidence of his other senses. It is a poem exploring the identity of self, a poetic autobiography which serves to locate the creative principle in oneself, to determine one's subject matter for a life's work. It involves the bringing into greater consciousness of all that was most deeply embedded and the result is the emerging discipline of awareness without which the novels could scarcely be imagined. It is a poem of an altogether original kind whose structure includes not only the direct recounting of his life in the epistles in a memorably lucid and vivid manner but also the poem of Marmion himself which illustrates, counterpoints, and deepens the autobiography almost in the manner of an 'objective correlative'. It is the emergence of a concrete and dominant poetic personality which roots the tale of Marmion in the earth of self. This, indeed, seems to have been Scott's intention since the memoir printed by Lockhart was written at about the time that *Marmion* was exercising him and since the introductions to the cantos were originally announced a year before the poem was

published as *Six Epistles from Ettrick Forest* (to be published as a separate volume). Further, the configuration of dates involving the emergence of *Waverley,* the Ashestiel Memoir, the *Six Epistles,* and *Marmion* shows how justified we are in regarding the poetry as remarkable not only for itself but also as the vital preparatory work for the novels. As the poetry was written, so the impetus to the novels grew. At some stage in the process, Scott came into his own. *Marmion* marks the time when he entered his imaginative prime and realized (as we may also deduce from the figure of the minstrel in his previous long poem) the creative instincts formed in his early life.

Thomas Crawford   (lecture date 1971)

SOURCE: "Scott as a Poet," in *Ètudes Anglaises,* Vol. XXIV, No. 4, October-December, 1971, pp. 478–91.

[*Crawford is a Scottish critic and educator and the author of* Scott *(1965), a book-length study of Sir Walter Scott. In the following essay, Crawford extends the ideas presented by Donald Davie in his1961 lecture. Like Davie, Crawford finds much of Scott's poetry to be innovative and finely crafted, though Crawford emphasizes the manner in which Scott is able to "ad-lib" on the folk song and popular lyric forms, as well as the interesting textures that are created in the scenes of the poems. Crawford also comments on the connection he perceives between Scott's poetry and novels.*]

At the time of that other Centenary of nearly forty years ago—the Centenary of Sir Walter's death, which was so widely observed in 1932—there was much shaking of heads at the decline in Scott's reputation. "Who reads Walter Scott now?" was the cry; "what can be done to stimulate interest, to renew his popularity?" The pundits read the signs, and there were even forecasts that the productions of the time—the Grierson edition of the Letters, the new biographies of John Buchan and Una Pope-Hennessy, such critical essays as Lord David Cecil's in the *Atlantic Monthly* or those edited by Sir Herbert Grierson in the volume *Sir Walter Scott Today*—were in fact the forerunners of a Scott revival. But, of course, it was not to be. If 1932 was almost, if not quite, the worst year of the Great Depression, it was certainly one of the most seminal years for the literary Left. It was, for example, the year of W. H. Auden's *The Orators*; and Auden's generation, brooding on slag-heaps and a remade humanity "free and equal as the shine from snow", were not in the mood to assess on his own terms a backward-looking Romancer afraid of Luddites and radical mobs. Moreover, 1932 was also a significant date in the development of the new elitism, when F. R. Leavis in *Scrutiny* was beginning his radical-mandarin attempt to chart a selective tradition—the main line of English poetry and of the English novel—from which Scott was to be so conspicuously excluded. Scott, indeed, was seen as a kind of nineteenth-century Hugh Walpole (Walpole, for the early Leavisites, was a symbol of all that was worst in the middlebrow commercial novel of that time)—like the H. G. Wells of *Kipps* or *Tono-Bungay* perhaps;

like Trollope even, or C. P. Snow at the present day, he was beyond the pale.

But even in the years immediately following 1932, the crusading years of the young Leavis, an entirely contrary trend was making itself felt. A critic whom some of us feel to be one of the three or four critics who really deserve to be called "great" in this Byzantine century of ours, was in his Moscow exile revaluing Scott and Balzac and Stendhal and publishing in the pages of *International Literature* and other Soviet periodicals those brilliant essays which later appeared in book form as *Studies in European Realism* and *The Historical Novel*. I am referring, of course, to Georg Lukács, who died in Budapest early in the present year. And in Scotland and beyond David Daiches was developing an approach which in essence is not so very different from Lukács, and which first reached publication in the introduction to an American edition of *The Heart of Midlothian,* and in the essay "Scott's Reputation as a Novelist" which appeared in the periodical *Nineteenth Century Fiction* during 1951. The modern reappraisal of Scott by academics both in Britain and America during the past few years is either a development, refinement or qualification of the positions of Lukács and Daiches, or else a sophisticated reaction against them.

Yet neither Lukács nor Daiches would, I think, extend this reappraisal to Scott's poetry to any significant extent; and what is true of them is even truer of their successors. Writing in 1957, for example, in the *Pelican Guide to English Literature,* Patrick Cruttwell declared:

> With the best will in the world, one cannot say much for the poems. They have historical interest . . . But now they seem intolerably faded and fustian. Their manner is a versifying of the Horace Walpole—Mrs. Radcliffe melodramatic-Gothick: burning tears flow from flashing eyes, breasts heave beneath corselets obviously filched from museums

and so on.

Or—another witness—John Lauber, in his volume on Scott in the Twayne Books series, published in 1965:

> Scott's poetry appears irretrievably faded today. His heroics no longer thrill; his rhetoric seems rant; and his sentiment, sentimentality. His language too often alternates between a rather stilted eighteenth-century poetic diction and obtrusive archaisms designed to lend the proper medieval tone to his work. The long narrative poems on which his poetic reputation rested appear flimsy and unsubstantial in structure, in characterization and in versification.

It surely cannot be gainsaid that Cruttwell and Lauber represent the prevailing view, and that any dissentient voices are regarded either as survivals from a bygone era of impressionistic belles-lettres, or else as just plain eccentric. As an example of the first, let me take the late Christina Keith, who in *The Author of Waverley* (1964) praised Scott's handling of the *sounds* of verse, claiming

that "his ear for sound is one of the finest in English literature, and far the finest in Scots," and that "all his best passages, alike in verse and prose, were written first for the ear". Following a well-established critical tradition, Miss Keith also drew attention to Scott's handling of colour—the "purples and gold of Perthshire" in *The Lady of the Lake,* and his magnificent presentation of light: red light, white moonlight with its background of night—scarlet and black, evanescence and cloudscapes reminiscent of Turner and Whistler. And as an example of the second, let me cite Donald Davie's British Academy lecture, published in the *Proceedings* of that body for 1961. Davie noted that Scott's octosyllabics (so often interspersed with lines of six syllables) build up to parallel climaxes, at the same time as his syntax builds up to similar climaxes. In their anxiety to condemn Scott for his facile imagery and stilted diction, Davie implies, his critics are almost ludicrously blind to his true originality, which is an originality of grammar. Scott's poetical rhetoric repeats identical constructions, he says, in order to produce syntactic augmentation. The traditional repetitive orderings of poetry are rhyme and metre, of course—and the orthodox critics have plenty to say about these—"mechanical rhymes", "lumbering, insensitive jog-trot", etc. But "syntactic augmentation" is an additional ordering added to the familiar ones: and when Scott puts the three orderings together and combines them with real *expertise,* then, says Davie:

> We recognise a poetry thoroughly achieved, structured through and through, and elegant variation, the saying of one thing many ways, brings with it for Scott this additional source of order.

In other words, Davie is claiming that the very things the *élitist* critics cite as evidence for lack of structure are in fact evidence *for* structure, that when you truly make the imaginative effort to understand the kind of poetry that Scott was writing, "elegant variation" and "the saying of one thing many ways" can indicate a sort of excellence which some blinkered minds are indisposed to admit.

It is my contention that Donald Davie is right and that further application of modern critical method to Scott's poems will lead not to the discovery that Scott is among the major poets of the world (clearly, he isn't), but at the very least to a further upgrading.

What merits, then, other than the poetry of grammar and the saying of the same thing many ways to which Davie has drawn attention, or the colour, light and cloud effects which Miss Keith has reminded us of—what additional merits are to be found in the longer poems of Scott? Scott's age (and I am well aware that I am perpetrating an enormous historical oversimplification when I say this) was one in which the lyrical impulse and the narrative impulse were intensely aroused and even in conflict with each other. It was at one and the same time an age of supreme poetry and of some of our very greatest novels—not so much "The Age of Wordsworth" as the old literary compendiums used to term it, as the age of those two diametrically opposed contemporaries—William Blake and Jane Austen. In poetry itself, it was an age both of great long poems and of great lyrics. Now it seems incontrovertibly true that we miss from the longer poems of the age the over-mastering narrative line of the rhetoricians and of traditional epic. Yet although "Romantic" long poems have this deficiency—if, indeed, it *is* a deficiency—they have their compensating merits. Instead of the overall planning and comprehensive onward drive of a Dante or a Milton, we find not one but three narrative "lines" of a somewhat different sort—first, the line of the traditional ballad, next the small-scale line of the simple oral tale, and thirdly what I am going to call the "line of free association", of the maunderings and convolutions of spontaneous reminiscence. The line of the simple tale has of course a long pre-history, back through the prose of Fielding and Defoe to Chaucer and Boccaccio and further back still, perhaps to the primitive tribe; but in the eighteenth and nineteenth centuries it returns to the establishment literature of "high culture" through the antiquarian movement and the folk revival, producing something qualitatively new in the process. Traditional folk narrative in verse has its own repertoire of inherited plots, motifs and techniques such as incremental repetition, and it may very well be extremely formal and ceremonious. In folk prose narrative, though there may exist a similar formal element ("Once upon a time", the three brothers who set off on a quest or the three sisters who are to be wooed in turn—in each case it is the third one, poor and despised, who is successful), yet there is also an amount of spontaneity and free variation which is far more fluid than the variation we find in a traditional "Child" ballad. The literary example I wish to name is, of course, in verse—Burns's *Tam o' Shanter*; and Burns is able to create this ease and fluency precisely because of the verse, as detailed critical analysis has shown. But it is significant for my argument here . . . that its immediate sources were two oral tales, which Burns himself has preserved for us in their *prose* form.

The best known narrative of free association and spontaneous reminiscence is in prose—Sterne's *Tristram Shandy,* but its first really startling *poetic* expression occurs again in Burns—this time in his verse epistles. Here are two stanzas from the *Second Epistle to Lapraik.* Burns is utterly tired out after a day's heavy labour in the fields, but he wills himself to reply to Lapraik, though his "awkwart" Muse pleads and begs to the contrary:

> Sae I gat paper in a blink,
> An' down gaed stumpie in the ink:
> Quoth I, "before I sleep a wink,
>   I vow I'll close it;
> An' if ye winna mak it clink,
>   By Jove, I'll prose it!"
>
> Sae I've begun to scrawl, but whether
> In rhyme, or prose, or baith thegither;
> Or some hotch-potch that's rightly neither,
>   Let time mak proof;
> But I shall scribble down some blether
>   Just clean aff-loof.

What must strike everyone is the astonishing verve of these lines, the brilliance of their colloquialism, so firmly root-ed in the previous vernacular tradition in Lowland Scotland, their disarming defiance of *anything* approaching the logic of heroic narrative. This is seen in Burns's deliberate glorying in "some hotch-potch", the offhand throwaway; he will simply scribble down some nonsense, quite extempore, and make of it a kind of action-poetry that recaptures and preserves for us the poet's own delight in the process of writing. Of course we are not dealing with narrative here but with the epistle, a different genre, and what concerns us is the effect that occurs when this spirit of spontaneity is transferred to narrative. Even so, and on the level of the epistle as a Literary Kind, Burns's apparent negation of planned rational composition is perfectly compatible with some very definite and categorical statements about life and its meaning. Burns's method is a free association which has its own sort of control, and in each epistle he counterposes some positive value to the hypocrisy and smug utilitarian calculation that he regards as the enemy of Life. We have to go to Byron in the following generation before we find an equal spontaneity, an equal "open-endedness", this time made into the organising principle of narrative works. I am referring, of course, to *Beppo* and *Don Juan.*

How does Scott fit into this picture? An examination of his longer poems shows that Scott was indebted to all three narrative lines; he employed both the two lines of folk narrative, that of the classical ballad and that of the oral tale, and his own form of the line of spontaneity. Since I have elsewhere examined, however briefly, the contribution made by the classical ballad to the structure of the longer poems and, indeed, of the novels, perhaps you will forgive me if I concentrate [here] upon the third narrative line, the line of spontaneity. One of the most amusing of his *juvenilia* shows Scott reacting with the instinctive spontaneity of the born occasional poet. At this time (aged 16) he was in love with the mysterious Jessie from Kelso, and often visited her when she was tending an invalid aunt in Edinburgh. If he arrived when the old lady was awake, he had to hide in a cramped closet—a large shelved cupboard crammed with hams and cheeses and domestic utensils:

> Though tired of standing all this time
>   I dare na stir a leg,
> Though wishing sair to stretch my arms
>   I canna move a peg.
>
> The glasses tremble at my breath
>   So close to me they stand,
> Whist jars are pressing at my feet
>   And jugs at either hand.
>   (**"The Prisoner's Complaint,"** Stzs. 5–6)

Like the Burns epistles, these stanzas are not narrative; but they show how Scott, right at the beginning of his career as a versifier, could draw on yet another reservoir of the unconstrained—the vigorous humour of popular lyric. Neither is my next quotation narrative; indeed, I've chosen it for a similar purpose, because it shows him in his maturity, at the very height of his powers, skilfully reacting to the built-in freedom of the Burns stanza itself (which we in Scotland like to call "Standard Habbie"). Here are four stanzas of the **"Epilogue to the Drama founded on 'St. Roman's Well'"**, spoken by Mr. Mackay in the character or Meg Dodds, who enters "encircled by a crowd of unruly boys, whom a town's-officer is driving off":

That's right, friend—drive the gaitlings back,
And lend yon muckle ane a whack;
Your Embro' bairns are grown a pack,
    Sae proud and saucy,
They scarce will let an auld wife walk
    Upon your causey.

The next stanza is about the disappearance of such well-known Edinburgh landmarks as the Old Tolbooth, and the ancient Town guard, known as "the Claught", as well as two well-known Edinburgh worthies of Meg Dodds' own time:

But whar's the gude Tolbooth gane noo?
Whar's the auld Claught, wi' red and blue?
Whar's Jamie Laing? and whar's John Doo?
    And whar's the Weigh-house?
Deil hae't I see but what is new,
    Except the Playhouse!

Yoursells are changed frae head to heel,
There's some that gar the causeway reel
With clashing hufe and rattling wheel,
    And horses canterin',
Whase father's daundered hame as weel
    Wi lass and lantern.

Mysell being in the public line,
I look for howffs I kenn'd lang syne,
Whar gentles used to drink gude wine,
    And eat cheap dinners;
But deil a soul gangs there to dine,
    Of saints and sinners!

She laments the passing of once-famous taverns, and their replacement by those new and revolting abominations—Hotels:

Fortune's and Hunter's gane, alas!
And Bayle's is lost in empty space;
And now if folk would splice a brace,
    Or crack a bottle,
They gang to a new-fangled place
    They ca' a Hottle.
            (Stzs. I, 3–6)

At all periods of his life Scott drew upon the living variety of Scottish traditional modes. He drew on the medieval Romances, on popular occasional verse, on Standard Habbie, on vernacular folk-song:

Donald Caird's come again!
Donald Caird's come again!

Tell the news in brugh and glen,

Donald Caird's come again.

Steek the amrie, lock the kist,
Else some gear may weel be mist;
Donald Caird finds orra things
Where Allan Gregor fand the tings;
Dunts of kebbuck, taits of woo,
Whiles a hen and whiles a sow,
Webs or duds frae hedge or yard—
'Ware the wuddie, Donald Caird!
            (St. 4)

And he also drew on folk-song's parodic tendency, as in his Tory and Legitimist gloss on the revolutionary songs about that symbol of democracy, the Tree of Liberty. Here it is—Stanza three of Scott's version of **"For a' that,"** which was sung at the first meeting of the Pitt Club of Scotland and published in the *Scots Magazine* for July 1814:

The Austrian Vine, the Prussian Pine
    (For Blucher's sake, hurra that),
The Spanish Olive, too, shall join,
    And bloom in peace, for a' that.
Stout Russia's Hemp, so surely twined
    Around our wreath we'll draw that,
And he that would the cord unbind,
    Shall have it for his gra-vat!

It is my contention that Scott's narrative structure in the longer poems is all of a piece with the flexible movement of the non-narratives we have been examining. Scott's narrative structure is a line of spontaneity within which there occurs that repetition, that saying of one thing many ways, which Donald Davie sees as characteristic of Sir Walter's verse. Now that variation—"elegant" or "inelegant" depending on your point of view—can at its best achieve a most pleasing vividness, as, for example, in the solid rendering of a person or of a concrete object or grouping of objects, or in the brightness of contrasting primary colours (as noted recently by Miss Keith, and earlier by Ruskin and others), or in the evanescence of illuminated mist or cloud, or in the loudness or clarity of sound, or in the rush and movement of action.

As an example of several of these features, let me take the description, from *The Lady of the Lake,* of Ellen Douglas in her skiff, startled by a horn blown by the hidden huntsman, Fitzjames:

But scarce again his horn he wound,
When lo! forth starting at the sound,
From underneath an aged oak,
That slanted from the islet rock,
A damsel guider of its way,
A little skiff shot to the bay,
That round the promontory steep
Led its deep line in graceful sweep,
Eddying, in almost viewless wave,
The weeping willow twig to lave,
And kiss, with whispering sound and slow,
The beach of pebbles bright as snow.

The boat had touch'd this silver strand,
Just as the Hunter left his stand,
And stood conceal'd amid the brake,
To view this Lady of the Lake.
The maiden paused, as if again
She thought to catch the distant strain.
With head upraised, and look intent
And eye and ear attentive bent,
And locks flung back, and lips apart,
Like monument of Grecian art,
In listening mood, she seem'd to stand,
The guardian Naiad of the strand.
And ne'er did Grecian chisel trace
A Nymph, a Naiad, or a Grace,
Of finer form, or lovelier face!
What though the sun, with ardent frown,
Had slightly tinged her cheek with brown,—
The sportive toil, which, short and light,
Had dyed her glowing hue so bright,
Served too in hastier swell to show
Short glimpses of a breast of snow:
What though no rule of courtly grace
To measured mood had train'd her pace,—
A foot more light, a step more true,
Ne'er from the heath-flower dash'd the dew;
E'en the slight harebell raised its head,
Elastic from her airy tread:
What though upon her speech there hung
The accents of the mountain tongue,—
Those silver sounds, so soft, so dear,
The list'ner held his breath to hear!

(Canto I, Stzs. 17, 18)

The effect of the octosyllabics is quite different from ordinary expository prose in that Scott's discursive description of the girl is stylized, yet at the same time there is an "ad lib" impression in the way the lines run on from rhyme to rhyme. Within the "ad libbing" the verse serves or organises in a more patterned way than in ordinary prose such subsidiary features as alliteration, inversion, poetic diction ("sportive toil" and "aged oak"), and such similes as "Like monument of Grecian art". If I may borrow a phrase from Northrop Frye, the "figurative centre of gravity" of Scotts' octosyllabics is the illustrative simile, rather the metaphors that characterise more compressed and concentrated forms. The poetry of grammar operates through repeated comparatives—"A foot more light, a step more true", and parallel "What though" clauses. The construction "What though no rule of courtly grace / To measured mood had train'd her pace" is mirrored, seven lines later, by "What though upon her speech there hung / The accents of the mountain tongue". There is even a very minor instance of the poetry of action or rather motion in the passage—not the rumbustious battle incident for which Scott is famous, but the more subtle movement of the pressed harebell—

E'en the slight harebell raised its head
Elastic from her airy tread.

I would claim, then, that in the rather ordinary passage I have examined Scott is creating in verse effects which his

prose does not render, as can be seen by comparing the description of Ellen with the first appearance of Jeanie Deans in *The Heart of Midlothian*. You will recollect that at the beginning of the novel Jeanie is paid homage by the Laird of Dumbiedikes, yet

the historian, with due regard for veracity, is compelled to answer that her personal attractions were of no uncommon description. She was short, and rather too stoutly made for her size, had grey eyes, light-coloured hair, a round good-humoured face, much tanned with the sun, and her only peculiar charm was an air of inexpressible serenity, which a good conscience, kind feelings, contented temper, and the regular discharge of all her duties spread over her features. There was nothing, it may be supposed, very appalling in the form or manners of this rustic heroine; yet, whether from sheepish bashfulness, or from want of decision and imperfect knowledge of his own mind on the subject, the Laird of Dumbiedikes, with his old laced hat and empty tobacco-pipe, came and enjoyed the beatific vision of Jeanie Deans day after day, week after week, year after year, without proposing to accomplish any of the prophecies of the stepmother (ch. 9).

(The stepmother, of course, prophesied marriage between Jeanie and Dumbiedikes.)

We have all of us been conditioned to regard poetry as a more compressed form of discourse than prose. Yet, of the two passages I have read to you, it is the prose description which is more tightly packed, and this despite the *tone,* the flexible conversational voice of the author in a particular relationship with the reader, backed up by an urbanity perhaps derived from Fielding. Ever so lightly that description of Jeanie is related to the dominant themes and ideas of the novel—appearance and reality (this plain girl is a real heroine of everyday life), conscience and the claims of duty. It is true there are certain similarities—Ellen Douglas, like Jeanie, is more than she appears at first glance, and she, too, is sunburnt. But the cross references in the verse passage do not relate to important, socially determined *ideas* like conscience and duty: they are rather to a literary tradition, the Pastoral Tradition.

My next passage has been chosen to illustrate Scott's impressionistic handling of light and dark. It is from Canto I of *The Lord of the Isles* (1815). In the castle of Artornish, on the mainland side of the Sound of Mull, a wedding seems about to take place between Edith, maid of Lorn, and her reluctant intended, Lord Ronald. A lonely bark labours its way towards the castle anchorage. If they glance at the vessel at all, those petty Hebridean warrior chiefs who are making their way to the festivities and who are described with such opulence,

'Twas with such idle eye
As nobles cast on lowly boor,
When, toiling in his task obscure,
They pass him careless by.

(St. 16, lines 3–6)

This is one of the key images of the poem, which is linked indeed to the preoccupations underlying the Ellen Douglas passage and the description of Jeanie Deans. It is of remarkable significance for the theme of the poem (common elsewhere in Scott)—the nature of Heroism. For the poor, battered undistinguished bark contains none other than the Bruce, at his fortunes' lowest ebb. In the comparison I have just quoted, the national hero is juxtaposed to the peasant whose labour is the foundation of the whole of society—to the common people who persist throughout history, performing "their toils obscure, and a' that", in ages of moneygrubbing and decadence as well as in ages of Heroism. You will recollect that the noble endurance of the ordinary fisher folk is one of the abiding values in *The Antiquary,* that it is the same with the lower class Covenanters in *Old Mortality,* while the scepticism and sterling worth of Cuddie Headdrigg in that novel are the touchstones by which both cavaliers and fanatics are judged. And you will also recollect that the unprepossessing exterior of Jeanie Deans, physically the reverse of Tom Jones's incomparable Sophia, conceals true heroism—exactly the same sort of heroism that in another age and in other circumstances blazed forth in the life and career of Scotland's national leader—the Bruce. All this, or something like it, seems implied in the simple mention of the nobles' indifferent glance towards the lowly boor.

To return now to the text of the poem. As they approach the anchorage, the Leader (the Bruce) takes the helm himself. The first visual impression is the phosphorescence of sea-fire:

> The helm, to his strong arm consign'd,
> Gave the reef'd sail to meet the wind,
> And on her alter'd way,
> Fierce bounding, forward sprung the ship,
> Like greyhound starting from the slip
> To seize his flying prey.
> Awaked before rushing prow,
> The mimic fires of ocean glow,
> Those lightnings of the wave;
> Wild sparkles crest the broken tide,
> And, flashing round, the vessel's sides
> With elvish lustre lave.
> While, far behind, their livid light
> To the dark billows of the night
> A gloomy splendour gave
> It seems as if old Ocean shakes
> From his dark brow the lucid flakes
> In envious pageantry,
> To match the meteor light that streaks
> Grim Hecla's midnight sky.

(In this stanza, incidentally, there is a direct borrowing from *The Ancient Mariner,* which Scott himself draws attention to in a note—when Coleridge's water-snakes reared, "the elvish light / Fell off in hoary flakes"; in Scott, "the vessel's sides / With elvish lustre lave".)

Scott continues:

> Nor lack'd they steadier light to keep
> Their course upon the darken'd deep;—
> Artornish, on her frowning steep
> 'Twixt cloud and ocean hung,
> Glanced with a thousand lights of glee,
> And landward far, and far to sea,
> Her festal radiance flung.
> By that blithe beacon-light they steer'd,
> Whose lustre mingled well
> With the pale beam that now appear'd,
> As the cold moon her head uprear'd
> Above the eastern fell.

Scott next moves on from description to sound:

> Thus guided, on their course they bore,
> Until they near'd the mainland shore,
> When frequent on the hollow blast
> Wild shouts of merriment were cast,
> And wind and wave and sea-birds' cry
> With wassail sounds in concert vie,
> Like funeral shrieks with revelry,
> Or like the battle-shout
> By peasants heard from cliffs on high,
> When triumph, Rage and Agony,
> Madden the fight and rout.
> Nor nearer yet, through mist and storm
> Dimly arose the Castle's form,
> And deepen'd shadow made,
> Far lengthen'd on the main below,
> Where, dancing in reflected glow,
> A hundred torches play'd,
> Spangling the wave with lights as vain
> As pleasures in this vale of pain,
> That dazzle as they fade.
> (Stzs. 21–3)

I have quoted enough to illustrate what seems to me the most impressive feature of Scott's longer poems: to the fluid attenuated medium of his octosyllabics are added quite novel effects of "texture", which we are aware of in the line-by-line, stanza-by-stanza process of reading, and which were created by Scott in the bygoing, as part of his authorial ad-libbing. I am making use of that distinction between structure and texture which was developed by the American poet and critic John Crowe Ransom on the analogy of the visual and plastic arts, where texture normally refers to the surface qualities of a work—rough or smooth, coarse or finely grained, and so on. According to Ransom and his school, while the structure (i.e., the prose paraphrase of the argument) is of great consequence for a poem and indeed a poem cannot exist without it, yet it is in "texture" that a poem's main value resides. The skeleton is there so that flesh and muscles and sinews may have support and the brain and the nervous system may decode and transmit their messages, and not the other way round. Texture is a matter of "local heterogeneous detail"; the poet can't predict it; and it is in the interplay of these meanings—the counterpoint of rhyme and assonance, the fugue of metaphor, the dance of the phonemes as the poem is read aloud or heard with our inward ear—it is in these as they interact with the paraphrasable prose "structure", that the *real* poem consists.

Now the extraordinary paradox of Walter Scott as a poet is that whereas at first sight his aim is *merely* to tell a story, with the verse *merely* serving as a vehicle to that end, yet it's in what the vehicle does to that story, in the interaction between structure and texture—that true originality consists. For example, the climax of *The Lord of the Isles* is the Bannockburn battle-piece, and the whole poem moves up to it, with anticipatory images that are part of the poem's texture. Thus in Canto I the bark (containing, as we have seen, the Bruce) struggles through the Sound of Mull in a comparison that looks forward directly to Bannockburn:

> And midway through the channel met
> Conflicting tides that foam and fret,
> And high their mingled billows jet,
> As spears, that, in the battle set,
>   Spring upward as they break.
>   (St. 18, lines 4–8)

And a passage I have already cited is like an epitome of the poem's violent conflicts of mood:

> When frequent on the hollow blast
> Wild shouts of merriment were cast,
> And wind and wave and sea-birds cry
> With wassail sounds in concert vie,
> Like funeral shrieks with revelry,
>   Or like the battle-shout
> By peasants heard from cliffs on high . . .
>   (St. 23, lines 3–9)

The most original feature is not that structure and texture are connected; this is true of every poem by every author, of every play, of every literary work. No; it is the precise way in which the two are linked that matters, the way in which, when reading a Scott poem, we are aware of the action as an unfolding experience made up of concrete "scenes" which are unities of sight and sound, at the same time as we are conscious of the fluent movement of the verse medium itself.

Now in the opinion of many literary historians, the 19th century was the age in which the centre of literary gravity shifted from poetry (which had been dominant up till then) towards the novel: for a century and more, the sort of job that had formerly been done by the greater poets was done by the greater novelists. In a brilliant and thoughtful study entitled *Poetry Towards Novel*, . . . John Speirs argues that it was the influence of the poets of the early nineteenth century that made this possible. Blake, Coleridge and Keats mediated between Shakespeare and the later novelists; Wordsworth furnished subjectivism; Crabbe and Byron both made their contribution.

What makes the 19th century novel so different from (and perhaps so immeasurably superior to) the novel of the 18th century is that poetry, the whole major tradition of English poetry, is taken into it and fused with it.

It is rather striking that Speirs (a Scotsman, the author of that well-known book *The Scots Literary Tradition*) says practically nothing about Scott, the author who above all others, and in advance of the great nineteenth century figures whom Speirs mentions—the Brontës, Hardy, Hawthorne, Melville and Dickens—embodies in his own career the whole movement of "Poetry into Novel." For it is in his novels that Scott is most creatively a poet. I do not mean by this that the lyrics scattered through the novels are better than those incorporated into the longer poems, nor am I talking mystically, claiming that there is a more mysteriously transcendental "Poetic Vision" in the novels than in the longer poems. No: what I mean is that there is real imaginative continuity and that the degree of difference between the poems and the novels can best be established in relation to this matter of *texture*.

Exactly as in the longer poems, the unit of a Scott novel is the Scene—a fusion of sight and sound, where description and dialogue (especially where the dialogue is in Scots) combine in a way never previously known in the novel, and where the prose medium (based ultimately on the spoken Anglo-Scots of the legal profession) can carry a vastly more complex range of effects than the octosyllabic couplet. There are few symbols, in the modern sense of the word, in the poems. But in the novels, characters are often symbolic. To take a simple example, in *Guy Mannering* Scott makes Meg Merrilies into a symbol by the combination of her bizarre, even eldritch appearance and her heightened rhetorical language. To take a more complex example in *The Heart of Midlothian* Jeanie Deans is both a realistically portrayed human being and an allegorical figure standing for Scotland, as Chris Guthrie does in Lewis Grassic Gibbon's *A Scots Quair*. And in *The Bride of Lammermoor* we have an entire novel that is poetically organized, with a poetic texture. Donald Cameron gives a brilliant judgement on *The Bride* as "a beautifully formed tale of tragic pride and the treachery of the self, smoothly interwoven with a Scottish peasant sense of the supernatural based on a penetrating insight into the social life of the time and the hidden processes of the mind [in "The Web of Destiny: The Structure of *The Bride of Lammermoor*", repr. in A. N. Jeffares, ed., *Scott's Mind and Art*, 1969]. Surely it is significant that Cameron instinctively chooses a metaphor of interweaving, a metaphor of texture, to describe the book. And of course one element in the texture is the panoply of antiquarian notes; another is the Shakespearian references which abound—in *The Bride of Lammermoor* they are principally to *Romeo and Juliet, Macbeth* and *Hamlet*. Ravenswood's pride is counterposed to Lady Ashton's, Lucy's passiveness counterpoints the Lord Keeper's legalistic deviousness and henpecked chicanery, Edgar's peculiar form of self-betrayal contrasts with Lucy's, as Donald Cameron has noted (Edgar's is based on lack of self-knowledge about love, though not about social necessity; Lucy's rests on sheer innate passivity). And all these contrasts, as we come to know them in an actual reading of the novel, in an engagement with the work, are a matter of texture.

Take Lucy Ashton's song in Chapter III, rightly regarded as one of Scott's finest lyrics. It has been said that the song is an expression of the *hamartia* in Lucy's character which is part cause of the novel's catastrophe. Yet it also makes an ironic forward-looking reference to Edgar Ravensword himself. For if Edgar is to survive he must *not* allow himself to be affected by this "Beauty's charming"; he must refrain from violent action against the Lord Keeper; he must stop his own ear against the singer and renounce the course which will be urged on him by both "the Marquis of A—" and Sir William—namely, to marry into the Ashtons for their "red gold". But Edgar's character is the reverse of what is necessary if he is to survive. His heart, hand and eye are anything but vacant, and he has just the sort of pride which, in the context of the novel, will bring about the destruction fatalistically prefigured by the shooting of the raven at the Mermaiden's fountain and by the sombre prophecy of the Kelpie's Flow.

Lucy Ashton's song is a fine lyric; if anything at all in Scott is poetic, this is it. At the same time, what it expresses is the very essence of the central *perception* achieved by the novel as narrative. It would seem to follow that our reading of the whole work must be a poetic process, an outgrowth of the emotion with which we respond to the song. The texture of *The Bride of Lammermoor* is a highly complicated movement of the surface, apparent as we read, which is the expression of those movements below the surface which we term "plot," "structure," "interplay of character," and which Cameron so deftly summarises in the sentence I read out a moment ago. This movement of the surface and these deeper motions constitute a *single* movement, a unity with an almost bewildering number of aspects, each of which it is possible to consider separately for the purposes of analysis, but which lose much of their significance unless finally related to the Whole. Not only does *The Bride of Lammermoor* have the most controlled structure of any novel by Scott; it also, I would claim, has the richest texture. And both the details of texture and the ultimates of structure are, in *The Bride of Lammermoor,* deeply poetic.

May I suggest finally that if Scott is to be recognized as in any sense a *great* poet, it is because of the poetry in the novels themselves, which can best be revealed by detailed analysis of this texture. Long ago, the matter was succinctly formulated by Ralph Fox in *The Novel and the People:*

> (Scott) was an innovator in one sense . . . his astonishing and fertile genius attempted to make the synthesis which the eighteenth century had failed to produce, in which the novel should express the poetry as well as the prose of life (1947 edn., p. 65).

Fox thought that Scott did not succeed in this, that he was "a glorious failure." It is my contention that in *The Bride of Lammermoor* he does succeed; that in *The Heart of Midlothian* he succeeds for two thirds of that novel's length; and that he succeeds intermittently, and often for long stretches at a time, in many other novels.

Jill Rubenstein (essay date 1972)

SOURCE: "The Dilemma of History: A Reading of Scott's *Bridal of Triermain,*" in *Studies in English Literature, 1500-1900,* Vol. XII, No. 4, Autumn, 1972, pp. 721-34.

[*Rubenstein is the author of* Sir Walter Scott: A Reference Guide *(1978), as well as other writings on Scott. In the following essay, she maintains that* The Bridal of Triermain *addresses the reconciliation of tradition with progress.*]

Most critics of Scott have followed the poet's own lead in regarding **The Bridal of Triermain** (1813) as little more than a trifle, but it is a much more serious and noteworthy poem than it initially appears, and Scott's relatively frivolous attitude toward it has tended to obscure its very real significance and merit. It illustrates, to a greater extent than any other of Scott's narrative poems, his continuing preoccupation with the conflicting values of tradition and progress. The theme of **The Bridal of Triermain** is the difficulty and the possibility of deriving the best values from both in order to create a viable social and moral order. This theme manifests itself in Scott's frequently reiterated concern for the virtues of moderation and the necessity of reconciliation.

The poem's structure develops organically from Scott's thematic concern with individual growth and the historical process, and form plays a central role in its overall effect. He creates a complicated narrative and temporal design. The action of the poem covers three widely separated historical periods—the Arthurian; the medieval, roughly five hundred years after King Arthur; and the not-quite-contemporary, thirty years or so before the actual writing of the poem. Although these three successive societies are clearly differentiated, they are also linked by the narrative mode. Scott gives us three narrators, each located at a separate point in time. These narrators, however, are not independent of each other; each tells a story that interlocks with the other two in an intricate pattern of reality, conscious fiction, and unconscious dream.

The prophetic bard Lyulph, a familiar type in Scott's narrative poetry, relates the Arthurian fable. The original impetus toward using Arthurian material came from William Erskine (at first supposed to have authored the anonymously published poem), but Scott seems to have gone far beyond both specific suggestion and his own reading. The King's amorous interlude with the fictive Guendolyn and the birth of Gyneth, their illegitimate daughter, are apparently Scott's own invention. The major source for the matter of Britain in Scott's library before 1813 was Richard Robinson's black letter translation of John Leyland's *Learned and True Assertion of the Original Life . . . of Prince Arthure, King of Great Britaine,* published in 1582. Robinson deals mainly with Arthur's ancestry, the round table, the betrayal of Mordred, and the burial at Glastonbury. With marked reluctance he alludes to Guenevere's failing in chastity, but he nowhere mentions Arthur's indulgence in the same. Gyneth is a name Scott could easily have derived from Celtic romance, and the only mention of Guendolyn in direct relation to Arthur occurs in the thirteenth-century Latin prose romances *Historia*

Meriadoci and *De Ortu Waluuanii,* where she is Arthur's wife. The name is probably derived from Geoffrey of Monmouth, where Merlin's wife is so named. There is no evidence that Scott had read these Latin sources, and since he considered himself an indifferent Latinist and regarded Latin as rather a chore, his acquaintance with them is unlikely. He has apparently combined several of the standard elements of romance, a genre to which he readily admitted his devotion, and embodied them in an Arthurian context. This strategy guarantees a certain amount of reader interest and, more importantly, fits neatly into the pattern of interlocking tri-temporal narration.

Lyulph places the Arthurian fable in remote historical perspective, "far distant 'mid the wrecks of time" (I, ix). As usual, the Arthurian age emerges as the archetypal example of patriotic glory:

> Ah, Minstrel! when the Table Round
> Arose, with all its warriors crown'd,
> There was a theme for bards to sound
>   In triumph to their string!
> Five hundred years are past and gone,
> But Time shall draw his dying groan
> Ere he behold the British throne
>   Begirt with such a ring!
>
>   (II, xii)

However, Scott rarely indulges himself in unalloyed romantic glorification of the past, and he does not hesitate to expose the underlying corruption of Camelot. Although he adopts a worldly attitude toward Arthur's dalliance with the supernaturally lovely Guendolyn, he by no means condones extramartial love affairs, even in the world of romance. To express his disapproval, he employs an urbane irony that satirizes by understatement. Arthur must balance his promise to his illegitimate daughter and his obligations to his wife:

> His vow, he said, should well be kept,
> Ere in the sea the sun was dipp'd;
> Then, conscious, glanced upon his queen;
> But she, unruffled at the scene
> Of human frailty, construed mild,
> Look'd upon Lancelot, and smiled.
>
>   (II, xv)

The last three lines effectively chastise Guenevere without any sense of overt condemnation by Scott. Arthur's knights emulate their king's marital faithlessness, and Scott approaches an unusual cynicism in his ironic praise of the three knights who refrain from the tournament:

> And still these lovers' fame survives
>   For faith so constant shown,—
> There were two who loved their neighbours' wives,
>   And one who loved his own.
>
>   (II, xviii)

In the last analysis, however, courage and wisdom surpass the taint of corruption, and the Arthurian period retains the glitter of romance.

The medieval Sir Ronald De Vaux of Triermain lives five hundred years after these events narrated by the bard Lyulph to his page. The coincidence of his name with the father of the heroine in Coleridge's *Christabel* casts some suspicion on Scott, but the possibility of even this small borrowing seems remote. The two Sir Rolands are probably the same historical personage, but although Scott heard *Christabel* as early as 1802, his own sources for Sir Roland are clear and unimpeachable. In his notes to the poem he cites the *History and Antiquities of Westmoreland and Cumberland* by Joseph Nicolson and Richard Burns (1777), a book which appears in the library at Abbotsford. The De Vaux (or de Vallibus) family is also mentioned in William Hutchinson's *Excursion to the Lakes in Westmoreland and Cumberland* (1786) to which Scott refers the reader in Note V on the Castle Rocks of St. John. Hutchinson's meditation on Lanercost Priory, founded by Robert de Vallibus in 1169, concerns the decline of veneration for the past and the accompanying growth of avarice and luxury and would have been sufficient in itself to grant the De Vaux family a certain degree of permanence in Scott's memory.

Sir Roland represents a transitional step between the very old and the new, and he appropriately combines a strain of modified Arthurian romance with a touch of modern pragmatism. His task exemplifies his transitional status. His trial is essentially an ordeal of delusion, and the appearance-reality theme supplements Scott's typical historical pattern of enlightened gradualism. Sir Roland must convert delusive appearance into reality, and only through a passionate act of faith and self-assertion can he discover the truth about the Vale of St. John. Enraged by being treated as a plaything by supernatural caprice, he hurls his axe at the enchanted crag. This act of violence converts appearance into reality and is the first step in the realization of his earlier dream of Gyneth, who had been enchanted into a five hundred year slumber by Merlin as a punishment for her lack of compassion. Sir Roland's consequent self-fulfillment is symbolized by the traditional laurel crown he wears at the end of his ordeal.

King Arthur was given immediate access to the magic castle; he saw it as an unequivocal reality. The medieval Sir Roland must surmount a series of barriers to gain the vision that was given freely to Arthur. To modern man, however, the vision is totally inaccessible:

> Know too, that when a pilgrim strays,
> In morning mist or evening maze,
>   Along the mountain lone,
> That fairy fortress often mocks
> His gaze upon the castled rocks
>   Of the Valley of Saint John;
> But never man since brave De Vaux
>   The charmed portal won.
> 'Tis now a vain illusive show,
> That melts whene'er the sunbeams glow
>   Or the fresh breeze hath blown.
>
>   (Conc., i)

Contemporary man lacks a quality of romance, imagination, or perhaps credulity that would permit him to see the

A portrait of Scott by Sir Edwin Landseer, 1824.

enchanted castle. This quality had markedly diminished even by Sir Roland's time, and it has totally disappeared in the late eighteenth century of the frame story. Sir Roland bridges the gap between an age of chivalric romance and an age of modern pragmatism, and his own values combine both qualities in an equilibrium that Scott obviously admires. That his society alone escapes corruption reflects one of Scott's most fundamental beliefs about the value of compromise in the development of history.

The third temporal level, the frame story of Arthur's love for the wealthy Lucy, presents a decadent contemporary society marked by false values and diminished vitality. Lucy's high-born peers, "incapable of doing aught, / Yet ill at ease with nought to do" (end, II, i), have fallen as far as possible from the imaginative energy of King Arthur's time. They have lost sight of nature for the sake of artifacts, man-made objects and distinctions of no intrinsic value. Arthur, however, who tells Gyneth's story as a lesson to Lucy, has the right idea; he prizes natural virtue and adornment in place of the artificial qualities that men have tacitly agreed to endow with value. He scorns the society's falsification of natural functions and appearances, the "lordlings and witlings" who disguise their "simple manly grace" with unnatural fashions and gadgets.

The diminished imaginative vitality of an apparently decadent, over-civilized age, however, brings incidental compensation in terms of a greater self-consciousness that becomes, in its best members, a greater self-awareness. The contemporary Arthur, the self-deprecating anti-hero, is significantly the only one of the three narrators who tells his story as a conscious fiction. The connections among these three narrators and their three stories provide a formal exemplification of Scott's ideas of the problems of historical continuity. Both the narrator of the frame story and the bard Lyulph regard their respective stories as true. The realistic and practical Arthur, on the other hand, gently mocks the minstrel tradition and questions the basic validity of romance, hinting that it may be the appropriate amusement of a decadent social order. He mockingly invokes a self-consciously romantic muse who wakes only "by dim wood and silent lake" and quotes Shakespeare out of context in self-dramatizing "notes of flame" (Intro. IIII, vi). Arthur states repeatedly that he tells his trifling story only to amuse Lucy, and he conscientiously shuns all opportunities for self-glorification in the guise of poetic license.

In organizing his poem into three interdependent and successive chronological periods, Scott demonstrates, with unwonted economy, his vision of the simultaneous unity and diversity unfolded by the historical process. Although each society maintains its uniqueness and individuality, the recurring similarities among them testify to the basic uniformity of human nature. The most obvious of these similarities is the repetition of the name of the hero. King Arthur combines all the highest virtues of an age of chivalry and romance, and, as king, he epitomizes his era. The contemporary Arthur also represents the best of *his* era, but his strengths belong more to the realm of common sense than of romance. Although the eighteenth-century

Arthur lives in a diminished age, he refuses to succumb to its fopperies. He retains the heroic qualities in historical perspective and knows that they are simultaneously admirable and somewhat ludicrous. When he offers "a lyre, a falchion, and a heart" (Intro., v) to Lucy, he realizes quite clearly that the lyre is an anachronism and the sword is virtually useless. Nevertheless, his devotion is real, and the gesture is redeemed from emptiness by Arthur's ability to maintain his integrity even while laughing at himself.

> **Scott repeatedly emphasizes that nature, like the past, is fundamental and undeniable. Art springs from and imitates nature, but it cannot limit it or replace it.**
>
> —*Jill Rubenstein*

Sir Roland, too, represents the best of his particular historical period. The magical damsels of Europe who offer him "sceptre, robe, and crown" identify him explicitly as "Arthur's heir" (III, xxxvi). His quest for Gyneth parallels the contemporary Arthur's wooing of Lucy, and both ladies improve in character as a result of the influence of their respective lovers. As possessors of all the currently prevailing virtues, the three heroes demonstrate both the differences and the similarities among their three societies.

The corruption that is prevalent in both the Arthurian and the contemporary periods provides another trans-temporal link. By contrast, Sir Roland's medieval world appears rather wholesome, perhaps because it can modify the chivalric and modern extremes without indulging in the excesses of either one. Scott's traditional marriage motif also transcends the chronological divisions, so that the "Bridal" of the title ambiguously encompasses and unifies the ill-fated affair between King Arthur and Guendolyn, the long-sought union of Sir Roland and Gyneth, and the off-stage marriage of Arthur and Lucy.

What unifies the three narratives even more closely, however, is the analogous theme that appears in each one, Scott's concept of the reformation wrought by the course of history. Each tale concerns the deplorable consequences of individual egotism and social extremism, and each delineates the process of maturation through time. The tripartite narrative structure develops from and contributes to this thematic focus.

Gyneth's supernatural sleep is the most obvious instance of the lapse of time bringing reformation. The five hundred years of her slumber purify her character of its less admirable elements and permit her finer qualities to assert themselves. She has become at peace with herself:

Doubt, and anger, and dismay,
From her brow had pass'd away,

Forgot was that fell tourney day,
For, as she slept, she smiled;
It seem'd that the repentant Seer
Her sleep of many a hundred year
With gentle dreams beguiled.
(III, xxxvii)

Merlin, who traditionally unites past, present, and future in the act of prophecy, is an appropriate admonisher. He plays the role of peacemaker, restoring violated humanistic values, and he comes as a reconciler to put an end to mindless conflict; he subjects Gyneth to the process of time which alone can render her an appropriate bride for the Knight of Triermain.

Sir Roland's ordeal through time also purges him of his initial arrogance. Scott asks "Where is the maiden of mortal strain / That may match with the Baron of Triermain?" (I, i) and proceeds to expound a ridiculously idealized list of the required characteristics of this unavailable maiden. Like Gyneth at the tournament, Sir Roland is denied the possibility of love by his exaggerated self-esteem. However, by the end of the poem, the Knight's values have shifted, for he resists the ego-temptations of African, Indian, Asian, and European maidens in favor of "the garland and the dame" (III, xxxix).

The contemporary Arthur, and particularly Lucy, also gain new insights into themselves and each other in the temporal course of the poem. Lucy initially asks for a poem of pure romance, and Scott presents her at the beginning as a proud coquette, unworthy of Arthur's love. Her request for a romance is consistent with her apparent shallowness and her membership in the decadent establishment. However, Lucy does love Arthur and does marry him, and this, of course, speaks well for her. He woos her, not with an idle romance, but with "some moral truth in fiction's veil" (Conc., ii) whose theme is the "punishment of maiden's pride" (Intro., I, viii), and she manages to make the intended application. The combination of truth and fiction effects the end that either truth or fiction alone could probably never achieve.

The marriage of Arthur and Lucy revitalizes both of them. The lapse of time in which the off-stage marriage takes place between the end of canto II and the introduction to canto III transposes them from the tame English countryside to the rugged Highland mountains, one of Scott's favorite juxapositions. The descriptions are revealing. Arthur commences his tale in a "popular bower, / Where dew lies long upon the flower . . ." (Intro., i). Even the stream that flows through it symbolizes weakness, indolence, and the wasted potential of the decadent aristocracy:

For here, compell'd to disunite,
Round petty isles the runnels glide,
And chafing off their puny spite,
The shallow murmurers waste their might.
(Intro., i)

In distinct contrast to this miniaturized and passive landscape, Scott emphasizes the limitlessness of the Highland

country. In a parallel passage to the one quoted above, the Highland stream conserves and augments, rather than dissipates its energy:

See how the little runnels leap,
In threads of silver down the steep,
To swell the brooklet's moan!
(Intro. III, iii)

As in many of the Waverley novels, the Highlands here represent a new source of vitality and a natural civilization undiminished by modern decadence. Just as Arthur's tale of long ago has helped Lucy to see herself more clearly, so the natural beauty of the Highlands allows them to bring the past to the enrichment of the present in the ideal solution to the dilemma of history:

But Lucy, we will love them yet,
The mountain's misty coronet,
The greenwood and the wold;
And love them more that of their maze
Adventure high of other days
By ancient bards is told.
(Conc., ii)

Lucy and Arthur must progress through time and symbolic space—both actual and fictive—to gain access to the self-knowledge on which their happiness depends. Scott consistently conceives of history this way in spatial as well as temporal dimensions.

This profound faith in the beneficent effects of the process of history would ordinarily imply an equally strong admiration of chronological progress. But *The Bridal of Triermain* is consistent with Scott's compromised primitivism and his ambivalent attitude toward the value of progress. In the early stages of civilization, natural energies are stronger, but they work for both good and evil indiscriminately:

The attributes of those high days
Now only live in minstrel lays;
For Nature, now exhausted, still
Was then profuse of good and ill.
Strength was gigantic, valour high,
And wisdom soar'd beyond the sky,
And beauty had such matchless beam
As lights not now a lover's dream.
(I, xix)

Although nature may be "exhausted" in a highly civilized society, the natural passions are consequently more subject to rational control. Thus, Scott refuses to make an overt value judgment between the merits of his two Arthurs. His attitude here remains consistent with his major works; the ideal condition for art, society, and individual conduct is a balance of discordant qualities which modify and enrich each other. This balance between natural energy and cultivation cannot be attained in a moment. Like the reformation of Gyneth and Lucy, it must grow naturally out of time and suffering and wisdom and the gradual mellowing effects of history.

In *The Bridal of Triermain* Scott deals with the necessity for moderation in terms of the dichotomy between nature and art. He uses it as an aesthetic and moral analogue of the historical dichotomy between past and present. Once again, the ideal emerges as a mutually sustaining interchange between the two. Scott repeatedly emphasizes that nature, like the past, is fundamental and undeniable. Art springs from and imitates nature, but it cannot limit it or replace it. He mocks the attempt to restrict art to the arbitrary limits of fashionable gentility:

> Laud we the gods, that Fashion's train
> Holds hearts of more adventurous strain.
> Artists are hers, who scorn to trace
> Their rules from Nature's boundless grace,
> But their right paramount assert
> To limit her by pedant art,
> Damning whate'er of vast and fair
> Exceeds a canvas three feet square.
>
> (Conc. II, ii)

The echo of *Cymbeline* [Act V, Scene v, Line 476] in the first line strengthens the grounds of Scott's scorn by its implicit contrast between artificial limitations and Shakespeare's unfettered imagination. Arthur's mockery of the minstrel tradition is also consistent with Scott's concern for aesthetic balance. Arthur belittles his own song for lack of authenticity, because, like the song of the mocking bird, it is an imitation twice removed from its source in reality, based on an artistic rather than a natural model.

In the Arthurian legend, as narrated by the bard Lyulph, Scott is equally vehement about the need to reconcile art and nature, this time in terms of personal conduct. His treatment of Guendolyn, King Arthur's mistress, and of Gyneth, their daughter, exemplifies the ideal of mutually modifying qualities in the individual. Both are *naturally* good, but each has been spoiled by a parent's *art*. Guendolyn's ancestry is significant:

> Her mother was of human birth,
> Her sire a Genie of the earth,
> In days of old deem'd to preside
> O'er lovers' wiles and beauty's pride,
> By youths and virgins worshipp'd long
> With festive dance and choral song,
> Till, when the cross to Britain came,
> On heathen altars died the flame.
> Now, deep in Wastdale solitude,
> The downfall of his rights he rued,
> And, born of his resentment heir,
> He train'd to guile that lady fair,
> To sink in slothful sin and shame
> The champions of the Christian name.
>
> (II, iii)

Scott uses Guendolyn's parentage as a symbolic expression of his constant concern with the impediments to historical progress. Her genie father, displaced by the new energies of Christianity, trained her to ensnare Christian knights by dissipating those energies in "slothful sin and shame." Here is the central element in Scott's historical vision—when the old cannot give way gracefully to the new, strife and destruction inevitably result. Guendolyn is as much a victim as a villain, and she suffers from her inability to reconcile the contrary elements of genie and woman in her nature:

> Her sire's soft arts the soul to tame
> She practised thus, till Arthur came;
> Then frail humanity had part,
> And all the mother claim'd her heart,
> Forgot each rule her father gave,
> Sunk from a princess to a slave.
>
> (II, iv)

Guendolyn's dilemma reaffirms the need for reconciliation in human as well as aesthetic terms. Her mistake is to *begin* with art, revert to humanity, and then resort once again to art. She fails to retain Arthur's affection because she regards them as separate resources and cannot simultaneously unite the advantages of both:

> Art she invokes to Nature's aid,
> Her vest to zone, her locks to braid; . . .
> Her storied lore she next applies,
> Taxing her mind to aid her eyes;
> Now more than mortal wise, and then
> In female softness sunk again.
>
> (II, iv)

The next stanza presents the problem in a more abstract metaphor, but the basic conflict remains the same. The gardener (whose function exemplifies the co-presence of art and nature) attempts to construct the picturesque garden to disguise its natural limitations. He plants labyrinths within the "narrow bound" to induce the stroller's belief that he is in unwalled natural setting. He provides varieties of copses, arbors, and flowers to mimic nature's prodigality. But the imitation of nature within the confines of art is itself limited by the demands of *human* nature for unconfined freedom:

> Vain art! vain hope! 'tis fruitless all!
> At length we reach the bounding wall,
> And, sick of flower and trim-dress'd tree,
> Long for rough glades and forest free.
>
> (II, v)

Art and nature can be combined only within a severely limited scope, which, after a time, necessarily becomes untenable. Man must learn to regard nature as fundamental and art as relatively superficial. Like the relationship between past and present, each has its appointed place; and we cannot scrap either nature or the past in the delusion that we have provided something better in its place. Art and the present depend on nature and the past for their very existence; and just as man eventually yearns for what lies beyond the garden's bounding wall, so too he needs a sense of his own past.

Gyneth's parentage is somewhat more promising than her mother's. As the daughter of Guendolyn and Arthur, she embodies a potentially fine combination of qualities. She resembles her mother in physical appearance, but she possesses her father's strength of will. The transition from Guendolyn to Gyneth is a progression toward the increasingly human:

> But 'twas a face more frank and wild,
> Betwixt the woman and the child,
> Where less of magic beauty smiled
>   Than of the race of men;
> And in the forehead's haughty grace
> The lines of Britain's royal race,
> Pendragon's, you might ken.
>
> (II, xiv)

Unfortunately, her mother's indoctrination temporarily negates the advantages of Gyneth's ancestry. Guendolyn's chronicles of "the faithlessness of men" (II, xxi) have made her daughter proud, pitiless, and somewhat bloodthirsty. Merlin justly punishes her, but he cannot punish pitilessness without himself pitying the object of his malediction. He reconciles punishment with mercy for two reasons:

> Yet, because they mother's art
> Warp'd thine unsuspicious heart,
> And for love of Arthur's race,
> Punishment is blent with grace.
>
> (II, xxvi)

Gyneth cannot really be blamed for her hardness of heart; it originates not in her own *nature* but in her mother's *art*. And she is, of course, Arthur's daughter, and Merlin shows a proper veneration for the historical continuity of Pendragon's line. Gyneth's five-hundred-year sleep dissipates the effects of her mother's art and allows her own better nature to assert itself.

Man's nature eventually rebels at artificial limitations and longs for its own actuality, but he can attain it only through time. The gradual process of maturation encompasses not only realization of one's own inner nature, but also an awareness of one's relationship to the objective world. "At length we reach the bounding wall" to discover the limits of our abilities and the shortcomings of both nature and society. This is the point where Sir Roland, King Arthur, and many of the Waverley heroes begin to grow up, to confront their various worlds as they exist in reality rather than in idealistic dream.

The historical sense teaches ultimately the value of adjustment, and nostalgia need not be accompanied by impotent devotion to the past. Arthur and Lucy escape imprisonment in an exhausted society through a consciously fictive re-creation of the past. They emerge, however, not futilely dedicated to what is lost, but reinvigorated by a more natural present. In this reconciliation, they attain the happiness in which Scott fervently believes as both a realistic possibility and the highest earthly human good.

Claire Lamont (lecture date 1975)

SOURCE: "The Poetry of the Early Waverly Novels," in *Proceedings of the British Academy,* Vol. LXI, 1976, pp. 315–36.

[*In the following lecture, delivered in 1975, Lamont studies the function, characteristics, and effectiveness of verse passages within Scott's early Waverly novels.*]

My subject this evening is the lyrics, songs, and ballad snatches in the early novels of Sir Walter Scott. I shall say a little about the songs in his longer poems, but talk primarily about the poetry of the novels, up to *The Bride of Lammermoor* of 1819. It has often been pointed out that Scott's novels contain some of his finest poetry. John Buchan, for instance, claimed [in *Sir Walter Scott,* 1932] that it is there that Scott attained 'his real poetic stature', and added 'in his greater lyrics Scott penetrated to the final mystery of the poet.' The short poems in the novels are quite different from Scott's narrative verse, 'that poetry of careless glance, and reckless rhyme' [John Ruskin, *Modern Painters,* 1856]. In the poetry of the novels there is seldom any carelessness, seldom any failure of eye or ear. The songs and ballad snatches in the novels are usually impersonal, and are in one way or another overheard. We are not now dealing with the minstrel tradition which welcomes the listener into the tale. The short songs are simply sung, and there is not usually a listener although there may be a hearer. Scott knew himself to be a storyteller; and in many places in his work he shows himself preoccupied with the task of the minstrel or bard; did he in a more private part of his mind know that he had that more elusive gift, as a lyric poet?

In talking about the poetry of the novels I have used various terms, songs, lyrics, ballad snatches. As regards the ballad, I shall be dealing with only one ballad which occurs in anything like its narrative completeness, Elspeth's ballad of the Red Harlaw in *The Antiquary.* The rest are ballad snatches which, in the way that Scott quotes and alters them, are half-way to existing as separate songs. There is also the question of ownership. Am I going to give Scott credit for composing what he merely quoted? I shall distinguish as carefully as I can, but it is notoriously difficult and sometimes even Scott himself would not have known with certainty. The fact that the songs in the novels are sung by fictitious singers renders the problem of 'authorship' more intricate. A fictitious character may be supposed either to compose or quote; and if he quotes he may do so from another fictitious character, or from a fictitious tradition. In practice, however, the origin of a song in Scott's novels is usually less important than the fact that the singer knew it and sang it at the right moment.

The verse romances, most of which were published before he produced his first novel, show Scott creating various settings for his interspersed songs. In *The Lay of the Last Minstrel* (1805) there are none until the last canto when a group of songs is sung at the feast to celebrate the marriage of the heroine. Scott confessed in a letter that he had been short of material for the last canto, 'so I was fain to eke it out with the songs of the minstrels'. It was a happy accident if it enabled him to discover his talent for writing songs in a context. In *Marmion* (1808) there are two songs. The first, Constance's song **'Where shall the lover rest'**, with its statement about the fates of the lover and the traitor, is clearly related to the poem as a whole. Perhaps more interesting is the relation of the other, the very different song in Canto V, the story of young Lochinvar. It is sung by Lady Heron, the wily Englishwoman who was King James's favourite, while the Court was assembling in preparation for battle. James was about to embark on the rash venture that led to the field of Flodden. The song tells of the victory of the bold man who rode off with his bride on the eve of her marriage to another.

> So daring in love, and so dauntless in war,
> Have ye e'er heard of gallant like young Lochinvar?

The song, with its irrepressible metre, suggests inexorable success for the man who boldly takes, and is not calculated to bring moderation to the counsels of the King.

There are many more songs in *The Lady of the Lake* (1810). One of the most beautiful is the song sung by the madwoman, Blanche, to warn the King of treachery ahead.

> The toils are pitched, and the stakes are set,
>   Ever sing merrily, merrily;
> The bows they bend, and the knives they whet,
>   Hunters live so cheerily.
> It was a stag, a stag of ten,
>   Bearing his branches sturdily;
> He came stately down the glen,
>   Ever sing hardily, hardily.
>
>   . . . . .
>
> He had an eye, and he could heed,
>   Ever sing warily, warily;
> He had a foot, and he could speed—
>   Hunters watch so narrowly.
>   (Canto IV, xxv)

The hearer is given information by one to whom he would not normally turn for counsel. The madwoman sees through disguise (she recognizes the 'stag of ten'), and presents herself to give her vital warning. The inspiration for Blanche came from a poor woman whom Scott had seen in the Pass of Glencoe many years earlier, and in the rather hasty filling in of her life story we can see the germ of a character like Madge Wildfire.

Equally interesting from the point of view of the songs in the novels are those sung by Edmund in *Rokeby* (1813). Here for the first time Scott has created a character to sing his songs who has a sustained part in the action of the poem. Edmund is a peasant boy who has joined a robber gang, and he sings hauntingly of the way of life of the outlaw community:

> 'And when I'm with my comrades met,
>   Beneath the greenwood bough,
> What once we were we all forget,
>   Nor think what we are now.
>
> CHORUS.
> Yet Brignal banks are fresh and fair,
>   And Greta woods are green,
> And you may gather garlands there
>   Would grace a summer queen.'—
>   (Canto III, xviii)

That song, Scott said, was one of his favourites. There are no such inset songs in *The Lord of the Isles,* though one wonders if Edith would not have sung in her disguise as a page, had he not been 'from earliest childhood mute'. But *The Lord of the Isles* appeared in 1815, six months after the first of the novels, *Waverley.*

As the songs I am talking about were sung, it should be asked whether Scott had in mind any particular music? Sometimes he had; for instance Constance's song in *Marmion* was inspired by the singing of Highland reapers in the Lowlands, and was written to fit a specific tune. Scott was not particularly musical, but could write to a tune if it were hummed over to him often enough. For the songs in the novels he did not usually have specific tunes in mind, but he often indicates what the reader should be hearing by a phrase or two of verbal description. One of Madge Wildfire's dying songs, for instance, 'rather resembled the music of the Methodist hymns' [*Tales of My Landlord*].

Before turning to the novels I should say a word about the manuscripts, as most of Scott's novel manuscripts survive. It is surprising to anyone looking at a Scott novel manuscript for the first time how smoothly the songs appear inset in their places. A closer look reveals that some of the songs we know from the printed texts are not present in the manuscript, for instance Glossin's rather uncharacteristic drinking-song in *Guy Mannering.* In some cases the song is clearly needed in the first draft of the manuscript, and was presumably sent on a separate sheet. In others there was apparently no expectation of a song, and its addition, presumably in proof, required some slight alteration of the text to accommodate it. But still the majority of the songs occur in the manuscript, with very little correction. Did Scott compose the songs as he wrote; or had he worked them out in his capacious memory earlier? Many years later in his *Journal* he recalled the speed at which passages in the novels were written: 'the pen passd over the whole as fast as it could move and the eye never again saw them excepting in proof'. He added immediately afterwards, 'Verse I write twice and sometimes three times over'.

By 1814 the songs and ballad snatches in Scott's work were so well known that they threatened the anonymity of the new novel, *Waverley.* There is a wide range of poetry in *Waverley.* Besides the narrator's snatches of quotation, all the main characters sing or write verses. I want to concentrate on the most famous singer in the novel, Davie Gellatley. Davie Gellatley is the Baron of Bradwardine's *innocent,* which Scott glosses as 'a natural fool'. He is the first person whom Edward Waverley met on his arrival at Tully Veolan, and on coming up to Waverley he sang 'a fragment of an old Scotch ditty', starting 'False love, and hast thou play'd me this . . .' The reader hardly notices that the heir to an English Jacobite family, newly signed on in the Hanoverian army, is being addressed as a faithless lover. When there was a pause in Davie's singing and dancing Waverley asked if Mr. Bradwardine were at home. The reply came:

> The Knight's to the mountain
>   His bugle to wind;
> The Lady's to greenwood
>   Her garland to bind.
> The bower of Burd Ellen
>   Has moss on the floor,
> That the step of Lord William
>   Be silent and sure.

This conveyed no information . . .

and Edward had to repeat his inquiry. And he finished up following Davie Gellatley down the garden. '"A strange guide this," thought Edward, "and not much unlike one of Shakespeare's roynish clowns . . ."' **'The Knight's to the mountain'** Scott wrote himself. While alluding to the absence of the Baron, it alludes also to the fact that the daughter's lover is entering the house. But the situation is rendered general and impersonal by the references to the knight and the greenwood, and to Lord William and Burd Ellen, archetypal lover and beloved of the ballad tradition. It is not surprising that to the young Englishman, who had in any case so much to learn about Scotland, 'This conveyed no information'.

Before his next meeting with Davie Gellatley Waverley learns something of his history from Rose Bradwardine, including that he had

> a prodigious memory, stored with miscellaneous snatches and fragments of all tunes and songs, which he sometimes applied, with considerable address, as the vehicles of remonstrance, explanation, or satire.

The source of Davie's songs was his elder brother, now dead, who had been folk-singer and composer—it was he who wrote

> Hie away, hie away,
> Over bank and over brae,
> Where the copsewood is the greenest,
> Where the fountains glisten sheenest, . . .

a song of escape from the world that had dashed his hopes. So that behind the character of Davie Gellatley Scott has created a folk-singer and poet. In Davie's songs we feel the inherent pathos of the oral tradition: the reason that we have songs to sing is that the elders who used to sing them have passed away.

The next meeting between Waverley and Davie Gellatley took place early in the morning; Waverley rose early and going out of doors found Davie with his dog.

One quick glance of his [Davie's] eye recognised Waverley, when, instantly turning his back, as if he had not observed him, he began to sing part of an old ballad:

> Young men will love thee more fair and more fast;
>   *Heard ye so merry the little bird sing?*
> Old men's love the longest will last,
>   *And the throstle-cock's head is under his wing.*
>
> The young man's wrath is like light straw on fire;
>   *Heard ye so merry the little bird sing?*
> But like red-hot steel is the old man's ire,
>   *And the throstle-cock's head is under his wing.*
>
> The young man will brawl at the evening board;
>   *Heard ye so merry the little bird sing?*
> But the old man will draw at the dawning the sword,
>   *And the throstle-cock's head is under his wing.*

Although this is introduced as 'part of an old ballad', Scott later admitted to having written it himself. Waverley has by now learned that Davie's songs indicate something he should know, and he tries by direct inquiry to get Davie to tell him outright. But Davie will not. He had after all turned his back on Waverley before singing it, pretending not to see him. The song refers apparently to the quarrel with the young Laird of Balmawhapple two days earlier; but that quarrel was of political origin, and the song's deeper allusion is to the Jacobites, at the time—the summer of 1745—coming together to rise against the government that Waverley serves. It is one of the hints that the rising is shortly to come to a head. But it is a dark one, couched in terms of the contrast between the young man and the old, the young man hasty, impetuous, and quickly dashed, the old man true, owning old loyalties, undeflected. The pace at which the contrast emerges is slowed down by the refrain, with its reference to the rhythms of the natural world. The imminent situation is sketched in terms of the psychological traits of its participants—Balmawhapple and the Baron of Bradwardine, but not only them.

The allusiveness of Davie's song contrasts with the explicitness of the Bard's song about the impending rising which Waverley hears at the feast at Glennaquoich, and which is subsequently translated from Gaelic for him by Flora Mac-Ivor. The Bard's song is historical, exhortatory, and sung in a communal setting. Yet for all the mass response to the performance of Mac-Murrough the Bard, in which Waverley shares, we feel that the poetry is with Davie.

For all the central part of the novel Davie Gellatley is out of our ken while we watch Waverley join the Jacobite army, march with it into England, and during the retreat from Derby become separated from it in a nocturnal skirmish. It is months later, after the battle of Culloden, that Waverley, alone, makes his way to the deserted and devastated Tully Veolan.

> While . . . he was looking around for some one who might explain the fate of the inhabitants, he heard a

voice from the interior of the building, singing, in well-remembered accents, an old Scottish song:

'They came upon us in the night,
And brake my bower and slew my knight;
My servants a' for life did flee,
And left us in extremitie.
They slew my knight, to me sae dear;
They slew my knight, and drave his gear;
The moon may set, the sun may rise,
But a deadly sleep has closed his eyes.'

Scott later added a note on this song: 'The first three couplets are from an old ballad, called the Border Widow's Lament'. This ballad, which derives from James Hogg, had been included in Scott's collection, *The Minstrelsy of the Scottish Border*: it is about the murder of a Border chieftain by the King of Scotland. In turning two stanzas of it into a song for Davie Gellatley Scott has made the King into an unspecified enemy, and has added two lines at the end which give a feeling of finality, rather than lamentation. It is a statement of emotion rather than of fact, which Waverley, fortunately, seems partly to realize. By this late stage in the novel he is much matured, and he understands Davie Gellatley much better than before. As Davie made to flee the intruder,

> Waverley, remembering his habits, began to whistle a tune . . . which Davie had expressed great pleasure in listening to, . . . Davie again stole from his lurking place . . .

Davie Gellatley's poetry is both a commentary on the action of the novel, and a measure of the growing maturity of its hero. And it is, I think, an indication of the relative optimism of *Waverley,* despite Culloden in the background, that the poor foolish singer plays a valuable part in saving the family that protects him, and that the dashing young hero learns to listen and communicate with him.

In *Waverley* Scott created for himself an opportunity to be a folk poet; in *The Antiquary* he provided himself with a similar opportunity to become a ballad singer. Although versions of a ballad on the Battle of Harlaw are known, old Elspeth's ballad of the Red Harlaw is unlike them, and is thought to be Scott's own work. It is interesting to see how it is introduced. The Antiquary, Mr. Oldbuck, wishes to get from the crazed old Elspeth a statement 'in a formal manner' of the events long in the past which she has just revealed to Lord Glenallan. Oldbuck, his nephew Hector, and the old wandering beggar Edie Ochiltree, approach Elspeth's hut for that purpose.

> As the Antiquary lifted the latch of the hut, he was surprised to hear the shrill tremulous voice of Elspeth chaunting forth an old ballad in a wild and doleful recitative:—

'The herring loves the merry moon-light,
  The mackerel loves the wind,
But the oyster loves the dredging sang,
  For they come of a gentle kind.'

A diligent collector of these legendary scraps of ancient poetry, his foot refused to cross the threshold when his ear was thus arrested, and his hand instinctively took pencil and memorandum-book. From time to time the old woman spoke as if to the children—'O aye, hinnies, whisht, whisht! and I'll begin a bonnier ane than that—

'Now haud your tongue, baith wife and carle,
  And listen, great and sma',
And I will sing of Glenallan's Earl
  That fought on the red Harlaw.'

And she continues with a ballad about the battle of Harlaw, fought in 1411, the battle which, in Scott's words, determined 'whether the Gaelic or the Saxon race should be predominant in Scotland'. As she sings she is held up by failure of memory and wandering thoughts, and then, when she gets to a passage of particular interest, by the need to explain it to her supposed auditors, for she imagines her grandchildren to be present.

'"To turn the rein were sin and shame,
    To fight were wond'rous peril,
What would ye do now, Rowland Cheyne,
    Were ye Glenallan's Earl?"'

'Ye maun ken, hinnies, that this Roland Cheyne, for as poor and auld as I sit in the chimney-neuk, was my forbear, and an awfu' man he was that day in the fight, but specially after the Earl had fa'en; for he blamed himself for the counsel he gave . . .'

One can imagine that historical ballads were frequently glossed in that manner when they were fulfilling one of their basic functions, that of preserving a family's history.

But what about her actual auditors? Hector is impatient, Oldbuck is overcome with the lust of the ballad collector, only Edie Ochiltree has any sympathy for her elderly and bereaved condition. Their voices disturb her, she stops singing and bids them enter; and they start the inquiries which they hope will lead to a confession of her complicity in the Glenallan tragedy. But old Elspeth refuses to make any admission, and in a last disjointed assertion of loyalty to her former mistress she falls dead. So the formal statement was not obtained, and in the end any proofs required are got from elsewhere. But has not Oldbuck in his antiquarian zeal missed something? He came for a statement, and got a ballad—a ballad about an earlier Glenallan whose downfall was brought about by the advice of Elspeth's ancestor.

'"Were I Glenallan's Earl this tide,
  And ye were Roland Cheyne,
The spur should be in my horse's side,
  And the bridle upon his mane.

'"If they hae twenty thousand blades,
  And we twice ten times ten,
Yet they hae but their tartan plaids,
  And we are mail-clad men."'

The Countess and Elspeth had been just as ruthless, and it was Elspeth who had given her mistress the fatal advice, which destroyed her son's happiness. And like her ancestor, Roland Cheyne, after the miscarriage of her advice she fought the more loyally. In view of the mental world in which Elspeth is still living is there any hope that she will submit to a magistrate's inquiry? And likewise is there any hope that Oldbuck will attempt to discover the significance of his much-prized historical ballad?

Probably the most famous of Scott's fictitious singers is Madge Wildfire in *The Heart of Midlothian*. Scott says that the initial inspiration for Madge Wildfire came from 'Feckless Fanny', a girl who had lost her senses on the death of her lover. Some details, for instance Madge's ducking near Carlisle, clearly come from the gipsy lore which had called forth the character of Meg Merrilies in *Guy Mannering*. Other influences on this story of the girl rendered mad by sorrow and singing in her madness are Wordsworth's mysterious madwomen, and the mad singers of German literature. And in the background, of course, there is Ophelia. The suggestion is made only to be qualified: 'Of all the mad-women who have sung and said, since the days of Hamlet the Dane, if Ophelia be the most affecting, Madge Wildfire was the most provoking'. Madge Wildfire, like Davie Gellatley, sings snatches of song to warn, predict, and explain, could the hearer only interpret her message. Madge seldom offers information—though sometimes she has vital information; she is usually led into betraying it by just that playing on her feelings and weaknesses which the Baron of Bradwardine forbids to be practised on Davie Gellatley. For Davie is a protected member of the household at Tully Veolan, whereas Madge is an outcast.

Miss Lascelles has drawn our attention to Scott's interest in a character from an 'alternative society', for instance the gipsy society of Meg Merrilies, a clearly defined way of life drawing on different traditions which may impinge on the rest of society for good or ill, but only according to its own laws [Mary Lascelles, 'Jane Austen and Walter Scott: A Minor Point of Comparison,' *Notions and Facts*, 1972]. *The Heart of Midlothian* shows his preoccupation with a character slightly different, the person who has left the ordinary society of which he was once a member, either voluntarily, as George Staunton, or because he was driven out of it, like Madge Wildfire and her mother. Edmund in **Rokeby** is one who voluntarily adopts the life of an outlaw, and can sing of it most attractively:

> Allen-a-Dale has no faggot for burning,
> Allen-a-Dale has no furrow for turning,
> Allen-a-Dale has no fleece for the spinning,
> Yet Allen-a-Dale has red gold for the winning.
> Come, read me my riddle! come, hearken my tale!
> And tell me the craft of bold Allen-a-Dale.
> (Canto III, xxx)

We must enjoy its bravado, but the desperate fate of Bertram in the same poem shows that its freedom is illusory, or at most only a young man's freedom. The flam-

boyant outlaw becomes mere robber at last. And what about the girl invited to join such a society?

> 'If, Maiden, thou wouldst wend with me,
>   To leave both tower and town,
> Thou first must guess what life lead we,
>   That dwell by dale and down.
> And if thou canst that riddle read,
>   As read full well you may,
> Then to the green wood shalt thou speed,
>   As blithe as Queen of May.'—
>
> CHORUS.
> Yet sung she, 'Brignal banks are fair,
>   And Greta woods are green;
> I'd rather range with Edmund there,
>   Than reign our English queen.'
> (Canto III, xvi)

The next song shows the next stage:

> 'A weary lot is thine, fair maid,
>   A weary lot is thine!
> To pull the thorn thy brow to braid,
>   And press the rue for wine!
> A lightsome eye, a soldier's mien,
>   A feather of the blue,
> A doublet of the Lincoln green,—
>   No more of me you knew,
>   My love!
> No more of me you knew.'
> (Canto III, xxviii)

The two songs represent 'innocence' and 'experience', and the emotional pull of each is equally balanced.

George Staunton, alias Robertson, with all the explanations proper to a novel, has left ordinary society, and has seduced a vain, giddy girl, Madge Murdockson, in a way that ensures that she will have to leave it too. He wrote for her the song which in the novel becomes, as it were, Madge's 'signature tune', cropping up here and there like wildfire. George made it for her at Lockington wake, a festival in Leicestershire:

> 'I'm Madge of the country, I'm Madge of the town,
> And I'm Madge of the lad I am blithest to own—
> The Lady of Beever in diamonds may shine,
> But has not a heart half so lightsome as mine.
>
> I am Queen of the Wake, and I'm Lady of May,
> And I lead the blithe ring round the May-pole today:
> The wild-fire that flashes so fair and so free
> Was never so bright, or so bonnie as me.'

The rest of the novel shows us the pathos of this 'Queen of the May'.

It is surprising to realize that the first snatch of song to be sung in *The Heart of Midlothian* is not sung by Madge Wildfire.

'The elfin knight sate on the brae,
  The broom grows bonnie, the broom grows fair;
And by there came lilting a lady so gay,
  And we daurna gang down to the broom nae
    mair.'

It is sung by Effie Deans, to cover her confusion at meeting her sister shortly after parting from Staunton. This little snatch, which betrays her apprehensiveness, is sung by the daughter of the strict Presbyterian who had no time for 'fule sangs'; Effie Deans, who like Madge Wildfire was to be ruined by bearing a child to George Staunton. In her description of the dancing where she met Staunton Effie comes close to the world of Madge Wildfire, with its singing, dancing, laughter, and vanity. Yet it is the other sister, Jeanie, who has more to do with Madge in the novel. In her efforts to save Effie, Jeanie meets the dark side of Madge's world. And there, in the midst of her alarm, Jeanie finds that Madge's vanity is mingled with something deeper, though she scarcely understands it. As the two of them leave the barn where Jeanie had been unwillingly detained on her journey to London, Madge likens them to characters from *The Pilgrim's Progress* and sings one of Bunyan's songs. Davie Deans's sectarian zeal had prevented his children from reading Bunyan, and Jeanie has to make what little she can of Madge's fancy. Jeanie's compassion ensures that she will always do what she can to help Madge, but her religion, to which she is so faithful, makes it difficult for her to recognize a groping in the same direction when it does not take the same path.

Madge's position gives her freedom from the restrictions of the ordinary world, whether confining or shaping and reassuring. It gives her the freedom to say some things which need saying in the novel. Jeanie, having stumbled unwittingly on the fact that Madge had had and lost a child, says '"I am very sorry for your misfortune—"' Only to be interrupted by Madge, '"Sorry? what wad ye be sorry for? The bairn was a blessing—"' There is a blessing in the bairn that the rigours of law and theology in the novel fail to recognize, and the spokesman is Madge Wildfire.

We see no more of Madge after she and Jeanie part until, on her return journey from London, Jeanie visits Madge on her deathbed in the workhouse in Carlisle. Madge is singing as she enters, and does not recognize her visitor. Jeanie calls her by name; Madge replies by summoning the nurse, '"Nurse—nurse, turn my face to the wa', that I may never answer to that name ony mair, and never see mair of a wicked world."' There follow three songs. The first is religious:

'When the fight of grace is fought,—
When the marriage vest is wrought,—
When Faith hath chased cold Doubt away,
And Hope but sickens at delay,—
When Charity, imprisoned here,
Longs for a more expanded sphere,
Doff thy robes of sin and clay;
Christian, rise, and come away.'

The first two lines are reminiscent of Meg Merrilies's 'Dirge' [in *Guy Mannering*]; the rest remind one of the last lines of Johnson's *The Vanity of Human Wishes*, a poem which Scott particularly admired. As Madge becomes weaker the style of her song changes:

'Cauld is my bed, Lord Archibald,
  And sad my sleep of sorrow;
But thine sall be as sad and cauld,
  My fause true-love! to-morrow.'

—a ballad snatch, with as usual a prophetic and monitory element. Then comes her final song:

Again she changed the tune to one wilder, less monotonous, and less regular. But of the words only a fragment or two could be collected by those who listened to this singular scene.

'Proud Maisie is in the wood,
  Walking so early;
Sweet Robin sits on the bush,
  Singing so rarely.
'"Tell me, thou bonny bird,
  When shall I marry me?"—
"When six braw gentlemen
  Kirkward shall carry ye."

* * *

'"Who makes the bridal bed,
  Birdie, say truly?"
"The gray-headed sexton
  That delves the grave duly."

* * *

'The glow-worm o'er grave and stone
  Shall light thee steady;
The owl from the steeple sing,
  "Welcome, proud lady."'

Asterisks between the second and third, and third and fourth stanzas in the manuscript and early printed editions indicate that other stanzas are supposedly missing. It is after all 'only a fragment or two'. One is left to imagine a longer question-and-answer ballad, but the fragment which the listeners could hear is just enough, and enough to give it full emotional intensity. The manuscript shows also that Scott first attempted the song in the past tense:

Proud Maisie was in the wood
  Walking so early
Sweet Robin sat on the bush
  Singing so rarely

but he changed the verbs to the present, probably as he wrote. If we feel entitled to apply this most impersonal song to its singer we see that it expresses her situation and character.

The lightning that flashes so bright and so free,
Is scarcely so blithe or so bonny as me.

The giddy singer of that song is here labelled with laconic finality 'Proud Maisie', and as for the wildfire:

'The glow-worm o'er grave and stone
    Shall light thee steady.'

The last novel that I want to mention is *The Bride of Lammermoor*. Lucy Ashton's song, in the third chapter, has often been claimed one of Scott's finest lyrics. Critics concur in the view that the song expresses the character of the singer, and that more than any other song in Scott's novels it is indicative of the theme and mood of the whole work. But a curious feature of this criticism is that so many agree in finding Lucy a weak and passive character. Perhaps John Buchan may be allowed to speak for those who have expressed that view: 'Lucy Ashton is a passive creature, a green-sick girl unfit to strive with destiny . . .' But is Lucy purely passive? No one would claim that she is strong, but is it not only in the company and under the power of her mother that she is weak?

Perhaps I may look at Lucy Ashton's song in more detail in its context. We have not met Lucy, though we have been told that she is seventeen, when her father, leaving his library where he had been meditating further vengeance on the Ravenswood family whom he has superseded, overhears his daughter sing the following song to her own accompaniment on the lute:

Look not thou on Beautys charming
Sit thou still when Kings are arming
Taste not when the wine-cup glistens
Speak not when the people listens
Stop thine ear against the singer
From the red gold keep thy finger
Vacant heart & hand & eye
Easy live and quiet die.

As Mr. Maxwell has pointed out [in 'Lucy Ashton's Song,' *Notes and Queries*, CXCV, 1950], the song has elements of both the ballad and the cavalier lyric, and apparently it advocates a rejection of active life. Sir William Ashton's first remark to his daughter indicates the same interpretation: "'So Lucy, . . . does your musical philosopher teach you to contemn the world before you know it? . . .'"

Look not thou on Beautys charming
Sit thou still when Kings are arming . . .

A series of commands, each rendered in one way or another negative. And then the final couplet, the consequence of the withdrawal advocated,

Vacant heart & hand & eye
Easy live and quiet die.

The song is in one sense worldly wisdom couched in terms of advice and command. But if that is the surface meaning there is a strong undertow in the opposite direction. In

another sense the whole poem can be cast in the conditional; *if* you withdraw from full participation in living, *then* all you will have is an easy life and a quiet death. You may buy peace, but at what cost.

Well, how does this relate to the character of the singer? The novelist comments, shortly after the conclusion of the song,

The words she had chosen seemed particularly adapted to her character; for Lucy Ashton's exquisitely beautiful, yet girlish features, were formed to express peace of mind, serenity, and indifference to the tinsel of worldly pleasure.

And the passage goes on to describe the gentleness of Lucy's character, and the affection in which she was held by all except her mother, who, believing her to be 'unfit for courts, or crowded halls', can only plan her daughter's withdrawal from life by marriage to 'some country laird'.

But, like many a parent of hot and impatient character, she was mistaken in estimating the feelings of her daughter, who, under a semblance of extreme indifference, nourished the germ of those passions which sometimes spring up in one night, like the gourd of the prophet, and astonish the observer by their unexpected ardour and intensity. In fact, Lucy's sentiments seemed chill, because nothing had occurred to interest or awaken them.

This passage, which occurs between the end of Lucy's song and her father's first remark, indicates that Scott did not want Lucy to appear solely passive. We are introduced to someone of an apparently passive temperament, but with strong hints that she could prove otherwise. With her character as with her song, there is a current pulling against the most obvious interpretation.

'So Lucy,' said her father, entering as her song was ended, 'does your musical philosopher teach you to contemn the world before you know it?—that is surely something premature.—Or did you but speak according to the fashion of fair maidens, who are always to hold the pleasures of life in contempt till they are pressed upon them by the address of some gentle knight?'

Lucy blushed, disclaimed any inference respecting her own choice being inferred from her selection of a song, and readily laid aside her instrument at her father's request that she would attend him in his walk.

Father and daughter take their walk in the park—this is all in the same chapter, chapter three. There they meet a forester, and there follows a conversation in which the forester complains that there has been no sport in the park since the Ashtons took over the estate. Skill in outdoor sports lay with the Ravenswoods; and the forester extols in particular the prowess of Edgar, Master of Ravenswood, who is, of course, to become Lucy's lover. There are only two songs sung in *The Bride of Lammermoor* and they are both in this chapter. As the forester goes off he sings a song:

The monk must arise when the matins ring,
  The abbot may sleep to their chime;
But the yeoman must start when the bugles sing,
  'Tis time, my hearts, 'tis time.

There's bucks and raes on Bilhope braes,
  There's a herd in Shortwood Shaw;
But a lily white doe in the garden goes,
  She's fairly worth them a'.

Hunting is often in Scott an analogue of the active life, of the life that must be lived although it is not without danger and cruelty. The second stanza alludes also to the tradition, particularly strong in medieval literature, of the Chase of Love, where the progress of love is described in terms of a stag-hunt.

But a lily white doe in the garden goes,
  She's fairly worth them a'.

The 'lily white doe' is of course Lucy Ashton. Although she can be brought to follow a hunt, Lucy is in the end not the pursuer but the pursued. After her long persecution by her mother and Dame Gourlay, the hurt to Lucy is described thus: 'the arrow was shot, and was rankling barb-deep in the side of the wounded deer'. But long before the 'lily white doe' of the song becomes the 'wounded deer' of the end of the novel, there is the hunting scene in chapter nine, Lord Bittlebrain's hunting party. In the course of it the stag turns at bay: 'the hunted animal had now in his turn become an object of intimidation to his pursuers'. Bucklaw is the hero of the occasion, and after rather awkwardly paying his compliments to Lucy goes on to explain to her the particular danger from a stag at bay, '. . . for a hurt with a buck's horn is a perilous and somewhat venomous matter,'—a lesson he will learn to his cost on his wedding night.

I think the songs in *The Bride of Lammermoor* are misread if we see Lucy Ashton as innately passive, that is before the strange passivity that comes over her just before her marriage to Bucklaw. We must remember the Lucy Ashton who engaged herself to her father's enemy in a moment of passion. Her tragedy is the result of her attempt to participate in life. As her father had suggested, she was awakened to life by the addresses of a gentle knight. Immediately the engagement causes trouble, because Lucy knows that her mother will oppose it. The reader is shown in what fear Lucy stands of her mother, and with what justification. The strength of the mother should not be mitigated by declaring the daughter impossibly weak. The mother in the source story, a story of the Stair family in the seventeenth century, was supposed to have had supernatural power, and Lady Ashton is said to have used 'diabolical' means to coerce Lucy to renounce Ravenswood. Lady Ashton is one of Scott's formidably strong women, successor to the Lady in *The Lay of the Last Minstrel,* and the Countess of Glenallan in *The Antiquary.* Bucklaw curiously enough recognizes Lady Ashton's strength:

'I'll be bound Lady Ashton understands every machine
for breaking in the human mind, and there are as many

as there are cannon-bits, martingals, and cavessons for young colts.'

Ravenswood never seems to appreciate it, and sees in Lucy's fears a softness of mind, which however attractive, amounted 'almost to feebleness'. Does he ever understand her last faltering words to him, '"It was my mother"'? I think it is a mistake for the reader to fail there too.

Perhaps I have given enough examples to be allowed to draw one or two conclusions. The lyric voice in Scott is curiously impersonal; it is not the impassioned 'I' that we associate with the lyric in the post-renaissance tradition. That is one reason why it is possible for the lyric and ballad impulses in Scott to be so inextricably linked. Miss Woolf in the introduction to her study of *The English Religious Lyric in the Middle Ages* has pointed out two kinds of anonymity in literature: the accidental anonymity whereby history has lost for us the name of an author whose cast of mind we recognize to be individual; and what she calls natural or genuine anonymity, where the unknown poet obtruded no individual peculiarities of style or thought, where personality is not known because it is not relevant. For a popular author in the early nineteenth century there was not much likelihood of either. Scott played with the idea of the first, but, paradoxically, seems on occasions to be searching for the second. Sometimes in his poetry Scott seems to have wanted to step out of his own personality and into a self-effacing tradition. This is when he creates and steps into the world of his fictitious singers. Even in very slight snatches of poetry Scott often hints just enough to deflect the reader from too closely associating it with himself: the short mottoes which he wrote to head chapters in the novels, from *The Antiquary* onwards, frequently have this disclaimer, 'Old Ballad' or 'Old Play'. What is being said is better vouched for by impersonal utterance than by personal affidavit.

A fair number of Scott's fictitious singers are mad, or crazed with age or grief, apparently not in ordinary command of speech or action. This annoyed Jeffrey, reviewing *The Lady of the Lake*:

The Maniacs of poetry have indeed had a prescriptive right to be musical, since the days of Ophelia downwards; but it is rather a rash extension of this privilege to make them sing good sense, and to make sensible people be guided by them. [*The Edinburgh Review,* XVI, 1810]

Can anything be said to counter Jeffrey's criticism? Is the mad singer of a sane song a mere literary convention, apt to become tiresome with over-use? Or is it, like any good convention, an indication of something more? Can the mad singer and his hearer tell us anything about the nature of poetry and its place in the rest of life? The mad singer raises the problem of consciousness in the writing of poetry: the poetic gift enables one to express something that one may not be consciously aware of; the linking of words and sound, the convention seems to indicate, may be beyond the conscious decision of the writer. In the individual this gift suggests a many-layered consciousness: one part of the singer's mind can produce a penetrating insight about life, while another is unable to cope with life's most mundane demands. It is an impulse 'rather part of us than ours' [Introduction to the third canto of *Marmion*]. I think this may indicate why Scott always jibbed at the idea of being a professional poet. In his longer poems he often adopts the figure of the conscious mover of men; in the short lyrics and songs he displays another gift, less amenable to times and seasons. The figure of the mad singer is there to defeat our inquiry about the source of the lyric impulse, deliberately to baffle rational inquiry.

The mad singers in the novels have hearers, and this is where the figure of the mad singer illustrates aspects of poetry in its relation to the rest of life. Throughout the novels I have been discussing the hearers are offered information by those to whom they would not normally go for it. Matured by tribulation they learn to listen; wrapped in their own certainties and mental categories they hear but fail to understand; like old Elspeth's grandchildren they creep out of the room to play. The mature character in these novels has to learn that society is many-layered, that one layer can see what another cannot, and that if he can recognize what separates and what links them he may discover that, almost in another language, there is some sort of common utterance. The relation of the hearers to the singers in Scott's novels is an elaboration of the ironic injunction, 'Stop thine ear against the singer'. One may have to hear and act on information whose accuracy is only certain after one has done so—requiring a leap of faith again not readily amenable to the rational mind.

If the mad singer and his hearer is one image of poetry in society, the fact of verse printed in a novel is another. The rest of the novel, in all its variety, is the 'life' in which the poetry occurs. The songs usurp the role of dialogue (often in Scott another sort of poetry)—you are told something and you cannot answer; you cannot even be sure that you have heard properly.

Cumulatively these songs suggest that truth is reached by sudden insights. What you are offered is this statement beside which you must put that. You relish the bravado of the outlaw's song, and then you must put beside it the sad little refrain of the next song, 'Adieu for evermore'. And there are the contrasting songs on the death of Madge Wildfire: the religious lyric seeing death as a new life, and the laconic ballad of Proud Maisie stating the finality of our death in nature. The tragic emotion is allowed to exist in Scott without relief. There may be hope, but somehow that is another song. We are given two emotions, and one is not allowed to contain the other; only the order in which we hear the songs may indicate the dominance of one note over another. They express the apparently conflicting emotions which exist concurrently and with equal strength in the mind.

It follows that one is defeated in any attempt to build a system from these songs. Nevertheless there is what I may call a bias in favour of action and living life to the full whatever the cost. Scott's ideal is the man of action; he himself would have wished to be a soldier had he not been prevented by lameness. As it is he is expert in the psychology of the active life, fighting, hunting, loving, and their almost inevitable consequences, death, loss, jealousy, remorse. It is interesting that when he writes of death in a way other than tragic it is in terms of action,

> Doff thy robes of sin and clay,
> Christian, rise, and come away.

Scott's poems and novels offer a wide range of effects. The lyric voice is only one of them, but it is one in which his fitful genius is particularly sustained. Perhaps I may end by quoting a passage from the Introduction to the third canto of *Marmion,* a favourite analogy between Scott's poetry and the Border landscape of his youth:

> It was a barren scene, and wild,
> Where naked cliffs were rudely piled;
> But ever and anon between
> Lay velvet tufts of loveliest green.

Nancy Moore Goslee (essay date 1988)

SOURCE: "Witch or Pawn: Women in Scott's Narrative Poetry," in *Romanticism and Feminism,* edited by Anne K. Mellor, Indiana University Press, 1988, pp. 115–36.

[*An American educator and critic, Goslee is the author of a study about Scott's poetry,* Scott the Rhymer *(1988). In the following essay, she contends that while most of the female characters in Scott's narrative poems are cast in narrow roles, a few of his women undermine gender stereotypes.*]

When Walter Scott reviewed Jane Austen's novel *Emma* in 1816, he praised it highly; but he also criticized Austen's overemphasis upon a mercenary lust for property, a prudence at odds with the sense of romance. Not only is this unfair to Austen's biting analyses of the marriage market, but it obscures Scott's own portrayals of similar pressures within the plots of the romantic novels he had begun to publish two years earlier. Even in the narrative poems, far more explicitly romantic than his novels, Scott shows how women and their property all too often become pawns in male plots. Three of his seven major narrative poems—*Marmion* (1808), *Rokeby* (1813), and *The Lord of the Isles* (1815)—modify the usual romance pattern of hero rescuing and winning fair lady by showing the women as heiresses who become pawns in realistically portrayed struggles over money or land. Strikingly, these poems alternate with those in which the women are apparently far more dominant, but dominant within a romantic or even mythic, more than realistic, mode. In Scott's first, third, and fifth poems—*The Lay of the Last Minstrel* in 1805, *The Lady of the Lake* in 1810, and *The Bridal of Triermain* in 1813—the dominant female figures are witches or enchantresses who lure men into their isolated castles, either to alienate them from social responsibility in a stable culture, or to replace them in that culture. Usually the members of the second group associate themselves with the mysterious natural powers of the deep forest or of the lakes—and thus seem only slightly displaced nature goddesses. Yet in the first group, too, the woman whose land is so desirable appears alien to the male consciousness which, as Sherry Ortner and others have argued, tends to define culture [Sherry Ortner, "Is Female to Male as Nature Is to Culture?" in *Woman, Society, and Culture,* edited by Michelle Zimbalist Ricardo and Louise Lamphere, 1974].

Scott's seventh and final narrative poem, the 1817 *Harold the Dauntless,* includes even more, and more clearly hostile, witches than do the earlier poems. More central to the reform of the sullen Danish hero, however, is a woman disguised as a male skald or minstrel. Such cross-dressing, as conventional in literature as it is unconventional in society, also appears in *Marmion* and in *The Lord of the Isles*. Yet in *Harold,* and even more strikingly in the immediately preceding *Lord of the Isles,* it becomes a way to modify, if not fully to abolish, the two extreme patterns of women as passive land to be possessed, or as active natural or supernatural powers. [In *Woman and the Demon,* 1982] Nina Auerbach has described how, "as feminist criticism gains authority, its new sense of power involves not the denial of mythology but the impulse toward it. . . . The mythologies of the past have become stronger endowments than oppressions." By looking at the changing status of enchantress, pawn, or woman dressed as mediating minstrel within three of these poems—two from the first group and one from the second—we can recognize Scott's own dramatic modification of those quasi-mythic patterns for his vast reading public, and ask whether those modifications move, for his women characters and for his women readers, from oppression toward endowment.

In both *The Lay of the Last Minstrel* and *The Bridal of Triermain,* Scott filters the magic of his enchantresses through several narrators. In a scholarly note to *The Lay,* he carefully distinguishes between the intelligence of the historical Lady of Buccleuch and the "vulgar" view of her as a witch. Yet in his seventeenth-century minstrel's lay, the lady successfully calls up spirits to avenge the death of her husband at the hands of a neighboring border clan, and to forestall her daughter's love for a member of that clan. Similarly, in *The Bridal of Triermain,* a modern narrator tells two intertwined, avowedly fantastic medieval romances, to charm an heiress into eloping with him. In the earlier of the soldier's two narratives, King Arthur himself spends an idyllic summer in an enchantress's wilderness castle. Like the Lady of Buccleuch, this enchantress seems closely associated with nature. Yet almost as soon as the women's power becomes manifested in these poems, it becomes limited.

At the center of the lay sung by Scott's "last" minstrel is a figure who struggles to control her world through both written and spoken magic. Analogous to the problematic powers and limits of the imaginative self confronted by Scott and his minstrel, the struggles of the Renaissance Lady of Buccleuch have a very immediate purpose: she deploys her magic to protect her family and border terrain

after her husband has been killed. As the minstrel begins his lay, he contrasts the physical power of the waiting soldiers in the castle hall to the intellectual, visionary power of the lady in her isolated tower. His shudder of horror at the lady's solitary incantations echoes that of the narrator in *Christabel* but asks protection for himself and for his listening audience who may explore such topics, not for other characters: "Jesu Maria, shield us well!" (l. l.). Yet if the lady's incantatory magic is powerful in calling spirits from the vasty deep and having them answer her, the answer of river and mountain spirits to the lady is one that announces an ethical view opposing her own: "Till pride be quelled and love be free," she will receive no more help from them. The pride is her own, in her self, her art, and her immediate family; the love is her daughter's for a member of the family that has just killed her husband. Although the lady uses her magic to help her take on the male role of leadership her son is too young to assume, these nature spirits express what Carol Gilligan would call a more profoundly female vision: they urge a vital reconciliation instead of a killing revenge, a quelling of the lady's pride and a freeing of her daughter's love [Gilligan, *In a Different Voice: Psychological Theory and Women's Development,* 1982].

Instead of listening to those vocal presences, however, the lady continues her proud and individual challenge to romantic and domestic love. She also continues her usurpation of male power: in order to defend her view of family integrity, she sends her retainer, Walter of Deloraine, for a book of spells buried in the grave of its author, the local but renowned male wizard whose name is also Scott. Even though usurping a male wizard's power, this further reliance on magic increases her resemblance to the witches or enchantresses of romance who may indeed have descended from fertility goddesses but who draw men away from the human, social, and domestic ordering of that fertility.

The godlike powers of the book's written spells become manifest only through speech. Yet whoever reads the book may speak the spells. Freed from the dead hand of their author, spells can be either reinterpreted or redirected against his original intentions. Within the narrative, however, those powers are denied to the Lady of Buccleuch. Instead, the malicious goblin Gilpin Horner suddenly enters Scott's book, as the modern Lady Dalkieth, wife of his present chieftain, had requested. Seizing the wizard's book, the goblin forces it to open. Thus forcing both the wizard's text and Scott's own text into disorder, the goblin seems an animate and demonic *aporia*. This "elvish dwarf," we suddenly learn at the end of canto 2, serves Margaret of Buccleuch's suitor Cranstoun. As shown by his entry into the baron's service, his defining characteristic is leaping playfully and disruptively from one realm to another. When Cranstoun was hunting in Redesdale's remote glens,

> He heard a voice cry, "Lost! lost! lost!"
> And, like tennis-ball by racket toss'd,
> A leap, of thirty feet and three,
> Made from the gorse this elfin shape.

Even though, as the minstrel drily comments, "Lord Cranstoun was some whit dismay'd," and rode "five good miles . . . To rid him of his company," the dwarf "was first at the castle door" and eventually finds employment. "Though small his pleasure to do good," his alertness and devotion have since then served the baron well.

Taken alone, this "marvel" might seem only an image of anarchic violence or of the id. Yet he is also a figure for some original imaginative energy or presence that breaks through the conventional patterns of understanding. Arising from the goblin's arbitrary acts is a pattern of relationships that confirms this second interpretation: a pattern that links page, book, and lady. The goblin's spontaneous substitution of himself for the "Mighty Book" requested by the lady arises from his own quick study of its "gramarye," its magical text. Following a bloody encounter between Cranstoun and the returning Deloraine, the goblin discovers the book and reads "one short spell." This is just enough, evidently, for him to perfect the shape-changing skill of "glamour," in which "All was delusion, nought was truth." Through the glamour of the written spell, then, he enters the lady's castle and thus replaces the book's latent and ambiguous power with his own malicious and energetic presence.

In a further exchange, that presence is even more explicitly linked to the lady than is the wizard's book she waits for. In an apparently spontaneous maliciousness, the goblin disguises himself as a playmate and leads the lady's "fair young child," the heir of Branksome Hall, into the woods. There, after frightening the child with "his own elvish shape," he abandons him. A band of English invaders soon discovers him and holds him for ransom. When the aggressive boy declares his own identity first by fighting off their dogs and then by announcing that he is "the heir of bold Buccleuch," the English reiterate his heritage: "I think our work is well begun, / When we have ta'en thy father's son" (stanza 19). Meanwhile, the goblin takes on his appearance and his place in the Buccleuch family:

> Although the child was led away,
> In Branksome still he seem'd to stay,
> For so the Dwarf his part did play.
> And in the shape of that young boy,
> He wrought the castle much annoy.
>   (3. 21)

The socially acceptable, masculine, and other-directed aggression shown by the real child is distorted by the goblin into a painful pinching and sudden outbursts of flame: his violence, like the lady's magic, is a violation of domestic peace because it dislocates acceptable roles. It is nevertheless the dark side of that society's socially accepted violence. This connection is suggested by the minstrel's sequence of images at the end of canto 2: from the dwarf's small bonfires to Margaret's musings on what she thinks is the evening star that "shakes its loose tresses on the night" to her recognition that the "star" is in fact the beacon-blaze of war, announcing the arrival of the English and rallying support as far as Edinburgh.

In the fourth canto, because the disguised goblin's efforts to avoid detection by the lady lead to his temporary banishment from Branxholm to another castle, that banishment makes the English forces' possession of her biological son both explicable and threatening from the lady's viewpoint. Yet the goblin is in his rebelliousness and in his magic a child of the witchlike lady. In replacing her biological son, the goblin frees her temporarily from the social chain that makes her only the mother of the new child-cheiftain. And like her, he expresses an anarchic, disruptive individuality through a transforming magic.

Though shaking the fabric of society, this rebellion does not, however, fully transform it. Instead, the wizard's "Mighty Book," left with Cranstoun when the dwarf enters the lady's castle, makes possible a larger change. Tutored by his now-returned goblin-page, Cranstoun uses the book's "gramarye" in canto 5 to enter Branksome, the Buccleuchs' castle. Although the goblin hopes that Cranstoun's presence in Branksome will lead to sexual anarchy, the lovers can control the fires of their own passion well enough to redirect both passion and magic. Disguised through gramarye as Deloraine, the Lady's knight whom he had earlier wounded, Cranstoun fights a second and more formal single combat. Substituting himself for Deloraine as family champion, he fights this time against an English champion, in order to free the lady's biological son. His disguise as a retainer of the Scott family, moreover, proves prophetic; once the lady learns of his generous service, she reluctantly quells her pride and gives love its freedom, allowing him to marry her daughter. Thus his interpretation of the book's spells completes and reorders the exchanges, almost the metaphorical substitutions, made by the maliciously energetic goblin and brings peace not only between the feuding Scottish border clans but even, temporarily, between Scots and English.

Unwilling to disturb this fragile peace, itself so nearly a kind of "glamour" or illusion in that normally violent society, both Cranstoun and the lady are discreet about the nature of their struggle. "Much of the story she did gain," the minstrel comments, his balanced lines including the pun that confirms the interchange in his own story between the energy of the goblin page and that of speech written on a page:

> . . . How Cranstoun fought with Deloraine,
> And of his page, and of the Book
> Which from the wounded knight he took. . . .
>   (5. 27)

Cranstoun, however, leaves "half his tale . . . unsaid"—the half concerning his own use of the book—as if narrating his own experiment with magic might commit the baron too fully to its practice, or as if narrative itself is that commitment to magic.

Because the lady, too, "car'd not . . . to betray / Her mystic arts in view of day," her conversation with Cranstoun after the combat is constrained. Yet she planned "ere midnight came, / Of that strange page the pride to tame, / From his foul hands the Book to save, / And send it back to Michael's grave" (5. 27). Her attribution of "pride" to the dwarf comes right after her own painful and public relinquishing of pride as her chastising nature spirits had demanded. She associates the goblin's expression of pride with the supplementary power of the book; but "pride" seems in both cases to be an independent self-assertion that makes use of the wizard's neutral spells. Her intention to return the book to the grave suggests that she is beginning to relinquish such independence for herself—or, at least, that she now sees her family's identity as defined more by loving alliance than by hostile self-assertion.

As the minstrel carefully rejects the "false slander" of "some bards" who claim that the lady would not enter the chapel for her daughter's wedding, he confirms this turn from individual pride and imaginative energy toward a communal harnessing of that energy:

> . . . I trust right well
> She wrought not by forbidden spell;
> For mighty words have signs and power
> O'er sprites in planetary hour. . . .
>
> (6. 5)

Instead, she assents to the sacramental words of her daughter's wedding. Dwindled from magician into domestic mother of the bride,

> The Ladye by the altar stood:
>
> . . . . .
>
> . . . On her head a crimson hood,
>
> . . . . .
>
> A merlin sat upon her wrist,
> Held by a leash of silken twist.

Both she and the hawk are hooded; its allusive name confirms it as the emblem of her present state of submission.

Finally, she loses even the demonic distortion of her power. Her intention to leash not only her own magic words but also the gramarye of Michael Scott's book meets, like all her attempts, a reverse that proves more socially generous in its twist. Before she can return the book to the wizard's grave, yet another exchange confirms the interdependence of goblin-page and book: the wizard leaves his grave, stalks through the wedding feast, and claims the still-malicious goblin as his own. When the shadowy figure says, "Gylbin, come!" the elvish page mutters, "Found! found! found!" and vanishes. Though apparently chastised, the goblin thus gains a paternal recognition and control, more than a total repression. With the dramatically if skeptically described return of its male author from the grave, moreover, the written text of Michael Scott seems to lose its threatening moral ambiguity and confirms the lovers' goal of an harmonious, cooperative, and social world. The domestic, nurturing values traditionally desired in women dominate the end of the poem, but at the cost of leashing other powers women might exercise: the power of "mighty words and signs," the power of the book.

Almost overlooked in this dramatic epiphany, the book itself is apparently left behind when the wizard and goblin vanish together. If we look for further references to it in the minstrel's tale, we find instead another, more sublime vanishing of a book in the renewed presence of its creator. Through a pilgrimage to Melrose, the border clans try to quiet the restless soul of the wizard, and the minstrel's narrative concludes with a tribute to divine presence over text, the singing of the *Dies Irae*. In the face of an apocalyptic divine presence, "shrivelling like a parched scroll, / The flaming heavens together roll" (6. 31). Scott as writer, however, has the last word. He is now free to circulate his own individual, private text, doubly validated by male wizard and minstrel. Yet because the minstrel's song has also shown not quite the interchangeability but the familial relationships of written text and goblin energy, he preserves his own anarchic originality of imagination and his own identity by defining his family origins. Even though he has distanced and delimited her power, he becomes like the dwarf-goblin a son of the witchlike lady whose magic he has chastised.

A male magician bursting from the earth also marks a radical censuring of female magic in *The Bridal of Triermain*. In this case the magician is the powerful Merlin. In *Triermain,* too, a mother's antisocial magic sharply contrasts to and is redeemed through a daughter's more docile and conventional behavior. In the later poem, however, the mother begins to lose control even before the child is born. Conversely, and surprisingly, the modern narrator accomplishes his purpose—charming an heiress to elope with him—before he has completed the part of his story that shows this redemptive domestication. In this brief yet complex pattern of interlocking narratives, the modern heiress is first told about a thirteenth-century border knight, Sir Roland de Vaux of Triermaine. Visited by a strangely beautiful huntress whom no one else sees, Sir Roland asks a local bard to explain who she is. The bard Lyulph's tale goes back 500 years, to reveal King Arthur's seduction by an enchantress; the visionary huntress now loved by Sir Roland is the daughter of that temporary union. Roland's journey to the dark tower where he can find and free the daughter, now herself enchanted, is a morally instructive allegory. Yet the modern heiress, perhaps ironically named Lucy, chooses to elope with the narrator before he tells her that allegory; instead, her choice is prompted by the bard's Arthurian seduction narrative and its pendant, the daughter's arrival at Arthur's court fifteen years later. Although the serious social consequences of elopement appear fully in Jane Austen's novels, the wonderful fantasy of the romance episodes in *Triermain* seems to have persuaded both Scott's fictional heiress Lucy and his readers to overlook such difficulties.

How, then, should we understand Lucy's response to the earlier stages of her suitor's narrative? Although his name is also Arthur, he seems to control his own powers of enchantment, not—like the king—falling victim to another's control. By examining more fully the steps backward into myth and then forward into the demythologizing of its enchantresses, we may understand more clearly the heiress's enthrallment by her Arthur-author's narrative imagination—and possibly her recognition and freedom from it.

Appropriately enough, Arthurian narrative then begins with the king's name and with a highly conventional romance motif: Arthur's yearning to escape his queen's bowers for "vent'rous quest . . . by wood or river." What is unconventional about this narrative is Arthur's active role in the quest and in the confrontation with a mysterious enchantress. When this Arthur rides out into the "desert wild," the king places himself, rather startlingly, in the role of an imitator of traditional romance models: he "journey'd like knight errant" (1.10). In the isolated Vale of St. John he finds a mysterious, silent castle. Like Launfal, he is led by a "band of damsels fair" to their enchantress-queen. Once inside the castle, he finds himself ironically, if happily, enclosed in another bower.

In canto 1 the queen's seductions appear entirely natural. She uses the same human beguilements Guinevere uses on Lancelot (2. 15) and she is entirely successful. Scott's multiple audiences, too, seem charmed into silence by the natural inevitability of this relationship. There is no sharp narrative break between the formal divisions of canto 1 and canto 2, where we might expect responses from the multiple internal listeners: from the page listening to the bard Lyulph's tale, perhaps from Roland listening to the page's report of that tale, or from Lucy listening to the modern Arthur's. By refusing to describe the nearly mutual seduction of Arthur and the enchantress Guendolen in detail and instead calling it a "common tale," the bard Lyulph offers a distinctly moral commentary. Yet by linking Arthur's "gliding" first into "folly" and then into "sin" with the way time "glides away" as he lingers at the castle, Lyulph slides over the moral problems his various audiences, known and unknown to him, might well consider.

In canto 2, when the mysterious queen fears that the king's "hour of waking" from his infatuation is "near," she must turn to her supernatural powers. These powers connect her to an earlier world of myth: Lyulph describes her as a sort of demi-nature-goddess, supernatural though closely connected to the processes of an external natural world, "wood or river." Although Guendolen's "mother was of mortal birth," "Her sire[,] a Genie of the earth," presided over courtship and fertility rituals until the coming of Christianity. Resentful of losing "his rights," "He trained to guile that lady fair, / To sink in slothful sin and shame, / The Champions of the Christian name" (2. 3).

Though he has lost territory to Christianity, the resentful genie has neither vanished, like Plutarch's gods at the birth of Christ, nor lost all power; the "guile" he teaches his daughter is described in stanza 4 as "Her sire's soft arts the soul to tame." As stanza 3 describes Guendolen's practice of those arts, it slides, like the transition between cantos, from natural seduction to magical snare. It also glides, however, from a naively realistic acceptance of the existence both of the genie and his daughter to a subtly stated questioning of their actuality:

Well skill'd to keep vain thoughts alive,
And all to promise, naught to give;
The timid youth had hope in store,
The bold and pressing gain'd no more.
As wilder'd children leave their home,
After the rainbow's arch to roam,
Her lovers barter'd fair esteem,
Faith, fame, and honour, for a dream.

(2. 3)

Characteristically, however, Scott gives the visionary woman a motivation. Thus, even though her explicit if mythological family history would seem to make her more obviously malevolent than Keats's and Shelley's similar figures, its very explicitness makes her less mysterious and more human. Further, it makes her failure to use her magic understandable. She promptly forgets "each rule her father gave," and is "Sunk from a princess to a slave." As in *The Lay,* the lady has learned her magical skills from her father and thus does not draw her powers only from an originally female source in a fecund but alien nature. Scott's careful fathering of those mythic powers drawn from nature does not prevent but divides and thus controls the fusion of female and natural otherness so weirdly present in the powers both of Thomas the Rhymer's Queen of Elfland and of Keats's Belle Dame. Because of this weakening, Guendolen can keep Arthur, as Meleager captures Guinevere, only for a summer. This is long enough to insure her own fertility (2. 6–7) but not to confirm her divinity. Instead of continuing as a receding goal for the dreamer and luring him to destruction as the dream-woman in *Alastor* will do only a year later, she herself becomes the pursuer who must seek to maintain her summer's dream of fulfillment, to keep the father of her expected child.

Only as the king actually leaves, having broken from her natural charms, does Guendolen remember enough of her magical art to set a trap. Yet her use of magic clarifies neither her powers nor Arthur's power to resist them. Like Comus or like his reputed mother Circe, she offers him a "cup of gold." To share the parting ritual, she drinks first. When the unsuspicious Arthur "lifted the cup," however, a "drop escaped the goblet's brink" and, "Intense as liquid fire from hell," burned his horse so severely that its leap carried the king out of the vale (2. 10). If Guendolen's ability to drink this fiery potion seems to confirm her own supernatural powers, Arthur's avoidance of it is less a moral or perceptual victory than a comic accident.

His judgment of the whole episode, like the audience's judgment, is made even more difficult by his retrospective view. When he "back on the fatal castle gazed," he sees only "A tufted knoll, where dimly shone / Fragments of rock and rifted stone" (2. 10). If Arthur had tasted the genie's drink, he might have been drawn permanently into Guendolen's Circe-like realm of enchantment and might himself have disappeared with the castle, folded into liminal elf-realm within, yet beyond, nature. On the other hand, the drink might simply have killed the king, preventing both his return and the fulfillment of his fantasy of a dallying escape into nature. As it is, the enchantress's power remains untested: he returns and follows the whole career told by the "history" of Geoffrey of Monmouth and the romances of later writers: giants captured, twelve battles won, and an almost-perfect kingdom established. In contrast to Keats's knight or the newly prophetic Thomas the Rhymer, Arthur seems not to have put on the enchantress' supernatural knowledge with her sexual power.

In some sense Scott's turn toward the female minstrel may reflect his own role as a male taking on the female role of novel-writing, and the female values of domestic morality.

—Nancy Moore Goslee

Again with no intervention from any later listener or narrator, Lyulph skips fifteen years or more, to focus in stanza 11 of canto 2 on the arrival of Arthur's hitherto unknown daughter at his Penrith court. Though one might expect the child of such a union to exercise her inherited magic and to pursue further the genies' vengeance against Christian culture, instead she pursues vengeance against Arthur's desertion of her mother. More aware of her mother as wronged mortal than as wrongdoing enchantress—a view more justified by outcome than by her mother's intention—she turns the summer tournament meant to marry her off into an exposure of the decadence of Arthur's court. In contrast to her mother's earlier career as a receding visionary object, Gyneth and her new wealth become entirely too present. Abandoning their earlier commitments, all but three knights fight for her and for the two kingdoms Arthur promises with her. The sordidness of their motives is rewarded by the violence of their deaths. Though Arthur has given Gyneth his "leading-staff" to stop the tournament before it changes into such violence, she refuses to stop the slaughter and to restore the apparent order Arthur would have preserved in his court and in himself. Her destructive use of his phallic staff forms an appropriate revenge against Arthur's apparent seduction and abandonment of her mother.

Yet Gyneth does not complete her bloody quest for a husband among "the bravest, proved and tried." Instead, male magic intervenes with a claim to retaliate against her "mother's art." Arthur first uses this phrase in stanza 22, in response to her charge of "the faithlessness of men." In stanza 26, an angry Merlin arrives to avenge his nephew's death in the melee and repeats the charge: "thy mother's art / Warp'd thine unsuspicious heart." Although Gyneth uses no magic but her beauty and her potential wealth, she now becomes the victim, or at least the object, of Merlin's own more powerful art. Even in his arrival on the scene, Arthur's enchanter usurps the powers of her mother's line:

> . . . rent by sudden throes,
> Yawn'd in mid lists the quaking earth,

> And from the gulf, tremendous birth!
> The form of Merlin rose!
>
> (2. 25)

Reborn from the earth, he has no use for women's powers of fertility; claiming the earth himself, he denies the power of the "Genie of the earth" who taught Guendolen her arts. Triply imprisoned by Merlin's spell—in sleep, in an enchanted chair, and in the mysterious castle hidden in the "Vale of Saint John," where she had come from—Gyneth is condemned to endure a more passive version of her mother's career.

Two slightly differing interpretations of this punishment are given at the end of the canto, one Christian and explicitly antifeminist, the second returning to the mythic pattern behind the romance to continue her guilt (2. 26). Because she has caused Arthur's knights to kill each other in a most un-Christian acting out of their greed, Merlin makes her an Eve causing a second fall—"all their woes"—of "the Red Cross champions" (2. 26). Even if it does recall her genie-grandfather's antagonism to Christianity, Merlin's condemnation is surely an elegaic whitewashing of the knights' behavior. Her "pride," moreover, has only mirrored Arthur's own. Claiming acknowledgment as his daughter, she plays upon his own too easy buying-off of her claims, so that the anarchic violence she creates is only too appropriate a dowry.

The second interpretation recalls the genie's intentions even more fully, yet returns sympathy to the prisoner. Completing his narrative to the page, Lyulph explains that Gyneth "still . . . bears her weird alone, / In the valley of Saint John." As a visionary image she has even more power than did her mother to draw knights astray: "her semblance oft will seem, / Mingling in a champion's dream, / Of her weary lot to plain, / And brave his aid to burst her chain." Her imprisonment creates a trial of solitary, not social bravery for the knights who are led either by her dream or by "her wondrous tale" to search for her (2. 28). Among those who see the castle, "few have braved the yawning door, / And those few return'd no more." As her story is gradually forgotten, Lyulph implies, her power to haunt dreams is also lessened, and thus "well nigh lost is Gyneth's lot" (stanza 28). Her very existence seems dependent upon the active imagination of narrator and dreamer.

To consider the active realization of the knights' dreams also implies a complex assessment of the functions of romance as a genre. With its "yawning door," the terrifying castle in the mysterious vale resembles a Lawrence-like nightmare of the absorbing, consuming womb, seen as alien, annihilating, tomblike. Once realized as an actual person and not as a vision, Gyneth in part shares the castle's role as a physical trap that threatens the separate consciousness, even the existence of the male questers. Yet she is in part freed from this role because in her sleep she too seems a virginal victim. Like the lady in *Comus,* imprisoned in her chair, she is immobilized. In sharp contrast to Comus, Merlin is trying to freeze, not to release, the natural fertility she represents. In greater fairness to

Merlin, we might say that he is trying to reassert control over the lust and avarice that Gyneth has called out in the court. Daughter of a nature deity and a Circe, Gyneth has herself been a Comus, turning Arthur's ordered tournament into a brutal antimasque; but with Merlin's greater powers, she becomes the helpless Lady.

[In *The Uses of Enchantment: The Meaning and Importance of Fairy Tales,* 1975] Bruno Bettelheim argues that the spell cast over the sleeping beauty is a necessary period of narcissism in puberty, for emotional development to catch up to physical maturity. He suggests that the old woman, the evil fairy, represents the feared yet necessary aspects of physical maturity for women. In this version, however, Merlin's sleep punishes Gyneth for not denying the witchcraft of natural fertility and process. She must become a victim in order to be saved from her own maternal sources of power. In some sense, too, her purging from enchantment represents a purging of the women in Arthur's court, whose bowers have distorted the social structures of male chivalry or at least of military alliance.

When that Arthurian narrative ends, we expect to hear how one of those haunted knights, Sir Roland de Vaux, sets off to rescue the princess from her centuries-long sleep. Yet, surprisingly, the modern heiress does not wait for a happy ending at this point: she decides to elope with the soldier who is telling her both romances. She may see herself as a princess whose wealth makes her only the object of suitors' quests; or perhaps she is asleep, charmed by this ambitious minstrel about whom we know little except his rather cynical portrayal of the king for whom he is named. The conclusion of the modern Arthur's story, however, suggests that the heiress has gambled well. For the romance-quest of Sir Roland is a Renaissance moral allegory. Each mysterious chamber of the magical castle houses women whose temptations are both sexual and psychological.

At the center of these enclosures, the goal of Scott's knight differs from those of Ariosto's, Tasso's, and Spenser's. Roland's attempt is closest to Guyon's, for he is a rescuer. Yet he rescues not a preceding male quester victimized by an enchantress, but a younger, less guilty version of the enchantress herself. With great precision Scott uses these analogues to earlier Renaissance romantic epics to recall Gyneth's parentage and to distinguish her from her mother. Rogero has adopted "wanton, womanish behavior . . . An Atys or Adonis for to be / Unto Alcina" (canto 7) [Ariosto, *Orlando Furioso*]; Rinaldo's "sword, that many a pagan stout had shent, / Bewrapt with flowers hung idly by his side" (16. 30) [Tasso, *Jerusalem Delivered*]; Verdant has cast aside his sword (2. 12. 80) [Spenser, *The Faerie Queene*]. Although Scott's poem echoes these lines closely, they do not describe Roland. Instead, the lines (2. 1) come from Lyulph's tale, the first narrative, and they describe King Arthur. Even more dramatically than Spenser shifts the balance of Tasso's narrative by making his main protagonist the rescuer instead of the victim, Scott shifts the balance of these sources by dividing them into two parts. Thus Rogero, Rinaldo, and Verdant are models for Arthur, and, even more strikingly, the Circean enchant-resses Alcina, Armida, and Acrasia are models for Guendolen. In all four cases, these dominant enchantresses unman their lovers by embowering them in passive enjoyment. The sword hanging unused is both an abandonment of social responsibility and evidence of their impotence in the personal, if not the physical relationship.

Far less effective than the other three, Scott's Guendolen is also more sympathetic. As we saw, Arthur eventually decides to rescue himself, and she even spills the Circean cup that might have enchained him more permanently. Alcina, Armida, and Acrasia are indeed conquered, but only with superior magic beyond the power of their passive victims. Even with that superior magic, only Spenser's Acrasia is firmly conquered. Though these Renaissance parallels surely make Guendolen's career as an enchantress seem less terrifying than those of the earlier Circes, they nevertheless make firmer the association of female sexuality, demonic enchantment, and a dangerously contagious, yet isolated and antisocial domesticity. If remote from normal society, the bower is feminizing for the heroes. Also, since these parallels with Ariosto, Tasso, and Spenser become far clearer in the third canto of *The Bridal,* we not only share the modern Arthur's tendency to interpret Roland's quest allegorically, but we also reread or recall the earlier Arthurian story of the first two cantos in a different way. In this retrospective process Guendolen's significance, if not her actions, seems more terrifying and thus the need for Gyneth's purgation seems stronger. Through this network of allusions both to the preceding Renaissance poems and to the preceding parts of this one, Gyneth is trapped in a kind of sedimented, hermeneutic guilt.

Just as the elemental functions of romance heroes—those of errant dallier and of rescuer—are split between Arthur and Roland, so the function of witch and passive "damsel" to be "from danger freed" (*Marmion,* 4. 4) are split between Guendolen and Gyneth, between mother and daughter. This generational distinction between the female figures should remind us of *The Lay,* in which the Lady of Buccleuch relinquishes her powers of witchcraft to make way for her daughter's conventional domesticity. Both through contrast with the now more moralistic and more misogynist reading of the Arthurian narrative and through his return to analogues of *Comus* and "The Sleeping Beauty," Scott works out Gyneth's purification. Roland, a somewhat more charming Guyon, brushes off all temptation. Purified by this testing, he finds the sleeping Gyneth also purified by her long sleep: "Doubt, and anger, and dismay, / From her brow had pass'd away" (3. 37). No longer the Circean enchantress whose refusal to use the warder created brute chaos in the tournament, she releases the warder into Roland's hands as she wakes up. As mentioned earlier, she now resembles the lady in *Comus,* temporary victim of a son of Circe (3. 38). Like Milton's lady, she seems far younger than all the Circean arguments or the furor at the tournaments had led us to expect. Though a pun only in French, the "ivory chair" in which her life has been suspended seems almost to symbolize the suspended processes of her own sexual development. That suspension redeems her from being condemned as an enchantress.

Further, Roland's trials have made him wary of holding her in thrall. Instead of the earlier bluff, forthright egotism that we might have expected from him, he plays neither Comus nor even the gently aggressive prince in tales of the sleeping beauty:

> Motionless a while he stands,
> Folds his arms and clasps his hands,
> Trembling in his fitful joy,
> Doubtful how he should destroy
>   Long-enduring spell.
> Doubtful, too, when slowly rise
> Dark-fring'd lids of Gyneth's eyes,
>   What those eyes shall tell.

At first reading the elided grammar of the line suggests that Gyneth wakes up, given the freedom to do so. Yet in a sense his hesitation does lead to that result. In his willingness to wait for her response, he reaches out "gently" to grasp her hand and kiss her. As he does so, "the warder" that had been in her hand "leaves his grasp." Neither the newly educated Sir Roland nor Gyneth, then, keeps that power over male aggression, which was in Arthur's hands civic rule and in Gyneth's became, in both Arthur's and Merlin's view, "her mother's art." As Roland inadvertently parallels Prospero's breaking of his wand, the last magic of the poem becomes a release from magic. When "the warder leaves his grasp," the "magic halls / Melt . . . away,

> But beneath their mystic rocks,
> In the arms of bold De Vaux,
>   Safe the princess lay.
> Safe and free from magic power,
> Blushing like the rose's flower
> Opening to the day . . .

Although the phrase "beneath their mystic rocks" suggests for a moment that both Roland and Gyneth have been swallowed up into the magic castle, Arthur's conclusion places them firmly in this world, far less haunted than Keats's wan knight on the cold hill's side. Arthur wraps up his fiction with a flurry of conventional phrases, as if afraid to confront their entrance into ordinary time too closely:

> Our lovers, briefly, be it said,
> Wedded as lovers wont to wed,
>   When tale or play is o'er—
> Lived long and blest, loved fond and true,
> And saw a numerous race renew
> The honours that they bore.

"Safe and free from magic power," Gyneth apparently retains none of her mother's art. One could say, in an extension of Virginia Woolf's thesis, that even though she was trapped in that castle, unconscious for five centuries, she had a room and a power of her own. Now this second-generation enchantress has neither. The image of the castle, Arthur tells Lucy, still occasionally haunts a lost traveler. Yet he attributes the power of making it more than illusion to the male quester, not to the in-house female

magician: "Never man since brave De Vaux / The charmed portal won." Thus the menacing power of an independent female imagination or an independent, aggressive female sexuality is redefined. The first now becomes the creation of a male moral and aesthetic criterion so compelling that Roland has in a sense realized his own fantasy by finding Gyneth: and the second becomes a passive blossoming out of sleeping innocence. Thus in both poems the independent enchantresses are simultaneously domesticated and demythologized. Even the love that one might expect to draw men into the lawless, alien, antisocial aspects of their magic is revised in both poems into a domesticating force made manifest through a younger generation.

In a second group of poems, Scott makes the chief woman character an heiress who is far more obviously a powerless pawn, a victim of male plots for ownership. Two of the three poems in this group I will mention only briefly; the tangled web of the plots spun by their villains would take more space than I have here. In *Marmion* and *Rokeby,* the villains plot to trick unwilling heiresses into marriage in order to control their land. They are thwarted not only by the heiresses themselves, but also by the men the heiresses love. In both cases the successful lover proves his character while in disguise. In the third of these "pawn" poems, *The Lord of the Isles,* it is the woman who assumes the disguise. By doing so, she succeeds, paradoxically, in bringing about the family-arranged political marriage that she had wanted all along. It was one, however, that her brother and her fiancé had tried to break off, the brother from changed political loyalties and the fiancé from changed personal loyalties. Thus Scott uses a conventional literary topos—a woman disguised as a boy, pursuing her lover—to correct an all-too-conventional social situation, the woman as pawn.

Yet in this poem both the heroine's venturesome experiment in transexual dressing and her final success in marriage are nearly undermined by her extreme passivity, even in her disguise. Shakespeare's disguised heroines in the romantic comedies manipulate both the language of the play and the entire plot. Scott's heroine quite explicitly denies herself even that control of language. Presumably to avoid being recognized, she disguises herself as a harp-playing but vocally mute minstrel. For Scott, as his last minstrel says in *The Lay,* the medieval minstrel who relied on music alone abdicated his true vocation in shaping, through language, a culture's vision of itself. His heroine Edith of Lorn, then, seems to free herself from her role as pawn—only to have her assumed role express an even stronger denial of female power to develop either a self or a supporting culture. Cultural self-definition, moreover, is central to the poem's historical milieu, the struggle of Robert the Bruce to restore Scottish independence from England.

As the poem moves from castle to wilderness, then back to civilization, that journey leads, as in many romances, to the education of the hero—here, both Robert the Bruce, the would-be king of Scotland, and MacDonald of the Isles, the would-not-be bridegroom. In a further use of romance convention, the disguised Edith travels for weeks with Bruce and Ronald. Unidentified as a woman, she is—even more outrageously—unrecognized by her former fiancé. Reading the situation literally and realistically, at least one reviewer was scandalized by what he saw as impropriety [*Eclectic Review,* May, 1815]. In the civilized settings of the first two cantos Scott does indeed treat the earlier relationship between Edith and Ronald realistically, though a part of that realism involves the effect of romantic circumstances upon the characters. From canto 3 on, this realism is modified, but not fully transformed, by the roles of women in two different romance conventions—the medieval quest, suggested in part by Edith's green clothing, and Elizabethan comedy, suggested by her male clothing. The specific nature of her disguise as minstrel adds still further complexity to this use of romance conventions.

In canto 1 her foster mother gently chides Edith for the "cold demeanor" that seems so inappropriate to the wedding clothes she already wears. Reminding her of "many a tower" that "Owns thy broad brother's feudal power" (1. 18), Morag reminds her how "auspicious" the morning is that will unite "the daughter of high Lorn" with "the heir of mighty Somerled." Only adding to this appropriateness is "Fame's heroic tale" (1. 10) of Ronald's military success. Yet while Edith, betrothed to him since childhood by family arrangement, is prepared to love him by those "lays" of his "achievement," Ronald has not been equally prepared for her; his response is "cold delay" (1. 11). Although arranged marriages of this sort often enough led to indifference on both sides, Edith's readiness to love leaves her doubly vulnerable. A willing pawn in the arrangements for the marriage, she wants it to be more than an arrangement and thus becomes an emotional victim. Although the early betrothal and the vast landscapes involved in the negotiations are characteristic of the medieval period, Edith's poignant demand for love—though surely not unknown earlier—also reflects the growing emphasis placed upon woman's sentiments and the frequent conflict of such sentiments with the economics of the marriage market in the late eighteenth and early nineteenth century.

With Bruce's storm-driven arrival and then his recognition, the realism of larger political conflicts and actual historical characters breaks in upon the realism of Edith's typical characterization. First defending the still-anonymous Bruce by the laws of hospitality, Ronald responds to a "long-suppress'd . . . spark" of nationalism, then defends him even more hotly when he recognizes Bruce's sister as a woman he had admired at an English tournament. When he speaks to Isabel Bruce, his language eclipses the place of Edith—his possessives, even his term "bride," are addressed confusedly to both women (2. 19). Further, once Lorn sees that Ronald and his Islesmen are no longer his allies against Bruce but now the king's supporters, he threatens to marry Edith to another, more reliable ally—and he also reveals how unfeelingly he had pressed for the earlier marriage in spite of seeing Ronald's obvious indifference:

> Was't not enough to Ronald's bower
> I brought thee, like a paramour,

> Or bond maid at her master's gate,
> His careless cold approach to wait?
> (2. 25)

Her vanishing, then her reappearance, disguised and silent, in a near-wasteland are only the outward correlatives of her status at the end of this scene.

Her choice of a minstrel's disguise makes a further ironic protest against her situation. During the first two cantos, the minstrels at Ardtornish have distinguished themselves by their readiness to sing the socially and politically appropriate, if emotionally inappropriate, aubades for her wedding day. In canto 2, Lorn supplies a "lay" for the resident minstrel to sing: its narrative is so insulting to Bruce that he virtually reveals himself to correct his own history. Sardonically, Bruce praises the minstrel who has "framed thy strains / To praise the hand that pays thy pains" (2. 14). Edith's disguise of a voiceless minstrel seems an effective criticism of the politically compromised art she has just heard.

Further, her role as disguised minstrel on Skye enables Bruce to work toward the kingship that will be fully confirmed, undisguised, at Bannockburn. Effective for others, however, her silent minstrelsy is not a disguise that lends her strength, as does Flora MacDonald's disguising of Bonnie Prince Charles on Skye in 1746, a narrative much in the minds of Scott's readers. Instead, confirming a variant of Sandra Gilbert's thesis about cross-dressing, her weakness becomes a way to teach others a way to regulate their strength [Gilbert, "Costumes of the Mind: Transvestism as Metaphor in Modern Literature," *Critical Inquiry* 7, No. 2 (Winter 1980)].

When Bruce and MacDonald pursue a stag to the edge of the bleak Loch Corriskin on the Isle of Skye, they encounter there the mute minstrel-page, dressed in green as if a kind of nature spirit. Though disguised as a boy, Edith acts like one of the more benevolent ladies of the lake in Arthurian romance, a myth Scott has already used playfully in his own *Lady of the Lake*. When Edith warns the men of an ambush by her own brother's forces, their successful struggle becomes an omen for the long guerilla struggles that lead toward independence. Though a human and not a magical nature-spirit, Edith mediates between these men and the landscape as if to prophesy that its sublimity is an image of the moral grandeur of their cause, and thus an image of their claim upon the land of Scotland as a whole. Scott's supplement to history—Bruce's detour to Skye—converts romance into a cause of actual history.

One reason for her failure to gain male strength through her disguise is that Scott reshapes and relocates episodes from Barbour's *Bruce* to draw out their resemblance to medieval romance. As he does so, he modifies the freedom of male cross-dressing available to the heroines of Elizabethan comedy with a more conventional, even archetypal woman's role from romance. For Edith, however, the role of the elfin queen or wilderness enchantress carries no radically transforming "gramarye." Instead, it emphasizes—yet, paradoxically, in a constructive way—her passivity as object.

Unlike Ellen Douglas in *The Lady of the Lake,* the disguised Edith by no means thinks of herself, even teasingly, as a nearly supernatural lady of the lake. With her "cap and cloak of velvet green" (3. 22), she wears fairies' clothing. She thus shares with the elfin world and with traditional ladies of the lake that border-figure role of mediating between the natural and the supernatural. Because of her male disguise, however, she does not assume the sexual power of a Circean fertility goddess, or even of a Guendolen in *The Bridal of Triermain*. Unlike the ladies of the lake, she is also a border figure between the sexes. As Ronald later recalls, the men who brought her to Skye and who plan to ambush Bruce call her "Amadine . . . (In Gaelic 'tis the Changeling)" (5. 18). Alluding to the tradition that the fairies steal human children and leave behind their own "changelings," these men half-consciously recognize her disguised sexual identity. Thus they do not quite credit her with male power, nor does she possess, except associatively or iconically, the powers of a Nimue or a Morgan le Fay. Instead, she preserves only the half-natural, half-supernatural otherness of both changeling and enchantress.

She does indeed function as a guardian spirit. Though she gives neither sword nor the gift of prophecy, she protects the heroes from ambush by warning them with an inarticulate cry. Yet the help she offers Bruce and MacDonald in the camp on Skye emerges not through any strength she gains or is freer to exercise in her masculine page's disguise. Nor does it emerge even through the sort of cool-headed, articulate, and yet ladylike manner apparently shown by Flora MacDonald. Instead, it works through the double weaknesses of womanhood and muteness. Unlike the militant Britomart or the highly articulate Rosalind, she reveals in her apparent androgyny only a passivity. Yet her passivity awakens others, literally on Skye and more figuratively in two later episodes, to the possibilities of tenderer emotions and attitudes than those normally shown in war. Her disguise works, then, not to make her more masculine but to make her companions recognize more domestically feminine and thus more compassionate human values in themselves.

In the second of the three episodes in which the changeling minstrel-page acts as an almost supernatural guardian for Bruce's cause, her vulnerability becomes a test of character for the men she encounters. When Edward Bruce sends the page "Amadine" ashore as an advance scout before their landing at Carrick, he explains the double advantage presented by the physically frail and apparently mute boy:

> Noteless his presence, sharp his sense,
> His imperfection his defence.
> If seen, none can his errand guess;
> If ta'en, his words no tale express.
> (5. 10)

Ironically, of course, the "imperfection" is not of tongue but of phallus; and because Edith is not in fact physically mute but is physically weak, she requires enormous courage to resist the pressures once she is captured. That resistance, however, passive as it is, both creates the delay needed by Bruce's forces and intensifies the sympathetic bond growing between her and MacDonald. Isabel continues to educate her brother in the task of honoring vows as a positive, if sometimes painful, way to stabilize and unify society. He in turn can educate Ronald, made more susceptible to tenderness by his guardianship of the nearly helpless page. Because Ronald has grown fond of the young minstrel-page who joined their forces on Skye, he can eventually accept the undisguised Edith as person more than as political pawn. Because Scott's Bruce also eventually supports the betrothal vows, he develops a higher morality than the historical king.

The question of what final freedom Edith has gained for herself is left deliberately and ironically ambiguous. When Bruce now urges MacDonald to honor his original engagement to Edith, he seems to base the political loyalties of his supporters upon personal honor and loyalty—an important unifying theme for the public and private plots of the poem. Yet as the narrator points out, "King Robert's eye / Might have some glance of policy": for his military campaign had destroyed Edith's brother, and now

> Ample, through exile, death, and flight,
> O'er tower and land was Edith's right;
> This ample right o'er tower and land
> Were safe in [MacDonald's] faithful hand.

So much for "Edith's right"; in reassuming her woman's clothing, she reassumes her role as pawn, though a happy one even as she loses "ample right o'er tower and land." Scott's repetition neatly and deliberately confirms the irony.

Before this return to a woman's clothing and identity becomes known to more than Bruce and his sister, however, Edith reassumes her minstrel's disguise and intervenes for a third time to act as guardian spirit for the king and for the Lord of the Isles. Here the problem of interpreting the role of the minstrel becomes even more acute. This intervention, like the earlier two, supplements history. When she sees the Scottish forces wavering at Bannockburn, Edith cries out in warning. Because the unarmed camp followers still believe her the mute minstrel page, they think her suddenly restored speech is a miracle—and they charge so vigorously that they shift the momentum of battle. The charge of camp followers comes from history—but the double fiction of the minstrel's miraculous speech is again Scott's own. This miraculous speech is in one way the full assertion of the more active male role that Edith's disguise as a minstrel page had promised her. Yet because that speech is effective only in the context of its earlier denial, its miraculousness seems an elegant fraud that has in reality defrauded Edith—and all other women—of audible speech. Women's speech, women's abilities, women's leadership—like Edith's leadership of the camp followers—will seem miraculous when freed from the apparently voluntary constraints society has placed upon their exercise. Or further, once we consider the "miracle" of the page regaining his voice a false miracle, then the articulate speech and the leadership may themselves be seen as only fictional possibilities, not real, if belatedly recognized, accomplishments. As mediating symbolic object in and of the landscape, the green-clad, silent minstrel takes on great power for the development of the male figures in the poem. As a woman in her own right, she subsides into a domestic silence, relinquishing her rights in marriage, and becomes identified with the silence of the land she no longer holds in her own name. A poem that Scott first called *The Nameless Glen,* an appropriate metaphor for the unappropriated and silent woman as well as for Loch Corriskin, he finally inscribes as **The Lord of the Isles,** to preserve that and other patriarchal titles.

In all of these poems, then, we can see a movement toward the center, from the extreme stereotypes of witch or pawn. The pawns gain some power through the virtues of domestic morality, and the witches must lose their power in order to share the same domesticity, whether they want it or not. This center of domestic morality, moreover, is the realm toward which the novel had been developing, especially in the hands of the women novelists writing in the genre from the 1790s through the following twenty years. So in some sense Scott's turn toward the female minstrel may reflect his own role as a male taking on the female role of novel-writing, and the female values of domestic morality. No wonder Jane Austen, when she heard the strong rumor that Scott had turned from his best-seller poems to novel-writing, said, "Walter Scott has no business to write novels, especially good ones. It is not fair. He has fame and profit enough as a poet, and should not be taking the bread out of other people's mouths" [a letter to Anna Austen, September 28, 1814]. Yet, finally, it is fair to say that even in his poems Scott employs the patterns of witch and pawn not simply for fame and profit, but in order both to criticize and to modify these half-stereotypical, half-mythic categories. If that modification costs his more interesting women too much independence, and especially too much power over "mighty words and signs," he at least seems more sensitive to the cost than one might at first have suspected.

FURTHER READING

Bibliography

Burr, Allston. *Sir Walter Scott: An Index Placing the Short Poems in His Novels and in His Long Poems and Dramas.* Cambridge, Mass.: Harvard University Press, 1936.
>   A guide to Scott's short verse compositions.

Corson, James Clarkson. *A Bibliography of Sir Walter Scott: A Classified and Annotated List of Books and Articles Relating to His Life and Works, 1797–1940.* Edinburgh: Oliver and Boyd, 1943, 428 p.
>   Exhaustive annotated bibliography of writings on Scott, categorizing the sources as bibliographical, biographical, literary, and literary and biographical combined.

Hillhouse, James T., and Welsh Alexander . "Sir Walter Scott." In *The English Romantic Poets & Essayists: A Review of Research and Criticism,* rev. ed., edited by Carolyn Washburn Houtchens and Lawrence Huston Houtchens, pp. 115–54. New York: Modern Language Association/New York University Press, 1966.
>   An extended bibliographical essay that surveys critical and biographical writings on Scott.

Rubenstein, Jill. *Sir Walter Scott: A Reference Guide,* edited by Marilyn Gaull. Boston: G. K. Hall & Co., 1978, 344 p.
>   An annotated bibliography of writings about Scott that were published between 1932 and 1977.

Biography

Grierson, Sir Herbert J. C. *Sir Walter Scott, Bart.* 1938. Reprint. New York: Haskell House Publishers, 1969, 300 p.
>   A highly regarded biography that supplements and corrects inaccuracies in Lockhart's study of Scott's life (see below).

Johnson, Edgar. *Sir Walter Scott: The Great Unknown.* 2 vols. New York: Macmillan, 1970.
>   The definitive modern biography of Scott.

Lockhart, John Gibson. *Memoirs of the Life of Sir Walter Scott, Bart.* 2d ed. 10 vols. Edinburgh: Robert Cadell, 1839.
>   An indispensable source of information about Scott's life and works, written by his son-in-law. Despite its inaccuracies, Lockhart's biography is considered one of the greatest biographies of an English literary figure.

Criticism

Crawford, Thomas. *Scott.* Rev. ed. Edinburgh: Scottish Academic Press, 1982.
>   Critical study of Scott, the first edition of which appeared in 1965. Includes an analysis of his poetry and fiction, as well as a bibliography of writings by and about the author.

Goslee, Nancy M. "*Marmion* and the Metaphor of Forgery." In *Scottish Literary Journal* 7, No. 1 (May 1980): 85–96.
>   Analyzes Marmion's act of forgery in order to "reveal the complexity of attitudes toward fiction" that Scott employs in the poem.

———. "Romance as Theme and Structure in *The Lady of the Lake.*" In *Texas Studies in Literature and Language: A Journal of the Humanities* XVII, No. 4 (Winter 1976): 737–57.
>   Discusses the romantic subplot of the poem and the manner in which Scott combines a love story with a tale of political struggles.

———. *Scott the Rhymer.* Lexington: University Press of Kentucky, 1988, 264 p.
>   Book-length study of Scott's poetry.

Guest, Ann M. "Imagery of Color and Light in Scott's Narrative Poems." In *Studies in English Literature* XII, No. 4 (Autumn 1972): 705–20.

Analyzes Scott's use of color as it pertains to the "description, mood creation, characterization, symbolism, and overall structure" of his verse.

McClatchy, J. D. "The Function of the *Marmion* Epistles." In *Studies in Scottish Literature* IX, No. 4 (April 1972): 256–63.

Argues that the interplay between the epistles and the narrative make *Marmion* "a poem about the workings of the imagination which produced it."

Noyes, Alfred. "The Poetry of Sir Walter Scott: A Re-evaluation." In *The Quarterly Review* 290, No. 592 (April 1952): 211–25.

Praises the "splendid objectivity" of Scott's verse and predicts a renewed appreciation for poet's work among contemporary readers.

Ross, Marlon B. "Scott's Chivalric Pose: The Function of Metrical Romance in the Romantic Period." In *Genre* XIX, No. 3 (Fall 1986): 267–97.

Analyzes Scott's poems as exemplars of the metrical romance and argues that the works reveal the "confusions and contradictions" of the Romantic period.

Rubenstein, Jill. "Symbolic Characterization in *The Lady of the Lake*." In *Dalhousie Review* 51, No. 3 (Autumn 1971): 366–73.

Finds that Scott's characters are "representative of various aspects of the . . . historical situation" depicted in the poem. Rubenstein contends that Scott uses these figures to stress the value of compromise, a position that he also endorses in his novels.

Smith, Goldwin. "Scott's Poetry Again." In *The Atlantic Monthly* 95, No. 3 (March 1905): 300–02.

Defends Scott's poetry in response to Arthur Symons's 1904 essay. Smith lauds Scott's narrative excellence and offers a brief assessment of each of the epic poems.

Smith, Iain Crichton. "Poetry in Scott's Narrative Verse." In *Sir Walter Scott: The Long-Forgotten Melody,* edited by Alan Bold, pp. 109–26. London: Vision Press Ltd., 1983.

Praises Scott's narrative verse for its descriptive accomplishments while conceding that the poems are not interesting as poetry or for their human insights.

Additional coverage of Scott's life and career is contained in the following sources published by Gale Research: *Concise Dictionary of British Literary Biography 1789–1832*; *DISCovering Authors*; *Dictionary of Literary Biography,* Vols. 93, 107, 116, 114; *Nineteenth-Century Literary Criticism,* Vol. 15; *World Literature Criticism*; and *Yesterday's Authors of Books for Children,* Vol. 2.

Christopher Smart
1722–1771

English poet and translator.

INTRODUCTION

An author who long excited interest as much for his life as for his poetry, Smart has been described variously as a misunderstood mystic in an age of reason, a religiously obsessed madman, and a hack writer who, with *A Song to David*, unaccountably stumbled into genius. Composed in the middle of the eighteenth century, when poetic conventions were still heavily influenced by neoclassical notions of order and decorum, the *Song* stands out as an exuberant celebration of life as well as a deeply felt expression of religious belief. Although this work remains the foundation on which Smart's artistic reputation rests, since the discovery and publication in 1939 of fragments of *Jubilate Agno,* an erratic but at times brilliant poetic experiment, critics have increasingly come to regard *A Song to David* less as an anomaly in Smart's career and more as the poet's most sustained and successful fusion of religious fervor and lyrical virtuosity.

Biographical Information

Born in Kent, Smart was the son of Peter Smart, steward to William, Viscount Vane. After his father's death in 1733, Smart, his mother, and his sisters came under the protection of the Vane family. A thwarted adolescent elopement with Anne Vane, the daughter of William's cousin Henry Vane, has been seen by a few biographers as early evidence of Smart's unstable behavior. As a young man, Smart's academic abilities attracted the notice and patronage of the Duchess of Cleveland, another relative of Lord Vane. Her support enabled Smart to attend Pembroke Hall, Cambridge, and provided him with an annual allowance of forty pounds. Smart distinguished himself at Cambridge not only by his scholarship but also by his reckless manner of living. In 1742 he earned his bachelor's degree and three years later became a fellow of the university. Although he was already displaying signs of the alcoholism and financial difficulties which were to plague him throughout his life, he nevertheless continued to show promise in his academic career, achieving his master's degree in 1747 and being elected to college office. He was involved in a few petty scandals due to his intemperate habits, but university officials did not take action against him until the discovery of his secret marriage to Anna Maria Carnan. Even then the break was not complete; his position was nominally retained to allow him to participate in the university's annual poetry competition, the Seatonian Prize, which he won five times between 1750 and 1755. (He did not compete in 1754.)

After leaving Cambridge at age twenty-seven, Smart attempted to earn a living in the literary world of London. He became a journeyman writer, primarily for his wife's stepfather, the well-known bookseller John Newbery. Smart edited and wrote for several periodicals of the day, including the *Student* and the *Midwife*; he wrote songs and other materials for theatrical entertainments; and he produced a prose translation of Horace for use by students. The income from these endeavors was small, and given his continued prodigality, Smart was often in financial difficulty. He became so desperate for money that in 1755 he contracted to write exclusively for the magazine the *Universal Visiter* for ninety-nine years in exchange for one-sixth of the profits. During this period Smart suffered several severe illnesses, possibly mental breakdowns. Unable to write the required pieces for the *Universal Visiter*, he was aided by his friend Samuel Johnson, who submitted his own work instead. In addition to Johnson, Smart had a number of other friends who were among the leading cultural figures of the day. In 1759, the famed actor David Garrick performed a benefit play to extricate Smart from his debts. But Smart's difficulties proved to be beyond the reach of his friends' help. His debts and continual drinking contributed to the collapse of his marriage; his wife and two daughters moved to Ireland, and he never saw them again.

It is unclear exactly when Smart's first attack of madness began, or how long it lasted. It is known that Smart was confined three times between the years 1756 and 1763, part of the time in private homes, part in state-run asylums. The extent of Smart's insanity is also unknown. It expressed itself in religious monomania, in the compulsion to pray aloud wherever and whenever the urge arose. Sympathetic contemporaries conceded that, although undoubtedly strange, Smart's behavior was by no means a threat to anyone. Johnson insisted, "I did not think he ought to be shut up. His infirmities were not noxious to society. He insisted on people praying with him; and I'd as lief pray with Kit Smart as with any one else. Another charge was, that he did not love clean linen; and I have no passion for it." It was during his confinement that Smart composed *Jubilate Agno, A Song to David,* and much of his *Translation of the Psalms of David.* An apocryphal tale holds that, lacking pen and paper, Smart scratched the verses of *A Song to David* with a key on the wainscot of his cell. After his final release from confinement, Smart lived in comparative comfort, partly on proceeds from his work, partly on the generosity of friends. However, in 1770 he was sent to the King's Bench Prison for debt, and it was here that he composed his last work, *Hymns, for the Amusement of Children.* Smart died the following year, still incarcerated in the prison.

Major Works

Smart's career has been broadly divided into three periods. The first period covers the miscellaneous poetry and prize-winning Seatonian odes; the second is marked by Smart's adoption of the lyric mode, culminating in *A Song to David*; and the last comprises the religious verse written after the *Song.*

Smart's early poems were the most highly regarded of his works during his lifetime; but modern critics generally consider them conventional exercises in standard poetic genres. "The Hop-Garden," perhaps the most notable piece in his first collection, *Poems on Several Occasions,* is a georgic modelled after those of Vergil but written in blank verse reminiscent of John Milton's. Smart's five Seatonian Prize odes are linked in form and theme; all are written in Miltonian blank verse and all emphasize a different attribute of the Supreme Being. Many commentators have pointed out that these pieces in particular among Smart's early work show signs of the devices he was later to utilize in his lyric poems, notably the use of cataloguing, in which the poet lists and brings together all of creation to sing God's praise. Furthermore, it is in the Seatonian poems that Smart began to invoke the image of David, the ancient Hebrew king and composer of the Psalms, a figure that Smart would repeatedly turn to as a model and source of inspiration.

Hymn to the Supreme Being, on Recovery from a Dangerous Fit of Illness has often been cited as marking a turning point in Smart's career. The nature of the illness referred to in the title is uncertain; many have surmised that it was his first incidence of madness. In this poem Smart describes his illness in terms of a spiritual crisis, and he strikes for the first time the subjective and intensely personal note that marks his later poetry. The poem also heralds the lyricism of Smart's subsequent work, signaling his freedom from the Miltonian poetic conventions that characterized his earlier pieces. *Jubilate Agno,* composed in the period from 1759 to 1763, during Smart's confinement for insanity, displays a radical departure from his earlier poetry. This work survives only in fragments consisting of several individual manuscript pages. It is divided in two sections; each verse in the first begins with the word "For," while each verse in the second section begins with "Let." Each "Let" line features a biblical, historical, or contemporary figure—often linked with an animal—who is exhorted to rejoice in God. Most "For" lines deal directly with Smart himself; in Robert P. Fitzgerald's phrase, the subjective "For" lines constitute "a kind of personal journal" of his confinement. Both sections, with their often obscure references and allusions, demonstrate the encyclopedic breadth of Smart's knowledge. Although, when it was rediscovered and first published in 1939, it was seen as a jumbled, chaotic pastiche of verses, it is now clear that Smart conceived *Jubilate Agno* after ancient Hebraic poetic models which had recently been brought to light by Bishop Robert Lowth's book, *Praelectiones de Sacra Poesi Hebraeorum (Lectures on the Sacred Poetry of the Hebrews,* 1753).

A Song to David is almost universally considered to be Smart's masterpiece. Published just after Smart's release from the asylum, the poem was long thought the product of an irrational, deranged mind. In fact the *Song* is carefully and coherently organized; much of the interest of the poem lies in the conjunction of its meticulous arrangement with its ecstatic personal emotion. The poem is an elaborate lyrical paean to the glory of God, describing how all creation comes together to worship Him. It has been suggested that Smart, in addressing his song to David, desired to become an English David himself, a supreme psalmist dedicated to the adoration of God.

Smart's *Hymns and Spiritual Songs* and translations of the *Psalms* show stylistic and thematic similarities to both *Jubilate Agno* and *A Song to David.* The *Psalms* are loose paraphrases of the biblical text, as Smart's stated intention was to Christianize the Old Testament verses. The *Hymns and Spiritual Songs,* strongly influenced by both the Bible and the Book of Common Prayer, celebrate the cycle of the Christian year, and—as in the case of the *Psalms* and *Jubilate Agno*—there is evidence that Smart hoped his efforts would be adopted for use in the Anglican church service. Smart's last work, *Hymns for the Amusement of Children,* was written during his imprisonment for debt. Despite the circumstances of their composition, these *Hymns* are simple and childlike poems celebrating Christian virtues and evoking an air of peace and comfort.

Smart translated the works of Horace both in prose and in verse, and he greatly admired Horace's "unrivalled peculiarity of expression," by which he meant both precision and unexpectedness of poetic language. Smart took to heart Horace's words in his *Ars Poetica* on the desirability of using words in an unusual fashion, or of coining new ones, and derived from Horace his own poetic maxim which he called "impression," which he described as "a talent or gift of Almighty God, by which a Genius is impowered to throw an emphasis upon a word or sentence in such a wise, that it cannot escape any reader of sheer good sense, and true critical sagacity." Although this technique is apparent in Smart's earlier poetry, critics have noted that its use is more frequent and more effective in *Jubilate Agno, A Song to David,* and his later work.

Critical Reception

Until recently, the main body of Smart's works received critical attention only for the insight it could provide into the mind of the man who could produce *A Song to David.* Many critics over the centuries dismissed Smart's early works as of limited importance, finding them marred by their close adherence to traditional forms. The Seatonian odes, for instance, have long been viewed as "uninspired but technically proficient," in the words of William H. Bond, and Smart has been regarded as merely a "facile versifier" in his early works. Smart's contemporaries, however, generally admired his early poetry; magazine reviews of the time speak glowingly of his promise.

Conversely, *A Song to David* received mixed critical reaction when it first appeared, for by this time Smart's malady was well known, and early commentators were reluctant to praise a madman. Interest in Smart's poetry waned sharply after the publication of *A Song to David,* and it was not until Robert Browning eulogized the *Song* in his *Parleyings with Certain People of Importance in Their Day* (1887) that Smart again received critical attention. Twentieth-century critics have noted that the same circumstance that hindered the poem's success in the eighteenth century—Smart's madness—enhanced its value in the nineteenth, when Romantic views prevailed regarding the close connection between madness and artistic inspiration. Some critics, in fact, have considered Smart as in certain respects a precursor of Romanticism.

Speculation over the influence of Smart's madness has abated in recent years, as critics have determined that, whether or not Smart was sane, he produced in *A Song to David* one of the most powerfully moving religious poems in English literature. Similarly, scholars of *Jubilate Agno* have uncovered thematic and structural patterns in the seeming chaos of the poem, leading to a reconsideration of not only this, but Smart's other works as well. Smart is now often regarded as among the most highly original poets of the eighteenth century.

PRINCIPAL WORKS

Poetry

*On the Eternity of the Supreme Being: A Poetical Essay 1750
*On the Immensity of the Supreme Being: A Poetical Essay 1751
*On the Omniscience of the Supreme Being: A Poetical Essay 1752
Poems on Several Occasions 1752
The Hilliad: An Epic Poem 1753
*On the Power of the Supreme Being: A Poetical Essay 1754
Hymn to the Supreme Being, on Recovery from a Dangerous Fit of Illness 1756
*On the Goodness of the Supreme Being: A Poetical Essay 1756
Poems by Mr. Smart. Viz. Reason and Imagination a Fable. Ode to Admiral Sir George Pocock. Ode to General Draper. An Epistle to John Sherratt, Esq. 1763
A Song to David 1763
Ode to the Right Honourable the Earl of Northumberland, on his being appointed the Lord Lieutenant of Ireland. Presented on the Birth-Day of Lord Warkworth. With some other pieces 1764
A Poetical Translation of the Fables of Phaedrus, with the Appendix of Gudius, And an accurate Edition of the Original on the opposite Page. To which is added, A Parsing Index for the Use of Learners 1765
A Translation of the Psalms of David, Attempted in the Spirit of Christianity, and Adapted to the Divine Service, with Hymns and Spiritual Songs for the Fasts and Festivals of the Church of England 1765
The Works of Horace, Translated into Verse: With a Prose Interpretation, for the Help of Students. And Occasional Notes. 4 vols. 1767
The Parables of Our Lord and Saviour Jesus Christ: Done into Familiar Verse, with Occasional Applications, for the Use and Improvement of Younger Minds 1768
Hymns, for the Amusement of Children 1770
The Poems of the Late Christopher Smart. 2 vols. 1791
†Rejoice in the Lamb: A Song from Bedlam 1939; also published as *Jubilate Agno* 1954
The Collected Poems of Christopher Smart. 2 vols. 1949
Poems by Christopher Smart 1950
The Poetical Works of Christopher Smart. 4 vols. 1980–87

*These works are collectively referred to as the Seatonian odes, or the Seatonian Prize poems.

†This work was written during the period 1759–1763; it survives only in fragments.

Other Major Works

The Works of Horace, Translated Literally into English Prose (prose) 1756
Hannah. An Oratorio. Written by Mr. Smart. The Musick Composed by Mr. Worgan. As Perform'd at the King's Theatre in the Hay-Market (libretto) 1764
Abimelech, an Oratorio. As It Is Performed at the Theatre Royal in the Hay-Market (libretto) 1768

CRITICISM

Robert Browning (poem date 1887)

SOURCE: "With Christopher Smart," in *Parleyings with Certain People of Importance in Their Day,* Smith, Elder & Co., 1887, pp. 79–95.

[*Browning was an English poet and playwright who is considered one of the outstanding poets of the nineteenth century. Much of his poetry is expressive of his metaphysical concerns with the nature of and relationship between love, knowledge, and faith. His work greatly influenced later poets such as Ezra Pound and T. S. Eliot. In the following poem, composed as an apostrophe to Smart, Browning marvels at the mind that could produce the singular achievement of* A Song to David.]

I

It seems as if . . . or did the actual chance
Startle me and perplex? Let truth be said!
How might this happen? Dreaming, blindfold led
By visionary hand, did soul's advance
Precede my body's, gain inheritance
Of fact by fancy—so that when I read
At length with waking eyes your Song, instead
Of mere bewilderment, with me first glance
Was but full recognition that in trance
Or merely thought's adventure some old day
Of dim and done-with boyishness, or—well,
Why might it not have been, the miracle
Broke on me as I took my sober way
Through veritable regions of our earth
And made discovery, many a wondrous one?

II

Anyhow, fact or fancy, such its birth:
I was exploring some huge house, had gone
Through room and room complacently, no dearth
Anywhere of the signs of decent taste,
Adequate culture: wealth had run to waste
Nowise, nor penury was proved by stint:
All showed the Golden Mean without a hint
Of brave extravagance that breaks the rule.
The master of the mansion was no fool
Assuredly, no genius just as sure!
Safe mediocrity had scorned the lure
Of now too much and now too little cost,
And satisfied me sight was never lost
Of moderate design's accomplishment
In calm completeness. On and on I went,
With no more hope than fear of what came next,
Till lo, I push a door, sudden uplift
A hanging, enter, chance upon a shift
Indeed of scene! So—thus it is thou deck'st,
High heaven, our low earth's brick-and-mortar
    work?

III

It was the Chapel. That a star, from murk
Which hid, should flashingly emerge at last,
Were small surprise: but from broad day I passed
Into a presence that turned shine to shade.
There fronted me the Rafael Mother-Maid,
Never to whom knelt votarist in shrine
By Nature's bounty helped, by Art's divine
More varied—beauty with magnificence—
Than this: from floor to roof one evidence
Of how far earth may rival heaven. No niche
Where glory was not prisoned to enrich
Man's gaze with gold and gems, no space but
    glowed
With colour, gleamed with carving—hues which
    owed
Their outburst to a brush the painter fed
With rainbow-substance—rare shapes never wed
To actual flesh and blood, which, brain-born once,
Became the sculptor's dowry, Art's response
To earth's despair. And all seemed old yet new:
Youth,—in the marble's curve, the canvas' hue,
Apparent,—wanted not the crowning thrill
Of age the consecrator. Hands long still
Had worked here—could it be, what lent them skill
Retained a power to supervise, protect,
Enforce new lessons with the old, connect
Our life with theirs? No merely modern touch
Told me that here the artist, doing much,
Elsewhere did more, perchance does better, lives—
So needs must learn.

IV

                        Well, these provocatives
Having fulfilled their office, forth I went
Big with anticipation—well nigh fear—
Of what next room and next for startled eyes
Might have in store, surprise beyond surprise.
Next room and next and next—what followed here?
Why, nothing! not one object to arrest
My passage—everywhere too manifest
The previous decent null and void of best
And worst, mere ordinary right and fit,
Calm commonplace which neither missed, nor hit
Inch-high, inch-low, the placid mark proposed.

V

Armed with this instance, have I diagnosed
Your case, my Christopher? The man was sound
And sane at starting: all at once the ground
Gave way beneath his step, a certain smoke
Curled up and caught him, or perhaps down broke
A fireball wrapping flesh and spirit both
In conflagration. Then—as heaven were loth
To linger—let earth understand too well
How heaven at need can operate—off fell
The flame-robe, and the untransfigured man
Resumed sobriety,—as he began,
So did he end nor alter pace, not he!

VI

Now, what I fain would know is—could it be
That he—whoe'er he was that furnished forth
The Chapel, making thus, from South to North,
Rafael touch Leighton, Michelangolo
Join Watts, was found but once combining so
The elder and the younger, taking stand
On Art's supreme,—or that yourself who sang
A Song where flute-breath silvers trumpet-clang,
And stations you for once on either hand
With Milton and with Keats, empowered to claim
Affinity on just one point—(or blame
Or praise my judgment, thus it fronts you full)—
How came it you resume the void and null,
Subside to insignificance,—live, die
—Proved plainly two mere mortals who drew nigh
One moment—that, to Art's best hierarchy,
This, to the superhuman poet-pair?
What if, in one point only, then and there
The otherwise all-unapproachable
Allowed impingement? Does the sphere pretend
To span the cube's breadth, cover end to end
The plane with its embrace? No, surely! Still,
Contact is contact, sphere's touch no whit less
Than cube's superimposure. Such success
Befell Smart only out of throngs between
Milton and Keats that donned the singing-dress—
Smart, solely of such songmen, pierced the screen
'Twixt thing and word, lit language straight from
    soul,—
Left no fine film-flake on the naked coal
Live from the censer—shapely or uncouth,
Fire-suffused through and through, one blaze of truth
Undeadened by a lie,—(you have my mind)—
For, think! this blaze outleapt with black behind
And blank before, when Hayley and the rest . . .
But let the dead successors worst and best
Bury their dead: with life be my concern—
Yours with the fire-flame: what I fain would learn
Is just—(suppose me haply ignorant
Down to the common knowledge, doctors vaunt)
Just this—why only once the fire-flame was:
No matter if the marvel came to pass
The way folks judged—if power too long
    suppressed
Broke loose and maddened, as the vulgar guessed,
Or simply brain-disorder (doctors said)
A turmoil of the particles disturbed
Brain's workaday performance in your head,
Spurred spirit to wild action health had curbed,
And so verse issued in a cataract
Whence prose, before and after, unperturbed
Was wont to wend its way. Concede the fact
That here a poet was who always could—
Never before did—never after would—
Achieve the feat: how were such fact explained?

VII

Was it that when, by rarest chance, there fell
Disguise from Nature, so that Truth remained

Naked, and whoso saw for once could tell
Us others of her majesty and might
In large, her lovelinesses infinite
In little,—straight you used the power wherewith
Sense, penetrating as through rind to pith
Each object, thoroughly revealed might view
And comprehend the old things thus made new,
So that while eye saw, soul to tongue could trust
Thing which struck word out, and once more adjust
Real vision to right language, till heaven's vault
Pompous with sunset, storm-stirred sea's assault
On the swilled rock-ridge, earth's embosomed brood
Of tree and flower and weed, with all the life
That flies or swims or crawls, in peace or strife,
Above, below,—each had its note and name
For Man to know by,—Man who, now—the same
As erst in Eden, needs that all he sees
Be named him ere he note by what degrees
Of strength and beauty to its end Design
Ever thus operates—(your thought and mine,
No matter for the many dissident)—
So did you sing your Song, so truth found vent
In words for once with you?

VIII

                    Then—back was furled
The robe thus thrown aside, and straight the world
Darkened into the old oft-catalogued
Repository of things that sky, wave, land,
Or show or hide, clear late, accretion-clogged
Now, just as long ago, by tellings and
Retellings to satiety, which strike
Muffled upon the ear's drum. Very like
None was so startled as yourself when friends
Came, hailed your fast-returning wits: "Health
    mends
Importantly, for—to be plain with you—
This scribble on the wall was done—in lieu
Of pen and paper—with—ha, ha!—your key
Denting it on the wainscot! Do you see
How wise our caution was? Thus much we stopped
Of babble that had else grown print: and lopped
From your trim bay-tree this unsightly bough—
Smart's who translated Horace! Write us now".
Why, what Smart did write—never afterward
One line to show that he, who paced the sward,
Had reached the zenith from his madhouse cell.

IX

Was it because you judged (I know full well
You never had the fancy)—judged—as some—
That who makes poetry must reproduce
Thus ever and thus only, as they come,
Each strength, each beauty, everywhere diffuse
Throughout creation, so that eye and ear,
Seeing and hearing, straight shall recognize,
At touch of just a trait, the strength appear,—
Suggested by a line's lapse see arise
All evident the beauty,—fresh surprise
Startling at fresh achievement? "So, indeed,

Wallows the whale's bulk in the waste of brine,
Nor otherwise its feather-tufts make fine
Wild Virgin's Bower when stars faint off to seed!"
(My prose—your poetry I dare not give,
Purpling too much my mere grey argument.)
—Was it because you judged—when fugitive
Was glory found, and wholly gone and spent
Such power of startling up deaf ear, blind eye,
At truth's appearance,—that you humbly bent
The head and, bidding vivid work goodbye,
Doffed lyric dress and trod the world once more
A drab-clothed decent proseman as before?
Strengths, beauties, by one word's flash thus laid
    bare
—That was effectual service: made aware
Of strengths and beauties, Man but hears the text,
Awaits your teaching. Nature? What comes next?
Why all the strength and beauty?—to be shown
Thus in one word's flash, thenceforth let alone
By Man who needs must deal with aught that's
    known
Never so lately and so little? Friend,
First give us knowledge, then appoint its use!
Strength, beauty are the means: ignore their end?
As well you stopped at proving how profuse
Stones, sticks, nay stubble lie to left and right
Ready to help the builder,—careless quite
If he should take, or leave the same to strew
Earth idly,—as by word's flash bring in view
Strength, beauty, then bid who beholds the same
Go on beholding. Why gains unemployed?
Nature was made to be by Man enjoyed
First; followed duly by enjoyment's fruit,
Instruction—haply leaving joy behind:
And you, the instructor, would you slack pursuit
Of the main prize, as poet help mankind
Just to enjoy, there leave them? Play the fool,
Abjuring a superior privilege?
Please simply when your function is to rule—
By thought incite to deed? From edge to edge
Of earth's round, strength and beauty everywhere
Pullulate—and must you particularize
All, each and every apparition? Spare
Yourself and us the trouble! Ears and eyes
Want so much strength and beauty, and no less
Nor more, to learn life's lesson by. Oh, yes—
The other method's favoured in our day!
The end ere the beginning: as you may,
Master the heavens before you study earth,
Make you familiar with the meteor's birth
Ere you descend to scrutinize the rose!
I say, o'erstep no least one of the rows
That lead man from the bottom where he plants
Foot first of all, to life's last ladder-top:
Arrived there, vain enough will seem the vaunts
Of those who say—"We scale the skies, then drop
To earth—to find, how all things there are loth
To answer heavenly law: we understand
The meteor's course, and lo, the rose's growth—
How other than should be by law's command!"
Would not you tell such—"Friends, beware lest
    fume

Offuscate sense: learn earth first ere presume
To teach heaven legislation. Law must be
Active in earth or nowhere: earth you see,—
Or there or not at all, Will, Power and Love
Admit discovery,—as below, above
Seek next law's confirmation!" But reverse
The order, where's the wonder things grow worse
Than, by the law your fancy formulates,
They should be? Cease from anger at the fates
Which thwart themselves so madly. Live and learn,
Not first learn and then live, is our concern.

Philip Hanson (essay date 1897)

SOURCE: "Christopher Smart," in *Temple Bar,* Vol. 112, No. 443, October, 1897, pp. 268–74.

[*In this originally unsigned essay, Hanson argues that Smart's* Translation of the Psalms *provides the "missing link" between the brilliance of* A Song to David *and the mediocrity of the poet's other works.*]

In the history of literature it is not uncommon for a man to have two distinct and different reputations, one while he is alive and the other after his death. Adam Smith was known to his contemporaries as a philosopher, and the *Wealth of Nations* was only a fragment of a projected great work on the 'Progress of Man.' The example of Johnson is trite. Christopher Smart has had something of the same fortune. Those who know his name to-day think of him as the author of the ***Song to David***; but during his life his reputation rested chiefly on a number of odes ***On the Eternity of God*** and kindred topics, whose quality is sufficiently described by saying that some of them were University prize poems, and the rest might have been. These productions were at the time much admired, while the ***Song to David*** was omitted from the first edition of Smart's collected works, as bearing too evident traces of mental derangement. That verdict was soon reversed, but it expresses well enough the eighteenth century aspect of a truth, viz., that a man of that time could hardly write a religious poem to suit the readers of this, unless his mind had undergone a great exaltation of some kind. Smart, while he was sane, wrote religious poems which hit the taste of the day, and more particularly of the judges for the Seaton prize poem at the University of Cambridge; while he was mad, or after he had been mad, he wrote a religious poem which those who know it now find admirable. Nowadays a poet will do well to hold fast to whatever share of sanity the gods may have granted him; but perhaps in the time of Pope and Gray and Collins and Mason a little madness was the best thing he could pray for.

However, mad or sane, Smart was a religious poet; his best-known works were on religious subjects, and one of his two biographers observes that "His piety was exemplary and fervent. In composing his religious poems he was frequently so impressed with the sentiments of devotion as to write particular passages on his knees." And we know, from those fragments of Johnson's conversation, which are probably the best-known references to Smart, that his madness also was religious in character:—

> My poor friend Smart showed the disturbance of his mind by falling upon his knees and saying his prayers in the street, or in any other unusual place.

> I did not think he ought to be shut up. His infirmities were not noxious to society. He insisted on people praying with him; and I'd as lief pray with Kit Smart as any one else. Another charge was, that he did not love clean linen; and I have no passion for it.

But it would be a mistake to conceive Smart as a tender spirit overburdened with the weight of religious conviction, a sort of companion soul to Cowper. A somewhat different picture of him is presented in this extract from a letter of Gray to Thomas Wharton:—

> Your mention of Mr. Vane reminds me of poor Smart (not that I, or any other mortal, pity him); about three weeks ago he was arrested here at the suit of a tailor in London for a debt of about £50 of three years' standing. The college had about £28 due to him in their hands, the rest (to save him from going to the castle, for he could not raise a shilling) Brown, May and Peele lent him upon his note. Upon this he remained confined to his room, lest his creditors here should snap him; and the fellows went round to make out a list of his debts, which amount in Cambridge to above £350; that they might come the readier to some composition, he was advised to go off in the night, and lie hid somewhere or other. He has done so, and this has made the creditors agree to an assignment of £50 per annum out of his income. . . . I must own, if you heard all his lies, impertinence and ingratitude in this affair, it would perhaps quite set you against him, as it has his only friend (Mr. Addison) totally, and yet one would try to serve him, for drunkenness is one great cause of this, and he may change it. (November 30th, 1747, Cambridge.)

Again, Gray writes from Cambridge in October 1751 to Horace Walpole:—

> We have a man here that writes a good hand, but he has little failings that hinder my recommending him to you. He is dirty, and he is mad; he sets out this week for Bedlam; but if you insist upon it, I don't doubt he will pay his respects to you.

The savagely contemptuous pity which Gray shows when he speaks of Smart is a remarkable contrast to the affectionate tone of Johnson, but the difference is not hard to account for. The utter recklessness and shiftlessness with which Smart always managed, or rather did not manage, his affairs was nothing outrageous or extraordinary to Johnson, much of whose life had been passed in Grub Street; like Smart's foul linen, it was an eccentricity with which he could himself sympathise; to Gray, whose linen, mental and bodily, was always in the best order, such habits were disgusting. Then the close connections of University life inevitably strengthen any natural antipathy;

Johnson, living in London, could see as much or as little of his friend as he liked, but Gray was probably forced to see him nearly every day. Mr. Gosse, who has unearthed from the records of Pembroke College a good deal of new information as to Smart's life while he was a fellow there, and whose *Gossip in a Library* contains almost all the facts that are known about him, thinks that some of his satiric verses referring to college life are pointed at Gray. It is also certain that he was, in his odes, an imitator of Gray. Any or all of these may have been the reasons for that peculiarly bitter tone which jars on us so much in Gray's references to Smart, and which no one else who writes about him has used.

It is certain, however, that drink had a great deal to do with Smart's misfortunes, and it may probably have helped to bring about his madness. Johnson, in the same conversation with Dr. Burney, which was quoted above, remarked on his intemperance:—

> He has partly as much exercise as he used to have, for he digs in the garden. Indeed, before his confinement, he used for exercise to walk to the ale-house, but he was carried back again.

Such is the picture of our poet which his friends have handed down to us—sketched in outline only, but it is of a type sufficiently striking and sufficiently familiar to be easily made out. A man of literary tastes, poetic ability, and deep religious feeling, whose disposition was so amiable that all who speak of him—with the notable exception of Gray—speak with manifest indulgence, and that many continued to help and support him even to the end of his life, he wasted his talents, sank into degrading habits of drunkenness, and died in a debtors' prison after suffering the extreme of want. It is a very familiar character, more essentially in the world of literature; and many such men have been excellent poets.

Any one who had formed a conception of Smart's poetry from a knowledge of his life and character, and from the eulogies of his contemporaries, would be much disappointed when he came to compare that conception with the reality. The great mass of it is dull to a degree; and it has been matter of wonder to many, Browning among the number, how the same man could be the author of the *Seaton Prize Odes* and of the *Song to David*. The fit of madness which coincided with or preceded the composition of the song may account for a good deal of the difference, but it need not be made to account for it all. One very obvious consideration is that the odes, being prize odes, were written to order; and Mr. Gosse has shown that Smart's position was even more unfavourable than that of the ordinary competitor, inasmuch as the continuance of his fellowship was made to depend on his continuing to win the prize. He actually did win it five times, and when he ceased to do so his name was taken off the college books. It may easily be conceived that poetry produced under these conditions was not likely to be above the standard of the time.

But a more important point is that nearly all Smart's work except the *Song to David*—his odes, his fables, and his little Georgic the **'Hop Garden'**—was imitative, and imitative of bad models. He was endeavouring to follow Gray, and Prior and Pope in things which they had done perhaps as well as they can be done, and which after all are not the things best worth doing. His genius was peculiarly ill-fitted for the laborious neatness characteristic of the period, and his first biographer (of 1791) notes that all his compositions were spoiled by haste. There will be more to say on this point later on, with regard to the ***Translation of the Psalms***.

In reading the ***Song to David,*** the first impression is one of vague magnificence, rich obscurity. The temptation to the careless reader is particularly strong to pass over phrase after phrase with a mental reference to the poet's madness. Some part of this obscurity remains even after the most careful reading, and a little of it is perhaps finally irreducible; but further examination and a reference to the argument soon dispel all idea of confusion, and we gradually realise that most of the difficulty is really due, not at all to any vagueness of thought, but rather to the careful working out of an elaborate plan within a very small space. The obscurity is like the obscurity of Thucydides; and if there is any trace of madness in the poem, it must be looked for in the exaggerated elaboration and exactitude of the construction. If Smart uses daring and elliptic phrases, it is partly indeed because that is the bent of his poetic genius, but even more because every one of his short six-line stanzas is forced to contain a complete and coherent thought, falling orderly into its place in the general development. Naturally the connections are not obvious, and are more often understood than expressed; if they are overlooked, as they may easily be, the poem appears a heap of glittering fragments. But the poet has been careful to guard against the dangers of his style by prefixing an argument, and with that and a little careful reading it is not difficult to appreciate the grandeur of the design. That design is, in brief, the delineation of the character of David from a religious point of view, and the exhibition of the purposes of Providence in David's connection with the Messiah. But no adequate idea, of course, of the excellence of the poem in this respect can be given by description of quotation.

A few quotations, however, are probably the best means of exhibiting Smart's other characteristic excellence—his magnificence of phrase and sound. The extracts given in the *Golden Treasury* and elsewhere have made a great many people familiar with a few of these phrases; but there are many more in the poem of equal beauty and grandeur. They recall nothing so much as the diction of Milton. Take, for example, this stanza descriptive of David:—

> Strong—in the Lord, who could defy
> Satan, and all his powers that lie
>   In sempiternal night;
> And hell, and horror, and despair
> Were as the lion and the bear
>   To his undaunted might.

Or again:—

> Strong is the lion—like a coal
> His eyeball—like a bastion's mole
>   His chest against the foes;
> Strong the gier-eagle on his sail,
> Strong against tide th' enormous whale
>   Emerges, as he goes.

. . . . .

> Beauteous the fleet before the gale,
> Beauteous the multitudes in mail,
>   *Ranked arms, and crested heads.*

There is the same crash of steel in that last line that we hear among Milton's angels. And in a softer key, here are two admirable stanzas on David's harping:

> Blest was the tenderness he felt,
> When to his graceful harp he knelt,
>   And did for audience call;
> When Satan with his hand he quell'd,
> And in serene suspense he held
>   The frantic throes of Saul.

> His furious foes no more maligned,
> As he such melody divined,
>   And sense and soul detained;
> Now striking strong, now soothing soft,
> He sent the godly sounds aloft,
>   Or in delight refrained.

That such simple, strong, and beautiful diction as this should have appeared in the year 1763 is sufficiently marvellous, and appears still more so when we compare it with the rest of Smart's poetry. But the key to the puzzle lies in a book which has been perhaps more completely forgotten than any other of Smart's works—his ***Translation of the Psalms***.

The ***Translation of the Psalms*** was not popular when it appeared, and has never attained popularity since; nor, in truth, does it deserve it. It is not good enough poetry to be preserved on its merits, and it is not a close enough translation of the Psalms to have any ecclesiastical value. In fact, Smart states in his introduction, with a curious abortive anticipation of the Higher Criticism, that "In this translation, all expressions that seem contrary to Christ are omitted, and evangelical matter put in their room." One example of this substitution is too delicious to be omitted; he renders the verses of the **2nd Psalm**—"He that sitteth in heaven shall laugh them to scorn; the Lord shall have them in derision. Then shall he speak to them in his wrath, and vex them in his sore displeasure"—as follows:—

> He that in Heaven supports his reign,
>   Of spotless virgin born,
> Shall give them blessing for disdain,
>   And charity for scorn.
> Then shall he make his day-spring shine
>   In evangelic peace,
> And sinners from the wrath divine
>   Through faith in him release.

David, the sweet singer, might have stared to find himself so sweetened.

But in spite of a great deal of dulness and many things that are ridiculous in this *Translation,* it supplies the missing link between the *Song to David* and Smart's other poems. The *Translation* was published in 1765, two years after the *Song,* but an Apology to the Subscribers for the delay in its appearance came out in 1763, so it is probable that much of it was done before the *Song* (which is quite short, only 516 lines) was begun. Many of the *Psalms* are in the same metre as the *Song,* and seem like weaker echoes of its phraseology, and in general their faults are not those of the other poems. We see the effect of a different model; the language of the Bible, which had been the inspiration of Milton, was the inspiration of Smart also, imperfect though his mastery of it might be. And that little announcement about the "expressions contrary to Christ" shows at least that Smart tried to conceive of David as a human character, and not as a mere conduit of inspiration. The likeness of detached phrases to the diction of the *Song to David* is occasionally striking: *e g.*:—

> The glorious pillars of thy reign
> No flight can reach, nor heav'ns contain,
>   Nor exaltation bound. . . .

When we find a man trained in verse-making and of a religious temperament, who has long and closely studied the magnificent language of the Psalms (for it is to be presumed that Smart's translation was at least aided by the Authorised Version), turning his attention to the character and career of David, which have always been recognised as peculiarly romantic, we can understand that he may rise to a height much above his usual level; and if we allow for a sudden and exceptional inspiration (whether produced by madness or not does not matter), such as comes to almost all poets once in a long while, then the excellence of the *Song to David* becomes comprehensible.

Christopher Smart, however, will always be a poet of one poem. His other works are only interesting as throwing light on this one. His life has an interest of its own, but it is an interest of a comparatively commonplace kind. The union of religious enthusiasm with moral weakness is not a rare phenomenon; but that such a character should have once reached such an expression as the *Song to David* in the midst of a career of sombre mediocrity is a curious example of the uncertainty of the poetic gift.

Cyril Falls   (essay date 1924)

SOURCE: "Christopher Smart," in *The Critic's Armoury,* Richard Cobden-Sanderson, 1924, pp. 109–20.

[*In this essay, Falls extols* A Song to David *as an inspired poem and far superior to the rest of Smart's output.*]

> His muse, bright angel of his verse,
> Gives balm for all the thorns that pierce,
>   For all the pangs that rage;
> Blest light, still gaining on the gloom,
> The more than Michal of his bloom,
>   The Abishag of his age.

We can but hope that Smart's words on David were true of himself. Great was his need of such consolation. A more miserable and, but for one bright flower budded in madness, a more worthless and barren life than his, were hard to conceive. Even of his madness we have no picture of a fine spirit wasting away in melancholy, like that of his greater and like-circumstanced contemporary, William Collins. When Dr. Johnson, good, kindly soul, went to visit him in Bedlam, he returned to tell Boswell that he was growing fat. Boswell suggested it might be for lack of exercise; but Johnson denied this, declaring that now he dug in the garden, whereas before, though he might walk as far as the ale-house, he was carried back. He added that he saw no reason for his confinement, since his maladies were not hurtful to society. He enumerated two: "He insisted on people praying with him; and I'd as lief pray with Kit Smart as anyone else. Another charge was that he did not love clean linen; and I have no passion for it." Johnson was probably right, but it is hard to see how confinement injured Smart, whilst it is at least to that confinement we owe his one marvellous poem, *A Song to David.*

Christopher Smart was born at Shipborne, on the northern edge of the Weald, then as now a pleasant land of woods and hopfields. Thence, in youth, he derived the impressions and the technical knowledge which he was to put into the poem—of all his work most popular in his own time—"The Hop-Garden." His father, says his earliest biographer, was of a good North-country family. He was steward to Lord Barnard, managing the Kentish estates of that nobleman. It is related that Christopher Smart was prematurely born. He was certainly precocious in other respects. A poem, "Ethelinda," is noted in his collected edition of 1791 as having been written at thirteen. Its poetic qualities, remarkable enough in a boy of that age, are far below those of many other *juvenilia* which could be cited, but there is about the piece a warmth of passion uncomfortable, whether artificial or not. During a holiday spent at Raby Castle he attracted the attention of the Duchess of Cleveland, who allowed him thenceforth a very small annuity. Under her patronage he entered Pembroke Hall, Cambridge, becoming a Fellow in 1745. Beyond, "farming" the Seatonian Prize Poem, which he won year after year, he appears not to have distinguished himself save by debts and dissipations. Then came Grub Street and magazine work; and, what was better, the friendship of Johnson, Goldsmith, and Garrick. He had been confined for madness in 1751; twelve years later he was again in Bedlam. It was during this latter incarceration that he wrote *A Song to David.* His wife, meanwhile, since he could not support her, had gone to live with relatives in Dublin. Released once more, he settled down to his dreary work with new resolution. But he could not long keep his head above water. It was in the King's Bench Prison that he died in 1771.

The origin of the "wainscot" legend about *A Song to David*:

From the sufferings of this ingenious Gentleman, we could not but expect the performance before us to be greatly irregular; but we shall certainly characterise it more justly, if we call it irregularly great. There is a grandeur, a majesty of thought, not without a happiness of expression in [*A Song to David*]. . . .

We meet with some passages, however, in this performance that are almost, if not altogether, unintelligible. Few Readers probably will see into the Author's reason for distinguishing his seven pillars or monuments of the six days creation, by the seven Greek letters he hath selected. . . .

It would be cruel, however, to insist on the slight defects and singularities of this piece, for many reasons; and more especially, if it be true, as we are informed, that it was written when the Author was denied the use of pen, ink, and paper, and was obliged to indent his lines, with the end of a key, upon the wainscot.

John Langhorne, in an unsigned review of A Song to David, *in* The Monthly Review, *London, Vol. XXVIII, April, 1763, pp. 320-21.*

The legend of *A Song to David* is that, being denied pens and paper, he inscribed the poem upon the panelled walls of his room with a key. The tale seems improbable, in view of the length of the *Song. A Song to David* was amazingly omitted from the edition of 1791 upon the ground that it contained too many "melancholy proofs of the estrangement of Smart's mind." Such, doubtless, would have been the considered verdict of the age, had the poem become sufficiently known to warrant one. To the critical intelligence of that day, starting with the knowledge that it had been written by a madman, or at least by a man in a mad-house, it must have appeared to bear the clearest signs of madness. Vastly has opinion veered since. Browning's admiration of it was little short of adoration. Rossetti called it "the only great *accomplished* poem of the last century." Mere folly this of a century which, though admittedly an age of prose, produced *The Rape of the Lock, The Passions, The Progress of Poesy* and the *Elegy, The Deserted Village,* all the poetry of Burns and Cowper. But it is typical of the first effect of bewildering loveliness which certain stanzas make upon the imaginative and romantic mind. There is something of mystery and enchantment, an immense attraction, hanging about its very name. It is the only work of Smart's of which more than the smallest fraction of the intelligent reading public has heard, till now. It may almost be said to have been both world-famous and unknown.

Spurred to endeavour, perhaps, by the recent bicentenary of Kit Smart's birth, two enthusiasts [Edmund Blunden and Percival Serle], one a well-known poet, have brought forth simultaneously, in England and Australia, new editions of *A Song to David*. Each editor has included cer-

tain other poems; and it is no tribute to the quality of Smart's work, apart from the immortal *Song,* that in no case have they hit upon the same. Each has resisted what must have been a strong temptation, of the sort which assails the historian of a weak or unpleasant character, urging him to protest against the common verdict and prove his man stronger or more kindly than has hitherto been held. The temptation in this case was to assert that Smart's miscellaneous poetry had merits undiscovered by previous critics. There is little attempt at literary white-washing in either book. Mr. Blunden holds the theory that Smart's work improved after his confinement, and backs it by making his extracts exclusively from the *Psalms of David* (published in 1765), the *Hymns and Spiritual Songs* thereto appended, and miscellaneous poems from 1763 onward. From the historical point of view, Mr. Blunden is undoubtedly right in taking his selections from Smart's religious poems for the most part. In them there do indeed appear sudden flashes of felicity that recall the *Song.* These stanzas, from **Psalm civ**, might well be taken to belong to it:

He taught the silver moon her way,
Her monthly and nocturnal sway,
    Where'er she wanes or glows;
The glorious globe that glides the skies
Is conscious of his early rise,
    And his descent he knows.

The lines of light and shade to mark
Is thine, thou bidst the night be dark,
    Beneath whose solemn gloom
The forest beasts forsake their den,
And all that shun the walks of men
    Their wonted haunts resume.

But they would never be taken to be among the best. The truth is that the *Song* in its eight-and-sixty stanzas contains perhaps fifteen or twenty which are the language of pure enchantment, which attain a beauty difficult to define because so far above common experience. The wonderful effect of the poem is caused by the scattering of these magic beauties among a far greater number of beauties of a lower order and by the length and sustained lyrical quality of the whole. It is like a long rope of pearls, with some superlative in size and shape strung at intervals along it; its beauty being to a great extent due to these and to its length. To find a single one of the smaller pearls only here and there, strung into the thread of Smart's other work, is indeed pleasant, but it does not give that work any real semblance to the *Song.* Mr. Blunden has discovered for us a considerable number of these pearls of secondary (though still high) quality amid the religious poems.

To us there is in its strange beauty and tenderness much unevenness, some obscurity—though no more than in many of the greatest of the world's poets—and not more than a hint of derangement. None the less is the poem the fruit of derangement. In what fashion this comes about can best be discovered by a glance at Smart's other work, wherein, if here and there appear evidences of talent, there is little or nothing that could conceivably be called genius.

Genius certainly we shall not find in his journalism, in all the skits, lampoons, and *facetiæ* published for his stepfather Newbery in his magazine *The Midwife,* or in any of his pseudonymous effusions over such signatures as Mary Midnight, Ferdinando Foot, or Martinius Macularius. He can turn an epigram neatly and re-tell an old story well. But many men of genius have failed to display it in journalism, and it is to his poetry we must turn for the discovery of his true bent. Here, for example, are the opening lines of **"The Hop-Garden"**:

> When to inhume the plants, to turn the glebe,
> And wed the tendrils to th' aspiring poles,
> Under what sign to pluck the crop, and how
> To cure, and in capacious sacks infold,
> I teach in verse Miltonian. Smile the muse.

Smile! If the lady has a sense of humour, which has never been effectively proved, she must have split her sides with laughter. Nor is there anything more "Miltonian" in that which follows than is to be found in these five lines. Yet they are not bad lines. **"The Hop-Garden"** is, in fact, a pleasant Georgic of a minor type, and perhaps the best of his productions saving the incomparable *Song*. Or take him in another vein, in *The Hilliad,* an attack upon the notorious John Hill, who had, in truth, used him very badly. *The Hilliad* is a satire, laboriously modelled upon *The Dunciad.* It is lively enough in parts, and just readable to the student of the period. Smart is, indeed, a typical minor poet of an uninteresting age. And it was not only that he could not write fine poetry; he did not always know fine poetry when he saw it. When he set about writing an Ode for Saint Cecilia's Day, he felt that he ought to apologize, in view of the recent efforts in that direction of Dryden and Pope. Amidst his apologies he ventures upon some criticism. The quatrain beginning

> Happy, happy, happy pair!

he declares to be "so far from being adapted to the majesty of an Ode, that it would make no considerable figure in a ballad." Now in all the poem it is just that delightful, haunting cadence which reveals to us fully the brilliancy of one of the greatest masters that ever made music of our English tongue. Yes, Smart, sane, was kin of a Lovibond or an Aaron Hill, with a certain small talent, but conventional.

Conventional! Is not that word the key to our mystery? What was it that turned this secondary poet and journalist, who drank too much beer and could not pay his debts, into an inspired lyrist? For the case is very rare. Many poets of little general merit have written a pretty short poem or two, but it is hard to find any who has produced one so splendid and so long as the *Song* whose other work is so far removed from it. We are tempted to follow Browning's theory that

> all at once the ground
> Gave way beneath his step, a certain smoke

> Curled up and caught him, or perhaps down broke
> A fireball wrapping flesh and spirit both
> In conflagration.

Smart's poetical outlook was, as it were, filmed over by the conventions of his time. **A *Song to David*** is free of them. There is little external evidence to connect it with one literary period rather than another. It comes forth straight from the man's inner consciousness. His mental derangement did not mar it; is it fanciful to suppose that it made it, that it wiped clean a slate whereon natural genius, urged by a vivid religious emotion, should write? The popular verdict, that the *Song* alone of all its author's work is great work, is perfectly correct. It appears equally true that in the Song alone we behold the real soul of the man himself—needs, weaknesses, sufferings swept aside. Nothing artificial, no bubble blown, as Palgrave seemed to think, in a "medley between inspiration and possession," is this, but a pure and undefiled outpouring of secret springs, tapped this once only, when the incrustations that clogged them were broken.

Whatever the seed, the flower remains, in its fashion, one of the finest we have to show. Mr. Blunden makes a strikingly sound criticism when he says that "the splendour seems Hebraic in origin." The poem is, in fact, a psalm. Smart made of his translation of the *Psalms of David* into English verse, as has been stated, a very fair success. The *Song to David,* on the other hand, was his own psalm, the astonishing pouring forth of his own spirit in prayer and praise. Coming from the depths of his own soul, it far surpasses the borrowed work. Yet it retains the very atmosphere of the Psalms, and it is that which makes his work so rare in our literature. If we turn to our other great religious poets, what do we find that they recall? George Herbert, the Anglican High Church of his day; Crashaw, the medieval Roman Catholic Church, with its saints and martyrs; Francis Thompson, the same Church seen through the eyes of a nineteenth-century mystic. But with Smart no Church is recalled. By him we are borne straight back to that Hebraic ecstasy which preceded the Christian faith and amidst which it was brought to birth.

> He sendeth the springs into the rivers: which run among the hills.
> All beasts of the field drink thereof: and the wild asses quench their thirst.
> Beside them shall the fowls of the air have their habitation: and sing among the branches.

That is surely the very note of Smart's *Song,* and a note that we shall hardly find so exactly reproduced in all English poetry.

The verses chosen by Palgrave are justly famous. The first, in particular—

> He sang of God—the mighty source
> Of all things—the stupendous force
>   On which all strength depends;
> From Whose right arm, beneath Whose eyes

All period, power, and enterprise
    Commences, reigns, and ends—

is splendid in its declamation. But they lack the subtler fascination of the "Adoration" stanzas, in some of which Smart is scarce more than half poet and all but half painter.

    With vinous syrup cedars spout,
    From rocks pure honey gushing out,
        For Adoration springs;
    All scenes of painting crowd the map
    Of nature; to the mermaid's pap
        The scaléd infant clings.

    The spotted ounce and playsome cubs
    Run rustling 'mong the flowering shrubs,
        And lizards feed the moss;
    For Adoration beasts embark,
    While waves upholding halcyon's ark
        No longer roar and toss.

What pictures he conjures up here for the mind's eye! These stanzas would have their fitting complement in drawings by an Albrecht Dürer. In the last eight words of the first-quoted Smart suggests his mystery, strangeness, romance, even his beauty of line. There are a dozen others which exhibit this keen and precise sense of the picturesque. Sometimes he crowds picture swift upon picture, picking out each with the few but flawless lines of a mastercraftsman.

    Beauteous the fleet before the gale,
    Beauteous the multitudes in mail,
        Ranked arms and crested heads;
    Beauteous the garden's umbrage mild,
    Walk, water, meditated wild,
        And all the bloomy beds.

The second and third lines call to mind Walter Pater's description of Leonardo's fragmentary drawing for "The Battle of the Standard"—"a waving field of lovely armour, the chased edgings running like lines of sunlight from side to side."

The celebration of the centenaries of famous men is an act of piety. Such occasions, however, are apt to throw the soberest of us momentarily off our balance. Our man of the moment waxes huge before our eyes, while his contemporaries and rivals recede and dwindle. Let us then beware on this occasion of making claims too extravagant for poor Kit Smart. Only let us remember that, if we dub him a man of one poem, that poem is a long, sustained effort, and that it must set him in a category above, say, a Wolfe, whose reputation rests upon eight stanzas. For the rest, is it not enough for us, and for his memory, to acknowledge with thankfulness that out of misery and squalor came forth this one joyous and splendid ode, which will never lack appreciation from the finest minds and the appreciation of which may be called one of the tests of finely critical judgment?

Raymond D. Havens (essay date 1938)

SOURCE: "The Structure of Smart's *Song to David,*" in *The Review of English Studies,* Vol. 14, No. 54, April, 1938, pp. 178–82.

[*In this essay, Havens identifies patterns of language, imagery, and numerology as ordering elements in* A Song to David.]

Certain structural features of Christopher Smart's ***Song to David,*** such as the repetition of "adoration" and "glorious," are so obvious as to attract immediate attention, but no one seems to have remarked, at least in print, that the poem is constructed throughout on one or another formal pattern. This attention to form extends even to the general divisions, which are made up almost entirely of stanzas grouped in threes, or sevens or their multiples—the mystic numbers. The ***Song*** begins with three stanzas of invocation, which are followed by fourteen (twice seven) describing David, by nine (thrice three) which give the subjects of which he sings, and by three recounting the results of his singing; then comes a group of nine consisting of an introductory stanza, seven devoted to the seven "pillars of the Lord," and a concluding stanza; then an introduction, a group of nine stanzas that summarizes the Biblical moral code, and a conclusion; then a stanza introductory to the three groups that follow, each of seven stanzas dealing with adoration; and finally five groups of three which treat of earthly delights and of the greater delight in each field to be found in God.

There can be no question as to most of these divisions, since nearly all are indicated by obvious verbal peculiarities or are pointed out in Smart's argument. This argument, prefixed to the poem and entitled "Contents," is a puzzling document, since it says nothing of groups of threes and sevens, since it sometimes recognizes and sometimes ignores these divisions which are clearly marked out in the poem itself, since it overlooks five stanzas [XXXVIII, XXXIX, XLIX, LXIV, and LXXI], and since it is misleading as to the subject-matter of one group [XL–XLVIII]. To be more specific: each of the stanzas LI–LXXI is distinguished from the rest of the poem by having the words "For ADORATION" at the beginning of one of its lines and, as if to emphasize the unity of the group, the word "adoration" is printed in capital letters; yet in the argument the first of these stanzas is joined to that which precedes although this preceding stanza does not contain the words "For ADORATION," and the last seven of the stanzas which do contain the words "For ADORATION" are treated as if they were independent of the preceding fourteen. Clearly Smart wrote the argument when in haste—perhaps at the request of the printer—and some time after he composed the poem, or when in such a mental state that he overlooked what he had originally emphasized, or when he did not think it worth while to call attention to the elaborate structure he had devised. There is a bare possibility that much of this structure was introduced unconsciously.

The first three stanzas of the poem constitute, as the argument asserts, an "Invocation." The fourth stanza begins, "Great, valiant, pious, good, and clean" and the first word and theme of the fifth stanza is "Great"; of the sixth, "Valiant"; of the seventh, "Pious"; and so on. The seventeenth stanza does not have the form of those that precede or those that follow, and its subject, David's "muse," links it with the subsequent rather than the antecedent group; yet it must be joined to the antecedent group if that is to consist of fourteen stanzas. Such slight irregularities are, like imperfect rimes and distorted accents, very common in poetry. The next stanza begins, "He sung of God" and the first word or words of each of the eight stanzas that follow announce one of the topics of David's song: "Angels," "Of man," "The world," and the like. Then come three stanzas of no apparent pattern devoted to the results of his singing.

The subject then changes abruptly with the announcement, "The pillars of the Lord are seven." The introductory stanza, of which this is the first line, is succeeded by seven others each of them beginning with a Greek letter which is the name of one of the pillars: Alpha, Gamma, Eta, Theta, Iota, Sigma, Omega. Why these particular letters—alternate vowels and consonants—were chosen is not clear. Their significance may lie in the fact that each of the stanzas which they begin deals with one of the days of creation; or it may perhaps be found in masonic symbolism. This group of seven stanzas dealing with "the pillars of knowledge" is logically concluded by a stanza addressed to David as "scholar of the Lord." Thus the seven with the introduction and conclusion make nine. Then comes a stanza introducing nine others which summarize the moral code of the Old Testament (with some borrowings from the New) and which, as in the preceding group, are followed by a single stanza addressed to David. In his Argument Smart asserts that XL—XLVIII are "an exercise upon the decalogue"—which would lead us to expect ten stanzas instead of nine. But verses like the following were not derived from the ten commandments:

> Act simply, as occasion asks;
> Put mellow wine in season'd casks;
>   Till not with ass and bull:
> Remember thy baptismal bond;
> Keep from commixtures foul and fond,
>   Nor work thy flax with wool.
>   (XLV)

Some lines, moreover, were clearly inspired by the teachings of Christ:

> Thou shalt not call thy brother fool;
> The porches of the Christian school
>   Are meekness, peace, and pray'r.
>   (XLI)

The next stanza, beginning "PRAISE above all," announces the theme of the three following groups, each of seven stanzas closely related to one another and set off from the remaining verses by verbal repetition and by thought. Each of these twenty-one stanzas has the words "For ADORA-

TION" at the beginning of one of its lines. Throughout the last seven stanzas these words come in the first line, where they are likewise found in the introductory stanza of the first group and the concluding stanza of the second. In the remaining verses of the first and second groups the words occur in the first line of the first stanza, the second line of the second, the third line of the third, and so on. It is hard to believe that Smart was not here striving for the sacred number seven since, as his stanza consists of only six lines, each of which has "For ADORATION" once, we should expect groups of six. In order to achieve the seven-stanza pattern, which he has used elsewhere in the poem and which is particularly suitable for biblical material, he added one stanza at the beginning of the first group and another at the end of the second. The first of these additions is clearly introductory and the last furnishes a kind of conclusion; at any rate, each stands apart from the intervening lines, which describe the beauty of plant and animal life as it changes in the course of the four seasons. To each of these seasons, significantly enough, three stanzas are given so that we have here a double pattern, two groups of seven stanzas sub-divided into four groups of three. The third of the "adoration" groups—which has "For ADORATION" in the first line of each stanza—is devoted to the five senses. As each of these has one stanza some piecing out is required here also. The sixth stanza treats of the purification and sanctification of the senses, but the last (LXXI), which says that sparrows and swallows find a home in the church, seems not to fit into the scheme, although it has the same verbal pattern as its predecessors.

The final section, like most of the rest, starts somewhat abruptly and has a pattern of its own. It consists of five groups of three stanzas each, the first and second stanza of each group beginning with the same adjective, which appears in the comparative degree at the commencement of the third stanza. Thus we have "Sweet . . . ," "Sweet . . . ," "Sweeter . . . ," "Precious . . . ," "Precious . . . ," "More precious . . . " In each group, furthermore, the first two stanzas deal with earthly delights and the third with the greater sweetness, strength, beauty . . . of human powers devoted to the worship of God. The adjectives with which the first and second stanzas of each group start often begin several of the other lines, but they do not commence all the lines of any stanza until the last group is reached. In this way a superb climax is achieved by the repetition of "Glorious" at the beginning of thirteen successive lines. It is like using the full orchestra in all its power for the first time at the conclusion of a symphony. And, like a great composer, Smart does not prolong his climax unduly or repeat a single theme too often. After the first line of the last stanza "glorious" disappears and there is no repetition of any kind.

It should be observed that all of these means of indicating structure are much alike. They are never refrains, or lines, or long phrases but words—usually one and never more than two words. And they are placed invariably at the beginning of a line and generally at the beginning of a stanza. The poem may well contain more of these devices than are here pointed out, and undoubtedly those here noticed may be explained more satisfactorily, but enough has been done to make clear that the most romantic poem of its time—ecstatic, sensuous, abrupt, and above all strange—was constructed with unusual attention to parallelism, formal design, and pattern—to the ordered beauty of classic and neo-classic art.

William Force Stead (essay date 1939)

SOURCE: An introduction to *Rejoice in the Lamb: A Song from Bedlam* by Christopher Smart, J. Cape, 1939, pp. 13–49.

[*Stead was the discoverer and first editor of the manuscript of* Jubilate Agno. *The following excerpt is taken from his introduction to the first edition of the work, which he called* Rejoice in the Lamb. *Stead views the poem as valuable principally for the light it sheds on Smart's composition of* A Song to David.]

This is a curiosity, an extraordinary document; but if it were nothing more, I would not have troubled to edit it. Bewildering at the first glance, it contains much that is intelligent and beautiful, which I believe will reward the reader who makes an allowance for absurdities and examines the obscurities. Imagine that the foundations had sunken under one of those fantastic gothic palaces built by the mad King of Bavaria, and that in consequence the doors, windows and turrets were all twisted askew. The design, when it became distorted, would have changed from the fantastic to the disconcerting. If you entered such a building you might be tempted to hurry through and out again, before its bizarre disproportions unsettled your reason. But if you were brave and patient enough to linger a little while within the tilting chambers and along the wavering corridors, you would begin to notice that some of the details were interesting and retained the marks of a master-craftsman. So it is in this strange composition, written by that Cambridge prodigal, Christopher Smart, while confined in a madhouse. The fundamental brainwork has broken down, the walls, as it were, are cracked; but not a few of the details are worth examining. There is plenty of rubbish, there are frequent intrusions of the meaningless and grotesque; yet amid all this, one is continually coming upon a revealing phrase which tells us what the poet had been thinking, reading, praying for, enduring and suffering. There are bright little thumbnail sketches, whimsical fancies, and here and there some bold gigantic images. There are fragments of wide and curious learning, with signs of a hundred friendships and of more than one love affair.

What sort of man was that distracted poet, famous chiefly as the author of *A Song to David*? Since a writer is a cause and his work is an effect, it is only natural to look for some relation between the two. Yet what relation can there be between the glorious *Song to David,* that skyscraper among eighteenth-century lyrics, and the feckless, drunken, crazy little man who wrote it? That Christopher Smart wrote *A Song to David,* no one has ever questioned, but what there was in the man which could produce such a poem no one has ever explained. Mr. Blunden has refuted the charge that Smart was 'a sot and a wastrel'; yet even if he had been (and he was not far from it) we might discover a glimmering of the hidden sources of the poem, had the poet left behind him a few letters or journals or recorded conversations which showed any deep spiritual strivings and yearnings in his nature; but nothing of the kind has ever been available.

Colonel Carwardine Probert, a man of letters, a scholar, and an early member of the Keats-Shelley Memorial Association (of which for a few years I have been Secretary), invited me to visit him at his home in Suffolk to look over some of his inherited treasures. He showed me old stained glass from a ruined priory; ancient monastic deeds and charters; documents relating to the Elizabethan Earl of Oxford; letters from William Hayley, the friend and biographer of Cowper, written to Colonel Probert's great-grand-father, the Reverend Thomas Carwardine (who flourished from 1734 to 1824); family portraits by Romney whom this ancestor, along with Hayley, had taken out to Italy, and sketches by the great masters which they collected on their Italian tour one hundred and fifty years ago. But it was the sixteen folio pages closely written on both sides in the handwriting of Christopher Smart (the manuscript printed in the following pages) to which my attention kept returning. Colonel Probert is not sure how these papers came into the possession of his family, but he believes they were left with the Reverend Thomas Carwardine at Colne Priory by William Hayley, when these two friends were discussing what could be done for Cowper in one of his attacks of madness, the subject of much of their correspondence. Apparently they regarded this manuscript by the demented Smart as a fair specimen of the nature of poetic insanity, and therefore of some value when they were dealing with Cowper, who had been attacked by the same disease. Hayley, by the way, visited William Collins's sister to inquire into the case of Collins; he was also the friend and patron of Blake, and thus became acquainted with various examples (four in all) of mad poets.

Colonel Probert is the soul of courtesy and consideration, as becomes one who for many years was a courtier in the best meaning of the word. Being skilled in fine points of honour, he was at first a little troubled about the propriety of printing a manuscript, the manifest absurdities of which might expose the writer to ridicule. But poor Smart has been dead for a long time now, and everyone who knows anything about him knows that he was insane. I confess that I am amused, and that I see no reason why one should not be amused, when, after mentioning a fish named dentex, the poet hastily adds, 'Blessed be the name Jesus for my teeth'. But one's amusement is tempered by a consciousness that the poor fellow was suffering. Here is a fine intellect, a highly aspiring spirit, all crumpled up and wrecked by some weakness in the body or will. If the result in places is grotesque enough to provoke our laughter, yet the whole is far more of a tragedy than a comedy, and when we survey the whole, our laughter will be subdued by sympathy and regret. That, I feel sure, is the way this strange work will be received.

Many will value it as supplying a bridge over the gulf between a splendid poem and an unhappy author. No claim need be made for it as literature, except that there are several passages and a number of individual lines which should appeal to those who appreciate the romantic and mystical. Students of poetry will value its revelation of the vast accumulation of poetic resources which Smart had to draw upon when writing *A Song to David*. Here are the beasts, the birds, the fish, the flowers, the precious stones, all in prodigal profusion, from which a selection was made for a much reduced but brilliant display in the rapturous *Song*. Broadly speaking, the theme of the two compositions is the same, the bringing together of the whole of creation in praise of the Creator.

. . . . .

If Smart had not been locked up in an asylum, he might never have written *A Song to David*.

In the lives of most of us the central point moves to and fro between the plane of thinking and willing, and the plane of merely existing and drifting. Maybe, we never retire very far into the sessions of sweet, silent thought, nor do we abandon ourselves entirely to the mood of rattlin', roarin' Willie; but while circumstances incline us toward one level or the other, most of us retain the power to alter our direction, to move the point of focus when occasion requires. Smart either had no such power, or little desire to exercise it; he drifted into the lower region and settled there. Perhaps he was guilty of bad taste rather than bad morals. Endowed with a warm, affectionate nature, which won the friendship of many good men; gifted, too, with a wondering tenderness toward animals, birds, and insects, and with a spirit which could rise into the ardours of worship and adoration, he remained lazily content with life in an alehouse parlour and the fleeting applause that greeted his waggery.

Not far from Coleridge in imagination and learning, he was even more ruinously weak in will. Coleridge searched himself, found out his faults, and in a measure resolved them; Smart did none of these things, probably because of a deficiency in analytical and constructive thought, two powers of the mind in which Coleridge excelled. Coleridge was always exploring the noumenal world with a view to discovering the unifying relations which sustain the whole; Smart saw things only in flashes. His mental processes were nearer to those of Blake, with whom a good deal of this document shows a kindred spirit. Cowper and Smart, compared as two victims of religious mania, exhibit contrasted self-portraits, the one all black, and the other all white, since Cowper, whose life was nearly blameless, became convinced that he was damned, while Smart, who had wandered so far astray, never doubted his inheritance in the New Canaan. Because he did not know himself, he hardly suspected his own faults, and went astray with a child's innocent conscience.

This manuscript is a panorama of the thoughts, or, more correctly, of the stream of ideas, which flowed through his mind during chastened, solitary years, when, if ever, he might have expressed regret for his wasted talents and for the pain he had caused his family. But of self-examination, or a contrite spirit, there is hardly a trace. Once, when he writes,

> For I am come home again, but there is nobody to
> kill the calf or to pay the musick,

one hears an echo from the Parable of the Prodigal Son; but he had just written, a few lines above,

> For I have abstained from the blood of the grape
> and that even at the Lord's table,

which means that he was more aware of abstinence than of self-indulgence. When he writes,

> God be gracious to the soul of Hobbes, who was no
> atheist, but a servant of Christ, and died in the
> Lord—I wronged him God forgive me,

he is writing as a penitent, but not as one who had examined his life and discovered his faults. There is a mysterious sentence,

> For I bless the children of Asher for the evil I did
> them & the good I might have received at their
> hands,

which possibly contains a reference to his wife and children, but may as well refer to anyone else, or no one in particular. These stray phrases amount to so little that it cannot be said that Smart recognized his failure and had determined to amend his habits.

How, then, did the solitary years in an asylum help him to write *A Song to David*? What did they do for him? Many things; they gave him the gift of quietness, they drove him in upon his own resources, they took the bottle away (which the prison later did not), they stilled the bubbling prattle of his wit and waggery, and in an enforced restraint upon the weak and foolish part of his nature, they allowed the deep and serious to emerge. Very strange and unexpected things began to come to the surface; many of them as grotesque as primitive animals in the early stages of evolution; but beautiful forms appeared as well, and the whole was dedicated to the glory of God. When he began this ill-proportioned song of praise, he had already entered upon a process which was to culminate in his masterpiece. One cannot read more than a page or two before meeting with signs of the work of an artist. Even such obscure creatures as the flea, the spider, and the beetle are shown as under a microscope and brought before us as notable citizens of the universe:

> Let Ethan praise with the Flea, his coat of mail, his
> piercer, and his vigour . . .
> Let Heman bless with the Spider, his warp and his
> woof, his subtlety and industry . . .
> Let Chalcol praise with the Beetle, whose life is
> precious in the sight of God, tho' his appearance
> is against him.

In the newly-found quiet he began to see clearly (probably he had always seen in some degree) an untold meaning in the things we hardly notice, or prefer to ignore; his flea with coat of mail and piercer is magnified into a warrior and a kinsman worthy of that extraordinary being which Blake revealed in his drawing of the Ghost of a Flea. When the more familiar creatures were exhausted, he began to delve deeply into the resources which he had been storing up through years of interest in natural phenomena, and the result is so overwhelming that the artist becomes lost in the collector. One is tempted to ask, But is it all genuine? Is he not writing nonsense and inventing names like Edward Lear? What of 'Chenomycon an herb which terrifies a goose' and 'The King of the Wavows a strange fowl'? They are not bogus; the first came from Pliny's *Natural History,* and the second had been exhibited in the George Tavern at Charing Cross. Though he is writing here as a collector rather than as an artist, it is well that he should bring his immense collection out of storage and so be able to examine it before making a selection for his masterpiece.

Closely related to this absorbing interest in multitudinous forms of life, is his interest in other departments of science, illustrated in numerous passages throughout. . . . He prays for the increase of the Cambridge collection of fossils; he mentions three successive Cambridge Professors of Geology; he is acquainted with new discoveries (as they were then) such as the barometer, the air-pump, electrical treatment of disease, and the diving bell. He knows the value of Peruvian bark (quinine) and a hundred medicinal herbs. He is concerned about the exact method of calculating the longitude (which had not yet been established). For some natural phenomena, such as the echo (which Gilbert White studied), for thunder and lightning (then being investigated by Benjamin Franklin), for the ascent of vapours and sap (studied by such men as Nehemiah Grew), for the nature of colours and light (as treated by Sir Isaac Newton), for the tides, and centripetal and centrifugal motion (which Newton had studied and Derham expounded in popular science): for these phenomena he crosses swords with the naturalists and resorts to a supernatural or mystical philosophy.

We are thus introduced to another region of his mind, one of its most important aspects, which had never seen the light of day in his crambo ballads, his fables, and his journalistic essays. As he unveiled his hidden life during these years of silence and confinement, there came up out of the deep places a mystical or occult philosophy derived from such writers as Pythagoras, Hermes, the Cabalists, Cornelius Agrippa, Eugenius Philalethes, and Henry More the Cambridge Platonist. Writings of this kind had been voluminous in the sixteenth and seventeenth centuries, but had fallen out of fashion with the coming of the Augustans. The literature is so extensive and there was so much give and take between its authors, that an editor should be careful not to attribute an image or an idea to one specific writer as though he were the only possible source. For instance, I have illustrated Smart's mystical interpretation of Jacob's Ladder by a passage from Eugenius Philalethes, his exposition of the occult significance of numbers by a passage from Cornelius Agrippa, and his use of the word 'centre' by a passage from Henry More; but the mystical interpretation of Jacob's Ladder was used by medieval theologians as well as by the occultists of the Renaissance; the mystical meaning of numbers was the common property of the Pythagoreans as well as the Cabalists, and the special meaning of 'centre' is found in the school of nature mystics to which Henry Vaughan belonged. My illustrations, therefore, are intended only to show the community of thought between Smart and the authors of these various kinds of esoteric philosophy. That he was acquainted with some of their writings, and found them congenial, is, I think, beyond question. One might describe him as the last of the Cambridge Platonists. He was not at home either in the orthodoxy or scepticism of his age; in the Cambridge of Henry More he might have been a different man.

That his sympathy lay with the mystics can be seen (apart from this manuscript) in those unexplained stanzas of *A Song to David*:

> The pillars of the Lord are sev'n,
> Which stand from earth to topmost heav'n . . .
> Alpha, the cause of causes, first . . .
> Gamma supports the glorious arch . . .

and that his interests had turned in this direction during his Cambridge days is suggested by an entry in the records of Pembroke College Library showing that he had borrowed Iamblichus's *Life of Pythagoras*. A study of these authors may have helped to unbalance his mind; but it need not have done so. Through the Hermetic and other esoteric philosophies there came to Henry Vaughan, his brother Thomas Vaughan, Henry More, and the like, beautiful trains of spiritual thought and vision. Some of that unearthly beauty shines through the broken lights of this manuscript, and burns without a shadow in the great *Song to David*. Nearly allied to these authors were Boehme and Swedenborg, who were studied by Blake; their affinities with the mystical writers familiar to Smart may account for lines in the following pages which could easily be attributed to Blake. Yet, of course, there need not have been any intermediaries between Smart and Blake, because genius is a miracle, and if there are beautiful mountains from which the nightingales come, and well-heads and springs of light from which poets and mystics fill their urns, Smart and Blake may have visited the same mountains and dipped their urns in the same springs. I am thinking of such lines as these:

> For the SUN is an intelligence and an angel of the human form.
> For the MOON is an intelligence and an angel in shape like a woman . . .
> For the Glory of God is always in the East, but cannot be seen for the cloud of the crucifixion . . .
> For GOD the father Almighty plays upon the HARP of stupendous magnitude and melody.
> For innumerable Angels fly out at every touch and . his tune is a work of creation.

For at that time malignity ceases and the devils
  themselves are at peace.
For this time is perceptible to man by a remarkable
  stillness and serenity of soul.

There are other ways in which he anticipates Blake: he
engaged in prophecies; he wrote of the cherub cat as a
'term of the Angel Tiger'; he believed in worshipping
naked in the rain; he wrote a little book of hymns for
children, far inferior to Blake's, yet showing the same
love of children and their innocence.

Other lines might have come from the seventeenth century
nature mystics:

For Flowers can see, and Pope's Carnations knew
  him . . .
For the flowers have their angels even the words of
  God's Creation . . .
For the ASCENT of VAPOURS is the return of
  thanksgiving from all humid bodies.

But what is one to make of this line?

For in my nature I quested for beauty, but God,
  God hath sent me to sea for pearls.

To quest for beauty sounds strange in the eighteenth century, though it might come naturally from Keats: God
sending him to sea for pearls is more difficult; I suppose
it is a crystallization of the belief that in God's wisdom
the heart may be sent to find its treasure in the deep sea
of affliction.

Thinking in flashes, he jotted down, like Blake, little sayings of gnomic wisdom:

There is a way to the terrestrial Paradise upon the
  knees . . .
For Ignorance is a sin, because illumination is to be
  had by prayer . . .
For Justice is infinitely beneath Mercy in nature and
  office . . .
For beauty is better to look upon than to meddle
  with and tis good for a man not to know a
  woman . . .
For TEA is a blessed plant and of excellent virtue . . .
For stuff'd guts make no musick; strain them strong
  and you shall have sweet melody.

These abrupt, disjointed utterings of a wisdom terrestrial
and celestial resemble Blake's method of writing in *The
Marriage of Heaven and Hell*, and the phrases have a
similar vitality and freshness. All through this manuscript
Smart shows himself in possession of a new instrument of
language. There is much in his earlier work which is admirable, much that is graceful and charming; some acute
observation, and ingenious rhymes; yet the phrasing is
often conventional, because he was not writing from the
centre of his own being, but in a style acquired from others. Now, when the superficial man was put under restraint, the hidden man, who could see through magical

---

An excerpt from *Jubilate Agno*:

For I will consider my Cat Jeoffry.
For he is the servant of the Living God, duly and
  daily serving him.
For at the first glance of the glory of God in the
  East he worships in his way.
For is this done by wreathing his body seven times
  round, with elegant quickness.
For then he leaps up to catch the musk, wch is the
  blessing of God upon his prayer.
For he rolls upon prank to work it in.
For having done duty and received blessing he
  begins to consider himself.
For this he performs in ten degrees.
For first he looks upon his fore-paws to see if they
  are clean.
For secondly he kicks up behind to clear away
  there.
For thirdly he works it upon stretch with the fore
  paws extended.
For fourthly he sharpens his paws by wood.
For fiftly he washes himself.
For sixthly he rolls upon wash.
For Seventhly he fleas himself, that he may not be
  interrupted upon the beat.
For Eightly he rubs himself against a post.
For Ninthly he looks up for his instructions.
For Tenthly he goes in quest of food.
For having consider'd God and himself he will
  consider his neighbour.
For if he meets another cat he will kiss her in
  kindness.
For when he takes his prey he plays with it to give
  it [a] chance.
For one mouse in seven escapes by his dallying.
For when his day's work is done his business more
  properly begins.
For keeps the Lord's watch in the night against the
  adversary.
For he counteracts the powers of darkness by his
  electrical skin & glaring eyes.
For he counteracts the Devil, who is death, by
  brisking about the life.

Christopher Smart, Jubilate Agno, *in* Rejoice in
the Lamb: A Song from Bedlam, *edited by William
Force Stead, Henry Holt and Company, 1939.*

---

eyes, came forth and brought his own language with him.
New phrases arose spontaneously and the lines were impelled by natural rhythms, forming a remarkable example
of eighteenth-century free verse.

Besides being conventional, Smart's earlier work in places had been deficient in technical refinements. How did
he become such a virtuoso when writing *A Song to David*?
Its splendid technique cannot be an accident, and I think

that we should include among the advantages of his con-finement the opportunity it gave him for reflecting upon the meaning-value of sounds and their translation into words. Smart's interest in music can be shown from var-ious sources, here and elsewhere; in these pages there are frequent references to musicians, Handel, Arne, Burney, Randall of Cambridge; also, there is a delightful passage in which the poet assigns to musical instruments their corresponding rhymes:

> For the trumpet rhimes are sound bound, soar more
>   and the like.
> For the Shawm rhimes are lawn fawn moon boon
>   and the like.
> For the harp rhimes are sing ring, string & the like.

These lines show that he was cultivating his ear for the musical value of words, and that the cultivation was car-ried on during these years of confinement. I have always admired the note of finality at the end of *A Song to David*:

> Thou at stupendous truth believ'd,
> And now the matchless deed's achiev'd,
>   DETERMIN'D, DAR'D, and DONE.

The sequence of words in this last line embraces the whole sweep of the cosmic drama; 'determin'd'—it is foreseen; 'dar'd'—it is undertaken; 'done'—it is accomplished. And the meaning is both accompanied and amplified by a cor-responding adaptation of sound; for in these final words the vowels are increasingly deepened, while the conso-nants keep up a drumming undertone only varied between d-t-r-m-n-d, d-r-d, and d-n. I am inclined to thank the asylum for that development in technique.

But what there can be no mistake about is that the years of confinement were his only period of 'recollection', when he could discover and uncover his deeper self; the only years in which he attained some unity of spiritual experi-ence, and during which the delicate flowers of light, gath-ered on his visits to Paradise upon his knees, were not gathered only to be destroyed by the folly which tore him to pieces when unrestrained.

For these reasons, I believe that if Smart had not been locked up in an asylum, he would never have written *A Song to David*.

Norman Callan (essay date 1949)

SOURCE: An introduction to *The Collected Poems of Christopher Smart, Volume 1*, Routledge and Kegan Paul, 1949, pp. xiii–xxxvi.

[*In the following excerpt, Callan broadly surveys Smart's work, attempting to identify the characteristics of the poet's style.*]

It is not an easy matter to dissociate the poetry Smart wrote from the life he lived. This is due in some measure to the sort of criticism which has been applied to his work since Browning included him in *Parleyings with Certain People,* but much more to Smart's own nature. Like Donne and Milton, he is persistently egocentric, but whereas they show the ego at grips with the great prob-lems of humanity, Smart's ego seems too often entangled in a pettifogging exhibitionism. His tone is so personal that unless the reader is prepared to make the effort to understand his personality he is continually subject to a feeling of irritation at the self-absorption everywhere apparent.

For a sympathetic approach to his poetry Smart's psy-chological development is therefore of some importance. He is one of those people who never outgrow the infe-riorities and assertiveness of childhood. He oscillates between extremes of self-belittlement and self-glorifica-tion; between

> For I am a little fellow . . .

and

>   . . . now the deed's
>   DETERMINED, DARED and DONE.

In his earlier poetry (this is particularly true of the Seato-nian poems) much of the reader's pleasure, though by no means all, comes from the sudden transitions from gran-diloquence to simplicity; from a passage of Miltonic 'el-evation' such as that in [*On the Goodness of the Supreme Being*] beginning

> Without thy aid, without thy gladsome beams
> The tribes of woodland warblers wou'd remain
> Mute on the bending branches . . .

to

> And though their throats coarse ruttling hurt the ear
> They mean it all for music . . .

In the later verse, the *Hymns for the Fasts and Festivals* and the *Hymns for Children* particularly, it is the second mood which predominates. Under the stress of emotional suffering, Smart seems to have turned more and more to his childhood; not only to the sights and sounds of the Medway countryside but to the emotional attitudes and the unquestioning acceptances of that time. No observa-tion is more true of Smart than Mr. Stead's that for all his recondite learning he lacked an analytical mind. In *Jubi-late Agno,* and to some extent in all the poetry which follows, he simplifies the problem of relating learning to understanding by viewing everything, from Pliny's natural history to the reformation of the calendar, in the light of a naïve literalness, which, however irritating it may be philosophically, often makes for moving poetry. His cat Jeoffrey is the servant of the Lord, who tells him he is a good cat, spinks and ouzels proclaim that they too have a Saviour, the writing of an Ode to a successful admiral is to be compared to the swiftness of the ship 'when Christ the seaman was on board'.

A directness of expression, which makes no distinction between analogy and identity, has been singled out as the most noteworthy characteristic of Smart's verse by critics from Browning to Mr. Middleton Murry. Used too exclusively this approach, however penetrating, leads to the ignoring of other good qualities in his poetry, qualities which are equally the product of childhood. Smart's childhood must have been a period of unusual sensitivity, heightened, one may suppose, by his early love for Anne Vane; and it is at moments when he succeeds in re-creating the intense perceptiveness of those years that his poetry glows. Enough has been written of the *Song to David* and the *Hymns* for anyone who has an acquaintance with those poems to know where to look for such moments: but elsewhere in his poetry they have not been generally recognized. They are to be found everywhere: in the *Fables*—

> The dew and herbage all around
> Like pearls and emeralds on the ground,
> The uncultur'd flowers that rudely rise,
> Where smiling freedom art defies,
> The lark in transport towering high,
> The crimson curtains of the sky . . .

in the pastoral pieces:

> Their scythes upon the adverse bank
> Glitter 'mongst th' entangled trees,
> Where the hazels form a rank,
> And court'sy to the courting breeze . . .

even amid the *facetiae* of **'The Pretty Barmaid,'** in such a line as

> Markt little hemispheres with stars.

Smart is a poet with the eye of a painter developed to an unusually high degree. He has the stereoscopic vision which makes the object leap to the eye, the painter's sense of physical texture, and his skill in 'composing' a picture:

> Then came Sleep, serene and bland,
> Bearing a death watch in his hand;
> In fluid air around him swims
> A tribe grotesque of mimic dreams.

He is a miniaturist rather than a painter of broad effects. One of his key words is 'little'—which takes us back once more to his childhood and to his sensitiveness about his small stature—and the careful reader will find his poetry full of minute arabesques, which owe something of their manner to Pope, who was another poet with a miniaturist's eye, but for the most part are so peculiar to Smart that it is not easy to compare them with anything else in English poetry.

This is Smart's strongest claim, and a more than sufficient one, for greater notice than he has hitherto received; but it is by no means the only one. There is, for instance, his versatility. He practised almost every 'kind' of poetry which a conventional age recognized as such, and gave to each his own personal inflexion. The **'Night Piece'**, for exam-

ple, had acquired almost a genre of its own since Lady Winchilsea's time, yet the kind of fantasy evident in the quatrain just quoted . . . is to be found in no other piece of the same type that I know of. **'The Fair Recluse'** affords a similar instance. This is a 'gothic' poem which derives from Pope's 'Unfortunate Lady' and perhaps from *Clarissa,* and most of it might have been written by any poet of the period: but there is one quatrain which is peculiarly Smart's own—

> Say, must these tears for ever flow,
> Can I from patience learn content,
> While solitude still nurses woe,
> And leaves me leisure to repent?

The tone of these not very striking lines is of some importance in understanding Smart's poetry. It looks back to the earlier [**'Eagle Confin'd in a College Court'**] and forward to the *Psalms*. From his early Cambridge days Smart undoubtedly suffered from a feeling—later all too unhappily actualized—that he was being persecuted, and it is this sense of a personal situation which gives his verse a cryptic emphasis whenever the subject affords an opportunity. Another instance is to be found in **'Reason and Imagination'**. By accepted canons of criticism this sort of thing should not happen: poetry is supposed to be a release from emotion, and I am not concerned to justify Smart's habit of identifying himself with a 'persecution situation' whenever he can. What I do wish to emphasize is that when he 'translates' from Psalm xc

> O be thou placable by pray'r,
> And stand between us and despair,
> How long wilt thou postpone?
> To these our off'rings as they burn,
> Do thou propitiate thy return,
> And let our tears atone.

the poetry is what it is because Smart sees his own position and that of persecuted Israel as one and the same.

> Smart is a poet with the eye of a painter developed to an unusually high degree. He has the stereoscopic vision which makes the object leap to the eye, the painter's sense of physical texture, and his skill in 'composing' a picture.
>
> —*Norman Callan*

The clearest illustration, however, of the 'difference' of Smart's poetry from that of his contemporaries is to be seen in the *Fables*. Again, they are poems of a recognized 'kind': the *Monthly Review* compared them generously with the *Fables* of Gay and Moore. Yet, though Gay was certainly one of Smart's heroes (Smart regarded himself as the inheritor of the tradition of the Scriblerus Club in the war on dullness), the comparison is not really helpful. For one thing, Smart identifies himself invariably with the underdog; but it is more important to notice that the *Fables* do not depend for their effect on any neat point or moral so much as on the way the allegorical figures, 'nature', the bees, the mandrake, 'imagination', and so on, develop a personality of their own. This pictorial individuality more often than not overlays the moral and turns the poem into a fantasy quite unlike Gay's witty cautions.

What may be called the grandiose characteristic of Smart's style also arose from his personality. It is true that the use of Miltonic blank verse whenever the grand manner seemed to be required by the subject had become almost obligatory by the middle of the century, and that the **'Hop Garden'** and the Seatonian poems owe something to *Cider* and the *Seasons* as well as to *Paradise Lost*; but there was an element in Smart's nature compounded about equally of bravado and an infinite capacity for astonishment which showed itself in other things besides his handling of the technicalities of inversion and periphrasis. It is to be found in the early pindaric ode **'To the King',** in the naïve outbursts of patriotism in *Jubilate Agno* and [**'Ode to General Draper'**], in the *Psalms,* and even in such a passage as this from the *Hymns*:

> I speak for all—for them that fly,
> And for the race that swim;
> For all that dwell in moist and dry,
> Beasts, reptiles, flow'rs and gems to vie
> When gratitude begins her hymn.

Most clearly of all it is to be seen in *A Song to David*. In this poem Smart succeeded completely, for perhaps the only time, in harmonizing the extremes of his temperament, bravado and gentleness, erudition and simplicity, the immense and the minute. The almost universal praise lavished on the *Song* has undoubtedly been justified. It has not always been well considered, however. In the first place it is questionable how far many of its encomiasts really understand it. Before I had read Mr. Stead's introduction to *Jubilate Agno* a knowledge of some of Kipling's stories had convinced me that Smart was expressing in the *Song* the *arcana* of Freemasonry; and since I am not of that fraternity I suspect not only myself of being insufficiently equipped to comprehend it but others also, and particularly those who say that it presents no difficulty to the patient reader. Secondly, enthusiasm for the *Song* has damaged Smart's reputation as a poet by fostering what Mr. Edmund Blunden calls the myth that the writer was a sot who by accident wrote one consummate poem, and so distracting attention from his other verse. Particularly this is true in the matter of Smart's versification. The *Song* is a product of his later years, when (as happened with Milton) his rhythms had become more strongly marked, perhaps more grand, but certainly less fluid. This stiffening characterizes almost everything he published after 1763, and because of the interest which has been focused on these later poems his skill in handling the long stanza in the early pindaric odes, and the flexibility of his rhythms in octosyllabic and heroic couplets have been largely ignored. This is a pity, for there are few of Smart's early pieces, however trivial their subject, where the delicacy of ear, which is one of the essential qualities of a true poet, is not evident. The more I read him, the more I seem to hear an anticipation of the rhythms of the late A. E. Housman, and although there is probably no direct connexion, I think that the similarity may lie in the fact that they are both poets who had fully absorbed the movement of the Latin hendecasyllabic line.

However this may be, that Smart was more than ordinarily interested in the technique of versification is clear from the introduction to his verse translation of Horace, and from the wide range of verse forms that he used. It is also evident from the *Jubilate Agno,* where, as Mr. Stead has pointed out, at least some of the apparent incoherence may be explained as experiment in new forms of verse in preparation for his rendering of the Psalms. One case of this may perhaps be instanced—a line which has been frequently cited as evidence of Smart's madness:

> Let Ross house of Ross rejoice in the the great
> flabber dabber flat clapping fish with hands.

Mr. Stead thinks there is a reference here to the floods clapping their hands and another commentator has suggested that 'Ross' may be the name of a fisherman Smart had met in his travels. I would not venture to disagree with either of them, but it has always seemed to me that in this line Smart was trying to re-create the visual and aural experience of watching a fisherman (or a fishmonger, for that matter) emptying a catch of fish. In this case, of course, the 'hands' would be human ones, and the syntactical disorder imposed by the need to create a special sound effect.

Of *Jubilate Agno* as a whole there is no room to speak. The publication of the poem in 1939 not only enriched English poetry with some exquisite lines and passages, but added considerably to our means of assessing Smart's poetry. Once more, and with even greater insistence, we are brought up against the problem of personality—the personality of a man who does not recognize that his misfortunes may in some degree be due to his own failings. The temptation to take sides, . . . is stronger than ever. Nevertheless, it is to be resisted. Enough harm has already been done by turning the *Song to David* into a miraculous *tour de force.* The balance will not be righted by portraying Smart as a persecuted mystic. To quote one of the more level-headed of the earlier commentators, 'Smart wrote enough to fill two volumes, and much of what he wrote is very good'. How good it remains for the reader . . . to discover.

Sophia B. Blaydes (essay date 1966)

SOURCE: *Christopher Smart as a Poet of His Time: A Re-Appraisal,* Mouton & Co., 1966, 182 p.

[*In the following excerpt, Blaydes discusses the intrinsic value of Smart's Seatonian poetry, as well as its relationship to the author's later work, particularly* A Song to David.]

Since the time of the Victorians many readers of the *Song to David* have had little, if any, interest in Smart's minor religious poetry. His Seaton poems were forgotten and shelved with other eighteenth-century literary fads; his work in the asylum, *Jubilate Agno,* was regarded as proof of his madness; his metrical version of the Psalms was, at most, considered a step towards the composition of the *Song*. Today, however, those who are familiar with Smart's work are discovering that it displays striking echoes of the *Song* in theme and technique. . . .

Smart's most popular and most acclaimed works were the five early prize Seaton poems. They were the first poems to state the ideas which were to become so prominent in the *Song*. Each Seaton poem is a statement of man's gratitude to God and a praise of God. Smart calls upon nature and man to praise and adore God. The poems, however, are not lyrical expressions of Smart's theology; they are instead blank-verse meditations. As such they bear the heavy burden of "Miltonics", that is, of inversion, suspension, compound epithets, parenthetical remarks. Despite the unwieldy style, the poems contain evidence of Smart's development as a poet. One of his most successful techniques, the catalogue, is introduced in these poems. Smart lists all those things which praise God, or which God has created, anticipating his later catalogues in the *Jubilate* and the *Song*. Lines and images occur which echo some of the finer lines of his later, more successful lyrics.

In the first Seaton poem, *On the Eternity of the Supreme Being* . . . Smart explains how, even after the destruction of the world, God its Creator will remain and be eternal, and how, through His goodness, He will permit man's soul to survive and share His eternity. The poem is simple, expressing its idea in a logical series of verse paragraphs. The idea of praise is important, but it is not as powerful as it is in his later work. . . .

> 'Tis then the human tongue new-tun'd shall give
> Praises more worthy the eternal ear.
>
> . . . . .
>
> Yet still let reason thro' the eye of faith
> View him with fearful love; let truth pronounce,
> And adoration on her bended knee
> With heav'n directed hands confess His reign,
> And let th' Angelic, Archangelic band
> With all the Hosts of Heav'n, cherubic Forms,
> And forms Seraphic, with their silver trumps
> And golden lyres attend:—'For Thou art holy,
> For thou are One, th' Eternal, who alone
> Exerts all goodness, and transcends all praise.' . . .

In these last lines of the poem, Smart emphasizes music and heavenly harmony, an idea which will later be fundamental to his poetry and theology. Adoration is skilfully related to music; later music will become the only vehicle for adoration. It is this idea which Smart retains in his composition of the *Song*. . . .

In the central portion of the first Seaton poem, Smart discusses the destruction of the earth. In doing so he employs a catalogue of those things which shall perish. The catalogue is not as artistic as those which will appear in the *Song,* but it is a noble first attempt. . . .

The poem, as the other Seaton poems, is unlike Smart's later work because it is not lyrical. It is in the accepted tradition of Milton, which emphasizes the ornate and pictorial. Since the style was originally designed for lofty subjects, it is appropriate enough here. However, Smart's poems which were composed in this style are submerged by it. It is only through the lyric that Smart is able to communicate his ideas adequately and artistically, since the form lends itself to the ideas which he is presenting. In the *Song* he praises God and attaches to the act of praise the medium of music, so that David, the great musician, becomes the symbol of one who has praised and adored God. The poem is itself a song and at the same time describes music as the proper vehicle of praise. The style which Smart employed in the Seaton poems is not musical; it is heavy, grand poetry. Within its confines Smart is unable to bring into play his ability to strike a major key and refine it with minor themes.

The second Seaton poem, *On the Immensity of the Supreme Being* . . . , begins on Smart's major theme, that is, that all things in themselves praise God. Although Smart's idea that God created all things and that they exist in adoration of Him is more beautifully expressed in the *Song,* it is developed in the Seaton poem with some of the devices which Smart retains for the later poem. He introduces images which are later revived in the *Song;* he applies the catalogue to delineate God's immensity; he allies prayer and music.

The poem opens with an invocation to God to "Awake my lute and harp—". These instruments later become the tools of Orpheus and then of David. Here they belong unmistakably to Smart. He then joins nature in a prayer. . . . The remainder of the poem is a catalogue of the beings and things which both testify to God's immensity by their existence and which join Smart in [his] prayer of thanksgiving. He progresses in each verse paragraph from one category to another—from sky to ocean to sea to the earth—and within each category he catalogues items which declare God's presence. . . .

As he recounts the evidence of God's presence, he mentions gems.

>   Thence will I go
> To undermine the treasure-fertile womb
> Of the huge *Pyrenean,* to detect
> The Agat and the deep-intrenched gem
> Of kindred Jasper—Nature in them both
> Delights to play the Mimic on herself;
> And in their veins she oft pourtrays the forms
> Of leaning hills, of trees erect, and streams
> Now stealing softly on, now thund'ring down
> In desperate cascade, with flow'rs and beasts
> And all the living landskip of the vale.

The passage is contrived because it appears that Smart forced the reflection of Nature in the gems. Later the gem becomes a vivid, true image. He says in the *Song,*

> Of gems—their virtue and their price,
> Which hid in earth from man's device,
>   Their darts of lustre sheathe;
> The jasper of the master's stamp,
> The topaz blazing like a lamp
>   Among the mines beneath.

The simplicity of the imagery in the *Song* reveals the extent of Smart's development. Another indication is the language, which is direct and clear, as opposed to the intricate and involved language of the Seaton poems. . . .

The poem ends in a flourish. In a way it anticipates the exultant ending of the *Song.*

> I see, and I adore—O God most bounteous!
> O infinite of Goodness and of Glory!
> The knee, that Thou has shap'd, shall bend to
>   Thee,
> The tongue, which Thou has tun'd, shall chant thy
>   praise,
> And thine own image, the immortal soul
> Shall consecrate herself to Thee for ever.

The poem closes with an affirmation of prayer, praise and God. Despite the repetition and alliteration, the lines do not possess the spirit of the climax of the *Song.*

The third prize poem, *On the Omniscience of the Supreme Being* . . . , is another expression of man's praise of God, but it is among Smart's worst poems. It is full of erudition, pomposity and didacticism. There are lines and images which are offensive, if not in bad taste. The poem is so unlike Smart, and it is so bad that one wonders who the judges were. . . .

The poem is among the worst of the eighteenth century. The idea is typically Smart, but its execution is not. It appears that the young poet must have suddenly become aware of his erudition; the poem is full of recondite terms and garbled lines. He has yet to learn to master the language and learning of his early years.

The fourth Seaton poem, *On the Power of the Supreme Being* . . . , describes the power of God through the earth and universe as it is revealed in storms, earthquakes, eruptions, and the like. These same things join man to praise God. Once again there is a catalogue of natural events in the atmosphere, beneath the ground, in the world of man. The language is more controlled than it was in the previous Seaton poem. Few images and words occur which seem inappropriate to poetry.

The poem also contains many poetic devices which Smart had been using in his other Seaton poems. Some are derived from the eighteenth century's conception of Milton's style; others are devices which Smart has begun to develop in these early poems. Among them, as we have seen, are the catalogues of nature, man and heaven. In addition, there are devices such as repetition, parallel construction, and elaborate alliteration. These early attempts reveal Smart's interest in the balance and sounds of words. Later, in the *Jubilate* and the *Song,* Smart refines these devices. The second sentence of the poem exemplifies this:

> 'Tis thy terrific voice, thou God of power,
> 'Tis thy terrific voice; all Nature hears it
> Awaken'd and alarm'd; she feels its force,
> In every spring she feels it, every wheel,
> And every movement of her vast machine.

The first two lines contain repetition; in addition there is alliteration in "thou" and "power". There is also assonance in the third line, rather obviously in "Awaken'd and alarm'd", and less so in "hears" and "feels". The next two lines contain repetition through the words "feels" and "every".

The final poem contains more examples of Smart's devices. *On the Goodness of the Supreme Being* relates all the terrestrial elements which join in a praise of God. The poem opens with an invocation to David, or Orpheus, to inspire Smart in his earthly praise of God.

> ORPHEUS, for so the Gentiles call'd thy name,
> Israel's sweet psalmist, who alone could wake
> Th'inanimate to motion; who alone
> The joyful hillocks, the applauding rocks,
> And floods with musical persuasion drew;
> Thou, who to hail and snow gav'st voice and
>   sound,
> And mad'st the mute melodious!—greater yet
> Was thy divinest skill, and rul'd o'er more
> Than art or nature; for thy tuneful touch
> Drove trembling Satan from the heart of Saul,
> And quell'd the evil Angel:—in this breast
> Some portion of thy genuine spirit breathe,
> And lift me from myself; each thought impure
> Banish; each low idea raise, refine,
> Enlarge, and sanctify;—so shall the muse
> Above the stars aspire, and aim to praise
> Her God on earth, as he is prais'd in heaven.

The passage anticipates the *Song* in many ways. First, the use of David as the Orpheus symbol is characteristic of Smart's later impression of the Hebrew psalmist. It is David who identifies God in all that the earth contains and who is able to create a magnificent hymn of praise through all of nature. . . . In the *Song* Smart identifies David as the link between the Hebraic and the Christian religion, so that Christianity is the heir to all that the Old Testament contains. It is only later that Smart evolves his particular concept that the Old Testament should be used by the church and therefore should be Christianized. His vehicle for Christianization is David. In the Seaton poem, however, David is invoked only for his great power of praise.

The passage also contains a description of David's power when he cured Saul. The three lines are used in the *Song* in stanza twenty seven:

Blest was the tenderness he felt
When to his graceful harp he knelt,
    And did for audience call;
When satan with his hand he quell'd,
And in serene suspense he held
    The frantic throes of Saul.

The last line of the passage in the Seaton poem illustrates Smart's use of parallelism and also his ability to echo other prayers. The line seems to convey the sacred spirit of the Lord's Prayer as it expresses Smart's wish to praise God on earth as he is praised in Heaven.

The poem contains Smart's favorite structural device, the catalogue. After the introductory verse paragraph, the poem becomes a series of catalogues, all of which are found in the second paragraph which concludes the poem. All the items in the catalogue are terrestrial, and Smart calls upon them, identifies them, and joins them in praise of God, as did David or Orpheus.

Within the long catalogue familiar images appear:

Without the aid of yonder golden globe
Lost were the garnet's lustre, lost the lilly,
The tulip and auricula's spotted pride;
Lost were the peacock's plumage, to the sight
So pleasing in its pomp and glossy glow.

The garnet had appeared in the fourth Seaton poem in a similar catalogue. The pride of the flowers and the beauty of the peacock appear later in the sixty-second stanza of the *Song*:

The pheasant shows his pompous neck;
And ermine, jealous of a speck,
    With fear eludes offence:
The sable, with his glossy pride,
For ADORATION is descried,
    Where frosts the wave condense.

The ideas are similar, and the language is comparable. . . .

The poem also contains some of the poetic devices which Smart later applied to his *Song*. There is heavy alliteration, repetition and parallelism. In the course of his catalogue, Smart says:

He hears and feeds their feather'd families,
He feeds his sweet musicians,—nor neglects
Th' invoking ravens in the greenwood wide;
And though their throats coarse ruttling hurt the ear,
They mean it all for music, thanks and praise
They mean, and leave ingratitude to man,—

The first line of the passage contains the obvious alliteration of "f's" with "feeds", "feather'd" and "families". There is also assonance with the vowel sounds: "hears", "feeds", "he", "families" and "sweet". There is repetition in the first two lines and also in the last two with the word "feeds". There is a trace of the Horatian use of unusual

words in Smart's noun "ruttling", which is a late Medieval word for "throaty noise". . . .

The last few lines of the poem are declamatory. They are comparable to the last lines of the third prize poem and to the last section of the *Song*.

O all-sufficient, all beneficent,
Thou God of goodness and of glory, hear!
Thou, who to lowliest minds dost condescend,
Assuming passions to enforce thy laws,
Adopting jealousy to prove thy love;
Thou, who resign'd humility uphold,
Ev'n as the florist props the drooping rose;
But quell tyrannic pride with peerless pow'r
Ev'n as the tempest rives the stubborn oak,
O all-sufficient, all-beneficent,
Thou God of goodness and of glory, hear!
Bless all mankind, and bring them in the end
To Heav'n, to immortality, and THEE!

Smart uses the device of repetition to evoke a declamatory and triumphant tone. The first two lines of the prayer are repeated exactly toward the end of the poem. Within the prayer are numerous repetitions of words and phrases: "Thou" and "Ev'n" are used as the first words of various lines. Parallel statements appear which also seem to elevate the pitch of the poem:

Assuming passions to enforce thy laws,
Adopting jealousy to prove thy love:

The statements are parallel grammatically, and at the same time appear to be paradoxes. It is a good conclusion; it does possess more spirit and more complex technique than the other Seaton poems.

The Seaton poems are early efforts. At times they are dull, partly because of the Miltonics and partly because of the form itself. At their best, they are good examples of eighteenth century poetry. At their best, also, they are anticipations of Smart's better work. His use and perfecting of the catalogue increase the interest of the poems. His experimentation with alliteration, repetition, and parallelism reveals the early attempts of a young poet. In substance the poems are fascinating because they reveal the early focus of Smart's religious feelings; even then he was beset with the idea of praise, gratitude and adoration. They had not yet been crystallized into a working religious philosophy, but they were describing a function which Smart felt was necessary in man's relationship with God.

The poems were successful during their own age. Today they are not. There is little desire for early youthful experiments, especially if they are laden with Miltonics. However, these poems do possess some merit as poetry. It is doubtful that they will ever reach a larger audience than they already have. The ideas are better stated in the *Song*. These poems are of interest because they reveal a development of Smart as a poet. They serve to disprove the fanciful Victorian notion that Smart metamorphosed into a religious poet; and they also disprove the eighteenth-century idea that Smart dissipated his genius while confined.

In the last year of his Seatonian successes, 1756, Smart wrote another religious poem, *Hymn to the Supreme Being: On Recovery from a Dangerous Fit of Illness.* . . .

The poem is the product of an ill man. Yet, it does possess some interesting elements. It is the last poem which Smart wrote before he was confined. The form is lyrical, anticipating Smart's rejection of other forms of poetry. The basis of the poem is derived from the principles and ideas which Smart had stated in the Seaton poems; here, however, they are stated in personal terms. In the eighth stanza Smart describes his first reaction after he had survived this illness.

> But soul-rejoicing health again returns,
>   The blood meanders gentle in each vein,
> The lamp of life renew'd with vigour burns,
>   And exil'd reason takes her seat again—
> Brisk leaps the heart, the mind's at large once
>   more,
> To love, to praise, to bless, to wonder and adore.

This, of course, is an echo of the Seaton poems. . . .

The poem contains the usual poetic devices, but they are not illuminating since they do not possess the complexity which is evident in some of the Seaton poems and in the *Song*. This *Hymn* is of interest because it is Smart's first application of the principles which he defined in the Seaton poems. The poem is a personal expression of gratitude and repentance.

As we have seen, the poetry which Smart wrote before his confinement anticipates his later work through its subject-matter and some of its devices. In the Seaton poems Smart developed his use of the catalogue; he defined his attitude toward God and life; and he struggled with alliteration and sound in order to create a kind of music in his praise of God. In the *Hymn* he had already turned to a more lyrical expression of his theme. The handicap of blank-verse, with its Miltonics, an unfortunate characteristic of the Seaton poems, was erased by the lyric from of the *Hymn*. Despite the change in form, the *Hymn* was not a successful poem because it was based upon a hasty compilation of some of the ideas and techniques of the Seaton poems and thus it became an inartistic expression of joy. Yet, with the *Hymn,* Smart was able to subjectify the essence of his theme, that not only was man to praise God with all of nature but also that he was to find joy in living by doing so. Smart's philosophy, or religion, is optimistic, and most appropriately expressed through the lyric form. . . .

Although they were early ventures, the five [Seaton] poems display techniques and ideas which became characteristic of his later work. Despite the unwieldy Miltonics, the poems are good examples of eighteenth-century religious poetry. In each, Smart employed the catalogue, a device which he later perfected in the *Song*. The catalogue enabled Smart to identify the general or ideal elements and beings of the cosmos and to either compare them with God or to attribute to God their existence. Nothing is so wonderful, powerful, as God, since He is the creator of all and therefore greater than all. Eventually, Smart arrived at the idea that all of God's creations not only reflected Him but also praised and adored Him through their very existence.

The same ideas, of course, appear in all of Smart's work, but the techniques were gradually polished. Through his work on the Psalms, Smart turned to the lyric for his poetic mode. In them he found the perfect vehicle for the theme of praise which he had developed. David, or Orpheus, was the man who, like Smart, saw the essential unity of God's creations. David was also the link between the Mosaic and Christian tradition. Finally he was God's finest musician. All of these elements converged and became the core of the *Song*. In addition, the *Psalms* became a kind of poetic exercise for Smart. He utilized the proper lyric forms and created within these forms a variety of poetry.

There is little doubt that Smart conformed to the poetics of his age, not because they were forced upon him but because he found that they were useful to him. He was able to create within their limitations with assurance and facility. It is only in the *Jubilate* that we find a deviation, but this is only in the form. The antiphonal structure of the poem is unique to Smart's age, but, of course, it is traditional to the Church. Smart returned to the lyric form, specifically, one which was popular in mid-eighteenth-century England. In the *Song,* Smart presented the techniques and philosophy which he had been developing for many years. None of it is startling technically or philosophically; the devices and theories were commonplace. It was their execution which was unusual. The complexity and brilliance of the poem is undeniable. At the same time one cannot deny the heritage of the poem, i.e., the will and beliefs of the author. . . .

Because of his confinement, Smart was rejected by one age and later honored by another. In both cases, the critics and readers refused to acknowledge that Smart was a poet who abided by the traditions of his age and created for that age. He cannot be considered a mystic like Blake, who in a kind of madness withdrew from the world. Nor can be considered a pre-Romantic merely because he was confined and considered an enthusiast. He was, and should be considered as, one of literature's few great religious lyricists, and perhaps the eighteenth century's only evidence that fine lyric poetry could be written and still conform to the conventions of its day.

Edward L. Hart (essay date 1967)

SOURCE: "Christopher Smart Must Slay the Dragon (A Note on Smart's Satire)," in *Literature and Psychology,* Vol. XVII, Nos. 2–3, 1967, pp. 115–19.

[In this essay, Hart demonstrates how the satire in Smart's work reveals a fear of cuckoldry and sexual impotence.]

A good deal of satire appears throughout the works of Christopher Smart, and the writers on Smart have taken adequate notice of how he is related in his own times to Butler, Dryden, Pope, Gay, and others in the general way satire functioned in the eighteenth century. My purpose here is to leave these areas of general concern and attempt to show how satire functioned personally for Smart in his statement of hopes for himself in life and how, as hope died, he used satire to condition himself to the acceptance of failure.

"The writer of comedy," wrote Mr. James Sutherland in the first chapter of *English Satire,* "accepts the natural and acquired folly and extravagence and impudence which a bountiful world provides for his enjoyment. It is, on the contrary, the mark of the satirist that he cannot accept and refuses to tolerate. Confronted with the same human short-comings as the writer of comedy . . . he is driven to protest." I shall follow this nice distinction of Sutherland in my use of the word *satire;* however, I point out in advance that in establishing the normal pattern of Smart's inclinations, I occasionally refer to passages that are not satiric, especially in the paragraphs that immediately fol-low.

That Smart had the normal desires and attitudes toward sexual fulfillment is easy enough to demonstrate from his work, and a demonstration of any contrary pattern would, I believe, be impossible. The ideal state of a meaningful and mutually rewarding pairing of the sexes is evident in his works from the earliest to the latest. He admires and is strongly attracted by female sexuality. Even in his early poem **"To Ethelinda,"** written at the age of thirteen, though we may take that age with a grain of salt since it might have been revised at an older age, there is attraction for him toward womanly charms. He has given some verses to Ethelinda, who has carried them in her bosom. The poem ends:

> That breast was ne'er designed by fate
> For verse, or things inanimate;
> Then throw them from that downy bed,
> And take the poet in their stead.

The breast was a particularly attractive part of the female anatomy to Smart. **"The Pretty Bar-Keeper of the Mi-tre"** may have been "not unravish'd," "wanton," and giv-en to the "forc'd blush," but the fact that "No handker-chief her bosom hid" makes her so attractive that even her moles become decorative in a passage that illustrates Mr. Norman Callan's comment [in ***The Collected Poems of Christopher Smart,*** 1949] that Smart had a "stereoscopic vision which makes the object leap to the eye": "Her heaving breasts with moles o'spread, / Markt, little hemi-spheres, with stars." Even Imagination, in the poem **"Rea-son and Imagination,"** is personified with a "swelling breast." The adjectives *heaving* and *swelling* do not con-note a passive admiration; and the activity connoted com-plements that found as fulfillment in many other places in

Smart, such, for example, as at the ends of the two com-panion poems **"A Noon-Piece"** and **"A Night-Piece"**; and this is so even though the biographer Devlin dismisses the endings by saying that they "tail off into improprieties which are neither here nor there" [Christopher Devlin, *Poor Kit Smart,* 1961]. What can one say to this, except to say that they are indeed here as well as there. **"A Noon-Piece"** ends:

> Lend, lend thine hand—O let me view
> Thy parting breasts, sweet avenue!
> Then—then thy lips, the coral cell
> Where all th' ambrosial kisses dwell!
> Thus we'll each sultry noon employ
> In day-dreams of ecstactic joy.

The young man in **"A Night-Piece,"** after he had "rapp'd at fair Elenor's door," "laid aside Virtue that night." For a member of either sex to be alone is, to Smart, unnatural, and in **"The Widow's Resolution,"** even though Sylvia has resigned herself to joyless widowhood at the begin-ning, by the end she learns that:

> Nature a disguise may borrow,
>   Yet this maxim true will prove,
> Spite of pride, and spite of sorrow
>   She that has an heart must love.

Smart's sensitivity to all things, human and non-human, was such that he wished for cows and bulls that same happy conclusion to love that should be accorded to man. Significantly, this excerpt is from the ***Jubilate Agno,*** in-dicating that his ideal relationship of the sexes lasted as an ideal into his later life. "Let Ephah rejoice with Bu-prestis," he wrote, "the Lord endue us with temperance & humanity, till every cow have her mate!" [Fragment B1, Line 15]. Lest anyone contend that at this stage in his life Smart thought the relationship of a cow and her mate was one thing and that of a human with his mate another, let me quickly add another line from ***Jubilate Agno***: "For they have separated [sic] me and my bosom, whereas the right comes by setting us together" (B1. 59). Though Smart may have assented consciously to separation, it is quite clear that there was an unconscious dissent.

The enforced separation of Smart and Anna-Maria, occa-sioned by Smart's confinement and Anna-Maria's remov-al to Ireland, is perhaps the best point at which to intro-duce the reversal in satire of the ideal culmination just presented. I have developed this positive side of Smart's values to the extent I have in order that their existence may be accepted and may give added sharpness to the satirical, negative side I present now.

If satire began in the phallic chorus as an exorcism of the evil of barrenness in order that fruitfulness might be as-sured, then some associations from its origin still cling to the satire of Smart. A fear of impotence may, I assume, make itself manifest by an attack in satirical terms upon that which it fears. In the early poems of Smart, impo-tence occurs as a theme far too often to be ignored. And in these early poems, it is probably only a fear of impo-

Samuel Johnson on Smart's madness:

[Tuesday 24 May 1763]—I have preserved the following short minute of what passed this day.

'Madness frequently discovers itself merely by unnecessary deviation from the usual modes of the world. My poor friend Smart shewed the disturbance of his mind, by falling upon his knees, and saying his prayers in the street, or in any other unusual place. Now although, rationally speaking, it is greater madness not to pray at all, than to pray as Smart did, I am afraid there are so many who do not pray, that their understanding is not called in question.'

Concerning this unfortunate poet, Christopher Smart, who was confined in a mad-house, he had, at another time, the following conversation with Dr. Burney.—BURNEY. 'How does poor Smart do, Sir; is he likely to recover?' JOHNSON. 'It seems as if his mind had ceased to struggle with the disease; for he grows fat upon it.' BURNEY. 'Perhaps, Sir, that may be from want of exercise.' JOHNSON. 'No, Sir; he has partly as much exercise as he used to have, for he digs in the garden. Indeed, before his confinement, he used for exercise to walk to the alehouse; but he was *carried* back again. I did not think he ought to be shut up. His infirmities were not noxious to society. He insisted on people praying with him; and I'd as lief pray with Kit Smart as any one else. Another charge was, that he did not love clean linen; and I have no passion for it.'

Samuel Johnson, in Boswell's Life of Johnson, *Volume I, edited by George Birkbeck Hill, Clarendon Press, 1934.*

tence that is the motivation, and the evil is to be warded off by being made fun of, as in **"A Story of a Cock and a Bull"**:—

> The cows proclaim'd in mournful lowing,
> The Bull's deficiency in wooing,
> And to their disappointed master,
> All told the terrible disaster.

This theme occurs again in the fables. We find it, for example, in **"The English Bull Dog, Dutch Mastiff, and Quail,"** where, with regard to greyhounds from Italy, he says, "By them my dames ne'er proved big-bellied, / For they, poor toads, are Farrinellied." The negative, impotence, is counterbalanced in the fables by the assertion of potency in the patent phallicism of **"Where's the Poker?"** and **"The Country Squire and the Mandrake."**

The themes we are now pursuing also occur in the miscellaneous poems. In **"To Lyce"** the reader is reminded "That Love hot as fire must be burnt to a coal, / As the Broomstick concludes in an Ember." In this context, the broomstick is certainly a phallic symbol, and its burning is the satirical equivalent of reduction to impotence. A final example, and that perhaps the most convincing of all, occurs in **"The Distressed Damsel,"** who makes the most unkindest cut of all, derision of a man who cannot perform as a man:

> You Fops, I invoke not to list to my song,
> Who answer no end, and to no sex belong,
> You echoes of echoes, and shadows of shade—
> For if I had you—I might still be a maid.

The implications to the woman of remaining a maid are stated in **"The Judgment of Midas,"** where Scandal is personified as a "wither'd, time-deflower'd old maid, / That ne'er enjoy'd love's ever sacred flame."

I shall not be so rash as to make definite claims concerning Smart's later physical condition, though that temptation will surely be resisted only with difficulty by others. I, like Antony, am just a plain blunt man and only speak right on. And that which I speak right on about concerns two things in the *Jubilate Agno,* one, the accusation of his wife of making him a cuckold, and the other, a preoccupation with horns in another sense.

Both of these subjects produce in Smart's poetry some of the really bitter reactions that are so rare in him. He seems, aside from these, almost saintlike, "Franciscan," in his lack of vanity, in his devotion, and in his resignation. Something must have provoked him mightily to have wrenched bitterness from him, and that something could as easily have been the enforced separation from his wife as physical impotence. The results would be indistinguishable.

For one whose philosophy of life viewed relations between the sexes as a proper fulfillment, enforced chastity must have been a lonely and a bitter experience. I am certainly not arguing that Anna-Maria should have stuck with him even though Smart demonstrated consistently an inability or an unwillingness to support her and their children. All I am trying to do is get inside the mind of Smart to learn, if possible, why he should accuse her of being unfaithful to him. The answer may be, simply, that he was frustrated by the disparity between the ideal and the actual. And, paradoxically, the ideal in this case is a physical relationship and the actual is a bitterly accepted chastity. The frustration leads to anger, and the anger to the invention of falsehoods. Whatever transformation eventually may have taken place within Smart during his confinement, at the time he wrote line 46 and those immediately following the B1 fragment of *Jubilate Agno* he was very bitter, as in noted by Mr. W. H. Bond in the notes to his [1954] edition.

Many examples of the cuckoldry theme are cited by Mr. Bond, but one will suffice here by way of illustration: "Let Milcah rejoice with the Horned Beetle who will strike a man in the face." And opposite in the *For* response is this: "For they throw my horns in my face and reptiles make themselves wings against me" (B1. 115). The prophetic fear of sexual incompletion of his early days has come to pass in *Jubilate Agno.* And potency appears only as an ironic barb aimed at his head; for the potency belongs to the adversary, and, therefore, it now becomes necessary to oppose it. This, instead of the proposed solution that he is espousing chastity for its own sake, may be what Smart had in mind when he wrote "For CHRISTO-

PHER must slay the Dragon with a PHEON's head" (B1. 58). The serpent and the dragon, one provided with wings and the other with a barbed head, are both certainly symbols of a potency that has become a threat through ironic reversal. This rationalization permits impotence to be accepted. And the woman is blamed for the reversal, which would have to be the case regardless of the justice or injustice of the charges. She is to blame simply because she is not there.

Some of the sexual sense of *horn* remains in the use of it in the C fragment. "For the horn on the forehead is a tower upon an arch" (C. 138). It is true that this horn has some additional values assigned to it, but basically it is still a symbol of potency:

> For it is instrumental in subjecting the woman.
> For the insolence of the woman has increased ever
>   since Man has been crest-fallen.
> For they have turned the horn into scoff and
>   derision without ceasing.
>
> (C. 140–142)

It is difficult to imagine what words could have expressed more fully Smart's sense of the failure of his marriage and of the woman's part in that failure. The derisive laughter of a woman over a man's failure, mortally wounding his bright dreams of fulfillment, rings hollowly through the lines. From this point on in his life there can be no more hope in that direction; and from this point on religious exaltation, also a theme growing steadily from the beginning of his writing, must assume the whole burden of hope. The difference in their religions, the fact that his wife was of a different faith raising their two daughters in her own faith, makes even a spiritual union impossible between Smart and his wife.

Even at the end, however, in the beautifully simple and emotionally kiln-cured lines of the *Hymns for the Amusement of Children,* he is not completely without satire, though the satire is very delicate, forgiving in the same breath that it condemns the anticipated jailer who will wrench from him his meager daily allowance at the debtors' prison where he is to die: "And give the wages of the day / To him that hunts my soul." Still, the condemnation is there. To end where we began, with a reference to Sutherland's definition of satire, we may certainly say that Smart, despite the beautiful equanimity of his disposition, does not accept his own situation with detachment. He is, as Sutherland says of the true satirist, "driven to protest."

Geoffrey H. Hartman (essay date 1974)

SOURCE: "Christopher Smart's 'Magnificat': Toward a Theory of Representation," in *The Fate of Reading and Other Essays,* University of Chicago Press, 1975, pp. 74–98.

[*In the following essay, which was first published in 1974, Hartman addresses questions regarding the nature of* verbal representation which arise from Smart's elaborate word-play in *Jubilate Agno.*]

> What is the consummation of perfect freedom? Not to be ashamed of one's self.
>
> Nietzsche

> For when men get their horns again, they will delight to go uncovered.
>
> C. Smart

THEORY AS PROLOGUE

When we present one person to another, a feeling of formality persists. It may be a residual awe, relating to exceptional presentations (of the child to elders in early or ritual circumstances) or it may be a more general sense of the distance between persons. The latter feeling would still have a psychological component, for the distance between persons is like that between self and other.

What if someone cannot be presented? The sense of distance has been thrown out of balance: either the self feels defective vis-a-vis the other, or the other appears magnified, unapproachable. The someone can be a something: certain subjects may not be introduced into discourse, certain taboos restrict or delimit the kinds of words used.

I introduce the example of words early, because words commonly help to present us. Should we feel that words are defective, or else that we are defective vis-a-vis them (words becoming the other, as is not unusual in poets who have a magnified regard for a great precursor or tradition), then a complex psychic situation arises. It is fair to assume, however, that the distance between self and other is always disturbed, or being disturbed; that there is always some difficulty of self-presentation in us; and that, therefore, we are obliged to fall back on a form of "representation."

Representation implies that the subject cannot be adequately "present" in his own person or substance, so that advocacy is called for. The reason for this "absence," compensated for by "representation," can be various. In legal or ritual matters, the subject may not be of age or not competent. But even when he is competent, of age, fully presentable, situations arise which produce a fiction of his having to be "seconded": in presentation at court (and sometimes in courts of law) he does not appear by himself but needs the support of someone already admitted into the superior presence.

The self does not, of course, disappear into its representative, for then the means would defeat the end, which remains self-presentation. Even in visionary poetry, which so clearly sublimes the self into the other, or exalts the other into quasi-supernatural otherness, the self persists in selfhood. Though Charles Lamb is right in remarking that Coleridge's "Ancient Mariner" "undergoes such trials as overwhelm and bury all individuality or memory of what he was—like the state of a man in a bad dream, one terrible peculiarity of which is that all consciousness of personality is gone," the spectral happenings in the poem actually doom the Mariner to survival. He is unable to die, or find release from his experience except in the "punctual agony" of storytelling.

Whether or not this doom of deathlessness is preferable to nothingness—"Who would lose," says Milton's "Belial," "Though full of pain, this intellectual being, / Those thoughts that wander through Eternity, / To perish rather, swallow'd up and lost / In the wide womb of uncreated night . . ."—the self can never be so sublimated, or so objectified, that only its representative is left. Even granted that self desires an absolute escape from self, what would be satisfied by that escape: indeed would anything of self be left to register the satisfaction? To urge questions of this kind is to approach psychoanalysis, but at the same time to link it with speculations on the sublime going back at least to Edmund Burke. These speculations ponder the vertiginous relation between self-loss and self-aggrandizement.

Let me return briefly to Coleridge's poem. Why does the Mariner kill the albatross? A fascinating question; but even the simplest answer, that it was willfulness, implies a drive on the Mariner's part for self-presence. The killing is a shadow of the Mariner's own casting. What follows his self-determining, self-inaugural act is, paradoxically, the presence of otherness. In seeking to "emerge," the self experiences separation anxieties, and these express themselves in motions akin to the defense mechanism of "beautiful indifference" (noted by Charcot in patients suffering from hysteria) as well as to the terror which may accompany isolation.

At the same time, there is a movement toward atonement (at-one-ment, reconciliation) in Coleridge's poem. "Representation" cannot be divorced from advocacy. You justify either the self or that which stands greatly against it: perhaps both at once. The situation could be likened to a trial, though not to one resulting in a definite verdict. The trouble with this line of inquiry is that too many metaphors come into play until one begins to move within art's own richness of thematic variation. Yet such metaphors as trial, court, theater, debut and so on, converge on the idea of a place of heightened demand and intensified consciousness. "The daemon," says Yeats, ". . . brings man again and again to the place of choice, heightening temptation that the choice may be as final as possible . . ." Let us consider the nature of this "place," imagined or real.

When Christopher Smart writes in *Jubilate Agno,* "For I pray the Lord Jesus to translate my MAGNIFICAT into verse and represent it," the pun (magnifi-cat) alluding to the "magnification" of the cat Jeoffery and of the animal kingdom generally, corroborates what Freud says about wit both submitting to and escaping the censor. To compare a hymn (the Magnificat) associated with the Virgin Mary to the gambols of Jeoffrey is blasphemous—except that the pun remains unexplicit and the poet, in any case, "gives the glory" to God by asking Christ to make his verses acceptable. Yet the anxiety, I believe, or the pressure resulting in this kind of wit, goes deeper. It is not one out-

rageously smart comparison which is at stake, but the legitimacy of artistic representation as a whole. The magnifi-cat theme expresses, in its marvelous mixture of humility and daring, the artist's sense that he is disturbing the "holy Sabbath" of creation by his recreation; that he is trespassing on sacred property or stealing an image of it or even exalting himself as a maker—in short, that he is magnifying mankind instead of "giving the glory" to God. Smart therefore atones the exposed, self-conscious self by "at-one-ing" it with the creature. He shows mankind "presenting" before God the animal creation it has exploited. And, in return, he asks that his verse-representation be "represented" before God by a mediator who enters the first line of his poem as "Lord, and Lamb." The opening of *Jubilate Agno* sets the pattern by compounding man and animal into ritual pairs:

> Let man and beast appear before him, and magnify his name together.
> Let Noah and his company approach the throne of Grace, and do homage to the Ark of their Salvation.
> Let Abraham present a Ram, and worship the God of his Redemption.
> Let Isaac, the Bridegroom, kneel with his Camels, and bless the hope of his pilgrimage.
>   (Fragment A, Lines 3–6)

Inspired by *Revelations,* Smart begins with a judgment scene: it envisages an ark that might survive a second flood. We find ourselves in a place of demand where everything must be "presented." The precise nature of the demand is not absolutely clear, and need not be the same in all works of art: perhaps it varies with historical circumstances, and perhaps it is the interpreter's task to make the relation between demand and response (demand and inner capability) perfectly clear. But artistic representation does seem to mediate a demand of this kind: one, moreover, not to be thought of as coming from outside, but rather, or also, from within. Again, whether "within" means the unconscious, or refers to a self-realizing instinct, may not be possible to determine generally but only in each case.

There is no way of being precise about this without engaging in considered acts of textual interpretation. We have to identify the nature of the challenge met by Smart and the "place" or "situation" he is in. It would be inadequate, for instance, to say of his "representation" of the animal creation that it springs from the same anxiety for the survival of the physical species that, according to Gertrude Levy's *The Gate of Horn* (1948), inspired the Cro-Magnon cave paintings at Lascaux. They may have had an apotropaic function, for they gather the essential traits of the hunted species into totemic sketches that intend to placate the Spirit of the hunted creature and so assure its fertile continuance. The creature is graphically "represented" by man to a Spirit in order for both human kind and the creature to survive.

Such recreative or reparative magic *is* relevant to Smart's poem; the analogy is too strong, and the theme of generation haunts too many of his verses. Yet it is only a beginning to specific interpretation. For we must add that in Smart the very *medium* of representation—visionary language itself—has become questionable, or subject to a demand which it cannot meet except by being renewed. His recreation of visionary categories is literally a re-creation: the source of vision is not exhausted but still operative through him. That, at least, is the claim he seems to make, or the test he puts himself to. The anxiety for survival has associated itself with an anxiety for language-source, liturgy, and the entire process of representation.

ENTHUSIASM AND ENTROPY

The fear that visionary language has lost its effectiveness may not be very different from the fear that nature grows old. Such "depletion anxieties" are linked to the not unrational feeling in us that our appetites—including that for presence—put a demand on the order of things which that order may not be able to satisfy; which, indeed, it may resent and reject. The "economy" of language use arising from depletion anxiety ranges from such devices of conservation as double-entendre, hermeticism, and classical restraint, to the complementary if opposite ones of revivalist forgery, radical innovation, and homeopathic promiscuity. You can write as sparse a hymn as Addison's famous "The spatious firmament on high" (1712), which, in spite of its source in Psalm 19, reflects Pascal's fright at the silence of the starry spaces; or you can fill the vacuum with the "clang expressions" of *Jubilate Agno,* till "barrenness becomes a thousand things" (Wallace Stevens).

Smart's aberrant verses would have been classified in their time as a product of "enthusiasm"; and this widespread and loosely knit religious movement was also a kind of counter-entropy. Affecting principally Puritans and Dissenters, it claimed to have uncovered a new source of truth, that of the individual in his privacy, who would know from "internal" grounds what revelation there was; but if that was all there was, then we were abandoned to individuality, and prone to the hell of unrelieved, sterile selfhood. The blessing proved to be the curse; the precious was also the accused object. "My selfhood, Satan, arm'd in Gold" (Blake). The danger in enthusiasm, moreover, was its inevitable closeness to fanaticism, for the enthusiast found it difficult not to impose his "internal" evidences on others, not to exhibit his "antitheatrical" truth. He sought out or compelled a like-minded community.

Enthusiasm in literature took many forms: it attacked, for example, the scientific "Religion of Nature" which affirmed the stability of the cosmos (nature would *not* grow old) at the cost of dehumanizing it and "untenanting Creation of its God" (Coleridge); and it overrode the pessimism of the neoclassic artist who felt he had come too late in history. The visionary or even the poet was felt to be superfluous in an Age of Reason; but the wish for originality, which enthusiasm abetted, increased in direct proportion to one's distance from the possibility. Yet the dilemma, even for the enthusiasts, was that originality and Original Sin were hard to tell apart.

Smart had to find, therefore, not only a well of visionary English but also an undefiled well. Every attempt to replenish, or imitate directly, the great source-books of secular and religious culture was open to the charge of false testimony—of giving glory to God as a cover for "representing" one's own passions. Today we have no problem with the first person singular, and fiction is inconceivable without a semblance of self-exposure. Enthusiasm in art has gone public and taken the name of confessionalism. Consequently, it is hard for us to appreciate Pascal's notorious maxim, "Le moi est haïssable," and the fact that he was so sensitive to the liaison between egotism and enthusiasm that he condemned even Montaigne:

> The stupid plan he has to depict himself, and this not incidentally and against his better judgment as it may happen to all us mortals, but by design and as a matter of principle. For to say foolish things by chance or weakness is an ordinary fault; but to say them intentionally, that is not tolerable, and moreover his kind of stuff. [*L'Apologie de la religion chrétienne*]

Yet Pascal is protesting too much, for the lines of confession (his *Mémorial*) found hemmed in his garments at his death showed how close he was to what his time, and the next century, castigated as enthusiasm:

> The year of grace 1654. Monday 23rd November. Feast of St. Clement, Pope and Martyr, and of others in the martyrology. Eve of Chrysogonous. Martyr and others. From about half past 10 in the evening until half past midnight. Fire. God of Abraham, God of Isaac, God of Jacob, not of philosophers and scholars. Certainty, certainty, heart-felt, joy, peace. God of Jesus Christ. God of Jesus Christ. *My God and your God.* Thy God shall be my God. The world forgotten and everything except God . . . Joy, joy, joy, tears of joy.
>
> [*Penseés*]

Apocalyptic visions, trances, egomania, or what Dr. Johnson was to call, memorably, the "hunger" and "dangerous prevalence" of imagination, were the diseases of enthusiasm against which Pascal and others erected their ideal of the "honnête homme," with his good sense, moderation, reasonable language. England, after the Puritan Revolution, imported this neoclassical ideal of correcting and improving not only the understanding but also speech itself, since an erroneous or corrupt language encourages intellectual and religious error. Swift's *Proposal for Correcting, Improving and Ascertaining the English Tongue* (1712) denounced the "Enthusiastick Jargon" of "Fanatick Times" (the Puritan Revolution and its epigones); and as Professor Wimsatt has noted in a remarkable essay on the "laughter" of the Augustans ["The Augustan Mode in English Poetry," in *Hateful Contraries,* 1966], behind all these calls for decorum there lurked a heightened sense of unreality, which was not dissimilar, perhaps, to experiences of spiritual vastation. The nearness of *flatus* and *afflatus,* of wind and inspiration, the manic-depressive cycle which all these doctors were seeking to cure, kept reasserting itself in epidemics of wit and farfetched conceits, in the incurable prevalence of the mock-heroic mode, in the hysterical style of the sublime ode, and the laughing, biting speech that joins Swift to a late Augustan poet called William Blake.

The wars of religion against enthusiasm are an old story. But why should so irreligious a poet as Keats complain of Wordsworth's *egotistical sublime?* Why is he so defensive with Moneta, denouncing to her "all mock lyrists, large self-worshipers, / And careless Hectorers in proud bad verse" (*The Fall of Hyperion,* I, 207–8)? The reason is that he could not give up the sublime. He feared that poetry without enthusiasm was no longer poetry; and he was all the more sensitive to the charge of self-inflation because he knew that to create a sublime mode not based on personal experience was to revert to a vacuous archaism, to that impersonation of impersonality which MacPherson and Chatterton succumbed to. The sublime had to be associated with personal experience: there was no other way. Something drives fiction to that recognition in the two hundred years which comprise *Paradise Lost,* the neoclassical reaction, the emergence of Romanticism, and that renewed valediction to the sublime which fails so gloriously in Browning's "Childe Roland" and Tennyson's "Morte D'Artur."

Let me add, before returning to Smart, that Freud also treats enthusiasm. He is our latest "doctor of the sublime," the twentieth century facing the gods or the pathology of ecstasy. A modern analytics of the sublime must begin with Boileau's remarks on Longinus, study Vico on the way to Burke, Kant, and Schopenhauer, and then admit that Freud is the inheritor of all these in his canny knowledge of the fortress against enthusiasm which polite society, or the soul itself, builds in the soul. Defense mechanisms cannot blossom when there is nothing—no fire or flood—to defend against.

Smart's poetic career is emblematic of the fate of enthusiasm. It divides neatly into two parts. Before 1756 he was "the ingenious Mr. Smart," a facile and brilliant practitioner of neoclassic modes of verse. But recovering from a serious fever he began "confessing God openly" by praying aloud whenever the impulse came. "I blessed God in St James's Park till I routed all the company" (B 1, 89). He was confined for insanity in 1757–58 and again from 1759–63. During his "illness" he produced two long poems as daring and personal as any the Romantics were to write. The *Song to David* (1763) was dismissed in its time as a "fine piece of ruins," while the *Jubilate Agno* was not published till 1939. Smart's contemporaries saw him as an excellent versifier misled by religious mania, and though he reverted to such modest tasks as translating Horace and composing hymns for children, he never reestablished himself in their eyes.

What is one to do, even today, with verses like "Let Lapidoth with Percnos the Lord is the builder of the wall of CHINA—REJOICE" (B 1, 97)? The marvelous thing here is not, despite appearances, "Enthusiasm, Spiritual Operations, and pretences to the Gifts of the Spirit, with the whole train of New Lights, Raptures, Experiences, and the like" [Samuel Taylor Coleridge, *Aids to Reflection*]. It is

the poet's total, consistent, critical rather than crazy, attack on the attenuated religious language of his day. "Percnos" is a bird of prey, like the Persian "Roc," punningly associated with the "Rock of Israel" in a previous line (B 1, 94), while "Lapidoth" (Judges 4:4) is linked to "Percnos-Roc" by an etymological pun which gives the Hebrew name a Latin root that means "stone" (*lapis, lapidis*). Add the "Wall of China" as the greatest stonework in the world, and the line as a whole is seen to "give the glory to the Lord." It says, in effect, "Let Rock with Rock, the Lord is the Rock of Rocks, rejoice."

"In this plenty," to quote Stevens once more, "the poem makes meanings of the rock." Visionary language knows itself as superfluous, redundant; yet its very breaking against the rock reveals a more than gratuitous splendor. The disparity between the sustained base (the unvarying ROCK or REJOICE) and Smart's ever-shifting, eclectic play of fancy, discloses a twofold problem of representation: the traditional one of ineffability, related to the belief that God is "dark with excessive bright," or not attainable through mortal speech; and the somewhat rarer view, that the fault lies with language, which has lost yet may regain its representational power. To the crisis which stresses the inattainability of the signified, Smart adds the impressively impotent splendor of the signifier.

This is too cold a description, however, of the agony of the signifier. The question is less whether language can represent than whether by doing so it seconds or comforts the creature. Representation, I have argued, contains the idea of advocacy; and in Christian theology it is Christ who preeminently acts as comforter and advocate. To rejoice in the "Lord, and the Lamb" is to rejoice in the hope that the Judge (Lord) will turn out to be the Comforter (Lamb).

Yet the premise of that comfort, hidden away for the most part in the "Songs of Innocence" of Smart's time—in children's poetry or catechistical emblem books—was that the creation (*res creatae,* Romans 1:20 and 8:19) would help the tormented or doubting spirit to be instructed. By a proliferation of types, emblems, analogies, and the like, the Christian was encouraged to "suck Divinity from the flowers of Nature," in Sir Thomas Browne's words. As long as instruction could be drawn from flower or beast, then "Man and Earth suffer together" (C, 155) while waiting to be redeemed. Smart's poetry serves to strengthen their bond, even if it is one of suffering. But in doing so, in seeking to "represent" the creature, the poet discovers that language too is a creature in need of reparation.

For Smart's animated diction is the other side of his feeling for the lost animal spirits of a language "amerced" of its "horn" (C, 118–62). His poem, therefore, blends theriomorphic and theomorphic as the animals named by Adam in the first act of divinely instituted speech are now named again, restitutively. Language is the rib taken from Adam's tongue to "helpmate" his solitude before Eve. And it is interesting that in *Jubilate Agno* Eve does not formally appear. Even Mary's "Magnificat," when mentioned in B 1, 43, exalts not the woman and mother but rather language in its creature-naming and creature-presenting function. So close is the bondage of language and the bondage of the creature that both are one for a poet who is their male comforter, their *logos*. His Magnificat consoles what originally was to console Adam, by "translating" and "representing" it.

CAT AND BAT

By magnifying Jeoffry, Smart is training the telescope of wit on an ordinary creature instead of on the heavens or a certifiably divine subject. The meditation on the creature (that is, on anything created, which included the heavens) was not uncommon; and a contemporary of Smart's, James Hervey, Methodist Rector of Weston-Favell, had popularized the genre by his *Meditations Among the Tombs* and *Contemplations of the Starry Heavens* (1746–47). Hervey provides his readers with a flattering humiliation of the spirit, a Urizenic (so Blake will call it) calculus of apparent human power and actual limitation. Hervey, in short, is second-rate Sir Thomas Browne and third-rate Book of Job. "I have often been charmed and awed," he writes,

at the sight of the nocturnal Heavens; even before I knew how to consider them in their proper circumstances of majesty and beauty. Something like magic, has struck my mind, on a transient and unthinking survey of the aethereal vault, tinged throughout with the purest azure, and decorated with innumerable starry lamps. I have felt, I know not what powerful and aggrandizing impulse; which seemed to snatch me from the low entanglements of vanity, and prompted an ardent sigh for sublimer objects. Methought I heard, even from the silent spheres, a commanding call, to spurn the abject earth, and pant after unseen delights.—Henceforward, I hope to imbibe more copiously this moral emanation of the skies, when, in some such manner as the preceding, they are rationally seen, and the sight is duly improved. The stars, I trust, will teach me as well as shine; and help to dispel, both Nature's gloom, and my intellectual darkness. . . .

I gaze, I ponder. I ponder, I gaze; and think ineffable things.—I roll an eye of awe and admiration. Again and again I repeat my ravished views, and can never satiate my immense field, till even Fancy tires upon her wing. I find wonders ever new; wonders more and more amazing.—Yet, after all my present inquiries, what a mere nothing do I know; by all my future searches, how little shall I be able to learn, of those vastly distant suns, and their circling retinue of worlds! Could I pry with Newton's piercing sagacity, or launch into his extensive surveys; even then my apprehensions would be little better, than those dim and scanty images, which the mole, just emerged from her cavern, receives on her feeble optic. . . . To fathom the depths of the Divine Essence, or to scan universal Nature with a critical exactness, is an attempt which sets the acutest philosopher very nearly on a level with the ideot.

["Contemplations of the Starry Heavens"]

This is also the period of Robert Blair's *The Grave* (1743) and Edward Young's *Night Thoughts* (1742–45). Smart's

meditation on Jeoffry is surely a criticism of such effusions. It replaces their self-regarding, didactic gloom with real observation, empathy, and a spirit as playful as that of the creature portrayed. The cat is the style; and the style, as a sustained song of innocence, is totally unchary. It leaps; it is prankish; not only in its "mixture of gravity and waggery," as when Smart avers "For the Lord commanded Moses concerning the cats at the departure of the Children of Israel from Egypt," but also in its semblance of plot.

The opening of the passage shows Jeoffry at his "exercises." These ordinary gambols turn into a ritual calisthenics curiously like the "Spiritual Exercises" of Ignatius of Loyola. When the poet "considers" his cat, the word "considers," which seems to have the Latin root for "star" in it, is a technical term from the tradition of the Spiritual Exercises (Compare "I have often been charmed and awed at the sight of the nocturnal Heavens; even before I knew how to consider them in their proper circumstances," and so forth). Here the term is applied *à rebours* to an uncelestial object; yet Jeoffry *is* a solar creature, worshipping at "the first glance of the glory of God in the East" and counteracting the powers of darkness "by his electrical skin and glaring eyes." The poet's consideration of Jeoffry is reinforced when Jeoffry "begins to consider himself" (B 2, 703) "in ten degrees"—"degrees" are also a term common to the genre of the Spiritual Exercises. In the argument prefaced to Smart's *A Song to David,* stanzas 65–71 constitute "An exercise upon the senses, and how to subdue them. . . . [with] An amplification in five degrees."

It is not my intent to turn Jeoffry the cat into a Christian soldier marching with Loyola. What the poem conveys is a spreading *consideration* from which nothing will eventually be excluded: Smart opens the covenant so that every creature—"The cat does not appear in the Bible," W. F. Stead, Smart's editor, notes drily—or at least the *names* of all created things may enter. "Let the Levites of the Lord take the Beavers of ye Brook alive into the Ark of the Testimony" (A, 16): the Beavers do not appear in the Bible either, but here they enter alive into an Ark which could have proved as deadly as in Exodus 25:9.

At this moment in time the covenant is merely the rainbow language before us, revived by Smart. But perhaps language is the only covenant. Smart renews the responsive prayer of the psalms and of the liturgy as if to provide the Church with a Book of Common Prayer genuinely "common." More and more of creation enters the Ark of Testimony as not only the verses pair ("Let . . . For") but also different orders of creation; and it becomes vain to distinguish in Smart responsive poetry and resurrected wit. Both deal with strange conjunctions, hidden echoes, powerful yokings together, the "grappling of the words upon one another" (B 2, 632). This principle of "clapperclaw," with its residual sexuality, sometimes extends itself into the phonation of single verses, which then seem built, like "clapperclaw," itself, out of the competing responsiveness of mutual parts. "Let Ross, house of Ross rejoice with the Great Flabber Dabber Flat Clapping Fish with hands" (D, 11).

Imagine the House of Ahab rejoicing with Moby Dick . . . We hear the voice of the hands, in this applause; indeed the animal body itself grows to be all voice and enters the language. "For the power of some animal is predominant in every language" (B 2, 627), writes Smart; and he exemplifies this by an outrageous onomatopoeic punning. "For the pleasantry of a cat at pranks is in the language ten thousand times over. / For JACK UPON PRANCK is in the performance of *peri* together or seperate" (B 2, 630–31). (Read *purr* for *pr* or *per*.) This covenant-language is quite literally the Ark where man and animal pair in amity, and the "Cherub Cat is a term of the Angel Tiger" (B 2, 725).

All creatures in Smart become flaming creatures, and the Great Chain of Being a Great Chain of Language. To characterize Smart as a late or parodic meditationist is not adequate, therefore. It does not clarify the nature of the demand on him or the burden of his response. "Gird up thy loins now, like a man, I will demand of thee and answer thou me," God thunders at Job. And Job is finally persuaded to put his finger on his mouth. James Hervey, and other pseudo-enthusiast worshippers of the whirlwind, put their deflating finger of inflated moralistic prose on our months. They make us kiss the rod. But Smart is not put out by Newton, Nature, or Nature's God. He escapes the stupor induced by Natural Religion—by the contemplation of Leviathan, Tiger, or the System of the World. And he does so by answering its "cunning alphabet" with his own force of language. I will demand of thee and answer thou me, means for Smart, girding up the loins of language and meeting the challenge of a divine text. The Bible is less a proof text than a shame text; and to escape this shame which affects, preeminently, the tongue, he must become David again and restore the Chain of Inspiration. "Rejoice in God, O ye Tongues . . ." The Great Chain of Being is honored not on account of order and hierarchy but only as it continues to electrify the tongue and represent the creature. In Smart's "consideration" everything stars; and the elation, or jubilation, of speech seems to sustain a demand put on it by the Book of God or the "cunning alphabet" of the Book of Nature.

Yet Bethlehem is not far from Bedlam. The madhouses of Smart's time had more than one King David in them, not to mention King Solomons and Queens of Sheba. The pressure on Smart of the divine text or of the need to respond to it by the creation of a New Song, that is, by a language covenant embracing the creature which had fallen with and away from man, heaps this Christopher as thoroughly as Melville's white whale "heaped" Ahab. When we read Smart's boast, "I am the Reviver of Adoration amongst English Men," we do not feel the tension of a pun that mounts up in stanzas 50 and following of the ***Song to David***:

> Praise above all—for praise prevails,
> Heap up the measure, load the scales . . .

This is followed by twenty stanzas centering on the repeated word "adoration." The method is indeed accumulative, additive, rather than calculating and accounting.

Double the "d" in "adoration" and the pun becomes visible.

A "Song to David" means dedicated to, or spoken toward, David, but also *add*ing itself by *ad*oration until measure and scale break and the account is closed. Smart's ad libitum at once acknowledges and destroys the Johnsonian morality of style; the Doctor's reservation, for instance, that "Sublimity is by aggregation" yet that it is impossible to add to the divine glory:

> The ideas of Christian theology are too simple for eloquence, too sacred for fiction, and too majestick for ornament. To recommend them by tropes and figures is to magnify by a concave mirror the sidereal universe.

> Omnipotence cannot be exalted; infinity cannot be amplified; perfection cannot be improved.
> [*Lives of the English Poets*]

Smart might have enjoyed William Blake's joshing of Dr. Johnson in *An Island in the Moon*:

> I say this evening we'll all get drunk. I say dash, an Anthem, an Anthem, said Suction

> Lo the Bat with Leathern Wing
> Winking & blinking
> Winking & blinking
> Winking & blinking
> Like Doctor Johnson

I quote only the more decent part. Compare cat and bat.

A SPECKLED LANGUAGE

Our delight in Smart is not a constant thing. Even in controlled sequences, like that on Jeoffry, where the catalogue (no pun intended) is less chaotic than usual, the poet's exuberance may fall into a near-infantile strain:

> For he rolls upon prank to work it in.
> For having done duty and received blessing he
>   begins to consider himself.
> (B 1, 702–3)

"Having done duty" may refer to Jeoffry's sunrise worship, but it could also be a euphemism, especially when followed by a lengthy description of a cat cleaning itself.

> For first he looks upon his fore-paws to see if they
>   are clean.
> For secondly he kicks up behind to clear away
>   there.
> For thirdly he works it upon stretch with fore paws
>   extended.
> (B 2, 705–7)

As every child knows, cleanliness is next to godliness, and Jeoffry provides an emblematic and charming illustration. Yet since Smart seems more wary of mentioning excrement than of mentioning the devil (B 2, 720ff.), and

Jeoffrey's ritual exorcism of dirt is continuous with his "dutiful" worship of God, the thought may arise as to what is being euphemistically "pranked" or "worked in" at the higher level of godliness, benevolence, or jubilant verse-making.

One could try to find that "foundation on slander" (or "on the devil") which Smart mentions in B 1, 170. "The furnace itself shall come up at the last" (B 1, 293) he also writes, alluding to Abraham's fearful vision. Whether at the bottom of it all is a lie or evil or detritus, a redemptive poet like Smart has to extend his *contrafactum* to embrace even the excrementitious. The "soil" needed to fertilize the soil works on language too. Yet Smart's consciousness that when the deep opens, or the foundation rises up, it is the "Adversary" who may appear—indeed the shadow-thought, perhaps there from the beginning, that the tongues invoked in the very first line of the poem might be used for the opposite of glorification—for slander or blasphemy or accusation—could help explain the *Jubilate*'s ritual or litany-like character, that apotropaic iteration which limits an otherwise emancipated verse line. Smart's verses are, as he implies, a "conjecture" (B 1, 173), a "cast" of the line or tongue whose outcome is uncertain enough to be the object of a wager like that between God and the Accuser (Satan) in the Book of Job.

The nature of Smart's anxiety about "slander" may never be clear to us. It may not have been clear to himself. It is an anxiety about the foundation, about origins, about genealogy; and so about the truth issuing from his own tongue:

> Let Ziba rejoice with Glottis whose tongue is
>   wreathed in his throat.
> For I am the seed of the WELCH WOMAN and speak
>   the truth from my heart.
> Let Micah rejoice with the spotted Spider, who
>   counterfeits death to effect his purposes.
> For they lay wagers touching my life.—God be
>   gracious to the winners.
>
>   (B 1, 91–92)

Yet Smart's anxiety about "tongues" may have produced too good a poetic defense mechanism. It is not immediately obvious that the animals here are cited for *their* defense mechanisms. "Let Abiezer, the Anethothite, rejoice with Phrynos who is the scaled frog. For I am like a frog in the brambles, but the Lord hath put his whole armour upon me" (B 1, 95). Euphemism and benediction feed the perpetual motion machine of Smart's poetry. "Let" and "For," and such punnable morphemes as "cat" and "ble" (bull), are linguistic simples, easily combined into phrases and sentences. They support the poet's run-on, combinatory technique, his compulsion to perpetual benevolence.

This may turn, also, by a momentum of its own, into a cat-and-mouse game with language, to see how much life can be eked out before the spirit fails and an adversary consciousness, or melancholia, penetrates:

> For the power of some animal is predominant in
>   every language.
> For the power and spirit of a CAT is in the Greek.
> For the sound of a cat is in the most useful
>   preposition κατ᾽ εὐχήν
> For the pleasantry of a cat at pranks is in the
>   language ten thousand times over.
> For JACK UPON PRANCK is in the performance of
>   περί together or seperate.
> For Clapperclaw is in the grappling of the words
>   upon one another in all the modes of
>   versification.
> For the sleekness of a Cat is in his ἀγλαίηφι.
> For the Greek is thrown from heaven and falls upon
>   its feet.
> For the Greek when distracted from the line is
>   sooner restored to rank & rallied into some form
>   than any other.
> For the purring of a Cat is his own τρύζει.
> For his cry is in οὐαί which I am sorry for.
> For the Mouse (Mus) prevails in the Latin.
> For Edi-mus, bibi-mus, vivi-mus—ore-mus.
>   (B 2, 627–39)

In brief, the overdetermination of simples like "cat" or "mus" keeps us within a sphere of childlike instruction. Smart's poem, at these points, is not so much a renovated liturgy as a marvelously inflated hornbook: a spiritual grammar rock ("Conjunction Junction, What's your function?") which averts discontinuity or catastrophic thoughts. However serious the content, the form remains propaedeutic; however dangerous Smart's insight, the verse recovers into business ("benevolence") as usual.

Despite Smart's delightful and outrageous wordplay, then, his resourcefulness may be a testing of the source, and his witty, promiscuous conjunctions may point to the fear of being cut off, by his family, or eternally by Satanic accusation. How else are we to understand that long fragment which is but a variation of "Let X, house of X, rejoice with creature Y"?

> Let Westbrooke, house of Westbrooke rejoice with
>   the Quail of Bengal. God be gracious to the
>   people of Maidstone.
>
> Let Allcock, house of Allcock rejoice with The
>   King of the a strange fowl. I pray for the whole
>   University of Cambridge especially Jesus College
>   this blessed day.
>
> Let Audley, house of Audley rejoice with The
>   Green Crown Bird. The Lord help on with the
>   hymns.
>
> Let Bloom, house of Bloom rejoice with
>   Hecatompus a fish with an hundred feet.
>
> Let Beacon, house of Beacon rejoice with
>   Amadavad a fine bird in the East Indies.
>
> Let Blomer, house of Blomer rejoice with Halimus
>   a Shrub to hedge with. Lord have mercy upon
>   poor labourers this bitter frost Decr. 29 N.S.
>   1762.
>
>   (D, 197–202)

Here the themes of house, foundation, fertility and rejoicing are interlaced with cries for help and mercy. The contiguity of "Maidstone" and "Allcock" is a parallel puzzle. "Without contaries," Blake wrote, "no progression," but what is progressive here except a verse that somehow keeps renewing itself?

I want to explore further the "wreathed" way in which Smart builds his verse. Take his basic words "Let" and "For." Though they "generate" sentences, they are really a *stutterance*: a verbal compromise-formation which at once "lets" (hinders) and forwards his song ("Let Forward, house of Forward rejoice with Immussulus a kind of bird the Lord forward my translation of the psalms this year" D, 220). "Let" is close to being a primal word with antithetical meanings; and the tension between these meanings—whether identified as control and permissiveness or contraction and expansiveness or chastity and promiscuity—can give an extraordinary twist effect to the verse. Sometimes the contraries are almost too close to be spotted ("*Let For*-ward . . ."); sometimes they seem apposites rather than opposites because of their position in the paired pattern of the verse ("Let . . . For . . ."); and sometimes they form a crisscross pattern varying in distance (how far is it from "Maidstone" to "Allcock"?).

Smart has left us hints of a poetics of pairing, opposition and distancing:

> For the relations of words are in pairs first.
> For the relations of words are sometimes in
>   oppositions.
> For the relations of words are according to their
>   distances from the pair.
>
> (B 2, 600–602)

It could roughly summarize the actual unfolding of verse sentences in Smart: words are in pairs first, "Let Jubal rejoice with Caecilia"; this pairing may also introduce a contrast, "the woman and the slow-worm" (B 1, 43). The contrast may be more pathetic as when "Let Jorim rejoice with the Roach" is followed by "God bless my throat & keep me from things stranggled" (B 1, 179). The oppositions Smart mentions can also be that of the "Let" verse and the "For" response. Relations of distance, finally, are clearest in a group of iterative or antiphonal verses. In

> Let Jubal rejoice with Caecilia, the woman and the
>   slow-worm praise the name of the Lord.
> For I pray the Lord Jesus to translate my
>   MAGNIFICAT into verse and represent it.
>
> (B 1, 43)

the first, relatively easy relation of words (Jubal and Caecilia being well-known patrons of music) becomes progressively more allusive and distant. Caecilia and the worm are linked by an etymological play on the Latin for the slow- or blind-worm (Caecilian, from *caecus*), but it needs more than curious learning to connect woman and worm with Mary's Magnificat through (1) the identification of Jesus as the seed of the woman who bruised the serpent's head (slow-worm / Caecilia; serpent / Eve); (2) the idea of

"translation," that is, transformation, as from low to high, or from one species to another; and (3) the pun on Magnificat which turns the word into a compound (Magnificat) and so establishes fully the relation between the "Let" and "For" verses through the paired opposition of lowly worm and magnified creature.

To refine this kind of analysis is to come ultimately on the *hendiadys* in covert or open form. Puns are condensed or covert two-in-one structures, while Smart's synthetic "compounding" of nouns or nounlike words provides a more open form of the hendiadys. Allcock and Maidstone, when interpreted as two-folds, are simply hendiadys; Magnificat is a somewhat more complex instance; Jorim seems atomic until we notice its Hebrew plural ending (creating, once again, uncertainty as to whether a creature is to be thought of as one or more than one); and "the woman and the slow-worm," as it emerges from the name "Caecilia," is an especially characteristic hendiadys. One begins to suspect every name, in this name-freighted poetry, of being potentially emanative: other parts of speech too seem often like the attributes or derived sounds of some magical noun. Smart composes as if he had a choice between analytic and synthetic language formation, as if he were writing a Hebrew-English or Hebrew-Greek-Latin-English. Something of this is certainly in his mind, since he shares in the pentecostal aim to reconcile Babel into a universal code of worship. But whatever it is he wishes to achieve, the hendiadys is indispensable. There are remarkable moments in which his verses "reproduce" or "replicate" by drawing two or even three words out of one, yet remain one-ly:

> Let Jorim rejoice with the Roach—God bless my
>   throat & keep me from things stranggled.
> Let Addi rejoice with the Dace—It is good to angle
>   with meditation.
> Let Luke rejoice with the Trout—Blessed be Jesus
>   in Aa, in Dee and in Isis.
>
> (B 1, 179–81)

In the first verse above, Roach, a monosyllable, if read on the analogy of Jorim, becomes disyllabic, with an aspirated ending (Ro-ach), so that the "stranggled" is not only thematically sustained by the image of the caught fish but equally by the throaty sound. In the following verses we see a proper noun, Addi, breaking up into three components that are sounds or rivers or both: Aa, Dee, Isis (A-D-I). Strictly speaking, we need only the "i" of Isis to complete Addi (itself a pun on the additive process?). But even the -sis may be accounted for if we read Isis as I-c's, and by a bit of scrabbling involve the second proper noun, Dace, also composed of the letter-sounds, A, D, and—this time—C. One name is A,D, plus I; the other A,D, plus C; so that Jesus (that famous fish, almost rhyming here with Isis, considering the closeness of I and J) comprehends both names, being blessed in A, in D, and in I, C's.

It is almost impossible to summarize Smart's poetic method. It is not, or not only, a "mad, philological vision of reality" [Moira Dearnley, *The Poetry of Christopher Smart,* 1969]. It does not, or not merely, subvert the referential aspect of words like Isis by deconstructing them as acoustic images or magical sounds. It is best seen as a sacred poetics driving to astonishing extremes the principle of antiphony or "parallelism of members" (Is-is!) discovered by Bishop Lowth in the Psalms. So, Jorim goes with the Roach and is paralleled by Addi with the Dace, and even by angle "with" meditation; while Addi and Dace and Isis can be shown to be "members" of Jesus. But how do you fit in Hecatompus with an hundred feet? "Why, then, I'le fit you!" And, indeed, there is a mad attempt to speak with tongues and write with all those feet, to re-member or re-present every last creature by a "pairing" that will exclude nothing from the "Ark" of testimony.

In society the simplest form of representation (in the sense of a normative presentation of the self) is by one's personal name. Names are a compromise, of course; for no name is unique; and Smart's use of single names (Abraham, Jorim, Dace, Hecatompus) makes them ambiguously individual and generic. Names, moreover, like all proper nouns, are curiously split in their semantic character. They tend to be both subsemantic (so conventional as to be meaningless, semantically neutral) and supersemantic (they can be analyzed or pseudoanalyzed into richly meaningful parts). The idea of naming, therefore, recapitulates the drama played out in Smart's verse. Names individualize and socialize: they are always a kind of two-in-one. "Christopher Smart" names a single person whose Christ-bearing (Christopher) wit and wound (Smart) are one like the "Lord, and the Lamb" (A, 1) are one.

Every individual is *impair*. He sticks out or should stick out. Yet selfhood is both a demand to be met and subject to accusation. Analysis could go from here in many directions: religious, sociological, or what I have called psychoesthetic. Smart invariably connects representability of the self (*by* language, *with* the creature, and *to* God) and the treatment of the impair (also the impaired). He first reduces the impair to an infantile charm or a linguistic simple (cat, mus, the opaque proper noun, and so forth). By this method he both acknowledges and comforts the isolation of each creature. The linguistic simple, at the same time, is given the chance to multiply or replicate, but the match that results also escapes divine assessment. It cannot be judged. Will you frown at "Rehob" because he "rejoices with Caucalis Bastard Parsley"? Or at the Wild Cucumber with which "Nebai" is asked to rejoice (C, 152, 160)? Such matchmakings are beyond good and evil.

It may be useful to summarize the ways of Smart with language because his comforting of creatureliness extends to language—to sounds and words, large and small. He delights in (1) morphemes which can be individualized as words (cat, Dee); (2) words that are reduplicative in structure and remain simples because quasi-reversible (Aa, David, Amadavad, Wavow, Immussulus); (3) self-replicating or redundant phrases which can expand into a whole verse, as in the following (D, 175) inspired by the very idea of "re": "Let Ready, house of Ready" (redundancy) "rejoice" (Re . . . Re . . . re . . .) "with Junco The Reed Sparrow" (Ready . . . Reed); (4) the categorical

hendiadys, which brings together, not as in the story of Noah, pairs of the same species but unmatable *res creatae.*

If the ark into which these pairs enter cannot be that of generation, it must be that of regeneration. But does regeneration involve or exclude generation? The new order here invoked, at once linguistic and ontic, coexists ambivalently with an older order which it neither subsumes nor yet suppresses. Smart's poetics of relation never quite turns into a poetics of translation. The name "Jesus" embraces the name "Isis" and the result is a speckled language. In the opening scene of the *Jubilate,* when Abraham presents a ram and Jacob his speckled drove, we cannot tell whether sexual generation is being sacrificed or consecrated.

THEORY AS EPILOGUE

A swallow is an emancipated owl, and a glorified bat . . . an owl that has been trained by the Graces . . . a bat that loves the morning light.

J. Ruskin, *Love's Meinie*

Let Shephatiah rejoice with the little Owl, which is the wingged Cat.

C. Smart

The newest movement in philosophy, which extends into literary studies, questions the idea of presence. It is said to be an illusion fostered by our tendency to privilege voice over the written word. Voice, for Jacques Derrida, is the egotistical sublime, and our desire for the proper name (*mot propre, nom unique*) a metaphysical comfort. The best voice can do is to become literature; that is, to subvert its referential or representational function by bruising itself on the limits of language.

Derrida moves within a philosophical context of his own, and it is confusing to juxtapose his theory and Smart's poetics. I apologize for this "perspective by incongruity," as Kenneth Burke would call it, but I see no better way of suggesting how complex yet empty the concept of representation may become. Even if one acknowledges that Derrida's very aim is to empty this concept, at least of its psychologistic and metaphysical pathos, the "nature" of representation remains a puzzle [see Derrida's "La différance" in his *Marges de la Philosophie,* 1972].

I have argued that representation supports the ideal of self-presence in its psychic and social aspects. "Vilest things become themselves in her," Shakespeare's Enobarbus says of Cleopatra. She is "beautiful in corruption," like Smart's "Eyed Moth" (B 1, 93); and Enobarbus may indeed be playing on the idea of life engendered by Nilotic slime. Yet toward this "becoming," this triumph over the shame of creaturely origin, artistic representation also aspires. It may turn out, of course, that representation is all there is, and that we will never experience a self-presence in which we see—and are seen—not as in a glass darkly but face to face. Yet who can decide how ultimate the category of substitution is, and in particular the substitution of representation for presence?

The tropes of literature, or similar kinds of imaginative substitution, could as easily be said to pursue that "presence" which "identifies" all creatures, as to defer it. Perhaps it does not matter which, since both pursuit and deferment are endless. That the identifying moment, like a snapshot, is too deathlike or ecstatic; that movement or troping must begin again; that the acute self-consciousness must be transcended by an act of what is commonly called imagination—all this is part of the psychopathology of ordinary life, or of that principle of "clapperclaw" which "joyces" language in Shakespeare, Smart, and even in Derrida.

It may be that the theory of representation finds a less problematic exponent in an intermediate figure, more congruous with Smart, and exerting through Proust some influence on French thought. Let me conclude, then, with a note on John Ruskin. His prose may be the best nature poetry in the language. Ruskin also "represents" the creature, though to his fellow-man rather than God. How sane he appears when placed beside Smart, even if touched by a madness and childishness similar to Smart's. There is probably no better antidote to the *Jubilate Agno* than Ruskin's celebration of robin and swallow in *Love's Meinie*.

These lectures, given by him as Slade Professor of Fine Art before the University of Oxford, are clearly acts of reparation toward robin and swallow and, indeed, all "lower classes" exploited by the Victorian combination of Wealth and Science. "That, then, is the utmost which the lords of land, and masters of science, do for us in their watch upon our feathered suppliants. One kills them, the other writes classifying epitaphs." The painters and monks, lumped together by Ruskin, do us no good either. "They have plucked the wings from birds, to make angels of men, and the claws from birds, to make devils of men." The emphasis on genetic development in Darwinian science seems equally pernicious to Ruskin, who fears that all such speculation on origins will distract us from the present, from the endangered beauty and aptness of the *living* creature.

But it is not the common creatures alone, the swallows, fissirostres, or split-beaks, which must be saved. The common words too must be "represented": English names in their vernacular being, winged expressions which lead Ruskin to reflect on the troubadours, Chaucer and the *Romance of the Rose*. The habitat of the creature is in literature and art as well as in wood and field. Nature and art are both endangered by the deadly Latin of modern anatomical analysis. We should not see the things of this world under the species of a false objectivity, or of its killing nomenclature, but through the medium of their own natures and the *lingua franca et jocundissima* of vernacular perception. Reading *Love's Meinie* I repent me for not being able to "translate" such words as "representation." "All of you who care for life as well as literature," Ruskin advises, "and for spirit,—even the poor souls of birds,—as well as lettering of their classes in books,— you, with all care, should cherish the old Saxon, English and Norman-French names of birds, and ascertain them with the most affectionate research."

Thomas F. Dillingham (essay date 1980)

SOURCE: "'Blest Light': Christopher Smart's Myth of David," in *The David Myth in Western Literature*, edited by Raymond-Jean Frontain and Jan Wojcik, Purdue University Press, 1980, pp. 120–33.

[*In the following essay, Dillingham analyzes the importance of the works of King David and Horace as models for Smart's poetry.*]

Christopher Smart's career is generally perceived as a paradigm of professional disorder, a kind of poetic junk shop littered with odd bits of undergraduate humor, Miltonic fustian, Grub Street hackwork, and only occasionally enriched with the poetic jewels in the creation of which Smart, as Robert Browning observed, "pierced the screen / 'Twixt thing and word, lit language straight from soul" [*Parleyings with Certain People of Importance in Their Day*, 1887]. The disorder of Smart's life is undeniable and can be seen by all in any of several more or less sympathetic biographies, as well as permanently impressed in the minds of any who read Boswell's report of Johnson's sometimes inaccurate but always affectionate remarks about his irregular friend. The incoherence of Smart's poetic output, however, is not as certain, although it is widely assumed.

Certainly there is variety, certainly there is inconsistency; there are probably more bad lines than good. The major division by theme and genre—the division, that is, between his secular and his religious or devotional poems— seems also to provide the line between good and bad. The poems we most value are those in which Smart makes us forget that language is an artfully manipulated veil between ourselves and the phenomenal world—those in which he achieves the orphic effect, persuading us that the mentioned objects leap and dance before us, enlivened by the poet's divinely inspired and empowered words. But Smart was neither a latter-day pagan, dabbling in mysteries, nor a wasteful hypocrite longing to disavow his secular poems or his classical heritage. Rather, he persists in his devotion to a personal myth of the poet as both servant and representative of God, as the voice of prophecy, inspiration, and thanksgiving. This expansive and inclusive myth embraces Orpheus and Horace, Milton and John Gay, religious fervor and sexual innuendo, devotion and dissipation, sublimity and wit. At the center of the myth is the complex figure of King David, the Psalmist whose poetry inspired the most voluminous as well as the best part of Smart's poetic work.

Smart's *A Song to David* celebrates, through description, the figure of the psalmist whose career forms the basis for Smart's myth of the poet, as well as his justification of his own career. While the adequacy of that justification is open to question, it is a mistake to ignore the effort to construct it which occupies Smart at various points in his life and provides some of the best moments of his poetry. The variety of Smart's output and his notorious "madness" have led to the critical fragmentation of his life and work into the stages or periods which take on normative as well as descriptive force. This fragmentation can be avoided if we recognize the persistent role of David both as the inspiration of Smart's best work and the somewhat idealized model of the life Smart would have liked to lead. The poetry and the life are closely linked, in this view, since Smart's myth of David projects a vision of a man whose whole being and every action are, in effect, poetry, and whose poems are only the most inspired, because verbal, expressions of that poetry—inspired by the voice of God himself. In this myth words and actions carry the force of divine will, and the equation gives the poems the peculiar energy we associate with Smart's successes. But Smart extends the authority of his myth beyond his purely devotional or Psalm-like poems in an effort to embrace all the words of all the poems he has written and all the poets he admires, thereby sanctifying poetry as prayer just as he sanctifies his cat Jeoffrey's antics as a form of devotion or adoration.

After enumerating David's virtues in the opening section of the *Song,* Smart begins his description of the Psalms with a reference to their special healing power:

> His muse, bright angel of his verse,
> Gives balm for all the thorns that pierce,
>   For all the pangs that rage;
> Blest light, still gaining on that gloom,
> The more than Michal of his bloom,
>   Th'Abishag of his age.

These lines, clearly, refer to the special place of the Psalms in David's mature life, to their smoothing, consoling power which mirrors his lost youthful vigor and warms his aged chill. The reference to the "muse" does double duty here, both reminding the reader of the divine inspiration inherent in the Psalms and referring metonymically to the Psalms as they affect the listener or reader who comes after. That the "Blest light" is "still gaining" on the surrounding gloom is welcome news to any who might feel oppressed by evil and darkness. It is also Smart's reassurance, both from and to himself (as we shall see), since he offers himself as a "restorer of adoration" in England and yet still needs the sustaining power of his myth in the face of his own afflictions.

In succeeding stanzas Smart enumerates the subject matter of David's songs, then returns to the characterization of the poet and his poems' effects:

> Blest was the tenderness he felt
> When to his graceful harp he knelt,
>   And did for audience call;
> When satan with his hand he quell'd,
> And in serene suspence he held
>   The frantic throes of Saul.
>
> His furious foes no more malign'd
> As he such melody divin'd,
>   And sense and soul detain'd;
> Now striking strong, now soothing soft,
> He sent the godly sounds aloft,
>   Or in delight refrain'd.

> When up to heaven his thoughts he pil'd
> From fervent lips fair Michal smil'd,
>   As blush to blush she stood;
> And chose herself the queen, and gave
> Her utmost from her heart, 'so brave,
>   And play his hymns so good.'

If stanza XVII emphasizes the reflexive virtues of the Psalms, these stanzas add to the consolatory balm the ability to suppress Satan and soothe the agony of one possessed, to disarm his foes by transforming their perception of him, and even to seduce (in a proper way and with chaste result) a beautiful young wife. Smart attributes other virtues to David as well, but it is these poetic strengths which act most centrally in the myth which unifies Smart's work, from the early Seatonian poems to the late verse translations of Horace and the paraphrases of the Psalms. To soothe inner pain and turmoil, to neutralize malignity and reveal inner goodness, to cement the loving relationship of souls to each other and to God—these are the special powers of the divinely inspired prophet and poet.

The peculiar succession of actions described in the verses just quoted—silencing the powers of darkness, soothing anger, and gaining the love of a good woman—may remind us of another myth of the poet. The songs of Orpheus soothe the guardians of the underworld and gain him, at least temporarily, a wife. That David is more successful is correct only from Smart's Christian viewpoint. Smart himself had made this same association in his Seatonian poem, *On the Goodness of the Supreme Being*:

> Orpheus, for so the Gentiles call'd thy name,
> Israel's sweet psalmist, who alone could wake
> Th'inanimate to motion; who alone
> The joyful hillocks, the applauding rocks,
> And floods with musical persuasion drew;
> Thou, who to hail and snow gav'st voice and
>   sound,
> And mad'st the mute melodious!—greater yet
> Was thy divinest skill, and rul'd o'er more
> Than art or nature; for thy tuneful touch
> Drove trembling Satan from the heart of Saul,
> And quell'd the evil Angel:—in this breast
> Some portion of thy genuine spirit breathe,
> And lift me from myself; each thought impure
> Banish; each low idea raise, refine,
> Enlarge, and sanctify;—so shall the muse
> Above the stars aspire, and aim to praise
> Her God on earth, as he is prais'd in heaven.

This euhemerist linkage of the pagan inventor of poetry (especially devotional poetry) with the ancestor of Christ himself, and of all Christian devotional poems, is not unique with Smart. He would have found it in a "life" of David published in 1740 by the Reverend Patrick Delany. Smart, interestingly, turns the Orphic control over inert objects of nature into metaphor, thus reflecting his own faith in language, properly directed toward adoration, as the means of imbuing all creation with spiritual force. By describing and praising God's works, David in effect makes them Godly for the listener and that, in spirit, is the true version of the Orphic myth as well as Smart's plan for his own work and his prescription for any poet who wishes to avoid vanity.

Regardless of the historical merits of the Orpheus-David association, its importance to Smart cannot be overestimated. Smart's educational background, and an important faction of literary opinion in his time, emphasized the primacy of classical poetry and saw the myths of Greece and Rome as the most appropriate subjects and decorative matter for serious poets. There was, of course, a counter-tradition which asserted the primacy of the poetry of the Bible as better suited to the edification of Christians. For a Cambridge scholar and Grub Street wit such as the young Christopher Smart, the efforts of Bishop Robert Lowth to reconcile these conflicting claims [in his *Lectures on the Sacred Poetry of the Hebrews,* 1753], recognizing the merits of both traditions and asserting the intrinsic value of poetry as a mode of adoration, must have come as a welcome patch for a troubled conscience. In his second lecture, Lowth defends the study of biblical poetry *as* poetry:

> It would not be easy, indeed, to assign a reason why the writings of Homer, of Pindar, and of Horace, should engross our attention and monopolize our praise, while those of Moses, of David and Isaiah pass totally unregarded. Shall we suppose that the subject is not adapted to a seminary, in which sacred literature has ever maintained a precedence? Shall we say, that it is foreign to this assembly of promising youth, of whom the greater part have consecrated the best portion of their time and labour to the same department of learning? Or must we conclude, that the writings of those men, who have accomplished only as much as human genius and ability could accomplish, should be reduced to method and theory; but that those which boast a much higher origin, and are justly attributed to the inspiration of the Holy Spirit, may be considered as indeed illustrious by their native force and beauty, but not as conformable to the principles of science, nor to be circumscribed by any rules of art?

Lowth here acknowledges the traditional tensions between artifice and inspiration as a prelude to his effort to demonstrate that they are not necessarily in conflict. The poets of the Bible proceed, as he demonstrates, with due attention to rhetoric and decorum, and he offers a solution to the mystery of Hebrew metrics which remains convincing today. Presumably, Smart needed no reassurance about the artistic excellence of biblical poetry, though he no doubt welcomed Lowth's arguments as a means of advancing the cause of adoration. Smart might well, however, have found Lowth's arguments useful from a different perspective. The reconciliation of inspiration and artifice adds a practical dimension to the association of David with Orpheus. By identifying Orpheus, the fountainhead of classical poetry, with David, the model for Christian adoration, Smart reconciles the two traditions and their combined influence on him, and finds a way around the opposition between "divine inspiration" and "art and nature." He can, as an accomplished and artful poet in the prevailing public mode of his time, nonetheless maintain

his inspirational role as "the poet of my God." David is not, then, merely a personal myth (or mania, as some might say) but embodies the terms by which Smart can proceed as a poet in both the secular and the devotional modes.

When Smart invokes David's help, it is not supernatural power he wants but the ability "to praise Her [the Muse's] God on earth, as he is prais'd in heaven." There is in this some of the conventional trope of unworthiness which accompanies most invocations of muses, and if it were an isolated case in Smart's work we might leave it at that. The wish to be able to worship and praise, the impulse to adoration, is so frequently expressed in Smart's work as to be a central part of his myth of David. In the lines already quoted from *On the Goodness of the Supreme Being,* Smart shows himself conscious of the "worldly" elements in his own nature which must be "refined" and "sanctified" if he is to achieve his aim. His plea, "in this breast / Some portion of thy genuine spirit breathe, / And life me from myself" is echoed and clarified in the *Song to David*:

> O David, highest in the list
> Of worthies, on God's ways insist,
>   The genuine word repeat:
> Vain are the documents of men,
> And vain the flourish of the pen
>   That keeps the fool's conceit.
>
> Praise above all—for praise prevails;
> Heap up the measure, load the scales,
>   And good to goodness add.

This segment of the poem introduces the sequence of stanzas which describe the various levels of creation engaged in adoration, and asserts David's primacy among them:

> For Adoration all the ranks
> Of angels yield eternal thanks,
>   And David in the midst.
>   [Ibid.]

David's possession of the "genuine spirit" makes it possible for him to repeat the "genuine word"—a word which is free of the "fool's conceit" that is characteristic of most of the vain productions of the human pen. Thus it is not the style of the poet which determines his worth but the purpose for which he writes that assures the perfection of his style. In this way Smart's myth of David helps him reconcile his quotidian existence with his religious ideals; like a penitent offering his sufferings for the glory of God, Smart sanctifies all his activities, all his poems, by including them in the category "adoration," through which he can most fully identify himself with David.

The fullest potential implication of Smart's myth of David may be traced in connection with the concept of the "genuine word" and its relation to what appears to be Smart's theory of language, as revealed in his poems and *Jubilate Agno.* Scattered references in the *Jubilate* suggest that Smart believed in a direct connection between objects or phenomena and the words which designate them. Further, the words themselves, when they are the right words, have sacred characteristics. Two examples from the *Jubilate* should suffice: "For Action and Speaking are one according to God and the Ancients" [Section B2, Line 562], and "The right names of flowers are yet in heaven. God make gardners better nomenclators" (B2.509). Smart's belief that names bear a direct relationship with their objects may be derived from the many biblical passages which impute active, creative power to God's "word," such as Psalm 119, or the first chapter of the Gospel of John. Smart, in *A Song to David,* paraphrases another such passage, the account from Genesis 1:27 of the creation of man: "So God created man in his own image, in the image of God created he him." In Smart's version an important verbal change takes place:

> Sigma presents the social droves,
> With him that solitary roves,
>   And man of all the chief;
> Fair on whose face, and stately frame
> Did God impress him hallow'd name,
>   For ocular belief.

The substitution of "name" for "image" cannot be dismissed as a bow to the exegencies of rhyme. The passage connects seeing with believing, and since the true names are all, in a sense, God's names, all the words of the poet have the power to evoke God's name by evoking true images of the works of God already impressed with his name. In the *Jubilate,* Smart claims that "my talent is to give an impression upon words by punching, that when the reader casts his eye upon 'em, he takes up the image from the mould wch I have made" (B2.404). Thus the poet's power is likened to the power of God's word, just as David is likened to Adam and to Christ (the Word). In biblical typology, David is the type of Christ; in Smart's myth he is also the type of the poet who engages in adoration, in which tradition Smart places himself: "For all good words are from GOD, and all others are cant" (B1.85), but "For the grace of God I am the Reviver of ADORATION amongst ENGLISH-MEN" (B2.332).

Familarity with the unifying character of the myth of David in relation to Smart's career helps clarify the importance and relevance of certain projects which might otherwise seem departures from his best modes. In particular, the late verse translation of the works of Horace and the paraphrase of the Psalms may be better understood and appreciated when seen in relation to the myth. The notion that Smart's career is "divided" by his madness into periods of shallow secular wit, on the one hand, and religious enthusiasm on the other is, if not dismissed, at least altered by reconsideration in light of the myth.

A recent study of Smart's work by Geoffrey Hartman describes the standard view of the fragmentation caused by his madness:

> Smart's poetic career is emblematic of the fate of enthusiasm. It divides neatly into two parts. Before 1756 he was "the ingenious Mr. Smart," a facile and brilliant practitioner of neoclassic modes of verse. But

recovering from a serious fever he began "confessing God openly" by praying aloud whenever the impulse came. "I blessed God in St. James's Park till I routed all the company" (B1.89). He was confined for insanity in 1757–58 and again from 1759–63. During his "illness" he produced two long poems as daring and personal as any the Romantics were to write. The *Song to David* (1763) was dismissed in its time as a "fine piece of ruins" while the *Jubilate Agno* was not published till 1939. Smart's contemporaries saw him as an excellent versifier misled by religious mania, and though he reverted to such modest tasks as translating Horace and composing hymns for children, he never reestablished himself in their eyes.

> [*The Fate of Reading,* 1975]

An understanding of his use of the David myth can show us that Smart himself did not consider his later tasks aberrant or "modest" at all; rather, there is continuity in his ongoing efforts to undermine the conventional opposition between "nature and art," the elements of his best secular verse, and "divine inspiration," the essential prerequisite of his poetry of adoration. Smart sees his translation of Horace's does as an enhancement of his own powers as a poet and as homage to a poet whom he explicitly identifies with David and, by extension, himself.

In his "Preface" to his four-volume *Works of Horace Translated Into Verse* (London, 1767), Smart remarks that "Genius is certainly that *great witness,* which God never suffered himself to be without even amongst the Heathens" (I, xiii). In a fascinating if mysterious passage, he attributes to Horace that same talent of "impression" which he claims for David and for himself: "*Impression* then, is a talent or gift of Almighty God, by which a Genius is empowered to throw an emphasis upon a word or sentence in such wise that it cannot escape any reader of sheer good sense, and true critical capacity" (I, xii). Not only does Smart come close to claiming divine inspiration for Horace, in spite of his heathen religion, but he further attributes to Horace the virtue he holds in highest esteem: gratitude. He describes Horace as "one of the most thankful men that ever lived," which judgment he derives "not only from the warmth of his language in his Odes and other works, but from the circumstances of his behavior to all his friends of all parties, with whom he always kept himself well to the last" (I, xxx). That Horace's gratitude is primarily directed to his friends, rather than the Christian God, is not necessarily an impossible limitation, since he shows gratitude to God by exercising his genius.

Smart frequently refers to the primacy of gratitude among virtues and the special evil of ingratitude. In *Hymns for the Amusement of Children,* the hymn to **"Gratitude"** is one of the most charming and contains an explicit statement of the special importance of gratitude to God. The speaker is **"Gratitude"** personified:

> I in Eden's bloomy bowers
>   Was the heav'nly gardner's pride,
> Sweet of sweets, and flower of flow'rs,
>   With the scented tinctures dy'd.

Hear, ye little children, hear me,
  I am God's delightful voice;
They who sweetly still revere me
  Still shall make the wisest choice.

In *Jubilate Agno,* Smart explicitly states that "the sin against the HOLY GHOST is INGRATITUDE" (B2. 306), and the theme recurs constantly in the *Psalms,* reinforced by Smart's practice (in the paraphrases) of elaborating on the themes in the originals which most appeal to him. In other words, Smart comes very near to crediting Horace with everything he might need for salvation, except the cross.

Smart's self-identification with Horace, like that with David, focuses on his wish to be a "reviver of adoration." He sees in Horace the same fruitful link between religion and poetry, and between divine inspiration and poetry. He responds strongly to the elements of piety and moral enlightenment in Horace's works, perhaps overemphasizing them. In this way not only Horace's matter but his urbane manner as well can be reconciled with Smart's religious fervor and subsumed under the categories of his myth of David. The crucial link is Horace's *Carmen Saeculare.* In his "Preface" Smart explains: "The Secular-Ode, that brightest monument of the *Heathen Psalmist* and Roman worship, I have laboured with all the art and address I am capable of" (I, x–xi). The appellation "Psalmist" must surely be the highest praise Smart can bestow, as it leads to association with King David. Also, the fact that the original ode was composed at the request of Augustus for a public religious celebration is important. The hymn is designed to be sung antiphonally by a pair of choirs of young boys and girls, precisely the kind of occasion, form, and means of performance for which Smart himself would most like to write. The poem expresses both gratitude and hopeful anticipation, and in its conclusion reflects upon itself as the instrument of thanksgiving and the means of drawing down the favor of the gods. Even in the work of the civilized and skeptical Horace, faith in the special powers of poetry suggests the continuing force of primitive belief in poetry's divine origins, a belief which is most fully expressed in poetic prayer and song. By assimilating Horace to his myth of David the Psalmist, Smart gives an added dimension to the possibilities of poetry, joining "enthusiasm" to artful and witty intelligence.

Smart's paraphrases of the Psalms are another major monument to his personal myth of David, and because they are, I think, generally undervalued where they are not ignored, I will attempt an account of them which may further illuminate Smart's unifying myth. Smart's purposes in writing metrical paraphrases of the Psalms differed importantly from his purposes in translating Horace, in spite of his near identification of the two poets with each other and his complete personal identification with both. The *Horace* is intended as a close translation to catch the spirit and as much of the art of the original as possible. Smart demonstrates his prosodic mastery, using a surprising variety of stanzas and rhythmic patterns to approximate the Horatian forms. The *Psalms,* on the other hand, is intended to replace the versions in the Anglican psalter and to be used in the Anglican service. Because they must

be simple and singable, Smart used variations on only three basic stanzas: the standard four-and five-line hymn stanzas and the six-line *Song to David* stanza (similar to the "romance six"), and translated loosely. As the title indicates, Smart's version is *A Translation of the Psalms of David, attempted in the Spirit of Christianity, and adapted to the Divine Service*.

Smart's deletions and expansions in his versions of the Psalms reveal his myth-making power at work, transforming David's vision in the light of subsequent Christian history and doctrine and, in a sense, transmuting David forward in time to union with the gentle soul of his eighteenth-century avatar, Christopher Smart. His most obvious alteration from the biblical Psalms is inserting Christ as a merciful mediator between man and the stern, vengeful Old Testament God who is invoked so often by King David. Christ's mercy and pastoral benevolence temper God's fierce justice. In Psalm 94, for example, the final verse describes God's reward for those who persecute the righteous: "He shall recompense them their wickedness, and destroy them in their own malice: yes, the Lord our God shall destroy them." In Smart's version this becomes:

Foes of their benign Creator,
  Would, as their own malice, fare,
Did not Christ the Mediator
  Plead his merits and his pray'r.
           [Psalm 94]

But less obvious and more intriguing, from our point of view, is Smart's pervasive intrusion into the poem. His identification with David is so complete that he pours his own sorrows into David's laments. In Psalm 105, for example, which describes the wanderings of the Israelites, verse 14 announces: "He suffered no man to do them wrong, but reproved even kings for their sakes." Although God reproves the kings for tyrannical acts which take advantage of the weakness of the homeless Israelites, no specific examples of tyranny are mentioned. Smart makes the passage more specific and more closely related to his own situation, but also, interestingly, to aspects of David's life:

No man could hurt their goods or lives
  As they their tents remov'd,
And for the virtue of their wives,
  He mighty kings reprov'd.
           [Psalm 105]

The association of tyrannical seizure of "goods" with the threat of adulterous lust reminds us that Smart, in *Jubilate Agno,* is obsessed with the idea that he has been cheated out of an inheritance, and that his wife has cuckolded him (cf. B1.56–60 and B1.74–76).

Another Psalm which seems to speak clearly to Smart's situation is 120, which begins, in the Prayer Book, simply: "When I was in trouble I called upon the Lord: and he heard me. Deliver my soul, O Lord, from lying lips and from a deceitful tongue." Smart's version shows his ten-

dency to raise the emotional tone of the Psalms by referring to specific situations and inserting more concrete
imagery:

> When strong calamity pervailed,
>   And all my mirth was mute,
> By pray'r the topmost heav'n I scal'd,
>   And Jesus heard my suit.
>
> Shield me from lips with lies replete,
>   Or which their word revoke;
> And from the language of the cheat,
>   Expert his thoughts to cloak.
>   **[Psalm 120]**

The psalm is especially poignant in view of Smart's probable state of mind in the madhouse:

> My soul her sorrows overcharge
>   Unto the last extreme,
> For while I still on peace enlarge
>   They question and blaspheme.
> I strive to work them up to peace
>   From horror and despair;
> But at the word their bands increase
>   And they their cross prepare.

This passage is extraordinary for several reasons. The
Prayer Book version reads: "My soul hath long dwelt
among them that are enemies unto peace. I labour for
peace, but when I speak to them thereof, they make ready
to battle." Smart makes explicit the implicit "horror and
despair" of his original, but his last two lines jolt us by
their deviation from "they make ready for battle." They
suggest either that Smart/David sees himself as interced-
ing with Christ's executioners or that Smart sees himself
preparing for his own crucifixion as a disciple of Christ,
caught in a pagan world. Or in a third, somewhat too
ingenious reading, the stanzas may refer to Smart's fellow
inmates in the asylum: Smart, trying to bring them out of
their horror to share his peace, finds them deaf to his
teaching and, by their continuing violence and stubborness,
preparing their own continuing crucifixion ("And they their
[own] cross prepare"). Given Smart's benevolence and
wish to bring all creatures to join in worship, this is not
an impossible alternative. We may remember his plea in
the *Jubilate*: "For I pray the Lord JESUS that cured the
LUNATICK to be merciful to all my brethren and sisters in
these houses" (B1.123).

Smart does not merely inflate the Psalms with random
associations and ornate words, despite the harsh rejection of his paraphrases by some critics. The extension of
the associations makes the poems more immediate to the
audience Smart has in mind. The language allows a complexity of meaning for which the Psalmist does not strive,
but which is consistent with Smart's notion of singing a
new psalm which will be England's own. His ability to
fuse disparate images and ideas cements the identification of his own life and beliefs with the ideal forms of
the "poet" which he perceives in his past. He places
himself in the two traditions—Horatian and "Davidic."

As a result of the fusion, he suggests an exciting possibility: the old dichotomy between art and passion need
not be an impassable gulf, but the two terms of a dialectic. Smart's myth of David—the scholar, the poet, the
thankful celebrant of his God—is also his myth of himself, his composite picture of the disparate—sometimes
tragic, sometimes buffoon-like—qualities of his own poetic personality.

Did you ever read Christopher Smart's
Song to David, **the only great**
accomplished **poem of the last century?**
The *un***accomplished ones are**
Chatterton's,—of course I mean earlier
than Blake or Coleridge, and without
reckoning so exceptional a genius as
Burns. . . . You will find Smart's poem a
masterpiece of rich imagery, exhaustive
resources, and reverberant sound.

—Dante Gabriel Rosetti, quoted in
Recollections of Dante Gabriel Rosetti *by*
T. Hall Caine, 1898.

James King (essay date 1984)

SOURCE: "The Revelation of Self in *Jubilate Agno* and
A Song to David," in *English Studies,* Netherlands, Vol.
65, No. 1, February, 1984, pp. 23–6.

[*In the essay below, King examines the "psychological
and structural interdependences" between* Jubilate Agno
and A Song to David, *focusing particularly on Smart's
identification with King David, a sinner who redeems
himself through poetry.*]

Although the structure of Christopher Smart's Davidic
poems, *Jubilate Agno* (composed *c.* 1759–63) and *A Song
to David* (1763), have been analyzed perceptively and the
background to these poems elucidated superbly, not much
attention has been paid to the psychological and structural
interdependences between the two poems. During the
mental instability he suffered from 1759–63, Smart probably focused his work on David because he saw him not
merely as the great poet of the psalms but also as a redeemed sinner who was a great poet. There is a tone, then,
of *apologia* and apology in Smart's decision to center his
work on David, who was the subject of heated debate
during Smart's confinement. If the ambiguity inherent in
using David as a central figure in a work of literature is
kept in mind, a theory can be constructed about Smart's
revelation of self in these two poems.

Smart composed *Jubilate Agno* at various times throughout the time at Bethnal Green. In these most anxious and
neurotic moments, Smart tried to arrange his perception of
the confusing panoply of God's goodness into some sort

of coherent ordering. In his use of the Hebraic structure of 'For' and 'Let', he attempted to impose order on the chaos of all the objects of the creation which entered his imagination. When he was moving out of this period of instability, Smart, now feeling himself a redeemed man, composed a rational, ordered poem to justify his previous effort. Since Smart had relied so heavily on David in his period of madness, he used David once more in the new ordered structure to explain and justify his ways to men. This helps to explain the remarkable change Smart was able to effect in his poetry at the end of his confinement. Smart viewed himself in *Jubilate Agno* as striving for redemption and in *A Song to David* as having arrived at the point of redemption. The redeemed sinner of the latter poem looks back upon the confusion in *Jubilate Agno*.

This new ordering can be seen in some of the ways in which material in *Jubilate Agno* is presented in much more structurally sounder ways in *A Song to David*. For example, the following sentiment, *'For I bless God for every feather from the wren in the sedge to the* CHERUBS *and their* MATES' [Fragment B, Line 122], is worked into stanza XIX of *A Song to David* where Smart recalled David's ability to sing of the angels:

> Angles—their ministry and meed,
> Which to and fro with blessings speed,
>   Or with their citterns wait;
> Where Michael with his millions bows,
> Where dwells the seraph and his spouse,
>   The cherub and her mate.

Daniel in the lions' den is mentioned by Smart in *Jubilate Agno* ('Let Daniel come forth with a Lion, and praise God with all his might through faith in Christ Jesus' A 13), but the iconographic association of David and the lion in *A Song* is used to characterize the Hebraic poet and to place his might next to his gentleness:

> O strength, O sweetness, lasting ripe!
> God's harp thy symbol, and thy type
>   The lion and the bee!
>
>   (XXXVIII)

There are many other examples of metamorphoses of material. Smart consciously used images in *Jubilate* in the well-ordered *A Song to David*.

Jubilate Agno is also an extremely defensive poem. It constantly attaches historical and contemporary figures to animals, flowers, and other created objects with the implication that their personalities can find salvation by direct association with the things the Lord has made.

> Rejoice in God, O ye Tongues; give the glory
>   to the Lord, and the Lamb,
> Nations, and languages, and every Creature,
>   in which is the breath of Life.
> Let man and beast appear before him, and
>   magnify his name together.
>
>   (A 1–3)

Smart is at pains in *Jubilate* to explain his reasons for writing such a poem:

> *For I am not without authority in my jeopardy,*
>   *which I derive inevitably from the*
>   *glory of the name of the Lord.*
>
>   (B 1)

The poet is justifying not only his existence and his reasons for composing *Jubilate Agno* but also his maladjustment, his insanity, his wretchedness. The poet who composed these sentiments in a time of instability feels called upon to put a rationale on such activity in *A Song to David*.

Smart imposes this rationale in three ways. First, he publishes before the text of his poem proper a prose outline which details his intent in writing the poem. The plan is an expansive one. It begins with the life of David, moves on to David's vast subject matter, his power over infernal spirits, stresses David's control over mental states ('An exercise upon the senses, and how to subdue them'), and finally arrives at the conclusion that David was the 'best poet' who ever lived. Although other eighteenth-century poets composed prose glosses for their poems as a matter of course, it is perhaps significant that this is the only one Smart ever contributed.

Second, there are numerous references to the idea of controlling or ordering material in *A Song to David*:

> 'Twas he the famous temple *plann'd* . . . (VII)
> Of vast *conception,* tow'ring tongue . . . (X),
> 'Twas then his thoughts *self-conquest prun'd* . . . (XI)
> *Constant*—in love to God the Truth . . . (XIV)
> *Controul* thine eye . . . (XLVII)
> Prevails his passions to *controul* . . . (LXIV)
>
>   (italics mine)

In *A Song* Smart is anxious to call his reader's attention to the fact that David was a poet very concerned with form in the universe, architecture, and poetry. By implication, Smart, the poet who identifies himself with David, is now concerned with such structural problems in his new, ordered poem which uses material originally developed in *Jubilate*.

Third, there are autobiographical elements in *A Song to David*. Special attention should be paid to Smart's gloss of verses XXVII through XXIX: 'He [David] obtains power over infernal spirits, and malignity of his enemies . . .' The reformed Smart comments more directly on this 'power over infernal spirits' in verse XXVIII:

> His furious foes no more malign'd
> As he such melody divin'd,
>   And sense and soul detain'd,
> Now striking strong, now soothing soft,
> He sent the godly sounds aloft,
>   Or in delight refrain'd.

David, through his poetry, conquered demonic foes. There is a very real sense of personal identification on Smart's part with this aspect of David's literary personality. Smart is writing the poem to show that he can write a coherent poem in tribute to a poet who also had to battle with contrary forces which threaten the existence of poetry. Smart calls his reader's attention to this when he says in his advertisement that the poem was 'composed in a Spirit of Affection and thankfulness to the great Author of the Book of gratitude, which is the *Psalms* of *David* the King'.

Smart also tips his autobiographical hand in verse XXX of *A Song*:

> The pillars of the Lord are seven,
> Which stand from earth to topmost heav'n;
>   His wisdom drew the plan;
> His Word accomplished the design,
> From brightest gem to deepest mine,
>   From Christ enthron'd to man.

There is a pun in the use of 'Word'. It refers to David's ability to write poetry, but it also signifies the second person of the Trinity, Christ, who is the Word made flesh and David's descendant. When Smart claims that David's Word has 'accomplished the design', he is forcefully suggesting that David's poem mirrors the mystery of the Incarnation and that David's controlled and ordered poetry makes divine wisdom accessible to mankind. In his own concern with imposing order over demonic powers in *A Song to David,* Smart is trying to write a poem that will carry on from David, that will in its turn be the Word in plan and design by a new David.

Jubilate Agno is manifestly unsuccessful in this regard. It is the disparate Word of God, a series of intricate, brightly-coloured mosaics, each sparkling with its own testimony to God. In *A Song to David* Smart is justifying his previous instability and his past poetic effort during that period in a meticulously controlled poem which leads carefully and guardedly to an explanation of the poet who feels called upon to praise the creation. *A Song to David* reveals a poet whose intensity never changes but whose architectonic unity is sharpened to explain and define the apparent ramblings in *Jubilate*. *Jubilate* reveals a *persona* for the poet terribly aware of the fabulous in all things; *A Song to David* reveals the same *persona,* who is almost identical with Smart, putting these same concerns into a penitential and rigorously articulated framework in testimony to Christ's ancestor, David.

The reader can feel the real sense of satisfaction Smart had at the end of his task in the latter poem—his feeling of having reformed himself and his previous poetic effort—when he declares in the very last lines: 'Determined, Dared, and Done'. David was a reformed sinner whose religious poetry captures the essence of the Word through words. In addressing a poem to David in which he attempts to follow David's lead, Smart mirrors David's accomplishment and redeems his previous poetic effort. Smart feels at the end of his poem of conscious order that he has succeeded in this attempt at personal and artistic salvation, and his identification with the full personality of David the poet and redeemed sinner is complete.

Edward Joseph Katz (essay date 1992)

SOURCE: "Transcendent Dialogic: Madness, Prophecy, and the Sublime in Christopher Smart," in *Compendious Conversations: The Method of Dialogue in the Early Enlightenment,* edited by Kevin L. Cope, Peter Lang, 1992, pp. 151–64.

[*In the following essay, Katz argues that by organizing language in his poetry, Smart both defines himself and gives form and shape to the inexpressible.*]

During the period extending from May 1757 to February 1763, Christopher Smart was confined to asylums for treatment of visual hallucinations and religious delusions, first at St. Luke's and later, after a brief recovery, at Potter's private house in Bethnal Green. The composition of *Jubilate Agno* (not published until 1939) dates from this time, and *A Song to David* reached the press only nine weeks after his discharge from Potter's. Smart's literary reception fluctuated in his own day and most of his contemporaries felt compelled to characterize the poet in terms describing either a borderline criminal or a pitiable eccentric. More recent commentators have reviewed documentation of Smart's symptoms and have applied to them a variety of modern psychological models to offer diagnoses of his mental condition. Literary criticism, though, has tended to probe more deeply in its exploration of the processes that underline Smart's work. Critics such as Lillian Feder have examined the dialectic underlying the poet's representation of madness; others, such as David B. Morris, have discussed Smart's poetics of prophecy in terms of the sublime [Lillian Feder, *Madness in Literature,* 1980; David B. Morris, *The Religious Sublime: Christian Poetry and Critical Tradition in Eighteenth-Century England,* 1972.]

It is my intention, however, to explore the significant points of contact between the strategies of self-representation and the idea of the sublime in Smart's poetry: for Smart's very conception of the sublime, in both *Jubilate Agno* and the *Song to David,* coheres precisely in an examination, and constitution, of the self in its relation to the ineffable. The sublime moment represents a confrontation with what cannot be accommodated by the mind, with what exceeds and calls into question the very identity of the self. The endeavor of the poetic imagination to circumscribe the ineffable in defiance of understanding, often through the accretion and representation of attributes of a vast and divine Other, is an effort to recover the self. Moreover, this strategy of circumscription and recovery—this constitution of the Other in order to establish identity—places the poet in a dialogical relationship to what he purports to describe. Smart's achievement in these works, then, reveals a dialogism which limns a rudimentary phenomenology of the sublime with a view to establishing a poetics of prophecy as hermeneutic, as a way of interpreting the self in its relation to the world and to God.

I

Admittedly, any treatment of Smart's work must come to terms with the issue of his madness. For, in his *Jubilate*

Agno, Smart openly confesses to his confinement and refers to his treatment there:

> FOR I pray the Lord JESUS that cured the LUNATICK to be merciful to all my brethren and sisters in these houses.

> FOR they work me with their harping-irons, which is a barbrous instrument, because I am more unguarded than others.

> [Fragment B, Lines 123–124]

By acknowledging his confinement, Smart sets aside for himself and others like him a space entirely their own, on the periphery of what might be considered normative existence. Human experience becomes disjointed, subject to the barbarism of those aligned against the individual who stands outside the pale. The poet is a marginalized figure and the realm he occupies one of torment.

However, as though to deny the pain of alienation, the poet blesses the day of his confinement:

> FOR I bless the thirteenth of August, in which I had the grace to obey the voice of Christ in my conscience.

> FOR I bless the thirteenth of August, in which I was willing to run all hazards for the sake of the name of the Lord.

> (B 49–50)

The poet's marginal status here becomes more magnified, despite his appeal to the divine: his decision to "be called a fool for the sake of Christ" (B 51) leads to an undefined risk, to a further isolation from others in the world. To the world, the poet is an outcast, whose behavior, whose very reliance upon and belief in God, represents a challenge to the norm: "Let Eli rejoice with Leucon," Smart writes, "he is an honest fellow, which is a rarity. For I have seen the White Raven and Thomas Hall of Willingham and am myself a greater curiosity than both" (B 25).

The greatest temptation for the pariah—and for the radical individualist in general—is the acquiescence to moral solipsism. But if the poet realizes that he is viewed as a prodigy, he nonetheless chooses to represent his social rejection in spiritual terms: "For I have adventured myself in the name of the Lord, and he hath mark'd me for his own" (B 21). To Smart, then, madness becomes a sign of radical Otherness—in both an ideological and spiritual sense, an acknowledgement of having been singled out to stand against the world.

Indeed, for the marginal figure, social assault must be endured to establish a credible voice with which to protect the primacy of the self, on the one hand, and to admonish the assailants, on the other. Thus, Smart writes that, despite the allurement of the mob (B 17),

> . . . it is the business of a man gifted in the word to prophecy good.

> FOR it will be better for England and all the world in a season, as I prophecy this day.

> (C 57–58)

The voice of the prophet serves as the wellspring of personal and social regeneration.

The poetic deployment of marginality and the prophetic voice enables Smart to develop in his ***Jubilate*** a discourse descriptive of what Mikhail Bakhtin, with regard to the novel, has termed "a concrete, socially embodied point of view, [and] not an abstract, purely semantic position" [*The Dialogic Imagination: Four Essays*]. Against the hypocrisy and spiritual morbidity of eighteenth-century English culture, the poet's cry rings out as an indictment. Through its biblical rhythms and syntax, its idiosyncratic and at times peculiarly naive tone, Smart's prophetic poetry comes to possess "a language with which it is organically united" [Bakhtin]. The discourse of the ***Jubilate,*** in its unique structure and diction, both sets itself apart from and absorbs other genres, such as religious poetry, spiritual autobiography, and social criticism; and this assimilative strategy, binding both form and content so closely, serves as a source of empowerment. Moreover, in casting himself as prophet, Smart envisions "the individual [as one who] acquires the ideological and linguistic initiative necessary to change the nature of his own image" and who destabilizes the received image of the world, in order to provide a reconstructed alternative.

Thus, Smart's use, during his years of confinement, of King David as his model poet-prophet reveals a search, as Allan J. Gedalof demonstrates, for "a dynamic focus of interest who is . . . an ideal agent for the articulation of [the poet's] sensibility and vision" ["The Rise and Fall of Smart's David," *Philological Quarterly* 60, 1981]. In ***A Song to David,*** Smart parallels himself with the Hebrew poet, observing David's initial rejection by Israel and his later conversion to prophetic wisdom:

> Wise—in recovery from his fall,
> Whence rose his eminence o'er all.
>   Of all the most reviled;
> The light of Israel in his ways,
> Wise are his precepts, prayer and praise,
>   And counsel to his child.

> (91–96)

Smart expands his identification with David in ***Jubilate,*** when in the longest line of the poem he declares,

> LET David bless with the Bear—The beginning of victory to the Lord—to the Lord the perfection of excellence—Hallelujah from the heart of God, and from the hand of the artist inimitable, and from the echo of the heavenly harp in sweetness magnifical and mighty.

> (A 41)

The "perfection of excellence" here issues "from the heart of God" and "from the hand of the artist." Despite, or rather because of, his marginality, the poet may align himself with the divine presence in benediction, in the common act of creation; for, as Smart suggest, the very dangers of alienation themselves confer a sort of power:

> LET Elizur rejoice with the Partridge, who is a prisoner of state and is proud of his keepers.

> FOR I am not without authority in my jeopardy, which I derive inevitably from the glory of the name of the Lord.
>
>   (B 1)

David's character in the *Song* reflects the central attributes given to him by eighteenth-century religious controversialists. He is great, valiant, and strong in the manner of the biblical hero; he is pious, serene, constant, and wise, as one would expect from God's chosen (*Song,* 19–21, 25–96). But literally at the heart of Smart's catalogue, two crucial traits appear: for David, Smart declares, is

> Sublime—invention ever young,
> Of vast conception, tow'ring tongue,
>   To God th' eternal theme;
> Notes from yon exaltations caught,
> Unrival'd royalty of thought,
>   O'er meaner strains supreme.
>
> Contemplative—on God to fix
> His musings, and above the six
>   The sabbath-day he blest;
> 'Twas then his thoughts self-conquest prun'd
> And heavenly melancholy tun'd,
>   To bless and bear the rest.
>
>   (55–66)

David's sublimity of character derives from his poetic originality and an aesthetics that captures the vastness of Creation. Moreover, it is in his "self-conquest," his conscious attempt to circumscribe the spirit through devotion, that the "heavenly melancholy" can be directed in praise of the sublime. Prayer and spiritual meditation constitute the internal dialogue which negotiates the boundaries of the altered self and situates it with respect to the Other.

Both God's creation and that of His poet-king reflect a nearly identical sublimity: in *Jubilate,* Smart writes that

> . . . GOD the father Almighty plays upon the HARP of stupendous magnitude and melody.

> FOR innumerable Angels fly out at every touch and his tune is a work of creation.

> FOR at that time malignity ceases and the devils themselves are at peace.
>
>   (B 246–248)

And in the *Song,* David's praise of God closely resembles Smart's benediction in the passage above:

> He sung of God—the mighty source
> Of all things—the stupendous force

> On which all strength depends;
> From whose right arm, beneath whose eyes,
> All period, pow'r, and enterprize
>   Commences, reigns, and ends.
>
>   (103–108)

These sequences strengthen Smart's identification with David; but equally important, the power that both of these passages ascribe to God are used by Smart, later in the *Song,* to describe the efficacy of David's own works:

> Blest was the tenderness he felt
> When to his graceful harp he knelt,
>   And did for audience call;
> When satan with his hand he quell'd,
> And in serene suspense he held
>   The frantic throes of Saul.
>
> His furious foes no more malign'd
> As he such melody divin'd,
>   And sense and soul detain'd;
> Now striking strong, now soothing soft,
> He sent the godly sounds aloft,
>   Or in delight refrain'd.
>
>   (157–168)

Thus, the dynamic here is twofold: Smart deploys his strategy of representation first to assume for himself completely the posture of prophet, who with David's messianic force can declare to the world the glory of God, and then to claim for poetry a sort of divine potency, revelatory of the transcendent value of the sublime. Smart's dialogism operates to secure the self through debate with its ideological opponents and through the determination of its spiritual identity in relation to the Other, ineffable and yet mysteriously immanent.

II

If Smart's representation of the self reveals the individual in temporary withdrawal in order to gain for himself the vantage of the periphery, his representation and deployment of the sublime mode reflect a return to the world—a return marked, however, by an understanding of the provisional nature of objectivity. In Smart's rudimentary phenomenology of the sublime, the decisive moment comes in the individual's confrontation with both the limitations of his inner resources and what lies beyond unmediated sensible apprehension. The transcendant moment for Smart begins with the experience of the natural world. The poet, then, assumes from the outset that nature reflects divine order. But as God's "scribe-evangelist" (*Jubilate,* B 327) any mere cataloguing of the divine attributes of creation fails to suffice for prophetic expression; rather, Smart desires to give meaning to these signs and symbols: "For the mind of man," he argues, "cannot bear a tedious accumulation of nothings without effect" (C 36).

All this is not to suggest that the catalogue, the accumulation of detail in representing the object of sensible and suprasensible perception, was not central to Smart's poetic technique. To the contrary, as nearly every critic of Smart has recognized, the poet owed a good deal of his poetics to Robert Lowth's *Lectures on the Sacred Poetry of the Hebrews* (1753; English translation, 1787), which stressed the use of parallelism and amplification in biblical verse of the sublime. From the catalogues of animals and plants in **Jubilate,** to the progression of the "Adoration" stanzas in the **Song** (301–426), the influence of Lowth's rhetorical theories of the sublime is unmistakable. Moreover, as Smart himself notes,

> . . . innumerable ciphers will amount to something . . .
>
> FOR infinite upon infinite they make a chain.
>
> FOR the last link is from man very nothing ascending to the first Christ the Lord of All.
>
> (*Jubilate,* C 35–38)

Clearly, Smart aims here at more than simple parallelism and amplification for the sake of approximating biblical tone; and, in any case, Lowth's treatment of these aspects of the sublime remains rather superficial, probing no further than a Longinian rhetoric of vast conception.

Yet elsewhere, in his chapter "The Sublimity of Sentiment," Lowth discusses the rhetorical sublime in far different terms. In the Book of Job and in the Psalms, Lowth argues,

> we find the idea of infinity perfectly expressed, though it be, perhaps, the most difficult of all ideas to impress upon the mind . . . The sacred writers have, therefore, recourse to description, amplification, and imagery, by which they give substance and solidity to what is in itself a subtile and unsubstantial phantom, and render an ideal shadow the object of our senses. These they do not describe in general or indefinite terms; they apply to them an actual line and measure . . . which the mind is indeed able to comprehend. When the intellect is carried beyond these limits, there is nothing substantial upon which it can rest . . . [The mind] imperceptibly glides into the void of infinity, whose vast and formless extent . . . impresses it with the sublimest and most awful sensations, and fills it with a mixture of admiration and terror.

Thus, Lowth claims, the Hebrew poets aimed to capture what lay beyond sensible and intellective perception, giving body to what was formerly "a subtile and unsubstantial phantom." Through metaphor and imagery, parallelism and amplification, they sought to circumscribe the ineffable and thus to suggest the order that the mind, by its very nature, is inadequate to comprehend. Ultimately, the intellect surrenders to its own insufficiency and slips into a state of reverence and awe before the sublime.

Still, the sublime moment depends for Lowth as much upon subjective experience as it inheres in the object itself. The problem of poetry, then, is to find a way of conveying to the reader not so much the object itself, but the impression it makes upon the perceiving subject. Again, Lowth writes:

Poetry itself is indebted for its origin . . . to the effects which are produced upon the mind and body, upon the imagination, the senses, the voice, and respiration, by the agitation of passion. Every affection of the human soul . . . is a momentary frenzy. When, therefore, a poet is able . . . to conceive any emotion of the mind so perfectly as to transfer to his own feelings the instinctive passion of another . . . such a one . . . may be said to possess the true poetic enthusiasm, or, as the ancients would have expressed it, "to be inspired; full of the god."

Thus, in the absence of affective response a poetry of the sublime is impossible: for as Lowth argues, "Some passions may be expressed without any of the sublime; the sublime also may exist where no passion is *directly* expressed: there is however no sublimity where no passion is *excited*" (italics mine). The poet, sensitive to the impressions made upon him by the object he perceives, translates experience so as to conjure it up in the reader: a poetics of inspiration—a poetry "full of the god," as it were—must communicate the ecstasy of the mind overwhelmed by its object.

In the **Song,** Smart follows Lowth in pointing to emotion as the source of the sublime moment (259–264): both a spiritual dread and an ecstatic beatitude issue forth from the excitation of the passions, which provide the as yet unordered material of religious experience. Yet as Smart observes earlier in the **Song,** "Open, and naked of offence, / Man's made of mercy, soul, and sense" (247–248): comprehension of the divine, insofar as it is possible, demands the full participation of man's threefold nature. As Karina Williamson observes in her appendix to Smart's **Hymns and Spiritual Songs,** within this conceptual framework, sense, soul and mercy correspond to the faculties of sensation, reason and spiritual intuition, respectively. Thus, in the sequence on the senses (379–414) found at the close of the **Song's** "Adoration" stanzas (301–426), Smart binds passion and intellect, sensation and spirit, in an expression of praise:

> For ADORATION, DAVID'S psalms
> Lift up the heart to deeds of alms;
>   And he, who kneels and chants,
> Prevails his passions to controul,
> Finds meat and med'cine to the soul,
>   Which for translation pants.
>
> (379–384)

The song of praise, which "above all . . . prevails" (295), demands the operation of the intellective faculties upon the shapeless mass of affective impressions: and just as the soul yearns for "translation" into immortality, so the mind seeks the "translation" of the ineffable into song. In both cases, the desire is to be filled with, or to comprehend, what exceeds the reach of the intellect.

As Lowth recognized, an associationist poetics relies heavily on imaginative sympathy, and here, too, Smart follows his lead, observing that

. . . my talent is to give an impression upon words by punching, that when the reader casts his eye upon 'em, he takes up the image from the mould which I have made.

(*Jubilate,* B 404)

Clearly, Smart conceives of language as the binding of poet and reader in common experience. Less obvious, perhaps, is his use of the metaphor of type-founding, which attests to the transformative power of the poet upon language itself: the word bears the poet's mark, his "impression," irrevocably; it belongs to the poet alone, until he bestows it, like a gift, upon the reader.

Language—and the language of poetry, in particular—refers, for Smart, to subjective experience; but, more importantly, the poet by ordering this experience possesses the capacity to inscribe meaning upon the objects of perception—that is, the poet lends to things in and beyond the world an apparent substance, an illusion of objectivity. As Smart observes in Fragment B of *Jubilate,*

FOR SOUND is propagated in the spirit and in all directions . . .

FOR a man speaks HIMSELF from the crown of his head to the sole of his feet.

(B 226–228)

FOR the VOICE is from the body and the spirit—and is a body and a spirit.

(B 239)

Poetic discourse sets up the self as the determinant of what exists beyond it—that is, the assertion of the self, the voicing of poetic identity, generates through linguistic reflexivity the context for interpretation and judgment. And Smart further develops this concept of self-reflexive language in the "Alphabet" sequences, when he declares that "I is identity" and later that "I is the organ of vision" (B 521, 546). For here his imitation of the Cabalistic practice of assigning specific meanings to letters takes on a new significance: the equation of the self with perception undergoes a metamorphosis, so that now the attempt of poetry to capture the sublime resembles more fully a projection of the self onto the object that it cannot adequately conceive. Once more, when Smart maintains that "the letter *lamed* which signifies God by himself is on the fibre of some leaf in every tree" (B 477), he does more than pun on the sounds of the English letter L and that of the Hebrew *lamed* (*el*) as one of the names of God. Rather, as the poet continues to locate the signification of *lamed* in "the grain of the human heart," "in the veins of all stones," and so on throughout all nature (B 477–491), it becomes increasingly clear that the poet, and not God, manipulates the forces of signification. The accumulation of divine attributes, moreover, points beyond the reflexivity of Smart's project to the insufficiency of language itself to voice what resists expression. And it is this failure of

language, coupled with the limitation of the intellect, that compels Smart to deploy the strategies of parallelism and amplification in an effort to circumscribe, or determine, the ineffable.

And yet, paradoxically, it is language, with all its imperfection, that for Smart bears the angelic nature of man. Thus, in the *Song to David,* the poet contrasts natural sublimity with the spiritual:

Strong is the lion—like a coal
His eyeball—like a bastion's mole
        His chest against the foes;
Strong, the gier-eagle on his sail;
Strong against tide, th' enormous whale
        Emerges as he goes.
But stronger still, in earth and air,
And in the sea, the man of pray'r;
        And far beneath the tide;
And in the seat to faith assign'd,
Where ask is have, where seek is find,
        Where knock is open wide.

(451–462)

Things in nature possess a strength of magnitude, but the power of the man of prayer exceeds even theirs. It is the language of prayer—the language, in Smart's terminology, of spirit and of prophecy—that enshrines faith and, therefore, yields access to or knowledge of that which exists outside, or in excess of, consciousness. Thus, in the passage from the *Song,* Smart points to prayer as a process of representation which, in essence, appears as objective knowledge: for the request is possession, the search is discovery, the knock is admittance. If the world seems unstable because the self constitutes the epistemological focus of experience, it nonetheless regains a profound coherence through the inscription of this discourse upon sensible and suprasensible perception. The prophetic, and hence poetic, act is in a real sense efficacious in the world, "For Action and Speaking are one" (B 562): the poet, in experiencing the sublime moment and giving it the substance of verse, finds in himself the order which eludes him. The rupture dividing the perceiving subject from perceived object is transcended through the projection of the self onto the world; and the very inscrutability of divine Creation necessitates the poetic act as a hermeneutic of empowerment.

For Smart, the prophetic gesture represents the recovery of self from the alienation threatened by the experience of the undifferentiated Other. Through the resolution of the sublime experience, the poet overcomes the decentering of knowledge—reinforced by associationism and eighteenth-century theorists of the mind—and is able to constitute, to interpret, both self and Other. Smart's poetry is a dialogic of resistance and empowerment: yet at the heart of his conception of the sublime lies the fundamental problem of faith—an insistence upon language and upon the poet's power to transform the unshaped mass of experience into coherent vision.

FURTHER READING

Bibliography

Mahoney, Robert, and Rizzo, Betty W. *Christopher Smart: An Annotated Bibliography 1743–1983.* New York: Garland Publishing, Inc., 1984, 671 p.
    A comprehensive work including annotations, notes, and a census of manuscripts.

Biography

Devlin, Christopher. *Poor Kit Smart.* Carbondale: Southern Illinois University Press, 1961, 200 p.
    The standard modern biography of Smart. Devlin interweaves biographical data with commentary on the style and meaning of Smart's poetry.

Sherbo, Arthur. *Christopher Smart: Scholar of the University.* East Lansing: Michigan State University Press, 1967, 303 p.
    Examines autobiographical data in Smart's poetry.

Criticism

Adams, Francis D. "*Jubilate Agno* and the 'Theme of Gratitude'." *Papers on Language and Literature* III, No. 3 (Summer 1967): 195–209.
    Argues that the poem's "comprehensive, though unfinished plan" is revealed by studying the theme of gratitude or praise.

Anderson, Frances E. *Christopher Smart.* New York: Twayne Publishers, 1974, 139 p.
    Survey of Smart's life, times, and poetry.

Bertelsen, Lance. "Journalism, Carnival, and *Jubilate Agno.*" *ELH* 59, No. 2 (Summer 1992): 357–84.
    Traces the influence on the composition of *Jubilate Agno* of "the madcap popular journalism and performances which engaged Smart's energy in the years immediately preceding his confinement to Bethnal Green."

Bond, William H. "Christopher Smart's *Jubilate Agno.*" *Harvard Library Bulletin* IV, No. 1 (Winter 1950): 39–52.
    Groundbreaking examination of the form of *Jubilate Agno* in which Bond discovers line-for-line correspondences between the "Let" and "For" sections.

Booth, Mark W. "Song Form and the Mind in Christopher Smart's Later Poetry." *Studies in Eighteenth-Century Culture* 15 (1985): 211–25.
    Explores the elements in Smart's poetry that "work to intercept discursive rational thought and to invoke another mentality."

Brittain, Robert. Introduction to *Poems by Christopher Smart,* edited by Robert Brittain, pp. 3–74. Princeton, N. J.: Princeton University Press, 1950.
    Valuable survey prefacing an important modern edition of Smart's major poetry. Brittain regards Smart as "fundamentally and foremost a writer of devotional lyrics."

Dearnley, Moira. *The Poetry of Christopher Smart.* New York: Barnes & Noble, 1969, 332 p.
    Examines in turn "the main phases in Smart's poetic activity—the secular work, the early religious verse, the mad poetry, and the religious verse written after madness" and relates the poetry to eighteenth-century literary conventions.

Fairchild, Hoxie Neale. "Four Christian Poets." In *Religious Trends in English Poetry, Volume II: 1740–1780, Religious Sentimentalism in the Age of Johnson,* pp. 131–90. New York: Columbia University Press, 1942.
    Refutes critics' judgment of Smart as a "hack writer" and *A Song to David* as an anomaly among his work. The *Song,* Fairchild maintains, was not "an isolated outburst but . . . the final expression of feelings which the poet had cherished from the beginning of his thwarted career."

Fitzgerald, Robert P. "The Form of Christopher Smart's *Jubilate Agno.*" *Studies in English Literature 1500–1900* VIII, No. 3 (Summer 1968): 487–99.
    Proposes that the poem is actually two works: the "For" section comprising "a kind of personal journal" and the "Let" section representing a draft of a work later abandoned in favor of *A Song to David.*

Gedalof, Allan J. "The Rise and Fall of Smart's David." *Philological Quarterly* 60, No. 3 (Summer 1981): 369–86.
    Examines the figure of King David in Smart's work, characterizing the biblical king as "an ideal agent for the articulation of Smart's sensibility and vision."

Greene, Donald J. "Smart, Berkeley, the Scientists and the Poets: A Note on Eighteenth-Century Anti-Newtonianism." *Journal of the History of Ideas* XIV, No. 3 (June 1953): 327–52.
    Posits a correlation between Smart's philosophy and that of Bishop Berkeley, and argues that Smart's anti-Newtonianism has a logical rather than a mystical basis.

Grigson, Geoffrey. *Christopher Smart.* London: Longmans, Green & Co., 1961, 44 p.
    Concise overview of Smart's major works, underscoring the effects of Smart's madness on his poetry.

Guest, Harriet. *A Form of Sound Words: The Religious Poetry of Christopher Smart.* Oxford: Clarendon Press, 1989, 239 p.
    Analysis of Smart's religious works, from the early Seatonian poems to the late hymns and spiritual songs.

Kumbier, William A. "Sound and Signification in Christopher Smart's *Jubilate Agno.*" *Texas Studies in Literature and Language* 24, No. 3 (Fall 1982): 293–312.
    An examination of *Jubilate Agno* that stresses Smart's preoccupation with language and forms of representation. Kumbier asserts that in *Jubilate Agno* the poet "transforms language into an instrument for mediating between mundane experience and that which . . . both informs and transcends it."

Saltz, Robert D. "Reason in Madness: Christopher Smart's Poetic Development." *Southern Humanities Review* 4, No. 1, (Winter 1970): 57–68.

> Discusses the evolution of Smart's "conception of the sublime poet as the conveyor of the apocalyptic vision."

Scott-Montagu, Elizabeth. "*Rejoice in the Lamb.*" *The Nineteenth Century and After* 125, No. 8 (June 1939): 707–10.

> Review of the initial publication of *Jubilate Agno*, praising the poem and commenting that it will significantly improve Smart's reputation.

Sherbo, Arthur. "Christopher Smart, Free and Accepted Mason." *The Journal of English and Germanic Philology* LIV, No. 4 (October 1955): 664–69.

> Examine's Smart's references to the Masons and his use of Masonic symbolism in *Jubilate Agno*.

Stonier, G. W. "Poor Christ Smart." *The New Statesman and Nation* XVII, No. 417 (18 February 1939): 354.

> Review of the first publication of *Jubilate Agno* that detects signs of Smart's madness evident in the poem.

Walsh, Marcus. Introduction to *The Poetical Works of Christopher Smart, Volume III: A Translation of the Psalms of David,* pp. xi–xxxix. Oxford: Clarendon Press, 1987.

> Includes background on the poems' composition and publication, their place in the tradition of psalm translation, and their critical reception.

Williamson, Karina. "Christopher Smart's *Hymns and Spiritual Songs.*" *Philological Quarterly* XXXVIII, No. 4 (October 1959): 413–24.

> Analyzes *Hymns and Spiritual Songs* according to eighteenth-century conventions of hymn writing.

———. Introduction to *The Poetical Works of Christopher Smart, Volume I: Jubilate Agno,* pp. xv–xxxi. Oxford: Clarendon Press, 1980.

> Provides an examination of the date, text, and sources of the poem, in addition to a biographical essay on Smart.

Wilson, Mona. "My Poor Friend Smart." *English: The Magazine of the English Association* II, No. ii (1939): 299–304.

> Finds in *Jubilate Agno* an affinity with the works of William Blake, as well as a "distorted semblance" of *A Song to David.*

François Villon
1431–1463?

(Born François de Montcorbier alias des Loges) French poet.

INTRODUCTION

Villon is considered one of the most significant French poets of the Middle Ages. His best known works, *Les Lais* (also called *Le Petit Testament* or *The Small Testament*) and *Le Testament* (also *Le Grand Testament* or *The Large Testament*) have been held up as exemplars of the popular Medieval verse form, the testament, which parodies the traditional legal will. The personal nature of his subject matter—especially his vivid descriptions of his life as a thief and vagabond on the streets of Paris—is deemed atypical for his time, and he is credited with imbuing the poetry of his age with vitality and realism.

Biographical Information

Born in France in 1431, Villon's real name was probably François de Montcorbier (after the village on the borders of Burgundy where his father was born) or des Loges (perhaps the name of his father's farm). Of his parents we know only that his father died while Villon was young, and that his mother was poor and illiterate. Villon was raised by Guillaume de Villon, a priest who was probably the poet's uncle. Under his patronage, Villon attended the University of Paris where he received both a Bachelor of Arts and later a Master of Arts. As a student he was often involved in thievery and mischief. In 1455, at the age 24, Villon killed a man, after which he fled Paris. As the murder was apparently a matter of self-defense, Villon received a pardon and returned to Paris six months later. On Christmas Eve, 1456, he participated in a robbery at the Collège de Navarre and fled Paris once again, this time for five years. Before leaving the city, he composed his first major poem, *Les Lais.* While wandering in exile in the provinces of France, Villon found a temporary patron in Charles, Duke of Orleans, who was himself a poet. According to Villon's poetry, he spent some time in the Duke of Orleans's prisons sentenced to death, but was pardoned in celebration of the birth of the Duke's daughter. During the summer of 1461 Villon suffered a particularly cruel imprisonment in Meung-sur-Loire under the order of the Bishop of Orleans, where he was apparently tortured and fed only bread and water. Upon his release in the fall of that year, the poet returned to Paris where he composed his major work, *Le Testament,* which expresses his bitterness toward the Bishop for this incarceration. In 1462, Villon was arrested under suspicion of committing another robbery, but was released due to lack of evidence. Shortly thereafter he was involved in a street brawl and, given his history of trouble with the law, was sentenced to death. While awaiting his sentence, Villon wrote his "Epitaphe Villon," also called "The Ballade des Pen-

Cy comence le grant codicille et testamēt maistre francois Villon

dus." The poet appealed his death sentence and on January 5, 1463 the court commuted his sentence to ten years banishment from Paris. No authentic mention was made of Villon again.

Major Works

Villon is known almost exclusively for his two testaments, *Les Lais* and *Le Testament*, the *ballades* which they contain, and for his epitaph. While his themes and forms were traditionally Medieval, his infusion of humor, pathos, and humanity into his verse was decidedly modern. His first testament, *Les Lais*, is said to genuinely evoke the atmosphere of Paris and the lives of common people during the Middle Ages. In this piece, Villon claims to be leaving Paris due to a troubled romance and he jokingly bequeaths mostly ridiculous items to his friends and enemies—a stolen duck, the sword and the breeches he has pawned, his broken heart. This work is noted by scholars for its clever wit and lighthearted tone. The larger *Testament* of 1461 is very different in sentiment and character from the first; this work is more serious and reflective. Villon reviews his life, his mistakes and disappointments, and the effect of his frequent imprisonments: sickness and poverty. Unlike traditional poetry of the day which was concerned with chivalry, mythology, and the lives of kings, Villon's work focuses on his own life, exploring a wide range of human emotions. Ezra Pound commented that in his poetry Villon "unconsciously proclaims man's divine right to be himself." Included within *Le Testament* are a number of *ballades*, which is a popular French verse form (not to be confused with the ballad) that follows a prescribed rhyme scheme and structure, with three stanzas and an *envoi* (a shorter closing stanza). *Ballades* such as "The Lament of La belle Heaulmière," and "Ballade of the Dead Ladies," are thought by some to best exemplify Villon's poetic genius. As another example of the intimacy and unflinching honesty of his work, "Villon's Epitaph," or "Ballade des Pendus," written under sentence of death, is a detailed and painful vision of himself dangling from the gallows among other hanged criminals.

Critical Reception

Villon's work was much disseminated and appreciated during his lifetime. The earliest edition of his work bearing a date appeared in 1489, with as many as twenty-seven editions appearing by 1542. From early on, critics have remarked less on the structure and composition of the poetry and more on the content, particularly the vivid descriptions of the medieval streets of Paris. Interest in Villon's work almost completely dissipated after the sixteenth century but was revived in the nineteenth as French and English scholars rediscovered Villon. In 1877, August Lognon's study *Etude biographique sur François Villon* revealed new biographical details of the poet's life and helped decipher obscure references in his work. Some critics, such as Robert Louis Stevenson in the *Cornhill Magazine* in 1877, criticized the poet as an insincere cad and a troublemaker whose poetic skills were not sufficient to redeem his work. Most critics agree that Villon's use of personal subject matter, informal language, and sharp wit made him a truly innovative poet. John Payne wrote of Villon in 1880: "The true son of his time, he rejected at once and for ever, with the unerring judgement of the literary reformer, the quaint formalities of speech, the rhetorical exaggerations and limitations of expressions . . . that dwarfed the thought and deformed the limbs of the verse of his day."

PRINCIPAL WORKS

Les Lais [also referred to as *Le Petit Testament*] 1456
Le Testament [commonly called *Le Grand Testament*] 1461
Le grand Testament Villon et le petit. Son codicille. Le jargon et ses balades 1489; reprinted 1924
Les oeuvres de Françoys Villon de Paris, reveues et remises en leur entier par Clément Marot 1533
Oeuvres 1932

The Complete Works of François Villon 1960
The Poems of François Villon 1982

* Dates provided for these works are those given by Villon on the original manuscript versions of his work.

CRITICISM

Henry Francis Cary   (essay date 1823)

SOURCE: "Early French Poets," in *The London Magazine,* Vol. VIII, October, 1823, pp. 436–38.

[*Below, Cary reviews the* Grand Testament *and the* Petit Testament.]

The praise bestowed by Boileau on Villon, and still more the pains taken by Clement Marot, at the instance of Francis the First, to edit his poems, would lead us to expect great things from them; but in this expectation most English readers will probably be disappointed. For while Alain Chartier is full as intelligible as Chaucer, and Charles Duke of Orleans more so, Villon (who wrote after both) can scarcely be made out by the help of a glossary. Even his editor, Marot, who, as he tells us in the preface, had corrected a vast number of passages in his poems, partly from the old editions, partly from the recital of old people who had got them by heart, and partly from his own conjectures, was forced to leave several others untouched, which he could neither correct nor explain. One cause of the difficulty, which we find in reading Villon, is assigned by Marot, in a sentence that shows his knowledge of the true principles of criticism.

> Quant à l'industrie des lays qu'il feit en ses testamens pour suffisamment la congnoistre et entendre, il faudroit avoir esté de son temps à Paris, et avoir congneu les lieux, les choses et les hommes dont il parle; la memoire desquelz tant plus se passera, tant moins se congnoistra icelle industrie des ses lays dictz. Pour ceste cause qui voudra faire une œuvre de longue durée, ne preigne son soubject, sur telles choses basses et particulieres. (**Les Œuvres de François Villon,** à Paris, 1723, small 8vo.)

As to the address with which he has distributed his legacies, in the poems called his Wills, to understand it sufficiently one should have been at Paris in his time, and have been acquainted with the places, the things, and the persons of whom he speaks; for by how much more the memory of these shall have been lost, so much less shall we be able to discover his dexterity in the distribution of these bequests. He who would compose a work that shall last, ought not to choose his subject in circumstances thus mean and particular.

The truth is, that Villon appears have been one of the first French writers who excelled in what they call Badinage, for which I do not know any adequate term in our language. It is something between wit and buffoonery. Less intellectual and refined than the one, and not so gross and personal as the other, in reconciling, it in some degree neutralizes both. To an Englishman it is apt to appear either ridiculous or insipid; to a Frenchman it is almost enough to make the charm of life.

One of the chief causes of Villon's popularity must however have arisen in the great number of French families whom he has mentioned in his two Wills, generally for the purpose of ridiculing certain individuals who belonged to them. A list of these, containing upwards of eighty names, is prefixed to these two poems.

His *Petit Testament,* which was written in 1456, he supposes to have been made on the following occasion. Being heartily tired of love, and thinking there was no other cure for it but death, he represents himself as determined on leaving this world, and accordingly draws up his will.

His *Grand Testament* was framed in a more serious conjuncture. In 1461 he was committed to prison at Melun, together with five accomplices, for a crime, the nature of which is not known. But whatever it were, he intimates that he was tempted into it by his mistress who afterwards deserted him. He remained in a dungeon and in chains, on an allowance of bread and water, during a whole summer, and was condemned to be hung; but Louis XI (who had then newly succeeded to the throne), in consideration, as it is said, of his poetical abilities, mercifully commuted his punishment into exile. He is, perhaps, the only man whom the muse has rescued from the gallows. The hardships he had suffered during his confinement brought on a premature old age; but they taught him, he says, more wisdom than he could have learned from a commentary on Aristotle's ethics.

> Travail mes lubres sentimens
> Aguisa (ronds comme pelote)
> Me monstrant plus que les commens
> Sur le sens moral d'Aristote.

> Trouble has sharpened my lubberly thoughts (before as round as a bullet); showing me more than the comments on Aristotle's Ethics could have done.

The first place at which he found a refuge was Saint Genou, near Saint Julien, on the road leading from Poitou into Bretagne. Here he was reduced to such extremity, that he was forced to beg his bread; and if the fear of his Maker had not restrained him, he declares he should have put an end to himself.

There is little known of what happened to him afterwards. He probably met with some lucky turn of fortune; for Rabelais mentions his having been in favour with Edward V of England, and his dying at an advanced age.

From what has been said of the peculiar vein of his genius, the reader will perceive, that it is scarcely capable of being fairly represented in another language. His happy

turns of expression, smart personalities, and witty inuendoes, would tell very indifferently at second hand. A short ballad out of the *Grand Testament,* being more general, may be attempted.

Ballade, des Dames du Temps Jadis.

> Dictes moy, ou, ne en quel pays
> Est Flora la belle Romaine,
> Archipiada, ne Thais
> Qui fut sa cousine Germaine?
> Echo parlant quand bruyt on maine
> Dessus riviere, ou sus estan
> Qui beauté eut trop plus que humaine?
> Mais ou sont les neiges d'antan?

> Ou est la tressage Heloïs?
> Pour qui fut chastré (et puy Moyne)
> Pierre Esbaillart à Sainct Denys
> Pour son amour eut cest essoyne.
> Semblablement ou est la Royne,
> Qui commanda que Buridan
> Fut jetté en ung sac en Seine?
> Mais ou sont les neiges d'antan?

> La Royne blanche comme ung lys
> Qui chantoit à voix de Sereine,
> Berthe au grand pied, Bietris, Allys,
> Harembouges qui tint le Mayne,
> Et Jehanne la bonne Lorraine
> Que Angloys bruslerent à Rouen.
> Ou sont ilz, vierge souveraine?
> Mais ou sont les neiges d'antan?

> Prince n'enquerez de sepmaine
> Ou elles sont, ne de cest an,
> Que ce refrain ne vous remaine
> Mais ou sont les neiges d'antan?

BALLAD, OF THE LADIES OF PAST TIMES.

> Tell me where, or in what clime,
> Is that mistress of the prime,
> Roman Flora? she of Greece,
> Thais? or that maid so fond,
> That, an ye shout o'er stream or pond,
> Answering holdeth not her peace?
> —Where are they?—Tell me, if ye know;
> What is come of last year's snow?

> Where is Heloise the wise,
> For whom Abelard was fain,
> Mangled in such cruel wise,
> To turn a monk instead of man?
> Where the Queen, who into Seine
> Bade them cast poor Buridan?
> —Where are they?—Tell me, if ye know;
> What is come of last year's snow?

> The Queen, that was as lily fair,
> Whose songs were sweet as linnets' are,
> Bertha, or she who govern'd Maine?

Alice, Beatrix, or Joan,
That good damsel of Loraine,
Whom the English burnt at Roan?
—Where are they?—Tell me, if ye know;
What is come of last year's snow?

   Prince, question by the month or year;
The burden of my song is here:
—Where are they?—Tell me, if ye know;
What is come of last year's snow?

While he was under sentence of death, he wrote some verses in which there is a strange mixture of pathos and humour. They begin thus:

Freres humains qui après nous vivez,
N'ayez les cueurs contre nous endurcis,
Car si pitié de nous pouvres avez,
Dieu en aura plustost de vous merciz;
Vous nous voyez cy attachez, cinq, six,
Quant de la chair, que trop avons nourrie
Elle est pieça devoree et pourrie,
Et nous les os, devenons cendre et pouldre;
De nostre mal personne ne s'en rie,
Mais priez Dieu que tous nous vueille absouldre.

O brethren, ye who live when we are gone,
Let not your hearts against us harden'd be;
For e'en as ye do pity us each one,
So gracious God be sure will pity ye;
Here hanging five or six of us you see;
As to our flesh, which once too well we fed,
That now is rotten quite and mouldered;
And we, the bones, do turn to dust and clay;
None laugh at us that are so ill bested,
But pray ye God to do our sins away.

The Epigram on himself, when he was condemned, is more ludicrous.

Je suis François (dont ce me poise)
Né de Paris, emprés Ponthoise,
Or d'une corde d'une toise
Sçaura mon col que mon cul poise.

Let us hope that it was no heinous offence for which he could suffer with so much gaiety.

The **Petit Testament** is very short, not much more than 200 verses. In the drollery, such as it is, of this fancied disposal of property, made with no other view than that of raising a laugh at the legatees, he has had a crowd of imitators. The **Grand Testament,** besides many items of the same kind, includes several ballads and rondels, which one of his commentators not unreasonably supposes to have been written separately, and afterwards classed under this common title, for they have no apparent connexion with the main subject.

His other writings consist chiefly of a few ballads in the language D'Argot, or, as we should call it, slang. Clement Marot found them unintelligible, and left them to be ex-

pounded by Villon's successors in the art of knavery. I have not heard that any of them have undertaken the task. Indeed it would be a betrayal of their secrets, as little for their common good, as if a Romish priest were to translate the invocations of the Saints, or a physician his recipes, out of the Latin into the vernacular tongue. Of the Repuës Franches, which has been sometimes attributed to him, it is decided that he is not the author but the hero.

Villon was born at Paris, in 1431, of mean parentage, as appears from the following stanza in his **Grand Testament:—**

Pauvre je suys de ma jeunesse
De pauvre et de petite extrace,
Mon pere, n'eut onq' grand' richesse,
Ne son ayeul nommé Erace,
Pauvreté tous nous suyt et trace,
Sur les tumbeaulx de mes ancestres
(Les ames desquelz Dieu embrasse)
On n'y voyt couronnes ne sceptres.

Poor am I, poor have alway been,
And poor before me were my race:
No wealth my sire possess'd, I ween,
And none his grandsire, hight Erace:
Poortith our steps doth ever trace:
O'er my forefathers' humble graves
(The souls of whom may God embrace)
No crown is hung, no seeptre waves.

The time of his death is not known.

Robert Louis Stevenson (essay date 1877)

SOURCE: "François Villon, Student, Poet, and House-breaker," in *The Cornhill Magazine,* Vol. XXXVI, No. 212, August, 1877, pp. 215–34.

[*Stevenson was a Scottish novelist and poet. His novels* Treasure Island *(1883),* Kidnapped *(1886), and* Dr. Jekyll and Mr. Hyde *(1886) were considered popular literary classics upon publication and firmly established his reputation as an inventive stylist and riveting storyteller. Stevenson is also noted for his understanding of youth, which is evident both in his early "boy's novels," as they were known, and in his much-loved* A Child's Garden of Verses *(1885). In the following excerpt, Stevenson probes Villon's biography and verse, and finds him a disreputable and insecure scoundrel and poet.*]

Perhaps one of the most curious revolutions in literary history is the sudden bull's-eye light cast by M. Longnon, only last winter, on the obscure existence of François Villon [in *Etude Biographique sur François Villon*]. His book is not remarkable merely as a chapter of biography exhumed after four centuries. To readers of the poet it will recall, with a flavour of satire, that characteristic passage in which he bequeaths his spectacles—with a humorous reservation of the case—to the hospital for blind paupers known as the Fifteen-Score. Thus equipped, let the blind paupers go and separate the good from the bad in the cemetery of the Innocents! For his own part the poet can see no distinction. Much have the dead people made of their advantages. What does it matter now that they have lain in state beds and nourished portly bodies upon cakes and cream? Here they all lie, to be trodden in the mud; the large estate and the small, sounding virtue and adroit or powerful vice, in very much the same condition; and a bishop not to be distinguished from a lamplighter with even the strongest spectacles.

Such was Villon's cynical philosophy. Four hundred years after his death, when surely all danger might be considered at an end, a pair of critical spectacles have been applied to his own remains; and though he left behind him a sufficiently ragged reputation from the first, it is only after these four hundred years that his delinquencies have been finally tracked home, and we can assign him to his proper place among the good or wicked. It is a staggering thought, and one that affords a fine figure of the imperishability of men's acts, that the stealth of the private inquiry office can be carried so far back into the dead and dusty past. We are not so soon quit of our concerns as Villon fancied. In the extreme of dissolution, when not so much as a man's name is remembered, when his dust is scattered to the four winds, and perhaps the very grave and the very graveyard where he was laid to rest have been forgotten, desecrated, and buried under populous towns,— even in this extreme let an antiquary fall across a sheet of manuscript, and the name will be recalled, the old infamy will pop out into daylight like a toad out of a fissure in the rock, and the shadow of the shade of what was once a man will be heartily pilloried by his descendants. A little while ago and Villon was almost totally forgotten; then he was revived for the sake of his verses; and now he is being revived with a vengeance in the detection of his misdemeanors. How unsubstantial is this projection of a man's existence, which can lie in abeyance for centuries and then be brushed up again and set forth for the consideration of posterity by a few dips in an antiquary's inkpot! This precarious tenure of fame goes a long way to justify those (and they are not few) who prefer cakes and cream in the immediate present.

François de Montcorbier, *alias* François des Loges, *alias* François Villon, *alias* Michel Mouton, Master of Arts in the University of Paris, was born in that city in the summer of 1431. It was a memorable year for France on other and higher considerations. A great-hearted girl and a poor-hearted boy made, the one her last, the other his first appearance on the public stage of that unhappy country. On the thirtieth of May the ashes of Joan of Arc were thrown into the Seine, and on the second of December our Henry Sixth made his Joyous Entry dismally enough into disaffected and depopulating Paris. Sword and fire still ravaged the open country. On a single April Saturday twelve hundred persons, besides children, made their escape out of the starving capital. The hangman, as is not uninteresting to note in connection with Master Francis, was kept hard at work in 1431; on the last of April and on the fourth of May alone, sixty-two bandits swung from Paris gibbets. A more confused or troublous time it would

have been difficult to select for a start in life. Not even a man's nationality was certain; for the people of Paris there was no such thing as Frenchmen. The English were the English indeed, but the French were only the Armagnacs, whom, with Joan of Arc at their head, they had beaten back from under their ramparts not two years before. Such public sentiment as they had, centred about their dear Duke of Burgundy, and the dear Duke had no more urgent business than to keep out of their neighbourhood. . . . At least, and whether he liked it or not, our disreputable troubadour was tubbed and swaddled as a subject of the English crown. On this account he may find some indulgence at the hands of Mrs. Grundy.

We hear nothing of Villon's father except that he was poor and of mean extraction. His mother was given piously, which does not imply very much in an old Frenchwoman, and quite uneducated. He had an uncle, a monk in an abbey at Angers, who must have prospered beyond the family average, and was reported to be worth five or six hundred crowns. Of this uncle and his money-box the reader will hear once more. In 1448 Francis became a student of the University of Paris; in 1450 he took the degree of Bachelor, and in 1452 that of Master of Arts. His *bourse,* or the sum paid weekly for his board, was of the amount of two sous. Now two sous was about the price of a pound of salt butter in the bad times of 1417; it was the price of half-a-pound in the worse times of 1419; and in 1444, just four years before Villon joined the University, it seems to have been taken as the average wage for a day's manual labour. In short, it cannot have been a very profuse allowance to keep a sharp-set lad in breakfast and supper for seven mortal days; and Villon's share of the cakes and pastry and general good cheer, to which he is never weary of referring, must have been slender from the first.

The educational arrangements of the University of Paris were, to our way of thinking, somewhat incomplete. Worldly and monkish elements were presented in a curious confusion, which the youth might disentangle for himself. If he had an opportunity, on the one hand, of acquiring much hair-drawn divinity and a taste for formal disputation, he was put in the way of much gross and flaunting vice upon the other. The lecture-room of a scholastic doctor was sometimes under the same roof with establishments of a very different and peculiarly unedifying order. The students had extraordinary privileges, which by all accounts they abused extraordinarily. And while some condemned themselves to an almost sepulchral regularity and seclusion, others fled the schools, swaggered in the street "with their thumbs in their girdle," passed the night in riot, and behaved themselves as the worthy forerunners of Jehan Frollo in the romance of *Notre Dame de Paris.* Villon tells us himself that he was among the truants, but we hardly needed his avowal. The burlesque erudition in which he sometimes indulged implies no more than the merest smattering of knowledge; whereas his acquaintance with blackguard haunts and industries, and the unaffected impudence of his corruption, could only have been acquired by early and consistent impiety and idleness. He passed his degrees, it is true; but some of us who have been to modern universities will make their own reflections on the value of the test. As for his three pupils, Colin Laurent, Girard Gossovyn, and Jehan Marceau—if they were really his pupils in any serious sense—what can we say but God help them? And sure enough, by his own description, they turned out as ragged, rowdy, and ignorant as was to be looked for from the views and manners of their rare preceptor.

At some time or other, before or during his university career, the poet was adopted by Master Guillaume de Villon, chaplain of Saint Benoît-le-Bétourné near the Sorbonne. From him he borrowed the surname by which he is known to posterity. It was most likely from his house, called the *Porte Rouge,* and situated in a garden in the cloister of St. Benoît, that Master Francis heard the bell of the Sorbonne ring out the Angelus while he was finishing his **Small Testament** at Christmastide in 1456. Towards this benefactor he usually gets credit for a respectable display of gratitude. But with his trap and pitfall style of writing, it is easy to make too sure. His sentiments are about as much to be relied on as those of a professional beggar; and in this, as in so many other matters, he comes towards us whining and piping the eye, and goes off again with a whoop and his finger to his nose. Thus, he calls Guillaume de Villon his "more than father," thanks him with a great show of sincerity for having helped him out of many scrapes, and bequeaths him his portion of renown. But the portion of renown which belonged to a young thief, distinguished (if, at the period when he wrote this legacy, he was distinguished at all) for having written some more or less obscene and scurrilous ballads, must have been little fitted to gratify the self-respect or increase the reputation of a benevolent ecclesiastic. The same remark applies to a subsequent legacy of the poet's library, with specification of one work which was plainly neither decent nor devout. We are thus left on the horns of a dilemma. If the chaplain was a godly, philanthropic personage, who had tried to graft good principles and good behaviour on this wild slip of an adopted son, these jesting legacies would obviously cut him to the heart. The position of an adopted son towards his adoptive father is one full of delicacy; where a man lends his name he looks for great consideration. And this legacy of Villon's portion of renown may be taken as the mere fling of an unregenerate scapegrace who has wit enough to recognise in his own shame the readiest weapon of offence against a prosy benefactor's feelings. The gratitude of Master Francis figures, on this reading, as a frightful *minus* quantity. If, on the other hand, those jests were given and taken in good humour, the whole relation between the pair degenerates into the unedifying complicity of a debauched old chaplain and a witty and dissolute young scholar. At this rate the house with the red door may have rung with the most mundane minstrelsy; and it may have been below its roof that Villon, through a hole in the plaster, studied, as he tells us, the leisures of a rich ecclesiastic.

It was, perhaps, of some moment in the poet's life that he should have inhabited the cloister of Saint Benoît. Three of the most remarkable among his early acquaintances are Catherine de Vausselles, for whom he entertained a short-lived affection and an enduring and most unmanly resent-

ment; Regnier de Montigny, a young blackguard of good birth; and Colin de Cayeux, a fellow with a marked aptitude for picking locks. Now we are on a foundation of mere conjecture, but it is at least curious to find that two of the canons of Saint Benoît answered respectively to the names of Pierre de Vaucel and Etienne de Montigny, and that there was a householder called Nicolas de Cayeux in a street—the Rue des Poirées—in the immediate neighbourhood of the cloister. M. Longnon is almost ready to identify Catherine as the niece of Pierre; Regnier as the nephew of Etienne, and Colin as the son of Nicolas. Without going so far, it must be owned that the approximation of names is significant. As we go on to see the part played by each of these persons in the sordid melodrama of the poet's life, we shall come to regard it as even more notable. Is it not Clough who has remarked that, after all, everything lies in juxtaposition? Many a man's destiny has been settled by nothing apparently more grave than a pretty face on the opposite side of the street and a couple of bad companions round the corner.

Catherine de Vausselles (or de Vaucel—the change is within the limits of Villon's licence) had plainly delighted in the poet's conversation; near neighbours or not, they were much together; and Villon made no secret of his court, and suffered himself to believe that his feeling was repaid in kind. This may have been an error from the first, or he may have estranged her by subsequent misconduct or temerity. One can easily imagine Villon an impatient wooer. One thing, at least, is sure: that the affair terminated in a manner bitterly humiliating to Master Francis. Indeed, if you run over on your fingers all the ridiculous mishaps by which a tender sentiment may be unworthily concluded and suppressed, you will scarcely imagine a more deplorable upshot than the one in question. In presence of his lady love, perhaps under her window and certainly with her connivance, he was unmercifully thrashed by one Noë le Joly—beaten, as he says himself, like dirty linen on the washing-board. The story oozed out and created infinite merriment among his friends: he became a byword in Paris. It is characteristic that his malice had notably increased between the time when he wrote the **Small Testament** immediately on the back of the occurrence, and the time when he wrote the **Large Testament** five years after. On the latter occasion nothing is too bad for his "damsel with the twisted nose," as he calls her. She is spared neither hint nor accusation, and he tells his messenger to accost her with the vilest insults. Villon, it is thought, was out of Paris when these amenities escaped his pen; or no doubt the strong arm of Noë le Joly would have been again requisition. So ends the love story, if love story it may properly be called. Poets are not necessarily fortunate in love; but they usually fall among more romantic circumstances and bear their disappointment with a better grace. Actual bastinado is a sad pass, and trying for a man's self-respect; but St. Paul was beaten with many stripes and could speak of them with pride. As for Master Francis he had not even the wit to hold his tongue; he must bear malice five years together and rail like a fish-woman against her whom he professed to love. What should have been at worst a five days' scandal in the Latin Quarter he has so cooked up and handed down that, after the lapse of four centuries, we can still hear Noë le Joly emphatically chastising, and still behold, in plausible imagination, a threadpaper poet reversed across his knee with squalls and agonies. Nor did he confine himself to mere reviling in the style of the rejected beggar. With a whine that is pre-eminently characteristic of the man, he declares this cruel fair one to be the cause of his misfortunes, and wishes to enscroll himself as one of the martyrs of love. One would not condemn a dog on the evidence of Master Francis; and besides, where a man is born a blackguard it requires no very elaborate chain of circumstances to put him in a blackguard way of life. But the whine is worth recording.

> Some charitable critics see no more than a *jeu d'esprit,* a graceful and trifling exercise of the imagination, in the grimy ballad of Fat Peg (*Grosse Margot*). I am not able to follow these gentlemen to this polite extreme. Out of all Villon's works that ballád stands forth in flaring reality, gross and ghastly, as a thing written in a contraction of disgust.
>
> —*Robert Louis Stevenson*

The neighbourhood of Regnier de Montigny and Colin de Cayeux was probably more instrumental in hurrying our poet towards disgrace, than either the contempt of Catherine or the strong arm of Noë le Joly. For a man who is greedy of all pleasures and provided with little money and less dignity of character, we may prophesy a safe and speedy voyage downward. Humble or even truckling virtue may walk unspotted in this life. But only those who despise the pleasures, can afford to despise the opinion of the world. A man of a strong, heady temperament, like Villon, is very differently tempted. His eyes lay hold on all provocations greedily, and his heart flames up at a look into imperious desire; he is snared and broached to by anything and everything, from a pretty face to a piece of pastry in a cookshop window; he will drink the rinsing of the wine cup, stay the latest at the tavern party; tap at the lit windows, follow the sound of singing, and beat the whole neighbourhood for another reveller, as he goes reluctantly homeward; and grudge himself every hour of sleep as a black, empty period when he cannot follow after pleasure. Such a person is lost if he have not dignity, or failing that, at least pride, which is its shadow and in many ways its substitute. Master Francis, although he was not so thick-skinned but he could smart under the affront of Noë le Joly's cudgelling, was, on the whole, singularly devoid of these incommodious and honourable qualities. I fancy he could follow his own eager instincts without much spiritual struggle. And we soon find him fallen among thieves in sober, literal earnest, and counting as friends the most disreputable people he could lay his hands on: fellows who stole ducks in Paris Moat; sergeants of the criminal court, and archers of the watch; blackguards who slept at night under the butchers' stalls, and for whom the aforesaid archers peered about carefully with lanterns; Regnier de Montigny, Colin de Caycux and their crew, all bound on a favouring breeze towards the gallows; the disorderly abbess of Port Royal who went about at fair time with soldiers and thieves, and conducted her abbey on the queerest principles; and most likely Perette Mauger, the great Paris receiver of stolen goods, not yet dreaming, poor woman! of the last scene of her career when Henry Cousin, executor of the high justice, shall bury her, alive and most reluctant, in front of the new Montigny gibbet. Nay, our friend soon began to take a foremost rank in this society. He could string off verses, which is always an agreeable talent; and he could make himself useful in many other ways. The whole ragged army of Bohemia, and whosoever loved good cheer without at all loving to work and pay for it, are addressed in contemporary verses as the "Subjects of François Villon." He was a good genius to all hungry and unscrupulous persons; and became the hero of a whole legendary cycle of tavern tricks and cheateries. At best, these were doubtful levities, rather too thievish for a school-boy, rather too gamesome for a thief. But he would not linger long in this equivocal border land. He must soon have complied with his surroundings. He was one who would go where the cannikin clinked, not caring who should pay; and from supping in the wolves' den, there is but a step to hunting with the pack. And here, as I am on the chapter of his degradation, I shall say all I mean to say about its darkest expression, and be done with it for good. Some charitable critics see no more than a *jeu d'esprit,* a graceful and trifling exercise of the imagination, in the grimy ballad of Fat Peg (*Grosse Margot*). I am not able to follow these gentlemen to this polite extreme. Out of all Villon's works that ballad stands forth in flaring reality, gross and ghastly, as a thing written in a contraction of disgust. M. Longnon shows us more and more clearly at every page that we are to read our poet literally, that his names are the names of real persons, and the events he chronicles were actual events. But even if the tendency of criticism had run the other way, this ballad would have gone far to prove itself. I can well understand the reluctance of worthy persons in this matter; for of course it is unpleasant to think of a man of genius as one who held, in the words of Marina to Boult—

> A place, for which the pained'st fiend
> Of hell would not in reputation change.

But beyond this natural unwillingness, the whole difficulty of the case springs from a highly virtuous ignorance of life. Paris now is not so different from the Paris of then; and the whole of the doings of Bohemia are not written in the sugar-candy pastorals of Murger. It is really not at all surprising that a young man of the fifteenth century, with a knack of making verses, should accept his bread upon disgraceful terms. The race of those who do, is not extinct; and some of them to this day write the prettiest verses imaginable. . . . After this, it were impossible for Master Francis to fall lower: to go and steal for himself would be an admirable advance from every point of view, divine or human.

And yet it is not as a thief, but as a homicide, that he makes his first appearance before angry justice. On June 5, 1455, when he was about twenty-four, and had been Master of Arts for a matter of three years, we behold him for the first time quite definitely. Angry justice had, as it were, photographed him in the act of his homicide; and M. Longnon, rummaging among old deeds, has turned up the negative and printed it off for our instruction. Villon had been supping—copiously we may believe—and sat on a stone bench in front of the church of St. Benoît, in company with a priest called Gilles and a woman of the name of Isabeau. It was nine o'clock, a mighty late hour for the period, and evidently a fine summer's night. Master Francis carried a mantle, like a prudent man, to keep him from the dews (*serain*), and had a sword below it dangling from his girdle. So these three dallied in front of St. Benoît, taking their pleasure (*pour soy esbatre*). Suddenly there arrived upon the scene a priest, Philippe Chermoye or Sermaise, also with sword and cloak, and accompanied by one Master Jehan le Mardi. Sermaise, according to Villon's account, which is all we have to go upon, came up blustering and denying God; as Villon rose to make room for him upon the bench, thrust him rudely back into his place; and finally drew his sword and cut open his lower lip, by what I should imagine was a very clumsy stroke. Up to this point, Villon professes to have been a model of courtesy, even of feebleness; and the brawl, in his version, reads like the fable of the wolf and the lamb. But now the lamb was roused; he drew his sword, stabbed Sermaise in the groin, knocked him on the head with a big stone, and then, leaving him to his fate, went away to have his own lip doctored by a barber of the name of Fouquet. In one version, he says that Gilles, Isabeau, and Le Mardi ran away at the first high words, and that he and Sermaise had it out alone; in another, Le Mardi is represented as returning and wresting Villon's sword from him: the reader may please himself. Sermaise was picked up, lay all that night in the prison of Saint Benoît, where he was examined by an official of the Châtelet and expressly pardoned Villon, and died on the following Saturday in the Hôtel Dieu. He was plainly not a man of execution like Noë le Joly; and on the whole, a poor, crapulous being, mused with drink.

This, as I have said, was in June. Not before January of the next year, could Villon extract a pardon from the king; but while his hand was in, he got two. One is for "François des Loges, alias (*autrement dit*) de Villon"; and the other runs in the name of François de Moncorbier. Nay, it appears there was a further complication; for in the narrative of the first of these documents, it is mentioned that he passed himself off upon Fouguet, the barber-surgeon, as one Michel Mouton. M. Longnon has a theory, that this unhappy accident with Sermaise was the cause of Villon's subsequent irregularities; and that up to that moment he had been the pink of good behaviour. But the matter has to my eyes a more dubious air. A pardon necessary for Des Loges and another for Montcorbier? and these two the same person? and one or both of them known by the *alias* of Villon, however honestly come by? and lastly, in the heat of the moment, a fourth name thrown out with an assured countenance? A ship is not to be trusted that sails

under so many colours. This is not the simple bearing of innocence. No—the young master was already treading crooked paths; already, he would start and blench at a hand upon his shoulder, with the look we know so well in the face of Hogarth's Idle Apprentice; already, in the blue devils, he would see Henry Cousin, the executor of high justice, going in dolorous procession towards Montfaucon, and hear the wind and the birds crying around Paris gibbet. . . .

John Payne (essay date 1880)

SOURCE: "François Villon," in *The Nineteenth Century*, Vol. VIII, No. XLIII, September, 1880, pp. 481–500.

[*Below, Payne discusses Villon's ability to portray common people and events of 15th-century Paris in a clear and realistic manner, making him "the first great poet of the people."*]

There are few names in the history of literature over which the shadow has so long and so persistently lain as over that of the father of French poetry. Up to no more distant period than the early part of the year 1877, it was not even known what was his real name, nor were the admirers of his genius in possession of any other facts relative to his personal history than could be gleaned, by a painful process of inference and deduction, from those works of the poet that have been handed down to posterity. The materials that exist for the biography of Shakespeare or Dante are indeed scanty enough, but they present a very harvest of fact and suggestion compared with the pitiable fragments upon which, until the publication of M. [Auguste] Longnon's *Etude Biographique sur Francois Villon* [1877], we had alone to rely for our personal knowledge of Villon. Even now the facts and dates, that M. Longnon has so valiantly and so ingeniously rescued for us from the vast charnel-house of mediæval history, are in themselves scanty enough; and it is necessary to apply to their connection and elucidation no mean amount of goodwill and faithful labour, before anything like a definite framework of biography can be constructed from them. Such as they are, however, they enable us for the first time to catch a glimpse of the strange mad life and dissolute yet attractive personality of the wild, reckless, unfortunate Parisian poet, whose splendid if erratic verse flames out like a meteor from the somewhat dim twilight of French fifteenth-century literature.

. . . . .

No work of Villon's, posterior to the *Greater Testament,* is known to us, nor is there any trace of its existence: indeed, from the date 1461, with which he himself heads his principal work, we entirely lose sight of him; and it may be supposed, in view of the condition of mental and bodily weakness in which we find him at that time, that he did not long survive its completion.

There can be no doubt that Villon was appreciated at something like his real literary value by the people of his time. Little as we know of his life, everything points to the conclusion that his writings were highly popular during his lifetime, not only among those princes and gallants whom he had made his friends, but among that Parisian public of the lower orders with whom he was so intimately identified. Allusions here and there lead us to suppose that his ballads and shorter pieces were known among the people long before they were collected into a final form; and it is probable that they were hawked about in MS. and afterwards printed on broadsheets in black letter, as were such early English poems as the *Childe of Bristowe* and the *History of Tom Thumb.* For a hundred years after his death the ballads were always differentiated from the rest in the colophons or descriptive headings of the various editions, in which the printers announce 'The Testament of Villon *and his Ballads,'* as if the latter had previously been a separate and well-known speciality of the poet; we may even suppose them to have been set to music and sung, as were the odes of Ronsard a hundred years later; and, indeed, many of them seem imperatively to call for such treatment. Who cannot fancy the **"Ballad of the Women of Paris,"** 'Il n'est bon bec que de Paris,' being sung about the streets by the students and gamins, or the orison for Master Cotard's soul being trolled out as a drinking-song by that jolly toper at some jovial reunion of the notaries and 'chicquanous' of his acquaintance?

> **The cry of the people rings out from Villon's verse—that cry of mingled misery and humour, sadness and cheerfulness, which, running through Rabelais and Régnier, was to pass unheeded till it swelled into the judgment-thunder of the Revolution.**
>
> —*John Payne*

The twenty-seven editions, still extant, that were published before 1542, are sufficient evidence of the demand (probably for the time unprecedented) that existed for his poems during the seventy or eighty years that followed his death; and it is a significant fact that the greatest poet of the first half of the sixteenth century should have applied himself, at the special request of Francis the First (who is said to have known Villon by heart), to rescue his works from the labyrinth of corruption and misrepresentation into which they had fallen through the carelessness of printers and the *insouciance* of the public, who seem to have had his verses too well by rote to trouble themselves to protest against misprints and misreadings. Marot's own writings bear evident traces of the care and love with which he had studied the first poet of his time, who, indeed, appears to have given the tone to all the rhymers, Gringoire, Martial d'Auvergne, Cretin, Coquillart, Jean Marot, who continued, though with no great brilliancy, to keep alive the sound and cadence of French song during the latter part of the fifteenth and the first years of the sixteenth centuries.

The advent of the poets of the Pleiad, and the deluge of Latin and Greek form and sentiment with which they flooded the poetic literature of France, seem at once to have arrested the popularity of the older poets. Imitations of Horace, Catullus, Anacreon, Pindar, took the place of the more spontaneous and original style of poetry founded upon the innate capacities of the language and that *esprit gaulois* that represented the national sentiment and tendencies. The memory of Villon, *enfant de Paris,* child of the Parisian gutter as he was, went down before the new movement, characterised at once by its extreme pursuit of refinement at all hazards and its neglect of those stronger and deeper currents of sympathy and passion for which one must dive deep into the troubled waters of popular life and popular movement. For nearly three centuries the name and fame of the singer of the ladies of old time remained practically forgotten, buried under wave upon wave of literary and political movement, all apparently equally hostile to the tendency and spirit of his work. We find, indeed, the three greatest spirits of the sixteenth and seventeenth centuries, Rabelais, Regnier and La Fontaine, evincing by their works and style, if not by any more explicit declaration, their profound knowledge and sincere appreciation of Villon; but their admiration had no influence whatever upon the universal consent with which the tastes and tendencies of their respective times appear to have agreed upon the complete oblivion of the early poet. The first half of the eighteenth century, indeed, produced three several editions of Villon; but the critics and readers of the age were little likely to prefer the high-flavoured and robust food, that Villon set before them, to the whipped creams, the rose and musk-flavoured confections with which the literary pastry-cooks of the day so liberally supplied them; and it was not till the full development, towards the end of the first half of the present century, of the Romantic movement (a movement whose causes and tendencies bore so great an affinity to that of which Villon in his own time was himself the agent), that he again began to be in some measure restored to his proper place in the hierarchy of French literature. Yet even then we can still remember the compassionate ridicule with which the efforts of Théophile Gautier to revindicate the memory of the great old poet were received, and how even that perfect and noble spirit, in whose catholic and unerring appreciation no spark of true genius or of worthy originality ever failed to light a corresponding flame of enthusiasm, was fain to dissimulate the fervour of his admiration under the translucid mask of partial depreciation, and to provide for his too bold enterprise of rehabilitation a kind of apologetic shelter by classing the first great poet of France with far less worthy writers, under the heading of 'Les Grotesques.' In the country of his birth Villon is still little read, although the illustrious poet Théodore de Banville has done much to facilitate the revival of his fame by regenerating the form in which his greatest triumphs were achieved; and it is perhaps, indeed, in England that his largest public (scanty enough as yet) may be expected to be found.

The vigorous beauty and reckless independence of Villon's style and thought, although a great, has been by no means the only obstacle to his enduring popularity. A hardly less effectual one has always existed in the evanescent nature of the allusions upon which so large a part of his work is founded. In his preface to the edition above referred to, Marot allows it to be inferred that, even at so comparatively early a period as 1533, the greater part of his references to persons and places of his own day had become obscure, if not altogether undecipherable, to all but those few persons of advanced age who may be said to have been almost his contemporaries. Nevertheless, when we have made the fullest possible allowance for obscurity and faded interest, there still remain in Villon's verse treasures of beauty, wit and wisdom, enough to insure the preservation of his memory as a poet as long as the remembrance of French poetry survives.

Villon's spirit and tendency are eminently romantic, in the sense that he employed modern language and modern resources to express and individualise the eternal elements of human interest and human passion as they appeared, moulded into new phases and invested with new colours and characteristics by the shifting impulses and tendencies of his time. He had, indeed, in no ordinary degree, the great qualification of the romantic poet; he understood the splendour of modern things, and knew the conjurations that should compel the coy spirit of contemporary beauty to cast off the rags and tatters of circumstance, the low and debased seeming in which it was enchanted, and tower forth, young, glorious and majestic, as the bewitched princess in the fairy tale puts off the aspect and vesture of hideous and repulsive eld at the magic touch of perfect love. The true son of his time, he rejected at once and for ever, with the unerring judgment of the literary reformer, the quaint formalities of speech, the rhetorical exaggerations and limitations of expression and the Chinese swathing of allegory and conceit that dwarfed the thought and deformed the limbs of the verse of his day and reduced poetry to a kind of Thibetan prayer-wheel, in which the advent of the Spring, the conflict of love and honour, the cry of the lover against the cruelty of his lady and the glorification of the latter by endless comparison to all things fit and unfit, were ground up again and again into a series of kaleidoscopic patterns, wearisome in the sameness of their mannered beauty, and from whose contemplation one rises with dazzled eyes and exhausted sense, longing for some cry of passion, some flower-birth of genuine sentiment, to burst the strangling sheath of affectation and prescription. Before Villon, the language of the poets of the time had become almost as pedantic, although not so restricted and colourless, as that of the seventeenth and eighteenth centuries. By dint of continual employment in the same grooves and in the same formal sense, the most forceful and picturesque words of the language had almost ceased to possess individuality or colour; for the phosphorescence that springs from the continual contact of words with thought and their reconstruction at the stroke of passion was wanting, not to be supplied or replaced by the aptest ingenuity or the most untiring wit. Villon did for French poetic speech that which Rabelais afterwards performed for its prose (and it is a singular coincidence, which I believe has not before been remarked, that the father of French poetry and the father of French prose were, as it were, predestined to the task they accomplished

A woodcut illustration for Villon's "Epitaph", from the 1489 edition, Le grant Testament Villon et le petit. Son codicille. Le jargon et ses balades.

by the name that was common to both, *François* or *French par excellence*). He restored the exhausted literary language of his time to youth and health by infusing into it the healing poisons, the revivifying acids and bitters of the popular speech, disdaining no materials that served his purpose, replacing the defunct forms with new phrases, new shapes wrung from the heart of the spoken tongue, plunging with audacious hand into the slang of the tavern and the bordel, the cant of the highway and the prison, choosing from the wayside heap and the street gutter the neglected pebbles and nodules in which he alone divined the hidden diamonds and rubies of picturesque expression, to be polished and facetted into glory and beauty by the regenerating friction of poetic employment.

Villon was the first great poet of the people: his love of the life of common things, the easy familiarity of the streets and highways, his intimate knowledge of and affection for the home and outdoor life of the merchant, the hawker, the artisan, the mountebank, nay, even the thief, the prostitute and the gipsy of his time, stand out in unmistakable characters from the lineaments of his work. The cry of the people rings out from his verse—that cry of mingled misery and humour, sadness and cheerfulness, which, running through Rabelais and Régnier, was to pass unheeded till it swelled into the judgment-thunder of the Revolution. The sufferings, the oppression, the *bonhomic,* the *gourmandise,* the satirical good humour of that French people that has so often been content to starve upon a jesting ballad or a mocking epigram, its gallantry, its perspicacity and its innate lack of reverence for all that symbolises an accepted order of things—all these stand out in their natural colours, drawn to the life and harmonised into a national entity, to which the poet gives the shape and seeming of his own individuality, unconscious that in relating his own hardships, his own sufferings, regrets and aspirations, he was limning for us the typified and foreshortened image and presentment of a nation at a cardinal epoch of national regeneration. 'He builded better than he knew.' His poems are a very album of types and figures of the day: as we read, the narrow, gabled streets, with their graven niches for saint and Virgin and their monumental fountains and gateways stemming the stream of traffic, rise before us, gay with endless movement of fur and satin clad demoiselles, with heart or diamond shaped head-dresses of velvet or brocade, fringed and broidered with gold and silver, sad-coloured burghers, gold-laced archers and jaunty clerks, 'whistling for lustihead,' with the long-peaked hood or liripipe falling over their shoulders and the short bright-coloured walking-cloak letting pass the glittering point of the dirk, shaven down-looking monks, 'breeched and booted like oyster-fishers,' and barefooted friars, purple-gilled with secret and unhallowed debauchery, light o' loves, distinguished by the tall helm or *hennin* and the gaudily coloured tight-fitting surcoat, square-cut to show the breasts, over the sheath-like petticoat, crossed by the demicinct or *châtelaine* of silver, followed by their esquires or bullies armed with sword and buckler, artisans in their jerkins of green cloth or russet leather, barons and lords in the midst of their pages and halberdiers, ruffling gallants brave in velvet and *orfévrerie,* with their boots of soft tan-coloured cordovan falling jauntily over the instep, as they press through a motley crowd of beggars and mountebanks, jugglers with their apes and carpet, *culs-de-jatte,* lepers with clap-dish and wallet, mumpers and chanters, truands and gipsies, jesters, fish-fags, cutpurses and swashbucklers, that rings anon with the shout of 'Noël!' as Charles the Seventh rides past, surrounded by his heralds and pursuivants, or Louis passes, with no attendants save his two dark henchmen, Tristan the Hermit and Oliver the Fiend, and nothing to distinguish him from the burghers with whom he rubs elbows save the row of images in his hat and the eternal menace of his unquiet eye. Anon we see the interior of the cathedral church at vespers, with its kneeling crowd of worshippers and its gold-grounded frescoes of heaven and hell, martyrdom and apotheosis, glittering vaguely from the swart shadow of

the aisles; the choir peals out, and the air gathers into a mist with incense, what while an awe-stricken old woman kneels apart before the altar in the Virgin's chapel, praying for that scapegrace son who has caused her such bitter tears and such poignant terrors. Outside, on the church steps, sit the gossips, crouched by twos and threes on the hem of their robes, chattering in that fluent Parisian tongue to which the Parisian poet gives precedence over all others. The night closes in, the dim cressets swing creaking in the wind from the ropes that stretch across the half-deserted streets, while the belated students hurry past to their colleges, with hoods drawn closely over their faces 'and thumbs in girdle-gear,' and the sergeants of the watch pace solemnly by, lantern-pole in one hand, and in the other the halberd wherewith they stir up the shivering wretches crouched for shelter under the deserted stalls of the street-hawkers, or draw across the entrances of the streets the chains that shall break the escape of the nocturnal brawler or the stealthy thief. Thence to the Puppet wineshop, where *truand* and light o' love, student and soldier, hold high revel, amidst the clink of beakers and the ever-recurring sound of clashing daggers and angry voices; or the more reputable tavern of La Pomme de Pin, where sits Master Jacques Raguyer, swathed in his warm mantle, with his feet to the blaze and his back resting against the piles of faggots that tower in the chimney corner; or the street in front of the Châtelet where we find Villon gazing upon the great flaring cressets that give light over the gateway of the prison with whose interior he was so well acquainted. Anon we come upon him watching, with yearning eyes and watering mouth, through some half-open window or door-chink, the roaring carouses of the debauched monks and nuns, or listening to the talk of La Belle Héaulmière and her companions in old age, as they crouch on the floor, under their curtains spun by the spiders, telling tales of the good times gone by, in the scanty, short-lived flicker of their fire of dried hemp-stalks. Presently Master Jehan Cotard staggers by, stumbling against the projecting stalls and roaring out some ranting catch or jolly drinking song, and the bully of La Grosse Margot hies him, pitcher in hand, to the Tankard Tavern, to fetch wine and victual for his clients. Presently the moon rises, high and calm, over the still churchyard of the Innocents, where the quiet dead lie sleeping soundly in the deserted charnels, ladies and lords, masters and clerks, bishops and water-carriers, all laid low in undistinguished abasement before the equality of Death. Once more the scene changes, and we stand by the thieves' rendezvous in the ruined castle of Bicêtre or by the lonely gibbet of Montfaucon, where the poet wanders in the 'silences of the moon,' watching with a terrified fascination the shrivelled corpses or whitened skeletons of his whilom comrades as they creak sullenly to and fro in the ghastly aureole of the midnight star. All Paris of the fifteenth century relives in the vivid hurry of his verse: one hears in his stanzas the very popular cries and watchwords of the street and the favourite oaths of the gallants and women of the day. We feel that all the world is centred for him in Paris, and that there is no landscape that for him can compare with those 'paysages de métal et de pierre' that he (in common with another ingrain Parisian, Baudelaire) so deeply loved. Much as he must have wandered over France, we find in his verse no hint of natural beauty, no syllable of description of land-scape or natural objects. In these things he had indeed no interest: flowers and stars, sun and moon, spring and summer unrolled in vain for him their phantasmagoria of splendour and enchantment over earth and sky: men and women were his flowers, and the crowded streets of the great city the woods and meadows, wherein, after his fashion, he worshipped beauty and did homage to art. Indeed, he was essentially the man of the crowd: his heart throbbed ever in unison with the mass in joy or sadness, crime or passion, lust or patriotism, aspiration or degradation.

It is astonishing, in the midst of the fantastic and artificial rhymers of the time, how quickly the chord of sensibility in our poet vibrates to the broad impulses of humanity—how, untainted by the selfish provincialism of the day, his heart warms towards the great patriot, Jacques Cœur, and sorrows over his unmerited disgrace—how he appreciates the heroism of Jeanne d'Arc, and denounces penalty upon penalty, that remind one of the seventy thousand pains of fire of the Arabian legend, upon the traitors and rebels that should 'wish ill unto the realm of France'—with what largeness of sympathy he anticipates the modern tender-ness over the fallen, and demonstrates how 'they were once honest verily,' till love, that befools us all, beguiled them to the first step upon the downward road—with what observant compassion he notes the silent regrets of the old and the poignant remembrances of those for whom all things fair have faded out—glozing with an iron pathos upon the 'nessun maggior dolore' of Dante, in the terrible stanzas that enshrine, in pearls and rubies of tears and blood, the passion and the anguish of La Belle Héaulmière.

The keenness of his pathos and the delicacy of his grace are as supreme as what one of his commentators magnificently calls 'la souveraine rudesse' of his satire. When he com-plains to his unyielding mistress of her 'hypocrite douceur' and her 'felon charms,' 'la mort d'un pauvre cœur,' and warns her of the inevitable approach of the days when youth and beauty shall no more remain to her, we seem to hear a robuster Ronsard sighing out his 'Cueil-lez, cueillez votre jeunesse'; when he laments for the death of Master Ythier's beloved, 'Two were we, having but one heart,' we must turn to Mariana's wail of wistful yet unreproachful passion for a more perfect lyric of regretful tenderness, a more pathetic dalliance with the simpleness of love; and when he appeals from the dungeon of Meung, or pictures himself and his companions swinging from the gibbet of Montfau-con, the tears that murmur through the fantastic fretwork of the verse are instinct with the salt of blood and the bitter-ness of death. Where can we look for a more poignant pathos than in his lament for his lost youth, or his picture of the whilom gallants of his early memories that now beg all naked, seeing no crumb of bread but in some window-place? or a nobler height of contemplation than that to which he rises, as he formulates the unalterable laws that make king and servant, noble and villein, equal in abasement before the unbending majesty of Death? or a sweeter purity of religious exaltation than in the ballad wherein, with the truest instinct of genius, using that mother's voice that can-not but be the surest passport to the Divine compassion, he soars to the very gates of heaven on the star-sown wings

of faith and song? He is one more instance of the poten-tiality of grace and pathos that often lurks in natures dis-tinguished chiefly for strength and passion. 'Out of the strong cometh sweetness,' and in few poets has the preg-nant fable of the honeycomb in the lion's mouth been more forcibly illustrated than in Villon.

Humour is with Villon no less pronounced a characteristic than pathos. Unstrained and genuine, it arises mainly from the continual contrast between the abasement of his life and the worthlessness of its possibilities, and the passion-ate and ardent nature of the man. He would seem to be always in a state of humorous astonishment at his own mad career and the perpetual perplexities into which his folly and recklessness have betrayed him; and this feeling constantly overpowers his underlying remorse and the anguish which he suffers under the pressure of the deplor-able circumstances wherein he continually finds himself involved. The *Spiel-trieb* or sport-impulse, that has been pronounced the highest attribute of genius, stands out with a rare prominence from his character, never to be alto-gether stifled by the most overwhelming calamities. The most terrible and ghastly surroundings of circumstance cannot avail wholly to arrest the ever-springing fountain of wit and *bonhomie* that wells up from the inmost nature of the man. In the midst of all his miseries, with his tears yet undried, he mocks at himself and others with an as-tounding good humour. In the dreary dungeon of the Me-ung moat, we find him bandying jests with his own per-sonified remorse, and, even whilst awaiting a shameful death, he seeks consolation in the contemplation of the comic aspects of the situation, as he will presently appear, upright in the air, swinging at the wind's will, with face like a thimble for bird-pecks and skin blackened by 'that ill sun that tans a man when he is dead.' It is a foul death to die, says he, yet we must all die some day, and it matters little whether we then find ourselves a lord rotting in a splendid sepulchre or a cutpurse strung up on Mont-faucon hill. He laughs at his own rascality and poverty, amorousness and gluttony, with an unequalled *naïveté* of candour, singularly free from cynicism, yet always man-ages to conciliate our sympathies and induce our pity rath-er than our reprobation. 'It is not to poor wretches like us,' he says, 'that are naked as a snake, sad at heart and empty of paunch, that you should preach virtue and tem-perance—as to us, God give us patience. You would do better to address yourselves to incite great lords and mas-ters to good deeds, who eat and drink of the best every day, and are more open to exhortation than beggars like ourselves that cease never from want.'

His faith in the saving virtues of meat and drink is both droll and touching. One feels, in all his verse, the distant and yearning respect with which the starveling poet re-gards all manner of victual, as he enumerates its various incarnations in a kind of litany or psalm of adorations in which they resemble the denominations and attributes of saints and martyrs to whom he knelt in unceasing and ineffectual prayer. Wines, hypocras, roast meats, sauces, soups, custards, tarts, eggs, pheasants, partridges, plovers, pigeons, capons, fat geese, pies, cakes, furmenty, creams and pasties and other *savoureux et friands morceaux,* defile in long and picturesque procession through his verse, like a dissolving view of Paradise, before whose gates he knelt and longed in vain. His ideal of perfect happiness is to 'break bread with both hands,' a potentiality of ecstatic bliss he attributes to the friars of the four Mendicant Orders; no delights of love or pastoral sweetness, 'not all the birds that singen all the way from here to Babylon' (as he says), could induce him to spend one day among the hard lying and sober fare of a country life; and the only enemy whom he refuses to forgive at his last hour is the Bishop of Orleans, who fed him so scurvily a whole summer long upon cold water and dry bread, 'not even manchets,' says he piteously. If he cannot come at his desire in the possession of the dainties for which his soul longs, there is still some sad pleasure for him in caressing in imagination the sacrosanct denominations of that 'bienheureux harnois de gueule' which hovers for him, afar off, in the rosy mists of an apotheosis. In this respect, as in no few others, he forcibly reminds one of another strange and noteworthy figure converted by genius into an eternal type, that 'Neveu de Rameau,' in whom the *reductio ad absurdum* of the whole sensualist philosophy of the eighteenth century was crystallised by Diderot into so poignant and curious a personality. Like Jean Rameau, the whole mystery of life seems to Villon to have resolved itself into the cabalistic science 'de mettre sous la dent,' that noble and abstract art of providing for 'the reparation of the region below the nose,' of whose alkahest and hermetic essence he so deplorably fell short; and as we make this unavoidable comparison, it is impossible not to be surprised into regret for the absence of some Diderot who might have rescued for us the singular individuality of the Bohemian poet of the fifteenth century.

Looking at the whole course of Villon's life, and the portrait he himself paints for us in such crude and unsparing colours, we can hardly doubt that, under different circumstances, had his life been consecrated by successful love and the hope of those higher things to whose nobility he was so keenly though unpractically sensitive, he might have filled a worthier place in the history of his time and have furnished a more honourable career than that of the careless Bohemian driven into crime, disgrace and ruin, by the double influence of his own unchecked desires and the maddening wistfulness of an unrequited love. However, to quote the words of the greatest critic of the nineteenth century: 'We might perhaps have lost the poet whilst gaining the honest man; and good poets are still rarer than honest folk, although the latter can hardly be said to be too common' [Théophile Gautier].

Hilaire Belloc (essay date 1903)

SOURCE: "Poets of the French Renaissance: Villon," in *The Living Age*, Vol. XX, No. 3089, September 19, 1903, pp. 763–65.

[*At the turn of the century Belloc was one of England's premier literary figures. His characteristically truculent stance as a proponent of Roman Catholicism and eco-* *nomic reform—and his equally characteristic clever humor—drew either strong support or harsh attacks from his audience, but critics have found common ground for admiration in his poetry. W. H. Auden called Belloc and his longtime collaborator G. K. Chesterton the best light-verse writers of their era, with Belloc's* Cautionary Tales *(1907) considered by some his most successful work in the genre. Here, Belloc compares and contrasts the medieval and renaissance qualities of Villon's poetry.*]

I have said that in Charles of Orleans the middle ages are at first more apparent than the advent of the Renaissance. His forms are inherited from an earlier time, his terminology is that of the long allegories which had wearied three generations, his themes recall whatever was theatrical in the empty pageantry of the great war. It is a spirit deeper and more fundamental than the mere framework of his writing which attaches him to the coming time. His clarity is new; it proceeds from natural things; it marks that return to reality which is the beginning of all beneficent revolutions. But this spirit in him needs examination and discovery, and the reader is confused between the mediæval phrases and the something new and troubling in the voice that utters them.

With Villon, the next in order, a similar confusion might arise. All about him as he wrote were the middle ages: their grotesque, their contrast, their disorder. His youth and his activity of blood forbad him any contact with other than immediate influences. He was wholly Northern; he had not so much as guessed at what Italy might be. The decrepit University had given him, as best she could, the dregs of her failing philosophy and something of Latin. He grew learned as do those men who grasp quickly the major lines of their study, but who, in details, will only be moved by curiosity or by some special affection. There was nothing patient in him, and nothing applied, and in all this, in the matter of his scholarship, as in his acquirement of it, he is of the dying middle ages entirely.

His laughter also was theirs. The kind of laughter that saluted that first Dance of Death which as a boy he had seen in new frescoes round the waste graveyard of the Innocents. His friends and enemies and heroes and buffoons were the youth of the narrow tortuous streets, his visions of height were the turrets of the palaces and the precipitate roofs of the town. Distance had never inspired him, for in that age its effect was forgotten. No one straight street displayed the greatness of the city, no wide and ordered spaces enhanced it. He crossed his native river upon bridges all shut in with houses, and houses bid the banks also. The sweep of the Seine no longer existed for his generation, and largeness of all kinds was hidden under the dust and rubble of decay. The majestic, which in sharp separate lines of his verse he certainly possessed, he discovered within his own mind, for no great arch or cornice, nor no colonnade had lifted him with its splendor.

That he could so discover it, that a solemnity and order should be apparent in the midst of his raillery whenever he desires to produce an effect of the grand, leads me to speak of that major quality of his by which he stands up out of his own time, and is clearly an originator of the great renewal. I mean his vigor.

It is all round about him, and through him, like a storm in a wood. It creates, it perceives. It possesses the man himself, and us also as we read him. By it he launches his influence forward and outward rather than receives it from the past. To it his successors turn, as to an ancestry, when they had long despised and thrown aside everything else that savored of the Gothic dead. By it he increased in reputation and meaning from his boyhood on for four hundred years, till now he is secure among the first lyric poets of Christendom. It led to no excess of matter, but to an exuberance of attitude and manner, to an inexhaustibility of special words, to a vividness of impression unique even among his own people.

He was poor; he was amative; he was unsatisfied. This vigor, therefore, led in his actions to a mere wildness; clothed in this wildness the rare fragments of his life have descended to us. He professed to teach, but he haunted taverns, and loved the roaring of songs. He lived at random from his twentieth year in one den or another along the waterside. Affection brought him now to his mother, now to his old guardian priest, but not for long; he returned to adventure—such as it was. He killed a man, was arrested, condemned, pardoned, exiled; he wandered and again found Paris, and again—it seems—stumbled down his old lane of violence and dishonor.

Associated also with this wildness is a curious imperfection in our knowledge of him. His very name is not his own—or any other man's. His father, if it were his father, took his name from Mont-Corbier—half noble. Villon is but a little village over beyond the upper Yonne, near the water-parting, within a day of the water-parting when the land falls southward to Burgundy and the sun in what they call "The Slope of Gold." From this village a priest, William, had come to Paris in 1423. They gave him a canory in that little church called "St. Bennets Askew," which stood in the midst of the University, near Sorbonne, where the Rue des Ecoles crosses the Rue St. Jacques today. Hither, to his house in the cloister, he brought the boy, a waif whom he had found, much at the time when Willoughby capitulated and the French recaptured the city. He had him taught, he designed him for the University, he sheltered him in his vagaries, he gave him asylum. The young man took his name and called him "more than father." His anxious life led on to 1468, long after the poet had disappeared.

For it is in 1461, in his thirtieth year, that Villon last writes down a verse. It is in 1463 that his signature is last discovered. Then not by death or, if by death, then by some death unrecorded, he leaves history abruptly—a most astonishing exit! . . . You may pursue fantastic legends, you will not find the man himself again. Some say a final quarrel got him hanged at last—it is improbable: no record or even tradition of it remains. Rabelais thought him a wanderer in England. Poitou preserves a story of his later passage through her fields, how still he drank and sang with boon companions, and of how, again, he killed a man . . . Maybe,

he only ceased to write; took to teaching soberly in the University, and lived in a decent inheritance to see new splendors growing upon Europe. It may very well be, for it is in such characters to desire in early manhood decency, honor, and repose. But for us the man ends with his last line. His body that was so very real, his personal voice, his jargon—tangible and audible things—spread outward suddenly a vast shadow upon nothingness. It was the end, also, of a world. The first Presses were creaking, Constantinople had fallen, Greek was in Italy, Leonardo lived, the sails of Vasco di Gama were ready—in that new light he disappears.

Of his greatness nothing can be said; it is like the greatness of all the chief poets, a thing too individual to seize in words. It is superior and exterior to the man. Genius of that astounding kind has all the qualities of an extraneous thing. A man is not answerable for it. It is nothing to his salvation; it is little even to his general character. It has been known to come and go, to be put off and on like a garment, to be given and taken away like a capricious gift.

But of its manner in expression it may be noted that, as his vigor prepared the flood of new verse, so in another matter he is an origin. Through him, first the great town—and especially Paris—appeared and became permanent in letters.

Her local spirit and her special quality had shone fitfully here and there for a thousand years—you may find it in Julian, in Abbo, in Joinville. But now, in the fifteenth century, it had been not only a town but a great town for more than a century—a town, that is, in which men live entirely, almost ignorant of the fields, observing only other men, and forgetting the sky. The keen edge of such a life, its bitterness, the mockery and challenge whereby its evils are borne, its extended knowledge, the intensity of its spirit—all these are reflected in Villon, and first reflected in him. Since his pen first wrote, acerbity has never deserted the literature of the capital.

It was not only the metropolitan, it was the Parisian spirit which Villon found and fixed. That spirit which is bright over the whole city, but which is not known in the first village outside; the influence that makes Paris Athenian.

The ironical Parisian soul has depths in it. It is so lucid that its luminous profundity escapes one—so with Villon. Religion hangs there. Humility—fatally divorced from simplicity—pervades it. It laughs at itself. There are ardent passions of sincerity, repressed and reacting upon themselves. The virtues, little practiced, are commonly comprehended, always appreciated, for the Faith is there permanent. All this you will find in Villon, but it is too great a matter for so short an essay as this.

Ezra Pound (essay date 1910)

SOURCE: "Montcorbier, *alias* Villon," in *The Spirit of Romance,* New Directions Books, 1910, pp. 166–78.

The century between Dante and Villon brought into the poetry of northern Europe no element which was distinctly new. The plant of the Renaissance was growing, a plant which some say begins in Dante; but Dante, I think, anticipates the Renaissance only as one year's harvest foreshadows the next year's Spring. He is the culmination of one age rather than the beginning of the next; he is like certain buildings in Verona, which display the splendor of the Middle Ages, untouched by any influence of the classic revival.

In architecture, mediæval work means line; line, composition and design: Renaissance work means mass. The Gothic architect envied the spider his cobweb. The Renaissance architect sought to rival the mountain. They raised successively the temple of the spirit and the temple of the body. The analogy in literature is naturally inexact; Dante, however, sought to hang his song from the absolute, the center and source of light; art since Dante has for the most part built from the ground.

General formulas of art criticism serve at best to suggest a train of thought, or a manner of examining the individual works of a period. Such formulas are not figures circumscribing the works of art, but points from which to compute their dimensions.

The Renaissance is not a time, but a temperament. Petrarch and Boccaccio have it. To the art of poetry they bring nothing distinctive: Petrarch refines but deenergizes. In England, Gower had written pleasantly, and "Romance," the romance of the longer narratives, had come to full fruit in Chaucer. Where Dante is a crystallization of many mediæval elements, his own intensity the cause of their cohesion, Chaucer comes as through a more gradual, gentler process, like some ultimate richer blossom on that bough which brought forth Beroul, Thomas, Marie, Crestien, Wace, and Gower. He is part, some will say, of the humanistic revolt. There was no abrupt humanistic revolt. Boccaccio and the rest but carry on a paganism which had never expired.

After all these fine gentlemen, guardians of the Arthurian Graal, prophets of Rome's rejuvenation, and the rest, had been laid in their graves, there walked the gutters of Paris one François Montcorbier, poet and gaol-bird, with no care whatever for the flowery traditions of mediæval art, and no anxiety to revive the massive rhetoric of the Romans. Yet whatever seeds of the Renaissance there may have been in Dante, there were seeds or signs of a far more modern outbreak in the rhymes of this Montcorbier, *alias* Villon.

The minstrelsy of Provence is as the heart of Sir Blancatz, and the later lords of song, in England and in Tuscany, have eaten well of it. From Provence the Tuscans have learned pattern; the Elizabethans a certain lyric quality; Villon carries on another Provençal tradition, that of unvarnished, intimate speech. I do not imply that Villon is directly influenced by Provence, but that some of his notes and fashions had been already sounded in Provence. Thus the tone of a tenzone of Arnaut Daniel's . . . suggests the tone of some of Villon's verses; even as the form of the Provençal canzon had suggested the form of the north French ballade.

Villon has been called gay. . . . This is, to my mind, an entire misconception of the character of the poet. I have read him throughout, and I protest that I cannot find one single spark of real lightheartedness. All is profoundly melancholy. He piles the bitterest reproaches on himself. If he laughs, it is not mirthfully; if he smiles, it is sadly.

—Walter Besant, in "Francois Villon," Studies in Early French Poetry, 1868.

Villon's abuse finds precedent in the lower type of sirvente, with this distinction, that Villon at times says of himself what the Provençals said only of one another. For precedent of Villon's outspokenness one need not seek so far as Provence. The French mystery plays are not written in veiled words. To witness, this passage from a Crucifixion play, when an angel says to God the Father:

> Père éternal, vous avez tort
> E ben devetz avoir vergogne.
> Vostre fils bien amis est mort
> E vous dormez comme un ivrogne.

> Father eternal, you are wrong
> And well should be shamed,
> Your well beloved son is dead
> And you sleep like a drunk.

Villon's art exists because of Villon. There is in him no pretence of the man sacrificed to his labor. One may define him unsatisfactorily by a negative comparison with certain other poets, thus: where Dante has boldness of imagination, Villon has the stubborn persistency of one whose gaze cannot be deflected from the actual fact before him: what he sees, he writes. Dante is in some ways one of the most personal of poets; he holds up the mirror to nature, but he is himself that mirror.

Villon never forgets his fascinating, revolting self. If, however, he sings the song of himself he is, thank God, free from that horrible air of rectitude with which Whitman rejoices in being Whitman. Villon's song is selfish through self-absorption; he does not, as Whitman, pretend to be conferring a philantropic benefit on the race by recording his own self-complacency. Human misery is more stable than human dignity; there is more intensity in the passion of cold, remorse, hunger, and the fetid damp of the mediæval dungeon than in eating water melons. Villon is a voice of suffering, of mockery, of irrevocable fact; Whitman is the voice of one who saith:

> Lo, behold, I eat water-melons When I eat water-
>   melons the world eats water-melons through me.
> When the world eats water-melons, I partake of the
>   world's water-melons.
> The bugs,
> The worms,
> The negroes, etc.,
> Eat water-melons; All nature eats water-melons.
> Those eidolons and particles of the Cosmos
> Which do not now partake of water-melons
> Will at some future time partake of water-melons.
> Praised be Allah or Ramanathanath Khrishna!

They call it optimism, and breadth of vision. There is, in the poetry of François Villon, neither optimism nor breadth of vision.

Villon is shameless. Whitman, having decided that it is disgraceful to be ashamed, rejoices in having attained nudity.

Goethe, when the joys of taxidermy sufficed not to maintain his self-respect, was wont to rejoice that there was something noble and divine in being *Künstler*. The artist is an artist and therefore admirable, or noble, or something of that sort. If Villon ever discovered this pleasant mode of self-deception, he had sense enough not to say so in rhyme. In fact, Villon himself may be considered sufficient evidence seriously to damage this artist-consoling theory.

Villon holds his unique place in literature because he is the only poet without illusions. There are *désillusionnés*, but they are different; Villon set forth without the fragile cargo. Vilon never lies to himself; he does not know much, but what he knows he knows: man is an animal, certain things he can feel; there is much misery, man has a soul about which he knows little or nothing. Helen, Heloise and Joan are dead, and you will gather last year's snows before you find them.

Thus the **"Ballade of Dead Ladies"**:

> Tell me now in what hidden way is
>   Lady Flora, the lovely Roman,
> Where is Hipparchia and where is Thaïs,
>   Neither of them the fairer woman,
> Where is Echo, beheld of no man,
>   Only heard on river and mere,
> She whose beauty was more than human?
>   But where are the snows of yester-year!

And where are Beatris, Alys, Hermengarde, and

> That good Joan whom Englishmen
> At Rouen doomed, and burned her there!
> Mother of God, where are they, where?
> But where are the snows of yester-year!

Of his further knowledge,

> I know a horse from a mule,
> And Beatrix from Bellet,
> I know the heresy of the Bohemians,
> I know son, valet and man.
> I know all things save myself alone.

Or in the *Grand Testament,*

> Je suis pecheur, je le scay bien
> Pourtant Dieu ne veut pas ma mort.

> I am a sinner, I know it well,
> However, God does not wish my death.

Or in the ballade quoted:

> Je cognois mort qui nous consomme,
> Je cognois tout fors que moi mesme.

> And I know Death that downs us all,
> I know all things save myself alone.

It is not Villon's art, but his substance, that pertains. Where Dante is the supreme artist, Villon is incurious; he accepts the forms of verse as unquestioningly as he accepts the dogma and opinion of his time. If Dante reaches out of his time, and by rising above it escapes many of its limitations, Villon in some way speaks below the voice of his age's convention, and thereby outlasts it. He is utterly mediæval, yet his poems mark the end of mediæval literature. Dante strives constantly for a nobler state on earth. His aspiration separates him from his time, and the ordinary reader from his work. The might of his imagination baffles the many. Villon is destitute of imagination; he is almost destitute of art; he has no literary ambition, no consciousness of the fame hovering over him; he has some slight vanity in impressing his immediate audience, more in reaching the ear of Louis XI by a ballade—this last under pressure of grave necessity.

Much of both the *Lesser* and the *Greater Testaments* is in no sense poetry; the wit is of the crudest; thief, murderer, pander, bully to a whore, he is honored for a few score pages of unimaginative sincerity; he sings of things as they are. He dares to show himself. His depravity is not a pose cultivated for literary effect. He never makes the fatal mistake of glorifying his sin, of rejoicing in it, or of pretending to despite its opposite. His "Ne voient pan qu'aux fenestres," is no weak moralizing on the spiritual benefits of fasting.

The poignant stanzas in which this line occurs, are comparable only to Lamb's graver and more plaintive, "I have had playmates, I have had companions."

Grand Testament

XXIX

Where are the gracious gallants
That I beheld in times gone by.
Singing so well, so well speaking,
So pleasant in act and in word.
Some are dead and stiffened,
Of them there is nothing more now.
May they have rest, but in Paradise,
And God save the rest of them.

XXX

And some are become
God's mercy! great lords and masters,
And others beg all naked
And see no bread, save in the windows;
Others have gone into the cloisters
Of Celestin and of Chartreuse,
Shod and hosed like fishers of oysters.
Behold the divers state among them all.

Villon paints himself, as Rembrandt painted his own hideous face; his few poems drive themselves into one in a way unapproached by the delicate art of a Daniel or a Baudeclaire. Villon makes excuses neither for God nor for himself; he does not rail at providence because its laws are not adjusted to punish all weaknesses except his own. There is, perhaps, no more poignant regret than that stanza in *Le Grand Testament,*

Je plaings le temps de ma jeunesse

I mourn the time of my youth,
When I made merry more than another,
Until the coming in of old age,
Which has sealed me its departure.
It is not gone on foot,
Nor on horseback; alas! and how then?
Suddenly it has flown away,
And has left me nothing worth.

XXIII

Gone it is, and I remain
Poor of sense and of savoir,
Sad, shattered, and more black than ripe
Sans coin or rent or anything mine own.

He recognizes the irrevocable, he blames no one but himself, he never wastes time in self-reproaches, recognizing himself as the result of irrevocable causes.

Necessitè faict gens mesprendre
E faim saillir le loup des boys.
Necessity makes men run wry,
And hunger drives the wolf from wood.

He has the learning of the schools, or at least such smattering of it as would be expected from a brilliant, desultory auditor, but his wisdom is the wisdom of the gutter. The dramatic imagination is beyond him, yet having lived himself, he has no need to imagine what life is. His poems are gaunt as the *Poema del Cid* is gaunt; they treat of actualities, they are untainted with fancy; in the *Cid* death is death, war is war. In Villon filth is filth, crime is crime; neither crime nor filth is gilded. They are not considered as strange delights and forbidden luxuries, accessible only to adventurous spirits. Passion he knows, and satiety he knows, and never does he forget their relation.

He scarcely ever takes the trouble to write anything he does not actually feel. When he does, as in the prayer made for his mother, the lament for Master Ythier's lost mistress, or the ballade for a young bridegroom, it is at the request of a particular person; and the gaunt method in which he expresses his own feelings does not desert him. Even here the expression is that of such simple, general emotion that the verses can hardly be regarded as dramatic; one almost imagines Villon asking Ythier or the bridegroom what they want written, and then rhyming it for them.

Thus this lay, or rather rondeau, which he bequeaths to Master Ythier who has lost his mistress:

Death, 'gainst thine harshless I appeal
That hath torn my leman from me,
Thou goest not yet contentedly
Though of sorrow of thee none doth me heal.
No power or might did she e'er wield,
In life what harm e'er did she thee
        Ah, Death!
Two we! that with one heart did feel,
If she is dead, how then, dividedly
Shall I live on, sans life in me.
Save as do statues 'neath thy seal
        Thou Death!

("Par coeur" in the last line of the original, has no equivalent in modern French or in English; to dine "par coeur," by heart, is to dine on nothing.)

The same tendencies are apparent in the following ballade, that which Villon made at the request of his mother, "to be prayed to our lady." I give here stanzas I and III from Rossetti's translation.

I

Lady of Heaven and Earth, and therewithal
Crowned empress of the nether clefts of Hell,—
I, thy poor Christian, on thy name do call,
Commending me to thee, with thee to dwell,
Albeit in nought I be commendable.
But all mine undeserving may not mar
Such mercies as thy sovereign mercies are;
Without the which (as true words testify)

No soul can reach thy Heaven so fair and far,
Even in this faith I choose to live and die.

III

A pitiful poor woman, shrunk and old,
I am, and nothing learned in letter-lore,
Within my parish-cloister I behold
A painted Heaven where harps and lutes adore,
And eke an Hell whose damned folk seethe full sore:
One bringeth fear, the other joy to me.
That joy, great goddess, make thou mine to be,—
Thou of whom all must ask it even as I;
And that which faith desires, that let it see,
For in this faith I choose to live and die.

Another interesting translation of this poem is to be found among the poems of the late J. M. Synge. For the ballade for the bridegroom I refer to Payne or Swinburne.

Villon is, if you will, dramatic in his **"Regrets of the Belle Heaumière,"** but his own life was so nearly that of his wasted armouress, that his voice is at one with hers. Indeed his own **"Je plains le temps de ma jeunesse"** might almost be part of this ballade. Here are stanzas 1, 5 and 10 of Swinburne's translation.

I

Meseemeth I heard cry and groan
That sweet who was the armourer's maid;
For her young years she made sore moan,
And right upon this wise she said;
'Ah fierce old age with foul bald head
To spoil fair things thou art over fain;
Who holdeth me? Who? Would God I were dead!
Would God I were well dead and slain!

V

And he died thirty years agone.
I am old now, no sweet thing to see;
By God, though when I think thereon,
And of that good glad time, woe's me,
And stare upon my changèd body
Stark naked, that has been so sweet,
Lean, wizen, like a small dry tree,
I am nigh mad with the pain of it.

X

So we make moan for the old sweet days,
Poor old light women, two or three
Squatting above the straw-fire's blaze,
The bosom crushed against the knee,
Like fagots on a heap we be,
Round fires soon lit, soon quenched and done,
And we were once so sweet, even we!
Thus fareth many and many an one.'

This ballade is followed in the *Testament* by the ballade of **"La Belle Heaumière aux filles de joie."**

> Car vieilles n'ont ne cours ne estre
> Ne que monnoye qu'on descrie,

> For old they have not course nor status
> More than hath money that's turned in,

is the tune of it.

In **"La Grosse Margot"** from "ce bourdel ou tenous nostre estat," Villon casts out the dregs of his shame.

Many have attempted to follow Villon, mistaking a pose for his reality. These experimenters, searchers for sensation, have, I think, proved that the "taverns and the whores" are no more capable of producing poetry than are philosophy, culture, art, philology, noble character, conscientious effort, or any other panacea. If persistent effort and a desire to leave the world a beautiful heritage, were greatly availing, Ronsard, who is still under-rated, and Petrarch, who is not, would be among the highest masters. Villon's greatness is that he unconsciously proclaims man's divine right to be himself, the only one of the so-called "rights of man" which is not an artificial product. Villon is no theorist, he is an objective fact. He makes no apology—herein lies his strength; Burns is weaker, because he is in harmony with doctrines that have been preached, and his ideas of equality are derivative. Villon never wrote anything so didactic in spirit as the "man's a man for a' that." He is scarcely affected by the thought of his time, because he scarcely thinks; speculation, at any rate, is far from him. But I may be wrong here. If Villon speculates, the end of his speculation is Omar's age-old ending: "Came out by the same door wherein I went." At any rate, Villon's actions are the result of his passions and his weaknesses. Nothing is "sicklied o'er with the pale cast of thought."

As a type of debauchee he is eternal. He has sunk to the gutter, knowing life a little above it; thus he is able to realize his condition, to see it objectively, instead of insensibly taking it for granted.

Dante lives in his mind; to him two blending thoughts give a music perceptible as two blending notes of a lute. He is in the real sense an idealist. He sings of true pleasures; he sings as exactly as Villon; they are admirably in agreement: Dante to the effect that there are supernormal pleasures, enjoyable by man through the mind; Villon to the effect that the lower pleasures lead to no satisfaction, "e ne m' a laissé quelque don." "Thenceforward was my vision mightier than the discourse," writes the Italian; and Dante had gone living through Hell, in no visionary sense. Villon lacked energy to clamber out. Dante had gone on, fainting, aided, erect in his own strength; had gone on to sing of things more difficult. Villon's poetry seems, when one comes directly from the *Paradiso,* more vital, more vivid; but if Dante restrains himself, putting the laments in the mouths of tortured spirits, they are not the less poignant. He stands behind his characters, of whom Villon might have made one.

Before we are swept away by the intensity of this gamin of Paris, let us turn back to the words set in the mouth of Bertrans of Altafort, "Thus is the counterpass observed in me," or to the lament of Francesca. Whoever cares at all for the art will remember that the words of this lament sob as branches beaten by the wind:

> nessun maggior dolore,
> che ricordarsi del tempo felice
> nella miseria; e ciò sa' I tuo dottore.

The whole sound of the passage catches in the throat, and sobs. Dante is many men, and suffers as many. Villon cries out as one. He is a lurid canto of the *Inferno,* written too late to be included in the original text. Yet had Dante been awaiting the execution of that death sentence which was passed against him, although we might have had one of the most scornful denunciations of tyranny the world has ever known, we should have had no ballade of stark power to match that which Villon wrote, expecting presently to be hanged with five companions:

Frères humains qui apres nous vivez.

Men, brother men, that after us yet live,
Let not your hearts too hard against us be;
For if some pity of us poor men ye give,
The sooner God shall take of you pity.
Here we are, five or six strung up, you see,
And here the flesh that all too well we fed
Bit by bit eaten and rotten, rent and shred,
And we the bones grow dust and ash withal;
Let no man laugh at us discomforted,
But pray to God that he forgive us all.

II

If we call upon you, brothers, to forgive,
You should not hold our prayer in scorn, though we
Were slain by law; ye know that all alive
Have not wit alway to walk righteously.

Dantes's vision is real, because he saw it. Vilon's verse is real, because he lived it; as Bartran de Born, as Arnaut Marvoil, as that mad poseur Vidal, he lived it. For these men life is in the press. No brew of books, no distillation of sources will match the tang of them.

D. B. Wyndham Lewis (essay date 1928)

SOURCE: "The Great Testament, with the Codicil and the Lesser Poems," in *Francois Villon: A Documented Survey,* Coward-McCann, Inc., 1928, pp. 333–40.

[Unrelated to the English author and painter Wyndham Lewis, D. B. Wyndham Lewis was a prominent English essayist, humorist, historian, and biographer. In the following excerpt, he defends Villon's poetry as high art of the most accomplished sort.]

Of [Villon's] scattered irregularities, his obscurities, his occasional untidiness of syntax, his wilful carelessness, his one or two verses left helpless in the air, dangling their legs, his demi-assonances, like the rhyming of *Grenobles* with *Doles, peuple* with *seule,* and *enfle* with *temple,* to take three instances, there is no need to make a howl. *Les poëtes font à leur guise,* as the goddess says in the play; adding, with enormous truth and aptitude, so far as Villon is concerned,

> Ce n'est pas la seule sottise
> Qu'on voit faire à ces messieurs-là.

[That is not the only folly we perceive emanating from those gentlemen.]

But those who would make him a slovenly improviser, throwing off his song carelessly and tossing together his verses as he felt inclined, do him wrong. The most superficial examination of the planning of the **Grand Testament** shows the arrangement of the whole work to be not haphazard, but, in spite of a few unimportant blemishes, rhythmic, subtle, and carefully studied: to take an example, that gradual crescendo of meditation on Death which rises a slow wave and bursts finally into the lovely melody of the **"Dead Ladies,"** falling back afterwards and dying in the **"Lament of the Belle Heaulmière,"** and her wailing for her lost youth; and again, that other slow lifting wave of religion and gratitude which swells and breaks in the **"Ballade to Our Lady"**; and once more, the mocking laughter of the **"Ballade of the Women of Paris,"** hardening and becoming harsh, and finally set in a bitter grimace as he passes to the **"Ballade of Fat Margot"**; and again, the first sad note, as of a passing-bell and the chant of *De Profundis,* in the song *"Au retour,"* deepening and growing more solemn and recollected thence to the end of the **Testament** and the **"Epitaph."** A poet of Villon's stature could do no less. His finest and most ecstatic work is set in the mass of the Testament with all the anxiety of the medieval craftsman. Well did Huysmans call him *ciseleur inimitable, joaillier non pareil.* And if his best verse is required to pass an academic test, it still emerges triumphant, fulfilling at once Pater's condition that all high poetry aspires towards music, and the corollary of M. Henri Bremond that all high poetry aspires towards prayer. As for his lesser flights, his gibes and fleers and mocks, Marcel Schwob, pointing out that more than half Villon's butts are rich Parisian financiers, tax-farmers, usurers, and money-merchants, the Marchands, Cornus, St. Amants, Baubignons, Baillys, Trascailles, Raguiers, Tarannes, Hesselins, Colombels, Charruaus, Louvieux, Marbeufs, Marles, Culdoes, Laurens, Gossouyns, and Marceaus, argues thence that he deliberately intended his work for a social satire or pamphlet, for at the latter part of the fifteenth century these financiers (and especially those of them who were usurers and speculators in food) were universally hated. But I do not think so much can be claimed for him, nor that he had anything more in his mind than personal dislikes and private hatreds. He was like his ancestor the disreputable poet Eumolpus in Petronius, one of those men of letters *quos odisse divites solent,* and he obviously returned cordially and fivefold this dislike. If there were some secure proof for Marcel Schwob's theory, it would certainly give Villon's least gibes a political distinction.

We may grant him, then, his moments of slackness, and moments also when his bright genius sulked and left him plugging along merely a pedestrian rhymer. But for the greatest part there is in his verses a mastery, a sureness, a rhythm, a sharp clarity, a relief, and above all a vigour, a breeze of life, which stamps him great. In every page of his works there strikes upon the eye some subtle arrangement of words, some final clear-cut picture, some melody, some round perfection which enlarges and satisfies not only the eye and the ear, but the mind also.

For example,

> Ou sont les gracieux gallans
> Que je suivoye ou temps jadis,
> Si bien chantans, si bien parlans,
> Si plaisans en faiz et en dis?

and again:

> Au moustier voy dont suis paroissienne
> Paradis paint, ou sont harpes et lus.

and again:

> Ryme, raille, cymballe, luttes,
> Comme fol, fainctif, eshontez;
>
> Frace, broulle, joue des fleustes,
> Fais, es villes et es citez,
> Farces, jeux, et moralitez;
> Gaigne au berlanc, au glic, aux quilles:
> Aussi bien va, or escoutezl
> Tout aux tavernes et aux filles.

and:

> Venez a son enterrement
> Quant vous orrez le carrillon,
> Vestus rouge com vermillon.

and once more:

> Filles, amans, jeunes gens et nouveaulx,
> Danceurs, saulteurs, faisans les piez de veaux,
> Vifs come dars, agus comme aguillon,
> Gousiers tintans cler comme cascaveaux . . .

In all these there is a running song, playing among the printed words and perceptible to the inner ear, woven in and out and flowing and returning, repeated like a fugue, a perpetual undercurrent: like the liquid music one hears (Pater *duce et auspice* Pater) in gazing at the paint and canvas of Giorgione's *Concert*.

> Sounds and sweet Ayrs, that give delight and hurt not.

I have chosen instances from the mass of his work. The three Great Ballades and some of the lesser are music absolute. Only a very great poet could have written any one of these three: the **"Ballade to Our Lady,"** like the rolling of minster organs at one of her feasts; the **"Ballade of the Hanged,"** which is like the *Dies Iræ*; the **"Ballade of Dead Ladies,"** a stringed symphony, shimmering and exquisite, heard afar off on a summer night, among the plashing of fountains.

Above all, there is his vigour. "It is all round him," says Mr. Belloc, "and through him, like a storm in a wood. It creates, it perceives. It possesses the man himself, and us also as we read him" [*The Living Age*, Sept. 19, 1903]. He bursts into a dying twilit world full of half-poets mumbling their worn-out formulæ, and creates the first modern poetry in Europe: modern, I mean, in that it is sharp and athrob with frank self-searching, eager, moody, fed from the poet's own heart's blood. Had he, as Clément Marot wished, lived and been formed and polished in the courts of princes he would have become, most probably, a polite little, smug little, precious little Court versifier, rhyming his uninspired conceits and turning out his quaint enamelled confections to order, like so many others. But in place of the faded decorations like tapestries, full of stiffly-grouped knights and ladies, of these his predecessors and contemporaries, Villon creates the poetry of Paris and sets down her soul and the pageant of her streets. Where they used over and over again the stilted, pompous phrase, the formal courtesy, the decorative, lifeless pattern, Villon crams into his verse the noisy brawl of the Town, its sights and sounds and life, its slang, its thieves' patter, foreign oaths left over from the wars, Latin of the University and the Church, rude jokes of the tavern, the drone of the Schools, scraps of street-songs ("Ma doulce Amour"—"Ouvrez vostre huys, Guillemette"), country patois, the mincing affectations of the genteel. Just as in

> Et quidam seros hiberni ad luminis ignes
> Pervigilat ferroque faces inspicat acuto;
> Interea longum cantu solata laborem
> Arguto conjunx percurrit perctine telas

> [Such a one works by night, by the light of his winter fire, cutting wood for torches with a sharp knife, while his wife, soothing her long labour with song, passes the noisy comb to and fro across the web.]

> (Vergil, *Georgics* I)

the acrid scent of wood-smoke rises at once to the nostrils and there is heard the swish of the comb through the threads, the crackling of the log fire, the rhythmic chopping of the knife on wood, and over all the crooning of an old dreamy song, so in

> Et aux pietons qui vont d'aguet
> Tastonnant par ces establis . . .

> [And to the foot-sergeants who go the rounds, groping past the stalls.]

there is heard the tramp of the Watch, the stumbling along the cobbles, the word of command, the rasp of halberds poked beneath the stalls, the grunted exchanges; and over all the vast murmur of the Town. And once more:

> Et Ysabeau qui dit: "Enné!"

For nearly five hundred years the girl Ysabeau, this cockney of medieval Paris, has been lisping *"Enné!"*—"Reelly!": so that you can hear the very inflection of her soft voice, and see the arched eyebrows, the cheap jewels, the pretty, silly, vapid face upturned to the mocking face of the poet. She is as alive as Galatea in the Bucolics, who so many centuries ago flung her apple at the shepherd Damoetas and fled to the willows. The apple (as a modern Vergilist, M. Bellessort, has finely said) is still rolling there, before our eyes. The willows are quivering; a girl's flushed, laughing face still peeps behind. So Ysabeau is still looking up and saying *"Enné!"*; the little affected fool. It is in the power of a poet to create, like this, a moment which is changeless, and to make Time stand still.

Of the greatness of Villon, says Gaston Paris, there is one supreme test. He wrote, in a French long ago obsolete and now sometimes barely intelligible, in an outmoded form, of an age long dead. The subject-matter of his verse lost centuries ago any actuality it had, and the values of his age have changed—though I may be excused for suggesting, rather quaintly, that its vital essence, its faith, is of course indestructible. Finally, some of his verse is concerned with persons or events so vague, so obscure, or so unpleasant that of themselves they would not arouse today the faintest interest. Yet his verse as you read it is alive, vibrant, as freshly coloured as when he first wrote it down, and ageless.

How true this is—and I have found it not possible to share all Gaston Paris' judgments on this poet one discovers by reading Villon as all good poetry should invariably be read: aloud. Such is the ecstasy of his creative force, the life he has breathed into his work, that it is seen and felt to be poetry absolute, stirring the soul and the imagination like a fanfare of silver trumpets, fulfilling the mind, vibrating, awakening that instant response which is the mark of high poetry. This is a test no lesser verse can pass. Villon possessed *le Verbe*, the Word, and the magic formula (Rabelais has it, too) by which words are changed into something beyond themselves and their arrangement transmuted into the language of another world; a language in which the very shape and size and colour and texture of words, their resonance, their position and significance, become as it were faëry, charged with tremendous, or mysterious, or ravishing music. Such music, I mean, as

> And we in dream behold the Hebrides,

and

> Formosam resonare doces Amaryllida silvas,

> [You teach the woods to resound with the name of lovely Amaryllis.]
>
>   (Vergil, *Bucolics* I)

and

> O western Wind, when wilt thou blow
> That the small rain down can rain?

and

> Tuba mirum spargens sonum,
>
> [Wondrous sound the trumpet flingeth.]
>
>   (From the *Dies Iræ*.)

and of course—

> Echo, parlant quant bruyt on maine
> Dessus riviere ou sus estan.
>
> [Echo, more than mortal-fair,
> That, when one calls by river-flow
> Or marish, answers out of the air.]
>
>   (Payne.)

Such alchemy, the Trismegistan Arcana, only great poets know, and Villon is one. *"Quel magique ruissellement de pierres!"* cries J. K. Huysmans, adoring his genius, *"Quel étrange fourmillement de feux! Quelles étonnantes cassures d'étoffes rudes et rousses! Quelles folles striures de couleurs vives et mornes!"*

There remains one final short thing to be said. He is a forerunner. "Through him first"—I quote Mr. Belloc again—"the great Town, and especially Paris, appeared and became permanent in letters. . . . Since his pen first wrote, a shining acerbity like the glint of a sword-edge has never deserted the literature of the capital. It was not only the metropolitan, it was the Parisian spirit which Villon found and fixed: that spirit which is so bright over the whole city, but which is not known in the first village outside; the influence that makes Paris Athenian."

This is a true judgment.

Grace Frank (essay date 1946)

SOURCE: "The Impenitence of François Villon," in *The Romanic Review*, Vol. XXXVII, No. 3, October, 1946, pp. 225–36.

[*In the following essay, Frank studies the believability of what she considers Villon's feigned penitence.*]

It has long been customary to think of François Villon as a great sinner who was truly remorseful and penitent on occasion. To be sure, since Siciliano put the famous phrase "je ris en pleurs" in its proper setting critics have recognized this contemporaneous cliché as a suitable *contrevérité* among the many others of the **"Ballade du concours de Blois"** rather than as the poet's description of himself. Nevertheless the romantic and sentimental conception of a Villon who wept over his sins and bitterly regretted them still persists. In the early days Marcel Schwob spoke of the *Testament* as "une œuvre de repentir" [in *Revue des Deux Mondes,* CXII, 1892], and Gaston Paris believed that at times Villon "se repentait de tout son cœur," that "les remords lui déchiraient le cœur" [*Francois Villon,* 1901]. More recently Champion called the poet's soul "repentante et insolente à la fois" [*Francois Villon,* 2nd ed., 1933]. Siciliano himself says that Villon experienced "le remords du péché et du crime" and sees him as "un pécheur repantant" [*Francois Villon,* 1934]. Cons refers to "ses repentances les plus amères" and contrasts "le Villon *réel,* un raillard pas mal cynique" with "le Villon *vrai* 'changé en lui-même,' grand, quasi pur" [*État présent des études sur Villon,* 1936].

But did Villon ever regret his sins? Was he ever contrite about what he himself had done? The tragic implications of his life and works seem to me to lie in the very fact that though he knew what was right, he weakly did what was wrong and with no regret whatsoever for his sins but only for the punishment visited upon him because of them. The poet is filled with self-pity, not remorse; he blames others, not himself, for his misfortunes. He knows well that all men are sinners and that sins can be washed away by penitence, that if he truly repents, God will forgive him. But there is little evidence that, despite this knowledge, he himself was ever a contrite and tortured sinner, admitting his guilt and promising to sin no more. He may acknowledge a few peccadilloes, but he rejoices inordinately when he escapes their consequences and indulges in self-pity only when caught, blaming poverty, necessity, the stars, fate and other persons, never himself, for whatever he may have done. An examination of his works will perhaps make this evident.

In the *Lais* the targets of Villon's wit are harshly, even cruelly, lampooned, but the poet does not yet feel obliged to excuse himself, and there is nothing in this work that anyone could regard as betraying a consciousness of guilt. Villon leaves various rich men some equivocal and humorously unneeded legacies with no obvious bitterness regarding their wealth or his own poverty. Indeed though at the end he professes to have very little money left after making his bequests, throughout the poem he has played the role of a well-endowed patron, pretending to give away swords, hauberks, *tentes et pavillons.* He innocently justifies the making of his will by the uncertainties incident to a projected journey, and the journey itself is attributed to nothing more serious than the behavior of his false lady.

It is the *Testament,* however, that is usually regarded as his "œuvre de repentir." Obviously in this poem Villon feels very sorry for himself and attempts to find excuses for his misfortunes, but, so far as I can see, he professes neither guilt nor remorse. He pities himself as a poor little clerk deprived of the steadying influence of some rich Alexander, disavowed by his own people, abused by his enemies, hungry, lean and old before his time because of mistreatment. He is deeply concerned with death and the ravages of time. He ascribes his troubles to Bishop Thibault d'Aussigny, to the rigors of the law, to poverty,

necessity, his false love, all the curs who have made him suffer. But does he say *peccavi?* A dispassionate reading of the work will hardly reveal the sinner torn by remorse so universally posited by our critics.

Villon knows that the Church tells us to pray for our enemies, but he prays only an equivocal prayer for his, actually cursing him (*Testament,* lines 16 ff.), and when he comes to praising the Son and Mother of God, it is for their help—and especially that of King Louis—in getting him out of trouble (49 ff.). He may say (105 ff.) "je suis pecheur, je le sçay bien," but he adds at once that God does not wish his death, only his conversion to the paths of righteousness and that if conscience stings him, even though he die in sin, God will pardon him. However, this is a large "if" which seems never to have been fulfilled, for he immediately states that, were the public weal to profit by his death, he would condemn himself, and then he expressly denies any guilt by insisting that on the contrary, dead or alive, he hurts neither young nor old (121–126). A little later he again exculpates himself and smilingly emphasizes his innocence by saying, "qui n'a mesfait ne le doit dire" (192).

To be sure, he admits that if he had studied in his foolish youth and dedicated himself to good conduct, he might now have his own house and a soft couch; alas, he adds, he fled school like a naughty child and in writing these words his heart almost breaks (201–208). Even while he pretends to weep over his lost youth, so soon departed, he admits that he had a better time then than others (169–170). Are these the thoughts of a contrite sinner, as is so often held? Does a penitent pretend to be broken-hearted over playing hooky and over failure through bad behavior to earn a comfortable bed? Is Villon really weeping over his lost youth here? Viewed in their context his tears have all the jesting mockery of some crocodile variety.

He soon speaks of himself as unfit to act as judge and vows that "de tous suis le plus imparfait," but it is obvious that this is feigned humility, as Thuasne rightly assumes, since "Loué soit le doulx Jhesu Crist" immediately follows (259 ff.). When later (294) Villon calls himself "pecheur" it is only in the general sense that all men are sinners. The "povre viellart" addressed in 424 who is prevented from committing some horrible deed by fear of God may or may not be Villon (critics differ); he is in any case no penitent.

As Villon begins the series of his actual bequests (833 ff.) he commends his soul to the Trinity and Nostre Dame, praying that it may be brought before the Throne, but he makes no confession of guilt. He admits that his "plus que pere," Guillaume de Villon, has pulled him out of many a scrape (849 ff.) and that his poor mother has had bitter sorrow and much sadness because of him, but he implies no serious misdemeanors, nothing worse than the students' fracas over the Pet au Deable. So too when he says that his attorney, Fournier, has won many a suit for him, he carefully adds that his cases were always just (1030 ff.). Of course the avowal of *paillardise* in the cynical **"Ballade de la Grosse Margot"** (1591 ff.) is accompanied by not a trace of remorse: "nous deffuyons onneur, il nous deffuit."

In the **"Belle leçon aux enfants perdus"** and the following **"Ballade de bonne doctrine"** (*Testament,* 1668 ff.) there is plenty of good advice sardonically offered: penitence comes too late if one gets caught and dies in infamy, a man is foolish to risk his life for so little, ill-gotten gains profit no one, etc. But then comes the mocking refrain that it makes no difference whether a man gains profit by good means or bad, in the end everything goes to the taverns and wenches. If Villon's heart is here torn with consciousness of sin, he manages without difficulty to conceal his wounds.

Villon frankly wishes posterity to think of him as a *bon follastre,* a good wanton, foolish and ribald but not criminal, and he pictures himself as a poor scholar unjustly driven into exile despite an appeal for clemency (1883 ff.). Before closing the testament he begs for the grace of an odd assortment of persons—monks, mendicants, fops, light women, brawlers, showmen—but definitely excludes and curses his enemies, the traitorous dogs who have made him suffer: let their ribs be crushed with heavy mallets (1968 ff.). And in the very last *ballade* concluding the whole poem he returns to his self-portrait of the *bon follastre,* pretending to die as a martyr of love, yet none the less, merry as a marlin, drinking a draught of good red wine as he leaves this world.

Now the *Testament* was written after Villon had murdered a man, however inadvertently, after he had remained in exile some seven months before being pardoned for this deed, after he had fallen foul of the law again by robbing the Collège de Navarre and had again gone into exile, after he had been associated with proved criminals, some of whom were hung for their crimes and whose language he wrote, after he had languished in the prison of Bishop Thibault for some unknown offense, possibly under sentence of death, and had been released only by a general freeing of prisoners at the time of King Louis's entry into Meung. The work exhibits bitterness toward his foes, a wide-ranging preoccupation with death, a tendency to make excuses for himself and to complain about his fate, but no sorrow for his evil life, no self-reproach, unless an unconvincing lament for his lost youth and references to the trouble caused his mother and protector can be so regarded. He regrets his own suffering, but he blames others, not himself, for it. Of true contrition and recantation our cynical *bon follastre* betrays no evidence.

His attitude toward himself emerges most clearly in the **"Debat du cuer et du corps de Villon,"** written when he was thirty years old and therefore at approximately the same time as the *Testament,* perhaps a little earlier. Villon shows here that he realizes he *ought* to feel the sting of conscience, that youth is no excuse, that he is lost, that he should seek honor, devote himself endlessly to reading and learning wisdom, that he *ought* to leave fools and foolish pleasures alone and be the master, not the servant, of his fate. But he rejects this sage advice of his better self and derisively snaps his fingers at it with his cynical "et

je m'en passeray." It may be objected that such admissions, humorously repulsed though they are, in themselves constitute an act of contrition. Perhaps. But they are accompanied by no reference to his actual crimes, no evidence of regret, no promise of reform. Instead, his wicked self always has the last word with the sardonic refrain that it can do without his better self's good counsel. And just as when Villon asks his friends to have pity on him and get him out of prison, blaming Fortune for his plight [*Poésies diverses* (*P.D.*), Foulet's fourth edition of *Oeuvres,* 1932, IX, 5, cf. also *P.D.* XIII], so here he does not blame himself: the fault is in his stars.

Even in the famous **"Epitaphe"** (*P.D.* XIV), one of the most realistically imaginative poems of all times, written with the gallows at his elbow, Villon reveals no contriteness. Once more in the clutches of the law and this time surely condemned to death, the poet shows humility and fear of punishment, he asks his fellow men for their pity and their prayers, he begs Jesus for absolution, he vividly paints a horrible picture of the hangman's victims. But does he repent? His only excuse is the morally feeble "tous hommes n'ont pas bon sens rassis." This is hardly a *mea culpa,* a recognition of personal guilt. And when Villon escapes the fate he so vividly and poignantly envisaged in his **"Epitaphe,"** when he writes his exultant **"Question au clerc du quichet"** (*P.D.* XVI), there is absolutely no trace of remorse. He says that if he had been related to the butchers and had thus had some claim on the man who judged him, he would never have had to submit to the question in his prison slaughterhouse; he insists that his punishment was arbitrary and that he was sentenced through trickery. Nor do we find a conscience-stricken poet in the labored **"Louenge a la court"** (*P.D.* XV), written at the same time, in which he extravagantly thanks the court for commuting his sentence. He wants his five senses and all his vile body to sing praises, he also begs for three days of grace so that he may put his affairs in order before going into exile, but though he calls his body "pire qu'ours, ne pourceau qui fait son nyt es fanges," he makes no confession of any sins nor does he give any pledge of reform or reparation.

In only one poem, so far as I know, does Villon play the role of a man who recognizes his own guilt, repents and promises to amend his ways. And this I believe was written with his tongue in his cheek, to make a good impression on some man who held him in bondage. Opinions about the so-called **"Ballade de bon conseil"** (*P.D.* I), which is addressed to "hommes faillis, bersaudez de raison," have varied little: most critics date it early and rightly consider it of little merit. Gaston Paris, Thuasne in his edition, Siciliano and Foulet, by the position he accords it, would all place it early; Paris and Thuasne regard it as mediocre, unworthy of the poet, and think it was written before Villon had gone over entirely to evil company, while he still entertained the sentiments of *un honnête homme*; Siciliano believes it a scholar's *pensum* written when the poet was very young. Jeanroy in his edition, without attempting to date the poem, speaks of it as "cette médiocre ballade, qu'on hésiterait à attribuer à Villon si elle n'était signée en acrostiche."

Champion, however, refers to the poem as "cette belle pièce" and places it late, after Villon's return to Paris in 1461 or 1462. Indeed Champion uses these lines as evidence that Villon during his exile had reflected much, had reformed, and intended henceforth to follow the paths of wisdom and piety.

Now there is nothing to bear out the assumption of Paris, Thuasne and Siciliano that this is an *œuvre de début,* written while the poet was *encore honnête homme,* or that a mediocre poem "calqué sur un texte connu" need be a scholar's *pensum.* On the other hand, there is good reason for putting the poem slightly later than Champion does, though without accepting his appraisal of its literary value.

That Villon associates himself with the *hommes faillis* is obvious from his use of the first person plural: *ne nous venjons, prenons en pacience, de bien faisons effort, reprenons cuer, ayons en Dieu confort, de nos maulx ont noz parens le ressort, ordre nous fault, ne laissons le vray port.* This is not the advice of an innocent youth, but an admission of membership in the group of wicked men he is addressing. As others have observed, the poem connects very closely in theme and phrase with the **"Belle leçon aux enfants perdus"** and the following **"Ballade de bonne doctrine"** of the *Testament* (1668 ff.). But a comparison of the **"Ballade de bon conseil"** with the poems of the *Testament* shows that, despite many similarities, there is one essential difference. Some of the same malefactors are in the poet's mind on both occasions, the concern with death is similar, and there is a like ring of *à quoi bon* in the two series of verbs that begin in *P.D.* I, 21 with "que vault piper, flater, rire en trayson" and in *T.* [*Testament*] 1700 with "ryme, raille, cymballe, luttes." But the essential difference is that in the *Testament* Villon assumes a light, ironical tone, whereas in the **"Ballade de bon conseil"** his words are deadly serious without a trace of his usual humor or his usual wry cynicism.

In the latter poem Villon calls his associates men who are wicked, justly tormented, unnatural, out of their senses, courting a detestable death through cowardice. They are not the fair lads with gluey fingers, his companions in pleasure, who are addressed in the *Testament,* but include poisoners and murderers not hinted at there. He urges these fallen men to recognize their errors, not to seek vengeance, to be patient and virtuous, to take heart, have faith in God, live in peace, end strife and achieve a favorable status in the world. They are not told, as in the *Testament,* that whatever they may do, good or ill, all their gains will go to the inns and girls. Nor are they warned in light, derisory banter against losing their skins on the gallows like Colin de Cayeux (*T.* [*Testament*] 1671–1675) or to keep away from the scorching heat that blackens the bodies of the hanged (*T.* 1722–1723). The lines of the **"Ballade de bon conseil"** are not laced with twisted laughter, but are heavy, pedantic and highly moral.

In its ponderous air of virtue it also differs from another poem with which it may be profitably compared, the **"Epistre a ses amis"** (*P.D.* IX) The **"Epistre"** calls on Villon's friends to get him out of prison, but these friends

are described as *gens d'esperit, ung petit estourdis,* not *hommes faillis.* Like those addressed in *T.* 1668 ff., they are light-hearted poets and musicians, dancers, girls, lovers, merry makers of song and rhyme, and unlike the wretches of *P.D.* I (as well as others mentioned in *T.* 1668 ff.) they are not thieves, gamblers, card sharpers and murderers. Since Villon is asking a favor of his friends here, rather than proffering advice, the difference in epithets may not be too significant. However, the bantering tone of the verses in the *Testament,* so entirely absent from *P.D.* I, obtains throughout *P.D.* IX. Though Villon is imploring help to get himself released from prison, though he feelingly refers to his sufferings, he can still joke about his fasting on feast days, about his teeth longer than a rake's from a dry-bread-and-water diet *sans* cake, and he can still thumb his nose at the end by remarking to his potential rescuers that even pigs rally around when one of them grunts.

Villon's association of himself with the *hommes faillis* in *P.D.* I, the echoes in this poem of lines from the *Testament,* the poet's concern with the fate of men who steal and murder, men like his comrades Regnier de Montigny and Colin de Cayeux who were put to death in 1457 and 1460 respectively, "par offenser et prendre autruy demaine," all seem to me to date this poem late. Moreover the series of verbs in the first person plural precludes the likelihood that it is the work of an innocent man. Indeed the whole poem suggests lines written in prison and a profession of guilt.

However, those who consider it mediocre and no better than a school exercise are surely right. The dull, virtuous tone, the uninspired phrases and the citation of apostolic authority recall the mannered poems which Villon wrote when he felt ill at ease in the presence of "the great." The poem he addressed to Marie d'Orléans (*P.D.* VIII), the **"Ballade pour Robert d'Estouteville"** (*T.* 1378 ff.), the **"Louenge a la court"** (*P.D.* XV) have the same awkward heaviness. I suggest therefore that the moralizing tone and the recognition of his own sinfulness, both so contrary to his usual attitude, were designed to impress some "higherup," that the references to *the hommes faillis,* so different from his other characterizations of his companions, were not intended for the eyes of his erring friends but for those of some jailor who had Villon in his power and who might be moved to a pardon by a confession of guilt and some symptoms of penitence.

It seems likely indeed that the poem was written in the Châtelet in Paris between November 2 and 7, 1462, after Villon had been imprisoned for some unknown theft and after, now caught, he had been charged with his old crime of participation in the robbery of the Collège de Navarre. The refrain about the evils that result from taking other men's property is exactly suited to this occasion; so are the intimations of a generally wicked life, such as Villon was known by this time to have led; so is the unusual atmosphere of contrition. Moreover, Villon was actually liberated from prison on this occasion after he had promised to make reparation to the Collège de Navarre by repaying 120 crowns in three annual installments. Thus the poem, so unlike his customary insolent and mocking verses, would correspond to the only occasion on which we know that the poet admitted guilt by offering to repair the damage he had done. However, of the true inner penitence of a sinner torn by consciousness of guilt and resolved to reform there is little evidence. This is rather a case of what Cons so well recognized when he said: "on peut croire que Villon a dû parfois faire de ses vers un usage pathétiquement intéressé pour garder ou reprendre sa liberté."

If the notion of a penitent Villon is abandoned, the essential psychological unity of the *Testament* becomes apparent. Most critics, while recognizing the fact that some earlier work may be incorporated in the poem, have usually accepted Villon's dating:

> Escript l'ay l'an soixante et ung,
> Que le bon roy me delivra
> De la dure prison de Mehun.
>
> (*T.* 81–83)

These scholars, noting differences of tone in various parts of the *Testament,* ascribe them to the poet's dual nature, to his being a penitent, however wicked, a sinner yet somehow "grand, quasi pur." If one substitutes for this picture of the penitent sinner that of a man who knew what was right but impenitently did what was wrong, a man who could jest at the pricks of conscience he *ought* to feel but did not feel, a man who regretted punishment rather than crime, then the true unity of spirit in the *Testament* becomes even more obvious.

Siciliano would contend, however, that Villon's date applies to only part of the poem and that the so-called dual nature of the poet does not exist, not at least simultaneously. The differences of tone and discrepancies of other sorts which he detects derive, he thinks, from different periods in the poet's life. The first 800 lines approximately were written later than the rest, according to this scholar. The main, "earlier" part of the *Testament,* from *ca.* line 800 to the end, he finds light-hearted and gay, a continuation in matter and spirit of the *Lais,* and he assumes it was written by a relatively care-free young man, begun perhaps while he was a prisoner at Meung. The "later" introduction, where Villon pictures himself as sick, old, desperate, abandoned by his own people, Siciliano would date from after 1464, perhaps even as late as 1476.

But surely this is an over-simplification. The hatred of Thibault and the joy at the poet's release from prison have the ring of contemporaneity. And why should the poet be care-free and gay while a prisoner? Moreover there is light-hearted jesting throughout the so-called "serious" introduction. Villon pictures himself there not only as "triste, failly, plus noir que meure" (179 ff.), but also as "foible . . . plus de biens que de santé" (73–74). Even in the midst of his references to poverty and death he can joke: it is better to be poor and alive than rich and dead like Jacques Cœur (285): he will die some day, but he hopes to have enjoyed himself first (419).

Siciliano finds discrepancies between the "earlier" and "later" parts in Villon's attitude toward love: he pretends to be an "amant martyr" in the "earlier" part (2001, 2015) while in the "later" he says he has to abandon love because his sad heart and famished stomach take him from amorous paths (195 ff.). Yet in line 712, which by hypothesis should belong to the "late" part, Villon says he is called "l'amant remys et regnyé" and Siciliano can only explain this stanza by the assumption that it is an attempt at "soldering." But what of the enumeration of the contradictions that his faithless lady would have him believe (689 ff.)? These do not sound like the jokes of the aged, disheartened, gravely penitent and morally matured sinner painted by Siciliano. Again in 729 ff. when the poet describes himself as nearing his end, spitting collops large as tennis balls, he lightly asks what this may mean and answers with his usual irony that it means Jenny will no longer think of him as a young gallant but as an impotent old nag. One might add that Villon's references to his infirmities and poverty, which supposedly characterize only the "late" introduction, may also be found in the posited "earlier" portion (cf. 1462, 1466, 1894–1896).

In short Siciliano's discrepancies do not seem to me to derive from different periods in the poet's life. The same "duality" that obtains in the *Testament* obtains in the nearly contemporaneous **"Debat du cuer et du corps."** It is not the duality of "je ris en pleurs" or of sinner and penitent. Our poet had good religious training and was himself sincerely religious up to a certain point. He knows what is right; he does what is wrong, and without remorse. When exiled or imprisoned he suffers and hates with all a poet's sensitivity. But he never loses his power of joking about his enemies and himself, he never loses his *joie de vivre.* And he never truly detests his sins, repents or recants.

Whether all the *Testament* was written at one time or not—and there is good reason to believe that some of the lyrical pieces like the ballade for Robert d'Estouteville (1378 ff.) and the rondeau for Ythier Marchant (978 ff.) were independently composed—nevertheless Siciliano's division into an introduction written late and a main will written early does not seem valid. It neglects the twisted irony of a man who can envisage with equanimity his evil self triumphing over the good counsels of his own conscience, a man who later could laugh in the very face of death and write:

> Je suis Françoys, dont il me poise,
> Né de Paris emprès Pontoise,
> Et de la corde d'une toise
> Sçaura mon col que mon cul poise.
>
> (*P.D.* XIII)

It seems quite certain to me that Villon never thought of himself as a criminal at all. The murder of Sermoise was not planned. The robbery of the Collège de Navarre—and doubtless other robberies—weighed lightly upon him. Whatever the charge that brought him into the power of Thibault, he resented the punishment as unfair and believed his release by King Louis no more than his due. When he was in prison for some minor theft on November 2, 1462 and was charged in addition with the old robbery of the Collège de Navarre of 1456, he soon gained his freedom. The sentence of death passed upon him at the end of 1462 must have struck him as wholly undeserved: it was imposed as a consequence of an insignificant broil in which a man was hurt, but in which Villon seems to have played a subordinate role. Doubtless the Châtelet was influenced on this occasion by his past record, his previous arrests and his association with notorious criminals, some of whom had been hanged, his "mauvaise vie," as the slightly later decree of banishment phrased it: so harsh a sentence for a relatively unimportant offense implies that Villon must have been regarded as an incorrigible. And yet again he was reprieved.

It seems obvious that in Villon's own mind the severity of his punishments always outweighed any sense of guilt. He excused himself on the score of need, of weakness, of fate, of the actions of his enemies. But he never conceded to himself that he deserved exile and imprisonment, least of all a sentence of death by hanging. Perhaps he was right, perhaps his weak character might have been fortified by less restraint and more understanding. Yet he seems always to have got off lightly enough, and repetition of misdeeds in the face of considerable clemency does suggest incorrigibility. Villon was probably more discerning when he wrote, "je congnois tout, fors que moy mesmes" (*P.D.* III). At any rate, incorrigible and impenitent as he probably was, it has well been said that "les fautes de Villon nous ont fait perdre un honnête homme dans le passé et nous ont donné un grand poète pour toujours."

John Fox (essay date 1962)

SOURCE: "Syntax and Vocabulary," in *The Poetry of Villon,* Thomas Nelson and Sons Ltd., 1962, pp. 78–111.

[*In this excerpt, Fox concerns himself with Villon's often curious word order and phrasing, which give the impression of realistic thought and speech patterns while retaining poetic qualities. Fox also examines Villon's expansive vocabulary.*]

It is impossible to read far into Villon's works without being struck by the concentrated, elliptical nature of his language. We have only to turn to the opening lines of his major work:

> En l'an de mon trentiesme aage,
> Que toutes mes hontes j'eus beues,
> Ne du tout fol, ne du tout sage,
> Non obstant maintes peines eues,
> Lesquelles j'ay toutes receues
> Soubz la main Thibault d'Aussigny . . .
> S'evesque il est, seignant les rues,
> Qu'il soit le mien je le regny.
>
> Mon seigneur n'est ne mon evesque,
> Soubz luy ne tiens, s'il n'est en friche . . .
>
> (*T* [*Testament*] 1–10)

It is at once made clear that Villon is writing about himself at the age of thirty, though his account in these opening lines reads more like a series of disconnected jottings than a properly arranged autobiography. We are at once taken into his confidence and find ourselves in the midst of his affairs, hearing of disgrace and suffering, but learning little or nothing of what it is really all about. An impression of near incoherence is created. He takes it for granted that his readers know who is writing—there is nothing corresponding to the 'Je, Françoys Villon, escollier' of the *Lais*—and he expects us to accept without question his remarks on the cruelty and injustice shown him by the bishop. Not a word on why he had been in prison. Here and elsewhere he gives his own obviously biased comments on episodes in his life without explaining just what had happened, a necessary reticence, no doubt, in view of his undeniably evil ways, which other sources, less discreet and less subjective, have revealed to us.

The language of this first stanza deserves closer attention:

> En l'an de mon trentiesme aage . . .

The meaning is quite clear: 'In the thirtieth year of my life . . .' but the construction is puzzling: 'In the year of my thirtieth . . . ?' Modern editors have explained that *aage* could mean 'year of one's life', but this does not solve the problem. The real difficulty is to know why Villon did not use the more common and logical construction: 'En l'an trentiesme de mon aage', the reading advocated by Gaston Paris even though not a single manuscript of Villon's work contains it. It is true that similar expressions from contemporary texts usually associate the numeral with *an* rather than with *aage*: 'ou XXXVIᵉ an de mon aage', 'en l'an XXXIXᵉ de l'aage d'icellui translateur', 'au XXXVᵉ an de mon aage', 'ou XVIᵉ an de son aage', etc. Only rarely does the numeral appear with *aage,* and then usually *an* is omitted altogether: 'en mon aage soixante et dixiesme'. The sole example resembling Villon's line which has been brought to light is the following, and the resemblance is only slight:

> La noble dame sur ce point trespassa,
> De quoy ce fut ung merveilleux dommage,
> Car jamais l'an en vie ne passa
> Avec six moys le quatorziesme aage . . .

but this may be accounted for by the exigencies of metre and rhyme. The free choice open to Villon ('En l'an trentiesme . . .' or 'En l'an de mon trentiesme . . .') was not available to this writer in these circumstances, and the parallel between this couplet and the line of Villon, to which both [Lucien] Foulet [in his 1932 edition of Villon's work, *Oeuvres,* 4th ed.] and [Louis] Thuasne [in his 1923 edition of *Oeuvres*] point, is misleading. The effect of Villon's order is to change the expression from a logical one: 'In the thirtieth year of my life', to a pleonastic one, 'In the year of my thirtieth year', so changing from one stylistic level, that of the written language, straightforward and syntactically logical, to that of the spoken language, which has at all times been fond of tautological constructions such as 'aujourd'hui' ('in the day of this day'), which in present-day popular French has become 'au jour d'aujourd'hui', cf. 'tout un chacun' ('un chascun' is used several times by Villon—*T* 596, 760, 1684, etc.), 'reculer en arrière', 'descendre en bas', etc. These constructions belong to conversation far more than to the written language, being sometimes of therapeutic value, as in the reinforcing of *hui* (*hodie*) by the addition of 'au jour d'', but more often conveying emphasis, turning a purely intellectual statement into an affective one. It has often been pointed out that Villon's opening line is reminiscent of that of the *Roman de la Rose*: 'Ou vintieme an de mon aage' but its very word order is enough to assign it to an altogether different type of literature, popular and not courtly. It is more of a parody than a simple reminiscence.

> Que toutes mes hontes j'eus beues . . .

'boire ses hontes', 'to drink one's disgrace', 'to drain the cup of one's disgrace' is a striking metaphor, introducing the confessions straightaway on a note of intimacy and familiarity.

> Ne du tout fol, ne du tout sage . . .

sums up very neatly Villon's attitude towards himself, about which we are to hear so much in the following stanzas: he is not entirely foolish, and so has not deserved the harsh treatment meted out to him, but neither is he altogether wise, for he has wasted his early years and been too intent on having a good time. This line also provides the first example in the *Testament* of the use of balance and contrast, of which Villon was so fond.

> Non obstant maintes peines eues,
> Lesquelles j'ay toutes receues
> Soubz la main Thibault d'Aussigny. . . .

The way this accusation is flung out in the opening lines makes it clear that Villon is quite unable to restrain his indignation, his resentment at the way he had been treated. The very mention of the name Thibault d'Aussigny deflects him from his purpose; he switches over abruptly from describing his sufferings to vituperating against the bishop. The very suddenness of the change is in itself an indication of the strength of his feelings.

'S'evesque il est . . .' Of course he was a bishop, as Villon knew only too well. This quick remark can have only a derogatory intent: 'If bishop he is . . .' that is, 'if we really must look on him as a bishop.' '. . . seignant les rues' (literally, 'signing the streets'), picturesque and pithy, is elliptical as are so many of Villon's expressions, and Thuasne has had to expand it considerably in his rendering: 'bénisant la foule en faisant le signe de la croix.'

'Qu'il soit le mien je le regny', the last line of the stanza, rounds it off neatly and drives the lesson home swiftly and surely, dispelling any shadow of doubt which may have lingered as to his true feelings for the bishop: I deny that he is my bishop, that is, that he has any jurisdiction over me—a point enlarged upon in the next stanza. However, something vital is missing from the whole of this passage.

These lines which have told us so much give us only half a sentence, less in fact, for there is no main verb. It is of no avail hunting for it in the second stanza, for Villon really has left his first sentence incomplete. This appears to have been something of a mania with him; the opening sentence of the *Lais* is also left hanging perilously in midair, and if we turn to the real beginning of the *Testament*, once the long lyrical passages of the introduction are over, we encounter a similar feature. Here, in the burlesque work, the traditional solemn opening of a will suddenly gives way to a mischievous thought:

> Ou nom de Dieu, Pere eternel,
> Et du Filz que vierge parit,
> Dieu au Pere coeternel,
> Ensemble et le Saint Esperit,
> Qui sauva ce qu' Adam perit
> Et du pery pare les cieulx . . .
> Qui bien ce croit, peu ne merit,
> Gens mors estre faiz petiz dieux.

> (*T* LXXX)

The construction closely resembles that of the first stanza of the *Testament*, with an abrupt and quite unexpected switch-over to an irreverent remark in the last two lines. One has the impression of listening to the poet as the thoughts pass quickly through his head and he gives them their first expression, imperfect, illogical perhaps to anyone preoccupied with grammar, yet clear and natural. We follow the workings of his lively mind moment by moment. We are with him as he composes, we are at his elbow, we feel the impact of his newly formed thoughts, addressed directly, so it seems, to us. He appears to write as he would think and speak. At times the chain of thought is pushed into the background, and a mischievous aside, which slid suddenly into his mind, comes to the fore. He develops it, plays around with it, then tiring of it, drops it and reverts to his main theme, the making of his will, but it is not long before we are off once more on another digression. The internal structure of stanza after stanza, passage after passage, reflects the disjointed nature of the *Testament* as a whole. Sometimes the aside is only very brief, but then it is often the more telling, as when the old harlot warns the young ones who have taken her place that when they too have aged, they will find that nobody is interested in them any more, except old priests (*T* 547).

This cruel, biting wit, this mind hopping swiftly and dexterously from one thought to another, are traits which the French people still possess, but none has ever been able to display them to better effect than Villon, not even the seventeenth-century master of this style, La Fontaine. Villon had an advantage in that he was not compelled to be explicit and grammatically logical as is the modern French writer. He did not have to trick out his sentences with an orderly array of tool-words: conjunctions, pronouns, prepositions and the like. He shapes language to his thoughts and feelings, and if a sentence is broken off suddenly, that is of no importance, for the moment he has said what he has to say, or hinted at it sufficiently, he has already passed on to the next thought crowding into his head. This moment-by-moment way of composing determines some of the salient features of his poetry: its rambling nature, full of digressions and contrary sentiments, 'mes lubres sentemens' as he calls them. We are promised the real beginning of the *Testament* after we have read not far from 800 lines, but yet another digression intervenes, and we are kept waiting for another 50 lines or so, a wait which can be borne patiently, moreover, for the digressions have a much greater interest—for the modern reader at least—than the actual string of legacies. However, it is only too easy to use terms such as 'spontaneity' in connection with Villon, and the fact that these three beginnings, that of the *Lais,* that of the introduction to the *Testament* and that of the *Testament* proper, are construed, or misconstrued, in this way, suggests deliberate intention. The beginning of the *Lais* gives the game away even more than does that of the *Testament*. In the latter the mention of the bishop's name arouses Villon's indignation to such an extent that he is impelled to abandon his first subject in order to inveigh against the bishop, so that the change here is very clearly motivated, but in the *Lais* there is nothing to jolt him out of his first train of thought. It is simply a matter of a loosely constructed sentence which has become too involved, so necessitating a new beginning in the second stanza:

> L'an quatre cens cinquante six,
> Je, Francoys Villon, escollier,
> Considerant, de sens rassis,
> Le frain aux dens, franc au collier,
> Qu'on doit ses œuvres conseillier,
> Comme Vegece le raconte,
> Sage Rommain, grant conseillier,
> Ou autrement on se mesconte . . .
> En ce temps que j'ay dit devant,
> Sur le Noel, morte saison,
> Que les loups se vivent du vent
> Et qu'on se tient en sa maison,
> Pour le frimas, pres du tison,
> Me vint ung vouloir de brisier
> La tres amoureuse prison
> Qui souloit mon cuer debrisier.
>
> (*L* [*Lais*] I–II)

Here no suddenly occurring thought or overpowering emotion obliges him to leave the first stanza incomplete, and he could so easily have completed it had he so desired. This is in fact a conscious art, not the purely undisciplined outpouring it appears, on the surface, to be. These incomplete openings and quick asides, like the very word order of the first line of the *Testament,* declare his intention of avoiding altogether a logically developed presentation, but this is no less an art than any other. To write as one speaks and thinks is far more difficult than may seem. To manage it at all is a rare achievement, and to manage it in rhymed verse of eight syllables in such a way as to make the arguments and feelings more, not less, forceful and convincing, is an even more formidable achievement. It is admittedly an art well suited to Villon, reflecting the nature of the man's mind, mercurial, penetrating, seeing all at a glance yet unable to concentrate for long on any one subject. It is an admirable expression of his personality, and the art can never be wholly separated from the man.

The longest piece that we have from him devoted entirely to a single topic and avoiding digressions of all kinds is the **"Épître à Marie d'Orléans,"** which contains a mere 132 octosyllabic lines. On two occasions Villon pretends that the *Testament* has been dictated by him to a clerk. This is doubtless a fiction, but it is a fiction well suited to the character of his work, suggesting that he himself never set pen to paper. But we must not allow ourselves to be deceived into thinking that this is all 'spontaneous', 'inspired' verse, where instinct replaces art, composed at tremendous speed in one or two days, and without effort of any kind. It has been maintained that art is the last word to use in connection with Villon. On the contrary it should surely be the first word, for writing in analogical, conversational style is an art in itself as rare in the age of the *Grands Rhétoriqueurs* as it is today. It is this art which gives his poetry its flavour and individuality, and makes it live as though he were there before our eyes, speaking directly to us.

Villon's syntax reveals to us not only the workings of his mind, but also the seeing quality of his eye, for with a few terse expressions he depicts a whole scene, imparting a photographic impression. He may mention only one or two seemingly incidental details, but they are chosen in such a way that the imagination is fired and the picture leaps into life. Here is a group of Parisiennes chatting busily together:

> Regarde m'en deux, trois, assises
> Sur le bas du ply de leurs robes,
> En ces moustiers, en ces eglises;
> Tire toy pres, et ne te hobes;
> Tu trouveras la que Macrobes
> Oncques ne fist tels jugemens. . . .
>
> (*T* 1543–8)

The **"Ballade de Mercy"** at the end of the *Testament* is addressed to the many types of people with whom he had rubbed shoulders in the streets of Paris; the crowds he had known and loved live and move again in this most vivid of verse:

> A Chartreux et a Celestins,
> A Mendians et a Devotes,
> A musars et claquepatins,
> A servans et filles mignotes
> Portans surcotz et justes cotes,
> A cuidereaux d'amours transsis
> Chaussans sans meshaing fauves botes,
> Je crie a toutes gens mercis.
>
> A filletes monstrans tetins
> Pour avoir plus largement d'ostes,
> A ribleurs, mouveurs de hutins,
> A bateleurs, traynans marmotes,
> A folz, folles, a sotz et sotes,
> Qui s'en vont siflant six a six,
> A vecyes et mariotes,
> Je crie a toutes gens mercis. . . .
>
> (*T* 1968–83)

Villon is an adept at finding the expression or adjective which really describes and is not used merely to fill out the line. [Georges] Lote has condemned the feeble choice of adjectives in so much medieval poetry [in his *Histoire du vers français*, Vol. 1, 1949; Vol. 2, 1951; Vol. III, 1955]. *Grant, bel* and such words are grossly overworked, just as *nice* is overworked in English; descriptions of castles, heroines, landscapes abound but they are all so stereotyped, so conventional in this age when no high store was set by originality. Villon is one of the few poets of his century who possess a real talent for observing directly through their own eyes, not through those of a rather effete literature. Lote acknowledges Villon's superiority in this respect, and quotes the following stanza describing the harlot in her old age. The italics are his:

> Le front ridé, les cheveux gris,
> Les sourcilz *cheus*, les yeulx estains,
> Qui faisoient regars et ris
> Dont mains meschans furent attains;
> Nez courbes de beauté loingtains,
> *Oreilles pendantes, moussues,*
> Le vis pally, mort et *destains*,
> Menton froncé, levres *peaussues* . . .
>
> (*T* LIV)

Editors of Villon's poetry sometimes quote, in their notes, expressions which seem to them to refer to something that Villon has seen and of which he has kept impression. Thus Thuasne, commenting on the line:

> S'evesque il est, seignant les rues . . .
>
> (*T* 7)

suggests that before his arrest, Villon must actually have seen the bishop blessing the crowds in the streets of Orléans. G. Atkinson, commenting on the image in the following lines:

> Mes jours s'en sont allez errant
> Comme, dit Job, d'une touaille
> Font les filetz, quant tisserant
> En son poing tient ardente paille . . .
>
> (*T* 217–20)

points out that it is a paraphrase of Job vii, 6: 'My days are swifter than a weaver's shuttle . . .', and adds: 'Villon's image is much more specific than the Biblical picture. He had *seen* the process of weaving.' The substitution of a precise image for a more general one is significant, as also is the knowledge revealed here and on a number of occasions of the exact nature of the work done by people of a variety of trades and of the terms they used. The sharp visual impact of his phraseology constantly surprises the reader and keeps him alert. On the other hand, it must be confessed that the imagination of some readers is rather too easily aroused. The mere line:

> L'emperieres au poing dorez
>
> (*T* 394)

conjures up the whole Orient for D. B. Wyndham Lewis: ' . . . the minarets; the coloured domes; the Liturgy of Chrysostom; the *ikonostasis* and its array of strange framed ovalfaced saints with hands vestments of solid gold and silver, studded with gems; the flowery Greek rites.' Such effusions can be tremendous fun to read, but they are of course concerned much more with the critic's imagination than with the poetry he is supposed to be writing about. The critic's business is with the text, but to dictate exactly how the imagination should react to the poetry, or to catalogue the images which he feels it ought to conjure up, is to say the least a vain enterprise.

Villon's syntax reveals to us not only the workings of his mind, but also the seeing quality of his eye, for with a few terse expressions he depicts a whole scene, imparting a photographic impression. He may mention only one or two seemingly incidental details, but they are chosen in such a way that the imagination is fired and the picture leaps into life.

—John Fox

Brevity is the soul of Villon's genius (but not that of his critics, it would seem). Reading through his poetry one frequently comes across examples of elliptical syntax, a peculiar telescoped style which, though not representing a complete departure from the fifteenth-century norm, is used far more consistently by him than by his contemporaries, many of whose works are extremely prolix and would have benefited greatly from a more concentrated expression. It is the same with details of syntax as with his thoughts and feelings: the beginning is there, but the end is not infrequently missing. 'Qui plus est' ('moreover') becomes 'Qui plus'. 'Somme toute' becomes 'Somme' (more common in the sixteenth century than in the fifteenth). His stanzàs are based on a climactic pattern which we have already encountered in the introduction to the *Testament*. The last line rounds the whole thing off and drives the point home. In this he is really following the tradition of concluding a stanza with a proverb, but he will generally substitute for the proverb a cutting expression of his own, again elliptical or paratactic in structure. Thus, having appointed his heirs who are to meet his debts and make sure that his legacies are distributed, he concludes in this way:

> De moy, dictes que je leur mande,
> Ont eu jusqu'au lit ou je gis.
>
> (*T* 775–6)

This brisk culmination snaps one's breath away its with very suddenness. It explains with a wry humour why these people have been chosen as heirs. The hearty, ribald laughter of the tavern echoes in this line. Another example: having bequeathed to one Mademoiselle de Bruyères the right to preach out-of-doors, Villon concludes the stanza with this stipulation:

> Mais que ce soit hors cymetieres,
> Trop bien au Marchié au fillé.
>
> *(T* 1513–14)

The last line shows the real point of this legacy, so far quite innocuous in appearance: at the Threadmarket adjoining the cemetery will be a suitable place for her preaching, since it was there, as everyone knew, that the prostitutes were to be found.

Describing a shed or hovel in which he took refuge at one time and where he seems to have put up a hook in lieu of a sign, Villon concludes:

> Qui que l'ait prins, point ne m'en loue:
> Sanglante nuyt et bas chevet!
>
> *(T* 1004–5)

Once more the last line is elliptical and has to be expanded in translation as have so many of Villon's lines: 'he certainly spent a beastly night in the place and had a low pillow' (i.e. slept on the ground).

Villon says what he has to say quickly, briefly, without undue wordiness, and the forceful impact of his verse is due largely to this habit. He captures beautifully the incomplete, untidy utterances of conversation. Indeed, on numerous occasions he deliberately turns his poetry into a conversation by inventing an interlocutor who objects to a statement he has just made; he then proceeds to demolish that objection, sometimes in a few lines (*T* III, LXXI, CXXXV), sometimes taking two or more stanzas (*T* LVIII–LXIV, LXXXII–LXXXIII): 'And if anyone should take me up on this . . .' (*T* 17), 'And if anyone should question me on this . . .' (*T* 725), 'And should anyone blame me for these words . . .' (*T* 571–2), 'If anyone asks me . . .' (*T* 809). He also addresses an imaginary audience (*T* XLIII, CLVI–CLVIII, CLIX, *T* 1692–1719, *T* 1968–95), sometimes adopting for this purpose a disguise such as that of the Belle Heaulmière, or else he anticipates objections and accusations as though following the line of thought his poetry creates in the reader (*T* 105–6, 185–92). He is particularly fond of poking questions at himself and then providing the answer, which may be anything in length from a couple of words to a couple of stanzas (*T* 174–6, 205–8, 225–48, 289–92, 327–8, 418–20, 609–12, 732–6, 759–60, 773–6, 914–17, 1100–1, 1283, 1355–61, 1655, 1737–43, 1815–16, 1919, 1930–2, 1934). Some of these questions are obviously supposed to come from his clerk, Firmin; for example, when he is appointing the various executors of the will, he gives their names in reply to his clerk's questions:

> Qui sera l'autre? G'y pensoye:
> Ce sera sire Colombel . . .
>
> *(T* 1930–1; cf. 1919, 1934)

It may well be that this clerk fulfilled a need felt by Villon

for another presence, someone, even if only imaginary, at whom he could fling his sarcasms and reflections. It is also worth nothing that one of the longer digressions in the early part of the *Testament* takes the form of a conversation between Alexander and Diomedes, with whom Villon identifies himself: he is a Diomedes who has never met his Alexander. This conversational style is in fact one of Villon's main methods of keeping his mind on the move from one idea or feeling to another; repartee, questions, objections, accusations act as a stimulus, constantly urging him on. The conversational nature of his style is reflected also in the use of exclamatory expressions such as 'Viore' and 'Dieu merci', which appear, on the surface, merely to fill the line out, though they are not out of place in this most lyric of poetry, subjective in thought and construction alike, and are in fact reflections of the particular art of Villon.

In medieval French, word order was far more of a stylistic device than it is nowadays. Examples of its use to provide stress abound in the earliest texts:

> Halt sunt li pui e tenebrus e grant

in the *Chanson de Roland* (l. 1830) emphasises the height of the hills more than would 'Li pui sunt halt . . .', and also gives a more strongly marked caesura. Similarly:

> Granz est la noise, si l'oïrent Franceis
>
> (l. 1005)

rather than 'La noise est granz . . .' stresses the loudness of the noise of battle. From late medieval French onwards, word order was to become more stereotyped, but even so the fifteenth-century writer still had far more choice in such matters than has his modern counterpart. However, in any study of this subject as it affects poetry, two factors must be constantly borne in mind. Firstly, certain word orders may appear to be based on stylistic considerations but are in fact due to the exigencies of rhyme or metre. Thus, when Villon writes:

> Pour ce que foible je me sens
>
> *(T* 73)

foible may appear to be thrown into prominence, but the placing of the word at the end of the line would not give him the rhyme he was seeking. Also, it cannot be said that he wrote:

> S'evesque il est, seignant les rues
>
> *(T* 7)

as a more emphatic form of 'S'il est evesque . . .', for this order would involve a syllable too many, so that in point of fact he had no choice in the matter. Similarly:

> Trop forte elle est pour telz enfans
>
> *(T* 1293)

would involve a syllable too many if written as 'Elle est trop forte . . .', and in the line:

Vostre je suis et non plus mien
>   (*PD* [*Poésies Diverses*] VIII, 86)

the first word certainly seems to be singled out for emphasis, but

Je suis vostre et non plus mien

would lack a syllable. Secondly, despite the freedom of choice open to the medieval writer in the sphere of word order, certain tendencies were followed from the earliest times. One was to place the past participle in front of its auxiliary. The **Testament** provides several instances:

Peu [nourri] m'a d'une petite miche
>   (*T* 13)—not 'M'a peu . . .'

Escript l'ay l'an soixante et ung . . .
>   (*T* 81)

Allé s'en est et je demeure . . .
>   (*T* 177)

Tollu m'as la haulte franchise . . .
>   (*T* 461)

Abusé m'a et fait entendre . . .
>   (*T* 689)

Degeté m'a de maint bouillon . . .
>   (*T* 853)

Villon was not influenced in such cases by the tendency of earlier medieval French to avoid using the regime form of the weak personal pronoun at the beginning of a line, since he writes:

Me vint ung vouloir de brisier . . .
>   (*L* 14)

not 'Ung vouloir me vint . . .' and between them the two testaments contain a number of such examples (*L* 28; *T* 95, 101, 148, 197, 327, 483, 996, 1010, 1413, 1480, 1592, 1675, 1773, 2015). On the other hand, this habit of inverting participle and auxiliary was allied to the long-established one of keeping a central position for the verb. Where a compound tense was involved, or a construction with an infinitive, it was the part of the verb indicating the person that was allotted the central position; usually it was made the second element of the sentence (cf. inversion of subject and verb after certain adverbs in modern French, and even after conjunctions such as *et* in Middle French), occasionally the third. Thus, for 'You are his master', Villon could not write 'Es son seigneur'. Theoretically he had the choice between 'Tu es son seigneur' as in modern French, or 'Son seigneur es', but the 4–6 division of decasyllabic verse made the former impossible and it is accordingly the latter he has used:

Son seigneur es, et te tiens son varlet
>   (*PD* XI, 34)

This order was dictated by a combination of syntactic convention and metrical requirements, not simply by a desire to lay emphasis on *seigneur*. There is a number of similar examples in Villon's poetry:

Mon seigneur n'est ne mon evesque . . .
>   (*T* 9)

Riens ne hayt que perseverance . . .
>   (*T* 104)

Griefz ne faiz a jeunes n'a vieulx . . .
>   (*T* 125)

Bons vins ont, souvent embrochiez . . .
>   (*T* 249)

Moue ne fait qui ne desplaise . . .
>   (*T* 440)

Rondement ayment toute gent . . .
>   (*T* 579; cf. *T* 717, 749, 758, 767, 801, 869, 895, 985, etc.)

Only rarely does one find a verb, positive or negative, as the first element of a line in Villon's poetry, unless it is an interrogative form, an imperative, a subjunctive expressing a hypothesis, or unless it completes a clause or sentence begun in the preceding lines:

Moy, povre mercerot de Renes,
Mourray je *pas?*
>   (*T* 417–18)

Dieu, qui les pelerins d'Esmaus
Conforta . . .
>   (*T* 99–100)

. . . en grant povreté . . .
Ne *gist* pas grant loyauté.
>   (*T* 150–2)

Griefz ne faiz a jeunes n'a vieulx
Soie sur piez ou soie en biere . . .
>   (*T* 125–6)

Excusez moy aucunement . . .
>   (*T* 149)

Of a total of over a hundred examples (a hundred positive, fourteen negative) which occur in the two testaments, only two do not fit in to any of the above categories, and even here the subject has already been given in the preceding lines:

Ont eu jusqu'au lit ou je gis;
>   (*T* 776)

We have seen above that this line was intended to have a startling effect.

Regrete huy sa mort et hier.

(*T* 431)

Foulet points out in the notes to his edition of Villon's poetry that this line is peculiar since it makes *hier* dissyllabic 'malgré l'usage constant de l'ancien français'. He draws attention to the reading of one manuscript (F): 'Regretant sa mort huy et hier', and this may well have been the original version, since the present participle, like the past participle, is frequently used by Villon at the beginning of a line.

Two questions arise from what precedes. The first is this: is word order in Villon's poetry ever influenced by stylistic considerations? The answer is certainly yes, and in more ways than one. . . . euphony was an important consideration with him, and he avoids, where possible, awkward clashes of sounds. Thus, although he writes in *PD* IX, 17: 'Quant mort sera', he does not follow the same order in *T* 1760: 'Or m*or*s sont ilz . . .' but prefers: 'Or sont ilz mors . . .' (also in *T* 485: 'Or est il mort . . .'). Similarly in *T* 11 he writes: 'Foy ne luy doy . . .', not 'Ne luy *doy* foy . . .'; and in *T* 259: 'Je ne suis juge . . .', not 'Ju*ge je* ne suis'. Balance and contrast are also important considerations; thus he does not write:

. . . Quant des cuisses
Plus ne sont cuisses, mais cuissetes.

but

. . . Quant des cuisses
Cuisses ne sont plus, mais cuissetes.

(*T* 523)

In addition, word order is used on occasion for purposes of emphasis, as in the numerous examples of overflow mentioned earlier. Also, it is noteworthy that, when speaking of poverty and the terrible hold it had on his life, he writes, not:

Je suis povre de ma jeunesse

but

Povre je suis de ma jeunesse . . .

(*T* 273)

But on the other hand, presenting himself as a sinner, without wishing to stress the fact any too heavily, he writes, not:

Pecheur je suis, je le sçay bien

but

Je suis pecheur, je le sçay bien,

(*T* 105)

and the 'je le sçay bien' makes it quite clear that he feels no need for stress: 'the fact is quite obvious enough' is the implication. In his version of the *carpe diem* theme, stress-

ing the folly of neglecting the joys of life until one is too old to appreciate them, he writes:

Viel je seray; vous, laide, sans couleur

(*T* 962)

not

Je seray viel . . .

whilst in the **"Ballade pour prier Nostre Dame,"** which he wrote for his mother, she is made to say, not:

Je suis femme povrette et ancïenne,

which would be a dull statement of fact devoid of emotive content, but

Femme je suis, povrette et ancïenne,

(*T* 893)

a word order which has also the effect of giving a more firmly marked caesura, although the lyric caesura that 'Je suis femme . . .' would entail is common enough in Villon's decasyllabic verse.

This brings us to the second question arising from these remarks on word order. Is it possible, and is it necessary, to distinguish between those instances where word order was intended by the poet to achieve a stylistic effect and those where grammatical conventions or metrical requirements give the reader an impression of stylistic effect, as in

Son seigneur es, et te tiens son varlet

The value of linguistic analysis of the type given above is that it enables us to get the poetry into a fairly true perspective. It throws light on the circumstances governing its composition, and prevents us from attributing to the poet what belonged to the period as a whole. Obviously, however, such considerations cannot be allowed to come between the poetry and our appreciation of it. We cannot postpone our reaction until the analysis has been made, as though it were some sort of postmortem examination. Stylistic effects sometimes derive not so much from the poet's intentions as from the metre he is using and the syntactic conventions he is following. They are thus inherent qualities of the system as a whole, but are no less real for that. Furthermore the stature of the poet is revealed when the effect of his poetry is enhanced by such matters as metre and rhyme, for this is by no means an inevitable occurrence. With lesser poets a line of verse is so often distorted, or allowed to fall flat, or to strain the understanding simply in order to achieve a suitable rhyme or the required number of syllables. There is very little straining of this kind with Villon; he is the complete master of his versification, and where he himself is not directly responsible for a stylistic effect, always and inevitably he is indirectly responsible. Thus if he had no choice between

Tu es son seigneur et te tiens son varlet

and

> Son seigneur es et te tiens son varlet

he could on the other hand have chosen between the latter and

> Tu es son maistre et te tiens son varlet

so that the wording as it stands does all the same involve a choice, as any line of poetry is ultimately bound to do, be the choice felicitous or otherwise. It is not simply a matter of some effects being accidental, and therefore spurious, and others deliberate, and therefore genuine. Whether the ultimate source is provided by the personal style of the poet himself or by the language of the period in which he is writing, each trait contributes towards the impression created by the whole. The flavour of any work is in part that of its period.

Not the least remarkable aspect of Villon's poetry is the very wide range of vocabulary it reveals. He handles words and phrases with an exuberance worthy of a writer of the Renaissance. He revels in the word matter for its own sake. His piling up of words in crisp, staccato formation contributes to the lilt and energy of his verse. The few doublets and *clichés* apart, each word is there with a purpose and has something to add to the overall pattern. The personality the poetry builds up for itself is thin, wiry, sharp of look and quick of manner. It has none of the rather dreary obesity characterising many a late medieval poet, such as Guillaume Alexis. All is grist to Villon's mill, whether it be names of chemicals or foods, lists of proverbs or occupations, dialect forms, thieves' slang, nationalities, names of heroes or heroines, whores and harlots. We may turn to the **"Ballade de Bonne Doctrine"** with its argot terms, its heaping up of nouns and verbs relating to a variety of professions, most of them of a dubious kind:

> Car ou soies porteur de bulles,
> Pipeur ou hasardeur de dez,
> Tailleur de faulx coings et te brusles
> Comme ceulx qui sont eschaudez,
> Traistres parjurs, de foy vuidez;
> Soies larron, ravis ou pilles:
> Ou en va l'acquest, que cuidez?
> Tout aux tavernes et aux files.
>
> Ryme, raille, cymballe, luttes,
> Comme fol, fainctif, eshontez;
> Farce, broulle, joue des fleustes;
> Fais, es villes et es citez,
> Farces, jeux et moralitez;
> Gaigne au berlanc, au glic, aux quilles:
> Aussi bien va, or escoutez!
> Tout aux tavernes et aux filles.
>
> (*T* 1692–1707)

The raciness and vigour of these lines are quite clear to any reader, even if the meaning is not. We may also turn to the **"Ballade des Langues Envieuses"** which lists a wide variety of substances in which, says Villon, certain jealous tongues should be fried; along with several minerals he places in this witches' brew the most loathsome things his extremely fertile mind could conjure up. These tongues have evidently done him harm in the past, but however fierce and nasty they may have been, they were clearly no match for Villon's pen:

> En realgar, en arcenic rochier,
> En orpiment, en salpestre et chaulx vive,
> En plomb boullant pour mieulx les esmorchier,
> En suye et poix destrempez de lessive
> Faicte d'estrons et de pissat de juifve,
> En lavailles de jambes a meseaulx,
> En racleure de piez et viels houseaulx,
> En sang d'aspic et drogues venimeuses,
> En fiel de loups, de regnars et blereaulx,
> Soient frittes ces langues envieuses!
>
> (*T* 1422–31)

An enumeration of a very different kind appears at the end of the *Lais*, which pokes fun at the pompous language of the Sorbonne:

> Lors je sentis dame Memoire
> Respondre et mectre en son aulmoire
> Ses especes collateralles,
> Oppinative faulce et voire,
> Et autres intellectualles,
>
> Et mesmement l'estimative,
> Par quoy prospective nous vient,
> Similative, formative . . .
>
> (*L* 284–91)

The **"Ballade des Proverbes"** accumulates popular sayings of the day:

> Tant grate chievre que mal gist,
> Tant va le pot a l'eaue qu'il brise,
> Tant chauffe on le fer qu'il rougist,
> Tant le maille on qu'il se debrise,
> Tant vault l'homme comme on le prise,
> Tant s'eslongne il qu'il n'en souvient,
> Tant mauvais est qu'on le desprise,
> Tant crie l'on Noel qu'il vient.
>
> (*PD* 11, 1–8)

In the *Ballades en Jargon,* Villon takes an obvious delight in handling the special, secret language of the Parisian underworld of his day, not to be confused with argot which, unlike the jargon or *jobelin,* did not necessarily strive to place itself beyond the comprehension of all but the initiated:

> Brouez, Benards, eschecquez a la saulve,
> Car escornez vous estes a la roue;
> Fourbe, joncheur, chascun de vous se saulve:
> Eschec, eschec, coquille si s'en broue!
> Cornette court: nul planteur ne s'i joue.
> Qui est en plant, en ce coffre joyeulx,

Pour ses raisons il a, ains qu'il s'escroue,
Jonc verdoiant, havre du marieulx!

This accumulative technique is an integral part of Villon's poetry, and appears throughout his work, in the lines on death, in the lists of foodstuffs, in the names of the heroes and heroines of the past, in the description of woman's beauty. It is used in various ways, sometimes merely facetiously, the better to bring out the point of a joke, sometimes more seriously, to underline the inevitability of fate, and sometimes with a bewildering mixture of the two, which imparts the cynicism to poems such as the **"Ballade de Bonne Doctrine"**. But this very technique reveals the fascination that Villon finds in words. He never tires of building them up into fantastic patterns. None the less, however brilliantly he uses this technique, it is far from being original. Similar features appear already in the *Chanson de Roland* and other *chansons de geste,* where poets revel in accumulating sonorous, mouth-filling words, for example in descriptions of armies:

Li amiralz ·x· escheles ajusted.
La premere est des jaianz de Malpruse,
L'altre est de Hums e la terce de Hungres,
E la quarte est de Baldise la lunge
E la quinte est de cels de Val Penuse
E la siste est de . . . Maruse
E la sedme est de Leus e d'Astrimonies,
L'oidme est d'Argoilles e la noefme de Clarbone
E la disme est des barbez de Fronde . . .

According to Leo Spitzer, names have a poetry of their own, for they are less ringed about with grammatical considerations than are other words, and in consequence exist more as sounds which appeal to our ears. He quotes as example Racine's

La fille de Minos et de Pasiphaé

and then applies his remarks to Villon's accumulation of names in the **"Ballade des Dames du Temps Jadis"**. Whatever its potentialities, this word-building technique inevitably lends itself to abuse, and the poets of the fourteenth and fifteenth centuries often overworked it, using it sometimes for no purpose other than to provide intricate leonine rhymes, or even simply to fill out a poem. With Villon it is never the case of a string of words or names serving merely as padding; always there is a motive, and always a rhythm and sound pattern appropriate to the context.

An outstanding feature of Villon's vocabulary, apart from its breadth, is its 'modernism'. Rather more than one hundred of the words he uses were, at the most, little over a century old; several old words appear in new forms unknown to writers of earlier centuries and which are still those of today; whilst about thirty which have come down to modern French appear in his poetry for the first time or were used only very rarely by his predecessors. A few others appear to have been invented by him, either in their actual form, or in the meaning and use allotted to them. The hundred or so words from the immediate past are mostly Latinisms and learned forms introduced into the language from the fourteenth century onwards.

It is characteristic of the many-sided and contradictory nature of this poet that, having pointed out how his syntax resembles that of ordinary speech, we should have to go on to speak about his use of Latinisms. To be sure, his language is not invariably that of conversation; he was by no means without erudition, and was capable of a formal style, at times oddly out of place, as in the opening lines of the **"Ballade pour prier Nostre Dame"**. This prayer is supposed to be uttered by his mother, poor, ignorant and illiterate:

. . . povrette et ancïenne,
Qui riens ne sçay; oncques lettre ne lus . . .
                                                        (*T* 893–4)

yet it begins in a pompous way with learned literary expressions:

Dame du ciel, *regente terrienne,*
Emperiere des *infernaux palus* . . .
                                                        (*T* 873–4)

If this poem is so celebrated today it is because of its latter section where Villon, having cast aside his learning, has reverted to a simpler style, more suited both to him and to the occasion, and far more moving:

Au moustier voy, dont suis paroissienne
Paradis paint, ou sont harpes et lus,
Et ung enfer ou dampnez sont boullus:
L'ung me fait paour, l'autre joye et liesse.
La joye avoir me fay, haulte Deesse,
A qui pecheurs doivent tous recourir,
Comblez de foy, sans fainte ne paresse:
En ceste foy je vueil vivre et mourir.
                                                        (*T* 895–902)

An occasional whiff of pedantry reminds us once again that his conversational style was not just simply 'spontaneous', 'natural', 'instinctive'. It is not that he was capable of this style and nothing else. He had to make a choice, and had to feel his way like any other in order to find the art best suited to his personality.

A look at some of the terms Villon may have introduced into French literature brings us back once more into contact with his more familiar style. Here are some examples of words which appear in his poetry for the first time, or are only rarely found earlier: *un tantinet* (*T* 1109), *la plupart* (*L* 117), *en effet* (*T* 587), *toutefois* (*T* 745, 805, 1217, *PD* VIII, 52), *corvée* (*T* 1031) in its extended sense of 'nuisance', 'bother', *altérer* (*L* 54) in its connection with thirst, *défaut* (*L* 59) in the sense of 'fault', and *en dépit de* (*T* 1803). There are good grounds for believing that *tantinet* originated amongst the people of Paris, whilst an abbreviation such as *la plupart* for *la plus grande partie de* (in *T* 1832 Villon uses *la plus partie de*), a transformation such as *toutefois* for earlier *toutes voies* (cf. Spanish *todavìa*), and extensions of meaning such as those involved in *corvée* and *altérer* all illustrate usages and developments common in speech. On the other hand, one old form used by Villon, *extrace* (*T*274) in place of the then relatively new borrowing from Latin, *extraction,* had a popular flavour retained to this day by the spoken language which uses forms such as *administrace* for *administration.*

Turning to the **Ballades en Jargon,** we find a host of strange words, and some familiar terms with new meanings. It is impossible to estimate Villon's originality in this sphere; he may well have coined some of these expressions himself, but we have no means of knowing. It is here that we encounter the first attested use of *niais* in its modern sense of 'simpleton'; formerly it had meant 'fledgling', having been derived from the noun *le nid*; *blanc* was used in the same sense, as an extension of its first metaphorical meaning of 'innocent', 'inexperienced' (cf. modern *blanc bec,* which like *niais* referred originally to a young bird); *rouge* on the other hand meant 'cunning', owing to the reputation for slyness enjoyed by red-haired people; criminals whose ears had been cut off are described as having been 'circumcised of their handles'—*des ances circoncis,* which seems not inappropriate in a language whose word for head had meant originally 'earthenware pot' (*tête<testa*)! Several expressions are obviously ironical: *être accolé* meant 'to be hanged'; *le mariage* meant 'hanging'; *montjoye* ('Hill of Joy', originally the name given to a hill near Paris where St Denis was martyred) meant 'gibbet'; *un ange* was a hangman's assistant; *dorer* meant 'to lie', literally 'to cloak beneath a bright exterior'—a little like English 'to gild the pill'; a *vendengeur* was a thief, as was also *gagneur,* recalling the euphemistic use of 'to win' in modern English. *Ne pas sçavoir oignons peller* may have had the same meaning as English 'not to know one's onions'; *babiller,* originally 'to stutter' (onomatopoetic, cf. English 'to babble') meant 'to spill the beans'; *rebigner,* originally 'to squint', meant 'to look at', 'to take a squint at'; while *pigeon,* yet another word for 'simpleton', recalls an American use of the word. *Beffleur,* 'a cheat', 'swindler', is of the same origin as English 'to baffle'; *estre sur les joncs,* meaning 'to be in prison', the floor of which was covered in rushes, reveals a semantic evolution analagous to that of English 'to be on the mat'—at least they share the same basic meaning, 'to be in trouble'! Although a few of these jargon terms are obvious enough: *la dure,* 'the ground', *la tarde* (cf. modern Spanish *la tarde*) 'the evening', *le contre,* 'companion', *le coffre,* 'prison', *le banc,* 'scaffold', *le pluc,* 'spoils', literally 'peel' (cf. modern French *épluchure*), large numbers remain obscure and can only be guessed at. Not only the meaning, but the very authorship of some of these poems is in doubt, so that one is in danger of attributing to Villon expressions which he never used in point of fact. None the less, enough is known about the poems in jargon which Villon definitely wrote, and about the jargon in general—racy, ironical, terse, absorbing expressions from a wide variety of sources—to show clearly that it had considerable influence on Villon. This is the school which fashioned his imagery, which imparted the pungency to his style and developed his feeling for words. The jargon contained special terms for even the commonest notions: some were archaic and had been forgotten by

most people or had survived only in the provinces; large numbers were based on metaphorical extension of meaning; some were adopted from other languages. What the *trobar clus* had been to the troubadours of Provence the jargon was to Villon and his associates. Although the two were at opposite ends of the social scale, the *trobar clus* sophisticated, literary rather than spoken, the jargon earthy and popular, the latter was, all the same, not nearly as wholly vulgar and coarse as one might imagine. Its heterogeneous nature, by no means ignorant of learned terms and expressions, betrays people of some education, and it is known that Villon was by no means the only cleric to haunt the underworld of fifteenth-century Paris.

The influence of *jobelin* may be seen in the peculiar and original use of metaphor in Villon's poetry. It is not necessarily a matter of direct borrowing from the language of the Coquillards, but concerns rather the basic approach to words, a continual readiness to use even the commonest terms metaphorically. The reader is constantly coming across a strange use of a word which contributes to the brisk slanginess of the language, and helps to build up an impression of freshness, of boundless life and vigour. The metaphor is frequently only trifling and not necessarily original, but the cumulative effect is considerable. Thus, in his quarrel with Grosse Margot, Villon gives her a blow on the nose with a piece of wood:

Dessus son nez luy en fais ung *escript*

(*T* 1609)

and in another ballade he refers to:

Serpens, lesars et telz nobles *oyseaulx*

(*T* 1440)

'Beeswax' is *estrons de mouche* (*T* 1199, literally 'bees' excrement'); 'physical love' is *contemplacion* when applied, mischievously, to the religious Orders (*T* 1165) and more conventionally *le jeu d'asne* (*T* 1566). Occasionally the meaning of such expressions has become obscured; thus a reference to the *caige vert* of an aged monk (*T* 1195) is generally taken to mean his mistress, but this is uncertain; there was, apparently, a brothel by the name of *La Caige* in the Paris of Villon's day, and the colour green may have been associated with such places, or may have symbolised prostitution. When Villon wanted to say: 'What a beating I was given', he wrote in fact: 'Such mittens there were at that marriage', and it was only a reference by Rabelais to the quaint custom of slapping people on the back with a mitten at marriage feasts—with the idea of implanting the occasion on their memories—that revealed the meaning of the line. The expression appears to be unique in medieval literature. These are but a few random examples of the peculiar metaphorical uses to which Villon puts his words. Metaphorical expressions with an altogether richer and deeper symbolical meaning occur frequently in his poetry, but these lighter, relatively insignificant ones help to create in the mind of the reader an impression of a springy, quick-fire inventiveness. Everything points to a fresh and lively mind, the very antithesis of the pedantic *Rhétoriqueurs* who ruled French poetry in the second half of the fifteenth century.

A writer of varying moods and uneven inspiration, Villon treats words in a number of ways. When facetiously inclined, he plays around with puns, using them, as he uses almost every device that language can offer, to ridicule those whom he disliked:

> Je ne suis son serf ne sa biche . . .
>   (*T* 12, *serf*='slave' or 'deer')

> Ne luy laisse ne cuer ne foye . . .
>   (*T* 911, *cuer* abstract or concrete)

> Qui luy laira escu ne targe . . .
>   (*T* 917, *escu*='coin' or 'shield')

> Qui n'entent ne mont ne vallee . . .
>   (*L* 99 *mont*='hill' or 'much', a variant of *mout*)

He is also fond of toying with antiphrasis in such a way that the reader never quite knows whether love means hate or black means white. At times the joke, such as it is, is plain enough:

> Et s'aucun, dont n'ay congnoissance
> Estoit allé de mort a vie . . .
>   (*T* 1860–1)

Villon is evidently looking on earthly life as death, and on life in the next world as true life. Sometimes a remark was for long taken at its face value: the reference to three poor orphans, for example, who in point of fact were, as we have seen, rich old money-lenders well known in the Paris of Villon's day. Sarcasm of this sort abounds in his poetry, and when poking fun at people he excels; but on the other hand, when he is writing out of duty, in praise of some benefactor, his words not infrequently assume a leaden quality and he trips up over them:

> Raison ne veult que je desacoustume,
> Et en ce vueil avec elle m'assemble,
> De vous servir, mais que m'y acoustume.
>   (*T* 1390–2)

These clumsy lines have not an ounce of feeling behind them. Opinions differ as to how this *ballade,* written for the provost Robert d'Estouteville, should be interpreted. Some claim that it is the usual, insulting Villon, for, they say, the unfortunate provost's wife is compared to a ploughed field! However much in character this may seem, it is not what the poem in fact says, and we must resist the temptation to out-Villon Villon by seeing some lubricous intention or thinly veiled insult beneath every remark. The entire *ballade* is put into the mouth of the provost, who is telling his wife of his love for her, and is certainly not casting aspersions on her moral behaviour. Villon simply makes the provost say: 'I do not lose the seed I sow in your field since the fruit resembles me. God ordained me to till and enrich it.' For once this is not thinly disguised insult, but heavy-handed flattery. At the beginning of the **Testament** the flat-

tery of Louis XI, to whom Villon owed his release from prison, is also clumsily worded and in no way heralds the lyric poetry to follow. The lines:

> . . . suis, tant que mon cuer vivra,
> Tenu vers luy m'humilier,
> Ce que feray jusques il mourra.
>   (*T* 85–7)

are, to say the least, awkward, for they appear to mean: 'I will honour the king until he dies.' It has been suggested that *il* of the last line may refer to *cuer,* meaning in that case 'until I die', which seems far more appropriate, but the fact remains that the line is ambiguous in a way that cannot have been intended. It is difficult to share Marot's regret that Villon was not a court poet; both the life and literature of court circles were altogether alien to his nature.

Villon was hopelessly lacking in inspiration when writing out of duty, or when he had nothing particular to say about his associates (which was rare) or about himself (which was even more rare). His poetry leaps to life whenever he is in springly mood or when he is breaking some victim on the wheel of his wit. But only when he is haunted by the fear of poverty, of suffering and death, does his poetry reach its greatest heights. At such moments his vocabulary, for all its scope and richness, becomes stark, ascetic almost. Vulgarisms and learned expressions alike are left on one side. Nothing could be simpler or more direct than:

> Freres humains qui après nous vivez,
> N'ayez les cuers contre nous endurcis . . .
>   (*PD* XIV, 1–2)

The word content of this verse is very plain, yet such is the art of Villon that it echoes for long in the memory even after the context has faded away:

> Deux estions et n'avions qu'ung cuer . . .

> Hé! Dieu, se j'eusse estudié
> Ou temps de ma jeunesse folle . . .

> Les aucuns sont morts et roidis,
> D'eulx n'est il plus riens maintenant . . .

> Hommes, icy n'a point de mocquerie,
> Mais priez Dieu que tous nous vueille absouldre!

Geoffrey Brereton   (essay date 1973)

SOURCE: "Francois Villon," in *An Introduction to the French Poets: Villon to the Present Day,* revised edition, Methuen & Co. Ltd., 1973, pp. 1–10.

[*Brereton is an English educator who has written extensively on French literature of the sixteenth, seventeenth, and eighteenth centuries. Here, in a revised version of an essay originally published in 1956, he praises Villon's poetic technique of combining the traditional* ballade *form with the modern tendency to write about highly personal subject matter.*]

Villon was the last of the great French poets of the Middle Ages and one of the few who can now be read without a considerable background knowledge of medieval culture. He loses, of course, something in the process. One may fail to recognize the traditional nature of the themes he is treating, one may miss catching in his comments on life and death echoes going back two hundred years before his lifetime and so not appreciate the interesting twists he gives them. One may, in particular, remain unaware of his masterly use of verse-forms which had been developing during more than three centuries, since the time of the Provençal troubadours. But though he belonged to his age and reflected its cynicism, its innocent obscenity, its piety, its learning (on a lowish level), and some of its literary conventions, he is more than a merely representative poet. He is both universal and personal enough to carry beyond his age—or, if one prefers it, to carry his age to ours.

If, as modern scholarship tends to show, he is not quite the remarkable special case he was once considered to be, he is none the less the only poet to have expressed the spirit of his time with what *seems* to be a completely personal voice. This, which distinguishes him from all his major contemporaries, is the quality which has ensured his survival and it matters very little whether he was experiencing for the first time the states of mind he communicates. The point is that he communicates them effectively and, to the extent that he does so, makes them his own. Behind the work there is undoubtedly a man. While it would be a mistake to try to visualize the man too clearly apart from the work, yet something is known of his life from external sources. Scanty though these are, they fit the rest of the picture.

He was born in Paris in 1431, the year when Joan of Arc was burnt at Rouen. His mother, according to his poems, was poor and illiterate. From his father, of whom no mention remains, he presumably took one of his two original names of Montcorbier and Des Loges. In later life he discarded them to adopt the name of a priest who befriended and educated him, Guillaume de Villon. Studying at Paris University, François Villon took the degrees of Bachelor, *Licencié,* and finally Master of Arts. Even after this, he continues to regard himself as a student, though of an unacademic kind. His first recorded conflict with the law occurred at the age of twenty-four, when he killed a priest called Philippe Chermoye in a brawl and fled from Paris. He returned with a pardon six months later, took part in a successful robbery at the Collège de Navarre and again left the capital, this time for five years. Just before going, he composed his first considerable poem, *Les Lais* (Christmas 1456).

During his wandering in the provinces he visited Orleans, Blois, and probably roved much further afield. He found a temporary patron in Charles, Duke of Orleans—himself a fine poet in the old courtly tradition—who included some

of Villon's verses in his own album of poems. He had relations with a gang of malefactors known as *les compagnons de la Coquille* and he continued to fall foul of the law. One of his own compositions suggests that he lay at one time in the Duke of Orleans's prisons under sentence of death but was saved by an amnesty granted to celebrate the birth of the Duke's daughter. He spent the summer of 1461 in prison at Meung-sur-Loire. This time his captor was the Bishop of Orleans. He was released in the autumn of that year to return once more to Paris and write his principal poem, ***Le Testament.***

There is no record of the crimes for which Villon suffered these punishments. He may even—though it seems unlikely—have been innocent. But, innocent or guilty, he was by now a marked man in the eyes of the authorities. In November 1462 he was arrested on suspicion of a new robbery. He was about to be released for lack of evidence when his share in the six-year-old affair of the Collège de Navarre was recalled. He was obliged to sign a promise to repay 120 gold crowns before they let him go. When, a few weeks later, he was concerned in a street brawl outside the office of a papal official, his evil reputation nearly destroyed him. He was sentenced to be hanged and it was no doubt while waiting to be executed that he composed the famous **"Epitaphe Villon"** or **"Ballade des pendus."** Meanwhile, he had chanced the desperate throw of an appeal. To his joy, it was granted. He was set free, but under penalty of ten years' banishment from the city and viscounty of Paris. This judgment, rendered on 5 January 1463, is the last authentic mention of François Villon.

Villon's poetry is not mere whining and whimpering of genius which occasionally changes its mood and sticks its fingers to its nose. It is rather the confession of a man who had wandered over the "crooked hills of delicious pleasure," and had arrived in rags and filth in the famous city of Hell.

—Robert Lynd in "Villon: The Genius of the Tavern," Old and New Masters, *1919.*

Two picturesque anecdotes of his later life were recounted by Rabelais writing some ninety years after. One describes him in banishment in England, chatting with Rabelaisian familiarity to Edward IV. The other depicts him living in his boisterous old age at Saint-Maixantd-de-Poitou. The interest of the anecdotes, which are certainly inventions, is that already by Rabelais's time Villon had become a legendary figure, famed for his ingenious pranks and his coarse wit. The legend has continued to grow, fed by the abundant material, rich in contrasting pathos and squalor, provided by Villon's own writings. As would be expected, few precise statements of fact can be obtained from such a source. What does emerge is the revelation of a character, drawn with great frankness.

The self-portrayed Villon was a man of some education who drifted into a life of crime and vagabondage through his incurable love of independence. In spite of his obscure parentage, he was not inevitably marked out as a social outcast, for with his benefactor Guillaume Villon and his studies behind him he should have found at least a humble security in some ecclesiastical charge—had he wanted it. On the other hand, he was not a heroic rebel. He became a criminal less from design than from lethargy. He needed money to keep himself alive and to spend on 'taverns and women', and crime appeared the easiest way of obtaining it. Even here, he was not very successful, as his various imprisonments show.

Imprisonment soured him, but brought no repentance. His occasional flashes of regret were for his carefree youth and for the material comforts which had eluded him through his own folly, not for any moral standard from which he had fallen short. He could indulge in self-pity and at the same time cock verbal snooks at the rich and prosperous. Here in fact is the only kind of pride discernible in him; he had kept himself free from the taint of conformism. This was his essential freedom, worth preserving at the cost of many grovellings to the powerful, of many months of captivity in dungeons.

So far we have the makings of a picaresque poet—as handy, because of his peculiar position, with his stabs of satire as he is with his knife—irreverent, racy, slangy, no more respectful of words than of persons so long as they serve his purpose—a highly flavoured 'character,' but, on the long view, a minor poet. What raises him to a higher level is his partly traditional preoccupation with two themes which, fundamentally, are one: the shortness of youth, the horror of old age and death. These haunt him, less as poetic commonplaces than as almost tangible realities, to be handled as concretely as Hamlet did Yorick's skull. Over all is his religious seriousness, colouring much that he wrote and giving to some of his verses a solemn tone, though to others—judged by modern standards—a grotesque one. On the whole, however, it would be mistaken to include religion among the motive-forces of Villon's art. He was soaked in the beliefs of his century and he echoed them as unquestioningly as a modern poet might echo, woven into his thought, the main tenets of Freudian psychology.

Villon has left some three thousand lines of verse which fall into three main divisions: ***Les Lais, Le Testament,*** and a small number of miscellaneous pieces. He used two different but related verse-forms which he handled with such ease and mastery that they seem to belong to him as his personal language. The first is an eight-line stanza on three rhymes. The lines are octosyllabic and are used for what might be called the narrative part of ***Les Lais*** and ***Le Testament***. These are the two opening stanzas of ***Les Lais***:

> L'an quatre cens cinquante six,
> Je, Françoys Villon, escollier,
> Considerant, de sens rassis,
> Le frain aux dens, franc au collier,
> Qu'on doit ses oeuvres conseillier,

> Comme Vegece le raconte,
> Sage Rommain, grant conseillier,
> Ou autrement on se mesconte—

> En ce temps que j'ay dit devant,
> Sur le Noel, morte saison,
> Que les loups se vivent de vent
> Et qu'on se tient en sa maison,
> Pour le frimas, pres du tison,
> Me vint ung vouloir de brisier
> La tres amoureuse prison
> Qui soulait mon cuer debrisier.

Villon's second verse-form is the *ballade,* a more stylized version of the first, with a similar rhyme-pattern. It had been a favourite with medieval French poets ever since it was established in the fourteenth century by Guillaume de Machaut and it was used in English by Machaut's contemporary, Chaucer. Villon writes it in several variations. At its simplest, it consists of three eight-line stanzas and a four-line *envoi,* as in the well-known **"Ballade des dames du temps jadis,"** with its refrain 'Mais où sont les neiges d'antan?'—or in the **"Ballade des menus propos,"** which ends thus:

> Je congnais cheval et mulet,
> Je congnais leur charge et leur somme,
> Je congnais Bietris et Belet,
> Je congnais get qui nombre et somme,
> Je congnais vision et somme,
> Je congnais la faulte des Boesmes,
> Je congnais le povoir de Romme,
> Je congnais tout, fors que moy mesmes.

> Prince, je congnais tout en somme,
> Je congnais coulourez et blesmes,
> Je congnais Mort qui tout consomme,
> Je congnais tout, fors que moy mesmes.

The same rhymes recur throughout and the last line of each stanza and of the *envoi* is always the same, making up the refrain. The *envoi* often begins with the word *Prince,* originally addressed to the presiding judge at the medieval literary festivals known as *puys.* More elaborate kinds of *ballade* could be built by increasing the number of stanzas, or the number of lines within the stanza.

In Villon's hands the *ballade* acquires much greater flexibility than its stereotyped form suggests. He uses it for his most impressive pieces—the peaks which suddenly rise above the chirpy running verse of ***Le Testament***—but also for poems where dignity would be as incongruous as a horse in the House of Commons. With this limited and traditional technical equipment he wrote almost the whole known body of his poetry.

Les Lais, as he says in the opening stanzas, already quoted, was written at Christmas 1456. He had just taken part in the robbery at the Collège de Navarre and was apparently contemplating a similar coup in the provinces, at Angers. Naturally he does not refer to this, but says that an unhappy love-affair is driving him from Paris. Knowing that he may be gone for some time and that life is uncertain, he makes a number of comic bequests to his friends and enemies. This explains the title of the poem, which is the same as the modern French *legs,* or legacy. It is sometimes called, less correctly, **Le Petit Testament**. The poem, a relatively short one of some three hundred lines, is a not entirely truthful balance-sheet of Villon's state of mind at the time and a half-mocking, half-serious farewell to his Parisian acquaintances. To his benefactor Guillaume Villon he leaves his reputation, to the woman who has treated him so harshly he leaves his heart, 'pâle, piteux, mort et transi', to his barber he leaves his hair-clippings and to his cobbler his old shoes. Many of his other jokes are topical and local and do not travel well to the reader of today. A few remain surprisingly fresh.

Villon at this point was clearly pleased with himself and life in general. In spite of his protestation that the torments of love have left him 'as dry and black as a sweep's brush', he is still perky, full of an impudent, street-boy wit. He has enjoyed making his mock legacies and is looking forward with some pleasure to the new adventures which await him outside the capital.

Le Testament is a two-thousand-line poem of a more impressive and bitter nature. Five years older than when he wrote **Les Lais,** Villon has just been released, a broken man, from the prison of the Bishop of Orleans. He may have felt that it was literally time to make his will. In any case, while still following very loosely the plan of **Les Lais,** he seems intent on bequeathing in his new poem all the fruits of his painfully-acquired experience. Moreover, by encrusting in **Le Testament** poems which he had written earlier, he seeks to give them a more permanent setting and so preserve them. Villon's 'last will and testament' thus has a triple sense. It contains a few mock bequests which ostensibly justify its name; it is his latest word on life; and it represents the body of poetry which he wishes to leave to future generations. The show-pieces in it are certain of the *ballades,* but, although these can be taken out and appreciated in isolation, most of them gain when read in their ingeniously woven context.

Thus the famous **"Ballade des dames du temps jadis"** is part of a sequence of reflections on the brevity of youth and the inevitable coming of Death the Leveller. Villon leads up to it by a terrifyingly realistic description of the physical changes which death brings—an obsession of the medieval mind which occurs again in the late Renaissance, then virtually disappears until Baudelaire. He follows it with the deservedly less-known **"Ballade des seigneurs du temps jadis,"** of which little but the refrain is worth remembering ('Mais où est le preux Charlemagne?'), and then, his pen having become stuck in this groove, with a *ballade* of similar import in pastiched 'Old French'. After this, he works back into the realistic vein of which he was a master and rhymes the regrets of la belle Heaulmière for her lost youth. Once beautiful, she is now a hideous old crone, and Villon omits no detail of her decay. And the moral, as she gives it to the younger women who still possess the beauty she has lost, is: Love while you are able, spare no man, take all the profit you can get.

Prenez a destre et a senestre;
N'espargnez homme, je vous prie:
Car vielles n'ont ne cours ne estre,
Ne que monnoye qu'on descrie.

It should be obvious that there was not a particle of romanticism in Villon's nature. But since many English readers will first have met him in translations of the great *ballades,* they must be warned that some of these translations deform the original by glamourizing it. There is no glamour in Villon. Sex, illness, hunger, cold, poverty, vice, are all described by him in the same flat and precise detail. His only escape from the concrete reality is, not into romanticism, but into humour, which sometimes resembles the cynical, snivelling laugh of the down-and-out. Any translation which makes him express fine sentiments is completely foreign to the original, and represents nothing but its form. There is, however, emotion in Villon, achieved in the hardest way of all: not by rhetoric which is a flourish from above, but by properly rooted pathos, rising from the lowest and grimiest feelings of humanity. His sense of the fundamental brotherhood of mankind, cutting right across distinctions of rank and wealth, is Villon's most positive quality. It saves him from total cynicism and every now and then exalts him above his material and enables him to write some tremendous poem such as the **"Epitaphe Villon,"** in which he imagines himself to be dangling from the gallows among other hanged criminals:

Freres humains qui après nous vivez,
N'ayez les cuers contre nous endurcis,
Car, se pitié de nous povres avez,
Dieu en aura plus tost de vous mercis.
Vous nous voiez cy attachez cinq, six:
Quant de la chair, que trop avons nourrie,
Elle est pieça devorée et pourrie,
Et nous, les os, devenous cendre et pouldre.
De nostre mal personne ne s'en rie;
Mais priez Dieu que tous nous vueille absouldre.
Se freres vous clamons, pas n'en devez
Avoir desdaing, quoy que fusmes occis
Par justice. Toutefois, vous sçavez
Que tous les hommes n'ont pas bon sens rassis;
Excusez nous, puis que sommes transsis,
Envers le fils de la vierge Marie,
Que sa grace ne soit pour nous tarie,
Nous preservant de l'infernale fouldre.
Nous sommes mors, ame ne nous harie;
Mais priez Dieu que tous nous vueille absouldre.

La pluye nous a debuez et lavez,
Et le soleil dessechiez et noircis;
Pies, corbeaulx, nous ont les yeux cavez,
Et arrachié la barbe et les sourcis.
Jamais nul temps nous ne sommes assis;
Puis ça, puis la, comme le vent varie,
A son plaisir sans cesser nous charie,
Plus becquetez d'oiseaulx que dez a couldre.
Ne soiez donc de notre confrairie;
Mais priez Dieu que tous nous vueille absouldre.

Prince Jhesus, qui sur tous a maistrie,
Garde qu'Enfer n'ait de nous seigneurie:
A luy n'ayons que faire ne que souldre.
Hommes, icy n'a point de mocquerie;
Mais priez Dieu que tous nous vueille absouldre.

With this poem, we are outside *Le Testament*. It is one of a score of pieces written on various occasions which do not fit into the framework of the longer poem. To show how these pieces came to be composed, it is interesting to recall that the **"Epitaphe,"** written when he expected to be hanged, was followed by a *ballade* of ecstatic gratitude to the judges who reprieved him (ending, typically, with a further request for three days' grace before the sentence of banishment should take effect); and then by a cheerful little *ballade* addressed to his gaoler, who had evidently taken a gloomy view of Villon's chances. 'What do you think now of my appeal?' he asks him. 'Was I wise or mad to try to save my skin?' And with that perky question François Villon disappears from the scene.

Because of his archaic though direct language and his remote period, Villon might appear to be isolated from [other French poets]. His work, as it reads today, has a strongly individualized flavour and nothing quite like it could be expected to occur again. He himself and his immediate material world were the centre of his poetry. His best writing seems to spring straight from experience, for his book-learning was undisgested and always remained a surface feature. The main trend of the fifteenth century was still that of courtly poetry, renewed by Alain Chartier (who died at about the time when Villon was born) and continued by Charles d'Orléans and by the 'rhetorical' poets who flourished at the court of Burgundy. When these write of their personal experience, they do so in a discreet and generalized way, subordinating the individual note to an art ruled by elaborate and sometimes exquisite conventions. Moreover, up to Charles d'Orléans, they are often writing for music, in the old troubadour tradition. Villon's verse, on the contrary, was not intended to be sung. Artistic considerations, in the narrower sense, do not influence him. He writes for the broad or knowing laugh, for the gasp of surprise or emotion, rather than for the more subtle reactions of the educated connoisseur. This leads him to put down everything, however trivial, however unflattering to himself, and to put it down raw. The only concealment which he attempted was of facts which might involve him with the law—a practical rather than an aesthetic consideration.

It has already been observed that Villon was no Romantic. If he is sometimes represented as one in popular works, the ultimate blame lies with Sir Walter Scott who *was* a Romantic and whose reconstructions of the Middle Ages have much to answer for. The real Romantic poet, as he appeared in the nineteenth century, is always an arranged figure even in his most intimate self-revelations. He cannot help being conscious of the contrast between himself and his environment. Villon seems to have lacked this self-consciousness. He accepts the environment as inevitable and, within it, remains unstudiedly himself. When he whines, it is not in revolt or in any exhibitionist spirit. It is a spon-

taneous abject whine forced out of him by misery. He is thus an example of that very rare writer, the subjective realist. His lyricism springs straight from his sensations. He seems unaware of more sophisticated conventions. Ultimately the difference between a poet of the fifteenth century and one of the nineteenth century lies in a changed attitude of society towards the writer. The good writer of any period always does what is expected of him. The great writer, like Villon manages to exceed expectations.

But if Villon has no equivalent in French literature, it is possible to find him certain affinities, particularly in Baudelaire and Verlaine. He is an early example—to use a much abused word—of the Bohemian poet. He is also—in France the two things have usually gone together—the first good Parisian poet, the first man to find all his material in the streets, the taverns, the personalities and transient happenings of that city. Others after him were inspired by the Paris of their time, but none absorbed its life more thoroughly than he did.

The intense local flavour of much of his work makes it at once more lively and less accessible to the modern reader. It is here, rather than in any fundamental difference between the medieval and the modern mentality, that the chief obstacle to appreciation may lie. But anyone who has the time and opportunity to study Villon's language and environment will be well rewarded. To read *Le Testament* in full is a lasting experience, and one which it is a pity to abandon to the specialist. Meanwhile the great *ballades,* which are admittedly the cream, can be enjoyed with the help of a few footnotes.

Ann Tukey Harrison (essay date 1980)

SOURCE: "The Theme of Authority in the Works of François Villon," in *The Centennial Review,* Vol. XXIV, No. I, Winter, 1980, pp. 65–78.

[*Below, Tukey Harrison comments on the respect for authority displayed in Villon's poetry.*]

Because of his life as an activist, both student and postgraduate, Francois Villon has often appeared to be engaged in a lifelong rebellion against all authority figures. He was supremely poor, often in difficulty with the law, and he wrote irreverently about many of the men of high station of his time and place; it is easy to conclude that he condemned authority out of hand. Yet, a close reading of his poems reveals a mixed set of attitudes expressed through the varied assortment of specific references to influential persons and powerful institutions interwoven with opinions of the author. Even the most recent Villonistes arrive at contrasting if not contradictory conclusions. Evelyn Vitz writes of "Villon's questioning of the traditional hierarchy and disbelief in its moral justification" [*The Crossroad of Intention: A Study of Symbolic Expression in the Poetry of François Villon,* 1974], while Barbara Nelson Sargent states that "Nulle part il ne met en question l'ordre social ou politique" [*Le Testament et Poésies diverses*, 1967, edited by

Sargent]. Vitz observes that "order is nowhere apparent in the world which Villon presents to us"; Sargent reaches a different point of view:

> Il va de soi qu'il y a un roi en France, qu'il y a des princes et des ducs, des officiers et des magistrats, des sergents et des géoliers, tout comme il va de soi qu'il y a des riches et des pauvres.

Clearly, the subject of Villon and authority is not a settled one.

That Villon was not anti-authoritarian is generally accepted, and the most common defense of this point is his refusal to condemn classes or power groups *ab initio* and *de natura*. Sargent can write

> Ses ironies, ses attaques, se dirigent non contre les institutions mais contre des individus indignes. (p. 6)

Similarly, David Kuhn notes that Villon is led

> . . . a distinguisher soigneusement entre l'autorité et les autorités—par exemple, entre l'évêque injuste et l'Eglise durable que ce dernier trahit, en opprimant celui qui, pour sa part, y reste fidele. [*La Poétique de François Villon*, 1967]

Persons are singled out for mockery or approval by turns; and society's systems are not automatically suspect any more than the intimacy of daily acquaintance is a guarantee of praise. Villon's resentments do not center on those who are above him because of their social class or the power they exercise in the abstract, but rather he always views them in connection with abuse of just treatment which he has experienced in an immediate and personal way.

Six kinds of authorities respected can be verified in the *Lais, Testament*, and miscellaneous writings: civil, religious, seigneurial, economic, educational, peer-family. Sometimes the authority sphere of a person to whom Villon refers is of more than one type: both civil and religious, as in the case of Thibaud d'Auxigny, Bishop of Orleans, who caused the poet to be imprisoned in the episcopal dungeons at Meung; or civil and seigneurial, as Robert d'Estouteville, a member of the nobility and Provost of Paris. Though Villon recognizes these classes, he reacts to each group and to individuals within each classification in varied and often contradictory ways. A brief review will illustrate.

1. Civil

A possible synonym of civil might be judiciary or municipal; and, the constant reference to magistrates, attorneys, sergeants of the local guard, jailers is surely a unifying procedure within both long poems. Daniel Poirion has commented that

> les personnages de sa comédie humaine ont tous eu quelque rapport—bon ou mauvais—avec le monde judiciaire . . . [preface to *François Villon, Oeuvres Poétiques,* 1965]

This serves as a kind of vortex around and through which the friends of the poet and the poet himself circulate.

Because Villon's tone is often readily discernible when he writes of this class and because of the painstaking reconstructions of his personal life, it is possible to identify the benevolent and malevolent figures of judicial authority. The bequest to Orfevre de Bois, the torturer, though ironic, reveals Villon's feelings unmistakably:

> *Item* I give the Woodworker
> A hundred spikes tails and heads
> Of ginger from the Saracens
> Not for fitting together boxes
> But for joining cunts and cocks
> And attaching hams and sausages
> So that milk rises to the tits
> And blood goes down to the balls.
> (CXI: 1118–1125)
> [*The Poems of François Villon*, translated by Galway Kinnell, 1977]

Villon loves the merciful and hates the capriciously cruel; he blesses those who facilitated defense or freedom while cursing any who personally, in the name of civil authority, tortured or imprisoned. The man who exercises power over the person in an abusive or noxious manner becomes the personal enemy of his victim. However, in all cases, the authority itself is left intact, accepted wholly, as its representatives are reviewed and judged individually.

2. Religious

Unlike civil authorities who are not treated collectively, clergy are named both individually and collectively. Villon cites the Church corporate once, early in *Le Testament,* recalling

> "But the Church asks and expects us
> To pray for our enemies"
> (IV: 29–30)

His tone is ironic, but context shows his true target to be Thibault d'Auxigny, and despite a mocking manner, the Church collective is not attacked at all.

Clerics and priests are friend or foe, depending on their relationship and interactions with Villon; their association with the Church itself is neutral, one trait among many:

> *Item* I give to Friar Baude
> Who lives in the Carmelites' hostel
> And looks virile and vigorous
> A helmet and two pikes
> So that De Tusca and his armed men
> Won't mess with his love nest
> He's so old, if he doesn't lay down his weapon
> He must be the Devil of Vauvert.
> (CXX: 1190–1197)

Item I leave to Chappelain
My chapel of simple tonsure
Which involves saying a dry Mass
In which you do hardly any reading
I'd have given him my curacy too
But the care of souls isn't his line,
He has no interest, he says, in confessions
Except of chambermaids and ladies.

(CLXXII: 1836–1843)

An abuser of power, the Bishop of Orleans, is denounced and threatened with reciprocal maltreatment, nothing more, nothing less. The Bishop should be punished by his logical and ultimate superior, and neither the bishopric nor the ecclesiastical chain of command is challenged. "God be to him as he's been to me." (II: 16)

The orders are condemned repeatedly as units: the Mendiants, the Filles-Dieu, and the Beguines are ridiculed in *Le Lais* and in *Le Testament,* where they are joined by the Turlupins-Turlupines. [In his edition of *The Complete Works of François Villon*, 1960] Anthony Boucher suggests that Villon's upbringing had made him a sworn enemy of the Mendicant Friars who were at loggerheads with the regular clergy allied with the University of Paris. Villon frequently expresses his criticism through references to the orders in the context of unsavory, immoral persons, a guilt by association, as in the **"Ballade de mercy"** (1968–1995) where the Chartreux, Celestins, Mendiants, and Devotes are men-tioned immediately before streetwalkers, torturers, montebanks. Or, in a more indirect passage, the prelude to the **"Ballade des femmes de Paris"** in stanza CXLIV (1507–1514):

Item since she knows her Bible
I leave it to Mademoiselle de Bruyeres
Her and her postgraduate girls
To go out and preach from the Gospels
And reform the girls on the streets
Who've got such stinging tongues
And not in the cemeteries either
Pick some place like the Thread Market.

Doctrine, the notion of faith, religious practices, current heresies, and the vast body of Christian literature also appear integrated into Villon's consciousness. He cites Biblical exempla and uses religious formulae or phrases easily: in the first fourteen stanzas of the *Testament* he refers to the Picard sect (37), the stories of Jacob (57), Solomon (58), Methuselah (64), the pilgrims of Emmaeus (99), the Psalter (45), the *Deus laudem* (48), the Virgin Mary (55), Jesus (23, 49) and God (16, 27, 32, 57, 76, 99, 106, 110). The oft-quoted prayer (**"Ballade pour prier Nostre Dame"** 873–909) he writes for his mother is a likely depiction of her reverence, and an earlier stanza summarizes his own personal *credo*:

I am a sinner I know it well
And yet God doesn't want me to die
But to change my ways and live right
And so with all others bitten by sin
Though in my sin I may be dead

Yet God and his mercy live
If my conscience gnaws
He is his grace forgives me.

(XIV: 105–112)

Villon reacts to the many forms of medieval religious authority in mixed fashion; he seems to accept the Church of which he was a formal part, he rejects the Mendicant clergy, and views clerics of his personal acquaintances as individuals. The doctrine he received or learned appears to be wholly accepted and unquestioned.

3. Seigneurial

The nobility are visible throughout Villon's work; although Parisian officials are often scorned, the aristocracy do not fare so ill. If a nobleman is criticized, it is generally with reference to his role in another sphere of authority (civil, for example, or religious). The lords mentioned may have been instruments of clemency: King Louis and the Duke of Orleans were each responsible for Villon's release from prison. They are presented in a tone of gentleness and respect matched by conventionally polite language of their circle, as the **"Requeste à Monseigneur de Bourbon"** and the **"Epitre à Marie d'Orléans"** illustrate. Villon can also assume the robust enthusiam of the common man, using everyday turns of phrase to express loyalty and well-wishing:

And Louis the good king of France

To whom God grant Jacob's luck
And Solomon's honor and glory
As for prowess he has plenty
And authority too, by my soul
And so that his memory may last
In this fleeting world
Such as it has of length and breadth
Let him live as long as Methuselah

And see twelve fine children all sons
Born of his precious royal blood
Conceived in the marriage bed
Doughty as the great Charles
And good as Saint Martial
May it turn out so for the ex-dauphin
I wish him no further trouble
And then paradise at the last.

(VII–IX: 56–72)

The thoughts are honestly expressed with no ironic intent, and the reference to Charlemagne hints of a deep nationalistic feeling in Villon, an awareness of France as a tradition and a people. The leader of the nation and its aristocrats are neither questioned nor resented in their status.

4. Economic

Rich men of national renown, such as Jacques Coeur, or of neighborhood repute, government officials with financially oriented functions, money lenders and changers are prominent members of the *Testament* cast, and the many tradesmen, merchants and petty Parisian entrepreneurs of the poet's immediate circle are remembered with good humor or ill will, depending on their particular transactions with Villon. This nobility of the purse does not receive unqualified admiration, but rather the opposite is more likely to be true. Villon seems to express deeper scorn for the more greatly moneyed, and he is inclined to show more cheery confidence in those who are marginally successful in business. The authority of accumulated wealth, like the authority of the torturer, resides in success gained at the expense of others. The continuing official condemnation of usury, Villon's participation in thievery, and his experience of economic inequity on a level and of a type reserved to the very poor may have provided him with awareness of the need for money coupled with suspicious or jealous hatred of the wealthy. Economic authority earns grudging respect at best, and this provides an interesting contrast with his attitude toward the nobility, perhaps due to Villon's lack of close contact with the latter.

5. Educational

Villon refers to education twice in the long **Testament**: first when lamenting his misspent youth, and second when scoffing at the three pseudo-orphans (Colin Laurens, Girart Gossouyn and Jean Marceau, in actuality wealthy usurers, speculators, and salt-traders). The second reference is longer, a four-stanza section dealing with the proposed education of the three "orphans." Villon, in designing a curriculum, chooses subjects according to the punning potential of educational and commercial vocabulary. His primary concern is to amuse and attack the three financiers, not to describe utopian education. One can conclude that though he perhaps regrets that he personally did not profit from opportunities within the educational system, he nowhere expresses any malice toward the practices of his time. Any failure he may have experienced therein is his own, not systemic.

6. Peer-Family

The word authority must be stretched to the utmost to accommodate the peer group and family; among the many meanings for "authority" found in the *American Heritage Dictionary,* three apply to this case: "an accepted source of advice," "power to influence or persuade," "a claim to be accepted or believed."

The poet mentions his family without hesitation, and he peoples his verse with peers or friends whose claims of affection he meets with broad humor and whom he teases with the pointed sarcasm of intimacy. His mother and the cleric from whom he took a name are addressed with kindness surpassing convention, and they receive a priority in the sequence of people to be remembered as well as honor by association: Villon's adopted father-figure with Job, his mother with the Virgin Mary. In tone, in situation within the text, and in the content of his lines, Villon shows deference and affection toward his parental kin.

Not only the ambiance of conviviality and friendship, but also the poems in slang, Villon's mastery of the language

of his peers the Coquillards, are evidence that the social authority of friendship like that of kinship was part of Villon's world. He has experienced adult comradeship and accepted responsibility for his companions; he is one of the most articulate advocates of peer loyalty.

From his family and friends Villon learned the rich assortment of proverbs and folk wisdom which he can string into the **"Ballade des proverbes"** or upon which he can base the **"Ballade des contre vérités"** or the **"Ballade du concours de Blois."** He knows the popular mind of his time and can alternately twit and quote it.

Although Villon does not write directly about the hierarchy of medieval social order or the existence of human institutions of authority, it is possible to observe his tacit assumption of what Vitz calls a *de facto* order. He implies (in the prayer ballade for his mother and elsewhere) recognition of God, Mary, and Jesus above all earthly law or action, and he acknowledges death as the great human leveler. In his world, Villon respects King and nobility; his antipathy towards torturers, usurers, the Mendicant orders, the bishop who imprisoned him is balanced by his sympathy for certain clerics and minor officials, prostitutes, his parent figures, and named friends. The institutions of state, church, school, economy are acceptable, but their agents are human and by nature capable of error.

What sets Villon apart from so many other artists of his and later periods is his sense of inner authority. He fairly revels in the license accorded Everypoet, and the proximity of death gives his words, even in his own eyes, value and significance beyond that attributed to idle opinions. He always writes with strong conviction, drawing on common sense or the lessons of experience, displaying at every turn a deep feeling for his own knowledge and valuing his own insights. Even in moments of confessed personal weakness and lament over what might have been, Villon accepts the burden of his own decisions; his ultimate tests are before his personal and individual court of last resort—and the authority he respects most conscientiously is his own. By making this confidence in his own judgment so vividly clear, he establishes his own forceful identity which attracts and holds the reader's respect as well as his interest.

Villon writes as one who never exercised any of the six types of authority reviewed above. He does not regret this or even note it, but his view is always that of the mass man who has felt the effects of the authorities without ever assuming the burden or reward of decision-making. As Sargent has also noted, he lacks totally the revolutionary's desire to rule the world in his turn, and he is neither anarchist nor reformer.

Furthermore, Villon has experienced prison and torture, the ultimate exercise of authority by one human being over another. (See Kuhn's more than thirty references or discussions of the impact of what he calls "l'expérience de Mehun.") Villon does not identify ever with the jailer, governor or judge: he naturally considers himself to be the jailed, exiled or convicted. Unlike Marot or Charles d'Orléans, for whom inner authority and civil authority have common cause, Villon is more likely to place himself among the wrongdoers whose major claim to fair treatment is their human nature or brotherhood, the ultimate trait of man before God in the presence of death.

Early in the *Testament* Villon recounts an exemplum about Diomedes the pirate brought before Alexander to be condemned to death. The pirate has the shabby, vermin-infested appearance of the thief, and the emperor asks why he is a thief. Villon gives to the pirate words of Villon's own defense for his own crimes:

> "Why do you call me a robber?
> Because I'm seen marauding about
> In a tiny skiff?
> If I could arm myself like you
> Like you I'd be an emperor."

> "But what can one expect? Fortune
> Whom I'm helpless against
> Who deals me such bad luck
> Sets the course of life I've taken
> Take this as some excuse
> And know that in great poverty
> It's said often enough
> Not many scruples remain."

(XVIII–XIX: 140–152)

The emperor decides to change Diomedes' fortune from bad to good, and it is done. The former thief never lied again but became a man of truth. The lesson is that if Villon were given a second chance and he "went wrong" again, he himself would be his harshest judge. But

> Necessity makes people err
> And hunger drives wolf from woods.

(XXI: 167–8)

The thief attributes his behavior (*tout ce gouvernement*) to his fortune, and states that given the accoutrements of the emperor (*armer*), he would act like the emperor, that is, more rationally and in a more civilized manner. The true criminals of the world are those in comfortable circumstances who have no necessity to do wrong and who still maltreat their fellow men. Society as it is ordered, including the caprice of fortune which establishes men in their stations, is acceptable; the world's heroes are the merciful emperor and those whose lives are honest in spite of horrendous surroundings. If persons of power were Alexanders, if the poverty, hunger, and necessity were removed by executive order changing bad fortune to good. Every poet would become the ideal *vray homme*. The resolution of society's ills falls not to Francois Villon but to authority (as it was then constituted) properly exercised.

The most important form of authority for Villon the poet must be literary, and his reactions to the authorities and traditions of his time are of ultimate interest to his readers. Furthermore, unlike the forms of authority mentioned above, in writing, Villon becomes a practitioner, an executive, an exerciser of authority, not merely an observer or

recipient. From the texts, his rhetorical erudition and cultural literacy are obvious. Not only was he schooled, but he delighted in following the literary conventions and traditions of his epoch. To the reader examining *Le Testament* in search of authority respected, the literary heritage Villon uses with pride as well as ease is impressive. Biblical lore, classical sources, scientific concepts, contemporary literature, popular song and ballad—*Le Testament* reads like a catalogue of the medieval scriptorium, just as the rhetorical variety and virtuosity exhibited in his slender volume of works is a worthy illustration of a fifteenth-century *Ars Rhetorica*.

Two sections are especially noteworthy within the *Testament*: the **"Ballade pour Robert d'Estouteville"** (1378–1405) and **"Le Contrediz de Franc Gontier"** (1473–1506), for they are reflections of the poet's acceptance and use of a major authority and his participation in literary activities of his time. The first is a love ballade, a bequest to Robert, with his wife's name (Ambroise de Lore) in acrostic. The theme, an extolling of married sexual love, and the refrain ("Ending in this, for this we are together.") are a-courtly, but fall directly within the influence of the *Roman de la Rose* and its neo-Platonic parentage. Villon's tactful references to allegorical figures ("Love inscribes it in her book" 1. 1384, "Reason doesn't wish me to break the habit . . ." 1. 1390; ". . . Fortune who's often roused to anger" 1. 1395) placed one in each stanza, his use of bird imagery ("the sparrow hawk" and "the thrush" in the first stanza), his final reliance on the imagery of sowing seed in fertile fields are three well chosen echoes of the *Rose*'s rhetoric, setting, and philosophical message. The relationship of the ballade's tone and language, given its explicitly sexual theme, to that of other parts of the *Testament* shows this poet's versatility and elegance. Villon gingerly skirts the subject of Church-enjoined procreation in terms that contrast strikingly with the naked physiological vulgarity of other stanzas. Only one line escapes the restrained and allusive phrasing: "Dieu m'ordonne que le vostre champ fouysse et fume." This sentence is placed in the third stanza, immediately pre-refrain. Given the normal change in tone of the *Envoi*, the pre-refrain position is the perfect setting for the only wry ribaldry, where its piquancy will be most effective. It is an adroit and swift thrust which is restrained and softened at once by the descending mood of the refrain and *Envoi*. Villon here establishes himself as master not only of his inherited tradition but also of rhetorical diversity and discipline.

"Le Contrediz de Franc Gontier" is placed less than one hundred lines and one bequest later, and it is a broad mockery of the content of a work by Philippe de Vitry. Villon here makes his own literary quarrel and reveals that he is an active participant in the world of *belles lettres* not an isolate, polemicist, or criminal turned versifier. Better than the so-called Concours de Blois verse, this ballade and its location in the *Testament* attest to Villon's professional affiliation and commitment: he considers himself to be a poet and man of letters, and part of a literary tradition whose forms, themes, and debates he acknowledges and engages in willingly.

From the preceding analysis, several points emerge. Villon is not anti-authoritarian, and there is ample evidence of authority respected in his writings. This implies conversely that the world he describes is neither completely chaotic nor disordered. His lack of explicit commentary on social hierarchy *per se,* his continuous and persistent evaluation of authority figures as individuals, and his use of the Alexander exemplum confirm an attitude toward authority that is receptive in principle and critical in practice. HIs sense of inner authority is strong, and though he never exercised power over others in a political or social sense, certainly his writing is an exercise in literary authority. Here is his true domain, of which he has been undisputed master for more than half a millenium. An examination of the theme of authority in his writings only reaffirms the primacy of literature and literary creation in the world of Villon.

Barbara N. Sargent-Baur (essay date 1992)

SOURCE: "Communication and Implied Audience(s) in Villon's *Testament,*" in *Neophilologus,* Vol. LXXVI, No. 1, January, 1992, pp. 35–40.

[*In the following essay, Sargent-Baur finds Villon addressing three separate audiences in the* Testament *and examines the various personas that Villon presents to this "plural audience."*]

By now, most careful readers are aware that behind every speech act as preserved in writing there is a speaking voice, an implied or explicit "I" from whom the text stems. This applies, as well, to compositions conceived as written from the outset. In the case of the *Testament* of François Villon the "I" of the narrator is very prominent indeed, to the point where the whole work takes on the character of a dramatic monologue with interspersed dialogue and debate. The personality and rôle of this narrator, his relations with the implied author and the historical author, have been much discussed, over a long period of time, and such investigations have in many cases been highly illuminating to modern readers of Villon's works.

My undertaking here is somewhat different. If the "I" of the narrative persona is much to the fore (as is the case in this work), so necessarily is an implied or expressed "you," singular or plural. Villon in fact, through divers means, frequently and quite explicitly conjures up a multifarious audience, one composed of types as well as individuals. I propose to explore some of the modalities through which the *Testament* narrator defines and evokes the *destinataires*—the sets of listening ears and reading eyes—who sooner or later are to take cognizance of this particular communication. Who is being addressed, and what does this element contribute to the whole economy of the *Testament*? Just as the narrator is much in evidence, so is his audience, which is sometimes named, sometimes apostrophized directly, sometimes drawn into the narration through conversational exchanges, questions, objections, challenges. This audience, of which the narrator is so conscious and of which in turn he makes us so conscious, is a fairly complex entity. The speaking voice addresses now one part of it, now another; or perhaps it would be more accurate to say that throughout the long poem there is communication on more than one level going on. There are inscribed hearers and readers within the *Testament*; there are implied hearers or readers observing from the outside as it were and appreciating the poet's fiction; there is a third, far more nebulous audience that one might call the poet's *alter ego,* or the Ideal Reader, or the student of the human condition, or simply mankind. To the various audiences the narrator presents different faces. What follows is an attempt to look at some of these faces, and some components of the plural audience that call them up, and see how they act and react together.

H. de Vere Stacpoole on Villon's literary standing:

Villon is the greatest and truest of French poets, and if you doubt my word look at his star which is only now in true ascension after nearly half a thousand years. He is the only French poet who is entirely real; all the rest are tinged with artifice, and his reality is never more vividly apparent than when it is conveyed in the most artificial and difficult form of verse.

The ballade in the hands of this supreme master is capable of producing the most astonishing results. It is now the perfect necklace that fits the throat of Thaïs, and, now the noose that swings from the gibbet. He only requires twenty-eight lines to say about women what Zola has prosily said in five volumes, and only twenty-eight lines to write the epitaph of all the women who have ever lived. Villon is the most modern of the moderns; his verse, with the gibbets removed, might have been written in the Paris of to-day, and in any civilization to follow ours he will hold the same high place; for it is his essential that the forms of his genius are the concretions of eternal principles, not the flowery expansions of ephemeral moods.

H. de Vere Stacpoole, "Fragments of Villon," in
Forum, *Vol. L, July, 1913.*

First, the narrator. He does not present himself as a poet; he applies to himself only the labels *escolier* and *follastre*. At the outset of the *Testament* is adumbrated the primary and recurrent persona of the narrator: he is self-identified as a man in fragile health, mindful of the approach of death and making appropriate preparation—a sort of fifteenth-century French Everyman, thinking the kinds of thoughts and performing the same legal acts that were being accomplished daily throughout France and elsewhere in his time. He is making his will. The articles thereof are the same as in real wills: bequests to individuals and institutions, prayers and requests for prayers, funeral arrangements, directions for the disposition of his body, and all the normal provisions for the proper execution of the will. Beyond the legal and theological considerations, this particular dying man (again in accordance with late-medieval practice) relates selected episodes of his life story and adds thereto his own understanding of what has happened to him, drawing on his own experience to shape lessons for others. There is in fact a fair amount of reflection and of advice-giving in this work of poetic fiction, just as there frequently is in genuine documents of the time. From start to finish, then, the *Testament* is a literary will; the first lines of the poem form the preamble to it; and the final ballade, announcing with its change of narrative voice the death of the testator, confirms the general leave-taking of the penultimate ballade and serves as a *post scriptum* to the whole. Will and poem are co-terminous; with the exception of the **"Ballade de conclusion"** with its post-mortem reverberations there is no poem outside the will. The corollary of this is that the narrative persona by and large is a testator.

Such being the case, we realize that by the nature of this document there is an inscribed audience. It is the same in type as that of every genuine will: the executors. They are the ones who are charged with carrying out the instructions, including the individual bequests; hence it is they who will be obliged to read the will in its entirety. In this they differ from the individual legatees, each of whom will be informed in due course of his or her own bequest and will not have to read the others—or even his or her own, for that matter. None of the bequests can go into effect until after the testator's death, a circumstance that, within the established givens of the poem, effectively blocks communication between the poet and all his readers.

It might be objected (to borrow one of Villon's own favorite procedures) that this reading exaggerates the role of the executors, who are not even mentioned until nine-tenths of the way through the poem. To this, Villon-like, one might reply that the word *testament* occurs as early as line 78:

> J'ay ce testament tres estable
> Fait, de derreniere voulenté,
> Seul pour tout et inrevocable.

Reading retroactively, we realize that the very first lines of this work create the expectation of a literary will (and the original audience must have been alert to this also):

> En l'an de mon trentïesme aage,
> Que toutes mes hontes j'euz beues,
> Ne du tout fol ne du tout saige . . .

Wills require executors as intermediaries between testator and beneficiaries, so that communication from the dead to the living—both legatees and the reading public—can take place. There are some pretty severe logical difficulties here; but they seem to have troubled the poet not at all. On the contrary, he is very much conscious of the advantages of such a fiction for candid and uninhibited expression. He can say—or rather, have his narrator say—anything and everything he has in his heart, a fact to which he draws attention by claiming a dying man's privilege:

> Qui meurt a ses loix de tout dire.
>
>   (728)

We might pause to notice that the situation evoked in the poem is not the sort of death-bed scene that involves friends and relations gathered round attending to the sufferer's last wishes and words; nor is it one of a public address from a scaffold (that will come in the **"Ballade des pendus"**). The narrator does not foresee an immediate audience, with one exception (to which I shall return). This is what one may call delayed communication; there will be an interval of indeterminate duration between the articulation of thought and its reception by the intended audience. The narrator can speak frankly because he is dying, and the more frankly that he knows he will not have to face the consequences of his speech. From this perspective . . . the *Testament* finds its place in a large category of semi-secret if not downright furtive communication; it is akin to the hidden diary, the mémoir held for posthumous publication, the anonymous broadside or lampoon, the graffito. Only if the named executors, or their alternates, carry out the charge laid upon them (and of which they are at present unaware) will the numerous legatees learn of their individual bequests and the spirit in which these are made. It is only through the executors' action, for instance, that the poet's mother will have a new prayer with which to address the Virgin, that La Grosse Margot (if she exists) will receive the poetic depiction of her life with the narrator, that Andry Courault will know Villon's send-up of modish pastoral poetry, that Robert d'Estouteville will be able to address his agricultural compliments to his lady wife.

Yet the relationship testator-executors-world at large appears in a new light when the executors are at last specified by name. The narrator's first three choices are rich officials, clearly far too grand to trouble themselves with Villon either living or dead. As alternates in case of refusal he proposes three other men, of lower status and of doubtful reputation. At this point the narrator, too, shows himself in a different guise: we realize that the executor clause is a joke, the channeling of the poetic testament to the eventual real readers through such individuals is also a joke, and the narrator stands revealed as having been a joker all along—at least in his character as testator. (But to grasp the joke is to belong to an *implied* audience; of this more anon.)

Leaving aside the executors, there are two more inscribed readers who will have early knowledge of the *Testament* in its entirety. The first is Jehan de Calais, the Paris notary charged with verifying the wills of (significantly) *lay* persons residing in Paris; on him the testator lavishes three whole octaves of instructions (ll. 1844–67) regarding the correction and clarification of this legal instrument. The second is dealt with more briskly; it is the young priest Thomas Tricot (1. 1955), pointedly substituted for the normal ecclesiastical judge whose duty it was to resolve testamentary disputes. Thomas is empowered to edit the will; the implication is that the *Testament* as we have it has passed through his hands and met with his approval. Although both Jehan de Calais and Thomas Tricot must perforce have access to the document as a whole, neither contributes much to the internal economy of the *Testament*. Nor does the narrator engage in any sort of direct address to them, or imply any personal relationship.

The case is very different with the testator's clerk, Fremin. This personage is by implication present through the entire process of composition. His is the unique listening ear that receives the dying man's instructions, his the writing hand that records them. By introducing Fremin, the poet answers our possibly not-yet-shaped question concerning the modality by which a dying man's words, wishes, and meditations can come to us. By introducing him late—over a quarter of the way through the whole work—Villon pretty brusquely demolishes the impression that I presume the reader has unconsciously formed, that of a poet directly and timelessly addressing all of humanity capable of understanding his language. We realize that communication is going on within the poem, and simultaneously with its composition. Fremin is first mentioned after the long dramatic monologue of the Belle Hëaulmiere, when the narrator informs us that he has had her remarks recorded by a scribe. This incoherence may well leave us puzzled, particularly since the scribe promptly disappears from the narrative for another 200 lines; but at least we are to some degree prepared for him when the narrator at length returns to the testamentary mode he had briefly adopted in the first stanza. The speaker resumes his persona of a testator, one who is ill and now indeed bedridden, who must dictate his last wishes to a scribe:

> Somme, plus ne diray q'un mot,
> Car commencer vueil a tester.
> Devant mon clerc Fremin qui m'ot,
> S'il ne dort, je vueil protester
> Que n'entens homme detester
> En ceste presente ordonnance . . .
>
> (777–82)

Then he addresses Fremin directly:

> Fremin, siez toy pres de mon lit,
> Que l'en ne me viengne espïer.
> Pren ancre tost, plume, pappier,
> Ce que nomme escriptz vistement,
> Puis fay le partout coppïer,
> Et vecy le commancement.
>
> (787–92)

We are being led to think that what follows (that is, all the rest of the *Testament*) is an oral communication, dictated by a testator, recorded by a clerk, and thus preserved until the testator's decease. This is perhaps acceptable, at least provisionally; yet problems remain. Three in particular are troublesome: Why are the addresses to the clerk—the "asides" so to speak (e.g. *Escryptz,* 1. 1927)—preserved in the document? Who has been recording the document up to the point where Fremin is mentioned? / And who is/ who are the character(s) evoked by the *je/nous,* the witnesses to Villon's demise, whose voices are heard in the **"Ballade de conclusion"**? This poem, we remember, marks the end of the *Testament:*

> Icy se clost le testament
> Et finist du povre Villon.
>
> (1996–97)

This ballade announces the death of the fictious testator, but only serves notice of his coming burial. The will, in consequence, is now in effect, ready to be carried out by the executors. The unidentified voices in the last stanzas serve to bridge the gap we have noted in the text, between the formulation of a man's wishes and the communication of those wishes (and reflections, and life story) to his contemporaries: his executors, and through them his beneficiaries, and beyond them whatever persons may see his will or hear of it. Only now (still following the fiction of the *Testament*) does the narrator's voice reach beyond the inscribed audience to the implied one, and address the general public, or at least that part of it that is within earshot, or can catch sight of the dictated text. We know perfectly well that all of this is a complicated game; the *Testament* is no legal instrument but a semi-autobiographical poetic composition. Those of Villon's contemporaries who were aware of his literary activities certainly knew this also. It was they, and more specifically his close friends, whom we can infer to be the real audience that the poet had in mind (at least intermittently) while writing the *Testament* from beginning to end. The references, the jokes, the plays on words, the name-dropping, the half-told tales, even the testamentary fiction—all these are brought up for their recognition and amusement. The wealth of topical allusions strongly suggests that Villon had an immediate audience in mind, one well known to him. It is this restricted circle of readers or listeners that is addressed, directly or indirectly. They furnish the element of difference, of contrast and even of debate and conflict, that is so prevalent a feature of the *Testament* from one end to the other.

Was Villon looking over their heads to generations unborn? Did he in any way suggest that he was addressing mankind in general? I am persuaded that this is so, at least in many passages. When he meditates on the human condition, assimilating the records of classical antiquity and the Bible to his own recent and present experiences, and taking up anew some of the age-old themes of literature, he moves away from 1461 into timelessness, and from a small, immediate audience to a much larger one. A good deal of the time he appears to be oblivious to all audience. When he asks his reiterated question *ou sont?*, when he commends to God the souls of the departed, when he wonders aloud whether he too will at least really die like everyone else, the presence or indeed existence of any listeners is temporarily blotted out. Villon speaks to himself then, dialoguing with his divided psyche. It is in those moments, when both the inscribed and the implied readers or hearers are forgotten, that, paradoxically, his speech can reach and move the widest possible public, these *freres humains* far more numerous and varied than his drinking companions or the imagined spectators at the gibbet of Monfaucon. He communicates with all of us, in fact.

FURTHER READING

Bibliography

Peckham, Robert D. *François Villon: A Bibliography.* New York: Garland, 1990.

Comprehensive bibliography of some 2000 foreign- and English-language sources, arranged chronologically by year, with an author and subject index.

Biography

Longon, Auguste. *Etude biographique sur François Villon d'après les documents inédits conservés aux Archives Nationales.* Paris: Henri Menu, 1877.
Earliest comprehensive biography of Villon. This french-language study is a seminal work of Villon scholarship.

Criticism

Aldington, Richard. "François Villon." In *French Studies and Reviews,* pp. 64–82. New York: The Dial Press, 1926.
Offers justification for Villon's repute as a genius.

Anacker, Robert. *François Villon.* New York: Twayne Publishers, 1968, 122 p.
Introductory monograph on Villon's life and works.

Besant, Walter. "François Villon." In *Studies in Early French Poetry,* pp. 114–43. London: Macmillan and Co., 1868.
Reviews Villon's life and the themes and style of his poetry.

———. "François Villon." *Temple Bar* L (May 1877): 91–103.
Updates the critic's earlier work on Villon (see above), taking newly discovered biographical information into account.

Chaney, Edward F. "A Glimpse of Villon's Paris." *Bulletin of the John Rylands Library, Manchester* 28, No. 2 (December 1944): 340–57.
Colorful description of Paris during Villon's lifetime.

Cholakian, Rouben C. "The (Un)naming Process in Villon's *Grand Testament.*" *French Review* 66, No. 2 (December 1992): 216–28.
Claims that Villon's *Testament* is an attempt to take control of his world by dispossessing his "heirs."

Collin, Rodney. "François Villon: A Modernist of the Middle Ages." *The Poetry Review* XXV, No. 3 (May–June 1934): 195–99.
Explores the ways in which Villon's poetic style differed from typical Medieval poetry.

Cox, E. Marion. "The Ballads of François Villon." *The Library* (London) VIII (1917): 53–74.
Argues that the *ballades* represent Villon's best work.

Du Bruck, Edelgard. "Villon Studies: 1961–1967." *Studies in Medieval Culture* IV, No. 3 (1974): 507–15.
Highlights outstanding Villon scholarship from 1961–1967.

Edelman, Nathan. "The Vogue of François Villon in France from 1828 to 1873." In *The Eye of the Beholder: Essays in French Literature,* pp. 1–30. Baltimore: The Johns Hopkins University Press, 1974.
Examines the rediscovery of Villon in France after centuries of neglect.

Lynd, Robert. "Villon: The Genius of the Tavern." In *Old and New Masters,* pp. 98–104. New York: Charles Scribner's Sons, 1919.
Argues that Villon was not as morally corrupt as some commentators have suggested and that he was, nonetheless, a poetic genius.

Omans, Glen. "The Villon Cult in England." *Comparative Literature* XVIII, No. 1 (Winter 1966): 16–35.
Summarizes English criticism of Villon.

Poetry Criticism
INDEXES

Literary Criticism Series
Cumulative Author Index

Cumulative Nationality Index

Cumulative Title Index

How to Use This Index

The main references

```
Calvino, Italo
  1923-1985.....CLC 5, 8, 11, 22, 33, 39,
                              73; SSC 3
```

list all author entries in the following Gale Literary Criticism series:

BLC = *Black Literature Criticism*
CLC = *Contemporary Literary Criticism*
CLR = *Children's Literature Review*
CMLC = *Classical and Medieval Literature Criticism*
DA = *DISCovering Authors*
DC = *Drama Criticism*
HLC = *Hispanic Literature Criticism*
LC = *Literature Criticism from 1400 to 1800*
NCLC = *Nineteenth-Century Literature Criticism*
PC = *Poetry Criticism*
SSC = *Short Story Criticism*
TCLC = *Twentieth-Century Literary Criticism*
WLC = *World Literature Criticism, 1500 to the Present*

The cross-references

```
See also CANR 23; CA 85-88;
  obituary CA 116
```

list all author entries in the following Gale biographical and literary sources:

AAYA = *Authors & Artists for Young Adults*
AITN = *Authors in the News*
BEST = *Bestsellers*
BW = *Black Writers*
CA = *Contemporary Authors*
CAAS = *Contemporary Authors Autobiography Series*
CABS = *Contemporary Authors Bibliographical Series*
CANR = *Contemporary Authors New Revision Series*
CAP = *Contemporary Authors Permanent Series*
CDALB = *Concise Dictionary of American Literary Biography*
CDBLB = *Concise Dictionary of British Literary Biography*
DLB = *Dictionary of Literary Biography*
DLBD = *Dictionary of Literary Biography Documentary Series*
DLBY = *Dictionary of Literary Biography Yearbook*
HW = *Hispanic Writers*
JRDA = *Junior DISCovering Authors*
MAICYA = *Major Authors and Illustrators for Children and Young Adults*
MTCW = *Major 20th-Century Writers*
NNAL = *Native North American Literature*
SAAS = *Something about the Author Autobiography Series*
SATA = *Something about the Author*
YABC = *Yesterday's Authors of Books for Children*

Literary Criticism Series
Cumulative Author Index

A. E. . . . . TCLC 3, 10
See also Russell, George William

Abasiyanik, Sait Faik 1906-1954
See Sait Faik
See also CA 123

Abbey, Edward 1927-1989 . . . . . . CLC 36, 59
See also CA 45-48; 128; CANR 2, 41

Abbott, Lee K(ittredge) 1947- . . . . . . CLC 48
See also CA 124; DLB 130

Abe, Kobo 1924-1993 . . . . . CLC 8, 22, 53, 81
See also CA 65-68; 140; CANR 24; MTCW

Abelard, Peter c. 1079-c. 1142 . . . CMLC 11
See also DLB 115

Abell, Kjeld 1901-1961 . . . . CLC 15
See also CA 111

Abish, Walter 1931- . . . . CLC 22
See also CA 101; CANR 37; DLB 130

Abrahams, Peter (Henry) 1919- . . . . . CLC 4
See also BW 1; CA 57-60; CANR 26;
DLB 117; MTCW

Abrams, M(eyer) H(oward) 1912- . . . CLC 24
See also CA 57-60; CANR 13, 33; DLB 67

Abse, Dannie 1923- . . . . CLC 7, 29; DAB
See also CA 53-56; CAAS 1; CANR 4, 46;
DLB 27

Achebe, (Albert) Chinua(lumogu)
1930- . , ... CLC 1, 3, 5, 7, 11, 26, 51, 75;
BLC; DA; DAB; WLC
See also BW 2; CA 1-4R; CANR 6, 26, 47;
CLR 20; DLB 117; MAICYA; MTCW;
SATA 40; SATA-Brief 38

Acker, Kathy 1948- . . . . CLC 45
See also CA 117; 122

Ackroyd, Peter 1949- . . . . CLC 34, 52
See also CA 123; 127; DLB 155

Acorn, Milton 1923- . . . . CLC 15
See also CA 103; DLB 53

Adamov, Arthur 1908-1970 . . . . . . CLC 4, 25
See also CA 17-18; 25-28R; CAP 2; MTCW

Adams, Alice (Boyd) 1926- . . . CLC 6, 13, 46
See also CA 81-84; CANR 26; DLBY 86;
MTCW

Adams, Andy 1859-1935 . . . . TCLC 56
See also YABC 1

Adams, Douglas (Noel) 1952- . . . CLC 27, 60
See also AAYA 4; BEST 89:3; CA 106;
CANR 34; DLBY 83; JRDA

Adams, Francis 1862-1893 . . . . NCLC 33

Adams, Henry (Brooks)
1838-1918 . . . . . . TCLC 4, 52; DA; DAB
See also CA 104; 133; DLB 12, 47

Adams, Richard (George)
1920- . . . . CLC 4, 5, 18
See also AITN.1, 2; CA 49-52; CANR 3,
35; CLR 20; JRDA; MAICYA; MTCW;
SATA 7, 69

Adamson, Joy(-Friederike Victoria)
1910-1980 . . . . CLC 17
See also CA 69-72; 93-96; CANR 22;
MTCW; SATA 11; SATA-Obit 22

Adcock, Fleur 1934- . . . . CLC 41
See also CA 25-28R; CANR 11, 34;
DLB 40

Addams, Charles (Samuel)
1912-1988 . . . . CLC 30
See also CA 61-64; 126; CANR 12

Addison, Joseph 1672-1719 . . . . LC 18
See also CDBLB 1660-1789; DLB 101

Adler, C(arole) S(chwerdtfeger)
1932- . . . . CLC 35
See also AAYA 4; CA 89-92; CANR 19,
40; JRDA; MAICYA; SAAS 15;
SATA 26, 63

Adler, Renata 1938- . . . . CLC 8, 31
See also CA 49-52; CANR 5, 22; MTCW

Ady, Endre 1877-1919 . . . . TCLC 11
See also CA 107

Aeschylus
525B.C.-456B.C. . . . CMLC 11; DA; DAB

Afton, Effie
See Harper, Frances Ellen Watkins

Agapida, Fray Antonio
See Irving, Washington

Agee, James (Rufus)
1909-1955 . . . . TCLC 1, 19
See also AITN 1; CA 108; 148;
CDALB 1941-1968; DLB 2, 26, 152

Aghill, Gordon
See Silverberg, Robert

Agnon, S(hmuel) Y(osef Halevi)
1888-1970 . . . . CLC 4, 8, 14
See also CA 17-18; 25-28R; CAP 2; MTCW

Agrippa von Nettesheim, Henry Cornelius
1486-1535 . . . . LC 27

Aherne, Owen
See Cassill, R(onald) V(erlin)

Ai 1947- . . . . CLC 4, 14, 69
See also CA 85-88; CAAS 13; DLB 120

Aickman, Robert (Fordyce)
1914-1981 . . . . CLC 57
See also CA 5-8R; CANR 3

Aiken, Conrad (Potter)
1889-1973 . . . CLC 1, 3, 5, 10, 52; SSC 9
See also CA 5-8R; 45-48; CANR 4;
CDALB 1929-1941; DLB 9, 45, 102;
MTCW; SATA 3, 30

Aiken, Joan (Delano) 1924- . . . . CLC 35
See also AAYA 1; CA 9-12R; CANR 4, 23,
34; CLR 1, 19; JRDA; MAICYA;
MTCW; SAAS 1; SATA 2, 30, 73

Ainsworth, William Harrison
1805-1882 . . . . NCLC 13
See also DLB 21; SATA 24

Aitmatov, Chingiz (Torekulovich)
1928- . . . . CLC 71
See also CA 103; CANR 38; MTCW;
SATA 56

Akers, Floyd
See Baum, L(yman) Frank

Akhmadulina, Bella Akhatovna
1937- . . . . CLC 53
See also CA 65-68

Akhmatova, Anna
1888-1966 . . . . CLC 11, 25, 64; PC 2
See also CA 19-20; 25-28R; CANR 35;
CAP 1; MTCW

Aksakov, Sergei Timofeyvich
1791-1859 . . . . NCLC 2

Aksenov, Vassily
See Aksyonov, Vassily (Pavlovich)

Aksyonov, Vassily (Pavlovich)
1932- . . . . CLC 22, 37
See also CA 53-56; CANR 12, 48

Akutagawa Ryunosuke
1892-1927 . . . . TCLC 16
See also CA 117

Alain 1868-1951 . . . . TCLC 41

Alain-Fournier . . . . TCLC 6
See also Fournier, Henri Alban
See also DLB 65

Alarcon, Pedro Antonio de
1833-1891 . . . . NCLC 1

Alas (y Urena), Leopoldo (Enrique Garcia)
1852-1901 . . . . TCLC 29
See also CA 113; 131; HW

Albee, Edward (Franklin III)
1928- . . . . . . CLC 1, 2, 3, 5, 9, 11, 13, 25,
53, 86; DA; DAB; WLC
See also AITN 1; CA 5-8R; CABS 3;
CANR 8; CDALB 1941-1968; DLB 7;
MTCW

Alberti, Rafael 1902- . . . . CLC 7
See also CA 85-88; DLB 108

Albert the Great 1200(?)-1280 . . . . CMLC 16
See also DLB 115

Alcala-Galiano, Juan Valera y
See Valera y Alcala-Galiano, Juan

Alcott, Amos Bronson 1799-1888 . . NCLC 1
See also DLB 1

Alcott, Louisa May
1832-1888 . . . NCLC 6; DA; DAB; WLC
See also CDALB 1865-1917; CLR 1, 38;
DLB 1, 42, 79; JRDA; MAICYA;
YABC 1

Aldanov, M. A.
See Aldanov, Mark (Alexandrovich)

Aldanov, Mark (Alexandrovich)
1886(?)-1957 . . . . TCLC 23
See also CA 118

Aldington, Richard 1892-1962...... **CLC 49**
See also CA 85-88; CANR 45; DLB 20, 36, 100, 149

Aldiss, Brian W(ilson)
1925-................. **CLC 5, 14, 40**
See also CA 5-8R; CAAS 2; CANR 5, 28; DLB 14; MTCW; SATA 34

Alegria, Claribel 1924-........... **CLC 75**
See also CA 131; CAAS 15; DLB 145; HW

Alegria, Fernando 1918-.......... **CLC 57**
See also CA 9-12R; CANR 5, 32; HW

Aleichem, Sholom .... **TCLC 1, 35**
See also Rabinovitch, Sholem

Aleixandre, Vicente 1898-1984 ... **CLC 9, 36**
See also CA 85-88; 114; CANR 26; DLB 108; HW; MTCW

Alepoudelis, Odysseus
See Elytis, Odysseus

Aleshkovsky, Joseph 1929-
See Aleshkovsky, Yuz
See also CA 121; 128

Aleshkovsky, Yuz .... **CLC 44**
See also Aleshkovsky, Joseph

Alexander, Lloyd (Chudley) 1924-.. **CLC 35**
See also AAYA 1; CA 1-4R; CANR 1, 24, 38; CLR 1, 5; DLB 52; JRDA; MAICYA; MTCW; SAAS 19; SATA 3, 49, 81

Alfau, Felipe 1902-............... **CLC 66**
See also CA 137

Alger, Horatio, Jr. 1832-1899..... **NCLC 8**
See also DLB 42; SATA 16

Algren, Nelson 1909-1981 .... **CLC 4, 10, 33**
See also CA 13-16R; 103; CANR 20; CDALB 1941-1968; DLB 9; DLBY 81, 82; MTCW

Ali, Ahmed 1910-................ **CLC 69**
See also CA 25-28R; CANR 15, 34

Alighieri, Dante 1265-1321 .... **CMLC 3**

Allan, John B.
See Westlake, Donald E(dwin)

Allen, Edward 1948-............. **CLC 59**

Allen, Paula Gunn 1939-.......... **CLC 84**
See also CA 112; 143; NNAL

Allen, Roland
See Ayckbourn, Alan

Allen, Sarah A.
See Hopkins, Pauline Elizabeth

Allen, Woody 1935-........... **CLC 16, 52**
See also AAYA 10; CA 33-36R; CANR 27, 38; DLB 44; MTCW

Allende, Isabel 1942-.... **CLC 39, 57; HLC**
See also CA 125; 130; DLB 145; HW; MTCW

Alleyn, Ellen
See Rossetti, Christina (Georgina)

Allingham, Margery (Louise)
1904-1966 .... **CLC 19**
See also CA 5-8R; 25-28R; CANR 4; DLB 77; MTCW

Allingham, William 1824-1889 ... **NCLC 25**
See also DLB 35

Allison, Dorothy E. 1949-........ **CLC 78**
See also CA 140

Allston, Washington 1779-1843.... **NCLC 2**
See also DLB 1

Almedingen, E. M. .... **CLC 12**
See also Almedingen, Martha Edith von
See also SATA 3

Almedingen, Martha Edith von 1898-1971
See Almedingen, E. M.
See also CA 1-4R; CANR 1

Almqvist, Carl Jonas Love
1793-1866 .... **NCLC 42**

Alonso, Damaso 1898-1990 .... **CLC 14**
See also CA 110; 131; 130; DLB 108; HW

Alov
See Gogol, Nikolai (Vasilyevich)

Alta 1942-....................... **CLC 19**
See also CA 57-60

Alter, Robert B(ernard) 1935-...... **CLC 34**
See also CA 49-52; CANR 1, 47

Alther, Lisa 1944-............... **CLC 7, 41**
See also CA 65-68; CANR 12, 30; MTCW

Altman, Robert 1925-............. **CLC 16**
See also CA 73-76; CANR 43

Alvarez, A(lfred) 1929-.......... **CLC 5, 13**
See also CA 1-4R; CANR 3, 33; DLB 14, 40

Alvarez, Alejandro Rodriguez 1903-1965
See Casona, Alejandro
See also CA 131; 93-96; HW

Alvaro, Corrado 1896-1956 ...... **TCLC 60**

Amado, Jorge 1912-..... **CLC 13, 40; HLC**
See also CA 77-80; CANR 35; DLB 113; MTCW

Ambler, Eric 1909-............ **CLC 4, 6, 9**
See also CA 9-12R; CANR 7, 38; DLB 77; MTCW

Amichai, Yehuda 1924- ...... **CLC 9, 22, 57**
See also CA 85-88; CANR 46; MTCW

Amiel, Henri Frederic 1821-1881 .. **NCLC 4**

Amis, Kingsley (William)
1922-...... **CLC 1, 2, 3, 5, 8, 13, 40, 44; DA; DAB**
See also AITN 2; CA 9-12R; CANR 8, 28; CDBLB 1945-1960; DLB 15, 27, 100, 139; MTCW

Amis, Martin (Louis)
1949-.................... **CLC 4, 9, 38, 62**
See also BEST 90:3; CA 65-68; CANR 8, 27; DLB 14

Ammons, A(rchie) R(andolph)
1926-........ **CLC 2, 3, 5, 8, 9, 25, 57**
See also AITN 1; CA 9-12R; CANR 6, 36; DLB 5; MTCW

Amo, Tauraatua i
See Adams, Henry (Brooks)

Anand, Mulk Raj 1905-........... **CLC 23**
See also CA 65-68; CANR 32; MTCW

Anatol
See Schnitzler, Arthur

Anaya, Rudolfo A(lfonso)
1937-................. **CLC 23; HLC**
See also CA 45-48; CAAS 4; CANR 1, 32; DLB 82; HW 1; MTCW

Andersen, Hans Christian
1805-1875 .... **NCLC 7; DA; DAB; SSC 6; WLC**
See also CLR 6; MAICYA; YABC 1

Anderson, C. Farley
See Mencken, H(enry) L(ouis); Nathan, George Jean

Anderson, Jessica (Margaret) Queale
.... **CLC 37**
See also CA 9-12R; CANR 4

Anderson, Jon (Victor) 1940- .... **CLC 9**
See also CA 25-28R; CANR 20

Anderson, Lindsay (Gordon)
1923-1994 .... **CLC 20**
See also CA 125; 128; 146

Anderson, Maxwell 1888-1959 ..... **TCLC 2**
See also CA 105; DLB 7

Anderson, Poul (William) 1926- .... **CLC 15**
See also AAYA 5; CA 1-4R; CAAS 2; CANR 2, 15, 34; DLB 8; MTCW; SATA-Brief 39

Anderson, Robert (Woodruff)
1917-...................... **CLC 23**
See also AITN 1; CA 21-24R; CANR 32; DLB 7

Anderson, Sherwood
1876-1941 .... **TCLC 1, 10, 24; DA; DAB; SSC 1; WLC**
See also CA 104; 121; CDALB 1917-1929; DLB 4, 9, 86; DLBD 1; MTCW

Andouard
See Giraudoux, (Hippolyte) Jean

Andrade, Carlos Drummond de ...... **CLC 18**
See also Drummond de Andrade, Carlos

Andrade, Mario de 1893-1945..... **TCLC 43**

Andreas-Salome, Lou 1861-1937... **TCLC 56**
See also DLB 66

Andrewes, Lancelot 1555-1626 .... **LC 5**
See also DLB 151

Andrews, Cicily Fairfield
See West, Rebecca

Andrews, Elton V.
See Pohl, Frederik

Andreyev, Leonid (Nikolaevich)
1871-1919 .... **TCLC 3**
See also CA 104

Andric, Ivo 1892-1975 .... **CLC 8**
See also CA 81-84; 57-60; CANR 43; DLB 147; MTCW

Angelique, Pierre
See Bataille, Georges

Angell, Roger 1920-.............. **CLC 26**
See also CA 57-60; CANR 13, 44

Angelou, Maya
1928- .... **CLC 12, 35, 64, 77; BLC; DA; DAB**
See also AAYA 7; BW 2; CA 65-68; CANR 19, 42; DLB 38; MTCW; SATA 49

Annensky, Innokenty Fyodorovich
1856-1909 .... **TCLC 14**
See also CA 110

Anon, Charles Robert
See Pessoa, Fernando (Antonio Nogueira)

Anouilh, Jean (Marie Lucien Pierre)
1910-1987 . . . . . . **CLC 1, 3, 8, 13, 40, 50**
See also CA 17-20R; 123; CANR 32;
MTCW

Anthony, Florence
See Ai

Anthony, John
See Ciardi, John (Anthony)

Anthony, Peter
See Shaffer, Anthony (Joshua); Shaffer,
Peter (Levin)

Anthony, Piers 1934- . . . . **CLC 35**
See also AAYA 11; CA 21-24R; CANR 28;
DLB 8; MTCW

Antoine, Marc
See Proust, (Valentin-Louis-George-Eugene-)
Marcel

Antoninus, Brother
See Everson, William (Oliver)

Antonioni, Michelangelo 1912- . . . . . **CLC 20**
See also CA 73-76; CANR 45

Antschel, Paul 1920-1970
See Celan, Paul
See also CA 85-88; CANR 33; MTCW

Anwar, Chairil 1922-1949 . . . . **TCLC 22**
See also CA 121

Apollinaire, Guillaume . . **TCLC 3, 8, 51; PC 7**
See also Kostrowitzki, Wilhelm Apollinaris
de

Appelfeld, Aharon 1932- . . . . **CLC 23, 47**
See also CA 112; 133

Apple, Max (Isaac) 1941- . . . . **CLC 9, 33**
See also CA 81-84; CANR 19; DLB 130

Appleman, Philip (Dean) 1926- . . . . . **CLC 51**
See also CA 13-16R; CAAS 18; CANR 6,
29

Appleton, Lawrence
See Lovecraft, H(oward) P(hillips)

Apteryx
See Eliot, T(homas) S(tearns)

Apuleius, (Lucius Madaurensis)
125(?)-175(?) . . . . **CMLC 1**

Aquin, Hubert 1929-1977 . . . . **CLC 15**
See also CA 105; DLB 53

Aragon, Louis 1897-1982 . . . . **CLC 3, 22**
See also CA 69-72; 108; CANR 28;
DLB 72; MTCW

Arany, Janos 1817-1882 . . . . **NCLC 34**

Arbuthnot, John 1667-1735 . . . . **LC 1**
See also DLB 101

Archer, Herbert Winslow
See Mencken, H(enry) L(ouis)

Archer, Jeffrey (Howard) 1940- . . . . **CLC 28**
See also BEST 89:3; CA 77-80; CANR 22

Archer, Jules 1915- . . . . **CLC 12**
See also CA 9-12R; CANR 6; SAAS 5;
SATA 4

Archer, Lee
See Ellison, Harlan (Jay)

Arden, John 1930- . . . . **CLC 6, 13, 15**
See also CA 13-16R; CAAS 4; CANR 31;
DLB 13; MTCW

Arenas, Reinaldo
1943-1990 . . . . **CLC 41; HLC**
See also CA 124; 128; 133; DLB 145; HW

Arendt, Hannah 1906-1975 . . . . **CLC 66**
See also CA 17-20R; 61-64; CANR 26;
MTCW

Aretino, Pietro 1492-1556 . . . . **LC 12**

Arghezi, Tudor . . . . **CLC 80**
See also Theodorescu, Ion N.

Arguedas, Jose Maria
1911-1969 . . . . **CLC 10, 18**
See also CA 89-92; DLB 113; HW

Argueta, Manlio 1936- . . . . **CLC 31**
See also CA 131; DLB 145; HW

Ariosto, Ludovico 1474-1533 . . . . **LC 6**

Aristides
See Epstein, Joseph

Aristophanes
450B.C.-385B.C. . . . . **CMLC 4; DA;
DAB; DC 2**

Arlt, Roberto (Godofredo Christophersen)
1900-1942 . . . . **TCLC 29; HLC**
See also CA 123; 131; HW

Armah, Ayi Kwei 1939- . . . . **CLC 5, 33; BLC**
See also BW 1; CA 61-64; CANR 21;
DLB 117; MTCW

Armatrading, Joan 1950- . . . . **CLC 17**
See also CA 114

Arnette, Robert
See Silverberg, Robert

**Arnim, Achim von (Ludwig Joachim von
Arnim)** 1781-1831 . . . . **NCLC 5**
See also DLB 90

Arnim, Bettina von 1785-1859 . . . . **NCLC 38**
See also DLB 90

Arnold, Matthew
1822-1888 . . . . . **NCLC 6, 29; DA; DAB;
PC 5; WLC**
See also A. E.
See also CDBLB 1832-1890; DLB 32, 57

Arnold, Thomas 1795-1842 . . . . . . **NCLC 18**
See also DLB 55

Arnow, Harriette (Louisa) Simpson
1908-1986 . . . . **CLC 2, 7, 18**
See also CA 9-12R; 118; CANR 14; DLB 6;
MTCW; SATA 42; SATA-Obit 47

Arp, Hans
See Arp, Jean

Arp, Jean 1887-1966 . . . . **CLC 5**
See also CA 81-84; 25-28R; CANR 42

Arrabal
See Arrabal, Fernando

Arrabal, Fernando 1932- . . . **CLC 2, 9, 18, 58**
See also CA 9-12R; CANR 15

Arrick, Fran . . . . **CLC 30**
See also Gaberman, Judie Angell

Artaud, Antonin 1896-1948 . . . . . **TCLC 3, 36**
See also CA 104

Arthur, Ruth M(abel) 1905-1979 . . . . **CLC 12**
See also CA 9-12R; 85-88; CANR 4;
SATA 7, 26

Artsybashev, Mikhail (Petrovich)
1878-1927 . . . . **TCLC 31**

Arundel, Honor (Morfydd)
1919-1973 . . . . **CLC 17**
See also CA 21-22; 41-44R; CAP 2;
CLR 35; SATA 4; SATA-Obit 24

Asch, Sholem 1880-1957 . . . . **TCLC 3**
See also CA 105

Ash, Shalom
See Asch, Sholem

Ashbery, John (Lawrence)
1927- . . . . . . **CLC 2, 3, 4, 6, 9, 13, 15, 25,
41, 77**
See also CA 5-8R; CANR 9, 37; DLB 5;
DLBY 81; MTCW

Ashdown, Clifford
See Freeman, R(ichard) Austin

Ashe, Gordon
See Creasey, John

Ashton-Warner, Sylvia (Constance)
1908-1984 . . . . **CLC 19**
See also CA 69-72; 112; CANR 29; MTCW

Asimov, Isaac
1920-1992 . . . . . . **CLC 1, 3, 9, 19, 26, 76**
See also AAYA 13; BEST 90:2; CA 1-4R;
137; CANR 2, 19, 36; CLR 12; DLB 8;
DLBY 92; JRDA; MAICYA; MTCW;
SATA 1, 26, 74

Astley, Thea (Beatrice May)
1925- . . . . **CLC 41**
See also CA 65-68; CANR 11, 43

Aston, James
See White, T(erence) H(anbury)

Asturias, Miguel Angel
1899-1974 . . . . **CLC 3, 8, 13; HLC**
See also CA 25-28; 49-52; CANR 32;
CAP 2; DLB 113; HW; MTCW

Atares, Carlos Saura
See Saura (Atares), Carlos

Atheling, William
See Pound, Ezra (Weston Loomis)

Atheling, William, Jr.
See Blish, James (Benjamin)

Atherton, Gertrude (Franklin Horn)
1857-1948 . . . . **TCLC 2**
See also CA 104; DLB 9, 78

Atherton, Lucius
See Masters, Edgar Lee

Atkins, Jack
See Harris, Mark

Atticus
See Fleming, Ian (Lancaster)

Atwood, Margaret (Eleanor)
1939- . . . . . **CLC 2, 3, 4, 8, 13, 15, 25, 44,
84; DA; DAB; PC 8; SSC 2; WLC**
See also AAYA 12; BEST 89:2; CA 49-52;
CANR 3, 24, 33; DLB 53; MTCW;
SATA 50

Aubigny, Pierre d'
See Mencken, H(enry) L(ouis)

Aubin, Penelope 1685-1731(?) . . . . **LC 9**
See also DLB 39

Auchincloss, Louis (Stanton)
1917- . . . . **CLC 4, 6, 9, 18, 45**
See also CA 1-4R; CANR 6, 29; DLB 2;
DLBY 80; MTCW

Auden, W(ystan) H(ugh)
1907-1973 . . . . . . CLC **1, 2, 3, 4, 6, 9, 11, 14, 43; DA; DAB; PC 1; WLC**
See also CA 9-12R; 45-48; CANR 5;
CDBLB 1914-1945; DLB 10, 20; MTCW

Audiberti, Jacques 1900-1965 . . . . . . CLC **38**
See also CA 25-28R

Audubon, John James
1785-1851 . . . . NCLC **47**

Auel, Jean M(arie) 1936- . . . . CLC **31**
See also AAYA 7; BEST 90:4; CA 103;
CANR 21

Auerbach, Erich 1892-1957 . . . . TCLC **43**
See also CA 118

Augier, Emile 1820-1889 . . . . NCLC **31**

August, John
See De Voto, Bernard (Augustine)

Augustine, St. 354-430 . . . . . CMLC **6; DAB**

Aurelius
See Bourne, Randolph S(illiman)

Austen, Jane
1775-1817 . . . . . NCLC **1, 13, 19, 33, 51; DA; DAB; WLC**
See also CDBLB 1789-1832; DLB 116

Auster, Paul 1947- . . . . CLC **47**
See also CA 69-72; CANR 23

Austin, Frank
See Faust, Frederick (Schiller)

Austin, Mary (Hunter)
1868-1934 . . . . TCLC **25**
See also CA 109; DLB 9, 78

Autran Dourado, Waldomiro
See Dourado, (Waldomiro Freitas) Autran

Averroes 1126-1198 . . . . CMLC **7**
See also DLB 115

Avicenna 980-1037 . . . . CMLC **16**
See also DLB 115

Avison, Margaret 1918- . . . . CLC **2, 4**
See also CA 17-20R; DLB 53; MTCW

Axton, David
See Koontz, Dean R(ay)

Ayckbourn, Alan
1939- . . . . CLC **5, 8, 18, 33, 74; DAB**
See also CA 21-24R; CANR 31; DLB 13;
MTCW

Aydy, Catherine
See Tennant, Emma (Christina)

Ayme, Marcel (Andre) 1902-1967 . . . CLC **11**
See also CA 89-92; CLR 25; DLB 72

Ayrton, Michael 1921-1975 . . . . CLC **7**
See also CA 5-8R; 61-64; CANR 9, 21

Azorin. . . . . CLC **11**
See also Martinez Ruiz, Jose

Azuela, Mariano
1873-1952 . . . . TCLC **3; HLC**
See also CA 104; 131; HW; MTCW

Baastad, Babbis Friis
See Friis-Baastad, Babbis Ellinor

Bab
See Gilbert, W(illiam) S(chwenck)

Babbis, Eleanor
See Friis-Baastad, Babbis Ellinor

Babel, Isaak (Emmanuilovich)
1894-1941(?) . . . . . . TCLC **2, 13; SSC 16**
See also CA 104

Babits, Mihaly 1883-1941 . . . . TCLC **14**
See also CA 114

Babur 1483-1530. . . . . LC **18**

Bacchelli, Riccardo 1891-1985 . . . . . CLC **19**
See also CA 29-32R; 117

Bach, Richard (David) 1936- . . . . CLC **14**
See also AITN 1; BEST 89:2; CA 9-12R;
CANR 18; MTCW; SATA 13

Bachman, Richard
See King, Stephen (Edwin)

Bachmann, Ingeborg 1926-1973. . . . . CLC **69**
See also CA 93-96; 45-48; DLB 85

Bacon, Francis 1561-1626 . . . . LC **18**
See also CDBLB Before 1660; DLB 151

Bacon, Roger 1214(?)-1292 . . . . . . CMLC **14**
See also DLB 115

Bacovia, George. . . . . TCLC **24**
See also Vasiliu, Gheorghe

Badanes, Jerome 1937- . . . . CLC **59**

Bagehot, Walter 1826-1877 . . . . . . NCLC **10**
See also DLB 55

Bagnold, Enid 1889-1981 . . . . CLC **25**
See also CA 5-8R; 103; CANR 5, 40;
DLB 13; MAICYA; SATA 1, 25

Bagritsky, Eduard 1895-1934 . . . . . TCLC **60**

Bagrjana, Elisaveta
See Belcheva, Elisaveta

Bagryana, Elisaveta. . . . . CLC **10**
See also Belcheva, Elisaveta
See also DLB 147

Bailey, Paul 1937- . . . . CLC **45**
See also CA 21-24R; CANR 16; DLB 14

Baillie, Joanna 1762-1851 . . . . NCLC **2**
See also DLB 93

Bainbridge, Beryl (Margaret)
1933- . . . . CLC **4, 5, 8, 10, 14, 18, 22, 62**
See also CA 21-24R; CANR 24; DLB 14;
MTCW

Baker, Elliott 1922- . . . . CLC **8**
See also CA 45-48; CANR 2

Baker, Nicholson 1957- . . . . CLC **61**
See also CA 135

Baker, Ray Stannard 1870-1946 . . . TCLC **47**
See also CA 118

Baker, Russell (Wayne) 1925- . . . . . . CLC **31**
See also BEST 89:4; CA 57-60; CANR 11,
41; MTCW

Bakhtin, M.
See Bakhtin, Mikhail Mikhailovich

Bakhtin, M. M.
See Bakhtin, Mikhail Mikhailovich

Bakhtin, Mikhail
See Bakhtin, Mikhail Mikhailovich

Bakhtin, Mikhail Mikhailovich
1895-1975 . . . . CLC **83**
See also CA 128; 113

Bakshi, Ralph 1938(?)- . . . . CLC **26**
See also CA 112; 138

Bakunin, Mikhail (Alexandrovich)
1814-1876 . . . . NCLC **25**

Baldwin, James (Arthur)
1924-1987 . . . . . . CLC **1, 2, 3, 4, 5, 8, 13, 15, 17, 42, 50, 67; BLC; DA; DC 1; SSC 10; WLC**
See also AAYA 4; BW 1; CA 1-4R; 124;
CABS 1; CANR 3, 24;
CDALB 1941-1968; DLB 2, 7, 33;
DLBY 87; MTCW; SATA 9;
SATA-Obit 54

Ballard, J(ames) G(raham)
1930- . . . . CLC **3, 6, 14, 36; SSC 1**
See also AAYA 3; CA 5-8R; CANR 15, 39;
DLB 14; MTCW

Balmont, Konstantin (Dmitriyevich)
1867-1943 . . . . TCLC **11**
See also CA 109

Balzac, Honore de
1799-1850 . . . . . NCLC **5, 35; DA; DAB; SSC 5; WLC**
See also DLB 119

Bambara, Toni Cade
1939- . . . . CLC **19, 88; BLC; DA**
See also AAYA 5; BW 2; CA 29-32R;
CANR 24, 49; DLB 38; MTCW

Bamdad, A.
See Shamlu, Ahmad

Banat, D. R.
See Bradbury, Ray (Douglas)

Bancroft, Laura
See Baum, L(yman) Frank

Banim, John 1798-1842 . . . . NCLC **13**
See also DLB 116

Banim, Michael 1796-1874 . . . . . . NCLC **13**

Banks, Iain
See Banks, Iain M(enzies)

Banks, Iain M(enzies) 1954- . . . . CLC **34**
See also CA 123; 128

Banks, Lynne Reid . . . . CLC **23**
See also Reid Banks, Lynne
See also AAYA 6

Banks, Russell 1940- . . . . CLC **37, 72**
See also CA 65-68; CAAS 15; CANR 19;
DLB 130

Banville, John 1945- . . . . CLC **46**
See also CA 117; 128; DLB 14

Banville, Theodore (Faullain) de
1832-1891 . . . . NCLC **9**

Baraka, Amiri
1934- . . . . CLC **1, 2, 3, 5, 10, 14, 33; BLC; DA; PC 4**
See also Jones, LeRoi
See also BW 2; CA 21-24R; CABS 3;
CANR 27, 38; CDALB 1941-1968;
DLB 5, 7, 16, 38; DLBD 8; MTCW

Barbauld, Anna Laetitia
1743-1825 . . . . NCLC **50**
See also DLB 107, 109, 142

Barbellion, W. N. P.. . . . . TCLC **24**
See also Cummings, Bruce F(rederick)

Barbera, Jack (Vincent) 1945- . . . . . . CLC **44**
See also CA 110; CANR 45

Barbey d'Aurevilly, Jules Amedee
1808-1889 . . . . NCLC **1; SSC 17**
See also DLB 119

Barbusse, Henri 1873-1935 . . . . **TCLC 5**
See also CA 105; DLB 65

Barclay, Bill
See Moorcock, Michael (John)

Barclay, William Ewert
See Moorcock, Michael (John)

Barea, Arturo 1897-1957 . . . . **TCLC 14**
See also CA 111

Barfoot, Joan 1946- . . . . **CLC 18**
See also CA 105

Baring, Maurice 1874-1945 . . . . **TCLC 8**
See also CA 105; DLB 34

Barker, Clive 1952- . . . . **CLC 52**
See also AAYA 10; BEST 90:3; CA 121;
129; MTCW

Barker, George Granville
1913-1991 . . . . **CLC 8, 48**
See also CA 9-12R; 135; CANR 7, 38;
DLB 20; MTCW

Barker, Harley Granville
See Granville-Barker, Harley
See also DLB 10

Barker, Howard 1946- . . . . **CLC 37**
See also CA 102; DLB 13

Barker, Pat 1943- . . . . **CLC 32**
See also CA 117; 122

Barlow, Joel 1754-1812 . . . . **NCLC 23**
See also DLB 37

Barnard, Mary (Ethel) 1909- . . . . **CLC 48**
See also CA 21-22; CAP 2

Barnes, Djuna
1892-1982 . . . **CLC 3, 4, 8, 11, 29; SSC 3**
See also CA 9-12R; 107; CANR 16; DLB 4,
9, 45; MTCW

Barnes, Julian 1946- . . . . **CLC 42; DAB**
See also CA 102; CANR 19; DLBY 93

Barnes, Peter 1931- . . . . **CLC 5, 56**
See also CA 65-68; CAAS 12; CANR 33,
34; DLB 13; MTCW

Baroja (y Nessi), Pio
1872-1956 . . . . **TCLC 8; HLC**
See also CA 104

Baron, David
See Pinter, Harold

Baron Corvo
See Rolfe, Frederick (William Serafino
Austin Lewis Mary)

Barondess, Sue K(aufman)
1926-1977 . . . . **CLC 8**
See also Kaufman, Sue
See also CA 1-4R; 69-72; CANR 1

Baron de Teive
See Pessoa, Fernando (Antonio Nogueira)

Barres, Maurice 1862-1923 . . . . **TCLC 47**
See also DLB 123

Barreto, Afonso Henrique de Lima
See Lima Barreto, Afonso Henrique de

Barrett, (Roger) Syd 1946- . . . . **CLC 35**

Barrett, William (Christopher)
1913-1992 . . . . **CLC 27**
See also CA 13-16R; 139; CANR 11

Barrie, J(ames) M(atthew)
1860-1937 . . . . **TCLC 2; DAB**
See also CA 104; 136; CDBLB 1890-1914;
CLR 16; DLB 10, 141; MAICYA;
YABC 1

Barrington, Michael
See Moorcock, Michael (John)

Barrol, Grady
See Bograd, Larry

Barry, Mike
See Malzberg, Barry N(athaniel)

Barry, Philip 1896-1949 . . . . **TCLC 11**
See also CA 109; DLB 7

Bart, Andre Schwarz
See Schwarz-Bart, Andre

Barth, John (Simmons)
1930- . . . . . . **CLC 1, 2, 3, 5, 7, 9, 10, 14,
27, 51, 89; SSC 10**
See also AITN 1, 2; CA 1-4R; CABS 1;
CANR 5, 23, 49; DLB 2; MTCW

Barthelme, Donald
1931-1989 . . . . . . **CLC 1, 2, 3, 5, 6, 8, 13,
23, 46, 59; SSC 2**
See also CA 21-24R; 129; CANR 20;
DLB 2; DLBY 80, 89; MTCW; SATA 7;
SATA-Obit 62

Barthelme, Frederick 1943- . . . . **CLC 36**
See also CA 114; 122; DLBY 85

Barthes, Roland (Gerard)
1915-1980 . . . . **CLC 24, 83**
See also CA 130; 97-100; MTCW

Barzun, Jacques (Martin) 1907- . . . . **CLC 51**
See also CA 61-64; CANR 22

Bashevis, Isaac
See Singer, Isaac Bashevis

Bashkirtseff, Marie 1859-1884 . . . **NCLC 27**

Basho
See Matsuo Basho

Bass, Kingsley B., Jr.
See Bullins, Ed

Bass, Rick 1958- . . . . **CLC 79**
See also CA 126

Bassani, Giorgio 1916- . . . . **CLC 9**
See also CA 65-68; CANR 33; DLB 128;
MTCW

Bastos, Augusto (Antonio) Roa
See Roa Bastos, Augusto (Antonio)

Bataille, Georges 1897-1962 . . . . **CLC 29**
See also CA 101; 89-92

Bates, H(erbert) E(rnest)
1905-1974 . . . . . . **CLC 46; DAB; SSC 10**
See also CA 93-96; 45-48; CANR 34;
MTCW

Bauchart
See Camus, Albert

Baudelaire, Charles
1821-1867 . . . . . **NCLC 6, 29; DA; DAB;
PC 1; SSC 18; WLC**

Baudrillard, Jean 1929- . . . . **CLC 60**

Baum, L(yman) Frank 1856-1919 . . . **TCLC 7**
See also CA 108; 133; CLR 15; DLB 22;
JRDA; MAICYA; MTCW; SATA 18

Baum, Louis F.
See Baum, L(yman) Frank

Baumbach, Jonathan 1933- . . . . . . **CLC 6, 23**
See also CA 13-16R; CAAS 5; CANR 12;
DLBY 80; MTCW

Bausch, Richard (Carl) 1945- . . . . . . **CLC 51**
See also CA 101; CAAS 14; CANR 43;
DLB 130

Baxter, Charles 1947- . . . . **CLC 45, 78**
See also CA 57-60; CANR 40; DLB 130

Baxter, George Owen
See Faust, Frederick (Schiller)

Baxter, James K(eir) 1926-1972 . . . . **CLC 14**
See also CA 77-80

Baxter, John
See Hunt, E(verette) Howard, (Jr.)

Bayer, Sylvia
See Glassco, John

Baynton, Barbara 1857-1929 . . . . . . **TCLC 57**

Beagle, Peter S(oyer) 1939- . . . . **CLC 7**
See also CA 9-12R; CANR 4; DLBY 80;
SATA 60

Bean, Normal
See Burroughs, Edgar Rice

Beard, Charles A(ustin)
1874-1948 . . . . **TCLC 15**
See also CA 115; DLB 17; SATA 18

Beardsley, Aubrey 1872-1898 . . . . . **NCLC 6**

Beattie, Ann
1947- . . . . **CLC 8, 13, 18, 40, 63; SSC 11**
See also BEST 90:2; CA 81-84; DLBY 82;
MTCW

Beattie, James 1735-1803 . . . . **NCLC 25**
See also DLB 109

Beauchamp, Kathleen Mansfield 1888-1923
See Mansfield, Katherine
See also CA 104; 134; DA

Beaumarchais, Pierre-Augustin Caron de
1732-1799 . . . . **DC 4**

**Beauvoir, Simone (Lucie Ernestine Marie
Bertrand) de**
1908-1986 . . . . **CLC 1, 2, 4, 8, 14, 31, 44,
50, 71; DA; DAB; WLC**
See also CA 9-12R; 118; CANR 28;
DLB 72; DLBY 86; MTCW

Becker, Jurek 1937- . . . . **CLC 7, 19**
See also CA 85-88; DLB 75

Becker, Walter 1950- . . . . **CLC 26**

Beckett, Samuel (Barclay)
1906-1989 . . . . . . **CLC 1, 2, 3, 4, 6, 9, 10,
11, 14, 18, 29, 57, 59, 83; DA; DAB;
SSC 16; WLC**
See also CA 5-8R; 130; CANR 33;
CDBLB 1945-1960; DLB 13, 15;
DLBY 90; MTCW

Beckford, William 1760-1844 . . . . **NCLC 16**
See also DLB 39

Beckman, Gunnel 1910- . . . . **CLC 26**
See also CA 33-36R; CANR 15; CLR 25;
MAICYA; SAAS 9; SATA 6

Becque, Henri 1837-1899 . . . . **NCLC 3**

Beddoes, Thomas Lovell
1803-1849 . . . . **NCLC 3**
See also DLB 96

Bedford, Donald F.
See Fearing, Kenneth (Flexner)

Beecher, Catharine Esther
1800-1878 . . . . **NCLC 30**
See also DLB 1

Beecher, John 1904-1980 . . . . **CLC 6**
See also AITN 1; CA 5-8R; 105; CANR 8

Beer, Johann 1655-1700 . . . . **LC 5**

Beer, Patricia 1924- . . . . **CLC 58**
See also CA 61-64; CANR 13, 46; DLB 40

Beerbohm, Henry Maximilian
1872-1956 . . . . **TCLC 1, 24**
See also CA 104; DLB 34, 100

Beerbohm, Max
See Beerbohm, Henry Maximilian

Beer-Hofmann, Richard
1866-1945 . . . . **TCLC 60**
See also DLB 81

Begiebing, Robert J(ohn) 1946- . . . . . **CLC 70**
See also CA 122; CANR 40

Behan, Brendan
1923-1964 . . . . **CLC 1, 8, 11, 15, 79**
See also CA 73-76; CANR 33;
CDBLB 1945-1960; DLB 13; MTCW

Behn, Aphra
1640(?)-1689 . . . . . . **LC 1, 30; DA; DAB;**
DC 4; PC 13; WLC
See also DLB 39, 80, 131

Behrman, S(amuel) N(athaniel)
1893-1973 . . . . **CLC 40**
See also CA 13-16; 45-48; CAP 1; DLB 7,
44

Belasco, David 1853-1931 . . . . **TCLC 3**
See also CA 104; DLB 7

Belcheva, Elisaveta 1893- . . . . **CLC 10**
See also Bagryana, Elisaveta

Beldone, Phil "Cheech"
See Ellison, Harlan (Jay)

Beleno
See Azuela, Mariano

Belinski, Vissarion Grigoryevich
1811-1848 . . . . **NCLC 5**

Belitt, Ben 1911- . . . . **CLC 22**
See also CA 13-16R; CAAS 4; CANR 7;
DLB 5

Bell, James Madison
1826-1902 . . . . **TCLC 43; BLC**
See also BW 1; CA 122; 124; DLB 50

Bell, Madison (Smartt) 1957- . . . . . . **CLC 41**
See also CA 111; CANR 28

Bell, Marvin (Hartley) 1937- . . . . . **CLC 8, 31**
See also CA 21-24R; CAAS 14; DLB 5;
MTCW

Bell, W. L. D.
See Mencken, H(enry) L(ouis)

Bellamy, Atwood C.
See Mencken, H(enry) L(ouis)

Bellamy, Edward 1850-1898 . . . . . . **NCLC 4**
See also DLB 12

Bellin, Edward J.
See Kuttner, Henry

Belloc, (Joseph) Hilaire (Pierre)
1870-1953 . . . . **TCLC 7, 18**
See also CA 106; DLB 19, 100, 141;
YABC 1

Belloc, Joseph Peter Rene Hilaire
See Belloc, (Joseph) Hilaire (Pierre)

Belloc, Joseph Pierre Hilaire
See Belloc, (Joseph) Hilaire (Pierre)

Belloc, M. A.
See Lowndes, Marie Adelaide (Belloc)

Bellow, Saul
1915- . . . . . . **CLC 1, 2, 3, 6, 8, 10, 13, 15,**
25, 33, 34, 63, 79; DA; DAB; SSC 14;
WLC
See also AITN 2; BEST 89:3; CA 5-8R;
CABS 1; CANR 29; CDALB 1941-1968;
DLB 2, 28; DLBD 3; DLBY 82; MTCW

Belser, Reimond Karel Maria de
See Ruyslinck, Ward

Bely, Andrey . . . . **TCLC 7; PC 11**
See also Bugayev, Boris Nikolayevich

Benary, Margot
See Benary-Isbert, Margot

Benary-Isbert, Margot 1889-1979 . . . **CLC 12**
See also CA 5-8R; 89-92; CANR 4;
CLR 12; MAICYA; SATA 2;
SATA-Obit 21

Benavente (y Martinez), Jacinto
1866-1954 . . . . **TCLC 3**
See also CA 106; 131; HW; MTCW

Benchley, Peter (Bradford)
1940- . . . . **CLC 4, 8**
See also AAYA 14; AITN 2; CA 17-20R;
CANR 12, 35; MTCW; SATA 3

Benchley, Robert (Charles)
1889-1945 . . . . **TCLC 1, 55**
See also CA 105; DLB 11

Benda, Julien 1867-1956 . . . . **TCLC 60**
See also CA 120

Benedict, Ruth 1887-1948 . . . . **TCLC 60**

Benedikt, Michael 1935- . . . . **CLC 4, 14**
See also CA 13-16R; CANR 7; DLB 5

Benet, Juan 1927- . . . . **CLC 28**
See also CA 143

Benet, Stephen Vincent
1898-1943 . . . . **TCLC 7; SSC 10**
See also CA 104; DLB 4, 48, 102; YABC 1

Benet, William Rose 1886-1950 . . . **TCLC 28**
See also CA 118; DLB 45

Benford, Gregory (Albert) 1941- . . . . **CLC 52**
See also CA 69-72; CANR 12, 24, 49;
DLBY 82

Bengtsson, Frans (Gunnar)
1894-1954 . . . . **TCLC 48**

Benjamin, David
See Slavitt, David R(ytman)

Benjamin, Lois
See Gould, Lois

Benjamin, Walter 1892-1940 . . . . . . **TCLC 39**

Benn, Gottfried 1886-1956 . . . . **TCLC 3**
See also CA 106; DLB 56

Bennett, Alan 1934- . . . . . **CLC 45, 77; DAB**
See also CA 103; CANR 35; MTCW

Bennett, (Enoch) Arnold
1867-1931 . . . . **TCLC 5, 20**
See also CA 106; CDBLB 1890-1914;
DLB 10, 34, 98, 135

Bennett, Elizabeth
See Mitchell, Margaret (Munnerlyn)

Bennett, George Harold 1930-
See Bennett, Hal
See also BW 1; CA 97-100

Bennett, Hal . . . . **CLC 5**
See also Bennett, George Harold
See also DLB 33

Bennett, Jay 1912- . . . . **CLC 35**
See also AAYA 10; CA 69-72; CANR 11,
42; JRDA; SAAS 4; SATA 41;
SATA-Brief 27

Bennett, Louise (Simone)
1919- . . . . **CLC 28; BLC**
See also BW 2; DLB 117

Benson, E(dward) F(rederic)
1867-1940 . . . . **TCLC 27**
See also CA 114; DLB 135, 153

Benson, Jackson J. 1930- . . . . **CLC 34**
See also CA 25-28R; DLB 111

Benson, Sally 1900-1972 . . . . **CLC 17**
See also CA 19-20; 37-40R; CAP 1;
SATA 1, 35; SATA-Obit 27

Benson, Stella 1892-1933 . . . . **TCLC 17**
See also CA 117; DLB 36

Bentham, Jeremy 1748-1832 . . . . . **NCLC 38**
See also DLB 107

Bentley, E(dmund) C(lerihew)
1875-1956 . . . . **TCLC 12**
See also CA 108; DLB 70

Bentley, Eric (Russell) 1916- . . . . . . **CLC 24**
See also CA 5-8R; CANR 6

Beranger, Pierre Jean de
1780-1857 . . . . **NCLC 34**

Berendt, John (Lawrence) 1939- . . . . **CLC 86**
See also CA 146

Berger, Colonel
See Malraux, (Georges-)Andre

Berger, John (Peter) 1926- . . . . . . **CLC 2, 19**
See also CA 81-84; DLB 14

Berger, Melvin H. 1927- . . . . **CLC 12**
See also CA 5-8R; CANR 4; CLR 32;
SAAS 2; SATA 5

Berger, Thomas (Louis)
1924- . . . . **CLC 3, 5, 8, 11, 18, 38**
See also CA 1-4R; CANR 5, 28; DLB 2;
DLBY 80; MTCW

Bergman, (Ernst) Ingmar
1918- . . . . **CLC 16, 72**
See also CA 81-84; CANR 33

Bergson, Henri 1859-1941 . . . . **TCLC 32**

Bergstein, Eleanor 1938- . . . . **CLC 4**
See also CA 53-56; CANR 5

Berkoff, Steven 1937- . . . . **CLC 56**
See also CA 104

Bermant, Chaim (Icyk) 1929- . . . . . . **CLC 40**
See also CA 57-60; CANR 6, 31

Bern, Victoria
See Fisher, M(ary) F(rances) K(ennedy)

Bernanos, (Paul Louis) Georges
1888-1948 . . . . **TCLC 3**
See also CA 104; 130; DLB 72

Bernard, April 1956- . . . . **CLC 59**
See also CA 131

Berne, Victoria
See Fisher, M(ary) F(rances) K(ennedy)

Bernhard, Thomas
1931-1989 . . . . CLC **3, 32, 61**
See also CA 85-88; 127; CANR 32;
DLB 85, 124; MTCW

Berriault, Gina 1926- . . . . CLC **54**
See also CA 116; 129; DLB 130

Berrigan, Daniel 1921- . . . . CLC **4**
See also CA 33-36R; CAAS 1; CANR 11,
43; DLB 5

Berrigan, Edmund Joseph Michael, Jr.
1934-1983
See Berrigan, Ted
See also CA 61-64; 110; CANR 14

Berrigan, Ted . . . . CLC **37**
See also Berrigan, Edmund Joseph Michael,
Jr.
See also DLB 5

Berry, Charles Edward Anderson 1931-
See Berry, Chuck
See also CA 115

Berry, Chuck . . . . CLC **17**
See also Berry, Charles Edward Anderson

Berry, Jonas
See Ashbery, John (Lawrence)

Berry, Wendell (Erdman)
1934- . . . . CLC **4, 6, 8, 27, 46**
See also AITN 1; CA 73-76; DLB 5, 6

Berryman, John
1914-1972 . . . . . . CLC **1, 2, 3, 4, 6, 8, 10,**
13, 25, 62
See also CA 13-16; 33-36R; CABS 2;
CANR 35; CAP 1; CDALB 1941-1968;
DLB 48; MTCW

Bertolucci, Bernardo 1940- . . . . CLC **16**
See also CA 106

Bertrand, Aloysius 1807-1841 . . . . NCLC **31**

Bertran de Born c. 1140-1215 . . . . . CMLC **5**

Besant, Annie (Wood) 1847-1933 . . . TCLC **9**
See also CA 105

Bessie, Alvah 1904-1985 . . . . CLC **23**
See also CA 5-8R; 116; CANR 2; DLB 26

Bethlen, T. D.
See Silverberg, Robert

Beti, Mongo . . . . CLC **27; BLC**
See also Biyidi, Alexandre

Betjeman, John
1906-1984 . . . CLC **2, 6, 10, 34, 43; DAB**
See also CA 9-12R; 112; CANR 33;
CDBLB 1945-1960; DLB 20; DLBY 84;
MTCW

Bettelheim, Bruno 1903-1990 . . . . . . CLC **79**
See also CA 81-84; 131; CANR 23; MTCW

Betti, Ugo 1892-1953 . . . . TCLC **5**
See also CA 104

Betts, Doris (Waugh) 1932- . . . . CLC **3, 6, 28**
See also CA 13-16R; CANR 9; DLBY 82

Bevan, Alistair
See Roberts, Keith (John Kingston)

Bialik, Chaim Nachman
1873-1934 . . . . TCLC **25**

Bickerstaff, Isaac
See Swift, Jonathan

Bidart, Frank 1939- . . . . CLC **33**
See also CA 140

Bienek, Horst 1930- . . . . CLC **7, 11**
See also CA 73-76; DLB 75

Bierce, Ambrose (Gwinett)
1842-1914(?) . . . . TCLC **1, 7, 44; DA;**
SSC 9; WLC
See also CA 104; 139; CDALB 1865-1917;
DLB 11, 12, 23, 71, 74

Billings, Josh
See Shaw, Henry Wheeler

Billington, (Lady) Rachel (Mary)
1942- . . . . CLC **43**
See also AITN 2; CA 33-36R; CANR 44

Binyon, T(imothy) J(ohn) 1936- . . . . CLC **34**
See also CA 111; CANR 28

Bioy Casares, Adolfo
1914- . . . CLC **4, 8, 13, 88; HLC; SSC 17**
See also CA 29-32R; CANR 19, 43;
DLB 113; HW; MTCW

Bird, Cordwainer
See Ellison, Harlan (Jay)

Bird, Robert Montgomery
1806-1854 . . . . NCLC **1**

Birney, (Alfred) Earle
1904- . . . . CLC **1, 4, 6, 11**
See also CA 1-4R; CANR 5, 20; DLB 88;
MTCW

Bishop, Elizabeth
1911-1979 . . . . . . CLC **1, 4, 9, 13, 15, 32;**
DA; PC 3
See also CA 5-8R; 89-92; CABS 2;
CANR 26; CDALB 1968-1988; DLB 5;
MTCW; SATA-Obit 24

Bishop, John 1935- . . . . CLC **10**
See also CA 105

Bissett, Bill 1939- . . . . CLC **18**
See also CA 69-72; CAAS 19; CANR 15;
DLB 53; MTCW

Bitov, Andrei (Georgievich) 1937- . . . CLC **57**
See also CA 142

Biyidi, Alexandre 1932-
See Beti, Mongo
See also BW 1; CA 114; 124; MTCW

Bjarme, Brynjolf
See Ibsen, Henrik (Johan)

Bjornson, Bjornstjerne (Martinius)
1832-1910 . . . . TCLC **7, 37**
See also CA 104

Black, Robert
See Holdstock, Robert P.

Blackburn, Paul 1926-1971 . . . . . . CLC **9, 43**
See also CA 81-84; 33-36R; CANR 34;
DLB 16; DLBY 81

Black Elk 1863-1950 . . . . TCLC **33**
See also CA 144; NNAL

Black Hobart
See Sanders, (James) Ed(ward)

Blacklin, Malcolm
See Chambers, Aidan

Blackmore, R(ichard) D(oddridge)
1825-1900 . . . . TCLC **27**
See also CA 120; DLB 18

Blackmur, R(ichard) P(almer)
1904-1965 . . . . CLC **2, 24**
See also CA 11-12; 25-28R; CAP 1; DLB 63

Black Tarantula, The
See Acker, Kathy

Blackwood, Algernon (Henry)
1869-1951 . . . . TCLC **5**
See also CA 105; DLB 153

Blackwood, Caroline 1931- . . . . CLC **6, 9**
See also CA 85-88; CANR 32; DLB 14;
MTCW

Blade, Alexander
See Hamilton, Edmond; Silverberg, Robert

Blaga, Lucian 1895-1961 . . . . CLC **75**

Blair, Eric (Arthur) 1903-1950
See Orwell, George
See also CA 104; 132; DA; MTCW;
SATA 29

Blais, Marie-Claire
1939- . . . . CLC **2, 4, 6, 13, 22**
See also CA 21-24R; CAAS 4; CANR 38;
DLB 53; MTCW

Blaise, Clark 1940- . . . . CLC **29**
See also AITN 2; CA 53-56; CAAS 3;
CANR 5; DLB 53

Blake, Nicholas
See Day Lewis, C(ecil)
See also DLB 77

Blake, William
1757-1827 . . . . NCLC **13, 37; DA; DAB;**
PC 12; WLC
See also CDBLB 1789-1832; DLB 93;
MAICYA; SATA 30

Blasco Ibanez, Vicente
1867-1928 . . . . TCLC **12**
See also CA 110; 131; HW; MTCW

Blatty, William Peter 1928- . . . . CLC **2**
See also CA 5-8R; CANR 9

Bleeck, Oliver
See Thomas, Ross (Elmore)

Blessing, Lee 1949- . . . . CLC **54**

Blish, James (Benjamin)
1921-1975 . . . . CLC **14**
See also CA 1-4R; 57-60; CANR 3; DLB 8;
MTCW; SATA 66

Bliss, Reginald
See Wells, H(erbert) G(eorge)

Blixen, Karen (Christentze Dinesen)
1885-1962
See Dinesen, Isak
See also CA 25-28; CANR 22; CAP 2;
MTCW; SATA 44

Bloch, Robert (Albert) 1917-1994 . . . CLC **33**
See also CA 5-8R; 146; CAAS 20; CANR 5;
DLB 44; SATA 12; SATA-Obit 82

Blok, Alexander (Alexandrovich)
1880-1921 . . . . TCLC **5**
See also CA 104

Blom, Jan
See Breytenbach, Breyten

Bloom, Harold 1930- . . . . CLC **24**
See also CA 13-16R; CANR 39; DLB 67

Bloomfield, Aurelius
See Bourne, Randolph S(illiman)

Blount, Roy (Alton), Jr. 1941- ..... **CLC 38**
See also CA 53-56; CANR 10, 28; MTCW

Bloy, Leon 1846-1917............ **TCLC 22**
See also CA 121; DLB 123

Blume, Judy (Sussman) 1938-... **CLC 12, 30**
See also AAYA 3; CA 29-32R; CANR 13,
37; CLR 2, 15; DLB 52; JRDA;
MAICYA; MTCW; SATA 2, 31, 79

Blunden, Edmund (Charles)
1896-1974 .... **CLC 2, 56**
See also CA 17-18; 45-48; CAP 2; DLB 20,
100, 155; MTCW

Bly, Robert (Elwood)
1926- .... **CLC 1, 2, 5, 10, 15, 38**
See also CA 5-8R; CANR 41; DLB 5;
MTCW

Boas, Franz 1858-1942.......... **TCLC 56**
See also CA 115

Bobette
See Simenon, Georges (Jacques Christian)

Boccaccio, Giovanni
1313-1375 .... **CMLC 13; SSC 10**

Bochco, Steven 1943-............. **CLC 35**
See also AAYA 11; CA 124; 138

Bodenheim, Maxwell 1892-1954 ... **TCLC 44**
See also CA 110; DLB 9, 45

Bodker, Cecil 1927- .... **CLC 21**
See also CA 73-76; CANR 13, 44; CLR 23;
MAICYA; SATA 14

Boell, Heinrich (Theodor)
1917-1985 .... **CLC 2, 3, 6, 9, 11, 15, 27,
32, 72; DA; DAB; WLC**
See also CA 21-24R; 116; CANR 24;
DLB 69; DLBY 85; MTCW

Boerne, Alfred
See Doeblin, Alfred

Boethius 480(?)-524(?) .... **CMLC 15**
See also DLB 115

Bogan, Louise
1897-1970 ...... **CLC 4, 39, 46; PC 12**
See also CA 73-76; 25-28R; CANR 33;
DLB 45; MTCW

Bogarde, Dirk .... **CLC 19**
See also Van Den Bogarde, Derek Jules
Gaspard Ulric Niven
See also DLB 14

Bogosian, Eric 1953- .... **CLC 45**
See also CA 138

Bograd, Larry 1953-............. **CLC 35**
See also CA 93-96; SATA 33

Boiardo, Matteo Maria 1441-1494 .... **LC 6**

Boileau-Despreaux, Nicolas
1636-1711 .... **LC 3**

Boland, Eavan (Aisling) 1944-... **CLC 40, 67**
See also CA 143; DLB 40

Bolt, Lee
See Faust, Frederick (Schiller)

Bolt, Robert (Oxton) 1924-1995 .... **CLC 14**
See also CA 17-20R; 147; CANR 35;
DLB 13; MTCW

Bombet, Louis-Alexandre-Cesar
See Stendhal

Bomkauf
See Kaufman, Bob (Garnell)

Bonaventura.................... **NCLC 35**
See also DLB 90

Bond, Edward 1934-....... **CLC 4, 6, 13, 23**
See also CA 25-28R; CANR 38; DLB 13;
MTCW

Bonham, Frank 1914-1989........ **CLC 12**
See also AAYA 1; CA 9-12R; CANR 4, 36;
JRDA; MAICYA; SAAS 3; SATA 1, 49;
SATA-Obit 62

Bonnefoy, Yves 1923-........ **CLC 9, 15, 58**
See also CA 85-88; CANR 33; MTCW

Bontemps, Arna(ud Wendell)
1902-1973 .... **CLC 1, 18; BLC**
See also BW 1; CA 1-4R; 41-44R; CANR 4,
35; CLR 6; DLB 48, 51; JRDA;
MAICYA; MTCW; SATA 2, 44;
SATA-Obit 24

Booth, Martin 1944-............. **CLC 13**
See also CA 93-96; CAAS 2

Booth, Philip 1925-.............. **CLC 23**
See also CA 5-8R; CANR 5; DLBY 82

Booth, Wayne C(layson) 1921-..... **CLC 24**
See also CA 1-4R; CAAS 5; CANR 3, 43;
DLB 67

Borchert, Wolfgang 1921-1947 ..... **TCLC 5**
See also CA 104; DLB 69, 124

Borel, Petrus 1809-1859........ **NCLC 41**

Borges, Jorge Luis
1899-1986 ... **CLC 1, 2, 3, 4, 6, 8, 9, 10,
13, 19, 44, 48, 83; DA; DAB; HLC;
SSC 4; WLC**
See also CA 21-24R; CANR 19, 33;
DLB 113; DLBY 86; HW; MTCW

Borowski, Tadeusz 1922-1951...... **TCLC 9**
See also CA 106

Borrow, George (Henry)
1803-1881 .... **NCLC 9**
See also DLB 21, 55

Bosman, Herman Charles
1905-1951 .... **TCLC 49**

Bosschere, Jean de 1878(?)-1953... **TCLC 19**
See also CA 115

Boswell, James
1740-1795 ...... **LC 4; DA; DAB; WLC**
See also CDBLB 1660-1789; DLB 104, 142

Bottoms, David 1949-............. **CLC 53**
See also CA 105; CANR 22; DLB 120;
DLBY 83

Boucicault, Dion 1820-1890...... **NCLC 41**

Boucolon, Maryse 1937-
See Conde, Maryse
See also CA 110; CANR 30

Bourget, Paul (Charles Joseph)
1852-1935 .... **TCLC 12**
See also CA 107; DLB 123

Bourjaily, Vance (Nye) 1922- .... **CLC 8, 62**
See also CA 1-4R; CAAS 1; CANR 2;
DLB 2, 143

Bourne, Randolph S(illiman)
1886-1918 .... **TCLC 16**
See also CA 117; DLB 63

Bova, Ben(jamin William) 1932-.... **CLC 45**
See also CA 5-8R; CAAS 18; CANR 11;
CLR 3; DLBY 81; MAICYA; MTCW;
SATA 6, 68

Bowen, Elizabeth (Dorothea Cole)
1899-1973 ...... **CLC 1, 3, 6, 11, 15, 22;
SSC 3**
See also CA 17-18; 41-44R; CANR 35;
CAP 2; CDBLB 1945-1960; DLB 15;
MTCW

Bowering, George 1935-........ **CLC 15, 47**
See also CA 21-24R; CAAS 16; CANR 10;
DLB 53

Bowering, Marilyn R(uthe) 1949-... **CLC 32**
See also CA 101; CANR 49

Bowers, Edgar 1924- .... **CLC 9**
See also CA 5-8R; CANR 24; DLB 5

Bowie, David .... **CLC 17**
See also Jones, David Robert

Bowles, Jane (Sydney)
1917-1973 .... **CLC 3, 68**
See also CA 19-20; 41-44R; CAP 2

Bowles, Paul (Frederick)
1910- .... **CLC 1, 2, 19, 53; SSC 3**
See also CA 1-4R; CAAS 1; CANR 1, 19;
DLB 5, 6; MTCW

Box, Edgar
See Vidal, Gore

Boyd, Nancy
See Millay, Edna St. Vincent

Boyd, William 1952-....... **CLC 28, 53, 70**
See also CA 114; 120

Boyle, Kay
1902-1992 ..... **CLC 1, 5, 19, 58; SSC 5**
See also CA 13-16R; 140; CAAS 1;
CANR 29; DLB 4, 9, 48, 86; DLBY 93;
MTCW

Boyle, Mark
See Kienzle, William X(avier)

Boyle, Patrick 1905-1982.......... **CLC 19**
See also CA 127

Boyle, T. C.
See Boyle, T(homas) Coraghessan

Boyle, T(homas) Coraghessan
1948- .... **CLC 36, 55; SSC 16**
See also BEST 90:4; CA 120; CANR 44;
DLBY 86

Boz
See Dickens, Charles (John Huffam)

Brackenridge, Hugh Henry
1748-1816 .... **NCLC 7**
See also DLB 11, 37

Bradbury, Edward P.
See Moorcock, Michael (John)

Bradbury, Malcolm (Stanley)
1932- .... **CLC 32, 61**
See also CA 1-4R; CANR 1, 33; DLB 14;
MTCW

Bradbury, Ray (Douglas)
1920- .... **CLC 1, 3, 10, 15, 42; DA;
DAB; WLC**
See also AITN 1, 2; CA 1-4R; CANR 2, 30;
CDALB 1968-1988; DLB 2, 8; MTCW;
SATA 11, 64

Bradford, Gamaliel 1863-1932..... **TCLC 36**
See also DLB 17

Bradley, David (Henry, Jr.)
1950- .... **CLC 23; BLC**
See also BW 1; CA 104; CANR 26; DLB 33

Author Index

Bradley, John Ed(mund, Jr.)
1958- .... **CLC 55**
See also CA 139

Bradley, Marion Zimmer 1930-..... **CLC 30**
See also AAYA 9; CA 57-60; CAAS 10;
CANR 7, 31; DLB 8; MTCW

Bradstreet, Anne
1612(?)-1672 ...... **LC 4, 30; DA; PC 10**
See also CDALB 1640-1865; DLB 24

Brady, Joan 1939- .... **CLC 86**
See also CA 141

Bragg, Melvyn 1939- .... **CLC 10**
See also BEST 89:3; CA 57-60; CANR 10,
48; DLB 14

Braine, John (Gerard)
1922-1986 .... **CLC 1, 3, 41**
See also CA 1-4R; 120; CANR 1, 33;
CDBLB 1945-1960; DLB 15; DLBY 86;
MTCW

Brammer, William 1930(?)-1978 .... **CLC 31**
See also CA 77-80

Brancati, Vitaliano 1907-1954..... **TCLC 12**
See also CA 109

Brancato, Robin F(idler) 1936-..... **CLC 35**
See also AAYA 9; CA 69-72; CANR 11,
45; CLR 32; JRDA; SAAS 9; SATA 23

Brand, Max
See Faust, Frederick (Schiller)

Brand, Millen 1906-1980.......... **CLC 7**
See also CA 21-24R; 97-100

Branden, Barbara .... **CLC 44**
See also CA 148

Brandes, Georg (Morris Cohen)
1842-1927 .... **TCLC 10**
See also CA 105

Brandys, Kazimierz 1916- .... **CLC 62**

Branley, Franklyn M(ansfield)
1915- .... **CLC 21**
See also CA 33-36R; CANR 14, 39;
CLR 13; MAICYA; SAAS 16; SATA 4,
68

Brathwaite, Edward Kamau 1930-... **CLC 11**
See also BW 2; CA 25-28R; CANR 11, 26,
47; DLB 125

Brautigan, Richard (Gary)
1935-1984 ... **CLC 1, 3, 5, 9, 12, 34, 42**
See also CA 53-56; 113; CANR 34; DLB 2,
5; DLBY 80, 84; MTCW; SATA 56

Braverman, Kate 1950- .... **CLC 67**
See also CA 89-92

Brecht, Bertolt
1898-1956 ...... **TCLC 1, 6, 13, 35; DA;
DAB; DC 3; WLC**
See also CA 104; 133; DLB 56, 124; MTCW

Brecht, Eugen Berthold Friedrich
See Brecht, Bertolt

Bremer, Fredrika 1801-1865 ..... **NCLC 11**

Brennan, Christopher John
1870-1932 .... **TCLC 17**
See also CA 117

Brennan, Maeve 1917-............ **CLC 5**
See also CA 81-84

Brentano, Clemens (Maria)
1778-1842 .... **NCLC 1**
See also DLB 90

Brent of Bin Bin
See Franklin, (Stella Maraia Sarah) Miles

Brenton, Howard 1942- .... **CLC 31**
See also CA 69-72; CANR 33; DLB 13;
MTCW

Breslin, James 1930-
See Breslin, Jimmy
See also CA 73-76; CANR 31; MTCW

Breslin, Jimmy .... **CLC 4, 43**
See also Breslin, James
See also AITN 1

Bresson, Robert 1901- .... **CLC 16**
See also CA 110; CANR 49

Breton, Andre 1896-1966... **CLC 2, 9, 15, 54**
See also CA 19-20; 25-28R; CANR 40;
CAP 2; DLB 65; MTCW

Breytenbach, Breyten 1939(?)- .. **CLC 23, 37**
See also CA 113; 129

Bridgers, Sue Ellen 1942- .... **CLC 26**
See also AAYA 8; CA 65-68; CANR 11,
36; CLR 18; DLB 52; JRDA; MAICYA;
SAAS 1; SATA 22

Bridges, Robert (Seymour)
1844-1930 .... **TCLC 1**
See also CA 104; CDBLB 1890-1914;
DLB 19, 98

Bridie, James.................... **TCLC 3**
See also Mavor, Osborne Henry
See also DLB 10

Brin, David 1950-............... **CLC 34**
See also CA 102; CANR 24; SATA 65

Brink, Andre (Philippus)
1935- .... **CLC 18, 36**
See also CA 104; CANR 39; MTCW

Brinsmead, H(esba) F(ay) 1922- .... **CLC 21**
See also CA 21-24R; CANR 10; MAICYA;
SAAS 5; SATA 18, 78

Brittain, Vera (Mary)
1893(?)-1970 .... **CLC 23**
See also CA 13-16; 25-28R; CAP 1; MTCW

Broch, Hermann 1886-1951....... **TCLC 20**
See also CA 117; DLB 85, 124

Brock, Rose
See Hansen, Joseph

Brodkey, Harold 1930-........... **CLC 56**
See also CA 111; DLB 130

Brodsky, Iosif Alexandrovich 1940-
See Brodsky, Joseph
See also AITN 1; CA 41-44R; CANR 37;
MTCW

Brodsky, Joseph .. **CLC 4, 6, 13, 36, 50; PC 9**
See also Brodsky, Iosif Alexandrovich

Brodsky, Michael Mark 1948- ..... **CLC 19**
See also CA 102; CANR 18, 41

Bromell, Henry 1947-............ **CLC 5**
See also CA 53-56; CANR 9

Bromfield, Louis (Brucker)
1896-1956 .... **TCLC 11**
See also CA 107; DLB 4, 9, 86

Broner, E(sther) M(asserman)
1930- .... **CLC 19**
See also CA 17-20R; CANR 8, 25; DLB 28

Bronk, William 1918-............ **CLC 10**
See also CA 89-92; CANR 23

Bronstein, Lev Davidovich
See Trotsky, Leon

Bronte, Anne 1820-1849......... **NCLC 4**
See also DLB 21

Bronte, Charlotte
1816-1855 .... **NCLC 3, 8, 33; DA;
DAB; WLC**
See also CDBLB 1832-1890; DLB 21

Bronte, Emily (Jane)
1818-1848 .... **NCLC 16, 35; DA; DAB;
PC 8; WLC**
See also CDBLB 1832-1890; DLB 21, 32

Brooke, Frances 1724-1789 .... **LC 6**
See also DLB 39, 99

Brooke, Henry 1703(?)-1783 .... **LC 1**
See also DLB 39

Brooke, Rupert (Chawner)
1887-1915 .... **TCLC 2, 7; DA; DAB;
WLC**
See also CA 104; 132; CDBLB 1914-1945;
DLB 19; MTCW

Brooke-Haven, P.
See Wodehouse, P(elham) G(renville)

Brooke-Rose, Christine 1926- ...... **CLC 40**
See also CA 13-16R; DLB 14

Brookner, Anita
1928- .... **CLC 32, 34, 51; DAB**
See also CA 114; 120; CANR 37; DLBY 87;
MTCW

Brooks, Cleanth 1906-1994 ..... **CLC 24, 86**
See also CA 17-20R; 145; CANR 33, 35;
DLB 63; DLBY 94; MTCW

Brooks, George
See Baum, L(yman) Frank

Brooks, Gwendolyn
1917- ...... **CLC 1, 2, 4, 5, 15, 49; BLC;
DA; PC 7; WLC**
See also AITN 1; BW 2; CA 1-4R;
CANR 1, 27; CDALB 1941-1968;
CLR 27; DLB 5, 76; MTCW; SATA 6

Brooks, Mel..................... **CLC 12**
See also Kaminsky, Melvin
See also AAYA 13; DLB 26

Brooks, Peter 1938-.............. **CLC 34**
See also CA 45-48; CANR 1

Brooks, Van Wyck 1886-1963...... **CLC 29**
See also CA 1-4R; CANR 6; DLB 45, 63,
103

Brophy, Brigid (Antonia)
1929- .... **CLC 6, 11, 29**
See also CA 5-8R; CAAS 4; CANR 25;
DLB 14; MTCW

Brosman, Catharine Savage 1934-.... **CLC 9**
See also CA 61-64; CANR 21, 46

Brother Antoninus
See Everson, William (Oliver)

Broughton, T(homas) Alan 1936- ... **CLC 19**
See also CA 45-48; CANR 2, 23, 48

Broumas, Olga 1949-.......... **CLC 10, 73**
See also CA 85-88; CANR 20

Brown, Charles Brockden
1771-1810 .... **NCLC 22**
See also CDALB 1640-1865; DLB 37, 59,
73

Brown, Christy 1932-1981 . . . . **CLC 63**
See also CA 105; 104; DLB 14

Brown, Claude 1937- . . . . **CLC 30; BLC**
See also AAYA 7; BW 1; CA 73-76

Brown, Dee (Alexander) 1908- . . **CLC 18, 47**
See also CA 13-16R; CAAS 6; CANR 11,
45; DLBY 80; MTCW; SATA 5

Brown, George
See Wertmueller, Lina

Brown, George Douglas
1869-1902 . . . . **TCLC 28**

Brown, George Mackay 1921- . . . . **CLC 5, 48**
See also CA 21-24R; CAAS 6; CANR 12,
37; DLB 14, 27, 139; MTCW; SATA 35

Brown, (William) Larry 1951- . . . . . . **CLC 73**
See also CA 130; 134

Brown, Moses
See Barrett, William (Christopher)

Brown, Rita Mae 1944- . . . . . **CLC 18, 43, 79**
See also CA 45-48; CANR 2, 11, 35;
MTCW

Brown, Roderick (Langmere) Haig-
See Haig-Brown, Roderick (Langmere)

Brown, Rosellen 1939- . . . . **CLC 32**
See also CA 77-80; CAAS 10; CANR 14, 44

Brown, Sterling Allen
1901-1989 . . . . **CLC 1, 23, 59; BLC**
See also BW 1; CA 85-88; 127; CANR 26;
DLB 48, 51, 63; MTCW

Brown, Will
See Ainsworth, William Harrison

Brown, William Wells
1813-1884 . . . . **NCLC 2; BLC; DC 1**
See also DLB 3, 50

Browne, (Clyde) Jackson 1948(?)- . . . **CLC 21**
See also CA 120

Browning, Elizabeth Barrett
1806-1861 . . . . . **NCLC 1, 16; DA; DAB;
PC 6; WLC**
See also CDBLB 1832-1890; DLB 32

Browning, Robert
1812-1889 . . **NCLC 19; DA; DAB; PC 2**
See also CDBLB 1832-1890; DLB 32;
YABC 1

Browning, Tod 1882-1962 . . . . **CLC 16**
See also CA 141; 117

Brownson, Orestes (Augustus)
1803-1876 . . . . **NCLC 50**

Bruccoli, Matthew J(oseph) 1931- . . **CLC 34**
See also CA 9-12R; CANR 7; DLB 103

Bruce, Lenny . . . . **CLC 21**
See also Schneider, Leonard Alfred

Bruin, John
See Brutus, Dennis

Brulard, Henri
See Stendhal

Brulls, Christian
See Simenon, Georges (Jacques Christian)

Brunner, John (Kilian Houston)
1934- . . . . **CLC 8, 10**
See also CA 1-4R; CAAS 8; CANR 2, 37;
MTCW

Bruno, Giordano 1548-1600 . . . . **LC 27**

Brutus, Dennis 1924- . . . . **CLC 43; BLC**
See also BW 2; CA 49-52; CAAS 14;
CANR 2, 27, 42; DLB 117

Bryan, C(ourtlandt) D(ixon) B(arnes)
1936- . . . . **CLC 29**
See also CA 73-76; CANR 13

Bryan, Michael
See Moore, Brian

Bryant, William Cullen
1794-1878 . . . . . . **NCLC 6, 46; DA; DAB**
See also CDALB 1640-1865; DLB 3, 43, 59

Bryusov, Valery Yakovlevich
1873-1924 . . . . **TCLC 10**
See also CA 107

Buchan, John 1875-1940 . . . **TCLC 41; DAB**
See also CA 108; 145; DLB 34, 70; YABC 2

Buchanan, George 1506-1582 . . . . **LC 4**

Buchheim, Lothar-Guenther 1918- . . . **CLC 6**
See also CA 85-88

Buchner, (Karl) Georg
1813-1837 . . . . **NCLC 26**

Buchwald, Art(hur) 1925- . . . . **CLC 33**
See also AITN 1; CA 5-8R; CANR 21;
MTCW; SATA 10

Buck, Pearl S(ydenstricker)
1892-1973 . . . . **CLC 7, 11, 18; DA; DAB**
See also AITN 1; CA 1-4R; 41-44R;
CANR 1, 34; DLB 9, 102; MTCW;
SATA 1, 25

Buckler, Ernest 1908-1984 . . . . **CLC 13**
See also CA 11-12; 114; CAP 1; DLB 68;
SATA 47

Buckley, Vincent (Thomas)
1925-1988 . . . . **CLC 57**
See also CA 101

Buckley, William F(rank), Jr.
1925- . . . . **CLC 7, 18, 37**
See also AITN 1; CA 1-4R; CANR 1, 24;
DLB 137; DLBY 80; MTCW

Buechner, (Carl) Frederick
1926- . . . . **CLC 2, 4, 6, 9**
See also CA 13-16R; CANR 11, 39;
DLBY 80; MTCW

Buell, John (Edward) 1927- . . . . **CLC 10**
See also CA 1-4R; DLB 53

Buero Vallejo, Antonio 1916- . . . **CLC 15, 46**
See also CA 106; CANR 24, 49; HW;
MTCW

Bufalino, Gesualdo 1920(?)- . . . . **CLC 74**

Bugayev, Boris Nikolayevich 1880-1934
See Bely, Andrey
See also CA 104

Bukowski, Charles
1920-1994 . . . . **CLC 2, 5, 9, 41, 82**
See also CA 17-20R; 144; CANR 40;
DLB 5, 130; MTCW

Bulgakov, Mikhail (Afanas'evich)
1891-1940 . . . . **TCLC 2, 16; SSC 18**
See also CA 105

Bulgya, Alexander Alexandrovich
1901-1956 . . . . **TCLC 53**
See also Fadeyev, Alexander
See also CA 117

Bullins, Ed 1935- . . . . **CLC 1, 5, 7; BLC**
See also BW 2; CA 49-52; CAAS 16;
CANR 24, 46; DLB 7, 38; MTCW

Bulwer-Lytton, Edward (George Earle Lytton)
1803-1873 . . . . **NCLC 1, 45**
See also DLB 21

Bunin, Ivan Alexeyevich
1870-1953 . . . . **TCLC 6; SSC 5**
See also CA 104

Bunting, Basil 1900-1985 . . . . **CLC 10, 39, 47**
See also CA 53-56; 115; CANR 7; DLB 20

Bunuel, Luis 1900-1983 . . **CLC 16, 80; HLC**
See also CA 101; 110; CANR 32; HW

Bunyan, John
1628-1688 . . . . . . **LC 4; DA; DAB; WLC**
See also CDBLB 1660-1789; DLB 39

Burckhardt, Jacob (Christoph)
1818-1897 . . . . **NCLC 49**

Burford, Eleanor
See Hibbert, Eleanor Alice Burford

Burgess, Anthony
. **CLC 1, 2, 4, 5, 8, 10, 13, 15, 22, 40, 62,
81; DAB**
See also Wilson, John (Anthony) Burgess
See also AITN 1; CDBLB 1960 to Present;
DLB 14

Burke, Edmund
1729(?)-1797 . . . . **LC 7; DA; DAB; WLC**
See also DLB 104

Burke, Kenneth (Duva)
1897-1993 . . . . **CLC 2, 24**
See also CA 5-8R; 143; CANR 39; DLB 45,
63; MTCW

Burke, Leda
See Garnett, David

Burke, Ralph
See Silverberg, Robert

Burney, Fanny 1752-1840 . . . . **NCLC 12**
See also DLB 39

Burns, Robert 1759-1796 . . . . **PC 6**
See also CDBLB 1789-1832; DA; DAB;
DLB 109; WLC

Burns, Tex
See L'Amour, Louis (Dearborn)

Burnshaw, Stanley 1906- . . . . . **CLC 3, 13, 44**
See also CA 9-12R; DLB 48

Burr, Anne 1937- . . . . **CLC 6**
See also CA 25-28R

Burroughs, Edgar Rice
1875-1950 . . . . **TCLC 2, 32**
See also AAYA 11; CA 104; 132; DLB 8;
MTCW; SATA 41

Burroughs, William S(eward)
1914- . . . . **CLC 1, 2, 5, 15, 22, 42, 75;
DA; DAB; WLC**
See also AITN 2; CA 9-12R; CANR 20;
DLB 2, 8, 16, 152; DLBY 81; MTCW

Burton, Richard F. 1821-1890 . . . . **NCLC 42**
See also DLB 55

Busch, Frederick 1941- . . . **CLC 7, 10, 18, 47**
See also CA 33-36R; CAAS 1; CANR 45;
DLB 6

Bush, Ronald 1946- . . . . **CLC 34**
See also CA 136

Bustos, F(rancisco)
See Borges, Jorge Luis

Bustos Domecq, H(onorio)
See Bioy Casares, Adolfo; Borges, Jorge
Luis

Butler, Octavia E(stelle) 1947- . . . . . **CLC 38**
See also BW 2; CA 73-76; CANR 12, 24,
38; DLB 33; MTCW

Butler, Robert Olen (Jr.) 1945- . . . . . **CLC 81**
See also CA 112

Butler, Samuel 1612-1680 . . . . **LC 16**
See also DLB 101, 126

Butler, Samuel
1835-1902 . . . . . . **TCLC 1, 33; DA; DAB;**
WLC
See also CA 143; CDBLB 1890-1914;
DLB 18, 57

Butler, Walter C.
See Faust, Frederick (Schiller)

Butor, Michel (Marie Francois)
1926- . . . . **CLC 1, 3, 8, 11, 15**
See also CA 9-12R; CANR 33; DLB 83;
MTCW

Buzo, Alexander (John) 1944- . . . . . . **CLC 61**
See also CA 97-100; CANR 17, 39

Buzzati, Dino 1906-1972 . . . . **CLC 36**
See also CA 33-36R

Byars, Betsy (Cromer) 1928- . . . . **CLC 35**
See also CA 33-36R; CANR 18, 36; CLR 1,
16; DLB 52; JRDA; MAICYA; MTCW;
SAAS 1; SATA 4, 46, 80

Byatt, A(ntonia) S(usan Drabble)
1936- . . . . **CLC 19, 65**
See also CA 13-16R; CANR 13, 33;
DLB 14; MTCW

Byrne, David 1952- . . . . **CLC 26**
See also CA 127

Byrne, John Keyes 1926-
See Leonard, Hugh
See also CA 102

Byron, George Gordon (Noel)
1788-1824 . . . . . **NCLC 2, 12; DA; DAB;**
WLC
See also CDBLB 1789-1832; DLB 96, 110

C. 3. 3.
See Wilde, Oscar (Fingal O'Flahertie Wills)

Caballero, Fernan 1796-1877 . . . . . **NCLC 10**

Cabell, James Branch 1879-1958 . . . **TCLC 6**
See also CA 105; DLB 9, 78

Cable, George Washington
1844-1925 . . . . **TCLC 4; SSC 4**
See also CA 104; DLB 12, 74

Cabral de Melo Neto, Joao 1920- . . . **CLC 76**

Cabrera Infante, G(uillermo)
1929- . . . . **CLC 5, 25, 45; HLC**
See also CA 85-88; CANR 29; DLB 113;
HW; MTCW

Cade, Toni
See Bambara, Toni Cade

Cadmus and Harmonia
See Buchan, John

Caedmon fl. 658-680 . . . . **CMLC 7**
See also DLB 146

Caeiro, Alberto
See Pessoa, Fernando (Antonio Nogueira)

Cage, John (Milton, Jr.) 1912- . . . . . **CLC 41**
See also CA 13-16R; CANR 9

Cain, G.
See Cabrera Infante, G(uillermo)

Cain, Guillermo
See Cabrera Infante, G(uillermo)

Cain, James M(allahan)
1892-1977 . . . . **CLC 3, 11, 28**
See also AITN 1; CA 17-20R; 73-76;
CANR 8, 34; MTCW

Caine, Mark
See Raphael, Frederic (Michael)

Calasso, Roberto 1941- . . . . **CLC 81**
See also CA 143

Calderon de la Barca, Pedro
1600-1681 . . . . **LC 23; DC 3**

Caldwell, Erskine (Preston)
1903-1987 . . . . **CLC 1, 8, 14, 50, 60;**
SSC 19
See also AITN 1; CA 1-4R; 121; CAAS 1;
CANR 2, 33; DLB 9, 86; MTCW

Caldwell, (Janet Miriam) Taylor (Holland)
1900-1985 . . . . **CLC 2, 28, 39**
See also CA 5-8R; 116; CANR 5

Calhoun, John Caldwell
1782-1850 . . . . **NCLC 15**
See also DLB 3

Calisher, Hortense
1911- . . . . **CLC 2, 4, 8, 38; SSC 15**
See also CA 1-4R; CANR 1, 22; DLB 2;
MTCW

Callaghan, Morley Edward
1903-1990 . . . . **CLC 3, 14, 41, 65**
See also CA 9-12R; 132; CANR 33;
DLB 68; MTCW

Calvino, Italo
1923-1985 . . . . . **CLC 5, 8, 11, 22, 33, 39,**
73; SSC 3
See also CA 85-88; 116; CANR 23; MTCW

Cameron, Carey 1952- . . . . **CLC 59**
See also CA 135

Cameron, Peter 1959- . . . . **CLC 44**
See also CA 125

Campana, Dino 1885-1932 . . . . **TCLC 20**
See also CA 117; DLB 114

Campbell, John W(ood, Jr.)
1910-1971 . . . . **CLC 32**
See also CA 21-22; 29-32R; CANR 34;
CAP 2; DLB 8; MTCW

Campbell, Joseph 1904-1987 . . . . . . **CLC 69**
See also AAYA 3; BEST 89:2; CA 1-4R;
124; CANR 3, 28; MTCW

Campbell, Maria 1940- . . . . **CLC 85**
See also CA 102; NNAL

Campbell, (John) Ramsey
1946- . . . . **CLC 42; SSC 19**
See also CA 57-60; CANR 7

Campbell, (Ignatius) Roy (Dunnachie)
1901-1957 . . . . **TCLC 5**
See also CA 104; DLB 20

Campbell, Thomas 1777-1844 . . . . **NCLC 19**
See also DLB 93; 144

Campbell, Wilfred . . . . **TCLC 9**
See also Campbell, William

Campbell, William 1858(?)-1918
See Campbell, Wilfred
See also CA 106; DLB 92

Campos, Alvaro de
See Pessoa, Fernando (Antonio Nogueira)

Camus, Albert
1913-1960 . . . . **CLC 1, 2, 4, 9, 11, 14, 32,**
63, 69; DA; DAB; DC 2; SSC 9; WLC
See also CA 89-92; DLB 72; MTCW

Canby, Vincent 1924- . . . . **CLC 13**
See also CA 81-84

Cancale
See Desnos, Robert

Canetti, Elias
1905-1994 . . . . **CLC 3, 14, 25, 75, 86**
See also CA 21-24R; 146; CANR 23;
DLB 85, 124; MTCW

Canin, Ethan 1960- . . . . **CLC 55**
See also CA 131; 135

Cannon, Curt
See Hunter, Evan

Cape, Judith
See Page, P(atricia) K(athleen)

Capek, Karel
1890-1938 . . . . . . **TCLC 6, 37; DA; DAB;**
DC 1; WLC
See also CA 104; 140

Capote, Truman
1924-1984 . . . . . . **CLC 1, 3, 8, 13, 19, 34,**
38, 58; DA; DAB; SSC 2; WLC
See also CA 5-8R; 113; CANR 18;
CDALB 1941-1968; DLB 2; DLBY 80,
84; MTCW

Capra, Frank 1897-1991 . . . . **CLC 16**
See also CA 61-64; 135

Caputo, Philip 1941- . . . . **CLC 32**
See also CA 73-76; CANR 40

Card, Orson Scott 1951- . . . . **CLC 44, 47, 50**
See also AAYA 11; CA 102; CANR 27, 47;
MTCW; SATA 83

Cardenal (Martinez), Ernesto
1925- . . . . **CLC 31; HLC**
See also CA 49-52; CANR 2, 32; HW;
MTCW

Carducci, Giosue 1835-1907 . . . . **TCLC 32**

Carew, Thomas 1595(?)-1640 . . . . **LC 13**
See also DLB 126

Carey, Ernestine Gilbreth 1908- . . . . **CLC 17**
See also CA 5-8R; SATA 2

Carey, Peter 1943- . . . . **CLC 40, 55**
See also CA 123; 127; MTCW

Carleton, William 1794-1869 . . . . . . **NCLC 3**

Carlisle, Henry (Coffin) 1926- . . . . . . **CLC 33**
See also CA 13-16R; CANR 15

Carlsen, Chris
See Holdstock, Robert P.

Carlson, Ron(ald F.) 1947- . . . . **CLC 54**
See also CA 105; CANR 27

Carlyle, Thomas
1795-1881 . . . . **NCLC 22; DA; DAB**
See also CDBLB 1789-1832; DLB 55; 144

Carman, (William) Bliss
1861-1929 .... TCLC 7
See also CA 104; DLB 92

Carnegie, Dale 1888-1955 .... TCLC 53

Carossa, Hans 1878-1956........ TCLC 48
See also DLB 66

Carpenter, Don(ald Richard)
1931- .... CLC 41
See also CA 45-48; CANR 1

Carpentier (y Valmont), Alejo
1904-1980 .... CLC 8, 11, 38; HLC
See also CA 65-68; 97-100; CANR 11;
DLB 113; HW

Carr, Caleb 1955(?)-.............. CLC 86
See also CA 147

Carr, Emily 1871-1945........... TCLC 32
See also DLB 68

Carr, John Dickson 1906-1977 ...... CLC 3
See also CA 49-52; 69-72; CANR 3, 33;
MTCW

Carr, Philippa
See Hibbert, Eleanor Alice Burford

Carr, Virginia Spencer 1929-....... CLC 34
See also CA 61-64; DLB 111

Carrere, Emmanuel 1957- .... CLC 89

Carrier, Roch 1937-........... CLC 13, 78
See also CA 130; DLB 53

Carroll, James P. 1943(?)-........ CLC 38
See also CA 81-84

Carroll, Jim 1951- .... CLC 35
See also CA 45-48; CANR 42

Carroll, Lewis .... NCLC 2; WLC
See also Dodgson, Charles Lutwidge
See also CDBLB 1832-1890; CLR 2, 18;
DLB 18; JRDA

Carroll, Paul Vincent 1900-1968.... CLC 10
See also CA 9-12R; 25-28R; DLB 10

Carruth, Hayden
1921- ...... CLC 4, 7, 10, 18, 84; PC 10
See also CA 9-12R; CANR 4, 38; DLB 5;
MTCW; SATA 47

Carson, Rachel Louise 1907-1964... CLC 71
See also CA 77-80; CANR 35; MTCW;
SATA 23

Carter, Angela (Olive)
1940-1992 ...... CLC 5, 41, 76; SSC 13
See also CA 53-56; 136; CANR 12, 36;
DLB 14; MTCW; SATA 66;
SATA-Obit 70

Carter, Nick
See Smith, Martin Cruz

Carver, Raymond
1938-1988 ... CLC 22, 36, 53, 55; SSC 8
See also CA 33-36R; 126; CANR 17, 34;
DLB 130; DLBY 84, 88; MTCW

Cary, Elizabeth 1585-1639......... LC 30

Cary, (Arthur) Joyce (Lunel)
1888-1957 .... TCLC 1, 29
See also CA 104; CDBLB 1914-1945;
DLB 15, 100

Casanova de Seingalt, Giovanni Jacopo
1725-1798 .... LC 13

Casares, Adolfo Bioy
See Bioy Casares, Adolfo

Casely-Hayford, J(oseph) E(phraim)
1866-1930 .... TCLC 24; BLC
See also BW 2; CA 123

Casey, John (Dudley) 1939-........ CLC 59
See also BEST 90:2; CA 69-72; CANR 23

Casey, Michael 1947-.............. CLC 2
See also CA 65-68; DLB 5

Casey, Patrick
See Thurman, Wallace (Henry)

Casey, Warren (Peter) 1935-1988... CLC 12
See also CA 101; 127

Casona, Alejandro................. CLC 49
See also Alvarez, Alejandro Rodriguez

Cassavetes, John 1929-1989....... CLC 20
See also CA 85-88; 127

Cassill, R(onald) V(erlin) 1919-... CLC 4, 23
See also CA 9-12R; CAAS 1; CANR 7, 45;
DLB 6

Cassity, (Allen) Turner 1929- .... CLC 6, 42
See also CA 17-20R; CAAS 8; CANR 11;
DLB 105

Castaneda, Carlos 1931(?)-........ CLC 12
See also CA 25-28R; CANR 32; HW;
MTCW

Castedo, Elena 1937- .... CLC 65
See also CA 132

Castedo-Ellerman, Elena
See Castedo, Elena

Castellanos, Rosario
1925-1974 .... CLC 66; HLC
See also CA 131; 53-56; DLB 113; HW

Castelvetro, Lodovico 1505-1571..... LC 12

Castiglione, Baldassare 1478-1529 ... LC 12

Castle, Robert
See Hamilton, Edmond

Castro, Guillen de 1569-1631........ LC 19

Castro, Rosalia de 1837-1885 ..... NCLC 3

Cather, Willa
See Cather, Willa Sibert

Cather, Willa Sibert
1873-1947 .... TCLC 1, 11, 31; DA;
DAB; SSC 2; WLC
See also CA 104; 128; CDALB 1865-1917;
DLB 9, 54, 78; DLBD 1; MTCW;
SATA 30

Catton, (Charles) Bruce
1899-1978 .... CLC 35
See also AITN 1; CA 5-8R; 81-84;
CANR 7; DLB 17; SATA 2;
SATA-Obit 24

Cauldwell, Frank
See King, Francis (Henry)

Caunitz, William J. 1933- .... CLC 34
See also BEST 89:3; CA 125; 130

Causley, Charles (Stanley) 1917-..... CLC 7
See also CA 9-12R; CANR 5, 35; CLR 30;
DLB 27; MTCW; SATA 3, 66

Caute, David 1936-.............. CLC 29
See also CA 1-4R; CAAS 4; CANR 1, 33;
DLB 14

Cavafy, C(onstantine) P(eter)
1863-1933 .... TCLC 2, 7
See also Kavafis, Konstantinos Petrou
See also CA 148

Cavallo, Evelyn
See Spark, Muriel (Sarah)

Cavanna, Betty .... CLC 12
See also Harrison, Elizabeth Cavanna
See also JRDA; MAICYA; SAAS 4;
SATA 1, 30

Cavendish, Margaret Lucas
1623-1673 .... LC 30
See also DLB 131

Caxton, William 1421(?)-1491(?)..... LC 17

Cayrol, Jean 1911-............... CLC 11
See also CA 89-92; DLB 83

Cela, Camilo Jose
1916- .... CLC 4, 13, 59; HLC
See also BEST 90:2; CA 21-24R; CAAS 10;
CANR 21, 32; DLBY 89; HW; MTCW

Celan, Paul ...... CLC 10, 19, 53, 82; PC 10
See also Antschel, Paul
See also DLB 69

Celine, Louis-Ferdinand
.... CLC 1, 3, 4, 7, 9, 15, 47
See also Destouches, Louis-Ferdinand
See also DLB 72

Cellini, Benvenuto 1500-1571 .... LC 7

Cendrars, Blaise .... CLC 18
See also Sauser-Hall, Frederic

Cernuda (y Bidon), Luis
1902-1963 .... CLC 54
See also CA 131; 89-92; DLB 134; HW

Cervantes (Saavedra), Miguel de
1547-1616 .... LC 6, 23; DA; DAB;
SSC 12; WLC

Cesaire, Aime (Fernand)
1913- .... CLC 19, 32; BLC
See also BW 2; CA 65-68; CANR 24, 43;
MTCW

Chabon, Michael 1965(?)- .... CLC 55
See also CA 139

Chabrol, Claude 1930-............ CLC 16
See also CA 110

Challans, Mary 1905-1983
See Renault, Mary
See also CA 81-84; 111; SATA 23;
SATA-Obit 36

Challis, George
See Faust, Frederick (Schiller)

Chambers, Aidan 1934- .... CLC 35
See also CA 25-28R; CANR 12, 31; JRDA;
MAICYA; SAAS 12; SATA 1, 69

Chambers, James 1948-
See Cliff, Jimmy
See also CA 124

Chambers, Jessie
See Lawrence, D(avid) H(erbert Richards)

Chambers, Robert W. 1865-1933... TCLC 41

Chandler, Raymond (Thornton)
1888-1959 .... TCLC 1, 7
See also CA 104; 129; CDALB 1929-1941;
DLBD 6; MTCW

Chang, Jung 1952-............... CLC 71
See also CA 142

Channing, William Ellery
1780-1842 .... NCLC 17
See also DLB 1, 59

Chaplin, Charles Spencer
1889-1977 . . . . **CLC 16**
See also Chaplin, Charlie
See also CA 81-84; 73-76

Chaplin, Charlie
See Chaplin, Charles Spencer
See also DLB 44

Chapman, George 1559(?)-1634 . . . . . . **LC 22**
See also DLB 62, 121

Chapman, Graham 1941-1989 . . . . . **CLC 21**
See also Monty Python
See also CA 116; 129; CANR 35

Chapman, John Jay 1862-1933 . . . . . **TCLC 7**
See also CA 104

Chapman, Walker
See Silverberg, Robert

Chappell, Fred (Davis) 1936- . . . . **CLC 40, 78**
See also CA 5-8R; CAAS 4; CANR 8, 33;
DLB 6, 105

Char, Rene(-Emile)
1907-1988 . . . . **CLC 9, 11, 14, 55**
See also CA 13-16R; 124; CANR 32;
MTCW

Charby, Jay
See Ellison, Harlan (Jay)

Chardin, Pierre Teilhard de
See Teilhard de Chardin, (Marie Joseph)
Pierre

Charles I 1600-1649 . . . . **LC 13**

Charyn, Jerome 1937- . . . . **CLC 5, 8, 18**
See also CA 5-8R; CAAS 1; CANR 7;
DLBY 83; MTCW

Chase, Mary (Coyle) 1907-1981 . . . . . . **DC 1**
See also CA 77-80; 105; SATA 17;
SATA-Obit 29

Chase, Mary Ellen 1887-1973 . . . . . . **CLC 2**
See also CA 13-16; 41-44R; CAP 1;
SATA 10

Chase, Nicholas
See Hyde, Anthony

Chateaubriand, Francois Rene de
1768-1848 . . . . **NCLC 3**
See also DLB 119

Chatterje, Sarat Chandra 1876-1936(?)
See Chatterji, Saratchandra
See also CA 109

Chatterji, Bankim Chandra
1838-1894 . . . . **NCLC 19**

Chatterji, Saratchandra . . . . **TCLC 13**
See also Chatterje, Sarat Chandra

Chatterton, Thomas 1752-1770 . . . . **LC 3**
See also DLB 109

Chatwin, (Charles) Bruce
1940-1989 . . . . **CLC 28, 57, 59**
See also AAYA 4; BEST 90:1; CA 85-88;
127

Chaucer, Daniel
See Ford, Ford Madox

Chaucer, Geoffrey
1340(?)-1400 . . . . **LC 17; DA; DAB**
See also CDBLB Before 1660; DLB 146

Chaviaras, Strates 1935-
See Haviaras, Stratis
See also CA 105

Chayefsky, Paddy . . . . **CLC 23**
See also Chayefsky, Sidney
See also DLB 7, 44; DLBY 81

Chayefsky, Sidney 1923-1981
See Chayefsky, Paddy
See also CA 9-12R; 104; CANR 18

Chedid, Andree 1920- . . . . **CLC 47**
See also CA 145

Cheever, John
1912-1982 . . . . . . **CLC 3, 7, 8, 11, 15, 25,
64; DA; DAB; SSC 1; WLC**
See also CA 5-8R; 106; CABS 1; CANR 5,
27; CDALB 1941-1968; DLB 2, 102;
DLBY 80, 82; MTCW

Cheever, Susan 1943- . . . . **CLC 18, 48**
See also CA 103; CANR 27; DLBY 82

Chekhonte, Antosha
See Chekhov, Anton (Pavlovich)

Chekhov, Anton (Pavlovich)
1860-1904 . . . . . **TCLC 3, 10, 31, 55; DA;
DAB; SSC 2; WLC**
See also CA 104; 124

Chernyshevsky, Nikolay Gavrilovich
1828-1889 . . . . **NCLC 1**

Cherry, Carolyn Janice 1942-
See Cherryh, C. J.
See also CA 65-68; CANR 10

Cherryh, C. J. . . . . **CLC 35**
See also Cherry, Carolyn Janice
See also DLBY 80

Chesnutt, Charles W(addell)
1858-1932 . . . . **TCLC 5, 39; BLC; SSC 7**
See also BW 1; CA 106; 125; DLB 12, 50,
78; MTCW

Chester, Alfred 1929(?)-1971 . . . . . . **CLC 49**
See also CA 33-36R; DLB 130

Chesterton, G(ilbert) K(eith)
1874-1936 . . . . **TCLC 1, 6; SSC 1**
See also CA 104; 132; CDBLB 1914-1945;
DLB 10, 19, 34, 70, 98, 149; MTCW;
SATA 27

Chiang Pin-chin 1904-1986
See Ding Ling
See also CA 118

Ch'ien Chung-shu 1910- . . . . **CLC 22**
See also CA 130; MTCW

Child, L. Maria
See Child, Lydia Maria

Child, Lydia Maria 1802-1880 . . . . **NCLC 6**
See also DLB 1, 74; SATA 67

Child, Mrs.
See Child, Lydia Maria

Child, Philip 1898-1978 . . . . **CLC 19, 68**
See also CA 13-14; CAP 1; SATA 47

Childress, Alice
1920-1994 . . **CLC 12, 15, 86; BLC; DC 4**
See also AAYA 8; BW 2; CA 45-48; 146;
CANR 3, 27; CLR 14; DLB 7, 38; JRDA;
MAICYA; MTCW; SATA 7, 48, 81

Chislett, (Margaret) Anne 1943- . . . . **CLC 34**

Chitty, Thomas Willes 1926- . . . . **CLC 11**
See also Hinde, Thomas
See also CA 5-8R

Chivers, Thomas Holley
1809-1858 . . . . **NCLC 49**
See also DLB 3

Chomette, Rene Lucien 1898-1981
See Clair, Rene
See also CA 103

Chopin, Kate
. . . . **TCLC 5, 14; DA; DAB; SSC 8**
See also Chopin, Katherine
See also CDALB 1865-1917; DLB 12, 78

Chopin, Katherine 1851-1904
See Chopin, Kate
See also CA 104; 122

Chretien de Troyes
c. 12th cent. - . . . . **CMLC 10**

Christie
See Ichikawa, Kon

Christie, Agatha (Mary Clarissa)
1890-1976 . . . . . . **CLC 1, 6, 8, 12, 39, 48;
DAB**
See also AAYA 9; AITN 1, 2; CA 17-20R;
61-64; CANR 10, 37; CDBLB 1914-1945;
DLB 13, 77; MTCW; SATA 36

Christie, (Ann) Philippa
See Pearce, Philippa
See also CA 5-8R; CANR 4

Christine de Pizan 1365(?)-1431(?) . . . . **LC 9**

Chubb, Elmer
See Masters, Edgar Lee

Chulkov, Mikhail Dmitrievich
1743-1792 . . . . **LC 2**
See also DLB 150

Churchill, Caryl 1938- . . . **CLC 31, 55; DC 5**
See also CA 102; CANR 22, 46; DLB 13;
MTCW

Churchill, Charles 1731-1764 . . . . **LC 3**
See also DLB 109

Chute, Carolyn 1947- . . . . **CLC 39**
See also CA 123

Ciardi, John (Anthony)
1916-1986 . . . . **CLC 10, 40, 44**
See also CA 5-8R; 118; CAAS 2; CANR 5,
33; CLR 19; DLB 5; DLBY 86;
MAICYA; MTCW; SATA 1, 65;
SATA-Obit 46

Cicero, Marcus Tullius
106B.C.-43B.C. . . . . **CMLC 3**

Cimino, Michael 1943- . . . . **CLC 16**
See also CA 105

Cioran, E(mil) M. 1911- . . . . **CLC 64**
See also CA 25-28R

Cisneros, Sandra 1954- . . . . . . **CLC 69; HLC**
See also AAYA 9; CA 131; DLB 122, 152;
HW

Clair, Rene . . . . **CLC 20**
See also Chomette, Rene Lucien

Clampitt, Amy 1920-1994 . . . . **CLC 32**
See also CA 110; 146; CANR 29; DLB 105

Clancy, Thomas L., Jr. 1947-
See Clancy, Tom
See also CA 125; 131; MTCW

Clancy, Tom . . . . **CLC 45**
See also Clancy, Thomas L., Jr.
See also AAYA 9; BEST 89:1, 90:1

Clare, John 1793-1864 . . . . . . **NCLC 9; DAB**
See also DLB 55, 96

Clarin
See Alas (y Urena), Leopoldo (Enrique Garcia)

Clark, Al C.
See Goines, Donald

Clark, (Robert) Brian 1932- . . . . **CLC 29**
See also CA 41-44R

Clark, Curt
See Westlake, Donald E(dwin)

Clark, Eleanor 1913- . . . . **CLC 5, 19**
See also CA 9-12R; CANR 41; DLB 6

Clark, J. P.
See Clark, John Pepper
See also DLB 117

Clark, John Pepper
1935- . . . . **CLC 38; BLC; DC 5**
See also Clark, J. P.
See also BW 1; CA 65-68; CANR 16

Clark, M. R.
See Clark, Mavis Thorpe

Clark, Mavis Thorpe 1909- . . . . **CLC 12**
See also CA 57-60; CANR 8, 37; CLR 30;
MAICYA; SAAS 5; SATA 8, 74

Clark, Walter Van Tilburg
1909-1971 . . . . **CLC 28**
See also CA 9-12R; 33-36R; DLB 9;
SATA 8

Clarke, Arthur C(harles)
1917- . . . . . . **CLC 1, 4, 13, 18, 35; SSC 3**
See also AAYA 4; CA 1-4R; CANR 2, 28;
JRDA; MAICYA; MTCW; SATA 13, 70

Clarke, Austin 1896-1974 . . . . **CLC 6, 9**
See also CA 29-32; 49-52; CAP 2; DLB 10,
20

Clarke, Austin C(hesterfield)
1934- . . . . **CLC 8, 53; BLC**
See also BW 1; CA 25-28R; CAAS 16;
CANR 14, 32; DLB 53, 125

Clarke, Gillian 1937- . . . . **CLC 61**
See also CA 106; DLB 40

Clarke, Marcus (Andrew Hislop)
1846-1881 . . . . **NCLC 19**

Clarke, Shirley 1925- . . . . **CLC 16**

Clash, The
See Headon, (Nicky) Topper; Jones, Mick;
Simonon, Paul; Strummer, Joe

Claudel, Paul (Louis Charles Marie)
1868-1955 . . . . **TCLC 2, 10**
See also CA 104

Clavell, James (duMaresq)
1925-1994 . . . . **CLC 6, 25, 87**
See also CA 25-28R; 146; CANR 26, 48;
MTCW

Cleaver, (Leroy) Eldridge
1935- . . . . **CLC 30; BLC**
See also BW 1; CA 21-24R; CANR 16

Cleese, John (Marwood) 1939- . . . . . **CLC 21**
See also Monty Python
See also CA 112; 116; CANR 35; MTCW

Cleishbotham, Jebediah
See Scott, Walter

Cleland, John 1710-1789 . . . . **LC 2**
See also DLB 39

Clemens, Samuel Langhorne 1835-1910
See Twain, Mark
See also CA 104; 135; CDALB 1865-1917;
DA; DAB; DLB 11, 12, 23, 64, 74;
JRDA; MAICYA; YABC 2

Cleophil
See Congreve, William

Clerihew, E.
See Bentley, E(dmund) C(lerihew)

Clerk, N. W.
See Lewis, C(live) S(taples)

Cliff, Jimmy . . . . **CLC 21**
See also Chambers, James

Clifton, (Thelma) Lucille
1936- . . . . **CLC 19, 66; BLC**
See also BW 2; CA 49-52; CANR 2, 24, 42;
CLR 5; DLB 5, 41; MAICYA; MTCW;
SATA 20, 69

Clinton, Dirk
See Silverberg, Robert

Clough, Arthur Hugh 1819-1861 . . **NCLC 27**
See also DLB 32

Clutha, Janet Paterson Frame 1924-
See Frame, Janet
See also CA 1-4R; CANR 2, 36; MTCW

Clyne, Terence
See Blatty, William Peter

Cobalt, Martin
See Mayne, William (James Carter)

Cobbett, William 1763-1835 . . . . . **NCLC 49**
See also DLB 43, 107

Coburn, D(onald) L(ee) 1938- . . . . . . **CLC 10**
See also CA 89-92

Cocteau, Jean (Maurice Eugene Clement)
1889-1963 . . . . **CLC 1, 8, 15, 16, 43; DA;
DAB; WLC**
See also CA 25-28; CANR 40; CAP 2;
DLB 65; MTCW

Codrescu, Andrei 1946- . . . . **CLC 46**
See also CA 33-36R; CAAS 19; CANR 13,
34

Coe, Max
See Bourne, Randolph S(illiman)

Coe, Tucker
See Westlake, Donald E(dwin)

Coetzee, J(ohn) M(ichael)
1940- . . . . **CLC 23, 33, 66**
See also CA 77-80; CANR 41; MTCW

Coffey, Brian
See Koontz, Dean R(ay)

Cohan, George M. 1878-1942 . . . . . **TCLC 60**

Cohen, Arthur A(llen)
1928-1986 . . . . **CLC 7, 31**
See also CA 1-4R; 120; CANR 1, 17, 42;
DLB 28

Cohen, Leonard (Norman)
1934- . . . . **CLC 3, 38**
See also CA 21-24R; CANR 14; DLB 53;
MTCW

Cohen, Matt 1942- . . . . **CLC 19**
See also CA 61-64; CAAS 18; CANR 40;
DLB 53

Cohen-Solal, Annie 19(?)- . . . . **CLC 50**

Colegate, Isabel 1931- . . . . **CLC 36**
See also CA 17-20R; CANR 8, 22; DLB 14;
MTCW

Coleman, Emmett
See Reed, Ishmael

Coleridge, Samuel Taylor
1772-1834 . . . . **NCLC 9; DA; DAB;
PC 11; WLC**
See also CDBLB 1789-1832; DLB 93, 107

Coleridge, Sara 1802-1852 . . . . . . **NCLC 31**

Coles, Don 1928- . . . . **CLC 46**
See also CA 115; CANR 38

Colette, (Sidonie-Gabrielle)
1873-1954 . . . . . . **TCLC 1, 5, 16; SSC 10**
See also CA 104; 131; DLB 65; MTCW

Collett, (Jacobine) Camilla (Wergeland)
1813-1895 . . . . **NCLC 22**

Collier, Christopher 1930- . . . . **CLC 30**
See also AAYA 13; CA 33-36R; CANR 13,
33; JRDA; MAICYA; SATA 16, 70

Collier, James L(incoln) 1928- . . . . . **CLC 30**
See also AAYA 13; CA 9-12R; CANR 4,
33; CLR 3; JRDA; MAICYA; SATA 8,
70

Collier, Jeremy 1650-1726 . . . . **LC 6**

Collier, John 1901-1980
See also CA 65-68; 97-100; CANR 10;
DLB 77; SSC 19

Collins, Hunt
See Hunter, Evan

Collins, Linda 1931- . . . . **CLC 44**
See also CA 125

Collins, (William) Wilkie
1824-1889 . . . . **NCLC 1, 18**
See also CDBLB 1832-1890; DLB 18, 70

Collins, William 1721-1759 . . . . **LC 4**
See also DLB 109

Colman, George
See Glassco, John

Colt, Winchester Remington
See Hubbard, L(afayette) Ron(ald)

Colter, Cyrus 1910- . . . . **CLC 58**
See also BW 1; CA 65-68; CANR 10;
DLB 33

Colton, James
See Hansen, Joseph

Colum, Padraic 1881-1972 . . . . **CLC 28**
See also CA 73-76; 33-36R; CANR 35;
CLR 36; MAICYA; MTCW; SATA 15

Colvin, James
See Moorcock, Michael (John)

Colwin, Laurie (E.)
1944-1992 . . . . **CLC 5, 13, 23, 84**
See also CA 89-92; 139; CANR 20, 46;
DLBY 80; MTCW

Comfort, Alex(ander) 1920- . . . . **CLC 7**
See also CA 1-4R; CANR 1, 45

Comfort, Montgomery
See Campbell, (John) Ramsey

Compton-Burnett, I(vy)
1884(?)-1969 . . . . . . **CLC 1, 3, 10, 15, 34**
See also CA 1-4R; 25-28R; CANR 4;
DLB 36; MTCW

Comstock, Anthony 1844-1915 .... **TCLC 13**
See also CA 110

Conan Doyle, Arthur
See Doyle, Arthur Conan

Conde, Maryse 1937- .... **CLC 52**
See also Boucolon, Maryse
See also BW 2

Condillac, Etienne Bonnot de
1714-1780 .... **LC 26**

Condon, Richard (Thomas)
1915- .... **CLC 4, 6, 8, 10, 45**
See also BEST 90:3; CA 1-4R; CAAS 1;
CANR 2, 23; MTCW

Congreve, William
1670-1729 .... **LC 5, 21; DA; DAB;
DC 2; WLC**
See also CDBLB 1660-1789; DLB 39, 84

Connell, Evan S(helby), Jr.
1924- .... **CLC 4, 6, 45**
See also AAYA 7; CA 1-4R; CAAS 2;
CANR 2, 39; DLB 2; DLBY 81; MTCW

Connelly, Marc(us Cook)
1890-1980 .... **CLC 7**
See also CA 85-88; 102; CANR 30; DLB 7;
DLBY 80; SATA-Obit 25

Connor, Ralph .... **TCLC 31**
See also Gordon, Charles William
See also DLB 92

Conrad, Joseph
1857-1924 .... **TCLC 1, 6, 13, 25, 43, 57;
DA; DAB; SSC 9; WLC**
See also CA 104; 131; CDBLB 1890-1914;
DLB 10, 34, 98; MTCW; SATA 27

Conrad, Robert Arnold
See Hart, Moss

Conroy, Pat 1945- .... **CLC 30, 74**
See also AAYA 8; AITN 1; CA 85-88;
CANR 24; DLB 6; MTCW

Constant (de Rebecque), (Henri) Benjamin
1767-1830 .... **NCLC 6**
See also DLB 119

Conybeare, Charles Augustus
See Eliot, T(homas) S(tearns)

Cook, Michael 1933- .... **CLC 58**
See also CA 93-96; DLB 53

Cook, Robin 1940- .... **CLC 14**
See also BEST 90:2; CA 108; 111;
CANR 41

Cook, Roy
See Silverberg, Robert

Cooke, Elizabeth 1948- .... **CLC 55**
See also CA 129

Cooke, John Esten 1830-1886 ..... **NCLC 5**
See also DLB 3

Cooke, John Estes
See Baum, L(yman) Frank

Cooke, M. E.
See Creasey, John

Cooke, Margaret
See Creasey, John

Cooney, Ray .... **CLC 62**

Cooper, Douglas 1960- .... **CLC 86**

Cooper, Henry St. John
See Creasey, John

Cooper, J. California. .... **CLC 56**
See also AAYA 12; BW 1; CA 125

Cooper, James Fenimore
1789-1851 .... **NCLC 1, 27**
See also CDALB 1640-1865; DLB 3;
SATA 19

Coover, Robert (Lowell)
1932- .. **CLC 3, 7, 15, 32, 46, 87; SSC 15**
See also CA 45-48; CANR 3, 37; DLB 2;
DLBY 81; MTCW

Copeland, Stewart (Armstrong)
1952- .... **CLC 26**

Coppard, A(lfred) E(dgar)
1878-1957 .... **TCLC 5**
See also CA 114; YABC 1

Coppee, Francois 1842-1908 ...... **TCLC 25**

Coppola, Francis Ford 1939-....... **CLC 16**
See also CA 77-80; CANR 40; DLB 44

Corbiere, Tristan 1845-1875 ..... **NCLC 43**

Corcoran, Barbara 1911-.......... **CLC 17**
See also AAYA 14; CA 21-24R; CAAS 2;
CANR 11, 28, 48; DLB 52; JRDA;
SAAS 20; SATA 3, 77

Cordelier, Maurice
See Giraudoux, (Hippolyte) Jean

Corelli, Marie 1855-1924......... **TCLC 51**
See also Mackay, Mary
See also DLB 34

Corman, Cid. .... **CLC 9**
See also Corman, Sidney
See also CAAS 2; DLB 5

Corman, Sidney 1924-
See Corman, Cid
See also CA 85-88; CANR 44

Cormier, Robert (Edmund)
1925- .... **CLC 12, 30; DA; DAB**
See also AAYA 3; CA 1-4R; CANR 5, 23;
CDALB 1968-1988; CLR 12; DLB 52;
JRDA; MAICYA; MTCW; SATA 10, 45,
83

Corn, Alfred (DeWitt III) 1943-.... **CLC 33**
See also CA 104; CANR 44; DLB 120;
DLBY 80

Corneille, Pierre 1606-1684.... **LC 28; DAB**

Cornwell, David (John Moore)
1931- .... **CLC 9, 15**
See also le Carre, John
See also CA 5-8R; CANR 13, 33; MTCW

Corso, (Nunzio) Gregory 1930-... **CLC 1, 11**
See also CA 5-8R; CANR 41; DLB 5, 16;
MTCW

Cortazar, Julio
1914-1984 ...... **CLC 2, 3, 5, 10, 13, 15,
33, 34; HLC; SSC 7**
See also CA 21-24R; CANR 12, 32;
DLB 113; HW; MTCW

Corwin, Cecil
See Kornbluth, C(yril) M.

Cosic, Dobrica 1921-.............. **CLC 14**
See also CA 122; 138

Costain, Thomas B(ertram)
1885-1965 .... **CLC 30**
See also CA 5-8R; 25-28R; DLB 9

Costantini, Humberto
1924(?)-1987 .... **CLC 49**
See also CA 131; 122; HW

Costello, Elvis 1955-.............. **CLC 21**

Cotter, Joseph Seamon Sr.
1861-1949 .... **TCLC 28; BLC**
See also BW 1; CA 124; DLB 50

Couch, Arthur Thomas Quiller
See Quiller-Couch, Arthur Thomas

Coulton, James
See Hansen, Joseph

Couperus, Louis (Marie Anne)
1863-1923 .... **TCLC 15**
See also CA 115

Coupland, Douglas 1961-.......... **CLC 85**
See also CA 142

Court, Wesli
See Turco, Lewis (Putnam)

Courtenay, Bryce 1933-........... **CLC 59**
See also CA 138

Courtney, Robert
See Ellison, Harlan (Jay)

Cousteau, Jacques-Yves 1910-...... **CLC 30**
See also CA 65-68; CANR 15; MTCW;
SATA 38

Coward, Noel (Peirce)
1899-1973 .... **CLC 1, 9, 29, 51**
See also AITN 1; CA 17-18; 41-44R;
CANR 35; CAP 2; CDBLB 1914-1945;
DLB 10; MTCW

Cowley, Malcolm 1898-1989 .... **CLC 39**
See also CA 5-8R; 128; CANR 3; DLB 4,
48; DLBY 81, 89; MTCW

Cowper, William 1731-1800....... **NCLC 8**
See also DLB 104, 109

Cox, William Trevor 1928- ... **CLC 9, 14, 71**
See also Trevor, William
See also CA 9-12R; CANR 4, 37; DLB 14;
MTCW

Coyne, P. J.
See Masters, Hilary

Cozzens, James Gould
1903-1978 .... **CLC 1, 4, 11**
See also CA 9-12R; 81-84; CANR 19;
CDALB 1941-1968; DLB 9; DLBD 2;
DLBY 84; MTCW

Crabbe, George 1754-1832....... **NCLC 26**
See also DLB 93

Craig, A. A.
See Anderson, Poul (William)

Craik, Dinah Maria (Mulock)
1826-1887 .... **NCLC 38**
See also DLB 35; MAICYA; SATA 34

Cram, Ralph Adams 1863-1942.... **TCLC 45**

Crane, (Harold) Hart
1899-1932 .... **TCLC 2, 5; DA; DAB;
PC 3; WLC**
See also CA 104; 127; CDALB 1917-1929;
DLB 4, 48; MTCW

Crane, R(onald) S(almon)
1886-1967 .... **CLC 27**
See also CA 85-88; DLB 63

Crane, Stephen (Townley)
1871-1900 ...... **TCLC 11, 17, 32; DA; DAB; SSC 7; WLC**
See also CA 109; 140; CDALB 1865-1917;
DLB 12, 54, 78; YABC 2

Crase, Douglas 1944- .... **CLC 58**
See also CA 106

Crashaw, Richard 1612(?)-1649...... **LC 24**
See also DLB 126

Craven, Margaret 1901-1980....... **CLC 17**
See also CA 103

Crawford, F(rancis) Marion
1854-1909 .... **TCLC 10**
See also CA 107; DLB 71

Crawford, Isabella Valancy
1850-1887 .... **NCLC 12**
See also DLB 92

Crayon, Geoffrey
See Irving, Washington

Creasey, John 1908-1973.......... **CLC 11**
See also CA 5-8R; 41-44R; CANR 8;
DLB 77; MTCW

Crebillon, Claude Prosper Jolyot de (fils)
1707-1777 .... **LC 28**

Credo
See Creasey, John

Creeley, Robert (White)
1926- ..... **CLC 1, 2, 4, 8, 11, 15, 36, 78**
See also CA 1-4R; CAAS 10; CANR 23, 43;
DLB 5, 16; MTCW

Crews, Harry (Eugene)
1935- .... **CLC 6, 23, 49**
See also AITN 1; CA 25-28R; CANR 20;
DLB 6, 143; MTCW

Crichton, (John) Michael
1942- .... **CLC 2, 6, 54**
See also AAYA 10; AITN 2; CA 25-28R;
CANR 13, 40; DLBY 81; JRDA;
MTCW; SATA 9

Crispin, Edmund .... **CLC 22**
See also Montgomery, (Robert) Bruce
See also DLB 87

Cristofer, Michael 1945(?)- .... **CLC 28**
See also CA 110; DLB 7

Croce, Benedetto 1866-1952 ...... **TCLC 37**
See also CA 120

Crockett, David 1786-1836 .... **NCLC 8**
See also DLB 3, 11

Crockett, Davy
See Crockett, David

Crofts, Freeman Wills
1879-1957 .... **TCLC 55**
See also CA 115; DLB 77

Croker, John Wilson 1780-1857 .. **NCLC 10**
See also DLB 110

Crommelynck, Fernand 1885-1970 .. **CLC 75**
See also CA 89-92

Cronin, A(rchibald) J(oseph)
1896-1981 .... **CLC 32**
See also CA 1-4R; 102; CANR 5; SATA 47;
SATA-Obit 25

Cross, Amanda
See Heilbrun, Carolyn G(old)

Crothers, Rachel 1878(?)-1958..... **TCLC 19**
See also CA 113; DLB 7

Croves, Hal
See Traven, B.

Crowfield, Christopher
See Stowe, Harriet (Elizabeth) Beecher

Crowley, Aleister................. **TCLC 7**
See also Crowley, Edward Alexander

Crowley, Edward Alexander 1875-1947
See Crowley, Aleister
See also CA 104

Crowley, John 1942-.............. **CLC 57**
See also CA 61-64; CANR 43; DLBY 82;
SATA 65

Crud
See Crumb, R(obert)

Crumarums
See Crumb, R(obert)

Crumb, R(obert) 1943-............ **CLC 17**
See also CA 106

Crumbum
See Crumb, R(obert)

Crumski
See Crumb, R(obert)

Crum the Bum
See Crumb, R(obert)

Crunk
See Crumb, R(obert)

Crustt
See Crumb, R(obert)

Cryer, Gretchen (Kiger) 1935-...... **CLC 21**
See also CA 114; 123

Csath, Geza 1887-1919.......... **TCLC 13**
See also CA 111

Cudlip, David 1933-.............. **CLC 34**

Cullen, Countee
1903-1946 ...... **TCLC 4, 37; BLC; DA**
See also BW 1; CA 108; 124;
CDALB 1917-1929; DLB 4, 48, 51;
MTCW; SATA 18

Cum, R.
See Crumb, R(obert)

Cummings, Bruce F(rederick) 1889-1919
See Barbellion, W. N. P.
See also CA 123

Cummings, E(dward) E(stlin)
1894-1962 ...... **CLC 1, 3, 8, 12, 15, 68;
DA; DAB; PC 5; WLC 2**
See also CA 73-76; CANR 31;
CDALB 1929-1941; DLB 4, 48; MTCW

Cunha, Euclides (Rodrigues Pimenta) da
1866-1909 .... **TCLC 24**
See also CA 123

Cunningham, E. V.
See Fast, Howard (Melvin)

Cunningham, J(ames) V(incent)
1911-1985 .... **CLC 3, 31**
See also CA 1-4R; 115; CANR 1; DLB 5

Cunningham, Julia (Woolfolk)
1916- .... **CLC 12**
See also CA 9-12R; CANR 4, 19, 36;
JRDA; MAICYA; SAAS 2; SATA 1, 26

Cunningham, Michael 1952- .... **CLC 34**
See also CA 136

Cunninghame Graham, R(obert) B(ontine)
1852-1936 .... **TCLC 19**
See also Graham, R(obert) B(ontine)
Cunninghame
See also CA 119; DLB 98

Currie, Ellen 19(?)-............... **CLC 44**

Curtin, Philip
See Lowndes, Marie Adelaide (Belloc)

Curtis, Price
See Ellison, Harlan (Jay)

Cutrate, Joe
See Spiegelman, Art

Czaczkes, Shmuel Yosef
See Agnon, S(hmuel) Y(osef Halevi)

Dabrowska, Maria (Szumska)
1889-1965 .... **CLC 15**
See also CA 106

Dabydeen, David 1955- .... **CLC 34**
See also BW 1; CA 125

Dacey, Philip 1939- .... **CLC 51**
See also CA 37-40R; CAAS 17; CANR 14,
32; DLB 105

Dagerman, Stig (Halvard)
1923-1954 .... **TCLC 17**
See also CA 117

Dahl, Roald
1916-1990 ...... **CLC 1, 6, 18, 79; DAB**
See also CA 1-4R; 133; CANR 6, 32, 37;
CLR 1, 7; DLB 139; JRDA; MAICYA;
MTCW; SATA 1, 26, 73; SATA-Obit 65

Dahlberg, Edward 1900-1977... **CLC 1, 7, 14**
See also CA 9-12R; 69-72; CANR 31;
DLB 48; MTCW

Dale, Colin..................... **TCLC 18**
See also Lawrence, T(homas) E(dward)

Dale, George E.
See Asimov, Isaac

Daly, Elizabeth 1878-1967........ **CLC 52**
See also CA 23-24; 25-28R; CAP 2

Daly, Maureen 1921-.............. **CLC 17**
See also AAYA 5; CANR 37; JRDA;
MAICYA; SAAS 1; SATA 2

Damas, Leon-Gontran 1912-1978 ... **CLC 84**
See also BW 1; CA 125; 73-76

Daniel, Samuel 1562(?)-1619........ **LC 24**
See also DLB 62

Daniels, Brett
See Adler, Renata

Dannay, Frederic 1905-1982 .... **CLC 11**
See also Queen, Ellery
See also CA 1-4R; 107; CANR 1, 39;
DLB 137; MTCW

D'Annunzio, Gabriele
1863-1938 .... **TCLC 6, 40**
See also CA 104

d'Antibes, Germain
See Simenon, Georges (Jacques Christian)

Danvers, Dennis 1947-............. **CLC 70**

Danziger, Paula 1944- .... **CLC 21**
See also AAYA 4; CA 112; 115; CANR 37;
CLR 20; JRDA; MAICYA; SATA 36,
63; SATA-Brief 30

Da Ponte, Lorenzo 1749-1838 .... **NCLC 50**

Dario, Ruben 1867-1916 .... **TCLC 4; HLC**
See also CA 131; HW; MTCW

Darley, George 1795-1846 .... **NCLC 2**
See also DLB 96

Daryush, Elizabeth 1887-1977.... **CLC 6, 19**
See also CA 49-52; CANR 3; DLB 20

Daudet, (Louis Marie) Alphonse
1840-1897 .... **NCLC 1**
See also DLB 123

Daumal, Rene 1908-1944 .... **TCLC 14**
See also CA 114

Davenport, Guy (Mattison, Jr.)
1927- .... **CLC 6, 14, 38; SSC 16**
See also CA 33-36R; CANR 23; DLB 130

Davidson, Avram 1923-
See Queen, Ellery
See also CA 101; CANR 26; DLB 8

Davidson, Donald (Grady)
1893-1968 .... **CLC 2, 13, 19**
See also CA 5-8R; 25-28R; CANR 4;
DLB 45

Davidson, Hugh
See Hamilton, Edmond

Davidson, John 1857-1909 .... **TCLC 24**
See also CA 118; DLB 19

Davidson, Sara 1943- .... **CLC 9**
See also CA 81-84; CANR 44

Davie, Donald (Alfred)
1922- .... **CLC 5, 8, 10, 31**
See also CA 1-4R; CAAS 3; CANR 1, 44;
DLB 27; MTCW

Davies, Ray(mond Douglas) 1944- .. **CLC 21**
See also CA 116; 146

Davies, Rhys 1903-1978 .... **CLC 23**
See also CA 9-12R; 81-84; CANR 4;
DLB 139

Davies, (William) Robertson
1913- ..... **CLC 2, 7, 13, 25, 42, 75; DA;
DAB; WLC**
See also BEST 89:2; CA 33-36R; CANR 17,
42; DLB 68; MTCW

Davies, W(illiam) H(enry)
1871-1940 .... **TCLC 5**
See also CA 104; DLB 19

Davies, Walter C.
See Kornbluth, C(yril) M.

Davis, Angela (Yvonne) 1944- ...... **CLC 77**
See also BW 2; CA 57-60; CANR 10

Davis, B. Lynch
See Bioy Casares, Adolfo; Borges, Jorge
Luis

Davis, Gordon
See Hunt, E(verette) Howard, (Jr.)

Davis, Harold Lenoir 1896-1960.... **CLC 49**
See also CA 89-92; DLB 9

Davis, Rebecca (Blaine) Harding
1831-1910 .... **TCLC 6**
See also CA 104; DLB 74

Davis, Richard Harding
1864-1916 .... **TCLC 24**
See also CA 114; DLB 12, 23, 78, 79

Davison, Frank Dalby 1893-1970 ... **CLC 15**
See also CA 116

Davison, Lawrence H.
See Lawrence, D(avid) H(erbert Richards)

Davison, Peter (Hubert) 1928- ..... **CLC 28**
See also CA 9-12R; CAAS 4; CANR 3, 43;
DLB 5

Davys, Mary 1674-1732 .... **LC 1**
See also DLB 39

Dawson, Fielding 1930- .... **CLC 6**
See also CA 85-88; DLB 130

Dawson, Peter
See Faust, Frederick (Schiller)

Day, Clarence (Shepard, Jr.)
1874-1935 .... **TCLC 25**
See also CA 108; DLB 11

Day, Thomas 1748-1789 .... **LC 1**
See also DLB 39; YABC 1

Day Lewis, C(ecil)
1904-1972 .... **CLC 1, 6, 10; PC 11**
See also Blake, Nicholas
See also CA 13-16; 33-36R; CANR 34;
CAP 1; DLB 15, 20; MTCW

Dazai, Osamu .... **TCLC 11**
See also Tsushima, Shuji

de Andrade, Carlos Drummond
See Drummond de Andrade, Carlos

Deane, Norman
See Creasey, John

**de Beauvoir, Simone (Lucie Ernestine Marie
Bertrand)**
See Beauvoir, Simone (Lucie Ernestine
Marie Bertrand) de

de Brissac, Malcolm
See Dickinson, Peter (Malcolm)

de Chardin, Pierre Teilhard
See Teilhard de Chardin, (Marie Joseph)
Pierre

Dee, John 1527-1608 .... **LC 20**

Deer, Sandra 1940- .... **CLC 45**

De Ferrari, Gabriella 1941- .... **CLC 65**
See also CA 146

Defoe, Daniel
1660(?)-1731 .... **LC 1; DA; DAB; WLC**
See also CDBLB 1660-1789; DLB 39, 95,
101; JRDA; MAICYA; SATA 22

de Gourmont, Remy
See Gourmont, Remy de

de Hartog, Jan 1914- .... **CLC 19**
See also CA 1-4R; CANR 1

de Hostos, E. M.
See Hostos (y Bonilla), Eugenio Maria de

de Hostos, Eugenio M.
See Hostos (y Bonilla), Eugenio Maria de

Deighton, Len .... **CLC 4, 7, 22, 46**
See also Deighton, Leonard Cyril
See also AAYA 6; BEST 89:2;
CDBLB 1960 to Present; DLB 87

Deighton, Leonard Cyril 1929-
See Deighton, Len
See also CA 9-12R; CANR 19, 33; MTCW

Dekker, Thomas 1572(?)-1632 .... **LC 22**
See also CDBLB Before 1660; DLB 62

de la Mare, Walter (John)
1873-1956 .... **TCLC 4, 53; DAB;
SSC 14; WLC**
See also CDBLB 1914-1945; CLR 23;
DLB 19, 153; SATA 16

Delaney, Franey
See O'Hara, John (Henry)

Delaney, Shelagh 1939- .... **CLC 29**
See also CA 17-20R; CANR 30;
CDBLB 1960 to Present; DLB 13;
MTCW

Delany, Mary (Granville Pendarves)
1700-1788 .... **LC 12**

Delany, Samuel R(ay, Jr.)
1942- ....**CLC 8, 14, 38; BLC**
See also BW 2; CA 81-84; CANR 27, 43;
DLB 8, 33; MTCW

De La Ramee, (Marie) Louise 1839-1908
See Ouida
See also SATA 20

de la Roche, Mazo 1879-1961 ...... **CLC 14**
See also CA 85-88; CANR 30; DLB 68;
SATA 64

Delbanco, Nicholas (Franklin)
1942- .... **CLC 6, 13**
See also CA 17-20R; CAAS 2; CANR 29;
DLB 6

del Castillo, Michel 1933- .... **CLC 38**
See also CA 109

Deledda, Grazia (Cosima)
1875(?)-1936 .... **TCLC 23**
See also CA 123

Delibes, Miguel .... **CLC 8, 18**
See also Delibes Setien, Miguel

Delibes Setien, Miguel 1920-
See Delibes, Miguel
See also CA 45-48; CANR 1, 32; HW;
MTCW

DeLillo, Don
1936- ..... **CLC 8, 10, 13, 27, 39, 54, 76**
See also BEST 89:1; CA 81-84; CANR 21;
DLB 6; MTCW

de Lisser, H. G.
See De Lisser, Herbert George
See also DLB 117

De Lisser, Herbert George
1878-1944 .... **TCLC 12**
See also de Lisser, H. G.
See also BW 2; CA 109

Deloria, Vine (Victor), Jr. 1933-.... **CLC 21**
See also CA 53-56; CANR 5, 20, 48;
MTCW; NNAL; SATA 21

Del Vecchio, John M(ichael)
1947- .... **CLC 29**
See also CA 110; DLBD 9

de Man, Paul (Adolph Michel)
1919-1983 .... **CLC 55**
See also CA 128; 111; DLB 67; MTCW

De Marinis, Rick 1934- .... **CLC 54**
See also CA 57-60; CANR 9, 25

Demby, William 1922- .... **CLC 53; BLC**
See also BW 1; CA 81-84; DLB 33

Demijohn, Thom
See Disch, Thomas M(ichael)

de Montherlant, Henry (Milon)
See Montherlant, Henry (Milon) de

Demosthenes 384B.C.-322B.C. ... **CMLC 13**

de Natale, Francine
See Malzberg, Barry N(athaniel)

Denby, Edwin (Orr) 1903-1983 ..... **CLC 48**
See also CA 138; 110

Denis, Julio
See Cortazar, Julio

Denmark, Harrison
See Zelazny, Roger (Joseph)

Dennis, John 1658-1734 .... **LC 11**
See also DLB 101

Dennis, Nigel (Forbes) 1912-1989 .... **CLC 8**
See also CA 25-28R; 129; DLB 13, 15;
MTCW

De Palma, Brian (Russell) 1940-.... **CLC 20**
See also CA 109

De Quincey, Thomas 1785-1859 ... **NCLC 4**
See also CDBLB 1789-1832; DLB 110; 144

Deren, Eleanora 1908(?)-1961
See Deren, Maya
See also CA 111

Deren, Maya .... **CLC 16**
See also Deren, Eleanora

Derleth, August (William)
1909-1971 .... **CLC 31**
See also CA 1-4R; 29-32R; CANR 4;
DLB 9; SATA 5

Der Nister 1884-1950 .... **TCLC 56**

de Routisie, Albert
See Aragon, Louis

Derrida, Jacques 1930-........ **CLC 24, 87**
See also CA 124; 127

Derry Down Derry
See Lear, Edward

Dersonnes, Jacques
See Simenon, Georges (Jacques Christian)

Desai, Anita 1937- ...... **CLC 19, 37; DAB**
See also CA 81-84; CANR 33; MTCW;
SATA 63

de Saint-Luc, Jean
See Glassco, John

de Saint Roman, Arnaud
See Aragon, Louis

Descartes, Rene 1596-1650 .... **LC 20**

De Sica, Vittorio 1901(?)-1974 ..... **CLC 20**
See also CA 117

Desnos, Robert 1900-1945 .... **TCLC 22**
See also CA 121

Destouches, Louis-Ferdinand
1894-1961 .... **CLC 9, 15**
See also Celine, Louis-Ferdinand
See also CA 85-88; CANR 28; MTCW

Deutsch, Babette 1895-1982 .... **CLC 18**
See also CA 1-4R; 108; CANR 4; DLB 45;
SATA 1; SATA-Obit 33

Devenant, William 1606-1649 .... **LC 13**

Devkota, Laxmiprasad
1909-1959 .... **TCLC 23**
See also CA 123

De Voto, Bernard (Augustine)
1897-1955 .... **TCLC 29**
See also CA 113; DLB 9

De Vries, Peter
1910-1993 .... **CLC 1, 2, 3, 7, 10, 28, 46**
See also CA 17-20R; 142; CANR 41;
DLB 6; DLBY 82; MTCW

Dexter, Martin
See Faust, Frederick (Schiller)

Dexter, Pete 1943-............ **CLC 34, 55**
See also BEST 89:2; CA 127; 131; MTCW

Diamano, Silmang
See Senghor, Leopold Sedar

Diamond, Neil 1941- .... **CLC 30**
See also CA 108

di Bassetto, Corno
See Shaw, George Bernard

Dick, Philip K(indred)
1928-1982 .... **CLC 10, 30, 72**
See also CA 49-52; 106; CANR 2, 16;
DLB 8; MTCW

Dickens, Charles (John Huffam)
1812-1870 ...... **NCLC 3, 8, 18, 26, 37,
50; DA; DAB; SSC 17; WLC**
See also CDBLB 1832-1890; DLB 21, 55,
70; JRDA; MAICYA; SATA 15

Dickey, James (Lafayette)
1923- .... **CLC 1, 2, 4, 7, 10, 15, 47**
See also AITN 1, 2; CA 9-12R; CABS 2;
CANR 10, 48; CDALB 1968-1988;
DLB 5; DLBD 7; DLBY 82, 93; MTCW

Dickey, William 1928-1994 ...... **CLC 3, 28**
See also CA 9-12R; 145; CANR 24; DLB 5

Dickinson, Charles 1951-.......... **CLC 49**
See also CA 128

Dickinson, Emily (Elizabeth)
1830-1886 ...... **NCLC 21; DA; DAB;
PC 1; WLC**
See also CDALB 1865-1917; DLB 1;
SATA 29

Dickinson, Peter (Malcolm)
1927-................... **CLC 12, 35**
See also AAYA 9; CA 41-44R; CANR 31;
CLR 29; DLB 87; JRDA; MAICYA;
SATA 5, 62

Dickson, Carr
See Carr, John Dickson

Dickson, Carter
See Carr, John Dickson

Diderot, Denis 1713-1784 .... **LC 26**

Didion, Joan 1934-..... **CLC 1, 3, 8, 14, 32**
See also AITN 1; CA 5-8R; CANR 14;
CDALB 1968-1988; DLB 2; DLBY 81,
86; MTCW

Dietrich, Robert
See Hunt, E(verette) Howard, (Jr.)

Dillard, Annie 1945-............ **CLC 9, 60**
See also AAYA 6; CA 49-52; CANR 3, 43;
DLBY 80; MTCW; SATA 10

Dillard, R(ichard) H(enry) W(ilde)
1937- .... **CLC 5**
See also CA 21-24R; CAAS 7; CANR 10;
DLB 5

Dillon, Eilis 1920-1994 .... **CLC 17**
See also CA 9-12R; 147; CAAS 3; CANR 4,
38; CLR 26; MAICYA; SATA 2, 74;
SATA-Obit 83

Dimont, Penelope
See Mortimer, Penelope (Ruth)

Dinesen, Isak .... **CLC 10, 29; SSC 7**
See also Blixen, Karen (Christentze
Dinesen)

Ding Ling .... **CLC 68**
See also Chiang Pin-chin

Disch, Thomas M(ichael) 1940-... **CLC 7, 36**
See also CA 21-24R; CAAS 4; CANR 17,
36; CLR 18; DLB 8; MAICYA; MTCW;
SAAS 15; SATA 54

Disch, Tom
See Disch, Thomas M(ichael)

d'Isly, Georges
See Simenon, Georges (Jacques Christian)

Disraeli, Benjamin 1804-1881 .. **NCLC 2, 39**
See also DLB 21, 55

Ditcum, Steve
See Crumb, R(obert)

Dixon, Paige
See Corcoran, Barbara

Dixon, Stephen 1936-..... **CLC 52; SSC 16**
See also CA 89-92; CANR 17, 40; DLB 130

Dobell, Sydney Thompson
1824-1874 .... **NCLC 43**
See also DLB 32

Doblin, Alfred .... **TCLC 13**
See also Doeblin, Alfred

Dobrolyubov, Nikolai Alexandrovich
1836-1861 .... **NCLC 5**

Dobyns, Stephen 1941-............ **CLC 37**
See also CA 45-48; CANR 2, 18

Doctorow, E(dgar) L(aurence)
1931- ..... **CLC 6, 11, 15, 18, 37, 44, 65**
See also AITN 2; BEST 89:3; CA 45-48;
CANR 2, 33; CDALB 1968-1988; DLB 2,
28; DLBY 80; MTCW

Dodgson, Charles Lutwidge 1832-1898
See Carroll, Lewis
See also CLR 2; DA; DAB; MAICYA;
YABC 2

Dodson, Owen (Vincent)
1914-1983 .... **CLC 79; BLC**
See also BW 1; CA 65-68; 110; CANR 24;
DLB 76

Doeblin, Alfred 1878-1957 .... **TCLC 13**
See also Doblin, Alfred
See also CA 110; 141; DLB 66

Doerr, Harriet 1910- .... **CLC 34**
See also CA 117; 122; CANR 47

Domecq, H(onorio) Bustos
See Bioy Casares, Adolfo; Borges, Jorge
Luis

Domini, Rey
See Lorde, Audre (Geraldine)

Dominique
See Proust, (Valentin-Louis-George-Eugene-)
Marcel

Don, A
See Stephen, Leslie

Donaldson, Stephen R.   1947-...... **CLC 46**
See also CA 89-92; CANR 13

Donleavy, J(ames) P(atrick)
1926- .... **CLC 1, 4, 6, 10, 45**
See also AITN 2; CA 9-12R; CANR 24, 49;
DLB 6; MTCW

Donne, John
1572-1631 .. **LC 10, 24; DA; DAB; PC 1**
See also CDBLB Before 1660; DLB 121,
151

Donnell, David   1939(?)-.......... **CLC 34**

Donoghue, P. S.
See Hunt, E(verette) Howard, (Jr.)

Donoso (Yanez), Jose
1924- .... **CLC 4, 8, 11, 32; HLC**
See also CA 81-84; CANR 32; DLB 113;
HW; MTCW

Donovan, John   1928-1992 .... **CLC 35**
See also CA 97-100; 137; CLR 3;
MAICYA; SATA 72; SATA-Brief 29

Don Roberto
See Cunninghame Graham, R(obert)
B(ontine)

Doolittle, Hilda
1886-1961 ..... **CLC 3, 8, 14, 31, 34, 73;
DA; PC 5; WLC**
See also H. D.
See also CA 97-100; CANR 35; DLB 4, 45;
MTCW

Dorfman, Ariel   1942-.... **CLC 48, 77; HLC**
See also CA 124; 130; HW

Dorn, Edward (Merton)   1929-... **CLC 10, 18**
See also CA 93-96; CANR 42; DLB 5

Dorsan, Luc
See Simenon, Georges (Jacques Christian)

Dorsange, Jean
See Simenon, Georges (Jacques Christian)

Dos Passos, John (Roderigo)
1896-1970 ..... **CLC 1, 4, 8, 11, 15, 25,
34, 82; DA; DAB; WLC**
See also CA 1-4R; 29-32R; CANR 3;
CDALB 1929-1941; DLB 4, 9; DLBD 1;
MTCW

Dossage, Jean
See Simenon, Georges (Jacques Christian)

Dostoevsky, Fedor Mikhailovich
1821-1881 ...... **NCLC 2, 7, 21, 33, 43;
DA; DAB; SSC 2; WLC**

Doughty, Charles M(ontagu)
1843-1926 .... **TCLC 27**
See also CA 115; DLB 19, 57

Douglas, Ellen.................... **CLC 73**
See also Haxton, Josephine Ayres;
Williamson, Ellen Douglas

Douglas, Gavin   1475(?)-1522........ **LC 20**

Douglas, Keith   1920-1944 .... **TCLC 40**
See also DLB 27

Douglas, Leonard
See Bradbury, Ray (Douglas)

Douglas, Michael
See Crichton, (John) Michael

Douglass, Frederick
1817(?)-1895 .... **NCLC 7; BLC; DA;
WLC**
See also CDALB 1640-1865; DLB 1, 43, 50,
79; SATA 29

Dourado, (Waldomiro Freitas) Autran
1926- .... **CLC 23, 60**
See also CA 25-28R; CANR 34

Dourado, Waldomiro Autran
See Dourado, (Waldomiro Freitas) Autran

Dove, Rita (Frances)
1952- .... **CLC 50, 81; PC 6**
See also BW 2; CA 109; CAAS 19;
CANR 27, 42; DLB 120

Dowell, Coleman   1925-1985........ **CLC 60**
See also CA 25-28R; 117; CANR 10;
DLB 130

Dowson, Ernest Christopher
1867-1900 .... **TCLC 4**
See also CA 105; DLB 19, 135

Doyle, A. Conan
See Doyle, Arthur Conan

Doyle, Arthur Conan
1859-1930 .... **TCLC 7; DA; DAB;
SSC 12; WLC**
See also AAYA 14; CA 104; 122;
CDBLB 1890-1914; DLB 18, 70; MTCW;
SATA 24

Doyle, Conan
See Doyle, Arthur Conan

Doyle, John
See Graves, Robert (von Ranke)

Doyle, Roddy   1958(?)-............ **CLC 81**
See also AAYA 14; CA 143

Doyle, Sir A. Conan
See Doyle, Arthur Conan

Doyle, Sir Arthur Conan
See Doyle, Arthur Conan

Dr. A
See Asimov, Isaac; Silverstein, Alvin

Drabble, Margaret
1939- ... **CLC 2, 3, 5, 8, 10, 22, 53; DAB**
See also CA 13-16R; CANR 18, 35;
CDBLB 1960 to Present; DLB 14, 155;
MTCW; SATA 48

Drapier, M. B.
See Swift, Jonathan

Drayham, James
See Mencken, H(enry) L(ouis)

Drayton, Michael   1563-1631........ **LC 8**

Dreadstone, Carl
See Campbell, (John) Ramsey

Dreiser, Theodore (Herman Albert)
1871-1945 ...... **TCLC 10, 18, 35; DA;
WLC**
See also CA 106; 132; CDALB 1865-1917;
DLB 9, 12, 102, 137; DLBD 1; MTCW

Drexler, Rosalyn   1926- .... **CLC 2, 6**
See also CA 81-84

Dreyer, Carl Theodor   1889-1968.... **CLC 16**
See also CA 116

Drieu la Rochelle, Pierre(-Eugene)
1893-1945 .... **TCLC 21**
See also CA 117; DLB 72

Drinkwater, John   1882-1937...... **TCLC 57**
See also CA 109; DLB 10, 19, 149

Drop Shot
See Cable, George Washington

Droste-Hulshoff, Annette Freiin von
1797-1848 .... **NCLC 3**
See also DLB 133

Drummond, Walter
See Silverberg, Robert

Drummond, William Henry
1854-1907 .... **TCLC 25**
See also DLB 92

Drummond de Andrade, Carlos
1902-1987 .... **CLC 18**
See also Andrade, Carlos Drummond de
See also CA 132; 123

Drury, Allen (Stuart)   1918-........ **CLC 37**
See also CA 57-60; CANR 18

Dryden, John
1631-1700 .... **LC 3, 21; DA; DAB;
DC 3; WLC**
See also CDBLB 1660-1789; DLB 80, 101,
131

Duberman, Martin   1930-.......... **CLC 8**
See also CA 1-4R; CANR 2

Dubie, Norman (Evans)   1945-...... **CLC 36**
See also CA 69-72; CANR 12; DLB 120

Du Bois, W(illiam) E(dward) B(urghardt)
1868-1963 ...... **CLC 1, 2, 13, 64; BLC;
DA; WLC**
See also BW 1; CA 85-88; CANR 34;
CDALB 1865-1917; DLB 47, 50, 91;
MTCW; SATA 42

Dubus, Andre   1936-... **CLC 13, 36; SSC 15**
See also CA 21-24R; CANR 17; DLB 130

Duca Minimo
See D'Annunzio, Gabriele

Ducharme, Rejean   1941-.......... **CLC 74**
See also DLB 60

Duclos, Charles Pinot   1704-1772 ..... **LC 1**

Dudek, Louis   1918- .... **CLC 11, 19**
See also CA 45-48; CAAS 14; CANR 1;
DLB 88

Duerrenmatt, Friedrich
1921-1990 ...... **CLC 1, 4, 8, 11, 15, 43**
See also CA 17-20R; CANR 33; DLB 69,
124; MTCW

Duffy, Bruce   (?)-................. **CLC 50**

Duffy, Maureen   1933- .... **CLC 37**
See also CA 25-28R; CANR 33; DLB 14;
MTCW

Dugan, Alan   1923-.............. **CLC 2, 6**
See also CA 81-84; DLB 5

du Gard, Roger Martin
See Martin du Gard, Roger

Duhamel, Georges   1884-1966 .... **CLC 8**
See also CA 81-84; 25-28R; CANR 35;
DLB 65; MTCW

Dujardin, Edouard (Emile Louis)
1861-1949 .... **TCLC 13**
See also CA 109; DLB 123

Dumas, Alexandre (Davy de la Pailleterie)
1802-1870 .. **NCLC 11; DA; DAB; WLC**
See also DLB 119; SATA 18

Dumas, Alexandre
    1824-1895 . . . . NCLC 9; DC 1

Dumas, Claudine
    See Malzberg, Barry N(athaniel)

Dumas, Henry L. 1934-1968 . . . . . CLC 6, 62
    See also BW 1; CA 85-88; DLB 41

du Maurier, Daphne
    1907-1989 . . . . CLC 6, 11, 59; DAB;
                           SSC 18
    See also CA 5-8R; 128; CANR 6; MTCW;
    SATA 27; SATA-Obit 60

Dunbar, Paul Laurence
    1872-1906 . . . . . . TCLC 2, 12; BLC; DA;
                    PC 5; SSC 8; WLC
    See also BW 1; CA 104; 124;
    CDALB 1865-1917; DLB 50, 54, 78;
    SATA 34

Dunbar, William 1460(?)-1530(?) . . . . LC 20
    See also DLB 132, 146

Duncan, Lois 1934- . . . . CLC 26
    See also AAYA 4; CA 1-4R; CANR 2, 23,
    36; CLR 29; JRDA; MAICYA; SAAS 2;
    SATA 1, 36, 75

Duncan, Robert (Edward)
    1919-1988 . . . . CLC 1, 2, 4, 7, 15, 41, 55;
                              PC 2
    See also CA 9-12R; 124; CANR 28; DLB 5,
    16; MTCW

Duncan, Sara Jeannette
    1861-1922 . . . . TCLC 60
    See also DLB 92

Dunlap, William 1766-1839 . . . . NCLC 2
    See also DLB 30, 37, 59

Dunn, Douglas (Eaglesham)
    1942- . . . . CLC 6, 40
    See also CA 45-48; CANR 2, 33; DLB 40;
    MTCW

Dunn, Katherine (Karen) 1945- . . . . . CLC 71
    See also CA 33-36R

Dunn, Stephen 1939- . . . . CLC 36
    See also CA 33-36R; CANR 12, 48;
    DLB 105

Dunne, Finley Peter 1867-1936 . . . . TCLC 28
    See also CA 108; DLB 11, 23

Dunne, John Gregory 1932- . . . . CLC 28
    See also CA 25-28R; CANR 14; DLBY 80

**Dunsany, Edward John Moreton Drax
Plunkett** 1878-1957
    See Dunsany, Lord
    See also CA 104; 148; DLB 10

Dunsany, Lord . . . . TCLC 2, 59
    See also Dunsany, Edward John Moreton
    Drax Plunkett
    See also DLB 77, 153

du Perry, Jean
    See Simenon, Georges (Jacques Christian)

Durang, Christopher (Ferdinand)
    1949- . . . . CLC 27, 38
    See also CA 105

Duras, Marguerite
    1914- . . . . . . CLC 3, 6, 11, 20, 34, 40, 68
    See also CA 25-28R; DLB 83; MTCW

Durban, (Rosa) Pam 1947- . . . . CLC 39
    See also CA 123

Durcan, Paul 1944- . . . . CLC 43, 70
    See also CA 134

Durkheim, Emile 1858-1917 . . . . . . TCLC 55

Durrell, Lawrence (George)
    1912-1990 . . . . CLC 1, 4, 6, 8, 13, 27, 41
    See also CA 9-12R; 132; CANR 40;
    CDBLB 1945-1960; DLB 15, 27;
    DLBY 90; MTCW

Durrenmatt, Friedrich
    See Duerrenmatt, Friedrich

Dutt, Toru 1856-1877 . . . . NCLC 29

Dwight, Timothy 1752-1817 . . . . . . NCLC 13
    See also DLB 37

Dworkin, Andrea 1946- . . . . CLC 43
    See also CA 77-80; CAAS 21; CANR 16,
    39; MTCW

Dwyer, Deanna
    See Koontz, Dean R(ay)

Dwyer, K. R.
    See Koontz, Dean R(ay)

Dylan, Bob 1941- . . . . . . CLC 3, 4, 6, 12, 77
    See also CA 41-44R; DLB 16

Eagleton, Terence (Francis) 1943-
    See Eagleton, Terry
    See also CA 57-60; CANR 7, 23; MTCW

Eagleton, Terry . . . . CLC 63
    See also Eagleton, Terence (Francis)

Early, Jack
    See Scoppettone, Sandra

East, Michael
    See West, Morris L(anglo)

Eastaway, Edward
    See Thomas, (Philip) Edward

Eastlake, William (Derry) 1917- . . . . . CLC 8
    See also CA 5-8R; CAAS 1; CANR 5;
    DLB 6

Eastman, Charles A(lexander)
    1858-1939 . . . . TCLC 55
    See also NNAL; YABC 1

Eberhart, Richard (Ghormley)
    1904- . . . . CLC 3, 11, 19, 56
    See also CA 1-4R; CANR 2;
    CDALB 1941-1968; DLB 48; MTCW

Eberstadt, Fernanda 1960- . . . . CLC 39
    See also CA 136

Echegaray (y Eizaguirre), Jose (Maria Waldo)
    1832-1916 . . . . TCLC 4
    See also CA 104; CANR 32; HW; MTCW

Echeverria, (Jose) Esteban (Antonino)
    1805-1851 . . . . NCLC 18

Echo
    See Proust, (Valentin-Louis-George-Eugene-)
    Marcel

Eckert, Allan W. 1931- . . . . CLC 17
    See also CA 13-16R; CANR 14, 45;
    SATA 29; SATA-Brief 27

Eckhart, Meister 1260(?)-1328(?) . . CMLC 9
    See also DLB 115

Eckmar, F. R.
    See de Hartog, Jan

Eco, Umberto 1932- . . . . CLC 28, 60
    See also BEST 90:1; CA 77-80; CANR 12,
    33; MTCW

Eddison, E(ric) R(ucker)
    1882-1945 . . . . TCLC 15
    See also CA 109

Edel, (Joseph) Leon 1907- . . . . . . CLC 29, 34
    See also CA 1-4R; CANR 1, 22; DLB 103

Eden, Emily 1797-1869 . . . . NCLC 10

Edgar, David 1948- . . . . CLC 42
    See also CA 57-60; CANR 12; DLB 13;
    MTCW

Edgerton, Clyde (Carlyle) 1944- . . . . CLC 39
    See also CA 118; 134

Edgeworth, Maria 1767-1849 . . . NCLC 1, 51
    See also DLB 116; SATA 21

Edmonds, Paul
    See Kuttner, Henry

Edmonds, Walter D(umaux) 1903- . . CLC 35
    See also CA 5-8R; CANR 2; DLB 9;
    MAICYA; SAAS 4; SATA 1, 27

Edmondson, Wallace
    See Ellison, Harlan (Jay)

Edson, Russell . . . . CLC 13
    See also CA 33-36R

Edwards, Bronwen Elizabeth
    See Rose, Wendy

Edwards, G(erald) B(asil)
    1899-1976 . . . . CLC 25
    See also CA 110

Edwards, Gus 1939- . . . . CLC 43
    See also CA 108

Edwards, Jonathan 1703-1758 . . . . LC 7; DA
    See also DLB 24

Efron, Marina Ivanovna Tsvetaeva
    See Tsvetaeva (Efron), Marina (Ivanovna)

Ehle, John (Marsden, Jr.) 1925- . . . . CLC 27
    See also CA 9-12R

Ehrenbourg, Ilya (Grigoryevich)
    See Ehrenburg, Ilya (Grigoryevich)

Ehrenburg, Ilya (Grigoryevich)
    1891-1967 . . . . CLC 18, 34, 62
    See also CA 102; 25-28R

Ehrenburg, Ilyo (Grigoryevich)
    See Ehrenburg, Ilya (Grigoryevich)

Eich, Guenter 1907-1972 . . . . CLC 15
    See also CA 111; 93-96; DLB 69, 124

Eichendorff, Joseph Freiherr von
    1788-1857 . . . . NCLC 8
    See also DLB 90

Eigner, Larry . . . . CLC 9
    See also Eigner, Laurence (Joel)
    See also DLB 5

Eigner, Laurence (Joel) 1927-
    See Eigner, Larry
    See also CA 9-12R; CANR 6

Eiseley, Loren Corey 1907-1977 . . . . . CLC 7
    See also AAYA 5; CA 1-4R; 73-76;
    CANR 6

Eisenstadt, Jill 1963- . . . . CLC 50
    See also CA 140

Eisenstein, Sergei (Mikhailovich)
    1898-1948 . . . . TCLC 57
    See also CA 114

Eisner, Simon
    See Kornbluth, C(yril) M.

Ekeloef, (Bengt) Gunnar
1907-1968 .... CLC 27
See also CA 123; 25-28R

Ekelof, (Bengt) Gunnar
See Ekeloef, (Bengt) Gunnar

Ekwensi, C. O. D.
See Ekwensi, Cyprian (Odiatu Duaka)

Ekwensi, Cyprian (Odiatu Duaka)
1921- .... CLC 4; BLC
See also BW 2; CA 29-32R; CANR 18, 42;
DLB 117; MTCW; SATA 66

Elaine .... TCLC 18
See also Leverson, Ada

El Crummo
See Crumb, R(obert)

Elia
See Lamb, Charles

Eliade, Mircea 1907-1986 .... CLC 19
See also CA 65-68; 119; CANR 30; MTCW

Eliot, A. D.
See Jewett, (Theodora) Sarah Orne

Eliot, Alice
See Jewett, (Theodora) Sarah Orne

Eliot, Dan
See Silverberg, Robert

Eliot, George
1819-1880 ..... NCLC 4, 13, 23, 41, 49;
DA; DAB; WLC
See also CDBLB 1832-1890; DLB 21, 35, 55

Eliot, John 1604-1690 .... LC 5
See also DLB 24

Eliot, T(homas) S(tearns)
1888-1965 ..... CLC 1, 2, 3, 6, 9, 10, 13,
15, 24, 34, 41, 55, 57; DA; DAB; PC 5;
WLC 2
See also CA 5-8R; 25-28R; CANR 41;
CDALB 1929-1941; DLB 7, 10, 45, 63;
DLBY 88; MTCW

Elizabeth 1866-1941 .... TCLC 41

Elkin, Stanley L(awrence)
1930-1995 ...... CLC 4, 6, 9, 14, 27, 51;
SSC 12
See also CA 9-12R; 148; CANR 8, 46;
DLB 2, 28; DLBY 80; MTCW

Elledge, Scott .... CLC 34

Elliott, Don
See Silverberg, Robert

Elliott, George P(aul) 1918-1980 ..... CLC 2
See also CA 1-4R; 97-100; CANR 2

Elliott, Janice 1931- .... CLC 47
See also CA 13-16R; CANR 8, 29; DLB 14

Elliott, Sumner Locke 1917-1991 ... CLC 38
See also CA 5-8R; 134; CANR 2, 21

Elliott, William
See Bradbury, Ray (Douglas)

Ellis, A. E. .... CLC 7

Ellis, Alice Thomas .... CLC 40
See also Haycraft, Anna

Ellis, Bret Easton 1964- .... CLC 39, 71
See also AAYA 2; CA 118; 123

Ellis, (Henry) Havelock
1859-1939 .... TCLC 14
See also CA 109

Ellis, Landon
See Ellison, Harlan (Jay)

Ellis, Trey 1962- .... CLC 55
See also CA 146

Ellison, Harlan (Jay)
1934- .... CLC 1, 13, 42; SSC 14
See also CA 5-8R; CANR 5, 46; DLB 8;
MTCW

Ellison, Ralph (Waldo)
1914-1994 .... CLC 1, 3, 11, 54, 86;
BLC; DA; DAB; WLC
See also BW 1; CA 9-12R; 145; CANR 24;
CDALB 1941-1968; DLB 2, 76;
DLBY 94; MTCW

Ellmann, Lucy (Elizabeth) 1956- .... CLC 61
See also CA 128

Ellmann, Richard (David)
1918-1987 .... CLC 50
See also BEST 89:2; CA 1-4R; 122;
CANR 2, 28; DLB 103; DLBY 87;
MTCW

Elman, Richard 1934- .... CLC 19
See also CA 17-20R; CAAS 3; CANR 47

Elron
See Hubbard, L(afayette) Ron(ald)

Eluard, Paul .... TCLC 7, 41
See also Grindel, Eugene

Elyot, Sir Thomas 1490(?)-1546 ..... LC 11

Elytis, Odysseus 1911- .... CLC 15, 49
See also CA 102; MTCW

Emecheta, (Florence Onye) Buchi
1944- .... CLC 14, 48; BLC
See also BW 2; CA 81-84; CANR 27;
DLB 117; MTCW; SATA 66

Emerson, Ralph Waldo
1803-1882 ..... NCLC 1, 38; DA; DAB;
WLC
See also CDALB 1640-1865; DLB 1, 59, 73

Eminescu, Mihail 1850-1889 ..... NCLC 33

Empson, William
1906-1984 .... CLC 3, 8, 19, 33, 34
See also CA 17-20R; 112; CANR 31;
DLB 20; MTCW

Enchi Fumiko (Ueda) 1905-1986.... CLC 31
See also CA 129; 121

Ende, Michael (Andreas Helmuth)
1929- .... CLC 31
See also CA 118; 124; CANR 36; CLR 14;
DLB 75; MAICYA; SATA 61;
SATA-Brief 42

Endo, Shusaku 1923- ..... CLC 7, 14, 19, 54
See also CA 29-32R; CANR 21; MTCW

Engel, Marian 1933-1985.......... CLC 36
See also CA 25-28R; CANR 12; DLB 53

Engelhardt, Frederick
See Hubbard, L(afayette) Ron(ald)

Enright, D(ennis) J(oseph)
1920- .... CLC 4, 8, 31
See also CA 1-4R; CANR 1, 42; DLB 27;
SATA 25

Enzensberger, Hans Magnus
1929- .... CLC 43
See also CA 116; 119

Ephron, Nora 1941- .... CLC 17, 31
See also AITN 2; CA 65-68; CANR 12, 39

Epsilon
See Betjeman, John

Epstein, Daniel Mark 1948- .... CLC 7
See also CA 49-52; CANR 2

Epstein, Jacob 1956- .... CLC 19
See also CA 114

Epstein, Joseph 1937-............. CLC 39
See also CA 112; 119

Epstein, Leslie 1938- .... CLC 27
See also CA 73-76; CAAS 12; CANR 23

Equiano, Olaudah
1745(?)-1797 .... LC 16; BLC
See also DLB 37, 50

Erasmus, Desiderius 1469(?)-1536.... LC 16

Erdman, Paul E(mil) 1932- .... CLC 25
See also AITN 1; CA 61-64; CANR 13, 43

Erdrich, Louise 1954-.......... CLC 39, 54
See also AAYA 10; BEST 89:1; CA 114;
CANR 41; DLB 152; MTCW; NNAL

Erenburg, Ilya (Grigoryevich)
See Ehrenburg, Ilya (Grigoryevich)

Erickson, Stephen Michael 1950-
See Erickson, Steve
See also CA 129

Erickson, Steve .... CLC 64
See also Erickson, Stephen Michael

Ericson, Walter
See Fast, Howard (Melvin)

Eriksson, Buntel
See Bergman, (Ernst) Ingmar

Ernaux, Annie 1940- .... CLC 88
See also CA 147

Eschenbach, Wolfram von
See Wolfram von Eschenbach

Eseki, Bruno
See Mphahlele, Ezekiel

Esenin, Sergei (Alexandrovich)
1895-1925 .... TCLC 4
See also CA 104

Eshleman, Clayton 1935-........... CLC 7
See also CA 33-36R; CAAS 6; DLB 5

Espriella, Don Manuel Alvarez
See Southey, Robert

Espriu, Salvador 1913-1985........ CLC 9
See also CA 115; DLB 134

Espronceda, Jose de 1808-1842... NCLC 39

Esse, James
See Stephens, James

Esterbrook, Tom
See Hubbard, L(afayette) Ron(ald)

Estleman, Loren D. 1952- .... CLC 48
See also CA 85-88; CANR 27; MTCW

Eugenides, Jeffrey 1960(?)- .... CLC 81
See also CA 144

Euripides c. 485B.C.-406B.C. ...... DC 4
See also DA; DAB

Evan, Evin
See Faust, Frederick (Schiller)

Evans, Evan
See Faust, Frederick (Schiller)

Evans, Marian
See Eliot, George

Evans, Mary Ann
See Eliot, George

Evarts, Esther
See Benson, Sally

Everett, Percival L. 1956- .... **CLC 57**
See also BW 2; CA 129

Everson, R(onald) G(ilmour)
1903- .... **CLC 27**
See also CA 17-20R; DLB 88

Everson, William (Oliver)
1912-1994 .... **CLC 1, 5, 14**
See also CA 9-12R; 145; CANR 20; DLB 5,
16; MTCW

Evtushenko, Evgenii Aleksandrovich
See Yevtushenko, Yevgeny (Alexandrovich)

Ewart, Gavin (Buchanan)
1916- .... **CLC 13, 46**
See also CA 89-92; CANR 17, 46; DLB 40;
MTCW

Ewers, Hanns Heinz 1871-1943 ... **TCLC 12**
See also CA 109

Ewing, Frederick R.
See Sturgeon, Theodore (Hamilton)

Exley, Frederick (Earl)
1929-1992 .... **CLC 6, 11**
See also AITN 2; CA 81-84; 138; DLB 143;
DLBY 81

Eynhardt, Guillermo
See Quiroga, Horacio (Sylvestre)

Ezekiel, Nissim 1924- .... **CLC 61**
See also CA 61-64

Ezekiel, Tish O'Dowd 1943- .... **CLC 34**
See also CA 129

Fadeyev, A.
See Bulgya, Alexander Alexandrovich

Fadeyev, Alexander .... **TCLC 53**
See also Bulgya, Alexander Alexandrovich

Fagen, Donald 1948- .... **CLC 26**

Fainzilberg, Ilya Arnoldovich 1897-1937
See Ilf, Ilya
See also CA 120

Fair, Ronald L. 1932- .... **CLC 18**
See also BW 1; CA 69-72; CANR 25;
DLB 33

Fairbairns, Zoe (Ann) 1948- .... **CLC 32**
See also CA 103; CANR 21

Falco, Gian
See Papini, Giovanni

Falconer, James
See Kirkup, James

Falconer, Kenneth
See Kornbluth, C(yril) M.

Falkland, Samuel
See Heijermans, Herman

Fallaci, Oriana 1930- .... **CLC 11**
See also CA 77-80; CANR 15; MTCW

Faludy, George 1913- .... **CLC 42**
See also CA 21-24R

Faludy, Gyoergy
See Faludy, George

Fanon, Frantz 1925-1961 ..... **CLC 74; BLC**
See also BW 1; CA 116; 89-92

Fanshawe, Ann 1625-1680 .... **LC 11**

Fante, John (Thomas) 1911-1983 ... **CLC 60**
See also CA 69-72; 109; CANR 23;
DLB 130; DLBY 83

Farah, Nuruddin 1945- .... **CLC 53; BLC**
See also BW 2; CA 106; DLB 125

Fargue, Leon-Paul 1876(?)-1947 ... **TCLC 11**
See also CA 109

Farigoule, Louis
See Romains, Jules

Farina, Richard 1936(?)-1966 .... **CLC 9**
See also CA 81-84; 25-28R

Farley, Walter (Lorimer)
1915-1989 .... **CLC 17**
See also CA 17-20R; CANR 8, 29; DLB 22;
JRDA; MAICYA; SATA 2, 43

Farmer, Philip Jose 1918- ...... **CLC 1, 19**
See also CA 1-4R; CANR 4, 35; DLB 8;
MTCW

Farquhar, George 1677-1707 .... **LC 21**
See also DLB 84

Farrell, J(ames) G(ordon)
1935-1979 .... **CLC 6**
See also CA 73-76; 89-92; CANR 36;
DLB 14; MTCW

Farrell, James T(homas)
1904-1979 .... **CLC 1, 4, 8, 11, 66**
See also CA 5-8R; 89-92; CANR 9; DLB 4,
9, 86; DLBD 2; MTCW

Farren, Richard J.
See Betjeman, John

Farren, Richard M.
See Betjeman, John

Fassbinder, Rainer Werner
1946-1982 .... **CLC 20**
See also CA 93-96; 106; CANR 31

Fast, Howard (Melvin) 1914- ...... **CLC 23**
See also CA 1-4R; CAAS 18; CANR 1, 33;
DLB 9; SATA 7

Faulcon, Robert
See Holdstock, Robert P.

Faulkner, William (Cuthbert)
1897-1962 ..... **CLC 1, 3, 6, 8, 9, 11, 14,
18, 28, 52, 68; DA; DAB; SSC 1; WLC**
See also AAYA 7; CA 81-84; CANR 33;
CDALB 1929-1941; DLB 9, 11, 44, 102;
DLBD 2; DLBY 86; MTCW

Fauset, Jessie Redmon
1884(?)-1961 .... **CLC 19, 54; BLC**
See also BW 1; CA 109; DLB 51

Faust, Frederick (Schiller)
1892-1944(?) .... **TCLC 49**
See also CA 108

Faust, Irvin 1924- .... **CLC 8**
See also CA 33-36R; CANR 28; DLB 2, 28;
DLBY 80

Fawkes, Guy
See Benchley, Robert (Charles)

Fearing, Kenneth (Flexner)
1902-1961 .... **CLC 51**
See also CA 93-96; DLB 9

Fecamps, Elise
See Creasey, John

Federman, Raymond 1928- ...... **CLC 6, 47**
See also CA 17-20R; CAAS 8; CANR 10,
43; DLBY 80

Federspiel, J(uerg) F. 1931- .... **CLC 42**
See also CA 146

Feiffer, Jules (Ralph) 1929- .... **CLC 2, 8, 64**
See also AAYA 3; CA 17-20R; CANR 30;
DLB 7, 44; MTCW; SATA 8, 61

Feige, Hermann Albert Otto Maximilian
See Traven, B.

Feinberg, David B. 1956-1994 ...... **CLC 59**
See also CA 135; 147

Feinstein, Elaine 1930- .... **CLC 36**
See also CA 69-72; CAAS 1; CANR 31;
DLB 14, 40; MTCW

Feldman, Irving (Mordecai) 1928- .... **CLC 7**
See also CA 1-4R; CANR 1

Fellini, Federico 1920-1993 ..... **CLC 16, 85**
See also CA 65-68; 143; CANR 33

Felsen, Henry Gregor 1916- .... **CLC 17**
See also CA 1-4R; CANR 1; SAAS 2;
SATA 1

Fenton, James Martin 1949- .... **CLC 32**
See also CA 102; DLB 40

Ferber, Edna 1887-1968 .... **CLC 18**
See also AITN 1; CA 5-8R; 25-28R; DLB 9,
28, 86; MTCW; SATA 7

Ferguson, Helen
See Kavan, Anna

Ferguson, Samuel 1810-1886 ..... **NCLC 33**
See also DLB 32

Fergusson, Robert 1750-1774 .... **LC 29**
See also DLB 109

Ferling, Lawrence
See Ferlinghetti, Lawrence (Monsanto)

Ferlinghetti, Lawrence (Monsanto)
1919(?)- .... **CLC 2, 6, 10, 27; PC 1**
See also CA 5-8R; CANR 3, 41;
CDALB 1941-1968; DLB 5, 16; MTCW

Fernandez, Vicente Garcia Huidobro
See Huidobro Fernandez, Vicente Garcia

Ferrer, Gabriel (Francisco Victor) Miro
See Miro (Ferrer), Gabriel (Francisco
Victor)

Ferrier, Susan (Edmonstone)
1782-1854 .... **NCLC 8**
See also DLB 116

Ferrigno, Robert 1948(?)- .... **CLC 65**
See also CA 140

Feuchtwanger, Lion 1884-1958 ..... **TCLC 3**
See also CA 104; DLB 66

Feuillet, Octave 1821-1890 ...... **NCLC 45**

Feydeau, Georges (Leon Jules Marie)
1862-1921 .... **TCLC 22**
See also CA 113

Ficino, Marsilio 1433-1499 .... **LC 12**

Fiedeler, Hans
See Doeblin, Alfred

Fiedler, Leslie A(aron)
1917- .... **CLC 4, 13, 24**
See also CA 9-12R; CANR 7; DLB 28, 67;
MTCW

Field, Andrew 1938- .... **CLC 44**
See also CA 97-100; CANR 25

Field, Eugene 1850-1895 .... **NCLC 3**
See also DLB 23, 42, 140; MAICYA;
SATA 16

Field, Gans T.
See Wellman, Manly Wade

Field, Michael . . . . **TCLC 43**

Field, Peter
See Hobson, Laura Z(ametkin)

Fielding, Henry
1707-1754 . . . . . . **LC 1; DA; DAB; WLC**
See also CDBLB 1660-1789; DLB 39, 84, 101

Fielding, Sarah 1710-1768 . . . . **LC 1**
See also DLB 39

Fierstein, Harvey (Forbes) 1954- . . . **CLC 33**
See also CA 123; 129

Figes, Eva 1932- . . . . **CLC 31**
See also CA 53-56; CANR 4, 44; DLB 14

Finch, Robert (Duer Claydon)
1900- . . . . **CLC 18**
See also CA 57-60; CANR 9, 24, 49; DLB 88

Findley, Timothy 1930- . . . . **CLC 27**
See also CA 25-28R; CANR 12, 42; DLB 53

Fink, William
See Mencken, H(enry) L(ouis)

Firbank, Louis 1942-
See Reed, Lou
See also CA 117

Firbank, (Arthur Annesley) Ronald
1886-1926 . . . . **TCLC 1**
See also CA 104; DLB 36

Fisher, M(ary) F(rances) K(ennedy)
1908-1992 . . . . **CLC 76, 87**
See also CA 77-80; 138; CANR 44

Fisher, Roy 1930- . . . . **CLC 25**
See also CA 81-84; CAAS 10; CANR 16; DLB 40

Fisher, Rudolph
1897-1934 . . . . **TCLC 11; BLC**
See also BW 1; CA 107; 124; DLB 51, 102

Fisher, Vardis (Alvero) 1895-1968. . . . **CLC 7**
See also CA 5-8R; 25-28R; DLB 9

Fiske, Tarleton
See Bloch, Robert (Albert)

Fitch, Clarke
See Sinclair, Upton (Beall)

Fitch, John IV
See Cormier, Robert (Edmund)

Fitzgerald, Captain Hugh
See Baum, L(yman) Frank

FitzGerald, Edward 1809-1883 . . . . **NCLC 9**
See also DLB 32

Fitzgerald, F(rancis) Scott (Key)
1896-1940 . . . . . . **TCLC 1, 6, 14, 28, 55;**
DA; DAB; SSC 6; WLC
See also AITN 1; CA 110; 123; CDALB 1917-1929; DLB 4, 9, 86; DLBD 1; DLBY 81; MTCW

Fitzgerald, Penelope 1916-. . . **CLC 19, 51, 61**
See also CA 85-88; CAAS 10; DLB 14

Fitzgerald, Robert (Stuart)
1910-1985 . . . . **CLC 39**
See also CA 1-4R; 114; CANR 1; DLBY 80

FitzGerald, Robert D(avid)
1902-1987 . . . . **CLC 19**
See also CA 17-20R

Fitzgerald, Zelda (Sayre)
1900-1948 . . . . **TCLC 52**
See also CA 117; 126; DLBY 84

Flanagan, Thomas (James Bonner)
1923- . . . . **CLC 25, 52**
See also CA 108; DLBY 80; MTCW

Flaubert, Gustave
1821-1880 . . . . **NCLC 2, 10, 19; DA;**
DAB; SSC 11; WLC
See also DLB 119

Flecker, (Herman) James Elroy
1884-1915 . . . . **TCLC 43**
See also CA 109; DLB 10, 19

Fleming, Ian (Lancaster)
1908-1964 . . . . **CLC 3, 30**
See also CA 5-8R; CDBLB 1945-1960; DLB 87; MTCW; SATA 9

Fleming, Thomas (James) 1927- . . . . **CLC 37**
See also CA 5-8R; CANR 10; SATA 8

Fletcher, John Gould 1886-1950. . . **TCLC 35**
See also CA 107; DLB 4, 45

Fleur, Paul
See Pohl, Frederik

Flooglebuckle, Al
See Spiegelman, Art

Flying Officer X
See Bates, H(erbert) E(rnest)

Fo, Dario 1926-. . . . . **CLC 32**
See also CA 116; 128; MTCW

Fogarty, Jonathan Titulescu Esq.
See Farrell, James T(homas)

Folke, Will
See Bloch, Robert (Albert)

Follett, Ken(neth Martin) 1949- . . . . **CLC 18**
See also AAYA 6; BEST 89:4; CA 81-84; CANR 13, 33; DLB 87; DLBY 81; MTCW

Fontane, Theodor 1819-1898 . . . . . **NCLC 26**
See also DLB 129

Foote, Horton 1916-. . . . . **CLC 51**
See also CA 73-76; CANR 34; DLB 26

Foote, Shelby 1916- . . . . **CLC 75**
See also CA 5-8R; CANR 3, 45; DLB 2, 17

Forbes, Esther 1891-1967. . . . . **CLC 12**
See also CA 13-14; 25-28R; CAP 1; CLR 27; DLB 22; JRDA; MAICYA; SATA 2

Forche, Carolyn (Louise)
1950- . . . . **CLC 25, 83, 86; PC 10**
See also CA 109; 117; DLB 5

Ford, Elbur
See Hibbert, Eleanor Alice Burford

Ford, Ford Madox
1873-1939 . . . . **TCLC 1, 15, 39, 57**
See also CA 104; 132; CDBLB 1914-1945; DLB 34, 98; MTCW

Ford, John 1895-1973. . . . . **CLC 16**
See also CA 45-48

Ford, Richard 1944-. . . . . **CLC 46**
See also CA 69-72; CANR 11, 47

Ford, Webster
See Masters, Edgar Lee

Foreman, Richard 1937-. . . . . **CLC 50**
See also CA 65-68; CANR 32

Forester, C(ecil) S(cott)
1899-1966 . . . . **CLC 35**
See also CA 73-76; 25-28R; SATA 13

Forez
See Mauriac, Francois (Charles)

Forman, James Douglas 1932-. . . . . . **CLC 21**
See also CA 9-12R; CANR 4, 19, 42; JRDA; MAICYA; SATA 8, 70

Fornes, Maria Irene 1930-. . . . . . **CLC 39, 61**
See also CA 25-28R; CANR 28; DLB 7; HW; MTCW

Forrest, Leon 1937- . . . . **CLC 4**
See also BW 2; CA 89-92; CAAS 7; CANR 25; DLB 33

Forster, E(dward) M(organ)
1879-1970 . . . . . **CLC 1, 2, 3, 4, 9, 10, 13,**
15, 22, 45, 77; DA; DAB; WLC
See also AAYA 2; CA 13-14; 25-28R; CANR 45; CAP 1; CDBLB 1914-1945; DLB 34, 98; DLBD 10; MTCW; SATA 57

Forster, John 1812-1876 . . . . **NCLC 11**
See also DLB 144

Forsyth, Frederick 1938-. . . . . . **CLC 2, 5, 36**
See also BEST 89:4; CA 85-88; CANR 38; DLB 87; MTCW

Forten, Charlotte L. . . . . **TCLC 16; BLC**
See also Grimke, Charlotte L(ottie) Forten
See also DLB 50

Foscolo, Ugo 1778-1827 . . . . **NCLC 8**

Fosse, Bob . . . . **CLC 20**
See also Fosse, Robert Louis

Fosse, Robert Louis 1927-1987
See Fosse, Bob
See also CA 110; 123

Foster, Stephen Collins
1826-1864 . . . . **NCLC 26**

Foucault, Michel
1926-1984 . . . . **CLC 31, 34, 69**
See also CA 105; 113; CANR 34; MTCW

Fouque, Friedrich (Heinrich Karl) de la Motte
1777-1843 . . . . **NCLC 2**
See also DLB 90

Fourier, Charles 1772-1837 . . . . . . **NCLC 51**

Fournier, Henri Alban 1886-1914
See Alain-Fournier
See also CA 104

Fournier, Pierre 1916-. . . . . **CLC 11**
See also Gascar, Pierre
See also CA 89-92; CANR 16, 40

Fowles, John
1926- . . . . . . **CLC 1, 2, 3, 4, 6, 9, 10, 15,**
33, 87; DAB
See also CA 5-8R; CANR 25; CDBLB 1960 to Present; DLB 14, 139; MTCW; SATA 22

Fox, Paula 1923-. . . . . **CLC 2, 8**
See also AAYA 3; CA 73-76; CANR 20, 36; CLR 1; DLB 52; JRDA; MAICYA; MTCW; SATA 17, 60

Fox, William Price (Jr.) 1926- ..... **CLC 22**
See also CA 17-20R; CAAS 19; CANR 11;
DLB 2; DLBY 81

Foxe, John 1516(?)-1587 .... **LC 14**

Frame, Janet .... **CLC 2, 3, 6, 22, 66**
See also Clutha, Janet Paterson Frame

France, Anatole .... **TCLC 9**
See also Thibault, Jacques Anatole Francois
See also DLB 123

Francis, Claude 19(?)- .... **CLC 50**

Francis, Dick 1920- .... **CLC 2, 22, 42**
See also AAYA 5; BEST 89:3; CA 5-8R;
CANR 9, 42; CDBLB 1960 to Present;
DLB 87; MTCW

Francis, Robert (Churchill)
1901-1987 .... **CLC 15**
See also CA 1-4R; 123; CANR 1

Frank, Anne(lies Marie)
1929-1945 .. **TCLC 17; DA; DAB; WLC**
See also AAYA 12; CA 113; 133; MTCW;
SATA-Brief 42

Frank, Elizabeth 1945- .... **CLC 39**
See also CA 121; 126

Franklin, Benjamin
See Hasek, Jaroslav (Matej Frantisek)

Franklin, Benjamin
1706-1790 .... **LC 25; DA; DAB**
See also CDALB 1640-1865; DLB 24, 43,
73

Franklin, (Stella Maraia Sarah) Miles
1879-1954 .... **TCLC 7**
See also CA 104

Fraser, (Lady) Antonia (Pakenham)
1932- .... **CLC 32**
See also CA 85-88; CANR 44; MTCW;
SATA-Brief 32

Fraser, George MacDonald 1925- .... **CLC 7**
See also CA 45-48; CANR 2, 48

Fraser, Sylvia 1935- .... **CLC 64**
See also CA 45-48; CANR 1, 16

Frayn, Michael 1933- ...... **CLC 3, 7, 31, 47**
See also CA 5-8R; CANR 30; DLB 13, 14;
MTCW

Fraze, Candida (Merrill) 1945- ..... **CLC 50**
See also CA 126

Frazer, J(ames) G(eorge)
1854-1941 .... **TCLC 32**
See also CA 118

Frazer, Robert Caine
See Creasey, John

Frazer, Sir James George
See Frazer, J(ames) G(eorge)

Frazier, Ian 1951- .... **CLC 46**
See also CA 130

Frederic, Harold 1856-1898 ...... **NCLC 10**
See also DLB 12, 23

Frederick, John
See Faust, Frederick (Schiller)

Frederick the Great 1712-1786 ...... **LC 14**

Fredro, Aleksander 1793-1876 ..... **NCLC 8**

Freeling, Nicolas 1927- .... **CLC 38**
See also CA 49-52; CAAS 12; CANR 1, 17;
DLB 87

Freeman, Douglas Southall
1886-1953 .... **TCLC 11**
See also CA 109; DLB 17

Freeman, Judith 1946- .... **CLC 55**
See also CA 148

Freeman, Mary Eleanor Wilkins
1852-1930 .... **TCLC 9; SSC 1**
See also CA 106; DLB 12, 78

Freeman, R(ichard) Austin
1862-1943 .... **TCLC 21**
See also CA 113; DLB 70

French, Albert 1943- .... **CLC 86**

French, Marilyn 1929- ...... **CLC 10, 18, 60**
See also CA 69-72; CANR 3, 31; MTCW

French, Paul
See Asimov, Isaac

Freneau, Philip Morin 1752-1832 .. **NCLC 1**
See also DLB 37, 43

Freud, Sigmund 1856-1939 .... **TCLC 52**
See also CA 115; 133; MTCW

Friedan, Betty (Naomi) 1921- ...... **CLC 74**
See also CA 65-68; CANR 18, 45; MTCW

Friedman, B(ernard) H(arper)
1926- .... **CLC 7**
See also CA 1-4R; CANR 3, 48

Friedman, Bruce Jay 1930- .... **CLC 3, 5, 56**
See also CA 9-12R; CANR 25; DLB 2, 28

Friel, Brian 1929- .... **CLC 5, 42, 59**
See also CA 21-24R; CANR 33; DLB 13;
MTCW

Friis-Baastad, Babbis Ellinor
1921-1970 .... **CLC 12**
See also CA 17-20R; 134; SATA 7

Frisch, Max (Rudolf)
1911-1991 ..... **CLC 3, 9, 14, 18, 32, 44**
See also CA 85-88; 134; CANR 32;
DLB 69, 124; MTCW

Fromentin, Eugene (Samuel Auguste)
1820-1876 .... **NCLC 10**
See also DLB 123

Frost, Frederick
See Faust, Frederick (Schiller)

Frost, Robert (Lee)
1874-1963 .... **CLC 1, 3, 4, 9, 10, 13, 15,
26, 34, 44; DA; DAB; PC 1; WLC**
See also CA 89-92; CANR 33;
CDALB 1917-1929; DLB 54; DLBD 7;
MTCW; SATA 14

Froude, James Anthony
1818-1894 .... **NCLC 43**
See also DLB 18, 57, 144

Froy, Herald
See Waterhouse, Keith (Spencer)

Fry, Christopher 1907- .... **CLC 2, 10, 14**
See also CA 17-20R; CANR 9, 30; DLB 13;
MTCW; SATA 66

Frye, (Herman) Northrop
1912-1991 .... **CLC 24, 70**
See also CA 5-8R; 133; CANR 8, 37;
DLB 67, 68; MTCW

Fuchs, Daniel 1909-1993 .... **CLC 8, 22**
See also CA 81-84; 142; CAAS 5;
CANR 40; DLB 9, 26, 28; DLBY 93

Fuchs, Daniel 1934- .... **CLC 34**
See also CA 37-40R; CANR 14, 48

Fuentes, Carlos
1928- ...... **CLC 3, 8, 10, 13, 22, 41, 60;
DA; DAB; HLC; WLC**
See also AAYA 4; AITN 2; CA 69-72;
CANR 10, 32; DLB 113; HW; MTCW

Fuentes, Gregorio Lopez y
See Lopez y Fuentes, Gregorio

Fugard, (Harold) Athol
1932- .... **CLC 5, 9, 14, 25, 40, 80; DC 3**
See also CA 85-88; CANR 32; MTCW

Fugard, Sheila 1932- .... **CLC 48**
See also CA 125

Fuller, Charles (H., Jr.)
1939- .... **CLC 25; BLC; DC 1**
See also BW 2; CA 108; 112; DLB 38;
MTCW

Fuller, John (Leopold) 1937- ...... **CLC 62**
See also CA 21-24R; CANR 9, 44; DLB 40

Fuller, Margaret .... **NCLC 5, 50**
See also Ossoli, Sarah Margaret (Fuller
marchesa d')

Fuller, Roy (Broadbent)
1912-1991 .... **CLC 4, 28**
See also CA 5-8R; 135; CAAS 10; DLB 15,
20

Fulton, Alice 1952- .... **CLC 52**
See also CA 116

Furphy, Joseph 1843-1912 .... **TCLC 25**

Fussell, Paul 1924- .... **CLC 74**
See also BEST 90:1; CA 17-20R; CANR 8,
21, 35; MTCW

Futabatei, Shimei 1864-1909 ...... **TCLC 44**

Futrelle, Jacques 1875-1912 ...... **TCLC 19**
See also CA 113

Gaboriau, Emile 1835-1873 ...... **NCLC 14**

Gadda, Carlo Emilio 1893-1973 .... **CLC 11**
See also CA 89-92

Gaddis, William
1922- ..... **CLC 1, 3, 6, 8, 10, 19, 43, 86**
See also CA 17-20R; CANR 21, 48; DLB 2;
MTCW

Gaines, Ernest J(ames)
1933- .... **CLC 3, 11, 18, 86; BLC**
See also AITN 1; BW 2; CA 9-12R;
CANR 6, 24, 42; CDALB 1968-1988;
DLB 2, 33, 152; DLBY 80; MTCW

Gaitskill, Mary 1954- .... **CLC 69**
See also CA 128

Galdos, Benito Perez
See Perez Galdos, Benito

Gale, Zona 1874-1938 .... **TCLC 7**
See also CA 105; DLB 9, 78

Galeano, Eduardo (Hughes) 1940- ... **CLC 72**
See also CA 29-32R; CANR 13, 32; HW

Galiano, Juan Valera y Alcala
See Valera y Alcala-Galiano, Juan

Gallagher, Tess 1943- .... **CLC 18, 63; PC 9**
See also CA 106; DLB 120

Gallant, Mavis
1922- .... **CLC 7, 18, 38; SSC 5**
See also CA 69-72; CANR 29; DLB 53;
MTCW

Gallant, Roy A(rthur) 1924- . . . . **CLC 17**
See also CA 5-8R; CANR 4, 29; CLR 30;
MAICYA; SATA 4, 68

Gallico, Paul (William) 1897-1976 . . . **CLC 2**
See also AITN 1; CA 5-8R; 69-72;
CANR 23; DLB 9; MAICYA; SATA 13

Gallup, Ralph
See Whitemore, Hugh (John)

Galsworthy, John
1867-1933 . . . . . . **TCLC 1, 45; DA; DAB;**
WLC 2
See also CA 104; 141; CDBLB 1890-1914;
DLB 10, 34, 98

Galt, John 1779-1839 . . . . **NCLC 1**
See also DLB 99, 116

Galvin, James 1951- . . . . **CLC 38**
See also CA 108; CANR 26

Gamboa, Federico 1864-1939 . . . . . . **TCLC 36**

Gandhi, M. K.
See Gandhi, Mohandas Karamchand

Gandhi, Mahatma
See Gandhi, Mohandas Karamchand

Gandhi, Mohandas Karamchand
1869-1948 . . . . **TCLC 59**
See also CA 121; 132; MTCW

Gann, Ernest Kellogg 1910-1991 . . . . **CLC 23**
See also AITN 1; CA 1-4R; 136; CANR 1

Garcia, Cristina 1958- . . . . **CLC 76**
See also CA 141

Garcia Lorca, Federico
1898-1936 . . . **TCLC 1, 7, 49; DA; DAB;**
DC 2; HLC; PC 3; WLC
See also CA 104; 131; DLB 108; HW;
MTCW

Garcia Marquez, Gabriel (Jose)
1928- . . . . **CLC 2, 3, 8, 10, 15, 27, 47, 55,**
68; DA; DAB; HLC; SSC 8; WLC
See also AAYA 3; BEST 89:1, 90:4;
CA 33-36R; CANR 10, 28; DLB 113;
HW; MTCW

Gard, Janice
See Latham, Jean Lee

Gard, Roger Martin du
See Martin du Gard, Roger

Gardam, Jane 1928- . . . . **CLC 43**
See also CA 49-52; CANR 2, 18, 33;
CLR 12; DLB 14; MAICYA; MTCW;
SAAS 9; SATA 39, 76; SATA-Brief 28

Gardner, Herb . . . . **CLC 44**

Gardner, John (Champlin), Jr.
1933-1982 . . . . . **CLC 2, 3, 5, 7, 8, 10, 18,**
28, 34; SSC 7
See also AITN 1; CA 65-68; 107;
CANR 33; DLB 2; DLBY 82; MTCW;
SATA 40; SATA-Obit 31

Gardner, John (Edmund) 1926- . . . . . **CLC 30**
See also CA 103; CANR 15; MTCW

Gardner, Noel
See Kuttner, Henry

Gardons, S. S.
See Snodgrass, W(illiam) D(e Witt)

Garfield, Leon 1921- . . . . **CLC 12**
See also AAYA 8; CA 17-20R; CANR 38,
41; CLR 21; JRDA; MAICYA; SATA 1,
32, 76

Garland, (Hannibal) Hamlin
1860-1940 . . . . **TCLC 3; SSC 18**
See also CA 104; DLB 12, 71, 78

Garneau, (Hector de) Saint-Denys
1912-1943 . . . . **TCLC 13**
See also CA 111; DLB 88

Garner, Alan 1934- . . . . **CLC 17; DAB**
See also CA 73-76; CANR 15; CLR 20;
MAICYA; MTCW; SATA 18, 69

Garner, Hugh 1913-1979 . . . . **CLC 13**
See also CA 69-72; CANR 31; DLB 68

Garnett, David 1892-1981 . . . . **CLC 3**
See also CA 5-8R; 103; CANR 17; DLB 34

Garos, Stephanie
See Katz, Steve

Garrett, George (Palmer)
1929- . . . . **CLC 3, 11, 51**
See also CA 1-4R; CAAS 5; CANR 1, 42;
DLB 2, 5, 130, 152; DLBY 83

Garrick, David 1717-1779 . . . . **LC 15**
See also DLB 84

Garrigue, Jean 1914-1972 . . . . **CLC 2, 8**
See also CA 5-8R; 37-40R; CANR 20

Garrison, Frederick
See Sinclair, Upton (Beall)

Garth, Will
See Hamilton, Edmond; Kuttner, Henry

Garvey, Marcus (Moziah, Jr.)
1887-1940 . . . . **TCLC 41; BLC**
See also BW 1; CA 120; 124

Gary, Romain . . . . **CLC 25**
See also Kacew, Romain
See also DLB 83

Gascar, Pierre . . . . **CLC 11**
See also Fournier, Pierre

Gascoyne, David (Emery) 1916- . . . . **CLC 45**
See also CA 65-68; CANR 10, 28; DLB 20;
MTCW

Gaskell, Elizabeth Cleghorn
1810-1865 . . . . **NCLC 5; DAB**
See also CDBLB 1832-1890; DLB 21, 144

Gass, William H(oward)
1924- . . . **CLC 1, 2, 8, 11, 15, 39; SSC 12**
See also CA 17-20R; CANR 30; DLB 2;
MTCW

Gasset, Jose Ortega y
See Ortega y Gasset, Jose

Gates, Henry Louis, Jr. 1950- . . . . . . **CLC 65**
See also BW 2; CA 109; CANR 25; DLB 67

Gautier, Theophile
1811-1872 . . . . **NCLC 1; SSC 20**
See also DLB 119

Gawsworth, John
See Bates, H(erbert) E(rnest)

Gaye, Marvin (Penze) 1939-1984 . . . **CLC 26**
See also CA 112

Gebler, Carlo (Ernest) 1954- . . . . **CLC 39**
See also CA 119; 133

Gee, Maggie (Mary) 1948- . . . . **CLC 57**
See also CA 130

Gee, Maurice (Gough) 1931- . . . . **CLC 29**
See also CA 97-100; SATA 46

Gelbart, Larry (Simon) 1923- . . . **CLC 21, 61**
See also CA 73-76; CANR 45

Gelber, Jack 1932- . . . . **CLC 1, 6, 14, 79**
See also CA 1-4R; CANR 2; DLB 7

Gellhorn, Martha (Ellis) 1908- . . **CLC 14, 60**
See also CA 77-80; CANR 44; DLBY 82

Genet, Jean
1910-1986 . . . **CLC 1, 2, 5, 10, 14, 44, 46**
See also CA 13-16R; CANR 18; DLB 72;
DLBY 86; MTCW

Gent, Peter 1942- . . . . **CLC 29**
See also AITN 1; CA 89-92; DLBY 82

Gentlewoman in New England, A
See Bradstreet, Anne

Gentlewoman in Those Parts, A
See Bradstreet, Anne

George, Jean Craighead 1919- . . . . . . **CLC 35**
See also AAYA 8; CA 5-8R; CANR 25;
CLR 1; DLB 52; JRDA; MAICYA;
SATA 2, 68

George, Stefan (Anton)
1868-1933 . . . . **TCLC 2, 14**
See also CA 104

Georges, Georges Martin
See Simenon, Georges (Jacques Christian)

Gerhardi, William Alexander
See Gerhardie, William Alexander

Gerhardie, William Alexander
1895-1977 . . . . **CLC 5**
See also CA 25-28R; 73-76; CANR 18;
DLB 36

Gerstler, Amy 1956- . . . . **CLC 70**
See also CA 146

Gertler, T. . . . . **CLC 34**
See also CA 116; 121

Ghalib 1797-1869 . . . . **NCLC 39**

Ghelderode, Michel de
1898-1962 . . . . **CLC 6, 11**
See also CA 85-88; CANR 40

Ghiselin, Brewster 1903- . . . . **CLC 23**
See also CA 13-16R; CAAS 10; CANR 13

Ghose, Zulfikar 1935- . . . . **CLC 42**
See also CA 65-68

Ghosh, Amitav 1956- . . . . **CLC 44**
See also CA 147

Giacosa, Giuseppe 1847-1906 . . . . . . **TCLC 7**
See also CA 104

Gibb, Lee
See Waterhouse, Keith (Spencer)

Gibbon, Lewis Grassic . . . . **TCLC 4**
See also Mitchell, James Leslie

Gibbons, Kaye 1960- . . . . **CLC 50, 88**

Gibran, Kahlil
1883-1931 . . . . **TCLC 1, 9; PC 9**
See also CA 104

Gibson, William 1914- . . **CLC 23; DA; DAB**
See also CA 9-12R; CANR 9, 42; DLB 7;
SATA 66

Gibson, William (Ford) 1948- . . . **CLC 39, 63**
See also AAYA 12; CA 126; 133

Gide, Andre (Paul Guillaume)
1869-1951 . . . . **TCLC 5, 12, 36; DA;**
DAB; SSC 13; WLC
See also CA 104; 124; DLB 65; MTCW

Gifford, Barry (Colby) 1946- . . . . **CLC 34**
See also CA 65-68; CANR 9, 30, 40

Gilbert, W(illiam) S(chwenck)
1836-1911 .... TCLC 3
See also CA 104; SATA 36

Gilbreth, Frank B., Jr. 1911- .... CLC 17
See also CA 9-12R; SATA 2

Gilchrist, Ellen 1935- .. CLC 34, 48; SSC 14
See also CA 113; 116; CANR 41; DLB 130;
MTCW

Giles, Molly 1942- .... CLC 39
See also CA 126

Gill, Patrick
See Creasey, John

Gilliam, Terry (Vance) 1940- .... CLC 21
See also Monty Python
See also CA 108; 113; CANR 35

Gillian, Jerry
See Gilliam, Terry (Vance)

Gilliatt, Penelope (Ann Douglass)
1932-1993 .... CLC 2, 10, 13, 53
See also AITN 2; CA 13-16R; 141;
CANR 49; DLB 14

Gilman, Charlotte (Anna) Perkins (Stetson)
1860-1935 .... TCLC 9, 37; SSC 13
See also CA 106

Gilmour, David 1949- .... CLC 35
See also CA 138, 147

Gilpin, William 1724-1804 .... NCLC 30

Gilray, J. D.
See Mencken, H(enry) L(ouis)

Gilroy, Frank D(aniel) 1925- .... CLC 2
See also CA 81-84; CANR 32; DLB 7

Ginsberg, Allen
1926- ...... CLC 1, 2, 3, 4, 6, 13, 36, 69;
DA; DAB; PC 4; WLC 3
See also AITN 1; CA 1-4R; CANR 2, 41;
CDALB 1941-1968; DLB 5, 16; MTCW

Ginzburg, Natalia
1916-1991 .... CLC 5, 11, 54, 70
See also CA 85-88; 135; CANR 33; MTCW

Giono, Jean 1895-1970 .... CLC 4, 11
See also CA 45-48; 29-32R; CANR 2, 35;
DLB 72; MTCW

Giovanni, Nikki
1943- ...... CLC 2, 4, 19, 64; BLC; DA;
DAB
See also AITN 1; BW 2; CA 29-32R;
CAAS 6; CANR 18, 41; CLR 6; DLB 5,
41; MAICYA; MTCW; SATA 24

Giovene, Andrea 1904- .... CLC 7
See also CA 85-88

Gippius, Zinaida (Nikolayevna) 1869-1945
See Hippius, Zinaida
See also CA 106

Giraudoux, (Hippolyte) Jean
1882-1944 .... TCLC 2, 7
See also CA 104; DLB 65

Gironella, Jose Maria 1917- .... CLC 11
See also CA 101

Gissing, George (Robert)
1857-1903 .... TCLC 3, 24, 47
See also CA 105; DLB 18, 135

Giurlani, Aldo
See Palazzeschi, Aldo

Gladkov, Fyodor (Vasilyevich)
1883-1958 .... TCLC 27

Glanville, Brian (Lester) 1931- ...... CLC 6
See also CA 5-8R; CAAS 9; CANR 3;
DLB 15, 139; SATA 42

Glasgow, Ellen (Anderson Gholson)
1873(?)-1945 .... TCLC 2, 7
See also CA 104; DLB 9, 12

Glaspell, Susan (Keating)
1882(?)-1948 .... TCLC 55
See also CA 110; DLB 7, 9, 78; YABC 2

Glassco, John 1909-1981 .... CLC 9
See also CA 13-16R; 102; CANR 15;
DLB 68

Glasscock, Amnesia
See Steinbeck, John (Ernst)

Glasser, Ronald J. 1940(?)- .... CLC 37

Glassman, Joyce
See Johnson, Joyce

Glendinning, Victoria 1937- .... CLC 50
See also CA 120; 127; DLB 155

Glissant, Edouard 1928- .... CLC 10, 68

Gloag, Julian 1930- .... CLC 40
See also AITN 1; CA 65-68; CANR 10

Glowacki, Aleksander
See Prus, Boleslaw

Glueck, Louise (Elisabeth)
1943- .... CLC 7, 22, 44, 81
See also CA 33-36R; CANR 40; DLB 5

Gobineau, Joseph Arthur (Comte) de
1816-1882 .... NCLC 17
See also DLB 123

Godard, Jean-Luc 1930- .... CLC 20
See also CA 93-96

Godden, (Margaret) Rumer 1907- ... CLC 53
See also AAYA 6; CA 5-8R; CANR 4, 27,
36; CLR 20; MAICYA; SAAS 12;
SATA 3, 36

Godoy Alcayaga, Lucila 1889-1957
See Mistral, Gabriela
See also BW 2; CA 104; 131; HW; MTCW

Godwin, Gail (Kathleen)
1937- .... CLC 5, 8, 22, 31, 69
See also CA 29-32R; CANR 15, 43; DLB 6;
MTCW

Godwin, William 1756-1836 ...... NCLC 14
See also CDBLB 1789-1832; DLB 39, 104,
142

Goethe, Johann Wolfgang von
1749-1832 .... NCLC 4, 22, 34; DA;
DAB; PC 5; WLC 3
See also DLB 94

Gogarty, Oliver St. John
1878-1957 .... TCLC 15
See also CA 109; DLB 15, 19

Gogol, Nikolai (Vasilyevich)
1809-1852 .... NCLC 5, 15, 31; DA;
DAB; DC 1; SSC 4; WLC
See also

Goines, Donald
1937(?)-1974 .... CLC 80; BLC
See also AITN 1; BW 1; CA 124; 114;
DLB 33

Gold, Herbert 1924- .... CLC 4, 7, 14, 42
See also CA 9-12R; CANR 17, 45; DLB 2;
DLBY 81

Goldbarth, Albert 1948- .... CLC 5, 38
See also CA 53-56; CANR 6, 40; DLB 120

Goldberg, Anatol 1910-1982 .... CLC 34
See also CA 131; 117

Goldemberg, Isaac 1945- .... CLC 52
See also CA 69-72; CAAS 12; CANR 11,
32; HW

Golding, William (Gerald)
1911-1993 .... CLC 1, 2, 3, 8, 10, 17, 27,
58, 81; DA; DAB; WLC
See also AAYA 5; CA 5-8R; 141;
CANR 13, 33; CDBLB 1945-1960;
DLB 15, 100; MTCW

Goldman, Emma 1869-1940 ...... TCLC 13
See also CA 110

Goldman, Francisco 1955- .... CLC 76

Goldman, William (W.) 1931- .... CLC 1, 48
See also CA 9-12R; CANR 29; DLB 44

Goldmann, Lucien 1913-1970 ...... CLC 24
See also CA 25-28; CAP 2

Goldoni, Carlo 1707-1793 .... LC 4

Goldsberry, Steven 1949- .... CLC 34
See also CA 131

Goldsmith, Oliver
1728-1774 ...... LC 2; DA; DAB; WLC
See also CDBLB 1660-1789; DLB 39, 89,
104, 109, 142; SATA 26

Goldsmith, Peter
See Priestley, J(ohn) B(oynton)

Gombrowicz, Witold
1904-1969 .... CLC 4, 7, 11, 49
See also CA 19-20; 25-28R; CAP 2

Gomez de la Serna, Ramon
1888-1963 .... CLC 9
See also CA 116; HW

Goncharov, Ivan Alexandrovich
1812-1891 .... NCLC 1

Goncourt, Edmond (Louis Antoine Huot) de
1822-1896 .... NCLC 7
See also DLB 123

Goncourt, Jules (Alfred Huot) de
1830-1870 .... NCLC 7
See also DLB 123

Gontier, Fernande 19(?)- .... CLC 50

Goodman, Paul 1911-1972 .... CLC 1, 2, 4, 7
See also CA 19-20; 37-40R; CANR 34;
CAP 2; DLB 130; MTCW

Gordimer, Nadine
1923- .... CLC 3, 5, 7, 10, 18, 33, 51, 70;
DA; DAB; SSC 17
See also CA 5-8R; CANR 3, 28; MTCW

Gordon, Adam Lindsay
1833-1870 .... NCLC 21

Gordon, Caroline
1895-1981 ... CLC 6, 13, 29, 83; SSC 15
See also CA 11-12; 103; CANR 36; CAP 1;
DLB 4, 9, 102; DLBY 81; MTCW

Gordon, Charles William 1860-1937
See Connor, Ralph
See also CA 109

Gordon, Mary (Catherine)
1949- .... CLC 13, 22
See also CA 102; CANR 44; DLB 6;
DLBY 81; MTCW

Gordon, Sol 1923- .... CLC 26
See also CA 53-56; CANR 4; SATA 11

Gordone, Charles 1925- .... **CLC 1, 4**
See also BW 1; CA 93-96; DLB 7; MTCW

Gorenko, Anna Andreevna
See Akhmatova, Anna

Gorky, Maxim .... **TCLC 8; DAB; WLC**
See also Peshkov, Alexei Maximovich

Goryan, Sirak
See Saroyan, William

Gosse, Edmund (William)
1849-1928 .... **TCLC 28**
See also CA 117; DLB 57, 144

Gotlieb, Phyllis Fay (Bloom)
1926- .... **CLC 18**
See also CA 13-16R; CANR 7; DLB 88

Gottesman, S. D.
See Kornbluth, C(yril) M.; Pohl, Frederik

Gottfried von Strassburg
fl. c. 1210- .... **CMLC 10**
See also DLB 138

Gould, Lois .... **CLC 4, 10**
See also CA 77-80; CANR 29; MTCW

Gourmont, Remy de 1858-1915.... **TCLC 17**
See also CA 109

Govier, Katherine 1948- .... **CLC 51**
See also CA 101; CANR 18, 40

Goyen, (Charles) William
1915-1983 .... **CLC 5, 8, 14, 40**
See also AITN 2; CA 5-8R; 110; CANR 6;
DLB 2; DLBY 83

Goytisolo, Juan
1931- .... **CLC 5, 10, 23; HLC**
See also CA 85-88; CANR 32; HW; MTCW

Gozzano, Guido 1883-1916 .... **PC 10**
See also DLB 114

Gozzi, (Conte) Carlo 1720-1806 .. **NCLC 23**

Grabbe, Christian Dietrich
1801-1836 .... **NCLC 2**
See also DLB 133

Grace, Patricia 1937- .... **CLC 56**

Gracian y Morales, Baltasar
1601-1658 .... **LC 15**

Gracq, Julien .... **CLC 11, 48**
See also Poirier, Louis
See also DLB 83

Grade, Chaim 1910-1982 .... **CLC 10**
See also CA 93-96; 107

Graduate of Oxford, A
See Ruskin, John

Graham, John
See Phillips, David Graham

Graham, Jorie 1951- .... **CLC 48**
See also CA 111; DLB 120

Graham, R(obert) B(ontine) Cunninghame
See Cunninghame Graham, R(obert)
B(ontine)
See also DLB 98, 135

Graham, Robert
See Haldeman, Joe (William)

Graham, Tom
See Lewis, (Harry) Sinclair

Graham, W(illiam) S(ydney)
1918-1986 .... **CLC 29**
See also CA 73-76; 118; DLB 20

Graham, Winston (Mawdsley)
1910- .... **CLC 23**
See also CA 49-52; CANR 2, 22, 45;
DLB 77

Grant, Skeeter
See Spiegelman, Art

Granville-Barker, Harley
1877-1946 .... **TCLC 2**
See also Barker, Harley Granville
See also CA 104

Grass, Guenter (Wilhelm)
1927- ..... **CLC 1, 2, 4, 6, 11, 15, 22, 32, 49, 88; DA; DAB; WLC**
See also CA 13-16R; CANR 20; DLB 75, 124; MTCW

Gratton, Thomas
See Hulme, T(homas) E(rnest)

Grau, Shirley Ann
1929- .... **CLC 4, 9; SSC 15**
See also CA 89-92; CANR 22; DLB 2; MTCW

Gravel, Fern
See Hall, James Norman

Graver, Elizabeth 1964- .... **CLC 70**
See also CA 135

Graves, Richard Perceval 1945- .... **CLC 44**
See also CA 65-68; CANR 9, 26

Graves, Robert (von Ranke)
1895-1985 ...... **CLC 1, 2, 6, 11, 39, 44, 45; DAB; PC 6**
See also CA 5-8R; 117; CANR 5, 36;
CDBLB 1914-1945; DLB 20, 100;
DLBY 85; MTCW; SATA 45

Gray, Alasdair (James) 1934- ...... **CLC 41**
See also CA 126; CANR 47; MTCW

Gray, Amlin 1946- .... **CLC 29**
See also CA 138

Gray, Francine du Plessix 1930-.... **CLC 22**
See also BEST 90:3; CA 61-64; CAAS 2;
CANR 11, 33; MTCW

Gray, John (Henry) 1866-1934 .... **TCLC 19**
See also CA 119

Gray, Simon (James Holliday)
1936- .... **CLC 9, 14, 36**
See also AITN 1; CA 21-24R; CAAS 3;
CANR 32; DLB 13; MTCW

Gray, Spalding 1941- .... **CLC 49**
See also CA 128

Gray, Thomas
1716-1771 ...... **LC 4; DA; DAB; PC 2; WLC**
See also CDBLB 1660-1789; DLB 109

Grayson, David
See Baker, Ray Stannard

Grayson, Richard (A.) 1951- .... **CLC 38**
See also CA 85-88; CANR 14, 31

Greeley, Andrew M(oran) 1928- .... **CLC 28**
See also CA 5-8R; CAAS 7; CANR 7, 43;
MTCW

Green, Brian
See Card, Orson Scott

Green, Hannah
See Greenberg, Joanne (Goldenberg)

Green, Hannah .... **CLC 3**
See also CA 73-76

Green, Henry .... **CLC 2, 13**
See also Yorke, Henry Vincent
See also DLB 15

Green, Julian (Hartridge) 1900-
See Green, Julien
See also CA 21-24R; CANR 33; DLB 4, 72;
MTCW

Green, Julien .... **CLC 3, 11, 77**
See also Green, Julian (Hartridge)

Green, Paul (Eliot) 1894-1981...... **CLC 25**
See also AITN 1; CA 5-8R; 103; CANR 3;
DLB 7, 9; DLBY 81

Greenberg, Ivan 1908-1973
See Rahv, Philip
See also CA 85-88

Greenberg, Joanne (Goldenberg)
1932- .... **CLC 7, 30**
See also AAYA 12; CA 5-8R; CANR 14,
32; SATA 25

Greenberg, Richard 1959(?)- .... **CLC 57**
See also CA 138

Greene, Bette 1934- .... **CLC 30**
See also AAYA 7; CA 53-56; CANR 4;
CLR 2; JRDA; MAICYA; SAAS 16;
SATA 8

Greene, Gael .... **CLC 8**
See also CA 13-16R; CANR 10

Greene, Graham
1904-1991 .... **CLC 1, 3, 6, 9, 14, 18, 27, 37, 70, 72; DA; DAB; WLC**
See also AITN 2; CA 13-16R; 133;
CANR 35; CDBLB 1945-1960; DLB 13,
15, 77, 100; DLBY 91; MTCW; SATA 20

Greer, Richard
See Silverberg, Robert

Gregor, Arthur 1923- .... **CLC 9**
See also CA 25-28R; CAAS 10; CANR 11;
SATA 36

Gregor, Lee
See Pohl, Frederik

Gregory, Isabella Augusta (Persse)
1852-1932 .... **TCLC 1**
See also CA 104; DLB 10

Gregory, J. Dennis
See Williams, John A(lfred)

Grendon, Stephen
See Derleth, August (William)

Grenville, Kate 1950- .... **CLC 61**
See also CA 118

Grenville, Pelham
See Wodehouse, P(elham) G(renville)

Greve, Felix Paul (Berthold Friedrich)
1879-1948
See Grove, Frederick Philip
See also CA 104; 141

Grey, Zane 1872-1939 .... **TCLC 6**
See also CA 104; 132; DLB 9; MTCW

Grieg, (Johan) Nordahl (Brun)
1902-1943 .... **TCLC 10**
See also CA 107

Grieve, C(hristopher) M(urray)
1892-1978 .... **CLC 11, 19**
See also MacDiarmid, Hugh
See also CA 5-8R; 85-88; CANR 33;
MTCW

Griffin, Gerald 1803-1840 .... NCLC 7

Griffin, John Howard 1920-1980.... CLC 68
See also AITN 1; CA 1-4R; 101; CANR 2

Griffin, Peter 1942- .... CLC 39
See also CA 136

Griffiths, Trevor 1935-......... CLC 13, 52
See also CA 97-100; CANR 45; DLB 13

Grigson, Geoffrey (Edward Harvey)
1905-1985 .... CLC 7, 39
See also CA 25-28R; 118; CANR 20, 33;
DLB 27; MTCW

Grillparzer, Franz 1791-1872...... NCLC 1
See also DLB 133

Grimble, Reverend Charles James
See Eliot, T(homas) S(tearns)

Grimke, Charlotte L(ottie) Forten
1837(?)-1914
See Forten, Charlotte L.
See also BW 1; CA 117; 124

Grimm, Jacob Ludwig Karl
1785-1863 .... NCLC 3
See also DLB 90; MAICYA; SATA 22

Grimm, Wilhelm Karl 1786-1859 .. NCLC 3
See also DLB 90; MAICYA; SATA 22

Grimmelshausen, Johann Jakob Christoffel
von 1621-1676 .... LC 6

Grindel, Eugene 1895-1952
See Eluard, Paul
See also CA 104

Grisham, John 1955- .... CLC 84
See also AAYA 14; CA 138; CANR 47

Grossman, David 1954- .... CLC 67
See also CA 138

Grossman, Vasily (Semenovich)
1905-1964 .... CLC 41
See also CA 124; 130; MTCW

Grove, Frederick Philip .... TCLC 4
See also Greve, Felix Paul (Berthold
Friedrich)
See also DLB 92

Grubb
See Crumb, R(obert)

Grumbach, Doris (Isaac)
1918- .... CLC 13, 22, 64
See also CA 5-8R; CAAS 2; CANR 9, 42

Grundtvig, Nicolai Frederik Severin
1783-1872 .... NCLC 1

Grunge
See Crumb, R(obert)

Grunwald, Lisa 1959-............. CLC 44
See also CA 120

Guare, John 1938- .... CLC 8, 14, 29, 67
See also CA 73-76; CANR 21; DLB 7;
MTCW

Gudjonsson, Halldor Kiljan 1902-
See Laxness, Halldor
See also CA 103

Guenter, Erich
See Eich, Guenter

Guest, Barbara 1920-............. CLC 34
See also CA 25-28R; CANR 11, 44; DLB 5

Guest, Judith (Ann) 1936-........ CLC 8, 30
See also AAYA 7; CA 77-80; CANR 15;
MTCW

Guevara, Che............... CLC 87; HLC
See also Guevara (Serna), Ernesto

Guevara (Serna), Ernesto 1928-1967
See Guevara, Che
See also CA 127; 111; HW

Guild, Nicholas M. 1944-......... CLC 33
See also CA 93-96

Guillemin, Jacques
See Sartre, Jean-Paul

Guillen, Jorge 1893-1984.......... CLC 11
See also CA 89-92; 112; DLB 108; HW

Guillen (y Batista), Nicolas (Cristobal)
1902-1989 ..... CLC 48, 79; BLC; HLC
See also BW 2; CA 116; 125; 129; HW

Guillevic, (Eugene) 1907-.......... CLC 33
See also CA 93-96

Guillois
See Desnos, Robert

Guiney, Louise Imogen
1861-1920 .... TCLC 41
See also DLB 54

Guiraldes, Ricardo (Guillermo)
1886-1927 .... TCLC 39
See also CA 131; HW; MTCW

Gumilev, Nikolai Stephanovich
1886-1921 .... TCLC 60

Gunn, Bill .... CLC 5
See also Gunn, William Harrison
See also DLB 38

Gunn, Thom(son William)
1929- .... CLC 3, 6, 18, 32, 81
See also CA 17-20R; CANR 9, 33;
CDBLB 1960 to Present; DLB 27;
MTCW

Gunn, William Harrison 1934(?)-1989
See Gunn, Bill
See also AITN 1; BW 1; CA 13-16R; 128;
CANR 12, 25

Gunnars, Kristjana 1948-.......... CLC 69
See also CA 113; DLB 60

Gurganus, Allan 1947-............ CLC 70
See also BEST 90:1; CA 135

Gurney, A(lbert) R(amsdell), Jr.
1930- .... CLC 32, 50, 54
See also CA 77-80; CANR 32

Gurney, Ivor (Bertie) 1890-1937... TCLC 33

Gurney, Peter
See Gurney, A(lbert) R(amsdell), Jr.

Guro, Elena 1877-1913.......... TCLC 56

Gustafson, Ralph (Barker) 1909-.... CLC 36
See also CA 21-24R; CANR 8, 45; DLB 88

Gut, Gom
See Simenon, Georges (Jacques Christian)

Guthrie, A(lfred) B(ertram), Jr.
1901-1991 .... CLC 23
See also CA 57-60; 134; CANR 24; DLB 6;
SATA 62; SATA-Obit 67

Guthrie, Isobel
See Grieve, C(hristopher) M(urray)

Guthrie, Woodrow Wilson 1912-1967
See Guthrie, Woody
See also CA 113; 93-96

Guthrie, Woody.................. CLC 35
See also Guthrie, Woodrow Wilson

Guy, Rosa (Cuthbert) 1928-........ CLC 26
See also AAYA 4; BW 2; CA 17-20R;
CANR 14, 34; CLR 13; DLB 33; JRDA;
MAICYA; SATA 14, 62

Gwendolyn
See Bennett, (Enoch) Arnold

H. D. .... CLC 3, 8, 14, 31, 34, 73; PC 5
See also Doolittle, Hilda

H. de V.
See Buchan, John

Haavikko, Paavo Juhani
1931- .... CLC 18, 34
See also CA 106

Habbema, Koos
See Heijermans, Herman

Hacker, Marilyn 1942- .... CLC 5, 9, 23, 72
See also CA 77-80; DLB 120

Haggard, H(enry) Rider
1856-1925 .... TCLC 11
See also CA 108; 148; DLB 70; SATA 16

Hagiwara Sakutaro 1886-1942 .... TCLC 60

Haig, Fenil
See Ford, Ford Madox

Haig-Brown, Roderick (Langmere)
1908-1976 .... CLC 21
See also CA 5-8R; 69-72; CANR 4, 38;
CLR 31; DLB 88; MAICYA; SATA 12

Hailey, Arthur 1920- .... CLC 5
See also AITN 2; BEST 90:3; CA 1-4R;
CANR 2, 36; DLB 88; DLBY 82; MTCW

Hailey, Elizabeth Forsythe 1938-... CLC 40
See also CA 93-96; CAAS 1; CANR 15, 48

Haines, John (Meade) 1924-....... CLC 58
See also CA 17-20R; CANR 13, 34; DLB 5

Haldeman, Joe (William) 1943-..... CLC 61
See also CA 53-56; CANR 6; DLB 8

Haley, Alex(ander Murray Palmer)
1921-1992 .... CLC 8, 12, 76; BLC; DA;
DAB
See also BW 2; CA 77-80; 136; DLB 38;
MTCW

Haliburton, Thomas Chandler
1796-1865 .... NCLC 15
See also DLB 11, 99

Hall, Donald (Andrew, Jr.)
1928- ....CLC 1, 13, 37, 59
See also CA 5-8R; CAAS 7; CANR 2, 44;
DLB 5; SATA 23

Hall, Frederic Sauser
See Sauser-Hall, Frederic

Hall, James
See Kuttner, Henry

Hall, James Norman 1887-1951 ... TCLC 23
See also CA 123; SATA 21

Hall, (Marguerite) Radclyffe
1886(?)-1943 .... TCLC 12
See also CA 110

Hall, Rodney 1935- .... CLC 51
See also CA 109

Halleck, Fitz-Greene 1790-1867 .. NCLC 47
See also DLB 3

Halliday, Michael
See Creasey, John

Halpern, Daniel 1945- . . . . **CLC 14**
See also CA 33-36R

Hamburger, Michael (Peter Leopold)
1924- . . . . **CLC 5, 14**
See also CA 5-8R; CAAS 4; CANR 2, 47;
DLB 27

Hamill, Pete 1935- . . . . **CLC 10**
See also CA 25-28R; CANR 18

Hamilton, Alexander
1755(?)-1804 . . . . **NCLC 49**
See also DLB 37

Hamilton, Clive
See Lewis, C(live) S(taples)

Hamilton, Edmond 1904-1977 . . . . . . **CLC 1**
See also CA 1-4R; CANR 3; DLB 8

Hamilton, Eugene (Jacob) Lee
See Lee-Hamilton, Eugene (Jacob)

Hamilton, Franklin
See Silverberg, Robert

Hamilton, Gail
See Corcoran, Barbara

Hamilton, Mollie
See Kaye, M(ary) M(argaret)

Hamilton, (Anthony Walter) Patrick
1904-1962 . . . . **CLC 51**
See also CA 113; DLB 10

Hamilton, Virginia 1936- . . . . **CLC 26**
See also AAYA 2; BW 2; CA 25-28R;
CANR 20, 37; CLR 1, 11; DLB 33, 52;
JRDA; MAICYA; MTCW; SATA 4, 56,
79

Hammett, (Samuel) Dashiell
1894-1961 . . . . **CLC 3, 5, 10, 19, 47;**
SSC 17
See also AITN 1; CA 81-84; CANR 42;
CDALB 1929-1941; DLBD 6; MTCW

Hammon, Jupiter
1711(?)-1800(?) . . . . **NCLC 5; BLC**
See also DLB 31, 50

Hammond, Keith
See Kuttner, Henry

Hamner, Earl (Henry), Jr. 1923- . . . **CLC 12**
See also AITN 2; CA 73-76; DLB 6

Hampton, Christopher (James)
1946- . . . . **CLC 4**
See also CA 25-28R; DLB 13; MTCW

Hamsun, Knut . . . . **TCLC 2, 14, 49**
See also Pedersen, Knut

Handke, Peter 1942- . . **CLC 5, 8, 10, 15, 38**
See also CA 77-80; CANR 33; DLB 85,
124; MTCW

Hanley, James 1901-1985 . . . **CLC 3, 5, 8, 13**
See also CA 73-76; 117; CANR 36; MTCW

Hannah, Barry 1942- . . . . **CLC 23, 38**
See also CA 108; 110; CANR 43; DLB 6;
MTCW

Hannon, Ezra
See Hunter, Evan

Hansberry, Lorraine (Vivian)
1930-1965 . . . . . . **CLC 17, 62; BLC; DA;**
DAB; DC 2
See also BW 1; CA 109; 25-28R; CABS 3;
CDALB 1941-1968; DLB 7, 38; MTCW

Hansen, Joseph 1923- . . . . **CLC 38**
See also CA 29-32R; CAAS 17; CANR 16,
44

Hansen, Martin A. 1909-1955 . . . . . **TCLC 32**

Hanson, Kenneth O(stlin) 1922- . . . . **CLC 13**
See also CA 53-56; CANR 7

Hardwick, Elizabeth 1916- . . . . **CLC 13**
See also CA 5-8R; CANR 3, 32; DLB 6;
MTCW

Hardy, Thomas
1840-1928 . . . . . . **TCLC 4, 10, 18, 32, 48,**
53; DA; DAB; PC 8; SSC 2; WLC
See also CA 104; 123; CDBLB 1890-1914;
DLB 18, 19, 135; MTCW

Hare, David 1947- . . . . **CLC 29, 58**
See also CA 97-100; CANR 39; DLB 13;
MTCW

Harford, Henry
See Hudson, W(illiam) H(enry)

Hargrave, Leonie
See Disch, Thomas M(ichael)

Harjo, Joy 1951- . . . . **CLC 83**
See also CA 114; CANR 35; DLB 120;
NNAL

Harlan, Louis R(udolph) 1922- . . . . . **CLC 34**
See also CA 21-24R; CANR 25

Harling, Robert 1951(?)- . . . . **CLC 53**
See also CA 147

Harmon, William (Ruth) 1938- . . . . . **CLC 38**
See also CA 33-36R; CANR 14, 32, 35;
SATA 65

Harper, F. E. W.
See Harper, Frances Ellen Watkins

Harper, Frances E. W.
See Harper, Frances Ellen Watkins

Harper, Frances E. Watkins
See Harper, Frances Ellen Watkins

Harper, Frances Ellen
See Harper, Frances Ellen Watkins

Harper, Frances Ellen Watkins
1825-1911 . . . . **TCLC 14; BLC**
See also BW 1; CA 111; 125; DLB 50

Harper, Michael S(teven) 1938- . . **CLC 7, 22**
See also BW 1; CA 33-36R; CANR 24;
DLB 41

Harper, Mrs. F. E. W.
See Harper, Frances Ellen Watkins

Harris, Christie (Lucy) Irwin
1907- . . . . **CLC 12**
See also CA 5-8R; CANR 6; DLB 88;
JRDA; MAICYA; SAAS 10; SATA 6, 74

Harris, Frank 1856(?)-1931 . . . . . . **TCLC 24**
See also CA 109

Harris, George Washington
1814-1869 . . . . **NCLC 23**
See also DLB 3, 11

Harris, Joel Chandler
1848-1908 . . . . **TCLC 2; SSC 19**
See also CA 104; 137; DLB 11, 23, 42, 78,
91; MAICYA; YABC 1

Harris, John (Wyndham Parkes Lucas)
Beynon 1903-1969
See Wyndham, John
See also CA 102; 89-92

Harris, MacDonald . . . . **CLC 9**
See also Heiney, Donald (William)

Harris, Mark 1922- . . . . **CLC 19**
See also CA 5-8R; CAAS 3; CANR 2;
DLB 2; DLBY 80

Harris, (Theodore) Wilson 1921-. . . . **CLC 25**
See also BW 2; CA 65-68; CAAS 16;
CANR 11, 27; DLB 117; MTCW

Harrison, Elizabeth Cavanna 1909-
See Cavanna, Betty
See also CA 9-12R; CANR 6, 27

Harrison, Harry (Max) 1925- . . . . . . **CLC 42**
See also CA 1-4R; CANR 5, 21; DLB 8;
SATA 4

Harrison, James (Thomas)
1937- . . . . **CLC 6, 14, 33, 66; SSC 19**
See also CA 13-16R; CANR 8; DLBY 82

Harrison, Jim
See Harrison, James (Thomas)

Harrison, Kathryn 1961- . . . . **CLC 70**
See also CA 144

Harrison, Tony 1937- . . . . **CLC 43**
See also CA 65-68; CANR 44; DLB 40;
MTCW

Harriss, Will(ard Irvin) 1922- . . . . . . **CLC 34**
See also CA 111

Harson, Sley
See Ellison, Harlan (Jay)

Hart, Ellis
See Ellison, Harlan (Jay)

Hart, Josephine 1942(?)- . . . . **CLC 70**
See also CA 138

Hart, Moss 1904-1961 . . . . **CLC 66**
See also CA 109; 89-92; DLB 7

Harte, (Francis) Bret(t)
1836(?)-1902 . . . . **TCLC 1, 25; DA;**
SSC 8; WLC
See also CA 104; 140; CDALB 1865-1917;
DLB 12, 64, 74, 79; SATA 26

Hartley, L(eslie) P(oles)
1895-1972 . . . . **CLC 2, 22**
See also CA 45-48; 37-40R; CANR 33;
DLB 15, 139; MTCW

Hartman, Geoffrey H. 1929- . . . . **CLC 27**
See also CA 117; 125; DLB 67

Hartmann von Aue
c. 1160-c. 1205 . . . . **CMLC 15**
See also DLB 138

Haruf, Kent 19(?)- . . . . **CLC 34**

Harwood, Ronald 1934- . . . . **CLC 32**
See also CA 1-4R; CANR 4; DLB 13

Hasek, Jaroslav (Matej Frantisek)
1883-1923 . . . . **TCLC 4**
See also CA 104; 129; MTCW

Hass, Robert 1941- . . . . **CLC 18, 39**
See also CA 111; CANR 30; DLB 105

Hastings, Hudson
See Kuttner, Henry

Hastings, Selina. . . . . **CLC 44**

Hatteras, Amelia
See Mencken, H(enry) L(ouis)

Hatteras, Owen. . . . . **TCLC 18**
See also Mencken, H(enry) L(ouis); Nathan,
George Jean

Hauptmann, Gerhart (Johann Robert)
1862-1946 . . . . TCLC 4
See also CA 104; DLB 66, 118

Havel, Vaclav 1936- . . . . CLC 25, 58, 65
See also CA 104; CANR 36; MTCW

Haviaras, Stratis . . . . CLC 33
See also Chaviaras, Strates

Hawes, Stephen 1475(?)-1523(?) . . . . . LC 17

Hawkes, John (Clendennin Burne, Jr.)
1925- . . . . . . CLC 1, 2, 3, 4, 7, 9, 14, 15,
27, 49
See also CA 1-4R; CANR 2, 47; DLB 2, 7;
DLBY 80; MTCW

Hawking, S. W.
See Hawking, Stephen W(illiam)

Hawking, Stephen W(illiam)
1942- . . . . CLC 63
See also AAYA 13; BEST 89:1; CA 126;
129; CANR 48

Hawthorne, Julian 1846-1934 . . . . . TCLC 25

Hawthorne, Nathaniel
1804-1864 . . . . NCLC 39; DA; DAB;
SSC 3; WLC
See also CDALB 1640-1865; DLB 1, 74;
YABC 2

Haxton, Josephine Ayres 1921-
See Douglas, Ellen
See also CA 115; CANR 41

Hayaseca y Eizaguirre, Jorge
See Echegaray (y Eizaguirre), Jose (Maria
Waldo)

Hayashi Fumiko 1904-1951 . . . . TCLC 27

Haycraft, Anna
See Ellis, Alice Thomas
See also CA 122

Hayden, Robert E(arl)
1913-1980 . . . . . . CLC 5, 9, 14, 37; BLC;
DA; PC 6
See also BW 1; CA 69-72; 97-100; CABS 2;
CANR 24; CDALB 1941-1968; DLB 5,
76; MTCW; SATA 19; SATA-Obit 26

Hayford, J(oseph) E(phraim) Casely
See Casely-Hayford, J(oseph) E(phraim)

Hayman, Ronald 1932- . . . . CLC 44
See also CA 25-28R; CANR 18; DLB 155

Haywood, Eliza (Fowler)
1693(?)-1756 . . . . LC 1

Hazlitt, William 1778-1830 . . . . . . NCLC 29
See also DLB 110

Hazzard, Shirley 1931- . . . . CLC 18
See also CA 9-12R; CANR 4; DLBY 82;
MTCW

Head, Bessie 1937-1986 . . . CLC 25, 67; BLC
See also BW 2; CA 29-32R; 119; CANR 25;
DLB 117; MTCW

Headon, (Nicky) Topper 1956(?)- . . . CLC 30

Heaney, Seamus (Justin)
1939- . . . . CLC 5, 7, 14, 25, 37, 74; DAB
See also CA 85-88; CANR 25, 48;
CDBLB 1960 to Present; DLB 40;
MTCW

Hearn, (Patricio) Lafcadio (Tessima Carlos)
1850-1904 . . . . TCLC 9
See also CA 105; DLB 12, 78

Hearne, Vicki 1946- . . . . CLC 56
See also CA 139

Hearon, Shelby 1931- . . . . CLC 63
See also AITN 2; CA 25-28R; CANR 18,
48

Heat-Moon, William Least . . . . CLC 29
See also Trogdon, William (Lewis)
See also AAYA 9

Hebbel, Friedrich 1813-1863 . . . . . NCLC 43
See also DLB 129

Hebert, Anne 1916- . . . . CLC 4, 13, 29
See also CA 85-88; DLB 68; MTCW

Hecht, Anthony (Evan)
1923- . . . . CLC 8, 13, 19
See also CA 9-12R; CANR 6; DLB 5

Hecht, Ben 1894-1964 . . . . CLC 8
See also CA 85-88; DLB 7, 9, 25, 26, 28, 86

Hedayat, Sadeq 1903-1951 . . . . TCLC 21
See also CA 120

Hegel, Georg Wilhelm Friedrich
1770-1831 . . . . NCLC 46
See also DLB 90

Heidegger, Martin 1889-1976 . . . . . . CLC 24
See also CA 81-84; 65-68; CANR 34;
MTCW

Heidenstam, (Carl Gustaf) Verner von
1859-1940 . . . . TCLC 5
See also CA 104

Heifner, Jack 1946- . . . . CLC 11
See also CA 105; CANR 47

Heijermans, Herman 1864-1924 . . . TCLC 24
See also CA 123

Heilbrun, Carolyn G(old) 1926- . . . . . CLC 25
See also CA 45-48; CANR 1, 28

Heine, Heinrich 1797-1856 . . . . NCLC 4
See also DLB 90

Heinemann, Larry (Curtiss) 1944- . . CLC 50
See also CA 110; CAAS 21; CANR 31;
DLBD 9

Heiney, Donald (William) 1921-1993
See Harris, MacDonald
See also CA 1-4R; 142; CANR 3

Heinlein, Robert A(nson)
1907-1988 . . . . . . CLC 1, 3, 8, 14, 26, 55
See also CA 1-4R; 125; CANR 1, 20;
DLB 8; JRDA; MAICYA; MTCW;
SATA 9, 69; SATA-Obit 56

Helforth, John
See Doolittle, Hilda

Hellenhofferu, Vojtech Kapristian z
See Hasek, Jaroslav (Matej Frantisek)

Heller, Joseph
1923- . . . . CLC 1, 3, 5, 8, 11, 36, 63; DA;
DAB; WLC
See also AITN 1; CA 5-8R; CABS 1;
CANR 8, 42; DLB 2, 28; DLBY 80;
MTCW

Hellman, Lillian (Florence)
1906-1984 . . . . . . CLC 2, 4, 8, 14, 18, 34,
44, 52; DC 1
See also AITN 1, 2; CA 13-16R; 112;
CANR 33; DLB 7; DLBY 84; MTCW

Helprin, Mark 1947- . . . . . CLC 7, 10, 22, 32
See also CA 81-84; CANR 47; DLBY 85;
MTCW

Helvetius, Claude-Adrien
1715-1771 . . . . LC 26

Helyar, Jane Penelope Josephine 1933-
See Poole, Josephine
See also CA 21-24R; CANR 10, 26;
SATA 82

Hemans, Felicia 1793-1835 . . . . . . NCLC 29
See also DLB 96

Hemingway, Ernest (Miller)
1899-1961 . . . . CLC 1, 3, 6, 8, 10, 13, 19,
30, 34, 39, 41, 44, 50, 61, 80; DA; DAB;
SSC 1; WLC
See also CA 77-80; CANR 34;
CDALB 1917-1929; DLB 4, 9, 102;
DLBD 1; DLBY 81, 87; MTCW

Hempel, Amy 1951- . . . . CLC 39
See also CA 118; 137

Henderson, F. C.
See Mencken, H(enry) L(ouis)

Henderson, Sylvia
See Ashton-Warner, Sylvia (Constance)

Henley, Beth . . . . CLC 23
See also Henley, Elizabeth Becker
See also CABS 3; DLBY 86

Henley, Elizabeth Becker 1952-
See Henley, Beth
See also CA 107; CANR 32; MTCW

Henley, William Ernest
1849-1903 . . . . TCLC 8
See also CA 105; DLB 19

Hennissart, Martha
See Lathen, Emma
See also CA 85-88

Henry, O. . . . . TCLC 1, 19; SSC 5; WLC
See also Porter, William Sydney

Henry, Patrick 1736-1799 . . . . LC 25

Henryson, Robert 1430(?)-1506(?) . . . . LC 20
See also DLB 146

Henry VIII 1491-1547 . . . . LC 10

Henschke, Alfred
See Klabund

Hentoff, Nat(han Irving) 1925- . . . . . CLC 26
See also AAYA 4; CA 1-4R; CAAS 6;
CANR 5, 25; CLR 1; JRDA; MAICYA;
SATA 42, 69; SATA-Brief 27

Heppenstall, (John) Rayner
1911-1981 . . . . CLC 10
See also CA 1-4R; 103; CANR 29

Herbert, Frank (Patrick)
1920-1986 . . . . . . CLC 12, 23, 35, 44, 85
See also CA 53-56; 118; CANR 5, 43;
DLB 8; MTCW; SATA 9, 37;
SATA-Obit 47

Herbert, George
1593-1633 . . . . LC 24; DAB; PC 4
See also CDBLB Before 1660; DLB 126

Herbert, Zbigniew 1924- . . . . CLC 9, 43
See also CA 89-92; CANR 36; MTCW

Herbst, Josephine (Frey)
1897-1969 . . . . CLC 34
See also CA 5-8R; 25-28R; DLB 9

Hergesheimer, Joseph
1880-1954 . . . . TCLC 11
See also CA 109; DLB 102, 9

Herlihy, James Leo   1927-1993 ...... **CLC 6**
See also CA 1-4R; 143; CANR 2

Hermogenes   fl. c. 175- .... **CMLC 6**

Hernandez, Jose   1834-1886 ...... **NCLC 17**

Herrick, Robert
    1591-1674 ..... **LC 13; DA; DAB; PC 9**
See also DLB 126

Herring, Guilles
See Somerville, Edith

Herriot, James   1916-1995 .... **CLC 12**
See also Wight, James Alfred
See also AAYA 1; CA 148; CANR 40

Herrmann, Dorothy   1941- .... **CLC 44**
See also CA 107

Herrmann, Taffy
See Herrmann, Dorothy

Hersey, John (Richard)
    1914-1993 ...... **CLC 1, 2, 7, 9, 40, 81**
See also CA 17-20R; 140; CANR 33;
    DLB 6; MTCW; SATA 25;
    SATA-Obit 76

Herzen, Aleksandr Ivanovich
    1812-1870 .... **NCLC 10**

Herzl, Theodor   1860-1904 .... **TCLC 36**

Herzog, Werner   1942- .... **CLC 16**
See also CA 89-92

Hesiod   c. 8th cent. B.C.- .... **CMLC 5**

Hesse, Hermann
    1877-1962 .... **CLC 1, 2, 3, 6, 11, 17, 25,
        69; DA; DAB; SSC 9; WLC**
See also CA 17-18; CAP 2; DLB 66;
    MTCW; SATA 50

Hewes, Cady
See De Voto, Bernard (Augustine)

Heyen, William   1940- .... **CLC 13, 18**
See also CA 33-36R; CAAS 9; DLB 5

Heyerdahl, Thor   1914- .... **CLC 26**
See also CA 5-8R; CANR 5, 22; MTCW;
    SATA 2, 52

Heym, Georg (Theodor Franz Arthur)
    1887-1912 .... **TCLC 9**
See also CA 106

Heym, Stefan   1913- .... **CLC 41**
See also CA 9-12R; CANR 4; DLB 69

Heyse, Paul (Johann Ludwig von)
    1830-1914 .... **TCLC 8**
See also CA 104; DLB 129

Heyward, (Edwin) DuBose
    1885-1940 .... **TCLC 59**
See also CA 108; DLB 7, 9, 45; SATA 21

Hibbert, Eleanor Alice Burford
    1906-1993 .... **CLC 7**
See also BEST 90:4; CA 17-20R; 140;
    CANR 9, 28; SATA 2; SATA-Obit 74

Higgins, George V(incent)
    1939- .... **CLC 4, 7, 10, 18**
See also CA 77-80; CAAS 5; CANR 17;
    DLB 2; DLBY 81; MTCW

Higginson, Thomas Wentworth
    1823-1911 .... **TCLC 36**
See also DLB 1, 64

Highet, Helen
See MacInnes, Helen (Clark)

Highsmith, (Mary) Patricia
    1921-1995 .... **CLC 2, 4, 14, 42**
See also CA 1-4R; 147; CANR 1, 20, 48;
    MTCW

Highwater, Jamake (Mamake)
    1942(?)- .... **CLC 12**
See also AAYA 7; CA 65-68; CAAS 7;
    CANR 10, 34; CLR 17; DLB 52;
    DLBY 85; JRDA; MAICYA; SATA 32,
    69; SATA-Brief 30

Higuchi, Ichiyo   1872-1896 ...... **NCLC 49**

Hijuelos, Oscar   1951- ...... **CLC 65; HLC**
See also BEST 90:1; CA 123; DLB 145; HW

Hikmet, Nazim   1902(?)-1963 .... **CLC 40**
See also CA 141; 93-96

Hildesheimer, Wolfgang
    1916-1991 .... **CLC 49**
See also CA 101; 135; DLB 69, 124

Hill, Geoffrey (William)
    1932- .... **CLC 5, 8, 18, 45**
See also CA 81-84; CANR 21;
    CDBLB 1960 to Present; DLB 40;
    MTCW

Hill, George Roy   1921- .... **CLC 26**
See also CA 110; 122

Hill, John
See Koontz, Dean R(ay)

Hill, Susan (Elizabeth)
    1942- .... **CLC 4; DAB**
See also CA 33-36R; CANR 29; DLB 14,
    139; MTCW

Hillerman, Tony   1925- .... **CLC 62**
See also AAYA 6; BEST 89:1; CA 29-32R;
    CANR 21, 42; SATA 6

Hillesum, Etty   1914-1943 .... **TCLC 49**
See also CA 137

Hilliard, Noel (Harvey)   1929- ...... **CLC 15**
See also CA 9-12R; CANR 7

Hillis, Rick   1956- .... **CLC 66**
See also CA 134

Hilton, James   1900-1954 .... **TCLC 21**
See also CA 108; DLB 34, 77; SATA 34

Himes, Chester (Bomar)
    1909-1984 .... **CLC 2, 4, 7, 18, 58; BLC**
See also BW 2; CA 25-28R; 114; CANR 22;
    DLB 2, 76, 143; MTCW

Hinde, Thomas .... **CLC 6, 11**
See also Chitty, Thomas Willes

Hindin, Nathan
See Bloch, Robert (Albert)

Hine, (William) Daryl   1936- .... **CLC 15**
See also CA 1-4R; CAAS 15; CANR 1, 20;
    DLB 60

Hinkson, Katharine Tynan
See Tynan, Katharine

Hinton, S(usan) E(loise)
    1950- .... **CLC 30; DA; DAB**
See also AAYA 2; CA 81-84; CANR 32;
    CLR 3, 23; JRDA; MAICYA; MTCW;
    SATA 19, 58

Hippius, Zinaida .... **TCLC 9**
See also Gippius, Zinaida (Nikolayevna)

Hiraoka, Kimitake   1925-1970
See Mishima, Yukio
See also CA 97-100; 29-32R; MTCW

Hirsch, E(ric) D(onald), Jr.   1928- ... **CLC 79**
See also CA 25-28R; CANR 27; DLB 67;
    MTCW

Hirsch, Edward   1950- .... **CLC 31, 50**
See also CA 104; CANR 20, 42; DLB 120

Hitchcock, Alfred (Joseph)
    1899-1980 .... **CLC 16**
See also CA 97-100; SATA 27;
    SATA-Obit 24

Hitler, Adolf   1889-1945 .... **TCLC 53**
See also CA 117; 147

Hoagland, Edward   1932- .... **CLC 28**
See also CA 1-4R; CANR 2, 31; DLB 6;
    SATA 51

Hoban, Russell (Conwell)   1925- .. **CLC 7, 25**
See also CA 5-8R; CANR 23, 37; CLR 3;
    DLB 52; MAICYA; MTCW; SATA 1,
    40, 78

Hobbs, Perry
See Blackmur, R(ichard) P(almer)

Hobson, Laura Z(ametkin)
    1900-1986 .... **CLC 7, 25**
See also CA 17-20R; 118; DLB 28;
    SATA 52

Hochhuth, Rolf   1931- .... **CLC 4, 11, 18**
See also CA 5-8R; CANR 33; DLB 124;
    MTCW

Hochman, Sandra   1936- .... **CLC 3, 8**
See also CA 5-8R; DLB 5

Hochwaelder, Fritz   1911-1986 ...... **CLC 36**
See also CA 29-32R; 120; CANR 42;
    MTCW

Hochwalder, Fritz
See Hochwaelder, Fritz

Hocking, Mary (Eunice)   1921- ..... **CLC 13**
See also CA 101; CANR 18, 40

Hodgins, Jack   1938- .... **CLC 23**
See also CA 93-96; DLB 60

Hodgson, William Hope
    1877(?)-1918 .... **TCLC 13**
See also CA 111; DLB 70, 153

Hoffman, Alice   1952- .... **CLC 51**
See also CA 77-80; CANR 34; MTCW

Hoffman, Daniel (Gerard)
    1923- .... **CLC 6, 13, 23**
See also CA 1-4R; CANR 4; DLB 5

Hoffman, Stanley   1944- .... **CLC 5**
See also CA 77-80

Hoffman, William M(oses)   1939- ... **CLC 40**
See also CA 57-60; CANR 11

Hoffmann, E(rnst) T(heodor) A(madeus)
    1776-1822 .... **NCLC 2; SSC 13**
See also DLB 90; SATA 27

Hofmann, Gert   1931- .... **CLC 54**
See also CA 128

Hofmannsthal, Hugo von
    1874-1929 .... **TCLC 11; DC 4**
See also CA 106; DLB 81, 118

Hogan, Linda   1947- .... **CLC 73**
See also CA 120; CANR 45; NNAL

Hogarth, Charles
See Creasey, John

Hogg, James   1770-1835 .... **NCLC 4**
See also DLB 93, 116

Holbach, Paul Henri Thiry Baron
    1723-1789 .... LC 14

Holberg, Ludvig   1684-1754 .... LC 6

Holden, Ursula   1921- .... CLC 18
    See also CA 101; CAAS 8; CANR 22

Holderlin, (Johann Christian) Friedrich
    1770-1843 .... NCLC 16; PC 4

Holdstock, Robert
    See Holdstock, Robert P.

Holdstock, Robert P.   1948- .... CLC 39
    See also CA 131

Holland, Isabelle   1920- .... CLC 21
    See also AAYA 11; CA 21-24R; CANR 10,
    25, 47; JRDA; MAICYA; SATA 8, 70

Holland, Marcus
    See Caldwell, (Janet Miriam) Taylor
    (Holland)

Hollander, John   1929- ...... CLC 2, 5, 8, 14
    See also CA 1-4R; CANR 1; DLB 5;
    SATA 13

Hollander, Paul
    See Silverberg, Robert

Holleran, Andrew   1943(?)- .... CLC 38
    See also CA 144

Hollinghurst, Alan   1954- .... CLC 55
    See also CA 114

Hollis, Jim
    See Summers, Hollis (Spurgeon, Jr.)

Holmes, John
    See Souster, (Holmes) Raymond

Holmes, John Clellon   1926-1988.... CLC 56
    See also CA 9-12R; 125; CANR 4; DLB 16

Holmes, Oliver Wendell
    1809-1894 .... NCLC 14
    See also CDALB 1640-1865; DLB 1;
    SATA 34

Holmes, Raymond
    See Souster, (Holmes) Raymond

Holt, Victoria
    See Hibbert, Eleanor Alice Burford

Holub, Miroslav   1923- .... CLC 4
    See also CA 21-24R; CANR 10

Homer
    c. 8th cent. B.C.- ..... CMLC 1, 16; DA;
                                        DAB

Honig, Edwin   1919- .... CLC 33
    See also CA 5-8R; CAAS 8; CANR 4, 45;
    DLB 5

Hood, Hugh (John Blagdon)
    1928- .... CLC 15, 28
    See also CA 49-52; CAAS 17; CANR 1, 33;
    DLB 53

Hood, Thomas   1799-1845........ NCLC 16
    See also DLB 96

Hooker, (Peter) Jeremy   1941- ...... CLC 43
    See also CA 77-80; CANR 22; DLB 40

Hope, A(lec) D(erwent)   1907- .... CLC 3, 51
    See also CA 21-24R; CANR 33; MTCW

Hope, Brian
    See Creasey, John

Hope, Christopher (David Tully)
    1944- .... CLC 52
    See also CA 106; CANR 47; SATA 62

Hopkins, Gerard Manley
    1844-1889 .. NCLC 17; DA; DAB; WLC
    See also CDBLB 1890-1914; DLB 35, 57

Hopkins, John (Richard)   1931- ...... CLC 4
    See also CA 85-88

Hopkins, Pauline Elizabeth
    1859-1930 .... TCLC 28; BLC
    See also BW 2; CA 141; DLB 50

Hopkinson, Francis   1737-1791 ...... LC 25
    See also DLB 31

Hopley-Woolrich, Cornell George   1903-1968
    See Woolrich, Cornell
    See also CA 13-14; CAP 1

Horatio
    See Proust, (Valentin-Louis-George-Eugene-)
    Marcel

Horgan, Paul (George Vincent O'Shaughnessy)
    1903-1995 .... CLC 9, 53
    See also CA 13-16R; 147; CANR 9, 35;
    DLB 102; DLBY 85; MTCW; SATA 13

Horn, Peter
    See Kuttner, Henry

Hornem, Horace Esq.
    See Byron, George Gordon (Noel)

Hornung, E(rnest) W(illiam)
    1866-1921 .... TCLC 59
    See also CA 108; DLB 70

Horovitz, Israel (Arthur)   1939- ..... CLC 56
    See also CA 33-36R; CANR 46; DLB 7

Horvath, Odon von
    See Horvath, Oedoen von
    See also DLB 85, 124

Horvath, Oedoen von   1901-1938... TCLC 45
    See also Horvath, Odon von
    See also CA 118

Horwitz, Julius   1920-1986........ CLC 14
    See also CA 9-12R; 119; CANR 12

Hospital, Janette Turner   1942- ..... CLC 42
    See also CA 108; CANR 48

Hostos, E. M. de
    See Hostos (y Bonilla), Eugenio Maria de

Hostos, Eugenio M. de
    See Hostos (y Bonilla), Eugenio Maria de

Hostos, Eugenio Maria
    See Hostos (y Bonilla), Eugenio Maria de

Hostos (y Bonilla), Eugenio Maria de
    1839-1903 .... TCLC 24
    See also CA 123; 131; HW

Houdini
    See Lovecraft, H(oward) P(hillips)

Hougan, Carolyn   1943- .... CLC 34
    See also CA 139

Household, Geoffrey (Edward West)
    1900-1988 .... CLC 11
    See also CA 77-80; 126; DLB 87; SATA 14;
    SATA-Obit 59

Housman, A(lfred) E(dward)
    1859-1936 ...... TCLC 1, 10; DA; DAB;
                                        PC 2
    See also CA 104; 125; DLB 19; MTCW

Housman, Laurence   1865-1959 ..... TCLC 7
    See also CA 106; DLB 10; SATA 25

Howard, Elizabeth Jane   1923- ... CLC 7, 29
    See also CA 5-8R; CANR 8

Howard, Maureen   1930- ..... CLC 5, 14, 46
    See also CA 53-56; CANR 31; DLBY 83;
    MTCW

Howard, Richard   1929- ...... CLC 7, 10, 47
    See also AITN 1; CA 85-88; CANR 25;
    DLB 5

Howard, Robert Ervin   1906-1936... TCLC 8
    See also CA 105

Howard, Warren F.
    See Pohl, Frederik

Howe, Fanny   1940- .... CLC 47
    See also CA 117; SATA-Brief 52

Howe, Irving   1920-1993........... CLC 85
    See also CA 9-12R; 141; CANR 21;
    DLB 67; MTCW

Howe, Julia Ward   1819-1910 ..... TCLC 21
    See also CA 117; DLB 1

Howe, Susan   1937- .... CLC 72
    See also DLB 120

Howe, Tina   1937- .... CLC 48
    See also CA 109

Howell, James   1594(?)-1666 .... LC 13
    See also DLB 151

Howells, W. D.
    See Howells, William Dean

Howells, William D.
    See Howells, William Dean

Howells, William Dean
    1837-1920 .... TCLC 7, 17, 41
    See also CA 104; 134; CDALB 1865-1917;
    DLB 12, 64, 74, 79

Howes, Barbara   1914- .... CLC 15
    See also CA 9-12R; CAAS 3; SATA 5

Hrabal, Bohumil   1914- .... CLC 13, 67
    See also CA 106; CAAS 12

Hsun, Lu
    See Lu Hsun

Hubbard, L(afayette) Ron(ald)
    1911-1986 .... CLC 43
    See also CA 77-80; 118; CANR 22

Huch, Ricarda (Octavia)
    1864-1947 .... TCLC 13
    See also CA 111; DLB 66

Huddle, David   1942- .... CLC 49
    See also CA 57-60; CAAS 20; DLB 130

Hudson, Jeffrey
    See Crichton, (John) Michael

Hudson, W(illiam) H(enry)
    1841-1922 .... TCLC 29
    See also CA 115; DLB 98, 153; SATA 35

Hueffer, Ford Madox
    See Ford, Ford Madox

Hughart, Barry   1934- .... CLC 39
    See also CA 137

Hughes, Colin
    See Creasey, John

Hughes, David (John)   1930- .... CLC 48
    See also CA 116; 129; DLB 14

Hughes, (James) Langston
   1902-1967 ..... **CLC 1, 5, 10, 15, 35, 44;**
      BLC; DA; DAB; DC 3; PC 1; SSC 6;
                                            WLC
   See also AAYA 12; BW 1; CA 1-4R;
      25-28R; CANR 1, 34; CDALB 1929-1941;
      CLR 17; DLB 4, 7, 48, 51, 86; JRDA;
      MAICYA; MTCW; SATA 4, 33

Hughes, Richard (Arthur Warren)
   1900-1976 .... **CLC 1, 11**
   See also CA 5-8R; 65-68; CANR 4;
      DLB 15; MTCW; SATA 8;
      SATA-Obit 25

Hughes, Ted
   1930- ... **CLC 2, 4, 9, 14, 37; DAB; PC 7**
   See also CA 1-4R; CANR 1, 33; CLR 3;
      DLB 40; MAICYA; MTCW; SATA 49;
      SATA-Brief 27

Hugo, Richard F(ranklin)
   1923-1982 .... **CLC 6, 18, 32**
   See also CA 49-52; 108; CANR 3; DLB 5

Hugo, Victor (Marie)
   1802-1885 .... **NCLC 3, 10, 21; DA;**
                                       DAB; WLC
   See also DLB 119; SATA 47

Huidobro, Vicente
   See Huidobro Fernandez, Vicente Garcia

Huidobro Fernandez, Vicente Garcia
   1893-1948 .... **TCLC 31**
   See also CA 131; HW

Hulme, Keri 1947- .... **CLC 39**
   See also CA 125

Hulme, T(homas) E(rnest)
   1883-1917 .... **TCLC 21**
   See also CA 117; DLB 19

Hume, David 1711-1776............. **LC 7**
   See also DLB 104

Humphrey, William 1924-......... **CLC 45**
   See also CA 77-80; DLB 6

Humphreys, Emyr Owen 1919-..... **CLC 47**
   See also CA 5-8R; CANR 3, 24; DLB 15

Humphreys, Josephine 1945-.... **CLC 34, 57**
   See also CA 121; 127

Hungerford, Pixie
   See Brinsmead, H(esba) F(ay)

Hunt, E(verette) Howard, (Jr.)
   1918- .... **CLC 3**
   See also AITN 1; CA 45-48; CANR 2, 47

Hunt, Kyle
   See Creasey, John

Hunt, (James Henry) Leigh
   1784-1859 .... **NCLC 1**

Hunt, Marsha 1946-............. **CLC 70**
   See also BW 2; CA 143

Hunt, Violet 1866-1942 .... **TCLC 53**

Hunter, E. Waldo
   See Sturgeon, Theodore (Hamilton)

Hunter, Evan 1926- .... **CLC 11, 31**
   See also CA 5-8R; CANR 5, 38; DLBY 82;
      MTCW; SATA 25

Hunter, Kristin (Eggleston) 1931-... **CLC 35**
   See also AITN 1; BW 1; CA 13-16R;
      CANR 13; CLR 3; DLB 33; MAICYA;
      SAAS 10; SATA 12

Hunter, Mollie 1922-............. **CLC 21**
   See also McIlwraith, Maureen Mollie
      Hunter
   See also AAYA 13; CANR 37; CLR 25;
      JRDA; MAICYA; SAAS 7; SATA 54

Hunter, Robert (?)-1734............. **LC 7**

Hurston, Zora Neale
   1903-1960 .... **CLC 7, 30, 61; BLC; DA;**
                                       SSC 4
   See also BW 1; CA 85-88; DLB 51, 86;
      MTCW

Huston, John (Marcellus)
   1906-1987 .... **CLC 20**
   See also CA 73-76; 123; CANR 34; DLB 26

Hustvedt, Siri 1955-............. **CLC 76**
   See also CA 137

Hutten, Ulrich von 1488-1523....... **LC 16**

Huxley, Aldous (Leonard)
   1894-1963 ..... **CLC 1, 3, 4, 5, 8, 11, 18,**
                         35, 79; DA; DAB; WLC
   See also AAYA 11; CA 85-88; CANR 44;
      CDBLB 1914-1945; DLB 36, 100;
      MTCW; SATA 63

Huysmans, Charles Marie Georges
   1848-1907
   See Huysmans, Joris-Karl
   See also CA 104

Huysmans, Joris-Karl.............. **TCLC 7**
   See also Huysmans, Charles Marie Georges
   See also DLB 123

Hwang, David Henry
   1957-................... **CLC 55; DC 4**
   See also CA 127; 132

Hyde, Anthony 1946-............. **CLC 42**
   See also CA 136

Hyde, Margaret O(ldroyd) 1917- ... **CLC 21**
   See also CA 1-4R; CANR 1, 36; CLR 23;
      JRDA; MAICYA; SAAS 8; SATA 1, 42,
      76

Hynes, James 1956(?)-............ **CLC 65**

Ian, Janis 1951- .... **CLC 21**
   See also CA 105

Ibanez, Vicente Blasco
   See Blasco Ibanez, Vicente

Ibarguengoitia, Jorge 1928-1983.... **CLC 37**
   See also CA 124; 113; HW

Ibsen, Henrik (Johan)
   1828-1906 .... **TCLC 2, 8, 16, 37, 52;**
                         DA; DAB; DC 2; WLC
   See also CA 104; 141

Ibuse Masuji 1898-1993........... **CLC 22**
   See also CA 127; 141

Ichikawa, Kon 1915-............. **CLC 20**
   See also CA 121

Idle, Eric 1943-.................. **CLC 21**
   See also Monty Python
   See also CA 116; CANR 35

Ignatow, David 1914-...... **CLC 4, 7, 14, 40**
   See also CA 9-12R; CAAS 3; CANR 31;
      DLB 5

Ihimaera, Witi 1944- .... **CLC 46**
   See also CA 77-80

Ilf, Ilya........................ **TCLC 21**
   See also Fainzilberg, Ilya Arnoldovich

Immermann, Karl (Lebrecht)
   1796-1840 .... **NCLC 4, 49**
   See also DLB 133

Inclan, Ramon (Maria) del Valle
   See Valle-Inclan, Ramon (Maria) del

Infante, G(uillermo) Cabrera
   See Cabrera Infante, G(uillermo)

Ingalls, Rachel (Holmes) 1940-..... **CLC 42**
   See also CA 123; 127

Ingamells, Rex 1913-1955 .... **TCLC 35**

Inge, William Motter
   1913-1973 .... **CLC 1, 8, 19**
   See also CA 9-12R; CDALB 1941-1968;
      DLB 7; MTCW

Ingelow, Jean 1820-1897 .... **NCLC 39**
   See also DLB 35; SATA 33

Ingram, Willis J.
   See Harris, Mark

Innaurato, Albert (F.) 1948(?)- .. **CLC 21, 60**
   See also CA 115; 122

Innes, Michael
   See Stewart, J(ohn) I(nnes) M(ackintosh)

Ionesco, Eugene
   1909-1994 .... **CLC 1, 4, 6, 9, 11, 15, 41,**
                         86; DA; DAB; WLC
   See also CA 9-12R; 144; MTCW; SATA 7;
      SATA-Obit 79

Iqbal, Muhammad 1873-1938 ..... **TCLC 28**

Ireland, Patrick
   See O'Doherty, Brian

Iron, Ralph
   See Schreiner, Olive (Emilie Albertina)

Irving, John (Winslow)
   1942-.................. **CLC 13, 23, 38**
   See also AAYA 8; BEST 89:3; CA 25-28R;
      CANR 28; DLB 6; DLBY 82; MTCW

Irving, Washington
   1783-1859 ..... **NCLC 2, 19; DA; DAB;**
                                       SSC 2; WLC
   See also CDALB 1640-1865; DLB 3, 11, 30,
      59, 73, 74; YABC 2

Irwin, P. K.
   See Page, P(atricia) K(athleen)

Isaacs, Susan 1943- .... **CLC 32**
   See also BEST 89:1; CA 89-92; CANR 20,
      41; MTCW

Isherwood, Christopher (William Bradshaw)
   1904-1986 .... **CLC 1, 9, 11, 14, 44**
   See also CA 13-16R; 117; CANR 35;
      DLB 15; DLBY 86; MTCW

Ishiguro, Kazuo 1954- ...... **CLC 27, 56, 59**
   See also BEST 90:2; CA 120; CANR 49;
      MTCW

Ishikawa Takuboku
   1886(?)-1912 .... **TCLC 15; PC 10**
   See also CA 113

Iskander, Fazil 1929-............. **CLC 47**
   See also CA 102

Ivan IV 1530-1584 .... **LC 17**

Ivanov, Vyacheslav Ivanovich
   1866-1949 .... **TCLC 33**
   See also CA 122

Ivask, Ivar Vidrik 1927-1992....... **CLC 14**
   See also CA 37-40R; 139; CANR 24

Jackson, Daniel
See Wingrove, David (John)

Jackson, Jesse 1908-1983 .... **CLC 12**
See also BW 1; CA 25-28R; 109; CANR 27;
CLR 28; MAICYA; SATA 2, 29;
SATA-Obit 48

Jackson, Laura (Riding) 1901-1991
See Riding, Laura
See also CA 65-68; 135; CANR 28; DLB 48

Jackson, Sam
See Trumbo, Dalton

Jackson, Sara
See Wingrove, David (John)

Jackson, Shirley
1919-1965 .... **CLC 11, 60, 87; DA;**
SSC 9; WLC
See also AAYA 9; CA 1-4R; 25-28R;
CANR 4; CDALB 1941-1968; DLB 6;
SATA 2

Jacob, (Cyprien-)Max 1876-1944 ... **TCLC 6**
See also CA 104

Jacobs, Jim 1942-................ **CLC 12**
See also CA 97-100

Jacobs, W(illiam) W(ymark)
1863-1943 .... **TCLC 22**
See also CA 121; DLB 135

Jacobsen, Jens Peter 1847-1885 .. **NCLC 34**

Jacobsen, Josephine 1908-........ **CLC 48**
See also CA 33-36R; CAAS 18; CANR 23,
48

Jacobson, Dan 1929- .... **CLC 4, 14**
See also CA 1-4R; CANR 2, 25; DLB 14;
MTCW

Jacqueline
See Carpentier (y Valmont), Alejo

Jagger, Mick 1944-.............. **CLC 17**

Jakes, John (William) 1932- .... **CLC 29**
See also BEST 89:4; CA 57-60; CANR 10,
43; DLBY 83; MTCW; SATA 62

James, Andrew
See Kirkup, James

James, C(yril) L(ionel) R(obert)
1901-1989 .... **CLC 33**
See also BW 2; CA 117; 125; 128; DLB 125;
MTCW

James, Daniel (Lewis) 1911-1988
See Santiago, Danny
See also CA 125

James, Dynely
See Mayne, William (James Carter)

James, Henry
1843-1916 ...... **TCLC 2, 11, 24, 40, 47;**
DA; DAB; SSC 8; WLC
See also CA 104; 132; CDALB 1865-1917;
DLB 12, 71, 74; MTCW

James, M. R.
See James, Montague (Rhodes)

James, Montague (Rhodes)
1862-1936 .... **TCLC 6; SSC 16**
See also CA 104

James, P. D. .... **CLC 18, 46**
See also White, Phyllis Dorothy James
See also BEST 90:2; CDBLB 1960 to
Present; DLB 87

James, Philip
See Moorcock, Michael (John)

James, William 1842-1910..... **TCLC 15, 32**
See also CA 109

James I 1394-1437 .... **LC 20**

Jameson, Anna 1794-1860 .... **NCLC 43**
See also DLB 99

Jami, Nur al-Din 'Abd al-Rahman
1414-1492 .... **LC 9**

Jandl, Ernst 1925- .... **CLC 34**

Janowitz, Tama 1957- .... **CLC 43**
See also CA 106

Jarrell, Randall
1914-1965 .... **CLC 1, 2, 6, 9, 13, 49**
See also CA 5-8R; 25-28R; CABS 2;
CANR 6, 34; CDALB 1941-1968; CLR 6;
DLB 48, 52; MAICYA; MTCW; SATA 7

Jarry, Alfred
1873-1907 .... **TCLC 2, 14; SSC 20**
See also CA 104

Jarvis, E. K.
See Bloch, Robert (Albert); Ellison, Harlan
(Jay); Silverberg, Robert

Jeake, Samuel, Jr.
See Aiken, Conrad (Potter)

Jean Paul 1763-1825 .... **NCLC 7**

Jefferies, (John) Richard
1848-1887 .... **NCLC 47**
See also DLB 98, 141; SATA 16

Jeffers, (John) Robinson
1887-1962 .... **CLC 2, 3, 11, 15, 54; DA;**
WLC
See also CA 85-88; CANR 35;
CDALB 1917-1929; DLB 45; MTCW

Jefferson, Janet
See Mencken, H(enry) L(ouis)

Jefferson, Thomas 1743-1826 .... **NCLC 11**
See also CDALB 1640-1865; DLB 31

Jeffrey, Francis 1773-1850....... **NCLC 33**
See also DLB 107

Jelakowitch, Ivan
See Heijermans, Herman

Jellicoe, (Patricia) Ann 1927- ...... **CLC 27**
See also CA 85-88; DLB 13

Jen, Gish .... **CLC 70**
See also Jen, Lillian

Jen, Lillian 1956(?)-
See Jen, Gish
See also CA 135

Jenkins, (John) Robin 1912- .... **CLC 52**
See also CA 1-4R; CANR 1; DLB 14

Jennings, Elizabeth (Joan)
1926- .... **CLC 5, 14**
See also CA 61-64; CAAS 5; CANR 8, 39;
DLB 27; MTCW; SATA 66

Jennings, Waylon 1937-........... **CLC 21**

Jensen, Johannes V. 1873-1950.... **TCLC 41**

Jensen, Laura (Linnea) 1948- ...... **CLC 37**
See also CA 103

Jerome, Jerome K(lapka)
1859-1927 .... **TCLC 23**
See also CA 119; DLB 10, 34, 135

Jerrold, Douglas William
1803-1857 .... **NCLC 2**

Jewett, (Theodora) Sarah Orne
1849-1909 .... **TCLC 1, 22; SSC 9**
See also CA 108; 127; DLB 12, 74;
SATA 15

Jewsbury, Geraldine (Endsor)
1812-1880 .... **NCLC 22**
See also DLB 21

Jhabvala, Ruth Prawer
1927- .... **CLC 4, 8, 29; DAB**
See also CA 1-4R; CANR 2, 29; DLB 139;
MTCW

Jiles, Paulette 1943-.......... **CLC 13, 58**
See also CA 101

Jimenez (Mantecon), Juan Ramon
1881-1958 .... **TCLC 4; HLC; PC 7**
See also CA 104; 131; DLB 134; HW;
MTCW

Jimenez, Ramon
See Jimenez (Mantecon), Juan Ramon

Jimenez Mantecon, Juan
See Jimenez (Mantecon), Juan Ramon

Joel, Billy .... **CLC 26**
See also Joel, William Martin

Joel, William Martin 1949-
See Joel, Billy
See also CA 108

John of the Cross, St. 1542-1591 .... **LC 18**

Johnson, B(ryan) S(tanley William)
1933-1973 .... **CLC 6, 9**
See also CA 9-12R; 53-56; CANR 9;
DLB 14, 40

Johnson, Benj. F. of Boo
See Riley, James Whitcomb

Johnson, Benjamin F. of Boo
See Riley, James Whitcomb

Johnson, Charles (Richard)
1948- .... **CLC 7, 51, 65; BLC**
See also BW 2; CA 116; CAAS 18;
CANR 42; DLB 33

Johnson, Denis 1949-............. **CLC 52**
See also CA 117; 121; DLB 120

Johnson, Diane 1934-........ **CLC 5, 13, 48**
See also CA 41-44R; CANR 17, 40;
DLBY 80; MTCW

Johnson, Eyvind (Olof Verner)
1900-1976 .... **CLC 14**
See also CA 73-76; 69-72; CANR 34

Johnson, J. R.
See James, C(yril) L(ionel) R(obert)

Johnson, James Weldon
1871-1938 .... **TCLC 3, 19; BLC**
See also BW 1; CA 104; 125;
CDALB 1917-1929; CLR 32; DLB 51;
MTCW; SATA 31

Johnson, Joyce 1935-............. **CLC 58**
See also CA 125; 129

Johnson, Lionel (Pigot)
1867-1902 .... **TCLC 19**
See also CA 117; DLB 19

Johnson, Mel
See Malzberg, Barry N(athaniel)

Johnson, Pamela Hansford
1912-1981 . . . . **CLC 1, 7, 27**
See also CA 1-4R; 104; CANR 2, 28;
DLB 15; MTCW

Johnson, Samuel
1709-1784 . . . . . **LC 15; DA; DAB; WLC**
See also CDBLB 1660-1789; DLB 39, 95,
104, 142

Johnson, Uwe
1934-1984 . . . . **CLC 5, 10, 15, 40**
See also CA 1-4R; 112; CANR 1, 39;
DLB 75; MTCW

Johnston, George (Benson) 1913- . . . **CLC 51**
See also CA 1-4R; CANR 5, 20; DLB 88

Johnston, Jennifer 1930- . . . . **CLC 7**
See also CA 85-88; DLB 14

Jolley, (Monica) Elizabeth
1923- . . . . **CLC 46; SSC 19**
See also CA 127; CAAS 13

Jones, Arthur Llewellyn 1863-1947
See Machen, Arthur
See also CA 104

Jones, D(ouglas) G(ordon) 1929- . . . . **CLC 10**
See also CA 29-32R; CANR 13; DLB 53

Jones, David (Michael)
1895-1974 . . . . **CLC 2, 4, 7, 13, 42**
See also CA 9-12R; 53-56; CANR 28;
CDBLB 1945-1960; DLB 20, 100; MTCW

Jones, David Robert 1947-
See Bowie, David
See also CA 103

Jones, Diana Wynne 1934- . . . . **CLC 26**
See also AAYA 12; CA 49-52; CANR 4,
26; CLR 23; JRDA; MAICYA; SAAS 7;
SATA 9, 70

Jones, Edward P. 1950- . . . . **CLC 76**
See also BW 2; CA 142

Jones, Gayl 1949- . . . . **CLC 6, 9; BLC**
See also BW 2; CA 77-80; CANR 27;
DLB 33; MTCW

Jones, James 1921-1977 . . . . **CLC 1, 3, 10, 39**
See also AITN 1, 2; CA 1-4R; 69-72;
CANR 6; DLB 2, 143; MTCW

Jones, John J.
See Lovecraft, H(oward) P(hillips)

Jones, LeRoi . . . . **CLC 1, 2, 3, 5, 10, 14**
See also Baraka, Amiri

Jones, Louis B. . . . . **CLC 65**
See also CA 141

Jones, Madison (Percy, Jr.) 1925- . . . **CLC 4**
See also CA 13-16R; CAAS 11; CANR 7;
DLB 152

Jones, Mervyn 1922- . . . . **CLC 10, 52**
See also CA 45-48; CAAS 5; CANR 1;
MTCW

Jones, Mick 1956(?)- . . . . **CLC 30**

Jones, Nettie (Pearl) 1941- . . . . **CLC 34**
See also BW 2; CA 137; CAAS 20

Jones, Preston 1936-1979 . . . . **CLC 10**
See also CA 73-76; 89-92; DLB 7

Jones, Robert F(rancis) 1934- . . . . **CLC 7**
See also CA 49-52; CANR 2

Jones, Rod 1953- . . . . **CLC 50**
See also CA 128

Jones, Terence Graham Parry
1942- . . . . **CLC 21**
See also Jones, Terry; Monty Python
See also CA 112; 116; CANR 35

Jones, Terry
See Jones, Terence Graham Parry
See also SATA 67; SATA-Brief 51

Jones, Thom 1945(?)- . . . . **CLC 81**

Jong, Erica 1942- . . . . . . **CLC 4, 6, 8, 18, 83**
See also AITN 1; BEST 90:2; CA 73-76;
CANR 26; DLB 2, 5, 28, 152; MTCW

Jonson, Ben(jamin)
1572(?)-1637 . . . . **LC 6; DA; DAB; DC 4;
WLC**
See also CDBLB Before 1660; DLB 62, 121

Jordan, June 1936- . . . . **CLC 5, 11, 23**
See also AAYA 2; BW 2; CA 33-36R;
CANR 25; CLR 10; DLB 38; MAICYA;
MTCW; SATA 4

Jordan, Pat(rick M.) 1941- . . . . **CLC 37**
See also CA 33-36R

Jorgensen, Ivar
See Ellison, Harlan (Jay)

Jorgenson, Ivar
See Silverberg, Robert

Josephus, Flavius c. 37-100 . . . . . **CMLC 13**

Josipovici, Gabriel 1940- . . . . **CLC 6, 43**
See also CA 37-40R; CAAS 8; CANR 47;
DLB 14

Joubert, Joseph 1754-1824 . . . . **NCLC 9**

Jouve, Pierre Jean 1887-1976 . . . . . . **CLC 47**
See also CA 65-68

Joyce, James (Augustine Aloysius)
1882-1941 . . . . **TCLC 3, 8, 16, 35, 52;
DA; DAB; SSC 3; WLC**
See also CA 104; 126; CDBLB 1914-1945;
DLB 10, 19, 36; MTCW

Jozsef, Attila 1905-1937 . . . . **TCLC 22**
See also CA 116

Juana Ines de la Cruz 1651(?)-1695 . . . **LC 5**

Judd, Cyril
See Kornbluth, C(yril) M.; Pohl, Frederik

Julian of Norwich 1342(?)-1416(?) . . . . **LC 6**
See also DLB 146

Juniper, Alex
See Hospital, Janette Turner

Just, Ward (Swift) 1935- . . . . **CLC 4, 27**
See also CA 25-28R; CANR 32

Justice, Donald (Rodney) 1925- . . **CLC 6, 19**
See also CA 5-8R; CANR 26; DLBY 83

Juvenal c. 55-c. 127 . . . . **CMLC 8**

Juvenis
See Bourne, Randolph S(illiman)

Kacew, Romain 1914-1980
See Gary, Romain
See also CA 108; 102

Kadare, Ismail 1936- . . . . **CLC 52**

Kadohata, Cynthia . . . . **CLC 59**
See also CA 140

Kafka, Franz
1883-1924 . . . . **TCLC 2, 6, 13, 29, 47, 53;
DA; DAB; SSC 5; WLC**
See also CA 105; 126; DLB 81; MTCW

Kahanovitsch, Pinkhes
See Der Nister

Kahn, Roger 1927- . . . . **CLC 30**
See also CA 25-28R; CANR 44; SATA 37

Kain, Saul
See Sassoon, Siegfried (Lorraine)

Kaiser, Georg 1878-1945 . . . . **TCLC 9**
See also CA 106; DLB 124

Kaletski, Alexander 1946- . . . . **CLC 39**
See also CA 118; 143

Kalidasa fl. c. 400- . . . . **CMLC 9**

Kallman, Chester (Simon)
1921-1975 . . . . **CLC 2**
See also CA 45-48; 53-56; CANR 3

Kaminsky, Melvin 1926-
See Brooks, Mel
See also CA 65-68; CANR 16

Kaminsky, Stuart M(elvin) 1934- . . . **CLC 59**
See also CA 73-76; CANR 29

Kane, Paul
See Simon, Paul

Kane, Wilson
See Bloch, Robert (Albert)

Kanin, Garson 1912- . . . . **CLC 22**
See also AITN 1; CA 5-8R; CANR 7;
DLB 7

Kaniuk, Yoram 1930- . . . . **CLC 19**
See also CA 134

Kant, Immanuel 1724-1804 . . . . . . **NCLC 27**
See also DLB 94

Kantor, MacKinlay 1904-1977 . . . . . . **CLC 7**
See also CA 61-64; 73-76; DLB 9, 102

Kaplan, David Michael 1946- . . . . . . **CLC 50**

Kaplan, James 1951- . . . . **CLC 59**
See also CA 135

Karageorge, Michael
See Anderson, Poul (William)

Karamzin, Nikolai Mikhailovich
1766-1826 . . . . **NCLC 3**
See also DLB 150

Karapanou, Margarita 1946- . . . . **CLC 13**
See also CA 101

Karinthy, Frigyes 1887-1938 . . . . . . **TCLC 47**

Karl, Frederick R(obert) 1927- . . . . . **CLC 34**
See also CA 5-8R; CANR 3, 44

Kastel, Warren
See Silverberg, Robert

Kataev, Evgeny Petrovich 1903-1942
See Petrov, Evgeny
See also CA 120

Kataphusin
See Ruskin, John

Katz, Steve 1935- . . . . **CLC 47**
See also CA 25-28R; CAAS 14; CANR 12;
DLBY 83

Kauffman, Janet 1945- . . . . **CLC 42**
See also CA 117; CANR 43; DLBY 86

Kaufman, Bob (Garnell)
1925-1986 . . . . **CLC 49**
See also BW 1; CA 41-44R; 118; CANR 22;
DLB 16, 41

Kaufman, George S. 1889-1961 . . . . . **CLC 38**
See also CA 108; 93-96; DLB 7

Kaufman, Sue . . . . CLC 3, 8
See also Barondess, Sue K(aufman)

Kavafis, Konstantinos Petrou   1863-1933
See Cavafy, C(onstantine) P(eter)
See also CA 104

Kavan, Anna   1901-1968 . . . . . . CLC 5, 13, 82
See also CA 5-8R; CANR 6; MTCW

Kavanagh, Dan
See Barnes, Julian

Kavanagh, Patrick (Joseph)
1904-1967 . . . . CLC 22
See also CA 123; 25-28R; DLB 15, 20;
MTCW

Kawabata, Yasunari
1899-1972 . . . . . CLC 2, 5, 9, 18; SSC 17
See also CA 93-96; 33-36R

Kaye, M(ary) M(argaret)   1909- . . . . . CLC 28
See also CA 89-92; CANR 24; MTCW;
SATA 62

Kaye, Mollie
See Kaye, M(ary) M(argaret)

Kaye-Smith, Sheila   1887-1956 . . . . . TCLC 20
See also CA 118; DLB 36

Kaymor, Patrice Maguilene
See Senghor, Leopold Sedar

Kazan, Elia   1909- . . . . CLC 6, 16, 63
See also CA 21-24R; CANR 32

Kazantzakis, Nikos
1883(?)-1957 . . . . TCLC 2, 5, 33
See also CA 105; 132; MTCW

Kazin, Alfred   1915- . . . . CLC 34, 38
See also CA 1-4R; CAAS 7; CANR 1, 45;
DLB 67

Keane, Mary Nesta (Skrine)   1904-
See Keane, Molly
See also CA 108; 114

Keane, Molly . . . . CLC 31
See also Keane, Mary Nesta (Skrine)

Keates, Jonathan   19(?)- . . . . CLC 34

Keaton, Buster   1895-1966 . . . . CLC 20

Keats, John
1795-1821 . . . . NCLC 8; DA; DAB;
PC 1; WLC
See also CDBLB 1789-1832; DLB 96, 110

Keene, Donald   1922- . . . . CLC 34
See also CA 1-4R; CANR 5

Keillor, Garrison . . . . CLC 40
See also Keillor, Gary (Edward)
See also AAYA 2; BEST 89:3; DLBY 87;
SATA 58

Keillor, Gary (Edward)   1942-
See Keillor, Garrison
See also CA 111; 117; CANR 36; MTCW

Keith, Michael
See Hubbard, L(afayette) Ron(ald)

Keller, Gottfried   1819-1890 . . . . NCLC 2
See also DLB 129

Kellerman, Jonathan   1949- . . . . CLC 44
See also BEST 90:1; CA 106; CANR 29

Kelley, William Melvin   1937- . . . . . . CLC 22
See also BW 1; CA 77-80; CANR 27;
DLB 33

Kellogg, Marjorie   1922- . . . . CLC 2
See also CA 81-84

Kellow, Kathleen
See Hibbert, Eleanor Alice Burford

Kelly, M(ilton) T(erry)   1947- . . . . . . CLC 55
See also CA 97-100; CANR 19, 43

Kelman, James   1946- . . . . CLC 58, 86
See also CA 148

Kemal, Yashar   1923- . . . . CLC 14, 29
See also CA 89-92; CANR 44

Kemble, Fanny   1809-1893 . . . . NCLC 18
See also DLB 32

Kemelman, Harry   1908- . . . . CLC 2
See also AITN 1; CA 9-12R; CANR 6;
DLB 28

Kempe, Margery   1373(?)-1440(?) . . . . . LC 6
See also DLB 146

Kempis, Thomas a   1380-1471 . . . . LC 11

Kendall, Henry   1839-1882 . . . . . . NCLC 12

Keneally, Thomas (Michael)
1935- . . . . . . CLC 5, 8, 10, 14, 19, 27, 43
See also CA 85-88; CANR 10; MTCW

Kennedy, Adrienne (Lita)
1931- . . . . CLC 66; BLC; DC 5
See also BW 2; CA 103; CAAS 20; CABS 3;
CANR 26; DLB 38

Kennedy, John Pendleton
1795-1870 . . . . NCLC 2
See also DLB 3

Kennedy, Joseph Charles   1929-
See Kennedy, X. J.
See also CA 1-4R; CANR 4, 30, 40;
SATA 14

Kennedy, William   1928- . . . CLC 6, 28, 34, 53
See also AAYA 1; CA 85-88; CANR 14,
31; DLB 143; DLBY 85; MTCW;
SATA 57

Kennedy, X. J. . . . . CLC 8, 42
See also Kennedy, Joseph Charles
See also CAAS 9; CLR 27; DLB 5

Kenny, Maurice (Francis)   1929- . . . . CLC 87
See also CA 144; NNAL

Kent, Kelvin
See Kuttner, Henry

Kenton, Maxwell
See Southern, Terry

Kenyon, Robert O.
See Kuttner, Henry

Kerouac, Jack . . . . . CLC 1, 2, 3, 5, 14, 29, 61
See also Kerouac, Jean-Louis Lebris de
See also CDALB 1941-1968; DLB 2, 16;
DLBD 3

Kerouac, Jean-Louis Lebris de   1922-1969
See Kerouac, Jack
See also AITN 1; CA 5-8R; 25-28R;
CANR 26; DA; DAB; MTCW; WLC

Kerr, Jean   1923- . . . . CLC 22
See also CA 5-8R; CANR 7

Kerr, M. E. . . . . CLC 12, 35
See also Meaker, Marijane (Agnes)
See also AAYA 2; CLR 29; SAAS 1

Kerr, Robert . . . . CLC 55

Kerrigan, (Thomas) Anthony
1918- . . . . CLC 4, 6
See also CA 49-52; CAAS 11; CANR 4

Kerry, Lois
See Duncan, Lois

Kesey, Ken (Elton)
1935- . . . . . . CLC 1, 3, 6, 11, 46, 64; DA;
DAB; WLC
See also CA 1-4R; CANR 22, 38;
CDALB 1968-1988; DLB 2, 16; MTCW;
SATA 66

Kesselring, Joseph (Otto)
1902-1967 . . . . CLC 45

Kessler, Jascha (Frederick)   1929- . . . . CLC 4
See also CA 17-20R; CANR 8, 48

Kettelkamp, Larry (Dale)   1933- . . . . CLC 12
See also CA 29-32R; CANR 16; SAAS 3;
SATA 2

Keyber, Conny
See Fielding, Henry

Keyes, Daniel   1927- . . . . CLC 80; DA
See also CA 17-20R; CANR 10, 26;
SATA 37

Khanshendel, Chiron
See Rose, Wendy

Khayyam, Omar
1048-1131 . . . . CMLC 11; PC 8

Kherdian, David   1931- . . . . CLC 6, 9
See also CA 21-24R; CAAS 2; CANR 39;
CLR 24; JRDA; MAICYA; SATA 16, 74

Khlebnikov, Velimir . . . . TCLC 20
See also Khlebnikov, Viktor Vladimirovich

Khlebnikov, Viktor Vladimirovich   1885-1922
See Khlebnikov, Velimir
See also CA 117

Khodasevich, Vladislav (Felitsianovich)
1886-1939 . . . . TCLC 15
See also CA 115

Kielland, Alexander Lange
1849-1906 . . . . TCLC 5
See also CA 104

Kiely, Benedict   1919- . . . . CLC 23, 43
See also CA 1-4R; CANR 2; DLB 15

Kienzle, William X(avier)   1928- . . . . CLC 25
See also CA 93-96; CAAS 1; CANR 9, 31;
MTCW

Kierkegaard, Soren   1813-1855 . . . . NCLC 34

Killens, John Oliver   1916-1987 . . . . . CLC 10
See also BW 2; CA 77-80; 123; CAAS 2;
CANR 26; DLB 33

Killigrew, Anne   1660-1685 . . . . LC 4
See also DLB 131

Kim
See Simenon, Georges (Jacques Christian)

Kincaid, Jamaica   1949- . . . CLC 43, 68; BLC
See also AAYA 13; BW 2; CA 125;
CANR 47

King, Francis (Henry)   1923- . . . . . CLC 8, 53
See also CA 1-4R; CANR 1, 33; DLB 15,
139; MTCW

King, Martin Luther, Jr.
1929-1968 . . . . CLC 83; BLC; DA; DAB
See also BW 2; CA 25-28; CANR 27, 44;
CAP 2; MTCW; SATA 14

King, Stephen (Edwin)
1947- . . . . . . **CLC 12, 26, 37, 61; SSC 17**
See also AAYA 1; BEST 90:1; CA 61-64;
CANR 1, 30; DLB 143; DLBY 80;
JRDA; MTCW; SATA 9, 55

King, Steve
See King, Stephen (Edwin)

King, Thomas 1943- . . . . **CLC 89**
See also CA 144; NNAL

Kingman, Lee. . . . . **CLC 17**
See also Natti, (Mary) Lee
See also SAAS 3; SATA 1, 67

Kingsley, Charles 1819-1875 . . . . . **NCLC 35**
See also DLB 21, 32; YABC 2

Kingsley, Sidney 1906-1995. . . . . . . **CLC 44**
See also CA 85-88; 147; DLB 7

Kingsolver, Barbara 1955- . . . . . . **CLC 55, 81**
See also CA 129; 134

Kingston, Maxine (Ting Ting) Hong
1940- . . . . **CLC 12, 19, 58**
See also AAYA 8; CA 69-72; CANR 13,
38; DLBY 80; MTCW; SATA 53

Kinnell, Galway
1927- . . . . **CLC 1, 2, 3, 5, 13, 29**
See also CA 9-12R; CANR 10, 34; DLB 5;
DLBY 87; MTCW

Kinsella, Thomas 1928- . . . . **CLC 4, 19**
See also CA 17-20R; CANR 15; DLB 27;
MTCW

Kinsella, W(illiam) P(atrick)
1935- . . . . **CLC 27, 43**
See also AAYA 7; CA 97-100; CAAS 7;
CANR 21, 35; MTCW

Kipling, (Joseph) Rudyard
1865-1936 . . . . . . **TCLC 8, 17; DA; DAB;**
PC 3; SSC 5; WLC
See also CA 105; 120; CANR 33;
CDBLB 1890-1914; DLB 19, 34, 141;
MAICYA; MTCW; YABC 2

Kirkup, James 1918- . . . . **CLC 1**
See also CA 1-4R; CAAS 4; CANR 2;
DLB 27; SATA 12

Kirkwood, James 1930(?)-1989 . . . . . . **CLC 9**
See also AITN 2; CA 1-4R; 128; CANR 6,
40

Kirshner, Sidney
See Kingsley, Sidney

Kis, Danilo 1935-1989 . . . . **CLC 57**
See also CA 109; 118; 129; MTCW

Kivi, Aleksis 1834-1872 . . . . **NCLC 30**

Kizer, Carolyn (Ashley)
1925- . . . . **CLC 15, 39, 80**
See also CA 65-68; CAAS 5; CANR 24;
DLB 5

Klabund 1890-1928. . . . . **TCLC 44**
See also DLB 66

Klappert, Peter 1942- . . . . **CLC 57**
See also CA 33-36R; DLB 5

Klein, A(braham) M(oses)
1909-1972 . . . . **CLC 19; DAB**
See also CA 101; 37-40R; DLB 68

Klein, Norma 1938-1989 . . . . **CLC 30**
See also AAYA 2; CA 41-44R; 128;
CANR 15, 37; CLR 2, 19; JRDA;
MAICYA; SAAS 1; SATA 7, 57

Klein, T(heodore) E(ibon) D(onald)
1947- . . . . **CLC 34**
See also CA 119; CANR 44

Kleist, Heinrich von
1777-1811 . . . . **NCLC 2, 37**
See also DLB 90

Klima, Ivan 1931- . . . . **CLC 56**
See also CA 25-28R; CANR 17

Klimentov, Andrei Platonovich 1899-1951
See Platonov, Andrei
See also CA 108

Klinger, Friedrich Maximilian von
1752-1831 . . . . **NCLC 1**
See also DLB 94

Klopstock, Friedrich Gottlieb
1724-1803 . . . . **NCLC 11**
See also DLB 97

Knebel, Fletcher 1911-1993 . . . . **CLC 14**
See also AITN 1; CA 1-4R; 140; CAAS 3;
CANR 1, 36; SATA 36; SATA-Obit 75

Knickerbocker, Diedrich
See Irving, Washington

Knight, Etheridge
1931-1991 . . . . **CLC 40; BLC**
See also BW 1; CA 21-24R; 133; CANR 23;
DLB 41

Knight, Sarah Kemble 1666-1727 . . . . . **LC 7**
See also DLB 24

Knister, Raymond 1899-1932 . . . . . . **TCLC 56**
See also DLB 68

Knowles, John
1926- . . . . **CLC 1, 4, 10, 26; DA**
See also AAYA 10; CA 17-20R; CANR 40;
CDALB 1968-1988; DLB 6; MTCW;
SATA 8

Knox, Calvin M.
See Silverberg, Robert

Knye, Cassandra
See Disch, Thomas M(ichael)

Koch, C(hristopher) J(ohn) 1932- . . . **CLC 42**
See also CA 127

Koch, Christopher
See Koch, C(hristopher) J(ohn)

Koch, Kenneth 1925- . . . . **CLC 5, 8, 44**
See also CA 1-4R; CANR 6, 36; DLB 5;
SATA 65

Kochanowski, Jan 1530-1584. . . . . **LC 10**

Kock, Charles Paul de
1794-1871 . . . . **NCLC 16**

Koda Shigeyuki 1867-1947
See Rohan, Koda
See also CA 121

Koestler, Arthur
1905-1983 . . . . **CLC 1, 3, 6, 8, 15, 33**
See also CA 1-4R; 109; CANR 1, 33;
CDBLB 1945-1960; DLBY 83; MTCW

Kogawa, Joy Nozomi 1935- . . . . **CLC 78**
See also CA 101; CANR 19

Kohout, Pavel 1928- . . . . **CLC 13**
See also CA 45-48; CANR 3

Koizumi, Yakumo
See Hearn, (Patricio) Lafcadio (Tessima
Carlos)

Kolmar, Gertrud 1894-1943 . . . . . . **TCLC 40**

Komunyakaa, Yusef 1947- . . . . **CLC 86**
See also CA 147; DLB 120

Konrad, George
See Konrad, Gyoergy

Konrad, Gyoergy 1933- . . . . . . **CLC 4, 10, 73**
See also CA 85-88

Konwicki, Tadeusz 1926- . . . . . **CLC 8, 28, 54**
See also CA 101; CAAS 9; CANR 39;
MTCW

Koontz, Dean R(ay) 1945- . . . . **CLC 78**
See also AAYA 9; BEST 89:3, 90:2;
CA 108; CANR 19, 36; MTCW

Kopit, Arthur (Lee) 1937- . . . . **CLC 1, 18, 33**
See also AITN 1; CA 81-84; CABS 3;
DLB 7; MTCW

Kops, Bernard 1926-. . . . . **CLC 4**
See also CA 5-8R; DLB 13

Kornbluth, C(yril) M. 1923-1958. . . . **TCLC 8**
See also CA 105; DLB 8

Korolenko, V. G.
See Korolenko, Vladimir Galaktionovich

Korolenko, Vladimir
See Korolenko, Vladimir Galaktionovich

Korolenko, Vladimir G.
See Korolenko, Vladimir Galaktionovich

Korolenko, Vladimir Galaktionovich
1853-1921 . . . . **TCLC 22**
See also CA 121

Kosinski, Jerzy (Nikodem)
1933-1991 . . . . **CLC 1, 2, 3, 6, 10, 15, 53,**
70
See also CA 17-20R; 134; CANR 9, 46;
DLB 2; DLBY 82; MTCW

Kostelanetz, Richard (Cory) 1940- . . **CLC 28**
See also CA 13-16R; CAAS 8; CANR 38

Kostrowitzki, Wilhelm Apollinaris de
1880-1918
See Apollinaire, Guillaume
See also CA 104

Kotlowitz, Robert 1924-. . . . . **CLC 4**
See also CA 33-36R; CANR 36

Kotzebue, August (Friedrich Ferdinand) von
1761-1819 . . . . **NCLC 25**
See also DLB 94

Kotzwinkle, William 1938- . . . **CLC 5, 14, 35**
See also CA 45-48; CANR 3, 44; CLR 6;
MAICYA; SATA 24, 70

Kozol, Jonathan 1936-. . . . . **CLC 17**
See also CA 61-64; CANR 16, 45

Kozoll, Michael 1940(?)- . . . . **CLC 35**

Kramer, Kathryn 19(?)- . . . . **CLC 34**

Kramer, Larry 1935- . . . . **CLC 42**
See also CA 124; 126

Krasicki, Ignacy 1735-1801 . . . . **NCLC 8**

Krasinski, Zygmunt 1812-1859 . . . . **NCLC 4**

Kraus, Karl 1874-1936. . . . . **TCLC 5**
See also CA 104; DLB 118

Kreve (Mickevicius), Vincas
1882-1954 . . . . **TCLC 27**

Kristeva, Julia 1941- . . . . **CLC 77**

Kristofferson, Kris 1936- . . . . **CLC 26**
See also CA 104

Krizanc, John 1956- . . . . **CLC 57**

Krleza, Miroslav 1893-1981......... **CLC 8**
See also CA 97-100; 105; DLB 147

Kroetsch, Robert 1927- ...... **CLC 5, 23, 57**
See also CA 17-20R; CANR 8, 38; DLB 53;
MTCW

Kroetz, Franz
See Kroetz, Franz Xaver

Kroetz, Franz Xaver 1946- .... **CLC 41**
See also CA 130

Kroker, Arthur 1945-............. **CLC 77**

Kropotkin, Peter (Aleksieevich)
1842-1921 .... **TCLC 36**
See also CA 119

Krotkov, Yuri 1917-............. **CLC 19**
See also CA 102

Krumb
See Crumb, R(obert)

Krumgold, Joseph (Quincy)
1908-1980 .... **CLC 12**
See also CA 9-12R; 101; CANR 7;
MAICYA; SATA 1, 48; SATA-Obit 23

Krumwitz
See Crumb, R(obert)

Krutch, Joseph Wood 1893-1970.... **CLC 24**
See also CA 1-4R; 25-28R; CANR 4;
DLB 63

Krutzch, Gus
See Eliot, T(homas) S(tearns)

Krylov, Ivan Andreevich
1768(?)-1844 .... **NCLC 1**
See also DLB 150

Kubin, Alfred 1877-1959 .... **TCLC 23**
See also CA 112; DLB 81

Kubrick, Stanley 1928-............ **CLC 16**
See also CA 81-84; CANR 33; DLB 26

Kumin, Maxine (Winokur)
1925- .... **CLC 5, 13, 28**
See also AITN 2; CA 1-4R; CAAS 8;
CANR 1, 21; DLB 5; MTCW; SATA 12

Kundera, Milan
1929- .... **CLC 4, 9, 19, 32, 68**
See also AAYA 2; CA 85-88; CANR 19;
MTCW

Kunene, Mazisi (Raymond) 1930-... **CLC 85**
See also BW 1; CA 125; DLB 117

Kunitz, Stanley (Jasspon)
1905- .... **CLC 6, 11, 14**
See also CA 41-44R; CANR 26; DLB 48;
MTCW

Kunze, Reiner 1933-.............. **CLC 10**
See also CA 93-96; DLB 75

Kuprin, Aleksandr Ivanovich
1870-1938 .... **TCLC 5**
See also CA 104

Kureishi, Hanif 1954(?)-.......... **CLC 64**
See also CA 139

Kurosawa, Akira 1910-............ **CLC 16**
See also AAYA 11; CA 101; CANR 46

Kushner, Tony 1957(?)- .... **CLC 81**
See also CA 144

Kuttner, Henry 1915-1958........ **TCLC 10**
See also CA 107; DLB 8

Kuzma, Greg 1944-................ **CLC 7**
See also CA 33-36R

Kuzmin, Mikhail 1872(?)-1936 .... **TCLC 40**

Kyd, Thomas 1558-1594....... **LC 22; DC 3**
See also DLB 62

Kyprianos, Iossif
See Samarakis, Antonis

La Bruyere, Jean de 1645-1696...... **LC 17**

Lacan, Jacques (Marie Emile)
1901-1981 .... **CLC 75**
See also CA 121; 104

**Laclos, Pierre Ambroise Francois Choderlos
de** 1741-1803 .... **NCLC 4**

Lacolere, Francois
See Aragon, Louis

La Colere, Francois
See Aragon, Louis

La Deshabilleuse
See Simenon, Georges (Jacques Christian)

Lady Gregory
See Gregory, Isabella Augusta (Persse)

Lady of Quality, A
See Bagnold, Enid

**La Fayette, Marie (Madelaine Pioche de la
Vergne Comtes** 1634-1693....... **LC 2**

Lafayette, Rene
See Hubbard, L(afayette) Ron(ald)

Laforgue, Jules
1860-1887 .... **NCLC 5; SSC 20**

Lagerkvist, Paer (Fabian)
1891-1974 .... **CLC 7, 10, 13, 54**
See also Lagerkvist, Par
See also CA 85-88; 49-52; MTCW

Lagerkvist, Par
See Lagerkvist, Paer (Fabian)
See also SSC 12

Lagerloef, Selma (Ottiliana Lovisa)
1858-1940 .... **TCLC 4, 36**
See also Lagerlof, Selma (Ottiliana Lovisa)
See also CA 108; SATA 15

Lagerlof, Selma (Ottiliana Lovisa)
See Lagerloef, Selma (Ottiliana Lovisa)
See also CLR 7; SATA 15

La Guma, (Justin) Alex(ander)
1925-1985 .... **CLC 19**
See also BW 1; CA 49-52; 118; CANR 25;
DLB 117; MTCW

Laidlaw, A. K.
See Grieve, C(hristopher) M(urray)

Lainez, Manuel Mujica
See Mujica Lainez, Manuel
See also HW

Lamartine, Alphonse (Marie Louis Prat) de
1790-1869 .... **NCLC 11**

Lamb, Charles
1775-1834 .. **NCLC 10; DA; DAB; WLC**
See also CDBLB 1789-1832; DLB 93, 107;
SATA 17

Lamb, Lady Caroline 1785-1828.. **NCLC 38**
See also DLB 116

Lamming, George (William)
1927- .... **CLC 2, 4, 66; BLC**
See also BW 2; CA 85-88; CANR 26;
DLB 125; MTCW

L'Amour, Louis (Dearborn)
1908-1988 .... **CLC 25, 55**
See also AITN 2; BEST 89:2; CA 1-4R;
125; CANR 3, 25, 40; DLBY 80; MTCW

Lampedusa, Giuseppe (Tomasi) di ... **TCLC 13**
See also Tomasi di Lampedusa, Giuseppe

Lampman, Archibald 1861-1899 .. **NCLC 25**
See also DLB 92

Lancaster, Bruce 1896-1963....... **CLC 36**
See also CA 9-10; CAP 1; SATA 9

Landau, Mark Alexandrovich
See Aldanov, Mark (Alexandrovich)

Landau-Aldanov, Mark Alexandrovich
See Aldanov, Mark (Alexandrovich)

Landis, John 1950-............... **CLC 26**
See also CA 112; 122

Landolfi, Tommaso 1908-1979... **CLC 11, 49**
See also CA 127; 117

Landon, Letitia Elizabeth
1802-1838 .... **NCLC 15**
See also DLB 96

Landor, Walter Savage
1775-1864 .... **NCLC 14**
See also DLB 93, 107

Landwirth, Heinz 1927-
See Lind, Jakov
See also CA 9-12R; CANR 7

Lane, Patrick 1939-.............. **CLC 25**
See also CA 97-100; DLB 53

Lang, Andrew 1844-1912......... **TCLC 16**
See also CA 114; 137; DLB 98, 141;
MAICYA; SATA 16

Lang, Fritz 1890-1976 .... **CLC 20**
See also CA 77-80; 69-72; CANR 30

Lange, John
See Crichton, (John) Michael

Langer, Elinor 1939- .... **CLC 34**
See also CA 121

Langland, William
1330(?)-1400(?) ...... **LC 19; DA; DAB**
See also DLB 146

Langstaff, Launcelot
See Irving, Washington

Lanier, Sidney 1842-1881 .... **NCLC 6**
See also DLB 64; MAICYA; SATA 18

Lanyer, Aemilia 1569-1645 ...... **LC 10, 30**
See also DLB 121

Lao Tzu .... **CMLC 7**

Lapine, James (Elliot) 1949-....... **CLC 39**
See also CA 123; 130

Larbaud, Valery (Nicolas)
1881-1957 .... **TCLC 9**
See also CA 106

Lardner, Ring
See Lardner, Ring(gold) W(ilmer)

Lardner, Ring W., Jr.
See Lardner, Ring(gold) W(ilmer)

Lardner, Ring(gold) W(ilmer)
1885-1933 .... **TCLC 2, 14**
See also CA 104; 131; CDALB 1917-1929;
DLB 11, 25, 86; MTCW

Laredo, Betty
See Codrescu, Andrei

Larkin, Maia
See Wojciechowska, Maia (Teresa)

Larkin, Philip (Arthur)
1922-1985 .... **CLC 3, 5, 8, 9, 13, 18, 33,**
39, 64; DAB
See also CA 5-8R; 117; CANR 24;
CDBLB 1960 to Present; DLB 27;
MTCW

Larra (y Sanchez de Castro), Mariano Jose de
1809-1837 .... **NCLC 17**

Larsen, Eric 1941- .... **CLC 55**
See also CA 132

Larsen, Nella 1891-1964 ..... **CLC 37; BLC**
See also BW 1; CA 125; DLB 51

Larson, Charles R(aymond) 1938-... **CLC 31**
See also CA 53-56; CANR 4

Lasker-Schueler, Else 1869-1945 .. **TCLC 57**
See also DLB 66, 124

Latham, Jean Lee 1902-........... **CLC 12**
See also AITN 1; CA 5-8R; CANR 7;
MAICYA; SATA 2, 68

Latham, Mavis
See Clark, Mavis Thorpe

Lathen, Emma .... **CLC 2**
See also Hennissart, Martha; Latsis, Mary
J(ane)

Lathrop, Francis
See Leiber, Fritz (Reuter, Jr.)

Latsis, Mary J(ane)
See Lathen, Emma
See also CA 85-88

Lattimore, Richmond (Alexander)
1906-1984 .... **CLC 3**
See also CA 1-4R; 112; CANR 1

Laughlin, James 1914-............ **CLC 49**
See also CA 21-24R; CANR 9, 47; DLB 48

Laurence, (Jean) Margaret (Wemyss)
1926-1987 .. **CLC 3, 6, 13, 50, 62; SSC 7**
See also CA 5-8R; 121; CANR 33; DLB 53;
MTCW; SATA-Obit 50

Laurent, Antoine 1952- .... **CLC 50**

Lauscher, Hermann
See Hesse, Hermann

Lautreamont, Comte de
1846-1870 .... **NCLC 12; SSC 14**

Laverty, Donald
See Blish, James (Benjamin)

Lavin, Mary 1912-...... **CLC 4, 18; SSC 4**
See also CA 9-12R; CANR 33; DLB 15;
MTCW

Lavond, Paul Dennis
See Kornbluth, C(yril) M.; Pohl, Frederik

Lawler, Raymond Evenor 1922- .... **CLC 58**
See also CA 103

Lawrence, D(avid) H(erbert Richards)
1885-1930 .... **TCLC 2, 9, 16, 33, 48;**
DA; DAB; SSC 4, 19; WLC
See also CA 104; 121; CDBLB 1914-1945;
DLB 10, 19, 36, 98; MTCW

Lawrence, T(homas) E(dward)
1888-1935 .... **TCLC 18**
See also Dale, Colin
See also CA 115

Lawrence of Arabia
See Lawrence, T(homas) E(dward)

Lawson, Henry (Archibald Hertzberg)
1867-1922 .... **TCLC 27; SSC 18**
See also CA 120

Lawton, Dennis
See Faust, Frederick (Schiller)

Laxness, Halldor .... **CLC 25**
See also Gudjonsson, Halldor Kiljan

Layamon fl. c. 1200-........... **CMLC 10**
See also DLB 146

Laye, Camara 1928-1980 ... **CLC 4, 38; BLC**
See also BW 1; CA 85-88; 97-100;
CANR 25; MTCW

Layton, Irving (Peter) 1912-..... **CLC 2, 15**
See also CA 1-4R; CANR 2, 33, 43;
DLB 88; MTCW

Lazarus, Emma 1849-1887....... **NCLC 8**

Lazarus, Felix
See Cable, George Washington

Lazarus, Henry
See Slavitt, David R(ytman)

Lea, Joan
See Neufeld, John (Arthur)

Leacock, Stephen (Butler)
1869-1944 .... **TCLC 2**
See also CA 104; 141; DLB 92

Lear, Edward 1812-1888 .... **NCLC 3**
See also CLR 1; DLB 32; MAICYA;
SATA 18

Lear, Norman (Milton) 1922- ...... **CLC 12**
See also CA 73-76

Leavis, F(rank) R(aymond)
1895-1978 .... **CLC 24**
See also CA 21-24R; 77-80; CANR 44;
MTCW

Leavitt, David 1961-.............. **CLC 34**
See also CA 116; 122; DLB 130

Leblanc, Maurice (Marie Emile)
1864-1941 .... **TCLC 49**
See also CA 110

Lebowitz, Fran(ces Ann)
1951(?)- .... **CLC 11, 36**
See also CA 81-84; CANR 14; MTCW

Lebrecht, Peter
See Tieck, (Johann) Ludwig

le Carre, John .... **CLC 3, 5, 9, 15, 28**
See also Cornwell, David (John Moore)
See also BEST 89:4; CDBLB 1960 to
Present; DLB 87

Le Clezio, J(ean) M(arie) G(ustave)
1940- .... **CLC 31**
See also CA 116; 128; DLB 83

Leconte de Lisle, Charles-Marie-Rene
1818-1894 .... **NCLC 29**

Le Coq, Monsieur
See Simenon, Georges (Jacques Christian)

Leduc, Violette 1907-1972......... **CLC 22**
See also CA 13-14; 33-36R; CAP 1

Ledwidge, Francis 1887(?)-1917 ... **TCLC 23**
See also CA 123; DLB 20

Lee, Andrea 1953- .... **CLC 36; BLC**
See also BW 1; CA 125

Lee, Andrew
See Auchincloss, Louis (Stanton)

Lee, Don L. .... **CLC 2**
See also Madhubuti, Haki R.

Lee, George W(ashington)
1894-1976 .... **CLC 52; BLC**
See also BW 1; CA 125; DLB 51

Lee, (Nelle) Harper
1926- ..... **CLC 12, 60; DA; DAB; WLC**
See also AAYA 13; CA 13-16R;
CDALB 1941-1968; DLB 6; MTCW;
SATA 11

Lee, Helen Elaine 1959(?)- .... **CLC 86**
See also CA 148

Lee, Julian
See Latham, Jean Lee

Lee, Larry
See Lee, Lawrence

Lee, Lawrence 1941-1990......... **CLC 34**
See also CA 131; CANR 43

Lee, Manfred B(ennington)
1905-1971 .... **CLC 11**
See also Queen, Ellery
See also CA 1-4R; 29-32R; CANR 2;
DLB 137

Lee, Stan 1922-................... **CLC 17**
See also AAYA 5; CA 108; 111

Lee, Tanith 1947-................. **CLC 46**
See also CA 37-40R; SATA 8

Lee, Vernon .... **TCLC 5**
See also Paget, Violet
See also DLB 57, 153

Lee, William
See Burroughs, William S(eward)

Lee, Willy
See Burroughs, William S(eward)

Lee-Hamilton, Eugene (Jacob)
1845-1907 .... **TCLC 22**
See also CA 117

Leet, Judith 1935- .... **CLC 11**

Le Fanu, Joseph Sheridan
1814-1873 .... **NCLC 9; SSC 14**
See also DLB 21, 70

Leffland, Ella 1931- .... **CLC 19**
See also CA 29-32R; CANR 35; DLBY 84;
SATA 65

Leger, Alexis
See Leger, (Marie-Rene Auguste) Alexis
Saint-Leger

Leger, (Marie-Rene Auguste) Alexis
Saint-Leger 1887-1975........ **CLC 11**
See also Perse, St.-John
See also CA 13-16R; 61-64; CANR 43;
MTCW

Leger, Saintleger
See Leger, (Marie-Rene Auguste) Alexis
Saint-Leger

Le Guin, Ursula K(roeber)
1929- ...... **CLC 8, 13, 22, 45, 71; DAB;**
SSC 12
See also AAYA 9; AITN 1; CA 21-24R;
CANR 9, 32; CDALB 1968-1988; CLR 3,
28; DLB 8, 52; JRDA; MAICYA;
MTCW; SATA 4, 52

Lehmann, Rosamond (Nina)
1901-1990 . . . . CLC 5
See also CA 77-80; 131; CANR 8; DLB 15

Leiber, Fritz (Reuter, Jr.)
1910-1992 . . . . CLC 25
See also CA 45-48; 139; CANR 2, 40;
DLB 8; MTCW; SATA 45;
SATA-Obit 73

Leimbach, Martha 1963-
See Leimbach, Marti
See also CA 130

Leimbach, Marti . . . . CLC 65
See also Leimbach, Martha

Leino, Eino . . . . TCLC 24
See also Loennbohm, Armas Eino Leopold

Leiris, Michel (Julien) 1901-1990 . . . CLC 61
See also CA 119; 128; 132

Leithauser, Brad 1953- . . . . CLC 27
See also CA 107; CANR 27; DLB 120

Lelchuk, Alan 1938- . . . . CLC 5
See also CA 45-48; CAAS 20; CANR 1

Lem, Stanislaw 1921- . . . . CLC 8, 15, 40
See also CA 105; CAAS 1; CANR 32;
MTCW

Lemann, Nancy 1956- . . . . CLC 39
See also CA 118; 136

Lemonnier, (Antoine Louis) Camille
1844-1913 . . . . TCLC 22
See also CA 121

Lenau, Nikolaus 1802-1850 . . . . . . NCLC 16

L'Engle, Madeleine (Camp Franklin)
1918- . . . . CLC 12
See also AAYA 1; AITN 2; CA 1-4R;
CANR 3, 21, 39; CLR 1, 14; DLB 52;
JRDA; MAICYA; MTCW; SAAS 15;
SATA 1, 27, 75

Lengyel, Jozsef 1896-1975 . . . . CLC 7
See also CA 85-88; 57-60

Lennon, John (Ono)
1940-1980 . . . . CLC 12, 35
See also CA 102

Lennox, Charlotte Ramsay
1729(?)-1804 . . . . NCLC 23
See also DLB 39

Lentricchia, Frank (Jr.) 1940- . . . . . . CLC 34
See also CA 25-28R; CANR 19

Lenz, Siegfried 1926- . . . . CLC 27
See also CA 89-92; DLB 75

Leonard, Elmore (John, Jr.)
1925- . . . . CLC 28, 34, 71
See also AITN 1; BEST 89:1, 90:4;
CA 81-84; CANR 12, 28; MTCW

Leonard, Hugh . . . . CLC 19
See also Byrne, John Keyes
See also DLB 13

Leopardi, (Conte) Giacomo
1798-1837 . . . . NCLC 22

Le Reveler
See Artaud, Antonin

Lerman, Eleanor 1952- . . . . CLC 9
See also CA 85-88

Lerman, Rhoda 1936- . . . . CLC 56
See also CA 49-52

Lermontov, Mikhail Yuryevich
1814-1841 . . . . NCLC 47

Leroux, Gaston 1868-1927 . . . . TCLC 25
See also CA 108; 136; SATA 65

Lesage, Alain-Rene 1668-1747 . . . . . . LC 28

Leskov, Nikolai (Semyonovich)
1831-1895 . . . . NCLC 25

Lessing, Doris (May)
1919- . . . . . CLC 1, 2, 3, 6, 10, 15, 22, 40;
DA; DAB; SSC 6
See also CA 9-12R; CAAS 14; CANR 33;
CDBLB 1960 to Present; DLB 15, 139;
DLBY 85; MTCW

Lessing, Gotthold Ephraim
1729-1781 . . . . LC 8
See also DLB 97

Lester, Richard 1932- . . . . CLC 20

Lever, Charles (James)
1806-1872 . . . . NCLC 23
See also DLB 21

Leverson, Ada 1865(?)-1936(?) . . . . TCLC 18
See also Elaine
See also CA 117; DLB 153

Levertov, Denise
1923- . . . . . . CLC 1, 2, 3, 5, 8, 15, 28, 66;
PC 11
See also CA 1-4R; CAAS 19; CANR 3, 29;
DLB 5; MTCW

Levi, Jonathan . . . . CLC 76

Levi, Peter (Chad Tigar) 1931- . . . . . CLC 41
See also CA 5-8R; CANR 34; DLB 40

Levi, Primo
1919-1987 . . . . CLC 37, 50; SSC 12
See also CA 13-16R; 122; CANR 12, 33;
MTCW

Levin, Ira 1929- . . . . CLC 3, 6
See also CA 21-24R; CANR 17, 44;
MTCW; SATA 66

Levin, Meyer 1905-1981 . . . . CLC 7
See also AITN 1; CA 9-12R; 104;
CANR 15; DLB 9, 28; DLBY 81;
SATA 21; SATA-Obit 27

Levine, Norman 1924- . . . . CLC 54
See also CA 73-76; CANR 14; DLB 88

Levine, Philip 1928- . . CLC 2, 4, 5, 9, 14, 33
See also CA 9-12R; CANR 9, 37; DLB 5

Levinson, Deirdre 1931- . . . . CLC 49
See also CA 73-76

Levi-Strauss, Claude 1908- . . . . CLC 38
See also CA 1-4R; CANR 6, 32; MTCW

Levitin, Sonia (Wolff) 1934- . . . . CLC 17
See also AAYA 13; CA 29-32R; CANR 14,
32; JRDA; MAICYA; SAAS 2; SATA 4,
68

Levon, O. U.
See Kesey, Ken (Elton)

Lewes, George Henry
1817-1878 . . . . NCLC 25
See also DLB 55, 144

Lewis, Alun 1915-1944 . . . . TCLC 3
See also CA 104; DLB 20

Lewis, C. Day
See Day Lewis, C(ecil)

Lewis, C(live) S(taples)
1898-1963 . . . . . CLC 1, 3, 6, 14, 27; DA;
DAB; WLC
See also AAYA 3; CA 81-84; CANR 33;
CDBLB 1945-1960; CLR 3, 27; DLB 15,
100; JRDA; MAICYA; MTCW;
SATA 13

Lewis, Janet 1899- . . . . CLC 41
See also Winters, Janet Lewis
See also CA 9-12R; CANR 29; CAP 1;
DLBY 87

Lewis, Matthew Gregory
1775-1818 . . . . NCLC 11
See also DLB 39

Lewis, (Harry) Sinclair
1885-1951 . . . . . CLC 4, 13, 23, 39; DA;
DAB; WLC
See also CA 104; 133; CDALB 1917-1929;
DLB 9, 102; DLBD 1; MTCW

Lewis, (Percy) Wyndham
1884(?)-1957 . . . . TCLC 2, 9
See also CA 104; DLB 15

Lewisohn, Ludwig 1883-1955 . . . . . . TCLC 19
See also CA 107; DLB 4, 9, 28, 102

Lezama Lima, Jose 1910-1976 . . . CLC 4, 10
See also CA 77-80; DLB 113; HW

L'Heureux, John (Clarke) 1934- . . . . CLC 52
See also CA 13-16R; CANR 23, 45

Liddell, C. H.
See Kuttner, Henry

Lie, Jonas (Lauritz Idemil)
1833-1908(?) . . . . TCLC 5
See also CA 115

Lieber, Joel 1937-1971 . . . . CLC 6
See also CA 73-76; 29-32R

Lieber, Stanley Martin
See Lee, Stan

Lieberman, Laurence (James)
1935- . . . . CLC 4, 36
See also CA 17-20R; CANR 8, 36

Lieksman, Anders
See Haavikko, Paavo Juhani

Li Fei-kan 1904-
See Pa Chin
See also CA 105

Lifton, Robert Jay 1926- . . . . CLC 67
See also CA 17-20R; CANR 27; SATA 66

Lightfoot, Gordon 1938- . . . . CLC 26
See also CA 109

Lightman, Alan P. 1948- . . . . CLC 81
See also CA 141

Ligotti, Thomas (Robert)
1953- . . . . CLC 44; SSC 16
See also CA 123; CANR 49

Li Ho 791-817 . . . . PC 13

Liliencron, (Friedrich Adolf Axel) Detlev von
1844-1909 . . . . TCLC 18
See also CA 117

Lilly, William 1602-1681 . . . . LC 27

Lima, Jose Lezama
See Lezama Lima, Jose

Lima Barreto, Afonso Henrique de
1881-1922 . . . . TCLC 23
See also CA 117

Limonov, Edward 1944-.......... **CLC 67**
See also CA 137

Lin, Frank
See Atherton, Gertrude (Franklin Horn)

Lincoln, Abraham 1809-1865..... **NCLC 18**

Lind, Jakov .... **CLC 1, 2, 4, 27, 82**
See also Landwirth, Heinz
See also CAAS 4

Lindbergh, Anne (Spencer) Morrow
1906-...................... **CLC 82**
See also CA 17-20R; CANR 16; MTCW;
SATA 33

Lindsay, David 1878-1945....... **TCLC 15**
See also CA 113

Lindsay, (Nicholas) Vachel
1879-1931........ **TCLC 17; DA; WLC**
See also CA 114; 135; CDALB 1865-1917;
DLB 54; SATA 40

Linke-Poot
See Doeblin, Alfred

Linney, Romulus 1930- .... **CLC 51**
See also CA 1-4R; CANR 40, 44

Linton, Eliza Lynn 1822-1898.... **NCLC 41**
See also DLB 18

Li Po 701-763.................. **CMLC 2**

Lipsius, Justus 1547-1606......... **LC 16**

Lipsyte, Robert (Michael)
1938-.................. **CLC 21; DA**
See also AAYA 7; CA 17-20R; CANR 8;
CLR 23; JRDA; MAICYA; SATA 5, 68

Lish, Gordon (Jay) 1934-.. **CLC 45; SSC 18**
See also CA 113; 117; DLB 130

Lispector, Clarice 1925-1977....... **CLC 43**
See also CA 139; 116; DLB 113

Littell, Robert 1935(?)- .... **CLC 42**
See also CA 109; 112

Little, Malcolm 1925-1965
See Malcolm X
See also BW 1; CA 125; 111; DA; DAB;
MTCW

Littlewit, Humphrey Gent.
See Lovecraft, H(oward) P(hillips)

Litwos
See Sienkiewicz, Henryk (Adam Alexander
Pius)

Liu E 1857-1909................ **TCLC 15**
See also CA 115

Lively, Penelope (Margaret)
1933-.................... **CLC 32, 50**
See also CA 41-44R; CANR 29; CLR 7;
DLB 14; JRDA; MAICYA; MTCW;
SATA 7, 60

Livesay, Dorothy (Kathleen)
1909-.................. **CLC 4, 15, 79**
See also AITN 2; CA 25-28R; CAAS 8;
CANR 36; DLB 68; MTCW

Livy c. 59B.C.-c. 17............ **CMLC 11**

Lizardi, Jose Joaquin Fernandez de
1776-1827 .... **NCLC 30**

Llewellyn, Richard
See Llewellyn Lloyd, Richard Dafydd
Vivian
See also DLB 15

Llewellyn Lloyd, Richard Dafydd Vivian
1906-1983 .... **CLC 7, 80**
See also Llewellyn, Richard
See also CA 53-56; 111; CANR 7;
SATA 11; SATA-Obit 37

Llosa, (Jorge) Mario (Pedro) Vargas
See Vargas Llosa, (Jorge) Mario (Pedro)

Lloyd Webber, Andrew 1948-
See Webber, Andrew Lloyd
See also AAYA 1; CA 116; SATA 56

Llull, Ramon c. 1235-c. 1316..... **CMLC 12**

Locke, Alain (Le Roy)
1886-1954 .... **TCLC 43**
See also BW 1; CA 106; 124; DLB 51

Locke, John 1632-1704 .... **LC 7**
See also DLB 101

Locke-Elliott, Sumner
See Elliott, Sumner Locke

Lockhart, John Gibson
1794-1854 .... **NCLC 6**
See also DLB 110, 116, 144

Lodge, David (John) 1935-........ **CLC 36**
See also BEST 90:1; CA 17-20R; CANR 19;
DLB 14; MTCW

Loennbohm, Armas Eino Leopold 1878-1926
See Leino, Eino
See also CA 123

Loewinsohn, Ron(ald William)
1937-...................... **CLC 52**
See also CA 25-28R

Logan, Jake
See Smith, Martin Cruz

Logan, John (Burton) 1923-1987..... **CLC 5**
See also CA 77-80; 124; CANR 45; DLB 5

Lo Kuan-chung 1330(?)-1400(?)...... **LC 12**

Lombard, Nap
See Johnson, Pamela Hansford

London, Jack.. **TCLC 9, 15, 39; SSC 4; WLC**
See also London, John Griffith
See also AAYA 13; AITN 2;
CDALB 1865-1917; DLB 8, 12, 78;
SATA 18

London, John Griffith 1876-1916
See London, Jack
See also CA 110; 119; DA; DAB; JRDA;
MAICYA; MTCW

Long, Emmett
See Leonard, Elmore (John, Jr.)

Longbaugh, Harry
See Goldman, William (W.)

Longfellow, Henry Wadsworth
1807-1882 ...... **NCLC 2, 45; DA; DAB**
See also CDALB 1640-1865; DLB 1, 59;
SATA 19

Longley, Michael 1939-........... **CLC 29**
See also CA 102; DLB 40

Longus fl. c. 2nd cent. -.......... **CMLC 7**

Longway, A. Hugh
See Lang, Andrew

Lopate, Phillip 1943-............ **CLC 29**
See also CA 97-100; DLBY 80

Lopez Portillo (y Pacheco), Jose
1920-...................... **CLC 46**
See also CA 129; HW

Lopez y Fuentes, Gregorio
1897(?)-1966 .... **CLC 32**
See also CA 131; HW

Lorca, Federico Garcia
See Garcia Lorca, Federico

Lord, Bette Bao 1938-............ **CLC 23**
See also BEST 90:3; CA 107; CANR 41;
SATA 58

Lord Auch
See Bataille, Georges

Lord Byron
See Byron, George Gordon (Noel)

Lorde, Audre (Geraldine)
1934-1992 .... **CLC 18, 71; BLC; PC 12**
See also BW 1; CA 25-28R; 142; CANR 16,
26, 46; DLB 41; MTCW

Lord Jeffrey
See Jeffrey, Francis

Lorenzo, Heberto Padilla
See Padilla (Lorenzo), Heberto

Loris
See Hofmannsthal, Hugo von

Loti, Pierre .... **TCLC 11**
See also Viaud, (Louis Marie) Julien
See also DLB 123

Louie, David Wong 1954- .... **CLC 70**
See also CA 139

Louis, Father M.
See Merton, Thomas

Lovecraft, H(oward) P(hillips)
1890-1937 .... **TCLC 4, 22; SSC 3**
See also AAYA 14; CA 104; 133; MTCW

Lovelace, Earl 1935-.............. **CLC 51**
See also BW 2; CA 77-80; CANR 41;
DLB 125; MTCW

Lovelace, Richard 1618-1657........ **LC 24**
See also DLB 131

Lowell, Amy 1874-1925.. **TCLC 1, 8; PC 13**
See also CA 104; DLB 54, 140

Lowell, James Russell 1819-1891.. **NCLC 2**
See also CDALB 1640-1865; DLB 1, 11, 64,
79

Lowell, Robert (Traill Spence, Jr.)
1917-1977 ... **CLC 1, 2, 3, 4, 5, 8, 9, 11,
15, 37; DA; DAB; PC 3; WLC**
See also CA 9-12R; 73-76; CABS 2;
CANR 26; DLB 5; MTCW

Lowndes, Marie Adelaide (Belloc)
1868-1947 .... **TCLC 12**
See also CA 107; DLB 70

Lowry, (Clarence) Malcolm
1909-1957 .... **TCLC 6, 40**
See also CA 105; 131; CDBLB 1945-1960;
DLB 15; MTCW

Lowry, Mina Gertrude 1882-1966
See Loy, Mina
See also CA 113

Loxsmith, John
See Brunner, John (Kilian Houston)

Loy, Mina .... **CLC 28**
See also Lowry, Mina Gertrude
See also DLB 4, 54

Loyson-Bridet
See Schwob, (Mayer Andre) Marcel

Lucas, Craig 1951- . . . . **CLC 64**
See also CA 137

Lucas, George 1944- . . . . **CLC 16**
See also AAYA 1; CA 77-80; CANR 30;
SATA 56

Lucas, Hans
See Godard, Jean-Luc

Lucas, Victoria
See Plath, Sylvia

Ludlam, Charles 1943-1987 . . . . . **CLC 46, 50**
See also CA 85-88; 122

Ludlum, Robert 1927- . . . . **CLC 22, 43**
See also AAYA 10; BEST 89:1, 90:3;
CA 33-36R; CANR 25, 41; DLBY 82;
MTCW

Ludwig, Ken . . . . **CLC 60**

Ludwig, Otto 1813-1865 . . . . **NCLC 4**
See also DLB 129

Lugones, Leopoldo 1874-1938 . . . . . **TCLC 15**
See also CA 116; 131; HW

Lu Hsun 1881-1936 . . . . . . **TCLC 3; SSC 20**
See also Shu-Jen, Chou

Lukacs, George . . . . **CLC 24**
See also Lukacs, Gyorgy (Szegeny von)

Lukacs, Gyorgy (Szegeny von) 1885-1971
See Lukacs, George
See also CA 101; 29-32R

Luke, Peter (Ambrose Cyprian)
1919-1995 . . . . **CLC 38**
See also CA 81-84; 147; DLB 13

Lunar, Dennis
See Mungo, Raymond

Lurie, Alison 1926- . . . . **CLC 4, 5, 18, 39**
See also CA 1-4R; CANR 2, 17; DLB 2;
MTCW; SATA 46

Lustig, Arnost 1926- . . . . **CLC 56**
See also AAYA 3; CA 69-72; CANR 47;
SATA 56

Luther, Martin 1483-1546 . . . . **LC 9**

Luzi, Mario 1914- . . . . **CLC 13**
See also CA 61-64; CANR 9; DLB 128

Lynch, B. Suarez
See Bioy Casares, Adolfo; Borges, Jorge
Luis

Lynch, David (K.) 1946- . . . . **CLC 66**
See also CA 124; 129

Lynch, James
See Andreyev, Leonid (Nikolaevich)

Lynch Davis, B.
See Bioy Casares, Adolfo; Borges, Jorge
Luis

Lyndsay, Sir David 1490-1555 . . . . . . **LC 20**

Lynn, Kenneth S(chuyler) 1923- . . . . **CLC 50**
See also CA 1-4R; CANR 3, 27

Lynx
See West, Rebecca

Lyons, Marcus
See Blish, James (Benjamin)

Lyre, Pinchbeck
See Sassoon, Siegfried (Lorraine)

Lytle, Andrew (Nelson) 1902- . . . . . . **CLC 22**
See also CA 9-12R; DLB 6

Lyttelton, George 1709-1773 . . . . **LC 10**

Maas, Peter 1929- . . . . **CLC 29**
See also CA 93-96

Macaulay, Rose 1881-1958 . . . . . **TCLC 7, 44**
See also CA 104; DLB 36

Macaulay, Thomas Babington
1800-1859 . . . . **NCLC 42**
See also CDBLB 1832-1890; DLB 32, 55

MacBeth, George (Mann)
1932-1992 . . . . **CLC 2, 5, 9**
See also CA 25-28R; 136; DLB 40; MTCW;
SATA 4; SATA-Obit 70

MacCaig, Norman (Alexander)
1910- . . . . **CLC 36; DAB**
See also CA 9-12R; CANR 3, 34; DLB 27

MacCarthy, (Sir Charles Otto) Desmond
1877-1952 . . . . **TCLC 36**

MacDiarmid, Hugh
. . . . **CLC 2, 4, 11, 19, 63; PC 9**
See also Grieve, C(hristopher) M(urray)
See also CDBLB 1945-1960; DLB 20

MacDonald, Anson
See Heinlein, Robert A(nson)

Macdonald, Cynthia 1928- . . . . . . **CLC 13, 19**
See also CA 49-52; CANR 4, 44; DLB 105

MacDonald, George 1824-1905 . . . . . **TCLC 9**
See also CA 106; 137; DLB 18; MAICYA;
SATA 33

Macdonald, John
See Millar, Kenneth

MacDonald, John D(ann)
1916-1986 . . . . **CLC 3, 27, 44**
See also CA 1-4R; 121; CANR 1, 19;
DLB 8; DLBY 86; MTCW

Macdonald, John Ross
See Millar, Kenneth

Macdonald, Ross . . . . . **CLC 1, 2, 3, 14, 34, 41**
See also Millar, Kenneth
See also DLBD 6

MacDougal, John
See Blish, James (Benjamin)

MacEwen, Gwendolyn (Margaret)
1941-1987 . . . . **CLC 13, 55**
See also CA 9-12R; 124; CANR 7, 22;
DLB 53; SATA 50; SATA-Obit 55

Macha, Karel Hynek 1810-1846 . . **NCLC 46**

Machado (y Ruiz), Antonio
1875-1939 . . . . **TCLC 3**
See also CA 104; DLB 108

Machado de Assis, Joaquim Maria
1839-1908 . . . . **TCLC 10; BLC**
See also CA 107

Machen, Arthur . . . . **TCLC 4; SSC 20**
See also Jones, Arthur Llewellyn
See also DLB 36

Machiavelli, Niccolo
1469-1527 . . . . **LC 8; DA; DAB**

MacInnes, Colin 1914-1976 . . . . . . **CLC 4, 23**
See also CA 69-72; 65-68; CANR 21;
DLB 14; MTCW

MacInnes, Helen (Clark)
1907-1985 . . . . **CLC 27, 39**
See also CA 1-4R; 117; CANR 1, 28;
DLB 87; MTCW; SATA 22;
SATA-Obit 44

Mackay, Mary 1855-1924
See Corelli, Marie
See also CA 118

Mackenzie, Compton (Edward Montague)
1883-1972 . . . . **CLC 18**
See also CA 21-22; 37-40R; CAP 2;
DLB 34, 100

Mackenzie, Henry 1745-1831 . . . . **NCLC 41**
See also DLB 39

Mackintosh, Elizabeth 1896(?)-1952
See Tey, Josephine
See also CA 110

MacLaren, James
See Grieve, C(hristopher) M(urray)

Mac Laverty, Bernard 1942- . . . . **CLC 31**
See also CA 116; 118; CANR 43

MacLean, Alistair (Stuart)
1922-1987 . . . . **CLC 3, 13, 50, 63**
See also CA 57-60; 121; CANR 28; MTCW;
SATA 23; SATA-Obit 50

Maclean, Norman (Fitzroy)
1902-1990 . . . . **CLC 78; SSC 13**
See also CA 102; 132; CANR 49

MacLeish, Archibald
1892-1982 . . . . **CLC 3, 8, 14, 68**
See also CA 9-12R; 106; CANR 33; DLB 4,
7, 45; DLBY 82; MTCW

MacLennan, (John) Hugh
1907-1990 . . . . **CLC 2, 14**
See also CA 5-8R; 142; CANR 33; DLB 68;
MTCW

MacLeod, Alistair 1936- . . . . **CLC 56**
See also CA 123; DLB 60

MacNeice, (Frederick) Louis
1907-1963 . . . . . . **CLC 1, 4, 10, 53; DAB**
See also CA 85-88; DLB 10, 20; MTCW

MacNeill, Dand
See Fraser, George MacDonald

Macpherson, James 1736-1796 . . . . . . **LC 29**
See also DLB 109

Macpherson, (Jean) Jay 1931- . . . . . . **CLC 14**
See also CA 5-8R; DLB 53

MacShane, Frank 1927- . . . . **CLC 39**
See also CA 9-12R; CANR 3, 33; DLB 111

Macumber, Mari
See Sandoz, Mari(e Susette)

Madach, Imre 1823-1864 . . . . **NCLC 19**

Madden, (Jerry) David 1933- . . . . **CLC 5, 15**
See also CA 1-4R; CAAS 3; CANR 4, 45;
DLB 6; MTCW

Maddern, Al(an)
See Ellison, Harlan (Jay)

Madhubuti, Haki R.
1942- . . . . **CLC 6, 73; BLC; PC 5**
See also Lee, Don L.
See also BW 2; CA 73-76; CANR 24;
DLB 5, 41; DLBD 8

Maepenn, Hugh
See Kuttner, Henry

Maepenn, K. H.
See Kuttner, Henry

Maeterlinck, Maurice 1862-1949 . . . **TCLC 3**
See also CA 104; 136; SATA 66

Maginn, William 1794-1842...... **NCLC 8**
See also DLB 110

Mahapatra, Jayanta 1928-......... **CLC 33**
See also CA 73-76; CAAS 9; CANR 15, 33

Mahfouz, Naguib (Abdel Aziz Al-Sabilgi)
1911(?)-
See Mahfuz, Najib
See also BEST 89:2; CA 128; MTCW

Mahfuz, Najib................. **CLC 52, 55**
See also Mahfouz, Naguib (Abdel Aziz
Al-Sabilgi)
See also DLBY 88

Mahon, Derek 1941-.............. **CLC 27**
See also CA 113; 128; DLB 40

Mailer, Norman
1923-...... **CLC 1, 2, 3, 4, 5, 8, 11, 14,
28, 39, 74; DA; DAB**
See also AITN 2; CA 9-12R; CABS 1;
CANR 28; CDALB 1968-1988; DLB 2,
16, 28; DLBD 3; DLBY 80, 83; MTCW

Maillet, Antonine 1929-.......... **CLC 54**
See also CA 115; 120; CANR 46; DLB 60

Mais, Roger 1905-1955 .... **TCLC 8**
See also BW 1; CA 105; 124; DLB 125;
MTCW

Maistre, Joseph de 1753-1821.... **NCLC 37**

Maitland, Sara (Louise) 1950-..... **CLC 49**
See also CA 69-72; CANR 13

Major, Clarence
1936-..........**CLC 3, 19, 48; BLC**
See also BW 2; CA 21-24R; CAAS 6;
CANR 13, 25; DLB 33

Major, Kevin (Gerald) 1949-....... **CLC 26**
See also CA 97-100; CANR 21, 38;
CLR 11; DLB 60; JRDA; MAICYA;
SATA 32, 82

Maki, James
See Ozu, Yasujiro

Malabaila, Damiano
See Levi, Primo

Malamud, Bernard
1914-1986 ...... **CLC 1, 2, 3, 5, 8, 9, 11,
18, 27, 44, 78, 85; DA; DAB; SSC 15;
WLC**
See also CA 5-8R; 118; CABS 1; CANR 28;
CDALB 1941-1968; DLB 2, 28, 152;
DLBY 80, 86; MTCW

Malaparte, Curzio 1898-1957 ..... **TCLC 52**

Malcolm, Dan
See Silverberg, Robert

Malcolm X................. **CLC 82; BLC**
See also Little, Malcolm

Malherbe, Francois de 1555-1628..... **LC 5**

Mallarme, Stephane
1842-1898 .... **NCLC 4, 41; PC 4**

Mallet-Joris, Francoise 1930-...... **CLC 11**
See also CA 65-68; CANR 17; DLB 83

Malley, Ern
See McAuley, James Phillip

Mallowan, Agatha Christie
See Christie, Agatha (Mary Clarissa)

Maloff, Saul 1922-................. **CLC 5**
See also CA 33-36R

Malone, Louis
See MacNeice, (Frederick) Louis

Malone, Michael (Christopher)
1942-...................... **CLC 43**
See also CA 77-80; CANR 14, 32

Malory, (Sir) Thomas
1410(?)-1471(?) ...... **LC 11; DA; DAB**
See also CDBLB Before 1660; DLB 146;
SATA 59; SATA-Brief 33

Malouf, (George Joseph) David
1934-................... **CLC 28, 86**
See also CA 124

Malraux, (Georges-)Andre
1901-1976 ...... **CLC 1, 4, 9, 13, 15, 57**
See also CA 21-22; 69-72; CANR 34;
CAP 2; DLB 72; MTCW

Malzberg, Barry N(athaniel) 1939-... **CLC 7**
See also CA 61-64; CAAS 4; CANR 16;
DLB 8

Mamet, David (Alan)
1947-......... **CLC 9, 15, 34, 46; DC 4**
See also AAYA 3; CA 81-84; CABS 3;
CANR 15, 41; DLB 7; MTCW

Mamoulian, Rouben (Zachary)
1897-1987 .... **CLC 16**
See also CA 25-28R; 124

Mandelstam, Osip (Emilievich)
1891(?)-1938(?) .... **TCLC 2, 6**
See also CA 104

Mander, (Mary) Jane 1877-1949... **TCLC 31**

Mandiargues, Andre Pieyre de...... **CLC 41**
See also Pieyre de Mandiargues, Andre
See also DLB 83

Mandrake, Ethel Belle
See Thurman, Wallace (Henry)

Mangan, James Clarence
1803-1849 .... **NCLC 27**

Maniere, J.-E.
See Giraudoux, (Hippolyte) Jean

Manley, (Mary) Delariviere
1672(?)-1724 .... **LC 1**
See also DLB 39, 80

Mann, Abel
See Creasey, John

Mann, (Luiz) Heinrich 1871-1950... **TCLC 9**
See also CA 106; DLB 66

Mann, (Paul) Thomas
1875-1955 .... **TCLC 2, 8, 14, 21, 35, 44,
60; DA; DAB; SSC 5; WLC**
See also CA 104; 128; DLB 66; MTCW

Manning, David
See Faust, Frederick (Schiller)

Manning, Frederic 1887(?)-1935 ... **TCLC 25**
See also CA 124

Manning, Olivia 1915-1980 ...... **CLC 5, 19**
See also CA 5-8R; 101; CANR 29; MTCW

Mano, D. Keith 1942- .... **CLC 2, 10**
See also CA 25-28R; CAAS 6; CANR 26;
DLB 6

Mansfield, Katherine
.... **TCLC 2, 8, 39; DAB; SSC 9; WLC**
See also Beauchamp, Kathleen Mansfield

Manso, Peter 1940- .... **CLC 39**
See also CA 29-32R; CANR 44

Mantecon, Juan Jimenez
See Jimenez (Mantecon), Juan Ramon

Manton, Peter
See Creasey, John

Man Without a Spleen, A
See Chekhov, Anton (Pavlovich)

Manzoni, Alessandro 1785-1873 .. **NCLC 29**

Mapu, Abraham (ben Jekutiel)
1808-1867 .... **NCLC 18**

Mara, Sally
See Queneau, Raymond

Marat, Jean Paul 1743-1793........ **LC 10**

Marcel, Gabriel Honore
1889-1973 .... **CLC 15**
See also CA 102; 45-48; MTCW

Marchbanks, Samuel
See Davies, (William) Robertson

Marchi, Giacomo
See Bassani, Giorgio

Margulies, Donald................. **CLC 76**

Marie de France c. 12th cent. -.... **CMLC 8**

Marie de l'Incarnation 1599-1672.... **LC 10**

Mariner, Scott
See Pohl, Frederik

Marinetti, Filippo Tommaso
1876-1944 .... **TCLC 10**
See also CA 107; DLB 114

Marivaux, Pierre Carlet de Chamblain de
1688-1763 .... **LC 4**

Markandaya, Kamala .... **CLC 8, 38**
See also Taylor, Kamala (Purnaiya)

Markfield, Wallace 1926-........... **CLC 8**
See also CA 69-72; CAAS 3; DLB 2, 28

Markham, Edwin 1852-1940 ...... **TCLC 47**
See also DLB 54

Markham, Robert
See Amis, Kingsley (William)

Marks, J
See Highwater, Jamake (Mamake)

Marks-Highwater, J
See Highwater, Jamake (Mamake)

Markson, David M(errill) 1927-.... **CLC 67**
See also CA 49-52; CANR 1

Marley, Bob..................... **CLC 17**
See also Marley, Robert Nesta

Marley, Robert Nesta 1945-1981
See Marley, Bob
See also CA 107; 103

Marlowe, Christopher
1564-1593 ..... **LC 22; DA; DAB; DC 1;
WLC**
See also CDBLB Before 1660; DLB 62

Marmontel, Jean-Francois
1723-1799 .... **LC 2**

Marquand, John P(hillips)
1893-1960 .... **CLC 2, 10**
See also CA 85-88; DLB 9, 102

Marquez, Gabriel (Jose) Garcia
See Garcia Marquez, Gabriel (Jose)

Marquis, Don(ald Robert Perry)
1878-1937 .... **TCLC 7**
See also CA 104; DLB 11, 25

Marric, J. J.
See Creasey, John

Marrow, Bernard
See Moore, Brian

Marryat, Frederick 1792-1848 .... **NCLC 3**
See also DLB 21

Marsden, James
See Creasey, John

Marsh, (Edith) Ngaio
1899-1982 .... **CLC 7, 53**
See also CA 9-12R; CANR 6; DLB 77;
MTCW

Marshall, Garry 1934- .... **CLC 17**
See also AAYA 3; CA 111; SATA 60

Marshall, Paule
1929- .... **CLC 27, 72; BLC; SSC 3**
See also BW 2; CA 77-80; CANR 25;
DLB 33; MTCW

Marsten, Richard
See Hunter, Evan

Martha, Henry
See Harris, Mark

Martial c. 40-c. 104 .... **PC 10**

Martin, Ken
See Hubbard, L(afayette) Ron(ald)

Martin, Richard
See Creasey, John

Martin, Steve 1945- .... **CLC 30**
See also CA 97-100; CANR 30; MTCW

Martin, Valerie 1948- .... **CLC 89**
See also BEST 90:2; CA 85-88; CANR 49

Martin, Violet Florence
1862-1915 .... **TCLC 51**

Martin, Webber
See Silverberg, Robert

Martindale, Patrick Victor
See White, Patrick (Victor Martindale)

Martin du Gard, Roger
1881-1958 .... **TCLC 24**
See also CA 118; DLB 65

Martineau, Harriet 1802-1876.... **NCLC 26**
See also DLB 21, 55; YABC 2

Martines, Julia
See O'Faolain, Julia

Martinez, Jacinto Benavente y
See Benavente (y Martinez), Jacinto

Martinez Ruiz, Jose 1873-1967
See Azorin; Ruiz, Jose Martinez
See also CA 93-96; HW

Martinez Sierra, Gregorio
1881-1947 .... **TCLC 6**
See also CA 115

Martinez Sierra, Maria (de la O'LeJarraga)
1874-1974 .... **TCLC 6**
See also CA 115

Martinsen, Martin
See Follett, Ken(neth Martin)

Martinson, Harry (Edmund)
1904-1978 .... **CLC 14**
See also CA 77-80; CANR 34

Marut, Ret
See Traven, B.

Marut, Robert
See Traven, B.

Marvell, Andrew
1621-1678 ..... **LC 4; DA; DAB; PC 10;
WLC**
See also CDBLB 1660-1789; DLB 131

Marx, Karl (Heinrich)
1818-1883 .... **NCLC 17**
See also DLB 129

Masaoka Shiki. .... **TCLC 18**
See also Masaoka Tsunenori

Masaoka Tsunenori 1867-1902
See Masaoka Shiki
See also CA 117

Masefield, John (Edward)
1878-1967 .... **CLC 11, 47**
See also CA 19-20; 25-28R; CANR 33;
CAP 2; CDBLB 1890-1914; DLB 10, 19,
153; MTCW; SATA 19

Maso, Carole 19(?)- .... **CLC 44**

Mason, Bobbie Ann
1940- .... **CLC 28, 43, 82; SSC 4**
See also AAYA 5; CA 53-56; CANR 11,
31; DLBY 87; MTCW

Mason, Ernst
See Pohl, Frederik

Mason, Lee W.
See Malzberg, Barry N(athaniel)

Mason, Nick 1945- .... **CLC 35**

Mason, Tally
See Derleth, August (William)

Mass, William
See Gibson, William

Masters, Edgar Lee
1868-1950 ...... **TCLC 2, 25; DA; PC 1**
See also CA 104; 133; CDALB 1865-1917;
DLB 54; MTCW

Masters, Hilary 1928- .... **CLC 48**
See also CA 25-28R; CANR 13, 47

Mastrosimone, William 19(?)- ...... **CLC 36**

Mathe, Albert
See Camus, Albert

Matheson, Richard Burton 1926- ... **CLC 37**
See also CA 97-100; DLB 8, 44

Mathews, Harry 1930- .... **CLC 6, 52**
See also CA 21-24R; CAAS 6; CANR 18,
40

Mathews, John Joseph 1894-1979... **CLC 84**
See also CA 19-20; 142; CANR 45; CAP 2;
NNAL

Mathias, Roland (Glyn) 1915- ...... **CLC 45**
See also CA 97-100; CANR 19, 41; DLB 27

Matsuo Basho 1644-1694 .... **PC 3**

Mattheson, Rodney
See Creasey, John

Matthews, Greg 1949- .... **CLC 45**
See also CA 135

Matthews, William 1942- .... **CLC 40**
See also CA 29-32R; CAAS 18; CANR 12;
DLB 5

Matthias, John (Edward) 1941- ...... **CLC 9**
See also CA 33-36R

Matthiessen, Peter
1927- .... **CLC 5, 7, 11, 32, 64**
See also AAYA 6; BEST 90:4; CA 9-12R;
CANR 21; DLB 6; MTCW; SATA 27

Maturin, Charles Robert
1780(?)-1824 .... **NCLC 6**

Matute (Ausejo), Ana Maria
1925- .... **CLC 11**
See also CA 89-92; MTCW

Maugham, W. S.
See Maugham, W(illiam) Somerset

Maugham, W(illiam) Somerset
1874-1965 ...... **CLC 1, 11, 15, 67; DA;
DAB; SSC 8; WLC**
See also CA 5-8R; 25-28R; CANR 40;
CDBLB 1914-1945; DLB 10, 36, 77, 100;
MTCW; SATA 54

Maugham, William Somerset
See Maugham, W(illiam) Somerset

Maupassant, (Henri Rene Albert) Guy de
1850-1893 ..... **NCLC 1, 42; DA; DAB;
SSC 1; WLC**
See also DLB 123

Maurhut, Richard
See Traven, B.

Mauriac, Claude 1914- .... **CLC 9**
See also CA 89-92; DLB 83

Mauriac, Francois (Charles)
1885-1970 .... **CLC 4, 9, 56**
See also CA 25-28; CAP 2; DLB 65;
MTCW

Mavor, Osborne Henry 1888-1951
See Bridie, James
See also CA 104

Maxwell, William (Keepers, Jr.)
1908- .... **CLC 19**
See also CA 93-96; DLBY 80

May, Elaine 1932- .... **CLC 16**
See also CA 124; 142; DLB 44

Mayakovski, Vladimir (Vladimirovich)
1893-1930 .... **TCLC 4, 18**
See also CA 104

Mayhew, Henry 1812-1887 ...... **NCLC 31**
See also DLB 18, 55

Mayle, Peter 1939(?)- .... **CLC 89**
See also CA 139

Maynard, Joyce 1953- .... **CLC 23**
See also CA 111; 129

Mayne, William (James Carter)
1928- .... **CLC 12**
See also CA 9-12R; CANR 37; CLR 25;
JRDA; MAICYA; SAAS 11; SATA 6, 68

Mayo, Jim
See L'Amour, Louis (Dearborn)

Maysles, Albert 1926- .... **CLC 16**
See also CA 29-32R

Maysles, David 1932- .... **CLC 16**

Mazer, Norma Fox 1931- .... **CLC 26**
See also AAYA 5; CA 69-72; CANR 12,
32; CLR 23; JRDA; MAICYA; SAAS 1;
SATA 24, 67

Mazzini, Guiseppe 1805-1872 .... **NCLC 34**

McAuley, James Phillip
1917-1976 .... **CLC 45**
See also CA 97-100

McBain, Ed
See Hunter, Evan

McBrien, William Augustine
1930- .... CLC 44
See also CA 107

McCaffrey, Anne (Inez) 1926-...... CLC 17
See also AAYA 6; AITN 2; BEST 89:2;
CA 25-28R; CANR 15, 35; DLB 8;
JRDA; MAICYA; MTCW; SAAS 11;
SATA 8, 70

McCall, Nathan 1955(?)-.......... CLC 86
See also CA 146

McCann, Arthur
See Campbell, John W(ood, Jr.)

McCann, Edson
See Pohl, Frederik

McCarthy, Charles, Jr. 1933-
See McCarthy, Cormac
See also CANR 42

McCarthy, Cormac 1933-..... CLC 4, 57, 59
See also McCarthy, Charles, Jr.
See also DLB 6, 143

McCarthy, Mary (Therese)
1912-1989 ... CLC 1, 3, 5, 14, 24, 39, 59
See also CA 5-8R; 129; CANR 16; DLB 2;
DLBY 81; MTCW

McCartney, (James) Paul
1942-.................... CLC 12, 35
See also CA 146

McCauley, Stephen (D.) 1955- ..... CLC 50
See also CA 141

McClure, Michael (Thomas)
1932-..................... CLC 6, 10
See also CA 21-24R; CANR 17, 46;
DLB 16

McCorkle, Jill (Collins) 1958-...... CLC 51
See also CA 121; DLBY 87

McCourt, James 1941-............. CLC 5
See also CA 57-60

McCoy, Horace (Stanley)
1897-1955 .... TCLC 28
See also CA 108; DLB 9

McCrae, John 1872-1918........ TCLC 12
See also CA 109; DLB 92

McCreigh, James
See Pohl, Frederik

McCullers, (Lula) Carson (Smith)
1917-1967 .... CLC 1, 4, 10, 12, 48; DA;
DAB; SSC 9; WLC
See also CA 5-8R; 25-28R; CABS 1, 3;
CANR 18; CDALB 1941-1968; DLB 2, 7;
MTCW; SATA 27

McCulloch, John Tyler
See Burroughs, Edgar Rice

McCullough, Colleen 1938(?)-...... CLC 27
See also CA 81-84; CANR 17, 46; MTCW

McElroy, Joseph 1930- .... CLC 5, 47
See also CA 17-20R

McEwan, Ian (Russell) 1948- ... CLC 13, 66
See also BEST 90:4; CA 61-64; CANR 14,
41; DLB 14; MTCW

McFadden, David 1940-.......... CLC 48
See also CA 104; DLB 60

McFarland, Dennis 1950- .... CLC 65

McGahern, John
1934- .... CLC 5, 9, 48; SSC 17
See also CA 17-20R; CANR 29; DLB 14;
MTCW

McGinley, Patrick (Anthony)
1937-...................... CLC 41
See also CA 120; 127

McGinley, Phyllis 1905-1978 ...... CLC 14
See also CA 9-12R; 77-80; CANR 19;
DLB 11, 48; SATA 2, 44; SATA-Obit 24

McGinniss, Joe 1942-............. CLC 32
See also AITN 2; BEST 89:2; CA 25-28R;
CANR 26

McGivern, Maureen Daly
See Daly, Maureen

McGrath, Patrick 1950-.......... CLC 55
See also CA 136

McGrath, Thomas (Matthew)
1916-1990 .... CLC 28, 59
See also CA 9-12R; 132; CANR 6, 33;
MTCW; SATA 41; SATA-Obit 66

McGuane, Thomas (Francis III)
1939-................ CLC 3, 7, 18, 45
See also AITN 2; CA 49-52; CANR 5, 24,
49; DLB 2; DLBY 80; MTCW

McGuckian, Medbh 1950-........ CLC 48
See also CA 143; DLB 40

McHale, Tom 1942(?)-1982....... CLC 3, 5
See also AITN 1; CA 77-80; 106

McIlvanney, William 1936-........ CLC 42
See also CA 25-28R; DLB 14

McIlwraith, Maureen Mollie Hunter
See Hunter, Mollie
See also SATA 2

McInerney, Jay 1955- .... CLC 34
See also CA 116; 123; CANR 45

McIntyre, Vonda N(eel) 1948- ..... CLC 18
See also CA 81-84; CANR 17, 34; MTCW

McKay, Claude
.... TCLC 7, 41; BLC; DAB; PC 2
See also McKay, Festus Claudius
See also DLB 4, 45, 51, 117

McKay, Festus Claudius 1889-1948
See McKay, Claude
See also BW 1; CA 104; 124; DA; MTCW;
WLC

McKuen, Rod 1933-............. CLC 1, 3
See also AITN 1; CA 41-44R; CANR 40

McLoughlin, R. B.
See Mencken, H(enry) L(ouis)

McLuhan, (Herbert) Marshall
1911-1980 .... CLC 37, 83
See also CA 9-12R; 102; CANR 12, 34;
DLB 88; MTCW

McMillan, Terry (L.) 1951-..... CLC 50, 61
See also BW 2; CA 140

McMurtry, Larry (Jeff)
1936- .... CLC 2, 3, 7, 11, 27, 44
See also AITN 2; BEST 89:2; CA 5-8R;
CANR 19, 43; CDALB 1968-1988;
DLB 2, 143; DLBY 80, 87; MTCW

McNally, T. M. 1961- .... CLC 82

McNally, Terrence 1939-...... CLC 4, 7, 41
See also CA 45-48; CANR 2; DLB 7

McNamer, Deirdre 1950-......... CLC 70

McNeile, Herman Cyril 1888-1937
See Sapper
See also DLB 77

McNickle, (William) D'Arcy
1904-1977 .... CLC 89
See also CA 9-12R; 85-88; CANR 5, 45;
NNAL; SATA-Obit 22

McPhee, John (Angus) 1931- ...... CLC 36
See also BEST 90:1; CA 65-68; CANR 20,
46; MTCW

McPherson, James Alan
1943-.................... CLC 19, 77
See also BW 1; CA 25-28R; CAAS 17;
CANR 24; DLB 38; MTCW

McPherson, William (Alexander)
1933-...................... CLC 34
See also CA 69-72; CANR 28

Mead, Margaret 1901-1978........ CLC 37
See also AITN 1; CA 1-4R; 81-84;
CANR 4; MTCW; SATA-Obit 20

Meaker, Marijane (Agnes) 1927-
See Kerr, M. E.
See also CA 107; CANR 37; JRDA;
MAICYA; MTCW; SATA 20, 61

Medoff, Mark (Howard) 1940- ... CLC 6, 23
See also AITN 1; CA 53-56; CANR 5;
DLB 7

Medvedev, P. N.
See Bakhtin, Mikhail Mikhailovich

Meged, Aharon
See Megged, Aharon

Meged, Aron
See Megged, Aharon

Megged, Aharon 1920-............. CLC 9
See also CA 49-52; CAAS 13; CANR 1

Mehta, Ved (Parkash) 1934- .... CLC 37
See also CA 1-4R; CANR 2, 23; MTCW

Melanter
See Blackmore, R(ichard) D(oddridge)

Melikow, Loris
See Hofmannsthal, Hugo von

Melmoth, Sebastian
See Wilde, Oscar (Fingal O'Flahertie Wills)

Meltzer, Milton 1915-............. CLC 26
See also AAYA 8; CA 13-16R; CANR 38;
CLR 13; DLB 61; JRDA; MAICYA;
SAAS 1; SATA 1, 50, 80

Melville, Herman
1819-1891 ..... NCLC 3, 12, 29, 45, 49;
DA; DAB; SSC 1, 17; WLC
See also CDALB 1640-1865; DLB 3, 74;
SATA 59

Menander
c. 342B.C.-c. 292B.C.... CMLC 9; DC 3

Mencken, H(enry) L(ouis)
1880-1956 .... TCLC 13
See also CA 105; 125; CDALB 1917-1929;
DLB 11, 29, 63, 137; MTCW

Mercer, David 1928-1980........... CLC 5
See also CA 9-12R; 102; CANR 23;
DLB 13; MTCW

Merchant, Paul
See Ellison, Harlan (Jay)

Meredith, George 1828-1909 . . . **TCLC 17, 43**
See also CA 117; CDBLB 1832-1890;
DLB 18, 35, 57

Meredith, William (Morris)
1919- . . . . **CLC 4, 13, 22, 55**
See also CA 9-12R; CAAS 14; CANR 6, 40;
DLB 5

Merezhkovsky, Dmitry Sergeyevich
1865-1941 . . . . **TCLC 29**

Merimee, Prosper
1803-1870 . . . . **NCLC 6; SSC 7**
See also DLB 119

Merkin, Daphne 1954- . . . . **CLC 44**
See also CA 123

Merlin, Arthur
See Blish, James (Benjamin)

Merrill, James (Ingram)
1926-1995 . . . . **CLC 2, 3, 6, 8, 13, 18, 34**
See also CA 13-16R; 147; CANR 10, 49;
DLB 5; DLBY 85; MTCW

Merriman, Alex
See Silverberg, Robert

Merritt, E. B.
See Waddington, Miriam

Merton, Thomas
1915-1968 . . **CLC 1, 3, 11, 34, 83; PC 10**
See also CA 5-8R; 25-28R; CANR 22;
DLB 48; DLBY 81; MTCW

Merwin, W(illiam) S(tanley)
1927- . . . **CLC 1, 2, 3, 5, 8, 13, 18, 45, 88**
See also CA 13-16R; CANR 15; DLB 5;
MTCW

Metcalf, John 1938- . . . . **CLC 37**
See also CA 113; DLB 60

Metcalf, Suzanne
See Baum, L(yman) Frank

Mew, Charlotte (Mary)
1870-1928 . . . . **TCLC 8**
See also CA 105; DLB 19, 135

Mewshaw, Michael 1943- . . . . **CLC 9**
See also CA 53-56; CANR 7, 47; DLBY 80

Meyer, June
See Jordan, June

Meyer, Lynn
See Slavitt, David R(ytman)

Meyer-Meyrink, Gustav 1868-1932
See Meyrink, Gustav
See also CA 117

Meyers, Jeffrey 1939- . . . . **CLC 39**
See also CA 73-76; DLB 111

Meynell, Alice (Christina Gertrude Thompson)
1847-1922 . . . . **TCLC 6**
See also CA 104; DLB 19, 98

Meyrink, Gustav . . . . **TCLC 21**
See also Meyer-Meyrink, Gustav
See also DLB 81

Michaels, Leonard
1933- . . . . **CLC 6, 25; SSC 16**
See also CA 61-64; CANR 21; DLB 130;
MTCW

Michaux, Henri 1899-1984 . . . . . . **CLC 8, 19**
See also CA 85-88; 114

Michelangelo 1475-1564 . . . . **LC 12**

Michelet, Jules 1798-1874 . . . . **NCLC 31**

Michener, James A(lbert)
1907(?)- . . . . **CLC 1, 5, 11, 29, 60**
See also AITN 1; BEST 90:1; CA 5-8R;
CANR 21, 45; DLB 6; MTCW

Mickiewicz, Adam 1798-1855 . . . . . **NCLC 3**

Middleton, Christopher 1926- . . . . . . **CLC 13**
See also CA 13-16R; CANR 29; DLB 40

Middleton, Richard (Barham)
1882-1911 . . . . **TCLC 56**

Middleton, Stanley 1919- . . . . **CLC 7, 38**
See also CA 25-28R; CANR 21, 46;
DLB 14

Middleton, Thomas 1580-1627 . . . . **DC 5**
See also DLB 58

Migueis, Jose Rodrigues 1901- . . . . . **CLC 10**

Mikszath, Kalman 1847-1910 . . . . . **TCLC 31**

Miles, Josephine
1911-1985 . . . . **CLC 1, 2, 14, 34, 39**
See also CA 1-4R; 116; CANR 2; DLB 48

Militant
See Sandburg, Carl (August)

Mill, John Stuart 1806-1873 . . . . . **NCLC 11**
See also CDBLB 1832-1890; DLB 55

Millar, Kenneth 1915-1983 . . . . **CLC 14**
See also Macdonald, Ross
See also CA 9-12R; 110; CANR 16; DLB 2;
DLBD 6; DLBY 83; MTCW

Millay, E. Vincent
See Millay, Edna St. Vincent

Millay, Edna St. Vincent
1892-1950 . . . . . . **TCLC 4, 49; DA; DAB;
PC 6**
See also CA 104; 130; CDALB 1917-1929;
DLB 45; MTCW

Miller, Arthur
1915- . . . . **CLC 1, 2, 6, 10, 15, 26, 47, 78;
DA; DAB; DC 1; WLC**
See also AITN 1; CA 1-4R; CABS 3;
CANR 2, 30; CDALB 1941-1968; DLB 7;
MTCW

Miller, Henry (Valentine)
1891-1980 . . . . **CLC 1, 2, 4, 9, 14, 43, 84;
DA; DAB; WLC**
See also CA 9-12R; 97-100; CANR 33;
CDALB 1929-1941; DLB 4, 9; DLBY 80;
MTCW

Miller, Jason 1939(?)- . . . . **CLC 2**
See also AITN 1; CA 73-76; DLB 7

Miller, Sue 1943- . . . . **CLC 44**
See also BEST 90:3; CA 139; DLB 143

Miller, Walter M(ichael, Jr.)
1923- . . . . **CLC 4, 30**
See also CA 85-88; DLB 8

Millett, Kate 1934- . . . . **CLC 67**
See also AITN 1; CA 73-76; CANR 32;
MTCW

Millhauser, Steven 1943- . . . . **CLC 21, 54**
See also CA 110; 111; DLB 2

Millin, Sarah Gertrude 1889-1968 . . **CLC 49**
See also CA 102; 93-96

Milne, A(lan) A(lexander)
1882-1956 . . . . **TCLC 6; DAB**
See also CA 104; 133; CLR 1, 26; DLB 10,
77, 100; MAICYA; MTCW; YABC 1

Milner, Ron(ald) 1938- . . . . **CLC 56; BLC**
See also AITN 1; BW 1; CA 73-76;
CANR 24; DLB 38; MTCW

Milosz, Czeslaw
1911- . . . **CLC 5, 11, 22, 31, 56, 82; PC 8**
See also CA 81-84; CANR 23; MTCW

Milton, John
1608-1674 . . . . . . **LC 9; DA; DAB; WLC**
See also CDBLB 1660-1789; DLB 131, 151

Min, Anchee 1957- . . . . **CLC 86**
See also CA 146

Minehaha, Cornelius
See Wedekind, (Benjamin) Frank(lin)

Miner, Valerie 1947- . . . . **CLC 40**
See also CA 97-100

Minimo, Duca
See D'Annunzio, Gabriele

Minot, Susan 1956- . . . . **CLC 44**
See also CA 134

Minus, Ed 1938- . . . . **CLC 39**

Miranda, Javier
See Bioy Casares, Adolfo

Mirbeau, Octave 1848-1917 . . . . **TCLC 55**
See also DLB 123

Miro (Ferrer), Gabriel (Francisco Victor)
1879-1930 . . . . **TCLC 5**
See also CA 104

Mishima, Yukio
. . . . . . **CLC 2, 4, 6, 9, 27; DC 1; SSC 4**
See also Hiraoka, Kimitake

Mistral, Frederic 1830-1914 . . . . . . **TCLC 51**
See also CA 122

Mistral, Gabriela . . . . **TCLC 2; HLC**
See also Godoy Alcayaga, Lucila

Mistry, Rohinton 1952- . . . . **CLC 71**
See also CA 141

Mitchell, Clyde
See Ellison, Harlan (Jay); Silverberg, Robert

Mitchell, James Leslie 1901-1935
See Gibbon, Lewis Grassic
See also CA 104; DLB 15

Mitchell, Joni 1943- . . . . **CLC 12**
See also CA 112

Mitchell, Margaret (Munnerlyn)
1900-1949 . . . . **TCLC 11**
See also CA 109; 125; DLB 9; MTCW

Mitchell, Peggy
See Mitchell, Margaret (Munnerlyn)

Mitchell, S(ilas) Weir 1829-1914 . . **TCLC 36**

Mitchell, W(illiam) O(rmond)
1914- . . . . **CLC 25**
See also CA 77-80; CANR 15, 43; DLB 88

Mitford, Mary Russell 1787-1855 . . **NCLC 4**
See also DLB 110, 116

Mitford, Nancy 1904-1973 . . . . **CLC 44**
See also CA 9-12R

Miyamoto, Yuriko 1899-1951 . . . . . **TCLC 37**

Mo, Timothy (Peter) 1950(?)- . . . . . . **CLC 46**
See also CA 117; MTCW

Modarressi, Taghi (M.) 1931- . . . . . . **CLC 44**
See also CA 121; 134

Modiano, Patrick (Jean) 1945- . . . . . **CLC 18**
See also CA 85-88; CANR 17, 40; DLB 83

Moerck, Paal
See Roelvaag, O(le) E(dvart)

Mofolo, Thomas (Mokopu)
1875(?)-1948 . . . . **TCLC 22; BLC**
See also CA 121

Mohr, Nicholasa 1935- . . . . . . **CLC 12; HLC**
See also AAYA 8; CA 49-52; CANR 1, 32;
CLR 22; DLB 145; HW; JRDA; SAAS 8;
SATA 8

Mojtabai, A(nn) G(race)
1938- . . . . **CLC 5, 9, 15, 29**
See also CA 85-88

Moliere
1622-1673 . . . . . **LC 28; DA; DAB; WLC**

Molin, Charles
See Mayne, William (James Carter)

Molnar, Ferenc 1878-1952 . . . . **TCLC 20**
See also CA 109

Momaday, N(avarre) Scott
1934- . . . . **CLC 2, 19, 85; DA; DAB**
See also AAYA 11; CA 25-28R; CANR 14,
34; DLB 143; MTCW; NNAL; SATA 48;
SATA-Brief 30

Monette, Paul 1945-1995 . . . . **CLC 82**
See also CA 139; 147

Monroe, Harriet 1860-1936 . . . . . . **TCLC 12**
See also CA 109; DLB 54, 91

Monroe, Lyle
See Heinlein, Robert A(nson)

Montagu, Elizabeth 1917- . . . . **NCLC 7**
See also CA 9-12R

Montagu, Mary (Pierrepont) Wortley
1689-1762 . . . . **LC 9**
See also DLB 95, 101

Montagu, W. H.
See Coleridge, Samuel Taylor

Montague, John (Patrick)
1929- . . . . **CLC 13, 46**
See also CA 9-12R; CANR 9; DLB 40;
MTCW

Montaigne, Michel (Eyquem) de
1533-1592 . . . . . . **LC 8; DA; DAB; WLC**

Montale, Eugenio
1896-1981 . . . . **CLC 7, 9, 18; PC 13**
See also CA 17-20R; 104; CANR 30;
DLB 114; MTCW

Montesquieu, Charles-Louis de Secondat
1689-1755 . . . . **LC 7**

Montgomery, (Robert) Bruce 1921-1978
See Crispin, Edmund
See also CA 104

Montgomery, L(ucy) M(aud)
1874-1942 . . . . **TCLC 51**
See also AAYA 12; CA 108; 137; CLR 8;
DLB 92; JRDA; MAICYA; YABC 1

Montgomery, Marion H., Jr. 1925- . . **CLC 7**
See also AITN 1; CA 1-4R; CANR 3, 48;
DLB 6

Montgomery, Max
See Davenport, Guy (Mattison, Jr.)

Montherlant, Henry (Milon) de
1896-1972 . . . . **CLC 8, 19**
See also CA 85-88; 37-40R; DLB 72;
MTCW

Monty Python
See Chapman, Graham; Cleese, John
(Marwood); Gilliam, Terry (Vance); Idle,
Eric; Jones, Terence Graham Parry; Palin,
Michael (Edward)
See also AAYA 7

Moodie, Susanna (Strickland)
1803-1885 . . . . **NCLC 14**
See also DLB 99

Mooney, Edward 1951-
See Mooney, Ted
See also CA 130

Mooney, Ted . . . . **CLC 25**
See also Mooney, Edward

Moorcock, Michael (John)
1939- . . . . **CLC 5, 27, 58**
See also CA 45-48; CAAS 5; CANR 2, 17,
38; DLB 14; MTCW

Moore, Brian
1921- . . . . **CLC 1, 3, 5, 7, 8, 19, 32; DAB**
See also CA 1-4R; CANR 1, 25, 42; MTCW

Moore, Edward
See Muir, Edwin

Moore, George Augustus
1852-1933 . . . . **TCLC 7; SSC 19**
See also CA 104; DLB 10, 18, 57, 135

Moore, Lorrie . . . . **CLC 39, 45, 68**
See also Moore, Marie Lorena

Moore, Marianne (Craig)
1887-1972 . . . . **CLC 1, 2, 4, 8, 10, 13, 19,
47; DA; DAB; PC 4**
See also CA 1-4R; 33-36R; CANR 3;
CDALB 1929-1941; DLB 45; DLBD 7;
MTCW; SATA 20

Moore, Marie Lorena 1957-
See Moore, Lorrie
See also CA 116; CANR 39

Moore, Thomas 1779-1852 . . . . **NCLC 6**
See also DLB 96, 144

Morand, Paul 1888-1976 . . . . **CLC 41**
See also CA 69-72; DLB 65

Morante, Elsa 1918-1985 . . . . **CLC 8, 47**
See also CA 85-88; 117; CANR 35; MTCW

Moravia, Alberto . . . . **CLC 2, 7, 11, 27, 46**
See also Pincherle, Alberto

More, Hannah 1745-1833 . . . . **NCLC 27**
See also DLB 107, 109, 116

More, Henry 1614-1687 . . . . **LC 9**
See also DLB 126

More, Sir Thomas 1478-1535 . . . . **LC 10**

Moreas, Jean . . . . **TCLC 18**
See also Papadiamantopoulos, Johannes

Morgan, Berry 1919- . . . . **CLC 6**
See also CA 49-52; DLB 6

Morgan, Claire
See Highsmith, (Mary) Patricia

Morgan, Edwin (George) 1920- . . . . . **CLC 31**
See also CA 5-8R; CANR 3, 43; DLB 27

Morgan, (George) Frederick
1922- . . . . **CLC 23**
See also CA 17-20R; CANR 21

Morgan, Harriet
See Mencken, H(enry) L(ouis)

Morgan, Jane
See Cooper, James Fenimore

Morgan, Janet 1945- . . . . **CLC 39**
See also CA 65-68

Morgan, Lady 1776(?)-1859 . . . . . . **NCLC 29**
See also DLB 116

Morgan, Robin 1941- . . . . **CLC 2**
See also CA 69-72; CANR 29; MTCW;
SATA 80

Morgan, Scott
See Kuttner, Henry

Morgan, Seth 1949(?)-1990 . . . . **CLC 65**
See also CA 132

Morgenstern, Christian
1871-1914 . . . . **TCLC 8**
See also CA 105

Morgenstern, S.
See Goldman, William (W.)

Moricz, Zsigmond 1879-1942 . . . . . **TCLC 33**

Morike, Eduard (Friedrich)
1804-1875 . . . . **NCLC 10**
See also DLB 133

Mori Ogai . . . . **TCLC 14**
See also Mori Rintaro

Mori Rintaro 1862-1922
See Mori Ogai
See also CA 110

Moritz, Karl Philipp 1756-1793 . . . . . . **LC 2**
See also DLB 94

Morland, Peter Henry
See Faust, Frederick (Schiller)

Morren, Theophil
See Hofmannsthal, Hugo von

Morris, Bill 1952- . . . . **CLC 76**

Morris, Julian
See West, Morris L(anglo)

Morris, Steveland Judkins 1950(?)-
See Wonder, Stevie
See also CA 111

Morris, William 1834-1896 . . . . **NCLC 4**
See also CDBLB 1832-1890; DLB 18, 35, 57

Morris, Wright 1910- . . . **CLC 1, 3, 7, 18, 37**
See also CA 9-12R; CANR 21; DLB 2;
DLBY 81; MTCW

Morrison, Chloe Anthony Wofford
See Morrison, Toni

Morrison, James Douglas 1943-1971
See Morrison, Jim
See also CA 73-76; CANR 40

Morrison, Jim . . . . **CLC 17**
See also Morrison, James Douglas

Morrison, Toni
1931- . . . . **CLC 4, 10, 22, 55, 81, 87;
BLC; DA; DAB**
See also AAYA 1; BW 2; CA 29-32R;
CANR 27, 42; CDALB 1968-1988;
DLB 6, 33, 143; DLBY 81; MTCW;
SATA 57

Morrison, Van 1945- . . . . **CLC 21**
See also CA 116

Mortimer, John (Clifford)
1923- . . . . CLC 28, 43
See also CA 13-16R; CANR 21;
CDBLB 1960 to Present; DLB 13;
MTCW

Mortimer, Penelope (Ruth) 1918- . . . . CLC 5
See also CA 57-60; CANR 45

Morton, Anthony
See Creasey, John

Mosher, Howard Frank 1943- . . . . . . CLC 62
See also CA 139

Mosley, Nicholas 1923- . . . . CLC 43, 70
See also CA 69-72; CANR 41; DLB 14

Moss, Howard
1922-1987 . . . . CLC 7, 14, 45, 50
See also CA 1-4R; 123; CANR 1, 44;
DLB 5

Mossgiel, Rab
See Burns, Robert

Motion, Andrew (Peter) 1952- . . . . . . CLC 47
See also CA 146; DLB 40

Motley, Willard (Francis)
1909-1965 . . . . CLC 18
See also BW 1; CA 117; 106; DLB 76, 143

Motoori, Norinaga 1730-1801 . . . . NCLC 45

Mott, Michael (Charles Alston)
1930- . . . . CLC 15, 34
See also CA 5-8R; CAAS 7; CANR 7, 29

Moure, Erin 1955- . . . . CLC 88
See also CA 113; DLB 60

Mowat, Farley (McGill) 1921- . . . . . CLC 26
See also AAYA 1; CA 1-4R; CANR 4, 24,
42; CLR 20; DLB 68; JRDA; MAICYA;
MTCW; SATA 3, 55

Moyers, Bill 1934- . . . . CLC 74
See also AITN 2; CA 61-64; CANR 31

Mphahlele, Es'kia
See Mphahlele, Ezekiel
See also DLB 125

Mphahlele, Ezekiel 1919- . . . . . CLC 25; BLC
See also Mphahlele, Es'kia
See also BW 2; CA 81-84; CANR 26

Mqhayi, S(amuel) E(dward) K(rune Loliwe)
1875-1945 . . . . TCLC 25; BLC

Mr. Martin
See Burroughs, William S(eward)

Mrozek, Slawomir 1930- . . . . CLC 3, 13
See also CA 13-16R; CAAS 10; CANR 29;
MTCW

Mrs. Belloc-Lowndes
See Lowndes, Marie Adelaide (Belloc)

Mtwa, Percy (?)- . . . . CLC 47

Mueller, Lisel 1924- . . . . CLC 13, 51
See also CA 93-96; DLB 105

Muir, Edwin 1887-1959 . . . . TCLC 2
See also CA 104; DLB 20, 100

Muir, John 1838-1914 . . . . TCLC 28

Mujica Lainez, Manuel
1910-1984 . . . . CLC 31
See also Lainez, Manuel Mujica
See also CA 81-84; 112; CANR 32; HW

Mukherjee, Bharati 1940- . . . . CLC 53
See also BEST 89:2; CA 107; CANR 45;
DLB 60; MTCW

Muldoon, Paul 1951- . . . . CLC 32, 72
See also CA 113; 129; DLB 40

Mulisch, Harry 1927- . . . . CLC 42
See also CA 9-12R; CANR 6, 26

Mull, Martin 1943- . . . . CLC 17
See also CA 105

Mulock, Dinah Maria
See Craik, Dinah Maria (Mulock)

Munford, Robert 1737(?)-1783 . . . . LC 5
See also DLB 31

Mungo, Raymond 1946- . . . . CLC 72
See also CA 49-52; CANR 2

Munro, Alice
1931- . . . . CLC 6, 10, 19, 50; SSC 3
See also AITN 2; CA 33-36R; CANR 33;
DLB 53; MTCW; SATA 29

Munro, H(ector) H(ugh) 1870-1916
See Saki
See also CA 104; 130; CDBLB 1890-1914;
DA; DAB; DLB 34; MTCW; WLC

Murasaki, Lady . . . . CMLC 1

Murdoch, (Jean) Iris
1919- . . . . . . CLC 1, 2, 3, 4, 6, 8, 11, 15,
22, 31, 51; DAB
See also CA 13-16R; CANR 8, 43;
CDBLB 1960 to Present; DLB 14;
MTCW

Murnau, Friedrich Wilhelm
See Plumpe, Friedrich Wilhelm

Murphy, Richard 1927- . . . . CLC 41
See also CA 29-32R; DLB 40

Murphy, Sylvia 1937- . . . . CLC 34
See also CA 121

Murphy, Thomas (Bernard) 1935- . . . CLC 51
See also CA 101

Murray, Albert L. 1916- . . . . CLC 73
See also BW 2; CA 49-52; CANR 26;
DLB 38

Murray, Les(lie) A(llan) 1938- . . . . . CLC 40
See also CA 21-24R; CANR 11, 27

Murry, J. Middleton
See Murry, John Middleton

Murry, John Middleton
1889-1957 . . . . TCLC 16
See also CA 118; DLB 149

Musgrave, Susan 1951- . . . . CLC 13, 54
See also CA 69-72; CANR 45

Musil, Robert (Edler von)
1880-1942 . . . . TCLC 12; SSC 18
See also CA 109; DLB 81, 124

Musset, (Louis Charles) Alfred de
1810-1857 . . . . NCLC 7

My Brother's Brother
See Chekhov, Anton (Pavlovich)

Myers, L. H. 1881-1944 . . . . TCLC 59
See also DLB 15

Myers, Walter Dean 1937- . . . CLC 35; BLC
See also AAYA 4; BW 2; CA 33-36R;
CANR 20, 42; CLR 4, 16, 35; DLB 33;
JRDA; MAICYA; SAAS 2; SATA 41, 71;
SATA-Brief 27

Myers, Walter M.
See Myers, Walter Dean

Myles, Symon
See Follett, Ken(neth Martin)

Nabokov, Vladimir (Vladimirovich)
1899-1977 . . . . . CLC 1, 2, 3, 6, 8, 11, 15,
23, 44, 46, 64; DA; DAB; SSC 11; WLC
See also CA 5-8R; 69-72; CANR 20;
CDALB 1941-1968; DLB 2; DLBD 3;
DLBY 80, 91; MTCW

Nagai Kafu . . . . TCLC 51
See also Nagai Sokichi

Nagai Sokichi 1879-1959
See Nagai Kafu
See also CA 117

Nagy, Laszlo 1925-1978 . . . . CLC 7
See also CA 129; 112

Naipaul, Shiva(dhar Srinivasa)
1945-1985 . . . . CLC 32, 39
See also CA 110; 112; 116; CANR 33;
DLBY 85; MTCW

Naipaul, V(idiadhar) S(urajprasad)
1932- . . . . . CLC 4, 7, 9, 13, 18, 37; DAB
See also CA 1-4R; CANR 1, 33;
CDBLB 1960 to Present; DLB 125;
DLBY 85; MTCW

Nakos, Lilika 1899(?)- . . . . CLC 29

Narayan, R(asipuram) K(rishnaswami)
1906- . . . . CLC 7, 28, 47
See also CA 81-84; CANR 33; MTCW;
SATA 62

Nash, (Fredric) Ogden 1902-1971 . . CLC 23
See also CA 13-14; 29-32R; CANR 34;
CAP 1; DLB 11; MAICYA; MTCW;
SATA 2, 46

Nathan, Daniel
See Dannay, Frederic

Nathan, George Jean 1882-1958 . . . TCLC 18
See also Hatteras, Owen
See also CA 114; DLB 137

Natsume, Kinnosuke 1867-1916
See Natsume, Soseki
See also CA 104

Natsume, Soseki . . . . TCLC 2, 10
See also Natsume, Kinnosuke

Natti, (Mary) Lee 1919-
See Kingman, Lee
See also CA 5-8R; CANR 2

Naylor, Gloria
1950- . . . . CLC 28, 52; BLC; DA
See also AAYA 6; BW 2; CA 107;
CANR 27; MTCW

Neihardt, John Gneisenau
1881-1973 . . . . CLC 32
See also CA 13-14; CAP 1; DLB 9, 54

Nekrasov, Nikolai Alekseevich
1821-1878 . . . . NCLC 11

Nelligan, Emile 1879-1941 . . . . TCLC 14
See also CA 114; DLB 92

Nelson, Willie 1933- . . . . CLC 17
See also CA 107

Nemerov, Howard (Stanley)
1920-1991 . . . . CLC 2, 6, 9, 36
See also CA 1-4R; 134; CABS 2; CANR 1,
27; DLB 5, 6; DLBY 83; MTCW

Neruda, Pablo
 1904-1973 ..... **CLC 1, 2, 5, 7, 9, 28, 62;**
 DA; DAB; HLC; PC 4; WLC
 See also CA 19-20; 45-48; CAP 2; HW;
 MTCW

Nerval, Gerard de
 1808-1855 ..... **NCLC 1; PC 13; SSC 18**

Nervo, (Jose) Amado (Ruiz de)
 1870-1919 .... **TCLC 11**
 See also CA 109; 131; HW

Nessi, Pio Baroja y
 See Baroja (y Nessi), Pio

Nestroy, Johann 1801-1862...... **NCLC 42**
 See also DLB 133

Neufeld, John (Arthur) 1938- ...... **CLC 17**
 See also AAYA 11; CA 25-28R; CANR 11,
 37; MAICYA; SAAS 3; SATA 6, 81

Neville, Emily Cheney 1919-....... **CLC 12**
 See also CA 5-8R; CANR 3, 37; JRDA;
 MAICYA; SAAS 2; SATA 1

Newbound, Bernard Slade 1930-
 See Slade, Bernard
 See also CA 81-84; CANR 49

Newby, P(ercy) H(oward)
 1918- .... **CLC 2, 13**
 See also CA 5-8R; CANR 32; DLB 15;
 MTCW

Newlove, Donald 1928- .... **CLC 6**
 See also CA 29-32R; CANR 25

Newlove, John (Herbert) 1938-..... **CLC 14**
 See also CA 21-24R; CANR 9, 25

Newman, Charles 1938- .... **CLC 2, 8**
 See also CA 21-24R

Newman, Edwin (Harold) 1919- .... **CLC 14**
 See also AITN 1; CA 69-72; CANR 5

Newman, John Henry
 1801-1890 .... **NCLC 38**
 See also DLB 18, 32, 55

Newton, Suzanne 1936- .... **CLC 35**
 See also CA 41-44R; CANR 14; JRDA;
 SATA 5, 77

Nexo, Martin Andersen
 1869-1954 .... **TCLC 43**

Nezval, Vitezslav 1900-1958 ...... **TCLC 44**
 See also CA 123

Ng, Fae Myenne 1957(?)-.......... **CLC 81**
 See also CA 146

Ngema, Mbongeni 1955- .... **CLC 57**
 See also BW 2; CA 143

Ngugi, James T(hiong'o)........ **CLC 3, 7, 13**
 See also Ngugi wa Thiong'o

Ngugi wa Thiong'o 1938-..... **CLC 36; BLC**
 See also Ngugi, James T(hiong'o)
 See also BW 2; CA 81-84; CANR 27;
 DLB 125; MTCW

Nichol, B(arrie) P(hillip)
 1944-1988 .... **CLC 18**
 See also CA 53-56; DLB 53; SATA 66

Nichols, John (Treadwell) 1940-.... **CLC 38**
 See also CA 9-12R; CAAS 2; CANR 6;
 DLBY 82

Nichols, Leigh
 See Koontz, Dean R(ay)

Nichols, Peter (Richard)
 1927- .... **CLC 5, 36, 65**
 See also CA 104; CANR 33; DLB 13;
 MTCW

Nicolas, F. R. E.
 See Freeling, Nicolas

Niedecker, Lorine 1903-1970.... **CLC 10, 42**
 See also CA 25-28; CAP 2; DLB 48

Nietzsche, Friedrich (Wilhelm)
 1844-1900 .... **TCLC 10, 18, 55**
 See also CA 107; 121; DLB 129

Nievo, Ippolito 1831-1861 .... **NCLC 22**

Nightingale, Anne Redmon 1943-
 See Redmon, Anne
 See also CA 103

Nik. T. O.
 See Annensky, Innokenty Fyodorovich

Nin, Anais
 1903-1977 ...... **CLC 1, 4, 8, 11, 14, 60;**
 SSC 10
 See also AITN 2; CA 13-16R; 69-72;
 CANR 22; DLB 2, 4, 152; MTCW

Nissenson, Hugh 1933-.......... **CLC 4, 9**
 See also CA 17-20R; CANR 27; DLB 28

Niven, Larry .... **CLC 8**
 See also Niven, Laurence Van Cott
 See also DLB 8

Niven, Laurence Van Cott 1938-
 See Niven, Larry
 See also CA 21-24R; CAAS 12; CANR 14,
 44; MTCW

Nixon, Agnes Eckhardt 1927-...... **CLC 21**
 See also CA 110

Nizan, Paul 1905-1940.......... **TCLC 40**
 See also DLB 72

Nkosi, Lewis 1936-......... **CLC 45; BLC**
 See also BW 1; CA 65-68; CANR 27

Nodier, (Jean) Charles (Emmanuel)
 1780-1844 .... **NCLC 19**
 See also DLB 119

Nolan, Christopher 1965-......... **CLC 58**
 See also CA 111

Norden, Charles
 See Durrell, Lawrence (George)

Nordhoff, Charles (Bernard)
 1887-1947 .... **TCLC 23**
 See also CA 108; DLB 9; SATA 23

Norfolk, Lawrence 1963-......... **CLC 76**
 See also CA 144

Norman, Marsha 1947- .... **CLC 28**
 See also CA 105; CABS 3; CANR 41;
 DLBY 84

Norris, Benjamin Franklin, Jr.
 1870-1902 .... **TCLC 24**
 See also Norris, Frank
 See also CA 110

Norris, Frank
 See Norris, Benjamin Franklin, Jr.
 See also CDALB 1865-1917; DLB 12, 71

Norris, Leslie 1921-............. **CLC 14**
 See also CA 11-12; CANR 14; CAP 1;
 DLB 27

North, Andrew
 See Norton, Andre

North, Anthony
 See Koontz, Dean R(ay)

North, Captain George
 See Stevenson, Robert Louis (Balfour)

North, Milou
 See Erdrich, Louise

Northrup, B. A.
 See Hubbard, L(afayette) Ron(ald)

North Staffs
 See Hulme, T(homas) E(rnest)

Norton, Alice Mary
 See Norton, Andre
 See also MAICYA; SATA 1, 43

Norton, Andre 1912- .... **CLC 12**
 See also Norton, Alice Mary
 See also AAYA 14; CA 1-4R; CANR 2, 31;
 DLB 8, 52; JRDA; MTCW

Norton, Caroline 1808-1877...... **NCLC 47**
 See also DLB 21

Norway, Nevil Shute 1899-1960
 See Shute, Nevil
 See also CA 102; 93-96

Norwid, Cyprian Kamil
 1821-1883 .... **NCLC 17**

Nosille, Nabrah
 See Ellison, Harlan (Jay)

Nossack, Hans Erich 1901-1978..... **CLC 6**
 See also CA 93-96; 85-88; DLB 69

Nostradamus 1503-1566............ **LC 27**

Nosu, Chuji
 See Ozu, Yasujiro

Notenburg, Eleanora (Genrikhovna) von
 See Guro, Elena

Nova, Craig 1945-.............. **CLC 7, 31**
 See also CA 45-48; CANR 2

Novak, Joseph
 See Kosinski, Jerzy (Nikodem)

Novalis 1772-1801 .... **NCLC 13**
 See also DLB 90

Nowlan, Alden (Albert) 1933-1983 .. **CLC 15**
 See also CA 9-12R; CANR 5; DLB 53

Noyes, Alfred 1880-1958 .... **TCLC 7**
 See also CA 104; DLB 20

Nunn, Kem 19(?)-................ **CLC 34**

Nye, Robert 1939- .... **CLC 13, 42**
 See also CA 33-36R; CANR 29; DLB 14;
 MTCW; SATA 6

Nyro, Laura 1947- .... **CLC 17**

Oates, Joyce Carol
 1938- ...... **CLC 1, 2, 3, 6, 9, 11, 15, 19,**
 33, 52; DA; DAB; SSC 6; WLC
 See also AITN 1; BEST 89:2; CA 5-8R;
 CANR 25, 45; CDALB 1968-1988;
 DLB 2, 5, 130; DLBY 81; MTCW

O'Brien, Darcy 1939-............. **CLC 11**
 See also CA 21-24R; CANR 8

O'Brien, E. G.
 See Clarke, Arthur C(harles)

O'Brien, Edna
 1936- ... **CLC 3, 5, 8, 13, 36, 65; SSC 10**
 See also CA 1-4R; CANR 6, 41;
 CDBLB 1960 to Present; DLB 14;
 MTCW

O'Brien, Fitz-James   1828-1862... NCLC 21
See also DLB 74

O'Brien, Flann....... CLC 1, 4, 5, 7, 10, 47
See also O Nuallain, Brian

O'Brien, Richard   1942-.......... CLC 17
See also CA 124

O'Brien, Tim   1946-........ CLC 7, 19, 40
See also CA 85-88; CANR 40; DLB 152;
   DLBD 9; DLBY 80

Obstfelder, Sigbjoern   1866-1900... TCLC 23
See also CA 123

O'Casey, Sean
   1880-1964 ...... CLC 1, 5, 9, 11, 15, 88;
                                           DAB
See also CA 89-92; CDBLB 1914-1945;
   DLB 10; MTCW

O'Cathasaigh, Sean
See O'Casey, Sean

Ochs, Phil   1940-1976............ CLC 17
See also CA 65-68

O'Connor, Edwin (Greene)
   1918-1968 .... CLC 14
See also CA 93-96; 25-28R

O'Connor, (Mary) Flannery
   1925-1964 .... CLC 1, 2, 3, 6, 10, 13, 15,
                       21, 66; DA; DAB; SSC 1; WLC
See also AAYA 7; CA 1-4R; CANR 3, 41;
   CDALB 1941-1968; DLB 2, 152;
   DLBD 12; DLBY 80; MTCW

O'Connor, Frank.......... CLC 23; SSC 5
See also O'Donovan, Michael John

O'Dell, Scott   1898-1989.......... CLC 30
See also AAYA 3; CA 61-64; 129;
   CANR 12, 30; CLR 1, 16; DLB 52;
   JRDA; MAICYA; SATA 12, 60

Odets, Clifford   1906-1963 .... CLC 2, 28
See also CA 85-88; DLB 7, 26; MTCW

O'Doherty, Brian   1934-.......... CLC 76
See also CA 105

O'Donnell, K. M.
See Malzberg, Barry N(athaniel)

O'Donnell, Lawrence
See Kuttner, Henry

O'Donovan, Michael John
   1903-1966 .... CLC 14
See also O'Connor, Frank
See also CA 93-96

Oe, Kenzaburo
   1935- .... CLC 10, 36, 86; SSC 20
See also CA 97-100; CANR 36; MTCW

O'Faolain, Julia   1932-....... CLC 6, 19, 47
See also CA 81-84; CAAS 2; CANR 12;
   DLB 14; MTCW

O'Faolain, Sean
   1900-1991 .... CLC 1, 7, 14, 32, 70;
                                         SSC 13
See also CA 61-64; 134; CANR 12;
   DLB 15; MTCW

O'Flaherty, Liam
   1896-1984 .... CLC 5, 34; SSC 6
See also CA 101; 113; CANR 35; DLB 36;
   DLBY 84; MTCW

Ogilvy, Gavin
See Barrie, J(ames) M(atthew)

O'Grady, Standish James
   1846-1928 .... TCLC 5
See also CA 104

O'Grady, Timothy   1951-.......... CLC 59
See also CA 138

O'Hara, Frank
   1926-1966 .... CLC 2, 5, 13, 78
See also CA 9-12R; 25-28R; CANR 33;
   DLB 5, 16; MTCW

O'Hara, John (Henry)
   1905-1970 ...... CLC 1, 2, 3, 6, 11, 42;
                                         SSC 15
See also CA 5-8R; 25-28R; CANR 31;
   CDALB 1929-1941; DLB 9, 86; DLBD 2;
   MTCW

O Hehir, Diana   1922- .... CLC 41
See also CA 93-96

Okigbo, Christopher (Ifenayichukwu)
   1932-1967 ..... CLC 25, 84; BLC; PC 7
See also BW 1; CA 77-80; DLB 125;
   MTCW

Okri, Ben   1959- .... CLC 87
See also BW 2; CA 130; 138

Olds, Sharon   1942-........ CLC 32, 39, 85
See also CA 101; CANR 18, 41; DLB 120

Oldstyle, Jonathan
See Irving, Washington

Olesha, Yuri (Karlovich)
   1899-1960 .... CLC 8
See also CA 85-88

Oliphant, Laurence
   1829(?)-1888 .... NCLC 47
See also DLB 18

Oliphant, Margaret (Oliphant Wilson)
   1828-1897 .... NCLC 11
See also DLB 18

Oliver, Mary   1935-............ CLC 19, 34
See also CA 21-24R; CANR 9, 43; DLB 5

Olivier, Laurence (Kerr)
   1907-1989 .... CLC 20
See also CA 111; 129

Olsen, Tillie
   1913- .... CLC 4, 13; DA; DAB; SSC 11
See also CA 1-4R; CANR 1, 43; DLB 28;
   DLBY 80; MTCW

Olson, Charles (John)
   1910-1970 ..... CLC 1, 2, 5, 6, 9, 11, 29
See also CA 13-16; 25-28R; CABS 2;
   CANR 35; CAP 1; DLB 5, 16; MTCW

Olson, Toby   1937- .... CLC 28
See also CA 65-68; CANR 9, 31

Olyesha, Yuri
See Olesha, Yuri (Karlovich)

Ondaatje, (Philip) Michael
   1943- .... CLC 14, 29, 51, 76; DAB
See also CA 77-80; CANR 42; DLB 60

Oneal, Elizabeth   1934-
See Oneal, Zibby
See also CA 106; CANR 28; MAICYA;
   SATA 30, 82

Oneal, Zibby .... CLC 30
See also Oneal, Elizabeth
See also AAYA 5; CLR 13; JRDA

O'Neill, Eugene (Gladstone)
   1888-1953 ...... TCLC 1, 6, 27, 49; DA;
                                      DAB; WLC
See also AITN 1; CA 110; 132;
   CDALB 1929-1941; DLB 7; MTCW

Onetti, Juan Carlos   1909-1994 ... CLC 7, 10
See also CA 85-88; 145; CANR 32;
   DLB 113; HW; MTCW

O Nuallain, Brian   1911-1966
See O'Brien, Flann
See also CA 21-22; 25-28R; CAP 2

Oppen, George   1908-1984 .... CLC 7, 13, 34
See also CA 13-16R; 113; CANR 8; DLB 5

Oppenheim, E(dward) Phillips
   1866-1946 .... TCLC 45
See also CA 111; DLB 70

Orlovitz, Gil   1918-1973 .... CLC 22
See also CA 77-80; 45-48; DLB 2, 5

Orris
See Ingelow, Jean

Ortega y Gasset, Jose
   1883-1955 .... TCLC 9; HLC
See also CA 106; 130; HW; MTCW

Ortese, Anna Maria   1914-........ CLC 89

Ortiz, Simon J(oseph)   1941-....... CLC 45
See also CA 134; DLB 120; NNAL

Orton, Joe .... CLC 4, 13, 43; DC 3
See also Orton, John Kingsley
See also CDBLB 1960 to Present; DLB 13

Orton, John Kingsley   1933-1967
See Orton, Joe
See also CA 85-88; CANR 35; MTCW

Orwell, George
   ..... TCLC 2, 6, 15, 31, 51; DAB; WLC
See also Blair, Eric (Arthur)
See also CDBLB 1945-1960; DLB 15, 98

Osborne, David
See Silverberg, Robert

Osborne, George
See Silverberg, Robert

Osborne, John (James)
   1929-1994 ..... CLC 1, 2, 5, 11, 45; DA;
                                      DAB; WLC
See also CA 13-16R; 147; CANR 21;
   CDBLB 1945-1960; DLB 13; MTCW

Osborne, Lawrence   1958- .... CLC 50

Oshima, Nagisa   1932- .... CLC 20
See also CA 116; 121

Oskison, John Milton
   1874-1947 .... TCLC 35
See also CA 144; NNAL

Ossoli, Sarah Margaret (Fuller marchesa d')
   1810-1850
See Fuller, Margaret
See also SATA 25

Ostrovsky, Alexander
   1823-1886 .... NCLC 30

Otero, Blas de   1916-1979......... CLC 11
See also CA 89-92; DLB 134

Otto, Whitney   1955-............. CLC 70
See also CA 140

Ouida .... TCLC 43
See also De La Ramee, (Marie) Louise
See also DLB 18

Ousmane, Sembene 1923- .... **CLC 66; BLC**
See also BW 1; CA 117; 125; MTCW

Ovid 43B.C.-18(?).........**CMLC 7; PC 2**

Owen, Hugh
See Faust, Frederick (Schiller)

Owen, Wilfred (Edward Salter)
1893-1918 ...... **TCLC 5, 27; DA; DAB;**
                                          WLC
See also CA 104; 141; CDBLB 1914-1945;
DLB 20

Owens, Rochelle 1936-............ **CLC 8**
See also CA 17-20R; CAAS 2; CANR 39

Oz, Amos 1939- ... **CLC 5, 8, 11, 27, 33, 54**
See also CA 53-56; CANR 27, 47; MTCW

Ozick, Cynthia
1928- .... **CLC 3, 7, 28, 62; SSC 15**
See also BEST 90:1; CA 17-20R; CANR 23;
DLB 28, 152; DLBY 82; MTCW

Ozu, Yasujiro 1903-1963 .... **CLC 16**
See also CA 112

Pacheco, C.
See Pessoa, Fernando (Antonio Nogueira)

Pa Chin .... **CLC 18**
See also Li Fei-kan

Pack, Robert 1929-.............. **CLC 13**
See also CA 1-4R; CANR 3, 44; DLB 5

Padgett, Lewis
See Kuttner, Henry

Padilla (Lorenzo), Heberto 1932-... **CLC 38**
See also AITN 1; CA 123; 131; HW

Page, Jimmy 1944-............... **CLC 12**

Page, Louise 1955-.............. **CLC 40**
See also CA 140

Page, P(atricia) K(athleen)
1916- .... **CLC 7, 18; PC 12**
See also CA 53-56; CANR 4, 22; DLB 68;
MTCW

Paget, Violet 1856-1935
See Lee, Vernon
See also CA 104

Paget-Lowe, Henry
See Lovecraft, H(oward) P(hillips)

Paglia, Camille (Anna) 1947-....... **CLC 68**
See also CA 140

Paige, Richard
See Koontz, Dean R(ay)

Pakenham, Antonia
See Fraser, (Lady) Antonia (Pakenham)

Palamas, Kostes 1859-1943 .... **TCLC 5**
See also CA 105

Palazzeschi, Aldo 1885-1974 ...... **CLC 11**
See also CA 89-92; 53-56; DLB 114

Paley, Grace 1922-.... **CLC 4, 6, 37; SSC 8**
See also CA 25-28R; CANR 13, 46;
DLB 28; MTCW

Palin, Michael (Edward) 1943- ..... **CLC 21**
See also Monty Python
See also CA 107; CANR 35; SATA 67

Palliser, Charles 1947-............ **CLC 65**
See also CA 136

Palma, Ricardo 1833-1919........ **TCLC 29**

Pancake, Breece Dexter 1952-1979
See Pancake, Breece D'J
See also CA 123; 109

Pancake, Breece D'J.............. **CLC 29**
See also Pancake, Breece Dexter
See also DLB 130

Panko, Rudy
See Gogol, Nikolai (Vasilyevich)

Papadiamantis, Alexandros
1851-1911 .... **TCLC 29**

Papadiamantopoulos, Johannes 1856-1910
See Moreas, Jean
See also CA 117

Papini, Giovanni 1881-1956...... **TCLC 22**
See also CA 121

Paracelsus 1493-1541.............. **LC 14**

Parasol, Peter
See Stevens, Wallace

Parfenie, Maria
See Codrescu, Andrei

Parini, Jay (Lee) 1948- .... **CLC 54**
See also CA 97-100; CAAS 16; CANR 32

Park, Jordan
See Kornbluth, C(yril) M.; Pohl, Frederik

Parker, Bert
See Ellison, Harlan (Jay)

Parker, Dorothy (Rothschild)
1893-1967 .... **CLC 15, 68; SSC 2**
See also CA 19-20; 25-28R; CAP 2;
DLB 11, 45, 86; MTCW

Parker, Robert B(rown) 1932-...... **CLC 27**
See also BEST 89:4; CA 49-52; CANR 1,
26; MTCW

Parkin, Frank 1940-.............. **CLC 43**
See also CA 147

Parkman, Francis, Jr.
1823-1893 .... **NCLC 12**
See also DLB 1, 30

Parks, Gordon (Alexander Buchanan)
1912- .... **CLC 1, 16; BLC**
See also AITN 2; BW 2; CA 41-44R;
CANR 26; DLB 33; SATA 8

Parnell, Thomas 1679-1718 .... **LC 3**
See also DLB 94

Parra, Nicanor 1914-........ **CLC 2; HLC**
See also CA 85-88; CANR 32; HW; MTCW

Parrish, Mary Frances
See Fisher, M(ary) F(rances) K(ennedy)

Parson
See Coleridge, Samuel Taylor

Parson Lot
See Kingsley, Charles

Partridge, Anthony
See Oppenheim, E(dward) Phillips

Pascoli, Giovanni 1855-1912 ...... **TCLC 45**

Pasolini, Pier Paolo
1922-1975 .... **CLC 20, 37**
See also CA 93-96; 61-64; DLB 128;
MTCW

Pasquini
See Silone, Ignazio

Pastan, Linda (Olenik) 1932- ...... **CLC 27**
See also CA 61-64; CANR 18, 40; DLB 5

Pasternak, Boris (Leonidovich)
1890-1960 ...... **CLC 7, 10, 18, 63; DA;**
                                 DAB; PC 6; WLC
See also CA 127; 116; MTCW

Patchen, Kenneth 1911-1972... **CLC 1, 2, 18**
See also CA 1-4R; 33-36R; CANR 3, 35;
DLB 16, 48; MTCW

Pater, Walter (Horatio)
1839-1894 .... **NCLC 7**
See also CDBLB 1832-1890; DLB 57

Paterson, A(ndrew) B(arton)
1864-1941 .... **TCLC 32**

Paterson, Katherine (Womeldorf)
1932- .... **CLC 12, 30**
See also AAYA 1; CA 21-24R; CANR 28;
CLR 7; DLB 52; JRDA; MAICYA;
MTCW; SATA 13, 53

Patmore, Coventry Kersey Dighton
1823-1896 .... **NCLC 9**
See also DLB 35, 98

Paton, Alan (Stewart)
1903-1988 ...... **CLC 4, 10, 25, 55; DA;**
                                      DAB; WLC
See also CA 13-16; 125; CANR 22; CAP 1;
MTCW; SATA 11; SATA-Obit 56

Paton Walsh, Gillian 1937-
See Walsh, Jill Paton
See also CANR 38; JRDA; MAICYA;
SAAS 3; SATA 4, 72

Paulding, James Kirke 1778-1860.. **NCLC 2**
See also DLB 3, 59, 74

Paulin, Thomas Neilson 1949-
See Paulin, Tom
See also CA 123; 128

Paulin, Tom..................... **CLC 37**
See also Paulin, Thomas Neilson
See also DLB 40

Paustovsky, Konstantin (Georgievich)
1892-1968 .... **CLC 40**
See also CA 93-96; 25-28R

Pavese, Cesare
1908-1950 ..... **TCLC 3; PC 13; SSC 19**
See also CA 104; DLB 128

Pavic, Milorad 1929-.............. **CLC 60**
See also CA 136

Payne, Alan
See Jakes, John (William)

Paz, Gil
See Lugones, Leopoldo

Paz, Octavio
1914- .... **CLC 3, 4, 6, 10, 19, 51, 65;**
                             DA; DAB; HLC; PC 1; WLC
See also CA 73-76; CANR 32; DLBY 90;
HW; MTCW

Peacock, Molly 1947-............. **CLC 60**
See also CA 103; CAAS 21; DLB 120

Peacock, Thomas Love
1785-1866 .... **NCLC 22**
See also DLB 96, 116

Peake, Mervyn 1911-1968........ **CLC 7, 54**
See also CA 5-8R; 25-28R; CANR 3;
DLB 15; MTCW; SATA 23

Pearce, Philippa .... **CLC 21**
See also Christie, (Ann) Philippa
See also CLR 9; MAICYA; SATA 1, 67

Pearl, Eric
See Elman, Richard

Pearson, T(homas) R(eid) 1956- .... **CLC 39**
See also CA 120; 130

Peck, Dale 1968(?)- .... **CLC 81**

Peck, John 1941- .... **CLC 3**
See also CA 49-52; CANR 3

Peck, Richard (Wayne) 1934- ...... **CLC 21**
See also AAYA 1; CA 85-88; CANR 19,
38; CLR 15; JRDA; MAICYA; SAAS 2;
SATA 18, 55

Peck, Robert Newton 1928-.... **CLC 17; DA**
See also AAYA 3; CA 81-84; CANR 31;
JRDA; MAICYA; SAAS 1; SATA 21, 62

Peckinpah, (David) Sam(uel)
1925-1984 .... **CLC 20**
See also CA 109; 114

Pedersen, Knut 1859-1952
See Hamsun, Knut
See also CA 104; 119; MTCW

Peeslake, Gaffer
See Durrell, Lawrence (George)

Peguy, Charles Pierre
1873-1914 .... **TCLC 10**
See also CA 107

Pena, Ramon del Valle y
See Valle-Inclan, Ramon (Maria) del

Pendennis, Arthur Esquir
See Thackeray, William Makepeace

Penn, William 1644-1718 .... **LC 25**
See also DLB 24

Pepys, Samuel
1633-1703 ..... **LC 11; DA; DAB; WLC**
See also CDBLB 1660-1789; DLB 101

Percy, Walker
1916-1990 .... **CLC 2, 3, 6, 8, 14, 18, 47,
65**
See also CA 1-4R; 131; CANR 1, 23;
DLB 2; DLBY 80, 90; MTCW

Perec, Georges 1936-1982 .... **CLC 56**
See also CA 141; DLB 83

Pereda (y Sanchez de Porrua), Jose Maria de
1833-1906 .... **TCLC 16**
See also CA 117

Pereda y Porrua, Jose Maria de
See Pereda (y Sanchez de Porrua), Jose
Maria de

Peregoy, George Weems
See Mencken, H(enry) L(ouis)

Perelman, S(idney) J(oseph)
1904-1979 ... **CLC 3, 5, 9, 15, 23, 44, 49**
See also AITN 1, 2; CA 73-76; 89-92;
CANR 18; DLB 11, 44; MTCW

Peret, Benjamin 1899-1959 .... **TCLC 20**
See also CA 117

Peretz, Isaac Loeb 1851(?)-1915... **TCLC 16**
See also CA 109

Peretz, Yitzkhok Leibush
See Peretz, Isaac Loeb

Perez Galdos, Benito 1843-1920 ... **TCLC 27**
See also CA 125; HW

Perrault, Charles 1628-1703 .... **LC 2**
See also MAICYA; SATA 25

Perry, Brighton
See Sherwood, Robert E(mmet)

Perse, St.-John .... **CLC 4, 11, 46**
See also Leger, (Marie-Rene Auguste) Alexis
Saint-Leger

Perutz, Leo 1882-1957 .... **TCLC 60**
See also DLB 81

Peseenz, Tulio F.
See Lopez y Fuentes, Gregorio

Pesetsky, Bette 1932-............. **CLC 28**
See also CA 133; DLB 130

Peshkov, Alexei Maximovich 1868-1936
See Gorky, Maxim
See also CA 105; 141; DA

Pessoa, Fernando (Antonio Nogueira)
1888-1935 .... **TCLC 27; HLC**
See also CA 125

Peterkin, Julia Mood 1880-1961.... **CLC 31**
See also CA 102; DLB 9

Peters, Joan K. 1945-............. **CLC 39**

Peters, Robert L(ouis) 1924-........ **CLC 7**
See also CA 13-16R; CAAS 8; DLB 105

Petofi, Sandor 1823-1849........ **NCLC 21**

Petrakis, Harry Mark 1923-........ **CLC 3**
See also CA 9-12R; CANR 4, 30

Petrarch 1304-1374................ **PC 8**

Petrov, Evgeny .... **TCLC 21**
See also Kataev, Evgeny Petrovich

Petry, Ann (Lane) 1908- ...... **CLC 1, 7, 18**
See also BW 1; CA 5-8R; CAAS 6;
CANR 4, 46; CLR 12; DLB 76; JRDA;
MAICYA; MTCW; SATA 5

Petursson, Halligrimur 1614-1674 .... **LC 8**

Philips, Katherine 1632-1664....... **LC 30**
See also DLB 131

Philipson, Morris H. 1926-........ **CLC 53**
See also CA 1-4R; CANR 4

Phillips, David Graham
1867-1911 .... **TCLC 44**
See also CA 108; DLB 9, 12

Phillips, Jack
See Sandburg, Carl (August)

Phillips, Jayne Anne
1952-............ **CLC 15, 33; SSC 16**
See also CA 101; CANR 24; DLBY 80;
MTCW

Phillips, Richard
See Dick, Philip K(indred)

Phillips, Robert (Schaeffer) 1938-... **CLC 28**
See also CA 17-20R; CAAS 13; CANR 8;
DLB 105

Phillips, Ward
See Lovecraft, H(oward) P(hillips)

Piccolo, Lucio 1901-1969.......... **CLC 13**
See also CA 97-100; DLB 114

Pickthall, Marjorie L(owry) C(hristie)
1883-1922 .... **TCLC 21**
See also CA 107; DLB 92

Pico della Mirandola, Giovanni
1463-1494 .... **LC 15**

Piercy, Marge
1936- .... **CLC 3, 6, 14, 18, 27, 62**
See also CA 21-24R; CAAS 1; CANR 13,
43; DLB 120; MTCW

Piers, Robert
See Anthony, Piers

Pieyre de Mandiargues, Andre 1909-1991
See Mandiargues, Andre Pieyre de
See also CA 103; 136; CANR 22

Pilnyak, Boris .... **TCLC 23**
See also Vogau, Boris Andreyevich

Pincherle, Alberto 1907-1990 ... **CLC 11, 18**
See also Moravia, Alberto
See also CA 25-28R; 132; CANR 33;
MTCW

Pinckney, Darryl 1953-........... **CLC 76**
See also BW 2; CA 143

Pindar 518B.C.-446B.C.......... **CMLC 12**

Pineda, Cecile 1942-............. **CLC 39**
See also CA 118

Pinero, Arthur Wing 1855-1934 ... **TCLC 32**
See also CA 110; DLB 10

Pinero, Miguel (Antonio Gomez)
1946-1988 .... **CLC 4, 55**
See also CA 61-64; 125; CANR 29; HW

Pinget, Robert 1919- .... **CLC 7, 13, 37**
See also CA 85-88; DLB 83

Pink Floyd
See Barrett, (Roger) Syd; Gilmour, David;
Mason, Nick; Waters, Roger; Wright,
Rick

Pinkney, Edward 1802-1828 ..... **NCLC 31**

Pinkwater, Daniel Manus 1941-.... **CLC 35**
See also Pinkwater, Manus
See also AAYA 1; CA 29-32R; CANR 12,
38; CLR 4; JRDA; MAICYA; SAAS 3;
SATA 46, 76

Pinkwater, Manus
See Pinkwater, Daniel Manus
See also SATA 8

Pinsky, Robert 1940-........ **CLC 9, 19, 38**
See also CA 29-32R; CAAS 4; DLBY 82

Pinta, Harold
See Pinter, Harold

Pinter, Harold
1930- ..... **CLC 1, 3, 6, 9, 11, 15, 27, 58,
73; DA; DAB; WLC**
See also CA 5-8R; CANR 33; CDBLB 1960
to Present; DLB 13; MTCW

Pirandello, Luigi
1867-1936 ...... **TCLC 4, 29; DA; DAB;
DC 5; WLC**
See also CA 104

Pirsig, Robert M(aynard)
1928- .... **CLC 4, 6, 73**
See also CA 53-56; CANR 42; MTCW;
SATA 39

Pisarev, Dmitry Ivanovich
1840-1868 .... **NCLC 25**

Pix, Mary (Griffith) 1666-1709....... **LC 8**
See also DLB 80

Pixerecourt, Guilbert de
1773-1844 .... **NCLC 39**

Plaidy, Jean
See Hibbert, Eleanor Alice Burford

Planche, James Robinson
    1796-1880 .... **NCLC 42**

Plant, Robert 1948- .... **CLC 12**

Plante, David (Robert)
    1940- .... **CLC 7, 23, 38**
    See also CA 37-40R; CANR 12, 36;
    DLBY 83; MTCW

Plath, Sylvia
    1932-1963 ..... **CLC 1, 2, 3, 5, 9, 11, 14,**
      17, 50, 51, 62; DA; DAB; PC 1; WLC
    See also AAYA 13; CA 19-20; CANR 34;
    CAP 2; CDALB 1941-1968; DLB 5, 6,
    152; MTCW

Plato
    428(?)B.C.-348(?)B.C..... **CMLC 8; DA;**
      DAB

Platonov, Andrei .... **TCLC 14**
    See also Klimentov, Andrei Platonovich

Platt, Kin 1911- .... **CLC 26**
    See also AAYA 11; CA 17-20R; CANR 11;
    JRDA; SAAS 17; SATA 21

Plick et Plock
    See Simenon, Georges (Jacques Christian)

Plimpton, George (Ames) 1927- ..... **CLC 36**
    See also AITN 1; CA 21-24R; CANR 32;
    MTCW; SATA 10

Plomer, William Charles Franklin
    1903-1973 .... **CLC 4, 8**
    See also CA 21-22; CANR 34; CAP 2;
    DLB 20; MTCW; SATA 24

Plowman, Piers
    See Kavanagh, Patrick (Joseph)

Plum, J.
    See Wodehouse, P(elham) G(renville)

Plumly, Stanley (Ross) 1939- ...... **CLC 33**
    See also CA 108; 110; DLB 5

Plumpe, Friedrich Wilhelm
    1888-1931 .... **TCLC 53**
    See also CA 112

Poe, Edgar Allan
    1809-1849 ..... **NCLC 1, 16; DA; DAB;**
      PC 1; SSC 1; WLC
    See also AAYA 14; CDALB 1640-1865;
    DLB 3, 59, 73, 74; SATA 23

Poet of Titchfield Street, The
    See Pound, Ezra (Weston Loomis)

Pohl, Frederik 1919- .... **CLC 18**
    See also CA 61-64; CAAS 1; CANR 11, 37;
    DLB 8; MTCW; SATA 24

Poirier, Louis 1910-
    See Gracq, Julien
    See also CA 122; 126

Poitier, Sidney 1927- .... **CLC 26**
    See also BW 1; CA 117

Polanski, Roman 1933- .... **CLC 16**
    See also CA 77-80

Poliakoff, Stephen 1952- .... **CLC 38**
    See also CA 106; DLB 13

Police, The
    See Copeland, Stewart (Armstrong);
    Summers, Andrew James; Sumner,
    Gordon Matthew

Polidori, John William
    1795-1821 .... **NCLC 51**
    See also DLB 116

Pollitt, Katha 1949- .... **CLC 28**
    See also CA 120; 122; MTCW

Pollock, (Mary) Sharon 1936- ...... **CLC 50**
    See also CA 141; DLB 60

Polo, Marco 1254-1324 .... **CMLC 15**

Pomerance, Bernard 1940- .... **CLC 13**
    See also CA 101; CANR 49

Ponge, Francis (Jean Gaston Alfred)
    1899-1988 .... **CLC 6, 18**
    See also CA 85-88; 126; CANR 40

Pontoppidan, Henrik 1857-1943 ... **TCLC 29**

Poole, Josephine .... **CLC 17**
    See also Helyar, Jane Penelope Josephine
    See also SAAS 2; SATA 5

Popa, Vasko 1922-1991 .... **CLC 19**
    See also CA 112; 148

Pope, Alexander
    1688-1744 ...... **LC 3; DA; DAB; WLC**
    See also CDBLB 1660-1789; DLB 95, 101

Porter, Connie (Rose) 1959(?)- ..... **CLC 70**
    See also BW 2; CA 142; SATA 81

Porter, Gene(va Grace) Stratton
    1863(?)-1924 .... **TCLC 21**
    See also CA 112

Porter, Katherine Anne
    1890-1980 ...... **CLC 1, 3, 7, 10, 13, 15,**
      27; DA; DAB; SSC 4
    See also AITN 2; CA 1-4R; 101; CANR 1;
    DLB 4, 9, 102; DLBD 12; DLBY 80;
    MTCW; SATA 39; SATA-Obit 23

Porter, Peter (Neville Frederick)
    1929- .... **CLC 5, 13, 33**
    See also CA 85-88; DLB 40

Porter, William Sydney 1862-1910
    See Henry, O.
    See also CA 104; 131; CDALB 1865-1917;
    DA; DAB; DLB 12, 78, 79; MTCW;
    YABC 2

Portillo (y Pacheco), Jose Lopez
    See Lopez Portillo (y Pacheco), Jose

Post, Melville Davisson
    1869-1930 .... **TCLC 39**
    See also CA 110

Potok, Chaim 1929- .... **CLC 2, 7, 14, 26**
    See also AITN 1, 2; CA 17-20R; CANR 19,
    35; DLB 28, 152; MTCW; SATA 33

Potter, Beatrice
    See Webb, (Martha) Beatrice (Potter)
    See also MAICYA

Potter, Dennis (Christopher George)
    1935-1994 .... **CLC 58, 86**
    See also CA 107; 145; CANR 33; MTCW

Pound, Ezra (Weston Loomis)
    1885-1972 ...... **CLC 1, 2, 3, 4, 5, 7, 10,**
      13, 18, 34, 48, 50; DA; DAB; PC 4; WLC
    See also CA 5-8R; 37-40R; CANR 40;
    CDALB 1917-1929; DLB 4, 45, 63;
    MTCW

Povod, Reinaldo 1959-1994 .... **CLC 44**
    See also CA 136; 146

Powell, Adam Clayton, Jr.
    1908-1972 .... **CLC 89; BLC**
    See also BW 1; CA 102; 33-36R

Powell, Anthony (Dymoke)
    1905- .... **CLC 1, 3, 7, 9, 10, 31**
    See also CA 1-4R; CANR 1, 32;
    CDBLB 1945-1960; DLB 15; MTCW

Powell, Dawn 1897-1965 .... **CLC 66**
    See also CA 5-8R

Powell, Padgett 1952-............. **CLC 34**
    See also CA 126

Powers, J(ames) F(arl)
    1917- .... **CLC 1, 4, 8, 57; SSC 4**
    See also CA 1-4R; CANR 2; DLB 130;
    MTCW

Powers, John J(ames) 1945-
    See Powers, John R.
    See also CA 69-72

Powers, John R. .... **CLC 66**
    See also Powers, John J(ames)

Pownall, David 1938-............. **CLC 10**
    See also CA 89-92; CAAS 18; CANR 49;
    DLB 14

Powys, John Cowper
    1872-1963 .... **CLC 7, 9, 15, 46**
    See also CA 85-88; DLB 15; MTCW

Powys, T(heodore) F(rancis)
    1875-1953 .... **TCLC 9**
    See also CA 106; DLB 36

Prager, Emily 1952-.............. **CLC 56**

Pratt, E(dwin) J(ohn)
    1883(?)-1964 .... **CLC 19**
    See also CA 141; 93-96; DLB 92

Premchand..................... **TCLC 21**
    See also Srivastava, Dhanpat Rai

Preussler, Otfried 1923-.......... **CLC 17**
    See also CA 77-80; SATA 24

Prevert, Jacques (Henri Marie)
    1900-1977 .... **CLC 15**
    See also CA 77-80; 69-72; CANR 29;
    MTCW; SATA-Obit 30

Prevost, Abbe (Antoine Francois)
    1697-1763 .... **LC 1**

Price, (Edward) Reynolds
    1933- .... **CLC 3, 6, 13, 43, 50, 63**
    See also CA 1-4R; CANR 1, 37; DLB 2

Price, Richard 1949- .... **CLC 6, 12**
    See also CA 49-52; CANR 3; DLBY 81

Prichard, Katharine Susannah
    1883-1969 .... **CLC 46**
    See also CA 11-12; CANR 33; CAP 1;
    MTCW; SATA 66

Priestley, J(ohn) B(oynton)
    1894-1984 .... **CLC 2, 5, 9, 34**
    See also CA 9-12R; 113; CANR 33;
    CDBLB 1914-1945; DLB 10, 34, 77, 100,
    139; DLBY 84; MTCW

Prince 1958(?)- .... **CLC 35**

Prince, F(rank) T(empleton) 1912- .. **CLC 22**
    See also CA 101; CANR 43; DLB 20

Prince Kropotkin
    See Kropotkin, Peter (Aleksieevich)

Prior, Matthew 1664-1721.......... **LC 4**
    See also DLB 95

Pritchard, William H(arrison)
    1932- .... **CLC 34**
    See also CA 65-68; CANR 23; DLB 111

Pritchett, V(ictor) S(awdon)
1900- .... CLC **5, 13, 15, 41; SSC 14**
See also CA 61-64; CANR 31; DLB 15,
139; MTCW

Private 19022
See Manning, Frederic

Probst, Mark 1925- .... CLC **59**
See also CA 130

Prokosch, Frederic 1908-1989.... CLC **4, 48**
See also CA 73-76; 128; DLB 48

Prophet, The
See Dreiser, Theodore (Herman Albert)

Prose, Francine 1947-............. CLC **45**
See also CA 109; 112; CANR 46

Proudhon
See Cunha, Euclides (Rodrigues Pimenta) da

Proulx, E. Annie 1935- .... CLC **81**

Proust, (Valentin-Louis-George-Eugene-) Marcel
1871-1922 .... TCLC **7, 13, 33; DA; DAB; WLC**
See also CA 104; 120; DLB 65; MTCW

Prowler, Harley
See Masters, Edgar Lee

Prus, Boleslaw 1845-1912 .... TCLC **48**

Pryor, Richard (Franklin Lenox Thomas)
1940- .... CLC **26**
See also CA 122

Przybyszewski, Stanislaw
1868-1927 .... TCLC **36**
See also DLB 66

Pteleon
See Grieve, C(hristopher) M(urray)

Puckett, Lute
See Masters, Edgar Lee

Puig, Manuel
1932-1990 ... CLC **3, 5, 10, 28, 65; HLC**
See also CA 45-48; CANR 2, 32; DLB 113;
HW; MTCW

Purdy, Al(fred Wellington)
1918- .... CLC **3, 6, 14, 50**
See also CA 81-84; CAAS 17; CANR 42;
DLB 88

Purdy, James (Amos)
1923- .... CLC **2, 4, 10, 28, 52**
See also CA 33-36R; CAAS 1; CANR 19;
DLB 2; MTCW

Pure, Simon
See Swinnerton, Frank Arthur

Pushkin, Alexander (Sergeyevich)
1799-1837 ..... NCLC **3, 27; DA; DAB; PC 10; WLC**
See also SATA 61

P'u Sung-ling 1640-1715 .... LC **3**

Putnam, Arthur Lee
See Alger, Horatio, Jr.

Puzo, Mario 1920- .... CLC **1, 2, 6, 36**
See also CA 65-68; CANR 4, 42; DLB 6;
MTCW

Pym, Barbara (Mary Crampton)
1913-1980............ CLC **13, 19, 37**
See also CA 13-14; 97-100; CANR 13, 34;
CAP 1; DLB 14; DLBY 87; MTCW

Pynchon, Thomas (Ruggles, Jr.)
1937- ..... CLC **2, 3, 6, 9, 11, 18, 33, 62, 72; DA; DAB; SSC 14; WLC**
See also BEST 90:2; CA 17-20R; CANR 22,
46; DLB 2; MTCW

Qian Zhongshu
See Ch'ien Chung-shu

Qroll
See Dagerman, Stig (Halvard)

Quarrington, Paul (Lewis) 1953-.... CLC **65**
See also CA 129

Quasimodo, Salvatore 1901-1968 ... CLC **10**
See also CA 13-16; 25-28R; CAP 1;
DLB 114; MTCW

Queen, Ellery.................. CLC **3, 11**
See also Dannay, Frederic; Davidson,
Avram; Lee, Manfred B(ennington);
Sturgeon, Theodore (Hamilton); Vance,
John Holbrook

Queen, Ellery, Jr.
See Dannay, Frederic; Lee, Manfred
B(ennington)

Queneau, Raymond
1903-1976 .... CLC **2, 5, 10, 42**
See also CA 77-80; 69-72; CANR 32;
DLB 72; MTCW

Quevedo, Francisco de 1580-1645.... LC **23**

Quiller-Couch, Arthur Thomas
1863-1944 .... TCLC **53**
See also CA 118; DLB 135, 153

Quin, Ann (Marie) 1936-1973....... CLC **6**
See also CA 9-12R; 45-48; DLB 14

Quinn, Martin
See Smith, Martin Cruz

Quinn, Simon
See Smith, Martin Cruz

Quiroga, Horacio (Sylvestre)
1878-1937 .... TCLC **20; HLC**
See also CA 117; 131; HW; MTCW

Quoirez, Francoise 1935-.......... CLC **9**
See also Sagan, Francoise
See also CA 49-52; CANR 6, 39; MTCW

Raabe, Wilhelm 1831-1910 ...... TCLC **45**
See also DLB 129

Rabe, David (William) 1940-... CLC **4, 8, 33**
See also CA 85-88; CABS 3; DLB 7

Rabelais, Francois
1483-1553 ...... LC **5; DA; DAB; WLC**

Rabinovitch, Sholem 1859-1916
See Aleichem, Sholom
See also CA 104

Racine, Jean 1639-1699 ...... LC **28; DAB**

Radcliffe, Ann (Ward) 1764-1823 .. NCLC **6**
See also DLB 39

Radiguet, Raymond 1903-1923 .... TCLC **29**
See also DLB 65

Radnoti, Miklos 1909-1944 .... TCLC **16**
See also CA 118

Rado, James 1939-.............. CLC **17**
See also CA 105

Radvanyi, Netty 1900-1983
See Seghers, Anna
See also CA 85-88; 110

Rae, Ben
See Griffiths, Trevor

Raeburn, John (Hay) 1941-........ CLC **34**
See also CA 57-60

Ragni, Gerome 1942-1991 .... CLC **17**
See also CA 105; 134

Rahv, Philip 1908-1973 .... CLC **24**
See also Greenberg, Ivan
See also DLB 137

Raine, Craig 1944-............... CLC **32**
See also CA 108; CANR 29; DLB 40

Raine, Kathleen (Jessie) 1908- ... CLC **7, 45**
See also CA 85-88; CANR 46; DLB 20;
MTCW

Rainis, Janis 1865-1929......... TCLC **29**

Rakosi, Carl.................... CLC **47**
See also Rawley, Callman
See also CAAS 5

Raleigh, Richard
See Lovecraft, H(oward) P(hillips)

Rallentando, H. P.
See Sayers, Dorothy L(eigh)

Ramal, Walter
See de la Mare, Walter (John)

Ramon, Juan
See Jimenez (Mantecon), Juan Ramon

Ramos, Graciliano 1892-1953 ..... TCLC **32**

Rampersad, Arnold 1941-.......... CLC **44**
See also BW 2; CA 127; 133; DLB 111

Rampling, Anne
See Rice, Anne

Ramsay, Allan 1684(?)-1758 .... LC **29**
See also DLB 95

Ramuz, Charles-Ferdinand
1878-1947 .... TCLC **33**

Rand, Ayn
1905-1982 ...... CLC **3, 30, 44, 79; DA; WLC**
See also AAYA 10; CA 13-16R; 105;
CANR 27; MTCW

Randall, Dudley (Felker)
1914-................... CLC **1; BLC**
See also BW 1; CA 25-28R; CANR 23;
DLB 41

Randall, Robert
See Silverberg, Robert

Ranger, Ken
See Creasey, John

Ransom, John Crowe
1888-1974 .... CLC **2, 4, 5, 11, 24**
See also CA 5-8R; 49-52; CANR 6, 34;
DLB 45, 63; MTCW

Rao, Raja 1909- .... CLC **25, 56**
See also CA 73-76; MTCW

Raphael, Frederic (Michael)
1931- .... CLC **2, 14**
See also CA 1-4R; CANR 1; DLB 14

Ratcliffe, James P.
See Mencken, H(enry) L(ouis)

Rathbone, Julian 1935- .... CLC **41**
See also CA 101; CANR 34

Rattigan, Terence (Mervyn)
1911-1977 .... CLC **7**
See also CA 85-88; 73-76;
CDBLB 1945-1960; DLB 13; MTCW

Ratushinskaya, Irina 1954- .... CLC **54**
See also CA 129

Raven, Simon (Arthur Noel)
1927- .... CLC **14**
See also CA 81-84

Rawley, Callman 1903-
See Rakosi, Carl
See also CA 21-24R; CANR 12, 32

Rawlings, Marjorie Kinnan
1896-1953 .... TCLC **4**
See also CA 104; 137; DLB 9, 22, 102;
JRDA; MAICYA; YABC 1

Ray, Satyajit 1921-1992........ CLC **16, 76**
See also CA 114; 137

Read, Herbert Edward 1893-1968.... CLC **4**
See also CA 85-88; 25-28R; DLB 20, 149

Read, Piers Paul 1941- ...... CLC **4, 10, 25**
See also CA 21-24R; CANR 38; DLB 14;
SATA 21

Reade, Charles 1814-1884 .... NCLC **2**
See also DLB 21

Reade, Hamish
See Gray, Simon (James Holliday)

Reading, Peter 1946- .... CLC **47**
See also CA 103; CANR 46; DLB 40

Reaney, James 1926- .... CLC **13**
See also CA 41-44R; CAAS 15; CANR 42;
DLB 68; SATA 43

Rebreanu, Liviu 1885-1944 .... TCLC **28**

Rechy, John (Francisco)
1934- .... CLC **1, 7, 14, 18; HLC**
See also CA 5-8R; CAAS 4; CANR 6, 32;
DLB 122; DLBY 82; HW

Redcam, Tom 1870-1933 .... TCLC **25**

Reddin, Keith..................... CLC **67**

Redgrove, Peter (William)
1932- .... CLC **6, 41**
See also CA 1-4R; CANR 3, 39; DLB 40

Redmon, Anne.................... CLC **22**
See also Nightingale, Anne Redmon
See also DLBY 86

Reed, Eliot
See Ambler, Eric

Reed, Ishmael
1938- ... CLC **2, 3, 5, 6, 13, 32, 60; BLC**
See also BW 2; CA 21-24R; CANR 25, 48;
DLB 2, 5, 33; DLBD 8; MTCW

Reed, John (Silas) 1887-1920 ...... TCLC **9**
See also CA 106

Reed, Lou........................ CLC **21**
See also Firbank, Louis

Reeve, Clara 1729-1807 .... NCLC **19**
See also DLB 39

Reich, Wilhelm 1897-1957....... TCLC **57**

Reid, Christopher (John) 1949-..... CLC **33**
See also CA 140; DLB 40

Reid, Desmond
See Moorcock, Michael (John)

Reid Banks, Lynne 1929-
See Banks, Lynne Reid
See also CA 1-4R; CANR 6, 22, 38;
CLR 24; JRDA; MAICYA; SATA 22, 75

Reilly, William K.
See Creasey, John

Reiner, Max
See Caldwell, (Janet Miriam) Taylor
(Holland)

Reis, Ricardo
See Pessoa, Fernando (Antonio Nogueira)

Remarque, Erich Maria
1898-1970 .... CLC **21; DA; DAB**
See also CA 77-80; 29-32R; DLB 56;
MTCW

Remizov, A.
See Remizov, Aleksei (Mikhailovich)

Remizov, A. M.
See Remizov, Aleksei (Mikhailovich)

Remizov, Aleksei (Mikhailovich)
1877-1957 .... TCLC **27**
See also CA 125; 133

Renan, Joseph Ernest
1823-1892 .... NCLC **26**

Renard, Jules 1864-1910 .... TCLC **17**
See also CA 117

Renault, Mary.............. CLC **3, 11, 17**
See also Challans, Mary
See also DLBY 83

Rendell, Ruth (Barbara) 1930- .. CLC **28, 48**
See also Vine, Barbara
See also CA 109; CANR 32; DLB 87;
MTCW

Renoir, Jean 1894-1979 .... CLC **20**
See also CA 129; 85-88

Resnais, Alain 1922-.............. CLC **16**

Reverdy, Pierre 1889-1960 .... CLC **53**
See also CA 97-100; 89-92

Rexroth, Kenneth
1905-1982 ...... CLC **1, 2, 6, 11, 22, 49**
See also CA 5-8R; 107; CANR 14, 34;
CDALB 1941-1968; DLB 16, 48;
DLBY 82; MTCW

Reyes, Alfonso 1889-1959 .... TCLC **33**
See also CA 131; HW

Reyes y Basoalto, Ricardo Eliecer Neftali
See Neruda, Pablo

Reymont, Wladyslaw (Stanislaw)
1868(?)-1925 .... TCLC **5**
See also CA 104

Reynolds, Jonathan 1942- .... CLC **6, 38**
See also CA 65-68; CANR 28

Reynolds, Joshua 1723-1792 .... LC **15**
See also DLB 104

Reynolds, Michael Shane 1937- .... CLC **44**
See also CA 65-68; CANR 9

Reznikoff, Charles 1894-1976 .... CLC **9**
See also CA 33-36; 61-64; CAP 2; DLB 28,
45

Rezzori (d'Arezzo), Gregor von
1914- .... CLC **25**
See also CA 122; 136

Rhine, Richard
See Silverstein, Alvin

Rhodes, Eugene Manlove
1869-1934 .... TCLC **53**

R'hoone
See Balzac, Honore de

Rhys, Jean
1890(?)-1979 .... CLC **2, 4, 6, 14, 19, 51**
See also CA 25-28R; 85-88; CANR 35;
CDBLB 1945-1960; DLB 36, 117; MTCW

Ribeiro, Darcy 1922- .... CLC **34**
See also CA 33-36R

Ribeiro, Joao Ubaldo (Osorio Pimentel)
1941- .... CLC **10, 67**
See also CA 81-84

Ribman, Ronald (Burt) 1932- ...... CLC **7**
See also CA 21-24R; CANR 46

Ricci, Nino 1959- .... CLC **70**
See also CA 137

Rice, Anne 1941- .... CLC **41**
See also AAYA 9; BEST 89:2; CA 65-68;
CANR 12, 36

Rice, Elmer (Leopold)
1892-1967 .... CLC **7, 49**
See also CA 21-22; 25-28R; CAP 2; DLB 4,
7; MTCW

Rice, Tim(othy Miles Bindon)
1944- .... CLC **21**
See also CA 103; CANR 46

Rich, Adrienne (Cecile)
1929- .... CLC **3, 6, 7, 11, 18, 36, 73, 76;
PC 5**
See also CA 9-12R; CANR 20; DLB 5, 67;
MTCW

Rich, Barbara
See Graves, Robert (von Ranke)

Rich, Robert
See Trumbo, Dalton

Richard, Keith.................... CLC **17**
See also Richards, Keith

Richards, David Adams 1950-...... CLC **59**
See also CA 93-96; DLB 53

Richards, I(vor) A(rmstrong)
1893-1979 .... CLC **14, 24**
See also CA 41-44R; 89-92; CANR 34;
DLB 27

Richards, Keith 1943-
See Richard, Keith
See also CA 107

Richardson, Anne
See Roiphe, Anne (Richardson)

Richardson, Dorothy Miller
1873-1957 .... TCLC **3**
See also CA 104; DLB 36

Richardson, Ethel Florence (Lindesay)
1870-1946
See Richardson, Henry Handel
See also CA 105

Richardson, Henry Handel......... TCLC **4**
See also Richardson, Ethel Florence
(Lindesay)

Richardson, Samuel
1689-1761 ...... LC **1; DA; DAB; WLC**
See also CDBLB 1660-1789; DLB 39

Richler, Mordecai
  1931- .... **CLC 3, 5, 9, 13, 18, 46, 70**
  See also AITN 1; CA 65-68; CANR 31;
  CLR 17; DLB 53; MAICYA; MTCW;
  SATA 44; SATA-Brief 27

Richter, Conrad (Michael)
  1890-1968 .... **CLC 30**
  See also CA 5-8R; 25-28R; CANR 23;
  DLB 9; MTCW; SATA 3

Ricostranza, Tom
  See Ellis, Trey

Riddell, J. H. 1832-1906 .... **TCLC 40**

Riding, Laura .... **CLC 3, 7**
  See also Jackson, Laura (Riding)

Riefenstahl, Berta Helene Amalia 1902-
  See Riefenstahl, Leni
  See also CA 108

Riefenstahl, Leni .... **CLC 16**
  See also Riefenstahl, Berta Helene Amalia

Riffe, Ernest
  See Bergman, (Ernst) Ingmar

Riggs, (Rolla) Lynn 1899-1954 .... **TCLC 56**
  See also CA 144; NNAL

Riley, James Whitcomb
  1849-1916 .... **TCLC 51**
  See also CA 118; 137; MAICYA; SATA 17

Riley, Tex
  See Creasey, John

Rilke, Rainer Maria
  1875-1926 .... **TCLC 1, 6, 19; PC 2**
  See also CA 104; 132; DLB 81; MTCW

Rimbaud, (Jean Nicolas) Arthur
  1854-1891 ..... **NCLC 4, 35; DA; DAB;
                              PC 3; WLC**

Rinehart, Mary Roberts
  1876-1958 .... **TCLC 52**
  See also CA 108

Ringmaster, The
  See Mencken, H(enry) L(ouis)

Ringwood, Gwen(dolyn Margaret) Pharis
  1910-1984 .... **CLC 48**
  See also CA 148; 112; DLB 88

Rio, Michel 19(?)- .... **CLC 43**

Ritsos, Giannes
  See Ritsos, Yannis

Ritsos, Yannis 1909-1990 ..... **CLC 6, 13, 31**
  See also CA 77-80; 133; CANR 39; MTCW

Ritter, Erika 1948(?)- .... **CLC 52**

Rivera, Jose Eustasio 1889-1928 ... **TCLC 35**
  See also HW

Rivers, Conrad Kent 1933-1968 ...... **CLC 1**
  See also BW 1; CA 85-88; DLB 41

Rivers, Elfrida
  See Bradley, Marion Zimmer

Riverside, John
  See Heinlein, Robert A(nson)

Rizal, Jose 1861-1896 .... **NCLC 27**

Roa Bastos, Augusto (Antonio)
  1917- .... **CLC 45; HLC**
  See also CA 131; DLB 113; HW

Robbe-Grillet, Alain
  1922- ...... **CLC 1, 2, 4, 6, 8, 10, 14, 43**
  See also CA 9-12R; CANR 33; DLB 83;
  MTCW

Robbins, Harold 1916- .... **CLC 5**
  See also CA 73-76; CANR 26; MTCW

Robbins, Thomas Eugene 1936-
  See Robbins, Tom
  See also CA 81-84; CANR 29; MTCW

Robbins, Tom .... **CLC 9, 32, 64**
  See also Robbins, Thomas Eugene
  See also BEST 90:3; DLBY 80

Robbins, Trina 1938- .... **CLC 21**
  See also CA 128

Roberts, Charles G(eorge) D(ouglas)
  1860-1943 .... **TCLC 8**
  See also CA 105; CLR 33; DLB 92;
  SATA-Brief 29

Roberts, Kate 1891-1985 .... **CLC 15**
  See also CA 107; 116

Roberts, Keith (John Kingston)
  1935- .... **CLC 14**
  See also CA 25-28R; CANR 46

Roberts, Kenneth (Lewis)
  1885-1957 .... **TCLC 23**
  See also CA 109; DLB 9

Roberts, Michele (B.) 1949- .... **CLC 48**
  See also CA 115

Robertson, Ellis
  See Ellison, Harlan (Jay); Silverberg, Robert

Robertson, Thomas William
  1829-1871 .... **NCLC 35**

Robinson, Edwin Arlington
  1869-1935 .... **TCLC 5; DA; PC 1**
  See also CA 104; 133; CDALB 1865-1917;
  DLB 54; MTCW

Robinson, Henry Crabb
  1775-1867 .... **NCLC 15**
  See also DLB 107

Robinson, Jill 1936- .... **CLC 10**
  See also CA 102

Robinson, Kim Stanley 1952- ...... **CLC 34**
  See also CA 126

Robinson, Lloyd
  See Silverberg, Robert

Robinson, Marilynne 1944- .... **CLC 25**
  See also CA 116

Robinson, Smokey .... **CLC 21**
  See also Robinson, William, Jr.

Robinson, William, Jr. 1940-
  See Robinson, Smokey
  See also CA 116

Robison, Mary 1949- .... **CLC 42**
  See also CA 113; 116; DLB 130

Rod, Edouard 1857-1910 .... **TCLC 52**

Roddenberry, Eugene Wesley 1921-1991
  See Roddenberry, Gene
  See also CA 110; 135; CANR 37; SATA 45;
  SATA-Obit 69

Roddenberry, Gene .... **CLC 17**
  See also Roddenberry, Eugene Wesley
  See also AAYA 5; SATA-Obit 69

Rodgers, Mary 1931- .... **CLC 12**
  See also CA 49-52; CANR 8; CLR 20;
  JRDA; MAICYA; SATA 8

Rodgers, W(illiam) R(obert)
  1909-1969 .... **CLC 7**
  See also CA 85-88; DLB 20

Rodman, Eric
  See Silverberg, Robert

Rodman, Howard 1920(?)-1985 ..... **CLC 65**
  See also CA 118

Rodman, Maia
  See Wojciechowska, Maia (Teresa)

Rodriguez, Claudio 1934- .... **CLC 10**
  See also DLB 134

Roelvaag, O(le) E(dvart)
  1876-1931 .... **TCLC 17**
  See also CA 117; DLB 9

Roethke, Theodore (Huebner)
  1908-1963 ...... **CLC 1, 3, 8, 11, 19, 46**
  See also CA 81-84; CABS 2;
  CDALB 1941-1968; DLB 5; MTCW

Rogers, Thomas Hunton 1927- ..... **CLC 57**
  See also CA 89-92

Rogers, Will(iam Penn Adair)
  1879-1935 .... **TCLC 8**
  See also CA 105; 144; DLB 11; NNAL

Rogin, Gilbert 1929- .... **CLC 18**
  See also CA 65-68; CANR 15

Rohan, Koda .... **TCLC 22**
  See also Koda Shigeyuki

Rohmer, Eric .... **CLC 16**
  See also Scherer, Jean-Marie Maurice

Rohmer, Sax .... **TCLC 28**
  See also Ward, Arthur Henry Sarsfield
  See also DLB 70

Roiphe, Anne (Richardson)
  1935- .... **CLC 3, 9**
  See also CA 89-92; CANR 45; DLBY 80

Rojas, Fernando de 1465-1541 ...... **LC 23**

**Rolfe, Frederick (William Serafino Austin
  Lewis Mary)** 1860-1913 ..... **TCLC 12**
  See also CA 107; DLB 34

Rolland, Romain 1866-1944 ...... **TCLC 23**
  See also CA 118; DLB 65

Rolvaag, O(le) E(dvart)
  See Roelvaag, O(le) E(dvart)

Romain Arnaud, Saint
  See Aragon, Louis

Romains, Jules 1885-1972 .... **CLC 7**
  See also CA 85-88; CANR 34; DLB 65;
  MTCW

Romero, Jose Ruben 1890-1952 ... **TCLC 14**
  See also CA 114; 131; HW

Ronsard, Pierre de
  1524-1585 .... **LC 6; PC 11**

Rooke, Leon 1934- .... **CLC 25, 34**
  See also CA 25-28R; CANR 23

Roper, William 1498-1578 .... **LC 10**

Roquelaure, A. N.
  See Rice, Anne

Rosa, Joao Guimaraes 1908-1967 ... **CLC 23**
  See also CA 89-92; DLB 113

Rose, Wendy 1948- .... **CLC 85; PC 13**
  See also CA 53-56; CANR 5; NNAL;
  SATA 12

Rosen, Richard (Dean) 1949- ...... **CLC 39**
  See also CA 77-80

Rosenberg, Isaac 1890-1918 ...... **TCLC 12**
  See also CA 107; DLB 20

Rosenblatt, Joe .... CLC 15
See also Rosenblatt, Joseph

Rosenblatt, Joseph 1933-
See Rosenblatt, Joe
See also CA 89-92

Rosenfeld, Samuel 1896-1963
See Tzara, Tristan
See also CA 89-92

Rosenthal, M(acha) L(ouis) 1917-... CLC 28
See also CA 1-4R; CAAS 6; CANR 4;
DLB 5; SATA 59

Ross, Barnaby
See Dannay, Frederic

Ross, Bernard L.
See Follett, Ken(neth Martin)

Ross, J. H.
See Lawrence, T(homas) E(dward)

Ross, Martin
See Martin, Violet Florence
See also DLB 135

Ross, (James) Sinclair 1908-....... CLC 13
See also CA 73-76; DLB 88

Rossetti, Christina (Georgina)
1830-1894 ..... NCLC 2, 50; DA; DAB;
PC 7; WLC
See also DLB 35; MAICYA; SATA 20

Rossetti, Dante Gabriel
1828-1882 ... NCLC 4; DA; DAB; WLC
See also CDBLB 1832-1890; DLB 35

Rossner, Judith (Perelman)
1935- .... CLC 6, 9, 29
See also AITN 2; BEST 90:3; CA 17-20R;
CANR 18; DLB 6; MTCW

Rostand, Edmond (Eugene Alexis)
1868-1918 ...... TCLC 6, 37; DA; DAB
See also CA 104; 126; MTCW

Roth, Henry 1906-........... CLC 2, 6, 11
See also CA 11-12; CANR 38; CAP 1;
DLB 28; MTCW

Roth, Joseph 1894-1939......... TCLC 33
See also DLB 85

Roth, Philip (Milton)
1933- ...... CLC 1, 2, 3, 4, 6, 9, 15, 22,
31, 47, 66, 86; DA; DAB; WLC
See also BEST 90:3; CA 1-4R; CANR 1, 22,
36; CDALB 1968-1988; DLB 2, 28;
DLBY 82; MTCW

Rothenberg, Jerome 1931-....... CLC 6, 57
See also CA 45-48; CANR 1; DLB 5

Roumain, Jacques (Jean Baptiste)
1907-1944 .... TCLC 19; BLC
See also BW 1; CA 117; 125

Rourke, Constance (Mayfield)
1885-1941 .... TCLC 12
See also CA 107; YABC 1

Rousseau, Jean-Baptiste 1671-1741 ... LC 9

Rousseau, Jean-Jacques
1712-1778 ..... LC 14; DA; DAB; WLC

Roussel, Raymond 1877-1933 ..... TCLC 20
See also CA 117

Rovit, Earl (Herbert) 1927-........ CLC 7
See also CA 5-8R; CANR 12

Rowe, Nicholas 1674-1718.......... LC 8
See also DLB 84

Rowley, Ames Dorrance
See Lovecraft, H(oward) P(hillips)

Rowson, Susanna Haswell
1762(?)-1824 .... NCLC 5
See also DLB 37

Roy, Gabrielle
1909-1983 .... CLC 10, 14; DAB
See also CA 53-56; 110; CANR 5; DLB 68;
MTCW

Rozewicz, Tadeusz 1921-........ CLC 9, 23
See also CA 108; CANR 36; MTCW

Ruark, Gibbons 1941- .... CLC 3
See also CA 33-36R; CANR 14, 31;
DLB 120

Rubens, Bernice (Ruth) 1923-... CLC 19, 31
See also CA 25-28R; CANR 33; DLB 14;
MTCW

Rudkin, (James) David 1936- ...... CLC 14
See also CA 89-92; DLB 13

Rudnik, Raphael 1933-............. CLC 7
See also CA 29-32R

Ruffian, M.
See Hasek, Jaroslav (Matej Frantisek)

Ruiz, Jose Martinez .... CLC 11
See also Martinez Ruiz, Jose

Rukeyser, Muriel
1913-1980 .... CLC 6, 10, 15, 27; PC 12
See also CA 5-8R; 93-96; CANR 26;
DLB 48; MTCW; SATA-Obit 22

Rule, Jane (Vance) 1931-.......... CLC 27
See also CA 25-28R; CAAS 18; CANR 12;
DLB 60

Rulfo, Juan 1918-1986.... CLC 8, 80; HLC
See also CA 85-88; 118; CANR 26;
DLB 113; HW; MTCW

Runeberg, Johan 1804-1877...... NCLC 41

Runyon, (Alfred) Damon
1884(?)-1946 .... TCLC 10
See also CA 107; DLB 11, 86

Rush, Norman 1933-.............. CLC 44
See also CA 121; 126

Rushdie, (Ahmed) Salman
1947- .... CLC 23, 31, 55; DAB
See also BEST 89:3; CA 108; 111;
CANR 33; MTCW

Rushforth, Peter (Scott) 1945- ..... CLC 19
See also CA 101

Ruskin, John 1819-1900......... TCLC 20
See also CA 114; 129; CDBLB 1832-1890;
DLB 55; SATA 24

Russ, Joanna 1937-.............. CLC 15
See also CA 25-28R; CANR 11, 31; DLB 8;
MTCW

Russell, George William 1867-1935
See A. E.
See also CA 104; CDBLB 1890-1914

Russell, (Henry) Ken(neth Alfred)
1927- .... CLC 16
See also CA 105

Russell, Willy 1947-.............. CLC 60

Rutherford, Mark .... TCLC 25
See also White, William Hale
See also DLB 18

Ruyslinck, Ward 1929-............ CLC 14
See also Belser, Reimond Karel Maria de

Ryan, Cornelius (John) 1920-1974 ... CLC 7
See also CA 69-72; 53-56; CANR 38

Ryan, Michael 1946- .... CLC 65
See also CA 49-52; DLBY 82

Rybakov, Anatoli (Naumovich)
1911- .... CLC 23, 53
See also CA 126; 135; SATA 79

Ryder, Jonathan
See Ludlum, Robert

Ryga, George 1932-1987 .... CLC 14
See also CA 101; 124; CANR 43; DLB 60

S. S.
See Sassoon, Siegfried (Lorraine)

Saba, Umberto 1883-1957 .... TCLC 33
See also CA 144; DLB 114

Sabatini, Rafael 1875-1950 .... TCLC 47

Sabato, Ernesto (R.)
1911- .... CLC 10, 23; HLC
See also CA 97-100; CANR 32; DLB 145;
HW; MTCW

Sacastru, Martin
See Bioy Casares, Adolfo

Sacher-Masoch, Leopold von
1836(?)-1895 .... NCLC 31

Sachs, Marilyn (Stickle) 1927- ..... CLC 35
See also AAYA 2; CA 17-20R; CANR 13,
47; CLR 2; JRDA; MAICYA; SAAS 2;
SATA 3, 68

Sachs, Nelly 1891-1970 .... CLC 14
See also CA 17-18; 25-28R; CAP 2

Sackler, Howard (Oliver)
1929-1982 .... CLC 14
See also CA 61-64; 108; CANR 30; DLB 7

Sacks, Oliver (Wolf) 1933- .... CLC 67
See also CA 53-56; CANR 28; MTCW

Sade, Donatien Alphonse Francois Comte
1740-1814 .... NCLC 47

Sadoff, Ira 1945-................. CLC 9
See also CA 53-56; CANR 5, 21; DLB 120

Saetone
See Camus, Albert

Safire, William 1929-............. CLC 10
See also CA 17-20R; CANR 31

Sagan, Carl (Edward) 1934-........ CLC 30
See also AAYA 2; CA 25-28R; CANR 11,
36; MTCW; SATA 58

Sagan, Francoise .... CLC 3, 6, 9, 17, 36
See also Quoirez, Francoise
See also DLB 83

Sahgal, Nayantara (Pandit) 1927-... CLC 41
See also CA 9-12R; CANR 11

Saint, H(arry) F. 1941- .... CLC 50
See also CA 127

St. Aubin de Teran, Lisa 1953-
See Teran, Lisa St. Aubin de
See also CA 118; 126

Sainte-Beuve, Charles Augustin
1804-1869 .... NCLC 5

Saint-Exupery, Antoine (Jean Baptiste Marie Roger) de
1900-1944 . . . . **TCLC 2, 56; WLC**
See also CA 108; 132; CLR 10; DLB 72;
MAICYA; MTCW; SATA 20

St. John, David
See Hunt, E(verette) Howard, (Jr.)

Saint-John Perse
See Leger, (Marie-Rene Auguste) Alexis
Saint-Leger

Saintsbury, George (Edward Bateman)
1845-1933 . . . . **TCLC 31**
See also DLB 57, 149

Sait Faik . . . . **TCLC 23**
See also Abasiyanik, Sait Faik

Saki . . . . **TCLC 3; SSC 12**
See also Munro, H(ector) H(ugh)

Sala, George Augustus . . . . **NCLC 46**

Salama, Hannu 1936- . . . . **CLC 18**

Salamanca, J(ack) R(ichard)
1922- . . . . **CLC 4, 15**
See also CA 25-28R

Sale, J. Kirkpatrick
See Sale, Kirkpatrick

Sale, Kirkpatrick 1937- . . . . **CLC 68**
See also CA 13-16R; CANR 10

Salinas (y Serrano), Pedro
1891(?)-1951 . . . . **TCLC 17**
See also CA 117; DLB 134

Salinger, J(erome) D(avid)
1919- . . . . . . **CLC 1, 3, 8, 12, 55, 56; DA;
DAB; SSC 2; WLC**
See also AAYA 2; CA 5-8R; CANR 39;
CDALB 1941-1968; CLR 18; DLB 2, 102;
MAICYA; MTCW; SATA 67

Salisbury, John
See Caute, David

Salter, James 1925- . . . . **CLC 7, 52, 59**
See also CA 73-76; DLB 130

Saltus, Edgar (Everton)
1855-1921 . . . . **TCLC 8**
See also CA 105

Saltykov, Mikhail Evgrafovich
1826-1889 . . . . **NCLC 16**

Samarakis, Antonis 1919- . . . . **CLC 5**
See also CA 25-28R; CAAS 16; CANR 36

Sanchez, Florencio 1875-1910 . . . . . **TCLC 37**
See also HW

Sanchez, Luis Rafael 1936- . . . . **CLC 23**
See also CA 128; DLB 145; HW

Sanchez, Sonia 1934- . . . **CLC 5; BLC; PC 9**
See also BW 2; CA 33-36R; CANR 24, 49;
CLR 18; DLB 41; DLBD 8; MAICYA;
MTCW; SATA 22

Sand, George
1804-1876 . . . . . **NCLC 2, 42; DA; DAB;
WLC**
See also DLB 119

Sandburg, Carl (August)
1878-1967 . . . . **CLC 1, 4, 10, 15, 35; DA;
DAB; PC 2; WLC**
See also CA 5-8R; 25-28R; CANR 35;
CDALB 1865-1917; DLB 17, 54;
MAICYA; MTCW; SATA 8

Sandburg, Charles
See Sandburg, Carl (August)

Sandburg, Charles A.
See Sandburg, Carl (August)

Sanders, (James) Ed(ward) 1939- . . . **CLC 53**
See also CA 13-16R; CAAS 21; CANR 13,
44; DLB 16

Sanders, Lawrence 1920- . . . . **CLC 41**
See also BEST 89:4; CA 81-84; CANR 33;
MTCW

Sanders, Noah
See Blount, Roy (Alton), Jr.

Sanders, Winston P.
See Anderson, Poul (William)

Sandoz, Mari(e Susette)
1896-1966 . . . . **CLC 28**
See also CA 1-4R; 25-28R; CANR 17;
DLB 9; MTCW; SATA 5

Saner, Reg(inald Anthony) 1931- . . . . **CLC 9**
See also CA 65-68

Sannazaro, Jacopo 1456(?)-1530 . . . . . . **LC 8**

Sansom, William 1912-1976 . . . . **CLC 2, 6**
See also CA 5-8R; 65-68; CANR 42;
DLB 139; MTCW

Santayana, George 1863-1952 . . . . . **TCLC 40**
See also CA 115; DLB 54, 71

Santiago, Danny . . . . **CLC 33**
See also James, Daniel (Lewis); James,
Daniel (Lewis)
See also DLB 122

Santmyer, Helen Hoover
1895-1986 . . . . **CLC 33**
See also CA 1-4R; 118; CANR 15, 33;
DLBY 84; MTCW

Santos, Bienvenido N(uqui) 1911- . . . **CLC 22**
See also CA 101; CANR 19, 46

Sapper . . . . **TCLC 44**
See also McNeile, Herman Cyril

Sappho fl. 6th cent. B.C.- . . . . . **CMLC 3; PC 5**

Sarduy, Severo 1937-1993 . . . . **CLC 6**
See also CA 89-92; 142; DLB 113; HW

Sargeson, Frank 1903-1982 . . . . **CLC 31**
See also CA 25-28R; 106; CANR 38

Sarmiento, Felix Ruben Garcia
See Dario, Ruben

Saroyan, William
1908-1981 . . . . . **CLC 1, 8, 10, 29, 34, 56;
DA; DAB; WLC**
See also CA 5-8R; 103; CANR 30; DLB 7,
9, 86; DLBY 81; MTCW; SATA 23;
SATA-Obit 24

Sarraute, Nathalie
1900- . . . . **CLC 1, 2, 4, 8, 10, 31, 80**
See also CA 9-12R; CANR 23; DLB 83;
MTCW

Sarton, (Eleanor) May
1912- . . . . **CLC 4, 14, 49**
See also CA 1-4R; CANR 1, 34; DLB 48;
DLBY 81; MTCW; SATA 36

Sartre, Jean-Paul
1905-1980 . . . . **CLC 1, 4, 7, 9, 13, 18, 24,
44, 50, 52; DA; DAB; DC 3; WLC**
See also CA 9-12R; 97-100; CANR 21;
DLB 72; MTCW

Sassoon, Siegfried (Lorraine)
1886-1967 . . . . **CLC 36; DAB; PC 12**
See also CA 104; 25-28R; CANR 36;
DLB 20; MTCW

Satterfield, Charles
See Pohl, Frederik

Saul, John (W. III) 1942- . . . . **CLC 46**
See also AAYA 10; BEST 90:4; CA 81-84;
CANR 16, 40

Saunders, Caleb
See Heinlein, Robert A(nson)

Saura (Atares), Carlos 1932- . . . . **CLC 20**
See also CA 114; 131; HW

Sauser-Hall, Frederic 1887-1961 . . . . **CLC 18**
See also Cendrars, Blaise
See also CA 102; 93-96; CANR 36; MTCW

Saussure, Ferdinand de
1857-1913 . . . . **TCLC 49**

Savage, Catharine
See Brosman, Catharine Savage

Savage, Thomas 1915- . . . . **CLC 40**
See also CA 126; 132; CAAS 15

Savan, Glenn 19(?)- . . . . **CLC 50**

Sayers, Dorothy L(eigh)
1893-1957 . . . . **TCLC 2, 15**
See also CA 104; 119; CDBLB 1914-1945;
DLB 10, 36, 77, 100; MTCW

Sayers, Valerie 1952- . . . . **CLC 50**
See also CA 134

Sayles, John (Thomas)
1950- . . . . **CLC 7, 10, 14**
See also CA 57-60; CANR 41; DLB 44

Scammell, Michael . . . . **CLC 34**

Scannell, Vernon 1922- . . . . **CLC 49**
See also CA 5-8R; CANR 8, 24; DLB 27;
SATA 59

Scarlett, Susan
See Streatfeild, (Mary) Noel

Schaeffer, Susan Fromberg
1941- . . . . **CLC 6, 11, 22**
See also CA 49-52; CANR 18; DLB 28;
MTCW; SATA 22

Schary, Jill
See Robinson, Jill

Schell, Jonathan 1943- . . . . **CLC 35**
See also CA 73-76; CANR 12

Schelling, Friedrich Wilhelm Joseph von
1775-1854 . . . . **NCLC 30**
See also DLB 90

Schendel, Arthur van 1874-1946 . . . **TCLC 56**

Scherer, Jean-Marie Maurice 1920-
See Rohmer, Eric
See also CA 110

Schevill, James (Erwin) 1920- . . . . **CLC 7**
See also CA 5-8R; CAAS 12

Schiller, Friedrich 1759-1805 . . . . **NCLC 39**
See also DLB 94

Schisgal, Murray (Joseph) 1926- . . . . . **CLC 6**
See also CA 21-24R; CANR 48

Schlee, Ann 1934- . . . . **CLC 35**
See also CA 101; CANR 29; SATA 44;
SATA-Brief 36

Schlegel, August Wilhelm von
1767-1845 .... **NCLC 15**
See also DLB 94

Schlegel, Friedrich 1772-1829 .... **NCLC 45**
See also DLB 90

Schlegel, Johann Elias (von)
1719(?)-1749 .... **LC 5**

Schlesinger, Arthur M(eier), Jr.
1917- .... **CLC 84**
See also AITN 1; CA 1-4R; CANR 1, 28;
DLB 17; MTCW; SATA 61

Schmidt, Arno (Otto) 1914-1979 .... **CLC 56**
See also CA 128; 109; DLB 69

Schmitz, Aron Hector 1861-1928
See Svevo, Italo
See also CA 104; 122; MTCW

Schnackenberg, Gjertrud 1953- ..... **CLC 40**
See also CA 116; DLB 120

Schneider, Leonard Alfred 1925-1966
See Bruce, Lenny
See also CA 89-92

Schnitzler, Arthur
1862-1931 .... **TCLC 4; SSC 15**
See also CA 104; DLB 81, 118

Schopenhauer, Arthur
1788-1860 .... **NCLC 51**
See also DLB 90

Schor, Sandra (M.) 1932(?)-1990 ... **CLC 65**
See also CA 132

Schorer, Mark 1908-1977 .... **CLC 9**
See also CA 5-8R; 73-76; CANR 7;
DLB 103

Schrader, Paul (Joseph) 1946- ...... **CLC 26**
See also CA 37-40R; CANR 41; DLB 44

Schreiner, Olive (Emilie Albertina)
1855-1920 .... **TCLC 9**
See also CA 105; DLB 18

Schulberg, Budd (Wilson)
1914- .... **CLC 7, 48**
See also CA 25-28R; CANR 19; DLB 6, 26,
28; DLBY 81

Schulz, Bruno
1892-1942 .... **TCLC 5, 51; SSC 13**
See also CA 115; 123

Schulz, Charles M(onroe) 1922- .... **CLC 12**
See also CA 9-12R; CANR 6; SATA 10

Schumacher, E(rnst) F(riedrich)
1911-1977 .... **CLC 80**
See also CA 81-84; 73-76; CANR 34

Schuyler, James Marcus
1923-1991 .... **CLC 5, 23**
See also CA 101; 134; DLB 5

Schwartz, Delmore (David)
1913-1966 ... **CLC 2, 4, 10, 45, 87; PC 8**
See also CA 17-18; 25-28R; CANR 35;
CAP 2; DLB 28, 48; MTCW

Schwartz, Ernst
See Ozu, Yasujiro

Schwartz, John Burnham 1965- .... **CLC 59**
See also CA 132

Schwartz, Lynne Sharon 1939- ..... **CLC 31**
See also CA 103; CANR 44

Schwartz, Muriel A.
See Eliot, T(homas) S(tearns)

Schwarz-Bart, Andre 1928- .... **CLC 2, 4**
See also CA 89-92

Schwarz-Bart, Simone 1938- .... **CLC 7**
See also BW 2; CA 97-100

Schwob, (Mayer Andre) Marcel
1867-1905 .... **TCLC 20**
See also CA 117; DLB 123

Sciascia, Leonardo
1921-1989 .... **CLC 8, 9, 41**
See also CA 85-88; 130; CANR 35; MTCW

Scoppettone, Sandra 1936- .... **CLC 26**
See also AAYA 11; CA 5-8R; CANR 41;
SATA 9

Scorsese, Martin 1942- .... **CLC 20, 89**
See also CA 110; 114; CANR 46

Scotland, Jay
See Jakes, John (William)

Scott, Duncan Campbell
1862-1947 .... **TCLC 6**
See also CA 104; DLB 92

Scott, Evelyn 1893-1963 .... **CLC 43**
See also CA 104; 112; DLB 9, 48

Scott, F(rancis) R(eginald)
1899-1985 .... **CLC 22**
See also CA 101; 114; DLB 88

Scott, Frank
See Scott, F(rancis) R(eginald)

Scott, Joanna 1960- .... **CLC 50**
See also CA 126

Scott, Paul (Mark) 1920-1978 .... **CLC 9, 60**
See also CA 81-84; 77-80; CANR 33;
DLB 14; MTCW

Scott, Walter
1771-1832 .... **NCLC 15; DA; DAB;**
                                PC 13; WLC
See also CDBLB 1789-1832; DLB 93, 107,
116, 144; YABC 2

Scribe, (Augustin) Eugene
1791-1861 .... **NCLC 16; DC 5**

Scrum, R.
See Crumb, R(obert)

Scudery, Madeleine de 1607-1701 ..... **LC 2**

Scum
See Crumb, R(obert)

Scumbag, Little Bobby
See Crumb, R(obert)

Seabrook, John
See Hubbard, L(afayette) Ron(ald)

Sealy, I. Allan 1951- .... **CLC 55**

Search, Alexander
See Pessoa, Fernando (Antonio Nogueira)

Sebastian, Lee
See Silverberg, Robert

Sebastian Owl
See Thompson, Hunter S(tockton)

Sebestyen, Ouida 1924- .... **CLC 30**
See also AAYA 8; CA 107; CANR 40;
CLR 17; JRDA; MAICYA; SAAS 10;
SATA 39

Secundus, H. Scriblerus
See Fielding, Henry

Sedges, John
See Buck, Pearl S(ydenstricker)

Sedgwick, Catharine Maria
1789-1867 .... **NCLC 19**
See also DLB 1, 74

Seelye, John 1931- .... **CLC 7**

Seferiades, Giorgos Stylianou 1900-1971
See Seferis, George
See also CA 5-8R; 33-36R; CANR 5, 36;
MTCW

Seferis, George .... **CLC 5, 11**
See also Seferiades, Giorgos Stylianou

Segal, Erich (Wolf) 1937- .... **CLC 3, 10**
See also BEST 89:1; CA 25-28R; CANR 20,
36; DLBY 86; MTCW

Seger, Bob 1945- .... **CLC 35**

Seghers, Anna .... **CLC 7**
See also Radvanyi, Netty
See also DLB 69

Seidel, Frederick (Lewis) 1936- ..... **CLC 18**
See also CA 13-16R; CANR 8; DLBY 84

Seifert, Jaroslav 1901-1986 ..... **CLC 34, 44**
See also CA 127; MTCW

Sei Shonagon c. 966-1017(?) ...... **CMLC 6**

Selby, Hubert, Jr.
1928- .... **CLC 1, 2, 4, 8; SSC 20**
See also CA 13-16R; CANR 33; DLB 2

Selzer, Richard 1928- .... **CLC 74**
See also CA 65-68; CANR 14

Sembene, Ousmane
See Ousmane, Sembene

Senancour, Etienne Pivert de
1770-1846 .... **NCLC 16**
See also DLB 119

Sender, Ramon (Jose)
1902-1982 .... **CLC 8; HLC**
See also CA 5-8R; 105; CANR 8; HW;
MTCW

Seneca, Lucius Annaeus
4B.C.-65. .... **CMLC 6; DC 5**

Senghor, Leopold Sedar
1906- .... **CLC 54; BLC**
See also BW 2; CA 116; 125; CANR 47;
MTCW

Serling, (Edward) Rod(man)
1924-1975 .... **CLC 30**
See also AAYA 14; AITN 1; CA 65-68;
57-60; DLB 26

Serna, Ramon Gomez de la
See Gomez de la Serna, Ramon

Serpieres
See Guillevic, (Eugene)

Service, Robert
See Service, Robert W(illiam)
See also DAB; DLB 92

Service, Robert W(illiam)
1874(?)-1958 ...... **TCLC 15; DA; WLC**
See also Service, Robert
See also CA 115; 140; SATA 20

Seth, Vikram 1952- .... **CLC 43**
See also CA 121; 127; DLB 120

Seton, Cynthia Propper
1926-1982 .... **CLC 27**
See also CA 5-8R; 108; CANR 7

Seton, Ernest (Evan) Thompson
1860-1946 . . . . TCLC 31
See also CA 109; DLB 92; JRDA; SATA 18

Seton-Thompson, Ernest
See Seton, Ernest (Evan) Thompson

Settle, Mary Lee 1918- . . . . CLC 19, 61
See also CA 89-92; CAAS 1; CANR 44;
DLB 6

Seuphor, Michel
See Arp, Jean

**Sevigne, Marie (de Rabutin-Chantal) Marquise
de** 1626-1696 . . . . LC 11

Sexton, Anne (Harvey)
1928-1974 . . . . CLC 2, 4, 6, 8, 10, 15, 53;
DA; DAB; PC 2; WLC
See also CA 1-4R; 53-56; CABS 2;
CANR 3, 36; CDALB 1941-1968; DLB 5;
MTCW; SATA 10

Shaara, Michael (Joseph, Jr.)
1929-1988 . . . . CLC 15
See also AITN 1; CA 102; 125; DLBY 83

Shackleton, C. C.
See Aldiss, Brian W(ilson)

Shacochis, Bob . . . . CLC 39
See also Shacochis, Robert G.

Shacochis, Robert G. 1951-
See Shacochis, Bob
See also CA 119; 124

Shaffer, Anthony (Joshua) 1926- . . . . CLC 19
See also CA 110; 116; DLB 13

Shaffer, Peter (Levin)
1926- . . . . . . CLC 5, 14, 18, 37, 60; DAB
See also CA 25-28R; CANR 25, 47;
CDBLB 1960 to Present; DLB 13;
MTCW

Shakey, Bernard
See Young, Neil

Shalamov, Varlam (Tikhonovich)
1907(?)-1982 . . . . CLC 18
See also CA 129; 105

Shamlu, Ahmad 1925- . . . . CLC 10

Shammas, Anton 1951- . . . . CLC 55

Shange, Ntozake
1948- . . . . CLC 8, 25, 38, 74; BLC; DC 3
See also AAYA 9; BW 2; CA 85-88;
CABS 3; CANR 27, 48; DLB 38; MTCW

Shanley, John Patrick 1950- . . . . CLC 75
See also CA 128; 133

Shapcott, Thomas W(illiam) 1935- . . CLC 38
See also CA 69-72; CANR 49

Shapiro, Jane . . . . CLC 76

Shapiro, Karl (Jay) 1913- . . CLC 4, 8, 15, 53
See also CA 1-4R; CAAS 6; CANR 1, 36;
DLB 48; MTCW

Sharp, William 1855-1905 . . . . TCLC 39

Sharpe, Thomas Ridley 1928-
See Sharpe, Tom
See also CA 114; 122

Sharpe, Tom . . . . CLC 36
See also Sharpe, Thomas Ridley
See also DLB 14

Shaw, Bernard . . . . TCLC 45
See also Shaw, George Bernard
See also BW 1

Shaw, G. Bernard
See Shaw, George Bernard

Shaw, George Bernard
1856-1950 . . . TCLC 3, 9, 21; DA; DAB;
WLC
See also Shaw, Bernard
See also CA 104; 128; CDBLB 1914-1945;
DLB 10, 57; MTCW

Shaw, Henry Wheeler
1818-1885 . . . . NCLC 15
See also DLB 11

Shaw, Irwin 1913-1984 . . . . CLC 7, 23, 34
See also AITN 1; CA 13-16R; 112;
CANR 21; CDALB 1941-1968; DLB 6,
102; DLBY 84; MTCW

Shaw, Robert 1927-1978 . . . . CLC 5
See also AITN 1; CA 1-4R; 81-84;
CANR 4; DLB 13, 14

Shaw, T. E.
See Lawrence, T(homas) E(dward)

Shawn, Wallace 1943- . . . . CLC 41
See also CA 112

Shea, Lisa 1953- . . . . CLC 86
See also CA 147

Sheed, Wilfrid (John Joseph)
1930- . . . . CLC 2, 4, 10, 53
See also CA 65-68; CANR 30; DLB 6;
MTCW

Sheldon, Alice Hastings Bradley
1915(?)-1987
See Tiptree, James, Jr.
See also CA 108; 122; CANR 34; MTCW

Sheldon, John
See Bloch, Robert (Albert)

Shelley, Mary Wollstonecraft (Godwin)
1797-1851 . . NCLC 14; DA; DAB; WLC
See also CDBLB 1789-1832; DLB 110, 116;
SATA 29

Shelley, Percy Bysshe
1792-1822 . . NCLC 18; DA; DAB; WLC
See also CDBLB 1789-1832; DLB 96, 110

Shepard, Jim 1956- . . . . CLC 36
See also CA 137

Shepard, Lucius 1947- . . . . CLC 34
See also CA 128; 141

Shepard, Sam
1943- . . . . CLC 4, 6, 17, 34, 41, 44; DC 5
See also AAYA 1; CA 69-72; CABS 3;
CANR 22; DLB 7; MTCW

Shepherd, Michael
See Ludlum, Robert

Sherburne, Zoa (Morin) 1912- . . . . . . CLC 30
See also AAYA 13; CA 1-4R; CANR 3, 37;
MAICYA; SAAS 18; SATA 3

Sheridan, Frances 1724-1766 . . . . LC 7
See also DLB 39, 84

Sheridan, Richard Brinsley
1751-1816 . . . . NCLC 5; DA; DAB;
DC 1; WLC
See also CDBLB 1660-1789; DLB 89

Sherman, Jonathan Marc . . . . CLC 55

Sherman, Martin 1941(?)- . . . . CLC 19
See also CA 116; 123

Sherwin, Judith Johnson 1936- . . . CLC 7, 15
See also CA 25-28R; CANR 34

Sherwood, Frances 1940- . . . . CLC 81

Sherwood, Robert E(mmet)
1896-1955 . . . . TCLC 3
See also CA 104; DLB 7, 26

Shestov, Lev 1866-1938 . . . . TCLC 56

Shiel, M(atthew) P(hipps)
1865-1947 . . . . TCLC 8
See also CA 106; DLB 153

Shiga, Naoya 1883-1971 . . . . CLC 33
See also CA 101; 33-36R

Shih, Su 1036-1101 . . . . CMLC 15

Shilts, Randy 1951-1994 . . . . CLC 85
See also CA 115; 127; 144; CANR 45

Shimazaki Haruki 1872-1943
See Shimazaki Toson
See also CA 105; 134

Shimazaki Toson . . . . TCLC 5
See also Shimazaki Haruki

Sholokhov, Mikhail (Aleksandrovich)
1905-1984 . . . . CLC 7, 15
See also CA 101; 112; MTCW;
SATA-Obit 36

Shone, Patric
See Hanley, James

Shreve, Susan Richards 1939- . . . . . . CLC 23
See also CA 49-52; CAAS 5; CANR 5, 38;
MAICYA; SATA 46; SATA-Brief 41

Shue, Larry 1946-1985 . . . . CLC 52
See also CA 145; 117

Shu-Jen, Chou 1881-1936
See Lu Hsun
See also CA 104

Shulman, Alix Kates 1932- . . . . CLC 2, 10
See also CA 29-32R; CANR 43; SATA 7

Shuster, Joe 1914- . . . . CLC 21

Shute, Nevil . . . . CLC 30
See also Norway, Nevil Shute

Shuttle, Penelope (Diane) 1947- . . . . . CLC 7
See also CA 93-96; CANR 39; DLB 14, 40

Sidney, Mary 1561-1621 . . . . LC 19

Sidney, Sir Philip
1554-1586 . . . . LC 19; DA; DAB
See also CDBLB Before 1660

Siegel, Jerome 1914- . . . . CLC 21
See also CA 116

Siegel, Jerry
See Siegel, Jerome

Sienkiewicz, Henryk (Adam Alexander Pius)
1846-1916 . . . . TCLC 3
See also CA 104; 134

Sierra, Gregorio Martinez
See Martinez Sierra, Gregorio

Sierra, Maria (de la O'LeJarraga) Martinez
See Martinez Sierra, Maria (de la
O'LeJarraga)

Sigal, Clancy 1926- . . . . CLC 7
See also CA 1-4R

Sigourney, Lydia Howard (Huntley)
1791-1865 . . . . NCLC 21
See also DLB 1, 42, 73

Siguenza y Gongora, Carlos de
1645-1700 . . . . LC 8

Sigurjonsson, Johann 1880-1919 . . . TCLC 27

Sikelianos, Angelos 1884-1951 .... **TCLC 39**

Silkin, Jon 1930- .... **CLC 2, 6, 43**
See also CA 5-8R; CAAS 5; DLB 27

Silko, Leslie (Marmon)
1948- .... **CLC 23, 74; DA**
See also AAYA 14; CA 115; 122;
CANR 45; DLB 143; NNAL

Sillanpaa, Frans Eemil 1888-1964... **CLC 19**
See also CA 129; 93-96; MTCW

Sillitoe, Alan
1928- .... **CLC 1, 3, 6, 10, 19, 57**
See also AITN 1; CA 9-12R; CAAS 2;
CANR 8, 26; CDBLB 1960 to Present;
DLB 14, 139; MTCW; SATA 61

Silone, Ignazio 1900-1978 .... **CLC 4**
See also CA 25-28; 81-84; CANR 34;
CAP 2; MTCW

Silver, Joan Micklin 1935- .... **CLC 20**
See also CA 114; 121

Silver, Nicholas
See Faust, Frederick (Schiller)

Silverberg, Robert 1935- .... **CLC 7**
See also CA 1-4R; CAAS 3; CANR 1, 20,
36; DLB 8; MAICYA; MTCW; SATA 13

Silverstein, Alvin 1933- .... **CLC 17**
See also CA 49-52; CANR 2; CLR 25;
JRDA; MAICYA; SATA 8, 69

Silverstein, Virginia B(arbara Opshelor)
1937- .... **CLC 17**
See also CA 49-52; CANR 2; CLR 25;
JRDA; MAICYA; SATA 8, 69

Sim, Georges
See Simenon, Georges (Jacques Christian)

Simak, Clifford D(onald)
1904-1988 .... **CLC 1, 55**
See also CA 1-4R; 125; CANR 1, 35;
DLB 8; MTCW; SATA-Obit 56

Simenon, Georges (Jacques Christian)
1903-1989 ...... **CLC 1, 2, 3, 8, 18, 47**
See also CA 85-88; 129; CANR 35;
DLB 72; DLBY 89; MTCW

Simic, Charles 1938-... **CLC 6, 9, 22, 49, 68**
See also CA 29-32R; CAAS 4; CANR 12,
33; DLB 105

Simmons, Charles (Paul) 1924- ..... **CLC 57**
See also CA 89-92

Simmons, Dan 1948- .... **CLC 44**
See also CA 138

Simmons, James (Stewart Alexander)
1933- .... **CLC 43**
See also CA 105; CAAS 21; DLB 40

Simms, William Gilmore
1806-1870 .... **NCLC 3**
See also DLB 3, 30, 59, 73

Simon, Carly 1945- .... **CLC 26**
See also CA 105

Simon, Claude 1913-...... **CLC 4, 9, 15, 39**
See also CA 89-92; CANR 33; DLB 83;
MTCW

Simon, (Marvin) Neil
1927- .... **CLC 6, 11, 31, 39, 70**
See also AITN 1; CA 21-24R; CANR 26;
DLB 7; MTCW

Simon, Paul 1942(?)- .... **CLC 17**
See also CA 116

Simonon, Paul 1956(?)- .... **CLC 30**

Simpson, Harriette
See Arnow, Harriette (Louisa) Simpson

Simpson, Louis (Aston Marantz)
1923- .... **CLC 4, 7, 9, 32**
See also CA 1-4R; CAAS 4; CANR 1;
DLB 5; MTCW

Simpson, Mona (Elizabeth) 1957-... **CLC 44**
See also CA 122; 135

Simpson, N(orman) F(rederick)
1919- .... **CLC 29**
See also CA 13-16R; DLB 13

Sinclair, Andrew (Annandale)
1935- .... **CLC 2, 14**
See also CA 9-12R; CAAS 5; CANR 14, 38;
DLB 14; MTCW

Sinclair, Emil
See Hesse, Hermann

Sinclair, Iain 1943-.............. **CLC 76**
See also CA 132

Sinclair, Iain MacGregor
See Sinclair, Iain

Sinclair, Mary Amelia St. Clair 1865(?)-1946
See Sinclair, May
See also CA 104

Sinclair, May................. **TCLC 3, 11**
See also Sinclair, Mary Amelia St. Clair
See also DLB 36, 135

Sinclair, Upton (Beall)
1878-1968 ...... **CLC 1, 11, 15, 63; DA;
DAB; WLC**
See also CA 5-8R; 25-28R; CANR 7;
CDALB 1929-1941; DLB 9; MTCW;
SATA 9

Singer, Isaac
See Singer, Isaac Bashevis

Singer, Isaac Bashevis
1904-1991 .... **CLC 1, 3, 6, 9, 11, 15, 23,
38, 69; DA; DAB; SSC 3; WLC**
See also AITN 1, 2; CA 1-4R; 134;
CANR 1, 39; CDALB 1941-1968; CLR 1;
DLB 6, 28, 52; DLBY 91; JRDA;
MAICYA; MTCW; SATA 3, 27;
SATA-Obit 68

Singer, Israel Joshua 1893-1944 ... **TCLC 33**

Singh, Khushwant 1915-........... **CLC 11**
See also CA 9-12R; CAAS 9; CANR 6

Sinjohn, John
See Galsworthy, John

Sinyavsky, Andrei (Donatevich)
1925- .... **CLC 8**
See also CA 85-88

Sirin, V.
See Nabokov, Vladimir (Vladimirovich)

Sissman, L(ouis) E(dward)
1928-1976 .... **CLC 9, 18**
See also CA 21-24R; 65-68; CANR 13;
DLB 5

Sisson, C(harles) H(ubert) 1914-..... **CLC 8**
See also CA 1-4R; CAAS 3; CANR 3, 48;
DLB 27

Sitwell, Dame Edith
1887-1964 .... **CLC 2, 9, 67; PC 3**
See also CA 9-12R; CANR 35;
CDBLB 1945-1960; DLB 20; MTCW

Sjoewall, Maj 1935-.............. **CLC 7**
See also CA 65-68

Sjowall, Maj
See Sjoewall, Maj

Skelton, Robin 1925-............. **CLC 13**
See also AITN 2; CA 5-8R; CAAS 5;
CANR 28; DLB 27, 53

Skolimowski, Jerzy 1938-........ **CLC 20**
See also CA 128

Skram, Amalie (Bertha)
1847-1905 .... **TCLC 25**

Skvorecky, Josef (Vaclav)
1924- .... **CLC 15, 39, 69**
See also CA 61-64; CAAS 1; CANR 10, 34;
MTCW

Slade, Bernard................ **CLC 11, 46**
See also Newbound, Bernard Slade
See also CAAS 9; DLB 53

Slaughter, Carolyn 1946-......... **CLC 56**
See also CA 85-88

Slaughter, Frank G(ill) 1908- ...... **CLC 29**
See also AITN 2; CA 5-8R; CANR 5

Slavitt, David R(ytman) 1935-.... **CLC 5, 14**
See also CA 21-24R; CAAS 3; CANR 41;
DLB 5, 6

Slesinger, Tess 1905-1945 .... **TCLC 10**
See also CA 107; DLB 102

Slessor, Kenneth 1901-1971........ **CLC 14**
See also CA 102; 89-92

Slowacki, Juliusz 1809-1849 ..... **NCLC 15**

Smart, Christopher
1722-1771 .... **LC 3; PC 13**
See also DLB 109

Smart, Elizabeth 1913-1986........ **CLC 54**
See also CA 81-84; 118; DLB 88

Smiley, Jane (Graves) 1949- .... **CLC 53, 76**
See also CA 104; CANR 30

Smith, A(rthur) J(ames) M(arshall)
1902-1980 .... **CLC 15**
See also CA 1-4R; 102; CANR 4; DLB 88

Smith, Anna Deavere 1950-........ **CLC 86**
See also CA 133

Smith, Betty (Wehner) 1896-1972... **CLC 19**
See also CA 5-8R; 33-36R; DLBY 82;
SATA 6

Smith, Charlotte (Turner)
1749-1806 .... **NCLC 23**
See also DLB 39, 109

Smith, Clark Ashton 1893-1961 .... **CLC 43**
See also CA 143

Smith, Dave................ **CLC 22, 42**
See also Smith, David (Jeddie)
See also CAAS 7; DLB 5

Smith, David (Jeddie) 1942-
See Smith, Dave
See also CA 49-52; CANR 1

Smith, Florence Margaret 1902-1971
See Smith, Stevie
See also CA 17-18; 29-32R; CANR 35;
CAP 2; MTCW

Smith, Iain Crichton 1928- .... **CLC 64**
See also CA 21-24R; DLB 40, 139

Smith, John 1580(?)-1631 .... **LC 9**

Smith, Johnston
See Crane, Stephen (Townley)

Smith, Lee 1944-.............. CLC **25, 73**
See also CA 114; 119; CANR 46; DLB 143;
DLBY 83

Smith, Martin
See Smith, Martin Cruz

Smith, Martin Cruz 1942-......... CLC **25**
See also BEST 89:4; CA 85-88; CANR 6,
23, 43; NNAL

Smith, Mary-Ann Tirone 1944-..... CLC **39**
See also CA 118; 136

Smith, Patti 1946- .... CLC **12**
See also CA 93-96

Smith, Pauline (Urmson)
1882-1959 .... TCLC **25**

Smith, Rosamond
See Oates, Joyce Carol

Smith, Sheila Kaye
See Kaye-Smith, Sheila

Smith, Stevie .... CLC **3, 8, 25, 44; PC 12**
See also Smith, Florence Margaret
See also DLB 20

Smith, Wilbur (Addison) 1933-..... CLC **33**
See also CA 13-16R; CANR 7, 46; MTCW

Smith, William Jay 1918- .... CLC **6**
See also CA 5-8R; CANR 44; DLB 5;
MAICYA; SATA 2, 68

Smith, Woodrow Wilson
See Kuttner, Henry

Smolenskin, Peretz 1842-1885.... NCLC **30**

Smollett, Tobias (George) 1721-1771 .. LC **2**
See also CDBLB 1660-1789; DLB 39, 104

Snodgrass, W(illiam) D(e Witt)
1926- .... CLC **2, 6, 10, 18, 68**
See also CA 1-4R; CANR 6, 36; DLB 5;
MTCW

Snow, C(harles) P(ercy)
1905-1980 .... CLC **1, 4, 6, 9, 13, 19**
See also CA 5-8R; 101; CANR 28;
CDBLB 1945-1960; DLB 15, 77; MTCW

Snow, Frances Compton
See Adams, Henry (Brooks)

Snyder, Gary (Sherman)
1930- .... CLC **1, 2, 5, 9, 32**
See also CA 17-20R; CANR 30; DLB 5, 16

Snyder, Zilpha Keatley 1927- ...... CLC **17**
See also CA 9-12R; CANR 38; CLR 31;
JRDA; MAICYA; SAAS 2; SATA 1, 28,
75

Soares, Bernardo
See Pessoa, Fernando (Antonio Nogueira)

Sobh, A.
See Shamlu, Ahmad

Sobol, Joshua.................... CLC **60**

Soderberg, Hjalmar 1869-1941 .... TCLC **39**

Sodergran, Edith (Irene)
See Soedergran, Edith (Irene)

Soedergran, Edith (Irene)
1892-1923 .... TCLC **31**

Softly, Edgar
See Lovecraft, H(oward) P(hillips)

Softly, Edward
See Lovecraft, H(oward) P(hillips)

Sokolov, Raymond 1941-.......... CLC **7**
See also CA 85-88

Solo, Jay
See Ellison, Harlan (Jay)

Sologub, Fyodor .... TCLC **9**
See also Teternikov, Fyodor Kuzmich

Solomons, Ikey Esquir
See Thackeray, William Makepeace

Solomos, Dionysios 1798-1857 ... NCLC **15**

Solwoska, Mara
See French, Marilyn

Solzhenitsyn, Aleksandr I(sayevich)
1918-...... CLC **1, 2, 4, 7, 9, 10, 18, 26,
34, 78; DA; DAB; WLC**
See also AITN 1; CA 69-72; CANR 40;
MTCW

Somers, Jane
See Lessing, Doris (May)

Somerville, Edith 1858-1949 ...... TCLC **51**
See also DLB 135

Somerville & Ross
See Martin, Violet Florence; Somerville,
Edith

Sommer, Scott 1951- .... CLC **25**
See also CA 106

Sondheim, Stephen (Joshua)
1930- .... CLC **30, 39**
See also AAYA 11; CA 103; CANR 47

Sontag, Susan 1933-... CLC **1, 2, 10, 13, 31**
See also CA 17-20R; CANR 25; DLB 2, 67;
MTCW

Sophocles
496(?)B.C.-406(?)B.C..... CMLC **2; DA;
DAB; DC 1**

Sordello 1189-1269............. CMLC **15**

Sorel, Julia
See Drexler, Rosalyn

Sorrentino, Gilbert
1929-......... CLC **3, 7, 14, 22, 40**
See also CA 77-80; CANR 14, 33; DLB 5;
DLBY 80

Soto, Gary 1952-........ CLC **32, 80; HLC**
See also AAYA 10; CA 119; 125; CLR 38;
DLB 82; HW; JRDA; SATA 80

Soupault, Philippe 1897-1990 ...... CLC **68**
See also CA 116; 147; 131

Souster, (Holmes) Raymond
1921- .... CLC **5, 14**
See also CA 13-16R; CAAS 14; CANR 13,
29; DLB 88; SATA 63

Southern, Terry 1926- .... CLC **7**
See also CA 1-4R; CANR 1; DLB 2

Southey, Robert 1774-1843 .... NCLC **8**
See also DLB 93, 107, 142; SATA 54

Southworth, Emma Dorothy Eliza Nevitte
1819-1899 .... NCLC **26**

Souza, Ernest
See Scott, Evelyn

Soyinka, Wole
1934- .... CLC **3, 5, 14, 36, 44; BLC;
DA; DAB; DC 2; WLC**
See also BW 2; CA 13-16R; CANR 27, 39;
DLB 125; MTCW

Spackman, W(illiam) M(ode)
1905-1990 .... CLC **46**
See also CA 81-84; 132

Spacks, Barry 1931-.............. CLC **14**
See also CA 29-32R; CANR 33; DLB 105

Spanidou, Irini 1946- .... CLC **44**

Spark, Muriel (Sarah)
1918- .... CLC **2, 3, 5, 8, 13, 18, 40;
DAB; SSC 10**
See also CA 5-8R; CANR 12, 36;
CDBLB 1945-1960; DLB 15, 139; MTCW

Spaulding, Douglas
See Bradbury, Ray (Douglas)

Spaulding, Leonard
See Bradbury, Ray (Douglas)

Spence, J. A. D.
See Eliot, T(homas) S(tearns)

Spencer, Elizabeth 1921-.......... CLC **22**
See also CA 13-16R; CANR 32; DLB 6;
MTCW; SATA 14

Spencer, Leonard G.
See Silverberg, Robert

Spencer, Scott 1945-.............. CLC **30**
See also CA 113; DLBY 86

Spender, Stephen (Harold)
1909-.............. CLC **1, 2, 5, 10, 41**
See also CA 9-12R; CANR 31;
CDBLB 1945-1960; DLB 20; MTCW

Spengler, Oswald (Arnold Gottfried)
1880-1936 .... TCLC **25**
See also CA 118

Spenser, Edmund
1552(?)-1599 .... LC **5; DA; DAB; PC 8;
WLC**
See also CDBLB Before 1660

Spicer, Jack 1925-1965 ...... CLC **8, 18, 72**
See also CA 85-88; DLB 5, 16

Spiegelman, Art 1948-............. CLC **76**
See also AAYA 10; CA 125; CANR 41

Spielberg, Peter 1929-............. CLC **6**
See also CA 5-8R; CANR 4, 48; DLBY 81

Spielberg, Steven 1947-........... CLC **20**
See also AAYA 8; CA 77-80; CANR 32;
SATA 32

Spillane, Frank Morrison 1918-
See Spillane, Mickey
See also CA 25-28R; CANR 28; MTCW;
SATA 66

Spillane, Mickey .... CLC **3, 13**
See also Spillane, Frank Morrison

Spinoza, Benedictus de 1632-1677 .... LC **9**

Spinrad, Norman (Richard) 1940-... CLC **46**
See also CA 37-40R; CAAS 19; CANR 20;
DLB 8

Spitteler, Carl (Friedrich Georg)
1845-1924 .... TCLC **12**
See also CA 109; DLB 129

Spivack, Kathleen (Romola Drucker)
1938- .... CLC **6**
See also CA 49-52

Spoto, Donald 1941-.............. **CLC 39**
See also CA 65-68; CANR 11

Springsteen, Bruce (F.) 1949- ...... **CLC 17**
See also CA 111

Spurling, Hilary 1940-............ **CLC 34**
See also CA 104; CANR 25

Spyker, John Howland
See Elman, Richard

Squires, (James) Radcliffe
1917-1993 .... **CLC 51**
See also CA 1-4R; 140; CANR 6, 21

Srivastava, Dhanpat Rai 1880(?)-1936
See Premchand
See also CA 118

Stacy, Donald
See Pohl, Frederik

Stael, Germaine de
See Stael-Holstein, Anne Louise Germaine
Necker Baronn
See also DLB 119

Stael-Holstein, Anne Louise Germaine Necker
Baronn 1766-1817 .... **NCLC 3**
See also Stael, Germaine de

Stafford, Jean 1915-1979 ... **CLC 4, 7, 19, 68**
See also CA 1-4R; 85-88; CANR 3; DLB 2;
MTCW; SATA-Obit 22

Stafford, William (Edgar)
1914-1993 .... **CLC 4, 7, 29**
See also CA 5-8R; 142; CAAS 3; CANR 5,
22; DLB 5

Staines, Trevor
See Brunner, John (Kilian Houston)

Stairs, Gordon
See Austin, Mary (Hunter)

Stannard, Martin 1947-........... **CLC 44**
See also CA 142; DLB 155

Stanton, Maura 1946- .... **CLC 9**
See also CA 89-92; CANR 15; DLB 120

Stanton, Schuyler
See Baum, L(yman) Frank

Stapledon, (William) Olaf
1886-1950 .... **TCLC 22**
See also CA 111; DLB 15

Starbuck, George (Edwin) 1931-.... **CLC 53**
See also CA 21-24R; CANR 23

Stark, Richard
See Westlake, Donald E(dwin)

Staunton, Schuyler
See Baum, L(yman) Frank

Stead, Christina (Ellen)
1902-1983 .... **CLC 2, 5, 8, 32, 80**
See also CA 13-16R; 109; CANR 33, 40;
MTCW

Stead, William Thomas
1849-1912 .... **TCLC 48**

Steele, Richard 1672-1729 .... **LC 18**
See also CDBLB 1660-1789; DLB 84, 101

Steele, Timothy (Reid) 1948-...... **CLC 45**
See also CA 93-96; CANR 16; DLB 120

Steffens, (Joseph) Lincoln
1866-1936 .... **TCLC 20**
See also CA 117

Stegner, Wallace (Earle)
1909-1993 .... **CLC 9, 49, 81**
See also AITN 1; BEST 90:3; CA 1-4R;
141; CAAS 9; CANR 1, 21, 46; DLB 9;
DLBY 93; MTCW

Stein, Gertrude
1874-1946 ...... **TCLC 1, 6, 28, 48; DA;**
DAB; WLC
See also CA 104; 132; CDALB 1917-1929;
DLB 4, 54, 86; MTCW

Steinbeck, John (Ernst)
1902-1968 ...... **CLC 1, 5, 9, 13, 21, 34,**
45, 75; DA; DAB; SSC 11; WLC
See also AAYA 12; CA 1-4R; 25-28R;
CANR 1, 35; CDALB 1929-1941; DLB 7,
9; DLBD 2; MTCW; SATA 9

Steinem, Gloria 1934-............. **CLC 63**
See also CA 53-56; CANR 28; MTCW

Steiner, George 1929-............. **CLC 24**
See also CA 73-76; CANR 31; DLB 67;
MTCW; SATA 62

Steiner, K. Leslie
See Delany, Samuel R(ay, Jr.)

Steiner, Rudolf 1861-1925 .... **TCLC 13**
See also CA 107

Stendhal
1783-1842 .... **NCLC 23, 46; DA; DAB;**
WLC
See also DLB 119

Stephen, Leslie 1832-1904 .... **TCLC 23**
See also CA 123; DLB 57, 144

Stephen, Sir Leslie
See Stephen, Leslie

Stephen, Virginia
See Woolf, (Adeline) Virginia

Stephens, James 1882(?)-1950 ...... **TCLC 4**
See also CA 104; DLB 19, 153

Stephens, Reed
See Donaldson, Stephen R.

Steptoe, Lydia
See Barnes, Djuna

Sterchi, Beat 1949-............... **CLC 65**

Sterling, Brett
See Bradbury, Ray (Douglas); Hamilton,
Edmond

Sterling, Bruce 1954-............. **CLC 72**
See also CA 119; CANR 44

Sterling, George 1869-1926 .... **TCLC 20**
See also CA 117; DLB 54

Stern, Gerald 1925- .... **CLC 40**
See also CA 81-84; CANR 28; DLB 105

Stern, Richard (Gustave) 1928-... **CLC 4, 39**
See also CA 1-4R; CANR 1, 25; DLBY 87

Sternberg, Josef von 1894-1969..... **CLC 20**
See also CA 81-84

Sterne, Laurence
1713-1768 ...... **LC 2; DA; DAB; WLC**
See also CDBLB 1660-1789; DLB 39

Sternheim, (William Adolf) Carl
1878-1942 .... **TCLC 8**
See also CA 105; DLB 56, 118

Stevens, Mark 1951- .... **CLC 34**
See also CA 122

Stevens, Wallace
1879-1955 .... **TCLC 3, 12, 45; DA;**
DAB; PC 6; WLC
See also CA 104; 124; CDALB 1929-1941;
DLB 54; MTCW

Stevenson, Anne (Katharine)
1933- .... **CLC 7, 33**
See also CA 17-20R; CAAS 9; CANR 9, 33;
DLB 40; MTCW

Stevenson, Robert Louis (Balfour)
1850-1894 ..... **NCLC 5, 14; DA; DAB;**
SSC 11; WLC
See also CDBLB 1890-1914; CLR 10, 11;
DLB 18, 57, 141; JRDA; MAICYA;
YABC 2

Stewart, J(ohn) I(nnes) M(ackintosh)
1906-1994 .... **CLC 7, 14, 32**
See also CA 85-88; 147; CAAS 3;
CANR 47; MTCW

Stewart, Mary (Florence Elinor)
1916- .... **CLC 7, 35; DAB**
See also CA 1-4R; CANR 1; SATA 12

Stewart, Mary Rainbow
See Stewart, Mary (Florence Elinor)

Stifle, June
See Campbell, Maria

Stifter, Adalbert 1805-1868...... **NCLC 41**
See also DLB 133

Still, James 1906-................ **CLC 49**
See also CA 65-68; CAAS 17; CANR 10,
26; DLB 9; SATA 29

Sting
See Sumner, Gordon Matthew

Stirling, Arthur
See Sinclair, Upton (Beall)

Stitt, Milan 1941-................ **CLC 29**
See also CA 69-72

Stockton, Francis Richard 1834-1902
See Stockton, Frank R.
See also CA 108; 137; MAICYA; SATA 44

Stockton, Frank R................ **TCLC 47**
See also Stockton, Francis Richard
See also DLB 42, 74; SATA-Brief 32

Stoddard, Charles
See Kuttner, Henry

Stoker, Abraham 1847-1912
See Stoker, Bram
See also CA 105; DA; SATA 29

Stoker, Bram .... **TCLC 8; DAB; WLC**
See also Stoker, Abraham
See also CDBLB 1890-1914; DLB 36, 70

Stolz, Mary (Slattery) 1920-....... **CLC 12**
See also AAYA 8; AITN 1; CA 5-8R;
CANR 13, 41; JRDA; MAICYA;
SAAS 3; SATA 10, 71

Stone, Irving 1903-1989........... **CLC 7**
See also AITN 1; CA 1-4R; 129; CAAS 3;
CANR 1, 23; MTCW; SATA 3;
SATA-Obit 64

Stone, Oliver 1946-.............. **CLC 73**
See also CA 110

Stone, Robert (Anthony)
1937- .... **CLC 5, 23, 42**
See also CA 85-88; CANR 23; DLB 152;
MTCW

Stone, Zachary
See Follett, Ken(neth Martin)

Stoppard, Tom
1937- . . . . . . **CLC 1, 3, 4, 5, 8, 15, 29, 34,
63; DA; DAB; WLC**
See also CA 81-84; CANR 39;
CDBLB 1960 to Present; DLB 13;
DLBY 85; MTCW

Storey, David (Malcolm)
1933- . . . . **CLC 2, 4, 5, 8**
See also CA 81-84; CANR 36; DLB 13, 14;
MTCW

Storm, Hyemeyohsts 1935- . . . . **CLC 3**
See also CA 81-84; CANR 45; NNAL

Storm, (Hans) Theodor (Woldsen)
1817-1888 . . . . **NCLC 1**

Storni, Alfonsina
1892-1938 . . . . **TCLC 5; HLC**
See also CA 104; 131; HW

Stout, Rex (Todhunter) 1886-1975 . . . **CLC 3**
See also AITN 2; CA 61-64

Stow, (Julian) Randolph 1935- . . **CLC 23, 48**
See also CA 13-16R; CANR 33; MTCW

Stowe, Harriet (Elizabeth) Beecher
1811-1896 . . . . . **NCLC 3, 50; DA; DAB;
WLC**
See also CDALB 1865-1917; DLB 1, 12, 42,
74; JRDA; MAICYA; YABC 1

Strachey, (Giles) Lytton
1880-1932 . . . . **TCLC 12**
See also CA 110; DLB 149; DLBD 10

Strand, Mark 1934- . . . . . . **CLC 6, 18, 41, 71**
See also CA 21-24R; CANR 40; DLB 5;
SATA 41

Straub, Peter (Francis) 1943- . . . . . . **CLC 28**
See also BEST 89:1; CA 85-88; CANR 28;
DLBY 84; MTCW

Strauss, Botho 1944- . . . . **CLC 22**
See also DLB 124

Streatfeild, (Mary) Noel
1895(?)-1986 . . . . **CLC 21**
See also CA 81-84; 120; CANR 31;
CLR 17; MAICYA; SATA 20;
SATA-Obit 48

Stribling, T(homas) S(igismund)
1881-1965 . . . . **CLC 23**
See also CA 107; DLB 9

Strindberg, (Johan) August
1849-1912 . . . . . . **TCLC 1, 8, 21, 47; DA;
DAB; WLC**
See also CA 104; 135

Stringer, Arthur 1874-1950 . . . . **TCLC 37**
See also DLB 92

Stringer, David
See Roberts, Keith (John Kingston)

Strugatskii, Arkadii (Natanovich)
1925-1991 . . . . **CLC 27**
See also CA 106; 135

Strugatskii, Boris (Natanovich)
1933- . . . . **CLC 27**
See also CA 106

Strummer, Joe 1953(?)- . . . . **CLC 30**

Stuart, Don A.
See Campbell, John W(ood, Jr.)

Stuart, Ian
See MacLean, Alistair (Stuart)

Stuart, Jesse (Hilton)
1906-1984 . . . . **CLC 1, 8, 11, 14, 34**
See also CA 5-8R; 112; CANR 31; DLB 9,
48, 102; DLBY 84; SATA 2;
SATA-Obit 36

Sturgeon, Theodore (Hamilton)
1918-1985 . . . . **CLC 22, 39**
See also Queen, Ellery
See also CA 81-84; 116; CANR 32; DLB 8;
DLBY 85; MTCW

Sturges, Preston 1898-1959 . . . . **TCLC 48**
See also CA 114; DLB 26

Styron, William
1925- . . . . **CLC 1, 3, 5, 11, 15, 60**
See also BEST 90:4; CA 5-8R; CANR 6, 33;
CDALB 1968-1988; DLB 2, 143;
DLBY 80; MTCW

Suarez Lynch, B.
See Bioy Casares, Adolfo; Borges, Jorge
Luis

Su Chien 1884-1918
See Su Man-shu
See also CA 123

Suckow, Ruth 1892-1960
See also CA 113; DLB 9, 102; SSC 18

Sudermann, Hermann 1857-1928 . . **TCLC 15**
See also CA 107; DLB 118

Sue, Eugene 1804-1857 . . . . **NCLC 1**
See also DLB 119

Sueskind, Patrick 1949- . . . . **CLC 44**
See also Suskind, Patrick

Sukenick, Ronald 1932- . . . . . **CLC 3, 4, 6, 48**
See also CA 25-28R; CAAS 8; CANR 32;
DLBY 81

Suknaski, Andrew 1942- . . . . **CLC 19**
See also CA 101; DLB 53

Sullivan, Vernon
See Vian, Boris

Sully Prudhomme 1839-1907 . . . . . . **TCLC 31**

Su Man-shu . . . . **TCLC 24**
See also Su Chien

Summerforest, Ivy B.
See Kirkup, James

Summers, Andrew James 1942- . . . . . **CLC 26**

Summers, Andy
See Summers, Andrew James

Summers, Hollis (Spurgeon, Jr.)
1916- . . . . **CLC 10**
See also CA 5-8R; CANR 3; DLB 6

**Summers, (Alphonsus Joseph-Mary Augustus)
Montague** 1880-1948 . . . . **TCLC 16**
See also CA 118

Sumner, Gordon Matthew 1951- . . . **CLC 26**

Surtees, Robert Smith
1803-1864 . . . . **NCLC 14**
See also DLB 21

Susann, Jacqueline 1921-1974 . . . . . . **CLC 3**
See also AITN 1; CA 65-68; 53-56; MTCW

Suskind, Patrick
See Sueskind, Patrick
See also CA 145

Sutcliff, Rosemary
1920-1992 . . . . **CLC 26; DAB**
See also AAYA 10; CA 5-8R; 139;
CANR 37; CLR 1, 37; JRDA; MAICYA;
SATA 6, 44, 78; SATA-Obit 73

Sutro, Alfred 1863-1933 . . . . **TCLC 6**
See also CA 105; DLB 10

Sutton, Henry
See Slavitt, David R(ytman)

Svevo, Italo . . . . **TCLC 2, 35**
See also Schmitz, Aron Hector

Swados, Elizabeth (A.) 1951- . . . . **CLC 12**
See also CA 97-100; CANR 49

Swados, Harvey 1920-1972 . . . . **CLC 5**
See also CA 5-8R; 37-40R; CANR 6;
DLB 2

Swan, Gladys 1934- . . . . **CLC 69**
See also CA 101; CANR 17, 39

Swarthout, Glendon (Fred)
1918-1992 . . . . **CLC 35**
See also CA 1-4R; 139; CANR 1, 47;
SATA 26

Sweet, Sarah C.
See Jewett, (Theodora) Sarah Orne

Swenson, May
1919-1989 . . . . **CLC 4, 14, 61; DA; DAB**
See also CA 5-8R; 130; CANR 36; DLB 5;
MTCW; SATA 15

Swift, Augustus
See Lovecraft, H(oward) P(hillips)

Swift, Graham (Colin) 1949- . . . . **CLC 41, 88**
See also CA 117; 122; CANR 46

Swift, Jonathan
1667-1745 . . . . . . **LC 1; DA; DAB; PC 9;
WLC**
See also CDBLB 1660-1789; DLB 39, 95,
101; SATA 19

Swinburne, Algernon Charles
1837-1909 . . . . . . **TCLC 8, 36; DA; DAB;
WLC**
See also CA 105; 140; CDBLB 1832-1890;
DLB 35, 57

Swinfen, Ann . . . . **CLC 34**

Swinnerton, Frank Arthur
1884-1982 . . . . **CLC 31**
See also CA 108; DLB 34

Swithen, John
See King, Stephen (Edwin)

Sylvia
See Ashton-Warner, Sylvia (Constance)

Symmes, Robert Edward
See Duncan, Robert (Edward)

Symonds, John Addington
1840-1893 . . . . **NCLC 34**
See also DLB 57, 144

Symons, Arthur 1865-1945 . . . . **TCLC 11**
See also CA 107; DLB 19, 57, 149

Symons, Julian (Gustave)
1912-1994 . . . . **CLC 2, 14, 32**
See also CA 49-52; 147; CAAS 3; CANR 3,
33; DLB 87, 155; DLBY 92; MTCW

Synge, (Edmund) J(ohn) M(illington)
1871-1909 . . . . **TCLC 6, 37; DC 2**
See also CA 104; 141; CDBLB 1890-1914;
DLB 10, 19

Syruc, J.
See Milosz, Czeslaw

Szirtes, George 1948-............. **CLC 46**
See also CA 109; CANR 27

Tabori, George 1914-............. **CLC 19**
See also CA 49-52; CANR 4

Tagore, Rabindranath
1861-1941 .... **TCLC 3, 53; PC 8**
See also CA 104; 120; MTCW

Taine, Hippolyte Adolphe
1828-1893 .... **NCLC 15**

Talese, Gay 1932-................ **CLC 37**
See also AITN 1; CA 1-4R; CANR 9;
MTCW

Tallent, Elizabeth (Ann) 1954- ..... **CLC 45**
See also CA 117; DLB 130

Tally, Ted 1952-................ **CLC 42**
See also CA 120; 124

Tamayo y Baus, Manuel
1829-1898 .... **NCLC 1**

Tammsaare, A(nton) H(ansen)
1878-1940 .... **TCLC 27**

Tan, Amy 1952- .... **CLC 59**
See also AAYA 9; BEST 89:3; CA 136;
SATA 75

Tandem, Felix
See Spitteler, Carl (Friedrich Georg)

Tanizaki, Jun'ichiro
1886-1965 .... **CLC 8, 14, 28**
See also CA 93-96; 25-28R

Tanner, William
See Amis, Kingsley (William)

Tao Lao
See Storni, Alfonsina

Tarassoff, Lev
See Troyat, Henri

Tarbell, Ida M(inerva)
1857-1944 .... **TCLC 40**
See also CA 122; DLB 47

Tarkington, (Newton) Booth
1869-1946 .... **TCLC 9**
See also CA 110; 143; DLB 9, 102;
SATA 17

Tarkovsky, Andrei (Arsenyevich)
1932-1986 .... **CLC 75**
See also CA 127

Tartt, Donna 1964(?)-............. **CLC 76**
See also CA 142

Tasso, Torquato 1544-1595 .... **LC 5**

Tate, (John Orley) Allen
1899-1979 .... **CLC 2, 4, 6, 9, 11, 14, 24**
See also CA 5-8R; 85-88; CANR 32;
DLB 4, 45, 63; MTCW

Tate, Ellalice
See Hibbert, Eleanor Alice Burford

Tate, James (Vincent) 1943- ... **CLC 2, 6, 25**
See also CA 21-24R; CANR 29; DLB 5

Tavel, Ronald 1940-............... **CLC 6**
See also CA 21-24R; CANR 33

Taylor, C(ecil) P(hilip) 1929-1981... **CLC 27**
See also CA 25-28R; 105; CANR 47

Taylor, Edward
1642(?)-1729 .... **LC 11; DA; DAB**
See also DLB 24

Taylor, Eleanor Ross 1920-......... **CLC 5**
See also CA 81-84

Taylor, Elizabeth 1912-1975 ... **CLC 2, 4, 29**
See also CA 13-16R; CANR 9; DLB 139;
MTCW; SATA 13

Taylor, Henry (Splawn) 1942-...... **CLC 44**
See also CA 33-36R; CAAS 7; CANR 31;
DLB 5

Taylor, Kamala (Purnaiya) 1924-
See Markandaya, Kamala
See also CA 77-80

Taylor, Mildred D. .... **CLC 21**
See also AAYA 10; BW 1; CA 85-88;
CANR 25; CLR 9; DLB 52; JRDA;
MAICYA; SAAS 5; SATA 15, 70

Taylor, Peter (Hillsman)
1917-1994 ..... **CLC 1, 4, 18, 37, 44, 50,
71; SSC 10**
See also CA 13-16R; 147; CANR 9;
DLBY 81, 94; MTCW

Taylor, Robert Lewis 1912-........ **CLC 14**
See also CA 1-4R; CANR 3; SATA 10

Tchekhov, Anton
See Chekhov, Anton (Pavlovich)

Teasdale, Sara 1884-1933.......... **TCLC 4**
See also CA 104; DLB 45; SATA 32

Tegner, Esaias 1782-1846......... **NCLC 2**

Teilhard de Chardin, (Marie Joseph) Pierre
1881-1955 .... **TCLC 9**
See also CA 105

Temple, Ann
See Mortimer, Penelope (Ruth)

Tennant, Emma (Christina)
1937-.................... **CLC 13, 52**
See also CA 65-68; CAAS 9; CANR 10, 38;
DLB 14

Tenneshaw, S. M.
See Silverberg, Robert

Tennyson, Alfred
1809-1892 .... **NCLC 30; DA; DAB;
PC 6; WLC**
See also CDBLB 1832-1890; DLB 32

Teran, Lisa St. Aubin de .... **CLC 36**
See also St. Aubin de Teran, Lisa

Terence 195(?)B.C.-159B.C...... **CMLC 14**

Teresa de Jesus, St. 1515-1582 ..... **LC 18**

Terkel, Louis 1912-
See Terkel, Studs
See also CA 57-60; CANR 18, 45; MTCW

Terkel, Studs................... **CLC 38**
See also Terkel, Louis
See also AITN 1

Terry, C. V.
See Slaughter, Frank G(ill)

Terry, Megan 1932-.............. **CLC 19**
See also CA 77-80; CABS 3; CANR 43;
DLB 7

Tertz, Abram
See Sinyavsky, Andrei (Donatevich)

Tesich, Steve 1943(?)-.......... **CLC 40, 69**
See also CA 105; DLBY 83

Teternikov, Fyodor Kuzmich 1863-1927
See Sologub, Fyodor
See also CA 104

Tevis, Walter 1928-1984 .... **CLC 42**
See also CA 113

Tey, Josephine.................. **TCLC 14**
See also Mackintosh, Elizabeth
See also DLB 77

Thackeray, William Makepeace
1811-1863 .... **NCLC 5, 14, 22, 43; DA;
DAB; WLC**
See also CDBLB 1832-1890; DLB 21, 55;
SATA 23

Thakura, Ravindranatha
See Tagore, Rabindranath

Tharoor, Shashi 1956- .... **CLC 70**
See also CA 141

Thelwell, Michael Miles 1939- ..... **CLC 22**
See also BW 2; CA 101

Theobald, Lewis, Jr.
See Lovecraft, H(oward) P(hillips)

Theodorescu, Ion N. 1880-1967
See Arghezi, Tudor
See also CA 116

Theriault, Yves 1915-1983........ **CLC 79**
See also CA 102; DLB 88

Theroux, Alexander (Louis)
1939-.................... **CLC 2, 25**
See also CA 85-88; CANR 20

Theroux, Paul (Edward)
1941-........ **CLC 5, 8, 11, 15, 28, 46**
See also BEST 89:4; CA 33-36R; CANR 20,
45; DLB 2; MTCW; SATA 44

Thesen, Sharon 1946-............. **CLC 56**

Thevenin, Denis
See Duhamel, Georges

Thibault, Jacques Anatole Francois
1844-1924
See France, Anatole
See also CA 106; 127; MTCW

Thiele, Colin (Milton) 1920- .... **CLC 17**
See also CA 29-32R; CANR 12, 28;
CLR 27; MAICYA; SAAS 2; SATA 14,
72

Thomas, Audrey (Callahan)
1935-.......... **CLC 7, 13, 37; SSC 20**
See also AITN 2; CA 21-24R; CAAS 19;
CANR 36; DLB 60; MTCW

Thomas, D(onald) M(ichael)
1935-................... **CLC 13, 22, 31**
See also CA 61-64; CAAS 11; CANR 17,
45; CDBLB 1960 to Present; DLB 40;
MTCW

Thomas, Dylan (Marlais)
1914-1953 ... **TCLC 1, 8, 45; DA; DAB;
PC 2; SSC 3; WLC**
See also CA 104; 120; CDBLB 1945-1960;
DLB 13, 20, 139; MTCW; SATA 60

Thomas, (Philip) Edward
1878-1917 .... **TCLC 10**
See also CA 106; DLB 19

Thomas, Joyce Carol 1938-........ **CLC 35**
See also AAYA 12; BW 2; CA 113; 116;
CANR 48; CLR 19; DLB 33; JRDA;
MAICYA; MTCW; SAAS 7; SATA 40,
78

Thomas, Lewis 1913-1993 .... **CLC 35**
See also CA 85-88; 143; CANR 38; MTCW

Thomas, Paul
    See Mann, (Paul) Thomas

Thomas, Piri 1928-............. **CLC 17**
    See also CA 73-76; HW

Thomas, R(onald) S(tuart)
    1913-........... **CLC 6, 13, 48; DAB**
    See also CA 89-92; CAAS 4; CANR 30;
    CDBLB 1960 to Present; DLB 27;
    MTCW

Thomas, Ross (Elmore) 1926-...... **CLC 39**
    See also CA 33-36R; CANR 22

Thompson, Francis Clegg
    See Mencken, H(enry) L(ouis)

Thompson, Francis Joseph
    1859-1907 .... **TCLC 4**
    See also CA 104; CDBLB 1890-1914;
    DLB 19

Thompson, Hunter S(tockton)
    1939-.................. **CLC 9, 17, 40**
    See also BEST 89:1; CA 17-20R; CANR 23,
    46; MTCW

Thompson, James Myers
    See Thompson, Jim (Myers)

Thompson, Jim (Myers)
    1906-1977(?) .... **CLC 69**
    See also CA 140

Thompson, Judith .... **CLC 39**

Thomson, James 1700-1748 ..... **LC 16, 29**
    See also DLB 95

Thomson, James 1834-1882 ...... **NCLC 18**
    See also DLB 35

Thoreau, Henry David
    1817-1862 ..... **NCLC 7, 21; DA; DAB;**
                                           WLC
    See also CDALB 1640-1865; DLB 1

Thornton, Hall
    See Silverberg, Robert

Thurber, James (Grover)
    1894-1961 .... **CLC 5, 11, 25; DA; DAB;**
                                           SSC 1
    See also CA 73-76; CANR 17, 39;
    CDALB 1929-1941; DLB 4, 11, 22, 102;
    MAICYA; MTCW; SATA 13

Thurman, Wallace (Henry)
    1902-1934 .... **TCLC 6; BLC**
    See also BW 1; CA 104; 124; DLB 51

Ticheburn, Cheviot
    See Ainsworth, William Harrison

Tieck, (Johann) Ludwig
    1773-1853 .... **NCLC 5, 46**
    See also DLB 90

Tiger, Derry
    See Ellison, Harlan (Jay)

Tilghman, Christopher 1948(?)-..... **CLC 65**

Tillinghast, Richard (Williford)
    1940-...................... **CLC 29**
    See also CA 29-32R; CANR 26

Timrod, Henry 1828-1867 .... **NCLC 25**
    See also DLB 3

Tindall, Gillian 1938-............. **CLC 7**
    See also CA 21-24R; CANR 11

Tiptree, James, Jr. .... **CLC 48, 50**
    See also Sheldon, Alice Hastings Bradley
    See also DLB 8

Titmarsh, Michael Angelo
    See Thackeray, William Makepeace

**Tocqueville, Alexis (Charles Henri Maurice
    Clerel Comte)** 1805-1859..... **NCLC 7**

Tolkien, J(ohn) R(onald) R(euel)
    1892-1973 .... **CLC 1, 2, 3, 8, 12, 38;**
                                    DA; DAB; WLC
    See also AAYA 10; AITN 1; CA 17-18;
    45-48; CANR 36; CAP 2;
    CDBLB 1914-1945; DLB 15; JRDA;
    MAICYA; MTCW; SATA 2, 32;
    SATA-Obit 24

Toller, Ernst 1893-1939 .... **TCLC 10**
    See also CA 107; DLB 124

Tolson, M. B.
    See Tolson, Melvin B(eaunorus)

Tolson, Melvin B(eaunorus)
    1898(?)-1966 .... **CLC 36; BLC**
    See also BW 1; CA 124; 89-92; DLB 48, 76

Tolstoi, Aleksei Nikolaevich
    See Tolstoy, Alexey Nikolaevich

Tolstoy, Alexey Nikolaevich
    1882-1945 .... **TCLC 18**
    See also CA 107

Tolstoy, Count Leo
    See Tolstoy, Leo (Nikolaevich)

Tolstoy, Leo (Nikolaevich)
    1828-1910 ...... **TCLC 4, 11, 17, 28, 44;**
                                    DA; DAB; SSC 9; WLC
    See also CA 104; 123; SATA 26

Tomasi di Lampedusa, Giuseppe 1896-1957
    See Lampedusa, Giuseppe (Tomasi) di
    See also CA 111

Tomlin, Lily .... **CLC 17**
    See also Tomlin, Mary Jean

Tomlin, Mary Jean 1939(?)-
    See Tomlin, Lily
    See also CA 117

Tomlinson, (Alfred) Charles
    1927-............. **CLC 2, 4, 6, 13, 45**
    See also CA 5-8R; CANR 33; DLB 40

Tonson, Jacob
    See Bennett, (Enoch) Arnold

Toole, John Kennedy
    1937-1969 .... **CLC 19, 64**
    See also CA 104; DLBY 81

Toomer, Jean
    1894-1967 ...... **CLC 1, 4, 13, 22; BLC;**
                                    PC 7; SSC 1
    See also BW 1; CA 85-88;
    CDALB 1917-1929; DLB 45, 51; MTCW

Torley, Luke
    See Blish, James (Benjamin)

Tornimparte, Alessandra
    See Ginzburg, Natalia

Torre, Raoul della
    See Mencken, H(enry) L(ouis)

Torrey, E(dwin) Fuller 1937-....... **CLC 34**
    See also CA 119

Torsvan, Ben Traven
    See Traven, B.

Torsvan, Benno Traven
    See Traven, B.

Torsvan, Berick Traven
    See Traven, B.

Torsvan, Berwick Traven
    See Traven, B.

Torsvan, Bruno Traven
    See Traven, B.

Torsvan, Traven
    See Traven, B.

Tournier, Michel (Edouard)
    1924-.................. **CLC 6, 23, 36**
    See also CA 49-52; CANR 3, 36; DLB 83;
    MTCW; SATA 23

Tournimparte, Alessandra
    See Ginzburg, Natalia

Towers, Ivar
    See Kornbluth, C(yril) M.

Towne, Robert (Burton) 1936(?)-.... **CLC 87**
    See also CA 108; DLB 44

Townsend, Sue 1946-........ **CLC 61; DAB**
    See also CA 119; 127; MTCW; SATA 55;
    SATA-Brief 48

Townshend, Peter (Dennis Blandford)
    1945-.................... **CLC 17, 42**
    See also CA 107

Tozzi, Federigo 1883-1920........ **TCLC 31**

Traill, Catharine Parr
    1802-1899 .... **NCLC 31**
    See also DLB 99

Trakl, Georg 1887-1914........... **TCLC 5**
    See also CA 104

Transtroemer, Tomas (Goesta)
    1931-.................... **CLC 52, 65**
    See also CA 117; 129; CAAS 17

Transtromer, Tomas Gosta
    See Transtroemer, Tomas (Goesta)

Traven, B. (?)-1969............. **CLC 8, 11**
    See also CA 19-20; 25-28R; CAP 2; DLB 9,
    56; MTCW

Treitel, Jonathan 1959- .... **CLC 70**

Tremain, Rose 1943-.............. **CLC 42**
    See also CA 97-100; CANR 44; DLB 14

Tremblay, Michel 1942-........... **CLC 29**
    See also CA 116; 128; DLB 60; MTCW

Trevanian .... **CLC 29**
    See also Whitaker, Rod(ney)

Trevor, Glen
    See Hilton, James

Trevor, William
    1928-............ **CLC 7, 9, 14, 25, 71**
    See also Cox, William Trevor
    See also DLB 14, 139

Trifonov, Yuri (Valentinovich)
    1925-1981 .... **CLC 45**
    See also CA 126; 103; MTCW

Trilling, Lionel 1905-1975 .... **CLC 9, 11, 24**
    See also CA 9-12R; 61-64; CANR 10;
    DLB 28, 63; MTCW

Trimball, W. H.
    See Mencken, H(enry) L(ouis)

Tristan
    See Gomez de la Serna, Ramon

Tristram
    See Housman, A(lfred) E(dward)

Trogdon, William (Lewis) 1939-
    See Heat-Moon, William Least
    See also CA 115; 119; CANR 47

Trollope, Anthony
    1815-1882 ..... NCLC 6, 33; DA; DAB;
                                        WLC
    See also CDBLB 1832-1890; DLB 21, 57;
    SATA 22

Trollope, Frances   1779-1863 ..... NCLC 30
    See also DLB 21

Trotsky, Leon   1879-1940........ TCLC 22
    See also CA 118

Trotter (Cockburn), Catharine
    1679-1749 .... LC 8
    See also DLB 84

Trout, Kilgore
    See Farmer, Philip Jose

Trow, George W. S.   1943-........ CLC 52
    See also CA 126

Troyat, Henri   1911-.............. CLC 23
    See also CA 45-48; CANR 2, 33; MTCW

Trudeau, G(arretson) B(eekman)   1948-
    See Trudeau, Garry B.
    See also CA 81-84; CANR 31; SATA 35

Trudeau, Garry B.................. CLC 12
    See also Trudeau, G(arretson) B(eekman)
    See also AAYA 10; AITN 2

Truffaut, Francois   1932-1984....... CLC 20
    See also CA 81-84; 113; CANR 34

Trumbo, Dalton   1905-1976 .... CLC 19
    See also CA 21-24R; 69-72; CANR 10;
    DLB 26

Trumbull, John   1750-1831....... NCLC 30
    See also DLB 31

Trundlett, Helen B.
    See Eliot, T(homas) S(tearns)

Tryon, Thomas   1926-1991 .... CLC 3, 11
    See also AITN 1; CA 29-32R; 135;
    CANR 32; MTCW

Tryon, Tom
    See Tryon, Thomas

Ts'ao Hsueh-ch'in   1715(?)-1763....... LC 1

Tsushima, Shuji   1909-1948
    See Dazai, Osamu
    See also CA 107

Tsvetaeva (Efron), Marina (Ivanovna)
    1892-1941 .... TCLC 7, 35
    See also CA 104; 128; MTCW

Tuck, Lily   1938-................ CLC 70
    See also CA 139

Tu Fu   712-770.................... PC 9

Tunis, John R(oberts)   1889-1975 ... CLC 12
    See also CA 61-64; DLB 22; JRDA;
    MAICYA; SATA 37; SATA-Brief 30

Tuohy, Frank.................... CLC 37
    See also Tuohy, John Francis
    See also DLB 14, 139

Tuohy, John Francis   1925-
    See Tuohy, Frank
    See also CA 5-8R; CANR 3, 47

Turco, Lewis (Putnam)   1934- ... CLC 11, 63
    See also CA 13-16R; CANR 24; DLBY 84

Turgenev, Ivan
    1818-1883 .... NCLC 21; DA; DAB;
                                SSC 7; WLC

Turgot, Anne-Robert-Jacques
    1727-1781 .... LC 26

Turner, Frederick   1943-.......... CLC 48
    See also CA 73-76; CAAS 10; CANR 12,
    30; DLB 40

Tutu, Desmond M(pilo)
    1931-................. CLC 80; BLC
    See also BW 1; CA 125

Tutuola, Amos   1920- ... CLC 5, 14, 29; BLC
    See also BW 2; CA 9-12R; CANR 27;
    DLB 125; MTCW

Twain, Mark
    ..... TCLC 6, 12, 19, 36, 48, 59; SSC 6;
                                        WLC
    See also Clemens, Samuel Langhorne
    See also DLB 11, 12, 23, 64, 74

Tyler, Anne
    1941-......... CLC 7, 11, 18, 28, 44, 59
    See also BEST 89:1; CA 9-12R; CANR 11,
    33; DLB 6, 143; DLBY 82; MTCW;
    SATA 7

Tyler, Royall   1757-1826.......... NCLC 3
    See also DLB 37

Tynan, Katharine   1861-1931 .... TCLC 3
    See also CA 104; DLB 153

Tyutchev, Fyodor   1803-1873 ..... NCLC 34

Tzara, Tristan .... CLC 47
    See also Rosenfeld, Samuel

Uhry, Alfred   1936-.............. CLC 55
    See also CA 127; 133

Ulf, Haerved
    See Strindberg, (Johan) August

Ulf, Harved
    See Strindberg, (Johan) August

Ulibarri, Sabine R(eyes)   1919- ..... CLC 83
    See also CA 131; DLB 82; HW

Unamuno (y Jugo), Miguel de
    1864-1936 .... TCLC 2, 9; HLC; SSC 11
    See also CA 104; 131; DLB 108; HW;
    MTCW

Undercliffe, Errol
    See Campbell, (John) Ramsey

Underwood, Miles
    See Glassco, John

Undset, Sigrid
    1882-1949 ... TCLC 3; DA; DAB; WLC
    See also CA 104; 129; MTCW

Ungaretti, Giuseppe
    1888-1970 .... CLC 7, 11, 15
    See also CA 19-20; 25-28R; CAP 2;
    DLB 114

Unger, Douglas   1952-............ CLC 34
    See also CA 130

Unsworth, Barry (Forster)   1930-.... CLC 76
    See also CA 25-28R; CANR 30

Updike, John (Hoyer)
    1932-...... CLC 1, 2, 3, 5, 7, 9, 13, 15,
    23, 34, 43, 70; DA; DAB; SSC 13; WLC
    See also CA 1-4R; CABS 1; CANR 4, 33;
    CDALB 1968-1988; DLB 2, 5, 143;
    DLBD 3; DLBY 80, 82; MTCW

Upshaw, Margaret Mitchell
    See Mitchell, Margaret (Munnerlyn)

Upton, Mark
    See Sanders, Lawrence

Urdang, Constance (Henriette)
    1922-....................... CLC 47
    See also CA 21-24R; CANR 9, 24

Uriel, Henry
    See Faust, Frederick (Schiller)

Uris, Leon (Marcus)   1924-...... CLC 7, 32
    See also AITN 1, 2; BEST 89:2; CA 1-4R;
    CANR 1, 40; MTCW; SATA 49

Urmuz
    See Codrescu, Andrei

Ustinov, Peter (Alexander)   1921-.... CLC 1
    See also AITN 1; CA 13-16R; CANR 25;
    DLB 13

Vaculik, Ludvik   1926-............. CLC 7
    See also CA 53-56

Valdez, Luis (Miguel)
    1940-................. CLC 84; HLC
    See also CA 101; CANR 32; DLB 122; HW

Valenzuela, Luisa   1938-... CLC 31; SSC 14
    See also CA 101; CANR 32; DLB 113; HW

Valera y Alcala-Galiano, Juan
    1824-1905 .... TCLC 10
    See also CA 106

Valery, (Ambroise) Paul (Toussaint Jules)
    1871-1945 .... TCLC 4, 15; PC 9
    See also CA 104; 122; MTCW

Valle-Inclan, Ramon (Maria) del
    1866-1936 .... TCLC 5; HLC
    See also CA 106; DLB 134

Vallejo, Antonio Buero
    See Buero Vallejo, Antonio

Vallejo, Cesar (Abraham)
    1892-1938 .... TCLC 3, 56; HLC
    See also CA 105; HW

Valle Y Pena, Ramon del
    See Valle-Inclan, Ramon (Maria) del

Van Ash, Cay   1918-.............. CLC 34

Vanbrugh, Sir John   1664-1726 ...... LC 21
    See also DLB 80

Van Campen, Karl
    See Campbell, John W(ood, Jr.)

Vance, Gerald
    See Silverberg, Robert

Vance, Jack.................... CLC 35
    See also Vance, John Holbrook
    See also DLB 8

Vance, John Holbrook   1916-
    See Queen, Ellery; Vance, Jack
    See also CA 29-32R; CANR 17; MTCW

Van Den Bogarde, Derek Jules Gaspard Ulric
    Niven   1921-
    See Bogarde, Dirk
    See also CA 77-80

Vandenburgh, Jane .... CLC 59

Vanderhaeghe, Guy   1951- .... CLC 41
    See also CA 113

van der Post, Laurens (Jan)   1906-... CLC 5
    See also CA 5-8R; CANR 35

van de Wetering, Janwillem   1931- .. CLC 47
    See also CA 49-52; CANR 4

Van Dine, S. S. .... TCLC 23
    See also Wright, Willard Huntington

Van Doren, Carl (Clinton)
1885-1950 .... **TCLC 18**
See also CA 111

Van Doren, Mark 1894-1972..... **CLC 6, 10**
See also CA 1-4R; 37-40R; CANR 3;
DLB 45; MTCW

Van Druten, John (William)
1901-1957 .... **TCLC 2**
See also CA 104; DLB 10

Van Duyn, Mona (Jane)
1921- .... **CLC 3, 7, 63**
See also CA 9-12R; CANR 7, 38; DLB 5

Van Dyne, Edith
See Baum, L(yman) Frank

van Itallie, Jean-Claude 1936-....... **CLC 3**
See also CA 45-48; CAAS 2; CANR 1, 48;
DLB 7

van Ostaijen, Paul 1896-1928 ..... **TCLC 33**

Van Peebles, Melvin 1932- ...... **CLC 2, 20**
See also BW 2; CA 85-88; CANR 27

Vansittart, Peter 1920-........... **CLC 42**
See also CA 1-4R; CANR 3, 49

Van Vechten, Carl 1880-1964 ...... **CLC 33**
See also CA 89-92; DLB 4, 9, 51

Van Vogt, A(lfred) E(lton) 1912-..... **CLC 1**
See also CA 21-24R; CANR 28; DLB 8;
SATA 14

Varda, Agnes 1928- .... **CLC 16**
See also CA 116; 122

Vargas Llosa, (Jorge) Mario (Pedro)
1936- .... **CLC 3, 6, 9, 10, 15, 31, 42, 85;**
DA; DAB; HLC
See also CA 73-76; CANR 18, 32, 42;
DLB 145; HW; MTCW

Vasiliu, Gheorghe 1881-1957
See Bacovia, George
See also CA 123

Vassa, Gustavus
See Equiano, Olaudah

Vassilikos, Vassilis 1933-......... **CLC 4, 8**
See also CA 81-84

Vaughan, Henry 1621-1695 .... **LC 27**
See also DLB 131

Vaughn, Stephanie................. **CLC 62**

Vazov, Ivan (Minchov)
1850-1921 .... **TCLC 25**
See also CA 121; DLB 147

Veblen, Thorstein (Bunde)
1857-1929 .... **TCLC 31**
See also CA 115

Vega, Lope de 1562-1635.......... **LC 23**

Venison, Alfred
See Pound, Ezra (Weston Loomis)

Verdi, Marie de
See Mencken, H(enry) L(ouis)

Verdu, Matilde
See Cela, Camilo Jose

Verga, Giovanni (Carmelo)
1840-1922 .... **TCLC 3**
See also CA 104; 123

Vergil
70B.C.-19B.C..... **CMLC 9; DA; DAB;**
PC 12

Verhaeren, Emile (Adolphe Gustave)
1855-1916 .... **TCLC 12**
See also CA 109

Verlaine, Paul (Marie)
1844-1896 .... **NCLC 2, 51; PC 2**

Verne, Jules (Gabriel)
1828-1905 .... **TCLC 6, 52**
See also CA 110; 131; DLB 123; JRDA;
MAICYA; SATA 21

Very, Jones 1813-1880.......... **NCLC 9**
See also DLB 1

Vesaas, Tarjei 1897-1970.......... **CLC 48**
See also CA 29-32R

Vialis, Gaston
See Simenon, Georges (Jacques Christian)

Vian, Boris 1920-1959 .... **TCLC 9**
See also CA 106; DLB 72

Viaud, (Louis Marie) Julien 1850-1923
See Loti, Pierre
See also CA 107

Vicar, Henry
See Felsen, Henry Gregor

Vicker, Angus
See Felsen, Henry Gregor

Vidal, Gore
1925- ..... **CLC 2, 4, 6, 8, 10, 22, 33, 72**
See also AITN 1; BEST 90:2; CA 5-8R;
CANR 13, 45; DLB 6, 152; MTCW

Viereck, Peter (Robert Edwin)
1916- .... **CLC 4**
See also CA 1-4R; CANR 1, 47, DLB 5

Vigny, Alfred (Victor) de
1797-1863 .... **NCLC 7**
See also DLB 119

Vilakazi, Benedict Wallet
1906-1947 .... **TCLC 37**

Villiers de l'Isle Adam, Jean Marie Mathias
Philippe Auguste Comte
1838-1889 .... **NCLC 3; SSC 14**
See also DLB 123

Villon, Francois 1431-1463(?) .... **PC 13**

Vinci, Leonardo da 1452-1519....... **LC 12**

Vine, Barbara .... **CLC 50**
See also Rendell, Ruth (Barbara)
See also BEST 90:4

Vinge, Joan D(ennison) 1948-...... **CLC 30**
See also CA 93-96; SATA 36

Violis, G.
See Simenon, Georges (Jacques Christian)

Visconti, Luchino 1906-1976....... **CLC 16**
See also CA 81-84; 65-68; CANR 39

Vittorini, Elio 1908-1966..... **CLC 6, 9, 14**
See also CA 133; 25-28R

Vizinczey, Stephen 1933-........... **CLC 40**
See also CA 128

Vliet, R(ussell) G(ordon)
1929-1984 .... **CLC 22**
See also CA 37-40R; 112; CANR 18

Vogau, Boris Andreyevich 1894-1937(?)
See Pilnyak, Boris
See also CA 123

Vogel, Paula A(nne) 1951-......... **CLC 76**
See also CA 108

Voight, Ellen Bryant 1943-........ **CLC 54**
See also CA 69-72; CANR 11, 29; DLB 120

Voigt, Cynthia 1942- .... **CLC 30**
See also AAYA 3; CA 106; CANR 18, 37,
40; CLR 13; JRDA; MAICYA;
SATA 48, 79; SATA-Brief 33

Voinovich, Vladimir (Nikolaevich)
1932-................... **CLC 10, 49**
See also CA 81-84; CAAS 12; CANR 33;
MTCW

Vollmann, William T. 1959-........ **CLC 89**
See also CA 134

Voloshinov, V. N.
See Bakhtin, Mikhail Mikhailovich

Voltaire
1694-1778 .... **LC 14; DA; DAB;**
SSC 12; WLC

von Aue, Hartmann 1170-1210 ... **CMLC 15**

von Daeniken, Erich 1935- .... **CLC 30**
See also AITN 1; CA 37-40R; CANR 17,
44

von Daniken, Erich
See von Daeniken, Erich

von Heidenstam, (Carl Gustaf) Verner
See Heidenstam, (Carl Gustaf) Verner von

von Heyse, Paul (Johann Ludwig)
See Heyse, Paul (Johann Ludwig von)

von Hofmannsthal, Hugo
See Hofmannsthal, Hugo von

von Horvath, Odon
See Horvath, Oedoen von

von Horvath, Oedoen
See Horvath, Oedoen von

von Liliencron, (Friedrich Adolf Axel) Detlev
See Liliencron, (Friedrich Adolf Axel)
Detlev von

Vonnegut, Kurt, Jr.
1922-...... **CLC 1, 2, 3, 4, 5, 8, 12, 22,**
40, 60; DA; DAB; SSC 8; WLC
See also AAYA 6; AITN 1; BEST 90:4;
CA 1-4R; CANR 1, 25, 49;
CDALB 1968-1988; DLB 2, 8, 152;
DLBD 3; DLBY 80; MTCW

Von Rachen, Kurt
See Hubbard, L(afayette) Ron(ald)

von Rezzori (d'Arezzo), Gregor
See Rezzori (d'Arezzo), Gregor von

von Sternberg, Josef
See Sternberg, Josef von

Vorster, Gordon 1924-............. **CLC 34**
See also CA 133

Vosce, Trudie
See Ozick, Cynthia

Voznesensky, Andrei (Andreievich)
1933-................... **CLC 1, 15, 57**
See also CA 89-92; CANR 37; MTCW

Waddington, Miriam 1917-........ **CLC 28**
See also CA 21-24R; CANR 12, 30;
DLB 68

Wagman, Fredrica 1937-........... **CLC 7**
See also CA 97-100

Wagner, Richard 1813-1883....... **NCLC 9**
See also DLB 129

Wagner-Martin, Linda 1936-....... **CLC 50**

Wagoner, David (Russell)
 1926- . . . . CLC 3, 5, 15
 See also CA 1-4R; CAAS 3; CANR 2;
 DLB 5; SATA 14

Wah, Fred(erick James) 1939- . . . . . . CLC 44
 See also CA 107; 141; DLB 60

Wahloo, Per 1926-1975 . . . . CLC 7
 See also CA 61-64

Wahloo, Peter
 See Wahloo, Per

Wain, John (Barrington)
 1925-1994 . . . . CLC 2, 11, 15, 46
 See also CA 5-8R; 145; CAAS 4; CANR 23;
 CDBLB 1960 to Present; DLB 15, 27,
 139, 155; MTCW

Wajda, Andrzej 1926- . . . . CLC 16
 See also CA 102

Wakefield, Dan 1932- . . . . CLC 7
 See also CA 21-24R; CAAS 7

Wakoski, Diane
 1937- . . . . CLC 2, 4, 7, 9, 11, 40
 See also CA 13-16R; CAAS 1; CANR 9;
 DLB 5

Wakoski-Sherbell, Diane
 See Wakoski, Diane

Walcott, Derek (Alton)
 1930- . . . . CLC 2, 4, 9, 14, 25, 42, 67, 76;
 BLC; DAB
 See also BW 2; CA 89-92; CANR 26, 47;
 DLB 117; DLBY 81; MTCW

Waldman, Anne 1945- . . . . CLC 7
 See also CA 37-40R; CAAS 17; CANR 34;
 DLB 16

Waldo, E. Hunter
 See Sturgeon, Theodore (Hamilton)

Waldo, Edward Hamilton
 See Sturgeon, Theodore (Hamilton)

Walker, Alice (Malsenior)
 1944- . . . . CLC 5, 6, 9, 19, 27, 46, 58;
 BLC; DA; DAB; SSC 5
 See also AAYA 3; BEST 89:4; BW 2;
 CA 37-40R; CANR 9, 27, 49;
 CDALB 1968-1988; DLB 6, 33, 143;
 MTCW; SATA 31

Walker, David Harry 1911-1992 . . . . CLC 14
 See also CA 1-4R; 137; CANR 1; SATA 8;
 SATA-Obit 71

Walker, Edward Joseph 1934-
 See Walker, Ted
 See also CA 21-24R; CANR 12, 28

Walker, George F.
 1947- . . . . CLC 44, 61; DAB
 See also CA 103; CANR 21, 43; DLB 60

Walker, Joseph A. 1935- . . . . CLC 19
 See also BW 1; CA 89-92; CANR 26;
 DLB 38

Walker, Margaret (Abigail)
 1915- . . . . CLC 1, 6; BLC
 See also BW 2; CA 73-76; CANR 26;
 DLB 76, 152; MTCW

Walker, Ted . . . . CLC 13
 See also Walker, Edward Joseph
 See also DLB 40

Wallace, David Foster 1962- . . . . CLC 50
 See also CA 132

Wallace, Dexter
 See Masters, Edgar Lee

Wallace, (Richard Horatio) Edgar
 1875-1932 . . . . TCLC 57
 See also CA 115; DLB 70

Wallace, Irving 1916-1990 . . . . . . CLC 7, 13
 See also AITN 1; CA 1-4R; 132; CAAS 1;
 CANR 1, 27; MTCW

Wallant, Edward Lewis
 1926-1962 . . . . CLC 5, 10
 See also CA 1-4R; CANR 22; DLB 2, 28,
 143; MTCW

Walley, Byron
 See Card, Orson Scott

Walpole, Horace 1717-1797 . . . . LC 2
 See also DLB 39, 104

Walpole, Hugh (Seymour)
 1884-1941 . . . . TCLC 5
 See also CA 104; DLB 34

Walser, Martin 1927- . . . . CLC 27
 See also CA 57-60; CANR 8, 46; DLB 75,
 124

Walser, Robert
 1878-1956 . . . . TCLC 18; SSC 20
 See also CA 118; DLB 66

Walsh, Jill Paton . . . . CLC 35
 See also Paton Walsh, Gillian
 See also AAYA 11; CLR 2; SAAS 3

Walter, Villiam Christian
 See Andersen, Hans Christian

Wambaugh, Joseph (Aloysius, Jr.)
 1937- . . . . CLC 3, 18
 See also AITN 1; BEST 89:3; CA 33-36R;
 CANR 42; DLB 6; DLBY 83; MTCW

Ward, Arthur Henry Sarsfield 1883-1959
 See Rohmer, Sax
 See also CA 108

Ward, Douglas Turner 1930- . . . . CLC 19
 See also BW 1; CA 81-84; CANR 27;
 DLB 7, 38

Ward, Mary Augusta
 See Ward, Mrs. Humphry

Ward, Mrs. Humphry
 1851-1920 . . . . TCLC 55
 See also DLB 18

Ward, Peter
 See Faust, Frederick (Schiller)

Warhol, Andy 1928(?)-1987 . . . . CLC 20
 See also AAYA 12; BEST 89:4; CA 89-92;
 121; CANR 34

Warner, Francis (Robert le Plastrier)
 1937- . . . . CLC 14
 See also CA 53-56; CANR 11

Warner, Marina 1946- . . . . CLC 59
 See also CA 65-68; CANR 21

Warner, Rex (Ernest) 1905-1986 . . . . CLC 45
 See also CA 89-92; 119; DLB 15

Warner, Susan (Bogert)
 1819-1885 . . . . NCLC 31
 See also DLB 3, 42

Warner, Sylvia (Constance) Ashton
 See Ashton-Warner, Sylvia (Constance)

Warner, Sylvia Townsend
 1893-1978 . . . . CLC 7, 19
 See also CA 61-64; 77-80; CANR 16;
 DLB 34, 139; MTCW

Warren, Mercy Otis 1728-1814 . . . NCLC 13
 See also DLB 31

Warren, Robert Penn
 1905-1989 . . . . CLC 1, 4, 6, 8, 10, 13, 18,
 39, 53, 59; DA; DAB; SSC 4; WLC
 See also AITN 1; CA 13-16R; 129;
 CANR 10, 47; CDALB 1968-1988;
 DLB 2, 48, 152; DLBY 80, 89; MTCW;
 SATA 46; SATA-Obit 63

Warshofsky, Isaac
 See Singer, Isaac Bashevis

Warton, Thomas 1728-1790 . . . . LC 15
 See also DLB 104, 109

Waruk, Kona
 See Harris, (Theodore) Wilson

Warung, Price 1855-1911 . . . . TCLC 45

Warwick, Jarvis
 See Garner, Hugh

Washington, Alex
 See Harris, Mark

Washington, Booker T(aliaferro)
 1856-1915 . . . . TCLC 10; BLC
 See also BW 1; CA 114; 125; SATA 28

Washington, George 1732-1799 . . . . . . LC 25
 See also DLB 31

Wassermann, (Karl) Jakob
 1873-1934 . . . . TCLC 6
 See also CA 104; DLB 66

Wasserstein, Wendy
 1950- . . . . CLC 32, 59; DC 4
 See also CA 121; 129; CABS 3

Waterhouse, Keith (Spencer)
 1929- . . . . CLC 47
 See also CA 5-8R; CANR 38; DLB 13, 15;
 MTCW

Waters, Frank (Joseph) 1902- . . . . . . CLC 88
 See also CA 5-8R; CAAS 13; CANR 3, 18;
 DLBY 86

Waters, Roger 1944- . . . . CLC 35

Watkins, Frances Ellen
 See Harper, Frances Ellen Watkins

Watkins, Gerrold
 See Malzberg, Barry N(athaniel)

Watkins, Paul 1964- . . . . CLC 55
 See also CA 132

Watkins, Vernon Phillips
 1906-1967 . . . . CLC 43
 See also CA 9-10; 25-28R; CAP 1; DLB 20

Watson, Irving S.
 See Mencken, H(enry) L(ouis)

Watson, John H.
 See Farmer, Philip Jose

Watson, Richard F.
 See Silverberg, Robert

Waugh, Auberon (Alexander) 1939- . . CLC 7
 See also CA 45-48; CANR 6, 22; DLB 14

Waugh, Evelyn (Arthur St. John)
1903-1966 ...... CLC 1, 3, 8, 13, 19, 27,
44; DA; DAB; WLC
See also CA 85-88; 25-28R; CANR 22;
CDBLB 1914-1945; DLB 15; MTCW

Waugh, Harriet 1944- .... CLC 6
See also CA 85-88; CANR 22

Ways, C. R.
See Blount, Roy (Alton), Jr.

Waystaff, Simon
See Swift, Jonathan

Webb, (Martha) Beatrice (Potter)
1858-1943 ....TCLC 22
See also Potter, Beatrice
See also CA 117

Webb, Charles (Richard) 1939- ...... CLC 7
See also CA 25-28R

Webb, James H(enry), Jr. 1946- .... CLC 22
See also CA 81-84

Webb, Mary (Gladys Meredith)
1881-1927 ....TCLC 24
See also CA 123; DLB 34

Webb, Mrs. Sidney
See Webb, (Martha) Beatrice (Potter)

Webb, Phyllis 1927- .... CLC 18
See also CA 104; CANR 23; DLB 53

Webb, Sidney (James)
1859-1947 ....TCLC 22
See also CA 117

Webber, Andrew Lloyd............. CLC 21
See also Lloyd Webber, Andrew

Weber, Lenora Mattingly
1895-1971 .... CLC 12
See also CA 19-20; 29-32R; CAP 1;
SATA 2; SATA-Obit 26

Webster, John 1579(?)-1634(?) .... DC 2
See also CDBLB Before 1660; DA; DAB;
DLB 58; WLC

Webster, Noah 1758-1843 .... NCLC 30

Wedekind, (Benjamin) Frank(lin)
1864-1918 ....TCLC 7
See also CA 104; DLB 118

Weidman, Jerome 1913-............. CLC 7
See also AITN 2; CA 1-4R; CANR 1;
DLB 28

Weil, Simone (Adolphine)
1909-1943 ....TCLC 23
See also CA 117

Weinstein, Nathan
See West, Nathanael

Weinstein, Nathan von Wallenstein
See West, Nathanael

Weir, Peter (Lindsay) 1944- .... CLC 20
See also CA 113; 123

Weiss, Peter (Ulrich)
1916-1982 .... CLC 3, 15, 51
See also CA 45-48; 106; CANR 3; DLB 69,
124

Weiss, Theodore (Russell)
1916- .... CLC 3, 8, 14
See also CA 9-12R; CAAS 2; CANR 46;
DLB 5

Welch, (Maurice) Denton
1915-1948 ....TCLC 22
See also CA 121; 148

Welch, James 1940- .... CLC 6, 14, 52
See also CA 85-88; CANR 42; NNAL

Weldon, Fay
1933- .... CLC 6, 9, 11, 19, 36, 59
See also CA 21-24R; CANR 16, 46;
CDBLB 1960 to Present; DLB 14;
MTCW

Wellek, Rene 1903- .... CLC 28
See also CA 5-8R; CAAS 7; CANR 8;
DLB 63

Weller, Michael 1942- .... CLC 10, 53
See also CA 85-88

Weller, Paul 1958- .... CLC 26

Wellershoff, Dieter 1925-.......... CLC 46
See also CA 89-92; CANR 16, 37

Welles, (George) Orson
1915-1985 .... CLC 20, 80
See also CA 93-96; 117

Wellman, Mac 1945- .... CLC 65

Wellman, Manly Wade 1903-1986 .. CLC 49
See also CA 1-4R; 118; CANR 6, 16, 44;
SATA 6; SATA-Obit 47

Wells, Carolyn 1869(?)-1942 ...... TCLC 35
See also CA 113; DLB 11

Wells, H(erbert) G(eorge)
1866-1946 .... TCLC 6, 12, 19; DA;
DAB; SSC 6; WLC
See also CA 110; 121; CDBLB 1914-1945;
DLB 34, 70; MTCW; SATA 20

Wells, Rosemary 1943-............ CLC 12
See also AAYA 13; CA 85-88; CANR 48;
CLR 16; MAICYA; SAAS 1; SATA 18,
69

Welty, Eudora
1909- ...... CLC 1, 2, 5, 14, 22, 33; DA;
DAB; SSC 1; WLC
See also CA 9-12R; CABS 1; CANR 32;
CDALB 1941-1968; DLB 2, 102, 143;
DLBD 12; DLBY 87; MTCW

Wen I-to 1899-1946 .... TCLC 28

Wentworth, Robert
See Hamilton, Edmond

Werfel, Franz (V.) 1890-1945 ...... TCLC 8
See also CA 104; DLB 81, 124

Wergeland, Henrik Arnold
1808-1845 .... NCLC 5

Wersba, Barbara 1932-............ CLC 30
See also AAYA 2; CA 29-32R; CANR 16,
38; CLR 3; DLB 52; JRDA; MAICYA;
SAAS 2; SATA 1, 58

Wertmueller, Lina 1928- .... CLC 16
See also CA 97-100; CANR 39

Wescott, Glenway 1901-1987....... CLC 13
See also CA 13-16R; 121; CANR 23;
DLB 4, 9, 102

Wesker, Arnold 1932- .. CLC 3, 5, 42; DAB
See also CA 1-4R; CAAS 7; CANR 1, 33;
CDBLB 1960 to Present; DLB 13;
MTCW

Wesley, Richard (Errol) 1945-....... CLC 7
See also BW 1; CA 57-60; CANR 27;
DLB 38

Wessel, Johan Herman 1742-1785 .... LC 7

West, Anthony (Panther)
1914-1987 .... CLC 50
See also CA 45-48; 124; CANR 3, 19;
DLB 15

West, C. P.
See Wodehouse, P(elham) G(renville)

West, (Mary) Jessamyn
1902-1984 .... CLC 7, 17
See also CA 9-12R; 112; CANR 27; DLB 6;
DLBY 84; MTCW; SATA-Obit 37

West, Morris L(anglo) 1916-..... CLC 6, 33
See also CA 5-8R; CANR 24, 49; MTCW

West, Nathanael
1903-1940 ..... TCLC 1, 14, 44; SSC 16
See also CA 104; 125; CDALB 1929-1941;
DLB 4, 9, 28; MTCW

West, Owen
See Koontz, Dean R(ay)

West, Paul 1930- .... CLC 7, 14
See also CA 13-16R; CAAS 7; CANR 22;
DLB 14

West, Rebecca 1892-1983 .. CLC 7, 9, 31, 50
See also CA 5-8R; 109; CANR 19; DLB 36;
DLBY 83; MTCW

Westall, Robert (Atkinson)
1929-1993 .... CLC 17
See also AAYA 12; CA 69-72; 141;
CANR 18; CLR 13; JRDA; MAICYA;
SAAS 2; SATA 23, 69; SATA-Obit 75

Westlake, Donald E(dwin)
1933- .... CLC 7, 33
See also CA 17-20R; CAAS 13; CANR 16,
44

Westmacott, Mary
See Christie, Agatha (Mary Clarissa)

Weston, Allen
See Norton, Andre

Wetcheek, J. L.
See Feuchtwanger, Lion

Wetering, Janwillem van de
See van de Wetering, Janwillem

Wetherell, Elizabeth
See Warner, Susan (Bogert)

Whalen, Philip 1923-........... CLC 6, 29
See also CA 9-12R; CANR 5, 39; DLB 16

Wharton, Edith (Newbold Jones)
1862-1937 ...... TCLC 3, 9, 27, 53; DA;
DAB; SSC 6; WLC
See also CA 104; 132; CDALB 1865-1917;
DLB 4, 9, 12, 78; MTCW

Wharton, James
See Mencken, H(enry) L(ouis)

Wharton, William (a pseudonym)
.... CLC 18, 37
See also CA 93-96; DLBY 80

Wheatley (Peters), Phillis
1754(?)-1784 .... LC 3; BLC; DA; PC 3;
WLC
See also CDALB 1640-1865; DLB 31, 50

Wheelock, John Hall 1886-1978 .... CLC 14
See also CA 13-16R; 77-80; CANR 14;
DLB 45

White, E(lwyn) B(rooks)
    1899-1985 . . . . **CLC 10, 34, 39**
    See also AITN 2; CA 13-16R; 116;
    CANR 16, 37; CLR 1, 21; DLB 11, 22;
    MAICYA; MTCW; SATA 2, 29;
    SATA-Obit 44

White, Edmund (Valentine III)
    1940- . . . . **CLC 27**
    See also AAYA 7; CA 45-48; CANR 3, 19,
    36; MTCW

White, Patrick (Victor Martindale)
    1912-1990 . . **CLC 3, 4, 5, 7, 9, 18, 65, 69**
    See also CA 81-84; 132; CANR 43; MTCW

White, Phyllis Dorothy James 1920-
    See James, P. D.
    See also CA 21-24R; CANR 17, 43; MTCW

White, T(erence) H(anbury)
    1906-1964 . . . . **CLC 30**
    See also CA 73-76; CANR 37; JRDA;
    MAICYA; SATA 12

White, Terence de Vere
    1912-1994 . . . . **CLC 49**
    See also CA 49-52; 145; CANR 3

White, Walter F(rancis)
    1893-1955 . . . . **TCLC 15**
    See also White, Walter
    See also BW 1; CA 115; 124; DLB 51

White, William Hale 1831-1913
    See Rutherford, Mark
    See also CA 121

Whitehead, E(dward) A(nthony)
    1933- . . . . **CLC 5**
    See also CA 65-68

Whitemore, Hugh (John) 1936- . . . . . **CLC 37**
    See also CA 132

Whitman, Sarah Helen (Power)
    1803-1878 . . . . **NCLC 19**
    See also DLB 1

Whitman, Walt(er)
    1819-1892 . . . . . **NCLC 4, 31; DA; DAB;**
                       PC 3; WLC
    See also CDALB 1640-1865; DLB 3, 64;
    SATA 20

Whitney, Phyllis A(yame) 1903- . . . . **CLC 42**
    See also AITN 2; BEST 90:3; CA 1-4R;
    CANR 3, 25, 38; JRDA; MAICYA;
    SATA 1, 30

Whittemore, (Edward) Reed (Jr.)
    1919- . . . . **CLC 4**
    See also CA 9-12R; CAAS 8; CANR 4;
    DLB 5

Whittier, John Greenleaf
    1807-1892 . . . . **NCLC 8**
    See also CDALB 1640-1865; DLB 1

Whittlebot, Hernia
    See Coward, Noel (Peirce)

Wicker, Thomas Grey 1926-
    See Wicker, Tom
    See also CA 65-68; CANR 21, 46

Wicker, Tom . . . . **CLC 7**
    See also Wicker, Thomas Grey

Wideman, John Edgar
    1941- . . . . **CLC 5, 34, 36, 67; BLC**
    See also BW 2; CA 85-88; CANR 14, 42;
    DLB 33, 143

Wiebe, Rudy (Henry) 1934- . . . **CLC 6, 11, 14**
    See also CA 37-40R; CANR 42; DLB 60

Wieland, Christoph Martin
    1733-1813 . . . . **NCLC 17**
    See also DLB 97

Wiene, Robert 1881-1938 . . . . **TCLC 56**

Wieners, John 1934- . . . . **CLC 7**
    See also CA 13-16R; DLB 16

Wiesel, Elie(zer)
    1928- . . . . . . **CLC 3, 5, 11, 37; DA; DAB**
    See also AAYA 7; AITN 1; CA 5-8R;
    CAAS 4; CANR 8, 40; DLB 83;
    DLBY 87; MTCW; SATA 56

Wiggins, Marianne 1947- . . . . **CLC 57**
    See also BEST 89:3; CA 130

Wight, James Alfred 1916-
    See Herriot, James
    See also CA 77-80; SATA 55;
    SATA-Brief 44

Wilbur, Richard (Purdy)
    1921- . . . . **CLC 3, 6, 9, 14, 53; DA; DAB**
    See also CA 1-4R; CABS 2; CANR 2, 29;
    DLB 5; MTCW; SATA 9

Wild, Peter 1940- . . . . **CLC 14**
    See also CA 37-40R; DLB 5

Wilde, Oscar (Fingal O'Flahertie Wills)
    1854(?)-1900 . . . . **TCLC 1, 8, 23, 41; DA;**
                  DAB; SSC 11; WLC
    See also CA 104; 119; CDBLB 1890-1914;
    DLB 10, 19, 34, 57, 141; SATA 24

Wilder, Billy . . . . **CLC 20**
    See also Wilder, Samuel
    See also DLB 26

Wilder, Samuel 1906-
    See Wilder, Billy
    See also CA 89-92

Wilder, Thornton (Niven)
    1897-1975 . . . . . **CLC 1, 5, 6, 10, 15, 35,**
                82; DA; DAB; DC 1; WLC
    See also AITN 2; CA 13-16R; 61-64;
    CANR 40; DLB 4, 7, 9; MTCW

Wilding, Michael 1942- . . . . **CLC 73**
    See also CA 104; CANR 24, 49

Wiley, Richard 1944- . . . . **CLC 44**
    See also CA 121; 129

Wilhelm, Kate . . . . **CLC 7**
    See also Wilhelm, Katie Gertrude
    See also CAAS 5; DLB 8

Wilhelm, Katie Gertrude 1928-
    See Wilhelm, Kate
    See also CA 37-40R; CANR 17, 36; MTCW

Wilkins, Mary
    See Freeman, Mary Eleanor Wilkins

Willard, Nancy 1936- . . . . **CLC 7, 37**
    See also CA 89-92; CANR 10, 39; CLR 5;
    DLB 5, 52; MAICYA; MTCW;
    SATA 37, 71; SATA-Brief 30

Williams, C(harles) K(enneth)
    1936- . . . . **CLC 33, 56**
    See also CA 37-40R; DLB 5

Williams, Charles
    See Collier, James L(incoln)

Williams, Charles (Walter Stansby)
    1886-1945 . . . . **TCLC 1, 11**
    See also CA 104; DLB 100, 153

Williams, (George) Emlyn
    1905-1987 . . . . **CLC 15**
    See also CA 104; 123; CANR 36; DLB 10,
    77; MTCW

Williams, Hugo 1942- . . . . **CLC 42**
    See also CA 17-20R; CANR 45; DLB 40

Williams, J. Walker
    See Wodehouse, P(elham) G(renville)

Williams, John A(lfred)
    1925- . . . . **CLC 5, 13; BLC**
    See also BW 2; CA 53-56; CAAS 3;
    CANR 6, 26; DLB 2, 33

Williams, Jonathan (Chamberlain)
    1929- . . . . **CLC 13**
    See also CA 9-12R; CAAS 12; CANR 8;
    DLB 5

Williams, Joy 1944- . . . . **CLC 31**
    See also CA 41-44R; CANR 22, 48

Williams, Norman 1952- . . . . **CLC 39**
    See also CA 118

Williams, Sherley Anne
    1944- . . . . **CLC 89; BLC**
    See also BW 2; CA 73-76; CANR 25;
    DLB 41; SATA 78

Williams, Shirley
    See Williams, Sherley Anne

Williams, Tennessee
    1911-1983 . . . . . **CLC 1, 2, 5, 7, 8, 11, 15,**
        19, 30, 39, 45, 71; DA; DAB; DC 4; WLC
    See also AITN 1, 2; CA 5-8R; 108;
    CABS 3; CANR 31; CDALB 1941-1968;
    DLB 7; DLBD 4; DLBY 83; MTCW

Williams, Thomas (Alonzo)
    1926-1990 . . . . **CLC 14**
    See also CA 1-4R; 132; CANR 2

Williams, William C.
    See Williams, William Carlos

Williams, William Carlos
    1883-1963 . . . . **CLC 1, 2, 5, 9, 13, 22, 42,**
                   67; DA; DAB; PC 7
    See also CA 89-92; CANR 34;
    CDALB 1917-1929; DLB 4, 16, 54, 86;
    MTCW

Williamson, David (Keith) 1942- . . . . **CLC 56**
    See also CA 103; CANR 41

Williamson, Ellen Douglas 1905-1984
    See Douglas, Ellen
    See also CA 17-20R; 114; CANR 39

Williamson, Jack . . . . **CLC 29**
    See also Williamson, John Stewart
    See also CAAS 8; DLB 8

Williamson, John Stewart 1908-
    See Williamson, Jack
    See also CA 17-20R; CANR 23

Willie, Frederick
    See Lovecraft, H(oward) P(hillips)

Willingham, Calder (Baynard, Jr.)
    1922-1995 . . . . **CLC 5, 51**
    See also CA 5-8R; 147; CANR 3; DLB 2,
    44; MTCW

Willis, Charles
    See Clarke, Arthur C(harles)

Willy
    See Colette, (Sidonie-Gabrielle)

Willy, Colette
See Colette, (Sidonie-Gabrielle)

Wilson, A(ndrew) N(orman) 1950- .. **CLC 33**
See also CA 112; 122; DLB 14, 155

Wilson, Angus (Frank Johnstone)
1913-1991 .... **CLC 2, 3, 5, 25, 34**
See also CA 5-8R; 134; CANR 21; DLB 15,
139, 155; MTCW

Wilson, August
1945- ...... **CLC 39, 50, 63; BLC; DA;**
DAB; DC 2
See also BW 2; CA 115; 122; CANR 42;
MTCW

Wilson, Brian 1942- .... **CLC 12**

Wilson, Colin 1931- .... **CLC 3, 14**
See also CA 1-4R; CAAS 5; CANR 1, 22,
33; DLB 14; MTCW

Wilson, Dirk
See Pohl, Frederik

Wilson, Edmund
1895-1972 .... **CLC 1, 2, 3, 8, 24**
See also CA 1-4R; 37-40R; CANR 1, 46;
DLB 63; MTCW

Wilson, Ethel Davis (Bryant)
1888(?)-1980 .... **CLC 13**
See also CA 102; DLB 68; MTCW

Wilson, John 1785-1854......... **NCLC 5**

Wilson, John (Anthony) Burgess 1917-1993
See Burgess, Anthony
See also CA 1-4R; 143; CANR 2, 46;
MTCW

Wilson, Lanford 1937- .... **CLC 7, 14, 36**
See also CA 17-20R; CABS 3; CANR 45;
DLB 7

Wilson, Robert M. 1944- .... **CLC 7, 9**
See also CA 49-52; CANR 2, 41; MTCW

Wilson, Robert McLiam 1964- ..... **CLC 59**
See also CA 132

Wilson, Sloan 1920- .... **CLC 32**
See also CA 1-4R; CANR 1, 44

Wilson, Snoo 1948-............... **CLC 33**
See also CA 69-72

Wilson, William S(mith) 1932- ..... **CLC 49**
See also CA 81-84

Winchilsea, Anne (Kingsmill) Finch Counte
1661-1720 .... **LC 3**

Windham, Basil
See Wodehouse, P(elham) G(renville)

Wingrove, David (John) 1954-...... **CLC 68**
See also CA 133

Winters, Janet Lewis .... **CLC 41**
See also Lewis, Janet
See also DLBY 87

Winters, (Arthur) Yvor
1900-1968 ....**CLC 4, 8, 32**
See also CA 11-12; 25-28R; CAP 1;
DLB 48; MTCW

Winterson, Jeanette 1959-........ **CLC 64**
See also CA 136

Wiseman, Frederick 1930-......... **CLC 20**

Wister, Owen 1860-1938 .... **TCLC 21**
See also CA 108; DLB 9, 78; SATA 62

Witkacy
See Witkiewicz, Stanislaw Ignacy

Witkiewicz, Stanislaw Ignacy
1885-1939 .... **TCLC 8**
See also CA 105

Wittgenstein, Ludwig (Josef Johann)
1889-1951 .... **TCLC 59**
See also CA 113

Wittig, Monique 1935(?)-.......... **CLC 22**
See also CA 116; 135; DLB 83

Wittlin, Jozef 1896-1976 .... **CLC 25**
See also CA 49-52; 65-68; CANR 3

Wodehouse, P(elham) G(renville)
1881-1975 ... **CLC 1, 2, 5, 10, 22; DAB;**
SSC 2
See also AITN 2; CA 45-48; 57-60;
CANR 3, 33; CDBLB 1914-1945;
DLB 34; MTCW; SATA 22

Woiwode, L.
See Woiwode, Larry (Alfred)

Woiwode, Larry (Alfred) 1941-... **CLC 6, 10**
See also CA 73-76; CANR 16; DLB 6

Wojciechowska, Maia (Teresa)
1927- .... **CLC 26**
See also AAYA 8; CA 9-12R; CANR 4, 41;
CLR 1; JRDA; MAICYA; SAAS 1;
SATA 1, 28, 83

Wolf, Christa 1929- .... **CLC 14, 29, 58**
See also CA 85-88; CANR 45; DLB 75;
MTCW

Wolfe, Gene (Rodman) 1931-....... **CLC 25**
See also CA 57-60; CAAS 9; CANR 6, 32;
DLB 8

Wolfe, George C. 1954- .... **CLC 49**

Wolfe, Thomas (Clayton)
1900-1938 .... **TCLC 4, 13, 29; DA;**
DAB; WLC
See also CA 104; 132; CDALB 1929-1941;
DLB 9, 102; DLBD 2; DLBY 85; MTCW

Wolfe, Thomas Kennerly, Jr. 1931-
See Wolfe, Tom
See also CA 13-16R; CANR 9, 33; MTCW

Wolfe, Tom .... **CLC 1, 2, 9, 15, 35, 51**
See also Wolfe, Thomas Kennerly, Jr.
See also AAYA 8; AITN 2; BEST 89:1;
DLB 152

Wolff, Geoffrey (Ansell) 1937- ..... **CLC 41**
See also CA 29-32R; CANR 29, 43

Wolff, Sonia
See Levitin, Sonia (Wolff)

Wolff, Tobias (Jonathan Ansell)
1945- .... **CLC 39, 64**
See also BEST 90:2; CA 114; 117; DLB 130

Wolfram von Eschenbach
c. 1170-c. 1220 .... **CMLC 5**
See also DLB 138

Wolitzer, Hilma 1930-............ **CLC 17**
See also CA 65-68; CANR 18, 40; SATA 31

Wollstonecraft, Mary 1759-1797...... **LC 5**
See also CDBLB 1789-1832; DLB 39, 104

Wonder, Stevie .... **CLC 12**
See also Morris, Steveland Judkins

Wong, Jade Snow 1922-........... **CLC 17**
See also CA 109

Woodcott, Keith
See Brunner, John (Kilian Houston)

Woodruff, Robert W.
See Mencken, H(enry) L(ouis)

Woolf, (Adeline) Virginia
1882-1941 .... **TCLC 1, 5, 20, 43, 56;**
DA; DAB; SSC 7; WLC
See also CA 104; 130; CDBLB 1914-1945;
DLB 36, 100; DLBD 10; MTCW

Woollcott, Alexander (Humphreys)
1887-1943 ....**TCLC 5**
See also CA 105; DLB 29

Woolrich, Cornell 1903-1968....... **CLC 77**
See also Hopley-Woolrich, Cornell George

Wordsworth, Dorothy
1771-1855 .... **NCLC 25**
See also DLB 107

Wordsworth, William
1770-1850 .... **NCLC 12, 38; DA; DAB;**
PC 4; WLC
See also CDBLB 1789-1832; DLB 93, 107

Wouk, Herman 1915-......... **CLC 1, 9, 38**
See also CA 5-8R; CANR 6, 33; DLBY 82;
MTCW

Wright, Charles (Penzel, Jr.)
1935- .... **CLC 6, 13, 28**
See also CA 29-32R; CAAS 7; CANR 23,
36; DLBY 82; MTCW

Wright, Charles Stevenson
1932- .... **CLC 49; BLC 3**
See also BW 1; CA 9-12R; CANR 26;
DLB 33

Wright, Jack R.
See Harris, Mark

Wright, James (Arlington)
1927-1980 .... **CLC 3, 5, 10, 28**
See also AITN 2; CA 49-52; 97-100;
CANR 4, 34; DLB 5; MTCW

Wright, Judith (Arandell)
1915- .... **CLC 11, 53**
See also CA 13-16R; CANR 31; MTCW;
SATA 14

Wright, L(aurali) R. 1939-......... **CLC 44**
See also CA 138

Wright, Richard (Nathaniel)
1908-1960 .... **CLC 1, 3, 4, 9, 14, 21, 48,**
74; BLC; DA; DAB; SSC 2; WLC
See also AAYA 5; BW 1; CA 108;
CDALB 1929-1941; DLB 76, 102;
DLBD 2; MTCW

Wright, Richard B(ruce) 1937- ...... **CLC 6**
See also CA 85-88; DLB 53

Wright, Rick 1945-............... **CLC 35**

Wright, Rowland
See Wells, Carolyn

Wright, Stephen Caldwell 1946- .... **CLC 33**
See also BW 2

Wright, Willard Huntington 1888-1939
See Van Dine, S. S.
See also CA 115

Wright, William 1930-............ **CLC 44**
See also CA 53-56; CANR 7, 23

Wroth, Lady Mary 1587-1653(?) ..... **LC 30**
See also DLB 121

Wu Ch'eng-en 1500(?)-1582(?)........ **LC 7**

Wu Ching-tzu 1701-1754 .... **LC 2**

Wurlitzer, Rudolph 1938(?)- ... **CLC 2, 4, 15**
See also CA 85-88

Wycherley, William 1641-1715 .... **LC 8, 21**
See also CDBLB 1660-1789; DLB 80

Wylie, Elinor (Morton Hoyt)
1885-1928 .... **TCLC 8**
See also CA 105; DLB 9, 45

Wylie, Philip (Gordon) 1902-1971 ... **CLC 43**
See also CA 21-22; 33-36R; CAP 2; DLB 9

Wyndham, John................... **CLC 19**
See also Harris, John (Wyndham Parkes
Lucas) Beynon

Wyss, Johann David Von
1743-1818 .... **NCLC 10**
See also JRDA; MAICYA; SATA 29;
SATA-Brief 27

Yakumo Koizumi
See Hearn, (Patricio) Lafcadio (Tessima
Carlos)

Yanez, Jose Donoso
See Donoso (Yanez), Jose

Yanovsky, Basile S.
See Yanovsky, V(assily) S(emenovich)

Yanovsky, V(assily) S(emenovich)
1906-1989 .... **CLC 2, 18**
See also CA 97-100; 129

Yates, Richard 1926-1992 ..... **CLC 7, 8, 23**
See also CA 5-8R; 139; CANR 10, 43;
DLB 2; DLBY 81, 92

Yeats, W. B.
See Yeats, William Butler

Yeats, William Butler
1865-1939 ..... **TCLC 1, 11, 18, 31; DA;**
DAB; WLC
See also CA 104; 127; CANR 45;
CDBLB 1890-1914; DLB 10, 19, 98;
MTCW

Yehoshua, A(braham) B.
1936- .... **CLC 13, 31**
See also CA 33-36R; CANR 43

Yep, Laurence Michael 1948- ...... **CLC 35**
See also AAYA 5; CA 49-52; CANR 1, 46;
CLR 3, 17; DLB 52; JRDA; MAICYA;
SATA 7, 69

Yerby, Frank G(arvin)
1916-1991 .... **CLC 1, 7, 22; BLC**
See also BW 1; CA 9-12R; 136; CANR 16;
DLB 76; MTCW

Yesenin, Sergei Alexandrovich
See Esenin, Sergei (Alexandrovich)

Yevtushenko, Yevgeny (Alexandrovich)
1933- .... **CLC 1, 3, 13, 26, 51**
See also CA 81-84; CANR 33; MTCW

Yezierska, Anzia 1885(?)-1970 ..... **CLC 46**
See also CA 126; 89-92; DLB 28; MTCW

Yglesias, Helen 1915- .... **CLC 7, 22**
See also CA 37-40R; CAAS 20; CANR 15;
MTCW

Yokomitsu Riichi 1898-1947 ...... **TCLC 47**

Yonge, Charlotte (Mary)
1823-1901 .... **TCLC 48**
See also CA 109; DLB 18; SATA 17

York, Jeremy
See Creasey, John

York, Simon
See Heinlein, Robert A(nson)

Yorke, Henry Vincent 1905-1974 ... **CLC 13**
See also Green, Henry
See also CA 85-88; 49-52

Yosano Akiko 1878-1942 .. **TCLC 59; PC 11**

Yoshimoto, Banana................ **CLC 84**
See also Yoshimoto, Mahoko

Yoshimoto, Mahoko 1964-
See Yoshimoto, Banana
See also CA 144

Young, Al(bert James)
1939- .... **CLC 19; BLC**
See also BW 2; CA 29-32R; CANR 26;
DLB 33

Young, Andrew (John) 1885-1971 .... **CLC 5**
See also CA 5-8R; CANR 7, 29

Young, Collier
See Bloch, Robert (Albert)

Young, Edward 1683-1765 .... **LC 3**
See also DLB 95

Young, Marguerite 1909- .... **CLC 82**
See also CA 13-16; CAP 1

Young, Neil 1945- .... **CLC 17**
See also CA 110

Yourcenar, Marguerite
1903-1987 .... **CLC 19, 38, 50, 87**
See also CA 69-72; CANR 23; DLB 72;
DLBY 88; MTCW

Yurick, Sol 1925- .... **CLC 6**
See also CA 13-16R; CANR 25

Zabolotskii, Nikolai Alekseevich
1903-1958 .... **TCLC 52**
See also CA 116

Zamiatin, Yevgenii
See Zamyatin, Evgeny Ivanovich

Zamora, Bernice (B. Ortiz)
1938- .... **CLC 89; HLC**
See also DLB 82; HW

Zamyatin, Evgeny Ivanovich
1884-1937 .... **TCLC 8, 37**
See also CA 105

Zangwill, Israel 1864-1926 .... **TCLC 16**
See also CA 109; DLB 10, 135

Zappa, Francis Vincent, Jr. 1940-1993
See Zappa, Frank
See also CA 108; 143

Zappa, Frank.................... **CLC 17**
See also Zappa, Francis Vincent, Jr.

Zaturenska, Marya 1902-1982 .... **CLC 6, 11**
See also CA 13-16R; 105; CANR 22

Zelazny, Roger (Joseph)
1937-1995 .... **CLC 21**
See also AAYA 7; CA 21-24R; 148;
CANR 26; DLB 8; MTCW; SATA 57;
SATA-Brief 39

Zhdanov, Andrei A(lexandrovich)
1896-1948 .... **TCLC 18**
See also CA 117

Zhukovsky, Vasily 1783-1852 .... **NCLC 35**

Ziegenhagen, Eric .... **CLC 55**

Zimmer, Jill Schary
See Robinson, Jill

Zimmerman, Robert
See Dylan, Bob

Zindel, Paul
1936- ...... **CLC 6, 26; DA; DAB; DC 5**
See also AAYA 2; CA 73-76; CANR 31;
CLR 3; DLB 7, 52; JRDA; MAICYA;
MTCW; SATA 16, 58

Zinov'Ev, A. A.
See Zinoviev, Alexander (Aleksandrovich)

Zinoviev, Alexander (Aleksandrovich)
1922- .... **CLC 19**
See also CA 116; 133; CAAS 10

Zoilus
See Lovecraft, H(oward) P(hillips)

Zola, Emile (Edouard Charles Antoine)
1840-1902 ...... **TCLC 1, 6, 21, 41; DA;**
DAB; WLC
See also CA 104; 138; DLB 123

Zoline, Pamela 1941- .... **CLC 62**

Zorrilla y Moral, Jose 1817-1893 .. **NCLC 6**

Zoshchenko, Mikhail (Mikhailovich)
1895-1958 .... **TCLC 15; SSC 15**
See also CA 115

Zuckmayer, Carl 1896-1977 .... **CLC 18**
See also CA 69-72; DLB 56, 124

Zuk, Georges
See Skelton, Robin

Zukofsky, Louis
1904-1978 .... **CLC 1, 2, 4, 7, 11, 18;**
PC 11
See also CA 9-12R; 77-80; CANR 39;
DLB 5; MTCW

Zweig, Paul 1935-1984 .... **CLC 34, 42**
See also CA 85-88; 113

Zweig, Stefan 1881-1942 .... **TCLC 17**
See also CA 112; DLB 81, 118

PC Cumulative Nationality Index

AMERICAN
Auden, W(ystan) H(ugh) **1**
Baraka, Amiri **4**
Bishop, Elizabeth **3**
Bogan, Louise **12**
Bradstreet, Anne **10**
Brodsky, Joseph **9**
Brooks, Gwendolyn **7**
Carruth, Hayden **10**
Crane, (Harold) Hart **3**
Cummings, E(dward) E(stlin) **5**
Dickinson, Emily (Elizabeth) **1**
Doolittle, Hilda **5**
Dove, Rita (Frances) **6**
Dunbar, Paul Laurence **5**
Duncan, Robert (Edward) **2**
Eliot, T(homas) S(tearns) **5**
Ferlinghetti, Lawrence (Monsanto) **1**
Forche, Carolyn (Louise) **10**
Frost, Robert (Lee) **1**
Gallagher, Tess **9**
Ginsberg, Allen **4**
Hayden, Robert E(arl) **6**
H. D. **5**
Hughes, (James) Langston **1**
Levertov, Denise **11**
Lorde, Audre (Geraldine) **12**
Lowell, Amy **13**
Lowell, Robert (Traill Spence Jr.) **3**
Madhubuti, Haki R. **5**
Masters, Edgar Lee **1**
McKay, Claude **2**
Merton, Thomas **10**
Millay, Edna St. Vincent **6**
Moore, Marianne (Craig) **4**
Plath, Sylvia **1**
Poe, Edgar Allan **1**
Pound, Ezra (Weston Loomis) **4**
Rich, Adrienne (Cecile) **5**
Robinson, Edwin Arlington **1**
Rose, Wendy **13**
Rukeyser, Muriel **12**
Sanchez, Sonia **9**
Sandburg, Carl (August) **2**
Schwartz, Delmore (David) **8**
Sexton, Anne (Harvey) **2**
Stevens, Wallace **6**
Toomer, Jean **7**
Wheatley (Peters), Phillis **3**
Whitman, Walt(er) **3**
Williams, William Carlos **7**
Zukofsky, Louis **11**

CANADIAN
Atwood, Margaret (Eleanor) **8**
Page, P(atricia) K(athleen) **12**

CHILEAN
Neruda, Pablo **4**

CHINESE
Li Ho **13**
Tu Fu **9**

ENGLISH
Arnold, Matthew **5**
Auden, W(ystan) H(ugh) **1**
Behn, Aphra **13**
Blake, William **12**
Bradstreet, Anne **10**
Bronte, Emily (Jane) **8**
Browning, Elizabeth Barrett **6**
Browning, Robert **2**
Coleridge, Samuel Taylor **11**
Day Lewis, C(ecil) **11**
Donne, John **1**
Eliot, T(homas) S(tearns) **5**
Graves, Robert (von Ranke) **6**
Gray, Thomas **2**
Hardy, Thomas **8**
Herbert, George **4**
Herrick, Robert **9**
Housman, A(lfred) E(dward) **2**
Hughes, Ted **7**
Keats, John **1**
Kipling, (Joseph) Rudyard **3**
Levertov, Denise **11**
Marvell, Andrew **10**
Page, P(atricia) K(athleen) **12**
Rossetti, Christina (Georgina) **7**
Sassoon, Siegfried (Lorraine) **12**
Sitwell, Dame Edith **3**
Smart, Christopher **13**
Smith, Stevie **12**
Spenser, Edmund **8**
Swift, Jonathan **9**
Tennyson, Alfred **6**
Wordsworth, William **4**

FRENCH
Apollinaire, Guillaume **7**
Baudelaire, Charles **1**
Mallarme, Stephane **4**
Merton, Thomas **10**
Nerval, Gerard de **13**
Rimbaud, (Jean Nicolas) Arthur **3**
Ronsard, Pierre de **11**
Valery, (Ambroise) Paul (Toussaint Jules) **9**
Verlaine, Paul (Marie) **2**
Villon, Francois **13**

GERMAN
Goethe, Johann Wolfgang von **5**
Holderlin, (Johann Christian) Friedrich **4**
Rilke, Rainer Maria **2**

GREEK
Sappho **5**

INDIAN
Tagore, Rabindranath **8**

IRISH
Day Lewis, C(ecil) **11**
Swift, Jonathan **9**

ITALIAN
Gozzano, Guido **10**
Martial **10**
Montale, Eugenio **13**
Pavese, Cesare **13**
Petrarch **8**

JAMAICAN
McKay, Claude **2**

JAPANESE
Ishikawa Takuboku **10**
Matsuo Basho **3**
Yosano Akiko **11**

LEBANESE
Gibran, Kahlil **9**

MEXICAN
Paz, Octavio **1**

NIGERIAN
Okigbo, Christopher (Ifenayichukwu) **7**

PERSIAN
Khayyam, Omar **8**

POLISH
Milosz, Czeslaw **8**

ROMAN
Ovid **2**
Vergil **12**

ROMANIAN
Celan, Paul **10**

RUSSIAN
Akhmatova, Anna **2**
Bely, Andrey **11**
Brodsky, Joseph **9**
Pasternak, Boris (Leonidovich) **6**
Pushkin, Alexander (Sergeyevich) **10**

SCOTTISH
Burns, Robert **6**
MacDiarmid, Hugh **9**
Scott, Walter **13**

SPANISH
Garcia Lorca, Federico **3**
Jimenez (Mantecon), Juan Ramon **7**

SYRIAN
Gibran, Kahlil **9**

WELSH
Thomas, Dylan (Marlais) **2**

PC Cumulative Title Index

"*A*" (Zukofsky) **11**:337-40, 345-46, 351, 356-58, 361-67, 369-73, 383, 385-93, 395-99
"*A*" *1-9* (Zukofsky) **11**:380
"*A*" *1-12* (Zukofsky) **11**:343-44, 367-68
"A Jenn de la Peruse, poète dramatique" (Ronsard) **11**:246
"A la Forest de Gastine" (Ronsard) **11**:228
"A la musique" (Rimbaud) **3**:258, 276, 283
"A la santé" (Apollinaire) **7**:44, 46-7
"A l'Italie" (Apollinaire) **7**:22
"A lo lejos" ("Far Off") (Jimenez) **7**:199
"A mi alma" (Jimenez) **7**:194
"A Philippes des-Portes Chartrain" (Ronsard) **11**:269-70
"A son ame" (Ronsard) **11**:244
"A une heure du matin" ("At One O'Clock in the Morning") (Baudelaire) **1**:59, 72
"A une passante" ("To a Passing Woman") (Baudelaire) **1**:45, 73
"A une raison" (Rimbaud) **3**:260
"Aaron" (Herbert) **4**:102, 114, 130
"Aaron Stark" (Robinson) **1**:460, 467
ABC of Economics (Pound) **4**:328
"L'abeille" (Valery) **9**:353, 387-88, 393-94
"Abel and Cain" (Baudelaire)
  See "Abel et Caïn"
"Abel et Caïn" ("Abel and Cain") (Baudelaire) **1**:68
"Abel's Bride" (Levertov) **11**:175
"Abnegation" (Rich) **5**:365
"Abode" (Milosz) **8**:215
"The Abominable Lake" (Smith) **12**:353
"The Abortion" (Sexton) **2**:349
"About the House" (Auden) **1**:21, 24
"About These Verses" (Pasternak) **6**:251

Above the Barriers (Pasternak)
  See *Poverkh barierov*
"Above These Cares" (Millay) **6**:235
"Abraham and Orpheus" (Schwartz) **8**:306, 308-09
"Absence" (Gozzano) **10**:178
"L'absence, ny l'oubly, ny la course du jour" (Ronsard) **11**:246
"Absolution" (Sassoon) **12**:241, 250, 252, 261, 276, 278, 280
"Abt Vogler" (Browning) **2**:37, 75, 80, 88, 95
"Abzählreime" (Celan) **10**:124-25
Academic Squaw: Reports to the World from the Ivory Tower (Rose) **13**:233, 238
"Acceptance" (Sassoon) **12**:259
"Accidentally on Purpose" (Frost) **1**:213
"Accomplishment" (Gallagher) **9**:59
An Account of a Weatherbeaten Journey (Matsuo Basho)
  See *Nozarashi kikō*
"Accountability" (Dunbar) **5**:133, 146
"Les accroupissements" (Rimbaud) **3**:284
"The Accuser" (Milosz) **8**:204
"Ach, um deine feuchten Schwingen" (Goethe) **5**:247
"The Ache of Marriage" (Levertov) **11**:169
"Achieving a Poem while Drinking Alone" (Tu Fu) **9**:327
"Achille's Song" (Duncan) **2**:115
"Acon" (H. D.) **5**:273
"Acquainted with the Night" (Frost) **1**:197, 205-06, 208
"An Acrostic" (Poe) **1**:446
"Ad Castitatem" (Bogan) **12**:117
"Adam" (Williams) **7**:350, 354
Adam & Eve & the City (Williams) **7**:350, 402
"Adam's Way" (Duncan) **2**:103
"The Addict" (Sexton) **2**:364
Additional Poems (Housman) **2**:176-77, 190

"Address for a Prize-Day" (Auden) **1**:8, 37
"Address of Beelzebub" (Burns) **6**:83-4, 88-9
"Address to a Louse" (Burns)
  See "To a Louse, on Seeing One on a Lady's Bonnet at Church"
"Address to Imagination" (Wheatley) **3**:335
"Address to the De'il" ("To the De'il") (Burns) **6**:49, 78, 83-4, 87
"Adelaide Abner" (Smith) **12**:310, 326
"L'adieu" (Apollinaire) **7**:48
"Adieu" (Rimbaud) **3**:273
"Adieu á Charlot" ("Second Populist Manifesto") (Ferlinghetti) **1**:181-82, 188
"Adieu, Mlle. Veronique" (Brodsky) **9**:2, 5
"Adolescence" (Dove) **6**:106
"Adolescence—III" (Dove) **6**:109
"Adolescencia" ("The Adolescent") (Jimenez) **7**:183, 209
"The Adolescent" (Jimenez)
  See "Adolescencia"
"Adonais" (Arnold) **5**:7
"Adonis" (H. D.) **5**:269, 304, 308
"Adonis" (Ronsard) **11**:251
"Advent" (Merton) **10**:340
"Advent" (Rossetti) **7**:290, 297
Advent (Rilke) **2**:280
"Advent, 1966" (Levertov) **11**:176
"Adventures" ("The Friend Who Is Sleeping") (Pavese) **13**:205
"Advocates" (Graves) **6**:144
"Ae Fond Kiss" (Burns) **6**:97
"Aeneas and Dido" (Brodsky) **9**:7
The Aeneid (Vergil) **12**:358, 361, 364-68, 371-73, 375-78, 380-99, 401-08
"The Aeolian Harp" ("The Eolian Harp") (Coleridge) **11**:51, 63, 73-4, 81-2, 88, 91, 97, 106-07, 109
"The Aesthetic Point of View" (Auden) **1**:12, 15

"Aether" (Ginsberg) **4**:81
"Affliction" (Herbert) **4**:118, 131
"Affliction I" (Herbert) **4**:111-12, 128, 131-32
"Affliction IV" (Herbert) **4**:112, 120
"The Affliction of Margaret----of----"
    (Wordsworth) **4**:402
"Afin qu'àtout jamais" (Ronsard) **11**:242
"Africa" (McKay) **2**:221
Africa (Blake) **12**:13
Africa (Petrarch) **8**:239-42, 246, 258, 260, 266-68, 278
"An African Elegy" (Duncan) **2**:103
"After a Flight" (Montale) **13**:158
"After a Flight" (Montefiore)
    See "Dopa una fuga"
"After a Journey" (Hardy) **8**:88, 93, 118, 135
"After a Long Illness" (Duncan) **2**:119
"After a Rain" (Pasternak) **6**:271
"After Apple-Picking" (Frost) **1**:193, 221-22
"After Dark" (Rich) **5**:364
"After Death" (Rossetti) **7**:269, 280, 287
"After Hearing a Waltz by Bartok" (Lowell) **13**:84
"After Many Days" (Dunbar) **5**:137
"After Mecca" (Brooks) **7**:63, 81
"After Paradise" (Milosz) **8**:209
After Parting (Bely)
    See *Posle razluki*
"After Rain" (Page) **12**:168, 178, 190
"After Reading *Mickey in the Night Kitchen*
    for the Third Time before Bed" (Dove) **6**:121
"After the Agony" (Atwood) **8**:6
"After the Cries of the Birds" (Ferlinghetti) **1**:173-74, 176
"After the Deluge" (Rimbaud)
    See "Après le déluge"
"After the Flood, We" (Atwood) **8**:12
"After the Funeral: In Memory of Anne
    Jones" ("In Memory of Ann Jones")
    (Thomas) **2**:390
"After the Persian" (Bogan) **12**:107, 118, 124-25, 129
"After the Surprising Conversions" (Lowell) **3**:202-03
"After the Winter" (McKay) **2**:228
"After Troy" (H. D.) **5**:268
"After Twenty Years" (Rich) **5**:384
"Afterimages" (Lorde) **12**:155
"Aftermath" (Plath) **1**:389
"Aftermath" (Sassoon) **12**:269, 289
Afternoon of a Faun (Mallarme)
    See *L'après-midi d'un faune*
"Afternoon on a Hill" (Millay) **6**:235-36
"Afternoon Rain in State Street" (Lowell) **13**:79
"The After-thought" (Smith) **12**:329-32
"Afterwards" (Hardy) **8**:101, 131
"Afterword" (Atwood) **8**:11
"Afterword" (Brodsky) **9**:25
"Afterword" (Carruth) **10**:71
"An Afterword: For Gwen Brooks"
    (Madhubuti) **5**:346
"Afton Water" (Burns)
    See "Sweet Afton"
"Again and Again and Again" (Sexton) **2**:353
"Again I Visited" (Pushkin)
    See "Vnov' Ya Posetil"
"Against System Builders" (Goethe) **5**:229
"Agatha" (Valery)
    See "Agathe; ou, La sainte du sommeil"

"Agathe; ou, La sainte du sommeil"
    ("Agatha") (Valery) **9**:357, 400-01
"The Age Demanded" (Pound) **4**:320
The Age of Anxiety: A Baroque Eclogue
    (Auden) **1**:14, 23, 33-4, 39
"The Ages of Man" (Bradstreet)
    See "The Four Ages of Man"
"An Agnostic" (Smith) **12**:352
"The Agony" (Herbert) **4**:100
"An Agony. As Now" (Baraka) **4**:16, 24
"Agosta the Winged Man and Rasha the Black
    Dove" (Dove) **6**:109
"Agrippina in the Golden House of Nero"
    (Lowell) **3**:222
"Agua sexual" ("Sexual Water") (Neruda) **4**:306
"Ah, Are You Digging on My Grave?"
    (Hardy) **8**:131
"Ah! Sun-Flower" (Blake) **12**:34
"Ahvan" (Tagore) **8**:415
"Aigeltinger" (Williams) **7**:370
"The Aim Was Song" (Frost) **1**:194
"Aimless Journey" (Tagore)
    See "Niruddesh yatra"
"Air" (Toomer) **7**:333
"Air de sémiramis" (Valery) **9**:365, 391-92
"Aire and Angels" (*Twice or thrice had I loved
    thee*) (Donne) **1**:130, 149
"The Airy Christ" (Smith) **12**:295, 330-31, 333
"Ajanta" (Rukeyser) **12**:204, 214, 219, 224
"Akatsuki no kane" ("The Morning Bell")
    (Ishikawa Takuboku) **10**:214
Akogare (*Longing*) (Ishikawa Takuboku) **10**:194, 212-16
"Al Aaraaf" (Poe) **1**:437, 449
"Al mio grillo" (Montale) **13**:138
"Al pintor Swaminathan" (Paz) **1**:354
Al que quiere! (Williams) **7**:344-45, 348-49, 377-79, 387-88, 398, 405-10
"Al soneto con mi alma" (Jimenez) **7**:192
"Ala bāb al-haykal" (Gibran) **9**:78
Al-ajnihah (Gibran) **9**:78
"Alas, a Prince" (Tu Fu) **9**:317
Al-'awāsif (Gibran) **9**:79-81
"Al-bahr" (Gibran) **9**:80
"L'albatros" (Baudelaire) **1**:65
Album de vers anciens, 1890-1900 (Valery) **9**:363, 365, 386-87, 390-91, 395
"The Alchemist" (Bogan) **12**:98, 103, 114
"Alchemy of the Word" (Rimbaud)
    See "Alchimie du verbe"
"Alchimie du verbe" ("Alchemy of the
    Word") (Rimbaud) **3**:261, 267, 274
Alcools (Apollinaire) **7**:6, 9-10, 12, 14-15, 38-46, 48-9
"Aleksandru" ("To Alexander") (Pushkin) **10**:421
Alexis und Dora (Goethe) **5**:240
"Alfansa" (Forche) **10**:134, 169-70
"Alfonso" (McKay) **2**:205
"Alfred the Great" (Smith) **12**:296, 316
"Al-hurūf al-nāriyah" (Gibran) **9**:78
"Alice" (Graves) **6**:139
"Alice Du Clos" (Coleridge) **11**:106
"Alice Fell" (Wordsworth) **4**:404, 415
"Al-jamāl" (Gibran) **9**:81
"All Clowns Are Masked and All Personae"
    (Schwartz) **8**:305
"All Guilt and Innocence Turned Upside
    Down" (Schwartz) **8**:285

"All in Green Went My Love Riding"
    (Cummings) **5**:87
"All kings and all their favourites" (Donne)
    See "The Anniversarie"
"All Life in a Life" (Masters) **1**:326, 328, 335-36, 342
"All Mountain" (H. D.) **5**:305
All My Pretty Ones (Sexton) **2**:346-47, 349-50, 353, 355, 360-61, 370
"All Nearness Pauses, While a Star Can
    Grow" (Cummings) **5**:109
"All of Us Always Turning Away for Solace"
    (Schwartz) **8**:305
"All Souls' Day" (Sassoon) **12**:258
All: The Collected Short Poems, 1923-1958
    (Zukofsky) **11**:348-49, 351, 354-56, 393-94
All: The Collected Shorter Poems, 1956-64
    (Zukofsky) **11**:349, 353, 356, 383, 390
"All the Dead Dears" (Plath) **1**:388, 407
"All the Fancy Things" (Williams) **7**:394
"All Worlds Have Halfsight, Seeing Either
    With" (Cummings) **5**:111
"All-destroyer" (Tagore)
    See "Sarvaneshe"
"Allégorie" (Baudelaire) **1**:56
"Alley Rats" (Sandburg) **2**:304
"Allie" (Graves) **6**:141
"The Allies" (Lowell) **13**:76, 78
"Allons adieu messieurs tachez de revenir"
    (Apollinaire) **7**:22
"Alloy" (Rukeyser) **12**:210
Almas de violeta (*Souls of Violet*) (Jimenez) **7**:199
Al-mawakib (Gibran) **9**:79-81
"Almost a Fantasy" (Montale) **13**:151
"Alone" (Poe) **1**:442-44
"Along History" (Rukeyser) **12**:228
"Along the Field as We Came By" (Housman) **2**:183
"Al-shā'ir" (Gibran) **9**:79
"The Altar" (Herbert) **4**:114, 120, 130
The Altar of the Past (Gozzano)
    See *L'altare del Passato*
L'altare del Passato (*The Altar of the Past*)
    (Gozzano) **10**:177
"Altarwise by Owl-light" (Thomas) **2**:388-89, 403, 406
"Einem alten Architekten in Rom" (Brodsky) **9**:2, 4
"Alternate Thoughts from Underground"
    (Atwood) **8**:40
Alturas de Macchu Picchu (*The Heights of
    Macchu Picchu; Macchu Picchu*) (Neruda) **4**:282, 284-85, 292-93
"Al-umm wa wahīduha" (Gibran) **9**:78
"Always the Mob" (Sandburg) **2**:302
"Am/Trak" (Baraka) **4**:39
"Am Was. Are Leaves Few This. Is This a or"
    (Cummings) **5**:107
"Amām 'arsh al-jamāl" ("The Daughter of the
    Forest") (Gibran) **9**:79
"Amaranth" (H. D.) **5**:305
Amaranth (Robinson) **1**:477-78, 482-83
"The Ambassador" (Smith) **12**:330, 339
"Ambassadors of Grief" (Sandburg) **2**:308
"Amen!" (Rossetti) **7**:268
"America" (McKay) **2**:212
"America" (Wheatley) **3**:363
America: A Prophecy, 1793 (Blake) **12**:13, 25-7, 63
"America, I Do Not Invoke Your Name in
    Vain" (Neruda)

See "América, no invoco tu nombre en vano"

"América, no invoco tu nombre en vano" ("America, I Do Not Invoke Your Name in Vain") (Neruda) **4**:292

"The American" (Kipling) **3**:161

"American Change" (Ginsberg) **4**:53, 84

"[American Journal]" (Hayden) **6**:188-89, 191-92, 195

American Journal (Hayden) **6**:194-96

"American Miscellany" (H. D.) **5**:268

"Ametas and Thestylis Making Hay-Ropes" (Marvell) **10**:269, 271, 294, 304

"L'amica di nonna speranza" ("The Friend of Grandmother Speranza"; "Grandmother Speranza's Friend") (Gozzano) **10**:177, 181-82

"L'amico che dorme" (Pavese) **13**:229

Les amies (Verlaine) **2**:432

"Among Those Killed in the Dawn Raid Was a Man Aged a Hundred" (Thomas) **2**:388

"Amor mundi" (Rossetti) **7**:282

Amores (*Erotic Adventures*; *Love-Poems*) (Ovid) **2**:234-35, 237-38, 242-43, 245, 251, 253-54, 258-59, 261

Amoretti (Spenser) **8**:329, 388-89

Amoretti and Epithalamion (Spenser) **8**:388

"Amour" (Verlaine) **2**:416-17, 425

"L'amour et le crâne" (Baudelaire) **1**:45

Amours (Ronsard) **11**:220-21, 246, 250, 254, 256, 258, 275, 277-78, 293

Amours de Cassandre (Ronsard) **11**:247-48

"Amours d'Eurymedon et de Calliree" (Ronsard) **11**:241

Amours diverses (Ronsard) **11**:270

"Amphibian" (Browning) **2**:80

Amplitude: New and Selected Poems (Gallagher) **9**:57-62

"Amravan" ("Mango Grove") (Tagore) **8**:416

"Amy's Cruelty" (Browning) **6**:23, 28, 32

"An den Wassern Babels" ("By the Waters of Babylon") (Celan) **10**:127-28

"Ananta jivan" ("Eternal Life") (Tagore) **8**:406

"Ananta maran" ("Eternal Death") (Tagore) **8**:406

"Anaphora" (Bishop) **3**:37, 56

An Anatomie of the World (Donne)
See *The First Anniversarie. An Anatomie of the World. Wherein By Occasion of the untimely death of Mistris Elizabeth Drury, the frailtie and decay of this whole World is represented*

"Ancestors" (Pavese) **13**:204

"Anchar" ("The Upas Tree") (Pushkin) **10**:373

"The Ancient Briton Lay Ynder His Rock" (Hughes) **7**:147

"Ancient discipline" (Pavese)
See "Disciplina antica"

"An Ancient Gesture" (Millay) **6**:232, 240

"The Ancient Heroes and the Bomber Pilot" (Hughes) **7**:132

"Ancient History" (Sassoon) **12**:258

"Ancient One" (Montale)
See "Antico, sono ubriacato della tua voce"

"The Ancient Sage" (Tennyson) **6**:407

"An Ancient to Ancients" (Hardy) **8**:121

"Ancient Wisdom Speaks" (H. D.) **5**:307

"Ancora ad Annecy" ("Still at Annecy") (Montale) **13**:138

& (*And*) (Cummings) **5**:75, 92-3, 95, 104-05

And (Cummings)
See &

"And a Few Negroes Too" (Madhubuti)
See "A Message All Blackpeople Can Dig (& A Few Negroes Too)"

"And a Wisdom as Such" (Duncan) **2**:115

"And Death Shall Have No Dominion" ("Death Shall Have No Dominion") (Thomas) **2**:379, 385, 389-90, 397

"And Did Those Feet in Ancient Time Walk upon England's Mountains Green?" (Blake) **12**:45

"And One for My Dame" (Sexton) **2**:363

"And Pass" (Toomer) **7**:332

"And So Goodbye to Cities" (Merton) **10**:334, 344

"And So Today" (Sandburg) **2**:307-08

"And the Children of Birmingham" (Merton) **10**:334, 341

". . .And the Clouds Return after the Rain" (Smith) **12**:331

"And There Was a Great Calm" (Hardy) **8**:119

"And What About the Children" (Lorde) **12**:139

"And with What Bodies Do They Come?" (Dickinson) **1**:102

"And You as Well Must Die" (Millay) **6**:211

"El andaluz universal" ("The Universal Andalusia") (Jimenez) **7**:205

"Andenken" ("Rememberance") (Holderlin) **4**:172, 178

"Andrea del Sarto" (Browning) **2**:37, 86, 88, 95

"Anecdote for Fathers" (Wordsworth) **4**:425-28

"Anecdote of the Jar" (Stevens) **6**:309, 326-27

"Anecdote of the Prince of Peacocks" (Stevens) **6**:309

Anew (Zukofsky) **11**:342, 347, 382-83

"L'ange du méridien" (Rilke) **2**:275

"Das angebrochene Jahr" (Celan) **10**:124

"Angel Boley" (Smith) **12**:352

The Angel of History (Forche) **10**:160, 169

"Angel Surrounded by Paysans" (Stevens) **6**:304

"L'angelo nero" ("The Black Angel") (Montale) **13**:134

"Angels of the Love Affair" (Sexton) **2**:365, 367

"The Anger of the Sea" (Ishikawa Takuboku)
See "Umi no ikari"

"Anger's Freeing Power" (Smith) **12**:295, 311, 330

"Anglais Mort à Florence" (Stevens) **6**:311

Angle of Ascent (Hayden) **6**:188, 190, 194

"The Angry God" (Ferlinghetti) **1**:183

"Angry Samson" (Graves) **6**:151

"The Anguish" (Millay) **6**:217

"Anima" (Carruth) **10**:85

Animal de fondo (*Animal of Depth*; *Animal of Inner Depths*) (Jimenez) **7**:183-84, 203, 211, 214

"Animal de luz" ("Animal of Light") (Neruda) **4**:289

Animal of Depth (Jimenez)
See *Animal de fondo*

Animal of Inner Depths (Jimenez)
See *Animal de fondo*

"Animal of Light" (Neruda)
See "Animal de luz"

"Animal, Vegetable, and Mineral" (Bogan) **12**:92, 99, 107, 125

The Animals in That Country (Atwood) **8**:3-4, 12, 15-16, 23

Animula (Eliot) **5**:194, 197-98, 203

"Anklage" (Goethe) **5**:248

"Ankor Wat" (Ginsberg) **4**:61

"Annabel Lee" (Poe) **1**:425, 429, 434, 438, 441, 444, 447-48

"Annandale Again" (Robinson) **1**:476

"Anne" (Valery) **9**:374, 392

"Anne Boleyn's Song" (Sitwell) **3**:315

"Anne Rutledge" (Masters) **1**:334, 348

"Annetta" (Montale) **13**:138

"The Anniad" (Brooks) **7**:53, 58, 61, 80, 102, 104

Annie Allen (Brooks) **7**:53-4, 56-8, 60-2, 68, 75, 78, 80-1, 85, 91, 96, 102, 104-05

"The Anniversarie" ("All kings and all their favourites") (Donne) **1**:130

The Anniversaries (*The First and Second Anniversaries*) (Donne) **1**:145-48, 155-56, 158

"Anniversario" ("Anniversary") (Montale) **13**:110

"The Anniversary" (Lowell) **13**:66, 97

"Anniversary" (Montale)
See "Anniversario"

Anno Domini MCMXXI (Akhmatova) **2**:3, 13-14, 18

"The Annunciation" (Merton) **10**:339

"Another Letter to My Husband" (Bradstreet) **10**:28

"Another New-yeeres Gift; or song for the Circumcision" ("The New Yeares Gift, or Circumcision Song") (Herrick) **9**:118, 120

"Another Space" (Page) **12**:180, 190, 197-98

"Another Spring" (Levertov) **11**:169-70

"Another Time" (Auden) **1**:18-19, 30, 34

"Another Year" (Williams) **7**:370

"The Answer" (Herbert) **4**:130

"An Answer to the Rebus" (Wheatley) **3**:363

"Antaryami" ("The Indweller") (Tagore) **8**:408

"An Antebellum Sermon" (Dunbar) **5**:120, 123, 133, 147

"Antenati" ("Forebears") (Pavese) **13**:217, 220, 225-26

"Antéros" (Nerval) **13**:181, 191-92, 194, 198

Anthology (Jimenez)
See *Antolojía poética (1898-1953)*

"Antico, sono ubriacato della tua voce" ("Ancient One") (Montale) **13**:115, 141

"Anti-Desperation" (Arnold) **5**:7

"Antigone" (Arnold) **5**:8

"Antiphon" (Herbert) **4**:103

"The Antiphon" (Levertov) **11**:198

"Anti-Vietnam War Peace Mobilization" (Ginsberg) **4**:76

Antolojía poética (1898-1953) (*Anthology*; *Selected Writings of Juan Ramon Jimenez*) (Jimenez) **7**:183-84

"anyone lived in a pretty how town" (Cummings) **5**:81

"Aphrodite Ode" (Sappho)
See "Ode to Aphrodite"

"Apogee of Celery" (Neruda)
See "Apogeo del apio"

"Apogeo del apio" ("Apogee of Celery") (Neruda) **4**:277

"Apollo at Pheræ" (Masters) **1**:329

"Apollo of the Physiologists" (Graves) **6**:152-53

"An Apollonian Elegy" (Duncan) **2**:105

"Apollo's Edict" (Swift) **9**:252

"The Apology of Demetrius" (Masters) **1**:343

"An Apology to the Lady Cartaret" (Swift) **9**:296

Apophoreta (Martial) **10**:230, 241

"The Apostrophe to Vincentine" (Stevens) **6**:309

"Apparent Failure" (Browning) **2**:68

"The Apparition" (Donne) **1**:130, 152

"The Apparition of His Mistress Calling Him to Elizium" (Herrick) **9**:93, 103, 133, 138-39

"Appendix to the Anniad Leaves from a Loose-Leaf War Diary" (Brooks) **7**:61

"Appetite" (Smith) **12**:310

"The Apple" (Page) **12**:168, 170

"An Apple Gathering" (Rossetti) **7**:260-61, 280

"Apple Tragedy" (Hughes) **7**:143, 159

"The Apple Woman's Complaint" (McKay) **2**:210

"Apples and Water" (Graves) **6**:141

"Appleton House" (Marvell)
   See "Upon Appleton House"

"The Applicant" (Plath) **1**:394, 400-01

"Apprehensions" (Duncan) **2**:110, 112

"An Apprentice Angel" (MacDiarmid) **9**:155

"Appuldurcombe Park" (Lowell) **13**:84

"Après le déluge" ("After the Deluge") (Rimbaud) **3**:261

L'après-midi d'un faune (*Afternoon of a Faun*) (Mallarme) **4**:186, 188, 190, 197, 207-08

"April Is the Saddest Month" (Williams) **7**:351, 354, 400

"Aquarelles" ("Water Color") (Verlaine) **2**:415

"The Aquarium" (Lowell) **13**:79

"Aquatre heures du matin" (Rimbaud) **3**:274

"Arabel" (Masters) **1**:328

"L'arca" ("The Ark") (Montale) **13**:113

"Arcady Unheeding" (Sassoon) **12**:240, 275

"Archibald Higbie" (Masters) **1**:333

"The Archipelago" (Holderlin)
   See "Der Archipelagus"

"Der Archipelagus" ("The Archipelago") (Holderlin) **4**:147-48, 164

"Architecture" (Stevens) **6**:293

"The Architecture: Passages 9" (Duncan) **2**:107

The Ardent Slingsman (Neruda)
   See *El hondero entusiasta, 1923-1924*

"La arena traicionada" ("The Land Betrayed") (Neruda) **4**:292-93

"The Argument of His Book" (Herrick) **9**:85, 95, 97, 101, 105, 107-10, 116, 132-34, 138-39, 141

"Ariadne" (H. D.) **5**:304

Arias tristes (*Sad Airs*) (Jimenez) **7**:199, 209

"Ariel" (Plath) **1**:381, 409, 413

Ariel (Plath) **1**:379-80, 383-84, 387, 389-91, 393-96, 405-07, 410-11

"Ariettes oubliées" ("Forgotten Arietta") (Verlaine) **2**:431

"Ariso" ("The Reefy Coast") (Ishikawa Takuboku) **10**:215

Aristophanes' Apology (Browning) **2**:96

"The Ark" (Montale)
   See "L'arca"

"Armageddon" (Tennyson) **6**:407-08, 413, 415-18

"Armor's Undermining Modesty" (Moore) **4**:267

"Arms" (Tagore)
   See "Bahu"

Ārogya (*Recovery; Recovery*) (Tagore) **8**:424, 426

"Arras" (Page) **12**:168, 170, 178, 180, 189-90, 197

"Arremba sulla strinata proda" (Montale) **13**:116

"Arrest of Antoñito the Camborio" (Garcia Lorca)
   See "Prendimiento de Antoñito el Camborio"

"Arrival at Santos" (Bishop) **3**:44

"The Arrival of the Bee Box" (Plath) **1**:410-13

"Arrow" (Dove) **6**:123

Ars Amandi (Ovid)
   See *Ars amatoria*

Ars amatoria (*Ars Amandi; Art of Love*) (Ovid) **2**:233-34, 238-39, 241-47, 253-55, 261

"Ars poetica" (Dove) **6**:121-22

"Ars poetica?" (Milosz) **8**:197, 201

"Arsenio" (Montale) **13**:107, 120, 124-25, 147, 164

Art of Love (Ovid)
   See *Ars amatoria*

"Art of Poetry" (Verlaine)
   See "L'Art poètique"

"The Art of Response" (Lorde) **12**:140

"L'Art poètique" ("Art of Poetry") (Verlaine) **2**:416-18, 428, 430-34

"L'arte povera" ("Poor Art") (Montale) **13**:138

"Artémis" (Nerval) **13**:173, 179, 181, 184-87, 195-96, 198

"Artemis Prologuises" (Browning) **2**:26

"Artificer" (Milosz) **8**:191

"Artillerie" ("Artillery") (Herbert) **4**:101, 129

"Artillery" (Herbert)
   See "Artillerie"

"The Artists' and Models' Ball" (Brooks) **7**:107

"As a Possible Lover" (Baraka) **4**:16

"As a World Would Have It" (Robinson) **1**:460

"As Any (Men's Hells Having Wrestled with)" (Cummings) **5**:108

"As Children Together" (Forche) **10**:144, 156-57, 168-69

"As Eagles Soar" (Toomer) **7**:340

"As Hermes Once" (Keats) **1**:279

"As I Ebb'd with the Ocean of Life" (Whitman) **3**:396-97, 421

"As I Grow Older" (Hughes) **1**:251

"As I Lay with My Head on Your Lap Camarado" (Whitman) **3**:379

"As I Sat Alone by Blue Ontario's Shore" (Whitman) **3**:377, 387

"As Is the Sea Marvelous" (Cummings) **5**:104

"As Lovers Do" (MacDiarmid) **9**:156

"As Loving Hind" (Bradstreet) **10**:35-6

"As My Blood Was Drawn" (Hayden) **6**:194

"As One Does Sickness Over" (Dickinson) **1**:94

"As Seen by Disciples" (Brooks) **7**:63

As Ten, as Twenty (Page) **12**:163-64, 167, 173, 193

"As virtuous men pass mildly away" (Donne)
   See "A Valediction: forbidding mourning"

"As Weary Pilgrim" ("A Pilgrim") (Bradstreet) **10**:8, 15, 28, 34, 36-7

"Asahya bhalobasa" ("Unendurable Love") (Tagore) **8**:405

"Ashar nairashya" ("Hope's Despari") (Tagore) **8**:405

Ashes (Bely)
   See *Pepel'*

"Ashes of Life" (Millay) **6**:206

"Ashurnatsirpal III" (Sandburg) **2**:323

Ash-Wednesday (Eliot) **5**:162-64, 170, 174, 186, 192, 194, 197-206, 209-10

"Ask Me No More" (Tennyson) **6**:366

Ask Your Mama: 12 Moods for Jazz (Hughes) **1**:249, 251-53, 261, 268, 270

Asolando (Browning) **2**:96

Asolando: Fancies and Facts (Browning) **2**:66-7, 88

"An Aspect of Love, Alive in the Fire and Ice" (Brooks) **7**:82, 88, 91, 94

"Aspen Tree" (Celan) **10**:112-13

"Asphalt Georgics" (Carruth) **10**:77, 91

"Asphodel, That Greeny Flower" (Williams) **7**:371, 375, 390-92, 402-03

"The Ass" (Smith) **12**:302-6, 319

"The Assassin" (Sexton) **2**:365 .

"Assassination Raga" (Ferlinghetti) **1**:173

"Assault" (Millay) **6**:236, 238

"Assay of the Infinite Man" (Neruda)
   See *Tentativa del hombre infinito*

"The Assertion" (Day Lewis) **11**:146

"Assommons les pauvres" ("Let's Beat Down the Poor") (Baudelaire) **1**:59

"Astigmatism" (Lowell) **13**:84

"Astronauts" (Hayden) **6**:194

"Astrophel: A Pastoral Elegy" (Spenser) **8**:365, 367, 387

"The Asylum" (Carruth) **10**:71, 82-4

"At a Bach Concert" (Rich) **5**:352, 387, 393

"At a Hasty Wedding" (Hardy) **8**:85

"At a Lunar Eclipse" (Hardy) **8**:89

"At a Party" (Bogan) **12**:106

"At a Solemn Musick" (Schwartz) **8**:289

"At a Window" (Sandburg) **2**:300

"At Baia" (H. D.) **5**:267

"At Candle-Lightin' Time" (Dunbar) **5**:122

"At Castle Boterel" (Hardy) **8**:118

"At Dawn" (Milosz) **8**:210

"At Daybreak" (Sassoon) **12**:247

"At Dusk" (Cummings) **5**:93, 106

"At Ithaca" (H. D.) **5**:268

"At Melville's Tomb" (Crane) **3**:90, 103

"At My Father's Grave" (MacDiarmid) **9**:156

"At One O'Clock in the Morning" (Baudelaire)
   See "A une heure du matin"

"At School" (Smith) **12**:330, 333

"At Sea" (Toomer) **7**:336

"At the Ball Game" (Williams) **7**:368, 385

"At the Caberet-Vert" (Rimbaud)
   See "Au caberet-vert"

"At the Faucet of June" (Williams) **7**:382-83, 387-89, 410

"At the Ferocious phenomenon of 5 O'clock I find Myself" (Cummings) **5**:93

"At the Fishhouses" (Bishop) **3**:42, 46, 48

"At the Gare Bruxelles-Midi" (Ferlinghetti) **1**:183

"At the Gates of the Tombs" (Sandburg) **2**:307

"At the German Writers Conference in Munich" (Dove) **6**:109

"At the Grave of Henry Vaughan" (Sassoon) **12**:246-47

"At the Hairdresser's" (Brooks) **7**:58, 68, 86, 102

"At the Head of This Street a Gasping Organ is Waving Moth-" (Cummings) **5**:93

"At the Indian Killer's Grave" (Lowell) **3**:202

"At the Loom: Passages 2" (Duncan) **2**:107

"At the National Black Assembly" (Baraka) **4**:28, 38

"At the Piano" (Hardy) **8**:93

"At the Tourist Centre in Boston" (Atwood) **8**:5, 23

At the Very Edge of the Sea (Akhmatova)
　See *U samovo morya*

"At The-Place-of-Sadness" (Gallagher) **9**:64

"At This Point" (Montale)
　See "A questo punto"

"At Waking" (Hardy) **8**:104

"Atavismo" (Pavese) **13**:209, 214

Atemwende (*Breath-Turning*) (Celan) **10**:96-7, 105, 110

"Atherton's Gambit" (Robinson) **1**:466

"Atlantic Oil" (Pavese) **13**:223

"Atlantis" (Crane) **3**:90, 97, 106, 110-11

"An Atlas of the Difficult World" (Rich) **5**:398

An Atlas of the Difficult World: Poems, 1988-1991 (Rich) **5**:398-99

"Attack" (Sassoon) **12**:266, 283-84, 286

"Attention, Attention" (Baraka) **4**:24

"The Attic Which Is Desire" (Williams) **7**:351, 399

"Attis" (Tennyson) **6**:363

"Atys, the Land of Biscay" (Housman) **2**:179, 181

"Au caberet-vert" ("At the Caberet-Vert") (Rimbaud) **3**:283

"Au Clair de la lune" (MacDiarmid) **9**:191

"Au lecteur" ("To the Reader") (Baudelaire) **1**:46, 57, 67, 70

"Au platane" (Valery) **9**:365, 394-96

"Au Roy" (Ronsard)
　See "Discours au Roy"

"Au Salon" (Pound) **4**:364

"Aubade" (Lowell) **13**:93

"Aubade" (Sitwell) **3**:297

"Aubade" (Smith) **12**:331

"Aubade: Harlem" (Merton) **10**:340

"Aubade: Lake Erie" (Merton) **10**:333, 340, 350

"Aubade—The Annunciation" (Merton) **10**:339

"Aube" (Rimbaud) **3**:261-62, 264

"L'aube spirituelle" (Baudelaire) **1**:56, 63

"Audley Court" (Tennyson) **6**:365

"Auf dem See" ("On the Lake") (Goethe) **5**:255

"Auguries of Innocence" (Blake) **12**:35-6

"Augurios" (Paz) **1**:361

"August" (Rich) **5**:371

"August First" (Carruth) **10**:91

"An August Midnight" (Hardy) **8**:112

"The Auld Farmer's New Year Morning Salutation" (Burns)
　See "The Auld Farmer's New Year Morning Salutation"

"The Auld Farmer's New Year's Day Address to His Auld Mare Maggie" (Burns) **6**:78

"Auld Lang Syne" (Burns) **6**:59, 75, 98-9

Aún (Neruda) **4**:289

"La aurora" ("Dawn") (Garcia Lorca) **3**:141

"Aurora Borealis" (Dove) **6**:110

Aurora Leigh (Browning) **6**:2, 6-7, 10-13, 21-3, 25-6, 31-2, 34-8, 40, 44, 46

"The Auroras of Autumn" (Stevens) **6**:338

Auroras of Autumn (Stevens) **6**:303, 335

"Aurore" (Valery) **9**:356, 363, 365, 367-68, 371, 394, 396

"Aus einer Sturmnacht" (Rilke) **2**:277

Ausgewahlte gedichte (Celan) **10**:102

"Aussi bien que les cigales" (Apollinaire) **7**:18, 22

"Aussöhnung" (Goethe) **5**:250-51

"The Author to her Book" (Bradstreet) **10**:7, 18, 27, 34

"The Author upon Himself" (Swift) **9**:295-96, 304, 306, 308-09

"The Author's Earnest Cry and Prayer" (Burns) **6**:78-9

"The Author's Manner of Living" (Swift) **9**:295

"Autobiography" (Ferlinghetti) **1**:177-80, 183-84, 187

Autobiography (Zukofsky) **11**:365

"Autochthon" (Masters) **1**:333

"Automne" (Apollinaire) **7**:42

"Automne malade" (Apollinaire) **7**:39, 42-3

"Autumn" (Lowell) **13**:97

"Autumn" (Neruda)
　See "Otoño"

"Autumn" (Pasternak) **6**:266

"Autumn" (Smith) **12**:345

"Autumn Cellars" (Montale) **13**:149-50

"Autumn Equinox" (Rich) **5**:351-52, 393

"Autumn Forest" (Pasternak) **6**:267

"Autumn Gold: New England Fall" (Ginsberg) **4**:54

"Autumn Lament" (Mallarme)
　See "Plainte d'automne"

"Autumn Sequence" (Rich) **5**:363, 382

"Avarice" (Herbert) **4**:102, 130

"Ave Imperatrix!" (Kipling) **3**:190

"Ave Maria" (Crane) **3**:84, 86

"Avenel Gray" (Robinson)
　See "Mortmain"

"Avenue of Limes" (Pasternak) **6**:267

"The Avenue of Poplars" (Williams) **7**:382

"Avondale" (Smith) **12**:352

"Avondall" (Smith) **12**:352

Avon's Harvest (Robinson) **1**:465-66, 468-69

"Awakening of the Waterfall" (Tagore)
　See "Nirjharer svapnabhanga"

"Away, Melancholy" (Smith) **12**:333

"Awful Music" (Merton) **10**:337

The Awful Rowing Toward God (Sexton) **2**:360, 367-68, 371-73

"The Ax-Helve" (Frost) **1**:215

"Aylmer's Field" (Tennyson) **6**:362

"L'azur" ("The Azure") (Mallarme) **4**:199-200, 208, 213

"The Azure" (Mallarme)
　See "L'azur"

"Azure and Gold" (Lowell) **13**:60

"Babočka" ("The Butterfly") (Brodsky) **9**:29

"Baby" (Sexton) **2**:367

"Baby Picture" (Sexton) **2**:370

"Babylon Revisited" (Baraka) **4**:18

"The Bacchae" (H. D.) **5**:305

"Bacchanales" (Ronsard) **11**:230-32, 234

"Bacchanalia" (Pasternak) **6**:267

"Back Again, Home" (Madhubuti) **5**:324, 329, 338

"Back from a Walk" (Garcia Lorca)
　See "Vuelta de paseo"

"The Back o' Beyond" (MacDiarmid) **9**:196

"Backdrop Addresses Cowboy" (Atwood) **8**:4, 16, 41

"The Backlash Blues" (Hughes) **1**:251, 257

"The Backside of the Academy" (Rukeyser) **12**:236

"Bad Dreams" (Browning) **2**:59

"The Bad Glazier" (Baudelaire)
　See "Le mauvais vitrier"

"Bad Man" (Hughes) **1**:270

"Bad Morning" (Hughes) **1**:241

"The Bad Season Makes the Poet Sad" (Herrick) **9**:89, 103, 109, 115

"Baha'u'llah in the Garden of Ridwan" (Hayden) **6**:185-86, 196, 198

"Bahu" ("Arms") (Tagore) **8**:407

"Baignée" (Valery) **9**:392

The Bak-Chesarian fountain: A Tale of the Tauride (Pushkin)
　See *Bakhchisaraiski Fontan*

The Bakhchisarai Fontan (Pushkin)
　See *Bakhchisaraiski Fontan*

Bakhchisaraiski Fontan (*The Bak-Chesarian fountain: A Tale of the Tauride; The Bakhchisarai Fontan*) (Pushkin) **10**:358, 365, 386-88, 411, 417, 419, 421

"Bal des pendus" (Rimbaud) **3**:281, 283

Baladas de primavera (*Ballads of Spring*) (Jimenez) **7**:184

Balākā (*A Flight of Cranes; A Flight of Swans; A Flight of Swans*) (Tagore) **8**:413-15, 418, 427

"Le balcon" ("The Balcony") (Baudelaire) **1**:45, 63

"The Balcony" (Baudelaire)
　See "Le balcon"

"Balder Dead" (Arnold) **5**:35, 37, 58-9, 62

"Balin and Balan" (Tennyson) **6**:376-77

"Ballad" (Pasternak) **6**:270

"Ballad Fourth: The Trogger" (Burns) **6**:78

"Ballad of Army Wagons" (Tu Fu) **9**:330

"The Ballad of Ballymote" (Gallagher) **9**:42

"A Ballad of Boding" (Rossetti) **7**:271

"The Ballad of Chocolate Mabbie" (Brooks) **7**:57, 68, 102, 104

"The Ballad of East and West" (Kipling) **3**:157, 182-83, 188

"Ballad of Faith" (Williams) **7**:363

"The Ballad of Jakko Hill" (Kipling) **3**:187

"The Ballad of Late Annie" (Brooks) **7**:102-04

"The Ballad of Launcelot and Elaine" (Masters) **1**:328

"The Ballad of Margie Polite" (Hughes) **1**:241, 243, 247

"Ballad of Missing Lines" (Rukeyser) **12**:228

"The Ballad of Nat Turner" (Hayden) **6**:176, 178-80, 186-87, 194-95, 198

"Ballad of Pearl May Lee" (Brooks) **7**:57, 68, 86, 103-04

"A Ballad of Remembrance" (Hayden) **6**:200

A Ballad of Remembrance (Hayden) **6**:183, 188, 194-95

"The Ballad of Rudolph Reed" (Brooks) **7**:62, 96

"The Ballad of Sue Ellen Westerfield"
(Hayden) **6**:196
"Ballad of the Black Sorrow" (Garcia Lorca)
See "Romance de la pena negra"
"The Ballad of the *Bolivar*" (Kipling) **3**:164
"The Ballad of the Children of the Czar"
(Schwartz) **8**:302, 305, 309
"Ballad of the Dark Trouble" (Garcia Lorca)
See "Romance de la pena negra"
"Ballad of the Five Senses" (MacDiarmid)
9:157, 193
"The Ballad of the Harp-Weaver" ("The Harp-
Weaver") (Millay) **6**:211, 225, 233
"The Ballad of the King's Jest" (Kipling)
3:182
"Ballad of The Ladies of Past Times" (Villon)
See "Ballade des Dames du Temps Jadis"
"Ballad of the Landlord" (Hughes) **1**:258,
267
"Ballad of the Little Square" (Garcia Lorca)
See "Ballada de la Placeta"
"The Ballad of the Lonely Masturbator"
(Sexton) **2**:352, 370
"The Ballad of the Long-Legged Bait"
(Thomas) **2**:382, 393, 402
"Ballad of the Moon, the Moon" (Garcia
Lorca)
See "Romance de la luna, luna"
"The Ballad of the Red Earl" (Kipling)
3:181-82
"Ballad of the Spanish Civil Guard" (Garcia
Lorca)
See "Romance de la Guardia Civil
Española"
"Ballad of the Summoned Man" (Garcia
Lorca) **3**:147
"The Ballad of the True Beast" (Hayden)
6:196-97
"Ballad of the World Extinct" (Celan)
See "Ballade von der erloschenen Welt"
"Ballad Written in a Clinic" (Montale)
See "Ballata scritta in una clinica"
"Ballada de la Placeta" ("Ballad of the Little
Square"; "Song of the Little Square")
(Garcia Lorca) **3**:125
"Ballade" (Dunbar) **5**:139-40
"Ballade de bon conseil" (Villon) **13**:394-95
"Ballade de bonne doctrine" (Villon) **13**:394-
95, 404-05
"Ballade de conclusion" (Villon) **13**:417
"Ballade de la Grosse Margot" ("Ballade of
Fat Margot"; "La Grosse Margot") (Villon)
13:389-90, 393
"Ballade de mercy" (Villon) **13**:399, 413
"Ballade des contre verites" (Villon) **13**:414
"Ballade des Dames du Temps Jadis" ("Ballad
of The Ladies of Past Times") (Villon)
13:374, 405, 409-10
"Ballade des femmes de Paris" ("Ballade of the
Women of Paris") (Villon) **13**:380, 390,
413
"Ballade des Langues Envieuses" (Villon)
13:404
"Ballade des menus propos" (Villon) **13**:409
"Ballade des Pendus" (Villon)
See "Epitaphe Villon"
"Ballade des proverbes" (Villon) **13**:404, 414
"Ballade des seigneurs du temps jadis" (Villon)
13:410
"Ballade du concours de Blois" (Villon)
13:392, 414
"La ballade du Mal Aimé" (Apollinaire)

See "La chanson du mal-aimé"
"Ballade of Dead Ladies" (Villon) **13**:387,
390-91
"Ballade of Fat Margot" (Villon)
See "Ballade de la Grosse Margot"
"Ballade of the Hanged" (Villon)
See "Epitaphe Villon"
"Ballade of the Women of Paris" (Villon)
See "Ballade des femmes de Paris"
"Ballade pour prier Nostre Dame" (Villon)
13:403, 405, 413
"Ballade pour Robert d'Estouteville" (Villon)
13:395, 415
"Ballade to Our Lady" (Villon) **13**:390-91
"Ballade vom Auszug der drei" (Celan)
10:126
"Ballade von der erloschenen Welt" ("Ballad
of the World Extinct") (Celan) **10**:125
Ballades en Jargon (Villon) **13**:404, 406
Ballads for Sale (Lowell) **13**:76, 84-5
Ballads of Spring (Jimenez)
See *Baladas de primavera*
"Ballata scritta in una clinica" ("Ballad
Written in a Clinic") (Montale) **13**:108,
131, 167
"Ballet" (Pavese)
See "Balletto"
"Balletto" ("Ballet"; "Dance") (Pavese)
13:205, 226
"Balloons" (Plath) **1**:391
Balustion's Adventure (Browning) **2**:85-6, 95
Banabani (*Voice of the Forest*) (Tagore) **8**:416
"Banaphul" ("Wild Flower") (Tagore) **8**:405
"Bandi" ("The Prisoner") (Tagore) **8**:407,
412
"The Bands and the Beautiful Children"
(Page) **12**:169, 177
"Banga bir" ("Bengali Heroes") (Tagore)
8:407
"The Bangs" (Montale)
See "La frangia dei capelli"
"Banishment" (Sassoon) **12**:267, 288
"A Banjo Song" (Dunbar) **5**:146
"The Banker's Daughter" (Lowell) **3**:218, 221
"Banking Coal" (Toomer) **7**:333
"Banneker" (Dove) **6**:105, 109
"The Banner Bearer" (Williams) **7**:389-90
"The Banners" (Duncan) **2**:102
"Banquet" (Gozzano) **10**:183
"The Banquet" (Herbert) **4**:134
"Bantams in Pine-Woods" (Stevens) **6**:293,
303, 327
"Baptism" (Herbert) **4**:100
"Baptism" (McKay) **2**:211
"Barbare" (Rimbaud) **3**:261
"The Bard" (Gray) **2**:134-35, 139, 143-44,
146, 148, 151-54
"The Bards" (Graves) **6**:140, 144
"Bards of Passion *and* of Mirth" (Keats)
1:312
"Barefoot" (Sexton) **2**:352
Barely and Widely, 1956-1958 (Zukofsky)
11:348
"Baroque Comment" (Bogan) **12**:90, 92, 97,
101
Barrack Room Ballads and Other Verses
(Kipling) **3**:155-56, 159-60, 163, 165, 167-
69, 177, 182, 187-89
"The Barrier" (McKay) **2**:212
"Base Details" (Sassoon) **12**:268, 277, 280
"Baseball and Writing" (Moore) **4**:242, 256,
259-60

"Baseball Canto" (Ferlinghetti) **1**:183
"The Basket" (Lowell) **13**:84, 95-6
"A Bastard Peace" (Williams) **7**:369
Le bateau ivre (*The Drunken Boat*) (Rimbaud)
3:249, 257-58, 268-70, 272-74, 282, 286
"A Bather" (Lowell) **13**:93-6
"Battalion-Relief" (Sassoon) **12**:269
"The Battle" (Brooks) **7**:67
"The Battle of Brunanburh" (Tennyson)
6:363, 369
The Battle of Marathon: A Poem (Browning)
6:19
"The Battle of Osfrontalis" (Hughes) **7**:123,
142, 160-61
"Baudelaire" (Schwartz) **8**:311, 319
"Bayn al-kharā'ib" (Gibran) **9**:79
"Bayonne Turnpike to Tuscarora" (Ginsberg)
4:54
"Be Still, My Soul, Be Still" (Housman)
2:184, 192
"Beach at Versilia" (Montale)
See "Proda di Versilia"
"Beachy" (Sandburg) **2**:300
"Beale Street Love" (Hughes) **1**:269
"The Bean Eaters" (Brooks) **7**:55-6, 62, 69,
100
The Bean Eaters (Brooks) **7**:56-8, 62-3, 67,
81, 86, 95-6, 98-9, 101-02, 105, 107
"The Bean-Stalk" (Millay) **6**:237, 239
"The Bear" (Frost) **1**:203-04
"The Bear and the Garden-Lover" (Moore)
4:261
"The Bearer of Evil Tidings" (Frost) **1**:202
Beast in View (Rukeyser) **12**:231-32
"The Beast's Confession to the Priest" (Swift)
9:281, 295
"Le beau navire" (Baudelaire) **1**:60
"La beauté" (Baudelaire) **1**:61, 65
"Beauté de femmes, leur faiblesse, et ces mains
pâles" (Verlaine) **2**:416
"The Beautiful American Word, Sure"
(Schwartz) **8**:302, 315
"A Beautiful Young Nymph Going to Bed.
Written for the Honour of the Fair Sex"
("Upon a Beautiful Young Nymph Going to
Bed") (Swift) **9**:257, 262, 267-69, 279, 281,
283-84, 286, 291, 295, 298, 301-03
"The Beauty" (Pushkin) **10**:371
Beauty (Jimenez)
See *Belleza*
"Beauty and the Beast" (Dove) **6**:108
"Beauty Shoppe" (Brooks) **7**:59, 102
"Beauty Who Took Snuff" (Pushkin) **10**:407
"Bebop Boys" (Hughes) **1**:267
"Because I Love You (Last Night"
(Cummings) **5**:105
"Because One Is Always Forgotten" (Forche)
10:138, 142, 144, 153, 155
Beckonings (Brooks) **7**:84, 94
"Bed Time" (Hughes) **1**:255
"The Bedpost" (Graves) **6**:141
"A Bedtime Story" (Hughes) **7**:159
"The Bee Meeting" (Plath) **1**:394, 410-13
"Beech" (Frost) **1**:197
"Beech, Pine, and Sunlight" (Lowell) **13**:64
Beechen Vigil and Other Poems (Day Lewis)
11:148
"Beehive" (Toomer) **7**:311, 320, 334
"The Beekeeper's Daughter" (Plath) **1**:389,
410-12
"Beeny Cliff" (Hardy) **8**:136

"Before a Midnight Breaks in Storm"
  (Kipling) **3**:183
"Before I Knocked and Flesh Let Enter"
  (Thomas) **2**:383, 402
"Before Knowledge" (Hardy) **8**:89
"Before the Altar" (Lowell) **13**:69, 83
"Before the Battle" (Sassoon) **12**:262
"Before the Birth of one of her Children"
  (Bradstreet) **10**:12, 18
"Before the Judgment" (Duncan) **2**:116
"Before the Storm" (Lowell) **13**:60-1
"Before the Trip" (Montale)
  See "Prima del viaggio"
"Before We Mothernaked Fell" (Thomas)
  2:402
"Before We Sinned (Incarnate Devil)"
  (Thomas) **2**:402
"Begat" (Sexton) **2**:366
"The Beggar to Mab, the Fairies' Queen"
  (Herrick) **9**:86
"The Beggars" (Wordsworth) **4**:377
"The Beginner" (Kipling) **3**:183
"Beginning a Poem of These States"
  (Ginsberg) **4**:81
"Beginnings" (Hayden) **6**:190
"The Beginnings" (Kipling) **3**:192
"Behind the Arras" (Dunbar) **5**:133
"Beiname" (Goethe) **5**:248
"The Being as Memory" (Carruth) **10**:71
"The Being as Moment" (Carruth) **10**:71
"The Being as Prevision" (Carruth) **10**:71
"Being Beauteous" (Rimbaud) **3**:261, 263-64
"Being of Beauty" (Rimbaud) **3**:263
"Being Young and Green" (Millay) **6**:236
Belaia staia (Akhmatova)
  See *Belaya staya*
Belaia staja (Akhmatova)
  See *Belaya staya*
Belaya staya (*Belaia staia*; *Belaia staja*; *White
  Flock*) (Akhmatova) **2**:3, 6, 11-12, 18
"Belfast Tune" (Brodsky) **9**:28
"La bell au bois dormant" (Valery) **9**:392
"La belle dame sans merci" (Keats) **1**:279,
  282, 304-05
"La belle Dorothée" ("Dorothée") (Baudelaire)
  1:49
"La belle époque" (Milosz) **8**:211
"La Belle Hequmière aux filles de joie"
  (Villon) **13**:389
"Belle lecon aux enfants perdus" (Villon)
  13:394-95
Belleza (*Beauty*) (Jimenez) **7**:202
"The Bells" (Poe) **1**:430-31, 439, 441
"The Bells" (Sexton) **2**:359
Bells and Pomegrantes (Browning) **2**:27, 70
"Bells in Winter" ("Bells of Winter") (Milosz)
  8:189, 205
Bells in Winter (Milosz) **8**:174
"Bells of Winter" (Milosz)
  See "Bells in Winter"
"The Bells that Signed" (Day Lewis) **11**:144
"Below" (Celan) **10**:118
"Belsen, Day of Liberation" (Hayden) **6**:194
"Belts" (Kipling) **3**:162
"Ben Jonson Entertains a Man from Stratford"
  (Robinson) **1**:462, 468, 487
"Bending the Bow" (Duncan) **2**:107
Bending the Bow (Duncan) **2**:104, 107, 113-
  116, 119, 125, 127
"Beneath a Cool Shade" (Behn) **13**:15
"Bénédiction" (Baudelaire) **1**:54, 70
"Bengali Heroes" (Tagore)

  See "Banga bir"
"Benjamin Pantier" (Masters) **1**:347
"Bennie's Departure" (McKay) **2**:225
"Ben's Last Fight" (Merton) **10**:345
"Berck-Plage" (Plath) **1**:390
"Bereavement" (Smith) **12**:351
"Bereft" (Hardy) **8**:131
"Berlin" (Ferlinghetti) **1**:167
"Berlin Is Hard on Colored Girls" (Lorde)
  12:142
The Berlin Songbook (Bely)
  See *Berlinsky pesennik*
Berlinsky pesennik (*The Berlin Songbook*)
  (Bely) **11**:7
"Bermudas" (Marvell) **10**:268-69, 271, 275,
  289, 311, 313-14
"Berry Holden" (Masters) **1**:324
"Bertha in the Lane" (Browning) **6**:17
"The Best of It" (Sassoon) **12**:248, 260
Le bestiaire; ou, Cortège d'Orphée (*Cortege of
  Orpheus*) (Apollinaire) **7**:48
Bestiary/Bestiario (Neruda) **4**:286-87
"Bestiary U.S.A." (Sexton) **2**:367
"Besy" ("The Devils") (Pushkin) **10**:413
"Betancourt" (Baraka) **4**:15
"Betrayal" (Pavese)
  See "Tradimento"
"The Betrothal" (Apollinaire)
  See "Les fiançailles"
"The Betrothal" (Millay) **6**:211
"Betrothed" (Bogan) **12**:127-28
"A Better Resurrection" (Rossetti) **7**:290
"Between Our Selves" (Lorde) **12**:139
Between Our Selves (Lorde) **12**:137, 156
"Between the Porch and the Altar" (Lowell)
  3:200, 203-04, 206
"Between Walls" (Williams) **7**:399, 402
"Beucolicks" (Herrick) **9**:89
"Beverly Hills, Chicago" (Brooks) **7**:81
"Beware, Madam!" (Graves) **6**:163
"Bewick Finzer" (Robinson) **1**:467
"Beyond the Alps" (Lowell) **3**:205, 211, 218,
  221
"Beyond the Last Lamp" (Hardy) **8**:125
"Bez nazvaniya" ("Nameless") (Pasternak)
  6:288
"Bezverie" ("Lack of Faith"; "Unbelief")
  (Pushkin) **10**:409, 411
"Bhagna mandir" ("The Ruined Temple")
  (Tagore) **8**:415
"Bhairavi gan" ("Composition in Bhairavi")
  (Tagore) **8**:407
Bhānu singha (Tagore) **8**:403
Bhanusigh Thakurer padavali (*Songs of
  Bhanusigh Thakur*) (Tagore) **8**:405
"Bhar" ("Burden"; "Weight") (Tagore) **8**:412
"Biafra" (Levertov) **11**:176, 194
"Bianca among the Nightingales" (Browning)
  6:23-4, 28, 32, 38, 40
"Bickford's Buddha" (Ferlinghetti) **1**:186-87
"Bien lion d'ici" (Baudelaire) **1**:49
"Bien que le trait de vostre belle face"
  (Ronsard) **11**:250
"Big Bessie Throws Her Son into the Street"
  (Brooks) **7**:63, 81
"Big Elegy" (Brodsky)
  See "The Great Elegy for John Donne"
"Big Fat Hairy Vision of Evil" (Ferlinghetti)
  1:167
"The Big Heart" (Sexton) **2**:368
"Big Momma" (Madhubuti) **5**:326, 344
"The Bight" (Bishop) **3**:50, 52-4

"Les bijoux" (Baudelaire) **1**:61
"The Billboard Painters" (Ferlinghetti) **1**:183
"Birches" (Frost) **1**:196, 221, 225, 227-28,
  230
"The Bird Frau" (Dove) **6**:108
"Bird of Air" (H. D.) **5**:287
"The Bird with the Coppery, Keen Claws"
  (Stevens) **6**:293, 304
"Birdbrain!" (Ginsberg) **4**:62, 76
"Birdcage Walk" (Merton) **10**:351
"Birds in the Night" (Verlaine) **2**:415
"Birds of Prey" (McKay) **2**:212
"Birmingham Sunday" (Hughes) **1**:252
"The Birth in a Narrow Room" (Brooks)
  7:54, 80
"Birth of a Genius among Men"
  (MacDiarmid) **9**:153
"The Birth of Christ" (Garcia Lorca)
  See "Nacimiento de Cristo"
"A Birthday" (Rossetti) **7**:276, 278, 280
"Bishop Blougram" (Browning) **2**:37
"Bishop Blougram's Apology" (Browning)
  2:43, 73
"The Bishop Orders His Tomb at St. Praxed's"
  (Browning) **2**:37, 48, 82, 94
"The Bitter River" (Hughes) **1**:251
Bixby Canyon to Jessore Road (Ginsberg)
  4:89
"The Black Angel" (Montale)
  See "L'angelo nero"
"Black Art" (Baraka) **4**:10, 19, 25, 40
"The Black Art" (Sexton) **2**:373
Black Arts (Baraka) **4**:18
"The Black Christ" (Madhubuti) **5**:339-40
"Black Cock" (Montale)
  See "Gallo cedrone"
"The Black Cottage" (Frost) **1**:193, 198
"BLACK DADA NIHILISMUS" (Baraka)
  4:9, 14
"Black Dancer in the Little Savoy" (Hughes)
  1:246
"Black Eagle Returns to St. Joe" (Masters)
  1:344
"Black Earth" (Moore) **4**:251
"The Black Goddess" (Graves) **6**:154
"Black Love" (Madhubuti) **5**:342
"Black Magic" (Sanchez) **9**:223, 234
*Black Magic: Sabotage, Target Study, Black
  Art; Collected Poetry, 1961-1967* (Baraka)
  4:6, 8, 16-18, 24, 26
"The Black Man Is Making New Gods"
  (Baraka) **4**:19
"Black March" (Smith) **12**:300-01, 308, 319,
  326
"Black Money" (Gallagher) **9**:36, 53
"Black Mother Woman" (Lorde) **12**:154,
  156-57
"Black Panther" (Hughes) **1**:251-52
"Black People!" (Baraka) **4**:19, 25-6
"The Black Pit" (Hayden) **6**:187
"Black Power Chant" (Baraka) **4**:19
Black Pride (Madhubuti) **5**:321, 336, 338-41,
  346
"Black Pudding" (Gallagher) **9**:64
"Black Sampson of Brandywine" (Dunbar)
  5:129, 131, 138
"Black Shroud" (Ginsberg) **4**:90
"Black Silk" (Gallagher) **9**:50, 59, 62
"Black Sketches" (Madhubuti) **5**:337
"Black Tambourine" (Crane) **3**:98
The Black Unicorn (Lorde) **12**:137-38, 141-
  42, 144, 148, 151, 153-55, 157-58, 160

"The Black Winds" (Williams)   **7**:383-85, 388-89

"Blackberrying" (Plath)   **1**:407-09

"Blackgirl Learning" (Madhubuti)   **5**:344

"Blackman/An Unfinished History" (Madhubuti)   **5**:326, 343, 345

Blacks (Brooks)   **7**:105

"The Blackstone Rangers" (Brooks)   **7**:88, 90-1

"Blackstudies" (Lorde)   **12**:147, 158

"Blanc" (Valery)   **9**:392

Blanco (Paz)   **1**:355-56, 358, 363, 368-69, 372, 374, 376-77

"The Blessed Virgin Mary Compared to a Window" ("A Window") (Merton)   **10**:330, 338

"Blighters" (Sassoon)   **12**:263, 277, 282

"Blind Panorama of New York" (Garcia Lorca)
   See "Panorama ceigo de Nueva York"

"Der blinde Sänger" (Holderlin)   **4**:147

"The Blinded Bird" (Hardy)   **8**:98

"Bliss" (Pushkin)   **10**:407

Bliznets v tuchakh (*The Twin In the Clouds*) (Pasternak)   **6**:263, 275

"blk/chant" (Sanchez)   **9**:204, 225, 234

"blk / wooooomen / chant" (Sanchez)   **9**:225

"Blödigkeit" (Holderlin)   **4**:148

"Bloodbirth" (Lorde)   **12**:157

"Bloodsmiles" (Madhubuti)   **5**:337

The Bloomingdale Papers (Carruth)   **10**:78-84

"The Blossom" (Blake)   **12**:7, 23, 33

"The Blossome" (Donne)   **1**:126, 130, 147

"The Blow" (Hardy)   **8**:94

"The Blow" (Neruda)
   See "El golpe"

"Blow and Counterblow" (Montale)
   See "Botta e riposta"

"The Blow-Fly" (Graves)   **6**:163

"Blowing Boy" (Page)   **12**:177

The Blue Estuaries: Poems, 1923-1968 (Bogan)   **12**:96-7, 100-03, 107, 112, 120-21

"The Blue from Heaven" (Smith)   **12**:302, 304, 319, 331, 333

"Blue Gem Creeper" (Tagore)
   See "Nilamanilata"

"The Blue Meridian" (Toomer)   **7**:309, 311-12, 324-26, 328-29, 336,-37, 340

"Blue Moles" (Plath)   **1**:389

"A Blue Ribbon at Amesbury" (Frost)   **1**:196

"A Blue Woman with Sticking out Breasts Hanging" (Cummings)   **5**:99, 103

"Bluebeard" (Millay)   **6**:205

"Blueberries" (Frost)   **1**:225

"The Blue-Flag in the Bog" (Millay)   **6**:233

"Blues at Dawn" (Hughes)   **1**:266

A Blues Book for Blue Black Magical Women (Sanchez)   **9**:207, 211-16, 218-20, 228-29, 234, 238-41, 243

"Boädicea" (Tennyson)   **6**:360, 363

"The Boat" (Sexton)   **2**:365

"The Boat of Life" (Ishikawa Takuboku)
   See "Inochi no fune"

"The Boat of the White Feather Bird" (Ishikawa Takuboku)
   See "Shiraha no toribune"

"Boat Ride" (Gallagher)   **9**:50-1, 58-60

"Boats on the Marne" (Montale)   **13**:146

"The Bobby to the Sneering Lady" (McKay)   **2**:226

"Bobo's Metamorphosis" (Milosz)   **8**:187

Le Bocage (Ronsard)   **11**:246

"Boccaccio: The Plague Years" (Dove)   **6**:109

"Body" (Tagore)
   See "Tanu"

Body of This Death (Bogan)   **12**:85-7, 103-04, 116, 119-20, 126-28

"Body of Waking" (Rukeyser)   **12**:217, 220

Body of Waking (Rukeyser)   **12**:217, 219-21, 224

"The Bohemian" (Dunbar)   **5**:125

"Le bois amical" (Valery)   **9**:391

"Bokardo" (Robinson)   **1**:468

"Bombardment" (Lowell)   **13**:78

"Bombinations of a Chimera" (MacDiarmid)   **9**:193

Bones of the Cuttlefish (Montale)
   See *Ossi di seppia*

"Bonfire" (Gallagher)   **9**:61-2

Bonheur (Verlaine)   **2**:417

La bonne chanson (Verlaine)   **2**:413-14, 419, 431-32

"The Bonnie Broukit Bairn" (MacDiarmid)   **9**:156, 160. 187

"Les bons chiens" (Baudelaire)   **1**:58-9

The Book of Ahania (Blake)   **12**:13

"Book of Ancestors" (Atwood)   **8**:28-9, 42

"The Book of Annandale" (Robinson)   **1**:460-61

The Book of Folly (Sexton)   **2**:355-56, 360, 365, 368

Book of Gypsy Ballads (Garcia Lorca)
   See *Primer romancero gitano*

"The Book of Hours of Sister Clotilde" (Lowell)   **13**:84

The Book of Los (Blake)   **12**:62-4

Book of Pictures (Rilke)
   See *Buch der Bilder*

Book of Questions (Neruda)
   See *Libro de las preguntas*

Book of Songs (Garcia Lorca)
   See *Canciones*

"The Book of the Dead" (Rukeyser)   **12**:203, 207, 213

The Book of the Dead (Rukeyser)   **12**:210

The Book of Thel (Blake)   **12**:19, 33-5, 37, 51

The Book of Urizen (*The First Book of Urizen*) (Blake)   **12**:15, 19, 35, 38, 60, 62

Book of Vagaries (Neruda)
   See *Extravagario*

A Book of Verses (Masters)   **1**:332, 342

"Booker T. Washington" (Dunbar)   **5**:131

"Boots" (Kipling)   **3**:192

The Borderers (Wordsworth)   **4**:416

The Borderland (Tagore)
   See *Prāntik*

Borderland (Tagore)
   See *Prāntik*

"Born in December" (Rukeyser)   **12**:224

"A Boston Ballad" (Whitman)
   See "Poem of Apparitions in Boston in the 73rd Year of These States"

"The Boston Evening Transcript" (Eliot)   **5**:153

"Botanical Gardens" (Masters)   **1**:330

"Botta e riposta" ("Blow and Counterblow"; "Thrust and Riposte") (Montale)   **13**:129, 131, 134, 147, 165

"Bottle Green" (Smith)   **12**:333

"Bound No'th Blues" (Hughes)   **1**:254

"A Boundless Moment" (Frost)   **1**:218

"Bournemouth" (Verlaine)   **2**:416

"Bova" (Pushkin)   **10**:407

"The Bowl and the Rim" (Graves)   **6**:128

"Bowls" (Moore)   **4**:265

"The Boy" (Tagore)   **8**:417

"Boy with a Sea Dream" (Page)   **12**:168, 170

"Boy with His Hair Cut Short" (Rukeyser)   **12**:223

"Boys. Black." (Brooks)   **7**:84

"A Boy's Summer Song" (Dunbar)   **5**:138

A Boy's Will (Frost)   **1**:192, 195, 197, 207, 213-14, 223-24

"Bracken Hills in Autumn" (MacDiarmid)   **9**:197

"Braid Scots: An Inventory and Appraisement" (MacDiarmid)
   See "Gairmscoile"

"Brandons Both" (Rossetti)   **7**:271

"Le brasier" ("The Brazier") (Apollinaire)   **7**:47

"Brass Keys" (Sandburg)   **2**:329

"Brass Spittoons" (Hughes)   **1**:241, 263, 265

Bratya Razboiniki (*The Brigand Brothers; The Brothers Highwaymen*) (Pushkin)   **10**:358, 365, 386

"Brawl" (Garcia Lorca)
   See "Reyerta"

"The Brazier" (Apollinaire)
   See "Le brasier"

"Brazil, January 1, 1502" (Bishop)   **3**:56

"Brazilian Fazenda" (Page)   **12**:178, 183, 190

"Bread" (Pasternak)   **6**:267

"Bread and Wine" (Holderlin)
   See "Brot und Wein"

Bread in the Wilderness (Merton)   **10**:352

"The Break" (Pasternak)   **6**:280-82

"The Break" (Sexton)   **2**:352-53

"Break, Break, Break" (Tennyson)   **6**:358

"Break of Day" (Sassoon)   **12**:244, 277

"Breake of Day" (Donne)   **1**:152

"Breaking Open" (Rukeyser)   **12**:221, 224, 230

Breaking Open (Rukeyser)   **12**:220, 224-25, 230

"The Breast" (Sexton)   **2**:352, 364

"Breasts" (Tagore)
   See "Stan"

"The Breathing" (Levertov)   **11**:171

"Breathing Landscape" (Rukeyser)   **12**:209

"The Breathing, the Endless News" (Dove)   **6**:122

Breathing the Water (Levertov)   **11**:200, 202-05, 209-10

Breath-Turning (Celan)
   See *Atemwende*

"Bredon Hill" (Housman)   **2**:160, 182-83, 185

"Brian the Still-Hunter" (Atwood)   **8**:19

"Briar Rose (Sleeping Beauty)" (Sexton)   **2**:354, 365, 368

"The Bridal Ballad" (Poe)   **1**:428, 432, 445, 447

The Bridal of Triermain (Scott)   **13**:297, 301-02, 311-12, 314, 317, 320

"Bride and Groom Lie Hidden for Three Days" (Hughes)   **7**:165, 168

"Bride Song" (Rossetti)   **7**:264

"The Bridegroom" (Kipling)   **3**:183

"The Bride-Night Fire" (Hardy)   **8**:99

The Bridge (Crane)   **3**:84-5, 87-90, 93-8, 100-01, 105-10

"The Bridge of Estador" (Crane)   **3**:100

The Brigand Brothers (Pushkin)
   See *Bratya Razboiniki*

"Bright Star" (Keats)   **1**:279

"Bright Sunlight" (Lowell)   **13**:64

"The Brigs of Ayr" (Burns) **6**:78

"Brilliant Sad Sun" (Williams) **7**:396, 409

"Bringers" (Sandburg) **2**:316-17, 324

"Bringing in New Couples" (Hughes) **7**:166

"Bringnal Banks are Wild and Fair For a' That" (Scott) **13**:278

"Brise marine" (Mallarme) **4**:208

"The British Church" (Herbert) **4**:100

"Brod und Wein" (Holderlin)
See "Brot und Wein"

"A Broken Appointment" (Hardy) **8**:88, 110

"The Broken Dark" (Hayden) **6**:181, 193-95

"Broken Jar" (Paz)
See "El cántaro roto"

"The Broken Pitcher" (Paz)
See "El cántaro roto"

"The Broken Tower" (Crane) **3**:90, 103, 111

"The Broken Wings" (Gibran) **9**:75

The Bronze Horseman (Pushkin)
See *Medny Vsadnik*

"The Bronze Horses" (Lowell) **13**:60, 62, 64, 73, 80, 82

"Bronze Tablets" (Lowell) **13**:76, 78

"Bronzeville Man with a Belt in the Back" (Brooks) **7**:106

"A Bronzeville Mother Loiters in Mississippi. Meanwhile a Mississippi Mother Burns Bacon" (Brooks) **7**:56, 62, 81, 86, 96, 98-9

"Bronzeville Woman in a Red Hat" (Brooks) **7**:58, 62

"The Brook" (Tennyson) **6**:357, 359

"Brook Farm" (Toomer) **7**:323

"Brooklyn Bridge Nocturne" (Garcia Lorca)
See "Ciudad sin sueño"

"Brot und Wein" ("Bread and Wine"; "Brod und Wein") (Holderlin) **4**:146-51, 161, 166, 169, 171, 176

"Brother, Do Not Give Your Life" (Yosano Akiko)
See "Kimi Shinitamô koto nakare"

"The Brothers" (Wordsworth) **4**:374, 380, 381, 393, 402, 414

The Brothers Highwaymen (Pushkin)
See *Bratya Razboiniki*

Brothers, I Loved You All: Poems, 1969-1977 (Carruth) **10**:69-70, 72-3, 91

"The Brown Menace or Poem to the Survival of Roaches" (Lorde) **12**:154-55, 158

"Brown River, Smile" (Toomer) **7**:324

"Brown's Descent" (Frost) **1**:195

"Bruce's Address" (Burns) **6**:55

"A Bruised Reed Shall He Not Break" (Rossetti) **7**:290; **50**:314

"Bubba" (Sanchez) **9**:240

Buch der Bilder (*Book of Pictures*) (Rilke) **2**:266-67

"The Buck in the Snow" (Millay) **6**:238

The Buck in the Snow, and Other Poems (Millay) **6**:213-14

Buckthorn (Akhmatova)
See *Podorozhnik*

Bucolic Comedies (Sitwell) **3**:293, 302-04, 307-08, 319, 322

"Bucolics" (Auden) **1**:23

Bucolics (Vergil)
See *Georgics*

"The Buddhist Painter Prepares to Paint" (Carruth) **10**:89

"Buenos Aires" (Lowell) **3**:214

"La bufera" ("The Storm") (Montale) **13**:113, 131

La bufera e altro (*The Storm and Other Things*; *The Storm and Other Things*) (Montale) **13**:103-04, 107, 113-14, 117-18, 122, 125, 131-33, 141, 148-49, 156, 160, 165-67

"Buffalo Bill's Defunct" (Cummings) **5**:93

"Le buffet" (Rimbaud) **3**:271, 283

"Build Soil: A Political Pastoral" (Frost) **1**:196, 199, 203, 217

"Builder Kachina" (Rose) **13**:236-37

"The Building of the Trophy" (Rose) **13**:235

"The Bull Moses" (Hughes) **7**:131, 140, 158

"Bull Song" (Atwood) **8**:25

"Bullfrog" (Hughes) **7**:165

"Bumming" (McKay) **2**:226

"The Bunch of Grapes" (Herbert) **4**:123, 125

"The Burden" (Kipling) **3**:183

"A Burden" (Rossetti) **7**:286

"Burden" (Tagore)
See "Bhar"

"The Burghers" (Hardy) **8**:99

"The Burglar of Babylon" (Bishop) **3**:48, 56

"The Buried Life" (Arnold) **5**:37-8, 41-5, 47, 49-50, 59, 64

"The Burly Fading One" (Hayden) **6**:196

"The Burning of Paper Instead of Children" (Rich) **5**:371, 393-95

"Burning Oneself Out" (Rich) **5**:360

"The Burning Passion" (MacDiarmid) **9**:153

"Burning the Christmas Greens" (Williams) **7**:360

"Burning the Tomato Worms" (Forche) **10**:132, 134, 142

"Burnt Lands" (Pavese) **13**:205

"Burnt Norton" (Eliot) **5**:164, 166-68, 171, 174, 177-85, 201, 210

"The Burnt-Out Spa" (Plath) **1**:389

"A Bus along St. Clair: December" (Atwood) **8**:40

"The Bush Garden" (Atwood) **8**:38-9

"Busie old foole" (Donne)
See "The Sunne Rising"

"But He Was Cool; or, He Even Stopped for Green Lights" (Madhubuti) **5**:329, 341

"But We've the May" (Cummings)
See "Song"

"'Butch' Weldy" (Masters) **1**:324

Butterflies (Gozzano)
See *Le farfalle*

"The Butterfly" (Brodsky)
See "Babočka"

"Butterfly Piece" (Hayden) **6**:194, 198

By Avon River (H. D.) **5**:302

"By God I Want above Fourteenth" (Cummings) **5**:94

"By Night When Others Soundly Slept" (Bradstreet) **10**:62

"By Rugged Ways" (Dunbar) **5**:131

By the Earth's Corpse (Hardy) **8**:121

"By the Fireside" (Browning) **2**:76, 78-9, 88

"By the Hoof of the Wild Goat" (Kipling) **3**:186

"By the Lake" (Sitwell) **3**:325

"By the Road" (Williams) **7**:382-83

By the Seashore (Akhmatova)
See *U samovo morya*

"By The Stream" (Dunbar) **5**:127

"By the Waters of Babylon" (Celan)
See "An den Wassern Babels"

"By Wauchopeside" (MacDiarmid) **9**:197, 199

"Bypassing Rue Descartes" (Milosz) **8**:200

"a C." (Montale) **13**:138

"Ca' the Yowes to the Knowes" (Burns) **6**:76

"Cabaret" (Hughes) **1**:237

"Cabaret Girl Dies on Welfare Island" (Hughes) **1**:247

"A Cabin in the Clearing" (Frost) **1**:212

"A Cabin Tale" (Dunbar) **5**:120

Cables to Rage (Lorde) **12**:140

"Cables to Rage, or I've Been Talking on This Street Corner a Hell of a Long Time" (Lorde) **12**:155

"Cables to the Ace" (Merton) **10**:337

Cables to the Ace; or, Familiar Liturgies of Misunderstanding (Merton) **10**:338, 345, 348, 351, 354

"Caboose Thoughts" (Sandburg) **2**:302

"Cadenus and Vanessa" (Swift) **9**:253-55, 296

"Cadenza" (Hughes) **7**:159

Caesar's Gate (Duncan) **2**:101

"Café" (Milosz) **8**:175

"Café at Rapallo" (Montale) **13**:148

"Caliban upon Setebos" (Browning) **2**:58-9, 88, 95

"The Call" (Herbert) **4**:130

"Call" (Lorde) **12**:139, 141

"Call Me Back Again" (Tagore)
See "Ebar phirao more"

"Callie Ford" (Brooks) **7**:62, 69

Calligrammes (Apollinaire) **7**:3, 9-10, 12, 35-6, 42, 44, 46, 48-9

"Calliope" (H. D.) **5**:304

"Callow Captain" (Graves) **6**:133

"The Calm" (Donne) **1**:122

"The Calm" (Gallagher) **9**:58

"Calmly We Walk Through This April's Day" (Schwartz) **8**:305-06

"Calverley's" (Robinson) **1**:466

"Calypso" (H. D.) **5**:306

"The Cambridge Ladies Who Live in Furnished Souls" (Cummings) **5**:94

"Cambridge, Spring 1937" (Schwartz) **8**:301

"Camelia" (Tagore) **8**:417

"Camp and Cloister" (Browning) **2**:26

"Camps of Green" (Whitman) **3**:378

"Can Grande's Castle" (Lowell) **13**:60

Can Grande's Castle (Lowell) **13**:60, 62-3, 65-6, 72-4, 79-83, 93

"The Canal's Drowning Black" (Hughes) **7**:148

"Canción tonta" ("Silly Song") (Garcia Lorca) **3**:136

Canciones (*Book of Songs*; *Songs*) (Garcia Lorca) **3**:118-19, 148-49

"Candle, Lamp, and Firefly" (Gallagher) **9**:59

"Candle-Lightin' Time" (Dunbar) **5**:122

Candles in Babylon (Levertov) **11**:198-201, 209

"The Candlestick" (Brodsky) **9**:3

Cane (Toomer) **7**:309-11, 319, 323-24, 326, 330, 332-33, 335, 339-41

"The Canonization" ("For Godsake hold your tongue, and let me love") (Donne) **1**:126, 130, 132-34

"El cántaro roto" ("Broken Jar"; "The Broken Pitcher") (Paz) **1**:361

"Canthara" (Williams) **7**:367

"Canti Romani" (Ferlinghetti) **1**:183

"Cantique des colonnes" ("Song of the Columns") (Valery) **9**:366, 394

"Canto a Bolivar" (Neruda) **4**:279-80

"Canto a las madres de los milicianos muertos" ("Song for the Mothers of Dead Militiamen"; "To the Mothers of the Dead Militia") (Neruda) **4**:278

"Canto a Stalingrado" (Neruda) **4**:279

"Canto C" (Pound) **4**:360-62

"Canto CI" (Pound) **4**:353

"Canto CIV" (Pound) **4**:357

"Canto CX" (Pound) **4**:353

"Canto CXIII" (Pound) **4**:353-54

"Canto CXV" (Pound) **4**:354

"Canto CXVI" (Pound) **4**:353-54

"Canto CXVIII" (Pound) **4**:353

"Canto CXX" (Pound) **4**:354

Canto general de Chile (*General Song*) (Neruda) **4**:279-82, 291-96

"Canto I" (Pound) **4**:334, 357

"Canto L" (Pound) **4**:360, 362

"Canto LI" (Pound) **4**:326

"Canto LXXIV" (Pound) **4**:345-49, 352, 354

"Canto LXXIX" (Pound) **4**:349

"Canto LXXV" (Pound) **4**:347, 349

"Canto LXXVI" (Pound) **4**:352-53

"Canto LXXVIII" (Pound) **4**:349

"Canto LXXX" (Pound) **4**:345, 349

"Canto LXXXI" (Pound) **4**:347, 349, 352, 356, 359

"Canto LXXXII" (Pound) **4**:349, 352

"Canto LXXXIII" (Pound) **4**:345, 348

"Canto LXXXIV" (Pound) **4**:345, 348

"Canto LXXXVI" (Pound) **4**:347

"Canto notturno di un pastore errante nell'Asia" ("Night Song of an Asiatic Wandering Shepherd") (Montale) **13**:109

"Canto sobre unas ruinas" ("Song over Some Ruins") (Neruda) **4**:309

"Canto VIII" (Pound) **4**:353

"Canto XCI" (Pound) **4**:354

"Canto XIV" (Pound) **4**:328, 358

"Canto XLI" (Pound) **4**:357

"Canto XLVII" (Pound) **4**:346-47, 349

"Canto XV" (Pound) **4**:358

"Canto XVI" (Pound) **4**:328

"Canto XXVI" (Pound) **4**:324

"Canto XXVIII" (Pound) **4**:325, 345

Cantos (Pound) **4**:332, 343-45, 350-54

"Cantos of Mutabilitie" ("Mutabilitie Cantos") (Spenser) **8**:344, 346, 375, 396

"Canzones" (Okigbo)
   See "Four Canzones (1957-1961)"

Canzoni (Pound) **4**:317

Canzoniere (*Rerum vulgarium fragmenta*; *Rime*; *Rime sparse*) (Petrarch) **8**:218, 220, 224-40, 242-45, 247-49, 251-65, 268-73, 276-78

The Cap and Bells (Keats) **1**:279, 311

"Cape Breton" (Bishop) **3**:39, 58-9

"A Cape Cod Lullaby" ("Lullaby of Cape Cod") (Brodsky) **9**:7, 19

"Cape Hatteras" (Crane) **3**:86-7, 90, 96, 106-10

"Cape Mootch" (Pasternak) **6**:251

"Capitol Air" (Ginsberg) **4**:62, 76, 83

"Cappadocian Song" (Carruth) **10**:89

"Captain Craig" (Robinson) **1**:460, 467, 483, 486

Captain Craig (Robinson) **1**:462-63, 470-72, 474, 490

The Captive of the Caucasus (Pushkin)
   See *Kavkazsky plennik*

"Caribbean Sunset" (Hughes) **1**:236

"Caritas" (Cummings) **5**:94

"Carlos among the Candles" (Stevens) **6**:295

"Carnegie Hall: Rescued" (Moore) **4**:242

"Carnevale di Gerti" (Montale) **13**:117

"Carol" (Merton) **10**:340

"Carousing Students" (Pushkin) **10**:407

"The Carpenters's Son" (Housman) **2**:192

"Carrefour" (Lowell) **13**:85

"A Carrion" (Baudelaire)
   See "Une charogne"

"Carta a Miguel Otero Silva, en Caracas, 1948" ("Letter to Miguel Otero Silva, in Caracas, 1948") (Neruda) **4**:293

"Carta de creencia" (Paz) **1**:376

"Cartographies of Silence" (Rich) **5**:378-79, 394-95

"Cartoons of Coming Shows Unseen Before" (Schwartz) **8**:291

"La casa dei doganieri" ("The Customs-Officer's House") (Montale) **13**:114

La casa dei doganieri (*House of the Customs Men*) (Montale) **13**:106, 138

Casa Guidi Windows: A Poem (Browning) **6**:2, 6-9, 16, 36, 38, 41, 46

"Casa in costruzione" ("House Under Construction") (Pavese) **13**:226

"Casa sul mare" ("House by the Sea") (Montale) **13**:137, 147, 164

"Casabianca" (Bishop) **3**:37, 56, 67

"La casada infiel" ("The Faithless Bride"; "The Faithless Wife"; "The Unfaithful Married Woman"; "The Unfaithful Wife") (Garcia Lorca) **3**:119, 132, 134

Case d'armons (Apollinaire) **7**:21-2

"Cassandra" (Bogan) **12**:110

"Cassandra" (Robinson) **1**:487

"Cassinus and Peter, a Tragic Elegy" (Swift) **9**:262, 270, 274, 279, 286, 288, 298, 302-03

"Căst rĕci" ("A Part of Speech") (Brodsky) **9**:7, 19

Căst rĕci (*Chast' rechi*; *A Part of Speech*) (Brodsky) **9**:6-8, 13-15, 26-7, 29-31

"Castástrofe en Sewell" ("Catastrophe at Sewell") (Neruda) **4**:294

"The Castaways" (McKay) **2**:221

"The Castle" (Graves) **6**:131, 135, 142, 144

"The Casualty" (Hughes) **7**:114

"The Cat and the Saxophone" (Hughes) **1**:236

"The Catalpa Tree" (Bogan) **12**:129, 131

"Catarina to Camoens" (Browning) **6**:16-17, 38

"Catastrophe at Sewell" (Neruda)
   See "Castástrofe en Sewell"

"A Catch of Shy Fish" (Brooks) **7**:105

Cathay (Pound) **4**:317, 364, 366

"Catherine of Alexandria" (Dove) **6**:107, 109

"Catherine of Siena" (Dove) **6**:107, 109

"Cato Braden" (Masters) **1**:33, 343

"Cats and a Cock" (Rukeyser) **12**:209

"Cattle Gredo" (Milosz) **8**:207

"Cattle Show" (MacDiarmid) **9**:160, 176

The Caucasian Captive (Pushkin)
   See *Kavkazsky plennik*

"Causerie" (Baudelaire) **1**:45, 66

"Cavalier Tunes" (Browning) **2**:26, 36

Cave Birds: An Alchemical Cave Drama (Hughes) **7**:153-58, 162-65, 171

"Cave Canem" (Millay) **6**:233

Cavender's House (Robinson) **1**:471-72, 475, 479, 483

"Cease, Cease, Aminta to Complain" (Behn) **13**:7

"La ceinture" (Valery) **9**:372, 374, 387, 396

"A Celebration" (Williams) **7**:345

Celestial Hoyden (Lowell) **3**:199

"The Celestial Poets" (Neruda)
   See "Los poetas celestes"

"Celestials at the Board of Projects" (Milosz) **8**:214

"Celia's Birthday Poem" (Zukofsky) **11**:342

"The Cellar of Memory" (Akhmatova) **2**:20

"A celle qui est trop gaie" (Baudelaire) **1**:44, 60-2

"Celle qui sort de l'onde" (Valery) **9**:392

"Cells" (Kipling) **3**:163

"The Celtic Fringe" (Smith) **12**:339

"Cemetery, Stratford Connecticut" (Rose) **13**:239

"La cena triste" ("The Sad Supper") (Pavese) **13**:205, 208

"The Census-Taker" (Frost) **1**:194

"Central Park" (Lowell) **3**:226

"Ceremonies for Candlemasse Eve" (Herrick) **9**:99

"Ceremonies for Christmasse" (Herrick) **9**:99, 104

"Ceremony after a Fire Raid" (Thomas) **2**:382, 388

"Certain Mercies" (Graves) **6**:152

"Certainty" (Paz) **1**:355

"César" (Valery) **9**:391

"Ceux qui luttent" (Smith) **12**:333

"Chaadayevu" ("To Chaadaev") (Pushkin) **10**:408

"Chacun sa chimère" (Baudelaire) **1**:58

"Chains" (Apollinaire)
   See "Liens"

Chaitāli (*The Last Harvest*) (Tagore) **8**:403, 409-10

"The Challenge" (Graves) **6**:137

"Le chambre double" ("The Double Chamber") (Baudelaire) **1**:54, 58

"Chameli-vitan" ("Jasmine Arbour") (Tagore) **8**:416

"Chance" (H. D.) **5**:304

"Chance Meeting" (H. D.) **5**:304

"Chance Topic" (Tu Fu) **9**:324, 327

"Chanchal" ("Restless") (Tagore) **8**:415

"The Change" (Hardy) **8**:93

"Change" (Pasternak)
   See "Peremena"

"Change Is Not Always Progress" (Madhubuti) **5**:344

"The Change: Kyoto-Tokyo Express" (Ginsberg) **4**:50, 63, 81

"Change of Season" (Lorde) **12**:154, 157

A Change of World (Rich) **5**:352-53, 358, 360, 362, 369, 375, 387-88, 392

"Change upon Change" (Browning) **6**:32

"The Changed Woman" (Bogan) **12**:94, 103

"The Changeful World" (MacDiarmid) **9**:183

Ch'ang-ku (Li Ho) **13**:44

"Channel Firing" (Hardy) **8**:119-21

"La chanson des ingénues" ("Songs of the Ingenues") (Verlaine) **2**:431

"La chanson du mal-aimé" ("La ballade du Mal Aimé"; "The Song of the Ill-beloved"; "The Song of the Poorly Beloved") (Apollinaire) **7**:3, 7-9, 11, 15, 22, 44, 46-9

"Chanson Juive" (Celan) **10**:127-28

"Chanson of a Lady in the Shade" (Celan) **10**:112

"Chanson un peu naïve" (Bogan) **12**:86, 90, 92, 101, 103

Chansons pour elle (Verlaine) **2**:417

"Chant d'automne" (Baudelaire) **1**:60, 62-3

"Chant de guerre parisien" (Rimbaud) **3**:255, 284

"Chant de l'horizon en champagne" (Apollinaire) **7**:22

"Chant de liesse" (Ronsard) **11**:262

"A Chant for Young/Brothas and Sistuhs" (Sanchez) **9**:218, 225

"Chant to Be Used in Processions around a Site with Furnaces" (Merton) **10**:334, 337

"Chantre" (Apollinaire) **7**:48

"Chaos in Motion and Not in Motion" (Stevens) **6**:307-10, 313

"Chaos Poem" (Atwood) **8**:24

"The Chapel-Organist" (Hardy) **8**:100, 124

"Chaplinesque" (Crane) **3**:98-100

"The Character of Holland" (Marvell) **10**:271

"The Character of the Happy Warrior" (Wordsworth) **4**:377

"The Charge of the Light Brigade" (Tennyson) **6**:359

"The Chariot" (Dickinson) **1**:84, 86

"Charioteer" (H. D.) **5**:268

"La charite" (Ronsard) **11**:236, 243, 263-64

"Charivari" (Atwood) **8**:38

"Charleston in the 1860s" (Rich) **5**:383

"A Charm" (Dickinson) **1**:112

Charmes; ou, Poèmes (Valery) **9**:355, 358, 365-67, 371, 374, 386-88, 390-96

"Une charogne" ("A Carrion"; "A Rotting Corpse") (Baudelaire) **1**:48

"The Chase" (Toomer) **7**:338, 340

"Chase Henry" (Masters) **1**:324

"Chasing the Paper-Shaman" (Rose) **13**:238

Chast' rechi (Brodsky)
See *Căst rĕci*

"Le chat" (Ronsard) **11**:280, 282

"Le châtiment de Tartuff" ("Tartuffe's Punishment") (Rimbaud) **3**:283

"Les chats blancs" (Valery) **9**:391

"Les chercheuses de poux" (Rimbaud) **3**:271, 276

"Les chères, mains qui furent miennes" (Verlaine) **2**:416

"Cherish You Then the Hope I Shall Forget" (Millay) **6**:211

"Cherry Blossoms" (Gallagher) **9**:65

"The Chestnut Casts His Flambeaux" (Housman) **2**:199

"Un cheval de race" (Baudelaire) **1**:59

"The Cheval-Glass" (Hardy) **8**:100

"La chevelure" (Baudelaire) **1**:45, 66-7, 69

"Chhabi" ("The Picture") (Tagore) **8**:414

"Chi vuol veder" (Petrarch) **8**:256

"Chiare fresche e dolci acque" (Petrarch) **8**:221, 230, 232-33, 235-36

"Chicago" (Sandburg) **2**:317, 322-23, 333, 335, 339

"The *Chicago Defender* Sends a Man to Little Rock" (Brooks) **7**:62

"The Chicago Picasso" (Brooks) **7**:82

Chicago Poems (Sandburg) **2**:300-02, 307-08, 312, 314, 316-18, 321, 333, 335-36, 338-39

"Chicago Poet" (Sandburg) **2**:339

"Chicory and Daisies" (Williams) **7**:373, 407

"The Child" (Carruth) **10**:71

"Child" (Sandburg) **2**:329

"Child of Europe" (Milosz) **8**:191-92

"Child Poems" (H. D.) **5**:305

"The Child Who Saw Midas" (Sitwell) **3**:308

"Childe Roland to the Dark Tower Came" (Browning) **2**:64, 85-6, 88

"Childe Rolandine" (Smith) **12**:302, 350, 354

"Childhood among the Ferns" (Hardy) **8**:125-26

"A Childish Prank" (Hughes) **7**:123, 143, 161

"Childless Father" (Wordsworth) **4**:374, 428

"Children of Darkness" (Graves) **6**:137

"The Children of the Night" (Robinson) **1**:459, 467, 486

The Children of the Night (Robinson) **1**:459, 462-63, 466, 474

"The Children of the Poor" (Brooks) **7**:55, 62, 75, 78

"The Children's Song" (Kipling) **3**:171

"A Child's Grave at Florence" (Browning) **6**:6

"Child's Talk in April" (Rossetti) **7**:274

The Chimeras (Nerval)
See *Les Chimères*

Les Chimères (*The Chimeras*) (Nerval) **13**:172, 174, 176, 179-80, 182, 184, 187, 191-92, 194-95

"The Chimney Sweeper" (Blake) **12**:7, 9, 34-5

Chinese Dynasty Cantos (Pound) **4**:352

Chinesisch-deutsche Jahres-und Tageszeiten (Goethe) **5**:251

"Chiron" (Holderlin) **4**:148, 166

Chitra (Tagore) **8**:408-09, 415, 418

"Chocorua to Its Neighbour" (Stevens) **6**:335

A Choice of Kipling's Verse Made by T. S. Eliot with an Essay on Rudyard Kipling (Kipling) **3**:175

"Cholera" (Dove) **6**:108

"The Choosers" (Smith) **12**:327

"The Choral Union" (Sassoon) **12**:242

"Choros Sequence from Morpheus" (H. D.) **5**:304

"Chorus" (Lorde) **12**:159

Chosen Defects (Neruda)
See *Defectos escogidos: 2000*

Chosen Poems: Old and New (Lorde) **12**:142, 146, 148, 154, 157

"Chrismus on the Plantation" ("Christmas on the Plantation") (Dunbar) **5**:133-34

"Le Christ aux Oliviers" (Nerval) **13**:173, 177, 181, 198

"Christ for Sale" (Lowell) **3**:203

"Christ Has Arisen" (Pushkin)
See "Khristos Voskres"

"Christ in Alabama" (Hughes) **1**:264

"Christ in Flanders" (Lowell) **3**:203

Christ is Arisen (Bely)
See *Hristos voskres*

Christ is Risen (Bely)
See *Hristos voskres*

"Christabel" (Coleridge) **11**:41-2, 51-3, 84-5, 90-1, 104, 110

"The Christian Statesman" (Masters) **1**:344

"Christiane R." (Goethe) **5**:246

"Christmas at Black Rock" (Lowell) **3**:201

"A Christmas Ballad" (Brodsky) **9**:2, 4

"A Christmas Card" (Merton) **10**:340

"Christmas Eve" (Sexton) **2**:363

"Christmas Eve under Hooker's Statue" (Lowell) **3**:200, 203

"Christmas Eve--Market Square" (Page) **12**:169

"Christmas in India" (Kipling) **3**:186

"Christmas in Simla" (Kipling) **3**:182

"Christmas on the Hudson" (Garcia Lorca)
See "Navidad en el Hudson"

"Christmas on the Plantation" (Dunbar)
See "Chrismus on the Plantation"

"Christmas Poem for Nancy" (Schwartz) **8**:316

"Christmas Tree--Market Square" (Page) **12**:169

Christmas-Eve (Browning) **2**:31-2, 44, 70-1

Christmas-Eve and Easter Day (Browning) **2**:33, 36, 70, 95

"Christs Incarnation" (Herrick) **9**:119

"Chrysallis" (Montale) **13**:151

"Chüeh-chü" (Tu Fu) **9**:323

"Chumban" ("The Kiss") (Tagore) **8**:407

"The Church" (Herbert) **4**:103, 113

"The Church and the Hotel" (Masters) **1**:343

"The Church Floore" (Herbert) **4**:109, 119

"The Church Militant" (Herbert) **4**:100, 130

"Church Monuments" (Herbert) **4**:100, 119

"Church Music" (Herbert) **4**:100, 131

"The Church of Brou" (Arnold) **5**:6, 9, 12, 50

"The Church Porch" (Herbert) **4**:100-01, 103, 107, 126

"Church-lock and Key" (Herbert) **4**:127

"Churchyard" (Gray)
See "Elegy Written in a Country Churchyard"

"Ciel brouillé" (Baudelaire) **1**:61, 66

"Un cigare allume que Fume" (Apollinaire)
See "Paysage"

"Cigola la carrucola del pozzo" (Montale) **13**:164

"Le cimetière marin" (Bishop) **3**:46

"Le cimetière marin" ("The Graveyard by the Sea") (Valery) **9**:348, 351-52, 355, 358, 361, 363-80, 382, 384, 387, 389-93, 395-96, 398

The Circle Game (Atwood) **8**:3, 12, 15, 18, 26-8

"Circulation of the Song" (Duncan) **2**:127

"Circumjack Cencrastus" (MacDiarmid) **9**:157

"Circumstance" (Lowell) **13**:94

"Cirque d'hiver" (Bishop) **3**:37

"The Cited" (Garcia Lorca)
See "Romance del emplazado"

"Cities and Thrones and Powers" (Kipling) **3**:183

"Citizen Cain" (Baraka) **4**:17, 24

"Città in campagna" ("City in the Country") (Pavese) **13**:227

"The City" (Pasternak)
See "Gorod"

"A City Dead House" (Whitman) **3**:379

"City in the Country" (Pavese)
See "Città in campagna"

"The City in the Sea" (Poe) **1**:426, 431, 434, 438, 443-45

"City Midnight Junk Strains for Frank O'Hara" (Ginsberg) **4**:47

"City of Monuments" (Rukeyser) **12**:230

"The City of the Dead" (Gibran) **9**:73

"The City Planners" (Atwood) **8**:13

"City Psalm" (Rukeyser) **12**:221

"City Trees" (Millay) **6**:207

"City Walk-Up, Winter 1969" (Forche) **10**:141, 144, 147, 157-58

"City without a Name" (Milosz) **8**:194-95

"City without Walls" (Auden) **1**:20

"The City's Love" (McKay) **2**:211

"Ciudad sin sueño" ("Brooklyn Bridge Nocturne"; "Unsleeping City (Brooklyn Bridge Nocturne)") (Garcia Lorca) 3:139-40
"Civil Rights Poem" (Baraka) 4:11, 19
"Clad All in Brown" (Swift) 9:256-57
"The Claim" (Browning) 6:14
"Clair de lune" ("Moonlight") (Apollinaire) 7:45-6
"Clair de lune" ("Moonlight") (Verlaine) 2:413, 420, 429
"Claribel" (Tennyson) 6:358-60, 365
"Clasping of Hands" (Herbert) 4:130
"Class Struggle" (Baraka) 4:30, 38
"Class Struggle in Music" (Baraka) 4:40
"Claud Antle" (Masters) 1:334
"Clay" (Baraka) 4:30
"Cleaning the Candelabrum" (Sassoon) 12:248, 259
"Clear, with Light Variable Winds" (Lowell) 13:94
"Cleared" (Kipling) 3:167
"The Clearing" (Baraka) 4:5, 15
"Cleon" (Browning) 2:36, 82, 95
"Cliff Klingenhagen" (Robinson) 1:467, 486
"Clifford Ridell" (Masters) 1:344-46
"The Climate of Thought" (Graves) 6:139, 143
"The Clinging Vine" (Robinson) 1:468
"The Clipped Stater" (Graves) 6:128, 137
"A Cloak" (Levertov) 11:176, 194
"La cloche fêlée" (Baudelaire) 1:65
"A Clock in the Square" (Rich) 5:352
"The Clock of Tomorrow" (Apollinaire)
    See "L'orloge de demain"
"The Clock Stopped" (Dickinson) 1:108
"The Clod and the Pebble" (Blake) 12:7
"Clorinda and Damon" (Marvell) 10:268, 271
"Closed for Good" (Frost) 1:213
"Clothes" (Sexton) 2:367
"Cloud" (Toomer) 7:338
The Clouds (Williams) 7:370
"The Clown Chastized" (Mallarme)
    See "Le pitre châtié"
Clown's Houses (Sitwell) 3:290, 294, 301-02
Cluster of Songs (Tagore)
    See *Gitāli*
Cluster of Songs (Tagore)
    See *Gitāli*
"Coal" (Lorde) 12:153
Coal (Lorde) 12:142, 148
"The Coal Picker" (Lowell) 13:84
"The Coastwise Lights" (Kipling) 3:162
"The Coats" (Gallagher) 9:60
"Cobwebs" (Rossetti) 7:278
"The Cocked Hat" (Masters) 1:325-26, 328-29, 342
"The Cocks" (Pasternak) 6:253
"Coconut Palm" (Tagore)
    See "Narikel"
"Cocotte" (Gozzano) 10:178
"The Code" (Frost) 1:195, 208, 226
"A Code of Morals" (Kipling) 3:190
"Coeur, couronne et miroir" ("Heart, Crown and Mirror") (Apollinaire) 7:32-6
"La coeur volé" ("The Tortured Heart") (Rimbaud) 3:270
"Cold in the Earth" (Bronte)
    See "Remembrance"
"Cold Iron" (Kipling) 3:171
"Colin Clout" (Spenser)
    See *Colin Clouts Come Home Againe*

Colin Clouts Come Home Againe ("Colin Clout") (Spenser) 8:336, 367, 387, 396
"The Coliseum" (Poe) 1:439
"The Collar" (Herbert) 4:102-03, 112-13, 130-31
"The Collar" (Herrick) 9:141
Collected Earlier Poems (Williams) 7:367-69, 374-75, 378, 382, 387-88, 392-94, 406-07, 409
Collected Early Poems (Pound) 4:355
Collected Later Poems (Williams) 7:370, 375
Collected Lyrics (Millay) 6:227
Collected Poems (Cummings) 5:82-4, 87, 107, 111
Collected Poems (Frost) 1:203
Collected Poems (Graves) 6:153, 165, 171
Collected Poems (Hardy) 8:89, 95-6, 98, 101, 118, 124
Collected Poems (MacDiarmid) 9;186
Collected Poems (Millay) 6:227
Collected Poems (Milosz) 8:190-91, 197-98, 202, 206-07, 214-15
    See *Czeslaw Milosz: The Collected Poems, 1931-1987*
Collected Poems (Moore) 4:235-36, 238, 247, 254, 271
The Collected Poems (Plath) 1:406
Collected Poems (Robinson) 1:467, 469, 480
Collected Poems (Rossetti)
    See *The Poetical Works of Christina Georgina Rossetti*
Collected Poems (Sassoon) 12:246-47
Collected Poems (Sitwell) 3:299, 301, 303-05, 308, 318-21, 325
Collected Poems (Stevens) 6:306
Collected Poems 1934 (Williams) 7:360, 372, 402
Collected Poems, 1938 (Graves) 6:166
Collected Poems, 1955 (Graves) 6:138, 140-43, 145
Collected Poems, 1909-1935 (Eliot) 5:173, 176, 179, 211
Collected Poems, 1912-1944 (H. D.) 5:297, 305
Collected Poems, 1923-1953 (Bogan) 12:93, 95-6, 120, 125
Collected Poems, 1929-1933 (Day Lewis) 11:123
Collected Poems, 1947-1980 (Ginsberg) 4:71-2, 76-9, 83-4, 86, 89
The Collected Poems of A. E. Housman (Housman) 2:175-76, 180
The Collected Poems of Christopher Smart (Smart) 13:347
Collected Poems of H. D. (H. D.) 5:268, 270, 276
The Collected Poems of Hart Crane (Crane) 3:89-90
The Collected Poems of Jean Toomer (Toomer) 7:340-41
The Collected Poems of Muriel Rukeyser (Rukeyser) 12:224, 226, 235
The Collected Poems of Octavio Paz, 1957-1987 (Paz) 1:374-76
The Collected Poems of Stevie Smith (Smith) 12:307, 309, 313-17, 320, 327, 346-47, 350, 352
The Collected Poems of Thomas Merton (Merton) 10:336-337, 345, 348, 351
The Collected Poems of Wallace Stevens (Stevens) 6:304

Collected Shorter Poems, 1927-1957 (Auden) 1:30
Collected Shorter Poems, 1930-1950 (Auden) 1:30
Collected Shorter Poems, 1946-1991 (Carruth) 10:89, 91
Collected Sonnets (Millay) 6:227
Collected Works (Akhmatova) 2:19
Collected Works (Rossetti)
    See *The Poetical Works of Christina Georgina Rossetti*
"Les collines" (Apollinaire) 7:12
"The Colloquies" (Gozzano) 10:175, 180
The Colloquies (Gozzano)
    See *I Colloqui*
"Colloquy in Black Rock" (Lowell) 3:201, 216-17, 227
"Collos. 3.3" (Herbert) 4:130
"La colombe poisnardée et le jet d'eau" (Apollinaire) 7:18, 20-2
"The Colonel" (Forche) 10:136, 138, 140, 145, 153, 167, 169
"Colonel Fantock" (Sitwell) 3:293, 301, 325
"The Colored Band" (Dunbar) 5:134, 147
"The Colored Soldiers" (Dunbar) 5:129-31, 133-34, 140
The Colossus, and Other Poems (Plath) 1:380-81, 84, 388-89, 391, 394, 396, 404, 407, 410, 414
"A Coloured Print by Shokei" (Lowell) 13:61
"A Coltrane Poem" (Sanchez) 9:225
"Columbian Ode" (Dunbar) 5:128
"Combat Cultural" (Moore) 4:259
"Come" (Smith) 12:316
"Come Break with Time" (Bogan) 12:87, 101, 105-06, 122
"Come Death" (Smith) 12:315
"Come Death (2)" (Smith) 12:314, 317, 319
"Come In" (Frost) 1:197, 213, 230
"Come on, Come back" (Smith) 12:295
"Come Republic" (Masters) 1:329, 343
"Come Thunder" ("Thunder Can Break") (Okigbo) 7:235
"The Comedian as the Letter C" (Stevens) 6:293, 295-96, 304, 306, 310, 330, 335
"The Comet at Yell'ham" (Hardy) 8:89
"Comfort" (Browning) 6:21
"Coming Down through Somerset" (Hughes) 7:166
"The Coming Fall" (Levertov) 11:185
"Coming Home" (Gallagher) 9:36
"The Coming of Arthur" (Tennyson) 6:408
"The Coming of the End (Moments of Vision)" (Hardy) 8:92
"Commander Lowell 1887-1950" (Lowell) 3:219, 235
"Comme Dieu Dispense de Graces" (Stevens) 6:294
"Comme on voit sur la branche" (Ronsard) 11:218, 234, 236, 240
"Comme un beau pré despouillè de ses fleurs" (Ronsard) 11:250
"The Commemorative Mound of the Decorated Tree" (Ishikawa Takuboku)
    See "Nishikigizuka"
"Comment against the Lamp" (Hughes) 1:266
"Commentary" (Milosz) 8:212-13
"A Common Ground" (Levertov) 11:169
"Communication in White" (Madhubuti) 5:340
"Communion" (Herbert) 4:100

"A Communist to Others" (Auden) **1**:15
"The Commuted Sentence" (Smith) **12**:327
"Company" (Dove) **6**:111, 119
"Company" (Smith) **12**:325
"Comparison" (Dunbar) **5**:125
"Compensation" (Dunbar) **5**:121
"The Complaint" (Wordsworth)
  See "The Complaint of the Forsaken Indian Woman"
"The Complaint of the Forsaken Indian Woman" ("The Complaint") (Wordsworth) **4**:347, 427-28
Complaints: Containing Sundrie Small Poemes of the Worlds Vanitie (Spenser) **8**:366
The Complete Collected Poems of William Carlos Williams, 1906-1938 (Williams) **7**:348, 355
The Complete Poems (Dickinson) **1**:102
Complete Poems (Sandburg) **2**:322-24, 328-29, 331, 333, 340
The Complete Poems, 1927-1979 (Bishop) **3**:50, 66
The Complete Poems of Marianne Moore (Moore) **4**:251, 254, 256, 270
The Complete Poem's of Paul Laurence Dunbar (Dunbar) **5**:120, 136
The Complete Poetical Works (Lowell) **13**:95
Complete Poetical Works of Samuel Taylor Coleridge (Coleridge) **11**:44, 71
"The Complete Works of Francois Villon" (Villon) **13**:413
"Complicity" (Gallagher) **9**:37
"Composition in Bhairavi" (Tagore)
  See "Bhairavi gan"
"Comrades Four" (McKay) **2**:225
"Conceit of Master Gysbrecht" (Browning) **2**:38
"Conceive a Man, Should He Have Anything" (Cummings) **5**:106
"The Concert" (Millay) **6**:215
"Conciliator, Who Had Never Believed" (Holderlin) **4**:178
"Conclusion" (Sassoon) **12**:258
"Concord River" (Rich) **5**:354
"The Condemned" (Page) **12**:174-75
A Coney Island of the Mind (Ferlinghetti) **1**:164-65, 167-77, 184, 187
"A Conference of the Powers" (Kipling) **3**:160
"Confession" (Baudelaire) **1**:61
"A Confession" (Milosz) **8**:197
"The Confessional" (Browning) **2**:30
"Confessions" (Browning) **6**:32
"Confessions of a Second-Rate, Sensitive Mind" (Tennyson) **6**:347
Configurations (Paz) **1**:355
"The Conflict" (Day Lewis) **11**:126, 150
"A Congratulatory Poem to Her Most Sacred Majesty on the Universal Hopes of All Loyal Persons for a Prince of Wales" (Behn) **13**:32
A Congratulatory Poem to . . . Queen Mary upon Her Arrival in England (Behn) **13**:9
"Conjuring in Heaven" (Hughes) **7**:159
"Connubii Flores, or the Well-Wishes at Weddings" (Herrick) **9**:86, 112
"The Conquererors" (Dunbar) **5**:131
"The Conqueror Worm" (Poe) **1**:437, 443
"Conscience" (Herbert) **4**:109, 129
"Conscience and Remorse" (Dunbar) **5**:115, 125
"Consciousness" (Milosz)
  See "Świadomość"
"Conscripts" (Sassoon) **12**:242, 280
"The Consecrating Mother" (Sexton) **2**:374
"Conseil d'ami" (Valery) **9**:391
"Consolation" (McKay) **2**:225
The Consolation of Philosophy (Boethius)
  See *The Consolation of Philosophy*
"Consorting with Angels" (Sexton) **2**:363
Constab Ballads (McKay) **2**:208, 210, 216, 221-22, 225-27
"Constancie" (Herbert) **4**:109
"Constantly Risking Absurdity" (Ferlinghetti) **1**:182
"Conte" (Rimbaud) **3**:261-63
"Contemplations" (Bradstreet) **10**:7-8, 19-21, 27-30, 35, 42, 65
"The Contender" (Hughes) **7**:155
"The Contention" (Sassoon) **12**:259
"Contest of the Bards" (Ginsberg) **4**:58-9
"The Continent" (Duncan) **2**:109-13
Continuation des amours (Ronsard) **11**:220, 230
"Continuum" (Levertov) **11**:207-09
"Contra mortem" (Carruth) **10**:83
Contra Mortem (Carruth) **10**:71
"Contre les bûcherons de la forêt de Gastine" (Ronsard) **11**:236-37, 242
"Le Contrediz de Franc Gontier" (Villon) **13**:415
"Contusion" (Plath) **1**:391, 394
"The Conundrum of the Workshop" (Kipling) **3**:167
"The Convalescent" (Gozzano) **10**:177
"The Convent Threshold" (Rossetti) **7**:267, 281-82, 291, 295-96, 298
"Conventionality" (Kipling) **3**:190
"The Convergence of the Twain" (Hardy) **8**:116
"The Conversation" (Masters) **1**:326
Conversation at Midnight (Millay) **6**:220, 223, 244
"Conversation in Moscow" (Levertov) **11**:197
"The Conversation of Prayer" (Thomas) **2**:390
"Conversation with a Fireman from Brooklyn" (Gallagher) **9**:44, 60
"Conversations with Jeanne" (Milosz) **8**:213
"Conversion" (Toomer) **7**:320, 334
"Convict" (Wordsworth) **4**:373
"Convivio!" (Williams) **7**:361
"A Cooking Egg" (Eliot) **5**:184
"Cook's Mountains" (Page) **12**:183, 190
"The Cool Web" (Graves) **6**:172
"cops" (Baraka) **4**:12
"A Coquette Conquered" (Dunbar) **5**:122
"Cor Mio" (Rossetti) **7**:278
El corazón amarillo (*The Yellow Heart*) (Neruda) **4**:287, 289
"El corazón de Pedro de Valdivia" ("The Heart of Pedro de Valdivia") (Neruda) **4**:293
"El corazón magellanico" ("The Magellanic Heart") (Neruda) **4**:281
"Corinna, Pride of Drury-Lane" (Swift) **9**:283-84
"Corinna's Going a-Maying" (Herrick) **9**:99-101, 104-05, 116, 120, 122-23, 125, 132, 137, 142, 145
"Coriolanus and His Mother" (Schwartz) **8**:282-83, 290-91, 297-98, 301, 308-09, 312
"The Corner of Night and Morning" (Lowell) **13**:64
"Cornet Solo" (Day Lewis) **11**:145
Cornhuskers (Sandburg) **2**:302, 304, 307, 309, 313-14, 316, 323, 338-39
"Cornish Heroic Song for Valda Trevlyn" (MacDiarmid) **9**:180, 183
"Corno Inglese" ("English Horn") (Montale) **13**:105
"A Corn-Song" (Dunbar) **5**:122
La Corona (Donne) **1**:136-39, 145, 147
"A Coronal" (Williams) **7**:345, 362
"The Coronet" (Marvell) **10**:267, 271, 274, 277, 293, 313-14
"Corpse Song" (Atwood) **8**:23, 25
"Correspondances" (Baudelaire) **1**:55, 65, 69-70
"Correspondences" (Rukeyser) **12**:226, 233
"La Corrida" (Hayden) **6**:194
"Cors de chasse" (Apollinaire) **7**:42
"The Cortege" (Gibran) **9**:73
"Cortège for Rosenbloom" (Stevens) **6**:293
Cortege of Orpheus (Apollinaire)
  See *Le bestiaire; ou, Cortège d'Orphée*
"The Cossack" (Pushkin) **10**:407
"The Cottage Dweller" (Tagore)
  See "Kutir-vasi"
"The Cottar's Saturday Night" (Burns) **6**:50, 57, 74, 79, 96
"Cotton Song" (Toomer) **7**:319, 321
"Cougar Meat" (Gallagher) **9**:59, 62
"Could Man Be Drunk for Ever" (Housman) **2**:195
Count Nulin (Pushkin)
  See *Graf Nulin*
"Counter-Attack" (Sassoon) **12**:256-57, 264-65, 277-78
Counter-Attack and Other Poems (Sassoon) **12**:242, 250, 253, 257-58, 260, 263-64, 266-69, 272, 276-77
"Counting the Beats" (Graves) **6**:136-37, 155
The Country between Us (Forche) **10**:136-38, 140, 143-46, 148, 150-53, 155, 157-59, 161, 165-66, 169
"A Country Burial" (Dickinson) **1**:79
"A Country Girl" (McKay) **2**:224
"A Country Life: To His Brother, Master Thomas Herrick" (Herrick) **9**:86, 110-13, 115
"The Country Life, to the Honoured Master Endimion Porter, Groome of the Bed-Chamber to His Majesty" (Herrick) **9**:101, 139, 144
Country Sentiment (Graves) **6**:127, 129, 132
"The Country Squire and the Mandrake" (Smart) **13**:348
"The Country Whore" (Pavese)
  See "La puttana contadina"
"The Countryside" (Pushkin)
  See "Derevnya"
Un coup de dés jamais n'abolira le hasard (*A Throw of the Dice Never Will Abolish Chance; A Throw of the Dice Will Never Abolish Chance*) (Mallarme) **4**:192, 199, 202-03, 208-09, 217-18
"Coup d'evential..." ("Rap of a Fan...") (Apollinaire) **7**:34-5
"Courage" (Akhmatova)
  See "Muzhestvo"
"Courtship" (Dove) **6**:112
"Cousin Kate" (Rossetti) **7**:270, 276, 280, 289, 291
"Coversation" (Tagore)
  See "Sambhashan"

Title Index

"The Cow in Apple-Time" (Frost) **1**:195, 197
"Cowley Rider" (Masters) **1**:334
"Cowper's Grave" (Browning) **6**:6, 21
"Cows: A Vision" (Gallagher) **9**:36
"The Cows at Night" (Carruth) **10**:85
"The Coy Mistress" (Marvell)
    See "To His Coy Mistress"
"The Crack" (Levertov) **11**:159
"A Cradle Song" (Blake) **12**:7, 10, 33
"Crag Jack's Apostasy" (Hughes) **7**:147
"La cravate et la montre" ("The Necktie and
    the Watch") (Apollinaire) **7**:32, 34-5
"Crazy Jane" (Day Lewis) **11**:159
"A Crazy Spiritual" (Ginsberg) **4**:79
"Creating the World" (Milosz) **8**:214
"The Creation" (Gibran) **9**:73
"Credat Judaeus" (Kipling) **3**:194
"Credences of Summer" (Stevens) **6**:306, 335,
    338
"Credo" (Robinson) **1**:485-86
"The Cremona Violin" (Lowell) **13**:60, 77, 96
"Crepuscolo di sabbiatori" ("The Sand-
    Diggrers' Twilight") (Pavese) **13**:226
Crepúsculario (*The Twilight Book*) (Neruda)
    4:276, 278
"Crépuscule" ("Twilight") (Apollinaire) **7**:40
"Le crépuscule du soir" ("Evening Twilight")
    (Baudelaire) **1**:58-9
"The Crimson Cyclamen" (Williams) **7**:350,
    354
"Cripples and Other Stories" (Sexton) **2**:363,
    365
A Critical Fable (Lowell) **13**:65, 74-6
"Critics and Connoisseurs" (Moore) **4**:232,
    257, 270
"De Critters' Dance" (Dunbar) **5**:145
"Croft" (Smith) **12**:333
"Cross" (Hughes) **1**:235, 243, 263-64
"The Crosse" (Donne) **1**:136
"The Crosse" (Herbert) **4**:111
"The Crossed Apple" (Bogan) **12**:101, 110-11
"Crossing Brooklyn Ferry" (Sexton) **2**:361
"Crossing Brooklyn Ferry" (Whitman) **3**:377,
    379, 391-93, 399-400, 410, 415
"Crossing the Atlantic" (Sexton) **2**:363
"Crossing the Bar" (Tennyson) **6**:359
Crossing the Water: Transitional Poems (Plath)
    1:391, 394, 396, 404
"The Cross-Roads" (Lowell) **13**:60, 76-7
"Crow Alights" (Hughes) **7**:130
"Crow and Mama" (Hughes) **7**:132
"Crow and the Birds" (Hughes) **7**:159
The Crow and the Heart (Carruth) **10**:70, 78,
    89
"Crow and the Sea" (Hughes) **7**:144
"Crow Blacker Than Ever" (Hughes) **7**:138
"Crow Communes" (Hughes) **7**:143
Crow: From the Life and Songs of the Crow
    (Hughes) **7**:129-30, 133, 137-39, 141-43,
    145, 152-53, 155-61, 163, 168-71
"Crow Frowns" (Hughes) **7**:159
"Crow Goes Hunting" (Hughes) **7**:142, 160-
    61
"Crow Hill" (Hughes) **7**:131, 150
"Crow Jane in High Society" (Baraka) **4**:16
"Crow on a Withered Branch" (Matsuo
    Basho) **3**:32
"Crow on the Beach" (Hughes) **7**:138, 144
"Crow Sickened" (Hughes) **7**:138
"Crow Song" (Atwood) **8**:25
"Crowdieknowe" (MacDiarmid) **9**:156
"Crowds" (Baudelaire)
    See "Les foules"
"Crowing-Hen Blues" (Hughes) **1**:256
"The Crown of Bays" (Smith) **12**:319
"The Crown of Gold" (Smith) **12**:295, 315
"Crown of Thorns" (Celan)
    See "Dornenkranz"
"Crowned Out" (Celan) **10**:113
Crowned with Dreams (Rilke) **2**:280
"Crowns and Garlands" (Hughes) **1**:252
"Crow's Account of St. George" (Hughes)
    7:161, 171
"Crow's Account of the Battle" (Hughes)
    7:133, 144, 152
"Crow's Account of the Battle" (Hughes)
    7:133, 144, 152
"Crow's Battle Fury" (Hughes) **7**:143
"Crow's Elephant Totem Song" (Hughes)
    7:138, 144
"Crow's Last Stand" (Hughes) **7**:123, 144
"Crow's Nerve Fails" (Hughes) **7**:144
"Crow's Playmates" (Hughes) **7**:144
"Crow's Theology" (Hughes) **7**:159, 161
"Crow's Undersong" (Hughes) **7**:167
"Crow's Vanity" (Hughes) **7**:144
"Crucibles of Love" (Graves) **6**:172
"The Crucifixion" (Akhmatova) **2**:15
"Crucifixion" (Garcia Lorca)
    See "Crucifixión"
"Crucifixión" ("Crucifixion") (Garcia Lorca)
    3:140
"The Cruell Maid" (Herrick) **9**:101
"Crusoe in England" (Bishop) **3**:48, 63-4,
    66-7, 70
"The Cry" (Levertov) **11**:198
"The Cry" (Masters) **1**:326
"Cry Ararat!" (Page) **12**:168, 190, 198
Cry Ararat! (Page) **12**:167, 179, 184, 190, 197
"Cry Faugh" (Graves) **6**:135
"The Cry of the Children" (Browning) **6**:6,
    17, 21, 27, 30, 42
"The Cry of the Human" (Browning) **6**:7, 21
"Cry to Rome: From the Chrysler Building
    Tower" (Garcia Lorca) **3**:141
"The Crystal Cabinet" (Blake) **12**:36
"Crystals Like Blood" (MacDiarmid) **9**:187
"Cuchualain" (Day Lewis) **11**:151
"Cuckoo Song" (H. D.) **5**:267
"Cudjoe Fresh from de Lecture" (McKay)
    2:224, 226
"Cuento de dos jardines" ("Story of Two
    Gardens"; "A Tale of Two Gardens") (Paz)
    1:361, 363
"The Cuirassiers of the Frontier" (Graves)
    6:133
"The Culprit" (Housman) **2**:162, 164, 169,
    179, 186
"Cultural Exchange" (Hughes) **1**:250, 252
"Culture and Anarchy" (Rich) **5**:386
Cup of Blizzards (Bely)
    See *Kubok metelej: Chetviortiia simfoniia*
The Cup of Snowstorms (Bely)
    See *Kubok metelej: Chetviortiia simfoniia*
"The Cure" (Graves) **6**:155
"A Cure of Souls" (Levertov) **11**:171
"The Curse" (Millay) **6**:211
"A Curse against Elegies" (Sexton) **2**:351
"A Curse for a Nation" (Browning) **6**:27
"Curtain" (Dunbar) **5**:119
"The Curve" (Levertov) **11**:176
"The Customs-Officer's House" (Montale)
    See "La casa dei doganieri"
"Cut" (Plath) **1**:385, 392
Cuttlefish Bones (Montale)
    See *Ossi di seppia*
"Cutty Sark" (Crane) **3**:84, 90, 106
"Le cygne" ("The Swan") (Baudelaire) **1**:45,
    66, 71
"Cyparissus" (Duncan) **2**:103
*Czeslaw Milosz: The Collected Poems, 1931-
    1987* (*Collected Poems*) (Milosz) **8**:190-91,
    197-98, 202, 206-07, 213-15
"D. R." (Zukofsky) **11**:351, 396
"Da una torre" ("From a Tower") (Montale)
    13:113
"Daddy" (Plath) **1**:382-83, 386-87, 392-93,
    395-97, 400-02, 406-07, 414
"The Daemon" (Bogan) **12**:100, 110
The Daffodil Murderer (Sassoon) **12**:252, 270,
    274-77
"Daguerreotype Taken in Old Age" (Atwood)
    8:39
"Un dahlia" (Verlaine) **2**:431
"Dahomey" (Lorde) **12**:160
"Les daimons" ("Demonology") (Ronsard)
    11:225, 279, 281-82
"Daisies Are Broken" (Williams) **7**:406
"The Daisy" (Tennyson) **6**:357, 360
"Daisy Frazer" (Masters) **1**:334
"Daisy's Song" (Keats) **1**:311
"Dakar Doldrums" (Ginsberg) **4**:72
"The Dalliance of the Eagles" (Whitman)
    3:397
"The Dam" (Rukeyser) **12**:210
Dam 'ah wabitisāmah (*A Tear and a Smile*;
    "Tears and Laughter") (Gibran) **9**:73, 75,
    77-8, 81
"Dämmerung" (Celan) **10**:124-25
"Damned Women" (Baudelaire)
    See "Femmes damnées"
"Damon Being Asked a Reason for Loveing"
    (Behn) **13**:18
"Damon the Mower" (Marvell) **10**:266, 293,
    295-97, 315
"The Dampe" (Donne) **1**:130
"The Dance" (Baraka) **4**:16
"The Dance" (Crane) **3**:84, 86, 88, 90
"Dance" (Pavese)
    See "Balletto"
"The Dance at the Phoenix" (Hardy) **8**:99
"Dance of Death" (Garcia Lorca)
    See "Danza de la muerte"
The Dance of Death (Auden) **1**:8
"Dance of the Macabre Mice" (Stevens)
    6:296
"Dance the Orange" (Hayden) **6**:196
"The Dancer" (H. D.) **5**:305
"Daniel Bartoli" (Browning) **2**:84
"Danny Deever" (Kipling) **3**:170-71, 179,
    188-89, 191
"Dans le restaurant" (Eliot) **5**:185
"Danse russe" (Williams) **7**:353, 367, 408
"Dante Études, Book Two" (Duncan) **2**:114-
    16, 127
"Danza de la muerte" ("Dance of Death")
    (Garcia Lorca) **3**:121
"Daphnaida" (Spenser) **8**:365, 367
"Daphnis and Chloe" (Marvell) **10**:265, 271,
    291-92, 301
"Darest Thou Now O Soul" (Whitman)
    3:378
"Darien" (Graves) **6**:137, 144, 168
"Dark Eye in September" (Celan) **10**:112
"The Dark Hills" (Robinson) **1**:468
The Dark One (Tagore)

See *Shyamali*
"Dark Song" (Sitwell) **3**:291
Dark Summer (Bogan) **12**:87, 89, 105-06, 120-23
"Dark Waters of the Beginning" (Okigbo) **7**:231
Dark World (Carruth) **10**:71, 91
"Darkling Summer, Ominous Dusk, Rumorous Rain" (Schwartz) **8**:319
"The Darkling Thrush" (Hardy) **8**:98, 105-06, 121, 131
"Darkness Chex George Whitman" (Ferlinghetti) **1**:183
"Darkness of Death" (Pasternak) **6**:253
"Darling! Because My Blood Can Sing" (Cummings) **5**:108
"Darling Daughters" (Smith) **12**:326
"Darling, It's Frightening! When a Poet Loves ..." (Pasternak) **6**:251
"Darling Room" (Tennyson) **6**:353
"Dat Dirty Rum" (McKay) **2**:222
"Dat ol' Mare o' Mine" (Dunbar) **5**:134
"A Daughter I" (Levertov) **11**:209
"A Daughter II" (Levertov) **11**:209
"The Daughter of the Forest" (Gibran)
See "Amām 'arsh al-jamāl"
Daughters of Fire (Nerval)
See *Les filles du feu*
"Daughters with Curls" (Stevens) **6**:292
"David and Bathsheba in the Public Garden" (Lowell) **3**:205-06, 215
"David's Lamentation for Saul and Jonathan" (Bradstreet) **10**:6
"Dawlish Fair" (Keats) **1**:311
"Dawn" (Dunbar) **5**:125, 128
"Dawn" (Garcia Lorca)
See "La aurora"
"Dawn Adventure" (Lowell) **13**:63
"Dawn after Storm" (Zukofsky) **11**:368
"Dawn Bombardment" (Graves) **6**:144
"Dawn Bombardment" (Graves) **6**:144
"The Dawn Wind" (Kipling) **3**:183
"Dawnbreaker" (Hayden) **6**:198
"The Dawning" (Herbert) **4**:102
"Dawn's Rose" (Hughes) **7**:138, 144, 159
"Day and Night" (Montale)
See "Giorno e notte"
Day by Day (Lowell) **3**:231-32
"The Day Dream" (Coleridge) **11**:91, 106
"The Day is Done" (Dunbar) **5**:126
"The Day Is Gone" (Keats) **1**:279
"The Day of Battle" (Housman) **2**:160
"The Day of Judgement" (Swift) **9**:259, 265, 281, 295
"Day or Night" (Rossetti) **7**:276
"Day Six O'Hare Telephone" (Merton) **10**:336
"The Day the Mountains Move" (Yosano Akiko)
See "Yama no ugoku hi"
"The Day They Eulogized Mahalia" (Lorde) **12**:156
"Daybreak" (Hughes) **1**:255
"Daystar" (Dove) **6**:111
"Las de l'amer repos" ("Weary of the Bitter Ease") (Mallarme) **4**:203
"Dea Roma" (Lowell) **3**:199-200
"Deacon Taylor" (Masters) **1**:323
"The Dead" (Day Lewis) **11**:147
"The Dead" (Montale)
See "I morti"
"Dead Are My People" (Gibran) **9**:73

"Dead before Death" (Rossetti) **7**:288
"The Dead Fox Hunter" (Graves) **6**:166
"The Dead King" (Kipling) **3**:182
The Dead Lecturer (Baraka) **4**:5-6, 16-17, 23, 31, 37
"Dead Musicians" (Sassoon) **12**:267
"The Dead Pan" (Browning) **6**:7, 19
The Dead Priestess Speaks (H. D.) **5**:305
"The Dead Princess and the Seven Heroes" (Pushkin)
See "Skazka o Mertvoy Tsarevne"
"Deaf Poem" (Gallagher) **9**:62
"The Dean of St. Patrick's to Thomas Sheridan" (Swift) **9**:295
"The Dean to Himself on St. Cecilia's Day" (Swift) **9**:295
"The Dean's Reasons" (Swift) **9**:295
"Dear Child of God" (Smith) **12**:335
"Dear Female Heart" (Smith) **12**:295
"Dear Little Sirmio" (Smith) **12**:331
"Dear Muse" (Smith) **12**:335
"Dear Patron of My Virgin Muse" (Burns) **6**:84
"Dear Toni..." (Lorde) **12**:157
"Death" (Herbert) **4**:113
"Death and Co." (Plath) **1**:397
"Death and Daphne" (Swift) **9**:260
"Death and Doctor Hornbook" (Burns) **6**:56, 88
"The Death and Dying Words of Poor Mailie" ("Elegy on Poor Mailie"; "Mailie's Dying Words and Elegy"; "Poor Mailie's Elegy") (Burns) **6**:52, 61, 63-4
"Death and Love" (Browning) **6**:16
"The Death Baby" (Sexton) **2**:373
"Death Carol" (Whitman) **3**:378
"The Death Dance" (Madhubuti) **5**:339
"Death Fugue" (Celan)
See "Todesfuge"
"Death in Mexico" (Levertov) **11**:205-06, 209
"A Death in the Desert" (Browning) **2**:36, 45, 72-73, 95
The Death Notebooks (Sexton) **2**:360-61, 367-68, 370-72
"Death of a Favorite Cat" (Gray)
See "Ode on the Death of a Favourite Cat, Drowned in a Tub of Gold Fishes"
"The Death of A. G. A." (Bronte) **8**:65, 74
"Death of a Young Son by Drowning" (Atwood) **8**:38-9
"Death of Antoñito the Camborio" (Garcia Lorca)
See "Muerte de Antoñito el Camborio"
"Death of Autumn" (Millay) **6**:236
"The Death of God" (Montale)
See "La morte di Dio"
"The Death of Lovers" (Baudelaire)
See "La mort des amants"
"The Death of Mr. Mounsel" (Smith) **12**:323
"The Death of Oenone" (Tennyson) **6**:360
"The Death of the Beloved" (Rilke) **2**:272-73
"The Death of the Fathers" (Sexton) **2**:356, 365-67
"The Death of the Firstborn" (Dunbar) **5**:140
"The Death of the Hired Man" (Frost) **1**:195, 197, 209, 216, 221, 226, 228-29
"Death of the Lord Protector" (Marvell)
See "Poem upon the Death of O. C."
"Death of the Lovers" (Baudelaire)
See "La mort des amants"
"The Death of the Other Children" (Atwood) **8**:39

"Death of the Poet" (Pasternak) **6**:268
"The Death of the Sheriff" (Lowell) **3**:200, 206
"The Death Room" (Graves) **6**:142, 144
"Death Shall Have No Dominion" (Thomas)
See "And Death Shall Have No Dominion"
"Death, That Struck when I Was Most Confiding" (Bronte) **8**:65
"Death the Barber" (Williams) **7**:388
"Death to Van Gogh's Ear!" (Ginsberg) **4**:63, 74-5
"A Death-Day Recalled" (Hardy) **8**:136
"Deaths and Entrances" (Thomas) **2**:380-82, 388, 390
"Debat du cuer et du corps de Villon" (Villon) **13**:394, 396
"The Debt" (Dunbar) **5**:120, 125
"A Decade" (Lowell) **13**:97
"Decay" (Herbert) **4**:102
"The Decay of Vanity" (Hughes) **7**:113
"December 1" (Milosz) **8**:215
"December 4th" (Sexton) **2**:372
"December 9th" (Sexton) **2**:352-53
"December 10th" (Sexton) **2**:364
"December 12th" (Sexton) **2**:352-53
"December 14th" (Sexton) **2**:353
"December 16th" (Sexton) **2**:352-53
"December 18th" (Sexton) **2**:352
"The Dedication" (Herbert) **4**:125
"Dedication" (Milosz) **8**:193
"Dedication for a Plot of Ground" (Williams) **7**:362, 394
"Dedication in Time" (Schwartz)
See "Time's Dedication"
"A Dedication of Three Hats" (Gray) **6**:166
"Dedications" (Rich) **5**:401
"The Deep Sea Cables" (Kipling) **3**:162
Deep Song (Garcia Lorca)
See *Poema del cante jondo*
"Deeply Morbid" (Smith) **12**:329, 346
"Deep-sea Fishing" (MacDiarmid) **9**:167
Defectos escogidos: 2000 (*Chosen Defects*; *Selected Failings*) (Neruda) **4**:287
"definition for blk / children" (Sanchez) **9**:224, 232
"Definition in the Face of Unnamed Fury" (Dove) **6**:111
"Definition of Creativity" (Pasternak) **6**:271
"The Definition of Love" (Marvell) **10**:264, 266, 271, 274, 277, 291, 294, 299-303, 312, 316, 319
"The Definition of Poetry" (Pasternak)
See "Opredelenyie poezii"
"The Definition of the Creative Power" (Pasternak) **6**:254
"Deher milan" ("Physcial Union") (Tagore) **8**:407
"Dehorning" (Hughes) **7**:166
"Dein Schimmer" (Celan) **10**:124-25
"Dejaneira" (Arnold) **5**:8
"Dejection: An Ode" (Coleridge) **11**:41, 52-3, 58, 69-73, 90-2, 105-09
"Delfica" (Nerval) **13**:181, 194
"Delight in Disorder" (Herrick) **9**:111-12, 115-16, 132, 135
"The Delinquent" (Dunbar) **5**:119
"Deliverance" (Graves) **6**:157
"Deliverance From a Fit of Fainting" ("Fit of Fainting") (Bradstreet) **10**:26, 61-2
"Della primavera trasportata al morale" (Williams) **7**:408
"Delphi" (H. D.) **5**:305

"Delta" (Montale)   **13**:134, 164
"Dem aufgehenden Vollmonde" (Goethe)
   5:249
"The Demiurge's Laugh" (Frost)   **1**:213
"Democracy" (Hughes)   **1**:241, 252, 258
"The Demon" (Pushkin)   **10**:406, 412-13, 418
"The Demon Lover" (Rich)   **5**:392
"Demonology" (Ronsard)
   See "Les daimons"
"Demos and Dionysus" (Robinson)   **1**:470,
   487
"An den Mond" (Goethe)   **5**:246-47
"Denial" (Herbert)   **4**:114, 119-20
"Denver Doldrum" (Ginsberg)   **4**:74
"Deola Thinking" (Pavese)   **13**:205
"Deola's Return" (Pavese)
   See "Ritorno di Deola"
Departmental Ditties (Kipling)   **3**:155-56, 159,
   165, 182, 190-91
"Departure" (Forche)   **10**:137, 144, 156, 169
"Departure" (Millay)   **6**:211
"Departure" (Plath)   **1**:388, 407-08
"Departure in the Dark" (Day Lewis)   **11**:145
"The Departure Song of the Divine Strings"
   (Li Ho)   **13**:51
Depends: A Poet's Notebook (Montale)
   See *Quaderno de quattro anni*
"Depression Before Spring" (Stevens)   **6**:313
"Depth of Love" (Graves)   **6**:172
"The Depths" (Apollinaire)
   See "Loin du pigeonnier"
"The Derelict" (Kipling)   **3**:183
"Derevnya" ("The Countryside") (Pushkin)
   10:421
Derivations: Selected Poems, 1950-1956
   (Duncan)   **2**:105-06
"Derniers vers" (Rimbaud)   **3**:285
*Les derniers vers de Pierre de Ronsard,
   gentilhomme vandomois* (Ronsard)   **11**:244,
   269, 274
"Des Beautés qui'il voudroit en s'amie"
   (Ronsard)   **11**:247
"Des Faux" ("Fakes") (Apollinaire)   **7**:46
"Des imagistes" (Williams)   **7**:345
"The Descent" (Williams)   **7**:403
"The Descent from the Cross" (Rossetti)
   7:264, 285
"The Descent of Odin, an Ode" (Gray)
   2:146, 148-49, 152
The Descent of Winter (Williams)   **7**:349, 352-
   53, 368, 400, 402
"A Descent through the Carpet" (Atwood)
   8:12, 19
"Description of a City Shower" ("Shower")
   (Swift)   **9**:252, 265, 275-79
"Description of the Morning" (Swift)   **9**:265
"Description without Place" (Stevens)   **6**:338
Descriptive Sketches (Wordsworth)   **4**:372
"El Desdichado" (Nerval)   **13**:174-75, 178-80,
   184-87, 195
"The Desert Music" (Williams)   **7**:374
The Desert Music, and Other Poems (Williams)
   7:371, 402-03
"Desert Places" (Frost)   **1**:213, 229
"The Deserted House" (Tennyson)   **6**:358
"The Deserted Plantation" (Dunbar)   **5**:117,
   123
"The Deserter" (Smith)   **12**:300, 330-31, 333
"Design" (Frost)   **1**:227-28
"Désir" (Apollinaire)   **7**:3
"Desire" (Hughes)   **1**:240
"Desire" (Toomer)   **7**:338

"Despite and Still" (Graves)   **6**:154
"Despondency, an Ode" (Burns)   **6**:71
"Destino del poeta" (Paz)   **1**:358
"Destiny" (Arnold)   **5**:43, 50
"The Destiny of Nations" (Coleridge)   **11**:49,
   63-4, 80
"The Destroyer" (Graves)   **6**:166
"Destroyers" (Kipling)   **3**:183
"La destruction" (Baudelaire)   **1**:63, 71
"Detail" (Williams)   **7**:369
"Der Deutsche dankt" (Goethe)   **5**:248
Deuxième édition du cinquiesme livre des odes
   (Ronsard)   **11**:246
"Development" (Browning)   **2**:96
"The Devil and the Lady" (Tennyson)   **6**:372,
   408-09
"The Devil at Berry Pomery" (Graves)   **6**:142,
   144
"The Devils" (Pushkin)
   See "Besy"
"The Devil's Advice to Story Tellers" (Graves)
   6:143
"The Devon Maid" (Keats)   **1**:311
"Devotion: That It Flow; That There Be
   Concentration" (Gallagher)   **9**:45, 59
"Devotion to Duty" (Sassoon)   **12**:257-58
"Devyatsat pyaty god" ("The Year 1905")
   (Pasternak)   **6**:265, 272
"Dharma prachar" ("Religious Propaganda")
   (Tagore)   **8**:407
"A Dialogue" (Herbert)   **4**:130
"A Dialogue between Old England and New"
   (Bradstreet)   **10**:5, 17, 21, 33
"A Dialogue between the Resolved Soul, and
   Created Pleasure" (Marvell)   **10**:265, 271,
   274, 277, 290-91, 294, 314
"A Dialogue between the Soul and Body"
   (Marvell)   **10**:265, 271, 274, 290, 313, 316
"A Dialogue between the Two Horses"
   (Marvell)   **10**:276
"A Dialogue between Thyrsis and Dorinda"
   (Marvell)   **10**:271, 314
"Dialogues of the Dogs" (Burns)
   See "The Twa Dogs"
"Diamantina" (Montale)   **13**:138
The Diamond Cutters, and Other Poems (Rich)
   5:350, 352-54, 358, 362-63, 368-69, 388, 392
Diario del '71 (Montale)   **13**:138, 144, 158
Diario del '71 e del '72 (*Diary of '71 and '72*)
   (Montale)   **13**:138-39, 152, 160, 168
Diario del '72 (Montale)   **13**:138, 144
Diaro de un poeta recien casado (*Diary of a
   Newly-Wed Poet*) (Jimenez)   **7**:197, 201-02,
   208, 212, 214
Diary of '71 and '72 (Montale)
   See *Diario del '71 e del '72*
"Diary of a Change" (Rukeyser)   **12**:218
"Diary of a Naturalist" (Milosz)   **8**:206
Diary of a Newly-Wed Poet (Jimenez)
   See *Diaro de un poeta recien casado*
"Diaspora" (Lorde)   **12**:138, 140
"Dichterberuf" (Holderlin)   **4**:169
"Dichtung" (Baraka)   **4**:17
"Dick, a Maggot" (Swift)   **9**:296
"The Dictators" (Neruda)   **4**:282
"The Dictatorship of the Proletariat" (Baraka)
   4:38-9
"Didactic Piece" (Bogan)   **12**:122
"Dido's Farewell to Aeneas" (Smith)   **12**:331
"An die Hofnung" (Holderlin)   **4**:148
"An die Jungen Dichter" ("To the Young
   Poets") (Holderlin)   **4**:165

"An die Natur" ("To Nature") (Holderlin)
   4:142
"Died of Wounds" (Sassoon)   **12**:262
"El dilitada guerra" ("The Drawn-Out War")
   (Neruda)   **4**:295
"Dinner Guest: Me" (Hughes)   **1**:252
"The Dinner Party" (Lowell)   **13**:79
"Dionysus in Doubt" (Robinson)   **1**:470
Dionysus in Doubt (Robinson)   **1**:470
*Dios deseado y deseante: Animal de fondo con
   numerosos poemas inéditos* (*God Desired and
   Desiring*) (Jimenez)   **7**:197, 207
"Diptych with Votive Tablet" (Paz)
   See "Preparatory Exercise (Dyptych with
   Votive Tablet)"
Directionscore: Selected and New Poems
   (Madhubuti)   **5**:330, 336, 346
"Directive" (Frost)   **1**:213, 227
"Director of Alienation" (Ferlinghetti)   **1**:187
"Dirge" (Smith)   **12**:292, 344
"A Dirge" (Tennyson)   **6**:359
"Dirge for a Town in France" (Merton)
   10:350
"Dirge for the New Sunrise (August 6, 1945)"
   (Sitwell)   **3**:327
"A Dirge upon the Death of the Right Valiant
   Lord, Bernard Stuart" (Herrick)   **9**:131
"Dis Aliter Visum" (Browning)   **2**:68
"The Disappointment" (Behn)   **13**:7, 10-11,
   13-14, 16, 25-6, 28
"A Disaster" (Hughes)   **7**:142, 160-61
"Disaster" (Valery)
   See "Sinistre"
"The Discharge" (Herbert)   **4**:109, 113, 120,
   129
"Disciplina antica" ("Ancient discipline")
   (Pavese)   **13**:226
"Discipline" (Herbert)   **4**:121
"Discipline" (Herbert)
   See "Throw Away Thy Rod"
"The Disclosure" (Levertov)   **11**:169
Discours (Ronsard)
   See *Discours des misères de ce temps*
"Discours à Pierre Lescot" (Ronsard)   **11**:266
"Discours au Roy" ("Au Roy") (Ronsard)
   11:244, 284, 291
"Discours de misères de ce temps" (Ronsard)
   11:248
Discours des misères de ce temps (*Discours*)
   (Ronsard)   **11**:224, 250
"Discours en forme d'élégie" (Ronsard)
   11:248
"The Discovery" (Hardy)   **8**:101
"The Discovery of the Madeiras" (Frost)
   1:196, 206
"Disembarking at Quebec" (Atwood)   **8**:36,
   40
"Disillusionment" (Hughes)   **1**:246
"The Disoblig'd Love" (Behn)   **13**:20
"Disorder Overtakes Us All Day Long"
   (Schwartz)   **8**:285
"Dispersal" (Sassoon)   **12**:259
"Displaced People" (Pavese)   **13**:218
"The Disquieted Muses" (Plath)
   See "The Disquieting Muses"
"The Disquieting Muses" ("The Disquieted
   Muses") (Plath)   **1**:388, 407
"The Dissolution" (Donne)   **1**:154
"Distance" (Milosz)
   See "Odlegtose"

Distances (Okigbo)   7:228, 234-35, 240-41, 243-47, 251, 253, 255
"The Distressed Damsel" (Smart)   13:348
"Dithyrambes" (Ronsard)   11:230-32
"Ditty" (Hardy)   8:90
Divagations (Mallarme)   4:202, 210
"The Diver" (Hayden)   6:187, 193, 198
"The Divine Image" (Blake)   12:5, 7, 33
Divine Poems (Donne)   1:158
"Diving into the Wreck" (Rich)   5:371, 374, 376, 394-95
Diving into the Wreck: Poems, 1971-1972 (Rich)   5:360, 362, 365, 367-68, 370-72, 384, 388-90, 393
"Divinità in incognito" (Montale)   13:133
"Divinitie" (Herbert)   4:108, 130
"Division" (Bogan)   12:98, 106, 121
"The Division" (Hardy)   8:93
"The Division of Parts" (Sexton)   2:351, 359-60, 367
"The Divorce Papers" (Sexton)   2:356, 367
"Divorce, Thy Name Is Woman" (Sexton)   2:359
"Divorcing" (Levertov)   11:197
"Do." (Cummings)   5:106
"Do Jōzefa Sadzika" ("To Joseph Sadzik") (Milosz)   8:190
"Do Not Touch" (Pasternak)   6:260
"Do Take Muriel Out" (Smith)   12:331, 337
"Do the Others Speak of Me Mockingly, Maliciously?" (Schwartz)   8:306
"Doc Hill" (Masters)   1:327
"Dock Rats" (Moore)   4:251
"The Doctor" (Smith)   12:330
"The Doctor of the Heart" (Sexton)   2:365
"Does It Matter?" (Sassoon)   12:267-68, 285
"Does the Road Wind Up-hill all the Way?" (Rossetti)   7:293
"Dog" (Ferlinghetti)   1:184
"A Dog Named Ego, the Snowflakes as Kisses" (Schwartz)   8:307, 314
"De Dog Rose" (McKay)   2:223
"Dog-Days" (Lowell)   13:64
"Dogs Are Shakespearean, Children Are Strangers" (Schwartz)   8:306, 312
"A Dog's Life" (MacDiarmid)   9:155
"The Doll" (Lowell)   13:84-5
The Dolphin (Lowell)   3:224, 229-30, 232-33, 239-41
A Dome of Many-Coloured Glass (Lowell)   13:60, 69
Domesday Book (Masters)   1:330-33, 335-36, 339
"Domestic Poem for a Summer Afternoon" (Page)   12:181
Domik v Kolomne (*The Little House of Kolomna*) (Pushkin)   10:366, 381-86, 391, 400
"Domination of Black" (Stevens)   6:293-94
"Don du poème" (Mallarme)   4:196
"Don Juan aux enfers" ("Don Juan in Hades") (Baudelaire)   1:47
"Don Juan in Hades" (Baudelaire)
  See "Don Juan aux enfers"
"The Donkey" (Smith)   12:318
"Donne perdute" ("Fallen Women") (Pavese)   13:225
Don't Cry, Scream (Madhubuti)   5:324-25, 328, 336, 338, 340-46
Don't Go Out of the Door (Li Ho)   13:42
"Don't Grow Old" (Ginsberg)   4:84
"Don't Wanna Be" (Sanchez)   9:229

"Doom Is the House without the Door" (Dickinson)   1:111
"Dooms-day" (Herbert)   4:131
"Doors, Doors, Doors" (Sexton)   2:349
"Dopa una fuga" ("After a Flight") (Montale)   13:134
"Dope" (Baraka)   4:40
"Dora" (Tennyson)   6:360
"Dora Markus" (Montale)   13:106, 113-14, 119
"Dora Williams" (Masters)   1:347
"La dormeuse" (Valery)   9:365-66, 374, 387, 392-93, 396
"Dornenkranz" ("Crown of Thorns") (Celan)   10:128-30
"Dorothée" (Baudelaire)
  See "La belle Dorothée"
"Dotage" (Herbert)   4:130
"The Double Chamber" (Baudelaire)
  See "Le chambre double"
"Double Feature" (Hayden)   6:194-95
"The Double Image" (Sexton)   2:350, 355-56, 359, 361-63, 372
The Double Image (Levertov)   11:163-64
"Double Monologue" (Rich)   5:374
"Double Ode" (Rukeyser)   12:225
Double Persephone (Atwood)   8:21
"The Double Voices" (Atwood)   8:16, 32
"The Dove Breeder" (Hughes)   7:116
"The Dove in Spring" (Stevens)   6:313
"Dover" (Auden)   1:16
"Dover Beach" (Arnold)   5:8, 13, 16-18, 35, 38, 47, 49, 53, 58, 64-5
"Dov'era il tennis" ("Where the Tennis Court Was") (Montale)   13:160
"Down" (Graves)   6:142, 144
"Down, Wanton, Down!" (Graves)   6:151, 153, 165
"Dr. Swift to Mr. Pope while He Was Writing the *Dunciad*" (Swift)   9:295
"The Draft Horse" (Frost)   1:213
A Draft of Eleven New Cantos (XXXI-XLI) (Pound)   4:321-22, 353, 357-58
A Draft of Shadows (Paz)
  See *Pasado en claro*
Drafts and Fragments of Cantos CX to CXVII (Pound)   4:352-54
"The Dragon and the Undying" (Sassoon)   12:278
"Dragonfly" (Bogan)   12:107-08
"A Drama of Exile" (Browning)   6:6, 20-1, 26, 31, 34, 46
Dramatic Lyrics (Browning)   2:26, 35, 66, 94
"Dramatic Poem: Voice of Silence" (Ishikawa Takuboku)
  See "Gekishi: Chimmoku no koe"
Dramatic Romances and Lyrics (Browning)   2:94
Dramatis Personae (Browning)   2:34, 45, 94-5
"The Drawn-Out War" (Neruda)
  See "El dilitada guerra"
"A Dream" (Blake)   12:7, 33-4
"The Dream" (Bogan)   12:111
"The Dream" (Browning)   6:19
"A Dream" (Burns)   6:89
"The Dream" (Sassoon)   12:267
"Dream" (Tagore)
  See "Svapna"
"The Dream, 1863" (Hayden)   6:180, 188
"Dream Boogie" (Hughes)   1:266
"A Dream Deferred" (Hughes)   1:266
"Dream Drumming" (Rukeyser)   12:222

The Dream of a Common Language: Poems, 1974-1977 (Rich)   5:373-76, 378, 384, 389
"A Dream of Comparison" (Smith)   12:330, 332-33, 345, 352
"A Dream of Fair Women" (Tennyson)   6:353, 359-60
"The Dream of Knowledge" (Schwartz)   8:297, 311
"A Dream of Nourishment" (Smith)   12:326
"A Dream of Whitman Paraphrased, Recognized, and Made More Vivid by Renoir" (Schwartz)   8:318
"Dream of Youth" (Tagore)
  See "Yauvan-svapna"
"A Dream or No" (Hardy)   8:135
"Dream Variations" (Hughes)   1:248
"A Dream within a Dream" (Poe)   1:434
"Dreamdust" (Hughes)   1:241
"The Dreame" (Donne)   1:147, 152
"The Dreame" (Herrick)   9:109
"The Dreamer" (Pushkin)   10:407
"The Dreamer" (Tennyson)   6:372
"Dreamers" (Sassoon)   12:284, 286
"The Dream-Follower" (Hardy)   8:108
"Dream-Land" (Poe)   1:433-34, 436, 438
"Dreams" (Poe)   1:436
"Dreams in War Time" (Lowell)   13:84
"Dressing to Wait a Table" (McKay)   2:205
"Dried Marjoram" (Lowell)   13:61
"The Drifter off Tarentum" (Kipling)   3:183
"The Drinker" (Lowell)   3:212
"A Drumlin Woodchuck" (Frost)   1:213
"Drummer Hodge" (Hardy)   8:121
"Drums" (Okigbo)   7:234
Drum-Taps (Whitman)   3:389, 414, 418
A Drunk Man Looks at the Thistle (MacDiarmid)   9:151-52, 158, 167-70, 173, 175, 181, 186, 189-93
"The Drunkard" (Sitwell)   3:299
The Drunken Boat (Rimbaud)
  See *Le bateau ivre*
"The Drunken Fisherman" (Lowell)   3:199-200, 202, 204, 212
"The Dry Salvages" (Eliot)   5:164-65, 167-69, 180-81, 183, 186, 210
"Dryads" (Sassoon)   12:240, 275
"Du coton dans les oreilles" (Apollinaire)   7:22
"Du liegst" (Celan)   10:98
"Du sei wei du" ("You Be Like You") (Celan)   10:100-01
"Dubrovnik October 14, 1980, 10:45 p. m." (Ginsberg)   4:62
"A Duck for Dinner" (Stevens)   6:322
"Due nel crepuscolo" ("Two in the Twilight") (Montale)   13:107, 150
"Due sigarette" ("Two Cigarettes") (Pavese)   13:225-28
"The Dug-Out" (Sassoon)   12:281, 283
Duineser Elegien (*Duino Elegies/Elegies*) (Rilke)   2:268-69, 279-82, 285-87, 294-95
Duino Elegies/Elegies (Rilke)
  See *Duineser Elegien*
"Dully Gumption's Addendum" (Hughes)   7:120
"Dulnesse" (Herbert)   4:112
"Duncan Gray" (Burns)   6:57, 59, 100
"The Dungeon" (Wordsworth)   4:373
"Duns Scotus" (Lowell)   3:201
"Duranta asha" ("Fierce Hope") (Tagore)   8:407
"Duration" (Paz)   1:355

"During a Transatlantic Call" (Lowell) **3**:241
"During Fever" (Lowell) **3**:206, 220, 243, 245
"During the Eichmann Trial" ("The Eichmann Trial") (Levertov) **11**:169, 193
"During the Passaic Strike of 1926" (Zukofsky) **11**:351, 396
"During Wind and Rain" (Hardy) **8**:88, 113
"Dusha" ("The Soul") (Pasternak) **6**:267, 285
"Dust Bowl" (Hughes) **1**:240
"Dust in the Eyes" (Frost) **1**:195
"Dust of Snow" (Frost) **1**:195, 218
"Dusting" (Dove) **6**:111, 113
"Dutch Graves in Bucks County" (Stevens) **6**:302
"Duty is my Lobster" (Smith) **12**:340
"The Dying Swan" (Tennyson) **6**:359, 389-91
"The Dykes" (Kipling) **3**:182
The Dynasts: A Drama of the Napoleonic Wars (Hardy) **8**:79-81, 85-7, 95-6, 104, 108, 111, 121-22
"Dytiscus" (MacDiarmid) **9**:157, 183
"E. P. Ode Pour L'Election de son Sepulchre" (Pound) **4**:319
"Each Bird Walking" (Gallagher) **9**:44
"Each of You" (Lorde) **12**:154
"Eagle Confin'd in a College Court" (Smart) **13**:341
Eagle or Sun? (Paz) **1**:354, 359
"Early Chronology" (Sassoon) **12**:245
"Early Evening Quarrel" (Hughes) **1**:247
"Early Lynching" (Sandburg) **2**:330
"Early March" (Sassoon) **12**:254, 259
"An Early Martyr" (Williams) **7**:353, 368
An Early Martyr, and Other Poems (Williams) **7**:350, 399, 402
"The Early Morning Light" (Schwartz) **8**:294
Early Poems (Crane) **3**:90-1
Early Poems, 1935-1955 (Paz) **1**:373, 375
Early Verse of Rudyard Kipling, 1877-99: Unpublished, Uncollected, and Rarely Collected Poems (Kipling) **3**:193
"The Earrings" (Montale)
   See "Gli orecchini"
"Ears in the Turrets Hear" (Thomas) **2**:379
"The Earth" (Sexton) **2**:372, 374
"Earth" (Toomer) **7**:333
"Earth Again" (Milosz) **8**:209
The Earth Gods (Gibran) **9**:71, 75, 80
"The Earth is Called Juan" (Neruda)
   See "La tierra se llama Juan"
"Earth Psalm" (Levertov) **11**:170
The Earth-Owl and Other Moon-People (Hughes) **7**:120
"Earth's Answer" (Blake) **12**:7, 35, 44
"Earthy Anecdote" (Stevens) **6**:294
"East Coker" (Eliot) **5**:164, 167-69, 171, 179-82, 198, 210
"East of Suez" (Kipling) **3**:179
East Slope (Paz)
   See *Ladera este*
"The East that is Now Pale, the East that is Now Silent" (Bely)
   See "Vostok pobledneuskii, vostok onemesvshii"
"East, West, North, and South of a Man" (Lowell) **13**:87
East Wind (Lowell) **13**:76, 84-5
"Eastbourne" (Montale) **13**:106, 109, 120-21, 128-29, 148, 152
"An East-End Curate" (Hardy) **8**:101
"Easter" (Herbert) **4**:100, 120
Easter Day (Browning) **2**:32, 45, 71-2, 75

"Easter Eve 1945" (Rukeyser) **12**:225
"Easter Hymn" (Housman) **2**:184
"Easter Wings" (Herbert) **4**:114, 120, 130
Eastern Slope (Paz)
   See *Ladera este*
"Eastern War Time" (Rich) **5**:398
"Eastport to Block Island" (Rich) **5**:352
"Eating Fire" (Atwood) **8**:27-8
"Ebar phirao more" ("Call Me Back Again") (Tagore) **8**:409
"Ébauche d'un serpent" ("Le serpent"; "Silhouette of a Serpent") (Valery) **9**:352-53, 365-67, 371, 374, 384, 387, 390, 394-99
Ebb and Flow (Ishikawa Takuboku) **10**:212-13, 215
Ecclesiastical Sketches (*Ecclesiastical Sonnets*) (Wordsworth) **4**:399
Ecclesiastical Sonnets (Wordsworth)
   See *Ecclesiastical Sketches*
"Echo" (Lorde) **12**:155
"Echo" (Rossetti) **7**:280-81
"Echo" (Tagore)
   See "Pratidhyani"
"The Echoing Green" (Blake) **12**:7
"L'eclatante victoire de Saarebrück" ("The Sinking Ship") (Rimbaud) **3**:283
"L'eclatante victorie de Sarrebruck" (Rimbaud) **3**:283
"El eclipse" (Jimenez) **7**:200
"Eclogue" (Ronsard) **11**:262
"Eclogue" (Stevens) **6**:333
"Eclogue 4" ("Messianic Eclogue") (Vergil) **12**:363, 370, 372, 382-85, 392
"Eclogue 6" (Vergil) **12**:365, 371
"Eclogue 10" (Vergil) **12**:370-71
"Eclogue IV: Winter" (Brodsky) **9**:22, 28-9
"An Eclogue, or Pastorall between Endymion Porter and Lycidas Herrick" (Herrick) **9**:86
"Eclogue V: Summer" (Brodsky) **9**:21, 28
"Eclogues" (Herrick) **9**:89
Eclogues (Petrarch) **8**:246
Eclogues (Vergil) **12**:365, 370-72, 375, 383, 388
"Ecologue" (Ginsberg) **4**:54, 82, 85, 89
"Ecoutez la chanson bien douce" (Verlaine) **2**:416
"The Ecstasy" (Carruth) **10**:71
"The Ecstasy" (Donne)
   See "The Extasie"
"Eddi's Service" (Kipling) **3**:183
"Edge" (Plath) **1**:391, 393, 397
"Edgehill Fight" (Kipling) **3**:183
"Edina, Scotia's Darling Seat!" (Burns) **6**:74
"Edinstvennye dni" ("Unequalled Days") (Pasternak) **6**:286
"Editorial Impressions" (Sassoon) **12**:268
"Edmonton, thy cemetery . . ." (Smith) **12**:293, 300
"Education" (Madhubuti) **5**:338
"Education a Failure" (Williams) **7**:370
"Edward Gray" (Tennyson) **6**:358
"Edward III" (Blake)
   See "King Edward the Third"
"The Eel" (Montale)
   See "L'anguilla"
"Eel" (Rukeyser) **12**:211
"The Eemis Stane" (MacDiarmid) **9**:158, 187
"The Effect" (Sassoon) **12**:285
"The Egg and the Machine" (Frost) **1**:203
"Egg-Head" (Hughes) **7**:116, 118, 135, 140, 161

"The Egoist" (Neruda)
   See "El egoísta"
"El egoísta" ("The Egoist"; "The Selfish One") (Neruda) **4**:290
"The Eichmann Trial" (Levertov)
   See "During the Eichmann Trial"
"Eight Drinking Immortals" (Tu Fu) **9**:330
"Eight Laments" (Tu Fu) **9**:333-38, 341-42
"Eight O'Clock" (Housman) **2**:162, 164, 169, 182
18 Poems (Thomas) **2**:378, 382, 384
"1887" (Housman) **2**:192, 194
"1805" (Graves) **6**:152
"The Eighth Crusade" (Masters) **1**:330
"Eighth Duino Elegy" (Rilke) **2**:291, 293
80 Flowers (Zukofsky) **11**:392
"84th Street, Edmonton" (Atwood) **8**:9
"Der Einzige" ("The Only One") (Holderlin) **4**:150, 156, 166
"Eldorado" (Poe) **1**:433, 439
"Eleanore" (Tennyson) **6**:350
"Elected Silence" (Sassoon) **12**:258
"Electra on Azalea Path" (Plath) **1**:410-11
"Electra-Orestes" (H. D.) **5**:305
"Electrical Storm" (Hayden) **6**:186, 194-95
Elegía (*Elegy*) (Neruda) **4**:287
"An Elegiac Fragment" (Duncan) **2**:101
"An Elegiac Poem on the Death of George Whitefield" ("On the Death of the Rev. Mr. George Whitefield") (Wheatley) **3**:336, 340, 343, 348
"Elegiac Stanzas" (Wordsworth) **4**:406-07
"Elegiacs" (Tennyson) **6**:385
"Elegie" (Goethe) **5**:248, 251
"Elegie IV: The Perfume" (Donne) **1**:130
"Elegie VIII: The Comparison" (Donne) **1**:124
"Elegie XI: The Bracelet" (Donne) **1**:122
"Elegie XII: His parting from her" (Donne) **1**:130
"Elegie XVI: On his mistris" ("On His Mistris") (Donne) **1**:130
"Elegie à Cassandre" (Ronsard) **11**:246, 248
"L'Elégie à Guillaume des Autels sur le Tumulte d'Amboise" (Ronsard) **11**:248
"Elegie à Hélène" (Ronsard) **11**:229
"l'elegie à J. Hurault, sieur de la pitardière" (Ronsard) **11**:249
"Elegie á Janet, peintre du Roi" (Ronsard) **11**:243, 247
"L'elégie à Lovs de Masures" (Ronsard) **11**:248
"Elégie à Marie Stuart" (Ronsard) **11**:224, 237
"Elegie A M. A. De Muret" (Ronsard) **11**:246, 248
"Elegie à son livre" (Ronsard) **11**:248
"Elegie au Seigneur Baillon, trésorier de l'Epargne du Roi" (Ronsard) **11**:249
"Elegie au Seigneur L'Huillier" (Ronsard) **11**:242
"Elegie du printemps" (Ronsard) **11**:242, 250
"Elegie du Verre à Jan Brinon" (Ronsard) **11**:247
"Elegie en forme d'épitaphe d'Antoine Chateignier" (Ronsard) **11**:246, 248
"An Elegie upon that Honourable and renowned Knight *Sir Philip Sidney*, who was untimely slaine at the Seige of *Zutphon*, Anno1586" (Bradstreet) **10**:31, 48, 54

"Elegie upon the untimely death of the incomparable Prince Henry" (Donne) **1**:122
Elegies (*Love Elegies*) (Donne) **1**:129-30, 147
Elegies (Jimenez)
  See *Elejías*
Elegies (Ovid)
  See *Tristia*
Elegies (Rilke) **2**:280-82, 285-87, 294
Elegies (Rukeyser) **12**:207, 211-13
"Elegies for Paradise Valley" (Hayden) **6**:191-92, 194-95
Elegies, Mascarades, et Bergerie (Ronsard) **11**:249-50
Elegies of Gloom (Ovid)
  See *Tristia*
"Elegija" ("Elegy") (Pushkin) **10**:413-14
"Elegy" (Pushkin)
  See "Elegija"
Elegy (Neruda)
  See *Elegía*
"Elegy before Death: At Settignano" (Day Lewis) **11**:151
"Elegy for a friend killed in the civil war" (Paz) **1**:352
"Elegy for Alto" (Okigbo) **7**:231, 235, 244
"An Elegy for D. H. Lawrence" (Williams) **7**:350, 354-55
"Elegy for Father Stephen" (Merton) **10**:344
"An Elegy for Five Old Ladies" (Merton) **10**:333, 343
"Elegy for John Donne" (Brodsky)
  See "The Great Elegy for John Donne"
"Elegy for N. N." (Milosz) **8**:186, 207
"Elegy: For Robert Lowell" (Brodsky) **9**:7, 8
"Elegy for Slit-Drum" (Okigbo) **7**:233, 235, 244
"Elegy for the Monastery Barn" (Merton) **10**:331, 342, 349
"Elegy for Y. Z." (Milosz) **8**:174, 198, 203
"Elegy of the Wind" (Okigbo) **7**:235
Elegy on Dead Fashion (Sitwell) **3**:295, 300, 304
"Elegy on Poor Mailie" (Burns)
  See "The Death and Dying Words of Poor Mailie"
"Elegy on the Death of Robert Ruisseaux" (Burns) **6**:67
"Elegy Written in a Country Churchyard" ("Churchyard") (Gray) **2**:134-37, 139-43, 145, 148, 151-52, 155
Elejías (*Elegies*) (Jimenez) **7**:184
"Element" (Page) **12**:168, 170
The Elemental Odes (Neruda)
  See *Odas elementales*
Elementary Odes (Neruda)
  See *Odas elementales*
"The Elements" (Bradstreet)
  See "The Four Elements"
"Eleonora Duse" (Lowell) **13**:91
"Elephants" (Moore) **4**:235, 260
"Elévation" (Baudelaire) **1**:46, 70
"Elevator Boy" (Hughes) **1**:263
"11/8" (Williams) **7**:368
"El-Hajj Malik El-Shabazz" (Hayden) **6**:176, 180-81, 187, 196
"The Elixir" (Herbert) **4**:134
"Elizabeth" (Poe) **1**:446
"Elizabeth Gone" (Sexton) **2**:359
"Elm" (Plath) **1**:390, 394
"Elsewhere" (Sassoon) **12**:252

Emblems of a Season of Fury (Merton) **10**:334, 343, 349-51
"Emblems of Conduct" (Crane) **3**:82
"Emergency Haying" (Carruth) **10**:91
"l'emigrant de Landor Road" (Apollinaire) **7**:42, 47
"Emilie vor ihrem Brauttag" ("Emily Before Her Wedding") (Holderlin) **4**:141
"Emily Before Her Wedding" (Holderlin)
  See "Emilie vor ihrem Brauttag"
"Emily Brosseau" (Masters) **1**:333
"Emily Sparks" (Masters) **1**:327, 347
Empedocles (Holderlin)
  See *Empedokles*
"Empedocles on Etna" (Arnold) **5**:5, 9-10, 12, 23, 35-6, 42-3, 45, 50-1, 56-7
Empedocles on Etna, and Other Poems (Arnold) **5**:2, 25, 30, 35, 42, 50, 55, 57
Empedokles (*Empedocles*) (Holderlin) **4**:146
"The Emperor of Ice-Cream" (Stevens) **6**:293, 296
"Employment I" (Herbert) **4**:100, 111
"Employment II" (Herbert) **4**:111, 131
"Employments" (Herbert) **4**:100
Empty Chestnuts (Matsuo Basho)
  See *Minashiguri*
Empty Mirror (Ginsberg) **4**:48, 73, 80, 91
"En bateau" (Verlaine) **2**:431
"Encounter" (Pavese) **13**:202
"Encoures au Lecteur" (Ronsard) **11**:249
"End" (Hughes) **1**:240
"The End" (Pasternak) **6**:268
"An End" (Rossetti) **7**:280
"The End of 1968" (Montale)
  See "Fine del '68"
The End of a Fine Epoch (Brodsky)
  See *Konets prekrasnoy epokhi*
"End of a Year" (Lowell) **3**:228
"The End of March" (Bishop) **3**:48-9, 72
"End of Play" (Graves) **6**:137
"The End of the Episode" (Hardy) **8**:91
"The End of the Search" (Masters) **1**:344
"End of the World: Weekend, near Toronto" (Atwood) **8**:13
"End of the Year" (Tagore)
  See "Varshashesh"
"End of the Year 1912" (Hardy) **8**:124
Endeavors of Infinite Man (Neruda)
  See *Tentativa del hombre infinito*
"An Ending" (Kipling) **3**:194
"Endless Life" (Ferlinghetti) **1**:180, 182-83, 185
Endless Life: Selected Poems (Ferlinghetti) **1**:180, 182, 184-85
"Ends" (Frost) **1**:213
"Endurance" (Forche) **10**:141-42, 144, 147, 156
Endymion: A Poetic Romance (Keats) **1**:275-79, 282, 288, 290-91, 308-09, 311, 313-14
"Enemies" (Sassoon) **12**:242
"Enfance" (Rimbaud) **3**:262, 265
"Engführung" ("The Straitening") (Celan) **10**:96, 99, 117
"The Engine Drain" (Smith) **12**:327
"England" (Moore) **4**:251
"The English Bull Dog, Dutch Mastiff, and Quail" (Smart) **13**:348
"The English Flag" (Kipling) **3**:157, 161
"English Horn" (Montale)
  See "Corno Inglese"
"English Idylls" (Tennyson) **6**:409
"English Lessons" (Pasternak) **6**:251

"An English Wood" (Graves) **6**:144, 166
The English Works of George Herbert (Herbert) **4**:103
"The Englishman in Italy" (Browning) **2**:62
"The Englishman in Sorrento" (Browning) **2**:38
"An Enigma" (Poe) **1**:446
"Enigma for an Angel" (Brodsky) **9**:2
"Enivrez-vous" (Baudelaire) **1**:58
Enoch Arden (Tennyson) **6**:360, 365
"Enough" (Moore) **4**:260
"Enter No (Silence Is the Blood Whose Flesh" (Cummings) **5**:111
"L'enterrement" (Verlaine) **2**:431
The Enthusiastic Slinger (Neruda)
  See *El hondero entusiasta, 1923-1924*
"Entrada a la madera" ("Entrance into Wood") (Neruda) **4**:277, 306-07
"Entrance into Wood" (Neruda)
  See "Entrada a la madera"
Entre la piedra y la flor (Paz) **1**:369
"Entwurf einer Hymne an die Madonna" (Holderlin) **4**:150
"Envy" (H. D.) **5**:305
"The Eolian Harp" (Coleridge)
  See "The Aeolian Harp"
"Ephemera" (Lowell) **13**:74
"Ephyphatha" (MacDiarmid) **9**:156
Epigrammata (Martial) **10**:243
"Epilogue" (Verlaine) **2**:432
"Epilogue to the Drama Founded on 'stSt. Roman's Welle'" (Scott) **13**:293
"Episode" (Valery) **9**:391
"Epistle Containing the Strange Medical Experiences of Karshish the Arab Physician" (Browning) **2**:36
"An Epistle to a Lady, Who Desired the Author to Make Verses on Her, in the Heroick Style" (Swift) **9**:256, 259-60, 281
"Epistle to a Young Friend" ("To A Young Friend") (Burns) **6**:71, 96
"Epistle to John Rankine, Enclosing Some Poems" (Burns) **6**:65, 83
"Epistle to Reynolds" (Keats) **1**:289, 305
"Epistle to William Simpson of Ochiltree, May 1785" ("To William Simpson of Ochiltree, May 1785") (Burns) **6**:69
"The Epistles" (Burns) **6**:49, 66-71, 79, 81
Epistles (Ovid)
  See *Heroides*
Epistolæ Heroidum (Ovid)
  See *Heroides*
"Epistre a ses amis" (Villon) **13**:395
"Epitaph" (Williams) **7**:345
"Epitaph for the Race of Man" (Millay) **6**:217, 230
"Epitaph on an Army of Mercenaries" (Housman) **2**:177
"An Epitaph upon a Child" (Herrick) **9**:129
"An Epitaph upon a Virgin" (Herrick) **9**:131
"Epitaphe Villon" ("Ballade des Pendus"; "Ballade of the Hanged") (Villon) **13**:390, 394, 408, 410-11, 417-18
"Epitaphs of the War" (Kipling) **3**:171, 192
"Epithalamie on Sir Clipseby Crew and His Lady" (Herrick)
  See "A Nuptiall Song, or Epithalamie on Sir Clipseby Crew and His Lady"
"An Epithalamie to Sir Thomas Southwell and His Ladie" (Herrick) **9**:86
"Epithalamion" (Herrick)

See "A Nuptiall Song, or Epithalamie on Sir Clipseby Crew and His Lady"
"Epithalamion" (Spenser) **8**:336, 389
"An Epithalamion, or mariage song on the Lady Elizabeth, and Count Palatine being married on St. Valentines day" (Donne) **1**:124
"The Epithalamium" (Housman) **2**:199
"An Epitome" (Sassoon) **12**:260
"Épître à Marie d'Orléans" (Villon) **13**:399, 413
"Equal Opportunity" (Lorde) **12**:140
"Equinox" (Lorde) **12**:157
"Ere Sleep Comes Down to Soothe the Weary Eyes" (Dunbar) **5**:121, 124
"The Eremites" (Graves) **6**:140
"Erige Cor Tuum ad Me in Coelum" (H. D.) **5**:307
"Erikönig" ("Erl-King") (Goethe) **5**:239, 254
"Erinnerung an Frankreich" (Celan) **10**:121
"Erl-King" (Goethe)
 See "Erikönig"
Erlkönig (Goethe) **5**:257
"L'ermite" ("The Hermit") (Apollinaire) **7**:46-7
"Ermunterung" (Holderlin) **4**:148
"Eroica" (Ginsberg) **4**:62
"L'eroismo" ("Heroism") (Montale) **13**:156
"Eros at Temple Stream" (Levertov) **11**:169
"Eros turannos" (Robinson) **1**:468, 490, 493-94, 497
Erotic Adventures (Ovid)
 See *Amores*
"Erwache, Friederike" (Goethe) **5**:246
"Es así" ("It Is So") (Neruda) **4**:311
"Es War Einmal" (Smith) **12**:312
Espacia (*Space*) (Jimenez) **7**:203, 213-14
España en el corazón: himno a las glorias del pueblo en la guerra (1936-1937) (*Spain at Heart*; *Spain in My Heart*; *Spain in the Heart*) (Neruda) **4**:278, 283, 287, 307-09, 311
"Especially When the October Wind" (Thomas) **2**:384
"L'espoir luit comme un brin de paille dans l'étable" (Verlaine) **2**:416
"Essay on Mind" (Browning) **6**:27
An Essay on Mind, with other Poems (Browning) **6**:19-20, 26
"Essay on Stone" (Carruth) **10**:83
"Essay on the Alliance of Education and Government" (Gray) **2**:136
"An Essay on War" (Duncan) **2**:105
"Esse" (Milosz) **8**:182, 187
La estación violenta (*The Season of Violence*; *The Violent Season*) (Paz) **1**:353, 359-60, 362
"Estate di San Martino" ("Indian Summer") (Pavese) **13**:244
"Una estatua en el silencio" ("A Statue in the Silence") (Neruda) **4**:289
"Estatura del vino" ("A Statute of Wine") (Neruda) **4**:277, 301
Esthétique du Mal (Stevens) **6**:300, 302
"Estimable Mable" (Brooks) **7**:94
Estío (Jimenez) **7**:212
Et moi aussi je suis peintre (*I Too Am a Painter*) (Apollinaire) **7**:34
"Etched Away" (Celan) **10**:97
"Été" (Valery) **9**:351, 373, 392
"Eternal Death" (Tagore)
 See "Ananta maran"

"Eternal Life" (Tagore)
 See "Ananta jivan"
Eternidades (Jimenez) **7**:187, 208, 212-13
"Eternity" (Crane) **3**:90
"An Eternity" (Williams) **7**:394
Eternity (Smart)
 See *On the Eternity of the Supreme Being*
"Ethelinda" (Smart)
 See "To Ethelinda"
"Eton" (Gray)
 See "Ode on a Distant Prospect of Eton College"
"Eton College Ode" (Gray)
 See "Ode on a Distant Prospect of Eton College"
"Euclid" (Millay) **6**:211
"Eugene Carman" (Masters) **1**:324
Eugene Onegin (Pushkin)
 See *Yevgeny Onegin*
"Eulalie" (Poe) **1**:441
"Eulenspiegelei" (Smith) **12**:327, 342
"Euphrosyne" ("Indifference") (Arnold) **5**:43
Eureka: A Prose Poem (Poe) **1**:422-24, 430-31, 437-38, 442-43, 450
Europe: A Prophecy, 1794 (Blake) **12**:13, 26, 35, 57, 61
"Eurydice" (H. D.) **5**:298, 304
"Evadne" (H. D.) **5**:267
"Eve" (Rossetti) **7**:264, 291
"Eve" (Williams) **7**:350, 354, 394-95
"The Eve of St. Agnes" (Keats) **1**:279, 282, 285-6, 288, 296, 298, 307-10
"The Eve of St. John" (Scott) **13**:269
"The Eve of St. Mark" (Keats) **1**:279, 304
"Evelyn Hope" (Browning) **2**:38
"Evelyn Ray" (Lowell) **13**:66, 91
"Even" (Burns) **6**:50
"Even If All Desires Things Moments Be" (Cummings) **5**:95
"Even Song" (Herbert) **4**:133
"Evening" (Merton) **10**:340
"Evening" (Wheatley)
 See "An Hymn to the Evening"
Evening (Akhmatova)
 See *Vecher*
"The Evening Bell" (Ishikawa Takuboku)
 See "Yube no kane"
"Evening Dance of the Grey Flies" (Page) **12**:190
Evening Dance of the Grey Flies (Page) **12**:181, 198-99
"Evening Fantasy" (Holderlin) **4**:140
"Evening in the Sanitarium" (Bogan) **12**:92, 99-101, 107, 121
"Evening of the Visitation" (Merton) **10**:339
"The Evening Sea" (Ishikawa Takuboku)
 See "Yūbe no umi"
"Evening Song" (Toomer) **7**:320
Evening Songs (Tagore)
 See *Sandhya sangit*
"Evening Star" (Bogan) **12**:98, 100
"Evening Star" (Poe) **1**:448
"The Evening That Love Enticed You Down into the Ballroom" (Ronsard)
 See "Le soir qu'amour vous fist en la salle descendre"
"Evening Twilight" (Baudelaire)
 See "Le crépuscule du soir"
"Evening Voluntary" (Wordsworth) **4**:408
"The Event" (Dove) **6**:110, 112, 114
"The Everlasting Gospel" (Blake) **12**:31

"Every Lovely Limb's a Desolation" (Smith) **12**:314
"Every Traveler Has One Vermont Poem" (Lorde) **12**:138
Everyone Sang (Sassoon) **12**:280, 284, 289
"Everything Came True" (Pasternak) **6**:266
Evgeni Onegin (Pushkin)
 See *Yevgeny Onegin*
"The Evil" (Rimbaud)
 See "Le mal"
"Evolution-Sustenance-Dissolution" (Tagore)
 See "Srishti-sthiti-pralaya"
"The Evolver" (Baraka) **4**:24
"Ex vermibus" (MacDiarmid) **9**:190
"Examination at the Womb-Door" (Hughes) **7**:159
"Examination of the Hero in a Time of War" (Stevens) **6**:318
"An Excellent New Ballad; or, The True English Dean to Be Hang'd for a Rape" (Swift) **9**:267
"Exchanging Hats" (Bishop) **3**:64
The Excursion, Being a Portion of "The Recluse" (*Prospectus to the Excursion*) (Wordsworth) **4**:377-78, 383, 392, 397-99, 402-03, 405-09
"Excuse" (Arnold)
 See "Urania"
"Exhortation" (Bogan) **12**:122
"The Exile's Return" (Lowell) **3**:200, 202, 234
"The Expatriate" (Forche) **10**:138, 141, 144, 156
"The Expatriates" (Sexton) **2**:359
"An Expedient-Leonardo da Vinci's-and a Query" (Moore) **4**:242
"Experience Is the Angled Road" (Dickinson) **1**:111
"The Expiration" ("So, so breake off this last lamenting kisse") (Donne) **1**:130
"Explaining a Few Things" (Neruda)
 See "Explico algunas cosas"
"The Explanation" (Kipling) **3**:183
"Explanation" (Pasternak) **6**:266
"Explanation and Apology, Twenty Years After" (Carruth) **10**:78
"Explico algunas cosas" ("Explaining a Few Things"; "I Explain a Few Things") (Neruda) **4**:297, 310-11
"The Explorers" (Atwood) **8**:13
"The Explorers" (Rich) **5**:362
"Expostulation and Reply" (Wordsworth) **4**:419
"Express" (Sandburg) **2**:340
"The Exstasie" ("The Ecstasy") (Donne) **1**:126, 128, 130, 135, 147, 152
"Extempore Effusion upon the Death of James Hogg" (Wordsworth) **4**:402
"Extracts from Addresses to the Academy of Fine Ideas" (Stevens) **6**:314
Extracts from an Opera (Keats) **1**:311
"Un extraño" (Gallagher) **9**:66
Extravagario (*Book of Vagaries*) (Neruda) **4**:290
Exultations (Pound) **4**:317
"Eye and Tooth" (Lowell) **3**:215
"The Eyeglasses" (Williams) **7**:381-83
"The Eye-Mote" (Plath) **1**:389
"Eyes and Tears" (Marvell) **10**:270-71
Eyes at the Back of Our Heads (Levertov)
 See *With Eyes at the Back of Our Heads*
"The Eyes of the Poor" (Baudelaire)

See "Les yeux des pauvres"
"Ezekiel Saw the Wheel" (Montale)   **13**:109, 129, 165
"Ezerskij" ("Yezersky") (Pushkin)   **10**:391, 394
Fables (Smart)   **13**:341
"The Fabulists, 1914-1918" (Kipling)   **3**:172
Façade (Sitwell)   **3**:294, 303, 306, 319, 322, 325, 328
"Face" (Toomer)   **7**:310, 333
"Face Lift" (Plath)   **1**:394
"Faces" (Whitman)   **3**:397
"Fackelzug" ("Torch Procession") (Celan)   **10**:127
The Fact of a Doorframe: Poems Selected and New, 1950-1984 (Rich)   **5**:388-89
"Faded Leaves" (Arnold)   **5**:13
Fadensonnen (*Thread-Suns*) (Celan)   **10**:96, 98
The Faerie Queene, Disposed into Twelve Bookes Fashioning XII Morall Vertues (Spenser)   **8**:323-25, 327-28, 330, 332-34, 337, 339, 341-47, 349-50, 354, 360-61, 363, 365, 369, 371-72, 374-78, 380-82, 384-85, 388-93, 395-97
"Fafnir and the Knights" (Smith)   **12**:302, 329
"The Failed Spirit" (Smith)   **12**:333
"A Failure" (Day Lewis)   **11**:147
"Faim" (Rimbaud)   **3**:271, 282
"Fair Choice" (Hughes)   **7**:135
"Fair Daffodils" (Herrick)
See "To Daffadills"
"Fair Elenor" (Blake)   **12**:31
"The Fair One in My Mind" (Tagore)
See "Manas-sundari"
"Fair Recluse" (Smart)   **13**:341
"The Fair Singer" (Marvell)   **10**:270-71, 294, 300
"The Fairie Temple: or, Oberons Chappell. Dedicated to Mr. John Merrifield, Counsellor at Law" ("Oberon's Chappell"; "The Temple") (Herrick)   **9**:86
Fairies and Fusiliers (Graves)   **6**:165
"The Fairy" (Blake)   **12**:34
"Fairy Land" (Poe)   **1**:440
"A Fairy Tale" (Lowell)   **13**:96
"Fairy Tales" (Pushkin)
See "Skazki"
Fairy Tales (Pushkin)
See *Skazki*
"Faith" (Herbert)   **4**:100, 119
"Faithfully Tinyig at Twilight Voice" (Cummings)   **5**:110
"The Faithless Bride" (Garcia Lorca)
See "La casada infiel"
"The Faithless Wife" (Garcia Lorca)
See "La casada infiel"
"Fakes" (Apollinaire)
See "Des Faux"
"The Falcon Woman" (Graves)   **6**:156, 172
"Fall" (Neruda)
See "Otoño"
"Fall 1961" (Lowell)   **3**:215
"Fall Festival" (Holderlin)   **4**:141
"Fall, Leaves, Fall" (Bronte)   **8**:68-9
The Fall of America: Poems of These States 1965-1971 (Ginsberg)   **4**:53-7, 59, 63-4, 66-7, 81
The Fall of Hyperion: A Dream (Keats)   **1**:287
"The Fall of Night" (Merton)   **10**:340
"The Fall of Rome" (Auden)   **1**:23
"The Fall of Zalona" (Bronte)   **8**:59
"Fall Time" (Sandburg)   **2**:316

"The Fallen Angels" (Sexton)   **2**:373
"The Fallen Tower of Siloam" (Graves)   **6**:137, 143
"Fallen Women" (Pavese)
See "Donne perdute"
"Falling Asleep over the 'Aeneid'" (Lowell)   **3**:205
The Falling Star's Path (Yosano Akiko)   **11**:301
"The Fallow Deer at the Lonely House" (Hardy)   **8**:124
"A False Step" (Browning)   **6**:23
"Falsetto" (Montale)   **13**:115-16
"Familiar Letter to Siegfried Sassoon" (Graves)   **6**:131
"Family" (Brooks)   **7**:93
Family Pictures (Brooks)   **7**:63-4, 66, 83, 91, 94-5
"Famous Poet" (Hughes)   **7**:114, 139
The Famous Tragedy of the Queen of Cornwall (Hardy)   **8**:95
"The Fan" (Montale)
See "Il ventaglio"
"Fanfara" (Montale)   **13**:134
"Fantoches" (Verlaine)   **2**:430
"Un fantôme" ("A Ghost") (Baudelaire)   **1**:64
"Far Away and Long Ago" (Stevens)   **6**:293
"Far in a Western Brookland" (Housman)   **2**:180
"Far Known to Sea and Shore" (Housman)   **2**:179
"Far Off" (Jimenez)
See "A lo lejos"
"Far Rockaway" (Schwartz)   **8**:291, 302-03, 305
"La farandola dei fanciulli" (Montale)   **13**:116
"Farewell" (Kipling)   **3**:189
"Farewell" (Smith)   **12**:301, 339
"Farewell" (Tagore)
See "Viday"
"A Farewell to Alexandria" (Bronte)   **8**:73
"A Farewell to America" (Wheatley)   **3**:341
"Farewell to Arcady" (Dunbar)   **5**:140
"Farewell to Barn and Stack and Tree" (Housman)   **2**:161
"A Farewell to Celadon, on His Going to Ireland" (Behn)   **13**:8
"Farewell to Florida" (Stevens)   **6**:297, 305
"Farewell to Heaven" (Tagore)
See "Svarga ha'ite biday"
"Farewell to love" (Donne)   **1**:147
"Farewell to Nancy" (Burns)   **6**:58
"Farewell to Poetry" ("His farwell unto Poetrie"; "Master Herrick's Farewell unto Poetry") (Herrick)   **9**:95, 102, 136
La farfalla di Dinard (Montale)   **13**:161
Le farfalle (*Butterflies*) (Gozzano)   **10**:177-78, 184
"The Farm Child's Lullaby" (Dunbar)   **5**:138
"The Farmer" (Williams)   **7**:384
"Farmer's Death" (MacDiarmid)   **9**:187, 191
"The Farmer's Wife" (Sexton)   **2**:350
Farmstead of Time (Celan)
See *Zeitgehöft*
"Farwell Frost, or Welcome the Spring" (Herrick)   **9**:109
"Fast-Anchor'd Eternal O Love!" (Whitman)   **3**:396
Fasti (*De Fastis*; *The Roman Calendar*) (Ovid)   **2**:238, 241, 243-45, 253-55, 260-61
De Fastis (Ovid)
See *Fasti*

"The Fat Man in the Mirror" (Lowell)   **3**:205
"Fat William and the Trains" (Sitwell)   **3**:301
"Fata Morgana" (Rossetti)   **7**:280
Fatal Interview (Millay)   **6**:213, 215-16, 218, 224, 230, 235, 239, 241, 243
"Fatal Sisters" (Gray)   **2**:135
"Father and Daughter" (Sanchez)   **9**:220-21, 229
"Father and Son" (Schwartz)   **8**:301-03, 305, 314
"Father Ch., Many Years Later" (Milosz)   **8**:181, 202, 205
"Father Explains" (Milosz)   **8**:207
"A Father for a Fool" (Smith)   **12**:333
"A Father out Walking on the Lawn" (Dove)   **6**:109
"Fatherhood" (Pavese)   **13**:203
"The Fathers" (Sassoon)   **12**:168, 282
"Father's Bedroom" (Lowell)   **3**:219-20
"Fatigue" (Lowell)   **13**:60
"The Faun" (Plath)   **1**:388
"The Faun Sees" (Zukofsky)   **11**:368
"La fausse morte" (Valery)   **9**:393, 396
"Faustina; or, Rock Roses" (Bishop)   **3**:60
"Faustus and Helen (II)" (Crane)   **3**:79, 80, 96, 98, 100
"Faustus and I" (Sexton)   **2**:367, 373
"The Fawn" (Millay)   **6**:214
"Fe Me Sal" (McKay)   **2**:225
"Fearless" (Tagore)
See "Nirbhay"
"Fears and Scruples" (Browning)   **2**:59
"Fears in Solitude" (Coleridge)   **11**:92, 94, 97-104
Fears in Solitude (Coleridge)   **11**:100
"A Feaver" ("A Fever"; "Oh do not die") (Donne)   **1**:126, 130, 153
"February" (Hughes)   **7**:147
"February Evening in New York" (Levertov)   **11**:167
"February Seventeenth" (Hughes)   **7**:162, 165
"Feeding Out Wintery Cattle at Twilight" (Hughes)   **7**:166
"Feeling and Precision" (Moore)   **4**:251
"The Felloe'd Year" (Graves)   **6**:137
"Femme et chatte" (Verlaine)   **2**:431
"Femmes damnées" ("Damned Women") (Baudelaire)   **1**:62
"Les fenêtres" (Apollinaire)   **7**:18, 36, 44
"Les fenêtres" (Baudelaire)   **1**:59
"Les fenêtres" ("The Windows") (Mallarme)   **4**:208
Ferishtah's Fancies (Browning)   **2**:59
"Fern" (Hughes)   **7**:121
"Fern Hill" (Thomas)   **2**:382, 385, 392, 396-99, 405
Ferrying Across (Tagore)
See *Kheya*
le Festin de Pierre (Moliere)
See *le Festin de Pierre*
"Festival of Spring" (Tagore)
See "Vasanter Kusumer mela"
"Fetchin' Water" (McKay)   **2**:216, 223
"Fêtes de la faim" (Rimbaud)   **3**:259
Fêtes galantes (Verlaine)   **2**:413-15, 424-25, 430-32
"Feuer-Nacht" (Bogan)   **12**:94, 121
"A Fever" (Donne)
See "A Feaver"
"Fever 103°" (Plath)   **1**:382, 386, 393
"A Few Figs from Thistles" (Millay)   **6**:208, 211, 234

A Few Figs from Thistles (Millay) 6:207, 211-12, 227, 230, 233-35, 237, 239
"Fiammetta Breaks Her Peace" (Dove) 6:109
"Les fiançailles" ("The Betrothal") (Apollinaire) 7:43-4, 46, 48
"Fiddler Jones" (Masters) 1:333
"Fidelity" (Wordsworth) 4:383
Fields of Wonder (Hughes) 1:240-44, 247, 268
"Fiend, Dragon, Mermaid" (Graves) 6:142, 145
"Fierce Hope" (Tagore)
    See "Duranta asha"
Fifine at the Fair (Browning) 2:42-4, 50, 72, 75, 80, 82, 96
"Fifteenth Farewell" (Bogan) 12:86
Fifth Decad of Cantos (Pound) 4:324
"Fifth Grade Autobiography" (Dove) 6:120
Fifty Poems (Cummings) 5:84, 107-08
"50-50" (Hughes) 1:247
55 Poems (Zukofsky) 11:341
"Fight to a Finish" (Sassoon) 12:267
"La figlia che piange" (Eliot) 5:153, 184
"La figue l'oeillet et la pipe a opium" (Apollinaire) 7:32
"The Figure in the Scene" (Hardy) 8:137
"Figures" (Hayden) 6:196
"Figurine" (Hughes) 1:245
"La fileuse" ("The Spinner") (Valery) 9:391
Les filles du feu (*Daughters of Fire*) (Nerval) 13:176-78, 192, 195
"Le fin de la journée" (Baudelaire) 1:54
"Final Call" (Hughes) 1:252
"the final solution" (Sanchez) 9:224
Fine Clothes to the Jew (Hughes) 1:237-38, 244, 246, 254-55, 258, 260, 262-63, 268-71
"Fine del '68" ("The End of 1968") (Montale) 13:134
"La fine dell'infanzia" (Montale) 13:115-16
"Finis" (Montale) 13:139
"Finisterne" (Montale) 13:156, 165-66
Finisterre (Montale) 13:103, 106, 127-30
"Fins" (Sandburg) 2:307
"The Fire" (Atwood) 8:39
"The Fire" (Brodsky) 9:2
"Fire" (Toomer) 7:333
"Fire and Ice" (Frost) 1:194, 197
"Fire Practice" (McKay) 2:225
"'Fire Stop Thief Help Murder Save the World'" (Cummings) 5:107
"The Firebombers" (Sexton) 2:365
"Fired" (Hughes) 1:247
"Firenze" (Ferlinghetti) 1:183
Fir-Flower Tablets (Lowell) 13:64, 74, 93
"First" (Kipling) 3:160
"The First American" (Toomer) 7:337
The First and Second Anniversaries (Donne)
    See *The Anniversaries*
The First Anniversarie. An Anatomie of the World. Wherein By Occasion of the untimely death of Mistris Elizabeth Drury, the frailtie and decay of this whole World is represented (*An Anatomie of the World*) (Donne) 1:122, 145-50, 152, 155-57
"The First Anniversary of the Government Under His Highness the Lord Protector" (Marvell)
    See "The First Anniversary of the Government under O. C."

"The First Anniversary of the Government under O. C." ("The First Anniversary of the Government Under His Highness the Lord Protector") (Marvell) 10:270-71, 290, 294, 305, 312, 318
The First Book of Urizen (Blake)
    See *The Book of Urizen*
The First Cities (Lorde) 12:137
The First Decade: Selected Poems (Duncan) 2:105-06
"First Elegy" (Rilke) 2:281, 286
"First Elegy" (Rukeyser) 12:219
The First Encounter (Bely)
    See *Pervoe svidanie*
"First Fig" (Millay) 6:227
"First Fight. Then Fiddle" (Brooks) 7:75
"First Georgic" (Vergil) 12:364
The First Half of "A"-9 (Zukofsky) 11:339, 396-97
"First Hymn to Lenin" (MacDiarmid) 9:177-78, 182
First Hymn to Lenin, and Other Poems (MacDiarmid) 9:158, 162, 171, 177, 196
"First Inclined to Take What It Is Told" (Brooks) 7:74
"First Lesson about Man" (Merton) 10:344-45
The First Meetings (Bely)
    See *Pervoe svidanie*
"First, Mills" (Hughes) 7:149
"First News from Villafranca" (Browning) 6:23-4
"First Objectives" (MacDiarmid) 9:154
"The First of All My Dreams Was of" (Cummings) 5:109
"The First Part" (Page) 12:190
"First Praise" (Williams) 7:405
"First Song" (Akhmatova)
    See "Pervaya pesenka"
"The First Sunday in Lent" (Lowell) 3:206
The First Symphony (Bely)
    See *Severnaia simfoniia: Pervia geroicheskaia*
"Der Fischer" (Goethe) 5:239
"The Fish" (Bishop) 3:37, 39, 42-3, 50-2, 54, 60, 66, 69, 75
"The Fish" (Moore) 4:236, 243, 252, 257
"Fish Crier" (Sandburg) 2:332, 338
"The Fish that Walked" (Sexton) 2:370, 373
"The Fisherman and the Fish" (Pushkin)
    See "Skazka o Rybake i Rybke"
The Fisherman's Art (Ovid)
    See *Halieutica*
"Fishing at Dawn" (Hughes) 7:120
"Fishing for Eel Totems" (Atwood) 8:12
"Fishing the White Water" (Lorde) 12:137
"Fishnet" (Lowell) 3:229
"Fit of Fainting" (Bradstreet)
    See "Deliverance From a Fit of Fainting"
"The Fitting" (Millay) 6:230, 239
"Five Aspects of Fear" (Levertov) 11:164
"The Five Day Rain" (Levertov) 11:169
"Five Flights Up" (Bishop) 3:48-9, 72
The Five Nations (Kipling) 3:192
"Five Songs" (Rilke) 2:273
"Five Things" (Goethe) 5:228
Five Variations on a Theme (Sitwell) 3:304
"Five Vignettes" (Toomer) 7:332
"Five-Finger Exercises" (Eliot) 5:185
"Le flacon" (Baudelaire) 1:45
"Le flambeau vivant" (Baudelaire) 1:56, 61
"Flame-Heart" (McKay) 2:216, 228
"Flammonde" (Robinson) 1:462, 468, 476

"Flashes and Dedications" (Montale)
    See "Flashes e dediche"
"Flashes e dediche" ("Flashes and Dedications") (Montale) 13:106, 166-67
"Flat-Foot Drill" (McKay) 2:225
"Flatted Fifth" (Hughes) 1:267
"The Flaw" (Lowell) 3:226-28
"A Flayed Crow in the Hall of Judgement" (Hughes) 7:165
"The Flea" (Donne) 1:134, 152
"Fleckno" (Marvell) 10:271, 294
"Flee on Your Donkey" (Sexton) 2:351, 363-64
Fleeting Moments (Tagore)
    See *Kshanikā*
Fleeting Moments (Tagore)
    See *Kshanikā*
Fleeting Thoughts (Tagore)
    See *Kshanikā*
Fleeting Thoughts (Tagore)
    See *Kshanikā*
"Fleming Helphenstine" (Robinson) 1:466
"The Flesh and the Spirit" (Bradstreet) 10:7-8, 13, 21, 29-30, 38
"Fletcher McGee" (Masters) 1:345
Les fleurs du mal (*The Flowers of Evil*) (Baudelaire) 1:44-51, 53-8, 60, 62-5, 67-71
"Flies Enter through a Closed Mouth" (Neruda)
    See "Por boca cerrada entran moscas"
"Flight" (Sexton) 2:347, 361
"Flight into Egypt" (Auden) 1:38
"The Flight into Egypt" (Merton) 10:330
A Flight of Cranes (Tagore)
    See *Balākā*
A Flight of Swans (Tagore)
    See *Balākā*
A Flight of Swans (Tagore)
    See *Balākā*
"Flight to the City" (Williams) 7:385, 387-88
"Flooding" (Celan) 10:105
"Florence" (Lowell) 3:213, 236
"Florida" (Bishop) 3:37
"Flow Gently Sweet Afton" (Burns)
    See "Sweet Afton"
"The Flower" (Herbert) 4:104, 109, 113, 118, 127, 131-32
"The Flower and the Rock" (Page) 12:178
"Flower in the Cranied Wall" (Tennyson) 6:358
"The Flowering of the Rod" (H. D.) 5:271-72, 274-75, 293, 296, 306, 309, 314-16
"The Flowers" (Kipling) 3:161, 167
The Flowers of Evil (Baudelaire)
    See *Les fleurs du mal*
"The Flume" (Bogan) 12:95, 121
"Flute Notes from a Reedy Pond" (Plath) 1:389
"Flute-Maker, with an Accompaniment" (Browning) 2:88
"Flutender" (Celan) 10:105
"The Fly" (Blake) 12:7, 34
"The Fly" (Brodsky) 9:29
"Flying Crooked" (Graves) 6:149, 151
"Flying out of It" (Ferlinghetti) 1:175
"Fog" (Sandburg) 2:301, 303
"The Foggy, Foggy Blue" (Schwartz) 8:317
"Folie de Minuit" (Lowell) 13:90-1
"Follies" (Sandburg) 2:303
"Folly" (MacDiarmid) 9:153
"Food for Fire, Food for Thought" (Duncan) 2:120-21

"Fool Errant" (Lowell) **13**:83
"Fool o' the Moon" (Lowell) **13**:67, 83, 86
"Footnote to Howl" (Ginsberg) **4**:65, 68, 70
Footprints (Levertov) **11**:189
"For" (Zukofsky) **11**:349
"For a Dead Lady" (Robinson) **1**:461, 490, 492-93
"For a Dead Vole" (Smith) **12**:317
"For a Fatherless Son" (Plath) **1**:397
"For a few Hopi Ancestors" (Rose) **13**:233
"For a Marriage" (Bogan) **12**:94
"For a Muse Meant" (Duncan) **2**:105
"For a Russian Poet" (Rich) **5**:383
"For a' that" (Scott) **13**:293
"For A' That and A' That" (Burns)
See "Is There for Honest Poverty"
"For a Young Artist" (Hayden) **6**:187, 189-90, 196, 198
"For Annie" (Poe) **1**:425, 434, 437, 444-45, 447
"For Black People" (Madhubuti) **5**:327, 345
"For Clarice" (Brooks) **7**:56
"For Deliverance from a Fever" (Bradstreet) **10**:36, 60
"For Each of You" (Lorde) **12**:157
"For Eleanor and Bill Monahan" (Williams) **7**:392-93
"For Eleanor Boylan Talking with God" (Sexton) **2**:371
"For George Santayana" (Lowell) **3**:219
"For God While Sleeping" (Sexton) **2**:351, 360-61, 371
"For Godsake hold your tongue, and let me love" (Donne)
See "The Canonization"
"For Hettie in Her Fifth Month" (Baraka) **4**:15
"For John, Who Begs Me Not to Enquire Further" (Sexton) **2**:347, 350, 357
"For John, Who Begs Me Not to Inquire Further" (Sexton) **2**:347, 350, 357
"For Johnny Pole on the Forgotten Beach" (Sexton) **2**:349-50, 353
"For Julia in Nebraska" (Rich) **5**:385
For Lizzie and Harriet (Lowell) **3**:224, 226
"For Memory" (Rich) **5**:395
"For Mr. Death Who Stands with His Door Open" (Sexton) **2**:367, 372
"For My Brother Reported Missing in Action, 1943" (Merton) **10**:331-32, 342, 349
"For My Lady" (Sanchez) **9**:209, 225
"For My Lover, Returning to His Wife" (Sexton) **2**:353, 372
"For Rhoda" (Schwartz) **8**:282
"For Sale" (Lowell) **3**:219-20
"For the Conjunction of Two Planets" (Rich) **5**:360
"For the Felling of a Tree in Harvard Yard" (Rich) **5**:359
"For the Marriage of Faustus and Helen" (Crane) **3**:81, 83, 90, 92, 95, 97
"For the One Who Would Not Take His Life in His Hands" (Schwartz) **8**:313
"For the One Who Would Not Take Man's Life In His Hands" (Schwartz) **8**:301, 313
"For the Record" (Lorde) **12**:140
"For the Restoration of My Dear Husband from a Burning Ague" (Bradstreet) **10**:26, 62
"For the Revolutionary Outburst by Black People" (Baraka) **4**:39
"For the Stranger" (Forche) **10**:144, 157, 168

For the Time Being (Auden) **1**:17, 23, 34, 36-7
"For the Union Dead" (Lowell) **3**:211-14, 223-24, 226, 232
For the Union Dead (Lowell) **3**:211-14, 223-24, 226, 232
"For the Year of the Insane" (Sexton) **2**:363
"For Tom Postell, Dead Black Poet" (Baraka) **4**:10-11, 19
"For Unborn Malcolms" (Sanchez) **9**:218-19, 224, 233
For You: Poems (Carruth) **10**:83
Force of Light (Celan)
See *Lichtzwang*
"The Force That through the Green Fuse Drives the Flower" (Thomas) **2**:384-84
"Ford Madox Ford" (Lowell) **3**:219
"Forebears" (Pavese)
See "Antenati"
"Foreign Flower" (Tagore)
See "Videshi phul"
"Foreigner" (Page) **12**:170
The Forerunner (Gibran) **9**:69, 71, 75, 79
" Forest Path" (Ishikawa Takuboku)
See "Mori no michi"
"La foret merveilleuse ou je vis donne un bal" (Apollinaire) **7**:3
"Le forgeron" (Rimbaud) **3**:277, 283, 285
"Forgotten Arietta" (Verlaine)
See "Ariettes oubliées"
"A Forgotten Miniature" (Hardy) **8**:137-38
"The Forlorn Sea" (Smith) **12**:326
"The Former Life" (Baudelaire) **1**:47
"The Forsaken" (Lowell) **13**:62
"The Forsaken Merman" (Arnold) **5**:5-8, 12-13, 17-18, 34-5, 38-9, 42, 49
"The Fortress" (Sexton) **2**:362
"Fortune..." (Ferlinghetti) **1**:183
45 Mercy Street (Sexton) **2**:356, 359, 367, 374
XLI Poems (Cummings) **5**:104
"Les foules" ("Crowds") (Baudelaire) **1**:59
Found Objects (Zukofsky) **11**:346
"The Fountain" (Wordsworth) **4**:374, 399
"A Fountain, a Bottle, a Donkey's Ear and Some Books" (Frost) **1**:194
"The Four Ages of Man" ("The Ages of Man") (Bradstreet) **10**:4, 17, 30, 45
"Four Auguries" (Atwood) **8**:27-8
"The Four Brothers" (Sandburg) **2**:302
"Four Canzones (1957-1961)" ("Canzones") (Okigbo) **7**:247-48
"Four Dancers at an Irish Wedding" (Gallagher) **9**:37
"The Four Elements" ("The Elements") (Bradstreet) **10**:11, 17, 41
"Four Evasions" (Atwood) **8**:24, 27-8
"The Four Gospels" (Goethe) **5**:229
"Four in a Family" (Rukeyser) **12**:223
"The Four Monarchies" (Bradstreet) **10**:4-5, 17-18, 20-1, 27, 31, 33-4, 40, 46-7
"4 Other Countries" (Zukofsky) **11**:348
"Four Preludes on Playthings of the Wind" (Sandburg) **2**:316, 340
The Four Quartets (Eliot) **5**:162-65, 174, 178-80, 182, 186, 196, 198, 200, 205-06, 208, 210-11
"The Four Seasons of the Year" ("Seasons") (Bradstreet) **10**:17, 44
"Four Sides to a House" (Lowell) **13**:61
The Four Years' Notebook (Montale)
See *Quaderno de quattro anni*

The Four Zoas: The Torments of Love and Jealousy in the Death and Judgement of Albion the Ancient Man (*Vala*) (Blake) **12**:13-21, 25-9, 32, 35-8, 41, 47, 49-50, 60-4, 73
"Fourth Georgic" (Vergil) **12**:365, 371
"The Fourth Month of the Landscape Architect" (Rich) **5**:384
"Fourth of July" (Hughes) **7**:119
"Fourth of July in Maine" (Lowell) **3**:226
The Fourth Symphony (Bely)
See *Kubok metelej: Chetviortiia simfoniia*
Fowre Hymnes (*Hymnes*) (Spenser) **8**:332, 334, 337, 390
"Fox Trot" (Sitwell) **3**:297, 303
"Foxhunt" (Hughes) **7**:166
"Fra Lippo Lippi" (Browning) **2**:37, 88, 95
Fra Rupert (Landor) **5**:95
"Fragment of an 'Antigone'" (Arnold) **5**:48-9
"Fragment Thirty-Six" (H. D.) **5**:268, 270
"Fragments du narcisse" (Valery) **9**:348, 365-66, 372, 393, 395-96
"Fragments from the Deluge" (Okigbo) **7**:231, 246, 255
"Frailty" (Herbert) **4**:135
"Frame" (Rich) **5**:396
"France" (Sassoon) **12**:276, 278
"France: An Ode" (Coleridge)
See "Ode to France"
La Franciade (Ronsard)
See *Les quatre premiers livres de la Franciade*
"Francis Furini" (Browning) **2**:72, 75, 84-5
"La frangia dei capelli" ("The Bangs") (Montale) **13**:111, 128
"Frederick Douglass" (Dunbar) **5**:131, 134, 143
"Frederick Douglass" (Hayden) **6**:176, 183, 188, 196, 199
"Free" (McKay) **2**:225
"Free Fantasia: Tiger Flowers" (Hayden) **6**:194-95
"Freedom" (Hughes) **1**:252
"Freedom Train" (Hughes) **1**:244
Freedom under Parole (Paz)
See *Libertad bajo palabra*
"Freedom's Plow" (Hughes) **1**:250, 258
The Freeing of the Dust (Levertov) **11**:197-98, 213
"Freeing the Boat" (Tu Fu) **9**:320
"A French Poem" (Merton) **10**:337
The French Revolution (Blake) **12**:13, 25, 63
"Frenzy" (Sexton) **2**:368
"Fresh Stain" (Gallagher) **9**:62, 64
"Friday the Thirteenth" (Ginsberg) **4**:75
"The Friend" (Smith) **12**:318
"The Friend of Grandmother Speranza" (Gozzano)
See "L'amica di nonna speranza"
"The Friend Who Is Sleeping" (Pavese)
See "Adventures"
"Friends" (Sexton) **2**:365
"The Frightened Man" (Bogan) **12**:86
"Frimaire" (Lowell) **13**:97
"A Frivolous Conversation" (Milosz) **8**:194
"Frog Autumn" (Plath) **1**:388
"The Frog Prince" (Smith) **12**:305, 323, 341
"A Frolick" (Herrick) **9**:103
"From a Notebook, October '68—May '69" ("Notebook") (Levertov) **11**:176, 180, 195
"From a Survivor" (Rich) **5**:360
"From a Tower" (Montale)

See "Da una torre"
"From a Train Window" (Millay) 6:214
"From an Old House in America" (Rich) 5:373-74, 394
"From Another Sore Fit" ("Sore Fit") (Bradstreet) 10:61-2
From Feathers to Iron (Day Lewis) 11:123-24, 128-30, 135, 138-39, 142, 148-52
"From House to Home" (Rossetti) 7:260-61, 276, 282, 284, 290
"From Memory" (Forche) 10:135
"From *Morpheus*" (H. D.) 5:270
"From My Notes for a Series of Lectures on Murder" (Smith) 12:343
From Snow and Rock, from Chaos: Poems, 1965-1972 (Carruth) 10:71, 91
"From Superstition" ("Out of Superstition") (Pasternak) 6:260
"From the Cave" (Lorde) 12:143
"From the Coptic" (Smith) 12:313-14
"From the Corpse Woodpiles, from the Ashes" (Hayden) 6:194-95, 198
"From the Garden" (Sexton) 2:351
"From the House of Yemanjá" (Lorde) 12:151
"From the Rising of the Sun" (Milosz)
    See "From Where the Sun Rises"
From the Rising of the Sun (Milosz)
    See *Gdziewschodzi stǫnce i kedy zapada*
"From *The School Anthology: Albert Frolov*" (Brodsky) 9:4
From the Sick-Bed (Tagore)
    See *Rogsajyae*
"From 'The Snow Lamp'" (Hayden) 6:194-95
From Threshold to Threshold (Celan)
    See *Von Schwelle zu Schwelle*
"From Where the Sun Rises" ("From the Rising of the Sun"; "The Rising of the Sun") (Milosz) 8:203-05
From Where the Sun Rises to Where It Sets (Milosz)
    See *Gdziewschodzi stǫnce i kedy zapada*
"Front Door Soliloquy" (Graves) 6:143
"Front the Ages with a Smile" (Masters) 1:335
"Frost at Midnight" (Coleridge) 11:51, 53, 57-8, 84, 89, 97, 100, 102-04
"The Frost of Death Was on the Pane" (Dickinson) 1:104
"Frosty Night" (Graves) 6:141
"The Frozen Greenhouse" (Hardy) 8:92
Das Frühwerk (Celan) 10:121
"The Fruit Shop" (Lowell) 13:78
"Fruitlands" (Toomer) 7:323
Fugitive (Tagore)
    See *Palātakā*
"El fugitivo" (Neruda) 4:292
"Fuite d'Enfance" (Smith) 12:325, 344
"Fulfilment" (Pasternak) 6:267
"Full Fathom Five" (Plath) 1:388-89
"Full Moon" (Graves) 6:136, 151
"Full Moon" (Hayden) 6:187, 194-95
"Full Moon and Little Frieda" (Hughes) 7:137, 142, 168
"Fumatori di carta" ("Smokers of Cheap Cigarettes") (Pavese) 13:225, 227
"The Funeral" (Brooks) 7:53, 87
"The Funeral of Bobo" (Brodsky) 9:8
"The Funerall" ("Who ever comes to shroud me do not harme") (Donne) 1:130
"A Funerall Elegie" (Donne) 1:146-47, 154-58; 24:151, 184-85, 188

"The Funerall Rites of the Rose" (Herrick) 9:126
"Fünf Gesänge" (Rilke) 2:265-69
"Funnel" (Sexton) 2:345, 350
"The Furies" (Masters) 1:329, 343
"The Furies" (Sexton) 2:367
"The Furious Voyage" (Graves) 6:130, 143
"The Furniture of a Woman's Mind" (Swift) 9:295
"Fürstin" (Goethe) 5:249
"Further Arrivals" (Atwood) 8:36, 39
A Further Range (Frost) 1:195-97, 202
"The Fury of Sundays" (Sexton) 2:367, 373
"The Fury of the Cocks" (Sexton) 2:371
"Fuscello teso" (Montale) 13:134
"The Future" (Arnold) 5:18, 43-5
"Future and Past" (Browning) 6:16
"Fuzzy-Wuzzy" (Kipling) 3:156, 158, 167, 186-87
"Gaiety" (Sitwell) 3:294
"Gairmscoile" ("Braid Scots: An Inventory and Appraisement") (MacDiarmid) 9:188-89, 193
"Gakusei" ("The Musical Voice") (Ishikawa Takuboku) 10:215
"Galatea Encore" (Brodsky) 9:25, 27
"The Gallery" (Marvell) 10:271, 300
"The Galley" (Kipling) 3:182
"The Galley-Slave" (Kipling) 3:157
"Gallo cedrone" ("Black Cock") (Montale) 13:108, 111
"The Galloping Cat" (Smith) 12:311
"Game after Supper" (Atwood) 8:3
"Ganymed" (Goethe) 5:247, 254
"Ganymede" (Holderlin) 4:148, 166
"Garden" ("Heat") (H. D.) 5:275, 303
"The Garden" (Marvell) 10:266, 268, 271-73, 277, 283-85, 287-92, 294, 297, 311, 313-14, 318
"The Garden" (Montale) 13:113, 151
    See "L'orto"
"Garden Abstract" (Crane) 3:81
"Garden by Moonlight" (Lowell) 13:64, 98
"The Garden of Boccaccio's" (Coleridge) 11:104-09
"The Garden of Earthly Delights" (Milosz) 8:181, 209
"The Garden of Gethsemane" (Pasternak) 6:285
"Garden of Love" (Blake) 12:7, 33
The Garden of the Prophet (Gibran) 9:75
"The Garden Seat" (Hardy) 8:100
"The Garden Wall" (Levertov) 11:169
"Gardener" (Graves) 6:151
Gardeners and Astronomers (Sitwell) 3:321
"The Gardener's Daughter" (Tennyson) 6:354
"Gareth and Lynette" (Tennyson) 6:373, 376
Garland of Songs (Tagore)
    See *Gitimālya*
"The Gates" (Rukeyser) 12:224
The Gates (Rukeyser) 12:220, 222, 225
The Gates of Paradise (Blake) 12:46
"The Gates of the Arsenal" (Milosz) 8:191
The Gates of Wrath: Rhymed Poems, 1948-1952 (Ginsberg) 4:55-7, 63, 79, 91
"Gather Ye Rosebuds while Ye May" (Herrick)
    See "To the Virgins, to Make Much of Time"
"Gathering Apricots" (Milosz) 8:212, 215
"Gathering Leaves" (Frost) 1:218

Gathering the Tribes (Forche) 10:132-35, 137, 141-43, 145, 148, 152, 156, 158, 165-66, 168-69
"GATSBY'S THEORY OF AESTHETICS" (Baraka) 4:19, 24
Gaudete (Hughes) 7:154-58, 161-65, 171
Gavriiliada (*The Gavriiliada*) (Pushkin) 10:364, 410-12
The Gavriiliada (Pushkin)
    See *Gavriiliada*
"Gay Chaps at the Bar" (Brooks) 7:70, 73, 89
"Gazing on the Great Peak" (Tu Fu) 9:329
"Gazing on the Peak" (Tu Fu) 9:328
"Gde, vysokaya, tvoy tsyganyonok" ("Where, Tall Girl, Is Your Gypsy Babe") (Akhmatova) 2:12
Gdziewschodzi stǫnce i kedy zapada (*From the Rising of the Sun*; *From Where the Sun Rises to Where It Sets*) (Milosz) 8:174-75, 178, 186, 188, 195-97, 206-07
Gedichte 1938-1944 (Celan) 10:121-24, 129
"Gegen-Strophen" (Rilke) 2:295
"Gehazi" (Kipling) 3:171, 182
"Gekishi: Chimmoku no koe" ("Dramatic Poem: Voice of Silence") (Ishikawa Takuboku) 10:213
"The Genealogy of My Hero" (Pushkin)
    See "Rodoslovnaya Moego Geroya"
"The General" (Sassoon) 12:268
"General Bloodstock's Lament for England" (Graves) 6:143
"The General Elliot" (Graves) 6:150
General Song (Neruda)
    See *Canto general de Chile*
"The Generals" (Ferlinghetti) 1:183
"Generation" (Page) 12:177
"Generation III" (Lorde) 12:143
"The Generations of Men" (Frost) 1:193
"Una generazione" (Pavese) 13:213
Genesis: Book One (Schwartz) 8:283-84, 301, 304, 308-10
"Genesis of After the Cries of the Birds" (Ferlinghetti) 1:186
"Genetic Expedition" (Dove) 6:122
"Genevieve" (Lorde) 12:140
"Genevieve and Alexandra" (Robinson) 1:470
"Génie" (Rimbaud) 3:261-62
"Genie's Prayer under the Kitchen Sink" (Dove) 6:123
"Gente che non capisce" ("People Who Don't Understand") (Pavese) 13:218, 227
"The Gentleman from Shallot" ("The Gentleman of Shallot") (Bishop) 3:37
"The Gentleman of Shallot" (Bishop)
    See "The Gentleman from Shallot"
"Gentleman-Rankers" (Kipling) 3:161
Geography III (Bishop) 3:48-9, 63, 66, 69, 73, 75
The Geography of Lograire (Merton) 10:334-35, 338, 348, 351
"Georgeline" (Rose) 13:236
"Georgia Dusk" (Toomer) 7:310, 319-20, 334
Georgics (*Bucolics*; *Pastorals*) (Vergil) 12:358-61, 364-66, 370-71, 373-77, 383, 385-86, 391-92
"Geraldine" (Bronte) 8:67, 73-4
"Germanien" (Holderlin) 4:149
"Gerontion" (Day Lewis) 11:151
"Gerontion" (Eliot) 5:160-62, 165, 171, 173, 183-85, 189, 195-97, 204, 209
Gesammelte Werke (Celan) 10:100-01, 124

"Gesang der Geister über den Wassern"
(Goethe) **5**:239
"Gethsemane" (Kipling) **3**:171
"Getting There" (Plath) **1**:412
"A Ghost" (Baudelaire)
See "Un fantôme"
"Ghost" (Lowell) **3**:203
"Ghost Crabs" (Hughes) **7**:137, 158-59
"A Ghost May Come" (Ginsberg) **4**:74
"Ghost of a Chance" (Rich) **5**:363, 370
"Ghosts" (Sexton) **2**:350
"Ghosts as Cocoons" (Stevens) **6**:297
"The Ghost's Leave-taking" (Plath) **1**:381,
388
"The Ghosts of James and Peirce in Harvard
Yard" (Schwartz) **8**:302
"The Ghost's Petition" (Rossetti) **7**:273
"Giant Toad" (Bishop) **3**:65
"Gibson" (Baraka) **4**:30
"The Gift" (H. D.) **5**:266, 270, 303
"Gift" (Milosz) **8**:209
"Gift" (Tagore)
See "Upahar"
"The Gift" (Williams) **7**:371
"The Gift of a Satin Brocade" (Tu Fu) **9**:318
"The Gift of God" (Robinson) **1**:462, 467-68
"The Gift of the Sea" (Kipling) **3**:183
"The Gift Outright" (Frost) **1**:212-13, 224
"Gift Poem" (Rukeyser) **12**:231
"Ginga no jo" ("Preface of the Galaxy")
(Matsuo Basho) **3**:13
"Giorno e notte" ("Day and Night")
(Montale) **13**:111
"Giovanni and the Indians" (Page) **12**:168
Gipsies (Pushkin)
See *Tsygany*
Gipsy Ballads (Lorca)
See *Primer romancero gitano*
"Girl Drowned in a Well" (Garcia Lorca)
3:139
"The Girl Who Loves to Shoot" (Smith)
12:326
"Girl's Song" (Bogan) **12**:90, 100
Gitāli (*Cluster of Songs; Cluster of Songs*)
(Tagore) **8**:413, 427
Gitanjali (*Song Offerings*) (Tagore) **8**:402,
412-14, 416, 418
Gitimālya (*Garland of Songs*) (Tagore) **8**:413
"Giuseppe Caponsacchi" (Browning) **2**:41
"Given to Li Po" (Tu Fu) **9**:330
"The Glance" (Herbert) **4**:132
"The Glass Air" (Page) **12**:178
The Glass Air (Page) **12**:189-90
"Gleneden's Dream" (Bronte) **8**:67
"Glimpse" (Hughes) **7**:153
"The Glory Is fallen Out of" (Cummings)
5:105
The Glory of the Nightingales (Robinson)
1:472-73, 475, 479, 483
"Glory of Women" (Sassoon) **12**:267
Glossolalia Poéma o zvuke (Bely) **11**:9, 11
"The Glove" (Browning) **2**:29, 38
"Glück der Entfernung" (Goethe) **5**:246
"The Glutton" (Graves) **6**:150
"Gnat-Psalm" (Hughes) **7**:136-37, 159
"Go, Fetch to Me a Pint o' Wine" (Burns)
6:76
The Goblet of Blizzards (Bely)
See *Kubok metelej: Chetviortiia simfoniia*
"Goblin Market" (Rossetti) **7**:259, 261, 266,
268, 272-73, 279-80, 282, 288-94, 298-304

Goblin Market, and Other Poems (Rossetti)
7:259, 261, 279, 296-97
"Goblin Revel" (Sassoon) **12**:240
The God (H. D.) **5**:303
"God and Devil" (Smith) **12**:331
God Desired and Desiring (Jimenez)
See *Dios deseado y deseante: Animal de
fondo con numerosos poemas inéditos*
"God Is a Distant, Stately Lover" (Dickinson)
1:93
"The God of Flowers" (Levertov) **11**:198
"The God of Youth" (Holderlin)
See "Der Gott der Jugend"
"God Speaks" (Smith) **12**:335
"God the Drinker" (Smith) **12**:326-27
"God the Eater" (Smith) **12**:326, 333
"God Works in a Mysterious Way" (Brooks)
7:74
Godbey (Masters) **1**:339
"The Goddess" (Levertov) **11**:159, 168
"God-Forgotten" (Hardy) **8**:104, 121
"Gods" (Sexton) **2**:373
"The Gods Are Here" (Toomer) **7**:336
"God's Education" (Hardy) **8**:121
"God's Funeral" (Hardy) **8**:131
"God's Providence" (Herrick) **9**:91
"God's World" (Millay) **6**:205, 215
"God's World" (Pasternak) **6**:268-69
Goethe's Works (Goethe) **5**:223
"Gog" (Hughes) **7**:126, 139
"The Go-goat" (Pavese)
See "Il Dio-Caprone"
"The Going" (Hardy) **8**:91, 113, 118, 133-35
"Going from the Capital to Feng-hsien,
Singing My Feelings" (Tu Fu) **9**:332
"Going To and Fro" (Lowell) **3**:215
*Going to War with All My Relations: New and
Selected Poems* (Rose) **13**:242
"Gold Coast Customs" (Sitwell) **3**:300, 305-
06, 308-09, 314, 316, 319-20, 325-26
"Gold Hair" (Browning) **2**:95
Gold in Azure (Bely)
See *Zoloto v lazuri*
"The Gold Key" (Sexton) **2**:364
"The Golden Age" (Behn) **13**:8, 22, 26, 32-4,
39
"The Golden Boat" (Tagore)
See "Sonar tari"
"The Golden Cockerel" (Reisman)
See "Skazka o Zolotom Petushke"
"The Golden Net" (Blake) **12**:36
"Golden Silences" (Rossetti) **7**:271
"The Golden Supper" (Tennyson) **6**:374
"The Goldsmith" (Sassoon) **12**:257
"Golgotha" (Sassoon) **12**:261-62
"Goliath of Gath. 1 Sam. Chap. XVII"
(Wheatley) **3**:354-55, 357-61
"Golos proshlogo" ("Voice of the Past") (Bely)
11:24
"El golpe" ("The Blow") (Neruda) **4**:288
"Gone" (Sandburg) **2**:303, 316
"Good Frend" (H. D.) **5**:297, 302
"Good Friday" (Donne)
See "Goodfriday 1613: Riding Westward"
"Good Friday" (Herbert) **4**:120
"Good Friday" (Rossetti) **7**:268, 283
"Good Friday: Rex Tragicus, or Christ Going
to His Crosse" (Herrick) **9**:109, 121
"The Good Life" (Hughes) **7**:119
"Good Morning, America" (Sandburg) **2**:330
Good Morning America (Sandburg) **2**:318-19,
321, 323

"Good Morning Revolution" (Hughes) **1**:268
"Good Night" (Williams) **7**:348
A Good Time Was Had by All (Smith)
12:292, 314-15, 317, 325
"Goodbye!" (Baraka) **4**:11
"Goodbye Christ" (Hughes) **1**:268
"Good-bye to the Mezzogiorno" (Auden)
1:17
"Goodfriday 1613: Riding Westward" ("Good
Friday") (Donne) **1**:139, 158-59
"Goo-dmore-ning(en" (Cummings) **5**:107
"The good-morrow" ("I wonder by my troth")
(Donne) **1**:125, 130-34, 147, 152-54
"Goody Blake and Harry Gill" ("Harry Gill")
(Wordsworth) **4**:381, 414
"Gorbunov and Gorchakov" (Brodsky) **9**:4-6,
10-12, 26-7
"Gorod" ("The City") (Pasternak) **6**:264
"Gorodok" ("The Town") (Pushkin) **10**:410
"Gospel" (Dove) **6**:117
"Gothic Letter on a Hot Night" (Atwood)
8:24
"Der Gott der Jugend" ("The God of Youth")
(Holderlin) **4**:142
"Gott im Mittelalter" (Rilke) **2**:275
"Das Göttliche" (Goethe) **5**:239
"Le goût du néant" (Baudelaire) **1**:68
"Gow's Watch" (Kipling) **3**:181
"Grace" (Herbert) **4**:111, 129
Grace Notes (Dove) **6**:120-22
"Grace's House" (Merton) **10**:340-41, 350,
353
Gracias Haus (Merton) **10**:341
Graf Nulin (*Count Nulin*) (Pushkin) **10**:366,
386, 390, 400-01
"The Grammarian's Funeral" (Browning)
2:37, 51
"Grand Marshal Kao's Dapple" (Tu Fu)
9:330
"The Grand Question Debated" (Swift) **9**:260
"Grand River Marshes" (Masters) **1**:330, 333
Le Grand Testament (Villon)
See *Le Testament*
"Une grande dame" (Verlaine) **2**:430-31
"Grandfather Arthur Winslow" (Lowell)
3:200
"Grandmother Speranza's Friend" (Gozzano)
See "L'amica di nonna speranza"
"Grandparents" (Lowell) **3**:217-20
"Granite and Steel" (Moore) **4**:259, 261
"Grape Sherbet" (Dove) **6**:106, 109
"Graph for Action" (Williams) **7**:369
"Grappa in September" (Pavese) **13**:218
"Gratitude" (Smart) **13**:361
"A Grave" (Moore) **4**:243, 251
"A Grave Illness" (Page) **12**:199
"Graves" (Sandburg) **2**:303
"The Graveyard by the Sea" (Valery)
See "Le cimetière marin"
"Gray Eyes" (Gallagher) **9**:51
"The Great Adventure of Max Breuck"
(Lowell) **13**:60, 96
"Great American Waterfront Poem"
(Ferlinghetti) **1**:188
"The Great Chinese Dragon" (Ferlinghetti)
1:176
"The Great Elegy for John Donne" ("Big
Elegy"; "Elegy for John Donne") (Brodsky)
9:2, 4, 10, 26
"The Great Figure" (Williams) **7**:399, 401,
410
"The Great Hunt" (Sandburg) **2**:300, 316

"The Great Palace of Versailles" (Dove)
6:111
"Great Snoring and Norwich" (Sitwell) 3:301
"Great Things" (Hardy) 8:112
"Great Unaffected Vampires and the Moon"
(Smith) 12:330-31
The Great Valley (Masters) 1:329, 332, 342-43
Greater Testament (Villon)
See *Le Testament*
"The Greek Women" (Merton) 10:349
"Green" (Verlaine) 2:415
"Green Flows the River of Lethe-O" (Sitwell)
3:309
"Green Grow the Rashes O" (Burns) 6:67,
74
"Green Lantern's Solo" (Baraka) 4:16
"The Green Man: For the Boston Strangler"
(Atwood) 8:7
"Green Memory" (Hughes) 1:267
"The Green Parrakeet" (Lowell) 13:88
"Green Song" (Sitwell) 3:312, 317
Green Song (Sitwell) 3:308, 320
The Green Wave (Rukeyser) 12:204-05, 209,
213
"Green Wood" (Pavese) 13:218
"The Greenest Continent" (Stevens) 6:317-19
"Les grenades" ("Pomegranates") (Valery)
9:387-90, 394, 396
"Grenades Are Not Free" (Sanchez) 9:235
"Grenzen der Menschheit" (Goethe) 5:239
"Los Grernios en el frente" ("The Unions at
the Front") (Neruda) 4:309
"The Grey Monk" (Blake) 12:35-7, 70
"Grey Sparrow" (Levertov) 11:160
The Grid of Language (Celan)
See *Sprachgitter*
"Grief" (Browning) 6:41
"A Grief Ago" (Thomas) 2:405
"Grief for Dead Soldiers" (Hughes) 7:114-15
"Grief Thief of Time" (Thomas) 2:405
"The Grindstone" (Frost) 1:197
"La Grosse Margot" (Villon)
See "Ballade de la Grosse Margot"
"Grosses Geburtstagsblaublau mit Reimzeug
und Assonanz" (Celan) 10:124
"Grotesques" (Graves) 6:142, 144
"Grotesques" (Lowell) 13:77
"The Ground Mist" (Levertov) 11:160
Ground Work: Before the War (Duncan)
2:114-17, 119, 125
Ground Work II: In the Dark (Duncan)
2:119, 127
"Growing Old" (Arnold) 5:13, 19, 23
"Grown-up" (Millay) 6:234-35
"The Growth of Lorraine" (Robinson) 1:461
"Grub First, Then Ethics" (Auden) 1:24
"The Guardian Angel" (Browning) 2:73
"A Guerilla Handbook" (Baraka) 4:16
"Guerre" (Rimbaud) 3:264
"A Guest Arrives" (Tu Fu) 9:323
Guide to Kulchur (Pound) 4:354, 359
"Guinness" (Hughes) 7:123
"The Gulf" (Levertov) 11:194
"Gulls" (Hayden) 6:185, 193-94
"Gulls" (Williams) 7:378
"Gum" (Toomer) 7:333
"Gunga Din" (Kipling) 3:157-58, 179, 187-89, 191
"Guns as Keys: And the Great Gate Swings"
(Lowell) 13:60, 64, 72, 81-2
"Gwin, King of Norway" (Blake) 12:60

The Gypsies (Pushkin)
See *Tsygany*
Gypsy Balladeer (Garcia Lorca)
See *Primer romancero gitano*
Gypsy Ballads (Garcia Lorca)
See *Primer romancero gitano*
"Gypsy Man" (Hughes) 1:270
"The Gypsy Nun" (Garcia Lorca)
See "La monja gitana"
"H" (Rimbaud) 3:261
"Ha chi je na I Am Coming" (Forche)
10:134
El habitante y su esperanza (*The Inhabitant
and His Hope*) (Neruda) 4:276, 281
"Hafen" (Celan) 10:105
"Haffār al-qubūr" (Gibran) 9:79
"The Hag Is Astride" (Herrick) 9:86
"Hagia Sophia" (Merton) 10:334
"Haiku" (Sanchez) 9:230
"Halahal" ("Poison") (Tagore) 8:405
"Halcyon" (H. D.) 5:304
"Half of Life" (Holderlin)
See "Hälfte des Lebens"
The Halfbreed Chronicles and Other Poems
(Rose) 13:235-36, 239-40
"The Half-moon Westers Low, My Love"
(Housman) 2:183
"Hälfte des Lebens" ("Half of Life"; "The
Middle of Life") (Holderlin) 4:143, 148,
167
Halieticon/On Fishing (Ovid)
See *Halieutica*
Halieutica (*The Fisherman's Art*; *Halieticon/On
Fishing*) (Ovid) 2:232, 242, 253
"Hallowe'en" (Burns) 6:50, 55, 57, 77, 91
"A Halt in the Desert" (Brodsky)
See "Ostanovka v pustyne"
"The Hambone and the Heart" (Sitwell)
3:295
"Hame" (MacDiarmid) 9:192
"The Hammers" (Lowell) 13:60, 78
"The Hand That Signed the Paper" (Thomas)
2:388
A Handful of Sand (Ishikawa Takuboku)
See *Ichiaku no suna*
"Handprints" (Rose) 13:238
"Hands" (Levertov) 11:159
The Hands of Day (Neruda)
See *Las manos del día*
"Hangman's Oak" (Millay) 6:217
"Hansel and Gretel" (Sexton) 2:364, 368
"The Happiest Day..." (Poe) 1:432
"Happiness" (Sandburg) 2:308, 332, 334
"Happiness in Herat" (Paz) 1:361
"Happy Warrior" (Wordsworth) 4:391
"Harbor" (Celan) 10:105
"Harbor Dawn" (Crane) 3:88-9
"Hard Daddy" (Hughes) 1:270
Hard Facts: Excerpts (Baraka) 4:29, 36-9
Hard Labor (Pavese)
See *Lavorare stanca*
"Hard Lines" (Zukofsky) 11:351
"Hard Luck" (Hughes) 1:255, 269
"Hard Times" (McKay) 2:209
"Hardcastle Crags" (Hughes) 7:149
"Hardcastle Crags" (Plath) 1:388
"Harlem Dance Hall" (Hughes) 1:247
"The Harlem Dancer" (McKay) 2:213-14
"Harlem Shadows" (McKay) 2:213
Harlem Shadows (McKay) 2:213-14, 227
"Harlem Sweeties" (Hughes) 1:247
"The Harm of Living" (Montale)

See "Il male di vivere"
"Harmonie du soir" (Baudelaire) 1:46, 68-9,
71
Harmonium (Stevens) 6:292, 294-95, 297-98,
300-01, 305, 309-11, 313-15, 329-30, 332-33,
336-37
Harold the Dauntles (Scott) 13:269, 281, 312
Harold's Leap (Smith) 12:335
"The Harp Song of the Dane Women"
(Kipling) 3:171, 183
"The Harp-Weaver" (Millay)
See "The Ballad of the Harp-Weaver"
The Harp-Weaver, and Other Poems (Millay)
6:211, 214-15, 224-25, 228, 230-31, 242
"Harriet Beecher Stowe" (Dunbar) 5:128
"Harriet's Donkey" (Lowell) 3:241
"The Harrowing of Hell" (Rilke) 2:275
"Harry Gill" (Wordsworth)
See "Goody Blake and Harry Gill"
"Harry Semen" (MacDiarmid) 9:180, 196-97
"Hartleap Well" (Wordsworth) 4:404, 414,
427-28
"Harvest" (Sitwell) 3:311
"Harvest Song" (Toomer) 7:311, 317, 320,
333, 335
"Harzreise im Winter" (Goethe) 5:247
"Hassan's Journey into the World" (Thomas)
2:402
"Hate Blows a Bubble of Despair into"
(Cummings) 5:107
"Hatem--, i.e. Goethe" (Goethe) 5:228
"Haunted" (Sassoon) 12:240
"Haunted House" (Graves) 6:142
"The Haunted Oak" (Dunbar) 5:131
"The Haunted Palace" (Poe) 1:424, 437-38,
443
"The Haunter" (Hardy) 8:93, 118, 135, 138
"Havana Rose" (Crane) 3:90
"Have Mercy upon Me My Soul" (Gibran)
9:73
"The Hawk in the Rain" (Hughes) 7:117-18,
121, 129, 165
The Hawk in the Rain (Hughes) 7:112-13,
115-20, 123, 131, 135-36, 139-41, 150, 162-63, 165-66
"Hawk Roosting" (Hughes) 7:113, 125, 140-41, 151, 164, 169
"The Hawks" (Montale) 13:149
"The Hawk's Cry in Autumn" (Brodsky)
9:27
"Hawthorne" (Lowell) 3:212, 216
"Hayāt al-hubb" (Gibran) 9:78
"The Hayswater Boat" (Arnold) 5:50
"The Hazel Grove" (Pasternak) 6:252
"He" (Ferlinghetti) 1:174-76
"He Abjures Love" (Hardy) 8:90
"He Has a Good Time There" (Duncan)
2:101
"He Heard the Newsboy Shouting 'Europe!
Europe!'" (Schwartz) 8:293
"He Is Last Seen" (Atwood) 8:10
"He Revisits His First School" (Hardy) 8:102
"The Head above the Fog" (Hardy) 8:97
"Head against White" (Atwood) 8:27
"Heart and Mind" (Sitwell) 3:312, 323
"The Heart and the Lyre" (Bogan) 12:126
"Heart, Crown and Mirror" (Apollinaire)
See "Coeur, couronne et miroir"
"The Heart of a Constab" (McKay) 2:216,
225-26
"The Heart of Pedro de Valdivia" (Neruda)
See "El corazón de Pedro de Valdivia"

"Heart Stirrings" (McKay) **2**:223
"Heartless Rhoda" (McKay) **2**:221
The Heart's Journey (Sassoon) **12**:258, 271, 289
"Heat" (H. D.)
   See "Garden"
"Heatwave" (Hughes) **7**:120
"L' héautontimorouménos" (Baudelaire) **1**:63
"Heaven" (Herbert) **4**:102, 114, 130
"Heaven" (Tagore)
   See "Svarga"
"Heaven Alive" (Garcia Lorca) **3**:141
"Heaven Is but the Hour" (Masters) **1**:344
"Heavenly City, Earthly City" (Duncan) **2**:105
Heavenly City, Earthly City (Duncan) **2**:100, 126
"Heavensgate" (Okigbo) **7**:250-51
Heavensgate (Okigbo) **7**:221-25, 228, 231-32, 236, 240, 242, 245, 247-48
"The Heavy Bear That Goes with Me" (Schwartz) **8**:290-91, 297, 306-09, 311, 313-14
"Heber" (Smith) **12**:327, 354
"Hector in the Garden" (Browning) **6**:16
"Hector Kane" (Robinson) **1**:476
"Hedge Island, a Retrospect and a Prophecy" (Lowell) **13**:72, 82
"He-goat God" (Pavese)
   See "Il Dio-Caprone"
"Heidenröslein" ("Rose on the Heath") (Goethe) **5**:254
The Heights of Macchu Picchu (Neruda)
   See *Alturas de Macchu Picchu*
"Heimkunft" ("The Homecoming") (Holderlin) **4**:141, 146
"Heine La Salle" (Masters) **1**:334
"Heine's Grave" (Arnold) **5**:34, 52, 63-4
"Helen" (H. D.) **5**:268, 300
Helen in Egypt (H. D.) **5**:276-84, 292-93, 297-301
"Helen of Troy" (Masters) **1**:325, 328, 342
"Hélène" (Valery) **9**:380
"Hélène, la reine triste" (Valery) **9**:380, 391
"Heliodora" (H. D.) **5**:270
Heliodora, and Other Poems (H. D.) **5**:267-68, 304-05
"Helios and Athene" (H. D.) **5**:290-92, 305
"Hell" (Graves) **6**:151
"The Hell Cantos" (Pound) **4**:328, 357, 360
"Hell Gate" (Housman) **2**:162, 165, 167, 199
"Helter Skelter; or, The Hue and Cry after the Attorneys Going to Ride the Circuit" (Swift) **9**:271
"Hemmed-in Males" (Williams) **7**:369
"Henceforth, from the Mind" (Bogan) **12**:105, 113
"Henry and Mary" (Graves) **6**:141
"Her Dead Brother" (Lowell) **3**:205-06
"Her Death and After" (Hardy) **8**:99
"Her Eyes" (Robinson) **1**:459
"Her/Flesh" (Cummings) **5**:95
"Her Immortality" (Hardy) **8**:131
"Her Kind" (Sexton) **2**:359
"Her Lips Are Copper Wire" (Toomer) **7**:320, 332, 340
Hercule Chrestien (Ronsard) **11**:273
"The Herd of Does" (MacDiarmid) **9**:156
Here and Now (Levertov) **11**:159, 163, 188
"Here she lies, a pretty bud" (Herrick)
   See "Upon a Child That Died"
"Heredity" (Hardy) **8**:129

"Here's to Opening and upward, to Leaf and to Sap" (Cummings) **5**:106
"The Heretic's Tragedy" (Browning) **2**:37, 59, 88
"Heriot's Ford" (Kipling) **3**:181
"Herman and Dorothea" (Goethe)
   See *Hermann und Dorothea*
Hermann und Dorothea ("Herman and Dorothea") (Goethe) **5**:223, 225-26, 236, 239, 257-59, 261
"Hermes" (H. D.) **5**:273
"Hermes of The Ways" (H. D.) **5**:303
"Hermetic Definition" (H. D.) **5**:281, 283, 285, 289, 297, 299
"The Hermit" (Apollinaire)
   See "L'ermite"
"The Hermit" (McKay) **2**:222
"The Hermit at Outermost House" (Plath) **1**:389
"Hero" (Madhubuti) **5**:342
"The Hero" (Moore) **4**:265
"The Hero" (Sassoon) **12**:242, 263, 277, 280, 283, 285
Hérodiade (*Herodias; Les Noces d'Hérodiade*) (Mallarme) **4**:188, 190, 196-97, 199-203, 208, 213, 218-25
Herodias (Mallarme)
   See *Hérodiade*
"Heroes Are Gang Leaders" (Baraka) **4**:10
Heroides (*Epistles; Epistolæ Heroidum; Heroines; Letters; Letters of the Heroines*) (Ovid) **2**:234, 238-39, 243-46, 253-54
Heroines (Ovid)
   See *Heroides*
"Heroism" (Montale)
   See "L'eroismo"
"Herrin" (Goethe) **5**:249
"Her-zie" (Smith) **12**:339
"Hesperides" (Tennyson) **6**:351
Hesperides: or, The Works Both Humane & Divine of Robert Herrick, Esq. (Herrick) **9**:85, 87, 89, 90, 92-6, 100, 102, 104-06, 108-10, 116-17, 122, 125, 127-29, 132-35, 138, 140, 143-46
"He-Who-Came-Forth" (Levertov) **11**:177
"Hey-Hey Blues" (Hughes) **1**:240
Hi no tori (Yosano Akiko) **11**:308
"Hibiscus on the Sleeping Shores" (Stevens) **6**:294-95, 305
"Hidden Door" (Ferlinghetti) **1**:166
"The High Malady" (Pasternak)
   See "Vysokaya bolesn"
"High to Low" (Hughes) **1**:258, 267
"Highway Patrol" (Ferlinghetti) **1**:187
"The Hill" (Masters) **1**:345
"The Hill and Grove at Bill-Borrow" (Marvell)
   See "Upon the Hill and Grove at Billborow"
"The Hill Wife" (Frost) **1**:195, 202, 229
The Hilliad (Smart) **13**:333
"Hill-Stone Was Content" (Hughes) **7**:149
"Himno entre ruinas" ("Hymn among the Ruins") (Paz) **1**:353, 360-61, 363
"L'hinne de Bacus" (Ronsard) **11**:230, 232-33
"Hippolytus" (H. D.) **5**:267
"Hippy Mo" (Smith) **12**:314, 327, 339
"The Hippopotamus" (Eliot) **5**:187
"Hiroshima, Watts, My Lai" (Hayden) **6**:190
"His Age, Dedicated to His Peculiar Friend, M. John Wickes, under the Name Posthumus" (Herrick) **9**:103, 107, 114-15
"His Anthem, to Christ on the Crosse" (Herrick) **9**:121

"His Blindness" (Browning) **6**:16
"His Confession" (Herrick) **9**:109, 117
"His Creed" (Herrick) **9**:104
"His Death" (Browning) **6**:16
"His Embalming to Julia" (Herrick) **9**:127, 129
"His farwell unto Poetrie" (Herrick)
   See "Farewell to Poetry"
"His Grange, or Private Wealth" (Herrick) **9**:89
"His Lachrimae, or Mirth, Turn'd to Mourning" (Herrick) **9**:108
"His Meditation upon Death" (Herrick) **9**:109
His Noble Numbers: or, His Pious Pieces, Wherein (amongst Other Things) He Sings the Birth of His Christ: and Sighes for His Saviours Suffering on the Crosse (*Noble Numbers, or Pious Pieces*) (Herrick) **9**:85, 87, 90-2, 94-5, 100-01, 104, 106, 109-10, 117-18, 122, 140-41
"His Own Epitaph" (Herrick) **9**:131
"His Poetry His Pillar" (Herrick) **9**:89, 106
"His Prayer for Absolution" (Herrick) **9**:94, 109, 117, 141
"His Prayer to Ben Jonson" (Herrick)
   See "Prayer to Ben Jonson"
"His Returne to London" (Herrick) **9**:89, 98, 108
"His Shield" (Moore) **4**:247-48, 261
"His Shining Helmet: Its Horsehair Crest" (Gallagher) **9**:62
"His Tears to Thamasis" (Herrick) **9**:108
"His Winding-Sheet" (Herrick) **9**:109
"His Words to Christ, Going to the Crosse" (Herrick) **9**:121
History (Lowell) **3**:224, 226, 228-29, 231-32
History of Peter I (Pushkin)
   See *The History of Peter the Great*
The History of Peter the Great (*History of Peter I*) (Pushkin) **10**:394
"History of the Poet as a Whore" (Madhubuti) **5**:329
"The History of the Twentieth Century" (Brodsky) **9**:19
"The History of the World: A T.V. Docu-Drama" (Ferlinghetti) **1**:184
"History on Wheels" (Baraka) **4**:29
"Hitherto Uncollected" (Moore) **4**:259
"The Hitlerian Spring" (Montale)
   See "La primavera Hitleriana"
"Hits and Runs" (Sandburg) **2**:316
"Hochbeglückt in deiner Liebe" (Goethe) **5**:247
"The Hock-Cart, or Harvest Home" (Herrick) **9**:141-42
"Hod Putt" (Masters) **1**:345
"Hölderlin" (Schwartz) **8**:316
"The Holdfast" (Herbert) **4**:123
"Holding Out" (Rich) **5**:357
"Holiday" (Sitwell) **3**:311-12, 326
"Holiday Inn Blues" (Ferlinghetti) **1**:187
The Hollow Men (Eliot) **5**:163, 171, 174, 180, 185, 191, 193, 198, 206, 209
"Holy Baptisme I" (Herbert) **4**:120
"The Holy Child's Song" (Merton) **10**:330, 340
"Holy Cross Day" (Browning) **2**:38, 63
"The Holy Fair" (Burns) **6**:49, 53, 57, 83-4, 86-8, 91, 94
"The Holy Grail" (Tennyson) **6**:407
"Holy Satyr" (H. D.) **5**:268

"Holy Scriptures I" (Herbert) **4**:126

"Holy Scriptures 2" (Herbert) **4**:133

"Holy Sonnet XIV: Batter my heart, three-person'd God" (Donne) **1**:138

Holy Sonnets (Donne) **1**:128, 136, 138-40

"Holy Spring" (Thomas) **2**:382, 390

"Holy Thursday" (Blake) **12**:5, 7, 23-4, 34-5

"Holy Willie's Prayer" (Burns) **6**:53, 65, 83, 85-6, 88-9, 96

Homage to Clio (Auden) **1**:17

"Homage to Literature" (Rukeyser) **12**:211

"Homage to Paul Robeson" (Hayden) **6**:192, 195

"Homage to Rimbaud" (Montale)
See "Omaggio a Rimbaud"

"Homage to Sextus Propertius" (Pound) **4**:317-18, 333, 363-66

"Homage to the Empress of the Blues" (Hayden) **6**:188, 196

"Homage to the Tree" (Tagore)
See "Vriksha-vandana"

"Homage to Yalta" (Brodsky) **9**:7

"Home" (Herbert) **4**:102, 130-31

"Home" (Lorde) **12**:138-39

"Home after Three Months Away" (Lowell) **3**:206, 209, 216, 221

"Home After Three Months Away" (Sexton) **2**:350

"Home at Grasmere" (Wordsworth) **4**:414

"Home Burial" (Frost) **1**:193, 195, 229

"Home Home Home" (Ferlinghetti) **1**:180

"Home Thoughts" (Sandburg) **2**:309

"The Homecoming" (Hardy) **8**:99

"The Homecoming" (Holderlin)
See "Heimkunft"

"Homecoming" (Sanchez) **9**:207, 209, 223

Homecoming (Sanchez) **9**:204, 206-07, 210-13, 215-16, 218-19, 222, 224, 229, 231-34, 237-38, 242

Homegirls and Hand Grenades (Sanchez) **9**:228, 230-31, 234-36, 238, 244

"Homeland" (Bely)
See "Rodine"

Homenaje a Pablo Neruda de los poetas espanoles: Tres cantos materiales (*Three Material Cantos*; *Three Material Songs*) (Neruda) **4**:277, 306

"Homenaje y profanaciones" (Paz) **1**:356-57

"Home-Thoughts" (McKay) **2**:228

"Hometown Piece for Messers Alston and Reese" (Moore) **4**:256, 259

El hondero entusiasta, 1923-1924 (*The Ardent Slingsman*; *The Enthusiastic Slinger*; *Man with a Sling*) (Neruda) **4**:276

Honey and Salt (Sandburg) **2**:336, 339

"Honey Bud" (Tagore)
See "Madhumanjari"

"The Hooks of a Corset" (Milosz) **8**:182, 197, 210

"Hope" (Milosz) **8**:187-88, 192

"Hope Is a Subtle Glutton" (Dickinson) **1**:111

Hopes and Impediments: Selected Essays (Achebe) **6**:1015

"Hope's Despari" (Tagore)
See "Ashar nairashya"

"The Hop-Garden" (Smart) **13**:330-31, 333, 342

"Hopi Overlay" (Rose) **13**:233

Horace (Smart)
See *The Works of Horace, Translated into Verse*

"Horace, *Lib.* 2 *Sat.* 6. Part of It Imitated" (Swift) **9**:297

"Horace to Leuconoë" (Robinson) **1**:459

"Horae Canonicae" (Auden) **1**:17

"An Horatian Ode upon Cromwell's Return from Ireland" ("Ode") (Marvell) **10**:259, 261-62, 264, 267-71, 275, 277, 289, 292, 294-95, 305-09, 311, 317-18

"Horatio Alger Uses Scag" (Baraka) **4**:30

"The Horn of Egremont Castle" (Wordsworth) **4**:377

"Horned Purple" (Williams) **7**:368

"Hornpipe" (Sitwell) **3**:297, 303

"L'horreur sympathique" (Baudelaire) **1**:55

"A Horrible Religious Error" (*Unedited Books of Poetry*) (Hughes) **7**:144

"Horse" (Hughes) **7**:143

"The Horse Show" (Williams) **7**:391, 394

"Horseman in Rain" (Neruda) **4**:282

"Horses" (Hughes) **7**:118

"Horses" (Sandburg) **2**:324

"Hortus" (Marvell) **10**:284, 286, 288

"Horus" (Nerval) **13**:180-81, 187-91

"Hospital / poem (for etheridge 9/26/69)" (Sanchez) **9**:225

"The Hostage" (Smith) **12**:329-30, 333

"Hôtel" (Apollinaire) **7**:48

"Hotel Bed" (Graves) **6**:143-44

"The Hour and the Ghost" (Rossetti) **7**:280

"House" (Browning) **2**:59, 66

"The House" (Sexton) **2**:361-62

"House by the Sea" (Montale)
See "Casa sul mare"

"House Guest" (Bishop) **3**:56

"The House in Main St." (Lowell) **13**:84

"A House of Mercy" (Smith) **12**:326, 334-35

"The House of Over-Dew" (Smith) **12**:330, 332-33

House of the Customs Men (Montale)
See *La casa dei doganieri*

"The House of the Dead" (Apollinaire)
See "La maison des mortes"

"The House on Bishop Street" (Dove) **6**:113

House on the Corner (Dove)
See *The Yellow House on the Corner*

"The House on the Hill" (Robinson) **1**:459

"House Under Construction" (Pavese)
See "Casa in costruzione"

"The Householder" (Browning) **2**:59

"The Housekeeper" (Frost) **1**:193

"Housewife" (Sexton) **2**:346, 370

"How" (Atwood) **8**:24

"The How and the Why" (Tennyson) **6**:347

"How Annandale Went Out" (Robinson) **1**:461

"How Cruel is the Story of Eve" (Smith) **12**:309

"How Do You See?" (Smith) **12**:325, 332-33, 352

"How Few, of All the Hearts That Loved" (Bronte) **8**:50, 74

"How I Came to Be a Graduate Student" (Rose) **13**:232

"How It Strikes a Contemporary" (Browning) **2**:80

"How Lilies Came White" (Herrick) **9**:143

"How Lucy Backslid" (Dunbar) **5**:122, 146

"How Many Bards" (Keats) **1**:313

"How Many Heavens" (Sitwell) **3**:312

"How Marigolds Came Yellow" (Herrick) **9**:102

"How Naked, How without a Wall" (Millay) **6**:238

"How Roses Came Red" (Herrick) **9**:143

"How Shall I Woo Thee" (Dunbar) **5**:126

"How Sweet I roam'd" (Blake) **12**:32, 36

"How the Wallflower Came First" (Herrick) **9**:102

"How to Die" (Sassoon) **12**:267, 285

"How to Enter a Big City" (Merton) **10**:337, 344

"How We Danced" (Sexton) **2**:366

"How Yesterday Looked" (Sandburg) **2**:305

"Howard Lamson" (Masters) **1**:338

"Howarth Churchyard" (Arnold) **5**:33-4, 52

"Howl" (Ginsberg) **4**:44-9, 51, 57-61, 63-5, 67-70, 73-5, 79

Howl, and Other Poems (Ginsberg) **4**:73, 87

"The Howling of Wolves" (Hughes) **7**:137, 142, 159

Hristos voskres (*Christ is Arisen*; *Christ is Risen*) (Bely) **11**:7, 24, 28, 31, 33

"Hsiang Consort" (Li Ho) **13**:51-2

Hugh Selwyn Mauberley (Pound) **4**:318-21, 330, 338-39, 341-42, 348

"Hugo at Théophile Gautier's Grave" (Lowell) **3**:224

"Huhediblu" (Celan) **10**:124

"L'Huillier, si nous perdons ceste belle Princess" (Ronsard) **11**:250

"The Human Abstract" (Blake) **12**:10, 34

"Human Affection" (Smith) **12**:310

"Human Applause" (Holderlin)
See "Menschenbeitfall"

Human Shows, Far Phantasies, Songs, and Trifles (Hardy) **8**:89

"A Humane Materialist . . ." (Smith) **12**:331

"Humanity I Love You" (Cummings) **5**:90

"The Humble Petition of Frances Harris" (Swift) **9**:251, 296

"The Humming-Bird" (Dickinson) **1**:79

"The Humours" (Bradstreet)
See "Of the Four Humours in Man's Constitution"

"Hunchback Girl: She Thinks of Heaven" (Brooks) **7**:53, 69, 80

"The Hunchback in the Park" (Thomas) **2**:394

"A Hundred Collars" (Frost) **1**:215

"Hunger" (Rich) **5**:374

"Hunger in the South" (Neruda) **4**:282

"The Hunter" (Williams) **7**:360

"Huntress" (H. D.) **5**:269

"The Huntress and Her Dogs" (MacDiarmid) **9**:191

Huntsman, What Quarry? (Millay) **6**:230-31, 233-34, 242

"Hurrah for Positive Science" (Whitman) **3**:384

"Hurrah for Thunder" (Okigbo) **7**:235, 247

"Hurry Up Please It's Time" (Sexton) **2**:367-68

"Hush'd Be the Camps To-day" (Whitman) **3**:418

"L'hylas" (Ronsard) **11**:235

"Hyme" (Donne)
See "Hymne to God my God, in my sicknesse"

Hymen (H. D.) **5**:266-70

"Hymme to God My God, in My Sicknesse" (Donne)
See "Hymne to God my God, in my sicknesse"

"Hymn" (Dunbar) **5**:137

"Hymn" (Poe) **1**:446

"Hymn among the Ruins" (Paz)
See "Himno entre ruinas"

"Hymn before Sunrise in the Vale of
Chamouni" (Coleridge) **11**:48-9, 53, 55-8,
92

"Hymn from a Watermelon Pavilion"
(Stevens) **6**:292

"Hymn of Not Much Praise for New York
City" (Merton) **10**:344

"Hymn to Adversity" (Gray)
See "Ode to Adversity"

"Hymn to Aphrodite" (Sappho)
See "Ode to Aphrodite"

"Hymn to Beauty" (Baudelaire)
See "Hymne à la beauté"

"Hymn to Beauty" (Spenser)
See "An Hymne in Honour of Beautie"

"An Hymn to Humanity" (Wheatley) **3**:338,
340-41, 348, 361, 363

"Hymn to Ignorance" (Gray) **2**:143, 155

"Hymn to Lanie Poo" (Baraka) **4**:15

"Hymn to Physical Pain" (Kipling) **3**:192

"An Hymn to the Evening" ("Evening")
(Wheatley) **3**:361, 363

"An Hymn to the Morning" ("Morning")
(Wheatley) **3**:361

"Hymn to the Seal" (Smith) **12**:295

"Hymn to the Supreme Being, on Recovery
from a Dangerous Fit of Illness" (Smart)
13:346

"Hymne" (Baudelaire) **1**:63

"Hymne à la beauté" ("Hymn to Beauty")
(Baudelaire) **1**:71

"Hymne de Calaïs et de Zetes" (Ronsard)
11:287

"Hymne de la Mort" (Ronsard) **11**:226-27,
244, 269, 272-74

"Hymne de l'autonne" (Ronsard) **11**:230,
232-34, 267, 279

"L'Hymne de l'hiver" (Ronsard) **11**:266

"Hymne de Pollux et de Castor" (Ronsard)
11:284, 287

"Hymne du printemps" (Ronsard) **11**:242

"An Hymne in Honour of Beautie" ("Hymn to
Beauty"; "Hymne of Beauty") (Spenser)
8:331, 337

"An Hymne in Honour of Love" ("Hymne of
Love") (Spenser) **8**:337

"Hymne of Beauty" (Spenser)
See "An Hymne in Honour of Beautie"

"An Hymne of Heavenly Beautie" (Spenser)
8:332, 336-37, 345

"An Hymne of Heavenly Love" (Spenser)
8:329, 332, 336-37, 345

"Hymne of Love" (Spenser)
See "An Hymne in Honour of Love"

"A Hymne to Christ, at the authors last going
into Germany" ("In what torne ship")
(Donne) **1**:139

"Hymne to God my God, in my sicknesse"
("Hyme"; "Hymme to God My God, in My
Sicknesse"; "Since I am comming") (Donne)
1:140, 158

"A Hymne to God the Father" ("Wilt thou
forgive") (Donne) **1**:138-39

"Hymnes" (Spenser) **8**:331

Hymnes (*Hymns*) (Ronsard) **11**:248

Hymnes (Spenser)
See *Fowre Hymnes*

"Hymnes in Honor of Love and Beauty"
(Spenser) **8**:331

Hymns (Ronsard)
See *Hymnes*

*Hymns and Spiritual Songs for the Fasts and
Festivals of the Church of England* (*Hymns
for the Fasts and Festivals*) (Smart) **13**:332,
340-42, 368

Hymns for Children (Smart)
See *Hymns for the Amusement of Children*

Hymns for the Amusement of Children (*Hymns
for Children*) (Smart) **13**:340, 349, 361

Hymns for the Fasts and Festivals (Smart)
See *Hymns and Spiritual Songs for the Fasts
and Festivals of the Church of England*

"Hymns to Death" (Ginsberg) **4**:58

Hyperion (Keats) **1**:278-79, 281-82, 284, 287-
91, 305, 309

Hyperions Schiksalslied (Holderlin) **4**:151

"Hypocrite Swift" (Bogan) **12**:95, 101, 125

"I Am" (Smith) **12**:314

"I Am a Beggar Always" (Cummings) **5**:100

"I Am a Victim of Telephone" (Ginsberg)
4:85

"'I Am Cherry Alive,' the Little Girl Sang"
(Schwartz) **8**:318

I Am in the Unstable Hour (Paz)
See *Vrindaban*

"I Am to My Own Heart Merely a Serf"
(Schwartz) **8**:306

I Colloqui (*The Colloquies*) (Gozzano) **10**:173,
176-81, 183-86

"I Did Not Know the Spoils of Joy"
(Schwartz) **8**:299

"I Do Confess Thou Art Sae Fair" (Burns)
6:81

"I don't love you" (Baraka) **4**:19

"I Dream a World" (Hughes) **1**:259

"I Dwell in Possibility" (Dickinson) **1**:102

"I Dwelled in Hell on Earth to Write This
Rhyme" (Ginsberg) **4**:79

"I Explain a Few Things" (Neruda)
See "Explico algunas cosas"

"I Found Her Out There" (Hardy) **8**:134

"I Found the Words to Every Thought"
(Dickinson) **1**:102

"I Had a Dream . . ." (Smith) **12**:295, 305-
06, 318, 345

"I Had No Human Fears" (Wordsworth)
4:420

"I Hate America" (Ginsberg) **4**:74

"I Have Longed to Move Away" (Thomas)
2:379, 389

"I Have Outlived My Desires" (Pushkin)
See "Ia Perezhil Svoi Zhelan'ia"

"I Hoed and Trenched and Weeded"
(Housman) **2**:192

"I Knew Not 'Twas So Dire a Crime"
(Bronte) **8**:72

"I Know" (Bely)
See "Znayu"

"I Know I Am but Summer" (Millay) **6**:225

"I Know This Vicious Minute's Hour"
(Thomas) **2**:405

"I Look into My Glass" (Hardy) **8**:90

"I May, I Might, I Must" (Moore) **4**:256

"I Never Hear That One Is Dead" (Dickinson)
1:94

"I Never Saw a Moor" (Dickinson) **1**:101

"I Plant in Your Favor This Tree of Cybele"
(Ronsard)

See "Je plante en la faveur cest arbre de
Cybelle"

"I Pressed My Hands Together..."
(Akhmatova) **2**:11

"I Reckon—When I Count at All—/First—
Poets" (Dickinson) **1**:96

"I Remember" (Smith) **12**:314, 320

"I Rode with My Darling" (Smith) **12**:327

"I Said" (H. D.) **5**:305

"I Said It" (Baraka) **4**:13

"I Save Your Coat, but You Lose It Later"
(Gallagher) **9**:44, 60

"I Saw Eternity" (Bogan) **12**:89, 100, 121

"I Saw in Louisiana a Live-Oak Growing"
(Whitman) **3**:402

"I Saw Thee on Thy Bridal Day" (Poe)
See "Song"

"I See around Me Tombstones Grey" (Bronte)
8:74

"I See the Boys of Summer" (Thomas) **2**:384

"I Shall Never See You Again" (Masters)
1:333, 338

"I Sing of Olaf Glad and Big" (Cummings)
5:88

"I Sing the Body Electric" (Whitman) **3**:385,
396

"I Sit by the Window" (Brodsky) **9**:8, 13

"I Sit in My Room" (Toomer) **7**:337

"I sonetti del ritorno" (Gozzano) **10**:188

"I Stood on Tiptoe" (Keats) **1**:291, 313

"I Stop Writing the Poem" (Gallagher) **9**:65

"I Take Care of You: A Lantern Dashes by in
the Glass" (Gallagher) **9**:50

"I Taste a Liquor Never Brewed" (Dickinson)
1:80

"I Tell You for Several Years of My Madness
I Heard the Voice of Lilith Singing in the
Trees of Chicago" (Carruth) **10**:85

"I to My Perils" (Housman) **2**:180

I Too Am a Painter (Apollinaire)
See *Et moi aussi je suis peintre*

"I, Too, Sing America" (Hughes) **1**:241, 258-
59

"I Travel as a Phantom Now" (Hardy) **8**:89

"I Vecchi" (Pound) **4**:317

"I' vo pensando" (Petrarch) **8**:227

"I Wandered Lonely as a Cloud"
(Wordsworth) **4**:388, 400

"I Was Reading a Scientific Article" (Atwood)
8:13

"I Will Be" (Cummings) **5**:93

"I Will Put Chaos into Fourteen Lines"
(Millay) **6**:243, 246

"I Will Sing You One-O" (Frost) **1**:195

"I Will Wade Out" (Cummings) **5**:91

"I Wish I Had Great Knowledge or Great
Art" (Schwartz) **8**:294

"I wonder by my troth" (Donne)
See "The good-morrow"

"I Would Have Been a Trumpet Player If I
Hadn't Gone to College" (Baraka) **4**:36

"I Would Not Paint—a Picture" (Dickinson)
1:102

"I Would Return South" (Neruda)
See "Quiero volver a sur"

"Ia Perezhil Svoi Zhelan'ia" ("I Have Outlived
My Desires") (Pushkin) **10**:412

Ibis (Ovid) **2**:238, 242, 244

"Ice Storm" (Hayden) **6**:194

"Ice Storm" (Hayden) **6**:193

Ichiaku no suna (*A Handful of Sand*; *One Handful of Sand*) (Ishikawa Takuboku) **10**:193, 200-02, 204-05, 210-11, 216

"The Idea of Order at Key West" (Stevens) **6**:305, 307, 325, 327

"Ideal Landscape" (Rich) **5**:393

"The Idiot Boy" (Wordsworth) **4**:372, 374, 381, 416-18, 426-27

"Idoto" (Okigbo) **7**:223, 225

Idylls of the Hearth (Tennyson) **6**:360

Idylls of the King (Tennyson) **6**:358, 360, 369, 374, 376, 379, 406-08

"If" (Kipling) **3**:176, 183-84, 188

"If Blood Were Not as Powerful as It Is" (Gallagher) **9**:59

"If I Am Too Brown or Too White for You" (Rose) **13**:241

"if i have made, my lady, intricate" (Cummings) **5**:87

"If I Were Tickled by the Rub of Love" (Thomas) **2**:384, 386, 401

"If in Beginning Twilight of Winter Will Stand" (Cummings) **5**:109-10

"If It Chance Your Eye Offend You" (Housman) **2**:184

"If It Were You" (Page) **12**:179

"If My Head Hurt a Hair's Foot" (Thomas) **2**:386, 407

"If Only" (Rossetti) **7**:280

"If There are Any Heavens My Mother Will (All by Herself) Have" (Cummings) **5**:88

"If We Must Die" (McKay) **2**:206-07, 211, 217, 220, 229

"If We Take All Gold" (Bogan) **12**:122

"If yet I have not all thy love" (Donne)
See "Lovers infinitenesse"

If You Call This Cry a Song (Carruth) **10**:77

Igitur (*Therefore*) (Mallarme) **4**:199, 201-03, 208

"Ike" (Dove) **6**:109

"Ikey (Goldberg)'s Worth I'm" (Cummings) **5**:82

"Il Dio-Caprone" ("The Go-goat"; "He-goat God") (Pavese) **13**:204, 207

"Il penseroso" (Gray) **2**:141

"Il pleut" ("It's Raining") (Apollinaire) **7**:20, 34

"Il reduce" (Gozzano) **10**:184-85, 190

"Il y a" (Apollinaire) **7**:22

"I'll tell thee now (dear love) what thou shalt doe" (Donne)
See "A Valediction: of the booke"

"Illic Jacet" (Housman) **2**:184

"Illinois Farmer" (Sandburg) **2**:316

Illuminations (Rimbaud)
See *Les illuminations*

Les illuminations (*Illuminations*) (Rimbaud) **3**:249, 254, 259-65, 279

The Illustrated Wilfred Funk (Ferlinghetti) **1**:186

"The Illustration" (Levertov) **11**:168

"Ilrumes et pluies" (Baudelaire) **1**:45

"I'm Wife....I'm Woman Now" (Dickinson) **1**:93

"The Image" (Day Lewis) **11**:146

"The Image of God" (Browning) **6**:20

"The Images" (Rich) **5**:385, 396

"Images for Godard" (Rich) **5**:366, 391

"Images of Angels" (Page) **12**:168-69, 177, 190

"Imagination" (Wheatley)
See "On Imagination"

"An Imitation of Spenser" (Blake) **12**:31

Imitations (Lowell) **3**:213, 223, 228, 232

"Imitations of Drowning" (Sexton) **2**:363

"Imitations of Horace" (Swift) **9**:265

"Immature Pebbles" (Zukofsky) **11**:355

"The Immigrants" (Atwood) **8**:38

"The Immortal Part" (Housman) **2**:179, 192

"Immortality Ode" (Wordsworth)
See "Ode: Intimations of Immortality from Recollections of Early Childhood"

"Impasse" (Hughes) **1**:260

"L'impenitent" (Verlaine) **2**:417

"The Impercipient" (Hardy) **8**:107-08, 112

"The Impossible Indispensibility of the Ars Poetica" (Carruth) **10**:86

"The Impossible Woman/Ideal" (Jimenez)
See "Quimérica"

"The Imprefect Lover" (Sassoon) **12**:258

"Impressionist Picture of a Garden" (Lowell) **13**:95

"Imprint for Rio Grande" (Toomer) **7**:337

"Impromptu on Lord Holland's House" (Gray)
See "On Lord Holland's Seat near Margate, Kent"

"The Improvisatore" (Coleridge) **11**:105

"In a Buggy at Dusk" (Milosz) **8**:205

"In a Caledonian Forest" (MacDiarmid) **9**:176

"In a Castle" (Lowell) **13**:70

"In a Gondola" (Browning) **2**:26

"In a Ship Recently Raised from the Sea" (Page) **12**:168, 184

"In a Station of the Metro" (Pound) **4**:355

"In a Time of Dearth" (Lowell) **13**:83

"In a Time of Revolution for Instance" (Ferlinghetti) **1**:188

"In a Troubled Key" (Hughes) **1**:254-55

"In a Waiting-Room" (Hardy) **8**:107

"In a Whispering Gallery" (Hardy) **8**:108

"In an Artist's Studio" (Rossetti) **7**:284-85

"In Blood's Domaine" (Duncan) **2**:120

"In Broken Images" (Graves) **6**:134-35, 137, 151, 153

"In casa del sopravissuto" ("In the Survivor's Home") (Gozzano) **10**:180, 183, 185, 189

"In Celebration of My Uterus" (Sexton) **2**:352-53

"In Country Heaven" (Thomas) **2**:395

"In Country Sleep" (Thomas) **2**:395

"In Distrust of Merits" (Moore) **4**:236, 238, 240, 249, 261, 267-69

In Dreams Begin Responsibilities, and Other Stories (Schwartz) **8**:281-82, 291, 294, 300-01, 305-07, 319

"In England" (Brodsky) **9**:8

"In Excelsis" (Lowell) **13**:91, 97

"In Explanation of Our Times" (Hughes) **1**:258

"In Golden Gate Park That Day" (Ferlinghetti) **1**:183

"In Harmony with Nature" (Arnold) **5**:31, 38, 49

"In Her Praise" (Graves) **6**:171-72

"In Honor of David Anderson Brooks, My Father" (Brooks) **7**:62

"In Honour of Du Bartas" (Bradstreet) **10**:2, 6, 52

"In Honour of that High and Mighty Princess, Queen Elizabeth, of Happy Memory" (Bradstreet) **10**:37, 56

"In Hospital" (Pasternak)
See "V bol'nitse"

"In Italy" (Brodsky) **9**:23

"In Just-" (Cummings) **5**:88, 104

"In Laughter" (Hughes) **7**:159

"In Lieu of the Lyre" (Moore) **4**:259

"In limine" (Montale) **13**:114-15, 165

"In Memoriam" (Brodsky) **9**:23

"In Memoriam" (Carruth) **10**:85

In Memoriam (Tennyson) **6**:354, 359-60, 362-64, 367-71, 379, 388, 392-94, 398-99, 403, 405-08, 412, 416

In Memoriam James Joyce (MacDiarmid) **9**:163-66, 173, 180, 182-84, 186

"In Memoriam: Wallace Stevens" (Duncan) **2**:114

"In Memory: After a Friend's Sudden Death" (Levertov) **11**:206

"In Memory of Ann Jones" (Thomas)
See "After the Funeral: In Memory of Anne Jones"

"In Memory of Arthur Winslow" (Lowell) **3**:218

"In Memory of Elena" (Forche)
See "The Memory of Elena"

"In Memory of My Dear Grandchild Elizabeth Bradstreet" (Bradstreet) **10**:27, 45

"In Memory of Radio" (Baraka) **4**:14

"In Memory of W. B. Yeats" (Auden) **1**:14

"In Michigan" (Masters) **1**:329

"In Mind" (Levertov) **11**:211-13

"In Montgomery" (Brooks) **7**:82

"In My Craft or Sullen Art" (Thomas) **2**:383

"In My Dreams" (Smith) **12**:343

In My Honor (Rilke) **2**:280

"In My Solitary Hours" (Bradstreet) **10**:62-3

"In Neglect" (Frost) **1**:192

In Our Terribleness (Some Elements and Meaning in Black Style) (Baraka) **4**:19-21

"In Our Time" (Rukeyser) **12**:216

In Parallel (Verlaine)
See *Parallèlement*

"In Paris in a Loud Dark Winter" (Ferlinghetti) **1**:165

In Praise of Krishna (Levertov) **11**:181

"In Praise of Limestone" (Auden) **1**:17, 20

"In Procession" (Graves) **6**:138

In Reckless Ecstasy (Sandburg) **2**:334

"In reference to her children" (Bradstreet) **10**:13, 26-7, 34-5, 43, 59

"In Shadow" (Crane) **3**:98-9

"In Sickness" (Swift) **9**:295

"In Silence" (Merton) **10**:347, 349

"In Sleep" (Montale)
See "Nel sonno"

"In Society" (Ginsberg) **4**:71

"In Summer" (Dunbar) **5**:139

"In Tall Grass" (Sandburg) **2**:324

"In Tenebris (I)" (Hardy) **8**:94, 110

"In Thankful Remembrance for My Dear Husband's Safe Arrival" (Bradstreet) **10**:60-1, 64

"In That Time when It Was Not the Fashion" (Gallagher) **9**:60

"In the Beach House" (Sexton) **2**:363

"In the Beginning" (Sanchez) **9**:228-29

"In the Beginning" (Thomas) **2**:403

In the Clearing (Frost) **1**:212-13, 224

"In the Courtroom" (Sanchez) **9**:225

"In the Dark and Cloudy Day" (Housman) **2**:193

"In the Days of Prismatic Color" (Moore) **4**:251-52, 257-58

"In the Deep Museum" (Sexton)   2:346, 348,
   351, 360-61
"In the Forest" (Pasternak)
   See "V lesu"
"In the Greenhouse" (Montale)
   See "Nella serra"
"In the Hands of a Blindman" (Gallagher)
   9:60
"In the Heart of Contemplation" (Day Lewis)
   11:144
"In the Hills" (Bely)   11:5
"In the M5 Restaurant" (Hughes)   7:162
"In the Mecca" (Brooks)   7:78, 81-2, 88-91
In the Mecca (Brooks)   7:62-3, 66, 81-3, 88,
   90-1, 94, 105, 107
"In the Moonlight" (Hardy)   8:124
"In the Naked Bed, in Plato's Cave"
   (Schwartz)   8:291, 297, 301-02, 308-09, 311,
   316
"In the Neolithic Age" (Kipling)   3:167
"In the Night" (Smith)   12:345
"In the Park" (Montale)   13:151
"In the Park" (Smith)   12:345, 352-54
"In the Pink" (Sassoon)   12:242, 262
"In the Public Garden" (Moore)   4:259
"In the Rain" (H. D.)   5:304
"In the Restaurant" (Hardy)   8:124
"In the Ruins of New York City" (Merton)
   10:344, 349
"In the Same Boat" (Kipling)   3:183
"In the Sconset Bus" (Williams)   7:409
"In the Shelter" (Day Lewis)   11:151
"In the Survivor's Home" (Gozzano)
   See "In casa del sopravissuto"
"In the Tents of Akbar" (Dunbar)   5:138
"In the Tradition" (Baraka)   4:40
"In the Underworld" (Rukeyser)   12:220
"In the Waiting Room" (Bishop)   3:59, 69-70
"In the White Giant's Thigh" (Thomas)
   2:395, 404
"In the Wilderness" (Graves)   6:128-29
"In the Wood" (Pasternak)   6:252-53, 259
"In This Age of Hard Trying, Nonchalance Is
   Good and ..." (Moore)   4:229, 270
"In Time of 'The Breaking of Nations'"
   (Hardy)   8:115, 121
"In Time of War" (Auden)   1:18
"In Valleys Green and Still" (Housman)
   2:180
"In Warsaw" (Milosz)   8:192
"In what torne ship" (Donne)
   See "A Hymne to Christ, at the authors last
      going into Germany"
"Inauguration Day: January 1953" (Lowell)
   3:214, 218, 222
"Incantation" (Milosz)   8:202
"Incantesimo" ("Spell") (Montale)   13:110
"Incense of the Lucky Virgin" (Hayden)
   6:195
"Incespicare" ("Stumbling") (Montale)
   13:134
"Inclusions" (Browning)   6:5-6, 15
"Incompatibilities" (Hughes)   7:113
"Incontro" ("Meeting") (Montale)   13:165
"Incontro" (Pavese)   13:217
"The Incorrigible Dirigible" (Carruth)   10:88
"The Independent Man" (Brooks)   7:53
Indian Journals, March 1962-May 1963
   (Ginsberg)   4:53, 56, 60
"Indian Serenade" (Montale)
   See "Serenata indiana"
"Indian Summer" (Pavese)

See "Estate di San Martino"
"Indiana" (Crane)   3:88, 106-07
"Indifference" (Arnold)
   See "Euphrosyne"
"The Indifferent" (Donne)   1:125
"The Indigo Glass in the Grass" (Stevens)
   6:324
"Indisciplina" ("Lack of Discipline") (Pavese)
   13:214, 226
"The Individual Man" (Duncan)   2:118
"The Indweller" (Tagore)
   See "Antaryami"
"Infant" (Smith)   12:310, 326
"Infant Joy" ("The Two-Days-Old Baby")
   (Blake)   12:7, 9, 33-4
"Infant Sorrow" (Blake)   12:7, 31, 34
"Infanta Marina" (Stevens)   6:311
"An Inference of Mexico" (Hayden)   6:194,
   198
"Ingoldsby Legends" (Browning)   2:36
The Inhabitant and His Hope (Neruda)
   See *El habitante y su esperanza*
"The Iniquity of the Fathers upon the
   Children" (Rossetti)   7:289-90
"Initiations" (Okigbo)   7:224-25, 232, 237
"Injudicious Gardening" (Moore)   4:266
"The Injury" (Williams)   7:360
The Inn Album (Browning)   2:68, 96
"Inochi no fune" ("The Boat of Life")
   (Ishikawa Takuboku)   10:213, 215
"The Insidious Dr. Fu Man Chu" (Baraka)
   4:15
"L'insinuant" (Valery)   9:395
"Insomniac" (Plath)   1:399
"Inspector General with an Ejection"
   (Bulgakov)
   See *"Inspector General* with an Ejection"
"Inspiration" (Lowell)   3:245
"Installation of the Duke of Grafton as
   Chancellor of Cambridge" (Gray)   2:143
"The Instant" (Levertov)   11:166, 168
"Instinct" (Pavese)
   See "L'istinto"
"Instructions to the Double" (Gallagher)
   9:58, 60
Instructions to the Double (Gallagher)   9:35-7,
   43, 53-4, 58
"Instructions to the Orphic Adept" (Graves)
   6:133
"Insufficiency" (Browning)   6:15
Intact Wind (Paz)
   See *Viento entero*
"Intercettazione telefonica" ("Wiretapping")
   (Montale)   13:133
"Intérieur" (Valery)   9:365, 396
"Interim" ("Prologue: An Interim") (Levertov)
   11:176, 195-96
"Interim" (Millay)   6:205-07, 214
"Intermezzo" (Montale)   13:106
"Intermission 3" (Brooks)   7:58, 62, 91, 104
"The Interrogation of the Man of Many
   Hearts" (Sexton)   2:352
"Interruption" (Graves)   6:137, 143-44
"Interview with a Tourist" (Atwood)   8:14
"Intimation of Immortality" (Smith)   12:313
"Intimations of Immorality" (Sappho)   5:418
"Intimations of Immortality" (Thomas)   2:392
" Intimations of Immortality" (Wordsworth)
   See "Ode: Intimations of Immortality from
      Recollections of Early Childhood"
"Into My Heart and Air That Kills"
   (Housman)   2:192

"Into My Own" (Frost)   1:213
"Into the Golden Vessel of Great Song"
   (Millay)   6:211
"Into the Tree" (Milosz)   8:198
"Introduction" (Blake)   12:7, 32, 34-5, 43-7
"The Intrusion" (Graves)   6:156
"Invective Against Swans" (Stevens)   6:294
Invectives (Verlaine)   2:419
Invisible Reality (Jimenez)
   See *La realidad invisible*
"L'invitation au voyage" (Baudelaire)   1:69
"Invitation to Miss Marianne Moore" (Bishop)
   3:44
"Invocation" (Levertov)   11:177
"Invocation" (Sitwell)   3:312
"Ione" (Dunbar)   125
"Iride" ("Iris") (Montale)   13:109, 111, 121-
   22, 130-31, 152, 166
"Iris" (Montale)
   See "Iride"
"The Irish Cliffs of Moher" (Stevens)   6:304
"Iron Hans" (Sexton)   2:365-68
"L'irrémédiable" (Baudelaire)   1:55
"L'Irréparable" (Baudelaire)   1:68
is 5 (Cummings)   5:77, 92, 95, 104
"Is It True?" (Sexton)   2:368, 374
"Is It Wise" (Smith)   12:343
"Is My Team Ploughing" (Housman)   2:180,
   193, 196
I's (Pronounced Eyes) (Zukofsky)   11:357
"Is There for Honest Poverty" ("For A' That
   and A' That") (Burns)   6:58, 83
"Is There No Way Out?" (Paz)
   See "¿No hay salida?"
"Isaac and Archibald" (Robinson)   1:467,
   486-87, 496
"Isabel" (Tennyson)   6:387
"Isabella" (Keats)   1:279, 282, 288-89, 296
"Isaiah LXII: 1-8" (Wheatley)   3:357
"The Island" (Forche)   10:138, 152, 161, 166
"Island" (Hughes)   1:244, 248
"An Island" (Robinson)   1:465, 467
"The Islanders" (Kipling)   3:179, 192
"The Islands" (H. D.)   5:268
"The Islands" (Hayden)   6:191, 193, 200
"Isolation: To Marguerite" (Arnold)   5:13, 18
"Isolationist" (Page)   12:170
"Israfel" (Poe)   1:438, 447-48
"L'istinto" ("Instinct") (Pavese)   13:205, 213
"It Is a Living Coral" (Williams)   7:369
"It Is a Spring Afternoon" (Sexton)   2:352
"It Is Everywhere" (Toomer)   7:337, 340
"It Is So" (Neruda)
   See "Es así"
"It Is the First Mild Day of March"
   (Wordsworth)
   See "Lines on the First Mild Day of March"
"It Must Give Pleasure" (Stevens)   6:329
"It Nods and Curtseys and Recovers"
   (Housman)   2:192-93
"It Was a Face Which Darkness Could Kill"
   (Ferlinghetti)   1:183
"It Was a' for Our Rightfu' King" (Burns)
   6:99
"It Was All Very Tidy" (Graves)   6:142, 144
"It Was Winter" (Milosz)   8:194
"Italia mia" (Petrarch)   8:267, 270
"Italian Morning" (Bogan)   12:106
"An Italian Visit" (Day Lewis)   11:150
"Italy and France" (Browning)   2:26
"Itching Heels" (Dunbar)   5:146
"It's a New Day" (Sanchez)   9:229

It's a New Day: Poems for Young Brothas and Sistuhs (Sanchez) **9**:207, 211-12, 215, 229, 237

"It's Nation Time" (Baraka) **4**:19, 26, 40

It's Nation Time (Baraka) **4**:19, 20, 26

"It's over a (See Just" (Cummings) **5**:108

"It's Raining" (Apollinaire)
   See "Il pleut"

"It's Time, My Friend, It's Time" (Pushkin)
   See "Pora, Moi Drug, Pora"

"It's Unbecoming" (Pasternak) **6**:265

I've Been a Woman (Sanchez) **9**:207, 211-12, 215-16, 218-22, 227, 229, 232, 238, 242

Iz shesti knig (Akhmatova) **2**:18

Jack Kelso: A Dramatic Poem (Masters) **1**:339

The Jacob's Ladder (Levertov) **11**:168, 193, 206

Jadis et naguère (Long Ago and Not So Long Ago) (Verlaine) **2**:416

"The Jaguar" (Hughes) **7**:118, 151, 163

"J'ai plus de souvenirs" (Baudelaire) **1**:67

"Jam Session" (Hughes) **1**:245

"Jamāl al-mawt" (Gibran) **9**:78

"James Wetherell" (Robinson) **1**:467

"The Jam-Pot" (Kipling) **3**:190

"January 1918" (Pasternak) **6**:261

"January 1919" (Pasternak) **6**:252

"A January Night" (Hardy) **8**:110

"Jardín de invierno" ("Winter Garden") (Neruda) **4**:287, 289-90

"El jardín triste se pierde" ("The Sad Garden Dissolves") (Jimenez) **7**:199

Jardines lejanos (Jimenez) **7**:209

"Jasmine Arbour" (Tagore)
   See "Chameli-vitan"

"Jaws" (Sandburg) **2**:330

"Jaybird" (Dunbar) **5**:144

"Jazzonia" (Hughes) **1**:246, 261

"Je plaings le temps de ma jeunesse" (Villon) **13**:388-89

"Je plante en la faveur cest arbre de Cybelle" ("I Plant in Your Favor This Tree of Cybele") (Ronsard) **11**:277

"Je suis bruslé, Le Gast, d'une double chaleur" (Ronsard) **11**:250

"Je suis l'empire à la fin de la décadence" (Verlaine) **2**:416

"The Jealous Man" (Graves) **6**:142, 144

"The Jerboa" (Moore) **4**:233, 236, 243

"Jeronimo's House" (Bishop) **3**:37, 47

"Jerusalem" (Blake) **12**:37

"Jerusalem" (Rich) **5**:383

Jerusalem: The Emanation of the Giant Albion (Blake) **12**:13, 20, 27, 29-32, 34-40, 43-4, 51-9, 61-75, 80

"Jessie Cameron" (Rossetti) **7**:280

"Jessie Mitchell's Mother" (Brooks) **7**:58, 62, 68, 96, 99-100, 102

"The Jester" (Hughes) **1**:235

"The Jester, A Ballad" (Bely)
   See "Shut, Bellada"

"Jester above It" (Bely)
   See "Shut Nad ney"

"Jesu" (Herbert) **4**:100

"The Jesus Papers" (Sexton) **2**:360

"Jesus Walking" (Sexton) **2**:360-61, 373

"Le jet d'eau" (Baudelaire) **1**:61

La jeune parque (The Young Fate) (Valery) **9**:346-48, 351-58, 361, 363-67, 369-74, 379-85, 387, 390-96, 401-03

"La jeune prêtre" (Valery) **9**:391

"Jeunesse" (Rimbaud) **3**:261, 263

"Jim and Arabel's Sister" (Masters) **1**:328

"Jim at Sixteen" (McKay) **2**:223

"Jim Brown on the Screen" (Baraka) **4**:19

Jim Crow's Last Stand (Hughes) **1**:250, 253

"Jitterbugs" (Baraka) **4**:12, 18

"Jivan devata" (Tagore) **8**:408

"Jivan madhyahna" ("Life's Noonday") (Tagore) **8**:407

"Jiving" (Dove) **6**:114, 117

"Joan and Darby" (Graves) **6**:156

"Joan of Arc" ("The Visions of the Maid of Orleans") (Coleridge) **11**:80, 83, 97

"Job" (Blake) **12**:38

"Jochanan Hakkadosh" (Browning) **2**:75

"Joggin' Erlong" (Dunbar) **5**:145

"John Anderson, My Jo" (Burns) **6**:78, 98

"John Barleycorn" (Burns) **6**:52

"John Brown" (Hayden) **6**:192, 195

"John Brown" (Robinson) **1**:468

"John Cowper Powys" (Masters) **1**:343

"John Dryden" (Carruth) **10**:74

"John Gorham" (Robinson) **1**:462, 468, 478

"John McLean (1879-1923)" (MacDiarmid) **9**:179

"Johnny Appleseed" (Masters) **1**:330

"Johnny Spain's White Heifer" (Carruth) **10**:74

"Joilet" (Sandburg) **2**:324

"Joke" (Bely)
   See "Shutka"

"A Joker" (Baudelaire)
   See "Un plaisant"

"La jolie rousse" ("The Pretty Redhead") (Apollinaire) **7**:3, 9, 49

"The Jolly Beggars" (Burns) **6**:55-6, 58, 78, 90-6

"Jonathan Edwards" (Lowell) **3**:212

"Jonathan Edwards in Western Massachusettes" (Lowell) **3**:216

"Jordan" (Herbert) **4**:102, 107, 113

"Jordan I" (Herbert) **4**:114, 129

"Jordan II" (Herbert) **4**:100, 114

"Joseph" (Forche) **10**:144, 156-57

"Joseph's Coat" (Herbert) **4**:130

"Le joujou du pauvre" ("The Poor Child's Toy") (Baudelaire) **1**:58

"Journal Night Thoughts" (Ginsberg) **4**:52, 69

"Journal of an Airman" (Auden) **1**:5

Journals: Early Fifties, Early Sixties (Ginsberg) **4**:60, 69

The Journals of Susanna Moodie (Atwood) **8**:10-12, 15, 21, 29, 31, 33, 35-6, 40

"Journey" (Millay) **6**:206

"Journey Home" (Page) **12**:178

"Journey North" (Tu Fu) **9**:332

"Journey of the Magi" (Eliot) **5**:171, 177, 194, 197, 203, 205, 209

Journey to a Known Place (Carruth) **10**:70

Journey to Love (Williams) **7**:371, 403

"The Journey to the Interior" (Atwood) **8**:36

"Joy" (Levertov) **11**:192

"The Joy and Agony of Improvisation" (Carruth) **10**:73

"Joy in Russia" (Bely) **11**:6

"Joys Faces Friends" (Cummings) **5**:110

"Juan Figueroa, Casa del Yodo 'Maria Elena,' Antofagasta" ("Juan Figueroa, Iodine Factory 'Maria Elena,' Antofagasta") (Neruda) **4**:294

"Juan Figueroa, Iodine Factory 'Maria Elena,' Antofagasta" (Neruda)
   See "Juan Figueroa, Casa del Yodo 'Maria Elena,' Antofagasta"

"Juan's Song" (Bogan) **12**:90, 92, 100

"Jubilate Agno" ("Rejoice in the Lamb") (Smart) **13**:339-40, 342-44, 346-48, 350-52, 355, 357-58, 360-69

"The Judgment" (Akhmatova) **2**:15

"Judgment" (Herbert) **4**:129

"The Judgment of Midas" (Smart) **13**:348

"Juice Joint: Northern City" (Hughes) **1**:243

"Julia" (Wordsworth) **4**:399

"Julian M. and A. G. Rochelle" ("The Prisoner") (Bronte) **8**:52

"Julia's Petticoat" (Herrick) **9**:143

"July 8, 1656" (Bradstreet) **10**:60

"July 1968" (Levertov) **11**:194

"July in Washington" (Lowell) **3**:214

"July Midnight" (Lowell) **13**:64

The Jungle Book (Kipling) **3**:162, 185, 188-89

"Das jüngste Gericht" (Rilke) **2**:277

"Junkman's Obbligato" (Ferlinghetti) **1**:165-66, 173

"Just Don't Never Give Up on Love" (Sanchez) **9**:234, 238, 244

"Just Lost, When I Was Saved!" (Dickinson) **1**:97

"Just Whistle a Bit" (Dunbar) **5**:137

"Justice" (Herbert) **4**:102

"Justice" (Hughes) **1**:252

"Justice II" (Herbert) **4**:131

"Justice Denied in Massachusetts" (Millay) **6**:223

"Juvat ire jugis" (Arnold) **5**:36

"K Liciniju" ("To Licinius") (Pushkin) **10**:408

"K Likomedu, na Skiros" ("On the Way to Lycomedes of Scyrus"; "To Lycomedes on Scyros") (Brodsky) **9**:5

"Ka 'Ba" (Baraka) **4**:18

"Kabi kahini" ("The Poet's Story") (Tagore) **8**:405

"Kaddish" (Ginsberg) **4**:49-50, 53, 59, 61, 64-5, 72, 74, 81, 83-6, 91

Kaddish, and Other Poems (Ginsberg) **4**:47

Kahini (Tagore) **8**:410

Kai oi (The Seashell Game) (Matsuo Basho) **3**:24

"Kalaloch" (Forche) **10**:133-35, 168

"Kaleidoscopes: Baroque" (Atwood) **8**:11

"Kalimpong" (Tagore) **8**:426

Kalpana (Tagore) **8**:410-11, 415

Kanashiki gangu (Sad Toys) (Ishikawa Takuboku) **10**:195-97, 200-01, 205, 210-11, 217

"Kansas City to St. Louis" (Ginsberg) **4**:54, 57

"Das kapital" (Baraka) **4**:30, 38

"Das Kapitäl" (Rilke) **2**:275

"Kapuzinerberg (Saltzberg)" (Bogan) **12**:100

Kari o komal (Sharps and Flats) (Tagore) **8**:406-07, 415

Katha (Tagore) **8**:410

"Käthe Kollwitz" (Rukeyser) **12**:228-30

"Die Kathedrale" (Rilke) **2**:275

"Katherine's Dream" (Lowell) **3**:201

Kavkazsky plennik (The Captive of the Caucasus; The Caucasian Captive; The Prisoner of the Caucasus) (Pushkin) **10**:357-58, 364-65, 371, 386-88, 395, 415-21

"Kay Rutledge" (Masters) **1**:334

"Keen" (Millay) **6**:225

"Keep a Pluggin' Away" (Dunbar) **5**:119

"Keeping Their World Large" (Moore) **4**:236, 268

"Keller Gegen Dom" (Williams) **7**:378

"Kellyburn Braes" (Burns) **6**:78

"Kept" (Bogan) **12**:105, 122

"Key West: An Island Sheaf" (Crane) **3**:90

"Khalil al-kāfir" (Gibran) **9**:78

Kheya (*Ferrying Across*) (Tagore) **8**:412-13, 415

"Khristos Voskres" ("Christ Has Arisen") (Pushkin) **10**:411-12

"Kid" (Hayden) **6**:196

"The Kids Who Die" (Hughes) **1**:243

"A Kike is the Most Dangerous" (Cummings) **5**:82, 84

"Killiecrankie" (Burns) **6**:78

"Killing the Spring" (Sexton) **2**:365

"Kilroy's Carnival" (Schwartz) **8**:311

"Kimi Shinitamô koto nakare" ("Brother, Do Not Give Your Life") (Yosano Akiko) **11**:320-26, 328-29

"Kin to Sorrow" (Millay) **6**:205

The Kind of Poetry I Want (MacDiarmid) **9**:180, 182, 184, 185-86

"Kind Sir: These Woods" (Sexton) **2**:358

"Kindness" (Plath) **1**:391, 393

"The King" (Kipling) **3**:161, 166

King Bolo (Eliot) **5**:174

"King Edward the Third" ("Edward III") (Blake) **12**:11, 61

"King Hamlet's Ghost" (Smith) **12**:311, 353

"A King in Funeral Procession" (Smith) **12**:315

King Jasper (Robinson) **1**:479, 483

"King of Carrion" (Hughes) **7**:153

"The King of Harlem" (Garcia Lorca) **3**:139

"The Kingdom of Poetry" (Schwartz) **8**:289, 308-09

"King-fisher" (Montale) **13**:139

The King's Daughter (Bely) **11**:32

"The King's Task" (Kipling) **3**:183

"The Kirk's Alarm" (Burns) **6**:78

"The Kiss" (Sassoon) **12**:262

"The Kiss" (Sexton) **2**:353

"The Kiss" (Tagore)
See "Chumban"

A Kist of Whistles: New Poems (MacDiarmid) **9**:182

"Kita no umi" ("The Northern Sea") (Ishikawa Takuboku) **10**:213

"Kitchenette Building" (Brooks) **7**:79

"Kite Flying" (McKay) **2**:223

"Kitty Hawk" (Frost) **1**:213

"The Kneeling One" (Gallagher) **9**:57

"The Knight" (Hughes) **7**:126

"The Knight" (Rich) **5**:370

"The Knight's to the Mountain" (Scott) **13**:305

"Knocking Donkey Fleas off a Poet from the Southside of Chi" (Madhubuti) **5**:323, 344

"Knotted Letter" (Gallagher) **9**:63

"Knowledge" (Bogan) **12**:101, 103, 120

"Knucks" (Sandburg) **2**:308, 324

"Kodachromes of the Island" (Hayden) **6**:183, 193, 196, 198

"Kôgao no shi" ("Rosy-Cheeked Death") (Yosano Akiko) **11**:324-26, 328

Kogda razglyaetsya (*When the Skies Clear*) (Pasternak) **6**:266-69, 284-85

"Kogda v mrachneyshey iz stolits" ("When in the Gloomiest of Capitals") (Akhmatova) **2**:12

Koigoromo ("Robe of Love") (Yosano Akiko) **11**:306-07

Konec prekrasnoj èpox (Brodsky)
See *Konets prekrasnoy epokhi*

Konets prekrasnoy epokhi (*The End of a Fine Epoch*; *Konec prekrasnoj èpox*) (Brodsky) **9**:7

Kora in Hell: Improvisations (Williams) **7**:344, 349, 374-75, 377, 379-81, 383-84, 394, 400, 405, 410

"The Kraken" (Tennyson) **6**:360, 389, 391, 406-10

"Kral Majales" (Ginsberg) **4**:82, 85

"Kronos; To Coachman Kronos" (Goethe)
See "An Schwager Kronos"

Kshanikā (*Fleeting Moments*; *Fleeting Moments*; *Fleeting Thoughts*; *Fleeting Thoughts*) (Tagore) **8**:411

"Kubla Khan" (Coleridge) **11**:41-7, 51, 59, 73, 75-9, 84-8, 90, 104, 107, 110

Kubok metelej: Chetviortiia simfoniia (*Cup of Blizzards*; *The Cup of Snowstorms*; *The Fourth Symphony*; *The Goblet of Blizzards*) (Bely) **11**:3, 6-7, 14-17, 22

"Kung Canto" (Pound) **4**:325

"Kure no kane" ("The Twilight Bell") (Ishikawa Takuboku) **10**:214

"The Kursaal at Interlaken" (Rich) **5**:359

"Kutir-vasi" ("The Cottage Dweller") (Tagore) **8**:416

"Kutoa Umoja" (Baraka) **4**:26

"Kwa Mamu Zetu Waliotuzaa (for our mothers who gave us birth)" (Sanchez) **9**:215-16, 221, 227, 229, 243

"Kyoko" ("Solitude") (Ishikawa Takuboku) **10**:213

"L.A. to Wichita" (Ginsberg) **4**:54

Laberinto (*Labyrinth*) (Jimenez) **7**:200-01, 211

"Labor and Management" (Baraka) **4**:13

"The Laboratory" (Browning) **2**:60

"The Laboring Skeleton" (Baudelaire)
See "Le squelette laboureur"

Labyrinth (Jimenez)
See *Laberinto*

Labyrinths, with Path of Thunder (*Path of Thunder*) (Okigbo) **7**:231, 233-35, 241-43, 248-49, 251-52, 254-56

"Lachrymae Christi" (Crane) **3**:82, 96-7, 102

"Lack of Discipline" (Pavese)
See "Indisciplina"

"Lack of Faith" (Pushkin)
See "Bezverie"

Ladera este (*East Slope*; *Eastern Slope*) (Paz) **1**:354, 346, 361-63, 374, 376

"The Ladies" (Kipling) **3**:164, 166, 174

"The Lads in Their Hundreds" (Housman) **2**:192

"The Lads of the Village" (Smith) **12**:330, 333

"Lady" (Carruth) **10**:74

"Lady Acheson Weary of the Dean" (Swift) **9**:295-96

"Lady Geraldine's Courtship" (Browning) **6**:10, 17-18, 26, 38-9, 42

"Lady Lazarus" (Plath) **1**:382, 386, 391, 395-97, 400-01, 406-07, 410, 413-14

"Lady of Cowrie Palace" (Li Ho) **13**:51-4

"The Lady of Shalott" (Tennyson) **6**:350, 358-59, 378, 380, 395, 409-10

The Lady of the Lake (Scott) **13**:257-58, 261, 267-68, 270-71, 273, 276-79, 281, 283, 285, 289, 291, 293, 304, 310-11, 319-20

"The Lady of the Well-Spring" (Smith) **12**:304, 306, 329, 341

"Lady's Boogie" (Hughes) **1**:266

"The Lady's Dressing Room" (Swift) **9**:257, 262, 268, 270, 273, 279, 281, 286-89, 291-92, 295, 298-99, 302-03

"Laeti et Errabundi" (Verlaine) **2**:417

"The Lag" (Rich) **5**:363

"Il lago di Annecy" (Montale) **13**:138

"Lais" (H. D.) **5**:268

Les Lais (*Lesser Testament*; *Le Petit Testament*; *Small Testament*) (Villon) **13**:374-75, 377, 387, 396-99, 402, 404-05, 408-10, 412-13

"Lake Boats" (Masters) **1**:330, 333

"The Lamb" (Blake) **12**:7, 9, 32, 62

"The Lambs of Grasmere" (Rossetti) **7**:266

"The Lament" (Burns) **6**:53

"Lament" (Hardy) **8**:135

"Lament" (Millay) **6**:211

"Lament" (Plath) **1**:410

"Lament" (Sexton) **2**:350

Lament for Ignacio Sánchez Mejías (Garcia Lorca)
See *Llanto por Ignacio Sánchez Mejías*

"Lament for Pasiphaé" (Graves) **6**:144

Lament for the Death of a Bullfighter (Garcia Lorca)
See *Llanto por Ignacio Sánchez Mejías*

"Lament of Mary Queen of Scots" (Burns) **6**:78

"Lament of the Belle Heaulmiere" ("Regrets of the Belle Heaumiere") (Villon) **13**:389-90

"Lament of the Drums" (Okigbo) **7**:224, 229-30, 244, 247, 254

"Lament of the Lavender Mist" (Okigbo) **7**:229, 248

"The Lament of the Masks: For W. B. Yeats: 1865-1939" (Okigbo) **7**:230, 245

"Lament of the Silent Sisters" (Okigbo)
See "Silences: Lament of the Silent Sisters"

"Lamentations" (Sassoon) **12**:267, 286

"The Lamentations of Jeremy, for the most part according to Tremelius" (Donne) **1**:139

Lamia, Isabella, The Eve of St. Agnes, and Other Poems (Keats) **1**:276, 279, 281, 296, 307-09, 311

Lancelot (Robinson) **1**:465, 468-70, 489, 491

"Lancer" (Housman) **2**:162

"The Land" (Kipling) **3**:171

"The Land Betrayed" (Neruda)
See "La arena traicionada"

"The Land of Dreams" (Blake) **12**:35

Land of Unlikeness (Lowell) **3**:199, 202, 213, 216-17, 232

"The Land Where All Is Gained" (Tagore)
See "Sab-peyechhir desh"

"Landcrab II" (Atwood) **8**:43

"Landlady, Count the Lawin" (Burns) **6**:81

"The Landscape" (Masters) **1**:333, 344

"Landscape" (Merton) **10**:349

"Landscape after a Battle" (Neruda)
See "Paisaje después de una batalla"

"Landscape I" (Pavese)
See "Paesaggio I"

"Landscape of the Heart" (Jimenez)
See "Paisaje del corozon"

"Landscape of the Star" (Rich) **5**:362

"Landscape of the Urinating Multitudes (Battery Place Nocturne)" (Garcia Lorca)
See "Paisaje de la multitud que orina"

"Landscape of the Vomiting Multitudes (Coney Island Dusk)" (Garcia Lorca)
See "Paisaje de la multitud que vomita"

"Landscape VI" (Pavese)
See "Paesaggio VI"

"Landscape VII" (Pavese)
See "Paesaggio VII"

"Landscape with Serifs" (Page)   **12**:183

"Landscapes" (Eliot)   **5**:166, 183

Landscapes of Living and Dying (Ferlinghetti)   **1**:180-81, 187

Language Lattice (Celan)
See *Sprachgitter*

"Language-Mesh" (Celan)
See "Sprachgitter"

"L'anguilla" ("The Eel") (Montale)   **13**:111

"Laodamia" (Wordsworth)   **4**:394, 399, 406-07

"Lapraik II" (Burns)
See "Second Epistle to John Lapraik"

"Lapse" (Dunbar)   **5**:126

"A Large Bad Picture" (Bishop)   **3**:37, 70-1

Large Testament (Villon)
See *Le Testament*

"Larme" (Rimbaud)   **3**:271

"Last" (Kipling)   **3**:160

Last and Lost Poems of Delmore Schwartz (Schwartz)   **8**:311, 319

"The Last Chantey" (Kipling)   **3**:161

"The Last Duchess" (Browning)   **2**:30

The Last Harvest (Tagore)
See *Chaitāli*

"Last Hill in a Vista" (Bogan)   **12**:104

"The Last Instructions to a Painter" (Marvell)   **10**:275

"The Last Invocation" (Whitman)   **3**:378

"Last Lines" (Bronte)   **8**:59

"Last Load" (Hughes)   **7**:166

"Last Looks at the Lilacs" (Stevens)   **6**:292

"The Last Meeting" (Sassoon)   **12**:262

"The Last Mowing" (Frost)   **1**:206

Last Octave (Tagore)
See *Shesh saptak*

"The Last of the Flock" (Wordsworth)   **4**:373, 415, 418

"Last Poems" (Tagore)
See "Śesh lekhā"

Last Poems (Browning)   **6**:23-4, 38, 40

Last Poems (Celan)   **10**:120

Last Poems (Housman)   **2**:161-67, 173-76, 180-81, 186, 191, 196, 199-201

"*Last Poems*: XX—The Night Is Freezing Fast" ("The Night Is Freezing Fast") (Housman)   **2**:196

"The Last Quatrain of the Ballad of Emmett Till" (Brooks)   **7**:62

"The Last Rhyme of True Thomas" (Kipling)   **3**:181-82

"The Last Ride Together" (Browning)   **2**:75

"The Last Signal" (Hardy)   **8**:131

"The Last Suttee" (Kipling)   **3**:183

"The Last Tournament" (Tennyson)   **6**:376

"The Last Turn of the Screw" (Smith)   **12**:295

Last Volume (Swift)   **9**:255

"The Last Word" (Tagore)
See "Shesh katha"

"Last Words" (Plath)   **1**:396, 407

"Last Words of the Dying Recruit" (McKay)   **2**:226

"Late" (Bogan)   **12**:122

"Late August" (Atwood)   **8**:28-9, 42

"Late Last Night" (Hughes)   **1**:243

Late Lyrics and Earlier with Many Other Verses (Hardy)   **8**:89, 123

"Later Life" (Rossetti)   **7**:278

"Lauda" (Milosz)   **8**:201

"Lauda" (Paz)   **1**:361

"The Laugh" (Graves)   **6**:156

"Laughing Corn" (Sandburg)   **2**:316

"Laughing Gas" (Ginsberg)   **4**:74, 81

"The Laughing Song" (Blake)   **12**:4, 7, 23

"Laughters" (Hughes)
See "My People"

"The Laureate" (Graves)   **6**:142, 144

"Lavorare stanca" ("Work Wearies") (Pavese)   **13**:203, 213, 225-27

Lavorare stanca (*Hard Labor; Work Is Tiresome; Work Wearies*) (Pavese)   **13**:201-02, 204-05, 210-14, 216-19, 222, 224-26, 228

"Law" (Lowell)   **3**:214

"The Law I Love Is Major Mover" (Duncan)   **2**:124

"The Laws of God, the Laws of Man" (Housman)   **2**:162, 179

The Lay of the Last Minstrel (Scott)   **13**:246, 248-51, 256, 258, 266, 269, 271, 273, 274-76, 279-83, 285, 303, 311-12, 315, 317-18

"Laying the Dust" (Levertov)   **11**:165

"Lazarus" (Robinson)   **1**:468

"Lead Soldiers" (Lowell)   **13**:78

"The Leaders" (Brooks)   **7**:63, 90

"Leaflets" (Rich)   **5**:396

Leaflets: Poems, 1965-1968 (Rich)   **5**:357, 365, 370-72, 383, 388-89, 396, 399

"Lear Is Gay" (Hayden)   **6**:187

"The Lea-Rig" (Burns)   **6**:82

"Learning to Write" (Lorde)   **12**:136

"Leather Jacket" (Page)   **12**:172

"Leather Leggings" (Sandburg)   **2**:302

Leaves of Grass (Whitman)   **3**:370, 378-79, 382, 384, 386-87, 389, 397-99, 401, 404-08, 410-14, 416-17

"Leave-taking Near Shoku" (Pound)   **4**:331

"Lebenslauf" (Holderlin)   **4**:147

"Lecture" (Milosz)   **8**:200

"Lecture I" (Milosz)   **8**:202

"Lecture IV" (Milosz)   **8**:203

"Lecture VI" (Milosz)   **8**:199

"Lecture VII" (Milosz)   **8**:202

"A Lecture upon the Shadow" (Donne)   **1**:135, 145, 147

"Leda and the Swan" (Montale)   **13**:150

Lee: A Dramatic Poem (Masters)   **1**:339

"Leech Gatherer" (Wordsworth)   **4**:390, 394

"Leffingwell" (Robinson)   **1**:466

"Left Behind" (Lowell)   **13**:97

"Legacies" (Browning)   **6**:16

"Legend" (Crane)   **3**:101

"A Legend of Porcelain" (Lowell)   **13**:61, 65

"Legende" (Celan)   **10**:126

Legends (Lowell)   **13**:60-3, 65, 74, 83, 93

"The Legion Club" (Swift)   **9**:281

"The Legs" (Graves)   **6**:151

"The Lemons" (Montale)   **13**:149

"Lenore" (Poe)   **1**:434, 438, 445

"Lenox Avenue: Midnight" (Hughes)   **1**:265

"Lent" (Herbert)   **4**:100

"The Lent Lily" (Housman)   **2**:184, 192

"A Leone Traverso" (Montale)   **13**:139

"Leonine Elegiacs" (Tennyson)   **6**:385-86

"leroy" (Baraka)   **4**:19, 23

"Lesbos" (Plath)   **1**:394

Lesser Testament (Villon)
See *Les Lais*

"The Lesson" (Levertov)   **11**:167

"The Lesson" (Lowell)   **3**:211

"Let America Be America Again" (Hughes)   **1**:250, 253

"Let Me Enjoy" (Hardy)   **8**:98

"Léthé" ("Le lethe") (Baudelaire)   **1**:72

"Le lethe" (Baudelaire)
See "Léthé"

"Lethe" (H. D.)   **5**:287, 304

"Let's Beat Down the Poor" (Baudelaire)
See "Assommons les pauvres"

"Let's, from Some Loud Unworld's Most Rightful Wrong" (Cummings)   **5**:109

"A Letter" (Bogan)   **12**:95, 127

"Letter" (Montale)
See "Lettera"

"Letter for Jan" (Lorde)   **12**:152

"A Letter from Phillis Wheatley" (Hayden)   **6**:189, 192, 195

"Letter from Prague, 1968-78" (Forche)   **10**:144, 156, 168-69

"A Letter Home" (Sassoon)   **12**:262

"A Letter in a Bottle" (Brodsky)   **9**:3, 4

"Letter of Advice to a Young Poet" (Swift)   **9**:272

"A Letter to a Brother of the Pen in Tribulation" (Behn)   **13**:7, 30

"Letter to a Wound" (Auden)   **1**:22

"A Letter to Dr. Martin Luther King" (Sanchez)   **9**:244

"A Letter to Her Husband, Absent upon Public Employment" (Bradstreet)   **10**:8, 28, 30, 34, 40, 65

Letter to Lord Byron (Auden)   **1**:22, 34

"Letter to Maxine Sullivan" (Carruth)   **10**:87

"Letter to Miguel Otero Silva, in Caracas, 1948" (Neruda)
See "Carta a Miguel Otero Silva, en Caracas, 1948"

"A Letter to My Friends" (Merton)   **10**:346-47

"A Letter to Sara Hutchinson" (Coleridge)   **11**:69-72, 91

"Letter to the Countesse of Huntingdon" (Donne)   **1**:130

"Letter to the Front" (Rukeyser)   **12**:228, 231-34

"Letter Written during a January Northeaster" (Sexton)   **2**:351

"Letter Written on a Ferry Crossing Long Island Sound" (Sexton)   **2**:351, 361

"Lettera" ("Letter") (Montale)   **13**:161

Letters (Duncan)   **2**:106

Letters (Ovid)
See *Heroides*

"Letters from a Land of Sinners" (Rich)   **5**:354

Letters from a Traveller's Pannier (Matsuo Basho)
See *Oi no obumi*

Letters from Iceland (Auden)   **1**:9, 13

"Letters from the Ming Dynasty" (Brodsky)   **9**:29

Letters of the Heroines (Ovid)
See *Heroides*

"Lettre-Océan" ("Ocean-Letter") (Apollinaire)   **7**:18, 25-9, 32, 34-7

"Letzter Abend" (Rilke)   **2**:267

"Levedad" ("Lightness") (Jimenez)   **7**:201

"Leviathan" (Neruda) **4**:282

"Lews estoilles envoyées à Monsieur de Pibrac en Polonne" (Ronsard) **11**:236-37, 239

"The Liar" (Baraka) **4**:17

"The Liars" (Sandburg) **2**:304

"Libation" (Levertov) **11**:197

Liber Spectaculorum (Martial) **10**:230

"Liberation Poem" (Sanchez) **9**:209

"The Liberators" (Neruda)
See "Los libertadores"

Libertad bajo palabra (*Freedom under Parole*; *Liberty behind the Words*) (Paz) **1**:353

"Los libertadores" ("The Liberators") (Neruda) **4**:292

"The Libertine" (Behn) **13**:4

"Liberty" (Pushkin)
See "Vol'nost': Oda"

"Liberty and Peace" (Wheatley) **3**:337, 341, 363

Liberty behind the Words (Paz)
See *Libertad bajo palabra*

Libro de las preguntas (*Book of Questions*) (Neruda) **4**:287, 290

Libro de poemas (*Poems*) (Garcia Lorca) **3**:117-18, 147-49

Libros inéditos de poesía (Jimenez) **7**:201

Lichee Nuts (Masters) **1**:338

Lichtzwang (*Force of Light*; *Light Compulsion*) (Celan) **10**:96, 98, 121

"Lidice" (Day Lewis) **11**:146

"(Liebeslied.)" ("(Lovesong.)") (Celan) **10**:123-24

"Liebhaber in allen Gestalten" (Goethe) **5**:246, 251

"Liens" ("Chains"; "Links") (Apollinaire) **7**:28, 49

Lieutenant Schmidt (Pasternak) **6**:265, 272

"Life" (Dunbar) **5**:121, 124-26, 130

"Life" (Herbert) **4**:100, 113

"Life and Death at Sunrise" (Hardy) **8**:124

"The Life and Genuine Character of Dr. Swift" (Swift) **9**:280, 295

"Life and Letters" (Rich) **5**:352

"Life at War" (Levertov) **11**:176, 194

Life in the Forest (Levertov) **11**:205, 207-10

"Life is More True than Reason Will Decieve" (Cummings) **5**:108

"Life Is Motion" (Stevens) **6**:333

"The Life of Lincoln West" (Brooks) **7**:85, 91-3

Life Studies (Lowell) **3**:205-09, 211-14, 216-19, 221, 223, 227, 230, 232-33, 242-43

"Life's Noonday" (Tagore)
See "Jivan madhyahna"

"A Lifetime Later" (Ferlinghetti) **1**:183

"The Light" (Ferlinghetti) **1**:183

"Light against Darkness" (Williams) **7**:385

"Light Becomes Darkness" (Williams) **7**:384, 388

"Light Becomes Where No Sun Shines" (Thomas)
See "Light Breaks Where No Sun Shines"

"Light Breaks Where No Sun Shines" ("Light Becomes Where No Sun Shines") (Thomas) **2**:304

Light Compulsion (Celan)
See *Lichtzwang*

"Light Love" (Rossetti) **7**:289

"A Light Snow-Fall after Frost" (Hardy) **8**:124

"A Lighted Cigar That Is Smoking" (Apollinaire)

See "Paysage"

"The Lighted House" (Day Lewis) **11**:145-46

"Lightness" (Jimenez)
See "Levedad"

"Lightnin' Blues" (Dove) **6**:117

Like a Bulwark (Moore) **4**:257

"Like Decorations in a Nigger Cemetery" (Stevens) **6**:308, 318

"Like Snow" (Graves) **6**:144, 172

"Like, This Is What I Meant" (Baraka) **4**:38

"Like This Together" (Rich) **5**:364, 382

"Lilacs" (Lowell) **13**:64, 67, 84-5, 98-9

"Lilian" (Tennyson) **6**:359

"Lilis Park" (Goethe) **5**:246

"The Lilly" (Blake) **12**:34-5

"The Lilly in a Christal" (Herrick) **9**:112-13, 115, 137-38, 144

"Limbo" (Coleridge) **11**:52, 85

"Limbo" (Graves) **6**:166

"Limitation of Perfection" (Tagore)
See "Purner abhav"

"Limitations" (Sassoon) **12**:245

"Limited" (Sandburg) **2**:312

"Limits" (Okigbo) **7**:241-42

Limits (Okigbo) **7**:223-28, 233-34, 246-48, 250-51

"I limoni" (Montale) **13**:114, 119, 122

"Lindau" (Montale) **13**:146

"Lineage" (Hughes) **7**:159

"The Liner She's a Lady" (Kipling) **3**:161

"Lines" (Williams) **7**:351-52

"Lines Above Tintern Abbey" (Wordsworth)
See "Lines Composed a Few Miles Above Tintern Abbey"

"Lines Composed a Few Miles Above Tintern Abbey" ("Lines Above Tintern Abbey"; "Tintern Abbey") (Wordsworth) **4**:373, 387, 391, 409-12, 418-19, 425-26, 428

"Lines Composed While Climbing the Left Ascent of Brockley Coomb, Somersetshire, May 1795" (Coleridge) **11**:82

"Lines for an Album" (Montale)
See "Per album"

"Lines for an Old Man" (Eliot) **5**:170

"Lines Left upon a Seat in a Yew-Tree, Which Stands near the Lake of Esthwaite, on a Desolate Part of the Shore, Commanding a Beautiful Prospect" (Wordsworth) **4**:373, 418

"Lines on an Autumnal Evening" (Coleridge) **11**:106

"Lines on the First Mild Day of March" ("It Is the First Mild Day of March") (Wordsworth) **4**:418

"Lines to a Movement in Mozart's E-Flat Symphony" (Hardy) **8**:114

"Lines Written after Detecting in Myself a Yearning toward the Large, Wise, Calm, Richly Resigned, Benignant Act Put on by a Great Many People after Having Passed the Age of Thirty Five" (Bogan) **12**:115

"Lines Written at a Small Distance from My House, and Sent by My Little Boy to the Person to Whom They Are Addressed" (Wordsworth) **4**:418

"Lines Written in an Asylum" (Carruth) **10**:84, 89

"Lines Written in Anticipation of a London Paper Attaining a Guaranteed Circulation of Ten Million Daily" (Sassoon) **12**:251-52

"Lines Written in Early Spring" (Wordsworth) **4**:418

"Lines Written in Kensington Gardens" (Arnold) **5**:19, 35, 49

"Lingard and the Stars" (Robinson) **1**:464

"Links" (Apollinaire)
See "Liens"

"The Linnet in the Rocky Dells" (Bronte) **8**:68-9

"Linoleum" (Gallagher) **9**:44, 56, 60

"The Lion in Love" (Moore) **4**:261

"The Lions" (Hayden) **6**:194, 197

"Lis" (Cummings) **5**:100

"Lisa May" (Dunbar) **5**:137

"Listen Here Blues" (Hughes) **1**:270

"Listenen to Big Black at S.F. State" (Sanchez) **9**:225

"The Litanie" (Donne) **1**:136-39, 147, 150

"Les litanies de satan" ("The Litanies of Satan") (Baudelaire) **1**:45, 71

"The Litanies of Satan" (Baudelaire)
See "Les litanies de satan"

"The Litany for Survival" (Lorde) **12**:137

"Literary Statement On Struggle!" (Baraka) **4**:30

"The Literate Farmer and the Planet Venus" (Frost) **1**:210

"Lithuanian Nocturne" (Brodsky) **9**:22-4, 27

"The Little Black Boy" (Blake) **12**:7-8

"The Little Boy Found" (Blake) **12**:7

"A Little Boy Lost" (Blake) **12**:7, 23, 33-5

"Little Boy Lost" (Smith) **12**:321, 325, 332

"Little Boy Sick" (Smith) **12**:318

"Little Boy Stanton" (Garcia Lorca) **3**:143

"Little Brown Baby" (Dunbar) **5**:142

"Little Exercise" (Bishop) **3**:49

"The Little Friend" (Browning) **6**:14

"Little Fugue" (Plath) **1**:390

"The Little Ghost" (Millay) **6**:206

"Little Gidding" (Eliot) **5**:165-67, 169-70, 181-83, 185, 193, 204-05, 208, 210-11

"The Little Girl Found" (Blake) **12**:7, 33-4, 61

"A Little Girl Lost" (Blake) **12**:7, 33-4, 61

"Little Girl, My String Bean, My Lovely Woman" (Sexton) **2**:363

"Little Girls" (Page) **12**:176-77

"Little Green Tree" (Hughes) **1**:243

"The Little Hill" (Millay) **6**:214, 233

The Little House of Kolomna (Pushkin)
See *Domik v Kolomne*

"Little Jim" (McKay) **2**:216, 222

"The Little June Book" (Stevens) **6**:332-33

"Little Lobeila's Song" (Bogan) **12**:100-01, 111

"Little Lyric" (Hughes) **1**:240

"Little Mattie" (Browning) **6**:24

"Little Old Letter" (Hughes) **1**:243

"The Little Old Women" (Baudelaire)
See "Les petites vielles"

"The Little Peasant" (Sexton) **2**:364, 368

Little Poems in Prose (Baudelaire)
See *Petits poèmes en prose: Le spleen de Paris*

"Little T. C." (Marvell)
See "The Picture of Little T. C. in a Prospect of Flowers"

"A Little Testament" (Montale)
See "Piccolo testamento"

"Little Tree" (Cummings) **5**:93

"A Little Uncomplicated Hymn" (Sexton) **2**:363

"The Little Vagabond" (Blake) **12**:7

"The Little White Rose" (MacDiarmid) **9**:154, 176, 186

"Littleblood" (Hughes) 7:153, 168-69
Liturgies intimes (Verlaine) 2:417-18
"Live" (Sexton) 2:351, 364
"Live Niggers--Stop Bullshitting" (Baraka)
    4:18
Live or Die (Sexton) 2:349, 351, 356, 362-65
"Lives" (Rukeyser) 12:207, 217, 228
"Living" (Levertov) 11:186
"Living Earth" (Toomer) 7:336-37
"Living in Sin" (Rich) 5:351, 369
Llanto por Ignacio Sánchez Mejías (*Lament for
    Ignacio Sánchez Mejías; Lament for the
    Death of a Bullfighter*) (Garcia Lorca)
    3:121-22, 124, 126, 128
"Llewellyn and the Tree" (Robinson) 1:462,
    468
"Lo! A Child Is Born" (MacDiarmid) 9:178-
    79
"The Load of Sugar-Cane" (Stevens) 6:293
"The Lockless Door" (Frost) 1:218
"Locksley Hall" (Tennyson) 6:354, 357, 359-
    60, 363
"Locus" (Hayden) 6:189, 194, 196
"The Locust Tree in Flower" (Williams)
    7:363
"Logos" (Hughes) 7:120, 159
"Loin Cloth" (Sandburg) 2:329
"Loin des oiseaux" (Rimbaud) 3:274
"Loin du pigeonnier" ("The Depths")
    (Apollinaire) 7:18, 21, 23
"Loitering with a Vacant Eye" (Housman)
    2:193
"Lollocks" (Graves) 6:137, 142, 144
"London" (Blake) 12:7, 25, 34
"London Bridge" (Robinson) 1:466, 468
Loneliness (Paz)
    See *Soledad*
"The Lonely Street" (Williams) 7:362
"Lonesome" (Dunbar) 5:119
Long Ago and Not So Long Ago (Verlaine)
    See *Jadis et naguère*
Long Division: A Tribal History (Rose) 13:232
"Long John Brown & Little Mary Bell"
    (Blake) 12:35
"Long Past Moncada" (Rukeyser) 12:231-32
"Long Screams" (Hughes) 7:150
"The Long Shadow of Lincoln: A Litany"
    (Sandburg) 2:334
"A Long Story" (Gray) 2:143, 152-53
"Long To'ds Night" (Dunbar) 5:147
"The Long Tunnel Ceiling" (Hughes) 7:148
"Longing" (Arnold) 5:42-3
Longing (Ishikawa Takuboku)
    See *Akogare*
"Longing for Heaven" (Bradstreet) 10:27, 30,
    42
"Longing Is Like the Seed" (Dickinson)
    1:111
"Look!" (Smith) 12:342
"Look for You Yesterday, Here You Come
    Today" (Baraka) 4:14-15
"Look on This Picture and on This" (Rossetti)
    7:277
"Look, Stranger, on This Island Now" (*On
    This Island*) (Auden) 1:7-8, 12, 22, 30
"Looking at a Picture on an Anniversary"
    (Hardy) 8:137-38
"Looking Forward" (Rossetti) 7:277
"Looking in a Mirror" (Atwood) 8:32, 38
"The Loom" (Masters) 1:333
"The Loop" (Masters) 1:329
"Loot" (Kipling) 3:160, 163, 174, 187

"Lord of Elbë, on Elbë Hill" (Bronte) 8:73
The Lord of the Isles (Scott) 13:277, 281, 288,
    294, 296, 304, 311-12, 318, 321
Lord Weary's Castle (Lowell) 3:200, 202-03,
    206-07, 211-12, 216-18, 224, 230-33
"Lorelei" (Plath) 1:388-89
"L'lorloge de demain" ("The Clock of
    Tomorrow") (Apollinaire) 7:32
"Losing Track" (Levertov) 11:160, 169
"Loss" (H. D.) 5:303
"The Loss of The Nabara" (Day Lewis)
    See "The Nabara"
"Lost" (Sandburg) 2:303
Lost Copper (Rose) 13:235, 237-38, 240
"The Lost Dancer" (Toomer) 7:336
"The Lost Ingredient" (Sexton) 2:350, 359
"Lost Love" (Graves) 6:129
"The Lost Mistress" (Browning) 2:38
"The Lost Wine" (Valery)
    See "Le vin perdu"
"The Lotos-Eaters" (Tennyson) 6:352, 358-
    60, 409-12
"Louenge a la court" (Villon) 13:394-95
"Love" (Herbert) ::100, 114
"Love III" (Herbert) 4:121
"Love among the Ruins" (Browning) 2:88
"Love and Friendship" (Bronte) 8:51
"Love and Harmony Combine" (Blake) 12:32
"Love Arm'd" ("Love in Fantastic Triumph
    Sat"; "Song") (Behn) 13:4, 7, 15, 23-5
"Love Despoiled" (Dunbar) 5:125
Love Elegies (Donne)
    See *Elegies*
"Love from the North" (Rossetti) 7:260, 278,
    280, 289
"Love in Barrenness" (Graves) 6:172
"Love in Fantastic Triumph Sat" (Behn)
    See "Love Arm'd"
"Love in the Museum" (Rich) 5:393
"Love is More Thicker than Forget"
    (Cummings) 5:108
"Love is the Only God" (Cummings) 5:107
"Love Joy" (Herbert) 4:122-23, 125
"A Love Letter" (Dunbar) 5:147
"Love Me!" (Smith) 12:346
"The Love Nut" (Ferlinghetti) 1:187
"The Love of Christ which Passeth
    Knowledge" (Rossetti) 7:268, 290
"The Love of the Lie" (Baudelaire) 1:72
"Love Poem" (Lorde) 12:158
"Love Poem" (Page) 12:177
Love Poems (Sanchez) 9:207, 212, 216, 218-
    21, 227, 229, 234, 237, 242
Love Poems (Sexton) 2:349, 351-53, 355, 364-
    65
Love Respelt (Graves) 6:154, 156
"Love Song" (Levertov) 11:159, 171
"Love Song" (Sexton) 2:363
"Love Song" (Williams) 7:345, 406-07
"A Love Song in the Modern Taste" (Swift)
    9:252, 268
"The Love Song of J. Alfred Prufrock" (Eliot)
    5:153-54, 157, 160, 206
"A Love Story" (Graves) 6:129, 133, 136-37,
    144, 163, 172
"Love Unknown" (Herbert) 4:109, 112, 123,
    129
"Love Winter When the Plant Says Nothing"
    (Merton) 10:334
"Love without Hope" (Graves) 6:141, 144,
    149-50

"Love You Right Back" (Brooks) 7:94
"Loveliest of Trees" (Housman) 2:184-85,
    192, 194-95
"Lovely Ladies" (Tu Fu) 9:330
"The Lovely Lady" (Tu Fu) 9:322
"A Lovely Love" (Brooks) 7:81, 96, 100-01
Love-Poems (Ovid)
    See *Amores*
"A Lover since Childhood" (Graves) 6:129
"Lover's Death" (Baudelaire)
    See "La mort des amants"
"Lovers infinitenesse" ("If yet I have not all
    thy love") (Donne) 1:130, 153
"Lovers of the Poor" (Brooks) 7:86, 88, 96
"The Lover's Tale" (Tennyson) 6:358, 373-
    74, 379-80
The Lovers Watch (Behn)
    See *La Montre; or, The Lover's Watch*
"Loves Alchymie" (Donne) 1:147, 159
"Love's Causes" (Browning) 6:17
"Love's Diet" (Donne) 1:127
"Love's Draft" (Dunbar) 5:126
"Love's Expression" (Browning) 6:17
"Love's Farewell" (Bronte) 8:57
"Loves Growth" (Donne) 1:153
"Love's New Creation" (Browning) 6:17
"Love's Obstacles" (Browning) 6:16
"Love's Refuge" (Browning) 6:17
"Love's Repetitions" (Browning) 6:17
"Loves Riddles" (Donne) 1:153
"Love's Sacrifice" (Browning) 6:17
"(Lovesong.)" (Celan)
    See "(Liebeslied.)"
"Loving the Killer" (Sexton) 2:352-53
"Low Tide" (Millay) 6:236
"Low to High" (Hughes) 1:258, 267
"The Lowest Place" ("The Lowest Room")
    (Rossetti) 7:274, 291
"The Lowest Room" (Rossetti)
    See "The Lowest Place"
"The Lowestoft Boat" (Kipling) 3:183
"Lub O' Mine" (McKay) 2:221
"Lucien Létinois" (Verlaine) 2:416
"Lucifer in the Train" (Rich) 5:354, 362, 393
The Lucky Bag (MacDiarmid) 9:158
"Lucretius" (Tennyson) 6:358, 360, 378, 380
"Lucy Gray" (Coleridge) 11:73-4
"Lucy Gray" (Wordsworth) 4:398, 404, 428
Lueurs des tirs (Apollinaire) 7:22
"Luke Havergal" (Robinson) 1:467, 475, 490-
    94
"Lullaby" (Dunbar) 5:122
"Lullaby" (Sexton) 2:359
"Lullaby" (Sitwell) 3:309, 311, 326
"Lullaby for Jumbo" (Sitwell) 3:303
"Lullaby of Cape Cod" (Brodsky)
    See "A Cape Cod Lullaby"
"Luna Habitabilis" (Gray) 2:155
Luna silvestre (Paz) 1:367
"Lundi rue Christine" (Apollinaire) 7:18, 36
"Lune de miel" (Eliot) 5:185, 191
Lupercal (Hughes) 7:115, 118-20, 123, 135-
    38, 140-41, 150, 158, 162-63, 165, 169
"Lustra" (Okigbo) 7:221, 225, 232, 239, 250
Lustra (Pound) 4:320, 365
"Lusts" (Verlaine)
    See "Luxures"
"Luxures" ("Lusts") (Verlaine) 2:416
Lyceia (Graves) 6:156
"Lycidas" (Arnold) 5:7
"The Lynching" (McKay) 2:205-06, 212, 217
"Lynching Song" (Hughes) 1:241

"La Lyre" (Ronsard) **11**:266

Lyrical Ballads (Coleridge) **11**:37, 59-60, 68, 91

Lyrical Ballads, with a Few Other Poems (Wordsworth) **4**:372-73, 375, 378, 380, 400, 412, 415-19, 425-29

"A Lyrick to Mirth" (Herrick) **9**:94, 103

Lyrics of Love and Laughter (Dunbar) **5**:119, 139

Lyrics of Lowly Life (Dunbar) **5**:117-18, 132, 136, 140

"Lysergic Acid" (Ginsberg) **4**:74, 81

"Lyubka" (Pasternak) **6**:253-54

"Ma bohème" ("My Bohemian Life") (Rimbaud) **3**:271, 276, 283

"Ma Man" (Hughes) **1**:270

"Macarius and the Pony" (Merton) **10**:351

"Macaw" (Bogan) **12**:86

Macchu Picchu (Neruda)
    See *Alturas de Macchu Picchu*

"Macpherson's Farewell" (Burns) **6**:55

"MacStatesman and Co." (MacDiarmid) **9**:176

"Mad Judy" (Hardy) **8**:102

"The Mad Maid's Song" (Herrick) **9**:87

"The Mad Monk" (Coleridge) **11**:69

"The Mad Mother" (Wordsworth) **4**:374, 380

"A Mad Negro Soldier Confined at Munich" (Lowell) **3**:205, 218, 222

"Mad Song" (Blake) **12**:31-2

"Madam and Her Might-Have Been" (Hughes) **1**:243

"Madam and the Wrong Visitor" (Hughes) **1**:243

"A Madame Sand" (Nerval) **13**:178

"Das Mädchen spricht" (Goethe) **5**:249

"Madeleine" (Apollinaire) **7**:32

"Mademoiselle Bistouri" (Baudelaire) **1**:58

"Mademoiselle Veronique" (Brodsky) **9**:10

"Madhouse Bells" (Browning) **2**:30

"Madhouse Cells" (Browning) **2**:26

"Madhumanjari" ("Honey Bud") (Tagore) **8**:416

The Madman, His Parables and Poems (Gibran) **9**:69, 71, 75, 77-80, 82

"Madness" (Baraka) **4**:27

"The Madonna" (Tennyson) **6**:353

"Madonna of the Evening Flowers" (Lowell) **13**:60, 64, 67, 96

"Madrid 1937" (Neruda) **4**:310

"Madrigal triste" (Baudelaire) **1**:61

"Madrigali privati" ("Private Madrigals") (Montale) **13**:106, 167

"Madurai" (Paz) **1**:361

"Le maestrine" ("The Schoolmistresses") (Pavese) **13**:221

"The Magellanic Heart" (Neruda)
    See "El corazón magellanico"

"Maggie a Lady" (Rossetti) **7**:291

"Magic" (Dove) **6**:113

"Magic" (Levertov) **11**:209

"The Magic Morning" (Smith) **12**:331

"Magna est Veritas" (Smith) **12**:333

The Magnetic Mountain (Day Lewis) **11**:123-26, 128-30, 135, 138-39, 143-45, 148, 151-52

"Magnolia Flower" (Hughes) **1**:237

"The Magnolia Shadow" (Montale)
    See "L'ombra della magnolia"

"Magnolias in Snow" (Hayden) **6**:194, 196

"Magpiety" (Milosz)
    See "Sroczość"

"Mahomets Gesang" (Goethe) **5**:247

Mahua (Tagore) **8**:415-16

"Maiden May" (Rossetti) **7**:277

"Maiden Song" (Rossetti) **7**:264, 274-76, 289

"The Maiden without Hands" (Sexton) **2**:365

"A Maiden's Pledge" (Hardy) **8**:98

"Maifest" ("May Festival") (Goethe) **5**:251

"Mailied" (Goethe) **5**:245

"Mailie's Dying Words and Elegy" (Burns)
    See "The Death and Dying Words of Poor Mailie"

"La maison des mortes" ("The House of the Dead") (Apollinaire) **7**:47

"Maithuna" (Paz) **1**:361, 368

"Le Majeur Ydow" (Smith) **12**:331

"Major Macroo" (Smith) **12**:309, 317

Majors and Minors (Dunbar) **5**:115, 117-18, 128, 132, 135-36, 142

"Making a Living" (Sexton) **2**:367

"Le mal" ("The Evil") (Rimbaud) **3**:283

"Malabaress" (Baudelaire) **1**:49

"Malachy Deagan" (Masters) **1**:343

"Malcolm" (Sanchez) **9**:224, 231

"Malcolm Spoke/Who listened? (This Poem Is for My Consciousness Too)" (Madhubuti) **5**:328, 341

"Il male di vivere" ("The Harm of Living") (Montale) **13**:105

"Le maline" (Rimbaud) **3**:283

"The Malingerer" (McKay) **2**:226

"Malmaison" (Lowell) **13**:71, 78, 84

"Malourène" (Apollinaire) **7**:48

"Mammy Hums" (Sandburg) **2**:324

"Man" (Herbert) **4**:100-01, 103

"The Man against the Sky" (Robinson) **1**:462, 471, 490, 492-94

The Man against the Sky (Robinson) **1**:462-63, 467-68, 474

"Man and Dog" (Sassoon) **12**:255

"Man and Wife" (Lowell) **3**:206, 209, 221, 245

"Man and Wife" (Sexton) **2**:363

Man Does, Woman Is (Graves) **6**:154

"The Man He Killed" (Hardy) **8**:102-03

"A Man I Am" (Smith) **12**:295

"Man in Black" (Plath) **1**:389

A Man in the Divided Sea (Merton) **10**:338, 346-47, 350

"Man into Men" (Hughes) **1**:241, 243

"Man is a Spirit" (Smith) **12**:297, 316

"A Man of the Middle Class" (Brooks) **7**:62

"The Man Seeking Experience Enquires His Way of a Drop of Water" (Hughes) **7**:116, 118

"The Man that are Falling" (Stevens) **6**:310

"Man, the Man-Hunter" (Sandburg) **2**:308

"Man the Master" (Merton) **10**:345

"Man Was Made to Mourn" (Burns) **6**:68

The Man Who Died Twice (Robinson) **1**:469, 472, 475, 477, 483, 489-90

"The Man Whose Pharynx Was Bad" (Stevens) **6**:294

"The Man with a Past" (Hardy) **8**:93

Man with a Sling (Neruda)
    See *El hondero entusiasta, 1923-1924*

"Man with One Small Hand" (Page) **12**:170

"The Man with the Blue Guitar" (Stevens) **6**:298, 323-24, 326, 337, 339

The Man with the Blue Guitar, and Other Poems (Stevens) **6**:304

"Manas-sundari" ("The Fair One in My Mind") (Tagore) **8**:408

"Mandalay" (Kipling) **3**:158, 160, 162, 167, 188-89, 192

"The Mandolin, the Carnation and the Bamboo" (Apollinaire)
    See "La mandoline, l'oeillet et le bambou"

"La mandoline, l'oeillet et le bambou" ("The Mandolin, the Carnation and the Bamboo") (Apollinaire) **7**:18, 20-2, 34, 36

"Mango Grove" (Tagore)
    See "Amravan"

"Manhattan May Day Midnight" (Ginsberg) **4**:84

"Mania di solitudine" ("Mania for solitude") (Pavese) **13**:225

"Mania for solitude" (Pavese)
    See "Mania di solitudine"

"Manicure" (Brooks) **7**:53

"The Man-Moth" (Bishop) **3**:37, 65

"The Manor Garden" (Plath) **1**:389

Las manos del día (*The Hands of Day*) (Neruda) **4**:288

"A Man's a Man for a' That" (Burns) **6**:60

"Man's Medley" (Herbert) **4**:101, 127

"Mantis" (Zukofsky) **11**:341, 347, 356, 392-99

"'Mantis,' an Interpretation" (Zukofsky) **11**:341, 356, 394

"Manual System" (Sandburg) **2**:304

"Manuelzinho" (Bishop) **3**:59-60

Many Inventions (Kipling) **3**:160

"The Many Mansions" (Levertov) **11**:201

"Many Swans" (Lowell) **13**:61, 64-5, 83

"The Map" (Bishop) **3**:37, 50-2

The Map of Love (Thomas) **2**:381, 390

"Maple and Sumach" (Day Lewis) **11**:144

El mar y las campanas (*The Sea and the Bells*) (Neruda) **4**:287-88

"Marburg" (Pasternak) **6**:270-71, 281

"The March of the Cameron Men" (Robinson) **1**:476

"March Twilight" (Bogan) **12**:111

"La marche impériale" (Valery) **9**:391

"Margaret" (Sandburg) **2**:303

"Margaret" (Wordsworth) **4**:399

"I mari del sud" (Pavese) **13**:210, 212, 216, 220-24, 228

"Maria Stuart" (Pasternak) **6**:267

"Mariana" (Tennyson) **6**:359, 364, 387, 389, 391, 406-09, 411

"Mariana in the South" (Tennyson) **6**:350

"Marichika" ("Mirage") (Tagore) **8**:407

"Marijuana Notation" (Ginsberg) **4**:79

"Marina" (Eliot) **5**:164, 195, 205-06, 210

"Marine" (Rimbaud) **3**:261

"Mariposa de obsidiana" ("Obsidian Butterfly") (Paz) **1**:364

"The Mark" (Bogan) **12**:87-8, 98, 106, 121

"Market" (Hayden) **6**:194, 196

Marmion (Scott) **13**:249-51, 256, 258, 261, 264, 266-68, 270-71, 273, 275-76, 279, 281-85, 287-90, 304, 311-12, 317-18

"Marriage" (Moore) **4**:230-31, 233, 243, 249, 251-52, 254-55, 258, 260-61

"Le marriage d'André Salmon" (Apollinaire)
    See "Poème lu au mariage d'André Salmon"

"The Marriage II" (Levertov) **11**:167

"A Marriage in the Sixties" (Rich) **5**:363

The Marriage of Heaven and Hell (Blake) **12**:12, 28, 36, 39-41, 47-51, 60-1, 64

"The Marriage of Hector and Andromache" (Sappho) **5**:414, 418

"The Marriage of Lord Fauconberg and Lady Mary Cromwell" (Marvell) **10**:270
"The Marriage Ring" (Blake) **12**:34
"The Married Man" (Kipling) **3**:192
"Marshall Washer" (Carruth) **10**:74
"Marsyas" (Masters) **1**:329
"Martha" (Lorde) **12**:140, 157
"A Martial Law Carol" (Brodsky) **9**:26-7
"Martirio de Santa Olalla" ("Martyrdom of Saint Eulalia") (Garcia Lorca) **3**:132, 146
"The Martyr Poets Did Not Tell" (Dickinson) **1**:96
"A Martyr: The Vigil of the Feast" (Rossetti) **7**:285
"The Martyrdom of Bishop Farrar" (Hughes) **7**:112
"Martyrdom of Saint Eulalia" (Garcia Lorca)
  See "Martirio de Santa Olalla"
"Une martyre" (Baudelaire) **1**:45, 48, 62
The Marvelous Arithmetics of Distance (Lorde) **12**:153
"Mary" (Blake) **12**:35, 43
"The 'Mary Gloster'" (Kipling) **3**:161, 167, 181
"Mary Morison" (Burns)
  See "Ye Are Na Mary Morison"
"Mary, Pity Women" (Kipling) **3**:161, 192
"Mary Winslow" (Lowell) **3**:206, 217-18
"Marz has Ruined Nature, for the Moment" (Stevens) **6**:297
"The Mask" (Baudelaire)
  See "Le masque"
"The Masked Face" (Hardy) **8**:119
"Masked Woman's Song" (Bogan) **12**:100-01
"Masks of Dawn" (Paz) **1**:359
"Le masque" ("The Mask") (Baudelaire) **1**:45, 65, 72
A Masque of Mercy (Frost) **1**:211
"The Masque of Plenty" (Kipling) **3**:181
A Masque of Reason (Frost) **1**:203-04, 206, 217
"Masquerade in the Park" (Akhmatova) **2**:6
"Masqueraders" (Page) **12**:178
"Mass for the Day of St. Thomas Didymus" (Levertov) **11**:198, 200-01
"The Master" (H. D.) **5**:306
"The Master" (Robinson) **1**:461, 465, 467
"Master Herrick's Farewell unto Poetry" (Herrick)
  See "Farewell to Poetry"
"Master Hugues of Saxe-Gotha" (Browning) **2**:37, 61, 88
"The Masters of the Heart Touched the Unknown" (Schwartz) **8**:292
"The Match" (Marvell) **10**:271, 300
"Maternità" (Pavese) **13**:213
"Mathilde in Normady" (Rich) **5**:352, 359
"Matinée d'ivresse" (Rimbaud) **3**:261, 263, 271-73, 281-82
"Matins" (Levertov) **11**:166
"Matros v Moskve" ("Sailor in Moscow") (Pasternak) **6**:283
"Mattens" (Herbert) **4**:119
"Mattens, or Morning Prayer" (Herrick) **9**:118
Matthias at the Door (Robinson) **1**:473-74, 479
"Mattino" (Pavese) **13**:230
"Maturity" (Ginsberg) **4**:87
Maud, and Other Poems (Tennyson) **6**:354, 356-57, 360, 363, 366, 373, 379-80, 383, 385, 387, 407

"Maude Clare" (Rossetti) **7**:260, 280, 291
"Mausfallen-Sprüchlein" (Morike) **1**:114
"Le mauvais moine" (Baudelaire) **1**:59
"Le mauvais vitrier" ("The Bad Glazier") (Baudelaire) **1**:67
"Mawu" (Lorde) **12**:143
"May" (Rossetti) **7**:265
"May 24, 1980" (Brodsky) **9**:24
"May 1943" (H. D.) **5**:307
"May Festival" (Goethe)
  See "Maifest"
"May It Be" (Pasternak) **6**:261
The May Queen (Tennyson) **6**:359
"Mayavada" ("Theory of Maya") (Tagore) **8**:408
"The Mayor of Gary" (Sandburg) **2**:304, 308
"The Maypole Is Up" (Herrick) **9**:102, 145
"May's Love" (Browning) **6**:24
"M.B." (Brodsky) **9**:10
"McAndrew's Hymn" (Kipling) **3**:161, 167, 170, 186, 192
Me Again: Uncollected Writings of Stevie Smith (Smith) **12**:314, 333-34, 340, 343-44, 346-47
"Me from Myself to Banish" (Dickinson) **1**:94
"Me Whoppin' Big-Tree Boy" (McKay) **2**:226
"Meadow Milk" (Bogan) **12**:110
"Meaning" (Milosz) **8**:215
"Meat without Mirth" (Herrick) **9**:98
"Le médaillon toujours ferme" (Apollinaire) **7**:22
Le médecin malgré lui (Williams) **7**:349
Medicamina Faciei (Ovid) **2**:238-39, 243, 251, 253, 258
Medieval Scenes (Duncan) **2**:109
"Meditation" (Baudelaire)
  See "Recueillement"
"A Meditation for His Mistresse" (Herrick) **9**:101
"A Meditation in Tuscany" (Browning) **6**:16
"Mediterraneo" (Montale) **13**:115
Medny Vsadnik (*The Bronze Horseman*) (Pushkin) **10**:367-68, 373-74, 385, 390-400, 414
"Medusa" (Bogan) **12**:85, 104-06, 111-12, 115, 117
"Medusa" (Dove) **6**:123
"Meeting" (Arnold) **5**:42
"Meeting" (Montale)
  See "Incontro"
"A Meeting" (Pasternak)
  See "Vstrecha"
"The Meeting" (Rukeyser) **12**:231
"A Meeting of Minds" (Lorde) **12**:135
"Meeting-House Hill" (Lowell) **13**:67
"Mein Karren knarrt nicht mehr" (Celan) **10**:124
"A Mei-p'i Lake Song" (Tu Fu) **9**:330-31, 333
"Melancholia en Orizba" ("Melancholy in Orizaba") (Neruda) **4**:281
"Melancholy" (Bely) **11**:6
"Melancholy in Orizaba" (Neruda)
  See "Melancholia en Orizba"
Melancolía (Jimenez) **7**:211
"Melancthon" (Moore) **4**:254
"Mélange adultère de tout" (Eliot) **5**:185
"Mémoire" (Rimbaud) **3**:262, 268
"Memorabilia" (Masters) **1**:343
"Memorandum Confided by a Yucca to a Passion-Vine" (Lowell) **13**:61, 64

"Memorial" (Sanchez) **9**:224
"Memorial II" (Lorde) **12**:140, 157
"Memorial for the City" (Auden) **1**:23
"Memorial Tablet" (Sassoon) **12**:269
"Memories..." (Jimenez)
  See "Recuerdos..."
"Memories of the Forest" (Ishikawa Takuboku)
  See "Mori no omoide"
"Memories of West Street and Lepke" (Lowell) **3**:206, 208, 220, 223, 237
"Memory" (Bogan) **12**:101, 120, 122
"A Memory" (Pavese) **13**:203
"Memory" (Sassoon) **12**:269
"Memory I" (Rossetti) **7**:277
"The Memory of Elena" ("In Memory of Elena") (Forche) **10**:136, 139, 152-53, 166, 169
"Memory of V. I. Ulianov" (Zukofsky) **11**:396
"A Memory Picture" (Arnold) **5**:49
"Men" (Toomer) **7**:336
Men and Women (Browning) **2**:66, 77, 94
"Men Loved Wholly beyond Wisdom" (Bogan) **12**:104, 126
Men, Women, and Ghosts (Lowell) **13**:63, 71, 73, 76, 79, 85, 93
"Mending Wall" (Frost) **1**:225, 227, 229
"Menons Klagen um Diotima" ("Menon's Lament for Diotime") (Holderlin) **4**:141-42
"Menon's Lament for Diotime" (Holderlin)
  See "Menons Klagen um Diotima"
"Menschenbeitfall" ("Human Applause") (Holderlin) **4**:165
"Menses" (Millay) **6**:233
"Menstruation at Forty" (Sexton) **2**:363 .
"The Mental Traveller" (Blake) **12**:36, 46, 48
"The Merchantmen" (Kipling) **3**:161
"Merely Statement" (Lowell) **13**:86
"Meriggiare pallido e assorto" ("Pale, Intent Noontide") (Montale) **13**:105
Merlin: A Poem (Robinson) **1**:462-63, 465, 468-71, 482-83, 488-89, 491
"Merlin and the Gleam" (Tennyson) **6**:389, 407
"The Mermaid's Children" (Lowell) **3**:241
"The Mermen" (Crane) **3**:90
Merope (Arnold) **5**:8, 12, 35, 37, 45, 47, 58-60, 62-3
"The Merry Guide" (Housman) **2**:180, 192
"The Merry Muses" (Burns) **6**:96
"Merveilles de la guerre" (Apollinaire) **7**:3, 22
"Mes bouguins refemés" (Mallarme) **4**:199
"Mes petites amoureuses" ("My Little Lovers") (Rimbaud) **3**:262, 284
"Mescaline" (Ginsberg) **4**:74, 81
"Un mese fra i bambini" ("A Month among Children") (Montale) **13**:134
Les meslanges (Ronsard) **11**:247, 266
"Message" (Forche) **10**:139, 144, 154-55
"The Message" (Levertov) **11**:171
"The Message" (Sassoon) **12**:248
"A Message All Blackpeople Can Dig (& A Few Negroes Too)" ("And a Few Negroes Too") (Madhubuti) **5**:329, 341
"Message for the Sinecurist" (Gallagher) **9**:62
"Message from the NAACP" (Baraka) **4**:11
"Message to a Black Soldier" (Madhubuti) **5**:339
"The Messenger" (Atwood) **8**:18
"The Messenger" (Merton) **10**:339

"The Messenger" (Sassoon) **12**:259

"A Messenger from the Horizon" (Merton) **10**:334

"Messianic Eclogue" (Vergil)
See "Eclogue 4"

"The Metal and the Flower" (Page) **12**:168, 178

The Metal and the Flower (Page) **12**:167, 171, 193

Die Metamorphose der Pflanzen (Goethe) **5**:239-40

Metamorphoses (*Metamorphosis; The Transformation/Transformations*) (Ovid) **2**:233, 238-241, 244-45, 260

"Les métamorphoses du vampire" ("The Metamorphoses of the Vampire") (Baudelaire) **1**:48, 71

"The Metamorphoses of the Vampire" (Baudelaire)
See "Les métamorphoses du vampire"

"Metamorphosis" (Sitwell) **3**:304

Metamorphosis (Ovid)
See *Metamorphoses*

"Metaphors of a Magnifico" (Stevens) **6**:311-12

"Métropolitain" (Rimbaud) **3**:265

"Mexican Divertimento" ("Mexican Divertissement") (Brodsky) **9**:12

"Mexican Divertissement" (Brodsky)
See "Mexican Divertimento"

"Mezzo Forte" (Williams) **7**:405

"La mia musa" ("My Muse") (Montale) **13**:139

"Mia vita a te non chiedo lineamenti" (Montale) **13**:139

"Miami You Are About to be Surprised" (Merton) **10**:351

"MIA's (Missing in Action and Other Atlantas)" (Sanchez) **9**:230, 235, 244

"Michael" (Wordsworth) **4**:380-81, 394, 399, 402, 412, 414, 425, 428

"Michel et Christine" (Rimbaud) **3**:264, 281

"Middle of a Long Poem on 'These States'" (Ginsberg) **4**:47

"The Middle of Life" (Holderlin)
See "Hälfte des Lebens"

"Middle Passage" (Hayden) **6**:176-81, 183, 187-88, 194, 196-200

"The Middle-Aged" (Rich) **5**:362-63, 367, 369

"Midnight Chippie's Lament" (Hughes) **1**:255

"A Midnight Interior" (Sassoon) **12**:246

"Midnight Nan at Leroy's" (Hughes) **1**:246

"Midnight on the Great Western" (Hardy) **8**:107

"Midnight Verses" (Akhmatova) **2**:16

"A Midnight Woman to the Bobby" (McKay) **2**:224

"Midway" (Graves) **6**:143

"Midwinter, Presolstice" (Atwood) **8**:2

"Mientras dura vida, sobra el tiempo" (Forche) **10**:135

"Might These be Thrushes Climbing through Almost (Do They)" (Cummings) **5**:108

"The Mighty Flight" (Baraka) **4**:26

"Mignonne, allons voir si la rose" (Ronsard)
See "Ode à Cassandre: 'Mignonne, allon voir'"

"Milk-Wort and Bog Cotton" (MacDiarmid) **9**:160, 176, 199

"The Mill" (Robinson) **1**:468, 475, 478

"The Miller's Daughter" (Tennyson) **6**:350

"The Mills of the Kavanaughs" (Lowell) **3**:204, 206-07, 215, 217, 224, 226, 231

The Mills of the Kavanaughs (Lowell) **3**:204, 206-07, 215, 217, 224, 226, 231

Milton (Blake) **12**:13, 27, 30, 36-8, 42, 44-5, 50, 62-5, 73, 75-80

Minashiguri (*Empty Chestnuts*) (Matsuo Basho) **3**:11

Mind Breaths: Poems, 1972-1977 (Ginsberg) **4**:61, 82

"The Mind Hesitant" (Williams) **7**:390

"The Mind, Intractable Thing" (Moore) **4**:243

"The Mind is an Enchanted Thing" (Moore) **4**:261

Mine the Harvest (Millay) **6**:226, 231-33, 237, 242

"Mineral" (Page) **12**:170

"Minesweepers" (Kipling) **3**:183

"Miniver Cheevy" (Robinson) **1**:462, 467, 478, 487, 496

"Minnie and Mattie" (Rossetti) **7**:274

Minstrels (Sitwell) **3**:290

"Minstrel's Song, on the Restoration of Lord Clifford the Shepherd" (Wordsworth) **4**:377

The Minstrelsy of the Scottish Border (Scott) **13**:249, 269, 278, 281, 306

"The Minute before Meeting" (Hardy) **8**:90

"Mirabeau Bridge" (Apollinaire)
See "Le pont Mirabeau"

"A Miracle for Breakfast" (Bishop) **3**:46, 57

"Miracles" (Whitman) **3**:381

"Mirage" (Tagore)
See "Marichika"

"Mirage of the Desert" (Masters) **1**:344

"The Mirages" (Hayden) **6**:193, 197

"Miranda Dies in the Fog, 1816" (Neruda)
See "Miranda muere en la niebla, 1816"

"Miranda muere en la niebla, 1816" ("Miranda Dies in the Fog, 1816") (Neruda) **4**:295

"The Mirror in Which Two Are Seen as One" (Rich) **5**:368

"The Mirrors" (Williams) **7**:370

Miscellaneous Poems (Marvell) **10**:257, 277, 311

Miscellanies (Swift) **9**:251, 253, 255, 275

A Miscellany of New Poems (Behn) **13**:7

"Mise en Scene" (Lowell) **13**:96

"Miserie" (Herbert) **4**:108, 121

"Misery" (Hughes) **1**:328

"The Misfit" (Day Lewis) **11**:147

"Misgiving" (Frost) **1**:195

"Miss Drake Proceeds to Supper" (Plath) **1**:398-99

"Miss Gee" (Auden) **1**:30

"Mississippi Levee" (Hughes) **1**:256

"Mississippi Mother" (Brooks) **7**:96

"Mito" ("Myth") (Pavese) **13**:210, 228-29

Mock Beggar Hall (Graves) **6**:127-28

"Mock Confessional" (Ferlinghetti) **1**:187

"Modern Love" (Keats) **1**:311

"Modern Poetry Is Prose (But It Is Saying Plenty)" (Ferlinghetti) **1**:182-83

"A Modern Sappho" (Arnold) **5**:12

"Modes of Being" (Levertov) **11**:197-98

"A Modest Proposal" (Hughes) **7**:118

"Modulations for a Solo Voice" (Levertov) **11**:209

"Moesta et Errabunda" (Baudelaire) **1**:70

Mohn und Gedächtnes (*Poppy and Memory*) (Celan) **10**:95

"Moment of Eternity" (MacDiarmid) **9**:193

"Mon Dieu m'a dit" (Verlaine) **2**:415

"Monax" ("The Monk") (Pushkin) **10**:407

"Monet's 'Waterlilies'" (Hayden) **6**:183, 195

"La monja gitana" ("The Gypsy Nun") (Garcia Lorca) **3**:132

"The Monk" (Pushkin)
See "Monax"

"The Monkeys" (Moore) **4**:270

The Monkey's Cloak (Matsuo Basho)
See *Sarumino*

The Monkey's Raincoat (Matsuo Basho)
See *Sarumino*

"The Monk's Walk" (Dunbar) **5**:121, 137-38, 141

"Monna Innominata" (Rossetti) **7**:271, 275, 280-81

"Le monocle de mon oncle" (Stevens) **6**:292, 295, 303, 327

"Monody" (Zukofsky) **11**:368

"Monody on the Death of Chatterton" (Coleridge) **11**:49, 52

"Monotone" (Sandburg) **2**:303

Montage of a Dream Deferred (Hughes) **1**:244-45, 247-48, 251, 253, 258, 261, 263, 265-68, 270

"The Months: A Pageant" (Rossetti) **7**:280

"Montparnasse" (Apollinaire) **7**:34

La Montre; or, The Lover's Watch (*The Lovers Watch*) (Behn) **13**:3

"The Monument" (Bishop) **3**:37, 41-3, 48-9, 72

"Monument" (Pushkin)
See "Pamjatnik"

"Monument of Love" (Jimenez) **7**:184

"The Moon" (Carruth) **10**:71

"Moon and Insect Panorama: Love Poem" (Garcia Lorca) **3**:141

"The Moon and the Yew Tree" (Plath) **1**:390, 409

Moon Crossing Bridge (Gallagher) **9**:62-5

"The Moon in Your Hands" (H. D.) **5**:275

"Moon Tiger" (Levertov) **11**:177

"Moonlight" (Apollinaire)
See "Clair de lune"

"Moonlight" (Verlaine)
See "Clair de lune"

"Moonlight Night" (Tu Fu) **9**:321

"Moonlight Night: Carmel" (Hughes) **1**:240

"Moonrise" (Plath) **1**:406

"Moonrise" (Sappho) **5**:416

"Moon-Set" (Carruth) **10**:85

"Moonstruck" (MacDiarmid) **9**:160

The Moor of Peter the Great (Pushkin)
See *The Negro of Peter the Great*

"Moortown" (Hughes) **7**:162

Moortown (Hughes) **7**:157-58, 162-63, 165, 171

"The Moose" (Bishop) **3**:58-60, 73, 75

"The Moose Wallow" (Hayden) **6**:194-95

"Morality" (Arnold) **5**:42

"More Clues" (Rukeyser) **12**:225

More Poems (Housman) **2**:167, 171-74, 176, 182-83, 188

More Poems, 1961 (Graves) **6**:154-56

"Mori no michi" (" Forest Path") (Ishikawa Takuboku) **10**:213

"Mori no omoide" ("Memories of the Forest") (Ishikawa Takuboku) **10**:212-13

"Moriturus" (Millay) **6**:236

"Morning" (Wheatley)
See "An Hymn to the Morning"

"Morning" (Williams) 7:352
"Morning After" (Hughes) 1:256
"The Morning Baking" (Forche) 10:142
"The Morning Bell" (Ishikawa Takuboku)
   See "Akatsuki no kane"
"Morning Express" (Sassoon) 12:275
"A Morning Imagination of Russia"
   (Williams) 7:350
"Morning, Noon, and Night" (Page) 12:173
"A Morning Ride" (Kipling) 3:194
"Morning Song" (Plath) 1:390
Morning Songs (Tagore)
   See *Prabhat sangit*
"The Morning Star" (Pavese)
   See "Lo steddazzu"
"Morning-Land" (Sassoon) 12:240
"La Mort de Narcisse" (Ronsard) 11:251
"La mort des amants" ("The Death of
   Lovers"; "Death of the Lovers"; "Lover's
   Death") (Baudelaire) 1:54, 73
"La mort des artistes" (Baudelaire) 1:45
"La Mort du Soldat est près des choses
   naturelles (5 Mars)" (Stevens) 6:294
"Le mort joyeux" (Baudelaire) 1:45
"Mortal Girl" (Rukeyser) 12:231
"Morte d'Arthur" ("The Passing of Arthur")
   (Tennyson) 6:354, 358-59, 409
"La morte di Dio" ("The Death of God")
   (Montale) 13:133
"I morti" ("The Dead") (Montale) 13:105,
   112
"Mortification" (Herbert) 4:100-01, 120, 127,
   133
"Mortmain" ("Avenel Gray") (Robinson)
   1:470
"Morts de quatre-vingt-douze et de quatre-
   vingt-treize" (Rimbaud) 3:283
"The Most of It" (Frost) 1:205-06, 230-31
"Most Things at Second Hand through Gloves
   We Touch" (Schwartz) 8:293
"Motet" No. 1 (Montale) 13:120-22
"Motet" No. 2 (Montale) 13:120, 122
"Motet" No. 3 (Montale) 13:118-20
"Motet" No. 4 (Montale) 13:120
"Motet" No. 5 (Montale) 13:118, 121-22,
   125, 127
"Motet" No. 6 (Montale) 13:121-22, 150
"Motet" No. 7 (Montale) 13:119, 122
"Motet" No. 8 (Montale)
   See "Mottetto" No. 8
"Motet" No. 9 (Montale) 13:119, 122-24
"Motet" No. 10 (Montale) 13:123
"Motet" No. 11 (Montale) 13:124-25
"Motet" No. 12 (Montale) 13:124
"Motet" No. 13 (Montale) 13:124
"Motet" No. 14 (Montale) 13:124
"Motet" No. 15 (Montale) 13:125
"Motet" No. 17 (Montale) 13:125-26
"Motet" No. 18 (Montale) 13:125, 127
"Motet" No. 19 (Montale) 13:126
"Motet" No. 20 (Montale) 13:126
"Motet XX" (Montale) 13:136
"The Mother" (Brooks) 7:67
"Mother" (Smith) 12:326
The Mother (Sitwell) 3:299
"Mother, among the Dustbins" (Smith)
   12:352
"Mother and Daughter" (Sexton) 2:365
"Mother and Poet" (Browning) 6:30-1
"Mother Dear" (McKay) 2:222
"Mother Hubberd's Tale" (Spenser)
   See "Prosopopoia; or, Mother Hubberds
   Tale"
"Mother in Wartime" (Hughes) 1:252
"Mother Marie Therese" (Lowell) 3:205
"Mother to Son" (Hughes) 1:241, 248-49, 262
Mother, What is Man? (Smith) 12:326
"Mother-Right" (Rich) 5:384
"The Moth-Signal" (Hardy) 8:99
"Motion and Rest" (Toomer) 7:338
"The Motive for Metaphor" (Stevens) 6:312-
   13, 340
"Motor Lights on a Hill Road" (Lowell)
   13:60
"A Motorbike" (Hughes) 7:162
"Motteti" (Montale) 13:105
"Mottetto" No. 8 ("Motet" No. 8) (Montale)
   13:105, 113, 122, 127
"Motto" (Hughes) 1:267
"Motto to the Songs of Innocence and of
   Experience" (Blake) 12:10
"Mount Zion" (Hughes) 7:147
"The Mountain" (Frost) 1:226
Mountain Interval (Frost) 1:197, 202, 207,
   215
"Mountains" (Auden) 1:17
"Mountains" (Hayden) 6:194, 196
"Mountains" (Hughes) 7:137
"The Mourner's Bench" (Masters) 1:339, 343
"Mournin' for Religion" (Masters) 1:344
"Mourning" (Marvell) 10:271, 301, 314
"The Mouth of the Hudson" (Lowell) 3:215
"The Mouth of Truth" (Ferlinghetti) 1:183
"Move Un-noticed to be Noticed: A
   Nationhood Poem" (Madhubuti) 5:345
"Movies" (Hughes) 1:266
"The Mower against gardens" (Marvell)
   10:266, 293, 297
"The Mower to the Glo-Worms" (Marvell)
   10:266, 296-97, 315
"The Mower's Song" (Marvell) 10:266, 296-
   97
Moya Rodoslovnaya (*My Geneology*) (Pushkin)
   10:391
"Mozart, 1935" (Stevens) 6:296
"Mr. Burnshaw and the Statue" ("The Statue
   at the World's End") (Stevens) 6:297, 321
"Mr. Edwards and the Spider" (Lowell)
   3:215
"Mr. Eliot's Sunday Morning Service" (Eliot)
   5:184
"Mr. Flood's Party" (Robinson) 1:478
"Mr. Mine" (Sexton) 2:352
"Mr. Nixon" (Pound) 4:320
"Mr. Over" (Smith) 12:297, 339
"Mr. Seurat's Sunday Afternoon" (Schwartz)
   See "Seurat's Sunday Afternoon along the
   Seine"
"Mr. Sludge, 'The Medium'" (Browning)
   2:72, 82
"Mr. Styrax" (Pound) 4:317
"Mrs. Alfred Uruguay" (Stevens) 6:304
"Mrs Arbuthnot" (Smith) 12:314
"Mrs. Benjamin Pantier" (Masters) 1:347
"Mrs Simpkins" (Smith) 12:344
"Mrs. Small" (Brooks) 7:62, 69, 96-8
"Mrs. Walpurga" (Rukeyser) 12:204
"Mrs. Williams" (Masters) 1:347
"Muerte de Antoñito el Camborio" ("Death of
   Antoñito the Camborio") (Garcia Lorca)
   3:131
"Mugging" (Ginsberg) 4:85
"Muiopotmos; or, the Fate of the Butterflie"
   (Spenser) 8:365, 367-68, 371
"La mujer desnuda" ("Nothingness")
   (Jimenez) 7:213-14
La mujer desnuda (1918-1923) (Jimenez)
   7:213
"Mulatto" (Hughes) 1:238, 263-64, 270
"Mulholland's Contract" (Kipling) 3:161
"The Munich Mannequins" (Plath) 1:384,
   391
"The Murder" (Brooks) 7:68
"The Murder" (Page) 12:178
The Murder of Lidice (Millay) 6:220
A Muriel Rukeyser Reader (Rukeyser) 12:234
Museum (Dove) 6:104-07, 109, 115-16, 118,
   121
"Mushrooms" (Atwood) 8:43
"Mushrooms" (Plath) 1:389, 404, 406, 408
"Music" (Herbert) 4:100
"Music" (Pasternak)
   See "Muzyka"
"Music Swims Back to Me" (Sexton) 2:359
"A Musical Instrument" (Browning) 6:23
"The Musical Voice" (Ishikawa Takuboku)
   See "Gakusei"
"The Musician" (Bogan) 12:124
"Musicks Empire" (Marvell) 10:313
"Mussel Hunter at Rock Harbour" (Plath)
   1:388, 407
"Mutabilitie Cantos" (Spenser)
   See "Cantos of Mutabilitie"
"Mutra" (Paz) 1:369
"Muzhestvo" ("Courage") (Akhmatova) 2:19
"Muzyka" ("Music") (Pasternak) 6:288
"Mwilu/or Poem for the Living" (Madhubuti)
   5:346
"My Bohemian Life" (Rimbaud)
   See "Ma bohème"
"My Cats" (Smith) 12:339
"My Comforter" (Burroughs) 8:51
"My Corn-cob Pipe" (Dunbar) 5:133
"My Daughter the Junkie on a Train" (Lorde)
   See "To My Daughter the Junkie on a
   Train"
"My Dear and Loving Husband" (Bradstreet)
   See "To My Dear and Loving Husband His
   Goeing into England"
"My Doves" (Browning) 6:21
"My Dreams Are a Field Afar" (Housman)
   2:182
"My Dreams, My Work, Must Wait till after
   Hell" (Brooks) 7:74
"My Fairy Godmother" (Hyde) 7:147
"My Father Moved through Dooms of Feel"
   (Cummings)
   See "My Father Moved through Dooms of
   Love"
"My Father Moved through Dooms of Love"
   ("My Father Moved through Dooms of
   Feel") (Cummings) 5:81, 89
"My Friend" (Gibran) 9:77
My Geneology (Pushkin)
   See *Moya Rodoslovnaya*
"My Grandmother's Love Letters" (Crane)
   3:98
"My Granny's Hieland Hame" (Burns) 6:98
"My Hat" (Smith) 12:331
"My Heart and I" (Browning) 6:23
"My Heart Goes Out" (Smith) 12:318, 325
"My Heart Was Full" (Smith) 12:333
"My Hero's Genealogy" (Pushkin)
   See "Rodoslovnaya Moego Geroya"

"My Kate" (Browning) **6**:23

"My Lady of the Castle Grand" (Dunbar)
5:134, 138

"My Lady's Lamentation and Complaint
against the Dean" (Swift) **9**:295-96

"My Last Afternoon with Uncle Devereux
Winslow" (Lowell) **3**:219, 222

"My Last Duchess" (Browning) **2**:37, 94

"My Life with the Wave" (Paz) **1**:354

"My Light with Yours" (Masters) **1**:333

"My Little Lovers" (Rimbaud)
See "Mes petites amoureuses"

"My Luve Is Like a Red, Red Rose" ("A Red,
Red Rose") (Burns) **6**:75, 77, 99

"My Mother Remembers That She Was
Beautiful" (Gallagher) **9**:58

"My Mother Would Be a Falconress"
(Duncan) **2**:127

"My Mountain Home" (McKay) **2**:222

"My Muse" (Montale)
See "La mia musa"

"My Muse" (Smith) **12**:312, 324, 336

"My Native Land, My Home" (McKay)
2:216, 224

"My New-Cut Ashlar" (Kipling) **3**:183

"My Own Sweet Good" (Brooks) **7**:55

"My People" ("Laughters") (Hughes) **1**:270

"My Portrait" (Pushkin) **10**:407

"My Pretty Dan" (McKay) **2**:221

"My Pretty Rose Tree" (Blake) **12**:34

"My Silks in Fine Array" (Blake) **12**:31

My Sister, Life (Pasternak)
See *Sestra moia zhizn*

"My Soldier Lad" (McKay) **2**:223

"My Songs" (Yosano Akiko)
See "Waga Uta"

"My Sort of Man" (Dunbar) **5**:131

"My Soul" (Bradstreet) **10**:60-1

"My Soul Accused Me" (Dickinson) **1**:94

"My Spectre around Me" (Blake) **12**:13

"My Spirit Will Not Haunt the Mound"
(Hardy) **8**:118

"My Star" (Browning) **2**:59

"My Sweet Brown Gal" (Dunbar) **5**:119

"My Voice Not Being Proud" (Bogan)
12:101, 120

"Mycerinus" (Arnold) **5**:13, 33-4, 37, 39, 48

"My-ness" (Milosz) **8**:179

"Myopia: A Night" (Lowell) **3**:215

"Myrtho" (Nerval) **13**:180

"Myself Was Formed—a Carpenter"
(Dickinson) **1**:96

"The Mysteries" (H. D.) **5**:305

"'Mystery Boy' Looks for Kin in Nashville"
(Hayden) **6**:196

Mystics and Zen Masters (Merton) **10**:352

"Mystique" (Rimbaud) **3**:260

"Myth" (Pavese)
See "Mito"

"Myth" (Rukeyser) **12**:228

"A Mythology Reflects its Region" (Stevens)
6:306

Na rannikh poezdakh (*On Early Trains*)
(Pasternak) **6**:282

"The Nabara" ("The Loss of The Nabara")
(Day Lewis) **11**:127, 130-31, 144

Nachtgesänge (*Nightsongs*) (Holderlin) **4**:142,
146, 148, 166

"Nacimiento de Cristo" ("The Birth of
Christ") (Garcia Lorca) **3**:141

"Nada" (Jimenez) **7**:202

"Nadezhdoi Sladostnoi" ("Sweet Hopes")
(Pushkin) **10**:412

"Nafsī muthqa ah bi athmāriha" (Gibran)
9:82

"Nah, im Aortenbogen" (Celan) **10**:101

"The Nail" (Hughes) **7**:143

"A Naive Poem" (Milosz)
See "The World"

Naivedya (Tagore) **8**:411-13

"Naked and Essential" (Montale) **13**:141

"A Name for All" (Crane) **3**:90, 104

"Nameless" (Pasternak)
See "Bez nazvaniya"

"Names" (Hayden) **6**:194

"The Nana-Hex" (Sexton) **2**:365

"The Nape of the Neck" (Graves) **6**:166

"Napoleon na El'be" ("Napoleon on the
Elba") (Pushkin) **10**:409, 421

"Napoleon on the Elba" (Pushkin)
See "Napoleon na El'be"

"Narcisse parle" ("Narcissus Speaks") (Valery)
9:350, 356, 363, 365, 385, 392, 395

"Narcissus Speaks" (Valery)
See "Narcisse parle"

"Narikel" ("Coconut Palm") (Tagore) **8**:416

Narraciones (Garcia Lorca) **3**:148

The Narrow Pond (Matsuo Basho)
See *Oku no hosomichi*

The Narrow Road to the Deep North (Matsuo
Basho)
See *Oku no hosomichi*

"I nascondigli" (Montale) **13**:138

"The Nation Is Like Ourselves" (Baraka)
4:19

"Nationality in Drinks" (Browning) **2**:59

"The Native Born" (Kipling) **3**:161-62

Native Land (Rich)
See *Your Native Land, Your Life*

"A Nativity (1914-18)" (Kipling) **3**:183, 189

"Natrabach i na cytrze" ("With Trumpets and
Zithers") (Milosz) **8**:186, 214

"Natural Resources" (Rich) **5**:374, 380, 384-
85

"Naturally" (Gallagher) **9**:43

"Nature" (Masters) **1**:336

"Nature and Free Animals" (Smith) **12**:323

"Nature morte" (Brodsky) **9**:4, 12

"Nature's Lineaments" (Graves) **6**:150-51

"Nature's Questioning" (Hardy) **8**:96

"Navidad en el Hudson" ("Christmas on the
Hudson") (Garcia Lorca) **3**:141

"Ne Plus Ultra" (Coleridge) **11**:52

"Near, as All That Is Lost" (Gallagher) **9**:64

"Near Keokuk" (Sandburg) **2**:332

"Near Lanivet, 1872" (Hardy) **8**:97, 125-26

"Near the Ocean" (Lowell) **3**:226-28, 233

Near the Ocean (Lowell) **3**:232

Necessities of Life: Poems, 1962-1965 (Rich)
5:356, 363-64, 370-71, 382, 388-89, 397

"The Neckan" (Arnold) **5**:12

"The Necktie and the Watch" (Apollinaire)
See "La cravate et la montre"

"Need: A Chorale for Black Women's Voices"
(Lorde) **12**:144, 154, 156, 158

"The Need of Being Versed in Country
Things" (Frost) **1**:229, 231

"A Needed Poem for My Salvation" (Sanchez)
9:208-09

"Negro Dancers" (Hughes) **1**:236

"The Negro Hero" (Brooks) **7**:86

"A Negro Love Song" (Dunbar) **5**:132, 142

The Negro of Peter the Great (*The Moor of
Peter the Great*; *The Nigger of Peter the
Great*) (Pushkin) **10**:394

"Negro Servant" (Hughes) **1**:247

"A Negro Speaks of Rivers" (Hughes) **1**:241-
42, 248, 258-59, 263, 268

"Negro Spiritual" (McKay) **2**:214

"Neither Out Far nor in Deep" (Frost) **1**:197,
218, 227-28

"Neither Sweet Pity, nor Lamentable
Weeping" (Ronsard)
See "Ny la douce pitie, ny le pleur
lamentable"

"Nel Mezzo del Commin di Nostra Vita"
(Duncan) **2**:103

"Nel parco di Caserta" (Montague) **13**:

"Nel parco di Caserta" (Montale) **13**:127

"Nel sonno" ("In Sleep") (Montale) **13**:107,
128, 150

"Nella serra" ("In the Greenhouse") (Montale)
13:110

"Nestor's Bathtub" (Dove) **6**:109

Neue Gedichte (*New Poems*) (Rilke) **2**:266-68,
275

Der neue Pausias und sein Blumenmädchen
(Goethe) **5**:239-40

"The Neurotic" (Day Lewis) **11**:147

"Neutral Tones" (Hardy) **8**:88, 126, 130

"Never Again Would Birds' Song Be the
Same" (Frost) **1**:231

"Never Such Love" (Graves) **6**:137

"Never to Dream of Spiders" (Lorde) **12**:143

"The New Age" (Smith) **12**:313, 316

New Collected Poems (Graves) **6**:166

"New Hampshire" (Eliot) **5**:166, 169

New Hampshire (Frost) **1**:215, 224

"New Heavens for Old" (Lowell) **13**:85, 88

"New Legends" (Graves) **6**:149

A New Lovesong for Stalingrad (Neruda)
See *Nuevo canto de amor a Stalingrado*

"New Morality" (Coleridge) **11**:102-03

New Poems (Arnold) **5**:12, 43, 50

New Poems (Montale) **13**:143-46

New Poems (Rilke)
See *Neue Gedichte*

New Poems (Rilke) **2**:280-81

New Poems, 1962 (Graves) **6**:154

"A New Psalm for the Chapel of Kilmarnock"
(Burns) **6**:89

"A New Reality Is Better Than a New
Movie!" (Baraka) **4**:30

"A New Record" (Duncan) **2**:103

"The New Sheriff" (Baraka) **4**:10, 15

"The New Sirens" (Arnold) **5**:5, 39

A New Song (Hughes) **1**:242, 250, 253-54, 268

The New Spoon River (Masters) **1**:333-34,
344-45

"New Stanzas" (Montale)
See "Nuove stanze"

"New Stanzas to Augusta" (Brodsky)
See "Novye stansy k Avguste"

"New Thoughts on Old Subjects" (Coleridge)
11:105

The New World (Masters) **1**:339

New Year Letter (Auden) **1**:16, 21, 23-24, 34

"The New Yeares Gift, or Circumcision Song"
(Herrick)
See "Another New-yeeres Gift; or song for
the Circumcision"

"New Year's Eve" (Hardy) **8**:104, 119

"New Year's Gift" (Herrick)

See "A New-Yeares Gift Sent to Sir Simeon Steward"

"New York 1962: Fragment" (Lowell)   **3**:215

"New York at Night" (Lowell)   **13**:79

"New York City 1970" (Lorde)   **12**:146, 158

The New York Head Shop and Museum (Lorde)   **12**:146-47, 154

"New York: Office and Denunciation" (Garcia Lorca)
See "Nueva York: Oficina y denuncia"

"Newcomer" (Okigbo)   **7**:233, 240

"News from Mount Amiata" (Montale)
See "Notizie dall'Amiata"

"Newsreel: Man and Firing Squad" (Atwood)   **8**:23

"A New-Yeares Gift Sent to Sir Simeon Steward" ("New Year's Gift") (Herrick)   **9**:102, 145

"Next to of Course God America I" (Cummings)   **5**:89

"A Nice Shady Home" (Stevens)   **6**:292

"Nick and the Candlestick" (Plath)   **1**:390

"Nicodemus" (Robinson)   **1**:476, 485

Die Niemandsrose (*The No One's Rose; The Nobody's Rose; No-man's Rose*) (Celan)   **10**:95, 98-99, 113, 117, 121

"Nigerian Unity/or Little Niggers Killing Little Niggers" (Madhubuti)   **5**:329, 341-42

"Nigger" (Sanchez)   **9**:223, 232

The Nigger of Peter the Great (Pushkin)
See *The Negro of Peter the Great*

"Nigger Song: An Odyssey" (Dove)   **6**:105;

"Niggy the Ho" (Baraka)   **4**:29, 38

"Night" (Blake)   **12**:7-8, 23, 33, 61

"Night" (Bogan)   **12**:96, 104

"Night" (Celan)   **10**:112

"Night" (Pasternak)
See "Noch'"

"Night" (Pavese)
See "La notte"

"Night" (Rilke)   **2**:275

"Night Bear Which Frightened Cattle" (Atwood)   **8**:39

"The Night Before" (Robinson)   **1**:460

"The Night before Great Babylon" (Sitwell)   **3**:310

"The Night Dances" (Plath)   **1**:388, 390

"Night, Death, Mississippi" (Hayden)   **6**:194, 196

"Night, Four Songs" (Hughes)   **1**:240

"Night in Maine" (Lowell)   **3**:226

"Night in the Old Home" (Hardy)   **8**:105

"The Night Is Freezing Fast" (Housman)
See "*Last Poems*: XX—The Night Is Freezing Fast"

"The Night My Father Got Me" (Housman)   **2**:191

"A Night Piece" (Smart)   **13**:341, 347

"Night Pleasures" (Pavese)
See "Piaceri notturni"

"Night Shift" (Plath)   **1**:388

"Night Song of an Asiatic Wandering Shepherd" (Montale)
See "Canto notturno di un pastore errante nell'Asia"

"Night Thoughts" (Smith)   **12**:337

"The Night-Blooming Cereus" (Hayden)   **6**:194-95, 198

The Night-Blooming Cereus (Hayden)   **6**:182, 184, 187, 190, 194

"Nightbreak" (Rich)   **5**:358

"Night-Flowering Cactus" (Merton)   **10**:334

"The Nightingale" (Coleridge)   **11**:85, 106

"Nightingale" (Keats)
See "Ode to a Nightingale"

"The Nightingales" (Williams)   **7**:345

"Nightmare" (Lowell)   **13**:78

"Nightmare" (Page)   **12**:168

"Night-Music" (Rukeyser)   **12**:209, 211

"Night-Piece" (Sassoon)   **12**:240

"The Night-Piece to Julia" (Herrick)   **9**:94, 132

"Nights and Days" (Rich)   **5**:375

Nightsongs (Holderlin)
See *Nachtgesänge*

"Night-Time in the Cemetery" (Smith)   **12**:316

"The Nihilist as Hero" (Lowell)   **3**:229

"Nilamanilata" ("Blue Gem Creeper") (Tagore)   **8**:416

"Nimmo" (Robinson)   **1**:468

"Nimrod in September" (Sassoon)   **12**:278

"Nina Replies" (Rimbaud)
See "Les reparties de Nina"

"Nine Poems for the Unborn Child" (Rukeyser)   **12**:228

"1909" (Apollinaire)   **7**:46-7

"1963" (Dove)   **6**:106

95 Poems (Cummings)   **5**:109-10

Ninfeas (*Water Lilies*) (Jimenez)   **7**:197, 199

"Ninth Elegy" (Rilke)   **2**:281, 286-87

"Ninth Elegy: The Antagonists" (Rukeyser)   **12**:223

"Ninth Psalm" (Sexton)   **2**:367

"The Ninth Symphony of Beethoven Understood at Last as a Sexual Message" (Rich)   **5**:360, 370

"Niobe in Distress for Her Children Slain by Apollo" (Wheatley)   **3**:338, 355, 357-60

Niobjeta ziemia (*Unattainable Earth*) (Milosz)   **8**:179, 211

"Nipping Pussy's Feet in Fun" (Smith)   **12**:339

"Nirbhay" ("Fearless") (Tagore)   **8**:415

"Nirjharer svapnabhanga" ("Awakening of the Waterfall") (Tagore)   **8**:406

"Niruddesh yatra" ("Aimless Journey") (Tagore)   **8**:408

"Nishikigizuka" ("The Commemorative Mound of the Decorated Tree") (Ishikawa Takuboku)   **10**:213

"No Buyers: A Street Scene" (Hardy)   **8**:101

"No Coward Soul Is Mine" (Bronte)   **8**:51, 60, 69-70

"¿No hay salida?" ("Is There No Way Out?") (Paz)   **1**:364

"No Hearing (Discovering)" (Lowell)   **3**:228

"No more" (Milosz)   **8**:190, 193

"No More Ghosts" (Graves)   **6**:132

"No More Marching" (Madhubuti)   **5**:339

The No One's Rose (Celan)
See *Die Niemandsrose*

"No Possom, No Sop, No Taters" (Stevens)   **6**:302

"No, Thank You, John!" (Rossetti)   **7**:267, 281, 291

No Thanks (Cummings)   **5**:106-07

Noah and the Waters (Day Lewis)   **11**:127-28, 144, 152-53

"The Nobel Prize" (Pasternak)
See "Nobelevskaya premiya"

"Nobelevskaya premiya" ("The Nobel Prize") (Pasternak)   **6**:268, 284

"The Noble Lady's Tale" (Hardy)   **8**:99

Noble Numbers, or Pious Pieces (Herrick)
See *His Noble Numbers: or, His Pious Pieces, Wherein (amongst Other Things) He Sings the Birth of His Christ: and Sighes for His Saviours Suffering on the Crosse*

"Noble Sisters" (Rossetti)   **7**:272, 274, 276, 280

"Nobody Comes" (Hardy)   **8**:101, 125

The Nobody's Rose (Celan)
See *Die Niemandsrose*

Les Noces d'Hérodiade (Mallarme)
See *Hérodiade*

"Noch'" ("Night") (Pasternak)   **6**:285

"Nocturnal Pleasures" (Pavese)
See "Piaceri notturni"

"A Nocturnal upon S. Lucies day, Being the shortest day" ("St. Lucies Day") (Donne)   **1**:130, 134, 149-50, 154

"Nocturne" (Pavese)
See "Notturno"

"Nocturne in a Deserted Brickyard" (Sandburg)   **2**:301, 303

"Nocturne of the Void" (Garcia Lorca)
See "Nocturno del hueco"

"Nocturne vulgaire" (Rimbaud)   **3**:264

"Nocturno de San Ildefonso" ("San Ildefonso Nocturne") (Paz)   **1**:370-72, 375

"Nocturno del hueco" ("Nocturne of the Void") (Garcia Lorca)   **3**:139

"Nodier raconte" (Pound)   **4**:317

"A Noiseless Patient Spider" (Whitman)   **3**:390

"Nomad Exquisite" (Stevens)   **6**:293

No-man's Rose (Celan)
See *Die Niemandsrose*

"Le non godute" (Gozzano)   **10**:184

"None with Him" (Rossetti)   **7**:276, 284

Nones (Auden)   **1**:23

"Nonsun Blob a" (Cummings)   **5**:109

"Noon Walk on the Asylum Lawn" (Sexton)   **2**:359

"Noone' Autumnal This Great Lady's Gaze" (Cummings)   **5**:107

"A Noon-Piece" (Smart)   **13**:347

"Nor We of Her to Him" (Smith)   **12**:326, 330

"Nora" (Toomer)   **7**:317

"Norma" (Sanchez)   **9**:234

"Norma y paraíso de los negros" ("Standards and Paradise of the Blacks") (Garcia Lorca)   **3**:150

"North American Time" (Rich)   **5**:395

"North and South" (McKay)   **2**:207

North & South (Bishop)   **3**:37, 39, 50

"North Labrador" (Crane)   **3**:83

North of Boston (Frost)   **1**:193-95, 202, 207, 214, 217, 223-26

"The North Sea Undertaker's Complaint" (Lowell)   **3**:216

"North Wind" (Montale)
See "Tramontana"

North Winter (Carruth)   **10**:70-71

"Northern Elegies" (Akhmatova)   **2**:4, 18

"The Northern Farmer" (Tennyson)   **6**:358, 360

"The Northern Farmer--Old Style" (Tennyson)   **6**:406

Northern Heroic (Bely)
See *Severnaia simfoniia: Pervia geroicheskaia*

"Northern Liberal" (Hughes)   **1**:252

"The Northern Sea" (Ishikawa Takuboku)
See "Kita no umi"

Northern Symphony (Bely)
  See *Severnaia simfoniia: Pervia geroicheskaia*
"Northumberland House" (Smith) **12**:296
Northwest Ecolog (Ferlinghetti) **1**:187
"Nossis" (H. D.) **5**:268
"Nostalgia" (Jimenez)
  See "Nostaljia"
"Nostaljia" ("Nostalgia") (Jimenez) **7**:201
"Not Every Day Fit for Verse" (Herrick)
  9:114
"The Not Impossible Him" (Millay)
  See "To the Not Impossible Him"
"Not Like Dante" (Ferlinghetti) **1**:182
"Not So Far as the Forest" (Millay) **6**:238
"Not So, Not So" (Sexton) **2**:373
"Not There" (Gallagher) **9**:59
"Not Waving but Drowning" (Smith) **12**:293,
  300, 307, 319-21, 324, 328, 331, 333, 337,
  347, 349, 354
Not Waving but Drowning (Smith) **12**:292-93
"Not with libations, but with Shouts and
  Laughter" (Millay) **6**:211, 244-46
"Notebook" (Levertov)
  See "From a Notebook, October '68—May
    '69"
Notebook 1967-68 (Lowell) **3**:223-26, 231-32,
  239-40
"The Notebook in the Gate-legged Table"
  (Lowell) **13**:84
The Note-Book of William Blake (Blake)
  12:11, 34-5
"Notes for a Little Play" (Hughes) **7**:130, 152
"Notes for a Speech" (Baraka) **4**:5
"Notes From Robin Hill Cottage" (Carruth)
  10:85
"Notes on a Conspiracy" (Rose) **13**:241
"Notes toward a Poem That Can Never Be
  Written" (Atwood) **8**:18, 43
Notes toward a Supreme Fiction (Stevens)
  6:310, 314, 324, 326-37, 329, 335, 337
"Nothing Down" (Dove) **6**:110, 112
Nothing for Tigers: Poems, 1959-1964 (Carruth)
  10:70
"Nothing Gold Can Stay" (Frost) **1**:194
"(Nothing Whichful About" (Cummings)
  5:108
"Nothingness" (Jimenez)
  See "La mujer desnuda"
"Notizie dall'Amiata" ("News from Mount
  Amiata") (Montale) **13**:106, 121, 127
"La notte" ("Night") (Pavese) **13**:230
"Notturno" ("Nocturne") (Pavese) **13**:230
"Noubousse" (Apollinaire) **7**:48
"November" (Hughes) **7**:119, 132-33, 136
"November Cotton Flower" (Toomer) **7**:319,
  333-34
"The Novices" (Levertov) **11**:169
"Novye stansy k Avguste" ("New Stanzas to
  Augusta") (Brodsky) **9**:4
"Now" (Sexton) **2**:352
"Now Air Is Air and Thing Is Thing: No
  Bliss" (Cummings) **5**:110
"Now Close the Windows" (Frost) **1**:197
"Now Does Our World Descend" (Cummings)
  5:111
"Now He Knows All There Is to Know: Now
  He Is Acquainted with the Day and Night"
  (Schwartz) **8**:319
"Now Hollow Fires" (Housman) **2**:189
"Now It Is You I Praise, Banner" (Rilke)
  2:273
"Now Pine-Needles" (Smith) **12**:318

"Now That I Am Never Alone" (Gallagher)
  9:62
"Now the Record Now Record" (Duncan)
  2:103
"Now This Cold Man" ("This Cold Man")
  (Page) **12**:168, 170, 178, 184
Nozarashi Diary (Matsuo Basho) **3**:6
Nozarashi kikō (*An Account of a
  Weatherbeaten Journey; Records of a
  Weather Exposed Skeleton*) (Matsuo Basho)
  3:11, 28
"The Nude Swim" (Sexton) **2**:352
"Nude Young Dancer" (Hughes) **1**:246
"Nueva York: Oficina y denuncia" ("New
  York: Office and Denunciation") (Garcia
  Lorca) **3**:141, 151
Nuevo canto de amor a Stalingrado (*A New
  Lovesong for Stalingrad*) (Neruda) **4**:279-80
"La nuit blanche" (Kipling) **3**:172
"Nuit blanche" (Lowell) **13**:89-90
"La nuit d'Avril, 1915" (Apollinaire) **7**:3
"Nullo" (Toomer) **7**:320, 330-31, 334
"Number Man" (Sandburg) **2**:322
"Number Three on the Docket" (Lowell)
  13:79, 84-5
"Numbers" (Hughes) **1**:267
"Numbers" (Smith) **12**:317
"Numbers, Letters" (Baraka) **4**:19
"Numpholeptos" (Browning) **2**:86, 88
"Nunc dimittis" (Brodsky) **9**:5
"A Nun's Complaint" (Rilke) **2**:270
"Nuns Fret Not" (Millay) **6**:242
"Nuns in the Wind" (Rukeyser) **12**:211
"Nuove stanze" ("New Stanzas") (Montale)
  13:106, 120-21
"A Nuptiall Song, or Epithalamie on Sir
  Clipseby Crew and His Lady" ("Epithalamie
  on Sir Clipseby Crew and His Lady";
  "Epithalamion") (Herrick) **9**:86, 102, 139
"Nursery Rhymes for Little Anglo-Indians"
  (Kipling) **3**:190
"Nurse's Song" (Blake) **12**:7, 21-2, 34
"Nursing Home" (Page) **12**:176
Nux (Ovid) **2**:244
"Ny la douce pitie, ny le pleur lamentable"
  ("Neither Sweet Pity, nor Lamentable
  Weeping") (Ronsard) **11**:278
"The Nymph and the Faun" (Marvell)
  See "The Nymph Complaining for the
    Death of Her Faun"
"The Nymph Complaining for the Death of
  Her Faun" ("The Nymph and the Faun")
  (Marvell) **10**:260-62, 266-67, 271, 274, 277,
  290, 294, 297, 301-02, 309-10, 315-16, 319,
  325
"O Captain! My Captain!" (Whitman) **3**:404,
  418, 422
"O Carib Isle!" (Crane) **3**:90
"O City, City" (Schwartz) **8**:302, 316
"O Daedalus, Fly Away Home" (Hayden)
  6:176, 179, 189
"O Dreams, O Destinations" (Day Lewis)
  11:145
"O Florida, Venereal Soil" (Stevens) **6**:305,
  339
"O Glorious France" (Masters) **1**:342
"O Happy Dogs of England" (Smith) **12**:318,
  330
"O Lady, when the Tipped Cup of the Moon
  Blessed You" (Hughes) **7**:113
"O Lay Thy Loof in Mine, Lass" (Burns)
  6:76

"O, Let Me in This Ae Night" (Burns) **6**:81
"O Love, Sweet Animal" (Schwartz) **8**:313
"O Love, the Interest Itself in Thoughtless
  Heaven..." (Auden) **1**:22
"O Mon Dieu, vous m'avez blessé d'amour"
  (Verlaine) **2**:416
"O Pug!" (Smith) **12**:301
"O saisons, ô châteaux!" (Rimbaud) **3**:275
"O Sweet Spontaneous" (Cummings) **5**:105
"O Taste and See" (Levertov) **11**:169
O Taste and See (Levertov) **11**:159, 169, 171,
  211
"O, Tempora! O Mores!" (Poe) **1**:449
"O to Be a Dragon" (Moore) **4**:249
"O Wander Not So Far Away!" (Burroughs)
  8:73
"O Wha's Been Here afore Me, Lass"
  (MacDiarmid) **9**:155, 160
"O Word I Love to Sing" (McKay) **2**:217,
  219
"O Ye Tongues" (Sexton) **2**:367, 372-73
Oak and Ivy (Dunbar) **5**:128, 132
"Obedience" (Herbert) **4**:119, 125-26
"Obermann Once More" (Arnold) **5**:19, 63-4
"Oberon's Chappell" (Herrick)
  See "The Fairie Temple: or, Oberons
    Chappell. Dedicated to Mr. John
    Merrifield, Counsellor at Law"
"Oberon's Feast" (Herrick) **9**:90
"Oberon's Palace" (Herrick) **9**:86, 90, 137
"Obituary for a Living Lady" (Brooks)
  7:66-7, 69
"The Objection to Being Stepped On" (Frost)
  1:215
"Oblique Prayers" (Levertov) **11**:198, 201
Oblique Prayers (Levertov) **11**:198, 200-02,
  209
"Oblivion" (Smith) **12**:317, 354
Observations (Moore) **4**:229-30, 244, 249-52
"The Observer" (Rich) **5**:370
"Obsidian Butterfly" (Paz)
  See "Mariposa de obsidiana"
Obus couleur de lune (Apollinaire) **7**:22
"Occasioned by Sir William Temple's Late
  Illness and Recovery" (Swift) **9**:250
Le occasioni (*The Occasions*) (Montale)
  13:103-05, 108-09, 113-14, 117-21, 126-28,
  131-32, 136, 141 , 160, 165-66
The Occasions (Montale)
  See *Le occasioni*
"Ocean Waves" (Tagore)
  See "Sindhu-taranga"
"Ocean-Letter" (Apollinaire)
  See "Lettre-Océan"
"Octavie" (Nerval) **13**:177
"October" (Frost) **1**:225
"October" (Hayden) **6**:193, 195
"October" (Lorde) **12**:154
"October" (Sassoon) **12**:240
"October Dawn" (Hughes) **7**:115
"October Trees" (Sassoon) **12**:248, 254
"An Octopus" (Moore) **4**:233, 252, 254-55,
  264
"Oda a Salvador Dali" ("Ode to Salvador
  Dali") (Garcia Lorca) **3**:136, 138, 143
"Oda a Walt Whitman" ("Ode to Walt
  Whitman") (Garcia Lorca) **3**:121, 127, 150
"Oda al edificio" (Neruda) **4**:285

"Oda al santísimo sacramento del altar: exposición y mundo" ("Ode to the Most Blessed Sacrament"; "Ode to the Most Holy Eucharist: Exposition and World"; "Ode to the Sacrament") (Garcia Lorca) **3**:136, 138, 143

"Oda solar al ejérito del pueblo" ("Solar Ode to the People's Army") (Neruda) **4**:309

Odas elementales (*The Elemental Odes*; *Elementary Odes*; *Odes to Simple Things*) (Neruda) **4**:285, 287

"Ode" (Marvell)
See "An Horatian Ode upon Cromwell's Return from Ireland"

"Ode" (Tennyson) **6**:357

"Ode" (Wordsworth) **4**:377, 399, 403-04, 407

"Ode à Cassandre: 'Mignonne, allon voir'" ("Mignonne, allons voir si la rose") (Ronsard) **11**:218-21, 234, 240

"Ode á Joachim du Bellay" (Ronsard) **11**:280

"Ode à Michel de l'Hospital" (Ronsard) **11**:258, 287-91

"Ode de la Paix" (Ronsard) **11**:283, 286, 289-91

"Ode for All Rebels" (MacDiarmid) **9**:171, 176

"An Ode for Him" (Herrick) **9**:86

"Ode for Music" (Gray) **2**:153, 155

"Ode: Intimations of Immortality from Recollections of Early Childhood" ("Immortality Ode"; " Intimations of Immortality") (Wordsworth) **4**:387-88, 390, 395, 401, 403, 411

"Ode: My Twenty-Fourth Year" (Ginsberg) **4**:73

"Ode: O Bosky Brook" (Tennyson) **6**:388-89

"Ode on a Distant Prospect of Eton College" ("Eton"; "Eton College Ode") (Gray) **2**:133-34, 137, 149-50, 153

"Ode on a Drop of Dew" (Marvell) **10**:269, 271, 277, 296, 313-14

"Ode on Indolence" (Keats) **1**:302-04, 307-08, 314

"Ode on Melancholy" (Keats) **1**:298-300, 306-07, 309, 312

"Ode on Spring" ("Ode on the Spring") (Gray) **2**:133, 135, 143, 145, 152

"Ode on the Death of a Favourite Cat, Drowned in a Tub of Gold Fishes" ("Death of a Favorite Cat") (Gray) **2**:133, 146, 148, 152

"Ode on the Pleasure Arising from Vicissitude" ("Ode on Vicissitude") (Gray) **2**:143, 152-53

"Ode on the Progress of Poesy" (Gray)
See "The Progress of Poesy"

"Ode on the Spring" (Gray)
See "Ode on Spring"

"Ode on Vicissitude" (Gray)
See "Ode on the Pleasure Arising from Vicissitude"

"Ode on Vicissitude" (Gray) **2**:143, 152-53

"Ode secrète" (Valery) **9**:394-96

"Ode to a Beloved Woman" (Sappho)
See "Ode to Anactoria"

"The Ode to a Girl" (Sappho) **5**:408

"Ode to a Grecian Urn" (Keats) **1**:281-82, 290-98, 300, 303-04, 307, 313-15

"Ode to a Nightingale" ("Nightingale") (Keats) **1**:281-83, 295-98, 301, 303, 305, 307-09, 314-15

"Ode to Adversity" ("Hymn to Adversity") (Gray) **2**:133, 135, 138-39, 141, 152

"Ode to Anactoria" ("Ode to a Beloved Woman"; "On Anactoria"; "Seizure") (Sappho) **5**:407, 411, 413

"Ode to Aphrodite" ("Aphrodite Ode"; "Hymn to Aphrodite"; "Ode to Venus") (Sappho) **5**:408, 411, 413, 431

"Ode to Apollo" (Keats) **1**:313

"Ode to Atthis" (Sappho) **5**:416

"Ode to Autumn" ("To Autumn") (Keats) **1**:282-83

"Ode to Dr. William Sancroft" (Swift) **9**:250

"Ode to Duty" (Wordsworth) **4**:401, 406-07

"Ode to Ethiopia" (Dunbar) **5**:124, 129, 131-34, 143

"Ode to Fame" (Masters) **1**:332

"Ode to Fear" (Day Lewis) **11**:147

"Ode to France" ("France: An Ode") (Coleridge) **11**:92, 94, 99-101

"Ode to Freedom" (Pushkin)
See "Vol'nost': Oda"

"Ode to General Draper" (Smart) **13**:342

"The Ode to Hesperus" (Sappho) **5**:418

"Ode to Liberty" (Pushkin)
See "Vol'nost': Oda"

"An Ode to Love" (Behn) **13**:30

"Ode to Mæcenas" ("To Mæcenas") (Wheatley) **3**:333, 340-41, 344-45, 348, 354, 356-57, 361-62

"Ode to Memory" (Tennyson) **6**:347, 359-60

"Ode to Neptune" (Wheatley) **3**:354, 357, 361

"Ode to Psyche" (Keats) **1**:295, 301, 305, 308-09, 314

"Ode to Salvador Dali" (Garcia Lorca)
See "Oda a Salvador Dali"

"An Ode to Sir Clipsebie Crew" (Herrick) **9**:103

"Ode to Sir William Temple" (Swift) **9**:250

"Ode to the Athenian Society" (*Sphinx: A Poem Ascrib'd to Certain Anonymous Authors: By the Revd. S—t*) (Swift) **9**:250

"An Ode to the Birth of Our Saviour" (Herrick) **9**:119-20

"Ode to the Departing Year" (Coleridge) **11**:49, 54, 93-4

"Ode to the Most Blessed Sacrament" (Garcia Lorca)
See "Oda al santísimo sacramento del altar: exposición y mundo"

"Ode to the Most Holy Eucharist: Exposition and World" (Garcia Lorca)
See "Oda al santísimo sacramento del altar: exposición y mundo"

"Ode to the Sacrament" (Garcia Lorca)
See "Oda al santísimo sacramento del altar: exposición y mundo"

"The Ode To Venus" (Sappho) **5**:408

"Ode to Venus" (Sappho)
See "Ode to Aphrodite"

"Ode to Walt Whitman" (Garcia Lorca)
See "Oda a Walt Whitman"

Odes (Gray) **2**:135

Odes (Ronsard) **11**:230, 234, 280, 287, 289, 291-92

Odes (Valery) **9**:365

Odes to Simple Things (Neruda)
See *Odas elementales*

"Odlegtose" ("Distance") (Milosz) **8**:189

"The Odour" (Herbert) **4**:102, 134

"Odysseus to Telemachus" (Brodsky) **9**:4

"Oeconomic divina" (Milosz) **8**:186-87

"Oedipus Crow" (Hughes) **7**:138

"Oenone" (Tennyson) **6**:359, 410-12

Oeuvres (Ronsard) **11**:247, 254, 269, 272, 276

Oeuvres complètes (Mallarme) **4**:198

Les Oeuvres de Francois Villon (Villon) **13**:373, 394

Oeuvres poétiques (Apollinaire) **7**:36

"Of Being" (Levertov) **11**:199, 202

"Of De Witt Williams on His Way to Lincoln Cemetery" (Brooks) **7**:85

"Of Distress Being Humiliated by the Classical Chinese Poets" (Carruth) **10**:87-88

"Of Dying Beauty" (Zukofsky) **11**:368

"Of Modern Poetry" (Stevens) **6**:324

"Of the Four Humours in Man's Constitution" ("The Humours") (Bradstreet) **10**:17, 41

Of the Progres of the Soule (Donne)
See *The Second Anniversarie. Of the Progres of the Soule. Wherein, By Occasion Of the Religious death of Mistris Elizabeth Drury, the incommodities of the Soule in this life, and her exaltation in the next, are Contemplated*

"Of the Vanity of All Worldly Creatures" (Bradstreet)
See "The Vanity of All Worldly Things"

Of the War (Duncan) **2**:104

"Off the Turnpike" (Lowell) **13**:78, 85

"Offering" (Tagore)
See "Utsarga"

An Offering to the Lares (Rilke) **2**:280

"Offices" (Page) **12**:173

"Often I Am Permitted to Return to a Meadow" (Duncan) **2**:120, 127

"Often Rebuked, yet Always Back Returning" (Bronte) **8**:50

"The Ogre" (Williams) **7**:349, 378, 393

"Ogres and Pygmies" (Graves) **6**:139, 142, 144, 151

"Oh" (Sexton) **2**:365

"Oh Christianity, Christianity" (Smith) **12**:325, 352

"Oh do not die" (Donne)
See "A Feaver"

"Oh Fair Enough Are Sky and Plain" (Housman) **2**:193

"Oh, See How Thick the Gold Cup Flowers" (Housman) **2**:183, 185, 196

"Oh Think Not I Am Faithful to a Vow" (Millay) **6**:211

"Oh You Sabbatarians!" (Masters) **1**:344

Oi no kobumi (Matsuo Basho) **3**:6

Oi no obumi (*Letters from a Traveller's Pannier*) (Matsuo Basho) **3**:12

Oku no hosomichi (*The Narrow Pond*; *The Narrow Road to the Deep North*) (Matsuo Basho) **3**:13, 27-30

"The Ol' Tunes" (Dunbar) **5**:122, 145

"The Old Adam" (Levertov) **11**:170

"Old Countryside" (Bogan) **12**:87, 94, 113

"The Old Cumberland Beggar" (Wordsworth) **4**:411-12, 428

"Old Dogs" (Smith) **12**:331-32

"Old Dwarf Heart" (Sexton) **2**:361

"Old England" (McKay) **2**:225

"Old Flame" (Lowell) **3**:212, 215

"Old Folk's Home, Jerusalem" (Dove) **6**:123

"The Old Front Gate" (Dunbar) **5**:122

"Old Furniture" (Hardy) **8**:105

"The Old Huntsman" (Sassoon) **12**:240, 242, 250, 252-53, 275-76

The Old Huntsman and Other Poems (Sassoon) **12**:249, 252, 256-57, 260, 263-64, 269, 272, 277

"The Old Italians Dying" (Ferlinghetti) **1**:182

"Old King Cole" (Robinson) **1**:468

"The Old King's New Jester" (Robinson) **1**:487

"Old Laughter" (Brooks) **7**:61

"Old Lines" (Montale)
See "Vecchi versi"

"The Old Man Travelling" (Wordsworth) **4**:374, 416

"Old Marrieds" (Brooks) **7**:53, 69, 79

"Old Mary" (Brooks) **7**:106

"An Old Memory" (Dunbar) **5**:140

"The Old Neighbour and the New" (Hardy) **8**:104

"Old Oak of Summer Chace" (Tennyson) **6**:356

"Old Park" (Jimenez) **7**:183

"Old Pictures in Florence" (Browning) **2**:37

"The Old Poet Moves to a New Apartment 14 Times" (Zukofsky) **11**:353

"The Old Pond" (Matsuo Basho) **3**:32

Old Possum's Book of Practical Cats (Eliot) **6**:174

"Old Song" (Crane) **3**:90

"The Old Stoic" (Bronte) **8**:60

"An Old Story" (Robinson) **1**:459

" Old Timers" (Sandburg) **2**:302

"Old Trails" (Robinson) **1**:462

"Old Walt" (Hughes) **1**:257

"An Old Woman" (Sitwell) **3**:312, 326

"The Old Woman and the Statue" (Stevens) **6**:297

"Old Words" (Sanchez) **9**:221

"An Old World Thicket" (Rossetti) **7**:277

The Oldest Killed Lake in North America (Carruth) **10**:91

"The Olive in Its Orchard" (Housman) **2**:189-90

"Omaggio a Rimbaud" ("Homage to Rimbaud") (Montale) **13**:111, 157

"L'ombra della magnolia" ("The Magnolia Shadow") (Montale) **13**:109-10, 118, 126

"Ombre Chinoise" (Lowell) **13**:94

Omniscience (Smart)
See *On the Omniscience of the Supreme Being*

"Omoide" ("Reminiscence") (Ishikawa Takuboku) **10**:213

"On a Bust" (Masters) **1**:342

"On a Certain Engagement South of Seoul" (Carruth) **10**:84, 89

"On a Clean Book" (Dunbar) **5**:125

"On a Conventicle" (Behn) **13**:7

"On a Copy of Verses Made in a Dream, and Sent to Me in a Morning before I Was Awake" (Behn) **13**:31

"On a Discovered Curl of Hair" (Hardy) **8**:137

"On a Fine Morning" (Hardy) **8**:108

"On a Heath" (Hardy) **8**:93

"On a Juniper Tree, Cut Down to Make Busks" (Behn) **13**:7, 27-8

"On a Raised Beach" (MacDiarmid) **9**:157, 172, 176, 180

"On a Sentence by Pascal" (Schwartz) **8**:285, 292

"On a Starry Night" (Dunbar) **5**:125-27

"On a Tree Fallen Across the Road" (Frost) **1**:213

"On Anactoria" (Sappho)
See "Ode to Anactoria"

"On Angels" (Milosz) **8**:201

"On Another's Sorrow" (Blake) **12**:7, 33

"On Being Asked to Write a Poem Against the War in Vietnam" (Carruth) **10**:77

"On Being Brought from Africa to America" (Wheatley) **3**:338, 340, 346, 349, 353, 362-63

"On Blake's Victory over the Spaniards" (Marvell)
See "On the Victory Obtained by Blake over the Spaniards"

"On Childhood" (Bradstreet) **10**:38

"On Christmas Eve" (Lowell) **13**:85

"On Desire. A Pindarick" (Behn) **13**:8, 10, 14

"On Duelling" (Graves) **6**:144

On Early Trains (Pasternak)
See *Na rannikh poezdakh*

"On Elgin Marbles" (Keats) **1**:279

"On Friendship" (Wheatley) **3**:363

"On Going Unnoticed" (Frost) **1**:205

"On Himselfe" (Herrick) **9**:87, 89, 131

"On His Mistris" (Donne)
See "Elegie XVI: On his mistris"

"On Imagination" ("Imagination"; "To Imagination") (Wheatley) **3**:336, 338, 353-55

"On Installing an American Kitchen in Lower Austria" (Auden) **1**:24

"On Julia's Clothes" (Herrick)
See "Upon Julia's Clothes"

"On Leaving Some Friends" (Keats) **1**:313

"On Looking at a Copy of Alice Meynell's Poems Given to Me Years Ago by a Friend" (Lowell) **13**:85, 89-90, 99-100

"On Lookout Mountain" (Hayden) **6**:180, 194

"On Lord Holland's Seat near Margate, Kent" ("Impromptu on Lord Holland's House") (Gray) **2**:143

"On Major General Lee" (Wheatley)
See "Thoughts on His Excellency Major General Lee"

"On Mr. J. H. in a Fit of Sickness" (Behn) **13**:8

"On My Son's Return out of England" (Bradstreet) **10**:36, 60

"On My Way Out I Passed over You and the Verrazano Bridge" (Lorde) **12**:138-39

"On Neal's Ashes" (Ginsberg) **4**:74

"On Obedience" (Duncan) **2**:114

"On Parting with My Wife, Jamina" (Milosz) **8**:211

"On Passing the New Menin Gate" (Sassoon) **12**:246

"On Poetry: A Rhapsody" (Swift) **9**:249

"On Portents" (Graves) **6**:149, 172-73

"On Reading John Cage" (Paz) **1**:355, 363, 374

"On Reading William Blake's 'The Sick Rose'" (Ginsberg) **4**:55

"On Recollection" ("Recollection") (Wheatley) **3**:332, 340, 361

"On Returning to Detroit" (Forche) **10**:144, 156

"On Scratchbury Camp" (Sassoon) **12**:259

"On Seeing Diana go Maddddddddd" (Madhubuti) **5**:344

"On the Author of . . . *The Way to Health* . . ." (Behn) **13**:8

"On the Beach at Night" (Whitman) **3**:401

"On the Beach at Ostia" (Ferlinghetti) **1**:184

"On the Death of Mr. Grinhill, the Famous Painter" (Behn) **13**:8

"On the Death of the Late Earl of Rochester" (Behn) **13**:8

"On the Death of the Rev. Mr. George Whitefield" (Wheatley)
See "An Elegiac Poem on the Death of George Whitefield"

"On the Death of the Reverend Dr. Sewall" (Wheatley) **3**:342

"On The Dedication of Dorothy Hall" (Dunbar) **5**:131, 134

"On the Departure Platform" (Hardy) **8**:90

"On the Edge" (Lorde) **12**:137

On the Eternity of God (Smart)
See *On the Eternity of the Supreme Being*

On the Eternity of the Supreme Being (*Eternity; On the Eternity of God*) (Smart) **13**:328, 343

"On the Extinction of the Venetian Republic" (Wordsworth) **4**:377

"On the First Discovery of Falseness in Amintas. By Mrs. B." (Behn) **13**:20-1

On the Goodness of the Supreme Being (Smart) **13**:340, 359-60

"On the Highest Pillar" (Montale)
See "Sulla colonna più alta"

"On the Hill and Grove at Billborow" (Marvell)
See "Upon the Hill and Grove at Billborow"

"On the Honourable Sir Francis Fane . . ." (Behn) **13**:8

"On the Idle Hill of Summer" (Housman) **2**:185

On the Immensity of the Supreme Being (Smart) **13**:343

"On the Lake" (Goethe)
See "Auf dem See"

"On the Mantelpiece" (Lowell) **13**:83

"On the Ocean Floor" (MacDiarmid) **9**:191

On the Omniscience of the Supreme Being (*Omniscience*) (Smart) **13**:344

On the Power of the Supreme Being (Smart) **13**:344

"On the Rhine" (Arnold) **5**:19, 43

"On the River Encountering Waters Like the Sea, I Wrote a Short Poem on the Spot" (Tu Fu) **9**:326

"On the Road" (McKay) **2**:205, 220

"On the Road Home" (Stevens) **6**:311-12

On the Sick-Bed (Tagore)
See *Rogsajyae*

"On the Spur of the Moment" (Tu Fu) **9**:323

"On the Threshold" (Gozzano) **10**:174

On the Trinity (Boethius)
See *On the Trinity*

"On the Victory Obtained by Blake over the Spaniards" ("On Blake's Victory over the Spaniards") (Marvell) **10**:270-71

"On the Way" (Robinson) **1**:468

"On the Way to Lycomedes of Scyrus" (Brodsky)
See "K Likomedu, na Skiros"

"On the Wide Heath" (Millay) **6**:215, 232, 238

"On the Works of Providence" (Wheatley)
See "Thoughts on the Works of Providence"

On This Island (Auden)
See "Look, Stranger, on This Island Now"

"On Virtue" ("Virtue") (Wheatley) **3**:361

"On Visiting the Tomb of Burns" (Keats) **1**:314

"On Walking Slowly After an Accident" (Smith) **12**:314, 316

"On Watching a World Series Game" (Sanchez) **9**:210, 225

"On Wenlock Edge" (Housman) **2**:180

"Once" (Celan) **10**:97

Once Again (Tagore)
See *Punascha*

"Once and Again" (Carruth) **10**:91

"Once by the Pacific" (Frost) **1**:221

"One Art" (Bishop) **3**:62-3, 66-8

"One Day in Spring" (Sitwell) **3**:311

One Handful of Sand (Ishikawa Takuboku)
See *Ichiaku no suna*

100 Selected Poems (Cummings) **5**:86

"125th Street and Abomey" (Lorde) **12**:155, 160

"One More Brevity" (Frost) **1**:213

"One Need Not Be a Chamber to Be Haunted" (Dickinson) **1**:94

"One Night Stand" (Baraka) **4**:6

"One of Many" (Smith) **12**:314, 331, 333

"One Ralph Blossom Soliloquizes" (Hardy) **8**:124

"One Sided Shoot-Out" (Madhubuti) **5**:321, 345

"One Soldier" (Rukeyser) **12**:231

"One Thousand Fearful Words for Fidel Castro" (Ferlinghetti) **1**:187

1x1 (Cummings) **5**:83, 107-08

"One Viceroy Resigns" (Kipling) **3**:181, 186

"One View of the Question" (Kipling) **3**:184

"One Volume Missing" (Dove) **6**:114

One Way Ticket (Hughes) **1**:241, 243, 247, 252, 260-61, 268

"One We Knew" (Hardy) **8**:99, 132

"One Word More" (Browning) **2**:66, 71, 95

"One-Eye, Two-Eyes, Three-Eyes" (Sexton) **2**:365

Onegin's Journey (Pushkin) **10**:400-01

"One-Legged Man" (Sassoon) **12**:242, 263

"One's-Self I Sing" (Whitman)
See "Song of Myself"

"Onirocritique" (Apollinaire) **7**:12

"Only a Curl" (Browning) **6**:24, 30

"Only a Few Left" (Madhubuti) **5**:340

"Only a Little Sleep, a Little Slumber" (Hughes) **7**:154

"Only Child" (Page) **12**:170, 175-76

"The Only One" (Holderlin)
See "Der Einzige"

"The Onset" (Frost) **1**:222

"Ontological Episode of the Asylum" (Carruth) **10**:89

"The Oon Olympian" (MacDiarmid) **9**:197

"Oonts" (Kipling) **3**:158

Open Eye, Open Heart (Ferlinghetti) **1**:186-88

"Open Sea" (Neruda) **4**:282

The Open Sea (Masters) **1**:333, 335

"Open the Door to Me, O" (Burns) **6**:75

The Opening of the Field (Duncan) **2**:103-04, 106, 113-14, 120, 122, 124-25, 127-28

"An Opera House" (Lowell) **13**:79

"The Operation" (Sexton) **2**:348, 350, 353, 361, 365

"Ophélie" (Rimbaud) **3**:283

"Opredelenyie poezii" ("The Definition of Poetry") (Pasternak) **6**:272, 285

Opus Posthumous (Stevens) **6**:306, 339

"Òpyt análiza chetyryokhstópnogo yàmba" (Bely) **11**:18

"Oracion" (Neruda) **4**:278

"The Oracle" (Merton) **10**:339

"The Oracles" (Housman) **2**:164

"Orange of Midsummer" (Lowell) **13**:97

"The Orange Tree" (Levertov) **11**:169

The Orators (Auden) **1**:4-5, 8-11, 16, 22, 25, 30-1, 37

"Orchard" (H. D.)
See "Priapus"

"Orders" (Duncan) **2**:125

"An Ordinary Evening in New Haven" (Stevens) **6**:338

"An Ordinary Girl" (Sirkis) **8**:417

"Ordinary Women" (Stevens) **6**:295

"The Ordination" (Burns) **6**:83, 88

"Oread" (H. D.) **5**:268, 275, 304

"Orestes-Theme" (H. D.) **5**:305

"Gli orecchini" ("The Earrings") (Montale) **13**:108, 128

"L'orgie Parisienne; ou, Paris se Repeuple" (Rimbaud) **3**:281

"Oriana" (Tennyson) **6**:359

"The Oriental Ballerina" (Dove) **6**:113

"Original Child Bomb" (Merton) **10**:337

"The Originators" (Merton) **10**:345

"Origins and History of Consciousness" (Rich) **5**:374

"Orlovu" ("To Orlov") (Pushkin) **10**:409

"Ornières" (Rimbaud) **3**:264

"The Orphan Reformed" (Smith) **12**:326

"L'Orphée" (Ronsard) **11**:251

"Orphée" (Valery) **9**:351

"L'orphelin" ("Réminiscence") (Mallarme) **4**:202

Orpheus (Rukeyser) **12**:207, 213-14, 220

"Orpheus. Eurydike. Hermes" (Rilke) **2**:295

"L'orto" ("The Garden") (Montale) **13**:109-10, 121-22, 133

"Osgar" (Pushkin) **10**:407

"Osiris and Set" (Duncan) **2**:103

"Osiris, Come to Iris" (Thomas) **2**:402

"Osobny zeszyt" ("The Separate Notebooks") (Milosz) **8**:186-87, 199, 204

Osorio (Coleridge)
See *Remorse*

Ossi di seppia (*Bones of the Cuttlefish*; *Cuttlefish Bones*) (Montale) **13**:103, 105-07, 109, 112-17, 119, 122, 126-27, 131, 133-34, 139, 141, 143, 160, 162-66

"Ostanovka v pustyne" ("A Halt in the Desert") (Brodsky) **9**:3, 5, 7

"Ostriches & Grandmothers" (Baraka) **4**:15

"The Other" (Sexton) **2**:365

"Others I Am Not the First" (Housman) **2**:179, 195

Otho the Great (Keats) **1**:279

"Otoño" ("Autumn"; "Fall") (Neruda) **4**:290

"An Otter" (Hughes) **7**:136, 140

"Our Bodies" (Levertov) **11**:169

"Our Bog Is Dood" (Smith) **12**:331, 333

"Our Cabal" (Behn) **13**:7, 20

Our Dead Behind Us (Lorde) **12**:137-39, 141-43, 148, 154-55, 157-58

"Our Lady of the Sackcloth" (Kipling) **3**:183

"Our Mothers" (Rossetti) **7**:286

"Our Prayer of Thanks" (Sandburg) **2**:316

"Our Storm" (Pasternak) **6**:271

"Our Whole Life" (Rich) **5**:391

"Ourselves or Nothing" (Forche) **10**:137, 143-44, 148, 154, 158-59, 161, 168

"Ourselves We Do Inter with Sweet Derision" (Dickinson) **1**:102

"Out" (Hughes) **7**:123, 149

"Out of Debt" (McKay) **2**:222

"Out of Superstition" (Pasternak)
See "From Superstition"

"Out of the Cradle Endlessly Rocking" (Whitman) **3**:378, 382, 391-92, 397, 401

"Out of the Watercolored Window, When You Look" (Schwartz) **8**:301

"Out on the Lawn I Lie in Bed..." (Auden) **1**:22

"Out, Out—" (Frost) **1**:227

"Out to the Hard Road" (Lorde) **12**:138

"Outcast" (McKay) **2**:213, 217, 221

The Outcasts (Sitwell) **3**:321

"The Outer Banks" (Rukeyser) **12**:224

"Outlines" (Lorde) **12**:137

"Outside a Gate" (Lowell) **13**:94

"The Oven Bird" (Frost) **1**:222

"Over 2,000 Illustrations" (Bishop) **3**:67

Over All the Obscene Boundaries: European Poems & Transitions (Ferlinghetti) **1**:183-85

"Over Cities" (Milosz) **8**:186

"Over Denver Again" (Ginsberg) **4**:57

"Over Sir John's Hill" ("Over St. John's Hill") (Thomas) **2**:395, 404

"Over St. John's Hill" (Thomas)
See "Over Sir John's Hill"

"Over Us If (as what Was Dusk Becomes" (Cummings) **5**:109

"The Overgrown Pasture" (Lowell) **13**:60, 78, 85

"Overheard" (Kipling) **3**:193

"Overheard" (Levertov) **11**:160

"Overland to the Islands" (Levertov) **11**:188, 192, 196

Overland to the Islands (Levertov) **11**:166, 188, 202

"Overlooking the River Stour" (Hardy) **8**:116-17

"Overpopulation" (Ferlinghetti) **1**:167, 175, 187

"Overture to a Dance of Locomotives" (Williams) **7**:345, 410

"Overtures to Death" (Day Lewis) **11**:144

Overtures to Death and Other Poems (Day Lewis) **11**:127-30, 144

"Ovid in Exile" (Graves) **6**:164

"Ovid, Old Buddy, I Would Discourse with You a While" (Carruth) **10**:88

"The Owl in the Sarcophagus" (Stevens) **6**:304

"Owl Song" (Atwood) **8**:25

Owl's Clover (Stevens) **6**:297-98, 317-20

"Owl's Song" (Hughes) **7**:160-61

"The Ox Tamer" (Whitman) **3**:377

"The Oxen" (Hardy) **8**:112, 121

"Oxford" (Auden) **1**:30

"Oysters" (Sexton) **2**:365

"Ozone" (Dove) **6**:121-23

Pacchiarotto (Browning) **2**:71

"A Pacific State" (Milosz) **8**:205

"A Packet of Letters" (Bogan) **12**:94

"Paesaggio I" ("Landscape I") (Pavese) **13**:204, 212, 220, 225-26

"Paesaggio II" (Pavese) **13**:212

"Paesaggio III" (Pavese) **13**:212

"Paesaggio V" (Pavese) **13**:212

"Paesaggio VI" ("Landscape VI") (Pavese) **13**:228

"Paesaggio VII" ("Landscape VII") (Pavese)
   13:204, 212
"Paesaggio VIII" (Pavese) **13**:212, 230
"The Pagan Isms" (McKay) **2**:219-20
A Pageant, and Other Poems (Rossetti) **7**:270
"Pagett, M. P." (Kipling) **3**:190
Paginas (Jimenez) **7**:208, 212
"The Pahty" ("The Party") (Dunbar) **5**:116,
   119, 122-23, 146
Paid on Both Sides (Auden) **1**:5, 8, 20, 30, 34
"Pain for a Daughter" (Sexton) **2**:363
"The Pains of Sleep" (Coleridge) **11**:41, 44
"Painted Steps" (Gallagher) **9**:45
"The Painting" (Williams) **7**:394
"Paisaje de la multitud que orina"
   ("Landscape of the Urinating Multitudes
   (Battery Place Nocturne)") (Garcia Lorca)
   3:140
"Paisaje de la multitud que vomita"
   ("Landscape of the Vomiting Multitudes
   (Coney Island Dusk)") (Garcia Lorca)
   3:140
"Paisaje del corazon" ("Landscape of the
   Heart"; "The Truth") (Jimenez) **7**:199
"Paisaje después de una batalla" ("Landscape
   after a Battle") (Neruda) **4**:309
"Las palabras" (Paz) **1**:358
"Palace" (Apollinaire)
   See "Palais"
"The Palace of Art" (Tennyson) **6**:353, 359-
   60, 370, 375, 378-80, 382, 409, 412
"The Palace of the Babies" (Stevens) **6**:293
"Palais" ("Palace") (Apollinaire) **7**:45-6, 48
Palātakā (*Fugitive; The Runaway, and Other
   Stories*) (Tagore) **8**:415
"Pale, Intent Noontide" (Montale)
   See "Meriggiare pallido e assorto"
"Pâline" (Apollinaire) **7**:48
"Palladium" (Arnold) **5**:8
"Pallas Athene" (Masters) **1**:344
"Palm" (Valery)
   See "Palme"
"Palm and Pine" (Kipling) **3**:179
"Palme" ("Palm") (Valery) **9**:363, 365, 367,
   393-94
"Pals" (Sandburg) **2**:303
"Paltry Nude" (Stevens) **6**:295
"The Paltry Nude Starts on a Spring Voyage"
   (Stevens) **6**:295
"Pamiatnik" (Pushkin)
   See "Pamjatnik"
"Pamjatnik" ("Monument"; "Pamiatnik")
   (Pushkin) **10**:408, 412, 415
"Pan and Luna" (Browning) **2**:88-9
"Panchishe vaisakh" ("Twenty-fifth of
   Vaisakh") (Tagore) **8**:415
"A Panegerick to Sir Lewis Pemberton"
   (Herrick) **9**:102
"A Panegyrick on the Dean in the Person of a
   Lady in the North" (Swift) **9**:262, 274, 295
"Panegyrique de la Renommée" (Ronsard)
   11:243
"The Pangolin" (Moore) **4**:235
"Panorama ceigo de Nueva York" ("Blind
   Panorama of New York") (Garcia Lorca)
   3:141
*The Panther and the Lash: Poems of Our
   Times* (Hughes) **1**:251-52, 257-58, 260, 262,
   268
"Pantomime" (Verlaine) **2**:430
"Paolo e Virginia" (Pavese) **13**:221

"The Papa and Mama Dance" (Sexton)
   2:349, 352-53
"Papà beve sempre" (Pavese) **13**:214
"Papa Love Baby" (Smith) **12**:315, 322, 325-
   26, 343
"The Paper Nautilus" (Moore) **4**:255
"The Paper Wind Mill" (Lowell) **13**:78
Paracelsus (Browning) **2**:26-31, 34, 42-3, 48,
   65-6, 73, 82, 91-3, 96
"Paradise" (Gallagher) **9**:64
"Paradise" (Herbert) **4**:114, 130
"Paradise on the Roofs" (Pavese) **13**:204
"Paradox" (Lowell) **13**:85
"Paragraphs" (Carruth) **10**:74-5, 83, 85
"Parajaya sangīt" ("Song of Defeat") (Tagore)
   8:405
Parallèlement (*In Parallel*) (Verlaine) **2**:414,
   416-17, 419, 425-26
"Paralytic" (Plath) **1**:391
"Paranoid" (Page) **12**:175
"Paraphrase" (Crane) **3**:102
"The Parasceve, or Preparation" (Herrick)
   9:117, 119
"Parchiarotto" (Browning) **2**:63, 71, 75
"The Parents: People Like Our Marriage,
   Maxie and Andrew" (Brooks) **7**:80
"Pärfum exotique" (Baudelaire) **1**:45
"Paris and Helen" (Schwartz) **8**:311
Paris Spleen (Baudelaire)
   See *Petits poèmes en prose: Le spleen de Paris*
"A Parisian Dream" (Baudelaire)
   See "Rêve parisien"
The Parisian Prowler (Baudelaire)
   See *Petits poèmes en prose: Le spleen de Paris*
"Park Bench" (Hughes) **1**:242
"The Parklands" (Smith) **12**:317
"Parleying with Charles Avison" (Browning)
   2:83
"Parleying with Gerard de Lairesse"
   (Browning) **2**:81, 83, 86
*Parleyings with Certain People of Importance in
   Their Day* (Browning) **2**:64, 85, 95-6
"Parlez-vous français" (Schwartz) **8**:302-03
"Parliament Hill Fields" (Plath) **1**:391
"Parlour-Piece" (Hughes) **7**:140
"Le parole" ("The Words") (Montale) **13**:134
"Parsley" (Dove) **6**:105, 110
"The Parson's Daughter and the Seminarist"
   (Bely) **11**:3
"A Part of Speech" (Brodsky)
   See "Căst reči"
A Part of Speech (Brodsky)
   See *Căst reči*
"Part of the Doctrine" (Baraka) **4**:18
"Part of the Seventh Epistle of the First Book
   of Horace Imitated and Addressed to the
   Earl of Oxford" (Swift) **9**:296
"Parted" (Dunbar) **5**:125, 140
"Parting" (Arnold) **5**:43, 55
Parts of a World (Stevens) **6**:299, 311, 318
"A Part-Sequence for Change" (Duncan)
   2:103
"The Party" (Dunbar)
   See "The Pahty"
"Les pas" (Valery) **9**:366, 374, 396
Pasado en claro (*A Draft of Shadows*) (Paz)
   1:369, 371-72, 374
"Passage" (Crane) **3**:82
"Passage" (Levertov) **11**:202
"Passage" (Okigbo) **7**:223-24, 231, 236-39,
   248-49, 251, 255
"Passage to India" (Whitman) **3**:378, 394-98

"Passages 13" (Duncan) **2**:116
"Passages 21" (Duncan) **2**:116
"Passages 25" (Duncan) **2**:25
"Passages 26" (Duncan) **2**:116
"Passages 27" (Duncan) **2**:116
"Passages 29" (Duncan) **2**:116
"Passages 31" (Duncan) **2**:117
"Passages 35 (Tribunals)" (Duncan) **2**:116,
   118
"Passages 36" (Duncan) **2**:115-17
"Passer mortuus est" (Millay) **6**:228
"Passing Chao-ling Again" (Tu Fu) **9**:322
"The Passing Cloud" (Smith) **12**:339
"Passing Losses On" (Frost) **1**:200
"The Passing of Arthur" (Tennyson)
   See "Morte d'Arthur"
*The Passion of Claude McKay: Selected Poetry
   and Prose, 1912-1948* (McKay) **2**:218
"Past" (Sanchez) **9**:219
"Past and Future" (Browning) **6**:16, 41
"Past and Present" (Masters) **1**:343
"The Past Is the Present" (Moore) **4**:237
"Pastoral" (Dove) **6**:120-21
"Pastoral" (Williams) **7**:367, 378
Pastoral (Williams) **7**:349
"Pastoral Dialogue" (Swift) **9**:261
"A Pastoral Pindaric . . ." (Behn) **13**:8
"A Pastoral to Mr. Stafford" (Behn) **13**:8, 32
"Pastorale" (Crane) **3**:98-9
Pastorale (Jimenez) **7**:184
"A Pastorall Song to the King" (Herrick)
   9:86
Pastorals (Vergil)
   See *Georgics*
"The Pasture" (Frost) **1**:197, 212, 225
"Patent Leather" (Brooks) **7**:58, 68, 79
"Paternità" ("Paternity") (Pavese) **13**:213,
   229
"Paternity" (Pavese)
   See "Paternità"
"Paterson" (Ginsberg) **4**:73-5
Paterson (Williams) **7**:350, 354-60, 362, 364-
   65, 370-75, 377, 379, 392-95, 402-03, 408-10
Paterson I (Williams) **7**:354, 357-58, 360, 365
Paterson II (Williams) **7**:363, 391-92
Paterson IV (Williams) **7**:363, 392
Paterson V (Williams) **7**:364-65, 370-71, 393
"Paterson: Episode 17" (Williams) **7**:360
"The Path" (Dunbar) **5**:125
"Path of Thunder" (Okigbo) **7**:228, 246-47,
   255
Path of Thunder (Okigbo)
   See *Labyrinths, with Path of Thunder*
"Paths and Thingscape" (Atwood) **8**:36
"Patience" (Graves) **6**:154
"Patience" (Lowell) **13**:60
"Patmos" (Holderlin) **4**:148, 150-51, 153,
   155-57, 159, 166, 172
"The Patriot" (Browning) **2**:60
"Patterns" (Lowell) **13**:60, 71, 76-7, 84-5, 89,
   96
"Paul and Virginia" (Gozzano) **10**:176, 178,
   180-84
Paul Celan: Poems (*Poems of Paul Celan*)
   (Celan) **10**:95-6, 107-08, 114
"Paul Robeson" (Brooks) **7**:92-3
"Paula Becker To Clara Westhoff" (Rich)
   5:379
Pauline: A Fragment of a Confession
   (Browning) **2**:25-6, 42-3, 48, 66, 90-2, 94
"Paul's Wife" (Frost) **1**:194
"A Pause for Thought" (Rossetti) **7**:280, 297

"Pauvre Lélian" (Verlaine) **2**:416
"Les pauvres à l'église" ("The Poor in Church") (Rimbaud) **3**:255
"Pavitra prem" ("Pure Love") (Tagore) **8**:407
"Pay Day" (Hughes) **1**:255
"Pay Day" (McKay) **2**:226
"Paying Calls" (Hardy) **8**:105
"Paysage" ("Un cigare allume que Fume"; "A Lighted Cigar That Is Smoking") (Apollinaire) **7**:32, 34-5
"Paysage Moralisé" (Auden) **1**:23
"Paysages belges" (Verlaine) **2**:415
"Peace" (Herbert) **4**:101, 134
"The Peace-Offering" (Hardy) **8**:93
"The Peacock Room" (Hayden) **6**:193-95, 198
"Pear Tree" (H. D.) **5**:275
"The Pearl" (Herbert) **4**:100, 128
"Pearl Horizons" (Sandburg) **2**:307
"The Peasant Whore" (Pavese)
    See "La puttana contadina"
"The Peasant's Confession" (Hardy) **8**:124
"Pedantic Literalist" (Moore) **4**:229
"Pedro as el cuando..." (Neruda) **4**:288
"Peele Castle" (Wordsworth)
    See "Stanzas on Peele Castle"
"Peers" (Toomer) **7**:336-37
"Pelleas and Ettarre" (Tennyson) **6**:376
"The Penitent" (Millay) **6**:211
Penny Wheep (MacDiarmid) **9**:151, 158, 166, 179, 188
"The Pennycandystore beyond the El" (Ferlinghetti) **1**:187
"Pensieri di Deola" (Pavese) **13**:214
"Penumbra" (Lowell) **13**:64
"People" (Toomer) **7**:336-37
"THE PEOPLE BURNING" (Baraka) **4**:12
"People Getting Divorced" (Ferlinghetti) **1**:183
"People Who Don't Understand" (Pavese)
    See "Gente che non capisce"
"People Who Have No Children" (Brooks) **7**:75
"People Who've Been There" (Pavese) **13**:218
The People, Yes (Sandburg) **2**:317-18, 320-23, 325-26, 328, 330, 333, 335-39, 341
Pepel' (*Ashes*) (Bely) **11**:3-4, 6-7, 24, 30-2
"Per album" ("Lines for an Album") (Montale) **13**:130
"Perdón si por mis ojos..." (Neruda) **4**:288
"Peremena" ("Change") (Pasternak) **6**:285
"The Perennial Answer" (Rich) **5**:351-52
"Perfect" (MacDiarmid) **9**:177
"The Perfect Sky" (Gallagher) **9**:59
"The Performers" (Hayden) **6**:195
"Perhaps No Poem But All I Can Say and I Cannot Be Silent" (Levertov) **11**:198
"The Permanent Tourists" (Page) **12**:178, 181-89
"Perpetuum Mobile: The City" (Williams) **7**:350
"Persephone" (Smith) **12**:331-32
"The Persian" (Smith) **12**:330
"The Persian Version" (Graves) **6**:143, 152
Personae (Pound) **4**:317
"Personae separatae" (Montale) **13**:
"Personae Separatae" (Montale) **13**:106, 126
"Personal" (Hughes) **1**:241, 259
"Personal Landscape" (Page) **12**:178, 190
"Personal Letter No. 2" (Sanchez) **9**:224, 232-33
"Personal Letter No. 3" (Sanchez) **9**:225

Pervaja simfonija (Bely) **11**:17
"Pervaya pesenka" ("First Song") (Akhmatova) **2**:9
Pervoe svidanie (*The First Encounter; The First Meetings*) (Bely) **11**:3, 7-11, 17-21, 28-9, 31-3
"Pesnia poslednei vstrechi" ("The Song of the Final Meeting/Song of the Last Meeting") (Akhmatova) **2**:11
"Peter" (Moore) **4**:257
Peter Bell (Wordsworth) **4**:399, 420
"Peter Quince at the Clavier" (Stevens) **6**:293, 295, 300-01
Le Petit Testament (Villon)
    See *Les Lais*
"Les petites vielles" ("The Little Old Women") (Baudelaire) **1**:45, 64
Petits poèmes en prose: Le spleen de Paris (*Little Poems in Prose*; *Paris Spleen*; *The Parisian Prowler*; *Poems in Prose from Charles Baudelaire*; *Prose Poems*; *Short Prose Poems*; *Le spleen de Paris*) (Baudelaire) **1**:48-9, 58-9
"Petrificada petrificante" (Paz) **1**:367
"Phaedra" (H. D.) **5**:267
"Phantasia for Elvira Shatayev" (Rich) **5**:377
"The Phantom Horsewoman" (Hardy) **8**:91, 136
"Phèdre" (Smith) **12**:331-32
"The Phenomenology of Anger" (Rich) **5**:371-72, 384, 394
"Phillis; or, The Progress of Love, 1716" (Swift) **9**:253
"Philomela" (Arnold) **5**:37-8, 41, 46-7
"The Philosophers" (Merton) **10**:337
"Philosophy" (Dunbar) **5**:144
"Phone Call from Mexico" (Page) **12**:198
"The Photograph" (Smith) **12**:308, 346
"Photograph of My Room" (Forche) **10**:144, 156
"The Photograph of the Unmade Bed" (Rich) **5**:366
"Photos of a Salt Mine" (Page) **12**:167-68, 189
"Phrases" (Rimbaud) **3**:263
"Physcial Union" (Tagore)
    See "Deher milan"
"Piaceri notturni" ("Night Pleasures"; "Nocturnal Pleasures") (Pavese) **13**:205, 226
"Piano after War" (Brooks) **7**:73
"Piccolo testamento" ("A Little Testament"; "A Small Will") (Montale) **13**:104, 113, 165-66, 168
Pickering MS (Blake) **12**:35-7, 43
"Pickthorn Manor" (Lowell) **13**:60, 77, 84
"Pictor Ignatus" (Browning) **2**:30
"The Picture" (Tagore)
    See "Chhabi"
"Picture of a Black Child with a White Doll" (Merton) **10**:341, 345
"A Picture of Lee Ying" (Merton) **10**:341
"The Picture of Little T. C. in a Prospect of Flowers" ("Little T. C.") (Marvell) **10**:271, 274, 277, 289, 294, 303-04
Picture Show (Sassoon) **12**:257-58, 269
"Pictures By Vuillard" (Rich) **5**:350
Pictures from Brueghel, and Other Poems (Williams) **7**:371-72, 374, 377, 392-93, 403, 408
Pictures of the Floating World (Lowell) **13**:73-4, 93-4, 96

Pictures of the Gone World (Ferlinghetti) **1**:167-69, 171-75, 186
"Pied Piper of Hamelin" (Browning) **2**:36, 63
"Piedra de sol" ("Sun Stone") (Paz) **1**:353
Piedra de sol (*Sun Stone*; *Sunstone*) (Paz) **1**:355-56, 358-59, 368-69, 371, 373, 375-77
"The Pier-Glass" (Graves) **6**:137, 142, 172
The Pier-Glass (Graves) **6**:128, 147, 150
"Piggy to Joey" (Smith) **12**:321
"Pike" (Hughes) **7**:136, 158
"The Pike" (Lowell) **13**:69
"A Pilgrim" (Bradstreet)
    See "As Weary Pilgrim"
"A Pilgrim Dreaming" (Levertov) **11**:209
"The Pilgrimage" (Herbert) **4**:109
"The Pillar of Fame" (Herrick) **9**:106
"Le pin" ("The Pine") (Ronsard) **11**:277
A Pindaric on the Death of Our Late Sovereign (Behn) **13**:8
A Pindaric Poem on the Happy Coronation of. . . James II (Behn) **13**:8
"Pindaric Poem to the Reverend Doctor Burnet" (Behn) **13**:32
"A Pindaric to Mr. P. Who Sings Finely" (Behn) **13**:8
"The Pine" (Ronsard)
    See "Le pin"
"The Pine Planters (Marty South's Reverie)" (Hardy) **8**:101
The Pink Church (Williams) **7**:370
"Pink Dog" (Bishop) **3**:65
"Pioggia d'agosto" (Gozzano) **10**:184-85
"The Piper" (Blake) **12**:9
Pippa Passes (Browning) **2**:28, 30, 35, 37, 67
"Il Pirla" (Montale) **13**:138
The Pisan Cantos (Pound) **4**:320, 337, 344-48, 352, 357-58, 360
"Le pitre châtié" ("The Clown Chastized") (Mallarme) **4**:202
"Pity Me Not" (Millay) **6**:225
"Pity 'Tis, 'Tis True" (Lowell) **13**:84
"Place for a Third" (Frost) **1**:194, 221
"The Place That Is Feared I Inhabit" (Forche) **10**:143
"Places" (Hardy) **8**:91, 104, 135-36
"A Plague of Starlings" (Hayden) **6**:185, 195
"The Plaid Dress" (Millay) **6**:234
"Plainte d'automne" ("Autumn Lament") (Mallarme) **4**:187
"Un plaisant" ("A Joker") (Baudelaire) **1**:59
"Plan for the Young English King" (Pound) **4**:364
Planet News: 1961-1967 (Ginsberg) **4**:51-2, 65-6
"Planetarium" (Rich) **5**:366, 370
"Planh for the Young English King" (Pound) **4**:364
"Planning the Garden" (Lowell) **13**:64
"Planning the Perfect Evening" (Dove) **6**:106
Plantain (Akhmatova)
    See *Podorozhnik*
"A Plantation Portrait" (Dunbar) **5**:147
"The Planters" (Atwood) **8**:36
Platero and I (Jimenez)
    See *Platero y Yo*
Platero and I: An Andalusion Elegy (Jimenez)
    See *Platero y Yo*
Platero y Yo (*Platero and I*; *Platero and I: An Andalusion Elegy*) (Jimenez) **7**:185-89, 191, 199-201, 203
"Plato Elaborated" (Brodsky) **9**:19, 20
"Playing Cards" (Atwood) **8**:5, 7

"Pleading" (McKay) **2**:223
"Please, Master" (Ginsberg) **4**:54, 90
"Pleasures" (Levertov) **11**:159, 164, 189
"Pleasure's Lament" (Tagore)
   See "Sukher vilap"
"Plegaria" ("Prayer") (Jimenez) **7**:198
"*Plessy vs. Ferguson*: Theme and Variations"
   (Merton) **10**:345
"Ploughing" (Pasternak) **6**:267
"Ploughing on Sunday" (Stevens) **6**:297, 333
"The Plumet Basilisk" (Moore) **4**:243
Plusieurs sonnets (Mallarme) **4**:214-15
"Plutonian Ode" (Ginsberg) **4**:61-2
Plutonian Ode: Poems, 1977-1980 (Ginsberg)
   4:61-2
"Po' Boy Blues" (Hughes) **1**:254, 270
"Podolie" (Apollinaire) **7**:48
Podorozhnik (*Buckthorn*; *Plantain*)
   (Akhmatova) **2**:3, 13, 18
"Poem" (Bishop) **3**:54-5, 70
"The Poem" (Lowell) **13**:83
"Poem" (Merton) **10**:349
"Poem" (Rukeyser) **12**:233
"Poem" (Sanchez) **9**:232
"The Poem" (Williams) **7**:399
"Poem 1" (Ferlinghetti) **1**:167
"Poem 2" (Ferlinghetti) **1**:173
"Poem 3" (Ferlinghetti) **1**:174
"Poem IV" (Auden) **1**:10
"Poem 4" (Ferlinghetti) **1**:174
"Poem 5" (Ferlinghetti) **1**:168, 172
"Poem V" (Rich) **5**:378
"Poem 6" (Ferlinghetti) **1**:168, 173-74
"Poem 7" (Ferlinghetti) **1**:187
"Poem VII" (Rich) **5**:378-79
"Poem 8" (Ferlinghetti) **1**:174
"Poem IX" (Auden) **1**:10
"Poem 10" (Ferlinghetti) **1**:172-73
"Poem 11" (Ferlinghetti) **1**:174-75
"Poem 13" (Ferlinghetti) **1**:169, 174
"Poem XIII" (Rich) **5**:379
"Poem 14" (Ferlinghetti) **1**:168, 170
"Poem 15" (Ferlinghetti) **1**:175
"Poem 16" (Ferlinghetti) **1**:175
"Poem 17" (Ferlinghetti) **1**:176
"Poem 18" (Ferlinghetti) **1**:174
"Poem 19" (Ferlinghetti) **1**:173, 175
"Poem 20" (Ferlinghetti) **1**:174, 176
"Poem XX" (Rich) **5**:379
"Poem 21" (Ferlinghetti) **1**:175
"Poem 22" (Ferlinghetti) **1**:169, 176
"Poem 23" (Ferlinghetti) **1**:172, 174
"Poem 24" (Ferlinghetti) **1**:168, 171, 175
"Poem XXV" (Auden) **1**:10
"Poem 25" (Ferlinghetti) **1**:169, 174-75
"Poem 26" (Ferlinghetti) **1**:174-75
"Poem 27" (Ferlinghetti) **1**:174
"The Poem as Mask: Orpheus" (Rukeyser)
   12:228
"Poem at Thirty" (Sanchez) **9**:224, 232-33,
   240
"Poem Beginning 'The'" ("The") (Zukofsky)
   11:366-69, 373-74, 381, 383-86, 390, 395
"A Poem Beginning with a Line by Pindar"
   (Duncan) **2**:121-22, 127
"Poem Catching Up with an Idea" (Carruth)
   10:88
"Poem for a Birthday" (Plath) **1**:381, 390
"A Poem for a Poet" (Madhubuti) **5**:327, 344
"A Poem for Anna Russ and Fanny Jones"
   (Baraka) **4**:39
"A Poem for Black Hearts" (Baraka) **4**:18-19

"Poem (for DCS 8th Graders—1966-67)"
   (Sanchez) **9**:224
"Poem for Etheridge" (Sanchez) **9**:225, 242
"A Poem for Max 'Nordau" (Robinson)
   1:459
"Poem for Maya" (Forche) **10**:142, 157
"A Poem for My Father" (Sanchez) **9**:220,
   225, 240
"A Poem for Negro Intellectuals (If There Bes
   Such a Thing)" (Madhubuti) **5**:329
"A Poem for Sterling Brown" (Sanchez)
   9:229
"A Poem for the End of the Century" (Milosz)
   8:213
"A Poem for Willie Best" (Baraka) **4**:10-11
*A Poem Humbly Dedicated to the Great Pattern
   of Piety and Virtue Catherine Queen
   Dowager* (Behn) **13**:8
"Poem (I lived in the first century of world
   wars. . . .)" (Rukeyser) **12**:222
"Poem in C" (Toomer) **7**:333
"Poem in October" (Thomas) **2**:382, 392, 404
"Poem in Prose" (Bogan) **12**:100, 107, 112
"Poem in Which I Refuse Contemplation"
   (Dove) **6**:120
"A Poem Looking for a Reader" (Madhubuti)
   5:323
"Poem No. 2" (Sanchez) **9**:220
"Poem No. 8" (Sanchez) **9**:242
"Poem No. 13" (Sanchez) **9**:213
"Poem of Apparitions in Boston in the 73rd
   Year of These States" ("A Boston Ballad")
   (Whitman) **3**:386
"Poem of Memory" (Akhmatova) **2**:16
"A Poem of Praise" (Sanchez) **9**:242
"Poem of the Body" (Whitman) **3**:385
Poem of the Cante Jondo (Garcia Lorca)
   See *Poema del cante jondo*
"Poem of the Daily Work of the Workmen
   and Workwomen of These States"
   (Whitman) **3**:385
The Poem of the Deep Song (Garcia Lorca)
   See *Poema del cante jondo*
"Poem of the Poet" (Whitman) **3**:386
"Poem of the Singers and of the Works of
   Poems" (Whitman) **3**:386
"Poem of These States" (Ginsberg) **4**:66
"A Poem of Walt Whitman, an American"
   (Whitman) **3**:384, 414
"Poem on His Birthday" (Thomas) **2**:391
"Poem, or Beauty Hurts Mr. Vinal"
   (Cummings) **5**:96
"Poem out of Childhood" (Rukeyser) **12**:231,
   235
"A POEM SOME PEOPLE WILL HAVE TO
   UNDERSTAND" (Baraka) **4**:16
"A Poem to Complement Other Poems"
   (Madhubuti) **5**:329, 342
"A Poem to Peanut" (Brooks) **7**:90
"A Poem Upon the Death of His Late
   Highness the Lord Protector" (Marvell)
   See "Poem upon the Death of O. C."
"Poem upon the Death of O. C." ("Death of
   the Lord Protector"; "A Poem Upon the
   Death of His Late Highness the Lord
   Protector"; "Upon the Death of the Lord
   Protector") (Marvell) **10**:270-71, 305, 312
Poem without a Hero: Triptych (Akhmatova)
   See *Poema bez geroya: Triptykh*
Poema bez geroya: Triptykh (*Poem without a
   Hero: Triptych*) (Akhmatova) **2**:4, 6-8, 16,
   18-21

Poema del cante jondo (*Deep Song*; *Poem of the
   Cante Jondo*; *The Poem of the Deep Song*)
   (Garcia Lorca) **3**:118, 123, 127, 129, 135,
   137
"Le poème de la mer" (Rimbaud) **3**:272
"Poème lu au mariage d'André Salmon" ("Le
   marriage d'André Salmon") (Apollinaire)
   7:48
Poèmes (*Poems*) (Ronsard) **11**:249
Poèmes saturniens (Verlaine) **2**:413-15, 430-32
"Poems" (Cooke) **6**:348, 394, 416
Poems (Arnold) **5**:12, 43, 50
Poems (Auden) **1**:4, 8, 10
Poems (Browning) **6**:14, 16-17, 19, 21, 25-7,
   32, 36-8, 41-2
Poems (Garcia Lorca)
   See *Libro de poemas*
Poems (Moore) **4**:228, 239, 250-51, 264
Poems (Poe) **1**:428, 437, 441
Poems (Ronsard)
   See *Poèmes*
Poems (Rossetti) **7**:265
Poems (Williams) **7**:367, 374, 395, 398
Poems (Wordsworth) **4**:375, 401, 415
Poems, 1953 (Graves) **6**:154-55
Poems, 1914-1926 (Graves) **6**:132
Poems, 1923-1954 (Cummings) **5**:85, 89
Poems, 1926-1930 (Graves) **6**:132
Poems, 1938-1945 (Graves) **6**:129
Poems, 1943-1947 (Day Lewis) **11**:147
"Poems about St. Petersburg, II" (Akhmatova)
   2:12
Poems and Fragments (Holderlin) **4**:171
The Poems and Letters of Andrew Marvell
   (Marvell) **10**:277
Poems and New Poems (Bogan) **12**:89, 91,
   107, 120, 124-26
Poems and Satires (Graves) **6**:135
Poems before Congress (Browning) **6**:6, 23,
   27, 36
Poems by Currer, Ellis, and Acton Bell (Bronte)
   8:46
Poems by Two Brothers (Tennyson) **6**:358
Poems, Chiefly in the Scottish Dialect (Burns)
   6:49
Poems, Chiefly Lyrical (Tennyson) **6**:347, 385,
   406-09
"Poems from the Margins of Thom Gunn's
   'Moly'" (Duncan) **2**:127
"Poems in Imitation of the Fugue" (Schwartz)
   8:289, 305
Poems in Prose from Charles Baudelaire
   (Baudelaire)
   See *Petits poèmes en prose: Le spleen de Paris*
Poems in Wartime (Day Lewis) **11**:145
"Poems of 1912-13" (Hardy) **8**:91-4, 132,
   137-8
Poems of Akhmatova (Akhmatova) **2**:16
The Poems of Francois Villon (Villon) **13**:412
"The Poems of Our Climate" (Stevens) **6**:299
Poems of Paul Celan (Celan)
   See *Paul Celan: Poems*
The Poems of Samuel Taylor Coleridge
   (Coleridge) **11**:70, 81, 83, 104
Poems of Shadow (Jimenez) **7**:183
"Poems of the Past and Present" (Hardy)
   8:121
Poems of the Past and Present (Hardy) **8**:123,
   125
Poems on Affairs of State (Marvell) **10**:311

Poems on Various Subjects, Religious and Moral, by Phillis Wheatley, Negro Servant to Mr. John Wheatley of Boston, in New England, 1773 (Wheatley) **3**:332-34, 336, 338, 345, 349-52, 356
Poems Selected and New (Page) **12**:180
Poems: Selected and New, 1950-1974 (Rich) **5**:384, 387
Poems upon Several Occasions, with a Voyage to the Island of Love (*Voyage to the Island of Love*) (Behn) **13**:3, 7-8, 16, 18
"Poesía" (Jimenez) **7**:183
"La poesía" ("Poetry") (Paz) **1**:353
Poesía (Jimenez) **7**:202
Poesías últimas escojidas (1918-1958) (Jimenez) **7**:214
"Poésie" (Valery) **9**:366, 394
Poesie (*Poetry*) (Pavese) **13**:207, 210, 215, 220-21, 223-30
Poesie e prose (Gozzano) **10**:184-85
Poesie edite e inedite (*Published and Unpublished Poems*) (Pavese) **13**:208, 219, 230
Poésies (*Various Poems of All Periods*) (Valery) **9**:399
Poésies complétes (Mallarme) **4**:206
Poésies diverses (Villon) **13**:394-95, 397, 402-03, 407, 411
"The Poet" (Carruth) **10**:84
"The Poet" (Day Lewis) **11**:146
"The Poet" (Dunbar) **5**:121, 136
"The Poet" (H. D.) **5**:306
"A Poet" (Hardy) **8**:90
"The Poet" (Rilke) **2**:280
"The Poet" (Tennyson) **6**:369
"The Poet and His Book" (Millay) **6**:220
"The Poet and His Song" (Dunbar) **5**:118, 121, 134
"Poet at Seventy" (Milosz) **8**:180, 197, 209
Poet in New York (Garcia Lorca)
  See *Poeta en Nueva York*
Poet in Our Time (Montale) **13**:146
"The Poet in the World" (Levertov) **11**:172-74
"The Poet Laments the Coming of Old Age" (Sitwell) **3**:317
"The Poet of Ignorance" (Sexton) **2**:368
"The Poet, to His Book" (Merton) **10**:337
Poeta en Nueva York (*Poet in New York*) (Garcia Lorca) **3**:120-21, 125, 136-38, 140, 143, 148-51
"Los poetas celestes" ("The Celestial Poets") (Neruda) **4**:293
"Les poètes de sept ans" ("The Poets of Seven Years") (Rimbaud) **3**:258
"Poetica" ("Poetics") (Pavese) **13**:228
Poetical Sketches (Blake) **12**:31-2, 36, 43, 60-1
The Poetical Works of Christina Georgina Rossetti (*Collected Poems; Collected Works*) (Rossetti) **7**:282-83
The Poetical Works of S. T. Coleridge (Coleridge) **11**:75
"Poetics" (Pavese)
  See "Poetica"
"Poetry" (Arnold) **5**:41
"Poetry" (Goethe) **5**:227
"Poetry" (Moore) **4**:232, 235, 249, 251, 254, 270-71
"Poetry" (Pasternak) **6**:252, 262, 272, 279, 282
"Poetry" (Paz)
  See "La poesía"

Poetry (Pavese)
  See *Poesie*
"Poetry for the Advanced" (Baraka) **4**:39
Poetry Is (Hughes) **7**:158
"Poetry is Not a Luxury" (Lorde) **12**:143
"Poetry Perpetuates the Poet" (Herrick) **9**:146
"Poets" (Herrick) **9**:91, 106
"The Poets are Silent" (Smith) **12**:354
"The Poet's Death Is His Life" (Gibran) **9**:73
"The Poets of Seven Years" (Rimbaud)
  See "Les poètes de sept ans"
"The Poet's Story" (Tagore)
  See "Kabi kahini"
"The Poet's Vow" (Browning) **6**:38-9
"The Point" (Hayden) **6**:193
"Point Shirley" (Plath) **1**:389
"Le poison" (Baudelaire) **1**:45, 61
"Poison" (Tagore)
  See "Halahal"
"A Poison Tree" (Blake) **12**:7
"Political Poem" (Baraka) **4**:10
"Political Relations" (Lorde) **12**:141
Poltava (Pushkin) **10**:366-69, 371, 373, 390-91, 394, 409, 411
"Pomade" (Dove) **6**:111, 113
"Pomegranates" (Valery)
  See "Les grenades"
"Pompilia" (Browning) **2**:41
"Le pont Mirabeau" ("Mirabeau Bridge") (Apollinaire) **7**:11, 21
"Les ponts" (Rimbaud) **3**:264
"Poor Art" (Montale)
  See "L'arte povera"
"The Poor Child's Toy" (Baudelaire)
  See "Le joujou du pauvre"
"A Poor Christian Looks at the Ghetto" (Milosz) **8**:191-92, 214
"The Poor in Church" (Rimbaud)
  See "Les pauvres à l'église"
"Poor Mailie's Elegy" (Burns)
  See "The Death and Dying Words of Poor Mailie"
"Poor Pierrot" (Masters) **1**:330, 333
"Poor Susan" (Wordsworth) **4**:374
"The Pope" (Browning) **2**:41, 72
"Poppies" (Sandburg) **2**:303
"Poppies in July" (Plath) **1**:381, 388
"Poppies in October" (Plath) **1**:384
Poppy and Memory (Celan)
  See *Mohn und Gedächtnes*
"Poppy Flower" (Hughes) **1**:240
"Populist Manifesto" (Ferlinghetti) **1**:176, 182, 188
"Por boca cerrada entran moscas" ("Flies Enter through a Closed Mouth") (Neruda) **4**:290
"Pora, Moi Drug, Pora" ("It's Time, My Friend, It's Time") (Pushkin) **10**:410
"Porter" (Hughes) **1**:242
"Portovenere" (Montale) **13**:151
"Portrait" (Bogan) **12**:87, 101, 103
"A Portrait" (Browning) **2**:59
"The Portrait" (Graves) **6**:144
"A Portrait" (Rossetti) **7**:296-97
"Portrait by a Neighbor" (Millay) **6**:233
"A Portrait in Greys" (Williams) **7**:409
"Portrait of a Lady" (Eliot) **5**:153, 161, 183, 185-86
"A Portrait of a Modern Lady" (Swift) **9**:259
"Portrait of a Women in Bed" (Williams) **7**:348, 367

"Portrait of an Old Woman on the College Tavern Wall" (Sexton) **2**:358
"Portrait of Georgia" (Toomer) **7**:310, 320, 334
"Portrait of Marina" (Page) **12**:168, 176, 189-90
"Portrait of the Author" (Pavese) **13**:205
"Portraits" (Cummings) **5**:94
"Die posaunenstelle" (Celan) **10**:98, 111
"The Posie" (Burns) **6**:76
"Positives: For Sterling Plumpp" (Madhubuti) **5**:346
"Posle grozy" (Pasternak) **6**:267-68, 285
Posle razluki (*After Parting*) (Bely) **11**:3, 25, 32-3
"Possessions" (Crane) **3**:83
"Possom Trot" (Dunbar) **5**:133
"Post aetatem nostram" (Brodsky) **9**:4
"A Postcard from the Volcano" (Stevens) **6**:297
"A Post-Impressionist Susurration for the First of November, 1983" (Carruth) **10**:88
"Postlude" (Williams) **7**:345
"A Post-Mortem" (Sassoon) **12**:248
Postscripts (Tagore)
  See *Punascha*
"The Posy" (Herbert) **4**:129
"The Pot of Flowers" (Williams) **7**:388
"Potato Blossom Songs and Jigs" (Sandburg) **2**:316
"Pouring the Milk Away" (Rukeyser) **12**:224
Poverkh barierov (*Above the Barriers*) (Pasternak) **6**:263, 268-69
"Power" (Lorde) **12**:155
"Power" (Rich) **5**:377
"Power" (Rukeyser) **12**:210
"The Power and the Glory" (Sassoon) **12**:246
Power Politics (Atwood) **8**:9, 12, 14-16, 21-4, 26, 31, 44
"Powers" (Milosz) **8**:202, 211
"Powhatan's Daughter" (Crane) **3**:86, 88, 105
Prabhat sangit (*Morning Songs*) (Tagore) **8**:405-06
"A Practical Program for Monks" (Merton) **10**:334
"Prairie" (Sandburg) **2**:303, 304, 307, 314, 316, 339
"Prairie Waters by Night" (Sandburg) **2**:316
"Praise II" (Herbert) **4**:121
"Praise III" (Herbert) **4**:125
"Praise for an Urn" (Crane) **3**:90, 100
Präntik (*The Borderland; Borderland*) (Tagore) **8**:422-24
"Pratidhyani" ("Echo") (Tagore) **8**:406
"Pravahini" ("The River") (Tagore) **8**:415
"The Prayer" (Browning) **6**:19
"The Prayer" (Herbert) **4**:102, 130
"Prayer" (Hughes) **1**:240
"Prayer" (Jimenez)
  See "Plegaria"
"Prayer" (Toomer) **7**:320-22, 334-35
"Prayer I" (Herbert) **4**:115
"Prayer for a Second Flood" (MacDiarmid) **9**:155-56, 197-98
"A Prayer of Columbus" ("A Thought of Columbus") (Whitman) **3**:379, 384, 395
"Prayer to Ben Jonson" ("His Prayer to Ben Jonson") (Herrick) **9**:86, 96
"Prayers of Steel" (Sandburg) **2**:302, 311
"Praying on a 707" (Sexton) **2**:373
"The Preacher: Ruminates behind the Sermon" (Brooks) **7**:53, 87, 94

"Preamble" (Rukeyser) **12**:209
"Precedent" (Dunbar) **5**:133
"The Precinct. Rochester" (Lowell) **13**:83
"Preciosa and the Wind" (Garcia Lorca)
   See "Preciosa y el aire"
"Preciosa y el aire" ("Preciosa and the Wind")
   (Garcia Lorca) **3**:146
"Precious Moments" (Sandburg) **2**:331
"Preface of the Galaxy" (Matsuo Basho)
   See "Ginga no jo"
Preface to a Twenty Volume Suicide Note
   (Baraka) **4**:5-6, 14-17, 27, 31, 37
The Prelude (Wordsworth)
   See *The Prelude; or, Growth of a Poets Mind:*
     Autobiographical Poem
The Prelude; or, Growth of a Poets Mind:
   Autobiographical Poem (*The Prelude*)
   (Wordsworth) **4**:397, 402-09, 412, 414, 421-
   27
"Prelude: The Troops" (Sassoon) **12**:264
"Prelude to a Fairy Tale" (Sitwell) **3**:295,
   300, 304
"Preludes" (Eliot) **5**:153
Premier livre des amours (Ronsard) **11**:246
Le premier livre des poemes (Ronsard) **11**:280
"Première soirèe" (Rimbaud) **3**:258, 283
"Les premières communions" (Rimbaud)
   3:260
"Prendimiento de Antoñito el Camborio"
   ("Arrest of Antoñito the Camborio")
   (Garcia Lorca) **3**:131
"Preparatory Exercise (Dyptych with Votive
   Tablet)" ("Diptych with Votive Tablet")
   (Paz) **1**:374
"Pres Spoke in a Language" (Baraka) **4**:39
"The Presence" (Graves) **6**:137
"Present" (Sanchez) **9**:219
Presented to Ch'en Shang (Li Ho) **13**:44
"Presented to Wei Pa, Gentleman in
   Retirement" (Tu Fu) **9**:322
"Pressure to Grow" (Baraka) **4**:30
"Pretty" (Smith) **12**:301, 318, 321, 328
"The Pretty Bar-Keeper of the Mitre" ("The
   Pretty Barmaid") (Smart) **13**:341, 347
"The Pretty Barmaid" (Smart)
   See "The Pretty Bar-Keeper of the Mitre"
"The Pretty Redhead" (Apollinaire)
   See "La jolie rousse"
"Priapus" ("Orchard") (H. D.) **5**:275, 303
"Prière du matin" (Verlaine) **2**:416
"The Priest" (H. D.) **5**:306
"Prigovor" ("The Sentence") (Akhmatova)
   2:8-9
"Prima del viaggio" ("Before the Trip")
   (Montale) **13**:134
"A Primary Ground" (Rich) **5**:361
"La primavera" (Jimenez) **7**:193-94
"La primavera Hitleriana" ("The Hitlerian
   Spring") (Montale) **13**:104, 109, 145, 148,
   165-66
"Prime" (Lowell) **13**:64, 67
Primer for Blacks (Brooks) **7**:83, 86
Primer romancero gitano (*Book of Gypsy
   Ballads*; *Gipsy Ballads*; *Gypsy Balladeer*;
   Gypsy Ballads; *Romancero gitano*) (Garcia
   Lorca) **3**:119-21, 127, 130, 133-34, 136-38,
   145-49
Primeras poesias (Jimenez) **7**:209
"The Primitive" (Madhubuti) **5**:322
"A Primitive Like an Orb" (Stevens) **6**:314,
   335
"The Primrose" (Donne) **1**:126, 130

"Primrose" (Herrick) **9**:125
"Primrose" (Williams) **7**:345
Prince Hohenstiel-Schwangau (Browning)
   2:43, 47, 82, 95
"The Prince's Progress" (Rossetti) **7**:262-64,
   279-80, 287, 289, 293-94, 296-98
The Prince's Progress, and Other Poems
   (Rossetti) **7**:261, 263, 266, 296
The Princess: A Medley (Tennyson) **6**:354,
   360, 364-65, 371, 409
The Princess and the Knights (Bely) **11**:24
De principiis (Gray)
   See *De principiis cogitandi*
De principiis cogitandi (*De principiis*) (Gray)
   2:154
"The Prisoner" (Bronte)
   See "Julian M. and A. G. Rochelle"
"The Prisoner" (Browning) **6**:26
"The Prisoner" (Paz)
   See "El prisonero"
"The Prisoner" (Tagore)
   See "Bandi"
The Prisoner of the Caucasus (Pushkin)
   See *Kavkazsky plennik*
"El prisonero" ("The Prisoner") (Paz) **1**:364-
   65
"The Prisoners" (Hayden) **6**:194-95
"The Prisoner's Complaint" (Scott) **13**:292
"The Prisoner's Dream" (Montale)
   See "Il Sogno del prigioniero"
"Private Madrigals" (Montale)
   See "Madrigali privati"
"Private Means is Dead" (Smith) **12**:309, 333
"The Probationer" (Page) **12**:176
"Procedures for Underground" (Atwood)
   8:13, 19
Procedures for Underground (Atwood) **8**:2-3,
   12, 15-16, 21
"Processionals, II" (Duncan) **2**:101
"Proda di Versilia" ("Beach at Versilia";
   "Versilian Shore") (Montale) **13**:112, 148
"Proem: To Brooklyn Bridge" (Crane) **3**:85,
   88, 90, 107, 109
"Proffitt and Batten" (Smith) **12**:339
"Les profondeurs" (Apollinaire) **7**:32, 34
"De profundis" (Browning) **6**:5, 23
"De profundis" (MacDiarmid) **9**:153
"Profusion du soir" (Valery) **9**:391
"The Progress of Beauty, 1720" (Swift)
   9:253, 257, 298-99
"The Progress of Poesy" ("Ode on the
   Progress of Poesy"; "The Progress of
   Poetry") (Gray) **2**:133, 135, 137, 139, 143-
   44, 146, 148-49, 151-55
"The Progress of Poetry" (Gray)
   See "The Progress of Poesy"
"The Progress of Poetry" (Swift) **9**:249
"Progression" (Smith) **12**:316
"Progressive Insanities of a Pioneer" (Atwood)
   8:4
"The Prohibition" ("Take heed of loving
   mee") (Donne) **1**:130
"Projected Slide of an Unknown Soldier"
   (Atwood) **8**:7
"The Prologue" (Bradstreet) **10**:2, 6, 11, 52
"Prologue" (Hughes) **7**:154
"Prologue" (Lorde) **12**:156
"Prologue" (Verlaine) **2**:432
"Prologue: An Interim" (Levertov)
   See "Interim"
"Prologue at Sixty" (Auden) **1**:20
"Prologue to King John" (Blake) **12**:31

"Prometheus" (Dunbar) **5**:146
"Prometheus" (Goethe) **5**:247, 254
"Prometheus" (Graves) **6**:137
Prometheus Bound, and Miscellaneous Poems
   (Browning) **6**:16, 18
Prometheus on His Crag (Hughes) **7**:155-56
"The Promise" (Toomer) **7**:338
"Promise and Fulfillment" (Dunbar) **5**:121
"Promontoire" (Rimbaud) **3**:264
"The Prophet" (Pushkin)
   See "Prorok"
The Prophet (Gibran) **9**:69-75, 80-2
"Prorok" ("The Prophet") (Pushkin) **10**:409,
   414
Prose Poems (Baudelaire)
   See *Petits poèmes en prose: Le spleen de Paris*
"Prosopèe de Louys de Ronsard" (Ronsard)
   11:282
"Prosopopoia; or, Mother Hubberds Tale"
   ("Mother Hubberd's Tale") (Spenser)
   8:335, 365, 368-71, 390
"Prospective Immigrants Please Note" (Rich)
   5:370
Prospectus to the Excursion (Wordsworth)
   See *The Excursion, Being a Portion of "The
     Recluse"*
"Prospice" (Browning) **2**:51, 66
"Protestant Easter" (Sexton) **2**:363
"Prothalamion" (Schwartz) **8**:290-91, 299,
   301-02, 304-05
Prothalamion; or, A Spousall Verse (Spenser)
   8:336, 390
"Proud Maisie" (Scott) **13**:272, 278, 280
"Proverbs of Hell" (Blake) **12**:36, 49-50
"Provide, Provide" (Frost) **1**:227-28, 231
"Providence" (Herbert) **4**:102, 134
Provinces (Milosz) **8**:212, 214-15
"Provincia deserta" (Pound) **4**:366
"Provisional Conclusions" (Montale) **13**:131
Provisional Conclusions (Montale) **13**:135
Prufrock and Other Observations (Eliot)
   5:152, 173, 184-85, 195, 204, 206
"Psalm" (Celan) **10**:98, 101, 118, 120
"A Psalm" (Merton) **10**:332
"Psalm II" (Ginsberg) **4**:81
"Psalm 2" (Smart) **13**:330
"Psalm 94" (Smart) **13**:362
"Psalm 104" (Smart) **13**:332
"Psalm 105" (Smart) **13**:362
"Psalm 120" (Smart) **13**:363
"Psalm Concerning the Castle" (Levertov)
   11:177
"Psalm Praising the Hair of Man's Body"
   (Levertov) **11**:171
"Psalms" (Smart)
   See *A Translation of the Psalms of David,
     Attempted in the Spirit of Christianity, and
     Adapted to the Divine Service*
Psalms of David (Smart)
   See *A Translation of the Psalms of David,
     Attempted in the Spirit of Christianity, and
     Adapted to the Divine Service*
"The Psychiatrist's Song" (Bogan) **12**:101,
   115
"Public Bar TV" (Hughes) **7**:120, 122
"Public Garden" (Lowell) **3**:199-200, 215
Published and Unpublished Poems (Pavese)
   See *Poesie edite e inedite*
"Puck of Pook's Hill" (Kipling) **3**:192
"Puck's Song" (Kipling) **3**:183, 192
"Pueblo Pot" (Millay) **6**:215
"Puella Mea" (Cummings) **5**:104

Title Index

"The Pulley" (Herbert) **4**:102

Punascha (*Once Again*; *Postscripts*) (Tagore) **8**:417

"The Puppets" (Page) **12**:184

Purabi (Tagore) **8**:415

"Pure Death" (Graves) **6**:137, 151

"Pure Love" (Tagore)
See "Pavitra prem"

"Purely Local" (Rich) **5**:352

"Purgatory" (Lowell) **3**:241

"Purner abhav" ("Limitation of Perfection")
(Tagore) **8**:414

"Purple Grackles" (Lowell) **13**:64, 67, 87,
98-9

"Pursuit" (H. D.) **5**:287-88

"La puttana contadina" ("The Country
Whore"; "The Peasant Whore") (Pavese)
13:210, 219

"Putting to Sea" (Bogan) **12**:123

"Pygmalion" (H. D.) **5**:270, 304

"Pygmies Are Pygmies Still, Though Percht on
Alps" (Brooks) **7**:55

"Pyrotechnics" (Bogan) **12**:117

"Pyrotechnics" (Lowell) **13**:83

"La pythie" (Valery) **9**:353, 365-66, 369, 373,
379, 393

Quaderno de quattro anni (*Depends: A Poet's
Notebook*; *The Four Years' Notebook*)
(Montale) **13**:128, 153, 156, 160, 168

"Quai D'Orleans" (Bishop) **3**:37

"The Quaker Graveyard at Nantucket (for
Warren Winslow, Dead at Sea)" (Lowell)
3:200-02, 204, 212, 217, 223, 233, 235-38

"Quaker Hill" (Crane) **3**:86, 90, 106

"Quand vous serez bien vieille" (Ronsard)
11:218-21

"Quando il soave mio fido conforto" (Petrarch)
8:235

"Quashie to Buccra" (McKay) **2**:215, 223

*Quatre de P. de Ronsard aux injures et
calomnies* (Ronsard) **11**:291

Les quatre premiers livres de la Franciade (*La
Franciade*) (Ronsard) **11**:226, 234, 246,
271, 283, 286-87, 290

"The Queen and the Young Princess" (Smith)
12:326, 352

"The Queen of Hearts" (Rossetti) **7**:272, 274

"Queen Worship" (Browning) **2**:26

"Queen-Anne's Lace" (Williams) **7**:374

"The Quest of the Purple-Fringed" (Frost)
1:218

"A Question" (Arnold) **5**:38

"The Question" (Rukeyser) **12**:225

"Question and Answer" (Browning) **6**:5

"Question au clerc du quichet" (Villon)
13:394

"A Question of Climate" (Lorde) **12**:136

"A Question of *Essence*" (Lorde) **12**:140

"Questions of Travel" (Bishop) **3**:55, 67

Questions of Travel (Bishop) **3**:48, 53, 59

"A questo punto" ("At This Point") (Montale)
13:158

Quia pawper amavi (Pound) **4**:317

"Quick I the Death of Thing" (Cummings)
5:108

"A Quickening: A Song for the Visitation"
(Merton) **10**:339

"The Quickening of St. John Baptist" (Merton)
10:339

"Quiero volver a sur" ("I Would Return
South") (Neruda) **4**:281

"Quiet Work" (Arnold) **5**:12, 36, 38, 49

"Quietness" (Williams) **7**:382

"Quimérica" ("The Impossible Woman/Ideal")
(Jimenez) **7**:197

"The Quip" (Herbert) **4**:100, 102, 108, 119,
130

"R. A. F." (H. D.) **5**:307

"The Rabbi" (Hayden) **6**:195, 198

"Rabbi Ben Ezra" (Browning) **2**:51, 75, 95

"The Rabbi's Song" (Kipling) **3**:183

"The Rabbit" (Millay) **6**:238

"The Rag Man" (Hayden) **6**:195

"Rages de césars" (Rimbaud) **3**:283

"The Ragged Schools of London" (Browning)
See "A Song for the Ragged Schools of
London"

"Railroad Avenue" (Hughes) **1**:237

"The Rain" (Levertov) **11**:176

"Rain" (Williams) **7**:349

"Rain Charm for the Duchy, a Blessed,
Devout Drench for the Christening of a
Prince Harry" (Hughes) **7**:171

"Rain Festival" (Tagore)
See "Varsha-mangal"

"The Rain, It Streams on Stone and Hillock"
(Housman) **2**:162

"Rain on a Grave" (Hardy) **8**:134

"Rain or Hail" (Cummings) **5**:88

"Rain-Song" (Dunbar) **5**:125

"Raise the Shade" (Cummings) **5**:89

"Raleigh Was Right" (Williams) **7**:360

"La rameur" (Valery) **9**:367, 395-96

"Rap of a Fan..." (Apollinaire)
See "Coup d'evential..."

"Rape" (Rich) **5**:361

"The Raper from Passenack" (Williams)
7:353, 368, 399

"Rapunzel" (Sexton) **2**:368

"Rapunzel, Rapunzel" (Smith) **12**:341

"Rational Man" (Rukeyser) **12**:220, 230

"The Raven" (Poe) **1**:419-20, 424, 427, 429-
34, 436, 439-40, 443-44, 447, 452-53

"The Raven: A Christmas Tale" (Coleridge)
11:109-17

The Raven, and Other Poems (Poe) **1**:437,
449

"The Ravine" (Carruth) **10**:85, 90

Rbaiyyat (Khayyam)
See *Rubáiyát*

"Re-Act for Action" (Madhubuti) **5**:338

"The Reader over My Shoulder" (Graves)
6:143, 151

"Reading Aloud" (Gallagher) **9**:60

"Reading Apollinaire by the Rouge River"
(Ferlinghetti) **1**:181, 187

"Reading Holderlin on the Patio with the Aid
of a Dictionary" (Dove) **6**:109

"Reading Myself" (Lowell) **3**:229

"Reading the Japanese Poet Issa" (Milosz)
8:189

"Reading the Will" (Kipling) **3**:190

"Reading Time: 1 Minute 26 Seconds"
(Rukeyser) **12**:206

"Readings of History" (Rich) **5**:355

"The Real Estate Agents Tale" (Lowell)
13:84

"Real Life" (Baraka) **4**:30

La realidad invisible (*Invisible Reality*)
(Jimenez) **7**:207

Reality Sandwiches (Ginsberg) **4**:67, 81

"Reapers" (Toomer) **7**:319, 333-34

"Reaping" (Lowell) **13**:60

"The Rear-Guard" (Sassoon) **12**:266

"Reason and Imagination" (Smart) **13**:341,
347

"Reawakening" (Pavese)
See "Risveglio"

"Le rebelle" (Baudelaire) **1**:55

"Rebellion" (Lowell) **3**:318

"The Rebels" (Ferlinghetti) **1**:184

"Rebirth" (Pushkin) **10**:408

"A Rebus by I. B." (Wheatley) **3**:338

"Recalling War" (Graves) **6**:137, 142, 144,
165

"The Recantation: An Ode. By S. T.
Coleridge" (Coleridge) **11**:94, 99

"Recessional" (Masters) **1**:333

"Recipe for Happiness in Khaboronsky"
(Ferlinghetti) **1**:183

"Recitative" (Crane) **3**:81, 83

Recklings (Hughes) **7**:120, 122-23

"The Recluse" (Smith) **12**:299, 331, 333

*The Recluse; or Views on Man, Nature, and on
Human Life* (Wordsworth) **4**:406-07, 409

"Recollection" (Wheatley)
See "On Recollection"

"Recollections of the Arabian Nights"
(Tennyson) **6**:347, 359, 389, 406, 408-09

Recollections of Tsarskoe-Selo (Pushkin)
See "Vospominanie v Tsarskom Sele"

"Reconciliation" (Day Lewis) **11**:147

"Reconciliation" (Milosz) **8**:213

"Reconciliation" (Sassoon) **12**:289

"Reconciliation" (Whitman) **3**:378

Records of a Weather Exposed Skeleton
(Matsuo Basho)
See *Nozarashi kikō*

"Recovering" (Rukeyser) **12**:225

"The Recovery" (Pushkin) **10**:408

Recovery (Tagore)
See *Ārogya*

Recovery (Tagore)
See *Ārogya*

"The Recruit" (Housman) **2**:196

"A Recruit on the Corpy" (McKay) **2**:226

"Recueillement" ("Meditation") (Baudelaire)
1:65

"Recuerdo" (Millay) **6**:215

"Recuerdos..." ("Memories...") (Jimenez)
7:199

"The Red Knight" (Lowell) **13**:84

"The Red Lacquer Music Stand" (Lowell)
13:78

"Red Poppy" (Gallagher) **9**:64

"A Red, Red Rose" (Burns)
See "My Luve Is Like a Red, Red Rose"

"Red Riding Hood" (Sexton) **2**:354, 364

Red Roses for Bronze (H. D.) **5**:270-71, 304

"Red Silk Stockings" (Hughes) **1**:269

"Red Slippers" (Lowell) **13**:79

"The Red Wheelbarrow" (Williams) **7**:378,
401-02, 409-10

"The Redbreast and the Butterfly"
(Wordsworth) **4**:376

"Red-Cotton Nightcap Country" (Browning)
2:96

"The Redeemer" (Sassoon) **12**:242, 249-51,
261-62, 276, 278, 287

"Redemption" (Herbert) **4**:119, 130

"Redwing" (Gallagher) **9**:62

"The Reefy Coast" (Ishikawa Takuboku)
See "Ariso"

"The Reflection: A Song" (Behn) **13**:18, 20-1

"Reflection in a Forest" (Auden) **1**:17

"Reflection in an Ironworks" (MacDiarmid)
9:155
"Reflections at Lake Louise" (Ginsberg)   4:84
"Reflections on a Scottish Slum"
(MacDiarmid)   9:181
"Reflections on Having Left a Place of
Retirement" (Coleridge)   11:81
"Refrain" (Dove)   6:117
"A Refusal to Mourn the Death, by Fire, of a
Child in London" (Thomas)   2:382-83, 386,
388, 390, 398, 400
"Regrets of the Belle Heaumiere" (Villon)
See "Lament of the Belle Heaulmiere"
"The Rehearsal" (Smith)   12:330
"Rejoice in the Lamb" (Smart)
See "Jubilate Agno"
Rekviem: Tsikl stikhotvorenii (Requiem: A
Cycle of Poems) (Akhmatova)   2:4, 7, 9, 15-
16, 19-20
"Relearning the Alphabet" (Levertov)
11:195-98
Relearning the Alphabet (Levertov)   11:176-78,
180, 193-94
"Religion" (Dunbar)   5:125
"Religious Isolation" (Arnold)   5:42
"A Religious Man" (Smith)   12:352
"Religious Musings" (Coleridge)   11:49-51,
53, 80-2, 93-6
"Religious Propaganda" (Tagore)
See "Dharma prachar"
"The Relique" (Donne)   1:126, 130
Remains of Elmet (Hughes)   7:146, 149, 162
"Rembrandt to Rembrandt" (Robinson)
1:487
"Remember" (Rossetti)   7:269, 280
"Rememberance" (Holderlin)
See "Andenken"
"Remembrance" ("Cold in the Earth")
(Bronte)   8:52, 56, 60, 65, 68, 74-5
"Remembrance Has a Rear and Front"
(Dickinson)   1:94
"Remembrance in Tsarskoe Selo" (Pushkin)
See "Vospominanie v Tsarskom Sele"
"Reminiscence" (Ishikawa Takuboku)
See "Omoide"
"Réminiscence" (Mallarme)
See "L'orphelin"
"Reminiscences at Tsarskoe Selo" (Pushkin)
See "Vospominanie v Tsarskom Sele"
"Remord posthume" (Baudelaire)   1:45
"Remorse" (Sassoon)   12:282
Remorse (Osorio) (Coleridge)   11:58
"Remorse Is Memory Awake" (Dickinson)
1:111
"Renascence" (Millay)   204-05, 207-08, 211,
214-15, 217, 221, 224, 226-27, 242
Renascence, and Other Poems (Millay)   6:204-
06, 225, 240
"Les reparties de Nina" ("Nina Replies")
(Rimbaud)   3:271
"Repas" (Valery)   9:391
"Repentance" (Herbert)   4:120
"The Repetitive Heart" (Schwartz)   8:292-93,
302
"Repining" (Rossetti)   7:287
"Repose of Rivers" (Crane)   3:83, 90, 96
"Repression of War Experience" (Sassoon)
12:264, 267, 288
"Reproach" (Graves)   6:140, 144
"Request for Requiems" (Hughes)   1:243
"A Request to the Graces" (Herrick)   9:88

"Requeste à Monseigneur de Bourbon"
(Villon)   13:413
Requiem (Rilke)   2:267, 279
Requiem: A Cycle of Poems (Akhmatova)
See *Rekviem: Tsikl stikhotvorenii*
"Requiem for the Death of a Boy" (Rilke)
2:279
"Requiescat" (Arnold)   5:12
Rerum vulgarium fragmenta (Petrarch)
See *Canzoniere*
"Rescue with Yul Brynner" (Moore)   4:242,
256, 259
Residence on Earth (Neruda)
See *Residencia en la tierra*
Residence on Earth and Other Poems (Neruda)
See *Residencia en la tierra*
Residencia en la tierra (Residence on Earth;
Residence on Earth and Other Poems;
Residencia en la tierra, Vol. 1, 1925-31;
Residencia en la tierra, Vol. 2, 1931-35;
Residencia I; Residencia II; Residencia III)
(Neruda)   4:277, 2809, 282-83, 285, 293,
295, 300-01, 304, 306
Residencia en la tierra, Vol. 1, 1925-31
(Neruda)
See *Residencia en la tierra*
Residencia en la tierra, Vol. 2, 1931-35
(Neruda)
See *Residencia en la tierra*
Residencia I (Neruda)
See *Residencia en la tierra*
Residencia II (Neruda)
See *Residencia en la tierra*
Residencia III (Neruda)
See *Residencia en la tierra*
"Resignation" (Arnold)   5:6, 18, 32, 34, 37-
41, 43, 47, 49-51, 54
"Resignation" (Dunbar)   5:133
"Resolution and Independence" (Wordsworth)
4:399, 404, 406, 411-12, 426
"The Resolve" (Levertov)   11:170
"Resolve" (Plath)   1:406
"Respectability" (Browning)   2:95
"The Respectable Burgher on 'The Higher
Criticism'" (Hardy)   8:124
Responce aux injures (Ronsard)   11:234
"Respondez!" (Whitman)   3:405
"Response" (Dunbar)   5:139
"A Responsory, 1948" (Merton)   10:333
"Ressurection, Imperfect" (Donne)   1:147
"Rest" (Rossetti)   7:277, 280
"Restless" (Tagore)
See "Chanchal"
"Restless Night" (Tu Fu)   9:319, 323
"Resurrection" (Atwood)   8:40
"Resurrection of the Right Side" (Rukeyser)
12:225
"Retired Ballerina, Central Park West"
(Ferlinghetti)   1:183
"The Retired Colonel" (Hughes)   7:140
"Retort" (Dunbar)   5:125, 127
"Return" (Forche)   10:136-41, 144-45, 152,
154-56, 162, 167
"The Return" (Hayden)   6:194
"Return" (Paz)
See "Vuelta"
"The Return" (Pound)   4:355-56, 365
The Return (Bely)
See *Vozvrat: Tretiia simfoniia*
Return (Paz)
See *Vuelta*

"The Return of the Goddess" (Graves)   6:137,
144
"Return to Kraków in 1880" (Milosz)   8:204
"A Return to Me" (Neruda)
See "Se vuelve a yo"
"Return to Oneself" (Neruda)
See "Se vuelve a yo"
"The Return to Work" (Williams)   7:369
"Returning" (Lowell)   3:226
"Returning North of Vortex" (Ginsberg)   4:76
"Returning to the Rhetoric of an Early Mode"
(Duncan)   2:109, 113
"Reuben Bright" (Robinson)   1:467, 496
"Reuben Pantier" (Masters)   1:347
"Reunion" (Forche)   10:137, 142-44, 147, 157,
168
"Le rêve d'un curieux" (Baudelaire)   1:54
"Rêve parisien" ("A Parisian Dream")
(Baudelaire)   1:47, 54
"Reveillé" (Housman)   2:164
"Reveille" (Hughes)   7:123, 159
"Revenge Fable" (Hughes)   7:132, 143
"Reverie" (Browning)   2:96
"Reversibilité" (Baudelaire)   1:56, 67
"Reversionary" (Smith)   12:314
"The Revolution at Market Hill" (Swift)
9:260
"Revolutions" (Arnold)   5:51
"Revulsion" (Hardy)   8:91
Rewards and Fairies (Kipling)   3:184
"Reyerta" ("Brawl") (Garcia Lorca)   3:131
"The Rhapsody of Life's Progress" (Browning)
6:6
"Rhapsody on a Windy Night" (Eliot)   5:153,
155, 171
"A Rhapsody on Poetry" (Swift)   9:281
"Der Rhein" ("The Rhine") (Holderlin)
4:143, 148, 153, 155, 173-74
"Rhénane d'automne" (Apollinaire)   7:42
"The Rhine" (Holderlin)
See "Der Rhein"
"Rhododendrons" (Gallagher)   9:60
"The Rhyme of the Duchess of May"
(Browning)   6:28
"The Rhyme of the Three Captains" (Kipling)
3:181-82
"The Rhyme of the Three Sealers" (Kipling)
3:182
Rhymed Ruminations (Sassoon)   12:252
Rhymes (Jimenez)
See *Rimas*
"Rhythm & Blues 1" (Baraka)   4:16
"Rhythm of Autumn" (Garcia Lorca)
See "Ritmo de otoño"
"Richard Bone" (Masters)   1:324
"Richard Cory" (Robinson)   1:467, 475, 486
"Richard Hunt's 'Arachne'" (Hayden)   6:186
"Richard Roe and John Doe" (Graves)   6:141
"The Riddle" (Auden)   1:34
"The Ride" (Smith)   12:315
"Ride to Aix" (Browning)   2:35
"Riding the Elevator into the Sky" (Sexton)
2:373
"Rigamarole" (Williams)   7:383, 389
"The Right of Way" (Williams)   7:387, 409,
411
"Right's Security" (Dunbar)   5:127
Rimas (Rhymes) (Jimenez)   7:197, 199
Rime (Petrarch)
See *Canzoniere*

"The Rime of the Ancient Mariner: A Poet's Reverie" ("The Rime of the Ancyent Marinere") (Coleridge) **11**:37-42, 44, 51, 53, 55, 58-69, 81, 84, 88-9, 92-7, 104, 106, 110, 117

"The Rime of the Ancyent Marinere" (Coleridge)
See "The Rime of the Ancient Mariner: A Poet's Reverie"

Rime sparse (Petrarch)
See *Canzoniere*

"Un rimorso" (Gozzano) **10**:188

The Ring and the Book (Browning) **2**:39-40, 42-4, 46-7, 53, 56, 63, 66-7, 73, 76-7, 82-3, 85, 88, 95

"The Ring and the Castle" (Lowell) **13**:60-1

"Ringing the Bells" (Sexton) **2**:350, 353

"Los ríos del canto" ("The Rivers of Song") (Neruda) **4**:293

"Riot" (Brooks) **7**:82, 88-9, 91

Riot (Brooks) **7**:63-4, 66, 82, 88, 91, 94

Ripostes (Pound) **4**:317, 355

"The Ripple" (Levertov) **11**:171

"A Ripple Song" (Kipling) **3**:183

"The Risen One" (Rilke) **2**:271 .

"The Rising of the Sun" (Milosz)
See "From Where the Sun Rises"

"Risveglio" ("Reawakening") (Pavese) **13**:229

"The Rites for Cousin Vit" (Brooks) **7**:66, 78, 81

"Rites for the Extrusion of a Leper" (Merton) **10**:345

"Ritmo de otoño" ("Rhythm of Autumn") (Garcia Lorca) **3**:125

"Ritorno di Deola" ("Deola's Return") (Pavese) **13**:229

"Ritratto" (Pound) **4**:317

"Ritratto d'autore" (Pavese) **13**:213

"Ritter" (Rilke) **2**:266-67

"The Ritual of Memories" (Gallagher) **9**:60

"The Ritual of Memories" (Gallagher) **9**:60

"The Rival" (Plath) **1**:390

"The Rivals" (Dunbar) **5**:122

"The River" (Arnold) **5**:19, 43

"The River" (Crane) **3**:84-6, 88-90, 95

"The River" (Tagore)
See "Pravahini"

The River (Hughes) **7**:163, 171

"The River God" (Smith) **12**:331, 337

"River Roads" (Sandburg) **2**:316

"River Stop" (Tu Fu) **9**:319

"River Village" (Tu Fu) **9**:319

"The Rivers of Song" (Neruda)
See "Los ríos del canto"

"The River's Story" (Tagore)
See "Tatinir katha"

"Riviere" ("Shores") (Montale) **13**:162

"Rizpah" (Tennyson) **6**:372-73, 377, 379, 381, 411

"The Road" (Sassoon) **12**:242

"The Road and the End" (Sandburg) **2**:300

"The Road Not Taken" (Frost) **1**:202, 205, 213, 221, 230

"Road to Mandalay" (Kipling) **3**:179

The Road to Ruin (Sassoon) **12**:252, 270

"The Road to Shelter" ("The Way of Refuge") (Gozzano) **10**:177

The Road to Shelter (Gozzano)
See *La via del refugio*

"Road Up" (Smith) **12**:317

"Roarers in a Ring" (Hughes) **7**:123

"Roast Opossum" (Dove) **6**:111

"The Robber" (MacDiarmid) **9**:155

"Robe of Love" (Yosano Akiko)
See *Koigoromo*

"Robert G. Ingersoll" (Masters) **1**:343

"Robert Gould Shaw" (Dunbar) **5**:121

"Robert Schumann, Or: Musical Genius Begins with Affliction" (Dove) **6**:108

"Robin Song" (Hughes) **7**:134

"The Rock" (Stevens) **6**:303, 313

"The Rock Below" (Graves) **6**:128-29

"The Rock of Rubies and the Quarry of Pearls" (Herrick) **9**:146

"Rockefeller is yo vice president, & yo mamma don't wear no drawers" (Baraka) **4**:30

"Rocky Acres" (Graves) **6**:151

"Rodine" ("Homeland") (Bely) **11**:24

"Rodoslovnaya Moego Geroya" ("The Genealogy of My Hero"; "My Hero's Genealogy") (Pushkin) **10**:391, 394

Rogsajyae (*From the Sick-Bed*; *On the Sick-Bed*) (Tagore) **8**:424-26

Rokeby (Scott) **13**:265, 267-68, 277-78, 281, 285, 304, 307, 311, 318

"Roland Hayes Beaten" (Hughes) **1**:241, 243, 252

"Rolling, Rolling" (Toomer) **7**:337

"Roman" (Rimbaud) **3**:271, 276

Roman Bartholow (Robinson) **1**:483, 489

The Roman Calendar (Ovid)
See *Fasti*

Roman Elegies (Goethe)
See *Römische Elegien*

Roman Elegies II (Brodsky) **9**:21

"Roman Fountain" (Bogan) **12**:99

"The Roman Road" (Smith) **12**:346

"Romance" (Robinson) **1**:495

"Romance de la Guardia Civil Española" ("Ballad of the Spanish Civil Guard"; "Romance of the Spanish Civil Guard") (Garcia Lorca) **3**:131, 148

"Romance de la luna, luna" ("Ballad of the Moon, the Moon") (Garcia Lorca) **3**:133

"Romance de la pena negra" ("Ballad of the Black Sorrow"; "Ballad of the Dark Trouble") (Garcia Lorca) **3**:133

"Romance del emplazado" ("The Cited") (Garcia Lorca) **3**:133

"Romance moderne" (Williams) **7**:345

"Romance of the Spanish Civil Guard" (Garcia Lorca)
See "Romance de la Guardia Civil Española"

"The Romance of the Swan's Nest" (Browning) **6**:32

"Romance sonámbulo" ("Sleepwalker Ballad"; "Somnambulent Ballad"; "Somnambulist Ballad") (Garcia Lorca) **3**:131, 133, 147

Romancero gitano (Garcia Lorca)
See *Primer romancero gitano*

Romances sans paroles (Verlaine) **2**:414-15, 418-19, 424, 431-32

"The Romantic" (Bogan) **12**:87, 100-01, 103

"The Romaunt of Margret" (Browning) **6**:32

"The Romaunt of the Page" (Browning) **6**:18, 32

"Rome-Sickness" (Arnold) **5**:19

Römische Elegien (*Roman Elegies*) (Goethe) **5**:239-40, 249, 255, 257

"Römische Sarkophage" (Rilke) **2**:278

"The Roofwalker" (Rich) **5**:363, 392-93, 395

"The Room of Mirrors" (Masters) **1**:344

"The Room of My Life" (Sexton) **2**:373

"Rooming-house, Winter" (Atwood) **8**:14

"Roosters" (Bishop) **3**:37, 46-8, 56-7, 60, 66

"Roots and Branches" (Duncan) **2**:103, 110

Roots and Branches (Duncan) **2**:102, 105-06, 109, 113-14, 119, 125

La rosa separada: obra póstuma (*The Separate Rose*) (Neruda) **4**:287

"The Rose" (Williams) **7**:386, 410

"Rose on the Heath" (Goethe)
See "Heidenröslein"

"Roseamond" (Apollinaire)
See "Rosemonde"

"Rosemonde" ("Roseamond") (Apollinaire) **7**:45, 47-8

"Rosenschimmer" (Celan) **10**:122

"Roses" (Dove) **6**:109

"Roses" (Sandburg) **2**:324

"Rosy-Cheeked Death" (Yosano Akiko)
See "Kôgao no shi"

"A Rotting Corpse" (Baudelaire)
See "Une charogne"

"Round the Turning" (Pasternak) **6**:267

"Round Trip" (Page) **12**:163

"De Route March" (McKay) **2**:225

"Route Marchin'" (Kipling) **3**:160

"A Route of Evanescence" (Dickinson) **1**:104

"Rowing" (Sexton) **2**:373

"The Rowing Endeth" (Sexton) **2**:371

"A Roxbury Garden" (Lowell) **13**:77-8, 96

"A Royal Princess" (Rossetti) **7**:272, 291

"Royauté" (Rimbaud) **3**:261-63

Rubáiyát (*Rbaiyyat*; *Ruba'iyat*) (Khayyam) **8**:143-45, 151-53, 157-70

Ruba'iyat (Khayyam)
See *Rubáiyát*

"Ruby Brown" (Hughes) **1**:249

"Rugby Chapel" (Arnold) **5**:33

"Ruin" (Garcia Lorca)
See "Ruina"

"Ruina" ("Ruin") (Garcia Lorca) **3**:139

"The Ruined Cottage" (Wordsworth) **4**:416, 418

"The Ruined Temple" (Tagore)
See "Bhagna mandir"

"The Ruines of Time" (Spenser) **8**:366-67, 371

"Rumpelstiltskin" (Sexton) **2**:364

"Runagate, Runagate" (Hayden) **6**:176, 178-80, 183, 185, 188, 194, 197-98

"The Runaway" (Frost) **1**:194

The Runaway, and Other Stories (Tagore)
See *Palātakā*

"The Runaway Slave at Pilgrim's Point" (Browning) **6**:30, 37-8, 42-3, 45

"Runes on Weland's Island" (Kipling) **3**:171

"Rupture" (Pasternak) **6**:260

Ruslan and Lyudmila (Pushkin)
See *Ruslan i Lyudmila*

Ruslan i Lyudmila (*Ruslan and Lyudmila*) (Pushkin) **10**:357-58, 363-64, 375, 381-82, 386-88, 398, 404-09

"Russia" (Williams) **7**:370

"Russian Sonia" (Masters) **1**:327

Rustic Elegies (Sitwell) **3**:294-95, 319

"Rusty Crimson (Christmas Day, 1917)" (Sandburg) **2**:331

"Ruth" (Wordsworth) **4**:380, 402

"Ru'ya" ("Vision") (Gibran) **9**:79

"Sabala" ("Woman of Strength") (Tagore) **8**:415

"A Sabbath Morning at Sea" (Browning) **6**:14

Sabotage (Baraka) **4**:38
"Sab-peyechhir desh" ("The Land Where All Is Gained") (Tagore) **8**:412
"Sacred Chant for the Return of Black Spirit and Power" (Baraka) **4**:27
"The Sacrifice" (Herbert) **4**:107, 117, 120
"The Sacrifice of Er-Heb" (Kipling) **3**:181
"The Sacrilege" (Hardy) **8**:99
Sad Airs (Jimenez)
　See *Arias tristes*
"The Sad Garden Dissolves" (Jimenez)
　See "El jardín triste se pierde"
"Sad Moments" (Gallagher) **9**:64
"Sad Strains of a Gay Waltz" (Stevens) **6**:296-97
"The Sad Supper" (Pavese)
　See "La cena triste"
Sad Toys (Ishikawa Takuboku)
　See *Kanashiki gangu*
"Sad Wine" (Pavese)
　See "Il vino triste"
"Sadie and Maude" (Brooks) **7**:67, 69
"Saffron" (Smith) **12**:295
Saga Diary (Matsuo Basho)
　See *Saga nikki*
Saga nikki (*Saga Diary*) (Matsuo Basho) **3**:29
"Sagesse" (H. D.) **5**:275
Sagesse (H. D.) **5**:282, 285
Sagesse (Verlaine) **2**:413, 415-19, 425-26, 430
"Said the Poet to the Analyst" (Sexton) **2**:358-59
"The Sail of Ulysses" (Stevens) **6**:326, 328
"Sailing after Lunch" (Stevens) **6**:297, 338
"Sailing Home from Rapallo" (Lowell) **3**:205, 220, 245
"A Sailor in Africa" (Dove) **6**:110
"Sailor in Moscow" (Pasternak)
　See "Matros v Moskve"
"The Sailor's Mother" (Wordsworth) **4**:398, 402
"Saint" (Graves) **6**:141, 144, 151
"A Saint about to Fall" (Thomas) **2**:408-09
"Saint Anthony and the Rose of Life" (Smith) **12**:308
"Saint Francis and Lady Clare" (Masters) **1**:325, 333
"Sainte" (Mallarme) **4**:201
"Sainte-Nitouche" (Robinson) **1**:460
La Saisiaz (Browning) **2**:66, 68, 71-2, 74
Une saison en enfer (*A Season in Hell*) (Rimbaud) **3**:249, 252-53, 260-66, 268, 270, 279, 286
"Sakyamuni Coming Out from the Mountain" (Ginsberg) **4**:49
"Sal" (Tagore) **8**:416
"La Salade" (Ronsard) **11**:240
The Salamander (Paz)
　See *Salamandra*
Salamandra (*The Salamander*) (Paz) **1**:353, 357, 360-62, 369
Salisbury Plain (Wordsworth) **4**:429
"The Sallow Bird" (Smith) **12**:326
"The Salmon Leap" (MacDiarmid) **9**:153
"Saltimbanque Elegie" (Rilke)
　See "Saltimbanques"
"Saltimbanques" ("Saltimbanque Elegie") (Rilke) **2**:278, 295
"Sambhashan" ("Coversation") (Tagore) **8**:417
"Samson" (Blake) **12**:31
"San Ildefonso Nocturne" (Paz)
　See "Nocturno de San Ildefonso"

"San Onofre, California" (Forche) **10**:141, 152-53, 155, 158
"The Sand Altar" (Lowell) **13**:95
Der Sand aus den Urnen (*Sand from the Urns*) (Celan) **10**:95, 121
"Sand Dunes" (Frost) **1**:203, 218
Sand from the Urns (Celan)
　See *Der Sand aus den Urnen*
"The Sand-Diggrers' Twilight" (Pavese)
　See "Crepuscolo di sabbiatori"
Sandhya sangit (*Evening Songs*) (Tagore) **8**:405-06
"Sandpiper" (Bishop) **3**:53-4
Sangschaw (MacDiarmid) **9**:151, 158, 166, 187, 190-91, 196
"Santa" (Sexton) **2**:365
"Santa Cruz Propostions" (Duncan) **2**:116
"Santarém" (Bishop) **3**:64-5
Saōgi (Yosano Akiko) **11**:310
Sarashina kikō (Matsuo Basho) **3**:26
"Sarcophagi I" (Montale) **13**:116
Sarumino (*The Monkey's Cloak*; *The Monkey's Raincoat*) (Matsuo Basho) **3**:3, 4, 29
"Sarvaneshe" ("All-destroyer") (Tagore) **8**:414
Satin-Legs Smith (Brooks)
　See "The Sundays of Satin-Legs Smith"
"Satires of Circumstance" (Hardy) **8**:124
Satires of Circumstance (Hardy) **8**:91, 97
"A Satirical Elegy on the Death of a Late Famous General" (Swift) **9**:256, 294, 307
Satirical Poems (Sassoon) **12**:258
Satura (Montale) **13**:131-34, 138, 143, 148, 152, 161, 167
"The Satyr in the Periwig" (Sitwell) **3**:294
"Satyre II" (Donne) **1**:144
"Satyre III" (Donne) **1**:125, 143, 147
Satyres (Donne) **1**:140-42, 145
"Saul" (Browning) **2**:36, 67-8, 72, 75
"Say, Lad, Have You Things to Do" (Housman) **2**:179, 192
"Scapegoats and Rabies" (Hughes) **7**:137
"Scar" (Lorde) **12**:139
"Schneebett" ("Snowbed") (Celan) **10**:114
Schneepart (Celan) **10**:96, 98
"The Scholar" (Baraka) **4**:23
"The Scholar-Gipsy" (Arnold) **5**:7, 13, 18-24, 33-5, 37, 47, 51, 53, 53, 59
"A School of Prayer" (Baraka) **4**:10, 18
"The School-Boy" (Blake) **12**:7, 34
Schoolboy Lyrics (Kipling) **3**:190, 193
"The Schoolmistresses" (Pavese)
　See "Le maestrine"
"An Schwager Kronos" ("Kronos; To Coachman Kronos") (Goethe) **5**:245, 247, 251
"Scirocco" ("Sirocco") (Montale) **13**:105, 125
"Scorpion" (Smith) **12**:301, 319, 333
Scorpion and Other Poems (Smith) **12**:299, 315
Scots Unbound (MacDiarmid) **9**:158, 175-76, 196
"Scots Wha Hae wi' Wallace Bled" (Burns) **6**:78
"Screw Guns" (Kipling) **3**:158
"Scrub" (Millay) **6**:235
"The Sculptor" (Plath) **1**:388-89
"Se vuelve a yo" ("A Return to Me"; "Return to Oneself") (Neruda) **4**:287
"The Sea" (Williams) **7**:385, 387
The Sea and the Bells (Neruda)
　See *El mar y las campanas*

"The Sea and the Mirror: A Commentary on Shakespeare's *Tempest*" (Auden) **1**:22, 34
"Sea Calm" (Hughes) **1**:236
"Sea Dreams" (Tennyson) **6**:360
Sea Garden (H. D.) **5**:266-67, 288-90, 303
"The Sea Horse" (Graves) **6**:154
"Sea Iris" (H. D.) **5**:289
"Sea Lily" (H. D.) **5**:288
"Sea Poppies" (H. D.) **5**:288
"Sea Surface Full of Clouds" (Stevens) **6**:304, 332
"Sea Unicorns and Land Unicorns" (Moore) **4**:233
"Sea Violet" (H. D.) **5**:289
"Sea-Blue and Blood-Red" (Lowell) **13**:60, 64, 66, 72, 81, 83
"The Sea-Elephant" (Williams) **7**:360
"The Sea-Fairies" (Tennyson) **6**:348, 359
"The Seafarer" (Pound) **4**:317, 331, 364
"The Seamless Garment" (MacDiarmid) **9**:177
"Sea-Nymph's Prayer to Okeanos" (Zukofsky) **11**:368
"The Search" (Herbert) **4**:101
"The Search" (Masters) **1**:343-44
"Searching, Not Searching" (Rukeyser) **12**:224
"Sea-Rose" (H. D.) **5**:288, 303
"Seascape" (Bishop) **3**:37
"Sea-Serpent" (MacDiarmid) **9**:193
The Seashell Game (Matsuo Basho)
　See *Kai oi*
"A Sea-Side Meditation" (Browning) **6**:20
A Season in Hell (Rimbaud)
　See *Une saison en enfer*
The Season of Violence (Paz)
　See *La estación violenta*
Season Songs (Hughes) **7**:157, 162, 171
"Seasons" (Bradstreet)
　See "The Four Seasons of the Year"
Seaton Prize Odes (Smart) **13**:329
"Sea-Wind" (Mallarme) **4**:187
The Second Anniversarie. Of the Progres of the Soule. Wherein, By Occasion Of the Religious death of Mistris Elizabeth Drury, the incommodities of the Soule in this life, and her exaltation in the next, are Contemplated (*Of the Progres of the Soule*) (Donne) **1**:122, 145-51, 155-57
"Second April" (Millay) **6**:206
Second April (Millay) **6**:211-12, 214-15, 233, 242-44
"The Second Best" (Arnold) **5**:42
The Second Birth (Pasternak) **6**:253-54, 268, 281
"Second Elegy" (Rilke)
　See "Second Song"
"Second Epistle to John Lapraik" ("Lapraik II") (Burns) **6**:68-70, 78
"Second Fig" (Millay) **6**:227
"Second Georgic" (Vergil) **12**:359, 365
"Second Glance at a Jaguar" (Hughes) **7**:136-37
"Second Hymn to Lenin" (MacDiarmid) **9**:158, 177, 180-81, 197
Second Hymn to Lenin, and Other Poems (MacDiarmid) **9**:156, 179, 196
The Second Jungle Book (Kipling) **3**:162, 185, 188-89
"Second Language" (Gallagher) **9**:60
Second livre des poemes (Ronsard) **11**:282
"Second Populist Manifesto" (Ferlinghetti)

See "Adieu á Charlot"
"The Second Sermon on the Warpland"
(Brooks) **7**:63
"Second Song" (Bogan) **12**:90, 129
"Second Song" ("Second Elegy") (Rilke)
2:273-74, 286
The Second Symphony (Bely)
See *Vtoraia simfoniia: Dramaticheskaia*
Second Year of Chang-ho (Li Ho) **13**:42
"Second-Class Constable Alston" (McKay)
2:205
"The Secret" (Merton) **10**:348
"Secret Festival; September Moon" (Levertov)
11:177
The Secret Meaning of Things (Ferlinghetti)
1:173-74, 176, 186-87
"Secret Music" (Sassoon) **12**:247
"Secretary" (Hughes) **7**:140
The Secrets of the Heart (Gibran) **9**:72
"Secrets of the Trade" (Akhmatova) **2**:5
Section: Rock-Drill, 85-95 de los cantares
(Pound) **4**:352, 357
Seeds for a Hymn (Paz)
See *Semillas para un himno*
"Seen by the Waits" (Hardy) **8**:130
Segund antolojía poética (Jimenez) **7**:178, 201
"Seizure" (Sappho)
See "Ode to Anactoria"
"Seldom yet Now" (Graves) **6**:156
Selected Failings (Neruda)
See *Defectos escogidos: 2000*
Selected letters (Williams) **7**:374
Selected Poems (Brooks) **7**:81, 102
Selected Poems (Duncan) **2**:102
Selected Poems (Frost) **1**:195
Selected Poems (H. D.) **5**:274
Selected Poems (Hayden) **6**:176, 178-79
Selected Poems (Lowell) **3**:226-27
Selected Poems (McKay) **2**:207, 228
Selected Poems (Milosz) **8**:174
Selected Poems (Montale) **13**:135
Selected Poems (Moore) **4**:240, 242, 253
Selected Poems (Rukeyser) **12**:210
Selected Poems (Sexton) **2**:347-48
Selected Poems (Sitwell) **3**:320
Selected Poems (Smith) **12**:293, 309, 350
*Selected Poems (1938-1958): Summer
Knowledge* (Schwartz)
See *Summer Knowledge: New and Selected
Poems, 1938-1958*
Selected Poems, 1957-1967 (Hughes) **7**:163
Selected Poems 1965-1975 (Atwood) **8**:23
Selected Poems, Joseph Brodsky (Brodsky) **9**:8
The Selected Poems of Langston Hughes
(Hughes) **1**:248, 258
Selected Poetry of Amiri Baraka/LeRoi Jones
(Baraka) **4**:31
The Selected Poetry of Hayden Carruth
(Carruth) **10**:84
Selected Writings of Juan Ramon Jimenez
(Jimenez)
See *Antolojía poética (1898-1953)*
"Selective Service" (Forche) **10**:137, 144, 146,
157, 165
"Self in 1958" (Sexton) **2**:351
"The Self Unsatisfied Runs Everywhere"
(Schwartz) **8**:285
"The Self-Betrayal Which Is Nothing New"
(Schwartz) **8**:294
"Self-Criticism and Answer" (Day Lewis)
11:128, 144
"Self-Dependence" (Arnold) **5**:19, 42-3, 49

"The Self-Hatred of Don L. Lee" (Madhubuti)
5:337
"The Selfish One" (Neruda)
See "El egoísta"
"Self-Praise" (Graves) **6**:139
"The Self-Unseeing" (Hardy) **8**:88, 129
"Selige Sehnsucht" (Goethe) **5**:248
"Selinda and Cloris" (Behn) **13**:30
"The Selves" (Page) **12**:198
"The Semblables" (Williams) **7**:360
Semillas para un himno (*Seeds for a Hymn*)
(Paz) **1**:353, 366
"Semper eadem" (Baudelaire) **1**:61, 72
"Semplicità" ("Simplicity") (Pavese) **13**:229
"The Sence of a Letter Sent Me, Made into
Verse; to a New Tune" (Behn) **13**:31
"Sensation" (Rimbaud) **3**:275, 283
"Sensation Time at the Home" (Merton)
See "A Song: Sensation Time at the Home"
"Sense and Conscience" (Tennyson) **6**:372-73
"The Sentence" (Akhmatova)
See "Prigovor"
"The Sentence" (Graves) **6**:157
"Sentences" (Milosz) **8**:189
"The Sentimental Surgeon" (Page) **12**:176
"The Separate Notebooks" (Milosz)
See "Osobny zeszyt"
The Separate Notebooks (Milosz) **8**:182, 195-
97
The Separate Rose (Neruda)
See *La rosa separada: obra póstuma*
"Les sept epées" ("The Seven Swords")
(Apollinaire) **7**:46
"Les sept vieillards" ("The Seven Old Men")
(Baudelaire) **1**:45, 65, 70
"September" (Hughes) **7**:113, 118
"September 1, 1939" (Auden) **1**:14, 25
"September on Jessore Road" (Ginsberg)
4:59
"Le Septiesme livre des poemes" (Ronsard)
11:246
"Sepulchre" (Herbert) **4**:120
Sequel to Drum-Taps (Whitman) **3**:418, 422
Sequences (Sassoon) **12**:247-48, 255, 257-60,
271
"The Seraphim" (Browning) **6**:6, 20, 22, 26-7
The Seraphim, and Other Poems (Browning)
6:14-15, 19, 26, 29, 31-2
"Serenade: Any Man to Any Woman"
(Sitwell) **3**:309, 311, 314
"Serenata indiana" ("Indian Serenade")
(Montale) **13**:107, 128
"The Sergeant's Weddin'" (Kipling) **3**:164,
192
"A Serious Step Lightly Taken" (Frost) **1**:203
"Sermon for Our Maturity" (Baraka) **4**:19
"A Sermon on the Warpland" (Brooks) **7**:63
"Le serpent" (Valery)
See "Ébauche d'un serpent"
"Le serpent qui danse" (Baudelaire) **1**:62
"A Servant to Servants" (Frost) **1**:193, 228
"La servante au grand coeur" (Baudelaire)
1:67-68
"Ses purs ongles très haut dèdiant leur onyx"
(Mallarme)
See "Sonnet en -yx"
"Sesenheimer Lyrik" (Goethe) **5**:245
"Śesh lekhā" ("Last Poems"; "Tagore's Last
Poems") (Tagore) **8**:424, 426-27
Sestina (Rukeyser) **12**:232
"Sestina: Altaforte" (Pound) **4**:356

"Sestina of the Tramp Royal" (Kipling)
3:160
Sestra moia zhizn (*My Sister, Life*) (Pasternak)
6:250-51, 254-55, 260, 263-65, 268-69, 271-
72, 278-80, 282, 285
"Set of Country Songs" (Hardy) **8**:127
"A Set of Romantic Hymns" (Duncan) **2**:103
"The Settlers" (Atwood) **8**:12
"Le seul savant, c'est encore Moïse" (Verlaine)
2:416
"Seurat's Sunday Afternoon along the Seine"
("Mr. Seurat's Sunday Afternoon")
(Schwartz) **8**:289-99, 317-18
"The Seven Ages" (Auden) **1**:39
"The Seven Old Men" (Baudelaire)
See "Les sept vieillards"
The Seven Seas (Kipling) **3**:159-62, 164, 167,
192-93
"Seven Songs Written during the Ch'ien-yüan
Era while Staying at T'ung-ku-hsien" (Tu
Fu) **9**:322
The Seven Storey Mountain (Merton) **10**:
"Seven Strophes" (Brodsky) **9**:22
"The Seven Swords" (Apollinaire)
See "Les sept epées"
"1777" (Lowell) **13**:78, 84
"A Seventeenth Century Suite" (Duncan)
2:115-16, 127
"Seventh Elegy" (Rilke) **2**:281, 286
"Seventh Psalm" (Sexton) **2**:367
73 Poems (Cummings) **5**:109-11
*Several Poems Compiled with Great Variety of
Wit and Learning, Full of Delight*
(Bradstreet) **10**:43-5, 51
"Several Voices Out of a Cloud" (Bogan)
12:100, 107, 124
Severnaia simfoniia: Pervia geroicheskaia (*The
First Symphony; Northern Heroic; Northern
Symphony; Simfonija (1-aga)*) (Bely) **11**:3,
12-15, 21
"A Sewerplant Grows in Harlem or I'm a
Stranger Here Myself When Does the Next
Swan Leave?" (Lorde) **12**:158
"Sext" (Auden) **1**:23
"Sextet" (Brodsky) **9**:19, 22
"Sexual Water" (Neruda)
See "Agua sexual"
"Shade of Fonvizin" (Pushkin) **10**:408
"The Shadow" (Lowell) **13**:60-1, 83
The Shadow of Cain (Sitwell) **3**:320, 327
"Shakespeare" (Arnold) **5**:49
"Shakespeare" (Pasternak) **6**:252
"Shakespeare in Harlem" (Hughes) **1**:239,
242, 246-47, 254-56, 268, 270
"Shakespeare Say" (Dove) **6**:109
"Shalom" (Levertov) **11**:170
"Shaman Mountain is High" (Li Ho) **13**:51
"Sharing Eve's Apple" (Keats) **1**:311
"The Sharp Ridge" (Graves) **6**:156
Sharps and Flats (Tagore)
See *Kari o komal*
"Shatabdir surya" ("Sunset of the Century")
(Tagore) **8**:412
"Shatter Me, Music" (Rilke) **2**:275
"She Being Brand-New" (Cummings) **5**:95
"She Said . . ." (Smith) **12**:326
She Steals My Heart (Li Ho) **13**:44
"She Tells Her Love while Half Asleep"
(Graves) **6**:144
"She, to Him" (Hardy) **8**:90
"The Sheaves" (Robinson) **1**:478
"A Sheep Fair" (Hardy) **8**:101

"Sheep in a Fog" (Plath) **1**:408-09
"The Sheep Went On Being Dead" (Hughes)
    7:149
"Sheltered Garden" (H. D.) **5**:269, 303
*The Shepheardes Calender: Conteyning Twelve
    Æglogues Proportionable to the Twelve
    Monethes* (Spenser) **8**:326-28, 335, 385-87
"The Shepherd" (Blake) **12**:7, 32
"The Shepherd" (H. D.) **5**:305
"Shesh katha" ("The Last Word") (Tagore)
    8:407
Shesh saptak (*Last Octave*) (Tagore) **8**:417
"Shiberia no uta" ("Song of Siberia")
    (Ishikawa Takuboku) **10**:213
"The Shield of Achilles" (Auden) **1**:23
"Shillin' a Day" (Kipling) **3**:191
Shipovnik tsevetyot (*The Wild Rose Flowers*)
    (Akhmatova) **2**:9
"Ships That Pass in the Night" (Dunbar)
    5:121
"Shiraha no toribune" ("The Boat of the
    White Feather Bird") (Ishikawa Takuboku)
    10:214
"Shiv and the Grasshopper" (Kipling) **3**:183
"Shizumeru kane" ("The Sunken Bell")
    (Ishikawa Takuboku) **10**:214
"Shoot It Jimmy" (Williams) **7**:383
"A Shooting Incident" (Smith) **12**:318, 346
"Shooting Script" (Rich) **5**:366-67, 378, 383,
    396-97
"Shop" (Browning) **2**:59
"Shores" (Montale)
    See "Riviere"
"The Shorewatchers' House" (Montale)
    13:150
"Short Poem" (Sanchez) **9**:212, 223
Short Prose Poems (Baudelaire)
    See *Petits poèmes en prose: Le spleen de Paris*
"A Short Recess" (Milosz) **8**:183, 186
"Short Summary" (Bogan) **12**:101
"The Shot" (Graves) **6**:143-44
"The Shot" (Pushkin)
    See "Vystrel"
"The Shovel Man" (Sandburg) **2**:332
"Shower" (Swift)
    See "Description of a City Shower"
"The Showings; Lady Julian of Norwich, 1342-
    1416" (Levertov) **11**:210
"The Shrine" (H. D.) **5**:270
A Shropshire Lad (Housman) **2**:159-67, 171-
    78, 180-81, 183-84, 186-88, 191-95, 197, 199-
    200
"The Shroud" (Millay) **6**:205
"Shūchō" (Ishikawa Takuboku) **10**:212
Shundeishū (*Spring Thaw*) (Yosano Akiko)
    11:305
"Shut, Bellada" ("The Jester, A Ballad")
    (Bely) **11**:24
"Shut Nad ney" ("Jester above It") (Bely)
    11:24
"Shut Out" (Rossetti) **7**:280
"Shut: Plamen" (Bely) **11**:24
"Shutka" ("Joke") (Bely) **11**:24
Shyamali (*The Dark One*) (Tagore) **8**:417
"Sibling Mysteries" (Rich) **5**:373, 384
"Sibrandus Schafnaburgensis" (Browning)
    2:59
"A Sibyl" (Atwood) **8**:25
Sibylline Leaves (Coleridge) **11**:57, 60, 97, 115
"Sic Transit" (Lowell) **3**:213
"The Sick" (Page) **12**:176

"The Sick King in Bokhara" (Arnold) **5**:6,
    39, 49
"Sick Leave" (Sassoon) **12**:267, 288
"Sick Love" (Graves) **6**:136-37, 142, 144,
    151, 169
"The Sick Rose" (Blake) **12**:7
"The Sickness unto Death" (Sexton) **2**:372
"Siena mi fe'; disfecemi Maremma" (Pound)
    4:319
"The Sigh" (Hardy) **8**:104
"Sigh" (Mallarme)
    See "Soupir"
"The Sigh That Heaves the Grasses"
    (Housman) **2**:183, 191
"Sighs and Groans" (Herbert)
    See "Sighs and Grones"
"Sighs and Grones" ("Sighs and Groans")
    (Herbert) **4**:120, 133-34,
"The Sign" (Masters) **1**:333, 337
"A Signiture. A Herold. A Span" (Brooks)
    7:90
"La Signorina Felicita" (Gozzano) **10**:176-77,
    180-83
"Signs and Tokens" (Hardy) **8**:111
"Die silbe schmerz" (Celan) **10**:102, 105
"Silence" (Eliot) **5**:217
"Silence" (Masters) **1**:325, 333, 342
"Silence and Tears" (Smith) **12**:341
"The Silence Answered Him Accusingly"
    (Schwartz) **8**:293
"Silences: Lament of the Silent Sisters"
    ("Lament of the Silent Sisters"; "Silent
    Sisters") (Okigbo) **7**:225, 228, 234, 244-47,
    251
"Silent Faces at Crossroads" (Okigbo) **7**:255
"Silent Service" (Sassoon) **12**:252
"Silent Sisters" (Okigbo)
    See "Silences: Lament of the Silent Sisters"
"Silhouette of a Serpent" (Valery)
    See "Ébauche d'un serpent"
"The Silken Tent" (Frost) **1**:196, 214
"Silly Song" (Garcia Lorca)
    See "Canción tonta"
"Silos" (Dove) **6**:120
"The Silver Tassie" (Burns) **6**:97
"Simaetha" (H. D.) **5**:266
Simfonija (1-aga) (Bely)
    See *Severnaia simfoniia: Pervia geroicheskaia*
Simfonija (2-aja) (Bely)
    See *Vtoraia simfoniia: Dramaticheskaia*
"Simon Lee" (Wordsworth) **4**:374, 416-17,
    425-26, 428
"Simon Surnamed Peter" (Masters) **1**:325,
    342
"Simple Autumnal" (Bogan) **12**:87-8, 106,
    121
"Simple Sonatina" (Gallagher) **9**:60
"Simplicity" (Pavese)
    See "Semplicità"
"Sin" (Herbert) **4**:100
"Sin I" (Herbert) **4**:130
"Since I am comming" (Donne)
    See "Hymne to God my God, in my
    sicknesse"
"Sindhu-taranga" ("Ocean Waves") (Tagore)
    8:407
"The Singer" (Levertov) **11**:183
"A Singer Asleep" (Hardy) **8**:125
"Singers" (Hughes) **7**:123
"Singing Nigger" (Sandburg) **2**:316
"Single Sonnet" (Bogan) **12**:90, 107

Sing-Song: A Nursery Rhyme-Book (Rossetti)
    7:291
"Sinistre" ("Disaster") (Valery) **9**:359, 381,
    399-401
"The Sinking Ship" (Rimbaud)
    See "L'eclatante victoire de Saarebrück"
"Sinners in the Hands of an Angry God"
    (Lowell) **3**:203
"The Sins of Kalamazoo" (Sandburg) **2**:308
"Sin's Round" (Herbert) **4**:114
"Sion" (Herbert) **4**:100
"Sir Galahad" (Masters) **1**:330, 333
"Sir Galahad" (Tennyson) **6**:359
"Siren Limits" (Okigbo) **7**:240-46
"Siren Song" (Atwood) **8**:23, 25-6, 41
"The Sirens' Welcome to Cronos" (Graves)
    6:144, 146
"Sirocco" (Montale)
    See "Scirocco"
"Sister Maude" (Rossetti) **7**:260, 270, 272-73,
    276, 280
"The Sisters" (Lowell) **13**:67
"Sisters in Arms" (Lorde) **12**:141, 151-53
"The Sitting" (Day Lewis) **11**:147
"The Situation in the West Followed by a
    Holy Proposal" (Ferlinghetti) **1**:172
"Six Lectures in Verse" (Milosz) **8**:199-200,
    202-03, 211
Six Odes (Auden) **1**:8
Six Quatrains Composed in Jest (Tu Fu)
    9:327
"Six Variations" (Levertov) **11**:183
"Six Years Later" (Brodsky) **9**:7, 8, 19, 26
"Six Young Men" (Hughes) **7**:113
"Six-Bit Blues" (Hughes) **1**:256
"The Sixteenth Floor" (Lowell) **13**:97
"Sixth Elegy" (Rilke) **2**:273
"Sixth Elegy. River Elegy" (Rukeyser)
    12:231-32
65 Poems (Celan) **10**:120
"The Size" (Herbert) **4**:100, 108
"Skazka o Mertvoy Tsarevne" ("The Dead
    Princess and the Seven Heroes"; "The Tale
    of the Dead Princess and the Seven Heroes")
    (Pushkin) **10**:382
"Skazka o Pope i o Rabotnike Yego Balde"
    ("The Tale of the Parson and His Man
    Balda") (Pushkin) **10**:382
"Skazka o Rybake i Rybke" ("The Fisherman
    and the Fish"; "The Tale of the Fisherman
    and the Fish") (Pushkin) **10**:382
"Skazka o Tsare Sultane" ("The Tale of the
    Tsar Sultan"; "Tsar Sultan") (Pushkin)
    10:381-83
"Skazka o Zolotom Petushke" ("The Golden
    Cockerel"; *The Tale of the Golden Cockerel*)
    (Pushkin) **10**:382-83
"Skazki" ("Fairy Tales") (Pushkin) **10**:408
Skazki (*Fairy Tales*) (Pushkin) **10**:381-86
"The Skeleton of the Future" (MacDiarmid)
    9:176, 179
"Sketch" (Sandburg) **2**:303, 335
"Sketches for a Portrait" (Day Lewis) **11**:148
"Skin Canoe" (Forche) **10**:134
"the skinny voice" (Cummings) **5**:99
"Skizze zu einem Sankt Georg" (Rilke) **2**:267
"Skunk Hour" (Lowell) **3**:209-11, 213-14,
    221, 223, 227, 235, 243-46
"Skunk Hour" (Sexton) **2**:350
"Skylarks" (Hughes) **7**:121-22, 136-37
"Skylights" (Gallagher) **9**:45

"Slabs of the Sunburnt West" (Sandburg)
  2:306, 308, 310-11, 314, 323, 330
Slabs of the Sunburnt West (Sandburg) **2**:306,
  308, 311, 314, 323
"The Sleep" (Browning) **6**:21
"Sleep" (Hughes) **1**:240
"Sleep" (Pushkin) **10**:407
"Sleep and Poetry" (Keats) **1**:280, 289, 291-
  92, 313
"Sleep at Sea" (Rossetti) **7**:293, 296-97
"Sleep Brings No Joy to Me" (Bronte) **8**:74
"The Sleep Worker" (Hardy) **8**:129
"The Sleeper" (Poe) **1**:434, 443-44
"The Sleepers" (Whitman) **3**:391, 396-97, 401
"Sleeping at Last" (Rossetti) **7**:287
The Sleeping Beauty (Carruth) **10**:75-8, 83-4,
  86, 91
The Sleeping Beauty (Sitwell) **3**:292-94, 298,
  300-01, 303, 307-08, 310, 316-17, 320, 324-
  25
"The Sleeping Fury" (Bogan) **12**:100, 104
The Sleeping Fury (Bogan) **12**:88-90, 105,
  109, 111, 120, 122-25, 131
"Sleeping on the Ceiling" (Bishop) **3**:37
"Sleepwalker Ballad" (Garcia Lorca)
  See "Romance sonámbulo"
"The Slippers of the Goddess of Beauty"
  (Lowell) **13**:67
"Slip-Shoe Lovey" (Masters) **1**:333, 336
"Slow through the Dark" (Dunbar) **5**:131
"A Slumber Did My Spirit Steal"
  (Wordsworth) **4**:420
"Small Comment" (Sanchez) **9**:224
"Small Garden near a Field" (Gallagher)
  9:62
"Small Hours" (Plath) **1**:391
"The Small Lady" (Smith) **12**:295
"Small Poems for the Winter Solstice"
  (Atwood) **8**:44
Small Testament (Villon)
  See *Les Lais*
"A Small Will" (Montale)
  See "Piccolo testamento"
"Smelt Fishing" (Hayden) **6**:196
"The Smile" (Blake) **12**:35, 43
"Smoke and Steel" (Sandburg) **2**:304, 316
Smoke and Steel (Sandburg) **2**:304-08, 313-
  14, 316, 321, 323, 338
"Smokers of Cheap Cigarettes" (Pavese)
  See "Fumatori di carta"
"Snail" (Hughes) **1**:241
"Snake" (Hughes) **1**:241
"Snake Hymn" (Hughes) **7**:159
"Snake River" (McKay) **2**:216
"Snakecharmer" (Plath) **1**:388-89
"Snapshots of a Daughter-in-Law" (Rich)
  5:370-72, 396
*Snapshots of a Daughter-in-Law: Poems, 1954-
  1962* (Rich) **5**:354, 358, 363, 369-72, 374,
  382, 388, 392
"Snarley-Yow" (Kipling) **3**:158
"Snow" (Frost) **1**:195, 215
"Snow" (Hayden) **6**:193, 196
"Snow" (Hughes) **7**:155
"Snow" (Rich) **5**:366
"The Snow Fairy" (McKay) **2**:228
"The Snow King" (Dove) **6**:108
"The Snow Lamp" (Hayden) **6**:189, 192
"Snow) Says! Says" (Cummings) **5**:106
"Snow White" (Sexton) **2**:368
"Snowbed" (Celan)
  See "Schneebett"

"Snowdrop" (Hughes) **7**:169
"Snowflakes as Kisses" (Schwarzweller) **8**:314
"The Snowman" (Page) **12**:167-68, 183
"So Much Depends" (Williams) **7**:362
"So, so breake off this last lamenting kisse"
  (Donne)
  See "The Expiration"
"So To Fatness Come" (Smith) **12**:326
"So We Grew Together" (Masters) **1**:326-26,
  328
Social Credit, An Impact (Pound) **4**:328
"Socrates' Ghost Must Haunt Me Now"
  (Schwartz) **8**:302, 315
"Soft Wood" (Lowell) **3**:211
"Softer-Mother's Tale" (Wordsworth) **4**:373
"Il Sogno del prigioniero" ("The Prisoner's
  Dream") (Montale) **13**:104
"Soho Cinema" (Lorde) **12**:140
"Sohrab and Rustum" (Arnold) **5**:9, 12-13,
  33, 35, 37, 45, 52, 62
"Un soir" (Apollinaire) **7**:46
"Le soir qu'amour vous fist en la salle
  descendre" ("The Evening That Love
  Enticed You Down into the Ballroom")
  (Ronsard) **11**:264-66
"Solar Ode to the People's Army" (Neruda)
  See "Oda solar al ejército del pueblo"
"Solde" (Rimbaud) **3**:261, 264
"Soldier, Soldier" (Kipling) **3**:163, 188-89
"The Soldiers" (Duncan) **2**:104
"Soldier's Song" (Burns) **6**:78
"Soledad" (Hayden) **6**:194, 196
Soledad (*Loneliness*) (Paz) **1**:366
"Soleil et chair" ("Sunlight and Flesh")
  (Rimbaud) **3**:251, 280, 283, 285
"Soliloquy of a Misanthrope" (Hughes) **7**:116
"Soliloquy of the Spanish Cloister" (Browning)
  2:37
"The Solitary Reaper" (Wordsworth) **4**:399,
  404
"Solitude" (Ishikawa Takuboku)
  See "Kyoko"
"Solitudes at Sixty" (Sassoon) **12**:259
"Solonique" (Apollinaire) **7**:48
"Solstice" (Lorde) **12**:153
"Som de escalina" (Eliot) **5**:201
"Sombre Figuration" (Stevens) **6**:298, 318,
  320
"Some Answers Are Cold Comfort to the
  Dead" (Schwartz) **8**:293
"Some Are Born" (Smith) **12**:316
"Some Foreign Letters" (Sexton) **2**:350, 361,
  363
"Some Foreign Wife" (Sexton) **2**:359
"Some Friends from Pascagoula" (Stevens)
  6:337
"Some Notes on Organic Form" (Levertov)
  11:160-62
Some Time (Zukofsky) **11**:343
"Some Verses Upon the Burning of Our
  House, July 10th, 1666" ("Verses Upon the
  Burning of Our House") (Bradstreet) **10**:8,
  19, 21, 27, 29-30, 34, 36-7, 42
"Someone Is Harshly Coughing as Before"
  (Schwartz) **8**:301
"Something for Hope" (Frost) **1**:200
"Something to Wear" (Levertov) **11**:165-66,
  168
"Something Was Happening" (Hughes) **7**:154
"Somewhere East o' Suez" (Kipling) **3**:189
"Somewhere I Have Never Travelled, Gladly
  Beyond" (Cummings) **5**:88

"Somewhere in Africa" (Sexton) **2**:364, 371
"Somnambulent Ballad" (Garcia Lorca)
  See "Romance sonámbulo"
"Somnambulist Ballad" (Garcia Lorca)
  See "Romance sonámbulo"
"Sonar tari" ("The Golden Boat") (Tagore)
  8:408
Sonar tari (Tagore) **8**:409, 418, 427
Sonetos espirituales (*Spiritual Sonnets*)
  (Jimenez) **7**:191-92, 194-96, 202, 211
Sonette (Goethe) **5**:248, 250
Sonette an Orpheus (*Die Sonette an
  Orpheus/Sonnets to Orpheus*) (Rilke) **2**:267-
  68, 277, 280-81, 283, 290, 293, 295
Die Sonette an Orpheus/Sonnets to Orpheus
  (Rilke)
  See *Sonette an Orpheus*
"Song" (Behn)
  See "Love Arm'd"
"Song" (Blake) **12**:6
"Song" (Bogan) **12**:86, 90, 103
"Song" (Bronte) **8**:62
"Song" ("But We've the May") (Cummings)
  5:109
"Song" (Donne) **1**:125
"Song" (H. D.) **5**:304
"Song" ("I Saw Thee on Thy Bridal Day")
  (Poe) **1**:432
"Song" (Rossetti) **7**:273, 276, 289
"Song" (Sitwell) **3**:313
"Song" (Williams) **7**:408
"Song Coming toward Us" (Forche) **10**:132
"Song for a Colored Singer" (Bishop) **3**:37
"Song for a Dark Girl" (Hughes) **1**:238, 243
"Song for a Lady" (Sexton) **2**:352
"Song for a Lyre" (Bogan) **12**:90, 92
"Song for a Phallus" (Hughes) **7**:132, 159,
  171
"Song for a Red Night Gown" (Sexton)
  2:352-53
"Song for a Slight Voice" (Bogan) **12**:90, 92
"Song for a Viola d'Amore" (Lowell) **13**:88,
  97
"A Song for J. H." (Behn) **13**:19
"Song for Nobody" (Merton) **10**:349
"A Song for Occupations" (Whitman) **3**:385,
  401-02
"Song for Our Lady of Cobre" (Merton) **10**:
"A Song for Simeon" (Eliot) **5**:194, 196-97,
  203, 205, 209
"Song for the Death of Averroës" (Merton)
  10:343
"Song for the Last Act" (Bogan) **12**:124
"Song for the Mothers of Dead Militiamen"
  (Neruda)
  See "Canto a las madres de los milicianos
  muertos"
"Song for the Next River" (Gallagher) **9**:35
"A Song for the Ragged Schools of London"
  ("The Ragged Schools of London")
  (Browning) **6**:7, 23
"Song for the Rainy Season" (Bishop) **3**:67
"A Song for the Year's End" (Zukofsky)
  11:349
"A Song from the Structures of Rime Ringing
  as the Poet Paul Celan Sings" (Duncan)
  2:117
"Song I" (Rilke) **2**:273
"A Song in the Front Yard" (Brooks) **7**:69
"Song: Lift-Boy" (Graves) **6**:142, 144
"The Song of a Rat" (Hughes) **7**:142, 155-56,
  159

"Song of Another Tribe" (Rukeyser) **12**:217

"Song of Defeat" (Tagore)
See "Parajaya saṅgīt"

"Song of Despair" (Neruda) **4**:301

"The Song of Diego Valdez" (Kipling) **3**:182

"The Song of God's Child" (Li Ho) **13**:51

"A Song of Joys" (Whitman) **3**:402

"A Song of Liberty" (Blake) **12**:33

"Song of Myself" ("One's-Self I Sing")
(Whitman) **3**:370, 394, 396-97, 399, 401-03,
405, 411-12, 414-17

"Song of Opposites" (Keats) **1**:312

"Song of P'eng-ya" (Tu Fu) **9**:321, 332

"A Song of Praise" (Sanchez) **9**:243

"Song of Siberia" (Ishikawa Takuboku)
See "Shiberia no uta"

"Song of the Answerer" (Whitman) **3**:386,
390

"Song of the Banjo" (Kipling) **3**:160-61

"Song of the Beautiful Ladies" (Tu Fu) **9**:320

"Song of the Bird" (Tagore)
See "Vihaṅger gan"

"The Song of the Cities" (Kipling) **3**:162

The Song of the Cold (Sitwell) **3**:320, 326

"Song of the Columns" (Valery)
See "Cantique des colonnes"

"Song of the Dead" (Kipling) **3**:160, 162

"A Song of the Dust" (Sitwell) **3**:327

"A Song of the English" (Kipling) **3**:160-62,
164

"The Song of the Exiles" (Kipling) **3**:194

"The Song of the Final Meeting/Song of the
Last Meeting" (Akhmatova)
See "Pesnia poslednei vstrechi"

"The Song of the Galley Slaves" (Kipling)
3:170

"Song of the Highest Tower" (Rimbaud)
3:259

"The Song of the Ill-beloved" (Apollinaire)
See "La chanson du mal-aimé"

"Song of the Little Square" (Garcia Lorca)
See "Ballada de la Placeta"

"Song of the Open Road" (Whitman) **3**:387

"The Song of the Poorly Beloved"
(Apollinaire)
See "La chanson du mal-aimé"

"The Song of the Red War-Boat" (Kipling)
3:183

"Song of the Son" (Toomer) **7**:310, 317, 319,
334

"The Song of the Sons" (Kipling) **3**:162

"A Song of the Soul of Central" (Hughes)
1:268

"Song of the Worms" (Atwood) **8**:19, 25

"Song of Women" (Masters) **1**:330, 333

Song Offerings (Tagore)
See *Gitanjali*

"Song over Some Ruins" (Neruda)
See "Canto sobre unas ruinas"

"A Song: Sensation Time at the Home"
("Sensation Time at the Home") (Merton)
10:345

"Song. 'Sweetest love, I do not goe'"
("Sweetest love, I do not goe") (Donne)
1:130

"Song: The Rev. MuBngwu Dickenson
Ruminates behind the Sermon" (Brooks)
7:94

"A Song to a Scotish Tune (Come My Phillis
Let Us Improve)" (Behn) **13**:18

"Song to a Scotish Tune (When Jemmy First
Began to Love)" ("When Jemmy First
Began to Love") (Behn) **13**:4, 7, 18, 32

A Song to David (Smart) **13**:328-34, 336-46,
352-54, 358, 360-65, 367-69

"Song to Ishtar" (Levertov) **11**:169

"A Song to No Music" ("Song without
Music") (Brodsky) **9**:4, 9, 12

"Song without Music" (Brodsky)
See "A Song to No Music"

"Songe D'Athalie" (Smith) **12**:331

"Songs" (Hughes) **1**:241

Songs (Garcia Lorca)
See *Canciones*

Songs and Satires (Masters) **1**:328, 335, 342

Songs and Sonets (Donne) **1**:130, 139, 145

Songs and Sonnets, second series (Masters)
1:321, 325, 332

"Songs for a Colored Singer" (Bishop) **3**:37,
46-7

"Songs from Cyprus" (H. D.) **5**:304

"Songs in a Cornfield" (Rossetti) **7**:275

Songs of Bhanusigh Thakur (Tagore)
See *Bhanusiṅgh Thakurer padavali*

Songs of Crow (Hughes) **7**:140

Songs of Experience (Blake) **12**:9-10, 23-5, 31,
33-5, 42-7, 61-2

Songs of Innocence (Blake) **12**:8-9, 19, 21-4,
32-4, 42, 61

*Songs of Innocence and of Experience: Shewing
the Two Contrary States of the Human Soul*
(Blake) **12**:8-11, 33-4, 42-3, 51

Songs of Jamaica (McKay) **2**:208, 210, 216,
221, 223-27

"Songs of the Hen's Head" (Atwood) **8**:41

"Songs of the Ingenues" (Verlaine)
See "La chanson des ingénues"

"Songs of the Runaway Bride" (Gallagher)
9:37

"Songs of the Transformed" (Atwood) **8**:23,
25-6

"The Sonne" (Herbert) **4**:109

"Sonnet" (Bogan) **12**:98, 110

"Sonnet II" (Thomas) **2**:388

"Sonnet III" (Thomas) **2**:388

"Sonnet VIII" (Thomas) **2**:388

"Sonnet X" (Thomas) **2**:388

"Sonnet XVI" (Browning) **6**:17

"Sonnet en -yx" ("Ses purs ongles très haut
dèdiant leur onyx") (Mallarme) **4**:214-15,
218

"Sonnet Entitled How to Run the World)"
(Cummings) **5**:106

"Sonnet héroïque" (Verlaine) **2**:416

"Sonnet— to My Mother" (Poe) **1**:439, 445-
46

Sonnets (Carruth) **10**:91

Sonnets (Rilke) **2**:280-82

Sonnets et madrigals pour astrée (Ronsard)
11:250

Sonnets for Hélène (Ronsard)
See *Sonnets pour Hélène*

"Sonnets from an Ungrafted Tree" (Millay)
6:224-25, 228, 230-32, 235, 239

Sonnets from the Portuguese (Browning)
6:4-6, 15-18, 22, 32, 36-9, 41-2, 46

Sonnets pour Hélène (*Sonnets for Hélène*)
(Ronsard) **11**:218, 220-22, 239, 242, 250,
254, 275-76, 278, 283

"Sono pronto ripeto, ma pronto a che?"
(Montale) **13**:139

"Sorapis, 40 anni fa" (Montale) **13**:138

Sordello (Browning) **2**:26-30, 34, 42, 50, 65-6,
73-6, 82, 92-6

"Sore Fit" (Bradstreet)
See "From Another Sore Fit"

The Sorrow Dance (Levertov) **11**:175-77, 191-
94

"SOS" (Baraka) **4**:20

"Sotto la pioggia" (Montale) **13**:122

"The Soul" (Pasternak)
See "Dusha"

"Soul, Be Calm" (Ishikawa Takuboku)
See "Tama yo shizume"

"A Soul, Geologically" (Atwood) **8**:3, 8, 19

"The Soul Has Bandaged Moments"
(Dickinson) **1**:94

"Soul in Space" (Rilke) **2**:275

"Soul's Desire" (Masters) **1**:342

"The Soul's Expression" (Browning) **6**:20, 26,
30

"The Souls of the Slain" (Hardy) **8**:120-21

Souls of Violet (Jimenez)
See *Almas de violeta*

"A Soul's Tragedy" (Browning) **2**:30, 37

"The Sound of the Trees" (Frost) **1**:197, 202

"Sound Poem I" (Toomer) **7**:333

"Sound Poem II" (Toomer) **7**:333

"Sound Sleep" (Rossetti) **7**:267, 280

"Sounds" (Browning) **6**:20

"Sounds Out of Sorrow" (Masters) **1**:333

"Soupir" ("Sigh") (Mallarme) **4**:187

Sour Grapes (Williams) **7**:344, 349, 367, 377,
381, 399-400, 409-10

Sources (Rich) **5**:389-90, 397

"Southeast Corner" (Brooks) **7**:58, 69, 80

"Souther Pacific" (Sandburg) **2**:302

"A Southern Night" (Arnold) **5**:8

"Souvenir de Monsieur Poop" (Smith) **12**:313

"Sow" (Plath) **1**:388, 404

"The Sowing of Meaning" (Merton) **10**:332

Space (Jimenez)
See *Espacia*

Spain (Auden) **1**:22

Spain at Heart (Neruda)
See *España en el corazón: himno a las glorias
del pueblo en la guerra (1936-1937)*

Spain in My Heart (Neruda)
See *España en el corazón: himno a las glorias
del pueblo en la guerra (1936-1937)*

Spain in the Heart (Neruda)
See *España en el corazón: himno a las glorias
del pueblo en la guerra (1936-1937)*

"The Spanish Needle" (McKay) **2**:228

"Spanish School" (Smith) **12**:316

"Spare Us from Loveliness" (H. D.) **5**:273

"Sparrow Hills" (Pasternak) **6**:258

"Spasskoye" (Pasternak) **6**:252, 259

"Spätherbst in Venedig" (Rilke) **2**:267, 277,
282, 288-90

"Speak, You Also" (Celan) **10**:99

"La Speakerine de Putney" (Smith) **12**:354

Speaking for Scotland (MacDiarmid) **9**:159

"Speaking of Love (of" (Cummings) **5**:105

"Special Starlight" (Sandburg) **2**:331

"Specimen of an Induction to a Poem" (Keats)
1:313

"Speech to the Young. Speech to the Progress-
Toward" (Brooks) **7**:91, 94

"Speeches for Doctor Frankenstein" (Atwood)
8:11

"Speech-Grille" (Celan)
See "Sprachgitter"

Speech-Grille, and Selected Poems (Celan)

See *Sprachgitter*
The Speed of Darkness (Rukeyser) **12**:216, 222, 228, 230
Spektorsky (Pasternak) **6**:253, 265, 283, 285
"Spell" (Montale)
　　See "Incantesimo"
"The Spell of the Rose" (Hardy) **8**:93, 136
"Spelling" (Duncan) **2**:104
"Spenser's Ireland" (Moore) **4**:258
"The Sphinx" (Hayden) **6**:186
Sphinx: A Poem Ascrib'd to Certain Anonymous Authors: By the Revd. S—t (Swift)
　　See "Ode to the Athenian Society"
"The Spinner" (Valery)
　　See "La fileuse"
"Spinster" (Plath) **1**:388
"The Spire Cranes" (Thomas) **2**:408
"Spirit of History" (Milosz) **8**:204
"The Spirit of Place" (Rich) **5**:386
The Spirit of Romance (Pound) **4**:352
Spirit Reach (Baraka) **4**:19-20, 26
"Spirit's Song" (Bogan) **12**:90, 92, 100, 124
"A Spiritual" (Dunbar) **5**:123
Spiritual Sonnets (Jimenez)
　　See *Sonetos espirituales*
"Spleen" (Baudelaire)
　　See "Le spleen"
"Le spleen" ("Spleen") (Baudelaire) **1**:55
"Spleen" (Verlaine) **2**:415
Le spleen de Paris (Baudelaire)
　　See *Petits poèmes en prose: Le spleen de Paris*
"Spoke Joe to Jack" (Cummings) **5**:88
"Spontaneous Me" (Whitman) **3**:387
Spoon River Anthology (Masters) **1**:321-42, 344-49
"The Spooniad" (Masters) **1**:327
"Sport" (Hughes) **1**:270
"Sprachgitter" ("Language-Mesh"; "Speech-Grille") (Celan) **10**:112, 115, 129-30
Sprachgitter (*The Grid of Language; Language Lattice; Speech-Grille, and Selected Poems; The Straightening*) (Celan) **10**:95-6, 121
"A Sprig of Rosemary" (Lowell) **13**:64
"Spring" (Blake) **12**:7, 32
"Spring" (Millay) **6**:236
"Spring" (Pasternak) **6**:251
"Spring" (Sitwell) **3**:311
"Spring" (Williams) **7**:345, 399
Spring and All (Williams) **7**:349, 351, 353, 355, 373-78, 381-83, 387-88, 400-02, 405-06, 409-11
"The Spring and the Fall" (Millay) **6**:225
"Spring Day" (Lowell) **13**:79
"Spring Flood" (Pasternak) **6**:266
"Spring in New Hampshire" (McKay) **2**:228
Spring in New Hampshire, and Other Poems (McKay) **2**:213, 228
"Spring in the Garden" (Millay) **6**:215
"Spring Lake" (Masters) **1**:343
"Spring Poem" (Atwood) **8**:24
"Spring Pools" (Frost) **1**:206
"Spring Prospect" (Tu Fu) **9**:322
"Spring Rain" (Pasternak) **6**:251
"Spring Season of Muddy Roads" (Brodsky) **9**:2
"Spring Song" (Baraka) **4**:39
Spring Thaw (Yosano Akiko)
　　See *Shundeishū*
"Spring Thunder" (Rich) **5**:383
"A Spring Wooing" (Dunbar) **5**:145
"Sprüche" (Goethe) **5**:248
"The Spur of Love" (MacDiarmid) **9**:189-90

"Le squelette laboureur" ("The Laboring Skeleton") (Baudelaire) **1**:45
"Srishti-sthiti-pralaya" ("Evolution-Sustenance-Dissolution") (Tagore) **8**:406
"Śroczość" ("Magpiety") (Milosz) **8**:187
"St. Brandan" (Arnold) **5**:12
"St. Launce's Revisited" (Hardy) **8**:136
"St. Lucies Day" (Donne)
　　See "A Nocturnal upon S. Lucies day, Being the shortest day"
"St. Praxed's Church" (Browning) **2**:30
"St. Simeon Stylites" (Tennyson) **6**:411
"Stagirius" (Arnold) **5**:38
"Stalin" (Lowell) **3**:223
"Stan" ("Breasts") (Tagore) **8**:407
"Stances de la fontaine de'Helene" (Ronsard) **11**:241
"The Standard Oil Co." (Neruda)
　　See "La Standard Oil Co."
"La Standard Oil Co." ("The Standard Oil Co.") (Neruda) **4**:296
"Standards and Paradise of the Blacks" (Garcia Lorca)
　　See "Norma y paraíso de los negros"
"Standomi un giorno solo a la fenestra" (Petrarch) **8**:253-57
"The Stand-To" (Day Lewis) **11**:146
"Stand-to: Good Friday Morning" (Sassoon) **12**:241, 251, 262, 280
"Stanza" (Bogan) **12**:103
"Stanzas" (Brodsky) **9**:4
"Stanzas from the Grande Chartreuse" (Arnold) **5**:18, 24, 33, 35, 52-3, 58
"Stanzas in Memory of Edward Quillinan" (Arnold) **5**:52
"Stanzas in Memory of the Author of 'Obermann'" (Arnold) **5**:42, 50, 52
"Stanzas on Peele Castle" ("Peele Castle") (Wordsworth) **4**:394, 410-11
"Stanzas to Bettine" (Browning) **6**:15
"Stanzas to Tolstoi" (Pushkin) **10**:409
"Stanzas Written at Night in Radio City" (Ginsberg) **4**:55
"The Star" (Masters) **1**:326, 333, 337, 342
The Star (Bely)
　　See *Zvezda*
"A Star in a Stone-Boat" (Frost) **1**:194, 221
"Starlight like Intuition Pierced the Twelve" (Schwartz) **8**:290-91
"The Starling" (Lowell) **13**:61
"The Starling" (Smith) **12**:326
"The Starred Coverlet" (Graves) **6**:156
"The Starry Night" (Sexton) **2**:350, 371-72
"Starry Night" (Sexton) **2**:350, 371-72
"Stars" (Hayden) **6**:184-85, 190, 194, 196
"The Star-Song: A Carroll to the King; Sung at White Hall" (Herrick) **9**:118, 119
"The Star-Splitter" (Frost) **1**:194
"Start Again Somewhere" (Gallagher) **9**:58
"Star-Talk" (Graves) **6**:166
"Starting from San Francisco" (Ferlinghetti) **1**:187
Starting from San Francisco (Ferlinghetti) **1**:166, 172-76, 187
Starting Point (Day Lewis) **11**:129
Starved Rock (Masters) **1**:332, 335, 338, 342-44
"Statement on Poetics" (Hayden) **6**:198
"Stations" (Hughes) **7**:137
"Stations" (Lorde) **12**:140
"Statue and Birds" (Bogan) **12**:94, 101, 127
"The Statue at the World's End" (Stevens)

See "Mr. Burnshaw and the Statue"
"Statue at Tsarskoye Selo" (Akhmatova) **2**:12
The Statue Guest (Pushkin)
　　See *The Stone Guest*
"The Statue in Stocks-Market" (Marvell) **10**:276
"The Statue in the Garden" (Lowell) **13**:61
"A Statue in the Silence" (Neruda)
　　See "Una estatua en el silencio"
"The Statue of Liberty" (Hardy) **8**:99
"A Statute of Wine" (Neruda)
　　See "Estatura del vino"
"Staying Alive" (Levertov) **11**:178-79, 195-96
"Stealing Trout on a May Morning" (Hughes) **7**:120, 170
"Steam Shovel Cut" (Masters) **1**:343
"Lo steddazzu" ("The Morning Star") (Pavese) **13**:229
Steeple Bush (Frost) **1**:200, 205-06, 217
"The Steeple-Jack" (Moore) **4**:256
"Stella's Birthday, March 13, 1718-19" (Swift) **9**:255, 297
"Stellenbosch" (Kipling) **3**:176
"The Stenographers" (Page) **12**:163, 173
"Stephen A. Douglas" (Masters) **1**:334
"Stepping Backward" (Rich) **5**:352
"Stepping Outside" (Gallagher) **9**:35
Stepping Outside (Gallagher) **9**:35
"Stepping Westward" (Wordsworth) **4**:395
Stevie Smith: A Selection (Smith) **12**:331, 348
Stikhotvoreniya (Bely) **11**:29
"Still at Annecy" (Montale)
　　See "Ancora ad Annecy"
"Still Do I Keep My Look, My Identity" (Brooks) **7**:71
"Still Falls the Rain" (Sitwell) **3**:310, 323, 326
"Still Life" (Hughes) **7**:121, 137
"Still Night" (Smith) **12**:317
"Stillborn" (Plath) **1**:391, 405
"Stillness" (Pasternak)
　　See "Tishina"
"Stimme des Volks" ("The Voice of the People") (Holderlin) **4**:166
"Stinging" (Cummings)
　　See "Sunset"
"Stings" (Plath) **1**:394, 410, 412-14
"Stixi na smert T. S. Èliota" ("Verses on the Death of T. S. Eliot") (Brodsky) **9**:2, 4
"The Stone" (Carruth) **10**:71
"The Stone from the Sea" (Celan) **10**:112
The Stone Guest (*The Statue Guest*) (Pushkin) **10**:394
"The Stonecarver's Poem" (Levertov) **11**:169
"The Stones" (Plath) **1**:389-90
"Stony Limits" (MacDiarmid) **9**:156, 176
Stony Limits (MacDiarmid) **9**:156, 158, 172-73, 175-76, 179-80, 182-84, 196, 200
"Stopping by Woods on a Snowy Evening" (Frost) **1**:194, 197, 208, 213-14, 221, 225
"La storia" (Montale) **13**:134
"Stories of Snow" (Page) **12**:164, 167-69, 172, 190, 197
Stories of the Sioux (Chief Standing Bear) **10**:333, 341-42
"The Storm" (Montale)
　　See "La bufera"
The Storm and Other Things (Montale)
　　See *La bufera e altro*
The Storm and Other Things (Montale)
　　See *La bufera e altro*
"The Storm Came" (Kipling) **3**:171, 183

"Storm Ending" (Toomer) **7**:317, 330-32

"Storm Warnings" (Rich) **5**:392, 396

"The Story of a Citizen" (Gallagher) **9**:60, 62

"A Story of a Cock and a Bull" (Smart) **13**:348

"The Story of Tommy" (Kipling) **3**:194

"Story of Two Gardens" (Paz)
    See "Cuento de dos jardines"

The Straightening (Celan)
    See *Sprachgitter*

"The Straitening" (Celan)
    See "Engführung"

"Strange Fits of Passion" (Wordsworth) **4**:420

The Strange Islands (Merton) **10**:331, 342, 347, 349, 351

"Strangeness of Heart" (Sassoon) **12**:254

"Stranger" (Merton) **10**:349

"The Stranger" (Rich) **5**:384

"Strategy" (Gallagher) **9**:59

"Straw Hat" (Dove) **6**:110, 114

"Strawberry Hill" (Hughes) **7**:119, 148

"The Strayed Reveller" (Arnold) **5**:5, 12, 39, 50

The Strayed Reveller, and Other Poems (Arnold) **5**:8, 31, 38-9, 42, 48

A Street in Bronzeville (Brooks) **7**:52-4, 56-8, 60-1, 67, 70, 75, 79-80, 85-7, 95, 102, 105

"Street Song" (Sitwell) **3**:311

Street Songs (Sitwell) **3**:308, 320

"Street Window" (Sandburg) **2**:309

"Streets" (Verlaine) **2**:415

"Strephon and Chloe" (Swift) **9**:257-58, 262, 270, 274, 286, 288, 294, 298, 301

"Stretcher Case" (Sassoon) **12**:242, 262

"The Stroke" (Dove) **6**:111

"The Stroke" (Smith) **12**:314

"Strong Men, Riding Horses" (Brooks) **7**:106

"A Strong New Voice Pointing the Way" (Madhubuti) **5**:346

"The Structure of Rime" (Duncan) **2**:126

The Structure of Rime (Duncan) **2**:126

"The Structure of Rime II" (Duncan) **2**:125

"The Structure of Rime XXVIII" (Duncan) **2**:114

"The Structure of the Plane" (Rukeyser) **12**:202

"Struggle" (Hughes) **7**:165-66

"Strumpet Song" (Plath) **1**:388

"The Student" (Moore) **4**:260

"The Studies of Narcissus" (Schwartz) **8**:311

"A Study" (Masters) **1**:342

"The Study of History" (Rich) **5**:365

"Study to Deserve Death" (Smith) **12**:318

"Stumbling" (Montale)
    See "Incespicare"

Stunden-Buch (*Stundenbuch/Das Stundenbuch/A Book for the Hours of Prayer*) (Rilke) **2**:277, 282, 288-90

Stundenbuch/Das Stundenbuch/A Book for the Hours of Prayer (Rilke)
    See *Stunden-Buch*

"Stupid Piety" (Goethe) **5**:229

"Stutgard" (Holderlin) **4**:147

"Style" (Baraka) **4**:9

"Style" (Moore) **4**:259

"Styx" (Duncan) **2**:119

"La suave agonie" (Valery) **9**:391-92

"Sub Contra" (Bogan) **12**:120

Sub Specie Aeternitatis (Hayden) **6**:194

"Sub Terra" (Williams) **7**:377

"A Subaltern" (Sassoon) **12**:242

"The Subalterns" (Hardy) **8**:111, 119

"Suburb" (Smith) **12**:317

"The Subverted Flower" (Frost) **1**:198

"The Succubus" (Graves) **6**:163

"Sudden Journey" (Gallagher) **9**:50

"The Sudder Bazaar" (Kipling) **3**:190, 194

"Suffer the Children" (Lorde) **12**:157

"Suffering" (Page) **12**:190

"Sugar Loaf" (Hughes) **7**:121

"Suicide" (Hughes) **1**:255

"The Suicide" (Millay) **6**:206

"Suicide Blues" (Rukeyser) **12**:228

"The Suicide in the Copse" (Graves) **6**:142, 144

"Suicide in the Trenches" (Sassoon) **12**:267, 285

"Suicide off Egg Rock" (Plath) **1**:389

"Suicide's Note" (Hughes) **1**:236

"A Suite for Augustus" (Dove) **6**:106

"Sukher vilap" ("Pleasure's Lament") (Tagore) **8**:405

"Sulla colonna più alta" ("On the Highest Pillar") (Montale) **13**:109, 111

"Sulla Greve" (Montale) **13**:152

"Sultry" (Lowell) **13**:95-6

"Sultry Rain" (Pasternak) **6**:257

"Summary" (Sanchez) **9**:224, 232

"Summer" (Rossetti) **7**:280

"Summer 1961" (Levertov) **11**:165

"Summer between Terms I" (Lowell) **3**:241

"Summer Is Over" (Cummings) **5**:108-09

"Summer Knowledge" (Schwartz) **8**:297-98, 312-19

Summer Knowledge: New and Selected Poems, 1938-1958 (*Selected Poems (1938-1958): Summer Knowledge*) (Schwartz) **8**:289-91, 296, 301-02, 305, 309, 311

"A Summer Night" (Arnold) **5**:36, 42, 49, 50

"Summer Night Piece" (Lowell) **13**:64, 67

"Summer Resort" (Page) **12**:173

"Summer time T. V. (is witer than ever)" (Sanchez) **9**:210-11, 213, 225

"Summer Wish" (Bogan) **12**:94-5, 98, 100, 106, 121-22

"Summer Words of a Sistuh Addict" (Sanchez) **9**:225

"A Summer's Dream" (Bishop) **3**:47

"Summertime and the Living..." (Hayden) **6**:194, 196

"Summit Beach, 1921" (Dove) **6**:121

"The Summons" (Auden) **1**:38

Summonses of the Times (Bely)
    See *Zovy vremen*

"The Sun" (Milosz) **8**:192, 207

"Sun" (Moore) **4**:243

"The Sun" (Sexton) **2**:351, 372

"The Sun Is near Meridan Height" (Bronte) **8**:73

"The Sun on the Letter" (Hardy) **8**:97

"The Sun Rising" (Donne)
    See "The Sunne Rising"

"Sun Stone" (Paz)
    See "Piedra de sol"

Sun Stone (Paz)
    See *Piedra de sol*

"Sunday" (Herbert) **4**:100

"Sunday" (Hughes) **1**:255

"Sunday" (Williams) **7**:351

"Sunday Morning" (Stevens) **6**:292, 301, 304, 306, 327, 336

"Sunday Morning" (Whitman) **3**:391

"Sunday Morning Apples" (Crane) **3**:83, 90, 100

"A Sunday Morning Tragedy" (Hardy) **8**:99

"The Sundays of Satin-Legs Smith" (*Satin-Legs Smith*) (Brooks) **7**:69, 79-80, 85

"Sundew" (Atwood) **8**:13

Sundry Phansies (Kipling) **3**:193

"The Sunflower" (Montale) **13**:138, 141, 149

"Sunflower Sutra" (Ginsberg) **4**:48, 50, 92

"Sung beneath the Alps" (Holderlin) **4**:142

"The Sunken Bell" (Ishikawa Takuboku)
    See "Shizumeru kane"

"Sunlight and Flesh" (Rimbaud)
    See "Soleil et chair"

"The Sunne Rising" ("Busie old foole"; "The Sun Rising") (Donne) **1**:125, 134, 145, 147, 152, 154

"Sunset" ("Stinging") (Cummings) **5**:70, 94

"Sunset" (Dunbar) **5**:138-39

"Sunset of the Century" (Tagore)
    See "Shatabdir surya"

"A Sunset of the City" (Brooks) **7**:68-9, 96

"Sunset Piece: After Reaching Rémy De Gourmont" (Cummings) **5**:71

Sunstone (Paz)
    See *Piedra de sol*

"Supper Time" (Hughes) **1**:255

"A Supplication for Love" (Browning) **6**:31

"Supposed Confessions of a Second-Rate Sensitive Mind" (Tennyson) **6**:406, 409

"Sur l'eau" (Valery) **9**:391-92

"Sur l'herbe" (Verlaine) **2**:430

"Survival as Tao, Beginning at 5:00 a.m." (Carruth) **10**:88

"Survival of the Fittest" (Gozzano) **10**:183

"The Survivor" (Graves) **6**:137, 142, 144

"Survivors" (Sassoon) **12**:267-68, 285

"Suspension" (Lorde) **12**:158

"Sussex" (Kipling) **3**:167, 192

"Svapna" ("Dream") (Tagore) **8**:410-11

"Svarga" ("Heaven") (Tagore) **8**:414

"Svarga ha'ite biday" ("Farewell to Heaven") (Tagore) **8**:409

"The Swan" (Baudelaire)
    See "Le cygne"

"The Swans" (Lowell) **13**:86

"The Swarm" (Plath) **1**:410, 412

"Sweeney among the Nightingales" (Eliot) **5**:184

"Sweet Afton" ("Afton Water"; "Flow Gently Sweet Afton") (Burns) **6**:77

"Sweet Boy, Give me Yr Ass" (Ginsberg) **4**:90

"A Sweet Flying Dream" (Ferlinghetti) **1**:183, 188

"Sweet Hopes" (Pushkin)
    See "Nadezhdoi Sladostnoi"

"Sweet Michel" (Browning) **2**:30

"The Sweet Primroses" (Hardy) **8**:130

"Sweetest love, I do not goe" (Donne)
    See "Song. 'Sweetest love, I do not goe'"

"Świadomość" ("Consciousness") (Milosz) **8**:209

"Switzerland" (Arnold) **5**:12-13

Sword Blades and Poppy Seed (Lowell) **13**:69-70, 76, 93

"Sygil" (H. D.) **5**:306

"The Syllable Pain" (Celan) **10**:102

"Le sylphe" (Valery) **9**:387, 391, 393

"Sylvia's Death" (Sexton) **2**:364, 370

"Sympathetic Portrait of a Child" (Williams) **7**:349

"Sympathy" (Dunbar) **5**:134
"Symptoms of Love" (Graves) **6**:155
T. V. Baby Poems (Ginsberg) **4**:47
"Table I" (Milosz) **8**:210
"Table II" (Milosz) **8**:210
"Tagore's Last Poems" (Tagore)
 See "Śesh lekhā"
"Take a whole holiday in honour of this" (Day Lewis) **11**:130
"Take heed of loving mee" (Donne)
 See "The Prohibition"
"Taken Aback" (McKay) **2**:221
"Taking In Wash" (Dove) **6**:111
"Taking Off My Clothes" (Forche) **10**:133, 135
"A Tale" (Bogan) **12**:85, 111, 127
"A Tale" (Coleridge) **11**:101
"A Tale of Starvation" (Lowell) **13**:60, 84
"The Tale of the Dead Princess and the Seven Heroes" (Pushkin)
 See "Skazka o Mertvoy Tsarevne"
"The Tale of the Female Vagrant" (Wordsworth) **4**:373, 419
"The Tale of the Fisherman and the Fish" (Pushkin)
 See "Skazka o Rybake i Rybke"
The Tale of the Golden Cockerel (Pushkin)
 See "Skazka o Zolotom Petushke"
"The Tale of the Parson and His Man Balda" (Pushkin)
 See "Skazka o Pope i o Rabotnike Yego Balde"
"The Tale of the Tsar Sultan" (Pushkin)
 See "Skazka o Tsare Sultane"
"A Tale of Two Gardens" (Paz)
 See "Cuento de dos jardines"
Talifer (Robinson) **1**:475, 477, 479, 483
"A Talisman" (Moore) **4**:232
"Talking Oak" (Tennyson) **6**:356
"Tam Glen" (Burns) **6**:59
"Tam o' Shanter" (Burns) **6**:55-8, 73-4, 76, 78, 81, 89, 96
"Tama yo shizume" ("Soul, Be Calm") (Ishikawa Takuboku) **10**:213
"Tamarlane" (Poe) **1**:428, 436-38, 442, 444-45, 448
Tamarlane, and Other Poems (Poe) **1**:428, 432, 437, 449
"Tanghi-Garu Pass" (Paz) **1**:361
"Tanu" ("Body") (Tagore) **8**:407
"Taproot" (Forche) **10**:142
"Tarakar atmahatya" (Tagore) **8**:405
Target Study (Baraka) **4**:38
"Tarrant Moss" (Kipling) **3**:183
"Tartuffe's Punishment" (Rimbaud)
 See "Le châtiment de Tartuff"
"A Task" (Milosz) **8**:206
The Tasking (Sassoon) **12**:271
"Tatinir katha" ("The River's Story") (Tagore) **8**:406
"The Tattooed Man" (Hayden) **6**:195
"Tavern" (Millay) **6**:205
"The Taxi" (Lowell) **13**:93
"T-Bar" (Page) **12**:177, 183, 188
"TCB" (Sanchez) **9**:225
"Tea at the Palaz of Hoon" (Stevens) **6**:304
"Teaching a Dumb Calf" (Hughes) **7**:166
"The Teamster" (Pavese) **13**:218
"The Tear" (Pushkin) **10**:407
A Tear and a Smile (Gibran)
 See *Dam 'ah wabitisāmah*
"Tear Gas" (Rich) **5**:393, 396

"Tears" (Sitwell) **3**:326
"Tears" (Whitman) **3**:379
"Tears and Laughter" (Gibran)
 See *Dam 'ah wabitisāmah*
The Tears of the Blind Lions (Merton) **10**:339
"Teatro Bambino" (Lowell) **13**:94
"The Technique of Perfection" (Graves) **6**:128
"Television Is a Baby Crawling Toward That Death Chamber" (Ginsberg) **4**:51, 76
"Television Poem" (Sanchez) **9**:210
"Tell Me" (Hughes) **1**:244
"Tell Me" (Toomer) **7**:335
Tell Me Again How the White Heron Rises and Flies Across the Nacreous River at Twilight Toward the Distant Islands (Carruth) **10**:86-7
Tell Me, Tell Me: Granite, Steel, and Other Topics (Moore) **4**:242, 259
"The Temper" (Herbert) **4**:100, 118
"The Temper I" (Herbert) **4**:101, 111
The Tempers (Williams) **7**:344, 348, 367, 378, 395, 398, 405
"Tempid: Bellosguardo" (Montale) **13**:126
"The Temple" (Herrick)
 See "The Fairie Temple: or, Oberons Chappell. Dedicated to Mr. John Merrifield, Counsellor at Law"
The Temple: Sacred Poems and Private Ejaculations (Herbert) **4**:99-102, 106, 110, 114-18, 120-21, 123, 126, 129, 132-33
"Il tempo passa" ("Time Goes By"; "Times Passes") (Pavese) **13**:209, 226
"The Temptation of St. Joseph" (Auden) **1**:38-39
Temy i variatsi (*Temy i var'iatsii*; *Themes and Variations*) (Pasternak) **6**:252, 255, 261, 264-65, 269, 271, 275, 277-81, 283
Temy i var'iatsii (Pasternak)
 See *Temy i variatsi*
"The Tenant" (Brodsky) **9**:2
Tender only To One (Smith) **12**:292, 326, 340, 343, 349
"Tenebrae" (Celan) **10**:101-02, 118
"Tenebrae" (Levertov) **11**:176
Tentativa del hombre infinito ("Assay of the Infinite Man"; *Endeavors of Infinite Man*; *Venture of the Infinite Man*) (Neruda) **4**:276
"Tentative Description of a Dinner to Promote the Impeachment of President Eisenhower" (Ferlinghetti) **1**:167
"Tenth Elegy" (Rilke) **2**:273, 286-87
"Tenth Muse" (Lowell) **3**:213
The Tenth Muse Lately sprung up in America (Bradstreet) **10**:2-3, 6-8, 12, 18, 20-1, 25-7, 29-31, 34, 37, 40-1, 43, 46, 51-2, 59
"Tenth Psalm" (Sexton) **2**:372
"Tenuous and Precarious" (Smith) **12**:312, 337
Tercera residencia, 1935-1945 (*The Third Residence*; *Third Residence*) (Neruda) **4**:291, 306
"Tercero antolojía poética" (Jimenez) **7**:195
"Terence, This Is Stupid Stuff" (Housman) **2**:193
"Terminal Day at Beverly Farms" (Lowell) **3**:219
"The Terrace at Berne" (Arnold) **5**:12, 19, 49
"The Terraced Valley" (Graves) **6**:135, 139, 143-44, 172
"Terror" (Levertov) **11**:169

"The Terror of Existing" (Montale)
 See "Il terrore di esistere"
"Il terrore di esistere" ("The Terror of Existing") (Montale) **13**:139
"Tess's Lament" (Hardy) **8**:85
Le Testament (*Le Grand Testament*; *Greater Testament*; *Large Testament*) (Villon) **13**:374-75, 377, 379, 387-90, 393-418
"Tête de faune" (Rimbaud) **3**:271
"Texas" (Lowell) **13**:86
"Thalamus" (MacDiarmid) **9**:168, 176-77
"Thamár y Amnón" (Garcia Lorca) **3**:120, 131-32, 134, 146
"Thank You, Fog" (Auden) **1**:31
"A Thanksgiving" (Auden) **1**:31
"Thanksgiving for a Habitat" (Auden) **1**:24
"Thanksgiving Ode" (Wordsworth) **4**:399
"Thanksgiving's Over" (Lowell) **3**:206
"That Day" (Sexton) **2**:353
"That Day That Was That Day" (Lowell) **12**:85
"That Kind of Thing" (Gallagher) **9**:61
"That Moment" (Hardy) **8**:94
"Their Frailty" (Sassoon) **12**:267
"Thekla's Answer" (Arnold) **5**:50
"Theme and Variation" (Hayden) **6**:186, 197
"Theme and Variations" (Pasternak) **6**:251
Themes and Variations (Pasternak)
 See *Temy i variatsi*
"Then I Saw What the Calling Was" (Rukeyser) **12**:223
"Theodore Dreiser" (Masters) **1**:343
"Theodore the Poet" (Masters) **1**:345
"Theology" (Dunbar) **5**:120, 125, 127
"Theology" (Hughes) **7**:123, 159
"Theory of Art" (Baraka) **4**:9
"Theory of Evil" (Hayden) **6**:194, 196
"Theory of Flight" (Rukeyser) **12**:207, 218, 225
Theory of Flight (Rukeyser) **12**:202-03, 206, 209-10, 226-27, 235-36
"Theory of Maya" (Tagore)
 See "Mayavada"
"There" (Verlaine) **2**:416
"There Are Blk/Puritans" (Sanchez) **9**:218
"There Has to Be a Jail for Ladies" (Merton) **10**:341
"There Is Only One of Everything" (Atwood) **8**:23, 28
"There Once Lived a Poor Knight" (Pushkin)
 See "Zhil Na Svete Rytsar' Bednyi"
"There Shines the Moon, at Noon of Night" (Bronte) **8**:75
"There Should be No Despair" (Bronte) **8**:68-9
"There Was a Child Went Forth" (Whitman) **3**:392, 396, 415
"There Was a Lad Was Born in Kyle" (Burns) **6**:76
"There Was a Poor Knight" (Pushkin)
 See "Zhil Na Svete Rytsar' Bednyi"
"There Was a Saviour" (Thomas) **2**:390
Therefore (Mallarme)
 See *Igitur*
"These" (Williams) **7**:360, 362-63
"These States: To Miami Presidential Convention" (Ginsberg) **4**:82
"Theseus and Ariadne" (Graves) **6**:136-37, 144, 146
"Thetis" (H. D.) **5**:267-68
"They" (Sassoon) **12**:241, 249, 263, 275, 277-78, 286

"They Are Not Missed" (Toomer) 7:338-39
"They Are Not Ready" (Madhubuti) 5:338
"They Eat Out" (Atwood) 8:6
"They'd Never Know Me Now" (Masters)
    1:344
"The Thin People" (Plath) 1:388, 406
"Things of August" (Stevens) 6:313
"Think No More, Lad: Laugh, Be Jolly"
    (Housman) 2:179, 183, 185
"Think of It" (Celan) 10:98
"The Thinker" (Williams) 7:353
"Thinking about El Salvador" (Levertov)
    11:198
"Thinking of Old Tu Fu" (Matsuo Basho)
    3:10
"Third Degree" (Hughes) 1:248
"The Third Dimension" (Levertov) 11:159
"Third Elegy" (Rilke) 2:271
"Third Georgic" (Vergil) 12:361
"Third Hymn to Lenin" (MacDiarmid)
    9:180-81, 197
"Third Psalm" (Sexton) 2:367
The Third Residence (Neruda)
    See *Tercera residencia, 1935-1945*
Third Residence (Neruda)
    See *Tercera residencia, 1935-1945*
"The Third Sermon of the Warpland"
    (Brooks) 7:88-9
"Third Song" (Rilke) 2:273
The Third Symphony (Bely)
    See *Vozvrat: Tretiia simfoniia*
"The Third World" (Ferlinghetti) 1:186
"Third World Calling" (Ferlinghetti) 1:183
"Thirteen Ways of Looking at a Blackbird"
    (Stevens) 6:293, 326-27
Thirty Poems (Merton) 10:338-39, 350-51
"Thirty Rhymes to Hermit Chang Piao" (Tu
    Fu) 9:326
"This Bread I Break" (Thomas) 2:379, 389
"This Cold Man" (Page)
    See "Now This Cold Man"
"This Compost" (Whitman) 3:410
"This Day" (Levertov) 11:198-99, 201
"This Florida: 1924" (Williams) 7:369
"This Frieze of Birds" (Page) 12:168
"This Is a Photograph of Me" (Atwood)
    8:12, 23
"This is Disgraceful and Abominable" (Smith)
    12:293, 309
"This Is Just to Say" (Williams) 7:363, 399,
    401
"This Is Noon" (Graves) 6:166
"This Is Their Fault" (Forche) 10:142
"This (Let's Remember) day Died Again and"
    (Cummings) 5:107
"This Life" (Dove) 6:108
"This Lime-Tree Bower My Prison"
    (Coleridge) 11:51, 53, 72, 83, 88-9, 97, 104,
    107
"This Near-At-Hand" (Rossetti) 7:276
"This Place Rumord to Have Been Sodom"
    (Duncan) 2:127
"This Side of Truth" (Thomas) 2:390
"This Urn Contains Earth from German
    Concentration Camps" (Lorde) 12:136
"This Was a Poet" (Dickinson) 1:96, 102
"Thistles" (Hughes) 7:121, 137
Thomas and Beulah (Dove) 6:104, 107, 110-
    20, 122
"Thomas at the Wheel" (Dove) 6:111
"Thompson's Lunch Room" (Lowell) 13:79
"Thorkild's Song" (Kipling) 3:183

"The Thorn" (Wordsworth) 4:381, 402, 412,
    416-17, 426, 428
"Thorn Piece" (Lowell) 13:85
"Those Times" (Sexton) 2:362-63, 370
"Those Various Scalpels" (Moore) 4:263-64,
    270
"Those Winter Sundays" (Hayden) 6:194-95
"The Thou" (Montale)
    See "Il tu"
"Thou Famished Grave, I Will Not Fill Thee
    Yet" (Millay) 6:242
"A Thought of Columbus" (Whitman)
    See "A Prayer of Columbus"
"The Thought-Fox" (Hughes) 7:120, 158,
    166, 168-69
"Thoughts about the Christian Doctrine of
    Eternal Hell" (Smith) 12:301, 325, 333
"Thoughts about the Person from Porlock"
    (Smith) 12:293, 330, 350
"Thoughts in 1932" (Sassoon) 12:252
"Thoughts on a Breath" (Ginsberg) 4:76
"Thoughts on His Excellency Major General
    Lee" ("On Major General Lee") (Wheatley)
    3:337
"Thoughts on the Works of Providence" ("On
    the Works of Providence") (Wheatley)
    3:332, 339, 358, 361, 363
"Thousand League Pool" (Tu Fu) 9:333
Thread-Suns (Celan)
    See *Fadensonnen*
"3 A.M. Kitchen: My Father Talking"
    (Gallagher) 9:53
"The Three Captains" (Kipling) 3:157
"The Three Decker" (Kipling) 3:161
"Three Desk Objects" (Atwood) 8:2, 13
"Three Ghosts" (Sandburg) 2:309
"The Three Grayes" (Coleridge) 11:117
"Three Green Windows" (Sexton) 2:363
*Three Hundred and Sixty Degrees of Blackness
    Comin at You* (Sanchez) 9:222
Three Material Cantos (Neruda)
    See *Homenaje a Pablo Neruda de los poetas
    espanoles: Tres cantos materiales*
Three Material Songs (Neruda)
    See *Homenaje a Pablo Neruda de los poetas
    espanoles: Tres cantos materiales*
"Three Meditations" (Levertov) 11:169
"Three Modes of History and Culture"
    (Baraka) 4:16
"Three Movements and a Coda" (Baraka)
    4:9, 19, 24
"Three Nuns" (Rossetti) 7:277
"Three Postcards from the Monastery"
    (Merton) 10:332
"Three Songs" (Crane) 3:106
The Three Taverns (Robinson) 1:465-66, 468
"Three Times in Love" (Graves) 6:172
"Three Travellers Watch a Sunrise" (Stevens)
    6:295
"Three United States Sonnets" (Cummings)
    5:94
"Threes" (Atwood) 8:21
"Three-year-old" (Tagore)
    See "Tritiya"
Thrones, 96-109 de los cantares (Pound)
    4:337-38, 352, 353, 357
"Through Corralitos under Rolls of Cloud"
    (Rich) 5:401
"Through Nightmare" (Graves) 6:137, 173
"Through the Looking Glass" (Ferlinghetti)
    1:173

"Throughout Our Lands" (Milosz) 8:187,
    194, 214
"Throw Away Thy Rod" ("Discipline")
    (Herbert) 4:103, 121
A Throw of the Dice Never Will Abolish Chance
    (Mallarme)
    See *Un coup de dés jamais n'abolira le
    hasard*
A Throw of the Dice Will Never Abolish Chance
    (Mallarme)
    See *Un coup de dés jamais n'abolira le
    hasard*
"Thrushes" (Hughes) 7:119, 169
"Thrushes" (Sassoon) 12:253
"Thrust and Riposte" (Montale)
    See "Botta e riposta"
"Thunder Can Break" (Okigbo)
    See "Come Thunder"
"Thunder, Momentarily Instantaneous"
    (Pasternak) 6:251
"A Thunder-Storm" (Dickinson) 1:79
"Thursday" (Millay) 6:208, 211
"Thyrsis" (Arnold) 5:7-8, 18-19, 21, 23-4, 33,
    36, 45, 47, 52, 55-6
"La tierra se llama Juan" ("The Earth is
    Called Juan") (Neruda) 4:294
"The Tiger" (Blake)
    See "The Tyger"
"Timbuctoo" (Tennyson) 6:358, 389, 407-08,
    413, 415-18
"Time Does Not Bring Relief" (Millay) 6:205
"Time Goes By" (Pavese)
    See "Il tempo passa"
"Time Lapse with Tulips" (Gallagher) 9:37
"A Time to Dance" (Day Lewis) 11:126
A Time to Dance and Other Poems (Day
    Lewis) 11:126-27, 129
"Times at Bellosguardo" (Montale) 13:147,
    152
"Time's Dedication" ("Dedication in Time")
    (Schwartz) 8:305, 307, 314
Time's Laughingstocks and Other Verses
    (Hardy) 8:93, 123
"Times Passes" (Pavese)
    See "Il tempo passa"
"Time's Revenges" (Browning) 2:33
"The Times Table" (Frost) 1:205
"Tintern Abbey" (Wordsworth)
    See "Lines Composed a Few Miles Above
    Tintern Abbey"
"Tiresias" (Tennyson) 6:361
Tiriel (Blake) 12:61
"Tirzey Potter" (Masters) 1:338
"Tishina" ("Stillness") (Pasternak) 6:286
"Tithonus" (Tennyson) 6:366, 411
"Title Divine Is Mine the Wife without the
    Sign" (Dickinson) 1:93
"To--- -- -----" (Poe) 1:436, 445
"To a Captious Critic" (Dunbar) 5:125, 127,
    135
"To a Clergyman on the Death of His Lady"
    (Wheatley) 3:357
"To a Common Prostitute" (Whitman) 3:416
"To a Contemporary Bunkshooter" (Sandburg)
    2:317, 330
"To a Contemporary Bunk-Shooter"
    (Sandburg) 2:317, 330
"To a Dreamer" (Pushkin) 10:407
"To a Friend" (Arnold) 5:12, 49
"To a Friend" (Herrick) 9:90
"To a Friend and Fellow-Poet" (MacDiarmid)
    9:183-84

"To a Friend Whose Work Has Come to Triumph" (Sexton) 2:370

"To a Gentleman on His Voyage to Great Britain for the Recovery of His Health" (Wheatley) 3:358

"To a Gipsy Child by the Sea-shore" (Arnold) 5:38, 49-50

"To a Giraffe" (Moore) 4:242-43

"To a Highland Girl" (Wordsworth) 4:404

"To a Husband" (Lowell) 13:74

"To a Jealous Cat" (Sanchez) 9:223, 232

"To a Lady and Her Children, On the Death of Her Son and Their Brother" (Wheatley) 3:363

"To a Lady on Her Remarkable Preservation in an Hurricane in North Carolina" (Wheatley) 3:354

"To a Lady on the Death of Three Relations" (Wheatley) 3:343, 348

"To a Louse, on Seeing One on a Lady's Bonnet at Church" ("Address to a Louse") (Burns) 6:65, 79

"To a Mountain Daisy, on Turning One Down with the Plough in April, 1786" (Burns) 6:50, 74

"To a Mouse, on Turning Her Up in Her Nest with the Plough, November, 1785" (Burns) 6:50, 65, 74, 80, 96

"To a Passing Woman" (Baudelaire)
See "A une passante"

"To a Poet" (Jimenez) 7:183

"To a Poet" (McKay) 2:206

"To a Poor Old Woman" (Williams) 7:390, 399

"To a Portrait in a Gallery" (Page) 12:168

"To a Republican Friend" (Arnold) 5:49

"To a Solitary Disciple" (Williams) 7:357, 378

"To a Strategist" (Moore) 4:266

"To a Winter Squirrel" (Brooks) 7:82

"To a Wreath of Snow" (Bronte) 8:67, 73

"To a Young Actress" (Pushkin) 10:407

"To A Young Friend" (Burns)
See "Epistle to a Young Friend"

"To a Young Girl" (Millay) 6:217

"To Alexander" (Pushkin)
See "Aleksandru"

"To Alexis, in Answer to His Poem against Fruition" (Behn) 13:26

"To All Brothers" (Sanchez) 9:224, 232

"To All Brothers: From All Sisters" (Sanchez) 9:221

"To All Gentleness" (Williams) 7:354

"To All Sisters" (Sanchez) 9:224, 231-32

"To Amintas, upon Reading the Lives of Some of the Romans" (Behn) 13:32

"To an Ancient" (Frost) 1:200

"To an Athlete Dying Young" (Housman) 2:180, 183, 185, 191-94, 198, 201

"To an Old Philosopher in Rome" (Stevens) 6:304, 324, 328

"To Anthea" (Herrick) 9:145

"To Anthea Lying in Bed" (Herrick) 9:137

"To Anthea, Who May Command Him Any Thing" (Herrick) 9:102

"To Any Dead Officer Who Left School for the Army in 1914" (Sassoon) 12:268, 277

"To Autumn" (Keats)
See "Ode to Autumn"

"To Autumn" (Keats) 1:298-302, 314-15

"To Be a Jew in the Twentieth Century" (Rukeyser) 12:234

"To Be in Love" (Brooks) 7:81-2

"To Be Liked by You Would Be a Calamity" (Moore) 4:250

"To Be Quicker for Black Political Prisoners" (Madhubuti) 5:330, 346

"To Be Sung on the Water" (Bogan) 12:90, 124

To Bedlam and Part Way Back (Sexton) 2:345-47, 349-50, 353, 355, 357-58, 360, 363, 367

"To Bennie" (McKay) 2:221

"To Blk/Record/Buyers" (Sanchez) 9:209, 217

"To Blossoms" (Herrick) 9:145

"To Bring the Dead to Life" (Graves) 6:143

"To Carl Sandburg" (Lowell) 13:67

"To Carry the Child" (Smith) 12:320

"To Cedars" (Herrick) 9:91

"To Chaadaev" (Pushkin)
See "Chaadayevu"

To . . . Christopher Duke of Albemarle (Behn) 13:8

"To Chuck" (Sanchez) 9:224, 233

To Circumjack Cencrastus (MacDiarmid) 9:151-53, 158, 171, 175-77, 197

"To Clarendon Hills and H.A.H." (McKay) 2:222

"To Conclude" (Montale) 13:146

"To Daddy" (Lowell) 3:226

"To Daffadills" ("Fair Daffodils") (Herrick) 9:101

"To Damon. To Inquire of Him If He Cou'd Tell Me by the Style, Who Writ Me a Copy of Verses That Came to Me in an Unknown Hand" (Behn) 13:30-1

"To Daphnie and Virginia" (Williams) 7:360, 363, 392

"To Dean Swift" (Swift) 9:295

"To Deism" (Wheatley) 3:354

"To Delmore Schwartz" (Lowell) 3:219, 222

"To Desire" (Behn) 13:24

"To Dianeme" (Herrick) 9:145

To Disembark (Brooks) 7:84, 93

"To Dispel My Grief" (Tu Fu) 9:326

"To Doctor Alabaster" (Herrick) 9:142

"To Don at Salaam" (Brooks) 7:84, 92

"To Earthward" (Frost) 1:197

"To Electra" (Herrick) 9:94

"To Elizabeth Ward Perkins" (Lowell) 13:90

"To Elsie" (Williams) 7:382, 384, 411

"To E.M.E." (McKay) 2:223

"To Enemies" (Bely) 11:24

"To Enter That Rhythm Where the Self is Lost" (Rukeyser) 12:227

"To Ethelinda" ("Ethelinda") (Smart) 13:331, 347

"To Evoke Posterity" (Graves) 6:143, 152

"To Fausta" (Arnold) 5:49

"To Find God" (Herrick) 9:109

"To Flowers" (Herrick) 9:102

"To Flush My Dog" (Browning) 6:6-7

"To Ford Madox Ford in Heaven" (Williams) 7:370

"To Galich" (Pushkin) 10:407

"To George Sand: A Recognition" (Browning) 6:26

"To God" (Herrick) 9:94-5, 109, 118

"To God, His Good Will" (Herrick) 9:118

"To God, on His Sicknesse" (Herrick) 9:144

"To Gurdjieff Dying" (Toomer) 7:338

"To Have Done Nothing" (Williams) 7:383, 389, 410

"To Helen" (Poe) 1:420, 424, 426, 428, 431, 438-39, 441, 443-45, 447

"To Her" (Pushkin) 10:408-09

"To Her Father with Some Verses" (Bradstreet) 10:27, 35

"To Her Most Honoured Father Thomas Dudley" (Bradstreet) 10:2

"To His Book" (Herrick) 9:106, 109

"To His Closet-Gods" (Herrick) 9:88

"To His Coy Mistress" ("The Coy Mistress") (Marvell) 10:259, 265, 269, 271, 273-74, 277-79, 281-82, 290-94, 297, 304, 310-11, 313

"To His Excellency General George Washington" (Wheatley) 3:337, 341

"To His Friend on the Untuneable Times" (Herrick) 9:89

"To His Girles" (Herrick) 9:107

"To His Girles Who Would Have Him Sportfull" (Herrick) 9:107

"To His Honor the Lieutenant Governor on the Death of His Lady" (Wheatley) 3:340

"To His Mistresses" (Herrick) 9:128, 146

"To His Paternall Countrey" (Herrick) 9:108

"To His Savior, a Child; a Present, by a Child" (Herrick) 9:120, 143

"To His Saviour, the New Yeers Gift" (Herrick) 9:95

"To His Saviours Sepulcher: His Devotion" (Herrick) 9:122

"To Homer" (Keats) 1:279, 314

"To Imagination" (Bronte) 8:54

"To Imagination" (Wheatley)
See "On Imagination"

"To John Goldie, August 1785" (Burns) 6:70, 78

"To Jos: Lo: Bishop of Exeter" (Herrick) 9:146

"To Joseph Sadzik" (Milosz)
See "Do Jōzefa Sadzika"

"To Juan at the Winter Solstice" (Graves) 6:137, 144, 146, 168, 171-72

"To Julia" (Herrick) 9:128, 143

"To Julia, in Her Dawne, or Day-breake" (Herrick) 9:143

"To Julia, the Flaminica Dialis, or Queen-Priest" (Herrick) 9:143

"To Keorapetse Kgositsile (Willie)" ("Willie") (Brooks) 7:83, 92, 105

"To Kevin O'Leary Wherever He Is" (Levertov) 11:189

"To Lady Crew, upon the Death of Her Child" (Herrick)
See "To the Lady Crew, upon the Death of Her Child"

"To Laurels" (Herrick) 9:127

"To Licinius" (Pushkin)
See "K Liciniju"

"To Live Merrily, and to Trust to Good Verses" (Herrick) 9:96, 103-05, 107, 114

"To Lord Byron" (Keats) 1:313

"To Lord Harley, on His Marriage" (Swift) 9:254

"To Lose the Earth" (Sexton) 2:363

"To Louise" (Dunbar) 5:121

"To Lucia at Birth" (Graves) 6:137

"To Lyce" (Smart) 13:348

"To Lycomedes on Scyros" (Brodsky)
See "K Likomedu, na Skiros"

"To Lysander at the Musick-Meeting" (Behn) 13:30

"To Lysander, on Some Verses He Writ, and Asking More for His Heart than 'Twas Worth" (Behn) **13**:30

"To Mæcenas" (Wheatley)
See "Ode to Mæcenas"

"To Marguerite" (Arnold) **5**:19, 64

"To Marguerite—Continued" (Arnold) **5**:13, 42-5, 49, 64

"To Mark Anthony in Heaven" (Williams) **7**:367

"To Matilda Betham" (Coleridge) **11**:58

"To Mr. Congreve" (Swift) **9**:250

"To Mr. Creech (under the Name of Daphnis) on His Excellent Translation of Lucretius" (Behn) **13**:8, 31

"To Mr. Delany, Nov. 10, 1718" (Swift) **9**:255

"To Mr R. W. 'If as mine is'" (Donne) **1**:124

"To Mrs. W. on Her Excellent Verses (Writ in Praise of Some I Had Made on the Earl of Rochester)" (Behn) **13**:8, 31

"To My Brother" (Bogan) **12**:117

"To My Brother" (Sassoon) **12**:261, 278

"To My Daughter the Junkie on a Train" ("My Daughter the Junkie on a Train") (Lorde) **12**:146-47, 154

"To My Dear and Loving Husband His Goeing into England" ("My Dear and Loving Husband"; "Upon My Dear and Loving Husband His Goeing into England") (Bradstreet) **10**:13, 36, 40, 63

"To My Ill Reader" (Herrick) **9**:89

"To My Lady Moreland at Tunbridge" (Behn) **13**:8, 29-30

"To My Mother" (Montale) **13**:112, 149, 152

"To Natal'ia" (Pushkin) **10**:404

"To Nature" (Holderlin)
See "An die Natur"

"To One in Paradise" (Poe) **1**:432-33, 437, 444, 446

"To One Who Was With Me in the War" (Sassoon) **12**:246

"To Orlov" (Pushkin)
See "Orlovu"

"To Perenna" (Herrick) **9**:136-37

"To Perilla" (Herrick) **9**:127-28

"To Pile Like Thunder to Its Close" (Dickinson) **1**:102

"To Pliuskova" (Pushkin) **10**:409

"To Raja Rao" (Milosz) **8**:195, 200

"To Robert Southey" (Coleridge) **11**:106

"To Robinson Jeffers" (Milosz) **8**:184, 199, 208

"To S. M., A Young African Painter, on Seeing His Works" (Wheatley) **3**:336, 338, 344, 362

"To Science" (Poe) **1**:437

"To See a World in a Grain of Sand" (Blake) **12**:36

"To Sleep" (Graves) **6**:137

"To Speak of Woe That Is in Marriage" (Lowell) **3**:221, 245

"To Stand (Alone) in Some" (Cummings) **5**:110

To Stay Alive (Levertov) **11**:178-80, 195

"To Stella, Visiting Me in My Sickness" (Swift) **9**:297

"To Stella, Who Collected and Transcribed His Poems, 1720" (Swift) **9**:255

"To Sylvia" (Herrick) **9**:97

"To T. A." (Kipling) **3**:191

"To The Airport" (Rich) **5**:382

"To the Countesse of Bedford. 'Madame, reason is'" (Donne) **1**:123

"To the Countesse of Bedford. 'This twilight of'" (Donne) **1**:124

"To the Cuckoo" (Wordsworth) **4**:403

"To the Daisy" (Wordsworth) **4**:376

"To the Dean, when in England, in 1726" (Swift) **9**:255

"To the De'il" (Burns)
See "Address to the De'il"

"To the Diaspora" (Brooks) **7**:84

"To the Dog Belvoir" (Smith) **12**:317

"To the Duke of Wellington" (Arnold) **5**:49

"To the Evening Star" (Blake) **12**:31

"To the Fair Clarinda Who Made Love to Me, Imagin'd More than Woman" (Behn) **13**:10, 13-14, 20, 22-3, 29

"To the Girl Who Lives in a Tree" (Lorde) **12**:154

"To the Honorable Edward Howard" (Behn) **13**:8

"To the Immaculate Virgin, on a Winter Night" (Merton) **10**:339

"To the King" (Smart) **13**:342

"TO THE KING, upon His Comming with His Army into the West" (Herrick) **9**:109

"TO THE KING, upon His Welcome to Hampton-Court" (Herrick) **9**:109

"To the Lady Crew, upon the Death of Her Child" ("To Lady Crew, upon the Death of Her Child") (Herrick) **9**:104, 131, 143

"To the Lark" (Herrick) **9**:98

To the Memory of . . . George Duke of Buckingham (Behn) **13**:9

"To the Memory of My Dear Daughter in Law, Mrs. Mercy Bradstreet" (Bradstreet) **10**:31

"To the Most Illustrious and Most Hopeful Prince, Charles" (Herrick) **9**:133

"To the Mothers of the Dead Militia" (Neruda)
See "Canto a las madres de los milicianos muertos"

"To the Muses" (Blake) **12**:31

"To the Not Impossible Him" ("The Not Impossible Him") (Millay) **6**:211, 235

"To the Peacock of France" (Moore) **4**:261

"To the Poet Who Happens to Be Black and the Black Poet Who Happens to Be a Woman" (Lorde) **12**:136

"To the Queene" (Herrick) **9**:116

"To the Reader" (Baudelaire)
See "Au lecteur"

"To the Right Honorable William, Earl of Dartmouth, His Majesty's Principal Secretary of State for North America" (Wheatley) **3**:337, 341, 343, 347, 350, 352

"To the Right Person" (Frost) **1**:200

"To the Road" (Dunbar) **5**:139

"To the Sea" (Pushkin) **10**:413

"To the Snake" (Levertov) **11**:205

"To the South: On Its New Slavery" (Dunbar) **5**:131

"To the Tune of the Coventry Carol" (Smith) **12**:316, 330

"To the University of Cambridge, in New England" (Wheatley) **3**:337, 340-41, 344-45, 353

"To the Unknown God" (Hardy) **8**:121

"To the Virgins, to Make Much of Time" ("Gather Ye Rosebuds while Ye May") (Herrick) **9**:100, 145

"To the Vision Seekers, Remember This" (Rose) **13**:241

"To the Water Nymphs Drinking at the Fountain" (Herrick) **9**:97

"To the White Fiends" (McKay) **2**:212, 216, 218, 229

"To the Wife of a Sick Friend" (Millay) **6**:217

"To the Young Poets" (Holderlin)
See "An die Jungen Dichter"

"To Those of My Sisters Who Kept Their Naturals" (Brooks) **7**:86

"To Tirzah" (Blake) **12**:7, 34-5

"To Urania" (Brodsky) **9**:25, 27

To Urania: Selected Poems 1965-1985 (Brodsky) **9**:20, 23-4, 26, 29, 30

"To V. L. Davydovu" (Pushkin)
See "V. L. Davydovu"

"To Victor Hugo of My Crow Pluto" (Moore) **4**:255, 259

"To Victory" (Sassoon) **12**:261, 263, 276

"To Virgil" (Tennyson) **6**:370

"To Waken an Old Lady" (Williams) **7**:345, 353, 360, 363

"To Walk on Hills" (Graves) **6**:143

"To W.G.G." (McKay) **2**:226

"To William Simpson of Ochiltree, May 1785" (Burns)
See "Epistle to William Simpson of Ochiltree, May 1785"

"To William Wordsworth Composed on the Night after His Recitation of a Poem on the Growth of the Individual Mind" (Coleridge) **11**:52-3, 58, 92, 106

"To Winkey" (Lowell) **13**:64

"To Winter" (Blake) **12**:32

"To You" (Whitman) **3**:381

"A Toccata of Galuppi's" (Browning) **2**:37, 88

"Today" (Baraka) **4**:30

"Today and Tomorrow" (Rossetti) **7**:275, 277

"Todesfuge" ("Death Fugue") (Celan) **10**:96, 102, 115-17, 120-21

"Todtnauberg" (Celan) **10**:98

"Tolerance" (Hardy) **8**:93

"Tolerance" (Pavese) **13**:205

"Tom May's Death" (Marvell) **10**:276

"Tom Merritt" (Masters) **1**:324

"Tom Snooks the Pundit" (Smith) **12**:333

"The Tomb of Edgar Poe" (Mallarme)
See "Le tombeau d'Edgar Poe"

"Tombeau de Charles IX" (Ronsard) **11**:243-44

"Le Tombeau de Marguerite de France, duchesse de Savoye" (Ronsard) **11**:243-44

"Le tombeau d'Edgar Poe" ("The Tomb of Edgar Poe"; "Le tombeau d'Edgard Poe") (Mallarme) **4**:203, 209

"Le tombeau d'Edgard Poe" (Mallarme)
See "Le tombeau d'Edgar Poe"

"The Tombstone-Maker" (Sassoon) **12**:242, 263

"Tomlinson" (Kipling) **3**:167, 182

"Tommy" (Kipling) **3**:187

"Too Blue" (Hughes) **1**:243

"Too Late" (Arnold) **5**:43, 56

Topoemas (Paz) **1**:363

"Torch Procession" (Celan)
See "Fackelzug"

The Torrent and the Night Before (Robinson) **1**:459, 474, 484-85

"Torso" (Brodsky) **9**:8

"The Tortured Heart" (Rimbaud)
See "La coeur volé"
"Totem" (Plath) **1**:391, 393, 399, 412
"Totò Merùmeni" (Gozzano) **10**:184-88, 190
"Tou Wan Speaks to Her Husband, Liu
Sheng" (Dove) **6**:107, 109
"The Touch" (Sexton) **2**:352
"The Tour" (Plath) **1**:399-401
"Tour 5" (Hayden) **6**:189, 194
"The Tourist and the Town" (Rich) **5**:353,
362
"Toward Siena" (Montale)
See "Verso Siena"
Toward the Cradle of the World (Gozzano)
See *Verso la cuna del mondo*
Toward the Gulf (Masters) **1**:330, 332, 335,
342-44
"Toward the Piraeus" (H. D.) **5**:268, 304
"Toward the Solstice" (Rich) **5**:374
"Towards a New Scotland" (MacDiarmid)
9:176
The Tower of Babel (Merton) **10**:344, 349
"The Tower of Siloam" (Graves) **6**:133
"The Town" (Pushkin)
See "Gorodok"
The Town down the River (Robinson) **1**:462-
63, 467, 474, 478, 490
"A Town Eclogue" (Swift) **9**:278
"Towns in Colour" (Lowell) **13**:79
"Tract" (Williams) **7**:348, 362, 378
"Tractor" (Hughes) **7**:166
"Tradimento" ("Betrayal") (Pavese) **13**:202,
226
"Tragedy of Teeth" (Kipling) **3**:194
"Train Time" (Bogan) **12**:107
"Trainor the Druggist" (Masters) **1**:347
"Trakat poetycki" ("Treatise on Poetry")
(Milosz) **8**:198-99, 204
"Tramontana" ("North Wind") (Montale)
13:105, 126
"A Trampwoman's Tragedy" (Hardy) **8**:99
"Trams" (Sitwell) **3**:301
"Transcedental Etude" (Rich) **5**:381
The Transformation/Transformations (Ovid)
See *Metamorphoses*
"Transformations" (Hardy) **8**:113
Transformations (Sexton) **2**:349, 354-55, 362,
364-65, 368
"Transgressing the Real" (Duncan) **2**:104
"Transitional" (Williams) **7**:392
Transitional Poem (Day Lewis) **11**:123-25,
128-31, 133-35, 137, 143-45, 148, 151
*A Translation of the Psalms of David,
Attempted in the Spirit of Christianity, and
Adapted to the Divine Service* ("Psalms";
Psalms of David) (Smart) **13**:330-32, 341-
42, 362
"Translations" (Rich) **5**:397
Translations, 1915-1920 (H. D.) **5**:304
The Translations of Ezra Pound (Pound)
4:331
"The Transport of Slaves from Maryland to
Mississippi" (Dove) **6**:108
Transport to Summer (Stevens) **6**:301-03
"The Trappist Abbey: Matins" (Merton)
10:332
"The Trappist Cemetery, Gethsemani"
(Merton) **10**:332-33, 342
"Trappists, Working" (Merton) **10**:332-33
"The Traveler" (Apollinaire)
See "Le voyageur"

"A Traveler at Night Writes His Thoughts"
(Tu Fu) **9**:324
"Traveling on an Amtrack Train Could
Humanize You" (Sanchez) **9**:234
"Traveling through Fog" (Hayden) **6**:194
"Traveller's Curse after Misdirection" (Graves)
6:137
"Traveller's Palm" (Page) **12**:181
"Treatise on Poetry" (Milosz)
See "Trakat poetycki"
"Tree" (Rukeyser) **12**:224
"Tree at My Window" (Frost) **1**:197, 205
"Tree Disease" (Hughes) **7**:120
"Tree Planting" (Tagore)
See "Vriksha-ropan"
"A Tree Telling of Orpheus" (Levertov)
11:177
"The Trees" (Carruth) **10**:71
"Trees" (Hughes) **7**:120
"Trees" (Williams) **7**:351
"La Treizieme" (Nerval) **13**:196
"Trespass Into Spirit" (Baraka) **4**:24
"A Triad" (Rossetti) **7**:272-73, 275, 291
"The Trial" (Sassoon) **12**:260
Tribunals (Duncan) **2**:106, 116, 127
"The Tribute" (H. D.) **5**:298, 304
Tribute to the Angels (H. D.) **5**:272, 274-75,
283-84, 286-87, 293-97, 308-09, 313, 315
"Trickle Drops" (Whitman) **3**:406
"Tricks with Mirrors" (Atwood) **8**:21-6
"Trickster 1977" (Rose) **13**:232
Trilogie der Leidenschaft (Goethe) **5**:250
Trilogy (*War Trilogy*) (H. D.) **5**:281, 283-86,
292-93, 2960-98, 304-07, 310-15
"Trinity Churchyard" (Rukeyser) **12**:225
"Trinity Peace" (Sandburg) **2**:304
"Trio for Two Cats and a Trombone" (Sitwell)
3:303, 306
Trionfi (*Triumphs*) (Petrarch) **8**:224-26, 238,
240, 243, 246, 252, 254, 257, 260, 273-78
"The Triple Fool" (Donne) **1**:125
"The Triple Fool" (Millay) **6**:243
"Tristesse d'un étoile" (Apollinaire) **7**:3
"Les tristesses de la lune" (Baudelaire) **1**:44-5
Tristia (*Elegies*; *Elegies of Gloom*; *Tristibus*)
(Ovid) **2**:233, 240-42, 244-45, 252-53, 255-
59
Tristibus (Ovid)
See *Tristia*
Tristram (Robinson) **1**:470-72, 474-75, 481,
489
"Tristram and Iseult" (Arnold) **5**:9, 12, 33-4,
42, 49, 64
"Tritiya" ("Three-year-old") (Tagore) **8**:415
Triumphal March (Eliot) **5**:168, 185
Triumphs (Petrarch)
See *Trionfi*
"The Triumphs of Bacchus" (Pushkin)
10:407
Les trois livres du recueil des nouvelles poesies
(Ronsard) **11**:248
Troisime livre des odes (Ronsard) **11**:283
"The Tropics in New York" (McKay) **2**:228
"Trouble in De Kitchen" (Dunbar) **5**:146
Troy Park (Sitwell) **3**:293-94, 298, 301, 303,
307-08, 320
"The Truce of the Bear" (Kipling) **3**:171, 182
"Las truchas" (Forche) **10**:134
"Truck-Garden-Market Day" (Millay) **6**:232
"True Confessional" (Ferlinghetti) **1**:187
"True Pearl--Belle of the Lo" (Li Ho) **13**:54

"True Recognition Often Is Refused"
(Schwartz) **8**:292
"True Romance" (Kipling) **3**:161
True Stories (Atwood) **8**:43
"True Tenderness" (Akhmatova) **2**:14
"The True, the Good, and the Beautiful"
(Schwartz) **8**:292
"Truganinny" (Rose) **13**:240
"Trumpet Player: 52nd Street" (Hughes)
1:241, 247, 249
"Truth" (Brooks) **7**:61
"The Truth" (Jimenez)
See "Paisaje del corozon"
"Truth" (McKay) **2**:215
"The Truth" (Montale) **13**:156
"Truth and Error" (Goethe) **5**:228
"Truth Is Not the Secret of a Few"
(Ferlinghetti) **1**:186
"Truth Kills Everybody" (Hughes) **7**:160
"The Truth the Dead Know" (Sexton) **2**:346,
361
"Tsar Sultan" (Pushkin)
See "Skazka o Tsare Sultane"
"Tsung-wu's Birthday" (Tu Fu) **9**:324
"Tsurugai Bridge" (Ishikawa Takuboku)
See "Tsurugaibashi"
"Tsurugaibashi" ("Tsurugai Bridge")
(Ishikawa Takuboku) **10**:213
Tsygany (*Gipsies*; *The Gypsies*) (Pushkin)
10:357-61, 365-66, 369, 371, 386-89, 391-92,
398, 410
"Il tu" ("The Thou") (Montale) **13**:132
"Tulips" (Page) **12**:176
"Tulips" (Plath) **1**:390, 395, 399-401, 405,
407, 409, 414
Tulips and Chimneys (Cummings) **5**:74-5,
77-8, 86, 91, 93-4, 104
"Tulpen" (Celan) **10**:122-23
"Tumbling-Hair" (Cummings) **5**:104
"Tumi o ami" ("You and Me") (Tagore)
8:414
"A Tune for Festive Dances in the Nineteen
Sixties" (Merton) **10**:345
"The Tunnel" (Crane) **3**:86, 88-90, 106-07,
110-11
"Il tuo volo" ("Your Flight") (Montale)
13:111
"Turin" (Gozzano) **10**:177, 180
"The Turkey in the Straw" (Williams) **7**:400
"The Turn of the Moon" (Graves) **6**:154, 156
"The Turncoat" (Baraka) **4**:5, 14
"Turning" (Rilke) **2**:280-81
"A Turning Wind" (Rukeyser) **12**:213
A Turning Wind (Rukeyser) **12**:211-12
"The Twa Dogs" ("Dialogues of the Dogs")
(Burns) **6**:51, 78, 83-4, 88
"The Twa Herds" (Burns) **6**:85
"Twelfth Night, Next Year, a Weekend in
Eternity" (Schwartz) **8**:294
"Twelve Articles" (Swift) **9**:260
"The Twelve Dancing Princesses" (Sexton)
2:365
"Twelve Months After" (Sassoon) **12**:288
Twentieth Century Harlequinade (Sitwell)
3:299-300, 302
"20th-century Fox" (Baraka) **4**:11
Twenty Love Poems and a Despairing Song
(Neruda)
See *Veinte poemas de amor y una canción
desesperada*
Twenty Love Poems and a Desperate Song
(Neruda)

See *Veinte poemas de amor y una canción desesperada*
Twenty Love Poems and a Song of Despair (Neruda)
See *Veinte poemas de amor y una canción desesperada*
Twenty Love Poems and One Song of Despair (Neruda)
See *Veinte poemas de amor y una canción desesperada*
Twenty Poems (Neruda)
See *Veinte poemas de amor y una canción desesperada*
"Twenty-fifth of Vaisakh" (Tagore)
See "Panchishe vaisakh"
Twenty-Five Poems (Thomas) **2**:378, 389
"Twenty-Four Hokku on a Modern Theme" (Lowell) **13**:66
"Twenty-four Poems" (Schwartz) **8**:302
"Twenty-Four Years" (Thomas) **2**:383
Twenty-One Love Poems (Rich) **5**:384, 395
"Twenty-two Rhymes" (Tu Fu) **9**:326
"Twice" (Rossetti) **7**:267, 275
Twice or thrice had I loved thee (Donne)
See "Aire and Angels"
"Twicknam Garden" (Donne) **1**:124, 130, 134
"Twilight" (Apollinaire)
See "Crépuscule"
"The Twilight Bell" (Ishikawa Takuboku)
See "Kure no kane"
The Twilight Book (Neruda)
See *Crepúsculario*
"Twilight Reverie" (Hughes) **1**:255
The Twin In the Clouds (Pasternak)
See *Bliznets v tuchakh*
"Two Amsterdams" (Ferlinghetti) **1**:183
"The Two April Mornings" (Wordsworth) **4**:374
"Two Children" (Graves) **6**:156
"Two Cigarettes" (Pavese)
See "Due sigarette"
"Two Egyptian Portrait Masks" (Hayden) **6**:185
"Two Eskimo Songs" (Hughes) **7**:153, 159
"The Two Fires" (Atwood) **8**:37
"Two Hands" (Sexton) **2**:371
"Two Hours in an Empty Tank" (Brodsky) **9**:2, 4
"Two in the Campagna" (Browning) **2**:68
"Two in the Twilight" (Montale)
See "Due nel crepuscolo"
"Two Legends" (Hughes) **7**:159
"Two Little Boots" (Dunbar) **5**:122, 129
"Two Look at Two" (Frost) **1**:194, 229, 231
"Two Night Pieces" (Sitwell) **3**:293
"The Two Parents" (MacDiarmid) **9**:156, 176
"Two Parted" (Rossetti) **7**:276
"Two Pendants: For the Ears" (Williams) **7**:360, 364, 394
"Two Poems" (Madhubuti) **5**:321
"The Two Roads" (Gozzano) **10**:177-78
"Two Scavengers in a Truck, Two Beautiful People in a Mercedes" (Ferlinghetti) **1**:183, 188
"Two Songs" (Rich) **5**:365
"Two Speak Together" (Lowell) **13**:96-7
"Two Stories" (Gallagher) **9**:36
"The Two Thieves" (Wordsworth) **4**:374, 388
"Two Tramps in Mud Time" (Frost) **1**:198, 221

"Two Views of a Cadaver Room" (Plath) **1**:389
"The Two Voices" (Tennyson) **6**:360
"Two-an'-Six" (McKay) **2**:208-09
"The Two-Days-Old Baby" (Blake)
See "Infant Joy"
Two-Headed Poems (Atwood) **8**:43
2000 (Neruda) **4**:287
"221-1424 (San Francisco suicide number)" (Sanchez) **9**:211, 224-25
"The Tyger" ("The Tiger") (Blake) **12**:6-7, 10, 25, 30, 34-5, 59-64
"The Typical American?" (Masters) **1**:343
"Typists" (Page) **12**:173
Tyrannus Nix? (Ferlinghetti) **1**:174
U samovo morya (*At the Very Edge of the Sea*; *By the Seashore*) (Akhmatova) **2**:15
"Uber Das Werden im Vergehen" (Holderlin) **4**:147
"Ulalume" (Poe) **1**:425-26, 428, 431, 434, 436, 439-40, 442-43, 447, 453
"The Ultimate Infidelity" (Gozzano) **10**:180
"The Ultimate Poem Is Abstract" (Stevens) **6**:314
"Ultimatum" (Sassoon) **12**:259
"Ulysses" (Graves) **6**:130, 137
"Ulysses" (Tennyson) **6**:354, 359, 366, 381, 383-84, 398, 409, 411
"Umi no ikari" ("The Anger of the Sea") (Ishikawa Takuboku) **10**:215
"Unable to Hate or Love" (Page) **12**:175
"Un'altra risorta" (Gozzano) **10**:185
"Un-American Investigators" (Hughes) **1**:252
Unattainable Earth (Milosz)
See *Niobjeta ziemia*
"Unbelief" (Pushkin)
See "Bezverie"
"The Unbeliever" (Bishop) **3**:48
"Unclassified Poems of Ch'in-chou" (Tu Fu) **9**:332
"The Uncle Speaks in the Drawing Room" (Rich) **5**:359, 392
"Uncollected Poems" (Crane) **3**:90
"Under" (Sandburg) **2**:300
Under a Soprano Sky (Sanchez) **9**:238-39, 245
"Under Sirius" (Auden) **1**:23
"Under Stars" (Gallagher) **9**:37, 58, 60
Under Stars (Gallagher) **9**:37, 42, 54, 58-60
"Under the Olives" (Graves) **6**:155-56
"Under the Rose" (Rossetti) **7**:266
"Under the Viaduct" (Dove) **6**:110
"Under the Waterfall" (Hardy) **8**:118
"Under Willows" (Rossetti) **7**:285
Undersong: Chosen Poems Old and New (Revised) (Lorde) **12**:153-58
"Understanding but not Forgetting" (Madhubuti) **5**:337-38, 340
"Underwear" (Ferlinghetti) **1**:183
"Undraped Beauty" (Tagore)
See "Vivasana"
Unedited Books of Poetry (Jimenez)
See "A Horrible Religious Error"
"Unendurable Love" (Tagore)
See "Asahya bhalobasa"
"Unequalled Days" (Pasternak)
See "Edinstvennye dni"
"The Unexplorer" (Millay) **6**:235
"The Unfaithful Married Woman" (Garcia Lorca)
See "La casada infiel"
"The Unfaithful Wife" (Garcia Lorca)
See "La casada infiel"

"The Unfortunate Lover" (Marvell) **10**:265-66, 271, 300, 302
"Ungratefulnesse" (Herbert) **4**:119, 133-34
"Unidentified Flying Object" (Hayden) **6**:196
"The Unions at the Front" (Neruda)
See "Los Grremios en el frente"
"A Unison" (Williams) **7**:360
"The United Fruit Company" (Neruda)
See "La United Fruit Company"
"La United Fruit Company" ("The United Fruit Company") (Neruda) **4**:296
U.S. One (Rukeyser) **12**:203-04, 211
"The Universal Andalusia" (Jimenez)
See "El andaluz universal"
"Universal Sorrow" (Tagore)
See "Vishvashoka"
"The Unknown" (Williams) **7**:369
"Unknown Girl in the Maternity Ward" (Sexton) **2**:349, 355
"Unresolved" (Levertov) **11**:198
"Les uns et les autres" (Verlaine) **2**:416
"An Unsaid Word" (Rich) **5**:359, 393
"Unsleeping City (Brooklyn Bridge Nocturne)" (Garcia Lorca)
See "Ciudad sin sueño"
"Unsounded" (Rich) **5**:359
"The Unsung Heroes" (Dunbar) **5**:131
"Unsuspecting" (Toomer) **7**:336
"Unto the Whole—How Add?" (Dickinson) **1**:103
"Gli uomini che si voltano" (Montale) **13**:133
"Up and Down" (Smith) **12**:316
"Up at a Villa-Down in the City, as Distinguished by an Italian Person of Quality" (Browning) **2**:38
"Up Hill" (Rossetti) **7**:261, 298
"The Up Rising" (Duncan) **2**:104
"Upahar" ("Gift") (Tagore) **8**:407
"The Upas Tree" (Pushkin)
See "Anchar"
"An Upbraiding" (Hardy) **8**:93
"Upon a Beautiful Young Nymph Going to Bed" (Swift)
See "A Beautiful Young Nymph Going to Bed. Written for the Honour of the Fair Sex"
"Upon a Child. An Epitaph" (Herrick) **9**:129-31
"Upon a Child That Died" ("Here she lies, a pretty bud") (Herrick) **9**:130-31
"Upon a Comely and Curious Maide" (Herrick) **9**:129
"Upon a fit of Sickness, Anno 1632" (Bradstreet) **10**:20, 26, 34, 59
"Upon Appleton House" ("Appleton House") (Marvell) **10**:260, 265-67, 269, 271-73, 289-91, 294, 298, 303-04, 314-15, 318
"Upon Ben Jonson" (Herrick) **9**:86
"Upon Her Blush" (Herrick) **9**:143
"Upon Himself" (Herrick) **9**:89, 109
"Upon Himselfe Being Buried" (Herrick) **9**:128, 131
"Upon His Kinswoman Mistris Elizabeth Herrick" (Herrick) **9**:131
"Upon His Last Request to Julia" (Herrick) **9**:108
"Upon Julia's Clothes" ("On Julia's Clothes") (Herrick) **9**:135-36
"Upon Julia's Recovery" (Herrick) **9**:102
"Upon Julia's Washing Her Self in the River" (Herrick) **9**:143

"Upon Meeting Don L. Lee, in a Dream" (Dove) **6**:104-05, 108

"Upon My Daughter Hannah Wiggin Her Recovery from a Dangerous Fever" (Bradstreet) **10**:34

"Upon My Dear and Loving Husband His Goeing into England" (Bradstreet)
See "To My Dear and Loving Husband His Goeing into England"

"Upon My Son Samuel His Going to England, November 6, 1959" (Bradstreet) **10**:26, 34, 36, 63

"Upon the Annunciation and Passion" (Donne) **1**:139

"Upon the Death of the Lord Protector" (Marvell)
See "Poem upon the Death of O. C."

"Upon the Hill and Grove at Billborow" ("The Hill and Grove at Bill-Borrow"; "On the Hill and Grove at Billborow") (Marvell) **10**:269

"Upon the Much Lamented, Master J. Warr" (Herrick) **9**:129

"Upon the Nipples of Julia's Breast" (Herrick) **9**:143

"Upon the Roses in Julias Bosome" (Herrick) **9**:143

"Upon Your Held-Out Hand" (Thomas) **2**:406

"Uptown" (Ginsberg) **4**:47

"The Urals" (Pasternak) **6**:268

"Urania" ("Excuse") (Arnold) **5**:43

Urbasi (Tagore) **8**:403

The Urn (Bely)
See *Urna*

Urna (*The Urn*) (Bely) **11**:3-4, 6-7, 24, 32-3

"Urvashi" (Tagore) **8**:409

"Us" (Sexton) **2**:352

"U.S. 1946 King's X" (Frost) **1**:200

"The Use of 'Tu'" (Montale) **13**:145

"Used Up" (Sandburg) **2**:303

"Useless" (Atwood) **8**:27

"Ustica" (Paz) **1**:355, 360-61

"Utsarga" ("Offering") (Tagore) **8**:409

"V bol'nitse" ("In Hospital") (Pasternak) **6**:266, 269, 286-87

"V. L. Davydovu" ("To V. L. Davydovu") (Pushkin) **10**:412

"V lesu" ("In the Forest") (Pasternak) **6**:280

"The Vacant Lot" (Brooks) **7**:69

"Vagabonds" (Rimbaud) **3**:261

"Vain and Careless" (Graves) **6**:141, 150

"Les vaines danseuses" (Valery) **9**:392

"Vaishnava kavita" ("Vaishnava Poetry") (Tagore) **8**:408

"Vaishnava Poetry" (Tagore)
See "Vaishnava kavita"

"Vaivén" (Paz) **1**:359

Vala (Blake)
See *The Four Zoas: The Torments of Love and Jealousy in the Death and Judgement of Albion the Ancient Man*

Vale Ave (H. D.) **5**:282

"The Vale of Esthwaite" (Wordsworth) **4**:417

"A Valediction: forbidding mourning" ("As virtuous men pass mildly away") (Donne) **1**:124, 126, 130, 135

"A Valediction Forbidding Mourning" (Rich) **5**:371, 395

"A Valediction: of my name, in the window" (Donne) **1**:152

"A Valediction: of the booke" ("I'll tell thee now (dear love) what thou shalt doe") (Donne) **1**:128, 130

"A Valediction: of weeping" (Donne) **1**:124, 130, 153

"A Valentine" (Poe) **1**:445

"Valentine" (Zukofsky) **11**:349

"Valentine Delivered by a Raven" (Gallagher) **9**:63

"Valentine I" (Bishop) **3**:36

"Valley Candle" (Stevens) **6**:338

"The Valley of the Shadow" (Robinson) **1**:490

"The Valley of Unrest" (Poe) **1**:438

"Valuable" (Smith) **12**:296

"Values in Use" (Moore) **4**:261

"Valvins" (Valery) **9**:392

"The Vampire" (Kipling) **3**:166

"Van Winkle" (Crane) **3**:100, 109

"Vanaspati" ("Vegetation") (Tagore) **8**:415

"Vandracour" (Wordsworth) **4**:399

"Vanishing Point: Urban Indian" (Rose) **13**:232

"Vanitie" (Herbert) **4**:120

"Vanitie I" (Herbert) **4**:132

"The Vanity of All Worldly Things" ("Of the Vanity of All Worldly Creatures") (Bradstreet) **10**:2, 6, 21

"Vanna's Twins" (Rossetti) **7**:291

"Variation and Reflection on a Poem by Rilke" (Levertov) **11**:206

"Variation and Reflection on a Theme by Rilke (The Book of Hours Book I Poem 7)" (Levertov) **11**:203

"Variation on a Theme by Rilke" (Levertov) **11**:202

"Variations on a Theme by Rilke (The Book of Hours Book I Poem 4)" (Levertov) **11**:203

"Variations on Two Dicta of William Blake" (Duncan) **2**:103

Various Poems of All Periods (Valery)
See *Poésies*

"Varsha-mangal" ("Rain Festival") (Tagore) **8**:411

"Varshashesh" ("End of the Year") (Tagore) **8**:411

"Vasanter Kusumer mela" ("Festival of Spring") (Tagore) **8**:406

"Vasundhara" ("The World") (Tagore) **8**:408

Vaudeville for a Princess, and Other Poems (Schwartz) **8**:285, 292-94, 318

"Vecchi versi" ("Old Lines") (Montale) **13**:108, 157

"La vecchia ubriaca" (Pavese) **13**:214

Vecher (*Evening*) (Akhmatova) **2**:3, 5-6, 11, 17

"Vechernyaya progulka" (Bely) **11**:22

"Vegetable Island" (Page) **12**:178

"Vegetation" (Tagore)
See "Vanaspati"

Veinte poemas de amor y una canción desesperada (*Twenty Love Poems and a Despairing Song*; *Twenty Love Poems and a Desperate Song*; *Twenty Love Poems and a Song of Despair*; *Twenty Love Poems and One Song of Despair*; *Twenty Poems*) (Neruda) **4**:276, 282, 284, 291, 299-305, 307

"Vendémiaire" (Apollinaire) **7**:10, 36, 44-6

Venetian Epigrams (Goethe) **5**:223

"Venice" (Pasternak) **6**:276

"The Venice Poem" (Duncan) **2**:105-06

"Il ventaglio" ("The Fan") (Montale) **13**:108, 128-29

"Vento e bandiere" ("Wind and Flags") (Montale) **13**:164

"Vento sulla mezzaluna" ("Wind on the Crescent") (Montale) **13**:110

Venture of the Infinite Man (Neruda)
See *Tentativa del hombre infinito*

"Vénus anadyomène" (Rimbaud) **3**:255

"Venus and the Ark" (Sexton) **2**:355

"Venus Transiens" (Lowell) **13**:66, 96

"Veracruz" (Hayden) **6**:193-94

"La verdad" (Jimenez) **7**:202

"Vermächtnis" (Goethe) **5**:248

"Vermont" (Carruth) **10**:73-4, 83

"Vernal Equinox" (Lowell) **13**:64

"Vers dorés" (Nerval) **13**:181

Vers et prose (Mallarme) **4**:207

"Vers nouveaux et chansons" (Rimbaud) **3**:285

"Verses on His Own Death" (Swift) **9**:265

"Verses on the Death of Dr. Swift" (Swift) **9**:258, 279-82, 294-95, 304, 306-08, 310

"Verses on the Death of T. S. Eliot" (Brodsky)
See "Stixi na smert T. S. Èliota"

"Verses Upon the Burning of Our House" (Bradstreet)
See "Some Verses Upon the Burning of Our House, July 10th, 1666"

"Verses Wrote in a Lady's Ivory Table-book" (Swift)
See "Written in a Lady's Ivory Table-book, 1698"

"Versilian Shore" (Montale)
See "Proda di Versilia"

Verso la cuna del mondo (*Toward the Cradle of the World*) (Gozzano) **10**:177, 184

"Verso la fede" (Gozzano) **10**:184

"Verso Siena" ("Toward Siena") (Montale) **13**:109

"Vertigo" (Rich) **5**:360

"Vertue" ("Virtue") (Herbert) **4**:100-01, 110, 113, 132-34

"Vespers" (Lowell) **13**:64, 67, 97

"Vestigia nulla retrorsum (In Memoriam: Rainer Maria Rilke 1875-1926)" (MacDiarmid) **9**:156, 176

"Les veuves" ("Widows") (Baudelaire) **1**:44, 58-9

La via del refugio (*The Road to Shelter*; *The Way of Refuge*) (Gozzano) **10**:179, 184-85, 188

"Vice" (Baraka) **4**:15

"Victoria's Tears" (Browning) **6**:14, 29

"Viday" ("Farewell") (Tagore) **8**:415

"Videshi phul" ("Foreign Flower") (Tagore) **8**:415

Viento entero (*Intact Wind*) (Paz) **1**:353, 356, 362-63, 369

"Le vierge, le vivace et le bel aujourdhui" (Mallarme) **4**:202, 206

"Vies" (Rimbaud) **3**:261-62

"Vietnam Addenda" (Lorde) **12**:155

"Le vieux saltimbanque" (Baudelaire) **1**:44, 58

"The View" (Holderlin) **4**:178

"The View" (Milosz) **8**:198

"A View across the Roman Campagna" (Browning) **6**:23

"View from an Empty Chair" (Gallagher) **9**:50

"View of Teignmouth in Devonshire" (Lowell) **13**:67
"View of the Pig" (Hughes) **7**:136, 140
"View of the Wilds" (Tu Fu) **9**:332
"Vigil Strange I Kept on the Field One Night" (Whitman) **3**:378
Vigils (Sassoon) **12**:258-59, 271
"Le vigneron champenois" (Apollinaire) **7**:22
"Vihanger gan" ("Song of the Bird") (Tagore) **8**:406
"Villa Adriana" (Rich) **5**:362
"The Village" (Carruth) **10**:71
"The Village" (Pushkin) **10**:408-09
"The Village Atheist" (Masters) **1**:335
"The Villagers and Death" (Graves) **6**:142
"Villes" (Rimbaud) **3**:261, 264-65
"Le vin perdu" ("The Lost Wine") (Valery) **9**:388, 390, 396
"The Vindictives" (Frost) **1**:206
"Vine" (Herrick) **9**:100, 109, 137
"The Vineyard" (Kipling) **3**:182
"Vino, primero, puro" (Jimenez) **7**:187
"Il vino triste" ("Sad Wine") (Pavese) **13**:224
The Violent Season (Paz)
 See *La estación violenta*
"The Virgin Carrying a Lantern" (Stevens) **6**:310
"The Virgin Mary to the Child Jesus" (Browning) **6**:29-30
"Virginia" (Eliot) **5**:166
"Virtue" (Herbert)
 See "Vertue"
"Virtue" (Wheatley)
 See "On Virtue"
"Vishvashoka" ("Universal Sorrow") (Tagore) **8**:417
"The Vision" (Burns) **6**:50
"Vision" (Gibran)
 See "Ru'ya'"
"The Vision" (Masters) **1**:342
"Vision" (Rimbaud) **3**:263
"Vision" (Sassoon) **12**:245
"Vision And Prayer" (Thomas) **2**:382, 387-88, 390
"Vision in the Repair Shop" (Graves) **6**:143
"A Vision of India" (Kipling) **3**:190
"A Vision of Poets" (Browning) **6**:7, 26, 38, 41
"The Vision of Sin" (Tennyson) **6**:359-60, 366, 378
A Vision of the Last Judgment (Blake) **12**:40-2
"The Visionary" (Bronte) **8**:52
Visions of the Daughters of Albion: The Eye Sees More Than the Heart Knows (Blake) **12**:35, 46, 57, 61, 63
"The Visions of the Maid of Orleans" (Coleridge)
 See "Joan of Arc"
"The Visit" (Baraka) **4**:17
"Visit to Toronto, with Companions" (Atwood) **8**:40
"The Visitation" (Graves) **6**:172
"Visiting the Ho Family Again" (Tu Fu) **9**:319
"The Visitor" (Forche) **10**:144, 153
"Visits to St. Elizabeth" (Bishop) **3**:47, 56
"Vitam quae faciunt beatiorem" (Martial) **10**:243
ViVa (*VV*) (Cummings) **5**:100, 104-07, 110-11
"Vivasana" ("Undraped Beauty") (Tagore) **8**:407

"Vnov' Ia Posetil" (Pushkin)
 See "Vnov' Ya Posetil"
"Vnov' Ya Posetil" ("Again I Visited"; "Vnov' Ia Posetil") (Pushkin) **10**:384, 414-15
"Vocation" (Levertov) **11**:198
"Voce giunta con le folaghe" ("Voice Coming with the Moorhens") (Montale) **13**:112
"Voeu à Phebus" (Ronsard) **11**:256
"The Voice" (Arnold) **5**:49
"A Voice" (Atwood) **8**:14
"The Voice" (Baudelaire) **1**:73
"The Voice" (Hardy) **8**:88, 117-18, 135
"Voice Arriving with the Coots" (Montale) **13**:146, 149
"Voice Coming with the Moorhens" (Montale)
 See "Voce giunta con le folaghe"
"Voice from the Tomb" (Smith) **12**:349
"The Voice of Rock" (Ginsberg) **4**:55
"The Voice of the Ancient Bard" (Blake) **12**:7
Voice of the Forest (Tagore)
 See *Banabani*
"Voice of the Past" (Bely)
 See "Golos proshlogo"
"The Voice of the People" (Holderlin)
 See "Stimme des Volks"
"Voices about the Princess Anemone" (Smith) **12**:298, 348-49
"Voicy le temps, Hurault, qui joyeux nous convie" (Ronsard) **11**:250
"Void in Law" (Browning) **6**:28, 32
"An vollen Büschelzweigen" (Goethe) **5**:247
"Vollmondnacht" (Goethe) **5**:247
"Vol'nost': Oda" ("Liberty"; "Ode to Freedom"; "Ode to Liberty") (Pushkin) **10**:408-09
"La volupté" (Baudelaire) **1**:71
"Von diesen Stauden" (Celan) **10**:122
Von Schwelle zu Schwelle (*From Threshold to Threshold*) (Celan) **10**:95, 121
"Voracities and Verities Sometimes Are Interacting" (Moore) **4**:261
"Vorobyev Hills" (Pasternak) **6**:251-54
"Vospominanie v Tsarskom Sele" (*Recollections of Tsarskoe-Selo*; "Remembrance in Tsarskoe Selo"; "Reminiscences at Tsarskoe Selo") (Pushkin) **10**:409, 421
"Vostok pobledneuskii, vostok onemesvshii" ("The East that is Now Pale, the East that is Now Silent") (Bely) **11**:32
"A Vow" (Ginsberg) **4**:56
"The Vow" (Lowell) **13**:86-7
"Vowels 2" (Baraka) **4**:24
"Le voyage" (Baudelaire) **1**:50, 60, 70, 73-4
"Le voyage à Cythère" ("Voyage to Cythera") (Baudelaire) **1**:65, 72-3
"Le Voyage de Tours, ou les amoureus Thoinet et Perrot" (Ronsard) **11**:260-61, 264
"The Voyage of Maeldune" (Tennyson) **6**:359, 369
"Voyage to Cythera" (Baudelaire)
 See "Le voyage à Cythère"
Voyage to the Island of Love (*The Consolation of Philosophy*; *On the Trinity*) (Behn)
 See *Poems upon Several Occasions, with a Voyage to the Island of Love*
"Voyagers" (Page) **12**:199
"Voyages" (Crane) **3**:90, 97, 104
"Voyages II" (Crane) **3**:80, 83, 96, 102
"Voyages III" (Crane) **3**:83
"Voyages IV" (Crane) **3**:83

"Voyages V" (Crane) **3**:83
"Le voyageur" ("The Traveler") (Apollinaire) **7**:48
"Les Voyelles" (Rimbaud) **3**:249, 268, 274
Vozvrat: Tretiia simfoniia (*The Return; The Third Symphony*) (Bely) **11**:3, 8-9, 14-17, 22
"Vriksha-ropan" ("Tree Planting") (Tagore) **8**:416
"Vriksha-vandana" ("Homage to the Tree") (Tagore) **8**:416
Vrindaban (*I Am in the Unstable Hour*) (Paz) **1**:361-63
"Vstrecha" ("A Meeting") (Pasternak) **6**:280
Vtoraia simfoniia: Dramaticheskaia (*The Second Symphony; Simfonija (2-aja)*) (Bely) **11**:3-4, 8-11, 13-16, 21, 27, 33
"Vue" (Valery) **9**:392
"Vuelta" ("Return") (Paz) **1**:370-72, 374
Vuelta (*Return*) (Paz) **1**:370-71, 374, 376
"Vuelta de paseo" ("Back from a Walk") (Garcia Lorca) **3**:139
VV (Cummings)
 See *ViVa*
"Vysokaya bolesn" ("The High Malady") (Pasternak) **6**:265
"Vystrel" ("The Shot") (Pushkin) **10**:414
"W. S. Landor" (Moore) **4**:242, 259
"Wadin' in de Crick" (Dunbar) **5**:144
"Wading at Wellfleet" (Bishop) **3**:49, 57
"Waga Uta" ("My Songs") (Yosano Akiko) **11**:302, 306
"The Wagoner" (Pavese) **13**:205
"The Waiting Head" (Sexton) **2**:350
"Wake-Up Niggers" (Madhubuti) **5**:329, 338
"Waking in the Blue" (Lowell) **3**:209, 221
"Waking in the Dark" (Rich) **5**:370, 392, 395
"Waking this Morning" (Rukeyser) **12**:230
"Wales Visitation" (Ginsberg) **4**:74, 93-4
"The Walk" (Hardy) **8**:93
"Walking in Paris" (Sexton) **2**:363
"Walking in the Blue" (Sexton) **2**:350
"The Walking Man of Rodin" (Sandburg) **2**:334
"Walking on the Prayerstick" (Rose) **13**:233
"The Wall" (Brooks) **7**:82
"The Wall" (Montale) **13**:148
"Walls" (Hughes) **7**:149
The Walls Do Not Fall (H. D.) **5**:272, 274-76, 293-95, 307, 309, 312, 314-15
"Walt Whitman" (Whitman) **3**:414
"Walter Bradford" (Brooks) **7**:92
"The Wanderer" (Pushkin) **10**:409
"The Wanderer" (Smith) **12**:326, 349-50, 354
"The Wanderer" (Williams) **7**:374, 382, 394
"The Wandering Jew" (Robinson) **1**:487
"The Wanderings of Cain" (Coleridge) **11**:89, 91
"Wandrers Sturmlied" (Goethe) **5**:237-39
"Wanting to Die" (Sexton) **2**:364
"War Pictures" (Lowell) **13**:76
War Trilogy (H. D.)
 See *Trilogy*
"The Ward" (Rukeyser) **12**:225
"Waring" (Browning) **2**:26
"Warning" (Hughes) **1**:252
"Warning to Children" (Graves) **6**:139, 143-44, 150
"A Warning to Those Who Live on Mountains" (Day Lewis) **11**:144
"Warnung" (Goethe) **5**:250

"The Warriors of the North" (Hughes)   7:132, 148

"The Warrior's Prayer" (Dunbar)   5:134

"Warum gabst du uns die tiefen Blicke" (Goethe)   5:246

"Was He Married?" (Smith)   12:333, 352

"Washerwoman" (Sandburg)   2:329

"The Wassaile" (Herrick)   9:104

The Waste Land (Eliot)   5:155-62, 165-67, 173-74, 176, 178-79, 183-89, 191-93, 198, 206-18

The Waste Land (Pound)   4:353

"Waste Paper Basket" (Tagore)   8:417

Watakushi no Oitach (Yosano Akiko)   11:309-11

"Watchful, A Tale of Psyche" (Smith)   12:303-05, 337

"The Water" (Carruth)   10:71

"Water" (Lowell)   3:212, 215

"Water and Marble" (Page)   12:178

"Water Color" (Verlaine)
   See "Aquarelles"

Water Lilies (Jimenez)
   See *Ninfeas*

"Water Music" (MacDiarmid)   9:154, 156, 158, 171, 176

"Water of Life" (MacDiarmid)   9:197-98

"Watercolor of Grantchester Meadows" (Plath)   1:388

"Watercolors" (Rose)   13:238

"The Watercourse" (Herbert)   4:114

"Watergate" (Baraka)   4:30

"The Watergaw" (MacDiarmid)   9:156, 160, 196

"Waterlily Fire" (Rukeyser)   12:221

Waterlily Fire: Poems, 1935-1962 (Rukeyser)   12:215-16

"Watermaid" (Okigbo)   7:232, 239

"The Way" (Lowell)   13:60, 83

"Way down the Ravi River" (Kipling)   3:194

Way of All the Earth (Akhmatova)   2:16

"The Way of Refuge" (Gozzano)
   See "The Road to Shelter"

The Way of Refuge (Gozzano)
   See *La via del refugio*

"The Way through the Woods" (Kipling)   3:171, 183, 186, 192

"Way-Out Morgan" (Brooks)   7:63

The Wayward and the Seeking: A Collection of Writing by Jean Toomer (Toomer)   7:341

We a BaddDDD People (Sanchez)   9:204, 206-08, 210-13, 216, 218-20, 224-27, 229, 234, 237-38, 240, 242

"We a BadddDDD People (for gwendolyn brooks/a fo real bad one)" (Sanchez)   9:209, 225, 237

"We Are Muslim Women" (Sanchez)   9:228

"We Are Seven" (Wordsworth)   4:374, 415, 420, 428

"We Lying by Seasand" (Thomas)   2:404

"We Real Cool" (Brooks)   7:62, 85, 90

"We Too" (H. D.)   5:268

We Walk the Way of the New World (Madhubuti)   5:326-27, 336, 343, 345-46

"We Wear the Mask" (Dunbar)   5:124, 130, 132, 135, 140, 142, 144

"The Weak Monk" (Smith)   12:333

"A Wearied Pilgrim" (Herrick)   9:108

"The Weary Blues" (Hughes)   1:236, 246, 248, 261, 269

The Weary Blues (Hughes)   1:236-37, 242, 244-46, 248, 258, 260, 262-64, 268-70

"Weary in Well-Doing" (Rossetti)   7:268

"Weary of the Bitter Ease" (Mallarme)
   See "Las de l'amer repos"

"The Weary Pund o' Tow" (Burns)   6:78

"The Weather-Cock Points South" (Lowell)   13:96

"Weathering Out" (Dove)   6:111

"Weathers" (Hardy)   8:124

"Webster Ford" (Masters)   1:344, 346,348

"The Wedding Photograph" (Smith)   12:316, 323

The Wedge (Williams)   7:370, 402

"The Weed" (Bishop)   3:37, 45, 75

"The Weeping Garden" (Pasternak)   6:268

"The Weeping Saviour" (Browning)   6:14

"Weggebeizt" (Celan)   10:106, 111

"Weight" (Tagore)
   See "Bhar"

Die Weise von Liebe und Tod des Cornets Christoph Rilke (Rilke)   2:266, 268

"Weiß sind die Tulpen" (Celan)   10:123

"Welcome and Parting" (Goethe)
   See "Willkommen und Abschied"

"Welcome Morning" (Sexton)   2:372

"The Welcome to Sack" (Herrick)   9:88, 94, 102

"Welcome to the Caves of Arta" (Graves)   6:153

"The Well" (Levertov)   11:168, 205-06

"The Well-Beloved" (Hardy)   8:91

"Welsh Incident" (Graves)   6:143, 150

"The Welsh Marches" (Housman)   2:159, 179

"We're few" (Pasternak)   6:252

"We're Not Learnen to Be Paper Boys (for the young brothas who sell Muhammad Speaks)" (Sanchez)   9:229

"The Wereman" (Atwood)   8:36

"An Werther" (Goethe)   5:250-51

Wessex Poems, and Other Verses (Hardy)   8:114, 123

"The West" (Housman)   2:167, 191, 199

"West and Away the Wheels of Darkness Roll" (Housman)   2:162

West-Östlicher Divan (Goethe)   5:223, 225, 229, 239, 247, 250

"West-Running Brook" (Frost)   1:203, 218, 220

West-Running Brook (Frost)   1:195, 203, 205, 213

"Wha Is That at My Bower-Door" (Burns)   6:77

"What Are Years" (Moore)   4:243

"What God Is" (Herrick)   9:94, 141

"What God Is Like to Him I Serve?" (Bradstreet)   10:34

"What Happened" (Duncan)   2:103

What Happened When the Hopi Hit New York (Rose)   13:239

"What It Cost" (Forche)   10:166

"What Lips My Lips Have Kissed" (Millay)   6:225

"What Shall I Give My Children?" (Brooks)   7:76

"What? So Soon" (Hughes)   1:266

"What Stillness Round a God" (Rilke)   2:275

"What the Bird with the Human Head Knew" (Sexton)   2:372

"What the Women Said" (Bogan)   12:110

"What Were They Like?" (Levertov)   11:176

"Whatever You Wish, Lord" (Jimenez)   7:184

What's O'Clock (Lowell)   13:66, 76, 84-5, 91, 93-4, 97-8

"What's That" (Sexton)   2:359

"Whe' Fe Do?" (McKay)   2:222-23

"Wheat-in-the-Ear" (Lowell)   13:96

"The Wheel" (Hayden)   6:194-95

"The Wheel of Being II" (Carruth)   10:71

"Wheesht, Wheesht, My Foolish Heart" (MacDiarmid)   9:156, 160

"When All My Five and Country Senses See" (Thomas)   2:392

"When de Co'n Pone's Hot" (Dunbar)   5:117, 122

"When Death Came April Twelve 1945" (Sandburg)   2:333

"When First I Saw" (Burns)   6:78

"When from Afar" (Holderlin)   4:174, 178

"When God Lets My Body Be" (Cummings)   5:99

"When Guilford Good" (Burns)   6:78

"When Hair Falls Off and Eyes Blur and" (Cummings)   5:105

"When He Would Have His Verses Read" (Herrick)   9:87, 96, 102, 109, 139, 145

"When I Buy Pictures" (Moore)   4:251, 266

"When I Die" (Brooks)   7:68

"When I Have Fears That I May Cease to Be" (Keats)   1:314

"When I Set Out for Lyonesse" (Hardy)   8:92, 112, 115

"When I Was One-and-Twenty" (Housman)   2:161, 192

"When I Watch the Living Meet" (Housman)   2:184

"When in the Gloomiest of Capitals" (Akhmatova)
   See "Kogda v mrachneyshey iz stolits"

"When Jemmy First Began to Love" (Behn)
   See "Song to a Scotish Tune (When Jemmy First Began to Love)"

"When Lilacs Last in the Dooryard Bloom'd" (Whitman)   3:378, 382, 396-97, 410, 418-19, 422

"When Lilacs Last in the Dooryard Bloomed" (Whitman)   3:378, 382, 396-97, 410, 418-19, 422

"When Malindy Sings" (Dunbar)   5:117, 119-21, 134, 146

"When Mrs. Martin's Booker T." (Brooks)   7:67, 69

"When Once the Twilight Locks No Longer" (Thomas)   2:402

"When Rain Whom Fear" (Cummings)   5:105

"When Serpents bargain for the Right to Squirm" (Cummings)   5:90, 107

"When Sir Beelzebub" (Sitwell)   3:303

"When Smoke Stood Up from Ludlow" (Housman)   2:184

"When Summer's End Is Nighing" (Housman)   2:165, 181

When the Skies Clear (Pasternak)
   See *Kogda razglyaetsya*

"When They Have Lost" (Day Lewis)   11:144

"When Under the Icy Eaves" (Masters)   1:328

"When Unto Nights of Autumn Do Complain" (Cummings)   5:104

"When We'll Worship Jesus" (Baraka)   4:29, 39

"When You Speak to Me" (Gallagher)   9:36

"When You've Forgotten Sunday" (Brooks)   7:53, 68

"Where Are the War Poets?" (Day Lewis)   11:131

"Where Shall the Lover Rest" (Scott)   13:304

"Where, Tall Girl, Is Your Gypsy Babe" (Akhmatova)
See "Gde, vysokaya, tvoy tsyganyonok"
"Where the Picnic Was" (Hardy) 8:136
"Where the Rainbow Ends" (Lowell) 3:200, 207
"Where the Tennis Court Was" (Montale)
See "Dov'era il tennis"
"Where's Agnes?" (Browning) 6:24
"Where's the Poker" (Smart) 13:348
"Whether on Ida's Shady Brow" (Blake) 12:11
"Which, Being Interpreted, Is as May Be, or, Otherwise" (Lowell) 13:91
"While Drawing in a Churchyard" (Hardy) 8:120-21
"Whip the World" (MacDiarmid) 9:187
Whipperginny (Graves) 6:127-28, 131
"The Whipping" (Hayden) 6:194-96
"Whiskers, A Philosophical Ode" (Pushkin) 10:407
"Whispers of Heavenly Death" (Whitman) 3:378
"Whistle and I'll Come tae Ye, My Lad" (Burns) 6:59
"The Whistle Cockade" (Burns) 6:82
Whistles and Whistling (Ishikawa Takuboku)
See *Yobuko to kuchibue*
"Whistling Sam" (Dunbar) 5:122, 146
"White and Green" (Lowell) 13:60, 69
"White and Violet" (Jimenez) 7:183
"White Arrow" (Toomer) 7:336
White Buildings (Crane) 3:81, 84, 87, 90
"The White City" (McKay) 2:211
The White Doe of Rylstone; or, The Fate of the Nortons (Wordsworth) 4:394, 402, 407
White Flock (Akhmatova)
See *Belaya staya*
"White Horses" (Kipling) 3:183
"The White House" (McKay) 2:210, 221, 229
"The White Man's Burden" (Kipling) 3:192
"White Shoulders" (Sandburg) 2:303
"White Shroud" (Ginsberg) 4:86, 90
White Shroud (Ginsberg) 4:86-7, 89-90
"The White Snake" (Sexton) 2:365
"The White Thought" (Smith) 12:292, 341, 354
"The White Troops" (Brooks) 7:73
"The White-Tailed Hornet" (Frost) 1:221
"Whitsunday" (Herbert) 4:118
Who Are We Now? (Ferlinghetti) 1:187-88
"Who But the Lord" (Hughes) 1:241
"Who Cares, Long as It's B-Flat" (Carruth) 10:85
"Who ever comes to shroud me do not harme" (Donne)
See "The Funerall"
"Who is this Who Howls and Mutters?" (Smith) 12:313, 336
"Who Knows" (Dunbar) 5:130
"Who Know's If the Moon's" (Cummings) 5:88
"Who Made Paul Bunyan" (Sandburg) 2:327
"Who Said It Was Simple" (Lorde) 12:153, 157
"Who Shot Eugenie?" (Smith) 12:333
"Who Will Survive America?/Few Americans/Very Few Negroes/No Crackers at All" (Baraka) 4:14, 19
"Whuchulls" (MacDiarmid) 9:197-98
"Why Did I Laugh Tonight" (Keats) 1:279, 305

"Why Did I Sketch"' (Hardy) 8:137
"Why do I" (Smith) 12:337
"Why East Wind Chills" (Thomas) 2:379
"Why I Am a Liberal" (Browning) 2:66
"Why Some Look Up to Planets and Heroes" (Merton) 10:334
"Whys/Wise" (Baraka) 4:40
"Wichita Vortex Sutra" (Ginsberg) 4:50, 53, 66, 82, 85
"The Widow at Windsor" ("The Widow o' Windsor"; "The Widow of Windsor") (Kipling) 3:161, 186-87, 191
"Widow La Rue" (Masters) 1:330, 333
"The Widow o' Windsor" (Kipling)
See "The Widow at Windsor"
"The Widow of Windsor" (Kipling)
See "The Widow at Windsor"
"Widower's Tango" (Neruda) 4:306
"Widowhood or the Home-Coming of Lady Ross" (Smith) 12:351-52
"Widows" (Baudelaire)
See "Les veuves"
"The Widow's Lament in Springtime" (Williams) 7:345, 353, 360, 363
"The Widow's Party" (Kipling) 3:160
"The Widow's Resolution" (Smart) 13:347
"Wie wenn am Feiertage ..." (Holderlin) 4:162, 165-66, 169
"A Wife at Daybreak I Shall Be" (Dickinson) 1:93
"Wife to Husband" (Rossetti) 7:267
Wild Dreams of a New Beginning (Ferlinghetti) 1:188
"Wild Flower" (Tagore)
See "Banaphul"
"Wild Grapes" (Frost) 1:215
"Wild Life Cameo, Early Morn" (Ferlinghetti) 1:182-83, 188
"Wild Orchard" (Williams) 7:345
A Wild Patience Has Taken Me This Far: Poems, 1978-1981 (Rich) 5:385, 389
The Wild Rose Flowers (Akhmatova)
See *Shipovnik tsevetyot*
"The Wild Sky" (Rich) 5:362
"The Wilderness" (Robinson) 1:459
"Wilderness" (Sandburg) 2:302
"The Wildflower" (Williams) 7:382, 386
"Wilfred Owen's Photographs" (Hughes) 7:133
"The Will" (Donne) 1:126
"Will Be" (Pasternak) 6:252
"Will Boyden Lectures" (Masters) 1:343
"Will Not Come Back" (Lowell) 3:226-27
"Will Out of Kindness of Their Hearts a Few Philosophers Tell Me" (Cummings) 5:93
"Will They Cry When You're Gone, You Bet" (Baraka) 4:18
The Will to Change: Poems, 1968-1970 (Rich) 5:365-67, 370-72, 383, 387-89, 391, 399
"Will Waterproof's Lyrical Monologue" (Tennyson) 6:360
"Will You Perhaps Consent to Be" (Schwartz) 8:305
"Willful Homing" (Frost) 1:197
William Blake's Prophetic Writing (Blake) 12:25
"William Bond" (Blake) 12:35, 43
William Carlos Williams: Selected Poems (Williams) 7:357
"William H. Herndon" (Masters) 1:334
"William Marion Reedy" (Masters) 1:325, 333, 342

"Willie" (Brooks)
See "To Keorapetse Kgositsile (Willie)"
"Willie Brew'd a Peck o' Maut" (Burns) 6:76
"Willie Wastle" (Burns) 6:78, 81
"The Willing Mistress" (Behn) 13:4, 14-16, 18-20, 29
"Willingly" (Gallagher) 9:58
Willingly (Gallagher) 9:42-4, 50-1, 53, 56, 58-62
"Willkommen und Abschied" ("Welcome and Parting") (Goethe) 5:247, 251
"Wilt thou forgive" (Donne)
See "A Hymne to God the Father"
"Wind" (Hughes) 7:118, 165
"Wind and Flags" (Montale)
See "Vento e bandiere"
"Wind and Silver" (Lowell) 13:94-5
"The Wind and the Rain" (Frost) 1:196
"Wind in Florence" (Brodsky) 9:14
"Wind on the Crescent" (Lewis) 13:
See "Vento sulla mezzaluna"
"A Window" (Merton)
See "The Blessed Virgin Mary Compared to a Window"
"The Windows" (Apollinaire) 7:36
"The Windows" (Herbert) 4:119, 131
"The Windows" (Mallarme)
See "Les fenêtres"
"Windröschen" (Celan) 10:122
"Winds" (Auden) 1:23
"The Winds" (Williams) 7:369
"The Winds of Orisha" (Lorde) 12:155
"The Wind's Prophecy" (Hardy) 8:115-17
"The Windy City" (Sandburg) 2:306, 308, 314
Wine from These Grapes (Millay) 6:214, 217, 232
"The Wine Menagerie" (Crane) 3:81, 90
"Wine: Passages 12" (Duncan) 2:108
"Wingfoot Lake" (Dove) 6:112
"Wings" (Hughes) 7:132, 137
"Wings of a God" (Levertov) 11:176
"Der Winkel von Hahrdt" (Holderlin) 4:148
"Wino" (Hughes) 7:123, 132, 137
"Winston Prairie" (Masters) 1:343
"Winter" (Celan) 10:129
"Winter" (Milosz) 8:210
"Winter, a Dirge" (Burns) 6:52
"Winter Evening" (Pushkin)
See "Zimniy Vecher"
"Winter Festivities" (Pasternak) 6:266
"Winter Garden" (Neruda)
See "Jardín de invierno"
"Winter in Dunbarton" (Lowell) 3:218-19
Winter Love (H. D.) 5:299-300
"Winter: My Secret" (Rossetti) 7:281
"The Winter Ship" (Plath) 1:389
"Winter Sleepers" (Atwood) 8:12
"Winter Swan" (Bogan) 12:95, 106, 122
Winter Trees (Plath) 1:396
"The Winter Twilight Glowing Black and Gold" (Schwartz) 8:295
Winter Words: Various Moods and Metres (Hardy) 8:89, 96, 124
"Wintering" (Plath) 1:410, 412-13
"A Winter's Day" (Dunbar) 5:126
"The Winter's Night" (Merton) 10:340, 351
"A Winter's Tale" (Thomas) 2:382, 385, 402
"Wintry" (Gozzano)
See "A Wintry Scene"
"A Wintry Scene" ("Wintry") (Gozzano) 10:177-78, 180

"Wintry Sky" (Pasternak)   **6**:250
"Wirers" (Sassoon)   **12**:267, 285
"Wiretapping" (Montale)
   See "Intercettazione telefonica"
"Wish: Metamorphosis to Hearldic Emblem"
   (Atwood)   **8**:32, 39
"Witch Burning" (Plath)   **1**:394
"Witch Doctor" (Hayden)   **6**:186, 196
"The Witch of Coös" (Frost)   **1**:197, 209, 220
"The Witch's Life" (Sexton)   **2**:373
"Witch-Woman" (Lowell)   **13**:61, 64
"With All Deliberate Speed" (Madhubuti)
   5:346
"With Eyes At The Back of Our Heads"
   (Levertov)   **11**:168
With Eyes at the Back of Our Heads (*Eyes at
   the Back of Our Heads*) (Levertov)   **11**:168,
   205
"With Happiness Stretch's across the Hills"
   (Blake)   **12**:36
"With Her Lips Only" (Graves)   **6**:151
"With Mercy for the Greedy" (Sexton)   **2**:346,
   348, 351, 370
"With Rue My Heart Is Laden" (Housman)
   2:180, 184, 192
"With Scindia to Delhi" (Kipling)   **3**:182
"With Seed the Sowers Scatter" (Housman)
   2:180
"With the World in My Bloodstream"
   (Merton)   **10**:345
"With Trumpets and Zithers" (Milosz)
   See "Natrabach i na cytrze"
"Without Benefit of Declaration" (Hughes)
   1:252
"Without Ceremony" (Hardy)   **8**:134-35
A Witness Tree (Frost)   **1**:196-97, 203, 205-06
"The Witnesses" (Auden)   **1**:22
"Wives in the Sere" (Hardy)   **8**:90
"Wm. Brazier" (Graves)   **6**:143
"Wodwo" (Hughes)   **7**:127-28, 155
Wodwo (Hughes)   **7**:120-23, 133-34, 136-38,
   140-42, 150, 157-60, 163, 171-72
"The Woman" (Carruth)   **10**:71
"The Woman" (Levertov)   **11**:213-14
"A Woman Alone" (Levertov)   **11**:210
"Woman and Tree" (Graves)   **6**:149
"A Woman Dead in Her Forties" (Rich)
   5:379-80, 394
"Woman of Strength" (Tagore)
   See "Sabala"
"A Woman Resurrected" (Gozzano)   **10**:177-
   78
"A Woman Speaks" (Lorde)   **12**:160
"A Woman Waits for Me" (Whitman)   **3**:372,
   387
"The Woman Who Raised Goats" (Gallagher)
   9:35-6, 59
"Woman with Girdle" (Sexton)   **2**:346, 350
"The Womanhood" (Brooks)   **7**:54
"Woman's Constancy" (Donne)   **1**:125
"Women" (Bogan)   **12**:101
"Women" (Rich)   **5**:370
"The Women of Dan Dance With Swords in
   Their Hands to Mark the Time When They
   Were Warriors" (Lorde)   **12**:159-60
"Women's Tug of War at Lough Arrow"
   (Gallagher)   **9**:37
"The Wonderful Musician" (Sexton)   **2**:365
"Woodcutting on Lost Mountain" (Gallagher)
   9:60
The Wooden Pegasus (Sitwell)   **3**:301-02
"The Woodpile" (Frost)   **1**:220, 222, 226, 228

"The Word" (Smith)   **12**:354
Word over All (Day Lewis)   **11**:144, 148
"The Words" (Montale)
   See "Le parole"
"Words" (Plath)   **1**:409
"Words" (Sexton)   **2**:372-73
"Words for Hart Crane" (Lowell)   **3**:219, 222
"Words in the Mourning Time" (Hayden)
   6:197-98
Words in the Mourning Time (Hayden)   **6**:179,
   181-83, 193, 195
"Work Gangs" (Sandburg)   **2**:304, 308
"Work in Progress" (MacDiarmid)   **9**:199
Work Is Tiresome (Pavese)
   See *Lavorare stanca*
"Work Wearies" (Pavese)
   See "Lavorare stanca"
Work Wearies (Pavese)
   See *Lavorare stanca*
"A Worker Reads History" (MacDiarmid)
   9:181
"A Working Party" (Sassoon)   **12**:257, 261-62,
   277-78, 284
"The Workingman's Drink" (Baudelaire)
   1:47
Works, 1735—Poems on Several Occasions
   (Swift)   **9**:256
The Works of Aphra Behn (Behn)   **13**:16, 18
The Works of George Herbert (Herbert)   **4**:107
The Works of Horace, Translated into Verse
   (*Horace*) (Smart)   **13**:361-62
The Works of William Blake (Blake)   **12**:51
"The World" (Herbert)   **4**:100
"The World" ("A Naive Poem") (Milosz)
   8:187, 192, 194, 207, 209
"The World" (Rossetti)   **7**:277
"The World" (Smith)   **12**:328
"The World" (Tagore)
   See "Vasundhara"
"The World and the Quietist" (Arnold)   **5**:38,
   49
"The World Is a Beautiful Place"
   (Ferlinghetti)   **1**:180, 182-83
"The World Is a Wedding" (Schwartz)   **8**:303
"The World Is Full of Remarkable Things"
   (Baraka)   **4**:23-4
The World of Gwendolyn Brooks (Brooks)
   7:64, 66, 105
"The World Outside" (Levertov)   **11**:168, 193
"World Soul" (Bely)   **11**:24
"Worlds" (Masters)   **1**:333
"Worlds Back of Worlds" (Masters)   **1**:343
"The World's Desire" (Masters)   **1**:333
"The Worms of History" (Graves)   **6**:137,
   142, 144
"The Wormwood Star" (Milosz)   **8**:201, 204
"The Worst Of It" (Sassoon)   **12**:248
"The Wound" (Hardy)   **8**:93
The Wound (Hughes)   **7**:155
"The Wounded Wilderness of Morris Graves"
   (Ferlinghetti)   **1**:165
"A Wreath" (Herbert)   **4**:127, 130
"Writing in the Dark" (Levertov)   **11**:199
"Writing to Aaron" (Levertov)   **11**:208
Writing Writing (Duncan)   **2**:106
"Written aboard a Boat on the Day of Little
   Cold Food" (Tu Fu)   **9**:320
"Written by Dr. Swift on His Own Deafness"
   (Swift)   **9**:295
'Written in a Lady's Ivory Table-book, 1698"
   ("Verses Wrote in a Lady's Ivory Table-
   book") (Swift)   **9**:251, 295

"Written in Emerson's Essays" (Arnold)
   5:38, 49
Xaipe: Seventy-One Poems (Cummings)
   5:82-3, 86, 107-08
Xenia (Martial)   **10**:230
Xenia (Montale)   **13**:132-33, 135-36, 138, 165,
   167
"Xenia I" (Montale)   **13**:144
"Xenia II" (Montale)   **13**:144
"Xenion" (Montale)   **13**:133-34
"Xenion" No. 7 (Montale)   **13**:134
"The Yachts" (Williams)   **7**:360, 368
"Yama no ugoku hi" ("The Day the
   Mountains Move") (Yosano Akiko)   **11**:321
"Yauvan-svapna" ("Dream of Youth")
   (Tagore)   **8**:407
"Yawm mawlidi" (Gibran)   **9**:78
"Ye Are Na Mary Morison" ("Mary
   Morison") (Burns)   **6**:99
"The Year 1905" (Pasternak)
   See "Devyatsat pyaty god"
"Year at Mudstraw" (Forche)   **10**:133
The Years as Catches (Duncan)   **2**:104, 109
"The Year's Awakening" (Hardy)   **8**:105
"A Year's Spinning" (Browning)   **6**:32
"A Year's Windfalls" (Rossetti)   **7**:262
"Yee Bow" (Masters)   **1**:327
"Yell'ham Wood's Story" (Hardy)   **8**:91
The Yellow Heart (Neruda)
   See *El corazón amarillo*
The Yellow House on the Corner (*House on the
   Corner*) (Dove)   **6**:104-09, 116, 118, 122
"Yellow Ribbons, Baghdad 1991" (Rose)
   13:241
"Yes" (Ferlinghetti)   **1**:187
"Yes" (Gallagher)   **9**:64-5
"Yes and It's Hopeless" (Ginsberg)   **4**:76, 85
"Yesterday" (Sitwell)   **3**:293
"Yestreen I Had a Pint o' Wine" (Burns)
   6:75
"Les yeux des pauvres" ("The Eyes of the
   Poor") (Baudelaire)   **1**:58
"Yeux Glauques" (Pound)   **4**:319
Yevgeny Onegin (*Eugene Onegin*; *Evgeni
   Onegin*) (Pushkin)   **10**:357-62, 366, 368-69,
   371, 374-83, 386, 391, 400-04, 406, 409
"Yezersky" (Pushkin)
   See "Ezerskij"
Yobuko to kuchibue (*Whistles and Whistling*)
   (Ishikawa Takuboku)   **10**:211
"Yonder See the Morning Blink" (Housman)
   2:179
"York: In Memoriam W. H. Auden"
   (Brodsky)   **9**:12
"You" (Cummings)   **5**:105
"You All Know the Story of the Other
   Woman" (Sexton)   **2**:352-53
"You and Me" (Tagore)
   See "Tumi o ami"
"You Are Happy" (Atwood)   **8**:25, 27
You Are Happy (Atwood)   **8**:20-4, 29, 31, 33,
   41-2
"You Be Like You" (Celan)
   See "Du sei wie du"
"You, Dr. Martin" (Sexton)   **2**:359, 365
"You Drive in a Circle" (Hughes)   **7**:137
"You Talk on Your Telephone; I Talk on
   Mine" (Gallagher)   **9**:59
"Young" (Sexton)   **2**:350
"Young Africans" (Brooks)   **7**:65, 91, 93
"A Young Birch" (Frost)   **1**:200

"The Young British Soldier" (Kipling)   **3**:158
"A Young Child and His Pregnant Mother"
    (Schwartz)   **8**:282, 302, 304
"The Young Cordwainer" (Graves)   **6**:144
The Young Fate (Valery)
    See *La jeune parque*
"Young Girls" (Page)   **12**:176
"Young Heroes" (Brooks)   **7**:92-3, 105
"The Young Housewife" (Williams)   **7**:348,
    363, 378, 409
"Young Love" (Marvell)   **10**:303-04
"Young Love" (Williams)   **7**:382, 410
"The Young Mage" (Bogan)   **12**:100
"A Young Man's Exhortation" (Hardy)
    8:108
"Young Singer" (Hughes)   **1**:236, 246
"Young Soul" (Baraka)   **4**:9
"Young Sycamore" (Williams)   **7**:372-77
"Your Face on the Dog's Neck" (Sexton)
    2:363
"Your Flight" (Montale)
    See "Il tuo volo"
"Your Last Drive" (Hardy)   **8**:134
Your Native Land, Your Life (*Native Land*)
    (Rich)   **5**:387-89
"You're" (Plath)   **1**:389-90
"Youth" (Akhmatova)   **2**:8
"Youth" (Zukofsky)   **11**:368
"Youth and Calm" (Arnold)   **5**:42, 51
"The Youth of Man" (Arnold)   **5**:19, 49
"The Youth of Nature" (Arnold)   **5**:19, 42,
    49, 51, 59
"Yube no kane" ("The Evening Bell")
    (Ishikawa Takuboku)   **10**:214
"Yūbe no umi" ("The Evening Sea")
    (Ishikawa Takuboku)   **10**:213, 215
"Za Ki Tan Ke Parlay Lot" (Lorde)   **12**:155
Zahme Xenien (Goethe)   **5**:223
"Zaporogue" (Apollinaire)   **7**:48
"Ein zärtlich jugendlicher Kummer" (Goethe)
    5:247
"Zauberspruch" (Celan)   **10**:124-25
Zeitgehöft (*Farmstead of Time*) (Celan)   **10**:96,
    111
"Der Zeitgeist" (Holderlin)   **4**:166
"The Zeppelin Factory" (Dove)   **6**:110
"Zero" (Gallagher)   **9**:58
"Zeroing In" (Levertov)   **11**:205
"Zeus over Redeye" (Hayden)   **6**:183, 194
"Zhil Na Svete Rytsar' Bednyi" ("There Once
    Lived a Poor Knight"; "There Was a Poor
    Knight") (Pushkin)   **10**:411
"Zimniy Vecher" ("Winter Evening")
    (Pushkin)   **10**:381
"Znayu" ("I Know") (Bely)   **11**:32
Zoloto v lazuri (*Gold in Azure*) (Bely)   **11**:3-6,
    22, 26, 31-2
"Zone" (Apollinaire)   **7**:6, 10-12, 14-15, 21,
    41, 44-8
"Zone" (Bogan)   **12**:126
"Zoo Keeper's Wife" (Plath)   **1**:399
Zovy vremen (*Summonses of the Times*) (Bely)
    11:31-2
"Zueignung" (Goethe)   **5**:257
"Zuleika" (Goethe)   **5**:228
Zvezda (*The Star*) (Bely)   **11**:7, 24, 30, 32

POETRY CRIT VOL 13

ISBN 0-8103-9274-7